PENGUIN LITERARY BIOGRAPHIES

LYTTON STRACHEY: A BIOGRAPHY

Michael Holroyd was born in 1935, studied science at Eton College and read literature at the Maidenhead Public Library. He has written biographies of Hugh Kingsmill, Lytton Strachey and Augustus John, and edited, with Robert Skidelsky, William Gerhardie's posthumous *God's Fifth Column*. From 1973 to 1974 he was Chairman of the Society of Authors, from 1976 to 1978 Chairman of the National Book League, and in 1985 became President of English P.E.N. Apart from his books, he has written scripts for radio and television, and lectured abroad for the British Council. He is married to the novelist Margaret Drabble and is at present working on the authorized biography of Bernard Shaw.

MICHAEL HOLROYD

Lytton Strachey: A Biography

PENGUIN BOOKS

Penguin Books Ltd, Harmondsworth, Middlesex, England
Viking Penguin Inc., 40 West 23rd Street, New York, New York 10010, U.S.A.
Penguin Books Australia Ltd, Ringwood, Victoria, Australia
Penguin Books Canada Limited, 2801 John Street, Markham, Ontario, Canada L3R 1B4
Penguin Books (N.Z.) Ltd, 182–190 Wairau Road, Auckland 10, New Zealand

—

The contents of *Lytton Strachey: A Biography* and *Lytton Strachey and the Bloomsbury
Group: His Work, Their Influence* were originally published by William Heinemann Ltd
in two volumes under the title: *Lytton Strachey: A Critical Biography* in 1967–68.
They were first published in the U.S.A. by Holt, Rinehart & Winston, Inc., under the
titles *Lytton Strachey; the Unknown Years, 1880–1910*, and *Lytton Strachey; the Years
of Achievement, 1910–1932*.

—

Lytton Strachey: A Biography published
in Penguin Books 1971
Reprinted with revisions 1979
Reprinted 1980, 1987

—

—

Set, printed and bound in Great Britain by
Cox & Wyman Ltd, Reading
Set in Intertype Lectura

CONTENTS

CONTENTS

PART II

PART III

CONTENTS

THE winter of 1963-4 was for me a crucial one. After two years' work, and a further two years of waiting, I had had my first book published: A Critical Biography of Hugh Kingsmill, the novelist, biographer and literary critic. But only two weeks after publication I was being threatened with an action for libel. The situation seemed perilous. My chief witness, Hesketh Pearson, who had first encouraged me to write, suddenly died. I could muster other supporters, but they would hardly figure as star witnesses. There was Malcolm Muggeridge, who had contributed a marvellous introduction to my book, but who had also attacked the Queen and whose appearance in court was guaranteed to stir up violent antipathy in any jury. There was John Davenport, the critic, who at that time had chosen to wear a prejudicial black beard. And there was William Gerhardie, the distinguished novelist, who had not actually published a novel for the last quarter of a century and who, besides denying that he spoke with a slight foreign intonation, would almost certainly turn up at the wrong court room or on the wrong day, however elaborate the precautions one took.

Altogether it was not a pleasant prospect. Yet my publisher, Martin Secker, who was nearing eighty, appeared to find the predicament wonderfully invigorating. It brought back to him, evidently, the good old fighting days of D. H. Lawrence, Norman Douglas and the early novels of Compton Mackenzie, all of whom he had sponsored. While the old man seemed splendidly rejuvenated, I, still in my twenties, tottered towards a nervous senility. For nights on end I would start awake from dreadful courtroom scenes — rhetorical but unavailing speeches from the dock — to the dreary horror of early morning and the next batch of solicitors' letters.

But out of this nightmare something else had been born.

The first of the sixteen publishers to whom I had submitted my Kingsmill manuscript was Heinemann. Fortunately it had fallen into the hands of James Michie, the poet and translator of the Odes of Horace. He had liked it, had sent for me, and gently explained that were his firm to make a practice of bringing out books about almost unknown writers by totally unknown authors, it would very soon be bankrupt. However, I might become better known myself were I to choose a less obscure subject. Had I any ideas?

This was just the opportunity for which I was looking. Kingsmill, along with Philip Guedalla, Emil Ludwig, André Maurois, Harold Nicolson and others, had been categorized as one of those imitators of Lytton Strachey, whose literary reputation he had helped to bring into disrepute. In order to demonstrate the injustice of this charge I had had to examine Strachey's books in some detail. To my surprise I found there was no biography of him, and no wholly satisfactory critical study of his work. Here, it seemed to me, there existed the real need for a book. James Michie agreed, and a contract was drawn up in which I undertook to make a revaluation of Strachey's place as a serious historian. It would be about seventy thousand words long and take me, I estimated, at least a year.

A year later I had arrived at a stalemate. I had read everything published by and about Strachey, and I had produced an almost complete manuscript. But I was very far from being satisfied. For I had come to the conclusion that Strachey was one of those historians whose work was so personal that it could only be illuminated by some biographical commentary. It was impossible, from published sources, to reconstruct any worthwhile biography. As for unpublished sources, Clive Bell had sounded an ominous warning. 'Lytton could love, and perhaps he could hate', he had written. 'To anyone who knew him well it is obvious that love and lust and that mysterious mixture of the two which is the heart's desire played in his life parts of which a biographer who fails to take account will make himself ridiculous. But I am not a biographer, nor can, nor should, a biography of Lytton Strachey be attempted for many years to come. It cannot be attempted till his letters have been published or at any rate made accessible, and his letters should not be published till those he cared for and those who thought he cared for them are dead. Most of his papers luckily are in safe and scholarly hands.'

This passage conjured up the picture of an almost impregnable stronghold through which I had to make a breach. But I had no doubt that within these fortifications lay solutions to many of the problems that my literary researches had raised. Why had Strachey been attracted to General Gordon almost, as it were, against his will? What was the peculiar mystery he hinted at in Albert the Prince Consort's marriage to Queen Victoria? What was the spell that obviously mesmerized him in Queen Elizabeth's powerful relationship with the Earl of Essex? There was something intensely subjective in such questions that could never be satisfactorily answered without a more certain knowledge of Strachey's own secret nature.

I knew none of the surviving members of the celebrated Bloomsbury Group, but I had been given the address of a certain Frances Partridge, a friend of Strachey's who had collaborated with him on the eight-volume edition of *The Greville Memoirs*. To write to her out of the blue and ask for assistance seemed as good a start as any.

I wrote. In her reply she explained that the person I should first get in touch with was James Strachey, Lytton's younger brother and literary executor. He was the key figure to any major critical and biographical study such as I wanted to carry out. For if he were prepared to cooperate then she too would be perfectly ready to help me, and so also, she implied, would most of Lytton's other friends.

I met James Strachey a fortnight later. In the meantime various unnerving rumours concerning him had reached me. He was a psychoanalyst, who had been analysed by Freud, had subsequently worked with him in Vienna, and who, during the last twenty years, had been engaged on a monumental translation of all the Master's works. This twenty-four volume edition, with all its maze of additional footnotes and introductions, was said to be so fine both as a work of art and of meticulous scholarship that a distinguished German publishing house was endeavouring to have it re-translated back into German as their own Standard Edition. He was married to another psychoanalyst, Alix Strachey, author of *The Unconscious Motives of War*, a once brilliant cricket player and avid dancer at the night clubs and now an authority on cowboys. Together, I was inaccurately informed by Osbert Sitwell, they had rented off the attics of their house to some unidentified people on whom they had practised their psycho-analytical experiments to an extent where the wretched tenants no longer knew anything except the amount of their rent and the date it was due.

It was therefore with deep qualms that I approached their red-brick Edwardian house, set in the beech woods of Marlow Common. I arrived at mid-day by a complicated system of trains and taxis, prepared for practically anything – but not for what I actually came across. Though it was cold and frosty outside, the temperature within the house seemed set at a steady eighty degrees Fahrenheit. No windows were open, and to prevent the suspicion of a draught cellophane curtains were drawn against them. There was an odour of disinfectant about the rooms. I felt I had entered a specially treated capsule where some rare variety of *homo sapiens* was exquisitely preserved.

James Strachey was an almost exact replica of Freud himself, though with some traces of Lytton's physiognomy – the slightly bulbous nose in particular. He wore a short white beard, because, he told me, of the difficulty of shaving. He had had it now for some fifty years. He also wore spectacles, one lens of which was transparent, the other translucent. It was only later that I learnt he had overcome with extraordinary patience and courage a series of eye operations that had threatened to put an end to his *magnum opus*. In a more subdued and somewhat less astringent form, he shared many of Lytton's remarkable qualities – his strange and subtle humour, his depth and ambiguity of silence, his sternly rational turn of mind, his shy emotionalism and something of his predisposition to vertigo. As he opened the front door to me, swaying slightly, murmuring something I failed to over-hear, I wondered for a moment whether he might be ill. I extended a hand, a gesture which might be interpreted either as a formality or an offer of assistance. But he retreated, and I followed him in.

Of all his Stracheyesque characteristics, it was his silence that I found most dismaying during our hour's 'interview', as he called it, before lunch. I could not tell whether he pro-duced these silences spontaneously, or whether they were in some manner premeditated. Had he heard what I said? Or did he disapprove of my remarks? Or again, was he pondering, indefinitely, upon some singular reply? It was impossible to tell. To fill the vacuum of soundlessness, I began jabbering nonsense.

His wife came in, austere and intellectual, very thin, with a deeply-lined parchment face and large deeply expressive eyes. We all drank a little pale sherry and then moved in procession past a sculptured bust of Lytton to the dining-room.

Lunch was a spartan affair. Though extremely generous in spirit, my hosts were by temperament ascetic, and lived very frugally. We ate spam, a cold potato each, and lettuce leaves. In our glasses there showed a faint blush of red wine from the Wine Society, but I was the only one who so much as sipped any. My hosts solemnly tipped theirs down the sink at the conclusion of the meal. After the spam, some cheese was quarried out from the cold storage, and some biscuits ex-tracted from a long row of numbered tins ranged like files along a shelf in the kitchen. Everything, spam, potato, lettuce, cheese and biscuits, was, like the windows, swathed in pro-tective cellophane.

During lunch we talked of psychoanalysis – not the subject but the word, its derivation and correct spelling. Should it have a hyphen? Did it need both the central 'o' and 'a'? It was a topic to which I could contribute little of brilliance.

After lunch, Alix Strachey excused herself. She was going upstairs to watch a television programme for children. Re-cently she had decided to learn physics, she explained for my benefit, and found these kindergarten classes very instructive. James said nothing. In silence we filed back the biscuits on the shelf, poured away the rest of the wine, re-inserted the cheese into its wrappings and into its frozen chamber. Then James announced that we were to visit the 'studio wilderness', a large building with a stone floor, standing some ten yards to the rear of the house. He put on boots, a scarf, gloves, a heavy belted overcoat down to his ankles, and we started out on our journey.

The 'studio wilderness' housed much of Lytton's library and collection of papers. The bookcase along one of its walls was filled with French and English volumes going back to the year 1841. In the middle of the building were two great wooden tables piled high with boxes and files, and on the floor were littered innumerable trunks and suitcases – all full of letters, diaries and miscellaneous papers. Cobwebs and a pall of dust blanketed everything. Spiders – of which I have a particular horror – scuttled about the walls and floor, or swam suspended from the ceiling. James stared at this carefully accumulated debris with a sort of fascinated wonder. He had made Herculean efforts to organize it all, but by now it had got the better of him. He felt sometimes like putting everything in the fire, or sending it off to the archives of some distant university. But instead he stored every item, however minimal, and had persistently done so for the last thirty years. It formed a peculiar family museum, with special emphasis on Lytton. He was waiting for a time when civilized opinion had advanced far enough to make the revelations which these papers contained acceptable to the public. One of the ways he would determine whether such a time had yet arrived was to be the reaction of any potential biographer. I was not the first to approach him. Several years before, Guy Boas, the teacher and author, had done so. But it had not worked out. Boas considered the material far too scandalous for publication. James Strachey suggested he might get the book printed in Holland, but Boas, not liking to risk it, had backed down. Then Michael Goodwin, editor of *Twentieth Century*, had applied, had even been permitted to start his research, but had soon vanished, driven, in James's opinion, insane by the whole project. Much pioneer work had been done by Professor C. R. Sanders. Finally, a certain Professor Merle had come over from Paris and been allowed to take back a large number of confidential microfilms of Lytton's letters in order to compose a thesis for the Sorbonne. So what I saw in front of me was only a fraction of the total quantity of material. There was still more besides, James added, in his study. We must go there now.

We travelled back and went upstairs. The study was a long rectangular room surrounded on three sides by books and gramophone records and a narrow window running above them. At the farther end of the room stood a desk on which lay the intimidating engines of James Strachey's *oeuvre*. Two massive metal radiators, to which I politely extended my hands, turned out to be stereophonic loudspeakers – James was an authority on classical music, especially Haydn, Mozart and Wagner, and contributed notes and commentaries for Glyndebourne. Above the fireplace hung a portrait of Lytton relaxing in a deck chair, painted by Carrington. Next to the fireplace was an armchair, draped in cellophane. James showed me more papers, including his own correspondence with Rupert Brooke, and several reels of microfilm that the French professor had not taken with him. 'Do you *still* want to write about Lytton?' he at length inquired. I replied that I did. 'I see,' was all he said.

I left the house late that afternoon in profound depression. The mass of unpublished material had exceeded my wildest dreams, and made my previous year's work seem all the more futile. But I could not think I had made a good impression. It appeared likely that I had been wasting my time.

Forty-eight hours later I received a letter from James. He and his wife had decided to assist me so far as possible. But there were practical difficulties. Since 'this Freud translation business is in a rather specially hectic state', they were both bound to avoid being diverted. Therefore, I would have to bring my own food and drink each day. There was also the problem of travel. I should have to journey up and down by a complex of trains and buses. However, if I could face such horrors as these, I was free to start whenever I liked – preferably before the snow set in. I would be allowed access to the 'studio wilderness', and permitted to inspect anything in the house itself.

So began what, for the next five years, was to prove not simply the composition of a large book, but a way of life and an education.

I started work at Marlow in October 1962. The hexagonal room where we had first had lunch was given over to me, and as soon as I entered it I would strip off as many clothes as I thought practicable, begin reading through the correspondence, copying out sections, taking notes. From time to time there was a knocking at the hatch which communicated with the kitchen. I would open it to find a steaming cup of coffee and a number 3 biscuit, presumably left by Alix. From time to time James would quietly manifest himself from the doorway on the other side of the room, stand there awhile regarding me, deposit some notebook or sheaf of papers he had just come across: then disappear. Apart from this there was little to disturb me – occasionally some music from the radiator-like loudspeakers upstairs, and very occasionally the sound of scuffling feet from the top floor tenants descending the stairs. Nothing else.

Very soon I realized that I had stumbled upon what must be reckoned one of the major caches of literary papers in modern times. Lytton was never an eloquent conversationalist and had been allergic to the telephone. But he had loved to write and to receive letters: he was one of the last great correspondents. Here, in holograph, typescript and microfilm, were nearly all his letters, preserved since the age of six, and the letters from his friends, many of them internationally famous as painters, philosophers, novelists and economists.

All this was tremendously exciting. But it posed for me equally tremendous problems – problems of how to treat this colossal quantity of unpublished documents and of how to organize my life around it. Near the very outset I had to make the difficult decision that the subject was worth several years of uninterrupted labour and a coverage of about half-a-million words. And I had to persuade my publisher that I had made the right decision. James Michie had left Heinemann, but I was fortunate in that David Machin, his successor, was equally sympathetic. I outlined to him my plan. I intended to try and accomplish four things – to provide a selection of the best of Lytton's letters; to attempt a completely original reappraisement of his work; to present a panorama of the social and intellectual environment of a remarkable generation; and to write a definitive biography. These four ingredients I would endeavour to shape into the polychromatic design of a huge conversation piece around the figure of Lytton Strachey. 'Discretion', Lytton himself had once said, 'is not the better part of biography.' I should not be discreet. My purpose was to fuse an imaginatively kindled re-creation of the inner life of my characters with the rigorous documentation and exactitude of strict biographical method.

Part of a biographer's research can have about it an inevitable sameness. When one has examined ten thousand letters, one may be forgiven for eyeing the next ten thousand with a certain lacklustre. Undoubtedly, while I was ploughing through Lytton's early and most plaintive correspondence, with its microscopic details of faulty digestion, illness, apathy, self-loathing and all the unhappy qualities that made up what he termed 'the black period' of his life, I did feel seriously infected with many of the same ailments. If symptoms like these were posthumously contagious, then my next subject must, I resolved, be some athlete of astonishing virility and euphoria. However, Lytton's unusual character, with its curious contradictions and complexities, soon began to exert over my imagination a potent spell. I became absorbed in his life, and over the years I was writing my book I do not think I was ever more than half aware of the outside world. The world in which I lived so intensely was that of the Bloomsbury Group during the early part of this century. My work held something of the excitement of an archaeological discovery. The vast *terra incognita* represented by the Strachey papers seemed like a miniature Pompeii, a whole way of life, that was gradually emerging into the light.

17

Luckily, too, the routine of my research was widely variegated. One of my most interesting finds took place in the basement of 51 Gordon Square, the Strachey family's home from 1919 to 1963. The house was being vacated, and had been bought by University College, London. But I had been given authority to explore everything. On my first visit I noticed a tablet in the entrance hall listing the various members of the family with the captions 'In' and 'Out'. The word 'Out' had been slotted against those who (some of them half a century ago) had died. By the time I finished reconnoitring the basement, the dustman had turned up to carry off the rubbish for burning, and I won a fierce tug-of-war with them for Lytton's bulky long-lost Fellowship dissertation, 120,000 words long, on Warren Hastings. Among other things I came across that day, was a letter in the illegible Gothic hand of Sigmund Freud, written on Christmas Day 1928, and setting forth in great detail his thoughts on Lytton's *Elizabeth and Essex*.

The research was enlivened, too, by a great deal of travel in order to record impressions of people and places. One of the first things I did on leaving Marlow was to fly to Paris. There I met Gabriel Merle, a charming and taciturn French scholar, who allowed me to carry off the microfilms he had been lent by James. These microfilms contained Lytton's correspondence with his family, with Virginia Woolf (unabridged) and with Duncan Grant and Maynard Keynes. The latter were especially valuable, since the originals had been placed under lock and key with a strict embargo that they were not to be seen until 1986. Having negotiated the customs and returned home, I hired from Kodaks a huge black machine, like an astronomer's telescope, and fed the reels of microfilm into it. For two months my life orbited round this monstrous object, which stood in the centre of my one-room flat, dwarfing the furniture. I ate, slept, washed and dressed under its shadow. And for twelve or fifteen hours a day I would sit projecting the films on to a screen, and copying down anything I needed.

Later on I travelled through France and inspected La Souco, the house overlooking Monte Carlo which had belonged to Lytton's brother-in-law, the painter Simon Bussy, and where Lytton had often stayed and worked. It was deserted when I called, with a notice that it was up for sale. So I boldly made my way in and explored until captured by a voluble French neighbour who accused me of being a burglar. My French not being up to providing a truthful explanation, I gave her to understand that I was a prospective purchaser, and in the guise of a man of wealth was lavishly entertained by her.

A number of people had disliked Lytton Strachey – Harold Nicolson, for instance. I went to see him in his rooms at the Albany one evening. He was sitting in a chair when I entered, open-eyed and apparently examining me very critically. He said nothing. I stood before him shuffling my feet, shifting my weight from one to the other, murmuring something about the uncontroversial weather. He continued to glare. Suddenly a sort of convulsion ran through him, and he blinked. 'I'm afraid I've been asleep,' he said. 'Would you like a drink?' I said that I would. But the question was evidently academic, more to satisfy his curiosity than my thirst. We began to talk. Lytton, he told me, had resembled a bearded and bitchy old woman, rude rather than witty in society, injecting with his unnaturally treble voice jets of stinging poison into otherwise convivial gatherings. After about a quarter of an hour he looked across at his own large empty glass, which stood on the table between us, and asked: 'Another drink?' Hesitantly I agreed. But once again he made no move, and since I could see no sign of drink in the room, we went on talking. Ten minutes later his gaze again fell on the glass, this time with a sort of dismayed incredulity. 'Do you want *another* drink?' His tone was so sharp I thought it prudent to refuse.

Next day I told this story to Duncan Grant. Without a word he leapt up and poured me out a strong gin and tonic. The time was half-past ten in the morning.

Another near-contemporary of Lytton's who was reputed to disapprove of him was Bertrand Russell. He invited me to Plas Penrhyn, his remote house in the north of Wales, high up on a hill overlooking the Irish sea. There, in the drawing-

19

room, he regaled me with mildly indecent stories of Frank Harris and Oscar Wilde, showed me the typescript of his then unpublished autobiography and several Strachey letters. Had he disliked Lytton? I asked. No, he answered, never. And so smiling, diminutive and gently nostalgic did he appear that it was scarcely possible to believe that he had fiercely upbraided Lytton for having degraded G. E. Moore's ethics into 'advocacy of a stuffy girls'-school sentimentalizing' – a piece of invective that earned him a withering rebuke from E. M. Forster.

When I first started on my quest for Lytton, Frances Partridge had intimated that James Strachey's approval would guarantee me the help of many other friends. And so it turned out. Over the years I met or corresponded with over a hundred people, and the great majority of these cooperated with me very fully. This was all the more remarkable in view of the highly inflammable material that was involved. For here was I, a total stranger from a completely different generation, proposing to investigate their past lives with a probing intimacy. It was only through detail, I argued, that the extraordinarily complicated relationship surrounding Lytton could be properly presented. I was setting out to do something entirely new in biography, to give Lytton's love-life the same prominence in my book as it had had in his career, to trace its effect on his work, and to treat the whole subject of homosexuality without any artificial veils of decorum – in exactly the same way as I would have treated heterosexuality. To have done otherwise would have been to admit tacitly a qualitative distinction, and tended to perpetuate prejudice rather than erode it. But my plan depended for its practicability on the cooperation of a band of mercurial octogenarians. It was for all of us a daunting prospect. 'Shall I be arrested?' one of them asked after reading through my typescript. And another, with deep pathos, exclaimed: 'When this comes out, they will never again allow me into Lord's.' In particular, it says much for the courage, candour and integrity of Duncan Grant and Roger Senhouse that, despite the shock of its unexpectedness, they did not object to what I had written. Each of them had been central to the understanding of a part of Lytton's life. But neither, perhaps, had appreciated the full extent of the role he played in Lytton's emotions until he read my account based largely on what Lytton wrote to other friends. It was hardly surprising that this sudden revelation of a new dimension to their friendship should be the cause of some agitation. But neither of them put any obstacle in my way, and Duncan Grant set his seal of approval on the first volume by drawing, for its jacket, a magnificent portrait of Lytton, which he later generously presented to me.

By the crucial winter of 1963–4, I had reached in my first volume what is for me always one of the most difficult stages in a book. I was two-thirds of the way through it. A great deal remained to be done, but the temptation to relax slightly, together with the accumulating strain of the Kingsmill affair, made the last third very arduous. I had often been haunted by fears that I would not be able to do the book, that it was beyond me. Now these fears multiplied alarmingly. Like a snail, I inched my way forward, writing in the mornings, typing or doing extra research work every afternoon. This last section of the book took me almost a year to finish, and by the time I had done so, my two index fingers, the only ones I used for typing, were raw.

I returned to Marlow in the autumn of 1964, taking with me the typescript of volume one. While James unhurriedly read through it in his study, I worked below preparing for the second volume. Occasionally, in the late afternoon, the electricity supply would fail, and the regime became candles in champagne bottles. James did not say much while he was reading the typescript, but when he had completed it his reaction was devastating. I had, he felt, been far too adversely critical of his brother. He suspected that I harboured an unconscious dişlike of him, probably on moral grounds. This suggestion seemed to me utterly fantastic, but there is no appeal against the accusation of an *unconscious* attitude. One's natural rejoinder – that one is totally *unconscious* of it – seems only to corroborate the allegation. For my own part, I had come to feel that James resented from an outsider any criticism – even in the form of qualified praise – of Lytton, to whom he had been very intimately attached. 'I'm in a bit of a conflict,' he told me. On the one hand, he explained, he had grown rather friendly towards me, but on the other he rather violently objected to many passages in the book. He didn't enjoy being unpleasant to someone he liked. What, therefore, were we to do?

What we agreed to do was to go through the book syllable by syllable, trying to hammer out a mutually acceptable text. In return for what he called 'a bribe' of five hundred pounds, I agreed not to publish this first volume until I had finished the whole work. Both volumes could then be brought out together or with only a short interval between them. Despite James's generosity, this was undeniably a hard blow. I felt like a marathon runner who, on completing the course, is asked whether he wouldn't mind immediately running round it all over again.

I returned to London, to my portable typewriter, the one-room flat and the start of another quarter of a million words. Over the next two and a half years, James went through both volumes, in microscopic detail, twice. I stayed with him and Alix a number of times in Marlow; he occasionally came to London; we exchanged about a hundred and fifty letters; he sent me over a hundred pages of closely-written notes. When he was especially cross, I noticed, he would switch from blue to red ink, and on one fearful occasion the envelope itself was addressed in red. Nothing escaped his attention. One character had 'short' not 'small' shin bones; 'extrovert' was a word that derived from Jung and not from Freud, and was therefore meaningless; another person's ability was not 'considerable' but *very* considerable'; 'pratter' was a mistyping of 'prattle'; and so on. These notes, queries and comments took up an infinite amount of James's time. But they were of incalculable value. By nature he was severely uncommunicative, yet now he was being provoked into divulging all sorts of information known to practically no other living person, that would, I believed, greatly enrich the biography. Sometimes, of course, we could not agree. In these cases I stuck to my guns and put James's dashing comments in the footnotes.

In April 1967, very shortly after having completed his final notes, James died suddenly of a heart attack. I felt stunned. I had thought he would live to at least a hundred. Although he would on occasions rant and rave over something I had or hadn't written, all our differences had been argued out in the best of spirits. His mind and scholarship could certainly appear daunting, but they were mixed with a humour and gentleness that were unforgettable, and that made working with him an education in civilized behaviour.

Readers of the biography might well deduce from some of the footnotes that James disliked the finished book. Happily this was not so. He was never one to pretend to opinions that were not absolutely his own, so that I knew it was true when he told me at the end he appreciated my seriousness of purpose and approved of the structure and length of the book. The figures and situations, though not always as he saw them, had seemed to force their way through, he said, by a kind of continuous pressure of permeation. And some of the narrative, especially towards the close, he praised highly. Since I had never blindly accepted his opinions, and since I knew his approbation extremely hard to win, nothing could have delighted me more.

*

James Strachey's wish was that my book on Lytton should be 'as viable as possible'. He would, I think, have approved of the changes I have made for this edition.

The central change has been to separate the biography from the literary criticism which now forms a companion volume. This should not suggest that the two are unconnected; the reason is primarily one of convenience for the reader. A knowledge of Lytton Strachey's life enables one, I believe, to read his books with new understanding. In places I have tried to use his own phrases, sentence rhythms and other stylistic qualities to show how and where the connection between the life and work are especially close.

Other alterations are of two main kinds. *In* has come new information from letters I had not seen when I originally wrote my book. *Out* have gone a number of errors revealed to me by readers and reviewers.

What I have written, I have re-written in those passages which betrayed my inexperience in dealing with some of the practical difficulties that confronted me. This should have the effect of tightening up the narrative. The result will be, I hope, that while the original version may continue to be useful primarily as a work of reference, the present re-organization may make for greater readability and enjoyment.

In the first edition of this book there are passages in Part II, Chapter 6, referring to Piers Noxall and his friendship with Carrington. I am asked to say that these passages have been understood to refer to Commander Bernard Penrose and I now recognize that they give an erroneous impression of his friendship with Carrington. The passages have been re-written in the light of information he has given me. I regret the inaccuracies in the first edition, though based upon information which at the time I had no reason to doubt, and any embarrassment I have caused Commander Penrose by reason of this inaccurate portrayal of him.

MICHAEL HOLROYD

ACKNOWLEDGEMENTS

My book has been possible by the kindness and cooperation of the late James Strachey, who, besides making accessible a formidable mass of unpublished material, answered the many questions which I put to him during the course of my work and also checked all the biographical facts of my typescript, though he is not to be held responsible for any of the opinions that I have expressed. Among others who have helped me in one way or another and to whom I would like to acknowledge my gratitude and indebtedness are: The Dowager Lady Aberconway, the late J. R. Ackerley, Mr Harold Acton, Lord Annan, the late Baroness Asquith of Yarnbury, Mrs Barbara Bagenal, the late Thomas Balston, the late Bishop Lumsden Barkway, Mr and Mrs J. L. Behrend, the late Clive Bell, Professor Quentin Bell, Mr Gerald Brenan, the Hon. Dorothy Brett, Mr Richard Carline, Mr Noel Carrington, Lord David Cecil, Lady Diana Cooper, Lord Cottesloe, Dr Lissant Cox, the late John Davenport, Mr James Dicker, Profesor Bonamy Dobrée, Mr and Mrs Guy Elwes, the late E. M. Forster, Mr Roderick W. B. Fraser, Mr Roger Fulford, Mr David Garnett, Mrs Angelica Garnett, the Hon. Robert Gathorne-Hardy, Mr William Gerhardie, Mrs Marjorie Gertler, Mrs Julia Gowing (née Strachey), Mr Duncan Grant, Mrs Karin Hall, Sir Roy Harrod, the late Christopher Hassall, Mr R. A. Hodgkin, Mr Basil Holroyd, the late Mr and Mrs Kenneth Holroyd, Mr Richard Hughes, Mrs Mary Hutchinson, the late Aldous Huxley, Miss Elizabeth Jenkins, Sir Caspar John, the late Dorelia John, the late C. H. B. Kitchin, Lady Pansy Lamb, Mr John Lehmann, Miss Rosamond Lehmann, Mr Robert Lescher, the late E. B. C. Lucas, the late F. L. Lucas, the late André Maurois, the late Professor H. O. Meredith, Mr Gabriel Merle, Mrs Dorothy Moore, Mr Raymond Mortimer, Lady Mosley, Lord Moyne. Dr A. N. L. Munby, Mrs U. Nares, the late Sir Harold Nicolson, Miss Lucy Norton, Miss Frances Partridge, the late Hesketh Pearson, Professor Lionel Penrose, Mr Alfred H. Perrin, the Hon. Wogan Philipps (Lord Milford), Mr. William Plomer, Mr Peter Quennell, Mrs Nancy Rodd, Sir John Rothenstein, Sir Steven Runciman, the late Lord Russell, Mr George Rylands, the late Lord Sackville, Miss Daphne Sanger, the late Siegfried Sassoon, Mr Alan Searle, the late Roger Senhouse, the late Sir John Sheppard, the Reverend F. A. Simpson, Professor George Kuppler Simson, Professor W. J. H. Sprott, Mrs Alix Strachey, the late Evelyn John St Loe Strachey, M.P., Mr John Strachey, the late Philippa Strachey, Mr and Mrs Richard Strachey, Sir Charles Tennyson, Dame Sybil Thorndike, Miss Marjorie H. Thurston, the late Iris Tree, Mrs Igor Vinogradoff, the late Boris von Anrep, the late Arthur Waley, Sir William Walton, Mrs Ursula Wentzel, Mrs Amabel Williams-

Ellis (*née* Strachey), the late John Dover Wilson, the late Leonard Woolf, Mr Wayland Young (Lord Kennet).

I should also like to record my thanks to the following: Chatto & Windus Ltd, the Chelsea Public and Reference Library, King's College Library, Cambridge, the National Book League, the Royal Society of Literature, the Society of Authors, and the Slade School of Fine Art.

I must also express my indebtedness to Mr David Machin for his unfailing patience and support over three long years; to Mr Roger Smith for his meticulous checking and preparing of my typescript for the printers; to Miss Jennifer Holden who helped to correct each page of my work and gave me many valuable suggestions; and to Mr Herbert Rees for his expert assistance at proof stage.

The writing of this book was largely made possible by the award, in 1963, of the Eugene F. Saxton Memorial Fellowship for the composition of the first volume; and, in 1965, for the second volume, of a Bollingen Foundation Fellowship.

I am grateful to the following for kindly granting me permission to quote from copyright sources: Lord Annan for *Leslie Stephen* (MacGibbon & Kee); the late Bishop Barkway for unpublished writings; Rupert Crew Ltd for *The Wandering Years* by Cecil Beaton (Weidenfeld & Nicholson); Professor Sir J. D. Beazley for unpublished writings; the Administratrix of the Estate of Sir Max Beerbohm for letters and *Mainly on the Air* (Heinemann and Alfred A. Knopf, Inc.); Professor Quentin Bell, Chatto & Windus Ltd and Harcourt, Brace & World, Inc, for *Old Friends* by Clive Bell, also Professor Bell for unpublished writings; A. P. Watt & Son for *Queen Victoria* by E. F. Benson (Longmans); A. M. Heath & Co. Ltd for *My Restless Years* by Hector Bolitho (Max Parrish); George Weidenfeld & Nicolson Ltd for *Memories* by C. M. Bowra; Hamish Hamilton Ltd for *South from Granada* by Gerald Brenan, also the author for unpublished writings; William Collins Sons & Co. Ltd for Ivor Brown's Introduction to *Queen Victoria* by Lytton Strachey (Collins Classics edition); Mrs Frances Partridge for unpublished writings by herself, the late Ralph Partridge and Carrington; Lord David Cecil, C.H., for an article in the *Dictionary of National Biography*; Mr John Stewart Collis for *An Artist of Life* (Cassell); Routledge & Kegan Paul Ltd and The Macmillan Company for *Enemies of Promise* by Cyril Connolly (copyright 1948 by Cyril Connolly); William Collins Sons & Co. Ltd for *Two Flamboyant Fathers* by Nicolette Devas; the Society of Authors for unpublished letters by Norman Douglas; Mrs T. S. Eliot for a review and unpublished letters by the late T. S. Eliot; Curtis Brown Ltd for *General Gordon* by Lord Elton (Collins); the late E. M. Forster, C.H., for unpublished writings; Sigmund Freud Copyright Ltd for an unpublished letter to Sigmund Freud; Mr Roger Fulford for unpublished writings; Mr David Garnett for *The Flowers of the Forest* and *The Familiar Faces* (Chatto and Windus); Mr William Gerhardie for *Resurrection* (Cassell) and unpublished writings; Mrs Marjorie Gertler for *Selected Letters* by Mark Gertler (Hart-Davis) and for unpublished letters by Mark Gertler; Mr Duncan Grant for an extract from an article and for unpublished writings; Professor G. B. Harrison for unpublished writings; Sir Roy Harrod for *The Life of John Maynard Keynes* (Macmillan); Mrs Dorelia John for *Chiaroscuro* by Augustus John (Cape); Martin Secker & Warburg Ltd and Farrar, Straus & Giroux, Inc., for *The Bloomsbury Group* by J. K. Johnstone (copyright © 1954 by Noonday Press); Sir Geoffrey Keynes for letters by J. M. Keynes; Associated Book Publishers Ltd for *Progress of a Biographer* (Methuen) and *The Return of William Shakespeare* (Eyre and Spottiswoode) by Hugh Kingsmill; the late C. H. B. Kitchin for unpublished writings; Laurence Pollinger Ltd (acting for the Estate of the late Mrs Frieda Lawrence) and The Viking Press, Inc. for letters by D. H. Lawrence (copyright 1932 by the Estate of D. H. Lawrence, 1960 by Angelo Ravagli and C. Montague Weekley) and Laurence Pollinger Ltd and Alfred A. Knopf, Inc. for 'None of That' by D. H. Lawrence; David Higham Associates Ltd for *The Whispering Gallery* by John Lehmann (Longmans); Mr Michael MacCarthy for *Memories* by Desmond MacCarthy (MacGibbon & Kee); Hamish Hamilton Ltd and Alfred A. Knopf, Inc. for *Forty Years with Berenson* by Nicky Mariano; Doubleday & Co. Inc. for *archy's life of mehitabel* by don marquis (copyright 1933 by Doubleday & Company Inc.); the late Kingsley Martin for *Father Figures* (Hutchinson); the late Professor H. O. Meredith for an unpublished letter; Mrs Igor Vinogradoff for *Ottoline: The Early Memoirs of Lady Ottoline Morrell* (Faber & Faber); Mr Raymond Mortimer for *Channel Packet* (Hogarth Press); and *Duncan Grant* (Penguin); Mr Beverley Nichols for unpublished writings; Sir Harold Nicolson for *The Development of English Biography* (Hogarth Press); Mrs Hesketh Pearson for *Beerbohm Tree* (Methuen) and *Modern Men and Mummers* (Allen & Unwin) by Hesketh Pearson; Mr. William Plomer for *At Home* (Cape) and a letter; William Collins Sons & Co. Ltd for *The Sign of the Fish* by Peter Quennell; Mr Kerrison Preston for *Letters from Graham Robertson* (Hamish Hamilton); Hamish Hamilton Ltd for *Summer's Lease* by John Rothenstein; Mr S. de R. Raleigh for letters by Sir Walter Raleigh; Dr. A. L. Rowse for a review; the late Bertrand Russell (Earl Russell, O.M.) for *Portraits from Memory* and *The Autobiography of Bertrand Russell* (Allen & Unwin and Little, Brown) and for unpublished letters; Mr Alan Searle for unpublished writings; Mr Roger Senhouse for unpublished writings; the Reverend F. A. Simpson for unpublished writings and *Louis Napoleon and the Fall of France* (Longmans); David Higham Associates Ltd for *Laughter in the Next Room* by Osbert Sitwell (Macmillan); David Higham Associates Ltd for *The Autobiography of Alice B. Toklas* by Gertrude Stein (The Bodley Head); Mr Frank Swinnerton for *The Georgian Literary Scene* (Dent); Professor Robert H. Tener for a letter; Dame Sybil Thorndike for unpublished writings; Sir Stanley Unwin for *The Truth About a Publisher* (Allen & Unwin); Longmans, Green & Co. Ltd for *Our Partnership* by Beatrice Webb and the Trustees of the Passfield Trust for Beatrice Webb's *Diary*; Mr Edmund Wilson for 'Lytton Strachey' from *The Shores of Light* (Farrar, Straus & Giroux, Inc. and W. H. Allen); Professor John

ACKNOWLEDGEMENTS

Dover Wilson, C.H., for an article and an unpublished letter; Mr Leonard Woolf for his own published and unpublished writings and those of Virginia Woolf.

PART I

'We begin life in a very odd manner – like shipwrecked sailors. The world is our desert Island.' *Lytton Strachey to Leonard Woolf* (July 1904)

ONE

Lancaster Gate

'To reconstruct, however dimly, that grim machine, would be to realize with some real distinctness the essential substance of my biography.' *Lytton Strachey, 'Lancaster Gate'* (1922)

1
PAPA AND MAMA

'THE Stracheys are most strongly the children of their fathers, not of their mothers,' Mrs St Loe Strachey wrote in 1930. ' "It does not matter whom they marry," said one of St Loe's aunts to me when I was quite young, "the type continues and has been the same for three hundred years." ' In the case of Lytton, St Loe's cousin, this dictum no longer holds true. 'You'd never think he was a general's son,' the head porter at the Great Gate of Trinity once remarked to Clive Bell, as the lanky, drooping silhouette of Strachey moved across the quadrangle. And even though the figure of Lieutenant-General Sir Richard Strachey, so stocky and dynamic, might not have fitted a head porter's impression of the typical British general, there was certainly little physical resemblance between him and his fifth son.

Richard Strachey, the third of six sons, had been born at Sutton Court near Chew Magna, Somerset, on 24 July 1817. His distinguished career in India showed the immense versatility of his temperament. Few men have done so much, often in ways unknown to the outside world, for the improvement of Indian administration. It was to him that India owed the initiation of her policy of the systematic extension of railways and canals which increased, to an incalculable extent, the wealth of the country and profoundly altered its condition. To him was due the conception of those measures of financial and

31

administrative decentralization pronounced by Sir Henry Maine to be by far the greatest and most successful reforms carried out in India in his time. He established the first adequate forest service in the country; he completely reorganized the public works department of which, in 1862, he became the head; he was the first to advise the amendment of the currency, the delay of which involved the country in considerable loss; and in his spare time he developed a very pretty talent for painting. His career in India extended altogether over thirty years and helped to fashion a stable form of government. By the time he eventually left in 1871, he commanded a position of very great power and importance. In public matters he had impressed those with whom he came into contact as being a man of strong mind, determined will. On the few occasions when he was indisputably in the wrong – as, for example, over the vexed topic of railway gauges – he could be obstinate and inflexible. But despite his outstanding success in public administration, his real leaning was towards science, and he liked to think that his more lasting achievements lay in this field. Of all his scientific investigations, the most zealous were in meteorology. He was also a fine geographical scholar, and was twice made President of the Royal Geographical Society.

Amid a society of prepotent personages Richard Strachey had more than held his own. He was not merely a soldier: he was also a scientist, civil administrator, explorer, engineer and mathematician. Yet, though his restless energy overflowed into so many, various channels, his imagination remained exclusively matter-of-fact, and his whole conception of life was of a perfectly unexceptional kind.

Richard Strachey's marriage to Jane Maria Grant took place on 4 January 1859. She was the daughter of Sir John Peter Grant and Henrietta Chichele, a prominent member of a rather more aristocratic Anglo-Indian family. She had been born on 13 March 1840, on board the East India Company's strong ship, *The Earl of Hardwicke*, in the middle of a violent storm off the Cape of Good Hope. Eighteen years later, in a sedate Indian withdrawing-room, she had met Richard Strachey for the first time, a black-haired man seated on a yellow sofa, and displaying 'the exact colours of a wasp'.

Physically they were not a well-matched pair. Whereas he, like most Stracheys, was rather short, highly methodical at work but of an abrupt social temperament, she was tall and stately in appearance, and of a more artistic bent.[1] They had in common, though, an abounding vitality, and since Richard Strachey's energies were directed mainly towards public and scientific matters, it was his wife's less diversified vigour which was experienced more keenly in the home. Certainly his paternal influence with the children seems to have declined sharply with time, while Lady Strachey became increasingly the dominating figure within the family, and most especially, of course, over her younger sons and daughters.

Lytton Strachey was born at Stowey House, Clapham Common, on 1 March 1880, the eleventh of thirteen children, three of whom died in infancy. He was christened Giles Lytton after a sixteenth-century ancestor, Giles Strachey, and his godfather, the first Earl of Lytton, Viceroy of India, who as 'Owen Meredith' achieved some distinction as a poet. For the first three years of his life, however, he appears to have been spiritually nameless, since his christening ceremony, which was combined with that of his younger sister Marjorie, was not performed until the second week of April 1883. As a young child he was high-spirited and loquacious – for the only time in his life. 'Giles is the most ridiculous boy I ever saw,' Lady Strachey wrote to her daughter Dorothy shortly after his third birthday: 'he said to me, "Yesterday in the streets I saw a cow eating the birds!" He then enacted a drama of which the punishment of the unnatural cow was the motive; as a policeman he flung himself on one knee and upraised his arms at the cow with a most fine dramatic gesture

1. James Strachey recalled that his father was actually as tall as his mother – that is, about five feet eight inches. But he held himself badly and therefore seemed smaller. Photographs of them together make him appear distinctly the shorter figure.

of Command; a terrific combat then ensued in which he wielded the peacock broom with might, and finally cried sternly, "Go to be dead!" and laid his broom on the floor saying, "Now the cow is dead." He never ceases talking for a single minute.'

As an infant Lytton was noticeably eccentric. He loved to march up and down Stowey House chanting what was apparently an epic poem full of high-sounding phrases, which always began the same way but varied unpredictably in its later stages. 'It is interspersed with morsels in rhyme called "Dickey Songs",' Lady Strachey noted in her diary on 25 March 1884, 'and sung by the "Bugyler" – the chief hero "Brynorma", the drummer boy is "Shiptenor", there is "Tellysin" and a "Calorum" and a "Sunsence"; as far as we can ascertain these names are entirely of his own construction. It looks rather as if he were one of the "many children" who could have written Ossian!'

Lytton's father was by this time nearing seventy, though Lady Strachey was still only forty-three. This wide discrepancy of age partly accounts for the differing roles which each played in the household and in the lives of their younger children. Terminating his short, rather impersonal letters in which the formality is relieved only by drawings of obscure botanical specimens to be seen at Kew, and which accompany mathematical booklets and packets of foreign stamps dispatched to Lytton, Richard Strachey invariably signed himself 'Your affnt father, Rd. Strachey'; while his mother, being much closer to him, wrote far longer and more frequent letters and remained, even when Lytton had fully grown up, 'ever darling, your loving Mama'. But while his father's remoteness only served to enhance, as time went on, Lytton's sense of admiration for him, the strong pressure of emotion laid upon him by his mother made him sometimes feel indifferent towards her, and in the long run anxious to set himself up free from her protection and complete in himself.

Although during former days out in India Richard Strachey had gained the reputation for being forceful and of a peppery temper, now in England he had grown rather mild in spirit, a

little vague and detached from all that was going on even in
the closest proximity. Lytton's earliest memories of him recalled little but the sheaves of papers, the voluminous sheets
covered with elaborate calculations, which, to the last, encumbered his desk. During the day he would sit working at
railway or atmospheric matters before this enormous desk in
his study; and Lytton was often sent up from the dining-room
to try and persuade him to descend for lunch. As Lytton grew,
so his father seemed to shrink into 'a little man with a very
beautiful head', as Leonard Woolf later described him, 'sitting
all day long, summer and winter, in a great armchair in front
of a blazing fire, reading a novel'.[2] Over the last few years of
his life Sir Richard was seldom seen without a novel in his
hand. Six a week were brought to him on a silver tray, and
these would apparently absorb him all evening until, shortly
after ten o'clock at night, Ellen, the maid, appeared with a
shawl to take him up to bed. Meanwhile Lady Strachey, as she
sat playing patience on the opposite side of the elaborately
tiled fireplace, kept an agonized eye on her husband to see if
he was going to be good or not. Occasionally, very occasionally, he *was* good, soon closed his book, rose with a smile
and shuffled off to bed on Ellen's arm. More often than not,
however, he was naughty and resolved to finish the chapter
before becoming aware that Ellen was in the room. Sometimes Ellen, after waiting patiently for several minutes, would
bend forward and gently whisper to him that it was late. No
notice whatever would be taken of this announcement. Silent
looks of sympathy were then exchanged between Ellen and
Lady Strachey, who shook her head in hopeless disapproval.
But never did she interfere or address any remark to Sir

2. James Strachey, who disputed some details in Leonard Woolf's description, told the author that the whole change in his father's life to
semi-invalidism only took place after 1897, when he was eighty. 'In that
year, which was when he was knighted, he made the journey by himself
from our then country house near Manningtree in Essex, I fancy, to Os-
borne for the investiture. He also took Pippa to the Naval Review at
Spithead that year. What happened was that he got an attack of dysen-
tery after a visit to Belgium, and nearly died. Though he recovered and
went on working, he was never so active again.'

Richard, and if the proceedings became unusually protracted, one of her daughters would put her book down, firmly advance and say 'Papa, it's bedtime!' Realizing that the game was up, Sir Richard would raise his spectacles over his forehead and with an engaging smile pretend that this was the first time he had heard of it. During the day he seemed at all times unaware of the terrific din which constantly surrounded him and which was unfailingly provided by his sons and daughters, sitting through it completely unmoved, Leonard Woolf recalls, and only 'occasionally smiling affectionately at it and them, when it obtruded itself unavoidably upon his notice, for instance, if in some deafening argument one side or the other appealed to him for a decision. He was usually a silent man, who listened with interest and amusement to the verbal hurricane around him; he was extraordinarily friendly and charming to an awkward youth such as I was, and he was fascinating when now and again he was induced to enter the discussion or recall something from his past.'

Part of this benevolent remoteness was occasioned by the increasing deafness which afflicted his later years and which forced him to relinquish several of the official appointments which he still held. Up to the age of ninety, he continued to go to the City and to the Meteorological Office. But he was a dangerous pedestrian, and on several occasions collided with hansom cabs – impacts which, though sometimes bringing on attacks of gout and causing the family the most acute anxiety, always left him in the highest spirits.

Even when Lytton was a young child his father took little active part in the everyday management of family affairs, for in this, as in most other respects, the household was staunchly Victorian. The Strachey tradition was seldom overtly stressed, but an assumption of its sufficiency saturated the atmosphere at Stowey House. The innermost feelings and ideas of the children were seldom contemplated and never discussed – a malpractice which tended in later years to produce in them an instinctive recoil from all kinds of emotional exhibitionism. Early in his life Richard Strachey had professed to be an atheist, though later he conceded being an agnostic.

36

The change was not of great significance, for in an age where materialism had assumed the disguise of Christian orthodoxy, atheists and agnostics appeared to share a fundamental quality: they were both conventionally religious. Although no tinge of scepticism or conscious hypocrisy found a place in Richard Strachey's make-up, he attached himself without question to the fashionable ideals and communal virtues of his day. An infinitely painstaking worker, he passed the last active period of his life in the invention and perfection of his instruments for measuring the most minute movements of the highest, least visible clouds, and in giving graphic expression to one or two laws of meteorology. The old man laboured with unmitigated, almost heroic endurance at these pursuits; but that the rules of ethics, the laws and customs of social morality, the psychological complexities of his own children could be subjected to a similarly minute scrutiny was a notion which would have struck him as perverse, a lapse from the recognized code of behaviour at once unwarranted and dangerous.

Placed beside her husband, Jane Maria Strachey appears at first sight to have been an unconventional figure. The quality which struck so many of her eminent contemporaries – among them Lord Lytton, Sir Henry Maine and Fitzjames Stephen – was that indefinable one of 'character'. Only a most remarkable woman would have been invited by Lord Bowen to sit beside him in the Court of Appeal, or asked by George Eliot to enter upon a sustained correspondence. Though she had no taste in the plastic arts, and was no intellectual, her personality was striking and agreeable. She was a figure in her own right – and not unaware of the fact. When on 22 June 1897, the date of Queen Victoria's Diamond Jubilee, she opened *The Times* and saw that her husband had been made Knight Grand Commander of the Star of India, she bitterly complained that this had been done without his first being asked. Previously he had declined other honours. And now she would be known as plain Lady Strachey – one of several – instead of *the* Mrs Richard Strachey.

From her earliest years she was addicted to literature, and

read especially French literature and Elizabethan drama with untiring relish. Her own publications consisted mostly of verse for children,[3] though she also edited her aunt's celebrated *Memoirs of a Highland Lady*, and in old age wrote 'Some Recollections of a Long Life'.[4] Some of her other tastes suggest enlightenment. A friend of Mrs Henry Fawcett, she worked to promote the Women's Progressive Movement; she loved classical music, sitting Lytton on her knee while she played songs on the piano; and she inspired him also with her passion for parlour games, amateur theatricals, puzzles, and with something of her zest for billiards, at which she was an expert player. For a number of the social conventions of her time she entertained scant respect, and long before women were generally permitted such habits she smoked, not just ordinary cigarettes, but those of the ultra-modern *American* variety. Even in her seventies she enjoyed particularly the company of young people, throwing herself into their amusements with the unquenchable vivacity of a girl of twenty. Indeed, she was much more 'advanced' in her old age than she had been in her youth – for which progress Lytton was largely responsible. She had been brought up an ordinary, passive Christian, but after reading John Stuart Mill's work *On Liberty* at the age of nineteen she became his fervent disciple. He was the guiding star of her youth, giving her a coherent scheme of thought and an intellectual basis for conduct newly permeated and vitalized by a fresh emotional enthusiasm, when

3. Lady Strachey's *Nursery Lyrics*, originally published in 1893 with illustrations by G. P. Jacomb Hood, was reprinted with additions in 1922 as *Nursery Lyrics and other Verses for Children* and illustrated by Philip Hagreen. *Poets on Poets* appeared in 1894. In 1887, she had brought out her children's anthology, *Lay Texts for the Young, in Both English and French*. A copy of this book was presented to Lytton when he was about fourteen. There are no religious authors included in the volume, and, presumably because he was too well known, no Shakespeare. Several of the quotations appear to contradict one another, but the chief qualities held up to be emulated are five in number: truth, reason, balance, virtue and aspiration.

4. *Nation and Athenaeum* XXXIV (5 Jan., 24 Feb. 1924), pp. 514–15, 730–31; XXXV (12 July, 30 Aug. 1924), pp. 473–4, 664–5. See also XXXIV, p. 514.

all she had been brought up to believe was shattered. From this faith she was eventually disabused by Lytton himself, who, reacting to the contrary influence of the philosopher G. E. Moore, came to regard the Utilitarian Mill, so far from being a champion of liberty, as totalitarian, intolerant and inquisitorial. In her anxiety to retain the affection of her son, Lady Strachey endeavoured to alter the course of her mind into more speculative channels. She tried when in her sixties to master the Greek language, and also to match the rather aggressive paganism which Lytton began to adopt as he grew up. 'I should not be surprised', she wrote hopefully to him on one occasion, 'if the decay of Christianity led to some really interesting appreciations of the New Testament that might stimulate perceptions which, like mine, have been blunted by ceaseless iteration and vitiated by the theological standpoint.' Her attempts to be modern were stamped by pathos. Lytton, appreciating the personal impulse which lay behind such affirmations of her desire to learn, treated what she said with kindness and respect. But to Maynard Keynes he wrote: 'Oh how dreadful to be a mother. How terrible to love so much and know so little! Will it always be like this to the end of the world?'

In public and political life she campaigned actively for the rights of women as citizens; but at home she instinctively put her husband before herself in every way, and preferred the scientists of her acquaintance – Galton, Huxley, Lubbock, Tyndall and others – to the artists and men of letters. Although she met many eminent writers, including Carlyle, Browning, Ruskin, Tennyson and George Eliot, her recorded observations on them reveal little genuine perception. She never, for example, noticed anything to suggest that the Carlyles were not on the very best of terms; and when Tennyson declared that *Troilus and Cressida* was probably Shakespeare's finest play, she merely registered shock. On the other hand some of the phrases she used in her letters to Lytton are quite vivid and arresting, and suggest a modest if undeveloped literary talent, swamped by the excessive conformity of an age in which women were still far from attaining reasonable emancipation.

Her trivial irregularities from the most petty conventions of the time were in themselves quite conventional idiosyncracies, showing how a strain of real originality, if stifled, may become squandered in the form of harmless social eccentricity.

One side of her nature had been furthered by experience at the total expense of the other, and from this ill-proportion seems to have arisen a curious lack of coordination. She was invariably dressed in long sweeping clothes of black satin, and, though rather statuesque in appearance, her movements were ungainly; though, too, her energy was unusually concentrated, in demeanour she was often vague and dream-like, and she would frequently enter some room, forget why she had come in and, after gazing round it in distraction for several minutes, be obliged to walk out empty-handed. She suffered also, this majestic-looking lady, from attacks of vertigo, which Lytton inherited, and after one such attack near Marble Arch was arrested by the police on suspicion of drunkenness. Her moods, too, were correspondingly unpredictable. Absent-minded and, like her husband, apparently unaware of what was going on around her for much of the time, she would all at once awake from her reverie and join in a discussion which the family had been carrying on in her presence for the previous hour, arguing her point of view with the most urgent and extreme passion, as if to make up for lost time.

Neither bohemian nor fashion-conscious, something of Lady Strachey's individual temperament was stamped on Stowey House and on the subsequent houses which the family were to occupy. For the children this lack of smartness was altogether delightful. They saw the overall dowdiness and confusion as a redeeming element – something human in the impersonal Victorian atmosphere – and took a ruthless joy in pointing out all the most blatant irregularities both to guests and to their mother. 'Our conventionality,' wrote Lytton, 'slightly mitigated by culture and intelligence, was impinged upon much more seriously by my mother's constitutional vagueness and immateriality, and by a vein in her of oddity and caprice. Her feeling for what was right and proper was unsupported by the slightest touch of snobbery; and, while it was very strong and quite unhesitating, it was surprisingly peculiar to herself. That her daughters should go into mourning for the German Emperor, for instance, appeared to her essential; but her own dresses were most extraordinary, designed by herself, quite regardless of fashion. She had all her children christened, but she never went to Church – except in the country, when she went with the utmost regularity. She was religious in the payment of calls; but the arrangements of her household, from the point of view of social life, were far below the standard.' From the point of view of domestic administration, her arrangements were more laborious than efficient, and amid the hubbub, the incessant *va-et-vient* of her large family, she would sit at her writing-desk littered with papers pursuing a slow and immensely elaborate system of household accounts.

The private education which Lady Strachey gave her sons and daughters was equally strange. Though they remained uninstructed and, in the case of the daughters at least, completely unenlightened regarding the facts of life, she read to them all the works of the bawdiest and most rollicking Elizabethan dramatists, together with such novels as *Tom Jones*, evidently unaware that they might be expected to comprehend only a fraction of what was going on. Many years later, however, when Lytton brought up the question of Shakespeare's sonnets, she sent two of his sisters – then in their twenties – out of the room, while she argued in favour of Shakespeare's purity, explaining to her silent and disbelieving son that the poet entertained no sexual feelings for the man whom he was addressing. Degradation and horror had no place in her life, and she somehow avoided coming into contact with the blood, lust and savagery of the Elizabethans of whom she was so fond. After all, she reasoned, it was only fiction; and between fiction and the facts of life there was a great salutary gulf for ever fixed. Her vivacious temperament responded automatically to their ribaldry, but they held for her no power of actuality. Similarly, she learnt long passages of Milton off by heart, and, enjoying the music of the poetry, paid not the least attention to the doctrines expressed in it. Despite being a freethinker, she liked to read South's sermons aloud to her children purely to give them an ear for rhythm in English prose. Literature, in short, might be an excellent recreation, but it could bear little intimate relation to her own and her family's lives. By the same token, for all the obvious pleasure she took in managing this large family, she remained extraordinarily ignorant of what any single one of them might be thinking or feeling. As a good and capable Victorian wife, she parodied on a smaller scale her husband's way of life, so that although she was keenly interested in public matters, together with Richard Strachey she presented a blank wall of unconscious indifference to the subjective problems of all her children.

2

ELEPHANTIASIS AND UNCLES

When Lytton was four years old the Stracheys moved from Stowey House to 69 Lancaster Gate, a rambling and portentous Victorian house just north of Kensington Gardens, where he was to spend the next twenty-five years of his life. 'My remembrances of Stowey House are dim and sporadic,' he wrote long afterwards in an unpublished essay which examines his early life in relation to the family and its heritage, '– Jim Rendel[5] with a penny in a passage – a miraculous bean at the bottom of the garden – Beatrice Chamberlain[6] playing at having tea with me, with leaves and acorns, under a tree. But my consecutive existence began in the nursery at Lancaster Gate – the nursery that I can see now, empty and odd and infinitely elevated, as it was when I stood in it for the first time at the age of four with my mother, and looked out of

5. James Meadows Rendel (1854–1937), Chairman of the Assam Bengal Railway and an expert on Poor Law administration, who married Lytton's eldest sister, Elinor.

6. Beatrice Chamberlain (1862–1918), the eldest daughter of Joseph Chamberlain and his first wife Harriet Kenrick, was a half-sister to Neville Chamberlain, later Prime Minister.

the window at the surprisingly tall houses opposite, and was told that this was where we were going to live. A calm announcement – received with some excitement, which was partly caused by the unusual sensation of extreme height, as I peered at the street below. The life that began then – my Lancaster Gate life – was to continue till I was twenty-eight – a man full grown – all the changes from childhood to adolescence, from youth to manhood, all the developments, the curiosities, the pains, the passions, the despairs, the delights, of a quarter of a century having taken place within those walls.'

A gloomy establishment, dark, badly planned, ugly both within and without, Lancaster Gate[7] filled Lytton with depression and discontent. He felt submerged by its solemn and prodigious bulk. The most remarkable aspect of the place was its physical size, which produced a lasting, nightmarish impression on the small child, difficult to convey in adult language. But it was not mere size alone which chilled him so, Lytton believed; 'it was size gone wrong, size pathological; it was a house afflicted with elephantiasis that one found one had entered, when, having mounted the steps under the porch, having passed through the front door and down the narrow dark passage with its ochre walls and its tessellated floor of magenta and indigo tiles, one looked upwards and saw the staircase twisting steeply up its elongated well – spiralling away into a thin infinitude, until, far above, one's surprised vision came upon a dome of pink and white glass, which yet one judged, with an unerring instinct, was not the top – no, not nearly, nearly the top.'[8]

Besides being of such gigantic proportions the Stracheys'

7. Today 69 Lancaster Gate is much altered. Though the shell of the building remains the same, the interior has been fused with the houses on either side and is unrecognizable. Since May 1959, the Stracheys' old home has been part of Douglas House, the large American Forces Club which now occupies Nos. 66–71 Lancaster Gate.

8. Lytton's unpublished autobiographical essay 'Lancaster Gate', written in 1922 for the Memoir Club, traces the influence of this house on himself as its long-term inhabitant. It is an attempt to spin out the web on which the pattern of his existence had been formed, and should be

new home was preposterously designed. There were, considering the vast area of space occupied, astonishingly few rooms. Lytton's father was the only member of the family to have a sitting-room of his own; while his daughters led an oddly communal existence in a tiny miserable apartment behind the dining-room, far higher than it was long or broad, and styled the 'young ladies' room'. For the boys there was not even this doleful sanctuary to withdraw into, and they enjoyed only the most precarious privacy. The house contained altogether seven layers of human habitation: a basement, a ground floor, and a drawing-room that filled out almost all the first floor and above which were placed four further floors of bedrooms. These were all small, of enormous height and, except for one on each floor that looked out on to the street, very dark, since there was no garden or even courtyard. So lugubrious indeed was the outlook from the two back rooms that the windows of most of them were made of pink and frosted glass, and their occupants never saw out of them at all. Borrowing an idea from her husband's office in the City, Lady Strachey had had 'reflectors' put up – vast plates of glassy material, slightly corrugated, which hung opposite the windows from chains. The actual windows themselves were so huge and cumbersome that no one could force them open, and little circular ventilators, working by means of cords and pulleys, had to be cut in the panes. All this created a weird impression on the young Lytton as he sat in his bedroom, dwarfed by its sombre altitude, or in the schoolroom at the end of the passage on the ground floor – the mammoth windows of pale ground glass with their complex machinery of string and ventilator, and a dim vision of discoloured yellow bricks, chains and corrugations looming through the London fog outside.

---

read as a truthful reconstruction not from the point of view of an estate agent's prospectus, but of his own psychological reactions to the place. He was always given to dramatic exaggerations of the circumstances of his life – as of other people's – and his magnification of Lancaster Gate (in contrast with which the proportions of every other house he lived in seemed tiny) came probably from an hysterical origin.

Apart from the universal height and darkness, there existed other alarming inconveniences. 'There was the one and only bathroom, for instance,' Lytton recorded, 'perched, with its lavatory, in an impossible position midway between the drawing-room and the lowest bedroom floors – a kind of crow's nest – to reach which, one had to run the gauntlet of stairs innumerable, and whose noises of rushing water were all too audible from the drawing-room just below.'

Already, by the late 1880s, it was obvious that the family was in decline. Now, as the Victorian age tottered towards its exhausted conclusion, and the first grumblings of serious reaction made themselves heard, they looked about and for the first time found themselves out of touch with the rising mood. But within the arid and forbidding precincts of Lancaster Gate everything remained as before, unchanged and unchangeable. Being invited there for the first time was an odd, sometimes even alarming experience, like stepping into another age, perhaps another world. The first chill was cast upon one by the butler who drew open the massive mahogany doors. Mercifully, there was more to him than met the eye. Uncouth and quite unpresentable – the promoted gardener's boy of Stowey House – Frederick was a gentle creature whose fearsome appearance, accentuated by a great mouth ill-concealed beneath his straggling moustache, belied his inner excellence. Later, he was replaced by a figure even more characteristic of the subtle *dégringolade* – Bastiani – 'a fat, black-haired, Italianate creature', as Lytton described him, 'who eventually took to drink, and could hardly puff up the stairs from the basement, and as he handed the vegetables, exuded an odour of sweat and whisky into one's face. He disappeared – after a scene of melodramatic horror – to be replaced by Mr Brooks who, we could only suppose, must have been a groom in earlier life, since all his operations were accompanied by a curious sound of *sotto voce* hissing.'

Hardly surprising, then, that the unprepared visitor would sometimes wonder whether he had strayed into an isolated colony of some undiscovered form of civilization, an Erewhon or Zuvendi. Conversely, the child who was brought up within

45

this drab mausoleum of a place took it for granted that here was the only world in existence. Indeed, Lytton hardly understood that anything else could be, though subconsciously he was aware that something was wrong with this world – that it was an unpleasant shape. An incubus descended upon his spirit as, gradually, the advanced state of decomposition infected the growing boy. His cheerfulness ebbed slowly away, his health mysteriously deteriorated. The disintegration of the home seemed to cast a physical and emotional spell on him.

The focal point of Lancaster Gate, which came to represent for Lytton the crowning emblem of a large family machine, was the monumental drawing-room. This great assembly hall, with its lofty eminence, its gigantic door, its glowing *portière* of pale green silk, its adumbrated sofas, instilled into him an almost religious awe. 'The same vitality, the same optimism, the same absence of nerves,' he wrote, 'which went to the deliberate creation of ten children, built the crammed high, hideous edifice that sheltered them. And so it was inevitable that the most characteristic feature of the house – its centre, its summary, the seat of its soul, so to speak – should have been the room which was the common meeting-place of all the members of the family – the drawing-room. When one entered that vast chamber, when, peering through its foggy distances, ill-lit by gas-jets, or casting one's eyes wildly towards the infinitely distant ceiling overhead, one struggled to traverse its dreadful length, to reach a tiny chair or a far-distant fireplace, conscious as one did so that some kind of queer life was clustered thick about one . . . then in truth one had come – whether one realized it or no – into an extraordinary holy of holies.'

Here, amid countless groups of relations and their friends, Lytton first grew mesmerized by the riddle of the Victorian age being played out before his eyes. If the drawing-room was a temple erected to the enigmatic spirit of Victorianism, its altar was undoubtedly the large, elevated and elaborate mantelpiece, an expanse of painted wood, designed by Halsey Ricardo, with pilasters and cornices and various marble and multicoloured tiles. Having reached this citadel through the waves of persons ebbing and flowing around it, one could see, from the vantage-point of a mottled hearth, that this was in no sense a romantic room. And yet there was something which continued to fascinate Lytton. It was not the size, or ugliness or absurdity of it alone which exerted so potent a spell upon his imagination, but the subtle way in which it expressed the whole complicated state of things. Like the age whose history will never be written, it was incredibly familiar to him yet at the same time even a little surprising, as though withholding perpetually some secret essential to his real understanding. 'Up to my last hour in it,' he later confessed, 'I always felt that the drawing-room was strange.'

By character and usage it was primarily a family room, built to contain not only Sir Richard and Lady Strachey and their ten children, but also all the other branches of the clan, in particular a large quantity of paternal uncles. The most senior of these, Sir Edward Strachey – the third baronet and father of St Loe Strachey, future editor of the *Spectator* – seldom left the fortified manor of Sutton Court in Somerset, behind whose walls he laboured gallantly at his *Materials to Serve for a History of the Strachey Family*. The second of Lytton's uncles, Colonel Henry Strachey, who had explored Tibet with Sir Richard and whose redoubtable tenacity was to carry him through to his ninety-sixth year, would, though blind, make his way up more frequently from Sutton Court, where for some time he acted as agent, and talk over old times with his brother. He was a very polite old gentleman, Lytton later remembered, and 'very dim, poor man, but his shoes exquisitely polished'. Yet another uncle, Sir John Strachey, who as finance minister to three successive Indian viceroys had fostered a measure for the introduction of metrical weights throughout India – a Trollopian edict that was never put into effect[9] – then, after disastrously underestimating the

9. The moving spirit behind this measure was in fact Lytton's father. See *Memorandum on the Introduction of Metric System in India* by Pitamber Plant, with a Foreword by Jawaharlal Nehru (Indian Government Publication, 1955). On the first page of this manual, the author remarks that Colonel R. Strachey's 'brilliant notes and memoranda (Appendices

cost of the war with Afghanistan, left India for England, visited Lancaster Gate regularly in the summer months from his house in Cornwall Gardens. He had by this time become a philosophic radical after the style of Mill, while, as an ardent supporter of Garibaldi, he spent his winters in Florence.

But perhaps the general state of decomposition which pressed in on Lytton as a boy was most strikingly embodied by his two junior uncles, William and George. Though both had shown signs of practical gifts when younger, their vein of pure eccentricity which, as an offshoot of thwarted creative talent – or the flower, perhaps, of originality gone to seed – was present in so many of the Stracheys, overran in time all traces of true ability. George, the youngest of all Lytton's uncles, had once possessed some aptitude for journalism and diplomacy, serving as H.M. Minister to the Court of the King of Saxony at Dresden. In his later years he contributed many articles to the *Spectator*, all of them decked in so richly prolix a style as to be unreadable. In the drawing-room of Lancaster Gate he presented Lytton with an exceedingly peculiar spectacle, 'bent double with age and eccentricity, hideously snuf-

B1, B2, B5), in particular his Minute of Dissent (B2) are classic in their quality, imbued with scholarship, practical wisdom and above all a noble earnestness which not only invokes admiration but inspires. No aspect of this complex subject has escaped his notice and none has received but the most patient and careful treatment. With ninety years separating his writings from now, it is remarkable that they are as much relevant and enlightening today, during our present consideration of the problem, as they were when the subject was in his care.' See also pp. 8, 20, 53–104. The combined labours of Sir John and Sir Richard Strachey had a strong and lasting influence over the policy and the constitution of the Indian Government in every department of affairs. Celebrated jointly in a Kipling poem, the two brothers had unrivalled opportunities, through a long course of years, of obtaining knowledge regarding India. In the Preface to the third edition of *India: Its Administration and Progress*, Sir John Strachey records that 'for many years we took part, often in close association, in its government, and it would be an affectation of humility to profess that this part was not an important one. There is hardly a great office in that state, from that of Acting-Viceroy, Lieutenant-Governor, or Member of Council downwards, which one or other of us has not held, and hardly a department of the administration with which one or other of us has not been intimately connected.'

fling and pouring out his opinion on architecture to anyone who ventured within his reach'.

The oddest uncle of all, however, was William Strachey. Notwithstanding his having lived in India only five years, and his association with the British Empire having been slight and undistinguished, he persevered in upholding Eastern customs with a far greater rigidity and finer disregard for common sense than any other member of the family. Having once visited Calcutta, he became convinced that the clocks there were the only reliable chronometers in the world, and in consequence kept his watch resolutely set by Calcutta time, organizing the remaining fifty-six years of his life accordingly. The results were often disconcerting for his friends and family in England. He breakfasted at afternoon tea and lived most of his waking hours by candlelight. On visits to Sutton Court, his strange nocturnal habits earned for him among the embedded Somerset folk an immense reputation in astrology. He had once bought a mechanical bed at the Paris Exhibition which upset the occupant at any appointed time of the morning. Using it for the first time, he was thrown out and into his bath standing next to the bed, and in a rage smashed the bed and clock, and resumed his old habits. At Lancaster Gate, his behaviour was equally memorable. During his youth he had been something of a man about town when, as he was probably well aware, his idiosyncrasies greatly enhanced his social prestige – though by now they were no longer assumed but had corroded their way into the very substance of his personality. He had been well known, too, at Holland House in the middle of the century, and having once exchanged the time of day with Palmerston, was now, in his later years, immoderately fond of attributing his own opinions to the late prime minister, introducing what he had to say with sentences commencing: 'I well remember Lord Palmerston once told me . . .' At the age of seventy he impressed his nine-year-old nephew Lytton as being an utterly fantastic figure, dressed always in spats and a coat and waistcoat of quaint cut and innumerable buttons – the very same that he might have worn in the forties – and, whatever the season or the prevailing weather conditions, attired in a pair of goloshes. When he died in his mid-eighties, he left Lytton a legacy consisting entirely of unworn and prettily coloured underclothes including 'some exquisite drawers or "pants" '.

But Lytton also owed much, in his tastes and capacities, to the Scottish side of his family. The Grants of Rothiemurchus traced their ancestry back to John Grant, Chief of Grant, who in 1539 had married Lady Marjorie Stuart, thereby making Lytton a potential claimant to the Scottish throne. The laird, Lady Strachey's eldest brother John Peter Grant, was rather remote from Lytton's London existence, but numerous other uncles and aunts often visited Lancaster Gate. Lytton's favourite was Uncle Trevor, a very friendly and uncomprehending fellow, married to a dusky native of India, Aunt Clementina, who was said to make chupatties on the drawing-room carpet. Together they brought up a large unfortunate family, the most unfortunate member of which ended his life being hugged by a bear. Besides Uncle Trevor, there was Uncle Bartle, a military gentleman who, on periods of leave from his regiment, edited a famous cookery book and compiled a learned volume on the orchids of Burma; Aunt Hennie, a most prominent and original figure who had been dropped on her head when an infant; and Uncles Charles and George who both had sons named Pat. 'White' Pat was presumed by the family to be a good character, 'Black' Pat a bad one, until, years later, 'White' Pat ran off with 'Black' Pat's wife. But most spectacular of all these material relations was 'Aunt Lell', the wife of Sir James Colvile. Two years older than Lady Strachey, she was utterly dissimilar to her – very sophisticated, a close friend of Robert Browning and a capable musician who had learnt the piano under Madame Schumann. Whenever Lady Strachey was away, Lytton would be left in the care of Aunt Lell 'a demi-lunatic, harmless and wonderfully funny', whose well-conducted social life, ebbing and flowing about her smart Park Lane house – so different from the knock-about regime of Lancaster Gate – immensely impressed him.

There was always at Lancaster Gate a large influx of these

uncles, their wives, children and friends, and of the other branches of the family in all their various combinations and permutations. But it was on Sunday afternoons, a time when the Victorian hostess particularly delighted to invite her guests and when Lytton's mother was invariably at home, that the family atmosphere, reinforced from without, reached its most bizarre pitch. 'Then the drawing-room,' wrote Lytton, 'gradually grew thick with aunts and uncles, cousins and connections, with Stracheys, Rendels, Plowdens, Battens, Ridpaths, Rowes. One saw that it had indeed been built for them — it held them all so nicely, so naturally, with their interminable varieties of age and character and class.' Since most of the Stracheys possessed peculiarly penetrating voices, and Lady Strachey's children inherited from her all the Scottish love of argument, the general volume of noise, the degree of turmoil and excited chatter on these weekly occasions was always terrific, and, though taken for granted by the family itself, bewildering for some of their more staid visitors. Despite the confusion which reigned over these gatherings, the British Raj was still very much in the air, while the multiplicity of sons and daughters, nephews and nieces, fathers and mothers and uncles and aunts was beyond computation, their striking resemblance to each other giving an effect of nightmare to the whole proceedings. On one such afternoon Bertrand Russell, whom Lady Strachey had met as a fellow member of a committee designed to secure votes for women, was invited to call. 'All the children', he records, 'were to my unpractised eyes exactly alike except in the somewhat superficial point that some were male and some were female. The family were not all assembled when I arrived, but dropped in one by one at intervals of twenty minutes (one of them I afterwards discovered was Lytton). I had to look round the room carefully to make sure that it was a new one that had appeared and not merely one of the previous ones that had changed his or her place. Towards the end of the evening I began to doubt my sanity, but kind friends afterwards assured me that things had really been as they seemed.'

At least as startling were the unannounced customs and the

51

general running of the house, to which all Stracheys, however sharply differentiated outside, unthinkingly conformed. Never before had any house acted as Lady Strachey's headquarters for more than a few consecutive years, and she had moved to Lancaster Gate with great regret. 'My ideal life', she once confided to Virginia Woolf, 'would be to live *entirely* in boarding houses.' And all the homes which she did inhabit rather resembled these establishments. When one of her sons or daughters invited a friend back to lunch, no one would pay the guest the very least attention. Innumerable Stracheys would sit in solemn silence round the dinner table, Sir Richard wrapped in a shawl at the centre of them reading a novel, and everything would proceed with a mysterious absence of human communication. Then, once the meal was completed, uproar broke out again.

The crowd of visiting relations was at its largest at about six every Sunday, and then it gradually thinned away. As at Stowey House, only the minimum of an appearance was kept up, and unless someone of importance stayed on, none of the family troubled to dress for the long and serious family dinner which followed at eight o'clock. The butler of the moment, assisted by a liveried boot-boy, waited upon them during these formidable sessions. 'At the end,' Lytton wrote, 'the three mystic bottles of port, sherry, and claret were put at the head of the table and solemnly circulated – the port, sherry, and claret having come from the grocer's round the corner.'

The rigours of formality and the excesses of communal inconsequence might be increased if, as often happened, someone did stay on – Sir Frederick Leighton, maybe, with his Olympian features and imposing manner of address, or Nina Grey with her faded airs of Roman Catholic aristocracy, or Fanny Stanley with her lodging-house garrulity, or even Mabel Batten, 'with that gorgeous bust on which the head of Edward the Seventh was wont to repose' – all of them carefully observed by the quiet, odd-looking youth whom they can seldom have noticed.

One of the most habitual visitors to Lancaster Gate during

these early years, Sir William Ward, was an amateur musician, and the memory of his several performances remained very vividly with Lytton all his life. Besides having been Governor of the Straits Settlements he was, Lytton explains, 'an executor, of astonishing brilliancy, on the pianoforte. Pressed to play, he would seat himself at the piano and dash into a Chopin waltz with the verve of a high-stepping charger, when suddenly a very odd and discordant sound, rising and falling with the music, would make itself heard. It was something between a snore and a whistle, and nobody could think what it could be. But the mystery was at last explained – the ex-Governor suffered, in moments of excitement, from a curious affection of the nose. While the family listened, a little hysterically, to this peculiar combination of sounds, all at once yet *another* sound – utterly different – burst upon their ears – the sound, this time, of rushing water. There was a momentary shock; and then we all silently realized that someone, in the half-way landing upstairs, was using the w.c.'

This admixture of heavy punctilio and extenuating farce, which made up the routine of life at Lancaster Gate, was unsettling to a sensitive boy such as Lytton; but it would be ridiculous to suggest that he was permanently miserable. To all outward appearances he was the very reverse, and his sisters remembered him as full of fun and laughter, 'giggling fairly continuously from the age of three to nineteen'. 'He indulged in all the customary jokes of childhood,' according to Pernel and Philippa Strachey, 'fanciful nicknames, endless conversations in dog French, acting, ragging, playing jokes on visitors, not practical but subtle and disconcerting. The round of fun was hectic and delirious, and Lytton's inventiveness seemed endless.' Yet, as in later life, his laughter and jokes were curiously segregated from the main tide of his feelings; they were cerebral, cut off from his darker emotions. His spirits bubbled brightly, but were cold to the touch. For beneath the bright surface of his gaiety, the clouds of tedium and aridity had already begun to thicken. 'It was not a question of unhappiness,' he explained, 'so much as of restriction and oppression – the subtle unperceived weight of the circumambient air.' The damp of the nineteenth century had entered into and warped his soul, causing a malady susceptible of no outright cure, but only a temporary relief when the mists of pessimism and loneliness would suddenly, miraculously, dissolve, the sun shine through and flood all his world with warmth and light. 'And', he wrote, 'there were moments, luckily, when some magic spring within me was suddenly released, and I threw off that weight, my spirit leaping up into freedom and beatitude.'

3

MARIE SOUVESTRE

The most free and pleasurable periods of Lytton's childhood were those he spent up in the Scottish Highlands. For many years his mother made a practice of taking her children up to the Doune,[10] the Grants' family home in Rothiemurchus, during part of the holidays. These were always happy excursions for Lytton, who found a deep satisfaction in escaping from the dank physiological oppression of Lancaster Gate, without any compensating chills of insecurity. He was like a bird suddenly released from behind the bars of its cage. Newly alive, he could go where he liked, do what he wanted. The old London life which had clung to him damply seemed to have crumbled to pieces like an old shell, a dried-up mould. He emerged from the dark recesses of Lancaster Gate like a butterfly liberated from its chrysalis, fluttering in the breeze over a fresh, wonderful universe of nature and sunlight. He never forgot this buoyant sense of liberation, and to the end of his life remained highly susceptible to the beauties of Rothiemurchus – 'its massive and imposing landscape, its gorgeous colouring, its hidden places of solitude and silence, its luxuriant vegetation, its wilderness of remote and awful splen-

10. The Doune was the home of the Grants the most celebrated of whom was Mrs Smith of Baltiboys, authoress of *Memoirs of a Highland Lady*. Her brother, Lady Strachey's father, Sir John Peter Grant, had modernized the house in the 1870s.

dour'. Though surrounded as usual by hordes of Grants and Stracheys, he could secure for himself here reasonable privacy, and he loved to take himself off for solitary, day-dreaming walks among the pine-woods and the mountains.[11]

An early diary shows Lytton on one of these summer holidays in Rothiemurchus playing on the grass with one of his cousins, eating strawberries ripe and fresh from the garden, riding ponies, dancing, playing cricket and robbers, vaulting streams and climbing the slopes of the Cairngorms. Altogether his time there comprised the mode of open-air, carefree and youthful living which he was to enhalo as an adult. In more easily recognizable sedentary moods he would listen to his mother as she recited to him extracts from the *Iliad*, and to his sister Dorothy reading from Walter Scott's *The Abbot*. And at other times he sat sketching the primeval forests and mountains or working out the puzzles which always fascinated him and with which his mother had a hard job to keep him supplied.

On other occasions, and more frequently as time went on, the family would rent a large country house for the summer in one of the Home Counties, Surrey or Essex, and here, amid a babble of young Stracheys, Lytton would play croquet and take an enthusiastic part in the amateur theatricals for which his mother and all her children cherished such an inordinate passion. But though he often enjoyed these country parties, they never cast the same happy spell over his imagination as the untamed hills and corries of the Highlands.

11. In his memoirs, *The Good Old Days* (1956), Lytton's cousin Patrick Grant wrote: 'During the summer months the house was packed, often with the whole Strachey family, my first cousins. Inspired perhaps by having read that famous book *The Fifth Form at St Dominic's*, Lytton Strachey and I decided we must produce and edit a magazine. Being almost unable to pronounce Dominican, I called it "The Domican". I have it still, and it represents, I think, Lytton's very first attemp[t]s at creative writing. Little did we guess that in the days to come he would become a famous author. His sister Pernel, afterwards I believe the Head of Newnham, was kind enough to write it out for us, and everyone, even including the butler, wrote stories or verses for it. Lytton's father, old Sir Richard, even painted a picture for us, but though it was a great success there was never a sequel to the first number.'

In the summer of 1886 Lytton was sent, with his younger sister Marjorie, to the Hyde Park Kindergarten and School at 24 Chilworth Street. Here he remained for some eighteen months, making excellent progress in all subjects, especially arithmetic. All his reports were good; he took a keen interest in his lessons and gave his teachers complete satisfaction. All in all he appears to have been a model pupil, and in the words of the headmistress, Miss E. Fisher Brown, 'worked exceedingly well and was very intelligent'.

In one of his earliest preserved letters, dated 7 May 1887, Lytton wrote to his mother: 'I have just begun French, it is very exciting. I know the French for Lion – it is Lion but pronounced differently. Marjorie smudged this letter.'

Lady Strachey, an ardent francophil, was delighted by this news. 'I am very glad you like French,' she answered; 'the further you go the more exciting you will find it. There are beautiful stories and books of all sorts in it.'

During the subsequent years Lytton's enthusiasm for French, and for the literature of France especially, grew under the active encouragement of his mother, who helped him to write French verses and often presented him on his birthdays with one of the French classics. She also saw to it that the first school which, indirectly, was to play a leading part in Lytton's early life and to help in shaping the course of his career, was a French girls' school near Wimbledon.

This state of affairs had come about in the following way. Many years earlier, while in Italy, Lady Strachey had met a Frenchwoman of great culture and distinction. Her name was Marie Souvestre, a daughter of the French writer Emile Souvestre – author of *Un Philosophe sous les Toits* – and she conducted a celebrated and fashionable school for girls at Fontainebleau, called Les Ruches. So impressed had Lady Strachey been by this woman's charm, stimulating intelligence and determination that those under her care should later go on to make their mark in the world, that soon afterwards she had sent her two eldest daughters, Elinor and Dorothy, to Les Ruches when they were each aged about sixteen. And when, shortly after Lytton was born, Marie Souvestre left France and became the headmistress-proprietor of Allenswood, at a little place named South Fields, not far from Wimbledon Common, both the younger Strachey daughters, Joan Pernel and Marjorie, were in due course entered there, while Dorothy was employed on the teaching staff, giving lessons on Shakespeare.

A brilliant and irreligious woman, Marie Souvestre was intimate with many of the radical and free-thinking set — John Morley, Joseph Chamberlain, Leslie Stephen, the Frederic Harrisons and numerous others. 'A remarkable woman,' Beatrice Webb described her in a diary entry for March 1889, 'with a gift of brilliant expression, and the charm of past beauty and present attractiveness. Purely literary in her training, and without personal experience of religious feeling or public spirit, she watches these characteristics in others with an odd combination of suspicion, surprise, and what one might almost call an unappreciative admiration. You feel that every idea is brought under a sort of hammering logic, and broken into pieces unless it be of very sound metal. If the idea belongs to the religious sphere and is proof against ridicule, it is laid carefully on one side for some future hostile analysis.'

The relationship between the Stracheys and Marie Souvestre during the 1880s and 1890s was very close. Comings and goings between Lancaster Gate and Allenswood were frequent, and sometimes the whole Strachey family spent part of their holidays at the school. Lytton, of course, was never enrolled as an official pupil of Marie Souvestre, but her influence on him was immensely important. During later adolescence, at a time when Lytton was bitterly critical of all mankind, 'cette grande femme', as he referred to her, was almost unique in that, throughout his often drastic and belligerent correspondence, he never once mentions her in a derogatory manner.

Of a naturally forceful personality, often galvanized into sudden, impulsive action, Marie Souvestre was approaching sixty when Lytton first got to know her, and was obliged to pay a certain amount of attention to her health. She was watched over with loving care by Mlle Samaia, a very tiny, dynamic woman who had been with her at Les Ruches, and whose adoration now took the practical form of seeing to it that she always breakfasted in her bedroom and was never vexed by having to look after the business side of running the school. Marie Souvestre was already by this time white-haired and rather stout. Her head was strikingly impressive, with clear-cut features, a strong almost masculine face, noble forehead and dark piercing eyes that hypnotized her pupils into imagining that she always knew exactly what was going on in their minds. She never married, appearing to find her emotional fulfilment in looking after her girls, many of whom served her well by distinguishing themselves in their later careers. To them she gave the whole of her emotive being, transforming the school into the very nucleus of her life. But she was by no means a typical headmistress, at least not by English standards. She entertained no veneration for outdoor sports, and proficiency in such pastimes left her cold. Games were encouraged at Allenswood solely as methods of exercise, designed to keep the body reasonably healthy. That was all. Unable to comprehend a deity who would pay any regard to such insignificant creatures as human beings, she was a declared atheist, a humanist and, in politics, fervently pro-Boer. And though she did not attempt to indoctrinate Lytton, it was not in her nature to conceal her strong feelings before adults or children.

Nor was Marie Souvestre scrupulously impartial in the attention she paid to her girls. Mrs Eleanor Roosevelt, who was a student at Allenswood during the 1890s, recalled that 'she had a very soft spot for Americans and liked them as pupils. This was not surprising as a number of her pupils turned out to be rather outstanding women.' In particular she was drawn to girls who were intelligent, attractive in appearance, or who possessed an instinctive appreciation for literature. Her voice, like Cordelia's, was 'soft, gentle and low, an excellent thing in woman', and she employed it with great feminine effect when reciting poems, plays or stories in French. Sometimes she would make the children read passages back to her. For her favourites, sitting on little chairs on either side of her library fireplace, the walls behind them lined with books and the room filled with flowers, and gazing forth on the wide expanse of lawn outside partially shaded from the heat of the sun by tall trees, these were moments of pure ecstasy, as they listened breathlessly to her voice and strove to imitate it. But those who were not similarly gifted would watch her striding up and down the room brandishing her pointer, and endure tortures as they waited with clammy hands and dry throats to make fools of themselves.

As the young and intelligent son of Lady Strachey, Lytton found himself automatically occupying a favoured position in Marie Souvestre's esteem, and he benefited enormously from the best that she, as the very embodiment of French culture, had to offer. The impression she produced on him was considerable and long-lasting. In the grace, the quick and witty brilliance of his literary style can be seen some reflection of her own peculiar charm and mental agility; while his views on public school education, his anti-religious convictions and his special feeling for French writers, in particular Racine, can be partly traced to her early influence. Dorothy, Lytton's elder sister, has given a vivid evocation of the emotional response which this ageing woman could still engender within a sensitive adolescent mind in her anonymously published novel, *Olivia*.[12] In this memorable book, Marie Souvestre is

12. *Olivia* by 'Olivia' (1949), the title of which was suggested by the Christian name of Dorothy's sister who died in infancy. The picture of Lancaster Gate and of Sir Richard and Lady Strachey which is given by Dorothy in the opening pages of this novel should be read with some care. Though outwardly friendly, there was a degree of antagonism between mother and daughter which arose from the fact that Dorothy had turned down several eminent offers of marriage and then become the wife of the indigent French artist Simon Bussy. Comparing Lady Strachey with aunt E. (Aunt Lell) who 'was sensitive to art to the very finger-tips of her beautiful hands, and successfully created about herself an atmosphere of *ordre et beauté, luxe, calme et volupté*', she presents her mother as being without taste, artistic or otherwise, and responsible for that solid comfort within Lancaster Gate from which 'the sensual element was totally lacking'. Her view, too, of Lady Strachey being 'perhaps incapable of the mystical illumination' and of her home being purely intellectual, may partly have been brought about by the fact that, alone of the family, Dorothy had no ear for music. So, when all the rest of them trooped off to a Joachim Quartet concert at St James's Hall, she

portrayed tenderly and with realism under the name of Mlle Julie, the joint principal of a girls' boarding school in France, Les Avons. On the first occasion that Mlle Julie makes her appearance, she is described giving a remarkable reading from Racine's *Andromaque*. 'I have heard many readers read Racine, and famous men among them, but I have not heard any who read him as well as Mlle Julie,' wrote Dorothy. 'She read simply and rapidly, without any of the actor's arts and affectations, with no swelling voice, with no gestures beyond the occasional lifting of her hand, in which she held a long ivory paper-cutter. But the gravity of her bearing and her voice transported me at once into the courts of princes and the presence of great emotions.'

After analysing the emotional excitement liberated in her by this characteristic recital, Dorothy concludes: 'What is certain is that it gave me my first conception of tragedy, of the terror and complication and pity of human lives. Strange that for an English child that revelation should have come through Racine instead of through Shakespeare. But it did.'

From another autobiographical passage in the novel, the reader is made to feel very forcibly the intoxicating enchantment which Marie Souvestre conveyed to all the Strachey family, and to understand the essential contrast in quality that lay between the influence of Lady Strachey — which, unsupported, might have led on to a subsequent reaction against literature in Lytton — and that of the French headmistress, which offered him further exciting adventures, and the revelation of a new heaven and a new earth. Despite her shrewdness and good sense, Lytton's mother had an extraordinarily ramshackle mind. The fashionable but limited social code under which she had originally been brought up remained a permanent obstacle to her capacity for absorbing any fresh ideas or unconventional emotions. Marie Souvestre, on the

---

was left alone in the house. The trouble continued: Simon Bussy was also unmusical, and so, perhaps as a result, was their daughter Janie. There was no piano at their home and no sound of music till fifty years later the radio set in, coinciding, oddly enough, with a late birth of musical interest.

other hand, was pleasantly free from any such inbred inhibitions, and she gave Lytton the promise of new, unknown aspects of life, appealing to something latent and undeveloped within him, something which lay crushed beneath the heavy, impersonal atmosphere of the family home. When she entered the drawing-room there and began to talk, everything changed and took on an added dimension, so that Lytton for the first time became aware of what he had always instinctively felt – that there existed somewhere beyond the boundaries of his home and his present knowledge an entirely different environment, far more congenial to his nature.

'I had no doubt been accustomed, or ought to have been accustomed, to good talk at home,' wrote Dorothy Strachey, comparing the atmosphere of Lancaster Gate with that of Les Ruches and Allenswood. 'But at home one was inattentive. . . . When one did listen to it, it was mostly political, or else took the form of argument. My mother and my aunt, who was often in the house, had interminable and heated discussions, in which my mother was invariably in the right and my aunt beyond belief inconsequent and passionate. We found them tedious and sometimes nerve-racking. My father, a man, in our eyes, of infinite wisdom and humour, did not talk much. . . . As for the people who came to the house, many of whom were highly distinguished, we admired them without listening to them. Their world seemed hardly to impinge upon ours.

'How different it was here! Mlle Julie was witty. Her brilliant speech darted here and there with the agility and grace of a humming-bird. Sharp and pointed, it would sometimes transfix a victim cruelly. No one was safe, and if one laughed with her, one was liable the next minute to be pierced with a shaft of irony. But she tossed her epigrams about with such evident enjoyment, that if one had the smallest sense of fun, one enjoyed them too, and it was from her that I, for one, learnt to realize the exquisite adaptation of the French tongue to the French wit.'

This description of Marie Souvestre's talk and personality might well serve as the basis for an appreciation of Lytton's mature prose style, and it conveys something of the enlivening zest with which she must have touched the growing boy. Her wit and cultivated intelligence 'capable of points of view, fond of the stimulus of paradox', communicated to him a burning literary exuberance never to be extinguished. 'To sit at table at her right hand', Dorothy summed up, 'was an education in itself.'

4

SPELLBOUND

Most of Lady Strachey's family inherited something of her love of letters; but in Lytton she soon recognized a boy of exceptional literary promise. Together the children composed copious quantities of verse, and Lytton would bring out programmes for the plays produced by his elder brothers and sisters, and illustrate their notebooks and magazines. His own first recorded quatrain was written at the age of five; and two years later he was busily engaged on an ingenious piece of poetry entitled 'Songs of Animals, Fishes and Birds'. He responded eagerly to his mother's inspirations, and with unusual application copied out the lyrics from Shakespeare, Marlowe and Blake which she taught him.

Versification was encouraged among the children as a hobby, and their best, most representative poems, which Lady Strachey collected together in a family book, are almost all playful, decorative pieces. But from among these many pages of light-hearted rhyming, one of Lytton's verses, written in April 1890, strikes an oddly discordant note. By any standards it expresses a strange and sombre sentiment for a boy of nine or ten – especially when one perceives that it is addressed to his sister who died in infancy.

> To me Life is a burden
>   But to thee
> The joyous pleasures of the world
>   Are all a gaiety.
>   But if thou did'st perceive my thoughts
>   Then thou would'st sigh and mourn,
>   Olivia, like me.

As in many large families, the children were encouraged to work in couples, and Lytton was usually paired off with his younger sister Marjorie. At one time or another he collaborated with her in producing a literary magazine, *The Gazelle Gazette*; a book of songs, *Carmina Exotica*; the beginning of a French comedy; and a play with a sea captain and a detective. A photograph of him taken at about the age of three shows a small figure gorgeously attired, chubby and with long dark locks reaching below his shoulders. For many years his mother dressed him in petticoats because she thought them prettier and less absurd than knickerbockers. In appearance he consequently resembled a girl more nearly than a boy, a peculiarity which is brought out by another photograph of the whole family, taken probably a year later, in which the likeness between Lytton and Marjorie is very striking.

Except for his mother and sisters there was no one towards whom he might turn for sympathetic companionship. The men in the Strachey household were either too old, or too remote and self-absorbed to have much personal contact with Lytton as a child. His elder brothers were seldom at Lancaster Gate. Richard John Strachey,[13] the eldest of all, was a commissioned officer in the Rifle Brigade, while Ralph Strachey,[14] having failed to get into the army owing to defective eyesight, ultimately became chief engineer in the East Indian Railway. The third son, Oliver Strachey,[15] was away for much of the year at Eton. In his daydreams, Lytton longed for a time when he too could play some part in these active, mas-

13. Richard John Strachey (1861–1935) became a colonel in the Rifle Brigade. In 1896 he married Grace, daughter of Field-Marshal Sir Henry Norman. They had no children.

14. Ralph Strachey (1868–1923) married Margaret Severs in 1901. Their first son is the novelist and writer of children's books, Richard Strachey. Their second son, John Strachey, is an artist and now lives in Antibes. Their only daughter, Ursula, who married Cyril Wentzel, an actor and barrister, was herself on the stage, and now works in the Foreign Office.

15. Oliver Strachey (1874–1960). Musician, civil servant and joint-author with his second wife, Ray Strachey, of *Keigwin's Rebellion* (1916). For his work in the Foreign Office and the War Office during both World Wars, where he was employed as their expert code-breaker, he was in 1943 awarded the C.B.E.

culine spheres of life, and for several years he kept a map on which he charted every movement which his brothers made about the world.

At home he still worshipped his father from afar, and was jubilant when, during the holidays, the old man occasionally took him to the circus, or to the Royal Naval Exhibition of 1891, or the Crystal Palace to see 'The Wonderful Performance of Wild Beasts', or even to inspect the *Stracheya tibetica* and other lesser botanical specimens at Kew. Sometimes on these expeditions, and greatly to his son's delight, Sir Richard Strachey would descend from his godlike silence into tomfoolery. Yet Lytton's filial veneration only emphasized the closer relationship for which he longed in vain and which, as an adult, he later tried to make good, tending in his friendships even with much younger men to become unnaturally dependent. Ironically, in his eagerness to attain a satisfactory companionship of mind and emotion, he would frequently act as his mother did towards himself – and with similar results. For he lavished on his most esteemed friends such a passionate intensity of adoration as to infect them with a feeling of guilt and inadequacy, even embarrassment, so that they shied away from his suffocating, alternately maternal and filial attentions. Years later, he was to write a letter to Maynard Keynes describing the total lack of affinity which then existed between himself and Professor Walter Raleigh: 'He [Raleigh] might be one's father.' The deplorable failure in human relationships could not, he felt, be expressed in more eloquent terms.

The prevailing atmosphere of femininity in which he grew up produced a definite retrograde effect upon Lytton's emotional development. While his mental faculties advanced swiftly, even precociously, his emotions were preserved in an almost static condition. An ingrained element of caution was nursed into a shrinking sense of shyness by the claustrophobic rigmarole of hushed literary dedication which was erected around him. He longed to join Oliver playing cricket, or teasing the peacock at the Doune, but his health, he was repeatedly reminded, was too fragile to permit anything so strenuous. His resistance to illness was certainly weak, and he was plagued by an unremitting succession of disorders throughout his life. But no one ever seemed to know what, fundamentally, was the cause of these maladies. As a child he was subjected to a variety of cures, each one more unsuccessful than its predecessor. At one time he was obliged to consume at every meal a plate of porridge; at another he was dosed with glasses of port; and for several months he was fed, almost exclusively, on raw meat. But, perhaps because his bad health was partly self-induced and not the result of a purely physical indisposition, no remedy, however farfetched, was to secure his lasting improvement.[16]

When he was nine years old Lytton was told by his mother that he was to be sent out of London to continue his education at a small private school on the south coast. The prospect filled him with a strange conflict of emotions – intense excitement and trepidation. He pined for the affection and comradeship of boys of his own age, and he yearned to escape from the onerous gloom of Lancaster Gate. Yet at the same time his pleasure was qualified by an opposing undercurrent of apprehension. Subconsciously, he already felt towards his family home something of the contradictory impulses of dependence and constitutional dislike. This ambiguous response remained with him and became more coherent throughout his life – even after he had left Lancaster Gate for ever. In the unpublished paper read to the Memoir Club in 1922, he reveals that during his adult years he persistently dreamt that he was back there again with all the family. Everything is unchanged. 'We are in the drawing-room, among the old furniture, arranged in the old way, and it is understood that we are to go on there indefinitely, as if we had never left it. The strange thing is that, when I realize that this has come about, that our successive wanderings have been a mere interlude, that we are once more permanently established at number 69, a feeling of intimate satisfaction

16. Lytton's illnesses seem to have started in his eighth year, after his younger brother James was born. They may well have been a means of attracting attention to himself.

comes over me. I am positively delighted. And this is strange because, in my working life, I have never for a moment, so far as I am aware, regretted our departure from that house, and if, in actuality, we *were* to return to it, I can imagine nothing which would disgust me more. So, when I wake up . . . I have the odd sensation of a tremendous relief at finding that my happiness of one second before was a delusion.'

The contrasting layers to his feelings which he describes in the recollection of these dreams exactly match his somewhat ambivalent attitude towards the Victorian age at large. Lancaster Gate, which became for him a personal symbol of Victorianism, also produced within him a deep sense of security. Its grim recesses inspired him neither with unqualified disapproval nor with real affection, but with an involuntary fascination comprising in part horror and in part an attachment which he never outgrew. A strong awareness of this redundant, rationally objectionable heritage was early ingrained into him. The huge, towering mansion exuded a faintly musty air of superannuated traditionalism; and many of the family embodied it – something indefinably antagonistic to youthful enjoyment, twisting and concealing the young boy's tastes and instincts.

It is only when a tradition is bankrupt that its efficacy is unduly insisted upon. The Stracheys of the late nineteenth and early twentieth century, many of whom displayed a tendency towards degeneracy and an increase of hereditary defects, schooled themselves in the past history of their family, placing special emphasis on those times when its prestige had stood highest – a practice which Lytton Strachey himself was for a short time to emulate. Some of his earliest letters, written at the ages of nine and ten, question his mother concerning details of the family pedigree. And she, after punctiliously filing this correspondence for posterity, would deal with each query at proper length.

The young tendrils of Lytton's creative spirit naturally sought the light of independence; but the conventional domestic society of the nineteenth century which had eclipsed his mother's artistic potential also cast its long last shadow over his own dawning imagination.

'What had happened', he told the members of the Memoir Club, 'was that a great tradition – the aristocratic tradition of the eighteenth century – had reached a very advanced state of decomposition. My father and my mother belonged by birth to the old English world of country-house gentlefolk – a world of wealth and breeding, a world in which such things as footmen, silver and wine were the necessary appurtenances of civilized life. But their own world was different: it was the middle-class professional world of the Victorians, in which the old forms still lingered, but debased and enfeebled, in which Morris wallpapers had taken the place of Adam pan-elling, in which the swarming retinue had been reduced to a boy in livery, in which the spoons and forks were bought at the Army and Navy Stores. And then, introducing yet another element into the mixture, there was the peculiar disin-tegrating force of the Strachey character. The solid bourgeois qualities were interpenetrated by intellectualism and eccen-tricity ...

'Disintegration and *dégringolade*, no doubt, and yet the total effect, materialized and enormously extended, was of a tremendous solidity. Lancaster Gate towered up above us, and around us, an imperturbable mass – the framework, almost the very essence – so it seemed – of our being. Was it itself, per-haps, one vast filth-packet, and we the mere *disjecta membra* of vanished generations, which Providence was too busy or too idle to clear away? So, in hours of depression, we might have unconsciously theorized; but nevertheless, in reality, it was not so. Lancaster Gate vanished into nothingness, and we survived.'

But while it lasted, the notion that this regime would, in the course of things, come to an end was for Lytton a dreadful idea and one not to be contemplated – like death itself. By the time the family's diminished income eventually brought about this catastrophe, it no longer mattered. The house had already cast its inextinguishable mesmeric spell upon him, so that, wherever he might travel, the same dream, only slightly varying in its details and always transporting him back within the sombre walls of Number 69, recurred with a curious iteration. Even at the age of nine the chance of moving beyond its encircling orbit was faintly disturbing. What lay beyond? What would, what *could* happen, when he went away from Lancaster Gate?

TWO

'Funny Little Creature'

'At school, friendship is a passion. It entrances the being; it tears the soul. All loves of after life can never bring its rapture, or its wretchedness; no bliss so absorbing, no pangs of jealousy or despair so crushing and so keen! What tenderness and what devotion; what illimitable confidence; infinite revelations of inmost thoughts; what ecstatic present and romantic future; what bitter estrangements and what melting reconciliations; what scenes of wild recrimination, agitating explanations, passionate correspondence; what insane sensitiveness, and what frantic sensibility; what earthquakes of the heart, and whirlwinds of the soul, are confined in that simple phrase – a schoolboy's friendship!' *Benjamin Disraeli,* 'Coningsby'

1
SEA AIR

LADY STRACHEY was determined that her sons and daughters should all distinguish themselves in their chosen careers. Yet, in spite of her lifelong addiction to literature, she remained, in the words of her daughter Dorothy, 'strangely devoid of psychology and strangely unconscious of persons'. Nowhere were these defects more incongruously expressed than in her efforts to arrange for Lytton an expedient education. She appreciated that, as a boy delicate in health and of a sensitive and impressionable mind, he might need special attention. But what that attention comprised she was never really sure. She seems to have been partly swayed in her judgement by the educational history of Lord Lytton, Lytton Strachey's godfather, whom she had first met in India a few years prior to her son's birth.[1] Their common love of literature had

1. Mary Stocks, whose family was closely associated with the Stracheys, puts forward an interesting speculation about Lytton Strachey's parent-

initially brought them into close contact, and as time went on they had become on increasingly confidential and affectionate terms. In an attempt to analyse her great admiration for him she once wrote: 'He was extremely unconventional, and not having been brought up at a public school, or in ordinary English society, was quite unable to understand the importance attached to conventionalities by the ordinary English public.' Undoubtedly she wanted Lytton to enjoy a similar enlightenment, and even to pursue a career comparable to that of the great Indian viceroy and poet.

Lytton was first sent, probably in the summer term of 1889, to a Mr Henry Forde, who took in a few boys for private teaching at his house at Parkstone, on Poole Harbour in Dorset. Here he was coached for the entrance examinations to the ordinary public schools, one of which, it was thought, he might attend once his stamina had sufficiently improved. His mother appears to have strongly believed at this time in the beneficial effects of Victorian 'sea air', and during the holidays, when the family did not go up to Rothiemurchus, she would make sure that Lytton visited some seaside resort, usually Torquay or Dover and once to Broadstairs where Lytton 'taught the waiter how to fold a napkin!' He remained at Parkstone, with one interval spent in travelling abroad, until the summer of 1893, and although he must have inhaled more recuperative ozone during these four years than throughout the rest of his life, no remarkable improvement in his general condition resulted from it.

Henry Forde was a rather pretentious, Dickensian character, extravagantly obsequious and literary-minded. He was harried continuously by an invalid wife, Grace, who resented the rival claims of her husband's few pupils to ill-health. 'What a trial the boys are, Henaree!' she would complain to him. 'Why don't you *whip* them?' The school reports which were

---

age: that he was not a Strachey at all but a Lytton, the illegitimate son of his godfather. See *My Commonplace Book* by Mary Stocks (Peter Davies, 1970). But Vincent Rendel describes this (*Times Literary Supplement*, 11 December 1970) as 'malicious nonsense' which he adds 'has not even found its way into "Holroyd".'

sent to Lady Strachey during these years sometimes contain more information about their own son who, in contrast to the sickly Lytton, was, they boasted, 'roughing it' at a boarding school at Tonbridge. A few of Henry Forde's comments on Lytton, however, are of interest. 'I do not consider Giles behind the average of the ordinary boy at his age,' he wrote (December 1890) to Lytton's mother, who was worried lest his repetitive illnesses and inability to study for long consecutive periods might prove too great a handicap to his scholastic progress, 'indeed I think he is rather in advance of it; but he is much behind what a boy of his powers should have reached, *if* he had had health.'

Most of the coaching which Lytton received at Parkstone was devised specifically to enable him to answer the type of question posed by the average examination paper of those days. Generally speaking, though he did not excel in the Classics as Henry Forde had thought he would, and though he developed a faculty for rapidly forgetting the technicalities of grammar, his progress was very satisfactory. In spite of the academic limitations imposed on his studies, many of the stylistic qualities later to characterize his biographical and critical writings were already in the process of being formed, and his literary flair soon made itself apparent. 'It would not at all surprise me, if he were to become literary,' Henry Forde told Lytton's mother shortly after his twelfth birthday, 'I do not mean merely fond of letters – that he is sure to be – but a contributor to them, a writer. He has an ear for, and a knack of hitting off queer and picturesque phrases and turns of expression, and I could quite easily fancy his developing a marked style of his own in the future, and one that would "stand out". He is a distinctly unusual and original kind of boy; and I should think had best be let develop his own way; his education should be chiefly directed to giving him help to evolve himself, not to forcing him into ordinary moulds. Owing to his bid-able-ness and – one must at present say – his timidity, he might be easily moulded after the average standard, with the result I believe of docking and thwarting what is special in him.'

Despite often looking pale and tired, Lytton seemed in good spirits for much of his time at Parkstone. He got on well with the other boys, and was usually glad to see them again after the holidays were over. He must have presented them with a curious spectacle on first acquaintance, and one not easy to accept. Tall for his age but terribly thin, he was habitually reserved in his manner. To match his odd appearance he had inherited more than a fair quota of the Strachey eccentricity, which he was already quite capable of exploiting both in what he did and what he wrote. This was soon recognized even within the family itself. 'When I read James the superscription of your letter,' Lady Strachey wrote to him on one occasion (1892) referring to his five-year-old brother, 'he said, "I know that's from Lytton, he's always so absurd"; and when he heard the contents he exclaimed, "He *is* a funny little creature!" '

While at Parkstone, Lytton entered clamorously into all the small school's activities. In his letters home, there are accounts of 'delightful bathes ... I can swim a little' (9 July 1893); of sailing in a big boat called *The Lulu*, striking a rock in the sea, and being stuck there till rescued at nine o'clock at night; of watching 'Mr Gladstone in a tug-boat going to pool. They actually rang the church bells!' (16 June 1889); of playing a 'lovely game of going round the room without touching the floor; it makes one get into a fever' (15 December 1889); of listening politely to Mr Forde as he read *Gulliver's Travels* — 'it is rather sickening but it can't be helped' (2 February 1890); and of starting 'a Small Naval and Military Exhibition which I hope will be a success' (7 June 1891).

He seems to have been particularly striking in the school's plays, which included a boisterous production of *Blue-Beard*, and several Shakespearian tableaux — Lytton playing Romeo in one, while in another 'I was Othello with my face blackened and a pillow and Cecil in bed being smothered'. His impersonation of female parts was especially convincing and sometimes well exploited in real life, as a letter to his mother on 27 March 1892 — written like an entry in *The Diary of a Nobody* — relates:

'On Sunday Dora was going to the Thompsons so she dressed me up in her short skirt and Mrs Forde's fashionable cape, bonet and she also put her boa round my neck wich hid my short hair behind we then went to the Thompsons and I was introduced by the name of Miss Miller – a friend of Dora's. After a little Mrs Thompson recognized me but as Mr Thompson had not come in yet so I was arranged with my back to the light. Soon Mr Thompson came in with a friend of his called Mr Pike, he is very frightened of ladies, so when the two entered I was introduced to them they were both unaware of what was going on. Soon the *whole* room was in suppressed laughter and the *unfortunate* Mr Pike didn't know what to do he grew redder and redder in the face and from red to purple and from purple to – I don't know what at last Miss Webb, perceiving his embarrassment said, "I think you'd [better] examine Miss Miller more carefully" – so he did – and then of course he recognized me.'

Though Henry Forde reported that Lytton 'eats with capital appetite' and did some 'spirited painting', his mother was disappointed with his continuing infirmity, and became fearful that he would fall behind in his work if he stayed too long at Parkstone. During the summer holidays of 1892, which the whole family spent at Holywell House near Wrotham, she told Lytton that she was arranging for him to go on a five-month stay with Uncle Charlie in Gibraltar, so that he would be able to inhale deeper and stronger quantities of 'sea air' and, even more important, escape the worst part of the English winter. He returned to Parkstone in September full of suppressed excitement which he communicated in a more ebullient form to the other boys.

This voyage did not start until nearly four months later, when, two days before Christmas, he and his sister Dorothy set sail on board the *Coromandel*. A diary which he now started tells how he began to feel seasick a few miles out of port, but effectively cured himself by drinking champagne – a tip given him by his father before embarking. Soon they reached Gibraltar, and Lytton noted that 'with the aid of spectacles I could see what the place looked like. All the houses were like toy houses scattered about the rock and to complete the smallness, the water became filled with little toy boats.'

Having 'affected a landing successfully', they went to live for the next month with their uncle, Charles Grant, a captain in the Black Watch; his wife, 'Aunt Aggie'; and their son, 'Black Pat' – a 'horribly snouted and absurdly mendacious' little boy of about the same age, with whom he got on very well. 'It is perfectly lovely here,' Lytton informed his mother. 'All kinds of flowers are in bloom, there are roses and oranges!' Together the two boys spent a delightful time, driving around the place in a cab 'like a four post bed', going to parties, playing bezique, climbing trees, inspecting the guns in the public park, watching football matches and the soldiers parading about the barracks, and being taught the Highland Fling by a Scottish piper named Smith. In company with Pat's mother and father, the two boys also crossed over into Spain where they visited an empty but 'most interesting' bull ring, after which they would play each morning at bull fights – 'We squat on the ground,' Lytton explained to his mother, 'and charge against each other.'

At the end of January the Black Watch was moved to Egypt, and Lytton travelled with the regiment on board the troopship H.M.S. *Himalaya*, reading and playing quoits for most of the passage, and attired in a diminutive variant of the Highland costume which occasioned favourable comment from the officers and men. At Alexandria, which Lytton disliked, they disembarked, travelling on by train to Cairo. The three weeks they spent here were among the happiest of the whole journey. The unfamiliar carnival atmosphere appealed enormously to Lytton's romantic imagination. The streets and buildings seemed like illustrations from some fabulous story book suddenly and mysteriously brought to life. 'It is a delight here,' he told his mother (6 February 1893). 'We don't know what is going to happen to us.' He explored the bazaars, the museums, the tomb of the Mamalukes, the Citadel Mosque, and Joseph's well, down which he and Pat dropped stones. The two boys went everywhere on donkeys

74

which were even more novel than four-post-bed cabs. 'The donkeys flew and I greatly enjoyed myself,' Lytton noted after his first ride. 'These donkeys would be priceless in England, they hold their heads up and never think of stopping till they are told to and even then sometimes they won't.'

One of the sights which Lytton had been particularly anxious to see were the Pyramids. 'Vast and grand and towering above all things near them, they rose against the blue sky solemn and majestic,' he wrote in his diary; but with the perverse taste of all children he appeared much more impressed by the modern hotel near by at which he stayed for a time – 'the most beautiful in the world' as he described it. His good opinion of the Pyramids revived however after a hectic expedition which the party made to inspect them close at hand. 'We were surrounded by Arabs,' he narrated, 'and one seized each arm and hauled us up the pyramid. The steps are from three to four feet high. My two Arabs helped me along very well and I rested two or three times during the ascent. ... Coming down was easier than going up I thought, but other people didn't. I simply jumped from step to step, the Arabs holding my hands.'

Almost immediately after this perilous ascent they were off again, this time to examine the Sphinx, whose feline, enigmatic expression, impenetrable as God, obviously fascinated Lytton. The account which he gave at the time of this excursion is especially interesting, since, being less well integrated than his adult-writing yet containing many of the same essential qualities, it shows the various individual strains which went to make up the composite pattern of his mature literary style – the wonderfully comic vision; the dramatic narrative gift; and the romantic and rhetorical rhapsodizing which, slightly over-pitched, never quite brings off the ambitious effect for which it strives. 'Aunt Aggie', he recounted, 'said she thought it would be a good idea to go to the Sphinx on camels, directly she mentioned this word fifteen camels were on us, all making the most awful noise when sitting down. We were all seized by at least four men who pulled us in four different directions. I got to a Camel and an Arab said it was a lady's one, which it was not, so I was hussled off and two men came and lifted me into the air and put me on a camel, at this moment the sheik interfered and I got on to the one that was supposed to have had a lady's saddle. It was a rather ghastly sensation when the camel got up and you thought you were going to tumble off. We walked on our camels to the Sphinx where we dismounted and walked to a place just opposite its face. Although its nose had entirely gone it looked as if all its features were there. What an exquisite face it is – how solemn – how majestic you look, your eyes looking out into the desert with that beautiful expression always on your face, so collosal and so perfect. You, who have been there for thousands and thousands of years, you, who have gazed and gazed at that endless sea of sand ever since you existed, tell me, oh! tell me how to look with that sublime expression on your face at all that comes and all that goes, careless of everything for ever.'

This single visit to the Sphinx seems to have produced a lasting impression on Lytton's mind. As he gazed up into the staring eyes of this strange, bland idol and wondered at the mystery that lay behind them, the first whisper of a poem went through him. Not composed in its final form until several years later, 'The Cat' remains the only one of his many verses to have been posthumously anthologized.[2] Looking into the great cat's eyes, he subsides into a demi-dream and is filled with a sense of exquisite enchantment, an almost mystical heightening of awareness:

> An ample air, a warmer June
> Enfold me, and my wondering eye

2. 'The Cat' was first printed on 12 June 1902 in the Supplement of the *Cambridge Review*, p. xxiii and signed 'G.L.S.' Subsequently it was reprinted in *Euphrosyne* (1905), an anthology anonymously compiled by Clive Bell. It has appeared more recently in Mona Gooden's *The Poet's Cat* (1946), and in *A Dictionary of Cat Lovers* (1949), an exhaustive symposium edited by Christabel Aberconway, containing scholarly notes on the 'Cat in Ancient Egypt', and on the belief in the sun and moon's influence upon the eyes of the cat. In these later publications, the word 'pagan' in the opening line of the second stanza quoted above has been changed to 'northern'.

Salutes a more imperial moon
  Throned in a more resplendent sky
Than ever knew this pagan shore.
  Oh, strange! For you are with me too,
And I who am a cat once more
  Follow the woman that was you.

Towards the end of February, Lytton left Cairo and returned by train to Alexandria. 'How interesting it's all been,'
he commented in his diary. 'How glad I am I came to Egypt and
saw all these wondrous sights.' To his great satisfaction he
remained in Alexandria only twenty-four hours, and then, on
27 February, embarked once more on the *Himalaya*, arriving
during the afternoon of the following day at Port Said. By 1
March, his thirteenth birthday, he was sailing along the Suez
Canal, suffering under the intense heat but thoroughly relish-
ing the sensation of celebrating a birthday at such an unexpected place. 'My birthday today,' he wrote, '– how odd – a
birthday in the Suez Canal. . . . Every now and then we pass a
little red-brick house with a brown roof and green trees
growing round it, they look so pretty. At 4 p.m. we arrived at
Suez, a wee town on the edge of the desert. We couldn't have
the birthday cake today as it was not iced.'

The *Himalaya* stopped long enough at Suez for Lytton to
watch a cricket match, collect some shells and ride a few more
donkeys. Then they were all off again, this time to Aden which
they reached in the second week of March. Here Lytton occupied himself with wandering through the exotic camel market
'crowded with camels in different attitudes', throwing stones
at an octopus and coins into the water for the little black
boys who 'dived down and brought up the sixpences in their
mouths, they swam exquisitely and were quite at home in
the water as in their boats'.

The party then continued its journey on to Mauritius, putting up at the town of Curepipe for two days of incessant
rain. Lytton was not impressed. 'The hills', he recorded, 'were
most extraordinary, they looked as if they were going to fall
down every minute, they were not at all grand, but looked
drunk and misshapen.'

77

Cape Town, on the other hand, where the *Himalaya* arrived on 23 April, was properly symmetrical, altogether better balanced and more pleasing. 'It is a most magnificent place,' Lytton decided, 'with palacial buildings and shops worthy of Bond Street but it is very small, everything is next door to everything else.' The six weeks which he now spent in Cape Town were tremendously exciting. His days were passed in climbing the slopes of Table Mountain which was 'exquisite and looked just as I'd expected it to be', setting off on fishing trips, playing croquet and billiards – at which he considered he had done exceedingly well whenever he failed throughout the entire course of a game to rip the cloth – and, helped by his cousin Pat, bringing out with the utmost industry an illustrated magazine, *The Comet*, which, he declared, was 'a great success, with poems and stories'.

Lytton's natural gift for treating grown-ups as his equals caused him to be made the hero of a farewell party given by the officers of the Black Watch, with whom he had spent so much of the voyage.[3] On 12 May, shortly before he was due to return to England, both he and Pat received an invitation to dine at the Mess. Lytton was attired for the occasion in 'my best Etons and a white waistcoat and a black tie'. Neither of them was allowed any alcoholic drinks throughout the evening, except to toast Queen Victoria's health, and so had to content themselves with lemon squash. After the Queen's health had been drunk, and much to the two boys' astonishment, the officers rose again to their feet. 'We did not know in the least what was happening,' Lytton confessed, 'and were going to follow their example, when they told us to sit down. Capt. Gordon then said, "I beg to propose the health of the Rt. Hon. Prime Minister Lytton Strachey and Field-Marshal Sir Patrick Grant!" "Hear, hear" was heard from several voices – soon afterwards we went into the anteroom.

'... Then it was discovered that it was very late and that if we did not hurry we should miss our train; so we hastily put on our coats and dashed out, Arthur Marindin accompanying us. As we left we were cheered by the officers! We ran

3. Dorothy Strachey had returned to England several weeks earlier.

with all speed to the station, my tie streaming in the breeze!'

A few days later Lytton sailed for England. He had thoroughly enjoyed being privileged to peep behind the scenes of military life.[4] Altogether his five months abroad, with their aura of heat and their perpetual stimulus of fresh excitement and companionship, comprised a carefree liberating interval in the dull routine of childhood – one which helped to quicken his lifelong passion for travel. 'I enjoyed the voyage very much indeed,' the final entry in his diary runs, 'it was so entertaining and interesting – oh! it is like some beautiful dream.'

2

'GLAD DAY, LOVE AND DUTY'

It was not long before Lytton was dropped back again into the greyness of Lancaster Gate. In the second week of June, he returned to Parkstone, where rumours of his adventures about the world had already made him a hero with the other boys. But for himself, the novelty was over, and the subsequent re-entry into the alternating routine of home and school palled on him. Mr Forde soon noticed a marked change both in his state of health and of mind. 'He certainly does look grown in every way: his cheeks are quite plump', he wrote to Lady Strachey. 'I am rather surprised to see that he is not at all tanned by the suns and seas of his journey. He bears his return to humdrum work and life like the philosophical boy he is; set to at his Virgil this morning as if he had only left off the day before, and is taking the ovation the boys are giving him – and which seems likely to continue for days, like a Roman Triumph – with dignity and as if it too were quite in its place and to be expected, and altogether is possessing his soul in blandness and calm. He is a most admirable boy.'

4. A few weeks later, Lytton became highly indignant on learning that his uncle was resigning his commission and returning to civilian life. 'I am most disgusted with Uncle Charlie for leaving the army', he announced to his mother.

Lytton's mother had also observed a general toughening in her son's physique and a consolidation of his air of quiet self-reliance. She was now determined that he·must be removed from the educational backwaters of Parkstone and sent off to a larger, more cosmopolitan institution. By August she had made the necessary arrangements, and informed Henry Forde that Lytton would not be returning to his care. 'We are very, very sorry to part with Giles,' he replied; 'we have all grown really fond of him. *I* also think it will be best for him, as he has grown so much stronger, to try his wings in a wider sphere, and more robust air . . .'

Lytton himself was not sorry to leave. Though he liked and got on well with some of the other boys, he had no great opinion of Henry Forde, and still less of his sickly complaining wife. Parkstone, it appears, was not much of a place. 'There is a dead mouse under the schoolroom I think, because of the dreadful smell — so bad we can't write our letters there!' After almost five years he was bored with it all, and looked forward to joining a real school. Had he known, however, the type of rigorous and unrelenting character-building to which he was shortly to be subjected, he might have viewed this new phase in his life with more alarm.

The New School, Abbotsholme, to which Lytton was sent in September, described itself as an advanced 'Educational Laboratory' which aimed at producing wholesome, healthy citizens by what was known as 'the natural method'. Despite the well-publicized modernity, no day-boys were admitted within its sacred precincts since, it was believed, they tended to befoul the moral climate of a school. For similar reasons it was not thought proper to develop the place as a co-educational academy, and it was modelled, for the most part, on nothing much more adventurous than the public-school tradition. Founded only four years previously by Dr Cecil Reddie, it originated what for a time was known as 'The New School Movement', and was the progenitor of the better-known Bedales, and the Landerziehungsheime Schule of Germany, respectively under Dr Badley and Dr Hermann Lietz, both of whom were temporarily assistant masters at Abbotsholme. Among its indirect but conspicuous offspring were L'Ecole des Roches, Salem and Gordonstoun.

For Lytton, Abbotsholme was a strange choice, and one that ran contrary to the excellent advice proffered some years earlier by Henry Forde.[5] For here, if anywhere, he ran the risk of being moulded after the average standard. Innovations there were in plenty, but they were more naïve than enlightened. The prospectus issued that year should in itself have sounded in Lady Strachey's ears an ominous warning. 'The aim', one passage ran, 'is to provide an ideal home and life for the sons of parents who can afford to have the best for their boys' physical, mental, and moral welfare, and who realize that Education spells Empire.' The fees amounted to about fifty pounds a term, but added charges were imposed on those parents whose children were found to possess certain deficiencies. These extra sums were in the nature of vicarious penalties, fines levied against parents as a reminder that 'the School is intended for boys who are in all respects normal'.

It seems likely, however, that Lady Strachey was persuaded in favour of Abbotsholme by the hypnotic personality of Dr Reddie himself. She was introduced to him by Charles Kegan Paul,[6] a mutual friend who, after serving as an assistant master at Eton, had been appointed one of the trustees of the New School. As founder and headmaster of Abbotsholme, Reddie was in all ways its moving spirit. A dynamic figure of sturdy proportions, stern, with piercing eyes and a thundering

5. There had been some question of sending Lytton to Eton, but Lady Strachey decided against this partly, it seems, because of her elder son Oliver's failure there, a love-letter from another boy having been discovered in his rooms. As an adult, Oliver was completely heterosexual and something of a womanizer – 'the most orthodox of all of us', as James Strachey described him.

6. Charles Kegan Paul (1828–1902) had been Vicar of Sturminster until 1874, when he was converted to publishing. He translated a number of books from the German and French, edited the letters of Mary Wollstonecraft and wrote a life of Godwin. His last publication was a volume of memoirs. In 1856 he had married Margaret Colvile, and was related, through marriage, to one of Lady Strachey's sisters.

flow of talk, he was worshipped by many of his pupils and held in extreme terror by others, including the teaching staff, none of whom – except the biology master – was permitted to marry. He was six foot tall, but rather stocky, owing apparently to his legs, which were shorter than they should have been. His autocratic assurance of manner and fierce idealism concealed from many the crankiness of his schemes for re-moulding national life, and producing from the gymnasium at Abbotsholme a higher type of human being. He was a man, or so he believed, whose mission was to rescue late Victorian England from degeneracy, by repopulating the country's key positions with Old Abbotsholmians. Lytton must have seemed poor material for such a grandiose plan of social reconstruction. But Dr Reddie, still in the experimental stages of building up what he defined as his 'organization of a normal tertiary (higher secondary) school for English boys of eleven to eighteen belonging to the directing classes', was anxious to amass the references of as many influential parents as possible, so that even the most unlikely specimen from a distinguished Anglo-Indian family was for him a welcome prize.

To appreciate exactly what Lytton experienced at Abbotsholme and how this may have contributed to his strong views both on the public-school system and on the genus of stern educational reformers – as later exemplified by the third essay of *Eminent Victorians* – something of the particular methods instigated by Dr Reddie should be explained. Initially he had based his ideas of a reconstituted society on the writings of Disraeli, Carlyle and Ruskin. But it was in Germany, he confessed in his familiar regal style, that 'notwithstanding our English prejudices, we at once observed strong evidence of superior intellectual life and social order'. In Germany too, he had first decided to put his theories of citizen-training into operation. As a schoolmaster, he had made a thorough study of 'Boy Nature' and convinced himself that he could divert the downward course of England's national life by incorporating with the ground plan of the public-school system those influences which modern culture and the up-to-date needs of society had shown to be desirable. By these far-seeing means, he was convinced that he could mould the pattern of a new English master race. Though many of the innovations which he planned were thought to be scandalously *avant-garde,* the main concept of his educational scheme was reactionary — to resurrect the legacy of more wholesome and puritanical days.

Dr Reddie was, in short, a Utopian, and the Abbotsholme of his dreams largely an empty fantasy. His ideal boys were to be cultural athletes, glorified all-rounders, who cast no shadows in the real world and who were divested of everything which vexes the spirit in its partnership with the flesh. Yet there was a morning light on his miniature experimental colony which gave it a pastoral charm lacking in most of the clinical Utopias. To keep alive this glow, reflected from the pure flame of his idealism, Dr Reddie sought out an idyllic setting: 'We must place first and foremost', ran his opening manifesto, 'the magnificent position of the school amid unparalleled scenery — mountains and sea, woods and fields, and gorgeous skies, with its spectacle spread out before us of one of the loveliest cities in the world. Next we must place the spacious grounds and stately buildings, an atmosphere of dignity and culture, and a free and open life. Such was the place.'

But it was within the building, and especially within the chapel, that Dr Reddie's spirit of sternly-checked emotionalism was most faithfully echoed. Here the corbels were carved with the heads not of saints but of redoubtable men of action and vision — Nelson and Shakespeare — while from the wall shone a five-pointed star, Solomon's seal, the sign of wisdom. Behind a simple altar cross (and in these post-Freudian days concealed by curtains from the public gaze) stood the statue of a naked youth transfixed in a Blakean pose. 'It was Dr Reddie's attempt to express something of his faith in his boys,' wrote a later headmaster, 'of their power to rise to great heights by truth and self-dedication.' In more secular matters he endeavoured to encourage these latent qualities by what he described as 'natural methods'. These 'natural methods' permeated the school, influencing even the most necessary and inevitably natural functions of the boys.

For on the question of lavatorial procedure, as on everything else, Dr Reddie held decided views. He dispensed with the decadent water-closet altogether, and reintroduced what he conceived to be the more natural method employed by the beasts of the field. Some concessions, however, were made to the higher status of the human being. The essential primitivism was modified by a degree, a not too exaggerated degree, of applied aesthetics. As they sat in a long military row, the boys looked over a neat dismal garden, flowerless but well-weeded.

When Lytton went to Abbotsholme, the school numbered just over forty boys. The School House itself had an imposing exterior, being a large country mansion in the Elizabethan-Victorian style, and surrounded by orchards and gardens. Altogether the Abbotsholme estate covered some one hundred and thirty acres, and was set on the western slope of Dove Ridge in Derbyshire, overlooking the river Dove. The country round about was remarkably fine and open, and, being nearly all permanent pasture, resembled a vast park. The nearest village – about a mile away – was Rocester, once a Roman camp, and later the seat of the Abbey from which Abbotsholme took its name.

Lytton's ordinary day, during the winter term of 1893, was divided into three main sections. His morning was devoted mainly to class-work indoors; his afternoon to physical and manual work out of doors; his evening to music, poetry, art and social recreation. Every morning reveille was sounded at five minutes to seven (in summer it was ten past six), and after a cold bath Lytton would fall in on the parade ground for military drill and work with the dumb-bells. From here he would hurry off to the chapel for a ten-minute thanksgiving service where he was able to recover a little before breakfast at twenty to eight. Twenty minutes later he was upstairs again standing by his bed while the dormitory was inspected by the masters. After dormitory parade, there came the first class of the day which was called Second School – First School in the summer being at six forty-five. These lessons differed from those of the ordinary public school in two respects: few of them exceeded three-quarters of an hour; and in the teaching of languages priority was given to German and French over the dead tongues, Latin and Greek. The classes which Dr Reddie took personally were often astonishing. Many a period supposedly given over to, say, physics or chemistry was sure to be occupied by the subject of hygiene, in which the importance of mental as well as bodily cleanliness was severely emphasized. 'On one occasion,' wrote Stanley Unwin, 'in a state of fury at our incompetence, he broke the pointer across the table and said that if we did not learn to think and to take more pains we should end by blacking the boots of the Germans.'

At midday the first of the outdoor activities began. Dr Reddie himself had been only moderately proficient at the usual English forms of sport such as cricket and rugger, and so the physical training at Abbotsholme consisted not just of mere games but also of useful manual labour which, he believed, promoted a less restricted social feeling than that enshrined by the traditional team spirit. As an exponent of what has been called 'the Gospel of Potato-digging' — originally conceived by Edward Carpenter — he strove to impress the minds of his pupils with the 'panoramic reflex of nature', and to banish from them the notorious psychological troubles afflicting those who lacked a hard and steady occupation employing body and mind together. This aim was to be secured by the muscular work involved in the agrarian occupations he set them, together with an indispensable programme of tonic exercises. Only these pursuits, Dr Reddie claimed, could 'stimulate the healthy growth of the body in supple grace and compact symmetry, and promote that frank, hearty, and instinctive appreciation of its beauty, which is essential to the true education. Moreover, to render the body strong, clean, and lovely is a religious duty. Therefore the claims of athletics will in no respect be ignored, but rather extended and rendered less artificial and mechanical.'

From twelve to one o'clock, when studies were interrupted by a brief lunch and a lengthy piano recital, and again from two o'clock to half-past four, Lytton was subjected to a variety of strenuous and unexpected tasks. Among the less arduous pastimes prescribed for these periods were drawing, carpentry, basket-making and bee-culture. In addition to this, and in order to rouse in him a manly interest in the subject of clothing and its proper relation to the human body, Lytton might at times be coached in the processes of boot-making and tailoring, or alternatively instructed in the preparation of butter so that he could acquire a sound knowledge in matters which directly affected his health. Simply to obviate the dangers of loafing, some Rugby Union football – Dr Reddie's own favourite team game – was also obligatory, as was a large minimum quota of tree-felling. Opportunity too was afforded him almost daily to learn on the farm lands the rudiments of agriculture and food-production. Bringing in the potato harvest, damming the streams in the Dingle, erecting pigeon houses, Lytton was said to be gleaning the ways of nature at first hand, benefiting from a true though little-regarded culture, and availing himself – should it prove necessary – of a sound preparation for colonial life.

Afternoon school lasted from half-past four till six o'clock, when the boys had their tea. This was followed by thirty minutes of freedom preparatory to the final part of the school day given over to artistic training. Since Dr Reddie himself admitted that he possessed 'neither talent, time, nor taste for literary composition; but on the contrary, feels a growing conviction that words and books, less by quality than by quantity, exert an exaggerated influence in our lives, producing new perils to body, mind, and character', Lytton's literary gifts received scant encouragement. Music, as the most social of the arts, was given the highest priority, and from seven to seven-thirty Lytton indulged in compulsory glee-singing under the tuition of the heavily bearded German professor of biology, his voice, by this stage of the day, being described as 'rather weak'. The hour's artistic training which succeeded this period, in so far as it was literary, was designed to stimulate his dormant aesthetic sensibilities by the simple process of making him learn off by heart those stirring incidents of history immortalized in verse. Each evening, too, the boys would assemble in Big School to meet the ladies, masters, and any visitors who might have arrived, and learn to amuse themselves in a sensible adult fashion. The day ended with a second ten-minute thanksgiving service in the chapel; and then, at ten minutes to nine, Lytton was at last allowed to go off to bed.

On the question of religious instruction the New School took very high ground indeed. On Sundays, Lytton was permitted to rise as late as half-past seven. Before breakfast he was obliged to attend a twenty-minute chapel service, and after the usual dormitory inspection and a period set aside for writing letters home, he would fall in at the full-dress Church Parade. This ceremony lasted until almost midday, and was followed, when the weather was wet, by a corollary in the form of a further three-quarters of an hour's celebration in the school chapel. This chapel was in fact seen as the source from which all other activities took their illumination. The services were intended to condense all the most elevated incentives of the place, by proclaiming to the captive congregation definite maxims of conduct associated with the actions of ideal figures, the whole series of illustrations being grouped round the Person and Life of Jesus Christ. Readings, however, were by no means confined to the Bible, but followed an individual pattern laid out by Dr Reddie in a publication of startling prolixity: 'The Abbotsholme Liturgy, with Special Services for Christmas, Good Friday, Easter, the Ascensions, Whit-tide, Trinity; also for Waterloo Day and Trafalgar Day; also David's Lament for Saul and Jonathan, the Seven Beatitudes, the Ten Laws, and a number of Canticles and a large number of the Psalms, all retranslated, pointed and noted; also part of the anthology in the school chapel.' No boy, were he Protestant, Catholic, Hindu or Mohammedan, was permitted to escape the frequent rigours of these Abbotsholme Services conducted under the strict regimen of their headmaster.

Dinner, at one o'clock, was followed by an organ recital, while the remainder of the afternoon was left officially free. In practice this was not the case for Lytton. As a contribution to

its religious purpose, the school was segregated into Fags,
Mids and Prefects, and as a new boy he naturally came into the
first category. This system, he might have been surprised to
learn as he busied himself about his unofficial duties throughout the long afternoon, had been set up by Dr Reddie in a
special effort to educate the boys' affections towards one
another. All boys 'are *trained* to understand their relation to
one another', Dr Reddie explained in his prospectus. 'At Abbotsholme this natural relation of boys to one another is
recognized and carefully organized.' To assist in this natural
organization the prefects were empowered to beat the fags.
The masters also, Dr Reddie continued, 'catch the same spirit
and learn to use the same methods. The result is greater
operation in the teaching and greater harmony in the boys'
deportment. Both are humanized.' In this way Abbotsholme
was conceived as a family unit, with Dr Reddie himself as God
the Father hammering home the school motto: 'Glad Day,
Love and Duty'. Involved in terrifying grandeur he ruled from
above, yet was an omnipresent force. During his time at Abbotsholme Lytton must certainly have witnessed, if not actually been the subject of, one of the occasional floggings
administered, with full Arnoldian gravity, by Dr Reddie before
the assembled school. These were awful and solemn ceremonies which impressed themselves for life on the more sensitive boys.

At a quarter-past five the so-called free time ended and
Lytton would join with the other boys in chanting re-
translated canticles and hymns from Dr Reddie's anthology;
while after tea he received an hour's religious instruction consisting, for the most part, of learning by heart portions of the
Gospels and selections from the Psalms. There followed yet
another hour's service in the chapel, before supper and lights
out.

By this system of all-round modern and religious instruction, based upon the high-flown principles of educational
science, and adapted to the special needs of the English cultured classes, did Dr Reddie aspire to instil in Lytton a lofty,
self-reliant moral character. The immediate results were not

encouraging. After the protective custody of Lancaster Gate and Parkstone the physical toughness needed to stand up to such a sentence of hard labour proved altogether beyond him. Something of the strain and exertion imposed by Dr Reddie's curriculum comes out in his letters home. 'I enjoy myself greatly on the whole. Of course there are some things which I don't much like, such as cold baths and paperchases! – but still I'm sure I shall get used to them' (5 October 1893); 'Yesterday [18 November] we had a run because we could not play football as it was snowing. So we sallied forth – oh! it was dreadfully cold, and the wind and the snow hit you – and altogether it was most unpleasant! ... I had my first round of boxing on Wednesday in which I was knocked flat on the ground!'; 'The baths *were* cold, I assure you! Everyday we change entirely into jersies and flannel knickers. One is allowed to put on as many jersies as you like – but no shirt or vest or draw!' (1 October 1893). 'I think you will get used to the cold bath in time,' his mother wrote to him hopefully. But already by the time her letter arrived at Abbotsholme, Lytton was in bed with a high fever. From this he recovered after some ten days' sedation, only to faint away with a spell of weakness and dizziness, being carried unconscious from the chapel back to the sick-room. His pulse became unusually rapid and he quickly lost weight. At this time he seems to have completely outgrown and overtaxed his strength, being already five feet two inches tall, but weighing only a few pounds over five stone. By December he had made a second recovery and, attired in a 'lovely' dress and wearing 'a beautiful yellow wig', gave a memorable performance as Hippolyta, Queen of Amazons, in *A Midsummer Night's Dream*.[7] 'I remember you very well,' Dr Reddie wrote to him twenty-eight years later; 'I still have that photograph of you as "a fascinating female" in the little play we gave, as we sat in the conservatory.'

From the term report which Lady Strachey was sent at

7. Earlier that term he had acted another female role in a school production of *My Turn Next*. 'I had on a beautiful red silk dress with flounces,' he proudly told his mother.

Christmas two interesting points emerge. First, Lytton was extremely eager to succeed in this new, masculine environment. He made a special effort to do well at athletics, drill and farming, but in each case lacked the necessary stamina. Secondly, Dr Reddie, in his anxiety that Lytton should not be removed from Abbotsholme, understated the physical deficiencies from which he suffered, and, so far as was consistent with his elevated principles, sheltered him from the full rigours of the New School's Spartan syllabus. Lytton's work was dismissed rather cursorily as 'good', and his health was cryptically described as 'fair'. 'I have not pressed this boy', he wrote. 'He neither needs it nor can he safely stand it. He has been twice ill this term, once when most were suffering from similar feverish colds in October, and again lately during the *hot weather* feeling faint for two days. He has otherwise been in good health and in excellent spirits – I believe the climate suits him – As regards work and general development, nothing more can be desired.'

Lytton returned to Abbotsholme in January 1894, when life proved even harder. Dressed only in shorts and a jersey he was expected during the most Arctic conditions to carry cheerfully on mending fences and gates, tarring railings, cleaning out the cowshed, wood-cutting and other endless jobs on the estate. 'He is not in the picture captioned potato digging,' one of Lytton's contemporaries at Abbotsholme, Gerald Brooke, told the author. 'It was a bitterly cold day with a wind from the snow-clad hills driving over the valley. It nearly put me out! Strachey was probably talking to matron in the sick-room.'[8]

Lytton was anxious to make some friends from among his companions at the school, but they almost all regarded him as something of an outcast. 'He was', another pupil, G. Lissant Cox, recalled, 'a strange bird from my point of view.' And this appears to have been the general verdict. 'My recollection of him is that he seemed to be older than I was, with a very

8. 'Sometime ago we have all been digging up potatoes in the field, we had to work pretty hard, because they all had to be got away before the frost came on' (Lytton Strachey to Lady Strachey, 29 October 1893).

grown-up air for a boy. He must have lived with grown-ups,' another Old Abbotsholmian remembered. 'I think he must have been much above the school average in taught knowledge. He could talk to anyone who would listen to him but not to me. I was only interested in bird's-nesting and outdoor activity which meant nothing to him. I remember seeing him talking about the play while he washed, then turning round stark naked to continue the discourse. He was circumcised but quite unconscious of the fact that he did not look like all other boys in the dormitory.'

During this, his second term, Lytton's health collapsed completely. It now became impossible to overlook his physical incompatibility with the bracing climate of the place. Before the end of the term he was removed altogether from the school and sent back home. His failure to endure the austerity of Abbotsholme threw him right back within the circumfluent effeminacy of Lancaster Gate. As in later life, his affability and sense of humour depended largely on his personal success, which liberated him from morbid self-preoccupation and enabled him to focus his mind upon external objects. In failure, he sank into hypersensitive awareness of his own insignificance and isolation, from which the only satisfactory outlet was hostility. When older, he would sometimes speak with intense dislike of the Abbotsholme regime, but secretly he would have loved to excel there, and it is perhaps significant that he never entirely broke off his connections with the school. When at Cambridge, he attended more than one of the annual Old Abbotsholmian dinners given at Christ's College, and received several personal visits from Dr Reddie himself, who always seemed dazed by the great height of his ex-pupil.

'Teachers and prophets', Strachey wrote in *Eminent Victorians*, 'have strange after-histories.' That of Dr Reddie was no exception. After Lytton had left, the fortunes of Abbotsholme were constantly bedevilled by sinister plots and counter-plots, the strain of which brought out in Dr Reddie the more tyrannical symptoms of paranoia. Weighed down by complex worries and responsibilities, he shed much of the high spirits that had formerly animated him during the holidays and made him unrecognizable to those who knew him only as a forbidding headmaster. Suspicious of everyone, he once dismissed five masters in a single term, convinced that they were conspiring to take control of his miniature kingdom under the leadership of a mysterious bankrupt Dutchman who, escaping from the bailiffs out of the window of an adjacent building which he had hoped to set up as a rival establishment to Abbotsholme, fled to Holland and was heard of no more. The greatest blow of all, however, fell with the declaration of war. Many parents who had previously supported the Germanic mode of school life now hurriedly withdrew their sons until at last, tenacious and perverse as ever, Dr Reddie was left in sole charge of two pupils. Various schemes, to which Lytton faithfully contributed, were implemented by the old boys, in order to reinstate the school. Though he did not send his old headmaster a copy of *Eminent Victorians* for fear that some passages in the pen-portrait of Dr Arnold might offend him, Lytton did forward him *Queen Victoria* and was warmly complimented for his courage in praising at such a time the Prince Consort, a German.

By the late 1920s a group of old boys finally persuaded Dr Reddie to sell the school, and under Colin Sharp it became more successful than ever before – and more orthodox. At this time Lytton contributed generously to an annuity given to the ex-headmaster on strict condition that he did not go near Abbotsholme ever again. It was a bitter pill for an ageing but still fiercely idealistic man to swallow. His stature declined noticeably, and during his few years of retirement he became a figure of increasing pathos and peculiarity. While his self-esteem shrank, so, symbolically, did his very name. As dr cecil reddie, a leading 'member of the league for abolition of capital-letters to save everybody's eyesight and to simplify education', he retired to welwyn-garden-city in hertfordshire, from where he wrote 'dear giles' a number of letters complaining of the invalid female relatives he was now forced to look after. He died, worn out but still undaunted, within a few days of Lytton himself.

3
'SCRAGGS'

'At school I used to weep – oh! for very definite things – bitter unkindness and vile brutality.' So wrote Lytton in a letter to Leonard Woolf, comparing the intense unhappiness he experienced as a schoolboy with his vaguer, more generalized feeling of sadness at university. The brazen religiosity of Abbotsholme, which so devastatingly inflamed his natural timidity, was soon succeeded in the summer of 1894 by the more traditional philistinism of Leamington College, then ranked as one of the minor public schools. At an age when the adolescent boy is growing increasingly aware of the physical side of his being, Lytton's painful awkwardness and odd appearance, were at once seized on by his new companions and brought home to him with all the malevolence at the disposal of the average schoolboy. Just as his younger brother had thought him 'absurd' and described him as a 'funny little creature' – comments which his mother had seen fit humorously to pass on to him on more than one occasion – so his schoolfellows immediately singled out his oddity for their special attentions. Enveloped by an atmosphere of unkindness which no discipline could dispel, he was given the nickname of 'Scraggs' and made a victim of the most savage bullying. 'I am not getting on very well at present,' he admitted, 'as on[e] of the boys (Phipps) as well as talking nasty things is rather a bully, which is rather painful.' The masters offered him little protection against this treatment, partly by reason of their ordinary human laziness and partly in the vague abstract belief that a totally uncivilized atmosphere, far from having any harmful effect, prepared a boy very adequately for the turmoil of the adult world.

Something of the distress which Lytton felt is expressed in one of the letters written to his mother at the beginning of June, just after he had recovered from a bout of illness. Naïvely and ambiguously phrased, hinting at rather than complaining of bullying, the picture of life at Leamington which emerges between the lines caused some alarm back at Lancaster Gate where Lady Strachey, feeling that the situation was moving beyond her province, placed her son's correspondence before her husband. In the answering letter which he addressed to Lytton on 4 June, Richard Strachey discloses some rather mixed feelings on the matter – a somewhat weary anxiety that his son should not have to be transferred every few months from one to yet another unsuitable school being counterbalanced by a fear lest various unmentionable atrocities might in the meantime be perpetrated against him. 'I am glad to hear that you are now off the Sick List and beginning again to get on to your work', he wrote. 'If you steadily stick at this you will find it in the end the best protection from annoyances such as you seem to have to submit to, from what you have written to your mother. I shall try as soon as possible to come up and see you, when you can explain if necessary more exactly what you have to complain of. Of course it is a very disagreeable position for a boy to be placed in to have to ask for protection against other boys, but there are some things which should not be put up with. If anything occurs that you feel any difficulty in writing about to your mother let me know or merely say that you think it better that I should see you and talk about it and I will come. As to mere petty bullying you may be able to grin and bear it – but certainly on no account put up with any absolute acts or attempts at indecency such as is well known are not unheard of at schools. You may feel quite confident that we will protect you completely against any unpleasant consequences to yourself if you resist all evil influences to the best of your ability, and do not hesitate to let it be known that you will not submit to what you feel you should resist.'

Lytton was both grateful and amused by his father's letter, which provided him with a much-needed sense of security and a resilience against his afflictions. What he wrote in reply shows clearly the extent and nature of this gratitude.

My dear Papa,

I think mine is a case of 'petty bullying' so I will to the best of my ability grin and bear it, which, I think, is the only thing to be done,

As to the other matter all I know is that conversations frequently take place without any regard to decency, but whether it is carried on further than this I do not know as I have only been here such a short time. But I hope that matters will clear up, and that I will have a happy issue out of my difficulties . . .

Your letter cheered me greatly for you see I am not *very* happy and its so nice to feel there's a place from where I can be sure of help in time of need.

After his first term the bullying diminished and Lytton was able gradually to integrate himself with the continuing flux of school life. Soon we hear of him entering chess competitions, joining 'a glee society and on Saturday evenings we sing glees, which is rather amusing' (21 October 1894), and being dragooned into the choir — 'every Sunday — arrayed in a white robe I stalk into the chapel — feeling most grand!' And he reassures his mother: 'Yes, things are getting smoother now which is a great comfort.' In particular the amateur theatricals, which he had always enjoyed and which enabled him to exploit his idiosyncrasies to popular effect, presented him at Leamington with a welcome means of self-escape. His correspondence home gives pictures of him at one time or another acting in Sheridan's farce *The Critic* ('I come in at the end as Tilburina, stark mad in white muslin, accompanied by my confidant stark mad in white calico'); and in a production of *The Frogs* by Aristophanes ('The Scene is Dionysus and his slave being rowed across the Styx by Charon, who I am'). But even on the stage he was liable to be brought abruptly back to a state of painful self-awareness, as when, one Speech Day, a parent-member of the audience, startled by his first entrance, exclaimed loudly: 'What terribly thin arms he's got!' However, his acting ability coupled with his freakish appearance could sometimes prove useful. Once when he was walking with his sister Philippa who had come down to visit him at the school, a strange man approached them and began making alarming advances towards her. Realizing that he was no match for the man in combat and hating to make any humourless exhibition of himself, Lytton straightway dropped into the role of a dangerous lunatic, playing the part with such a pageant of convincing jabber and gesticulation that the stranger fled in terror.

Although Lytton's spirits greatly improved in the three years he spent at Leamington, various illnesses continued to plague him. During the notoriously cold winter of 1894-5, he was allowed to miss early school at seven o'clock and stayed comfortably in bed until breakfast an hour later. 'I also have milk and cod-liver oil at all hours of the day,' he told his mother. Despite these precautions his health again broke down during the following winter, this time so completely that he had to be taken away for the whole of the 1896 Easter term. After this setback he was only allowed by the family doctor to return once special arrangements had been made for his welfare. These included extra food – 'My luxurious tea,' he reported happily, 'is eyed by my fellows with looks of covetousness.' – and indoor classes restricted to the morning so that he might inhale fresh air every afternoon to dispel the vapours. About this time, too, he learnt to ride a bicycle 'with some fluency though I have not yet mastered the art of mounting', and in the latter part of the day would go off for long solitary excursions about the countryside. On one of these afternoon bicycle trips he caught sight of a figure who was to play a minor part in his *Queen Victoria* and recorded the encounter in mock-Pepysian fashion: 'I also went to see the Prince of Wales, who had been on a visit to the Warwicks,' he wrote to his mother (21 May 1895). 'His Royal Highness was so gracious as to take off his august hat to me, and I returned the compliment. My lady Warwick looked very pretty but it struck me that her hat was not of quite the latest fashion.'

Considering the number of classes he missed over the years, his scholastic achievements are impressive. His reports show him to have excelled in mathematics, French and English; to have been fairly good at Classics, but quite useless at science. In the late summer of 1895, when he was fifteen and a half, he took the Oxford and Cambridge Lower Certificate Examination, passing in seven subjects altogether and being awarded First Classes in Arithmetic and English. Lady Strachey, who had been in a great state of anxiety as to how he would emerge from this, the first major test of his academic abilities, was delighted with the result. 'The Exam is for boys of sixteen years of age and a First or Second Class is given in *each* subject,' the headmaster explained in a letter notifying her of the good news. 'I am very pleased to say that Lytton obtained a First Class in Arithmetic and English, and a Second Class in Latin, Greek, French, Additional Mathematics and Scripture Knowledge – thus passing in seven subjects while five are only necessary for the Certificate. I think the result is highly satisfactory, and is due to the steady way in which he has worked. If he had been a stronger boy and able to bear more pressure, he might have got a First Class in other subjects. I think he might work for this next year and take the Higher Certificate the year after.'

Within twelve months of going to Leamington, Lytton had settled down quite comfortably. Much to the relief of the whole family, the occasional letters which Richard Strachey received from this time onwards contained nothing more alarming than bulletins of the latest botanical developments taking place in his son's window-box, while Lytton's correspondence to his mother tells of cricket matches, plays, natural history expeditions that were 'distinctly unnatural and could never become history', and all the usual topics of school life, including, not surprisingly, editing the school magazine. Many of his comments reveal his inability to enter into the boys' more hearty and athletic pursuits. He did, however, learn to skate and 'Now', he informed his sister Philippa, 'I am certainly able to fly at a descent rate, but occasionally falling, when performing the most brilliant feats.' At most of the other forms of sport his failure was less spectacular if quite as complete, and he spent much of his free time instead composing an Ibsenesque tragedy 'which is not only bloodthirsty, but dull, so dull that I cannot read it myself'. Nevertheless he was obviously better suited to such sedentary occupations, and these, together with his fondness for using lengthy, out-of-the-way words, made him an object of contempt, amusement, surprise and sometimes even admiration to his contemporaries. In general, he was less at home with the boys than with the masters, some of whom he would occasionally invite to supper in his room.

Lytton's passage up the school hierarchy from this time on was very rapid. He gave up studying science, but finished in the latter part of 1896 top both of the Classical School and of the Mathematical Sets. Already, by the autumn of 1895 he had been made head of his house and showered with a multitude of rather empty privileges: he was entitled to wear a tin mitre on his cap, to sport a walking-stick, and empowered to take roll-calls and read the lesson in chapel – his faltering and falsetto maiden performance, taken from the First Epistle of Paul the Apostle to Timothy, being an exhortation to widows. 'The agility of my voice', he wrote to Philippa, 'is not particularly convenient in this respect; as at one moment it is plunged in the depths below, and at the next is soaring with the lark at Heaven's gate – much to the alarm of the congregation.'

Lytton's house at Leamington College consisted of some thirty pupils. As head boy, he was one of its five prefects, and allowed a room of his own.

'My four colleagues', he confided to his mother, 'are *not* specimens of great brilliancy. Gaitskill is quite a fool.

'F— is not so bad, but, I should think, devoid of all moral qualities.

'Clarke is mild and inoffensive.

'P— is a thick headed lout—

'And then there is myself!'

It was characteristic of Lady Strachey, an avowed agnostic, to ensure that her son went to schools where a special emphasis was laid on Christian teaching. The religiosity of Leamington, however, was mercifully of a less muscular variety than that of Abbotsholme. The school visitor was the Lord Bishop of Worcester; three of its vice-presidents were also of the higher clergy; the headmaster, described by Lytton as 'somewhat of a crock', was the Very Reverend R. Arnold Edgell; while of the half-dozen assistant masters two had seen fit to take orders. For this ecclesiastical body of men Lytton had not a good word: with one exception, the Reverend (later Bishop) E. J. Bidwell — 'an excellent man as well as being a clergyman' — who soon perceived that the young Lytton was pleasingly different from the average boy.[9]

The upshot of being encircled for so long by representatives of the Church of England, whose pompous mummery and faked emotions jarred incessantly upon him, was that Lytton, while still at Leamington, discarded his automatic acceptance of Christianity, and embraced a rather hostile and high-principled form of agnosticism. His letters home are sprinkled liberally with contemptuous references to the men of God whose arduous business it was to instruct him. A few examples of these passages, sometimes a little priggish or over-extravagantly aimed at farce, will convey clearly enough the tenor of his mind.

7 October 1895

'We've had rather a painful missionary down here, converting us to the true faith! He religiously presented me with tracts, which I religiously presented to the waste paper basket! ... The general opinion here is that the man has done more harm than good by making the boys think of things they would never have before, and which they'd do very well without.'

9. In a letter to *The Times* (25 January 1932, p. 17), four days after Lytton's death, Bishop Bidwell wrote: 'It is stated in his obituary notice that Lytton Strachey was educated "privately". As a matter of fact, he was a pupil of mine when I was chaplain and a form master at old Leamington College, which then ranked as one of the minor public schools. I never saw or heard of him after he left till upwards of two years ago, when, seeing my name and address in a communication to your columns, he wrote me a most delightful letter, of the sort that gladdens the heart of an old schoolmaster. He said that he had been wanting to express his gratitude (I am afraid little deserved) for years, but had lost track of me when I went abroad. He describes himself as my "somewhat wayward pupil". He certainly was, as I quickly perceived, different from the average boy, but my recollections of him as a boy are entirely pleasing, and I deeply regret his premature passing.' In his letter replying to Lytton (11 April 1929), Bidwell had written: 'I cannot tell you how pleased I was to get your letter. It is comforting to be remembered after all these years. Yes, I recall you perfectly as a boy, but mea maxima culpa I never identified the youth I knew with the celebrity of today.'

31 May 1896

'Two of the masters are engaged to be married – one of them Mr Jones, the mathematical wallah – is engaged to a sister of one of the boys. The other Mr Suthery (classics) to an unknown. I am sorry to say the latter is going to be a clergyman – not so the former.'

10 November 1896

'Mr Suthery, the master who has distinguished himself by becoming a clergyman, preached on Sunday, not remarkably.'

23 November 1896

'Yesterday a special clergyman, very much like a goat, came to preach on Foreign Missions. He meandered through many a path of idiocy, and then quite suddenly – and luckily – stopped. I think he was seized with a sudden desire to go to Thibet and begin converting Grand Lhamas, or we would be listening with rapt attention to his bland remarks e'en now.'

Lytton's mother accepted these uncharitable outpourings without comment, slightly apprehensive that her own politer agnosticism should be taken up and given such a satirical and facetious twist. But when he turned his strong anti-Christian bias from life to literature she was more responsive. It was now, for the first time, that Lytton began to read Gibbon, whose literary style delighted him as much as his distinctive dislike of religion. During his last term at Leamington he concocted an amusing parody of Gibbon's balanced Corinthian rhetoric, which is nicely overweighted by the triviality of the fairy story to which it is applied: 'The Decline and Fall of Little Red Riding Hood.' In this tale, Lytton's most considerable piece of writing up to the age of seventeen, Red Riding Hood is shown, having been warned by her mother against the terrible beasts of the forest, setting out for her grandmother's house. She has not gone far when all at once she is terrified to behold 'the crafty eye, the sinister jowl, and the gaunt form of a wolf, aged alike in years and in deceit'. This cunning and malign creature soon banishes her fears, however, by chiv-

alrously offering her flowers, and then, learning of her destination, conjures up a scheme of devastating evil – 'as harmless
in appearance as it was diabolical in reality'. He races off to
the grandmother's cottage and there enters into a battle from
which he quickly emerges victorious:

'At last, having traversed twice as quickly as Red Riding
Hood a road twice as short as that which she had taken, he
arrived in triumph at the house of the redoubtable though
comatose octogenarian. History does not reveal the details
of the interview. It can only be gathered that it was a short
and stormy one. It is known for certain, however, that the
wolf obtained at the same moment a victory and a meal, and
that when Little Red Riding Hood entered her grandmother's
abode, the arch deceiver, occupying the bed, and arrayed in
the nightgown of his unfortunate victim, was prepared to receive the child with a smile of outward welcome and of
inward derision.'

Once Red Riding Hood arrives at the house, the celebrated
dialogue, amusingly recast, between her and the wolf leads
swiftly on to the climax of the story. Having made the girl
exclaim with innocent wonderment: 'What big teeth you
have!' Lytton polishes off the ending with a single short paragraph couched in his rotund imitation-Gibbonian prose:

' "The better," answered the wolf, seeing the culmination of
his plan coincide with the humour of the situation, "the
better to eat you with, my dear!" Suiting the action to the
word, he leapt out of bed and with incredible savageness
threw himself upon his victim. Then he divested himself of his
borrowed raiment and slipped quietly out of the cottage.'

An even more significant taste was for the works of Plato.
Here alone was Lytton able to discover something that tallied
intimately with the passionate and mysterious emotions which,
from the age of fourteen, had secretly risen up within him.
Once he had relinquished Christianity, Plato's *Symposium* became for him a new Bible. In this dramatic dialogue he found
a philosophy of love, at once sympathetic yet strict, which
seemed wonderfully pertinent to his own confused state of
mind. A short diary which he kept during part of November

1896 shows him reading the *Symposium* 'with a rush of mingled pleasure and pain ... of surprise, relief, and fear to know that what I feel now was felt 2,000 years ago in glorious Greece. Would I had lived then, would I had sat at the feet of Socrates, seen Alcibiades, wondrous Alcibiades, Alcibiades, the abused, but the great, felt with them all!'

The love affairs that excited Lytton at Leamington were almost certainly platonic and inconclusive. Yet they stirred within him feelings of so violent and complicated a kind that the memory of them persisted for ever in his mind where they came to represent for him the ideal, limitless, intimate companionship which he sought to recapture in adult life. In this sense, these schoolboy infatuations may be said to have conditioned nearly all his later love relationships. Without any natural power of ingratiating himself within ordinary human society, he enhaloed those who seemed to sail through the heavy seas of life, untroubled by ugly apprehensions, calm, graceful and self-assured. This, indeed, was how he would like to have felt and appeared – splendidly handsome, immediately popular and magnificently unperplexed. But since he could never bring about any such miraculous metamorphosis to transform his nervous spirit and sickly body into this vision of his ideal self, he did the next best thing: he endeavoured to mislay his remorseless sense of self-contempt in the all-embracing, all-absorbing contemplation of someone near to him with whom he could identify his romantic day-dreams, and even, for short ecstatic periods, assimilate his own being. While still in his first year at Leamington, he conceived a dumb, idyllic devotion to one of the older boys, whose celestial image, by eclipsing Lytton's own personality as the foremost object in his mental and emotional horizon, induced a state of temporary self-oblivion, and cast over his world an incredible, twilight aura of happiness. Magically, he felt himself released from the prison of his own hateful physique. This was his first real passion and it involved what he always considered to be his purest emotions – admiration, adoration and worship all wreathed and encircled by a wondering, inarticulate state of mind – 'that good kind exquisite abolition of oneself in such a heaven-born hero', as he subsequently described the sensation to Leonard Woolf. '. . . . Part of it, don't you think, came from what we certainly can never get again – that extraordinary sense of corporal hugeness of our God? To be able to melt into a body literally twice as big as one's own.'

At the age of sixteen Lytton experienced another delirious passion – 'the second of my desperate businesses at school', as he later called it. In many essential respects this relationship was similar to the first – unrequited, and focused upon someone utterly different from himself, who for a time dominated his life and dissipated his morbid introspection. Lytton's weak constitution cut him off from the athletic pursuits of youth, and stimulated his desire to enshrine those who practised them with ease and efficiency. His choice of hero on this second occasion fell on a dashing young batsman, head of the averages, a rather plump, amiable boy named George Underwood, very freckled and with red hair that intoxicated Lytton during the bright summer months. Owing to his mathematical rather than his sporting talent, Lytton succeeded in getting himself appointed as scorer to the cricket eleven, travelling round with them to the opposing schools, and lying in the long tickling grass under the sun amusing himself, and proudly assessing the quantities of runs that the glamorous Underwood amassed. Altogether it was a rapturous affair, entirely one-sided, which left him with a strong feeling of nostalgia in after-years. As late as September 1931, some four months before his death, Lytton recalled this romantic friendship in his diary with a sharpness of detail which suggests that the vision of it had often reappeared before his mind's eye.

'I was older and enormously devoted and obsessed,' he wrote; 'he was very sweet and very affectionate, but what he really liked was going off somewhere with Ruffus Clarke and the chic older boys, while I was left in the lurch, ruminating and desperate. How I loathed Ruffus Clarke! – a biggish, calm, very fair-haired boy, wicked and irresistible. I based my objections on purely moral grounds. I was a romantic prig, and the only wonder is how poor Underwood put up with me for a moment. ...

'Ruffus Clarke and Fell! I can see them with absolute distinctness. Both with that curious softness which some boys of about seventeen seem to be able to mingle with their brutality. Fell was handsome, dark and slightly sinister, though not nearly so sinister as his younger brother, who, sandy and hatchet-faced, had devilry written all over him. Ruffus Clarke didn't care about prestige or anything else. As for me, I never knew what really happened – nobody told me – I couldn't even guess.'

From the observations he made about Plato's *Symposium*, Lytton appears to have been drawn most sympathetically to the character of Alcibiades – the man who, unlike Socrates, was never harmoniously composed in his striving after a rather abstract and intellectual beauty, but who, while sensitive to the appeal of this disciplined philosophy, was also susceptible to carnal pleasures and the lure of political ambition. Like Alcibiades, Lytton was of a fundamentally divided nature. Emotionally he might be fired by enforced restraint, deriving a masochistic thrill from the subservient role he was obliged to adopt in his various passionate friendships. Since these early affairs were not translated into physical terms, Lytton was protected from slow disillusionment and made free to indulge himself in pleasantly will-less broodings, enlivened with a highly romantic turn of morality. Intellectually, however, he viewed the situation in a different light, realizing that the type of boy to whom he was fatally attracted tended to despise him, as indeed he despised himself, for being weak – though he might be kind and patient with his weakness. The hero accepted his submissive devotion; he took without thought his tremulous, abject offering, mixed with contempt as it was in his mind. And when the infatuation had faded into nothing, this contempt remained, cold and real inside Lytton, reinforcing the agony of his own self-contempt, and forming in its residue the very fuel of his ambition.

This repeated pattern of alternating submission and

mortification produced within Lytton a poison of accumulating resentment which was to find its most powerful outlet in *Eminent Victorians*. A ludicrously ineffectual schoolboy, he remained outwardly timid as, inwardly, his spirit grew more anarchical and sure. Even as an adolescent, the lustful germ of ambition fretted within him, making him restless, discontented. By the end of 1896, being no longer in love with his cricketer, he was eager to quit this 'semi-demi public school'. That holiday, there was much excited bustle and activity at Lancaster Gate, where preparations were in full swing for a family performance of Ibsen's *John Gabriel Borkman*, of which William Archer's translation had just appeared. Lytton himself played the part of Vilhelm Foldal, the ageing government clerk, with great success. This minor triumph added to his confidence and strengthened his determination to leave Leamington once and for all. Without great difficulty he prevailed upon his mother to write to the headmaster and inform him that her son would not be returning after the Easter holidays.

Arnold Edgell was appalled by Lady Strachey's sudden decision, and did all in his power to change her mind, even persuading the school doctor to support his plea on the grounds that an extended stay at Leamington would benefit Lytton's health. But Lady Strachey was adamant, no doubt detecting that the headmaster's arguments came very largely from a simple wish to add to the school's rather meagre list of scholars and exhibitioners.

Lytton himself was delighted. The years were moving on and he was resolved not to be left behind. At Leamington now he was only wasting his days, marking time. On 1 March 1897, his seventeenth birthday, he wrote to his mother: 'I am quite appalled by my great age. The man who instituted birthdays was a criminal.'

The following month he left Leamington for the last time, prepared to enter a new, challenging sphere of life, in which he was determined to excel, and where those who had despised him in the past should be forced to acknowledge his sovereignty. Yet sovereignty and the possession of power would never be enough. He would always push through curtains to privacy and want some whispered words alone. Therefore he went, dubious but elate; apprehensive of intolerable pain; yet, so he felt, bound in his adventuring to conquer after huge suffering, bound surely to discover in the end his twofold desire for ascendancy and perfect, fulfilled love.

THREE

Liverpool

'The truth is I want *companionship*.' *Lytton Strachey, Diary*
(April 1898).

'Have you noticed that one's always waggling between two
extremes – one's own opinion of oneself, and everyone else's.
Sometimes I get so fascinated by the latter that I'm quite
carried away and begin to act up to it, as if I really thought it
true ... We are all cupboards – with obvious outsides which
may be either beautiful or ugly, simple or elaborate, interesting or unamusing – but with insides mysteriously the same –
the abodes of darkness, terror and skeletons.' *Lytton Strachey
to John Sheppard* (1902).

1
PREPARATIONS

FOR six months after leaving Leamington College Lytton
prepared himself both physically and academically for the university life that awaited him. Every week he would go off to
perform isometrics before a Scottish doctor who had devised
an elaborate system of weights and pulleys to develop his
muscles. He also studied under the tuition of his sister Dorothy, the part-time mistress at Allenswood, who coached him
in English, History and French.

There were times during these months when he bitterly regretted his decision to quit school. He missed the comradeship, the endless activity, colour and excitement. Now,
buried alive in the towering edifice of Lancaster Gate, a vague
and universal feeling of unhappiness preserved him dimly, like
a dried-up flower on a pad of blotting paper. In the blackest
moments of depression, a sickening sense of his own inadequacy would rise up high into his lungs and stifle him. From
the critical age of puberty, his emotions had turned inwards
and now fed on themselves. Even the splendours of Rothie-

murchus no longer eased his dissatisfaction as once they had. Nature was too vapid, too vegetable. She had only sublimities and vastitudes and water and leaves. His desires were for something more intimate: for affection, for the right to an answering smile, an eye that understood, for the limbs of one person.

The impression which Lytton felt that he communicated to other people at this time was far from amiable. He was tortured by a need and inability to impress people. To those who did not succeed in drawing him out and proving their intellectual sympathy, he was cold and hostile. Mistrustful of all strangers who, he suspected, might be laughing at him, he felt their presence like a separating wall; and so as to avoid becoming vulnerable to their disapproval he retreated into a limbo of remote absorption, forbidding and unconciliatory. He hated what he considered to be the smug and trivial mediocrity of most people. What right had they, his obvious intellectual inferiors, to feel so self-satisfied? He did not admire them, and he refused to compromise with their ways. Already, at seventeen, he longed to consume them all utterly, to make them squirm and twist in their seats with his derision. And even from his silence they felt the radiating scintilla of his contempt – and returned it.

Something of the impression he conveyed has been recorded by Graham Robertson, who first met him about this time and felt for him a strong dislike which was equally strongly reciprocated. 'I so seldom actively dislike anyone that, when I do, the change and novelty are quite a little treat to me,' Graham Robertson wrote to a friend many years later, recalling the incident. 'This boon was vouchsafed to me in full measure by Lytton Strachey. This statement is really unfair both to him and to myself, as he was a mere boy of eighteen or nineteen when we came across each other, with all his laurels yet ungathered and his character (presumably) unformed, but in its unformed condition it was, to me, singularly objectionable, and we violently disliked each other – if violence in any form could be attributed to so limp and flaccid a being as was the Lytton of those days. As to the "strong, deep voice" mentioned by Max as reserved for his intimates, my meeting with him during a three days' stay with his family ... I suppose his parents, brothers and sisters must be reckoned among his intimates, but I never heard him address them otherwise than in a breathless squeak of an asthmatic rabbit. Voices were not the family strong point. I think they all talked so continuously as to have exhausted the small allotment of voice originally accorded to them.

'Lytton certainly made good later on and must have developed considerably in after years, but we never met again, I think by mutual consent, except once, when his charming father dragged the reluctant Lytton with him.'

In September Lytton took and passed the Preliminary Examination of the Victoria University of Manchester. To Dorothy Strachey, who had written to offer her congratulations, he replied jokingly: 'Let me add my congratulations for your admirable coaching, and also let me bring before you the fact that it is AGAINST MY PRINCIPLES to fail in an examination.'

Since Lytton was still rather young to go up directly to Oxford, his mother decided that he should first attend a smaller university. Luckily, the family had a special connection with Liverpool University College (as it then was) through Lytton's cousin, Sir Charles Strachey, who had married Ada Raleigh, sister of that most spirited of professional critics, Professor Walter Raleigh. It was because of Raleigh's position as King Alfred Professor of English Literature there that Lytton was sent by his mother in October 1897 to Liverpool University College, where he was to remain for the next two years.

2

FIVE BURLY MEN

The subjects that Lytton studied at Liverpool were Greek, Latin, mathematics, history and English literature. 'Five burly men spend their days in lecturing me,' he told his mother, 'so I really ought to be well instructed.' The best lecturer of all these, he added, was Walter Raleigh himself, who taught him English literature: 'He is thoroughly good.'

Lytton soon grew friendly with Raleigh who, besides being his foremost lecturer, also became the most influential figure in his life before he went up to Cambridge. His wife too delighted Lytton with her outspokenness and frank iconoclasm. 'What do you think of Mrs Raleigh?' he once asked a friend. 'Don't you like her brimstone and vitriol? Have you talked to her about [Bertrand] Russell? They hate each other like poison; he's a moralist, and she's an anarchist. And secretly I'm on her side.' Raleigh's own disposition was one likely to appeal to most young men of intelligence and literary sensibility. He came as a distinct relief from the more pedantic, fussy type of don. It was difficult to think of anyone less capable of that sort of pedagogic brutality which finds some place in all universities. There existed also much that was similar in their two temperaments. Both loved literature but distrusted academic pedantry. Both admired men of action more than men of letters. Both, in spite of irregular and romantic imaginations, became scholarly classical critics.

In Raleigh's mercurial personality Lytton found much that tallied with his own mixed feelings towards the world. Now nearing his forties, Raleigh had already written books on *The English Novel*, on *Robert Louis Stevenson* and on *Style* all of which the young Lytton had read and liked – and was now working on a study of Milton. His writing, however, though painstaking and often charming, lacked ballast and real originality. He had the flair of the artist for a fine phrase, but tended to suppress his buoyant powers of imagination in the supposed interests of promoting sound literary instruction. In contrast to this rather sober application, he nourished a secret inner faith, he once admitted, 'not in refinement and scholarly elegance, those are only a game, but in blood feuds, and the chase of wild beasts, and marriage by capture. In carrying this last savage habit into effect there would be an irresistible dramatic temptation to select the bluest lady of them all.'

This quotation, with its fanciful longing for a state of super-reality heightened with appropriately wry melodramatic side-effects, reveals the frustrated soul of a don; for in proportion as most dons feel themselves futile they admire the man of action. Yet Raleigh was a don with just a dash of genius, who had landed up in what was, by and large, his most equitable position in the world. Such an interpretation of his character he himself would have found quite unacceptable, even unrecognizable. Despite a fine professional career at Liverpool, and later at the universities of Glasgow and Oxford, he had induced within himself a totally fallacious conviction that, by virtue of his over-bold spirit, he was for ever being threatened with dismissal from one academic post after another. It was a psychological device by which he reconciled himself to his steady doctrinal career. On one side he recoiled in instinctive distaste from the remorseless insensitivity of the world at large; and on the other he rebelled against the miserably safe, cloistered existence to which he was forced to subscribe. In place of the crude and sordid extramural reality, he substituted a mental vision of some Elysian fairyland whose sportive joys were perpetually being denied him. His response to literature was genuine and personal, but he always believed that 'the word was cousin to the deed'. The self-contempt which rose up within him whenever he allowed his thoughts to centre on his own career took the literary form of debunking parasitic writing – the name by which he used to refer to his own criticism. Books on books, being disconnected or at least two removes from action, must by their very nature be trivial, since the principal value of all literature lay in recording and paying homage to great exploits. In his clearer moments literature meant more to him in itself than a means of purging his own sense of inadequacy, which, when it turned outwards and focused upon the lives of soldiers, sailors and airmen, was given a humility at once naïve and touching.

Up to this point the parallel between Raleigh and Lytton was close. Had Lytton become a don – as could well have happened – he might have produced a literary corpus very

111

similar to Raleigh's. But Raleigh possessed one accomplishment which sweetened the otherwise bitter inefficacy of his career and lifted him high out of the troughs of melancholia. When alone, immersed in the unenviable drudge of authorship, surrounded by dead and dusty volumes of reference, his freedom of expression faltered and grew intermittent; but in friendly conversation, with its lively interplay of thought and feeling, his delightful exuberance and wit were at once released and would flow from him freely and easily. He loved an audience and excelled before a good one, however large or small, for only then could he translate literature back into terms of the actual movement of life going on around him. Few people who heard him lecture ever forgot the gaiety, the sparkle, the keen and pervading subtlety of his performances. Raleigh was one of those rare people who can address a large audience or a single individual with the same magical effect. Even his mannerisms, so well known, never jarred. First one saw the spread of his ready smile announcing that he was coming out with something he knew to be good, and enlivening the anticipation of all who recognized it; next, in a single sentence, he would deliver his observation, clever, epigrammatic, conclusive; and then he would stop suddenly, as if in a delighted astonishment at his own fluency, and would glance about him as though to compliment everyone near by for their cleverness in drawing out of him such unexpected depths: 'There! You've got it! That's the point!' Lytton, whose appreciation of the stage was inborn, was delighted by these accomplishments. 'Uncle Raleigh's voice is well suited for Blank Verse. Deep and Booming,' he told his mother after a series of especially fine lectures, with readings, which Raleigh had given on Elizabethan lyrics.

The Raleighs took a special interest in Lytton while he was at Liverpool, and would often invite him round to dinner, or take him out to concerts and theatres. The dissatisfaction which both men felt in themselves acted during these years as something of a common bond. But though there was nothing dismaying about Raleigh's fervent and genial temperament, Lytton often left his company reflecting on his own introvert wretchedness, his contrasting lack of charm and energy. This outward diffidence was swollen by an inwardly accumulating intellectual arrogance, which tended to rouse some hostility among the 'bloods', that class of popular sportsmen whom above all others he wished to conciliate, while yet affecting to despise them. His low vitality, squeaky voice and long, ungainly body preyed more than ever on his mind, and made him behave in public with inept self-consciousness. In the company of a single, intimate friend he could be relaxed and happy, affectionate and kind. But whenever two or more were gathered together he felt as if he were on show, being stared at like some queer zoological specimen. His morbidity would then intensify, and though he wanted desperately to shine superior even to Raleigh, to occupy, by unanimous acclaim, the very centre of the stage, he was still more moved by the fear of failure, of public humiliation, his vanity and lack of supporting conceit conspiring to paralyse him into long periods of motionless non-competitive silence.

Both in his letters to his mother and in an occasional diary entry Lytton gave thumb-nail sketches of some of the other dons whose lectures he attended. The most eccentric of these was undoubtedly John Macdonald Mackay, Rathbone Professor of Ancient History. 'Professor Mackay is very weird and somewhat casual,' he wrote shortly after arriving at Liverpool. 'The first difficulty is to hear what he's saying as he speaks in a most extraordinary sing-song. When that has been mastered the connection must be traced between the lecture and Roman History. Lastly, but most important, to prevent and curb shrieks of laughter.' The professor himself, however, never scrupled to curb his own outbursts of merriment, and as he soon grew particularly friendly with Lytton – having been at Balliol with his cousin St Loe Strachey – his peculiar mannerisms became rather embarrassing. 'Mackay's lecture on Greek History,' Lytton noted later on. 'This was dull today. M is rather too much inclined to think himself funny and laugh at his own jokes. He *will* look at me when he means to be witty, which is most inconvenient as I feel that I must smile and yet do not like pandering.'

Another don, hardly less colourful, was Assistant Professor P. Hebblethwaite, whose lectures on Greek impressed Lytton as being penetrating and humorous. 'H is quite a character,' he observed, 'very stout and lame of a leg; with handsome features and grey beard and hair. His eye-glasses are a constant source of amusement to me; and his continual "Yes?" which is quite unintended to be answered.'

The other dons were men of more ordinary stamp, and Lytton's opinion of them seems to have varied according as to how much he liked the subject on which they were lecturing him. At mathematics he had always been proficient, and he described Professor Frank Carey, the mathematical don, as 'thoroughly good'. His least favourite subject was almost certainly Latin. He found these lectures were consistently dull, while Professor Herbert Strong, who delivered them, was, he informed Lady Strachey, the least likeable of all his five burly instructors.

3

THE MELANCHOLY OF ANATOMY

The two years which Lytton spent at Liverpool were among the most bleak of his whole life. In his solitude he would often grow nostalgic for Leamington, and murmur to himself homilies on divine comradeship. Boredom and isolation engulfed him. He was quite unable either to excel as he had once dreamed of doing, or to find those few intimate friends whose presence would have rendered his lonely existence endurable. 'My life is a turmoil of dullness,' he confessed in his diary. 'My days are spent in a wild excitement over the most arrant details. The putting on of boots is thrilling; the taking off of a coat, hat and gloves more so; the walk to the College and back a very procession of agitations. And all carried on with a feverish haste, and a desire to be done with it. As for letters – the expectation of one, no matter from whom, is the subject of frenzy.'

His daily programme had about it a depressing sameness.

Each week-day he rose at about eight o'clock and after breakfast he attended intermittently from half-past nine to half-past one his various lectures at the college. The afternoons were left completely free. With his allowance of one pound a month, given to him by his mother, Lytton hired a bicycle which he called 'the Graphic'. After lunch he would set off for prodigious rides far away from Liverpool out into the country, or else to explore some distant second-hand book shop, trying all the time to forget the chilling routine of university life. In under a year he succeeded in travelling during these afternoons and the week-ends a thousand miles on the Graphic. This feat – an eloquent testimony of his urge to escape from the place – was all the more remarkable since on Tuesdays, Thursdays and Saturdays he had to be back in Liverpool before half-past six to undergo a course of strengthening exercises under the direction of a certain Dr Blüm, who, Lytton explained, 'is a Swede, and decent enough. The system is entirely different from the Macphearson, and much more scientific. No pulleys, no weights, merely movements of the arms, legs and body, he presses in the opposite direction. Thus the resistance is regulated by the man himself.' Most evenings Lytton would spend alone in his room, writing up the day's lectures, and composing poetry; and at about eleven he retired to bed.

During his years at Liverpool, Lytton lodged at Number 80 Rodney Street – just across the road from where Gladstone was born. It was a sombre, dignified street of Georgian houses, full of rather sombre and dignified professional men with their middle-class families. Typical of this district were Lytton's landlords, Dr and Mrs Alexander Stookes. At first they had been apprehensive of having a young student in the house, fearing that he would be rowdy and irresponsible. But contrary to their fears Lytton turned out to be a model lodger, unobtrusive and invariably polite in suffering himself to be introduced to all their unliterary friends, the medical fraternity of Liverpool. Their relief and gratitude were manifest. 'The boy has proved a delightful companion and no trouble to either of us,' Dr Stookes wrote to Lady Strachey after Lytton's first term. 'We could hardly have imagined that it would have been possible to have a stranger guest with so little friction.'

With Dr Stookes himself – whom he nicknamed 'Spookes' – Lytton eventually grew quite friendly. Together they would discuss literature, religion, sociology and all manner of other subjects. As an uncompromising admirer of Ruskin, Dr Stookes considered that Lytton's literary taste was not sufficiently catholic, mainly, it appears, because Lytton – under Walter Raleigh's influence – much preferred the works of Stevenson to those of Ruskin, whose endless over-emphasis he found tedious. It was Dr Stookes also who first introduced him to some of the country's most urgent social problems, escorting him round a number of Liverpool's worst slums. 'Nearly every street is a slum in this town, except those with the fine shops,' Lytton recorded in his diary. 'There is nothing intermediate. Hardly anyone lives in the town if they can possibly help it. Pitt Street was painful to me in the extreme; it stank; dirty 'furriners' wandered in groups over it; and a dingy barrel organ rattled its jargon in the yard.'

The sordid scenes he witnessed during these expeditions deeply offended his sense of the aesthetic and the humane, making on him a lasting impression that imbued his writing on the squalor of the Crimean War – composed many years later for his 'Florence Nightingale' – with an unusual simplicity and austere power. Sometimes he would venture out to these gloomy slums on his own, when the dirt and drabness of the atmosphere filled him with loathing, seeming as it did to mirror his own internal wretchedness. 'In the afternoon walked down to the docks and thence to the landing-stage,' one diary entry runs. 'The crowds of people were appalling. The landing-stage blocked; and *all* hideous. It gave me the shivers and in ten minutes I fled. My self-conscious vanity is really most painful. As I walk through the streets I am agonized by the thoughts of my appearance. Of course it is hideous, but what *does* it matter? I only make it worse by peering into people's faces to see what they are thinking. And the worst of it is I hate myself for doing it. The truth is I want companionship.'

In a vain endeavour to find this companionship Lytton joined several of the undergraduate societies. Tempted by the promise of light refreshments, he told his mother, 'I attended the University College Christian Union meeting, thus becoming acquainted with some of the students. A very good thing I thought, but why Christian? A prayer terminated the proceedings. The undergraduates are not, I think particularly enlightened, but as yet I have only spoken to the less advanced ones.' A little later in his first term he was elected to the debating society, where he had higher hopes of meeting some kindred intellectual spirits. The first gathering he attended did not promise well. 'The subject is very dull,' he wrote to his mother, 'viz: "The Eastern Foreign Policy of the Government." So easy to attack; so tedious to defend!' For several months Lytton continued to go to these debates without ever taking an active part in them. Then, in March 1898, much to his dismay, he was scheduled to make his first speech, in defence of the use of slang. 'The day of the debate on slang,' he noted in his diary. 'I was alarmed, as I had only been able to scribble a few remarks by 2.30. The debate was at 4.30 with a tea at 4. I managed to put down some absurd notes and then, palpitating with horror, started off for the College. I arrived late of course. The tea was in the Ladies' Debating Room which was a most charming apartment. I stood dumbly and swallowed a cup of tea. Then, after a long pause, while everyone else was talking, we adjourned to the literature room, which was soon pretty well filled. I was horrified to see the swells of the place such as Grundy, Burnett, etc., accumulated there.' Luckily Lytton's opponents in the debate opened the proceedings with the proposition that slang was undesirable, so that he spoke last, seconding a Miss Hoare, a lady with flaxen hair and a twang. For half an hour he sat there hardly hearing what was being said and excruciated with a dreadful fear until it was time for him to rise and address the meeting. Then, despite his trepidation, all went well. 'Fortunately for me,' he modestly explained afterwards, 'I have come to be considered a funny man, so that the audience began to laugh even before I spoke. Perhaps my appearance accounted for this however. I stumbled through my very short oration somehow, and was relieved that it should have gone down so well.'

After this initial address, Lytton delivered several other successful speeches to the society. But though the strangeness of his manner and personal appearance enhanced these oratorical performances on the debating platform, he experienced it keenly as a barrier to all that he most desired from life, lust and power, love and humanity. He wanted to be a superman, and he felt he was a freak. His humour, however, often came to the rescue, reducing into ridicule the superior adjustment of others to the humdrum and taking the sting out of his own humiliation. He was adept at anticipating and neutralizing the derision of bystanders, and, by the same token, minimizing to himself the shock he had sustained — transferring it even to other people. 'The other day as I was sitting in the drawing-room with my back to the light,' he narrated to his mother on one occasion, 'a lady visitor who had been to inspect the twins, suddenly entered. Rushing up to me she said, "Oh my dear Dr Stookes, I really must congratulate you on your *charming* children! So pretty; so sweet!" Without a word I slowly rose to my full majestic height and the lady, giving one gasp of horror, fled wildly from the room!'

Some companionship he did eventually find to relieve his solitude, though it was far from being the ideal, passionate union for which he yearned. One new friend was Lumsden Barkway, later bishop of St Andrews. 'He is the son of a presbyterian clergyman, and is going in for that profession himself,' Lytton informed his mother. 'But he tries his best not to be bound down, and takes an interest in pictures and such. He is rather melancholy, and has hardly ever been out of the suburb of Liverpool where he lives.' Another friend whom he met at this time was a Miss Combe, the 'austerely flighty' headmistress of a large girls' school, whose sister had married Oliver Strachey's friend, Roger Fry. Miss Combe was — or of necessity became – an ardent cyclist with an inexhaustible fund of pastoral sagas (she would prattle on effusively about 'spring foliage' and 'autumn tints') and their friendship was conducted almost exclusively from two bicycles. Despite a number of unchaperoned and 'not altogether unsuccessful' bicycle trips together, Lytton did not really warm to Miss Combe. 'Women are such strange creatures,' he remarked. 'Miss Combe is not so pleasant. She appeared to me to possess the qualities of a groveller.'

Throughout his two years at Liverpool he met no one who responded intimately to his odd, secretive personality, no one who answered his innermost needs. 'Miss C is not good enough,' he concluded; 'besides I want someone who can go out for walks with me at any time. Barkway? Dear me, is that all University College can give me? If I could only make friends with Grundy or Bird![1] But my "habitual reserve" is too much for them. Well, well, well, perhaps I shall find someone some day. And then I am sure he – or she – will not belong to University College. Talking of shes, I think it is too much that one cannot speak to a member of "the sex" without being looked upon askance by somebody or other. If only people were more sensible on this point, half the so called immorality would come to an end at once. I wonder if I shall ever "fall in love". I can't help smiling at the question – if they only knew – if they only knew! But it is tragedy also.'

4

DIARIES AND DECISIONS

On 3 March, two days after his eighteenth birthday, Lytton began a new diary. All his earlier endeavours, he confessed, had been unsuccessful. 'Many times before I have got a book and written in it my thoughts and actions,' he explained. 'But my previous attempts have been crowned with failure; in as

1. Allan Wilson Grundy and Lancelot William Bird, two senior undergraduates who, in 1898, were both awarded B.A. degrees in the Faculty of Arts.

much as after 2, 3, or possibly 4 entries the diary came to an end. Another effort! God knows there is small enough reason for it. My other autobiographical writings were the outcome of excitements really quite out of the commonplace; but this is *begun*, at any rate, in the veriest dog days imaginable.'

This latest diary was his longest and most successful to date, covering a period of about six weeks. Though it contains some amusing sketches, many of its pages make depressing reading, being filled with much sentimental rhetoric and exuding a stagnant air of sick resignation. One of the opening passages reveals elaborately Lytton's obsessive lack of confidence and of self-knowledge, and the wavering uncertainty he felt in the course of his own future. 'My character', he wrote, 'is not crystallized. So there will be little recorded here that is not transitory, and there will be much here that is quite untrue. The inquisitive reader, should he peep between the covers, will find anything but myself, who perhaps after all do not exist but in my own phantasy.' Unable to contemplate directly his own hated image, he uses Shakespeare as a convenient looking-glass. 'Had Shakespeare any character? of his own, that is to say?' The answer, he goes on, is that he had not, and that Shakespeare was 'a cynic in his inmost heart of hearts'. Assumed superior cynicism, the endemic consolation of those spirits too shy to assert themselves in the full company of others, is a condition of egocentricity most prevalent among adolescents. The usual front of envious contempt which accompanies this type of youthful disillusion is very clearly exhibited in the next passage from the diary, in which Lytton pretends to rejoice in his enforced isolation, preferring it to the vulgar conviviality of the extrovert. 'Better so, perhaps; in fact necessarily so. And there are quite sufficient of the other sort.'

The purpose of keeping this diary was to redress the balance between the glamour of his private dreams and the degradation of the public spectacle he made. Within its pages Lytton was tortured by no fear of making an exhibition of himself, of boring others instead of impressing them. It was, he points out, 'a safety valve to my morbidity'. Although no longer bullied as he once had been at school, his sense of loneliness was more overwhelming, for in the larger multifarious world of the university he remained unknown and disregarded. As always when deeply unhappy, his microscopic inward gaze could not avoid focusing sharply on his appearance, and he gave expression to his misery in terms of anguished physical self-disgust: 'When I consider that I am now 18 years of age a shudder passes through my mind, and I hardly dare look at the creature those years have made me.'

This feeling of wretchedness, which dominated so much of his time at Liverpool, was further deepened by his repeated failure to get any of the poetry he was now writing accepted by the university magazine, *The Sphinx*. The poems which he submitted – sonnets and epigrams – are less personal than his diary entries; they are sometimes competently done, but seldom original. The first of his verses ever to be printed did not appear until he had gone up to Cambridge. But though eventually coming out in *The Granta* and not *The Sphinx*, they were in fact written while Lytton was still at Liverpool and belong to this period. Entitled 'On being asked for a description of a Roundel', this piece illustrates the commendable degree of metrical skill which Lytton, at his best and least ambitious, had by now attained.

> A Roundel is a thing that's not
> So *very* irksome to compose.
> It's something that one throws off hot –
> A Roundel is.
> The first thing needful, I suppose,
> Is some slight sentiment or plot,
> Then start off with a fitting close
> Add rhymes (with luck you'll find a lot)
> And, my inquiring friend, – who knows? –
> Perhaps you may have here just what
> A Roundel is.

Not all Lytton's endeavours, however, were crowned with failure. At the end of March 1898, he took the Intermediate B.A. examination and learnt two months later that he had passed in all subjects – Mathematics, Ancient History, Greek,

Latin and English literature. That summer, Lady Strachey arranged for him to spend some weeks with a French family, the Renons, who lived at Loches, about a hundred and thirty miles south-west of Paris, on the gently flowing Indre.

Early in June, with his baggage and his bicycle, Lytton set out, travelling first by train to Paris where he spent one night and then on the next day via Tours, to Loches itself. Twenty-four hours after arriving there he wrote back a long letter to his mother describing all the adventures on this, his first journey abroad to be undertaken alone:

Yesterday morning I sallied forth from the hotel, and, marching down the Avenue de l'Opéra found myself opposite the Hôtel du Louvre.... After making a tour of the building seven or eight times I found an entrance, and, giving up my umbrella to a gendarme, was soon lost among the majestic remnants of the Ancient World. I found it all too difficult to tear myself away. ... But at length, seizing my umbrella, I dashed into a chabriolet which conveyed me successfully to Saint [indecipherable]. The price of a commissionaire to look after the luggage was 5 francs – too much – so I essayed the perilous task myself. What need be said of the wild journey through the metropolis of the great Republic, the fearful jolts of the vehicle threatening at every moment to snatch me from my bicycle which I still held clasped to my breast? Twice we were nearly killed; twice we escaped death by a hairsbreadth. We reached the Gare d'Orléans a quarter of an hour before time and ... proceeded to Tours (changing at St-Pierre) where I had lunch, and took a walk in the town which appeared charming. Thence to Loches. I was met by a jeune homme aged 19, a son of M. Renon. We then drove in an omnibus here – 6 miles – where I was received by the family circle with open arms. M. Renon, Madame, Mademoiselle (15?) et bébé (fils 10). The rest of the family I have not seen, and I am not sure whether they exist. The house is charming, quite small, with all the rooms opening out of doors. My room is on the ground floor, and can only be approached by a door leading into the garden. Everyone is as polite as peculiar – much more gentle (in its true sense) than in England in corresponding circumstances. I am lured on to talk, and can understand fairly well, though the speed distresses me ...

Joining more readily than was customary for him in the casual but almost compulsory conviviality that went on,

Lytton soon became acquainted with the rest of the family who were constantly in and out of the house, in particular M. Renon's jovial younger brother who lived with his wife two miles off at Persusson. 'Apparently he is the youngest of the brothers and the best off,' Lytton wrote. 'He has only one child I *think*; and cultivates the vine also.' Of several of the guests who were entertained by the Renons Lytton would make short pen-portraits which he then introduced into his letters home. 'On Thursday M. le Curé and les deux Anglais came to dinner. The Curé has white fuzzy hair, a red face, a black gown, and an ecclesiastical hat. Les deux Anglais are called Ross and Chamberlain. Ross is short, wears eye-glasses, and knows the whole of Bradshaw by heart. Chamberlain is the image of the rest of the family . . .'

The scheme of Lytton's life at Loches was happy and simple. He spent most of the day reading Gibbon, walking for short distances in the cool of the day, composing a hilarious blank verse tragedy, catching frogs in the garden pond and, during the evening, playing cards. Every day, too, he repeatedly mislaid, until finally breaking altogether, his spectacles. He also inspected the dungeons at Loches where Louis XI confined his unfortunate friends, describing them as very terrible, 'most gloomy and ghastly, with the walls covered with the inscriptions of the prisoners'.

Despite his general mood of contentedness, the un-English way in which the Renons organized their time struck Lytton as eccentric. 'Life here is more like that on board ship than anything else,' he explained to his mother. 'I rise from my couch at 8.30. At 9 I have a petit déjeuner of coffee au lait and toast and butter. At 11.30 Déjeuner, consisting of lots of vegetables, soup, a small quantity of meat and strawberries. At half-past six is dinner, pretty well the same as déjeuner . . . I don't much approve of the French system of meals which elongates the afternoon abnormally and abolishes the morning and evening. Before déjeuner I do "traductions" which are quite harmless and amusing. After déjeuner I sleep for one hour – the rarity of meals rendering a vast absorption necessary when there is one.'

On Sundays Lytton would go with the rest of the family to church. There, as a highly critical member of the congregation, he observed dispassionately the various Catholic rites and ceremonies, welcoming only those opportunities which the *pain bénit* afforded him of augmenting his infrequent meals. Ill-satisfied, by and large, with the entertainment, he would later write up for his mother accounts of these services, some of which read more like theatre reviews of amateur musical productions. 'I sat behind the altar, at the very back of the building. From this position the show appeared tawdry. The robes of the Curé were truly splendid, but the tinsel, and the sham marble wallpaper were incongruous. A young man played vilely on the harmonium and the singing rivalled that of an English village church. On the whole I was not impressed, though I ate the holy bread like a martyr.' As for the Roman Church in general, he was sadly disappointed with it. It was tawdry and vulgar. 'On the whole,' he reassured Lumsden Barkway, 'I think I shall remain protestant.'

Far more to Lytton's taste were the pagan and pleasure-loving festivities celebrated later in the day. Often during these Sunday afternoons in summer a fair was set up in the market-place at Loches where the whole town, reinforced by the floating population of several villages near by, would assemble to enjoy themselves late into the long warm evenings. The sight of all this merrymaking exhilarated Lytton. Yet in his descriptions of the revelry he is, however sympathetic and exultant, always the spectator, never an active participant. 'An awning had been erected beneath which the people were dancing to the sound of clockwork music. It was a most amusing spectacle. The paysannes with their white lace caps, and handkerchiefs tied round their waists to keep their dresses clean, hanging on to their partners with both arms round their necks. When the music stopped they kissed and parted! It was a great relief to see all this happening on a Sunday.'

It had been Lytton's original intention to spend a month or six weeks at Loches, but he found the gentle pace of life there so congenial that eventually he stayed on a full two months. 'France is not so bad as it might be,' he admitted to Lumsden

Barkway. 'I was not so absolutely dumb as I expected to be; the country is charming and the people most kind and polite. The only drawback I have discovered as yet is in what I call the "sanitary arrangement". It is dark and dank, and full of bluebottles! I hardly dare to venture in – most inconvenient.'

He returned to civilization in the early part of August, joining his family at Ardeley Bury, 'a really delightful country house' near Stevenage in Hertfordshire. Here he spent several pleasant weeks doing nothing very much except reading Lecky, Tacitus, Thucydides, Thackeray and *Paradise Lost* which, he told Lumsden Barkway, was 'the best thing in the English language!'

In the first week of October, Lytton returned once more to Liverpool. Having passed his Intermediate B.A. examination, he was now confronted with the decision of whether to read history at Oxford or at Cambridge. In the past the family had assumed that he would go up to Cambridge, but more recently his mother had decided that he should prepare himself for entry into the Civil Service, and that to do this he ought to follow his brother, Oliver, up to Balliol College. 'If your object is the Civil Service,' she wrote to him (4 December 1898), 'you are likely to be better prepared for the examination at Oxford than at Cambridge. So we have settled it that way. Your father met Mr A. L. Smith – the Balliol tutor – at the Royal Society dinner, and he says you are to go to him and he will put you through your paces, and advise accordingly – which is his function; and this you will do during the Christmas holidays. We propose that you should enter at the next October term, and go up for the entrance exam before the Easter term.'

Although Lytton greatly preferred the prospect of studying at Cambridge, he acquiesced meekly enough in his mother's decision. At the same time Professor Mackay, learning that Lady Strachey was considering removing her son from Liverpool at the earliest possible moment and installing him at a private tutory, himself made a sudden dash up to Lancaster Gate and succeeded in persuading her to let him remain at University College for at least another two terms. He also suggested that her son should take a Balliol scholarship in the following November. But to this Lady Strachey would not agree, and finally a compromise solution was reached: Lytton would take his Responsions in March and then, in June, try for a Christ Church scholarship which, if obtained, would automatically make him eligible for entry to Balliol in the Michaelmas term of 1899. Throughout all these shifting and involved negotiations Lytton – despite his strong feelings on the matter – seems to have been little more than a passive spectator.

These new arrangements for his academic future were communicated to Lytton at the start of the winter holidays. Not surprisingly he was very subdued, and his spirits were further depressed by the ordeal of a family Christmas at Lancaster Gate, which appears to have been celebrated by the Stracheys one day earlier than customary, and which was something that in later life Lytton always strove to avoid. 'My time has been spent as follows,' he informed Lumsden Barkway, '– Dec. 16th–Dec. 24th. Preparations for Christmas festivities, and visits to the National Gallery. Dec. 24th. Official Christmas (very terrible). Dec. 25th. My cousin Charles and his wife Ada (sister of Raleigh) came to dinner (at which I ate and drank *far* too much). They afterwards sang a charming song called the "Kensit Battle Hymn" written by Charlie and Raleigh. *Delightful!* Dec. 25th–28th. Severe illness resulting from Xmas festivities.' The next day some of the family left London and moved to the Bank House in the High Street at Guildford, which belonged to one of Lytton's uncles who temporarily went to fill the vacuum at Lancaster Gate. 'The house is over a shop,' Lytton explained to Lumsden Barkway, ' – rather peculiar, isn't it? – but charming for all that, though the beds are rather short and hard.'

When he returned to Liverpool in the New Year, the course of his studies was altered so that he might prepare himself for the Christ Church scholarship in which his special subject was to be the Early Roman Empire, with eighteenth-century England thrown in as an extra. In view of the development of his prose style, the comments which he made at this time on

Gibbon's method of treating Christianity are of particular interest. 'I have been reading the Great Gibbon lately,' he wrote to his mother in February, 'and have just finished the two chapters on Christianity. They are the height of amusement – his attitude throughout so unimpeachably decorous; but I can't help thinking it all rather unfortunate. If he had not been so taken up with his scorn of superstition, he might have paid some attention to the extraordinary change which was coming over the world, the change from the pagan idea to the christian idea, which, however unsound the doctrines that contributed to its success, was still dominating Europe (I suppose) at the time Gibbon wrote. He might at least have cast a glance at the old paganism that had gone for ever. But he never touches more than the externals. I suppose his mind was unable to appreciate the real spirit of Christianity. The whole subject of the Roman Empire is so wildly and extraordinarily interesting that I am hardly able to contain myself when I think of it.'

On 21 March, Lytton travelled up to Oxford, spending four days in a bleak lodging house, No. 4 St John Street, while he took his Responsions. He hated exposure to public scrutiny, and in front of the Balliol tutor for Responsions, J. L. Strachan-Davidson, he cut a weirdly unprepossessing figure, accentuating the natural oddness of his appearance with a nervous unpredictable manner. This ordeal over, he returned for ten days to Lancaster Gate, bringing with him his Presbyterian friend, Lumsden Barkway, who had just won a scholarship to a theological college. 'I wish I were you!' Lytton told him. 'I have Oxford still before me. Alas.' The rest of this vacation was spent more happily with his cousin, Pat Grant, in Winchester.

By the end of April he was back at Liverpool for the Easter term. Three weeks later he visited Cambridge for a few days in company with Walter Raleigh, who 'gave a most witty lecture on Chesterfield'. The more rural and informal atmosphere of Cambridge appealed to him far more than Oxford, and he wished deeply that his mother had decided to send him here instead. Already he seemed to belong to its peculiar environment, to have assimilated himself with its community, and his letters home are full of social calls paid on friends and relations. 'On Sunday I lunched in Clough Hall where the Sidgwicks[2] were present, also the Freshfields[3] who were staying with them. On Monday I had dinner with Miss Stephen[4] in Sidgwick Hall. The Raleighs also came and paid Pernel a visit in her chamber.'

In the third week of June Lytton left University College, Liverpool, for the last time. Although his years there had not been happy or particularly successful, he felt little excitement at leaving, for he no longer faced the future with quite the same brave spirit which had infused his last days at Leamington. 'The thought of final departure is indeed painful,' he wrote to his mother (12 June 1899). 'Packing will be a sad business.' Paradoxically, Lady Strachey, who was happier at her son's departure from Liverpool, felt generally well pleased with his progress there. Most important of all, he had passed all his crucial examinations, and this in spite of being persistently incapacitated by sickness. It had been a very creditable performance. 'I think the Liverpool plan has been a success on

2. Henry Sidgwick (1838–1900), the philosopher and free-thinker, who wrote textbooks on ethics and political economy, advocated higher education for women, and, in the words of John Maynard Keynes, 'never did anything but wonder whether Christianity was true and prove that it wasn't and hope that it was. He even learnt Arabic in order to read Genesis in the original, not trusting the authorized translators, which does seem a little sceptical. And he went to Germany to see what Ewald had to say and fell in love with a professor's daughter, and wrote to his dearest friends about the American Civil War.'
His wife, Eleanor Mildred Sidgwick (1845–1936), the Principal (1892–1910) of Newnham College, was a sister of Arthur Balfour, the Prime Minister.

3. Douglas William Freshfield, mountain climber and author, and his wife Augusta, sister of Mrs Cornish and eldest daughter of the Hon. W. Ritchie, later Advocate General of Calcutta, were friends of the Stracheys. Their house in London was in these years a hub of cultivated society.

4. Miss Katherine Stephen, a cousin of Vanessa and Virginia Stephen, became Principal of Newnham, where Lytton's sister Pernel was studying. Athena Clough, her successor and Pernel's predecessor as Principal, was then a tutor there.

the whole,' she told him, 'and I am sure you have been better off than you would have been at a private Tutory.'

At the end of June, Lytton again went to Oxford, where he took the Christ Church scholarship examination. From here he travelled up alone to Rothiemurchus, where he stayed in lodgings, having meals with and being looked after by one of his aunts, until early August. 'In the evening, when the sun is setting, one cannot help being a little sad,' he wrote in the course of a rather stilted rhapsody addressed to Lumsden Barkway, but one which nevertheless does convey something of his very genuine pangs of nostalgia, 'it is the sadness of regret. The days of childhood, with their passionate pains and pleasures, are with us; days nearer to us, too, with their precious moments of bitterness and love; and the present day that is fading beneath the hills for ever.' His examinations no longer seemed so important, only slightly absurd. He idled pleasantly through these summer days indulging himself in delicious retrospective emotions, and soon he was feeling both happier and more philosophically sad than at any time since leaving school. It was all very satisfactory, to float along in a timeless chimera of recaptured sensations. 'Here, among the mountains,' he wrote, 'the Vision of Balliol itself seems to dwindle and appear insignificant.'

The actuality of Balliol was also, unknown to Lytton, fast dwindling. While he was in Rothiemurchus the result of his entrance examination came through. In the course of a long letter to Lady Strachey, J. L. Strachan-Davidson wrote:

'We have read the papers, and have come to the conclusion that the Essay is decidedly promising, but that the Classical work is insufficient. The Latin Translation was fair but the Greek was not up to the mark, and the Latin Prose was bad.

'I am not sure that this disappointment will not prove all for the best. I was struck by the extreme shyness and nervousness displayed by Mr Strachey, and much doubt whether he would be happy in a large College like Balliol. I am afraid that the pace would be too quick for him, and that he would find himself outside of the life and society of the place.'

Lytton would probably be happier, Strachan-Davidson

continued, at some smaller college in Oxford. As a suitable alternative to Balliol he suggested Lincoln College which, with his own special recommendation, would almost certainly accept him. This college, he explained, consisted of about sixty-five undergraduates, most of whom had not passed through the great public schools, and its more modest and intimate climate would, for that reason, be far better for a boy like Lytton, silent, maladroit and of a literary turn.

Lady Strachey was both angry and bitterly disappointed at this exclusion of her son from Balliol, based, she felt convinced, more on a superficial and inaccurate estimate of his character than on the quality of his written work. She rejected absolutely the notion that Lytton would be better placed at Lincoln College, and in her reply to Strachan-Davidson she drew a shrewd analysis of Lytton's peculiar personality.

I am sure you are mistaken in your diagnosis of his disposition, [she wrote] though I am not surprised at the impression produced. He has a very unfortunate manner which was no doubt at its worst in circumstances where a certain amount of nervousness is not inexcusable; but as a matter of fact it is more manner than anything else; he is both self-reliant and equable in a rather unusual degree. He has hitherto got on exceedingly well with other boys and young men wherever he has been placed, so that I should not feel very anxious about his eventually settling down comfortably in such a society as that of Balliol. At any rate, in sending him to College we look for the advantage to be gained by a larger, fuller life than would be obtained in one of the smaller colleges.

Up in Scotland Lytton received the news of his non-acceptance by Balliol with mixed feelings. On first reading Strachan-Davidson's letter it seemed to him as if the 'comble des horreurs' had indeed arrived. He hated failure of any kind and, as he had told his sister Dorothy, it was AGAINST HIS PRINCIPLES to miss the mark in an examination. But once he let his mind dwell on the possible life which, so unexpectedly, might now await him at Cambridge, he felt far happier. By this time his mother had made up her mind to send him to Trinity, which, with over six hundred undergraduates, was the largest college in Cambridge. The prospect delighted Lytton, and he wrote to assure her that 'the idea of Trinity is indeed pleasant'. As for Lady Strachey herself, once she had overcome her initial disappointment she was reconciled, even optimistic about the new plan. She could no longer see her son so clearly in the role of Lord Lytton, but perhaps, might he not just conceivably be another Lord Tennyson? 'I think you are to be congratulated on the change,' she told him, 'especially as it is a sign from above that you are to be a poet – the coming man in that line could never have been allowed to be anywhere but at Cambridge.'

Lytton returned to Lancaster Gate early in August and then moved down with the family to Selham House, near Petworth. There, surrounded by books and sisters, he spent his mornings preparing assiduously for the Previous Examination (then commonly known as the 'little-go'), and reading – in particular Swinburne, who was 'VERY GOOD', and Boswell's *Johnson* which he considered 'most delightful' – while the afternoons were usually passed bicycling in the country with his sister Pippa. Together they inspected the pictures at Petworth House, which Lytton pronounced to be 'excellent',[5] and visited Arundel Park – 'a most pleasant spot – very hilly and wooded. In the town of Arundel we were nearly arrested and thrown into jail for wheeling our bicycles on the pavement.' On another joint expedition they reached Witley, about fifteen miles off, where they called on Arthur Melville, the painter.[6] 'Mr M is painting what I daresay may be a chef-

5. The third Earl of Egremont's great collection of Turner's paintings, which he began in 1802. Turner often stayed at Petworth in the 1830s, working on his famous 'colour poems'. Sir John Rothenstein has written that 'at Petworth, the genius of Turner blossomed with an unprecedented brilliance ... the last of the inhibitions that the busy world imposed on Turner were resolved, and he was free to see the world as light and movement. ... Turner's sojourn at Petworth must ever be valued as one of the most fruitful episodes in the history of English painting.' There are, of course, many other things at Petworth besides the Turners. Lytton was particularly struck by two Holbein portraits – of Henry VIII and Edward VI.

6. Arthur Melville (1855–1904), Scottish figure and landscape painter. He died at Witley of typhoid contracted in Spain almost exactly five years after Lytton met him. For a long time he had been a friend of the

d'ouvre – the crucifixion', Lytton wrote to Lumsden Barkway. 'Most unlike anything you ever saw before on that
subject – Realistic. Very bright colours on the top half, and
shadow over the bottom. It is just the moment before the sun
sets, and the crowd is coming away – the three crosses at the
back – the Christ full in the light of the setting sun – his head
forward – and *bright* red hair covering his face. It is rather
magnificent and appalling I think. In the foreground in the
crowd is a Roman Centurion on horseback. It is all very striking. There were some other most charming things – landscapes chiefly. He is a quaint man.'

But dominating all other thoughts during these weeks was
the fearful, exquisite vision of Cambridge. 'As to Cambridge,'
he admitted to Lumsden Barkway, 'I am looking forward to it
with more dread than you. Though I am sure it will be charming in the long run – but the beginning I fear will be painful –
as most beginnings are to me.'

Towards the end of September, Lytton left Petworth and,
having in the course of the following month passed both
parts of the little-go, he was admitted as a pensioner at Trinity. At about the same time, too, a letter from Walter Raleigh arrived at the college announcing that among its
freshmen that Michaelmas would be a certain ex-pupil of his,
an undergraduate of remarkable distinction.

Stracheys. 'I remember him from at least 1893,' James Strachey told the
author. 'In that summer when we had Syston Court, near Bristol, Arthur
Melville made huge posters almost eight feet high of brown paper and
other coloured paper in the most modern style to advertise "Mr Pecunia
Sackum", a play written and acted by Lytton and Marjorie. He was a
leading member of the Glasgow school – specially as a water-colourist in
the impressionistic manner.'

FOUR

Fratribus

I think that in the chronicle of Age
   The richest Chapter bears the name of Youth,
For in that fair and still unspotted page
      Shines the incalculable jewel, Truth.

I think that Beauty, breathing on Youth's breast,
   Alone can teach us what the Schools ignore
— How piled-up goods can never reach the Best
   — How words are much, but eyes and hearts much more.

I think that with these Twain there ever dwells
   Love, who for them with hands of gentle night
And deep, mysterious, and passionate spells
   Has built a Heaven in this world's despite.

Lytton Strachey (undated)

1
A NEW ANIMAL

Now, for the fifth time in six years, Lytton had to face the terrifying ordeal of being a new member of a strange community. But on this occasion, owing partly to Walter Raleigh's thoughtfulness which helped to determine his immediate circle of friends, the agony of his isolation did not persist for long. At Cambridge he seemed to know from the first that he had entered a milieu which in many respects exactly suited him. The civilized sunny atmosphere was very wonderful after the damp breezes of Liverpool; and he was soon flourishing. His letters home are unusually cheerful, almost jovial: 'Ho! Ho! Ho! How proud I was as I swept through the streets of Cambridge yesterday, arrayed for the first time in cap and gown!' he wrote to his mother on 3 October. 'To my great surprise and delight the gown is blue!

133

Lovely!' And again, a fortnight later, he was writing in the same ecstatic vein: 'I am enjoying myself deeply, though I have been here only a week and am just beginning to enter into things. Everyone is the pique of politeness and kindness.'[1]

Apart perhaps from Walter Headlam, the classical scholar, Lytton knew no one on arriving at Trinity until he came across his Liverpool friend Lumsden Barkway, who was studying near by at the Westminster Theological College. In these first weeks, before Lytton had made any new friends from among his fellow undergraduates, the two of them would go off on bicycle rides together, and have tea in Lytton's rooms. These rooms, like everything else at Cambridge, immediately delighted him. After an initial inspection he informed his mother that 'they are very nice – on the 2nd floor – the sitting-room facing the Court [New Court], the bedroom the backs – with a beautiful view of weeping willows'. The following term he was transferred from these rooms to rather darker ones on the ground floor of New Court. These he did not care for so much and since, in the opinion of his mother, they were detrimental to his health, arrangements were made early in 1901 for him to lodge at a set of first-floor attics on Staircase K (where Byron had had rooms, in the topmost one of which he was said to have kept a bear) within the southeast corner turret of the Great Court of Trinity – 'nice and rather quaint with sloping roofs, etc.' Here, in what for unknown reasons used to be known as 'mutton-hole corner', he remained for almost five years.

Probably the only Cambridge phenomena which did not meet with his approval were the dons. His tutor at Trinity was J. D. Duff[2] whom he nicknamed 'Plum Duff', explaining to his mother that he 'cooes like a dove', and that he was fond of

1. Lytton first went up to Trinity at the end of September to take his little-go. This was presumably after the beginning of the Michaelmas term, but before the beginning of 'full-term'.

2. Duff was an Apostle. He was devoted to Lytton and on his account, James Strachey told the author, 'put up with my subsequent unsatisfactoriness'.

engaging him in long soothing talks 'chiefly about persons —
ranging from Heine to Sidney Lee'. The professor under
whom he learnt history, (Sir) Stanley Leathes — 'Mr Stand-at-
ease'[3] — was, however, the reverse of soporific, 'rather severe,
and hideously ugly, but very much on the spot'. Every week
Lytton had to take him an essay which was read aloud while
Lytton squirmed — altogether a most painful experience, but
one which he later turned to good use, adapting it as a means
of checking his literary compositions.

With his long limp body, his congenital short-sight, startling pale complexion and rather prim, secretive manner,
Lytton was certainly a formidable-looking undergraduate.
'His impact upon Cambridge when he came up was of a man
from a different planet,' Professor H. O. Meredith told the
author, 'human, but not of our humanity, who belonged in
his speech, gestures, poses and opinions to no recognized
category of adolescence or maturity. The Strachey "voice"
(which became so deservedly famous: faint echoes of it are
still discoverable in contemporary society) was only one of
his "differentials". His ways of standing, or sitting in a chair,
or helping himself to bread and butter — briefly everything
about him differentiated him from the crowd. The impression
was *not* however (*at least not primarily*) one of originality:
there was about him not much suggestion of a genius and still
less of a crank. He gave rather the feeling of one who brought
with him the ways and manners of an unsurmised and different
civilization.'

Inevitably such a man charmed some and irritated others.
Though a few of the 'bloods' were actively annoyed by his
freakish personality and on one occasion attempted to duck
him in the fountain, their numbers were never very great. Nor
were the charmed numerous. The most usual reaction was to
be more or less strongly intrigued: here was a new animal in
their midst, alien yet inoffensive, whom it was not easy to
accept and quite impossible to ignore.

Despite the disturbing sensation he produced, the Cam-

3. This name originated from his having been so announced by the
butler at the door of the Lancaster Gate drawing-room.

bridge community, with its high proportion of vocational bachelors[4] accommodated Lytton far better than anything he had hitherto experienced. Within a few short weeks he had already struck up several new and permanently valuable friendships; and during the six years he was resident there, the number of his friends increased as his personal prestige and influence within the university steadily widened. These often lifelong companionships – similar in some respects to those of Edward FitzGerald – were, as Desmond MacCarthy once observed, more like loves. And for this reason, part at least of his career at Trinity is best seen in relation to those who were closest to him.

2

ONCE UPON A MIDNIGHT

Among the freshmen at Trinity that Michaelmas were three with whom Lytton soon became closely associated: Clive Bell, Leonard Woolf and Saxon Sydney-Turner. Early in Lytton's second term, and together with one other undergraduate, A. J. Robertson,[5] these five marshalled themselves into a small society which, in the opinion of Clive Bell in whose rooms it met, formed the original source of the celebrated Bloomsbury Group. 'The Reading Club consists of 5 members,' Lytton wrote to his mother soon after its formation (February 1900). 'Myself, Robertson, Sydney-Turner (very distinguished and with immense knowledge of English Literature), Bell (a curious mixture of sport and reading) and

4. Dons had only recently been permitted to marry and continue to hold their fellowships and many of the younger ones could not afford a wife. Undergraduates in Strachey's class, Noël Annan has written, 'were solemnly warned of the guileful way in which they might be entrapped by the tobacconist's daughter, and every college was a bachelor community. Such communities provide elaborate justifications for their ethos, and in this case the justification came from the classics.'

5. A. J. Robertson was a brother in the flesh (i.e. as opposed to an Apostolic brother) of D. H. Robertson, the economist and father of James Robertson, the conductor.

Woolf (nothing particular). Last night we read J[ohn] G[abriel] B[orkman] – my Foldal being considered very life-like. I died of internal laughter every 5 minutes. Last time we did The Return of the Druses and next time we do the Cenci – so you see our taste is catholic. They are all very amusing and pleasant.'

With Robertson, whom he originally described as 'a most entertaining personage ... very tall, with a round cherubic face', Lytton's friendship did not develop far after he made the discovery that his father was a clergyman. But he quickly introduced into the group a sixth member, Thoby Stephen, who, he informed his mother (18 October 1899), 'looked a charmer, and the image of the others.[6] He has rooms in Whewell's Court. .... He is rather strange but I think sensible and the best I have yet met.'

Only an unremittingly earnest band of young men could have survived such an arduous overture to lifelong friendship. They called themselves the Midnight Society since it was their custom to meet each Saturday night at twelve o'clock. Having first strengthened themselves for their late-night marathon 'with whisky or punch and one of those gloomy beef-steak pies which it was the fashion to order for Sunday lunch', Clive Bell recounts, they would proceed 'to read aloud some such trifle as *Prometheus Unbound*, *The Cenci*, *The Return of the Druses*, *Bartholomew Fair* or *Comus*. As often as not it was dawn by the time we had done; and sometimes we would issue forth to perambulate the courts and cloisters, halting on Hall steps to spout passages of familiar verse, each following his fancy as memory served.' Finally, feeling as though a poetic apocalypse had opened, they would disperse in silent awe and weariness, and wander back to their cosy, masculine rooms.

Perhaps the most unlikely member of the group was Clive Bell himself. 'A gay and amiable dog', as Maynard Keynes retrospectively described him, and a 'bubbler' in the opinion of Frank Swinnerton, he was full of boyish high spirits. His

6. For two generations the Stracheys and the Stephens had been on cordial terms, and had a number of friends in common.

hair was golden-brown and covered his scalp with a waving luxuriance. The large, spacious, pink and polished face was fresh, though a little moonlike, and his forehead even now, before baldness had begun prematurely to set in, was intellectual in its smooth and lofty elevation. When he came up to Trinity from Marlborough most of his confrères had belonged to the affluent hunting and shooting set; and on the first occasion that the ascetic Leonard Woolf caught sight of him, he was strutting through Great Court arrayed in full sporting finery down to the hunting horn and the whip carried by the whipper-in.

When Bell was his natural, breezy self, speechifying on about the hunt or the shoot in his unreflecting 'so-happy-that-I-don't-care-whether-I-impress-you-or-not' sort of mood, Lytton was swept off his feet and thought him splendid. But whenever he recollected himself and set out to play the part of the literary gentleman, he struck Lytton as more than slightly ridiculous. These literary and artistic pretensions were erected on the grandest scale imaginable. In due course Clive Bell planned to deliver himself of a *magnum opus,* the importance of which seemed to justify the eternal postponement of its composition. The magnitude of his aspirations astonished and displeased Lytton, whose own romantic ideals they seemed to parody: 'He's really rather a mystery,' he told Leonard Woolf (July 1905), ' – what can be his *raison d'être?* He takes himself in deadly earnest, I've discovered, as Art Critic and litterateur. Very queer – and he likes, or says he likes, such odd things – Gluck, Racine, Pope and Gibbon. If it's mere imitation of us, the question remains – why the dickens should he imitate us? For he's not under our control, like Lamb.[7] He's even independent of the Goth.[8] His stupidity is of course gross, yet he can be occasionally almost witty.'

7. Walter R. M. Lamb, the elder brother of Henry Lamb the painter, was appointed Secretary of the Royal Academy in 1913 and later knighted. He was also author of *The Royal Academy* (1935). At this time he was anxious to be elected to the Cambridge Conversazione Society, to which both Lytton and Leonard Woolf belonged, but he was in fact never chosen.

8. 'The Goth' was Lytton's nickname for Thoby Stephen.

Booming and rubicund, Bell was a good talker, though he sometimes spoke with a little too much self-satisfaction for every taste. Yet Lytton, a prey to parallel uncertainties, was not deceived: 'He's modest and retiring,' he explained to a friend; 'he's also quite unrestrained in general conversation.' In short, Bell's was not an easy character to understand, and one's feelings for him were always fluctuating according to his mood. Eventually, after knowing him for some five or six years, Lytton concluded on 1 July 1905 that

his character has several layers, but it is difficult to say which is the *fond*. There is the country gentleman layer, which makes him retire into the depths of Wiltshire to shoot partridges. There is the Paris decadent layer, which takes him to the quartier latin where he discusses painting and vice with American artists and French models. There is the eighteenth-century layer, which adores Thoby Stephen. There is the layer of innocence which adores Thoby's sister. There is the layer of prostitution, which shows itself in an amazing head of crimped straw-coloured hair. And there is the layer of stupidity, which runs transversely through all the other layers.

Altogether he was one of those curious and instructive cases of mistaken vocation. If only he had been content with the part for which nature had so palpably intended him – the country magnate, destined to marry an ugly wife and die at the age of eighty-four having spent his life doing excellent work prodding up his turnips in Wiltshire. But no; he *would* be an art critic!

Clive Bell had first got to know the other members of the group through Saxon Sydney-Turner, whose rooms happened to be near his own, and he soon became friendly with Thoby Stephen. Certainly the reassuring presence within this bleak intellectual fraternity of someone like Thoby Stephen, with his disdainful athletic prowess and love of the open air, must greatly have facilitated Clive Bell's first bold, faltering footsteps in the mysterious new world of the *literati*. The two of them would smoke cigars and discuss points of hunting, watched by the others who, struggling between envy and disapprobation, deemed them both very worldly. 'Lytton, however, liked us for that,' Clive Bell shrewdly observed; while

Leonard Woolf noticed that 'in those early days, and indeed for many years afterwards, intellectually Clive sat at the feet of Lytton and Thoby'.

Thoby Stephen, the most mundane figure in the society after Clive Bell, was the eldest son of Sir Leslie Stephen. Over six feet tall and of a somewhat ponderous build, he was not ungraceful. He gave the impression of a sublime physical magnificence which put some of his friends in mind of Samuel Johnson, without the Doctor's infirmities yet with the same monumental brand of common sense, the same depth of character. But perhaps the single quality which above all others endeared him to Lytton was his natural and wholly unselfconscious charm. So vividly did this charm affect all the members of the Midnight Society that it called forth in them an element of hero-worship – romantic feelings which were heightened by his tragic death from typhoid at the age of twenty-six. 'His face was extraordinarily beautiful and his character was as beautiful as his face,' wrote Leonard Woolf some fifty years after he had died, and continued: 'It [his charm] was, no doubt partly physical, partly due to the unusual combination of sweetness of nature and affection with rugged intelligence and a complete lack of sentimentality, and partly to those personal flavours of the soul which are as unanalysable and indescribable as the scents of flowers or the overtones of a line of great poetry.'

A photograph taken of him at this time shows a pair of fine, light eyes, but his face, with its long nose and thick sensual mouth, is a little heavy. It was really his strong masculinity both of appearance and manner, coming as a relief from the bashful, disembodied intellectuality of the Cambridge élite, that particularly enchanted Lytton, who saw him as 'a heroic figure'. In a letter (1 July 1905) written to an Oxford undergraduate, B. W. Swithinbank, he gives the fullest description of his admired friend and unfolds something of the idolatrous feeling which Thoby inspired: 'He has a wonderful and massive frame,' Lytton wrote, 'and a face hewn out of the living rock. His character is as splendid as his appearance, and as wonderfully complete. In fact, he's monolithic. But, if it were not for his extraordinary sense of humour, he would hardly be of this world. We call him the Goth; and when you see him I'm sure you'll agree that he's a survival of barbaric grandeur. He'll be a judge of great eminence, and, in his old age, a sombre family potentate. One day we composed each other's epitaphs. He said that mine should be "The Universal Exception"; and mine for him was "The Forlorn Hope".'

Despite a strong sense of humour which helped to differentiate him from the usual muscular Christian or 'ape', as Lytton first described him to Pernel, and despite a fluent style of conversation and of writing, Thoby's mind was not especially quick, and afforded an excellent foil to any clever wild Stracheyesque exaggeration. Lytton venerated and idealized Thoby more than any other of his friends. Different in almost every respect from himself, he represented what was finest but for ever unobtainable in life, the perfect human specimen; and as an aesthetic ideal, Lytton deified him. 'Don't you think that if God had to justify the existence of the world,' he once asked Leonard Woolf, 'it would be done if he were to produce the Goth?'

In Leonard Woolf the Midnight Society had someone altogether different. Since he was naturally proficient at lessons, the general inefficiency of the masters at Arlington House, his private school, could not prevent him from winning a scholarship to St Paul's at the age of fourteen. But before leaving he had already given irrefutable evidence of a severely disciplinarian streak of puritanism, by dealing the low moral tone of the place an edifying blow from which it must have taken several terms to recover its normal equilibirum. The Spartan austerity of public-school life proved more to his liking, and he did well both at games and work. During these years he was tutored by a fanatical High Master, F. W. Walker, whose ambition it was, by means of an intensive cramming of Greek and Latin composition, to turn any pupil of rudimentary intelligence into an apparently brilliant classical scholar. As a result of these battery methods, Leonard won an exhibition to Trinity which he later converted into a foundation scholarship of a hundred pounds a year.

As a freshman he was, so he later confessed, in a curious psychological state. Having inherited a highly-strung intellect from his father, and rejected his mother's squeamish sentimentality, he had grown up into a rather dry, nervously unemotional young man, in appearance lean, with a long predatory nose and pale ascetic lips. His humanitarian principles were symptomatic of the repressed sensitivity which, in moments of stress, found an outlet in the involuntary trembling of his hands. As with the majority of men who appear to be guided by exclusively rationalistic motives, the pendulum of his expressed emotions swung through a fairly small arc. He understood the complexities and predicaments in other people's lives not so much from the imaginative echo of his own feelings, but by laboriously deducing and evaluating them through a process of ratiocination. To Lytton's delight, he never actively believed in God, considering the whole paraphernalia of prayer as 'one of the oddest freaks in human psychology'. For him the pathos and the beauty of religious supplication was always to strike a dumb note on the piano; and he was correspondingly deaf to other such emotional appeals. His humanitarianism had a social, economic or political emphasis which effectively divorced it from the immediate affairs of the individual human being. At the same time, indications of his subdued and latent sensibility are everywhere to be seen in the pages of his memoirs, notably in the fine etchings he made of his friends.

In his dealings with women, the puritan self-discipline of his early years brought out a repressive fastidiousness which applied the final stranglehold to that genuine poetic element within him vainly struggling to free itself. With his strong ethical feelings, he fitted well into the thin intellectual gatherings at Cambridge, and it was he whom Lytton singled out from among his new friends to act as his confessor, the one man to whom, during his first three years at Cambridge, he confided almost all his secret thoughts and passions. Such an outlet to his feelings would, Lytton felt, provide the relief which his early diaries had failed to give him. For diaries, as he now knew, tended to redouble one's self-preoccupation.

Through communion with a sympathetic but objective friend, he might, on the other hand, succeed in transferring – perhaps even permanently – some part of that onerous burden of isolation which afflicted him. The reasoning was sound; but the choice of Leonard Woolf was only partially successful. He had, of course, much to recommend him – a good brain, a lack of doctrinal religious prejudice, a detachment of manner. But his puritanism stood out as an insuperable obstacle to complete and spontaneous confidence. Often Lytton would tease him about it, suggesting that he should join a League for the Advancement of Social Purity, or refusing to send him 'an Etude quasi sadiste' which he had written, 'as I'm afraid you might think it improper'. Leonard Woolf always reacted indignantly to such jibes: Lytton's remark about a League for the Advancement of Social Purity was *not* amusing; of course he must send him the poem. But whenever Lytton tested him with some especially spicy or obscene piece of gossip, he would sense Leonard's fractional yet uncontrollable recoil. No amount of teasing or criticism could bring about that spirit of absolute unrestricted toleration for which he sought: 'It is hopeless', he told his brother James, his next confessor but one, '– what can one expect in even a remote future, when *Woolf* thinks that people ought to be "punished" for incest.'

The remaining member of the Midnight Society, Saxon Sydney-Turner, in several respects resembled Lytton more closely. As undergraduates, both were retiring, scholarly and widely read, their minds, like protective antennae, cautiously exploring every inch in their immediate vicinity. But the periodic inclination felt by Lytton to withdraw from the boisterous vulgarity of life overcame Sydney-Turner to a far more extravagant degree. During his first term up at Trinity he had shown himself to be charming and animated. But then, for no specific reason that his friends were able to ascertain, he suddenly broke down, relinquishing almost all participation in what went on around him. As Lytton himself once remarked, he was still-born into the Midnight; it was only in those first months that he had really lived. 'When I first knew him he was a wild and unrestrained freshman,' he told B. W. Swithinbank, 'who wrote poems, never went to bed, and declaimed Swinburne and Sir Thomas Browne till four o'clock in the morning in the Great Court at Trinity. He is now ... quite pale and inanimate, hardly more than an incompletely galvanized dead body.' Those who had not known him early on sometimes found him a colossal bore, a sort of automaton of a man. But Lytton remained staunchly loyal to him, albeit – as was his habit and the fashion of the times – denouncing him mercilessly to his other friends.

There was always some part of Lytton's nature which rebelled against the need he sometimes felt for academic reassurance; in Sydney-Turner there was no such division, little compensatory yearning for the fulfilment of human love or individual supremacy. There seemed consequently something ghost-like and insubstantial about him. He moved quietly, indecisively, amid the shadows, until the last years of his life, when in retirement from the Treasury, he took dramatically and disastrously to gambling. Tête-à-tête with Lytton or another confrère of the Midnight Society he would talk interminably on the most uninteresting subjects imaginable – cricket shop, or the technique of Wagner, or the use by Tacitus of the dative case. By strangers he was paralysed completely, languishing into long indefinite silences. From his early twenties, he seemed intent upon suffocating his soul, quietly, efficiently, and without even a brief struggle. Everything around him was kept in a static, monochromatic condition. The furniture in his room never varied, was never moved. He ate little, without relish and at unpredictable times. This slow process of self-murder was given physical expression by the increasing number of ailments which afflicted him and which were entirely symptomatic of his state of being, not, as was partly the case with Lytton, causative.

Signs of the self-destruction which he was determined to perpetrate seemed to be reflected in his fading appearance: short, thin, with an anaemic pallor and pale, straw-coloured hair. A portrait of him painted by Vanessa Bell in 1908 shows a sombre, precise figure, seated slightly bent before a pianola, and peering through his spectacles at some sheet of music with an expression of rapt, self-oblivious concentration. Small, bloodless and *effacé*, he might, Lytton always felt, have been a tragic figure on the grand scale, *if only he appeared aware of his tragedy.*

Nothing stands still; yet Sydney-Turner wholeheartedly, and Lytton fitfully, wished that it did. At times indeed, when his will-power began to crumble, Lytton felt that he might go under in precisely the same way as his friend. 'It would never do to become Turnerian,' he wrote to his brother James (October 1912), 'and I feel it's a danger that hangs over all of us.' And to Saxon himself a few years earlier he had written: 'Time and Space for you do not exist, and perhaps not for me either, who feel myself fleeting towards your philosophy. What this is you have never told me, but it occurred to me the other day, and though it made me feel very ill, perhaps I agree.' Even in his most wretched and pessimistic moments, however, Lytton never collapsed as Sydney-Turner had done.

Probably Sydney-Turner was the most exact and scholarly-minded member of the Midnight; and despite his taciturn nature, his Cambridge friends remained fond of him, showing by their continued affection that though he had tried to smother his soul out of existence, he had only succeeded in burying it alive. And occasionally Lytton and the others might catch a glimpse of the Saxon they had first known and who now lay entombed beneath a meticulously constructed carapace. 'He looks sometimes', wrote Leonard Woolf, 'like a little schoolboy whom life has bullied into unconsciousness.' And Lytton observed that 'he looks like some puzzled night-animal blinking in the unaccustomed daylight. Sometimes, even now, for a few moments, one realizes as one watches him that he still possesses a mystical supremacy and a sort of sibylline power' (1 July 1905).

One other friend Lytton made during his first months at Trinity, never so close but of almost equal value. This was George Trevelyan, the historian, who was some four years older than himself. Often he would be invited over to Trevelyan's rooms for breakfast and a lengthy walk; and when, on one occasion, he inquired whether – owing to another engagement – he might have the food without the exercise, he was curtly told: 'No walk, no breakfast.' Lytton found him very earnest, 'and somewhat patristic towards me,' as he told Pernel. '... On Thursday I went to Breakfast – painful meal – with George Trevelyan. He is indeed eager – also somewhat piteous I think – and very virulent. I am to go again tomorrow! This although I insulted bim by saying that I thought anyone who had been a Home Ruler was a fool!'

At other times the two of them would go off on bicycle rides together, Trevelyan talking most of the time about Cromwell, Milton, the scenery, Oxford, Cardinal Newman, and the Early Christians. 'He is most friendly and kind,' Lytton wrote to his mother (March 1900), 'and very like what I imagined his father to be.'[9] But in time, this kindness, with its overtones of heavily affectionate, avuncular authority – so welcome when he still felt lonely and unknown in Cambridge – began to pall on him. It was excessive, patronizing. And even tedious too, when, for instance, Trevelyan chose to explain that the pleasure which people derived from dancing came, not from the mere exercise, but from the legitimate physical contact it afforded partners of the opposite sex. Lytton did not like dancing, but it was hopeless to try and explain that his tastes lay in a different direction. 'He is very – I think *too* – earnest; and paternally kind', Lytton wrote to his mother in the spring of 1900. And in subsequent years his opinion does not seem substantially to have altered.

9. Sir G. O. Trevelyan (1838–1928), nephew and biographer of Lord Macaulay, was an eminent historian and parliamentarian. His works include *The Early History of Charles James Fox* (1880) and a history of the American Revolution in six stupendous volumes (1899–1914). He was also an Apostle.

3

PALPITATIONS, FRENCH AND ENGLISH

The Midnight Society temporarily folded up in the autumn of 1900, owing to Lytton's invalid health. He had come through the previous winter, for him, remarkably well. No chances, however, were taken, and, during the Easter vacation he was sent, with his sister Pippa as chaperon, to the Albion Hotel, Broadstairs, where the bracing sea-climate, Lady Strachey felt, should do much to pull him round. Although in no way seriously ill, his stay there took on the air of a patient recovering from some major operation – convalescent teas in the hotel lounge followed by slow, hypochondriac parades along the front to examine the sea.

'Broadstairs itself is charming,' he reported (19 April 1900). 'The sun has been out all day and the wind is easily avoidable. ... I feel already revived ...

'The trippers are not as yet aggressive though somewhat amusing. We took a slight walk along the sands this evening.'

Later that month he returned to Trinity for the Easter term, during which, and from this time onwards, he was excused all chapel services – though whether owing to conscience or health is not certain. For other reasons too this was a happy term. Spring was in the air, and the world revolved merrily. There was always something going on. He went to listen to Stephen Phillips declaiming his *Paolo and Francesca*[10] in a sonorous monotone which hushed into expectancy the rustling lace and jangling ornaments of his almost exclusively female audience, but sent Lytton himself off to sleep. Less soporific, though rather more disagreeable, was a Newnham lecture which he attended, given by Edmund Gosse on Leigh Hunt. 'Law! He *did* think himself clever!' Lytton wrote to Pernel. After 3 sentences he suddenly said, "I was never in such a

10. At that time Stehen Phillips's *Paolo and Francesca* had not been publicly performed. It opened under George Alexander at the St James' Theatre in February 1902.

draught in the whole course of my life!" Katherine [Stephen] and Sharpley ran forward and screwed ventilators (apparently). And after a long time he said, "Oh, it really doesn't matter." Grossly rude, I thought.' This term, too, every Wednesday and Thursday, he went to lectures on Early Florentine Art given by Roger Fry. 'They are very interesting and good though somewhat abstruse,' he commented in a letter to his mother (15 May 1900).

When the summer vacation came he joined his family at a country house they had rented at Kingston Lisle Park, Wantage. 'The place here is lovely', he told Lumsden Barkway, ' – in the Berkshire downs near the White Horse – a beautiful park and beautiful country.' It was while on holiday here during the hot weather of July that he was attacked by violent palpitations of the heart, which lasted intermittently until early September. A doctor was immediately called in to examine him, but could ascertain no specific physical cause for these attacks, which he put down to 'nerves'.[11] Sir Richard Strachey was also laid up at the time, and two nurses moved into the house, which was converted into a rather rough-and-ready sanatorium. Doses of digitalis and bromide were prescribed for Lytton, who was advised to rest for two or three months and, whenever practicable, to travel abroad during his future vacations. 'The disease is mysterious', he explained to Lumsden Barkway from his sick-bed, ' – of no very definite nature – fainting and general weakness. Nothing is radically wrong say the doctors, but it has been settled that I shall not go back to Cambridge next term so as to make a complete recovery. This is I suppose the wisest thing – but I am very, very sad at the thought of it.'

Instead of returning therefore to Cambridge for the Michaelmas term he remained at home, attended by a train of female relatives, who forbade him the least exertion, even

11. It seems possible that he was suffering from what is called paroxysmal tachycardia. The cause of this condition is not accurately known, though it is probably of nervous origin and can be aggravated by physical wear and tear. The symptoms are sometimes very alarming, but it is not considered in itself dangerous, and may be treated with quinidine sulphate tablets. I know, since I now suffer from it myself.

reading. 'Everyone and thing missed you last term,' wrote Leonard Woolf, to whom, in his letterless condition at darkest Lancaster Gate among eternal women, Lytton had cried out for the lifeblood of Trinity gossip, 'and I am sure the temporary death of the Midnight Society might have been avoided if we had had you to back up those members who are not afraid of late hours.'

By the middle of October Lytton already felt much improved. He had been moved to a nursing home in Queen's Gate Terrace[12] where Dr Roland Brinton, the family physician, gave him a thorough examination before reporting to Lady Strachey (18 October 1900) that 'he is more jovial and takes his food really well. I told him he could have a little light literature – after the business of the day is over – and before it is time for him to settle down for the night. He still has occasional attacks of palpitations – and his heart certainly has a tumultuous action – but I can find no reason to think that there is any structural disease there. So I feel fairly confident that all his uncomfortable sensations will disappear.

'He likes a little claret – but a pint bottle lasts him two days – so there is no excess.'

After six weeks of alternate resting, eating, drinking and professional massage, Lytton's weight increased from nine to eleven stone, and his mother was obliged to order an entirely new outfit, since his old clothes now failed conspicuously to meet across his manly chest. 'I feel much stronger,' he assured Lumsden Barkway (23 November 1900), ' – but not yet quite natural or ordinary – something of a portent or monster still . . . last Summer still remains a nightmare.'

By the beginning of December he felt well enough to travel to St-Jean-de-Luz, near Biarritz, in the Basses Pyrénées. His mother went with him so that the journey should not be troublesome, and having deposited him in the Hôtel d'Angleterre, and introduced him to some cousins living near by, she returned again to England.

'Blue sea and fresh air' there was, he told Leonard Woolf,

12. This was what used to be called a 'Rest Cure' – invented in the 1880s by an American doctor called Weir Mitchell.

'and heat enough for anyone. The country is Basque and rather strange, with bullock-carts and things at every town – flooded with English of course which makes it more or less unpleasant. The only man of amusement (barring a decayed millionaire and a gouty Baron) is an Oxford person who teaches little boys and in intervals writes poems for the *Spectator*. ... He gives me his poems to read (bad enough), and good advice (rather worse) and his views on Shakespeare (quite ridiculous). We talked the other day of people we should like to meet – I mentioned Cleopatra. He said, "I should rather see Our Lord to anyone else." I had to reply, "Oh, I put him on one side as inhuman."

'The people at the hotel are more than fearful. I often wish I was a snake and could wriggle on the ground. I have cousins here, whom I lunch with, and so manage to exist.'

The hotel was extraordinarily dull, especially at meals, when the few residents would seat themselves in order at a long table and stare hopelessly into a looking-glass opposite. On the table stood tall pots with some strangled, artificial chrysanthemums peeping out of the top, tall napkins and a few bleak cruet-stands. More dismal still was the conversation. Besides the tireless subject of Christianity, Lytton would listen daily at breakfast, lunch and dinner to monotonous golf and social gossip in appalling French. 'I have no one on my right,' he wrote to Lumsden Barkway describing the other inmates, 'on my left an old Irish squire of sorts – dull as ditchwater but good-natured enough – as I suppose all dullards are. He repeats indefinitely, and I dare say winds himself before he hops into bed at night. Next him an old maid – thin, and rather pitiful, then her two nieces – vulgar, *very* good, and *very, very* stupid. Poor people! At the head of the table a Captain (Caulfield by name) in the Navy – but *I* believe the Marines – or even Horse Marines. Terrible! Impossible to mention anyone who is not his bosom friend. As conceited as a cock-a-doodle-do, and as brainless. These are the English inhabitants of this house. Oh! I've forgotten one – Miss Roper, who looks like a governess, but who isn't, and wears curious tails to her jackets, and talks sensibly enough. I fear I am rude to some of them sometimes. I often want to make faces, and sometimes do – when nobody's looking. Oh dear me! I live in hope of someone rich and strange walking in at the door.' To lend further substance to this hope he joined the English Club, where there was a fire, a few papers and a good many more Anglo-Saxon dullards, drinking and golfing.

The town itself, with its old narrow streets, its quay, its square, and the ancient galleried church where Louis XIV was married, enchanted him. But nothing happened there, or it seemed, ever had happened. Increasingly, Lytton would escape into the delightful country. 'Imagine the colouring of late autumn,' he wrote, 'the warmth of midsummer, and the fresh air of early spring.' Often he went for long walks to surrounding villages and 'once I got on to a merry-go-round at a fair and revolved to my heart's content'.

His happiest hours were spent bicycling among the hills and trees and streams. He loved the wide expanse of sea and the mountains, both, it seemed to his youthful romantic imagination, the chosen voices of liberty. One day he went to Biarritz which, as a fashionable seaside resort, was more towny and paradey, though with a splendid sea-front and magnificent waves coming up in a continual procession. 'Their thunder was enormous, and their foam beautiful,' he wrote to Lumsden Barkway. 'Have you noticed the resemblance between them and Beethoven's music? I heard a Symphony by that great man the day before I came here – oh! marvellous! – but appalling is the only word to describe it properly – it grinds you to powder. I shudder with emotion while I hear it – and so you see it is like the ocean. Talking of great volumes of sound, isn't it extraordinary that some poetry really makes as much noise as anything else? I mean Milton for instance – the *quantity* of sound appears to me often as vast as that of a full symphony of Beethoven or the enormous roaring of the sea ...

'Coming back in the train the sunset was miraculous – hardly credible – dark purply grey – rose – pale saffron – altogether with the mountains an effect of great peace. I wondered why all the heads I passed were not turned towards it – but nature grows familiar and so I suppose contemptible to country-dwellers – and this is one of the advantages of travelling – one is woken up to the marvel of things.'

Lytton's day-to-day existence was made much more congenial by the hospitality of his cousins, Mrs King[13] – Lady Strachey's first cousin – Irish and gay and bright, and her daughter Janie – married to a young Irishman named McGusty[14] – an attractive and amusing girl with gold hair, a pink and white complexion and a rather skull-like face. In the course of his stay they introduced him to some of the inhabitants at St-Jean-de-Luz. There was a fat Dutch-Englishman called Boreel, with a made-up pseudo-handsome wife; and several bachelors – 'or people who ought to be bachelors – generals, bankers, loungers of all sorts. The man of business is Bellairs – half French and half English – talks French with an English accent, and English with a French, as Janie says, lays down the law on everything, says "damn it my dear fellow" a good deal, and is altogether a windy but not unimaginative fool. . . . Have I mentioned Mr Penny? a commercial gentleman staying here with a wife and child. He has, as he says, "knocked about all over the world", and now I suppose is settling down. His wife leads a sad life I fear, for even to us he is liable to give long lectures on the Roman Catholic religion and how to drive an omnibus. He is a Master of Platitude.'

Most interesting of all these new acquaintances were the Lilburnes, an amusing old Englishman and his deformed Spanish wife. Regularly once a week, and chaperoned by his cousins, Lytton went off to gamble at their roulette table, an occupation which he described as 'very soothing'. The chief attraction of these sessions was the opportunity which they afforded his social curiosity and powers of sharp, comic

13. Annie King was the daughter of Elizabeth Grant of Rothiemurchus (Mrs Smith of Baltiboys).

14. 'The two families live in a block of three villas one of which is empty – but you never know which one, so that you very often ring and knock in vain until a head, poked out of the window, tells you to go to the next (or next but one) house. Peculiar!' (Lytton to Pippa Strachey, 30 November 1900.)

observation. On one occasion a note of keen excitement was introduced into the party by the unexpected arrival of ex-Queen Nathalie of Servia, at that time living in retirement near by. Lytton noted with amused disapproval the ripple of thrilled obsequiousness produced by her regal entry into the Salle de Jeu: 'As the game was proceeding, suddenly "la Reine" was whispered, and everyone rising to their feet, Her Majesty, accompanied by her suite, entered the apartment. She looked pleasant and stupid – rather bulky and well-dressed – stayed for so long that I was late for dinner and consequently fined a franc and relegated to a side-table. People kissed her gloved hand when saying How-do-you-do, and curtseyed and shook hands at the same time on her leaving. I must say if I were a retired sovereign I should give up such airs and graces, and try to slip into a room like an ordinary mortal.'

By the end of the year Lytton had entirely recovered from the palpitations and misery of the summer. He spent a mild Christmas dining with his cousins off turkey, champagne and plum pudding, supported a pine tree in the hotel, and received a novel present from his mother in distant England – 'a *minute* Milton (2 inches by 3) complete, on India Paper – and too charming for words. I carry it in my pocket, so that I may take it out and admire it at intervals.'

On 9 January 1901 he travelled back to London by himself, and a little later returned to Trinity where the Midnight Society once again resumed its nocturnal readings, Lytton taking the part of Cleopatra in *Antony and Cleopatra*. In the months and years which followed, Lady Strachey was scrupulous in carrying out the doctor's recommendation, seeing to it that some part at least of every vacation Lytton spent either abroad, in the country, or by the sea. During March she took him down to the Belvedere Mansion Hotel, in Brighton, where he collaborated with his sister Marjorie on an incredibly involved but harmless literary composition entitled *Lachrymae Ostreorum*. This piece was made up from alternate lyrics, transcribed in red ink and called Pearls, and blue-black chunks of blank verse on which the coloured lyrics were strung and which were termed Cables. The lyrics were all written jointly in the usual way of a collaboration, but the Cables were stitched separately in sections. An additional complication in structure and in the texture of the poem, revolved round the three languages in which it was written, only one of them – English – containing any meaning whatever. The verses cast in mock-Italian and mock-German were never intended to carry any real sense, but simply to sound as if they did.

In the intervals between working at this collaboration Lytton read Walter Pater, whose laborious and anaemic refinements of scholarship and taste, achieving only an imitation of true literary style, he greatly disliked. 'As for Pater,' he wrote to Lumsden Barkway, 'though I have not read much of him he appears to me so deathly – no motion, no vigour – a waxen style. . . . And after all does he say so very much that is worth hearing? In short I do not like the man.' In the evenings his mother would read out to him from *The Ring and the Book,* which engrossed him far more. 'What a work!' he commented. 'No one but R B could ever have dreamt of writing it.' By Henry James, whose early novels Lady Strachey was also very fond of reading aloud, he was even more fascinated, opening one of his letters to Leonard Woolf in imitation of the master: 'In settling the great question, at any rate, is there more than one answer of the many which, as a serious solution, can add more than nothing to an after all admitted ignorance? Do not, in their hubbub, the thousand vociferations only succeed in missing the failure by which they are self-condemned by satisfactorily proving even to the least experienced auditor the correctness of the one? Will you not agree that boredom is, essentially, life? Sleep, I think, and death are the only states of which a limited consciousness can speak without it.'

Brighton, with its integrated mixture of charm and vulgarity, he liked to represent as some strange Anglo-Saxon Venice. 'This place is most peculiar,' he informed Lumsden Barkway, 'rather oppressive, and very bracing. A regular metropolis on the sea – powdered boatmen, carriages in pairs, fashions and frivolity. Such a parade! two piers with kiosks and mosques, and I don't know how many theatres, music-halls and Alhambras! Of such things I have only explored one – an Aquarium where I went with my small brother who comes down for week-ends. The fishes and things were amusing and weird enough – it was all underground and there were various terrible side-shows – such as the "Strange Lady" with pale individuals trying in vain to attract the attention of passers by. Some of them rang bells I believe – but in vain.'

With the determinedly unexotic Belvedere Mansion Hotel, however, he was very far from delighted. The cold, antique surroundings here grated incessantly upon him. 'Brighton I dare say is killing me,' he complained to Leonard Woolf. 'The waits between the courses are so long and the courses themselves so exceedingly scrappy. This all round. Easter thick upon us with its attendant horrors. Everyone appears to be fat, smug, happy and *bourgeois*. They roll, of course, in money. Beasts!'

The summer holidays that year Lytton again spent with the family, this time at Cuffnells, a country house with vast and spacious gardens, near Lyndhurst, ten miles from Southampton. Much of this vacation was occupied in writing an essay on Warren Hastings[15] for the Greaves Prize at Trinity, and in attempting to learn German. In his solitary moments he was 'reading Keats in raptures' and going off for long walks in the warm summer countryside, of the beauty of which he seems to have been made more sensitively aware by the slow-moving, pictorial verse, steeped in desire and regret. His state of happiness over these weeks was increased by the presence of the Stephen family, including, of course, the radiant and adored Thoby, whom he saw several times, once at a fair where he was sporting himself very splendidly among village boys and coconuts. 'Here it is delicious,' he told Leonard Woolf, 'the New Forest – beautiful trees and weather. The Goth within five miles with his family. It is a school they live in, and the Goth at night retreats to the dormitory where he magnificently sleeps among the small surrounding beds.'

Once or twice, to his great delight, he was invited across by

15. See *Lytton Strachey and the Bloomsbury Group*, pp. 65–7.

Thoby to the Stephen schoolhouse where, for the first time, he met his two aloof and lovely sisters, Vanessa – later to marry Clive Bell – and Virginia – who subsequently married Leonard Woolf – together with Adrian, their brother, and the awe-inspiring, patriarchal Leslie Stephen – 'quite deaf and rather dangerous' – who insisted on Lytton repeating all his falsetto remarks down a formidable ear-trumpet.[16] 'It is a nice though wild family,' Lytton wrote to Leonard Woolf, ' – 2 sisters very pretty – a younger brother Adrian, and Leslie with his ear-trumpet and tam-o'-shanter. What is rather strange is the old man – older than he really is – among so young a family. He is well kept in check by them, and they are well bustled by him. They know each other very well I think.'

During the Christmas vacation of 1901, Lytton was packed off to the south of France in company with two of his sisters, Dorothy and Marjorie. The three of them travelled down by train, breaking their journey for a few exciting days in Paris where they rushed about continuously, saw the Louvre, Luxembourg, Théâtre Français, the Opéra (*Lohengrin*), Notre Dame, the Sainte Chapelle, and snapped up a few books on the *quais*. They then resumed their progress south, and arrived shortly before Christmas at Menton. Here they put up at a comfortable Victorian house, Villa Himalaya, which had been rented by Lady Colvile, Lady Strachey's elder sister.

The blue sea, the sky and the land were all so enchanting that he dreaded returning to England and winter. He was perpetually occupied in a most civilized and enjoyable manner – two *déjeuners*, one at ten and the second at twelve; expeditions of all sorts and at all hours; reading and writing

16. In an unpublished fragment, Virginia Woolf later recalled that she had been taken across to see the Stracheys by her father. 'Lady Strachey was in high glee. She had been routing about among the books, and had discovered a first edition, I think of Ben Jonson. "Look at that, Sir Leslie! Look at that!" she exclaimed, thrusting the book before him and pointing to an inscription on the title page, "Ex dono Auctoris". My father looked and admired, but a little grimly I thought and on the way home he said to me, "I didn't like to tell Lady Strachey, but the accent should be on the second syllable of auctoris, not the first".'

scattered in between. 'This place is more charming than can be imagined,' he delightedly told his mother (29 December 1901) soon after arriving. And on the same day he wrote off to Lumsden Barkway: 'This is heavenly! Yes, heavenly! The best of what one imagines the Riviera! ... The country is of course perfect. Mountains! Yes! And some with snow! They tower! The sea glows and shimmers and swells! The sky is a marvel! ... we continue our rounds of pleasure – among which I don't think I mentioned to you the fascination of food. Omelettes! Wines – sparkling and sweet like ginger-beer! Rolls! All quite absolute! Especially after one has been toiling on legs or donkeys up precipitous paths under tropical suns. One falls on food voracious as lions.'

A more leisured note is struck in another letter written to Leonard Woolf: 'One sees villas here with boats going out – and idleness is the first necessity. To work is to die – I always think. It's the very admission of time and space – our fearful limitations – but to dream! Italy is at hand too. Roman arches come upon one. Boys play in gardens. I turned the Cape the other day, and there was Monte Carlo. One wouldn't go there.'

His attitude to Monte Carlo, examined from a cautious distance, was somewhere between that of a very old maid and a Wordsworthian poet. 'Monte Carlo with its abominations in rococo architecture,' he wrote, 'painted women, and stay-laced men, goes down to perfect seas and is backed by magnificent mountains. Nature is best – the natives next best – when they're young, with complexions which you never see in England, recalling Brittanyan shrimps.' In short, it was a study in incompatible contrasts – breathtaking scenery and hideous, cheap modern buildings. He went there several times (despite the *caveat* to Leonard Woolf), gambled and lost a little, listened to the orchestra, wandered through the Royal Palace with its beautiful garden, and saw the delicious orangeries, the trees crowded together on bright grass, the stark drop of the wall to the sea a thousand feet below. With his sisters he also attended a luxurious New Year's garden party given by Sir Thomas Hanbury, a wealthy benefactor of the neighbourhood, at his ornate Italian villa – balconies in all directions and commanding every view – marble floors – bronze statuettes – and a celebrated garden going down in terraces inevitably to the sea. 'It was most pleasant wandering about,' he wrote to Lumsden Barkway. 'A band played and there were ices – imagine – New Year's day – Aerial summer!'

Despite the necessity for idleness, Lytton spent some of his leisure hours writing a riotous three-act tragedy to be performed by the Midnight Society in the Lent term. In such an atmosphere, work did not come easily. 'The air is strangely lowering,' he told Leonard Woolf who had inquired after the progress of the play. 'I write the tragedy and walk – either strollingly or up steep hills to absurd villages.' The particular village to which this passage indirectly refers was Eze-en-haut, which hangs dramatically from a cliff top between Cap Ferrat and Monte Carlo. 'Dorothy and I made an expedition the day before yesterday to a place called Eza or Eze,' he wrote to his mother (29 December 1901), 'which is a minute village perched on the very top of a perpendicular hill. There are the ruins of a Moorish Castle there, also the foundations of a temple to Isis, now converted to a Church to the Holy Virgin.' One other village also caught his imagination. This was Castellar, 'in the depths – or heights? — of the hills. Very small and pleasant. With 4,000 children all shrieking and yelling – also a damp, tinsel R.C. Church – also one room of a mediaeval palace belonging to a family whose last descendant was hung from its own window in the time of the Revolution.'

Although, as Lytton once informed a friend, he had always nursed an obsession for paganism – outraged by the re-conversion work done at Eze – he generally preferred it to be Greek rather than Roman. He crossed the Italian border only twice during his stay at Menton, and on the first occasion detected no change between the two countries except that 'Italian roads are worse than the French – and that's the only difference'.

But on his second crossing, the barbarism of the ancient Romans suddenly seems to have communicated itself to him with unexpected force. A few hours later, once this strange and insidious chill had passed and he was back in twentieth-century France, he tried rationally to analyse the peculiar sensation which had come over him. For the amusement of Leonard Woolf, he also set the story down on paper, the romantic variations and facetiae in his description acting as a defence against the risk of being thought absurd. Together with Dorothy and Marjorie, he told his friend, he had reached Ventimiglia, 'an old Roman post, with a high mound which was once an amphitheatre commanding views up to snow-mountains through a valley, and on the other side the long Provençal shore. Italy pleases me – and this is still to a great extent it. But everything is strange, almost lurid with contrasts, and the sense of abounding life. Coming down a winding hill-road through a valley, we heard the other day the noises of a butchery. The surroundings were so bathed in country peace, the sky was so blue, the vegetation so green and florid, that the sound struck as a horror. I imagined, in some recess, whence – believe it! – rose shouts of fiendish human exultations, an obscene and reeking sacrifice to a still remembered pagan god. Above us perhaps loomed (beneath the walls of Madonna's edifice) the hoary temple of Isis; who knows whether through the remoteness of these secluded years some worship had not lingered; some mystic propitiation and reconciliation of the hideous mysteries of life and death.'

4

CHARACTERS

THE permanent death of the Midnight Society[17] was eventu-

17. This statement is based upon an account given by Clive Bell in his memoirs, *Old Friends*. It is possible that he may have over-emphasized the significance of the Midnight because of his extreme bitterness at not being elected to the Apostles. In the present chapter, the author has used the Midnight partly for aesthetic purposes, and partly because it was the first society to which Lytton belonged and, for a year or more, the chief one. After he had been introduced into the Apostles by R. G. Hawtrey in 1902, the Midnight completely ceased to exist. But even before this, its

159

ally brought about by the regular week-end visits from London of three former undergraduates, Desmond Mac-Carthy, Bertrand Russell and E. M. Forster, all of whom got to know Lytton well during his early years at Cambridge. After the company of MacCarthy, especially, it was difficult to carry on with the solemn formality of a prepared literary reading. He would bring along his friend, the philosopher G. E. Moore, not primarily to debate questions of philosophy but to play with vigour upon the piano, and to sing. And after the musical entertainment, MacCarthy himself would come forward with a string of stories, often, admittedly, unfinished, but always specifically designed so as to delight his particular audience. There was a natural and easy worldliness about him that was tremendously refreshing in the rarefied university atmosphere; and when he and Moore had done with their cabaret performance, the volumes of Swinburne, *Bartholomew Fair* and *The Cenci* would frequently remain unopened.

MacCarthy's reputation as a brilliant raconteur was rooted partly in his skill as a practised listener. In these late-night gatherings he achieved the difficult feat of talking just enough to suggest a flow of beguiling conversation. So winning and unegotistical was his personality that many of his new friends were mesmerized into attributing to him their own most witty remarks, like men inebriated with selfless generosity. He was at his best with people to whom he owed no special obligation. On these Saturday visits to Trinity, the apparent play of his soft Irish humour, the seeming grace and pertinence of his speech, cast about him an aura of warm, social well-being.

---

place had already been taken by the X Society – a play-reading club that met earlier on Saturday evenings. Leonard Woolf, Saxon Sydney-Turner, Thoby Stephen and Clive Bell belonged to it, together with a lot of miscellaneous characters such as Walter Lamb, D. S. Robertson (later Regius Professor of Greek), Hubback and Philby (the Arabian traveller and father of the 'Third Man' in the Burgess–Maclean affair). This group was still going strong after 1902 – 'I know because I went to a meeting much later,' James Strachey informed the author, 'when I was up for a week-end from St Paul's and they read *Love for Love*, much to my excitement.'

In later years, as literary editor of *The Speaker*, the *New Quarterly* and the *New Statesman* he was punctilious in giving Lytton and other of his personal long-standing friends the commissions that they needed. At the same time other, less intimately known reviewers for these papers were sometimes reduced to a state of impoverished despair by his vague, invariably courteous procrastination; and one of them, A. G. Macdonell, was eventually moved to retaliate by drawing a satirical pen portrait of him as Charles Ossory in his celebrated, overrated, comic novel, *England, Their England*.

As he seemed to like everyone, so everyone liked him. He soon took to the shy, remote figure of Lytton and began to draw him out. But it was a long business. At first Lytton remained stubborn and suspicious, unused to such genial treatment. He had, moreover, an automatic feeling of disdain for those who could command instant popularity, and he did not feel really at home in MacCarthy's vague and expansive presence. In due course he began to thaw out, responding to the older man's charm and endearing sartorial eccentricities – thick-lined suits, a flannel shirt and large blue tie. 'I liked him much better than before,' Lytton was able to tell Leonard Woolf by December 1904. 'He seemed to understand a good deal, and want to be liked.'

But in general conversation, MacCarthy only superficially represented his elusive self. Suiting his talk to his audience, he could be relied on to please under any circumstances. He was never malicious – a rare thing in wit – his musical tone of voice put everyone at their ease, and his imitations of the famous were hilarious. Since his skill lay in subtly impersonating his audience, his stories, while they lasted, both amused and soothed Lytton. But when they trailed off, and MacCarthy had left, he again felt the burden of his solitude, now even more severely reasserted. 'The curious thing', he observed, 'is that when one's with him [MacCarthy] it all seems very amusing, and that afterwards one can only look back on a dreary waste.' And in a letter to Maynard Keynes, he later (18 November 1905) described the same bewildering paradox. 'He's a curious figure – very dull and amusing. Also rather desolate.'

This feeling of desolation is understandable once one appreciates that talking with MacCarthy meant little more than carrying on an animated dialogue with oneself – in Lytton's case the one person from whom he wished to escape. The temporary euphoria induced by MacCarthy's succession of stories was like that caused by a series of mixed drinks – immediately intoxicating, filling one with an artificial *amour propre*, and swiftly succeeded by a hangover of redoubled self-abasement. For MacCarthy did not need anyone *in particular*, only the stimulus of *any* reasonably illuminating companion to bring him alive, to retrieve his chameleon personality from the dark of a featureless oblivion. And in the sombre light of Lytton's rather passive company, his mind glowed as a bright though indistinct reflection.

As an entertainer MacCarthy was unrivalled. On more personal matters, Lytton found that he could never confide in him, seldom expose to his sympathetic understanding, so soft and hazy, his own poignant, unique secrets. Despite his brilliance as a raconteur, he could be rather ·tiresome on more serious subjects, when his will struggled to assert itself and interfered with the elegant, easy variations of his mind. 'The thing is to keep him off literature,' Lytton once explained to Virginia Woolf, 'and insist on his doing music-hall turns: if only he'd make that his profession he'd make thousands. Can't you see him coming on in a macintosh?'

To the end of Lytton's life, MacCarthy remained a loyal and useful friend. Yet much of the pseudo-intimacy of their relationship, especially in these early years, depended upon the illusion that they closely resembled each other, whereas in truth their natures were greatly dissimilar. Educated at Eton and Trinity, MacCarthy's charm attracted numerous friends; he was seldom alone; a heavy blanket of popularity suffocated his talent. The strength of the Eton education – which he retrospectively recommended for Lytton – lies, then as now, in the comparative freedom it allows the boys; its weakness is to be found in the dogged lack of encouragement given to any pursuits other than team games, and, in a more diluted form, the odd scholarship examination. Both the strength and weakness of this system conceal for the boy of developing imagination subtle dangers which lurk like rocks under the calm surface of the water. MacCarthy was impaled inextricably at the harbour mouth within sight of land and of the open sea beyond. His faltering individuality was not resilient enough to withstand the tide of his pleasant vices. He was plagued by a rueful sense of disappointment at never having progressed further, a feeling which in itself became something of an indulgence. 'One of Nature's Oppidans', as John Davenport once called him, he grew into the kind of person many take to be a typical Etonian of the best variety – intelligent, diplomatic without being obviously dishonest, rather indolent by temperament, indulgent, and passionless. His volumes of literary and dramatic criticism reflect genuine catholicity of taste, but as in the rooms of an old house illuminated throughout by a low voltage, there are no memorable highlights. We may peer at the magnificent pictures suspended from the walls, but all too little penetrates the consoling twilight. What might have been vivid is vague. One longs to have the picture presented in clear, sharp focus, to escape from the impression of gently dissolving uniformity. By contrast, Lytton – a born rebel tug – is all simulated sparkle and brilliance. Here one moves nearer the portraits to inspect them more closely in all their glorious striking colours, and then – phut! – the lights fuse altogether. And by the time they flash on again, one is being hurriedly conducted through to the next room where, in due course, the same process of exhilaration and anti-climax will repeat itself.

Bertrand Russell, who used to travel down with MacCarthy, was of an altogether different stamp, and his differing attitude to Lytton sheds new light upon his character. Small and thin, with a pleasant, slightly dry smile, his luminous intelligence seemed to shine directly through his large dark eyes. Some of his near-contemporaries, notably D. H. Lawrence, were to dismiss him as being all 'Disembodied Mind'. But though his passions appeared to come to him in the form of ideas, so that he passed from one to the other instead of from one coordinated experience to another, there was something more positive and substantial to him than mere donnish fastidiousness and lack of Lawrentian animal zest.[18] A totally unpsychological thinker, he was always a bad judge of people. Like Lytton, he observed the general human predicament with absolute clarity. Even though he knew that life was carried on in the most complex and irrational of fashions, he held that the remedy was simple – namely, to carry it on more rationally. To this end, and often with great courage, he quixotically crusaded. The dazzling clarity and quickness of his mind was exceeded by the violence of his moral passions. As a young man he suffered greatly from loneliness, and to bridge the gulf of his failure to communicate with people he invented a number of little stories he was fond of bringing out. Extremely honest in his criticism of himself, he was consumed by envy of the success of others. He wanted to be as popular as Wells or Einstein, and also a great power for good in the world.

Russell greatly appreciated Lytton's sense of humour, and on reading *Eminent Victorians* in Brixton gaol, recorded that 'It caused me to laugh so loud that the officer came to my cell, saying I must remember that prison is a place of punishment.' [19] At the same time it struck him as significant that while he himself was incarcerated for his humanitarian beliefs, the feebly romantic Lytton – though ostensibly sharing these

18. 'By the way, do you bring out the fact that Bertie has the most marvellous mental apparatus, perhaps, ever? I mean as a mere machine. Lawrence's view of him, incidentally, was extraordinarily obtuse. Bertie was full of *passionate* emotions (which led him into trouble of all sorts).' (James Strachey to the author, October 1966.)

19. On 20 May 1918, Lytton wrote to Lady Ottoline Morrell: 'I sent a copy [of *Eminent Victorians*] to Alys [Russell], and oddly enough next morning had a letter from Alys saying how much she had enjoyed it. If it pleases him as well, I think it really will suit all tastes.' Bertrand Russell's reaction to the book was reported to Lytton by Ottoline a few days later. 'Thank you very much for passing on Bertie's message,' he replied (26 May 1918). 'I am delighted that he should have liked the book, and that he found it entertaining. If you're writing will you thank him from me, and say that I think it a great honour that my book should have made the author of *Principia Mathematica* laugh aloud in Brixton Gaol?'

beliefs – should be employing his secluded leisure to fabricate, after the outdated rhetorical style of Macaulay, literary compositions largely irrelevant to the current crises, and which, though clever and amusing, were also palpably exaggerated and imbued with the sentimentality of a stuffy girls' school. Russell's own mind was far more speculative than Lytton's, but his vision, though wonderfully sharp, was restricted in depth of focus. He could always understand an academic better than a simple man, for the limit of his wisdom was marked by his inability to account for prejudice and stupidity.

Something of the acuteness and over-simplification of Russell's mind was evident in his qualified dislike of Lytton. While MacCarthy apparently had a genius for discovering only the best in others, Russell judged people by altogether different standards. He found Lytton's wit diverting, but his amusement did not blind him to other facets of his character which he could only deplore. Russell was less objective than he liked to make out, and several personal reasons for his antipathy suggest themselves. In later years he and Lytton may be said to have temporarily been rivals for the friendship of Lady Ottoline Morrell. Russell, in the opinion of Gerald Brenan, considered Lytton to be fundamentally unpractical and frivolous over most major political and sociological issues, an attitude which he took to denote the essential shallowness of his mind. It may also have been, as James Strachey believed, that Russell resented the greater influence exerted over Lytton as an undergraduate by the author of *Principia Ethica* than by the joint-author of *Principia Mathematica*. G. E. Moore and Russell admired the power of each other's intellect, but their friendship never grew really easy or close. According to Frances Partridge, Moore sometimes rebuked Desmond MacCarthy for inviting Russell to his select reading parties during the Cambridge vacations, since he felt that his own patient, inquiring method of analysis was seriously disrupted by Russell's quick-fire, censorious and – so Moore sometimes felt – invalid arguments. Russell, indeed, must have been aware of this coolness in his colleague, for, as Alan

Wood recounts, he once asked him: 'You don't like me, do you, Moore?' Moore deliberated with characteristic conscientiousness for several minutes, and then replied in a single pregnant monosyllable: 'No.' After which the two philosophers went on chatting amiably enough about other matters. Certainly Russell never actively disliked Moore – no one could – but he seems to have returned Moore's cerebral disapprobation, to some extent resenting the great esteem in which his rival was held by Lytton and other disciples.This indirect aversion was aggravated by moral considerations in the particular case of Lytton who, he considered, had perverted Moore's original doctrine so as to condone and even exalt his own homosexuality.

The increasing eccentricity that Lytton was, in the opinion of Russell, to exhibit at Cambridge had a debilitating effect upon his genuine talent and ability, while his growing affectation overlaid what was honest and truly admirable in his personality. Russell thought he saw clearly that Lytton's basic failure as a literary artist lay in the emphasis which he tended to place not on truth, but on dramatically appealing and often rather obvious effect. He disliked, too, the lordly and arrogant tone which the young Lytton sometimes chose to adopt towards human affairs in general, as when he expostulated: 'I can't believe people think about life. There's nothing in it.' Yet Russell condemned such an outburst without apprehending the personal impulse from which it sprang. After years of loneliness and dissatisfaction magnified by a deep sense of personal inadequacy, Lytton felt it imperative to establish some strong, easily remembered impression upon those around him. He desired more than ever to occupy the centre of the stage, and his ineradicable self-consciousness was best exploited by theatrical means. There was an underlying pathos, too, in his mannered behaviour, of which Russell and many of his other friends were unaware. By making his voice squeak with more deliberate affectation, by dressing rather oddly, by encouraging 'a small rather dismal moustache',[20] he

20. This description appears in an essay which Desmond McCarthy wrote in about 1934, and which is included in the sixth volume of his

may have hoped to convey the notion that his idiosyncrasies were not innate but arbitrarily chosen, not ugly but amusing.

These undergraduate mannerisms were often disconcerting, especially to E. M. Forster. Forster liked Lytton, but found him an alarming young man, in whose presence he was for many years unable to feel at ease. His long unresponsive silences, which he spread like an airless eiderdown on all frivolous chatter, and the piercing little shrieks with which he would greet any vaguely mystical or other observation that he considered to be patently absurd, slightly unnerved Forster, who felt that he placed perhaps too high a value on boredom. He neither warmed to Lytton with the spontaneous bonhomie of Desmond MacCarthy, nor disapproved of him with the didactic heterosexuality of Bertrand Russell; for both he and Lytton possessed too oddly esoteric natures to respond freely and openly with each other. Indeed, Forster's contact with all the members of the Midnight Society seemed only intermittent, for already he was, as Maynard Keynes aptly described him, 'the elusive colt of a dark horse'. Of middle height and ivory pale complexion, the grave and modest sincerity of his manner, and his mild, implacable courtesy suggested at times that he was more intent upon self-communion than on conversation with his friends, and provoked in some of them an exaggerated, if impotent, boisterousness, generated in a desperate effort to ferry over the moat of invariable social calm around him, or perhaps only connect with his perpetually retiring personality. Naturally withdrawn, even in his twenties, he seemed to combine the bashful demureness of a spinster with the more abstract preoccupations of a don.

---

collected essays, entitled *Memories*. James Strachey, however, took issue with this statement. 'What do you think you mean by this? What can you mean? A wispy moustache which grew with difficulty? One like Hitler's? It certainly wasn't like Sir Gerald Nabarro's. Not an R.A.F. moustache. Nor a cavalry moustache. But, as you might see from photographs, a thick one, not in the least straggly. In those days far from unusual. This is a good example of your unceasing desire to run Lytton down – in this case to make people think he was impotent – which, believe me, he wasn't.'

But despite his discreet evasiveness, Forster's sensibility and subtle intelligence were clearly apparent to those who knew him best, and he reacted towards Lytton with the wariness and unspoken intimacy of one intelligent man to another. In some of his letters to other, mutual friends, Lytton sometimes criticized Forster rather uncharitably – his quaint timidity, his amiable, prematurely old-maidish liberalism, and so on. But it is clear that what he really objected to was having a mirror held up to reflect the more negative features of his own image. 'Excessive paleness is what I think worries me most,' he wrote to Leonard Woolf. 'The Taupe [Forster] in his wonderful way I imagine saw this about me, and feeling that he himself verged upon the washed-out, shuddered.'

Forster was by no means the only person severely castigated in Lytton's correspondence as an undergraduate. No one escapes, and almost all his new friends are slated at one time or another without mercy. For though these carefully composed epistles of his Cambridge years contain many items of real amusement, they are not the writings of a happy person, but of someone hypersensitive and very insecure. The feeling which they induce is one of acute depression. He was more apprehensive than the average child. The over-protection of his mother, so abruptly succeeded by the bullying which at school he almost inevitably drew down upon himself, had left him with the instinctive feeling – which his intellect nevertheless rejected strongly – that he was safe only by her side, and that the rest of the world's population was potentially dangerous. Timid and self-conscious, yet at the same time absolutely determined to correct the effect of these shortcomings, he met people with a mixture of distrust and hostility, so that even now, surrounded by many new well-disposed friends of about the same age, he could still never be certain that they *really* liked him. For this reason there is often something unnaturally forced about his human relationships. He is too impatient for intimacy, seldom prepared to allow his feelings to ripen gradually, for fear that procrastination will ruin everything and merely help perpetuate his sense of deprivation. His life, after coming up to

Trinity, was for the most part dominated jointly by two types of people. First, there was the man who approximated to the ideal and who excited his lust and adoration; secondly, there was the person to whom he confessed these feelings, and whose sympathy, commiseration and encouragement, he could never do without. In some cases the borderline between these two is not absolutely distinct; but despite several variations within this pattern, the theme always remains essentially the same. Thus his emotions and his intellect, his imagination and his will, were kept separate, never fused together, so that for many years his loves and friendships brought him more disillusion than real happiness.

During this period of his life Lytton tried to forearm himself against disappointment by stressing the shortcomings of others. Before comparative strangers he thought it quite fatal to admit anything short of omniscience, and for some half-dozen years the highest word of praise which he was likely to bestow on any living person was 'tolerable'.

Among others who share the somewhat risky distinction of appearing in his correspondence at this time were C. P. Sanger,[21] a gnomelike figure, universally loved, with bright sceptical eyes, rather older than Lytton, who had shown exceptional promise at Trinity and was now a brilliant barrister; Walter Lamb, rather short and conceitedly obsequious, whom Lytton nicknamed 'the Corporal' and who, he said, was 'like a fellow with one leg who's not only quite convinced that he's got two but boasts of his walking exploits'; R. C. Trevelyan (usually referred to as Bob Trevy), the whimsical, bookish poet and elder brother of George Trevelyan, whose writing Lytton thought tedious and whom he described as 'amusing but vague to a degree'; and J. E. McTaggart, the redoubtable Hegelian philosopher, whose rooms Lytton, in company with Leonard Woolf, Saxon Sydney-Turner and a few other chosen undergraduates, would visit every Thursday evening. A brilliant lecturer, severely

21. C. P. Sanger, the barrister and conveyancer, author of *The Structure of Wuthering Heights* and a highly edudite edition of Jarman *On Wills*.

169

neurotic and a sufferer from agoraphobia,[22] McTaggart completely bowled over Lytton before he came under the still greater force of Moore. As a character, he was intimidating and shyly eccentric, his rapt capacity for silence and immobility being apparently limitless. But for his brand of philosophy Lytton eventually seems to have had little use, and after hearing him lecture on the nature of good and evil, he soliloquized:

> McTaggart's seen through God
> And put him on the shelf;
> Isn't it rather odd
> He doesn't see through himself

5

BLANK, BLANK, BLANK

BECAUSE of his wide range of interests and literary predilections, Lytton's academic performance at Cambridge was conspicuously uneven. After matriculating in the Michaelmas term of 1899, he was made in the following year an Exhibitioner. In between prose and verse compositions, and the meetings of the Midnight and other societies, he was reading history in a rather desultory manner, and in June 1901 he took the first part of his History Tripos. 'My tripos begins tomorrow,' he wrote to his mother (21 May 1901), 'and lasts till Thursday. I am calm and with the aid of chocolate will I hope weather it.' To the general disappointment, he only obtained a Second Class. 'It was exactly what I expected', he wrote to Lumsden Barkway, ' – and I think on the whole inevitable.'

22. In the first volume of his autobiography, *Father Figures* (1966), Kingsley Martin writes: 'McTaggart was an extraordinary figure in my day. He suffered from agoraphobia, and walked with a strange, crab-like gait, keeping his backside to the wall, as if afraid that someone would kick it – and maybe they did at school. He talked very quickly and was very hard to follow. ... He invited questions, but answered them so sharply and decisively that few were encouraged to ask another.'

The next year was, academically, Lytton's most successful. Early in the Lent term he embarked on the longest and most complex exercise in verse that he had hitherto undertaken. Entitled 'Ely: An Ode', the piece is without poetic value or direct personal interest, and was written specifically for the Chancellor's Medal which is awarded each year for the best ode or poem in heroic verse and of less than two hundred lines submitted by a resident undergraduate. 'Ely' is an impeccably executed versification set in the strophes, antistrophes and epode of the difficult Pindaric mould. The subject of Lytton's entry was the cathedral of Ely, and throughout the composition one feels that he is on his very best behaviour. It is, in fact, the only Cambridge poem in which he addresses God with a capital 'G'. Characteristically he left himself very little time to complete this ode. 'Ely, if it is, will have to be written by next Saturday,' he told his mother (26 January 1902). 'I think of making a pilgrimage, and dream of strophes, antistrophes and epodes.' But all went well and a week later he was able to write: 'Ely was sent in yesterday! I fear too hurried. But beautifully arranged with strophes, antistrophes and epode!' The next month Lytton learnt that he had won the award, narrowly beating Sheppard of King's into second place.[23] 'I could dance with joy,' his mother wrote to him from Lancaster Gate, 'and we are all in the greatest delight.'[24] On 2 June the family delight was further increased when they came up to Cambridge and heard Lytton read his winning ode in the Senate House.

Meanwhile, after passing another examination in the early spring, he had been admitted as a scholar of Trinity in company with Thoby Stephen and some others. 'The ceremony was not particularly impressive,' he commented in a

23. Later Sir John Sheppard, and provost of King's.
24. In a letter to his mother, Lytton wrote: 'I am going to get for my prize Merivale's Roman Empire (bound and stamped) and Swinburne's works – *au naturel*. This will be rather more than £10 – but I thought the magnificence of twenty-nine volumes was not to be resisted.' There was no collected edition of Swinburne's works in those days. Besides these twenty-nine unbound separate volumes, Lytton finally bought an obligatorily bound two-volume edition of Shelley.

letter to his mother (28 April 1902), 'in fact particularly absurd. We all had to be dressed in black with white ties and bands – mystical articles which much increased the ludicrosity of the performance. We all assembled at the Lodge first, where the Master received us in his usual charming method. We then proceeded to Chapel. Various grinning dons occupied the pews. Each scholar advanced and read aloud his name in a book, and then knelt down on both knees before the Master, placing his hands between his, while he (the M) said in latin, "I admit thee a scholar of this College." But the whole thing was hurried over as quickly as possible – no pomp or even pomposity.'

This summer of 1902 marked the climax of Lytton's scholastic career at Cambridge. Towards the end of July a seal was set on his triumph by one of his father's now infrequent letters.

My dear Lytton

As I wished to make you a present as a token of our pleasure at your recent success at Trinity College – and especially on your getting the Chancellor's Medal, I thought that no more appropriate gift could be found than a portrait of your mother to whom so much of your literary training is in truth due.

Your affnt father
Rd. Strachey

In view of his having been made a scholar of Trinity, it was generally expected that Lytton would obtain a First Class in Part II of the History Tripos and then go on to become a Fellow of the College. Already, by the autumn of 1902, he had a particular Fellowship dissertation in mind and asked his mother to find out from Sir John Strachey – his uncle and the author of *Hastings and the Rohilla War* (1892) – whether he considered Warren Hastings and the Begums of Oude a good subject; and whether, too, should he embark on it, there existed any opportunities for original research work. Lady Strachey herself thought the subject a fine one; the only drawback, so far as she could see, being that it would involve Lytton spending a lot of time at the British Museum. In October she wrote off to Sir John Strachey who promptly replied that he was sure that Lytton could make a most valuable monograph out of Hastings's encounter with the Begums. 'Lytton's idea seems to me an excellent one,' he wrote back. 'With the exception of Stephen's *Nundkomar*[25] and my own Rohillas there has been, in my belief, little or no original research into the history of these times. I never looked into the great mass of Hastings's papers at the British Museum or the India Office Records for any time after that with which I was concerned, but there can be no doubt that they are a mine out of which a vast amount of knowledge can be dug. Unless someone unknown – which is not very likely I suppose – has been at work since my time nobody I believe, except myself, has ever seriously examined any part of the British Museum papers . . .'

But first there was the second part of the History Tripos. Lytton took this in the early summer of 1903, and once again, to everyone's dismay, he obtained only Second Class Honours. In a personal letter to Lady Strachey (30 June 1903), J. D. Duff described the result as a great disappointment and a complete surprise to him. 'That he is a First Class man is a point on which I feel no doubt at all,' he wrote. 'Of course I have never seen his work, except an Essay on Warren Hastings some years ago; but I judge from our personal intercourse, and say that in quality of intellect he is superior to any pupil I have had in my four years; and I have had dozens of Firsts and Double Firsts.

'Nor do I think it was a matter of health. He was not pressed for time: most men have only one year for the second part of that Tripos: and he kept well during the two years and I don't think he suffered during the examination.

'From what he has said to me, I believe the real reason to be that his Tripos involved a good deal of task work, books to be got up and definite facts to remember, and that he did not do this work. I had no notion of this beforehand, though perhaps I should have found it out.'

Though Lytton himself affected not to care overmuch

25. *The Story of Nuncomar and the Impeachment of Sir Elijah Impey* (1885) by Sir James Fitzjames Stephen.

about this Tripos result[26], his failure did entail one serious and very practical danger: that a Double Second might in due course prejudice the Fellowship Electors against him. They were a body of about sixteen dons representing all subjects, and all keen for their own candidates. Two, probably, would represent history; but all heard the evidence for each candidate before voting. 'I think Lytton might do so good a Dissertation as to overcome this prejudice', Duff told Lady Strachey, 'but it will undoubtedly be felt and expressed.'

Lady Strachey was also anxious lest Lytton's indifferent degree should act as an impediment against his entering the Civil Service, her original choice of career for him when he was applying to Balliol, and one which she now enthusiastically revived. Cambridge at this time trained a large proportion of its undergraduates for careers in public service, and several of Lytton's friends at one time or another were conscripted into some branch of the Civil Service — A. R. Ainsworth, Ralph Hawtrey and Robin Mayor going to the Education Office; Theodore Llewelyn Davies and Saxon Sydney-Turner to the Treasury; Maynard Keynes for a couple of years to the India Office; and Leonard Woolf, for seven, to the Ceylon Civil Service. But competition was keen and most of Lytton's associates were awarded Firsts or Double Firsts. 'Personally,' wrote G. M. Trevelyan to Maynard Keynes, 'I think it most distressing the way the civil service swallows nearly all the best Cambridge men.'

Lytton would have agreed with this opinion, for he felt no great urge himself to join any particular branch of the Civil Service. His mother however was determined that he should join the Board of Education, as it was then called, and Lytton once again appeared to fall in with her wishes. For the next few months she waged an energetic campaign on his behalf. After several abortive attempts she succeeded in arranging a confidential interview with J. W. Mackail, who had worked in the Education Department for some twenty years and had

26. 'Do you know, I *am* rather proud of my B.A. gown with its voluminous folds and its strings – little as I could have imagined such a thing possible.' Lytton Strachey to John Sheppard (23 June 1903).

recently been made an assistant secretary. He assured her that the lack of a First Class degree was by no means an insurmountable obstacle to appointment, since these things were still largely arranged by private influence.

Now the campaign began in earnest. While both his parents sent off letters to their various influential friends and relations, Lytton busied himself getting testimonials from the dons under whom he had studied. The letters of recommendation written by them for this occasion are naturally enough all very flattering. But, after all allowances are made for the goodwill, generosity and spirit of helpfulness normally motivating such testimonials, they do show that he was held in unusually high esteem among those of an older generation. J. D. Duff, more well-meaning than well-informed, wrote again along the lines of his earlier letter to Lady Strachey:

'I have known Mr Strachey well during his four years of residence. His character has always been excellent; and in point of intellect I consider him not inferior to any among the two hundred men who have been my pupils during the last four years.'

Stanley Leathes, who had been an examiner for both parts of the History Tripos, wrote of him as an undergraduate whose abilities deserved a higher place than that recorded in his official examination results:

'He is a man of unusually wide culture, of considerable originality, and unusual literary gifts . . . he is in every sense a well-educated man, and worthy to rank with first-class men, as is shown by his being elected to a Scholarship at Trinity. I think that his intelligence, wide reading, versatility, and cultivation would render him a good public servant in the Education Department. His intellectual capacity is far above his University degree.'

From the University of Glasgow, where he was now Professor of English Language and Literature, Walter Raleigh added a more personal note in support of Lytton's application:

'I have known Mr Strachey for years and I cannot think of anyone among my numerous past pupils, whom I should prefer to him for work requiring ability, tact and judgement. He has a mind of rare power and distinction, a character of great decision, and a temper so reasonable and gentle that it is a delight to work with him. I hope that he may be successful in obtaining the appointment that he seeks, where I am sure he would quickly gain the confidence and esteem of all who should have to do with him.'

Appropriately enough the briefest and most ambiguous of all Lytton's testimonials was contributed by a doctor of divinity, the Reverend William Cunningham,[27] later archdeacon of Ely, who managed on this occasion to discharge his responsibilities in a single sentence remarkable for its unambitious wording:

'I have known Mr G. L. Strachey well during his period of residence at Cambridge; he has impressed me as a man of unusual ability, and I believe that he might be thoroughly trusted to discharge the duties of a responsible position with earnestness and accuracy.'

Not long after Lytton had successfully canvassed these opinions, Lady Strachey got in touch with Sidney Webb, who was at that time especially influential as chairman of the London County Council's technical education board; and he in turn introduced her at a dinner given on 18 November to Sir Robert Laurie Morant, Permanent Secretary of the Board of Education. As a result of a talk they then had together, Morant agreed to interview Lytton once he returned to London for the vacation. Lady Strachey was jubilant. Her efforts seemed at last to have led to the very brink of a successful outcome. 'I believe I have done the trick,' she wrote to

27. Dr William Cunningham (1849–1919), familiarly known as 'Parson Bill', a pioneer though rather indifferent historian, who, in October 1901, had succeeded Stanley Leathes as Lytton's director of studies. 'William Cunningham was an imposing figure as he passed slowly across the Court in the shadow of his great archdeacon's hat,' wrote G. M. Trevelyan, 'looking like some high personage of Trollope's Barchester; but his capacious mind was evolving the new science of Economic History as an academic study, which has since grown to such great proportions.' His best-known work is *The Growth of English Industry and Commerce*.

Lytton the day after meeting Sir Robert Morant. '... I have little doubt that if he finds you satisfactory he will give you an appointment when there is a vacancy. He asked me every detail concerning you and said you were very young. He said he preferred to have in the office men who had read for the bar, but that is not essential.'

What exactly transpired at Lytton's meeting with Sir Robert Morant is not now known. All that can be said with certainty is that he did not at any time join the Board of Education and that afterwards Lady Strachey once and for all abandoned her idea of a career for him in the Civil Service. Moreover, the similarity between this unsuccessful petition and his previous, equally fruitless application to go up to Balliol is very striking. In both cases it is his mother who, as the originator and driving force behind the scheme, brings it as near completion as is within the power of a third party. Though there exist marginal academic obstacles, both plans ultimately depend upon the personal impression created by Lytton himself at a single confidential interview. And though, as the written testimonials from his various tutors show, he was capable of producing over a period of time a highly favourable impression on older people occupying positions of authority, it was without doubt the uninspiring, maladroit figure he cut in these interviews that finally damned his chances of being appointed to vacancies that he was not, from the start, notably keen on filling. Pure shyness or an obstinate line of subterfuge? Either would account for these failures, and both reactions could be characteristic.

Whatever the reason, the practical consequences were irrevocable. With the possibility of a career in public service gone, Lytton now prepared himself to pursue yet another of his mother's vicarious schemes – a Fellowship. Once again he was not entirely pleased with the prospect laid out before him. He had no great desire to metamorphose into a don, to enter that faded world of weak bodies and spent minds, that half-life passed in accumulating knowledge which would be of no use to others, and only of use to himself in so far as it

might numb his discontent with existence. He would, he liked
to imagine, rather enjoy the high seas of life

> Than sit, with eyes grown spectacled and smug,
> Hands soft, feet planted slippered on the rug,
> To note, infer, insinuate and opine!

But Cambridge itself he loved as no other place save perhaps
the wild, natural beauty, open skies and riotous vegetation of
Rothiemurchus. And with rooms at Trinity he could escape
the ponderable gloom of Lancaster Gate. Besides, what assured future *could* there be for him beyond the university?

'After Cambridge,' he wrote to Leonard Woolf, 'blank,
blank, blank.'

FIVE

Beetles and Water-spiders

'I feel I should go mad when I think of your set, Duncan Grant and Keynes and Birrell. It makes me dream of beetles. In Cambridge I had a similar dream. I had felt it slightly before in the Stracheys. But it came full upon me in Keynes and in Duncan Grant. And yesterday I knew it again in Birrell – you must leave these friends, these beetles.' *D. H. Lawrence in a letter to David Garnett* (19 April 1915)

'I can see us as water-spiders, gracefully skimming, as light and reasonable as air, the surface of the stream without any contact at all with the eddies and currents underneath.' *John Maynard Keynes, 'My Early Beliefs'* (1938)

1

ANARCHISTS AT TALK

DURING his full six years in residence at Cambridge Lytton joined several clubs within the university apart from the Midnight and the Sunday Essay Society. There was, for example, the Shakespeare Society at Trinity to which a number of his friends – Walter Lamb, Thoby Stephen, Leonard Woolf and others – also belonged. And there was the Union Society, at whose debates he remained for the most part silent. 'I, I fear, am no orator,' he explained to his mother.

The most celebrated of all the university societies, to which he was elected in his third year up at Trinity, was the 'Cambridge Conversazione Society', better known as the 'Apostles' or simply 'the Society'. Unlike the Midnight, the X, and all other such groups, the Apostles were not confined to Trinity: they covered the whole university, and at that time particularly King's. Lytton had hardly known any King's men before he was elected. But from this time onwards, his circle of friends expanded appreciably. For the Apostles differed from the usual undergraduate societies in the fact that members did not cease to belong once they had graduated or gone down. Although they had no say in the elections, many of the older brethren would still regularly attend the meetings, and it was as a result of this that Lytton was able really to get to know people such as Desmond MacCarthy, C. P. Sanger, Bertrand Russell, G. E. Moore, Goldie Dickinson and others. If one takes the spring of 1902 as a watershed, one begins to find a change in his writings and in the views he held. It wasn't simply a question of these Apostolic meetings. Almost every week-end one or two of the older brethren would turn up. Lytton would meet them at tea or dinner on the Saturday – and Sunday breakfasts were always an event.

Since its original foundation almost a century earlier, the Apostles had been – and still are – a 'secret' body, though having unerringly attracted to themselves a far greater volume of publicity than could ever be bestowed on less perseveringly clandestine fraternities. At the same time, there was a quite practical reason for this concealment. Although it was known to readers of memoirs none of the undergraduates realized that the society still existed. Consequently, the Apostles were protected from those who aspired to be elected, and who would behave in peculiar ways to achieve this end.

Lytton jubilantly proclaimed his election, which officially took place on 1 February 1902, in a heavily marked 'Private and Confidential' letter to his mother – who already knew much of the eminence and mystique of the Society, and was overjoyed at the news.[1]

'My dearest Mama – This is to say – before I am committed to oaths of secrecy – that I am now a Brother of the Society of Apostles – How I dare write the words I don't know! – I was apparently elected yesterday, and today the news was gently broken. The members – past and present – are

1. Lady Strachey had also been told something of the Apostles by various friends and relations – Walter Raleigh, Sir Henry Maine, James Fitzjames Stephen and Arthur Strachey, all past members – and had grown fearfully keen that Lytton should be elected. Before he went up to Cambridge, she had passed on to him all she knew of the Society.

sufficiently distinguished. Tennyson was one of the early ones. But I shall know more when I visit the Ark – or closet in which the documents of the Society are kept. It is a veritable Brotherhood – the chief point being personal friendship between the members. The sensation is a strange one. Angels are Apostles who have taken wings – viz, settled down to definite opinions – which they may do whenever they choose. I feel I shall never take wings. This has once occurred with the apparent result that the Ap. was eventually transported for life! Another person whom I don't know called Sheppard (King's) was elected at the same time as me. We meet each other tonight! . . .'

The Society had been founded as a small, comparatively humble debating club in St John's College. But during the 1820s it fell under the control of two formidable undergraduates, F. D. Maurice and John Stirling, who transferred its rendezvous to the larger and more fashionable Trinity. Once established in this new headquarters, the nature of its business soon underwent radical alteration. Its members, from now on selected only with the extremest caution, met behind locked doors on Saturdays, when, after tea and anchovy toast, they would read papers, often on moral topics, and hold troubled, militant discussions.

'The society', wrote Sir Roy Harrod, friend and hagiographer of Maynard Keynes, 'was very skilful in its choice of members.' Tennyson, who describes it in canto 87 of his *In Memoriam*, was, as Lytton had told his mother, an early member, and so was Arthur Hallam. But Tennyson's association with the Society was unhappy, and when his turn came to read a paper on 'Ghosts', embarrassment so overcame him that he tore the paper to pieces, the evening's entertainment ended in disaster, and he was summarily removed from the favour of the élite. Among other near-contemporaries Kinglake, Edward FitzGerald and Thackeray were not admitted into the circle; while Kemble, an authority on Anglo-Saxon, Sunderland, who died insane, and Venables, who failed to achieve any form of distinction whatever, were prominent at its gatherings.

181

The inner world of the Apostles was sacrosanct. Accounts of its workings given by two nineteenth-century brethren, Dean Merivale and Henry Sidgwick, 'show that its nature and atmosphere have remained fundamentally unaltered throughout its existence', wrote Leonard Woolf, who was elected in the same year as Lytton. Dean Merivale, a contemporary of poor Tennyson, describes its activities as follows:

'Our common bond has been a common intellectual taste, common studies, common literary aspirations, and we have all felt, I suppose, the support of mutual regard and perhaps some mutual flattery. We soon grew, as such youthful coteries generally do, into immense self-conceit. We began to think that we had a mission to enlighten the world upon things intellectual and spiritual. We had established principles, especially in poetry and metaphysics, and set up certain idols for our worship ... we piqued ourselves on the name of the "Apostles" – a name given us, as we were sometimes told, by the envious and jeering vulgar, but to which we presumed that we had a legitimate claim, and gladly accepted it. We lived, as I said, in constant intercourse with one another, day by day, meeting over our wine or our tobacco; but every Saturday evening we held a more solemn sitting, when each member of the society, about twelve in number, delivered an essay on any subject, chosen by himself, to be discussed and submitted to the vote of the whole number. Alas! alas! what reckless joyous evenings those were. What solemn things were said, pipe in hand; how much serious emotion was mingled with alternate bursts of laughter, how everyone hit his neighbour, intellectually, right and left, and was hit again, and no mark left on either side; how much sentiment was mingled with how much humour!'

The testimony of Henry Sidgwick, a close friend of the parents of Maynard Keynes, who was elected in 1856–7, shows only too clearly that, some three decades later, though their intellectual pugilism, their weird cerebral shadow-boxing, could be just as exhaustive, their collective sense of humour had become no laughing matter:

'Absolute candour was the only duty that the tradition of

the society enforced. No consistency was demanded with opinions previously held – truth as we saw it then and there was what we had to embrace and maintain, and there were no propositions so well established that an Apostle had not the right to deny or question, if he did so sincerely and not from mere love of paradox. The gravest subjects were continually debated, but gravity of treatment, as I have said, was not imposed, though sincerity was. In fact it was rather a point of the apostolic mind to understand how much suggestion and instruction may be derived from what is in form a jest – even in dealing with the gravest matters.'

This unencumbered sincerity and funereal merriment formed part of the close bond which continued to unite Apostles of the mid-nineteenth century and later, long after they had gone down from Cambridge, and which was given elevated expression by several of the elect. Jack Kemble announced that the world was one great thought, and he was thinking it; while his colleague, Venables, would often extemporize with genuine amazement on their good fortune at being exalted so far above the general rank and file of humanity, and wonder why in heaven they had been gifted to such excess over 'those cursed idiotic oxford (they spelt the hated word with a tiny "o") brutes'. And Lytton too felt something of the same fiercely partisan convictions, lamenting over the rival university like Christ over Jerusalem. 'It's all or nothing with us,' he wrote on one occasion to Maynard Keynes (4 November 1905), 'Oxford's the glorification of the half-and-half.'

This denunciation of Oxford had a serious meaning. Under Gerald Balfour,[2] brother of the Prime Minister and himself a senior politician, Alfred Lyttelton,[3] a Conservative cabinet

2. Gerald Balfour (1853–1945) was a Fellow of Trinity and member of Parliament for Central Leeds (1885–1906). Among the appointments he held were Chief Secretary for Ireland (1895–1900) and President of the Board of Trade (1900–1905). A popular man of great social charm.

3. Alfred Lyttelton (1857–1913), lawyer, stateman and popular socialite, who was head of the Colonial Office (1903–5) but whose chief eminence was as a cricketer. His play, remarked W. G. Grace, was 'the champagne of cricket'.

minister, and Henry Cust the distinguished art-historian, the Apostles had for a time gradually evolved into a more urbane group, and it was only in about 1890, with the election of Goldie Dickinson, Robin Mayor[4] and McTaggart, that it had finally reacted against this 'top hat epoch' and reintroduced more austere doctrines. By the time Lytton and Sheppard joined, the principles and aims were once again well-defined. They sought to establish a rival influence to that of the eclectic, worldly climate of Benjamin Jowett's Balliol.[5] Above the splendour and prestige of political advancement they venerated solitary self-development, and held abstract contemplation to be of more value than direct action.

Lytton warmly approved of this philosophy, but by temperament he was never wholly akin to it. He honestly believed that a lust for fame contaminated the pure search for truth, that a love of power distorted human affections. Yet personally he was not altogether unambitious. He therefore welcomed a way of life and standard of conduct that discouraged for all the worldly success he secretly cherished but felt he could never attain. If others, more fitted for social and political triumphs, disdained such prizes, then his friendships might never be poisoned by envy. Self-effacement did have an authentic appeal to him; but obscurity was a constant irritant. He was never truly Apostolic as men like Ralph Hawtrey,[6] G. E. Moore, Lionel Penrose, Frank Ramsey

4. Robert John Grote Mayor (1869–1947), Old Etonian, Fellow of King's and a prominent Civil Servant. Married Beatrice Meinertzhagen (1912), was assistant secretary at the Board of Education (1907–19) and became principal secretary (1919–26).

5. Benjamin Jowett (nicknamed 'the Jowler'), Master of Balliol from 1870 to 1893, who said that he wanted to 'inoculate England' with his college alumni, and who became one of the supreme influences in Victorian England. Arrogant and temperamental, with a shrill voice, squat figure and owl-like features, he was famous for his succinct rudeness and pithy conversational rebuffs. A formidable if erratic scholar and divine, he was Regius Professor of Greek at Oxford and responsible for a frigidly asexual translation of Plato.

6. Sir Ralph Hawtrey (b. 1879), economist at the Treasury (1904–45) and author of many books. President of the Royal Economic Society (1946–8). Married Hortense Emilia D'Arányi – one of the musical sisters.

C. P. Sanger, W. J. H. Sprott and James Strachey were, but, in Apostolic jargon, slightly 'tinged with the phenomenal'. He revered the Society, and considered the values they upheld to be the real ones. But world-wide renown was later to make him a happier, more beneficent being. He was right to be ambitious. Fame suited him. For only when he was famous could he effectively carry out his real ambition – the education of the public to more humane views.

A few days after their election Lytton and Sheppard attended their first formal meeting and inscribed their names in the official society ledger. 'I am number 239,' Lytton informed his mother (10 February 1902). 'We have previously inspected the ark in which the papers and books of the Society are kept. It is a charming cedar-wood chest – presented by Oscar Browning.[7] A paper of Arthur's[8] is preserved in it – also a speech by Uncle Raleigh. The minute books are very amusing. The procedure is as follows. A subject is chosen on which the next paper is to be read; but as a matter of fact the paper need have nothing to do with the subject chosen. ... Everyone speaks (though in a purely conversational way) in turn after the paper is read. There were a good many distinguished

---

'I retain a vivid recollection of him [Lytton Strachey] and of his personality,' he wrote to the author (23 April 1963). At Cambridge he was chiefly known as a mathematician, and had great arguments with Moore, Russell and Harry Norton on metaphysics (logic and epistemology).

7. Oscar Browning, C.B.E. (1837–1923), historian and historical biographer. Educated at Eton and King's College, Cambridge. In 1859 he had been made a Fellow of King's, and the following year took up a post as assistant master at Eton. Returned to King's in 1876 as lecturer in history. Hugely fat, he was a notorious socialite and 'character', a 'genius flawed by abysmal fatuity', as E. F. Benson once called him. His last years were spent in Rome, where he was appointed president of the Academy of Arts. Among his many friends was Oscar Wilde. 'Do you know Oscar Browning?' Wilde asked Robert Ross (circa 13 October 1888). 'You will find him everything that is kind and pleasant.' There is a biography of the legendary 'O.B.' by H. E. Wortham, called Victorian Eton and Cambridge (1956).

8. Sir Arthur Strachey (1855–1901), the second son of Lytton's uncle, Sir John Strachey. At Trinity Hall he had taken a degree in law, after which he went out to India and was made Chief Justice of the High Court at Allahabad. He died in Simla.

persons present — among them Goldie Dickinson — and I, being the last elected, had to speak last. They seemed fairly amused.[9] We then voted on this (which, though you wouldn't expect it, seemed to be the main point at issue) — Shall we be anti-vivisectionists? Most I think (including me) said no. Sometimes people add notes to their negatives or affirmatives — and this is what makes the minute books amusing ... everything's so mysterious, one doesn't always know exactly the thing that's wanted. What at present alarms me is the thought that I, as junior member, will have, at the annual dinner in June, to fulfil the function of Vice-President, and return thanks for the health of the Society proposed by the President, who will probably be either Sir Richard Jebb or the Earl of Carlisle!'

The papers which Lytton read out to his fellow Apostles during the first two or three years of his membership show something of a discrepancy. At their best they dredge up to the light of day the sour effluence of a bitter, repressed revolutionary spirit. Probably the most outspoken of them was 'Christ or Caliban?' (25 October 1902), a Swinburnian essay in which Caliban symbolized freedom from all restraint, and Christ the bleak plane of modern civilization. In essence it is a tract against the kind of hide-bound Victorian society which had turned its back on his own deepest problems and silently decreed that he should be branded a misfit. This old rule still persisted, merciless and uncomprehending, still enforced its senseless restrictions upon the free play of the human spirit. And while it remained, a strange feeling of revolt bubbled and surged up dangerously within him.

Yet even before his fellow Apostles, Lytton could not speak all his mind. The true gist of his meaning can only be interpreted between the lines of his speeches; and it is not quite clear how fully aware he was of the conceptions which lay at the root of some of them. The absurd overtones of a piece like 'Christ or Caliban?' with its Lawrentian enhaloment of the 'savage races' is to some extent offset by a vein of slightly

9. Lytton's paper was entitled 'Dignity, Romance and Vegetarianism'.

self-conscious humour running through it. At the same time the repressed, crusading spirit which informs his words is as real as Rousseau's passionate call to mankind to throw off its chains and revert to the natural primitive life. As real and as romanticized. Like Rousseau, Lytton did not have a truly speculative mind; he was not really interested in religious, philosophical or even historical theory, and his papers have the same network of sentimental fallacies and inconsistencies, saved however from ultimate absurdity by the unanalysed force of feeling which thrusts its way through every line – a belief in the superabundant importance of the individual, his dignity and his rights. 'Christ or Caliban?' contains little of Rousseau's paranoiac fire and morbidity, but it is written with a pallor and execration of its own. The iron chains of Rousseau are replaced by *démodé* elastic braces, and the whole fulminating composition unwittingly lends itself to a series of cartoons in the style of Max Beerbohm – Lytton as Greek slave, Roman gladiator, or British flyweight. For example:

'I, at any rate, would be willing with all the alacrity in the world to put myself back into one or other of those more violent ages where railways and figleaves were equally unknown. – "But if you were a slave?" I would be willing to risk that, for I should perhaps creep in to see the first performance of the Birds, or I might be doorkeeper at the Globe, or with some luck I might get to a Gladiatorial show. – How terrible! But supposing you were a gladiator yourself. You wouldn't enjoy that! – Perhaps not; but at any rate I should die a violent death . . . at least I should have no braces . . .

'We still have our field sports, we still hunt; and if I had ever been allowed to choose my life anywhere in my own age I should have been a stout athletic boxer . . .

'But if external help is lacking, is there no chance of some swift internal disintegration? Is there no possibility of a break-up so general and so complete that the entire reorganization of society would be a necessary sequence? Personally, I welcome every endeavour, conscious or unconscious, to bring about such an end. I welcome thieves, I welcome murderers, above all I welcome anarchists. I prefer anarchy to the Chinese Empire. For out of anarchy good may come, out of the Chinese Empire nothing.'

Several of his other Apostolic harangues strike the same fiercely iconoclastic note. 'Shall we be Missionaries?' (undated) was an attack on imperialism: 'I believe, indeed, that some Englishmen do sincerely hold that if England conquered the whole world the greatest possible amount of good would be produced.' Another paper, 'Is Death Desirable?' (January 1903) reaffirms his settled agnosticism: 'It is no longer, for me at any rate, either interesting or profitable to pretend to believe in the immortality of the soul ... immortality has been relegated simply to the position of a mere possibility, absolutely devoid of any particle of probability.' In other papers which ignore metaphysics and concern themselves exclusively with the benefits of *this* life, such as 'Will it come all right in the end?' (undated), a distinctly sybaritic tone is adopted: 'It *is* lust that makes the world go round.' And in line with this anarchical hedonism is an amusing take-off of prudery in art and morals, 'Ought the Father to grow a Beard?' (10 May 1902), where Lytton feigns horror at the growing fashion of naked chins, the failure of so many modern young people, even of quite good family and schooling, to wear a decent covering of whiskers over their stark fleshy faces. 'And that rounded chin, that soft repletion of flesh and fat, is it not more hateful than ever was the bristling and curling hair? More bare, more vile, more loathsome, more incomparably lewd?'

But in contrast to all this belligerence and declared apostasy, the papers which Lytton read out on the subjects of aesthetics and human relationships are orthodox, even diffident. In company with Clive Bell he had begun to develop by this time a rather literary appreciation for the visual arts, but his taste was, and always remained, conservative. In 'Ought Art to be always Beautiful?' (undated), one of his earlier papers, he spoke out against Manet and the Impressionist school of painting, arguing that although it was theoretically possible for good painting not to treat a subject inherently beautiful in itself, in practice it must always be otherwise. His aesthetic concepts on the art of the theatre are sounder, but hardly revolutionary, as another paper, 'When is a Drama not a Drama?' (undated) illustrates: 'My theory is that the essential point about a drama is that it should be composed of two parts, during the first of which the states of mind of the characters should be entirely different from their states of mind during the second. The transition from the first part to the second is the culminating point of the drama – the climax.' Such a well-tried theory of dramatic art was not unknown even in the Greek theatre, and probably represented what he was endeavouring, rather academically, to put into practice in a three-act Euripidean tragedy on which he was working at about this time.[10]

But perhaps the least revolutionary of all his papers are those which deal directly with human relationships. Altogether different from so much that he wrote in private letters to his closest friends, these personal reflections are qualified, mild, almost apologetic. In 'Does Absence Make the Heart Grow Fonder?' (19 November 1904), he wrote: 'I cannot help confessing that if I had the chance of marrying in quite the ordinary way the person whom I wanted to, I wouldn't hesitate for a moment.' But the chances of this actually happening, he felt, were remote. For as he admitted a year later – 'Shall we take the Pledge?' (December 1905) – 'My acquaintance among women is small; I know very few with anything approaching intimacy; and I must confess that I have never been in love with one.'

There were altogether only some half-dozen undergraduate members of the Society when Lytton and Sheppard were elected. For them, the greatest delight of belonging to the Society was the freedom of speech which it not only allowed but actually encouraged. At last, after years of silent con-

10. In November 1903, Lytton had read a translation of *Iphigenia in Tauris*, and written to his mother: 'I long to write the tragedy as sketched by him [Euripides].' Preserved among his papers are two undated plays in manuscript, 'Iphigenia in Aulis' in three acts, and 'Iphigenia in Tauris', a fragment of one uncompleted act.

straint, one might say out loud something of what one felt
and thought; and this was a marvellous release from the
polite suppressions of Victorian 'mupple-class' deportment, a
sudden expanding joy not so easy to appreciate these days. 'It
was a principle in discussion that there were to be no *taboos,*
no limitations, no barriers to absolute speculation,' wrote
Bertrand Russell in his autobiography. 'We discussed all
manner of things, no doubt with a certain immaturity, but
with a detachment and interest scarcely possible in later
life.'

Truth – that was what they were after; and truth they knew
could never be beguiled by mere mental ingenuity. Above all
they must be candid, speak their minds openly, confess their
doubts with sincerity and irreverence, and generally behave
with the rational good sense so lacking in ordinary mortals.
'We were at an age', wrote Maynard Keynes in 'My Early
Beliefs', a paper delivered in 1938 to the Memoir Club, 'when
our beliefs influenced our behaviour, a characteristic of the
young which it is easy for the middle-aged to forget.'

If one looks into it, the whole system of the Apostles
appears curiously analogous to a religious system; clearly is,
in fact, a parody of religion. One can perceive without
difficulty the distinctive characteristics of all religions in the
dogma, the ritual procedures and unspoken faith which made
up the nucleal sanctity of the Society. Not to be Apostolic
was not to exist. The formalities of a meeting and of an election were designed to caricature all the mystique of a religious service. There was no pulpit, but the hearthrug fulfilled
a similar function and was spoken of in exactly the same respectful fashion. In place of a blessing the brethren used a
curse. There was, too, an impressive mumbo jumbo, secret
words and secret meanings of words – 'whales', for instance,
which referred to the sardines now consumed in lieu of the
original anchovies, and which were held to have been the
object of some fantastic law of transubstantiation. And there
was a complete mystical hierarchy from 'embryos' – those
who were in the running for election – up the scale to
'angels'.

A religious secrecy also, full of paradox and mystery, fed their legend. Theoretically, they wanted everyone to be Apostolic; yet very few there were who were admitted to the Cambridge Conversazione Society. For the uninitiated, it was terrible, fascinating, exciting, to imagine exactly what these latter-day Apostles were up to, each Saturday night, behind those locked and bolted doors.

2

FATHER FIGURES

Although the Society had not altered much over seventy years, some minor changes of emphasis had gradually evolved. During the nineteenth century the congregation of brethren were frequently uplifted by transcendental politics. But by the turn of the century the debates had become the battleground of the younger Cambridge philosophers, J. E. McTaggart, A. N. Whitehead,[11] Bertrand Russell and G. E. Moore. True, there was still a small political element within the group, but it was very far from being in the ascendant. The ethical and metaphysical speculations that dominated their discussions were too elevated and too immaterial to preserve any very solid contact with the mundane affairs of party politics. And, at the beginning of the Edwardian era, this philosophical influence so overshadowed all other preoccupations that fierce radicals like George Trevelyan and Nathaniel Wedd[12] would sometimes doze off to sleep during the involved proceedings; while Leonard Woolf's anxiety to

11. Alfred North Whitehead, O.M., F.R.S. (1861–1947), mathematician and philosopher. Colleague of Bertrand Russell, with whom he wrote *Principia Mathematica*. Author of many distinguished books on mathematics and science In his later days he was chiefly famous for his philosophical writings.

12. Nathaniel Wedd, Fellow of King's College, where he was for many years Classical Lecturer and Assistant Tutor. Also member of council of Newnham College. Lionel Trilling, in his study of E. M. Forster, writes that 'the decisive influence on Forster was his classics tutor, Nathaniel Wedd, a cynical, aggressive, Mephistophelean character who affected red ties and blasphemy',

make arrangements for G. E. Moore to be appointed president of the Board of Education found little active support among his confederates and none at all from Moore himself, who was the last person to be offered, let alone to accept, such an appointment. For Lytton, politics was little more than, in Keynes's words, 'a fairly adequate substitute for bridge'.

Lytton spent as much of his time as possible in the company of other Apostles, his 'new and important friends' as he described them in a letter to Lumsden Barkway. In the Easter vacation of 1902 he was invited to a reading-party at Ventnor on the Isle of Wight, with a select band of brothers, including Charles Sanger, Robin Mayor, Desmond MacCarthy – who turned up late – G. E. Moore and his future brother-in-law, A. R. Ainsworth.[13]

Lytton looked forward to the Isle of Wight, so pleasantly small, with quantities of sea all round and chalk downs. It is all disgracefully regular. The party stays at the Blackgang Chine Hotel, where rooms are to be had at two guineas a week; and there they follow a daily Apostolic programme of work and entertainment. The mornings are consecrated to serious writing and reading – Moore pens philosophy; Ainsworth reads Plato and *Anna Karénine* in French, and Lytton *Père Goriot*, *Madame Bovary* and then Montaigne's essays, Swinburne's poems and Webster's plays – the afternoons are usually given over to walking to Carisbrooke, Freshwater and elsewhere, and the evenings to amusements – conversations on philosophy and literature, or games of jacoby or picquet. This is the most peaceful part of the day – Moore at the piano singing Brahms in his low German tenor, the tall, bespectacled Bob Trevelyan, with his craggy face and nebulous mind, standing by him swaying vaguely with the melody; MacCarthy in front of the fire deep in a rocking chair, his feet on the mantelpiece; Ainsworth still poring over his *Anna Karénine*;

13. Alfred Richard Ainsworth, C.B. (1879–1959), who after leaving Cambridge took a job as lecturer at Manchester University (1902–3) and then at Edinburgh University (1903–7), later becoming a Deputy Secretary at the Board of Education.

Lytton himself perfectly motionless, hovering on the interminable brink of some illness, of some precipitate loss of temper.

'Can you imagine the scene?' he writes to Leonard Woolf. 'We have a sitting-room to ourselves – a table in the middle, very uncomfortable red plush chairs, pictures of whores on the walls, a piano (at/on which Moore plays and sings) a marble mantelpiece, and 43 red and yellow glass ornaments. ... We are all very nice and happy I presume – though sometimes your humble servant sinks into demi-depression.'

These troughs of melancholia are occasioned by a succession of unforeseen calamities. Frequent attacks of indigestion interrupt his reading during the mornings and eventually reduce him to a noisome diet of bread and milk. In the afternoons he is regularly chilled to the bone as, together with the rest of the party, he makes his way joylessly across the cold blustery countryside, along twisting hillocks and sunken Victorian villages. And finally, over the course of several evenings he nearly quarrels with Ainsworth – 'I don't like the personification of irrelevance' – and waxes especially angry on being told by him that George Trevelyan shares Bernard Shaw's low opinion of Webster. 'My view of the world,' he tells Leonard Woolf, 'becomes black when I think of it.'

Between such fits of darkest anger and discomfort, Lytton wastes away in a gehenna of boredom, and is soon looking forward to his eventual departure. The tedium and 'utter drivelling imbecility' of the party, however, moderates just before the end, when Goldie Dickinson and Roger Fry turn up. 'The latter – as of course you know – is a sort of art-critic,' he reminds Lumsden Barkway. 'He began as a scientist but threw up that for painting. His quaker relations were a good deal agitated and fussed, and his father offered to increase his allowance by £100 if he'd promise not to study from the nude. But the charming offer was refused.'

Among the general un-Apostolic population of the world Lytton felt increasingly ill-at-ease. In July 1902 he went with some of his family to Oxfordshire to stay with three sisters, Ianthe, Ina and Angelica Homere – 'my Greek Lady friends' as he used to call them – who had lived next door to the Stracheys in No. 70 Lancaster Gate, but who now subsisted in moderate comfort on the wrecks of a fortune lost by their father in earnest speculation on the stock market. After the old man's death, his three daughters – the severely practical and embittered Ianthe, the nondescript Ina, and Angelica, a nymphomaniac of great beauty apparently infatuated with the dazed and cautious Lytton – had moved to a modest house between Kingham and Chipping Norton into which they took paying guests. The peaceful routine of life at Kingham rapidly provoked in Lytton an intense lack of feeling as he sat 'under the evening gnats under a tree on a lawn. . . . The sound of a brass band is only wafted to me occasionally'. 'For me I dribble on among ladies, whom I *cannot* fall in love with,' he complained to Leonard Woolf (July 1902). 'One of them is beautiful, young, charming – oughtn't I to be in love with her? We go for walks together, read each other sonnets, sit out together at nights, among moons, stars, and the whole romantic paraphernalia – oughtn't I to be in love? We talk about it. Oughtn't I? It's *my* disease, I'm afraid, not to be.'

His existence grew fractionally more tolerable when, at the end of the month, he visited Walter and Lucie Raleigh at a quasi-farmhouse abutting on the village green of Stanford-in-the-Vale in Berkshire. 'We sit out of doors and bicycle,' he wrote to his mother (3 August 1902). 'Uncle R writes his book in the morning – on Wordsworth. It is chiefly to deal with the technical points – poetic diction and such-like – so it ought to be very interesting to those who like such questions. We have been to two Clergyman tea-parties. One to Mr Cornish of Childrey, who so far failed to know who I was as to ask me whether I too was a Scotch Professor.' But even with the Raleighs things were not quite as they should have been. The general air of clergymen and bicycles reminded him unpleasantly of Liverpool. Uncle Raleigh, of course, was very brilliant; his talk bubbled away like champagne. Yet something was wrong. Raleigh, after all, was an Apostle, but with an important difference; he was a *Victorian* Apostle, and for this simple reason curiously out of date, tuned in, as it were, to some foreign wavelength from Lytton and his undergraduate friends. What was this difference between the opposing generations? They, the older generation, were altruists and enthusiasts; he was a disillusioned egoist. Their high-minded integrity seemed somehow theoretical, their idealism insensitive. They were always so eager to offer up real suffering individuals for the sake of some noble abstraction, some nice point of principle. How fond they were of sacrificing the actual here and now to some invisible, un-get-at-able future! Yet Raleigh was one of the best of them. '*He* is very eminent, but frantically taken up with a book on Wordsworth,' he told Leonard Woolf (August 1902), 'and at other times paralysing conversationally. She jabbers *sans cesse* – rather amusingly – altogether conceitedly – of persons more than things.' To complete Lytton's dismay he found that the farmhouse also contained four children. Like most fundamentally shy persons he liked to avoid all contact with '*le petit peuple*', though on this occasion he was pleased to note that one of them was 'most inviting' – a future embryo perhaps?

A week later, he was a critical spectator along the route of Edward VII's much-postponed coronation. Plush ceremonies and gorgeous trooping always appealed to his romantic imagination. Parades of this sort were a kind of civic ballet in the streets, not a dogmatic assertion of militarism or power. Yet he was not in the festive vein. He admitted of no false sentiment.

'Their Majesties of England had the honour to be cheered by me on Saturday,' he informed Leonard Woolf (11 August 1902). 'A purely mechanical stimulus. Kitchener looked almost absurdly proud. Roberts of course absolute: To have been in the Abbey would have repaid. My mother reports sumptuosities of dresses and trains unspeakable – also other things.'[14]

The last weeks of this summer vacation were spent at Verd-

14. This almost certainly refers to the surprising presence in Westminster Abbey of a number of Edward VII's favourites, past and present – among them Sarah Bernhardt, Mrs George Keppel, Mrs Hartmann, Lady Kilmorey and Mrs Arthur Paget.

ley Place, a country house near Fernhurst in Sussex, rented by the Stracheys. Here Lytton read Renan and Gibbon, played a little gentle croquet 'with a personage called Pearsall Smith – a literary, American gent – Bertie Russell's brother-in-law, who lives near by', and finally, before a select congregation presided over by an 'oily young clergyman', went through a ceremony of Christian confirmation. 'It was truly edifying,' he told Saxon Sydney-Turner, 'taking the body and blood of our Saviour into one's tum-tum. I assure you I felt a better, wiser, and happier man.'[15]

In the Michaelmas term his devotion to the true religion was handsomely rewarded on being elected secretary to the Society. 'The position is eminent and interesting,' he proudly wrote off to his mother (15 November 1902), 'as the S. has to keep a good many of the Society's papers, and generally arrange matters. I have got a book begun by Harry Wilson of biographies of brothers, which I hope to go on with. Much is mysterious and difficult to find out about the beginning part (1820, etc.). There is also a photograph book which we want to make as complete as possible.'

The special advantage of belonging to the Society was that, as a young undergraduate, Lytton might get to know some of the older members. In particular he encountered two distinguished Apostles who are reputed to have influenced his mind considerably and with whom he remained closely associated for some years after leaving Cambridge: Goldsworthy Lowes Dickinson and George Edward Moore.

The influence exercised by an older man upon a younger is very often no more than the sign of some latent simi-

15. Although Lytton describes this confirmation ceremony, it may be an apocryphal event, since no one else has recorded it or has any memory of it. His nephew, Richard Strachey, was born and christened at Verdley Place (now owned by the Imperial Chemical Industries). 'One of the sights was seeing the General (who for some reason had to function as a stand-in Godfather) being asked by the Vicar, as part of the service: "Do you believe in God the Father Almighty, maker of heaven and earth? And in Jesus Christ his only Son our Lord? who was, etc., etc.," and answering at the end "I do". His face was a sight.' (James Strachey to the author. October 1966.)

larity of temperament already existing between them. The similarity between Lowes Dickinson and Lytton is in several respects striking. Like Lytton at Abbotsholme and early Leamington, Lowes Dickinson had hated his schooldays at Charterhouse, where his physical unfitness had made him an object to be despised not only by the other boys but also by himself. At Cambridge, however, where he could choose his companions with more freedom, he had been happier; and later, as a Fellow of King's, he was able to observe the barbarous panorama of life from a more comfortable distance. Yet the self-contempt originally generated at school still lingered on. For a time he struggled to purge this unhappy feeling by setting himself up in the outside world as a citizen of some public value, a social servant propagating through example and precept the virtues of good citizenship. His endeavours to become immersed in a manly and useful occupation lasted only a few years during which he laboured on a cooperative farm, lectured in the provinces and studied medicine with the view to becoming a doctor. Back at Cambridge again he resigned himself to his unavoidable destiny with a sense of relief, leaving the community to make out as best it could. Here, secluded and safe, he should have been in his natural element, for, as one of his critics put it, 'his hatred of school had not sprung from any aversion to the young of his own sex'. But even now a simmering self-contempt continued to fret and ruffle his academic retirement. At the onset of the 1914–18 war he was to sketch out the idea of the League of Nations and in the following years devoted most of his energies to the furtherance of this scheme designed to establish a better-behaved Europe. But these activities, towards which, in his papers to the Apostles, he already showed signs of moving, could only lead on to eventual disillusionment. He was trying to create a world modelled after the disciplined and cloistered pattern of Cambridge, to expand a form of Apostolicism into an international world society, only to find that, on a far greater and more horrific scale, it was already set irremediably after the savage ways of Charterhouse.

In women Lowes Dickinson took no serious or sustained

interest. His misogyny was indeed celebrated, and he used to say of the female graduates who attended his lectures that he could never tell them apart: they all resembled cows.

Though exasperated sometimes by his mellowed sentimentalism, Lytton respected Lowes Dickinson; G. E. Moore he admired deeply. The one, a wonderful, sympathetic listener, acted as a perfect conversational foil, bringing out the latent brilliance of those around him; the other was a far more palpable and salient figure, whose Socratic method of thinking forced its way into the very blood-stream of his audience. 'What a brain the fellow has!' Dickinson wrote of him in a letter to R. C. Trevelyan. 'It desiccates mine! Dries up my lakes and seas and leaves me an arid tract of sand. Not that *he* is arid – anything but: he's merely the sun. One ought to put up a parasol – I do try to, one of humour, but it has so many rents in it.'

As a boy, Moore had been of a less dominating personality, reserved, and a little overshadowed by his brother, Thomas Sturge Moore, the poet, who was, he later admitted, 'a far readier talker than I and far more fertile of ideas'. One of the junior members of a large Victorian family, his early years were comparatively sheltered and uneventful. Both his father, Daniel, and his grandfather, George, after whom he was named, had been physicians. Daniel had married twice, producing one daughter by his first marriage, and three more daughters and four sons – of whom George was the third – by his later marriage to Henrietta Sturge. The Sturges, an old Gloucestershire family, had through four successive generations figured as prominent Quakers until, according to hearsay, Henrietta's parents were expelled from the local Friends' meeting, the members of which objected to the marriage of cousins. In any event there were no residual elements of orthodox Quakerism in George's upbringing to condition his unworldliness as a man; and he spent his childhood at Hastings Lodge – a detached, typically middle-class and suburban red-brick house on Sydenham Hill, Upper Norwood – enshrouded by an atmosphere of devout Baptist puritanism. At the age of twelve, however, he had passed through an ultra-evangelical phase, waxing for a time so zealous as a Jesus-lover that he went about preaching to people on the highway, until his brother Thomas was obliged to take him sharply in hand and convert him to agnosticism.

After leaving Dulwich College, where he and his brother were educated as day boys, Moore went up in 1892 to Trinity College, and was later elected to a Prize Fellowship given unconditionally for a period of six years. Lytton initially got to know him well on his own election to the Apostles when the philosopher was twenty-nine, some seven years older than he. From the first, Moore inspired in him a reverence that was profound. Though they saw a lot of each other, Lytton seems always to have preserved a rather awed, if not humour-less, respect for Moore, and never to have developed any really close familiarity with him. In a letter to Leonard Woolf (April 1905), he describes Moore as 'quite inaccessible on his cold, restrictive searchlight heights'. For some time he cherished the hope that Moore might marry his sister Pippa. And many years later he told a friend that of all the eminent people he had encountered in the course of his life, only Moore impressed him as being, without question, really great.

'About the greatest men', one of Lytton's aphorisms reads, 'there is always something incredible.' In the case of Moore this was especially true. To an extraordinary degree the philosopher fulfilled Lytton's ideal of genius. The passionate incandescent purity of his thought seemed to imbue and transfigure his countenance with a sublime beauty. He was still young enough to share many of Lytton's own enthusiasms, yet went his way apparently unconscious of the risk of ridicule, and without a trace of intellectual arrogance. A philosopher by divine vocation, he was sincerely perplexed less by the extraordinarily intricate problems of ethical analysis than by the ordinary day-to-day *mores* and shibboleths of society, with which he was sometimes inevitably obliged to come in contact. Among those whom he did not know well, he was shy and naïve. Even the ordeal of penning a simple, chatty letter in answer to one of his friends would fill him with im-

199

potent, baffled despair. 'The reason I haven't written, in spite of wanting to, is that I don't know what to say,' he once confessed in belated reply to Leonard Woolf. 'I have begun three letters to you already before this one; but I wouldn't finish them because they were so bad. I'm afraid I have nothing to say, which is worth saying; or, if I have, I can't express it.'

Moore's inability in this context to find anything to say was the simple result of his possessing no natural powers of fancy or invention by means of which he might elaborate with elegant sophistication on phenomenal affairs that neither interested him nor struck him as being of any intrinsic importance. In conversation he was neither witty nor brilliantly quick. Every word uttered in his presence was pondered over and subjected by him to an astringent linguistic analysis as part of the cumulative process of formulating an accurate interpretation of the complete sentence. An incorrectly employed word or an ambiguously distended infinitive, Leonard Woolf recalls, would draw from him a gasp of astonishment as at some shocking obscenity; he was incredulous, scandalized; he gazed at the speaker as if one or other of them must surely be mad. And later he would confess hopelessly: 'I *simply* don't understand *what* he means!' If a man could not define *exactly* what he meant, then he must be presumed to have meant nothing at all. In ludicrous contrast to this articulate, grammarian slowness was the lightning speed of his intelligence. He responded with immediate delight to Lytton's impeccable snake-like witticisms and highly individual stiletto stabs of humour. 'There was no question of his being shocked,' records Sir Roy Harrod in the course of an analysis of Moore's paramount influence over the Apostles, 'and the young had no inhibitions in his presence. When Strachey made one of his subtle, perhaps cynical, perhaps shocking, utterances, the flavour of which even his clever undergraduate friends did not at first appreciate at its full value, Moore was to be seen shaking with laughter ... the veneration which his young admirers accorded him almost matched that due to a saint.'

Happy and at ease amid the congenial company of his Cambridge friends, Moore joined in whatever they were doing with wholehearted passion. Whether it was the evaluation of ethical dogma, or the singing of a Beethoven song, or an energetic game of fives, or just a tide of pure uncontrollable laughter, he would be caught up into it with a breathless total concentration, the sweat pouring from his face, enthralled as a boy, oblivious to all else. An interesting line of argument always claimed his rapt attention to the exclusion of more mundane matters, and when he was with Lytton, Maynard Keynes, Desmond MacCarthy and Bertrand Russell, his pipe, alternately gripped in his hand and clenched between his teeth, would remain unlit all evening, though he might have exhausted a full box of matches in repeatedly burning his fingers. Lytton and the other Apostles were charmed by such endearing traits – his wonderful unselfconscious freshness, sudden captivating passions, the strong radiating beam of his mind – and they responded spontaneously to his simple and unworldly temperament. Many of them, notably Leonard Woolf, have testified to the enchanting sweetness of his personality, the aura of 'divine absurdity' which emanated from his commanding presence and shone most powerfully from his amazingly beautiful face, with its high domed forehead, its ethereal expression, its delightful and infectious smile. Guileless and sensitive himself, he could never comprehend guile or cynicism in others. His thought had the absolute directness of a child, both its strength and limitation, its muddle, its sudden tender sensibility and ruthlessness.

Still slim in those days, Moore seemed indeed not of this miserable planet, but a prophet nourished with wisdom and goodness from some far-off mysterious source, enhaloed with transcendental illumination. And in 1902, while his apostles watched and waited to be directed by this Messiah towards their new promised land, Moore himself was hard at work on the book which, the following year, was to make his name and match and even exceed his admirers' greatest expectations, the celebrated *Principia Ethica*. Meanwhile: 'One has a few moments that are tolerable,' wrote Lytton, ' – one breathes, as it were, again; one remembers things, but one hardly hopes. I hope for the New Age – that is all – which will cure all our woes, and give us new ones, and make us happy enough for Death.'

3

A ROSE-WATER REVOLUTION

Early in the year 1903, Lytton's attention was temporarily diverted from the affairs of the Society by a family event which shook the régime of Lancaster Gate to its foundations. A destitute though talented French painter, Simon Bussy, who had arrived in England the previous year with a letter of introduction from Auguste Bréal, taken a studio near by in Kensington, and become a frequent visitor at the Stracheys' home where he did portraits of several of the family, suddenly announced his engagement to Lytton's sister Dorothy. Before the death of Queen Victoria such undesirable unions were traditionally brought off by secret elopement or not at all. But Lady Strachey was a woman of greater enlightenment than the stereotyped Victorian matriarch; and besides, the more tolerant climate of the Edwardian era had already begun to invade the country, carrying with it a slight thaw in the frigid moral and social code of the nineteenth century. No one denied that Simon Bussy could paint very nicely; nevertheless, the advanced liberalism of his future mother-in-law faltered and finally broke down altogether at the sight of him *actually cleaning up his plate with pieces of bread*. Dorothy was almost forty at this time, and it was thought proper tactics to employ an unspoken adult censorship with her in place of any more aggressive form of persuasion. But all the silent disapprobation in the world was to no avail. With what Lytton later called 'extraordinary courage' she remained adamant. She was absolutely determined to marry her penurious French artist and no amount of maternal embarrassment could alter her determination. Disapproving, resigned, yet not without some impartial humour, Lady Strachey broke the catastrophic news to Lytton in a letter dated 8 February 1903:

> You will doubtless be more astonished than pleased to hear that Dorothy is engaged to marry S. Bussy. She is very much bent on it, and of course must do as she chooses, and we must all do our best to help her with it. The terrible feature of the case is the smallness of means, but this will doubtless improve as years go on. If you ever have occasion to mention him do say he is an artist of genius, one of the rising young painters of the modern school in France – which is strictly true ...
>
> P.S. Oh la! la!
> P.P.S. I now understand the expression in her portrait.

By the very same post Lytton received a letter from Dorothy herself announcing the same news in rather a different fashion:

> Dearest Lyt,
> Please give me your fraternal blessing. I am going to marry Simon Bussy. Most people I am afraid will think it exceedingly wild, but in reality it is an action of the highest wisdom. (vide Maeterlinck.)
> We shall have 2d. a year but we shall be very gay and sensible – and live if possible in a minute house near Roquebrune.

Lytton found it hard at first to get on with his future brother-in-law. To begin with there was the language barrier: Bussy could speak little English, and Lytton refused altogether to utter a syllable of French. And then, of course, like most Frenchmen, the poor fellow had no brain. No doubt he painted pictures very charmingly, but as everyone knew, artists had no need of brains – they never understood what they were doing anyway. What, he wondered, did his astounding sister see in this Frenchman? He was very *spirituel*, had a great deal of *esprit*, and – *bouffe!* – nothing more that he or anyone else could detect. Still, on principle, he supported Dorothy rather than his mother. Her act was a significant step in the disintegration and *dégringolade* of Lancaster Gate, a break-through of supreme importance in the Strachey anthropology. Parental dismay was made manifest at the marriage later in the year, when, under a feeble plea of difference of nationality, a full-scale wedding ceremony was dispensed with, and the family merely forgathered instead at a stiff and uneasy party in the mammoth drawing-room.[16]

Despite the revolutionary nature of this development – a cut clean across those fetters of convention which had held their parents' generation prisoners – life for Lytton was at first to carry on very much as before. 'The boredom of respectable, or unrespectable, persons (especially ladies) is so intense that my soul sinks far below my stomach, below my bottom, below my boots', he wrote to Sheppard (22 March 1903). 'The people who enter this house are mainly respectable, and nearly all females, which if you come to think of it is écrasant.' In preference to returning home during the Easter vacation, he goes off with another of Moore's reading-parties to Penmenner House, at the Lizard in Cornwall. Among other Apostles who attend are Leonard Wolf, C. P. Sanger and Desmond MacCarthy – who turns up late. 'Others expected later,' Lytton informs his mother (3 April 1903), 'including Bob Trevelyan, whose play[17] has just come out. I have read it – it is, I'm afraid, sad stuff. Moore has also brought the last volume of Charles Booth's new book – on religion in London.[18] It looks very interesting and full of details – which are the charming things.

'The country is at present grey. We are quite close to the sea. The house seems very comfortable. We have two sitting-rooms. There is another party of young gents from Oxford in the house.'

'Nose to nose with the sea', among geraniums and tiger-lilies Lytton languishes in contentment. The sun shines, the

16. Sir Richard Strachey in fact turned out to be extremely generous to the Bussys. He bought La Souco, a fine villa in the South of France, and gave it to them as a wedding-present.

17. Cecilia Gonzaga.

18. Life and Labour of the People of London. 3rd Series. Religious Influences, volume 7. Part of an eighteen-volume social survey – one of the first of its kind – compiled under the direction of Charles Booth, a philanthropic shipowner. He and his wife, Mary Macaulay, were close friends of Beatrice Potter before her marriage to Sidney Webb, of whose socialism they disapproved.

blue sea stretches away in almost every possible direction, Moore sings and laughs as seldom before, the Oxford gents leave and all is very pleasant, comfortable and lazy – no ill-nesses, no arguments and no necessity to shave. On most bright days the brethren take themselves off for communal strolls along the coast, eating sandwiches among the rocks, while a few of the more intrepid ones paddle, and the others have bad fits of the giggles. One afternoon they walk to Mul-lion, a village about seven miles away, to watch Desmond MacCarthy and Bob Trevelyan play in a football match for the Lizard.

Back the following month at Cambridge, Lytton was obliged to start studying more seriously for the second part of his Tripos. It was a bleak and lifeless term. Trinity seemed absolutely dead, though in other parts of the university the fierce academic radicalism of George Trevelyan – heralding the more fashionable wave of socialism which was to capture the undergraduates of two or three years later – stirred within him an amused curiosity. 'The only excitement is at King's,' he wrote to his mother (19 May 1903), 'where the whole college is racked by the social work and agnosticism question – viz, it wants to do work among the Poor, but can only find Clergy to help it to do so. But it doesn't like Clergy, so that it's in a quandary. I don't like Clergy, but then I don't want to do work among the Poor.

'Cambridge is flooded by so-called "working-men" im-ported by George Trevelyan for the day, who have to be en-tertained at various meals.'

By the second week of June his Tripos was over, and he was able to plunge into dissipation – two garden-parties at Newn-ham and a visit from his cousin, Duncan Grant.

The summer vacation that year was distinctly un-Apostolic. Seldom had his family seemed more tedious and remote. 'I find them a little difficult and on the whole a little dull to talk to', he wrote to Leonard Woolf, ' – I'd always rather be doing something else.' Every day for a fortnight he walked to the British Museum, looking through the Hastings papers. 'My life depends on what I find there,' he told Saxon Sydney-Turner.

Fortunately, his initial researches were encouraging, and in October he returned again to Cambridge to work on his Fellowship dissertation.

And so began what, very distinctly, was to be the second part of his university career.

4

THE GOOD LIFE

By far the most significant event of the year 1903 for all Apostles was the autumn publication of G. E. Moore's *Principia Ethica*. Its impact was enormous. 'I expected when I read it,' Lytton told John Sheppard (11 October 1903), 'to see posters in the streets announcing the Death of Herbert Spencer and the Fall of Kant. But there was only something about the Duke of Devonshire.' Moore's views on moral questions had, of course, been known for some time, but the algebraic passion of his book came as a revelation. Discussion of its ethical concepts dominated, for a time, everything else. The effect on Lytton personally was instantaneous. He saw Moore as another Plato, and *Principia Ethica* as a new and better *Symposium*. On 11 October he wrote a long, rhapsodic letter from Lancaster Gate, which conveys something of the tremendous enthusiasm which swept over him:

Dear Moore,

I have read your book, and want to say how much I am excited and impressed. I'm afraid I must be mainly classed among 'writers of Dictionaries, and other persons interested in literature', so I feel a sort of essential vanity hovering about all my 'judgements of fact'. But on this occasion I am carried away. I think your book has not only wrecked and shattered all writers on Ethics from Aristotle and Christ to Herbert Spencer and Mr Bradley, it has not only laid the true foundations of Ethics, it has not only left all modern philosophy bafoueé – these seem to me small achievements compared to the establishment of that Method which shines like a sword between the lines. It is the scientific method deliberately applied, for the first time, to Reasoning. Is that true? You perhaps shake your head, but henceforward who will be able to tell lies one thousand times as easily as before? The truth, there can be no doubt, is really now upon the march. I date from Oct. 1903 the beginning of the Age of Reason.

The last two chapters interested me most, as they were newer to me than the rest. Your grand conclusion made me gasp – it was so violently definite. Lord! I can't yet altogether agree. I think with some horror of a Universe deprived for ever of real slaughters and tortures and lusts. Isn't it possible that the real Ideal may be an organic unity so large and of such a nature that it is, precisely, the Universe itself? In which case Dr Pangloss was right after all.

... Dear Moore, I hope and pray that you realize how much you mean to us. It was very pleasant to be able to feel that one came into the Dedication.[19] But expression is so difficult, so very difficult, and there are so many cold material obstructions, that the best of Life seems to be an act of faith.

This is a confession of faith, from

> your brother
> Lytton Strachey

From the language which he employs, it is obvious that this letter is very far from being mere flattery, and that it constitutes an attempt at giving some coherence to the extraordinarily optimistic but as yet unsettled emotions to which *Principia Ethica* had given rise. For once, all Lytton's correspondence to other friends strikes exactly the same eulogistic note. 'The last two chapters – glory alleluiah!' he exclaimed in a letter to Leonard Woolf (October 1903). 'And the wreckage! That indiscriminate heap of shattered rubbish among which one spies the utterly mangled remains of Aristotle, Jesus, Mr Bradley, Kant, Herbert Spencer, Sidgwick and McTaggart! Plato seems the only person who comes out even tolerably well. Poor Mill has, simply, gone.'

Moore was the Homer, not the Einstein, of modern ethics. His *Principia Ethica* is known to philosophers for its initial chapters; but to Lytton and the younger Apostles it was for

---

19. Doctoribus Amicisque Cantabrigiensibus
Discipulus Amicus Cantabrigiensis
Primitias
D. D. D.
Auctor.

the delicate uplift of the conclusion that it came to be especially revered. Compared with the unworldliness of its last pages, Keynes once observed, the New Testament was a handbook for politicians. The final two chapters – which Lytton singled out in his letters to Leonard Woolf and to Moore himself – 'Ethics in Relation to Conduct' and 'The Ideal' – are certainly different in tone from the rest of the book. The rigmarole of meticulous argument, of cross-examination, assertion and counter-assertion, becomes less concentrated, while, particularly in the last chapter of all, the judgements grow more frankly personal, and Moore's forceful and passionate spirit shines through with ever-increasing vividness. Moral conduct, or duty, is defined as the obligation to select that action which will achieve more good than any alternative action. In so far as the goodness arising from the probable results of any specific act should be calculated in advance of that act being performed, this concept of moral conduct may be summarized as the intelligent prediction of practical consequences.

In the final chapter of all, 'The Ideal', Moore presents those things which, to his mind, are intrinsically good. In a crucial passage he writes: 'By far the most valuable things, which we know or can imagine, are certain states of consciousness which may be roughly described as the pleasures of human intercourse and the enjoyment of beautiful objects. No one probably, who has asked himself the question, has ever doubted that personal affection and the appreciation of what is beautiful in Art or Nature, are good in themselves.' This personal if rather haphazard choice of good things, together with an equally arbitrary list of what is bad – love of ugliness, hatred of beauty and the consciousness of pain – is defended by means of an argument to the effect that since good and bad are familiar to us through intuition, and since these particular qualities strike Moore's own intuition very obviously as being respectively good and bad, then it follows that they must be so.

It is only thus in the last resort that Moore appeals directly to the intuition. His mind was purely literal and speculative, not richly imaginative, and it operated along a straight, two-dimensional plane in tackling problems which were essentially multi-dimensional. It is as if Newton had been entrusted with the composition of Blake's prophetic writings; one is aware of a truly remarkable and powerful mind at work, but the achievement is in some respects terribly inadequate. His world was largely a conceptual one, almost a verbal one at times, and he handled words as a mathematician uses symbols and formulae. To explore the sort of issues which so fascinated him, one must of necessity take as the basis of one's perceptions and experiments the single real unit which exists in this life – the individual human being. Though in the last instance Moore was compelled to relate his search for truth to his own being, his basic unit as a philosopher comprised a network of impersonal linguistic principles upon which, with fine precision, he spun his closely reasoned theories. Anyone not possessing his incorruptible integrity and unassailable tenacity of purpose would have led himself into a morass of confusion before completing a dozen pages of a book which attempted to express the soul of a poet by means of the rigid mental apparatus of a logician. As time went on he was to experience greater and greater difficulty in transforming, diminishing and breaking up his valid intuitional promptings into clear, static components of philosophical jargon. The more he laboured, the more fantastically complex the problems which confronted him loomed.[20] For he was like a man endlessly, impossibly, engaged in trying to explain immortality in terms

20. After his second book, *Ethics*, was published, Moore sent Lytton a disarming letter (20 September 1912) that proclaims something of the chaos and bewilderment which were overcoming him. 'I feel very grateful for your remarks about my Ethics,' he wrote. 'I've been longing to hear something about it, and haven't heard a single word yet, except for one sentence from [W. R.] Sorley the other day. All your criticisms seem to me perfectly just, except that the particular passage which you say you found so baffling, doesn't seem to me so very difficult. But there were others in that chapter which I couldn't follow myself when I read the book through. I was fearfully bothered for want of space towards the end. If it hadn't been for that, I think I really should have brought out the main points more clearly and also made a better thing out of the last chapter.'

of a sequence of time, or to reduce eternity to an orderly chronological progression of feelings and events.

Moore's influence upon Lytton and the younger Cambridge Apostles can be categorized under three distinct headings: the philosophical, the literary, and the personal. Despite its wide reputation as a source-book of ideas and ideals among the Bloomsbury Group, the actual philosophical content of *Principia Ethica* exerted little precise influence on Lytton. But to a limited extent it does seem to have acted as a guide to 'good-as-an-end' and 'good-as-a-means' or the means to good, which clarified the whole subject and, being theoretically sound, was of some realistic and even practical help to him in life. The literary effect of this book upon him was more negligible, though it certainly did exist for a time and is well illustrated by the style of some early papers he wrote for various university societies. His later critical and biographical prose, with its alternating flow of rhetorical queries and bright responses, reads in places like facile parody of Moore's insistence that the thinker's first logical step was to formulate clear questions in order to establish clear answers.

Undoubtedly the main effect which *Principia Ethica* produced on Lytton was of a personal nature, and he may be said to have seen in Moore's philosophical writing an extension, minutely expounded and defined, of his beguiling personality. The doctrines expressed in Moore's work served not to unify the Apostles but to differentiate one from another. Each one measured off from this hedonic calculus a different point. Maynard Keynes, for example, accepted what was for him the religious attitude of *Principia Ethica* as practised by the older Apostles, but ignored Moore's views on moral consequences. Leonard Woolf later adapted and applied Moore's method of defining duty to an historical and political purpose, believing that the historian, by investigating the communal psychology of the past, might attain an understanding which would enable him to forecast the results of future policies. Lytton, in paying particular attention to the final chapter of *Principia Ethica* with its elevating accent upon the merits of human intercourse, turned his back upon ethics in relation to conduct. The impact which Moore had on him was pre-eminently not one of morals but of morale. By absorbing 'The Ideal' he could coordinate those two disparate sides of his nature, the romantic and the classical or intellectual. For Moore employed a severely rationalistic argument to support what Lytton felt to be an entirely sympathetic emotional appeal. No wonder he announced that the Age of Reason had at last dawned.[21] He saw in Moore a supreme cerebral force, simple yet subtle and effective, which severed at one stroke the umbilical cord binding art to orthodox morality, and which gave the arts a free and independent life.

Principia Ethica lit up for Lytton that remote region of the soul where morals melt into aesthetics. In the New Age which this book heralded, his own physical and psychological peculiarities would count for little. Indeed, in such a world they might be counted attributes. Moore was the prophet of that divine companionship for which he so urgently longed. Above all else Principia Ethica spelt out one word to Lytton: friendship. And it is not perhaps surprising at a time of criminal intolerance and incomprehension that it especially meant to him the glorification of that friendship which, throughout the Victorian Age of Unreason, had dared not speak its name. On several occasions he was on the very point of asking Moore whether he ever experienced any homosexual feeling; but in the end could never quite pluck up the courage. 'Dear Moore,' he had written, 'I hope and pray that you realize how much you mean to us.' Moore, however, seems to have been characteristically unaware of the personal interpretation which Lytton and some other Apostles elected to place on his work. He was the prophet: the crusaders must be other men, Lytton himself and more like him – Maynard Keynes, for example. 'Our great stumbling-block in the business of introducing the world to Moorism is our horror of half-measures,' Lytton once wrote to Keynes (8 April 1906). 'We can't be

21. 'The scientific method has been introduced once and for all into Reasoning, and henceforward it will be almost impossible to go back. The Age of Reason has now begun.' Lytton Strachey to John Sheppard (undated).

content with telling the truth – we must tell the whole truth; and the whole truth is the Devil. Voltaire abolished Christianity by believing in god. It's madness of us to dream of making dowagers understand that feelings are good, when we say in the same breath that the best ones are sodomitical. If we were crafty and careful, I dare say we'd pull it off. But why should we take the trouble? On the whole I believe that our time will come about a hundred years hence, when preparations will have been made, and compromises come to, so that, at the publication of our letters, everyone will be, finally, converted.'

Such highflown, semi-serious predictions are in fact less valid forecasts of the future than eloquent reminders of the Victorian past. Lytton turned a blind eye to the puritanical element in Moore's teaching, and extracted from it a message answering his own most imperative needs. Expressed as an equation, this was: aesthetic experience + personal relations = the good life. For him the book was a foretaste of a liberated existence where the generally acknowledged virtues were to be largely coincident with his own mental attributes and emotional predisposition.

Lytton was a natural disciple as a young man. But because he did not efface himself and respond at a very profound level to those who in turn dominated his life, because he was as much fascinated by their position of authority as by their actual creeds, an undercurrent of resentment flowed against the stream of his intense but immature hero-worship. He did not like himself, and by the same token tended to despise those who thought highly of him. His early passionate surrender to people older than himself – Marie Souvestre, Professor Walter Raleigh, and even Goldie Dickinson – usually cooled off after a relatively short time. He set each one up as an intellectual and cultural god, and as gods they failed him. Moore was really the last and greatest of these deified intellectual human beings. From Moore he gained a sense of reassurance which compensated in some degree for his invalidism, and gave him a prophetic hope of happiness and the success he so coveted. Frail and unprepossessing though his body might be, he was now confirmed in his ownership of a subtle and agile mind which was in itself a considerable weapon. There were many times when he exulted in thin but intense high spirits, of forced-up Rabelaisian rhetoric, when the pressure of his ideal longings mingled with his physical desires and banished all other feelings. 'I think I am now only excited by physical desires,' he once told Moore (5 February 1909). But these moments were interspersed with others, during which he demanded from his friends only the strictest intellectual standards.

Like a cripple who has just learnt to walk with sticks, Lytton sometimes needed but no longer sought for someone to aid him after Moore. From this time onwards, though he was to be absorbed by various other trends of thought, though he always remained *emotionally* dependent upon stronger, younger men, he felt no wish to adopt another intellectual mentor. At last he was gaining enough outward confidence to stand up for himself, to create, in due course, his own place in human society and ultimately in the pantheon of literature.

5

HASTINGS'S CREATURE

Lytton's friendships among other undergraduates may be conveniently segregated into two chronological halves. During his first three years at Cambridge most of his close friends belonged to his own college, Trinity. In his last three years he made so many excursions into King's College that when, some time after he had gone down, one of the university papers published a reproduction of Henry Lamb's early portrait above the caption 'Lytton Strachey (*King's*)' hardly anyone was aware of the error. All the members of the original Midnight Society had gone down long before Lytton himself left — Thoby Stephen to set up house in Gordon Square with his brother and two sisters after the death of their father; Clive Bell to shoot at animals in British Columbia, and subsequently to work at a dissertation in Paris on British policy during the Congress of Verona; Saxon Sydney-Turner to an attic in Somerset House; and, last of all, Leonard Woolf to the Civil Service station at Hambantota, Ceylon, where he became as Lytton put it to Moore 'absolute Lord there of a million blacks'. His own college now depressed him. 'Trinity is like a dead body in a high state of putrefaction,' he wrote in his last year there. 'The only interest of it is in the worms that come out of it.' And so he turned for companion-ship to the other colleges, especially King's.

One of the most intimate of his new friends was John Shep-pard, whom Lytton used to call Frank – 'my first, last, and only Frank!' With his white hair and diminutive frame, Shep-pard often gave the impression of being prematurely middle-aged, but there was always something light-hearted and theatrical about his manner which at once delighted Lytton. By leaning on a stick and affecting a slight limp he could appear positively senile at times, yet his vivid conversation and cher-ubic features always contrasted ludicrously with his perform-ance. The zest and whimsicality of his character were memorably caught, too, in his infectious laughter which he produced as a nasal, high-pitched blast, a sort of gasping preposterous explosion which held in it a note of mingled pro-test and incredulity. He could never be relied on to present himself as only twenty-four hours older than on the previous day. 'He is generally, I think, about his fifteenth birthday,' wrote one interviewer from *The Granta*, 'but sometimes he has just passed his hundred and fifteenth.' Though less obviously brilliant, less quick and supple in articulation than, say, May-nard Keynes, also of King's, whose arrogance and contempt for fools was often too apparent in his irascible tone of voice, Sheppard was equally effective in debate,[22] and his acting on the stage was energetic and original.

They first saw each other at the Decemviri, an under-graduate society that used to meet in one another's rooms for coffee and debate. One evening the subject for debate was 'that this house would rather be Drake than Shakespeare'. The

22. Sheppard became president of the Cambridge Union.

motion was proposed by Donald Robertson, a great Alpine climber, a young man of splendid physique and a scholar of Trinity, who gave a spirited account of the life of action and adventure. After he had sat down, a pair of heavy curtains, up to then closed and concealing a window-seat, were drawn open, and a high-pitched voice cried out: 'Utterly ridiculous!' These were the first words of Lytton's that Sheppard heard. The tall frail figure, with his faintly absurd brown moustache and his sensitive eloquent hands, went on to speak of the supreme value of all the things for which Shakespeare stands. Sheppard and the others were held spellbound, for the first time understanding something 'which some of us, I suppose, have never forgotten'.

There was much in Sheppard's personality to appeal to Lytton, and for almost two years he remained the chief figure in his emotional life. Together they used to go off to the rooms of a middle-aged widow, near Emmanuel College, to be instructed in the art of dancing. In turn each of them would solemnly circle the room in the arms of this unsmiling lady whose equally dismal sister sat in the corner strumming out sepulchral melodies upon the piano. These classes, however, were not a success; and on attending their first ball at Lancaster Gate,[23] both pupils were hopelessly outclassed by their partners, and were obliged to retire early and ignominiously from the floor.

Sheppard had a fine scholarly mind, but appeared to do little work as an undergraduate, much preferring those athletic pursuits for which he possessed no aptitude whatever. Like Lytton he worshipped Thoby Stephen, and loved to chide him with being a 'muscular Christian', for which taunt he would be exquisitely chased round the Great Court at Trinity, or the fountain at King's. But Lytton, whose admiration for athleticism was more furtive and inverted, did not approve; and he rigorously set out to make Sheppard a person fit for his affection. 'I can only send you my love', he told him

23. Lytton and Sheppard had decided to take up dancing in order to equip themselves for a special Dance that Lancaster Gate was giving before Dorothy Strachey's marriage.

(31 July 1903). But the affair was not so simple as that. 'If I hadn't liked Lytton,' Sheppard told the author, 'I couldn't have endured it.' His amiable sentimentality and vague disregard for things of the mind brought out the worst didactic side of Lytton. He alternately teased and scarified Sheppard for consorting with his intellectual inferiors. Friendship, he would explain, was all very well; but not friendship with *anyone*. He would grow jealously possessive, objecting to his friend going off on walks with other people, especially non-Apostles. Yet, unless removed entirely from temptation, Sheppard remained incorrigible, and ruthlessly tolerant towards people. He couldn't seem to help it; he actually *liked* everyone.

Lytton's tactics tended to produce more alarm than love. 'What frightens *me*', he wrote to Sheppard (22 March 1903), 'is the idea that you're sometimes frightened of *me*. I'm almost sure you are. That desolates me – you believe it? – and makes me want to kick down the walls of the Universe. My dear soaring Pig, put me at as high a figure as you like, you know quite well that for *you* I'm not in the market at all – I'm simply a gift.'

Occasionally Lytton would relent, and vary his approach to Sheppard by exhortation – 'Shall we all of us go to sleep for centuries, and wake up like young giants? Or never at all?' – by prophetic confidences – 'Most of the time I suffer a dull pain in the bowels. When I die and my stomach is opened, my intestines will be found knotted into more horrible contortions than have ever been known ... my knotted entrails are entwined in spiritual convolutions. My dear child, do my entrails begin to bore you?' – or sometimes by visions of pure romance – 'What quality is it that contains at once this simplicity and this majesty, this softness and this strength? ... It is what all of Us – the terribly intelligent, the unhappy, the artistic, the divided, the overwhelmed – most intimately worship, and most passionately, most vainly love'.

Sheppard greatly relished Lytton's humour, but felt dubious of his humanity. 'I am human,' Lytton reassured him (3 April 1903), 'too human, and I can hardly control my thoughts.' He tried, also, to explain for Sheppard the paradox between his yielding heart and critical mind. 'Dear Frank . . . it's so much easier to say filthy things than charming ones, which one may feel just as much if not more. It'd take fourteen years to say *everything* one thought about *anyone*. So one just says the things which are amusingest and of course the nastiest as well. All this, when one doesn't have any really very definite feelings either of like or dislike about the person. Because when the feelings are fairly engaged – la!' But Sheppard, though amused, was not convinced.

In the winter vacation of 1903–4 the two of them went down to the Mermaid Inn at Rye, where they spent a week together, reading, talking, walking to Romney and Winchelsea and keeping an unavailing eye open for the legendary Henry James who lived at Lamb House, a few yards off. Surrounded only by retired field officers, clergymen, and the occasional antiquarian golfer, there was little chance that even Sheppard would stray towards other sympathetic companionship. 'The inhabitants of the inn seem to be mostly military gents', Lytton wrote to his mother (17 December 1903). 'There is a parson who drinks champagne and plays billiards, but is otherwise the dullest man in Europe.'

This Christmas was, however, one of the last occasions on which Lytton and Sheppard managed to preserve any really close harmony, though they continued as more casual friends for many years. Sheppard was given up by Lytton as an impenitent sentimentalist, worse perhaps than Goldie Dickinson; so much so, in fact, that for a while he even displayed all the symptoms of falling in love with one of Lytton's sisters. There was no reasoning with him. In many of Lytton's letters to other friends from this time on, poor Sheppard is severely castigated for his lack of rigidly-applied high intellect, and for being hopelessly out of date. Lytton's enchantment had passed; and the one-sided infatuation once over was mercilessly purged. Already, by the following July, he told Leonard Woolf: 'I'm fairly bored by him, and as frigid as if he were a lovely young lady.'

Since the University Library did not stock several of the

books which he needed for his Fellowship dissertation, Lytton spent part of the Lent and almost all the Easter term of 1904 up in London working at the British Museum. 'I shall not be up,' he told Saxon Sydney-Turner, 'as the B. Museum and India Office are imperative. Whether I shall ever get to Cambridge next (Easter) term God knows. I suppose I shall somehow. I shall be a mere ghost till the damned dissertation is written.' He did spare some time, however, to accept an invitation in March to the wedding of George Trevelyan and Janet Ward. These solemn celebrations, garnished with some unusual rites, were staged in Oxford of all places, and did not in the least disappoint Lytton's most gloomy expectations. 'Have you heard of the arrangements for the Trevelyan-Ward wedding?' he inquired in a note to Pippa (9 February 1904). 'Bride and bridegroom wanted *Office*, Bride's mother (Mrs Humphry Ward) wanted *Church;* compromise arrived at – An Oxford Unitarian Chapel with a service drawn up by Bride, Bgroom, and B's mother – at present chiefly Emerson. The happy pair are to lead the Simple Life, and will go to Oxford in a special train.' Lytton himself travelled down from Lancaster Gate with several members of his family, and the following day wrote up an account of the proceedings in the course of a long letter to Leonard Woolf (20 March 1904): 'My mother said we were a "cultured crowd" and we were. Mostly matrons, in grey silk and hair – Henry James, Sheppard, Hawtrey, Theodore L. D.,[24] etc., filled in the gaps. The lunch was free, and at separate tables, but the whole train was interconnected, so that there was a good deal of moving about. A High char-à-banc, with a horn, drove us from the station; flags were waved of course, and there was some cheering. . . . Mr Edward Carpenter officiated. He began with an address composed of quotations and platitudes, during which, as Miss Souvestre said, the bride and bridegroom looked at the windows as much as they could. . . . On the platform going away, as Sheppard and I were talking, I turned round – and there

24. Theodore Llewelyn Davies of the Treasury, a good-looking, austere, highly intellectual contemporary of Lytton's at Trinity.

was Cornford.[25] He was in the most antique of toppers, and was travelling third. I suppose I looked at the hat too much, for at last he said, "I thought it would do my top hat good to have an airing – I haven't worn it for 7 years." Then he looked at Sheppard's and added, "Yours looks comparatively new." "Yes," I just remarked, "but then you see Sheppard isn't quite as old as you are." He positively blushed and stepped into his non-special train.

'The bride and bridegroom were almost completely hideous. But I suppose one must let copulation thrive. The service was practically all balls in both senses.'

Ten days later, in another letter to Leonard Woolf, he appended a postscript summarizing to his mind the whole *mésalliance*: 'I didn't tell you Henry James's *mot* on the occasion – "The ordinary service binds, and makes an impression – it's like a seal; this was nothing more than a wafer." '

At the start of the Easter vacation, Lytton went down to a reading-party at Hunter's Inn, not far from Lynton on the north coast of Devon, with Moore, Sanger, Ainsworth, Leonard Woolf, Desmond MacCarthy and a few other meticulously selected Apostles. 'This place is more like a hotel than an Inn,' he wrote to Pippa (4 April 1904). 'There is a large party of Oxford men with an elderly tutor; also an antique male and less antique female. The country is highly beautiful, the weather tolerable. We go for long walks, and usually quarrel about the way.'

On 8 April he left Hunter's Inn some time during the afternoon and following a brilliant short cut on his way to the South of France across a vast and misty common, he arrived an hour later, triumphant but lost, on an unknown road on the other side. After a long walk he at last encountered a

25. Professor F. M. Cornford (1874–1943), then lecturer in classics at Trinity and later Laurence Professor of Ancient Philosophy. Author of several works on the cosmology of Plato. Married Frances, the well-known poetess, and granddaughter of Charles Darwin. Perhaps his most enduring work is a skit on university politics entitled *Microcosmographia Academica* (1908).

group of three men sitting in a field skinning a dead pig. They seemed surprised when this lanky and lugubrious stranger, evidently held in suspense between curiosity and a sense of nausea, shouted across to them in a reedy treble, to ask for the station. 'The tavern?' they queried. By the time Lytton eventually arrived at Woody Bay Station his train had already long since vanished. But there was a fire in the waiting-room where he sat for three hours dozing and dreaming of the interminable journey which lay ahead. 'For the next four hundred years,' he wrote morosely from this dreary railway waiting-room to Moore, 'I shall be voyaging.'

The following day he was in Paris, where at the Hôtel St James he met Marie Souvestre 'bursting with Alfred de Vigny'. That evening he went to the Théâtre Antoine. 'The house was completely full, and very appreciative and quite stupid,' he wrote back to his mother (13 April 1904). 'The French bourgeois are I think on the whole more maddening than the English aristocracy; they are equally conceited, but infinitely more pedantic. An abbé and a vieille girl in the train here talked and colloqued together for several hours about education and classical literature with such a horrible wealth of platitude that I longed for cricket shop of the most degraded kind.'

On 12 April he arrived at La Souco, the little house in Roquebrune where the Bussys had recently installed themselves. Immediately he was enchanted with the place: so small, so pretty, so charmingly proportioned and coloured that it might have come from an illustration out of some children's story book. 'The house is perfectly divine,' he informed his mother (13 April 1904), who had not yet visited Dorothy since her unfortunate marriage. 'The pink of beauty reigns – marble staircases, Chippendale chairs, Louis XIV Cabinets, impressionist pictures, and the best view in Europe. . . . My bedroom looks out on to the neighbouring banker's and baron's garden, whose chief object is a gigantic red umbrella under which the bankers and barons sit.'

On the same day he wrote to Leonard Woolf with almost equal enthusiasm and in greater detail. 'It is a most extraordinary place. The house is 3 inches square[26] – and a dream of beauty. The floors are tiled with smooth red hexagonal tiles, and partially covered with matting; the walls are white, the furniture replete with every beauty. A few impressionist pictures are on the walls. If the whole place was taken up and plunged 400 miles away from everywhere and everything but the flowers and the frogs, I could live in it for ever; as it is there are too many Germans whirling past it through the air – too many terrific English driving tandems from Mentone just below and just above us.'

In England, Lytton could be prevailed upon to speak precious little French; in France itself he seldom uttered a single word. Conversation with his brother-in-law was consequently out of the question. Besides, even if he did speak the language, what was there to talk about? From his sister, on the other hand, the rebel of the family, he expected great things once he had presented her with a copy of Moore's *Principia Ethica*. To his dismay, however, she informed him after reading through it that in her view the last chapter omitted all the difficulties, and was untrue. This, it seemed to Lytton, was most discouraging for posterity. If intelligent females could not recognize the underlying truth of Moore's teaching, then who could? Perhaps, though, they were too bound up these days with the feminist movement to see things steadily and see them whole. It was understandable. Naturally he too believed, if more tepidly, that women should be given the vote – the poor things wouldn't have much else before long. Yet Dor-

26. To anyone not having been brought up in Lancaster Gate, La Souco might have appeared quite a fair-sized villa. It had originally been built by the Roquebrune carpenter for his own occupation, but was bought for the Bussys before it was finished, and has been extended since then – one main addition being a garage. Visiting it in August 1964, the author was surprised to find that it had three spacious ground-floor rooms plus a dark and narrow kitchen, and three bedrooms, balconies and a bathroom upstairs. The villa lies just off the Grande Corniche below Roquebrune village, and looks directly across to Monte Carlo bay. It has a steep terraced garden, now wildly overgrown, a number of olive trees and one towering cypress. Adjoining the house are a large studio and a patio with muralled walls. La Souco has recently been bought by the Belgian ex-ambassador to Canada.

othy's failure to hold opinions and feelings coincident with his own irritated Lytton. Probably, he reasoned, stupidity was infectious, and she had caught a bad dose of it from her French husband. Their exclusive heterosexual contentment irked him to an unreasonable degree. How insensitive they must be, he thought, to feel so happy with each other. Their show of love made him feel an outsider. What right had people without a tithe of his intellectual talent and 'goodness' of feeling to enjoy such felicity? Really, the world was too extraordinary. Only the dull, it seemed, lived happily. 'I must say that I am sometimes a little annoyed at their affectionateness,' he expostulated to Leonard Woolf (13 April 1904). 'Wouldn't you be? Two people loving each other so much – there's something devilishly selfish about it. Couples in the road with their silly arms round their stupid waists irritate me in the same way. I want to shake them.'

Surrounded by foreign peasants and enormous goats, Lytton missed the conversation of his friends. Always highly susceptible to boredom, it was for him not merely a negation of excitement, but something more positive and overwhelming, infecting every particle of his being like a malignant cancer. 'This is a wonderful, fascinating country,' he told Leonard Woolf, 'but as for living in it – ! I don't think I could live anywhere out of England – I should always be moving on.'

Turning from the euphoria of stupidity and the blank tedium everywhere around him, he soon resigned himself to working on his long dissertation. Almost every day he pressed resolutely along with it; but here too he was confronted by monotony. The task of perpetually renewing his original enthusiasm, of elucidating in detail for the benefit of crass pedagogic examiners information already so stalely familiar to himself was unbelievably enervating. Depression and ennui ate into the very marrow of his bones. 'I am lost', he confessed, 'over Warren.' But still, day after day, he forced himself methodically to go on with it.

Early in May Lytton returned to England, dividing the next six weeks between Lancaster Gate and the British Museum. By the second week of June, he had completed the bulk of his research work on Hastings, and was free to go off for a few days' rest, staying at Ivy Lodge, near Tilford, three miles from Farnham in Surrey, with Bertrand Russell, his wife Alys and her brother Logan Pearsall Smith, who was then working on his *Life and Letters of Sir Henry Wotton*. 'Everyone talks without stopping on every subject,' he wrote to his mother (16 June 1904). 'Ping Pong S reads poetry aloud in a wailing voice, which is rather depressing. I believe he thinks all poetry should be mildly melancholy, and has no more idea of drama than a cow. Russell is writing a chapter on the Improper Infinitive.' Through the Russells he also met C. F. G. Masterman, the author and Liberal politician − 'a beast, I think, mainly,' Lytton told Sheppard,'. . . . slimy and kind and christian and foolish. Limited horribly. Also rather nice.'

On his return he resumed for the next few weeks his work at Lancaster Gate, inching his way forward with the Warren Hastings thesis like a mole burrowing towards the light. 'My dissertation is assuming most unwieldy proportions,' he told Maynard Keynes (14 July 1904). 'You don't know how superb one feels − writing a real book, with real chapters.' In fact he had at this time been asked by Methuen, the publishers, to write another 'real book' on 'Holland House and its Circle', but refused the offer since he could afford to think of nothing but the Hastings, and felt that in any case Methuen were not willing to pay him enough money for what would be an arduous and risky undertaking.

On 15 July, he moved out of London to Morhanger Park, a country house at Sandy in Bedfordshire, within half an hour of Cambridge. He now immersed himself completely in the final stages of his work. 'I want to see everyone very much,' he wrote to Keynes; all the same he could not spare the time to go into Cambridge, not even to hear C. P. Sanger read a paper to the Society on copulation: 'I feel', he told Keynes (21 August 1904), 'that if I left off writing for a single second all would be lost.' Instead, he invited a few of his friends, Sheppard, Moore and one or two others, to visit him at his retreat. But he begged them not to disturb him. Best of all they should emulate the unobtrusive example of his father. 'Be prepared for doing nothing but sit in the garden and read novels,' he warned Moore (8 August 1904). 'Won't you like that? I am ploughing on with my dissertation; it's now very boring! But it looks beautiful all typewritten out.' As each sheet was finished it was passed to his sister, Pippa, who typed it out neatly on foolscap. At one point the table on which Lytton was working, bent low by the accumulation of reference books, collapsed with a bang, distributing the un-numbered papers all over the floor and giving rise to a general panic and pandemonium. But the chaos was soon sorted out by a cluster of female relatives, and the slow dispiriting pro-gress resumed.

The side issues of his work seemed at times to interest him more than the thesis itself. As he struggled along he began to observe and note his alternating moods and the physical re-sponses to which they gave rise with all the devotion of a true hypochondriac. 'I am in a fairly hellish state which makes me seem rather magnificent to myself,' he wrote and told Leo-nard Woolf (July 1904). 'Horrible illnesses attack me, and I sometimes think all's lost. But really perhaps the only sup-remacy is the supremacy of effort. I feel occasionally like an unchained tiger. ... But by God! one does have hours of hideous collapse! Also, I find, of a sort of wonderful, sub-limated sentimentality. ... I have it often at breakfast when my stomach is all wobbly with being up so early. I don't know — I seem to have a physical feeling in my abdomen of spiritual affection. But perhaps it is merely lust.'

Despite prolonged hard work, he had left his final con-centrated effort rather late and now had serious doubts as to whether the thesis would be completed in time, especially since it was turning out to be longer than he had originally planned. From this time on he could afford neither to see nor even to write to his friends, making only one exception to ask Maynard Keynes for a copy of Rosebery's *Life of Pitt* in a pale wan scrap of a letter which, he admitted (21 August 1904), 'should have been part of Chapter V, with quotations from Sir Eyre Coote, and information upon William Markham —

hush! – I think he *must* have been Hastings' creature – and the police of Benares.'

With a couple of days to spare, the dissertation was finished, and Lytton went off until the end of the month to join C. P. Sanger in Caernarvonshire, passing the final hours going through his typescript and making a number of minor corrections and emendations. Sanger's company, as always, suited him very well, but never more so than now in his rather exhausted, anxious state. For Sanger's penetrating intellect, with its swift bird-like flashes, never obtruded upon his natural gift for friendship; in a unique way his acute and critical mind was coupled with a warm, unambitious temperament to make up a truly sweet personality with which Lytton could relax and yet be entertained. To a rather lesser degree Lytton responded to Sanger as he did to Moore; he had something of the same beneficence, the same mystic fusion of heart and mind. Refreshed by this short holiday in Wales he returned to Trinity on 1 September to assemble with the other Fellowship candidates. 'I handed in my Dissertation all right, having corrected everything – with one exception remembered afterwards – and added a note on the spelling of proper names,' he wrote to his mother (2 September 1904). 'I find that there are about seven other people going in for fellowships, which is fewer than usual, and that there will be perhaps four fellowships – which is more than usual. There are very few people up, and those who are seem to be declining into perpetual melancholy.'

When he returned a few days later to Morhanger Park Lytton was in a state of well-concealed, hopeful expectation. Although the opposition likely to be encountered from the scientists was stiff, his chances of obtaining a Fellowship would never be better. But for the moment, being utterly sick of Warren Hastings and the whole subject of Anglo-Indian politics, he tried to turn his mind away from all the complicated historical issues which had been occupying it so unremittingly during the previous months. Compulsory reading that autumn for all Apostles was the posthumously selected essays of Henry Sidgwick, who, half a century ago, had refertilized the spirit of the Society in a fashion similar to Moore's. From these miscellaneous papers Lytton returned again to Sidgwick's *Methods of Ethics* to which Moore had paid generous acknowledgement in his *Principia Ethica*. But Sidgwick's arguments, Lytton found, were never so pointed or so formidably marshalled as Moore's. 'He [Sidgwick] seems to make hardly any false propositions, and the whole thing seems to be extraordinarily weighty and interesting,' he told Leonard Woolf (September 1904). 'But Lord! What a hopeless confused jumble of inarticulate matter. It is a vast vegetable mass of inert ponderosity, out of which the Yen[27] had beaten and welded, and fused his peerless flying-machine. Don't you think Sidgwick contains the embryonic Moore?'

In the third week of September, Lytton returned once more to Trinity to compose an essay for the Fellowship Examination in the form of a dialogue between Johnson, Gibbon and Adam Smith on the uses and abuses of universities, and to dine at the Master's Lodge with the other candidates. It was now that the awful news was broken to him that the electors, headed by a don with the sinister name of Moriarty, had referred his dissertation to a clergyman! – none other than that high-minded Tory divine, the Rev. William Cunningham, the doctor of divinity who had the previous year provided him with such a cryptic testimonial for the Board of Education. It seemed a disastrous omen.

He was sure by now that all was lost. Ten days later he arrived back at Trinity to be told by Cunningham that, as suspected, he had failed to win the Fellowship. 'Things are less satisfactory than I think might have been hoped,' he wrote off to his mother (12 October 1904), whom he had earlier forewarned of his likely lack of success. 'Cunningham's main objection to my dissertation was that its subject did not allow sufficient scope for original treatment. That is to say, the main point of view from which it is proper to regard H's administration has now been satisfactorily established by James Fitzjames and Uncle John, and hence all that a sub-

27. The Yen was Lytton's nickname for G. E. Moore.

sequent worker has to do is to follow along the line which they have indicated. This, Cunningham thought, I had done exceedingly well; but he saw no evidence to show that a man who was not first class might not have done the work which I had done. ... The Reverend Doctor was very kind, and persisted strongly that my work was well and thoroughly done – but he thought that it had not brought out the qualities which were to be looked for in a fellowship candidate.'

The restrained tone of this letter, with its unemphatic wording, gives no indication of the terrible despondency that now engulfed him. He believed that Cunningham's objections to his dissertation were trivial and confused: his work had been absolutely original in that it gave for the first time an account of the complex and involved Benares incident as it had actually occurred, with his personal reasons – supported by new and unpublished evidence – for believing that everything had happened as he described it. What could be more original than that? He did not, however, make it clear to his mother – or even apparently admit to himself – that Cunningham's objection was not simply to the effect that his dissertation carried on a line of research already begun by Sir James Stephen and Sir John Strachey – a purpose that was *prima facie* logical and justifiable and did not necessarily exclude originality – but that the affair of Cheyt Sing – especially when (as in this instance) severed from that episode concerning the Begums of Oude – was considerably less important and less difficult of treatment than those of Nuncomar and the Rohilla War. Nor had it ever aroused anything approaching the storm of controversy excited by those two matters.

Lytton had worked harder on his dissertation than he liked to admit to his friends. He wanted to be elected a Fellow of Trinity almost, as it were, against his will, and certainly without any apparent effort. Besides, it was AGAINST HIS PRINCIPLES to fail in an examination. His immediate disappointment was so bitter that he could barely endure to remain a single day longer in Cambridge. 'My misery is complete,' he confided to Leonard Woolf who was himself preparing to leave Cambridge having done relatively poorly in

the Civil Service examination. 'I have never felt more utterly
desolate and now can hardly imagine that I shall be able to
stick out the term. However, I presume it will at any rate
never be worse than this, as there is absolutely not a soul or a
cat in the place. ... Shall we ever recover? Is this the end of
all? Well, Lord have mercy upon us!'

Leonard Woolf, for his part, felt less pessimistic, and he
endeavoured to raise Lytton's spirits. After reading the typescript of his dissertation, he replied (October 1904): 'W.H., I
thought, was enthralling, but I believe I see what those asses
mean. It's too enthralling, and not enough like a dissertation.
It's a little too graceful for them, and if you made it all seem
more laborious and magnified all the points, they would have
elected you.'

Lytton at once responded to this encouragement. It
seemed obvious that he knew more about the original approach and treatment of history than his examiners. A letter
which he dispatched about this time to Leonard Woolf illustrates very clearly that the crushing arrogance and absurdly
infantile pride which many people found so offensive in him
was simply the reverse side of the coin whose face was abject
unhappiness. 'Yes; our supremacy is very great, and you've
raised my spirits vastly by saying so,' he told Leonard Woolf
early in the Michaelmas term. 'I sometimes feel as if it were
not only we ourselves who are concerned, but that the desti-
nies of the whole world are somehow involved in ours. We
are – oh! in more ways than one – like the Athenians of the
Periclean Age. We are the mysterious priests of a new and
amazing civilization. We are greater than our fathers; we are
greater than Shelley; we are greater than the eighteenth century; we are greater than the Renaissance; we are greater than
the Romans and the Greeks. What is hidden from us? We have
mastered all. We have abolished religion, we have founded
ethics, we have established philosophy, we have sown our
strange illumination in every province of thought, we have
conquered art, we have liberated love. It would be pleasant to
spend our days in a perpetual proclamation of our
magnificence.'

So Lytton wrote at a time when his misery and disappointment were complete; for the more wretched he felt, the more far-fetched and high-falutin had to be his claims, to lift him above the abyss of failure. Read in its biographical context, this affirmation of supremacy shows itself to be little more than the whistling of an ambitious man, trying to keep up his spirits in the dark.

A few days after Cunningham had pronounced his fatal verdict, Lytton decided to leave for the consoling wilds of Rothiemurchus. There, amid the trees, the lakes and mountains, the vast impersonal forces of nature, he could forget his petty troubles and frustrations. 'I have banished almost everything from my mind,' he wrote to Leonard Woolf (October 1904) after only a few hours there. Following this oblivion, his appetite for life returned. Something, he reasoned, might still be constructed out of the ruins. Cunningham had told him that there would probably be very few Fellowships next year and that it would be an outside chance if he got one. But at the same time he had urged him to go on with the work he had already done – remould his account of Benares and add to it a reconstruction of the Begums of Oude incident. To do this would certainly be more worth his while than beginning again on some other subject. If he pursued his researches, Cunningham had said, the result would be most useful to future historians, and even if it didn't win him a Fellowship, the thesis ought to be published. Methuen were already interested in it. Besides, what else could he do? There seemed no alternative. He must try again. 'On the whole,' he wrote to his mother (12 October 1904). 'I believe this is the best thing I can do.' Perhaps, one day, G. L. Strachey's 'Warren Hastings' would be acknowledged as a *magnum opus* – a fine revenge for the disregard of the Trinity electors.

Also, there was always that outside chance.

6

A VERY QUEER GENTLEMAN

The dissentient who persists steadfastly enough in his uncon-
formity at length dictates the norm of behaviour. When he
first went up to Trinity Lytton was a lonely, frail creature, so he
felt, ashamed of his own awkwardness and freakish appearance. But in his final two years he had grown to be so
much of a fashionably intellectual force that his influence is
said to have left its mark on at least three generations of
undergraduates, who strove to tune their voices in with the
Master's high-pitched glandular key.

Anxious not to be forced into the shades of oblivion by
his physical and emotive peculiarities Lytton was determinedly outspoken, above all on matters of religion. He
would go about the streets and rooms of Cambridge exclaim-
ing 'Damn God!' and other daring oaths and blasphemies,
waiting in complacent disbelief for the Old Testament Lord
God of Hosts to do his stuff and hurl down a thunderbolt. It
was an example of the ludicrous postures into which an unnaturally restrictive and superstitious society can distort an
otherwise highly intelligent human being.

To all Lytton's behaviour – some of it on the surface disconcertingly flippant – there was an extremely serious object. He
was, even now, seeking to jolt people out of their automatic
conventional morality and persuading them to accept more
enlightened attitudes. It says an immense amount for
the amazing power of his personality that, as Noël Annan
has pointed out, although he showed no signs of publishing
anything except the isolated book review, he was recognized
by so many as an arbiter. He was unauthorized, but taken as
an authority, and his influence became extraordinarily wide.
'My own view is that Lytton's Cambridge years had an important effect on the subsequent mental life in England: especially
on the attitude of ordinary people to religion and sex,' James
Strachey told the author. 'The young men in my years
(though also interested in socialism) were far more open-

230

minded on both those topics than their predecessors – and I believe they handed on what they derived from Lytton, and this (taken in conjunction with Freud, who was totally unknown till much later) is, I think, what has resulted in the reform of the general attitude to sex.'

Undoubtedly Lytton was the nucleus of that revitalized anti-religious group which now sprang up within the university. Clear evidence of his potent influence upon other undergraduates is provided by their letters to him, in which they studiously aimed at hitting off the same style of brash, pornographic pessimism. Beyond his own set and around Cambridge at large his sinister reputation for pagan decadence and wickedness spread alarmingly. 'You must be careful next term for "the College" is really enraged with us,' Leonard Woolf wrote to him in the summer vacation of 1903. 'They think you are a witch and given up to the most abandoned and horrible practices and are quite ready to burn us alive at the slightest provocation. One of Barlow's acquaintances, a scholar of the college, it is now a well-known fact, once went to tea with you and came out white to the lips and trembling. "The conversation," he said, "was too horrible! And the pictures and atmosphere." '

Lytton was secretly delighted. At last his presence was being felt; at last he was considered someone worthy to be reckoned with. The authorities, his foes, were being encouraged by nothing more aggressive than the force of mere words to adopt an attitude of transparent medievalism that must, he reasoned, forfeit them much support. Nor was Leonard Woolf exaggerating that mysteriously evil prestige which hung around him and aroused such hostility. Some confirmation of what he had written in his letter is recorded by a humorous article in *The Granta* – one of a series entitled 'People I have not met' – based on his by now notorious heathenism. The imaginary interviewer finds Strachey reclining on a sofa, robed in a négligé costume consisting mostly of silk pyjamas, with his eyes half-closed over the *oeuvre* of some French poet. Several bottles of *absinthe* and similar concoctions stand near by, and from these he frequently and with trembling hands replenishes his glass. The room is wreathed in swirling clouds of smoke from the heavy black tobacco cigarettes at which he draws deeply in between drinks. 'As I came in,' the interviewer wrote, 'he directed towards me the listless gaze of his cold, glassy eyes, but made no attempt to simulate the least interest in my presence.' The fictitious colloquy proceeds quietly, with Strachey still lying on the sofa, his hands bright yellow and his cheeks white and hollow, until without warning everything accelerates to a sudden climax. Rising to his feet, Strachey is seen to dance about the room 'after the manner of a lunatic who imagines himself to be an inebriated Bacchante in a frenzy of Greek orgy, but cannot find any liquor of sufficient strength to give the necessary realism to his performance'. This exhibition of mild exercise quickly exhausts him, and he falls back mumbling that he has found what he has been searching for all his life, an original sin – 'a corkscrew to open the bottle of an hitherto untasted draught of life'. Finally, before relapsing into bad verse, he terminates the interview with a last cryptic utterance: 'Oh virtue, virtue, life's a squiggle.' From which it would appear, Clive Bell commented, 'that his reputation was not purely literary after all'.

The scene brings to mind Oscar Wilde's rooms some thirty years earlier at Oxford. Their similar renown at university for picturesque, effete sinfulness was based partly on distinctive tastes which they held in common. As undergraduates each of them displayed a deep and lasting fascination for the stage; each won a much-coveted prize for rather indifferent, insincere poetry; fell out with the religious authorities of the day, and eventually – despite a contrary reputation for brilliant intellectuality – failed to obtain a Fellowship. In both cases their homosexuality was tied to an exaggerated self-preoccupation which, with its accompanying passion for the applause of others, acted as the limiting factor in their creative output. They evolved ingenious aesthetic theories which were more fanciful than truly imaginative, and which, for all their craftsmanlike expertise, never convince one as being profoundly original. Their strangely divided natures spoke through two antithetical literary styles; the sugary, ornamental fairy-tales and melodramas of Wilde, roughly equivalent to Lytton's own shrill thin romanticism, were the weaker strain. Like Wilde, Lytton was usually best at his most succinct; the crisp, spare irony of *Eminent Victorians* is anticipated perfectly by Wilde's study in green, his memoir of Griffiths Wainwright, *Pen, Pencil and Poison.*

In their lives too there is a parallel. It was the penalty of this dual nature that their charm was entangled with an ugly thoughtlessness. In the course of his life Lytton's unique and memorable personality, his reserved, steely strength, stamped itself indelibly on a remarkable number of people, sometimes altering the whole course of their lives and inspiring in them an intense and enduring devotion. '*Je n'ai jamais rencontré quelqu'un qui dominât la vie comme lui,*' wrote Francis Birrell of him. '*Souvent silencieux et morose, généralement en proie à quelque malais, il était constamment environné d'une atmosphère de déférence.*' For such people he represented the virtues of tolerance, enlightenment and humanity. Yet at the same time, the humanitarianism for which he stood was erected against a scathing contempt for the mass of humankind – the ugly, the boring, the stupid, the ambitious, the powerful and the ordinary. Towards these classes of persons he sometimes reacted with unselfconscious brutality, his rude and abrupt behaviour being quite as extraordinary as the warmth and kindness he lavished upon those he liked. From his deficiencies, his very lack of vitality, he had constructed a character of astonishing force. By deliberately withdrawing his personality from the reach of those around him he was able to cast a withering blight upon any social gathering of which he disapproved or which wearied him. Under the inspired tension of his silence the very fires would seem gradually to fade into dead ashes, the room grow chill. 'How dull everyone is!' he once exclaimed in the middle of a picnic: and even the birds on the trees stopped their singing in discouragement.

To attract this displeasure was a dismaying, sometimes a terrifying experience. He seldom scrupled to hide his boredom or the awful outward manifestations of his extreme shyness. Once, when he had persuaded Leonard Woolf to invite a well-known literary man to dinner so that they might be introduced to each other, he was so overpowered with ennui after five minutes' conversation that he retired completely into himself and, determined to take no further part in the proceedings, fell into a deep and tortuous silence, 'fixing his eyes upon his food or upon the ceiling and tying his legs into even more complicated knots than usual'. His habitual diffidence before strangers would sometimes blossom among mere acquaintances into a cutting callousness. 'Mr Strachey, do you realize it's five years since we met?' inquired Constant Lambert, then a clever, charming but rather noisy young man; to which he received the purring unexpected reply: 'Rather a nice interval, don't you think?'[28] At parties he had no small talk whatever, and his grim lack of response to any form of trivial chatter was often devastating. Like most inhibited people he could, on occasion, be arrantly outspoken. At the end of a solemn, lengthy lecture delivered in candlelight by A. C. Benson on the critic and historian, John Addington Symonds, he swayed to his feet like a languid jack-in-the-box and piped up from the back of the hall: 'But tell me, had Symonds *any* brain?' His capacity for disturbing repartee was difficult to match. When a taxi driver, having driven him home, suddenly turned to him and expostulated, 'I should never have agreed to take you had I known *this* was the house you wanted,' Lytton did not trouble himself to ask what on earth the man could have meant, but simply retorted: 'Has anyone ever told you what a *bore* you are?'

Humbug and grandiloquence he was especially swift to deflate, as on one notable occasion when he petrified a party of Highland sportsmen. A *Punch* artist had been pompously deprecating the practice of lynching Negroes and by way of a worldly-wise comment, added: 'But you know what it is they lynch them for.' 'Yes', replied Lytton. 'But are you sure the white women mind it as much as all that?'

28. Lytton had made an unsuccessful pass at the heterosexual Constant Lambert when they first met.

This quick contemptuous temper was a natural outlet for his seething self-dissatisfaction, sharpened to a fine edge by continual ill-health. Outward circumstances were sometimes less a cause than an excuse for his offensiveness; for, like Samuel Rogers, he seems to have felt that, with his weak voice, he could only be heard when he said unkind things. He never exploded with anger or indignation, but with perfect cold control planted his dagger in the heart of a chosen adversary. Perhaps the most striking example of his unprovoked rudeness took place a few years after leaving Cambridge, and had as its victim the poet and Chinese scholar Arthur Waley. At that time Waley was suffering from defective eyesight and unable to read. To enable himself to play chess, which as a substitute for reading he very much enjoyed, he used to tie a label round the bishops so that he could distinguish them more easily from the pawn pieces. Entering a room where Waley was bent low over this chess board, Lytton glanced at the labels fluttering from the bishops and remarked: 'I see you're not only blind, Waley, but also half-witted!'

Many such remarks, intended as humorous sallies, were never meant to hurt, for at heart Lytton had a kindly nature. But, in these early days, he was often unaware of the diabolical effect his manner produced upon others. Whenever it was pointed out to him that he had unwittingly offended someone, he would feel intensely remorseful, going to some lengths to apologize and set matters right again.

Like Wilde's dandyism and bold check suits, Lytton's sartorial devices, which later came to a head under the influence of Augustus John, were both a means of drawing attention to himself and of emphasizing in the most theatrical manner his departure from the conventions of the past. Yet his eccentricities were less easy-going than Wilde's. He had a devout horror of high fashion and during the autumn of 1904 was compelled sharply to rebuke such a close friend as Leonard Woolf for his brown boots and green collar. Since aesthetics were inextricably bound up with ethics in the public imagination, and many people judged others simply by their clothes, Lytton's unconventional views were often strictly and formidably applied. Wilde had made an art of disconformity; Lytton set out to make of it an asset. He chafed against his own eternal adolescence – of which his unbroken teenage voice was a perpetual reminder – instead, like Wilde, of sinking complacently within it. In his last year or two at Cambridge, he made himself into something of a philosopher-clown. And for a time, his clothes became very unlike what most people would have expected the son of a Victorian general to wear. A farmer's wife who let lodgings told Bertrand Russell that Lytton had once come to her to ask whether she could take him in. 'At first sir,' she said, 'I thought he was a tramp, and then I looked again and saw he was a gentleman, but a very queer one.'[29]

Cambridge temporarily became for Lytton the home from home for which he had been searching. Within a single year at University he established himself as an integral part of a small but intimate community. The all-male society of Trinity and King's was a convenient niche, but it appealed, as he himself came to realize, only to the more timid and unadventurous side of his nature, those weaker elements within him which he was resolutely determined to overcome. Now, in the autumn of 1904, he reigned over a tiny kingdom; but it was not enough. He longed for – and dreaded – some wider sphere of activity. But what? Until he could decide upon a fixed course for the future, supremacy over a small university group was preferable to the role of a wandering nonentity in the world at large.

As was the custom then, they all addressed each other by

29. James Strachey disagreed with the author that his brother was ever at all eccentric – an epithet which he interpreted as being purely derogatory. As an alternative to this, he took the view that Lytton was 'quite unshakeably rooted in commonplace sanity and reality', and that therefore a comparison with Oscar Wilde was unjust ('the only resemblance I can see is that they were both buggers'). His clothes too, James Strachey wrote, 'were always perfectly conventional except during the rather short Lamb-Augustus [John] period. My own very rarely used Savile Row tailor (an old gentleman now) told me a couple of years ago of his pride in having persuaded Lytton to go back to ordinary smart clothes (such as you see him wearing in the photograph with the globe). I think you get this from Bertie.'

surname, never by Christian name, though nicknames were considered quite proper. With his heightened physical awareness Strachey was responsible for inventing many of these nicknames himself. Maynard Keynes, to his evident dislike, was dubbed 'Pozzo', possibly, it has been suggested, on account of his figure, though probably after the devious Corsican diplomat, Pozzo di Borgo; Forster was familiarly known as 'the Taupe' because of his resemblance to a mole, in stature, in the snug richness of his apparel, and in the strength and silence with which he constructed his formidable works; Thoby Stephen was rechristened 'the Goth' owing to his monolithic appearance and character; the inscrutable, far-seeing wisdom of G. E. Moore was suggested by 'the Yen'; the second-rate officiousness of Walter Lamb was implied by 'the Corporal'. Despite looks which lent themselves easily to caricature, Lytton's friends never gave him a lasting nickname, possibly owing to their understanding of his painful physical self-conscious.[30] Such names expanded the general atmosphere of conviviality without really breaking the conventions of upper-middle-class reticence. In much the same spirit of prudent intimacy, of prim anti-puritanism, Lytton declared a little later that 'certain Latin technical terms of sex were the correct words to use, that to avoid them was a grave error, and, even in mixed company, a weakness, and the use of synonyms a vulgarity'. It is partly indicative of his undeveloped character, as well as of the indeterminate Edwardian age in general, that though sex was placed so high on the agenda of discussion, all deliberations should be carried on with the aid of a dead language.

Lytton gave as his reason for staying up a further year at Cambridge the need of the Society to be put back on its feet again. Its members were sadly depleted, and there seemed no one else capable of selecting desirable embryos. Moreover, the Michaelmas term of 1904 marked the end of Moore's six-

30. For a short time at the beginning of the war, David Garnett used to call Lytton 'the Cowboy', because of the wide-brimmed hat he then liked to wear. But the name did not stick. And at Cambridge, Leonard Woolf called him by a shorter version of his surname – 'the Strache'.

year tenure of his Prize Fellowship. To the dismay of his admirers, the most elevated angel of them all showed no inclination to remain at Trinity, but retired in September with A. R. Ainsworth to live in Edinburgh. 'He has gone,' Lytton wrote to Keynes during the Christmas vacation (11 January 1905). 'The wretched creature said he had no intention of coming to Cambridge next term, but that he would have to in the May term, as he's examining the Tripos. This is rather disappointing, isn't it?'

Just as Moore had succeeded McTaggart as the dominating influence among the young Apostles, so now Lytton and subsequently Maynard Keynes supplanted Moore. And, by the same token, metaphysical speculation soon began to retreat as the popular basis for intellectual discussion before its bastard offspring, psychological gossip, in much the same fashion as political idealism had earlier given way to metaphysics. Although Lytton possessed a clear head for argument, his mind was not especially well adapted to contend with labyrinthine reasoning and the abstract circumlocutions of ethics. Some of the changes in thought and habit which were foisted on the Society while Lytton was one of the supreme undergraduate members are elucidated by Bertrand Russell in his autobiography. 'The tone of the generation some ten years junior to my own was set mainly by Lytton Strachey and Keynes,' he wrote. 'It is surprising how great a change in mental climate those ten years had brought. We were still Victorian; they were Edwardian. We believed in ordered progress by means of politics and free discussion. The more self-confident among us may have hoped to be leaders of the multitude, but none of us wished to be divorced from it. The generation of Keynes and Lytton did not seek to preserve any kinship with the Philistine. They aimed rather at a life of retirement among fine shades and nice feelings, and conceived of the good as consisting in the passionate mutual admirations of a clique of the élite. This doctrine, quite unfairly, they fathered upon G. E. Moore, whose disciples they professed to be ...'

Owing largely to Moore's puritanical attitude towards

BEETLES AND WATER-SPIDERS

pleasure, the prevailing mood of the Apostles had been one of serious and studied gloom. For hours they would remain, as Maynard Keynes describes the scene, 'sunk deep in silence and in basket chairs on opposite sides of the fireplace in a room which was at all times pitch dark'.[31] There, in the smoky obscurity they sat upon their waists, with their buttocks protruding far beyond the edge of their chairs, their toes on the fender, interminably discussing philosophy and God and their livers and their hearts and the hearts of their friends – all broken. Though it was only later in life that Lytton was to make a fetish of pleasure, he did during the last years or so of his time at Cambridge introduce a brighter note into these Apostolic proceedings. Occasionally the meetings got out of control and were enlivened by cushion fights and thrilling games of blind man's buff. Lytton loved puns and ingenious ribald jokes. Yet his high spirits seemed something of an artificial contrivance and his wit a magic fountain playing bravely and prettily amid the surrounding night, but from which no one could assuage a real thirst. Despite his joking and his inventiveness, the pleasure-loving mask which he assumed was more a distraction from the disappointments of existence than the manifestation of a genuinely happy nature, for his deepest convictions were still pessimistic. It was these convictions, these 'good states of mind' as they were now called, that he liked to ventilate in the company of his special friends. For in spite of all his discontent, his illnesses and unrequited affections, somehow, way down within him, the magic fountain played irresistibly on. It was curious, almost

31. Of the above passage, based on Maynard Keynes's 'My Early Beliefs', and the previous passage taken from the first volume of Bertrand Russell's autobiography, James Strachey frankly disapproved. 'Of course,' he wrote to the author, 'you swallow Bertie's jaundiced story without a word of hesitation. It's quite untrue that metaphysical and logical arguments were out. When I was a brother, Maynard, Norton and Hawtrey (who came up very regularly) had constant hard headed arguments about such things as sense-perception or truth or internal relations; and Whitehead, Sanger, Russell and Moore turned up often enough to affect the sort of conversation. . . . And equally of course you accept without reservation Maynard's forty years' later bleatings.'

distressing, how in the face of such numerous complaints — his own deficiencies and the infuriating shortcomings of those near him — he still enjoyed himself so much.

In the opinion of Bertrand Russell and some others, the new note of gaiety that Lytton injected into the Society acted as a salutary antidote to the immature and over-solemn priggishness of some of the elder brethren. And there were other, more crucial departures from the past. The Apostles 'repudiated entirely', in Keynes's own words, 'customary morals, conventions, and traditional wisdom. We were, that is to say, in the strict sense of the term, immoralists.' Bertrand Russell is even more specific. 'After my time the Society changed in one respect,' he records in his autobiography. 'There was a long drawn out battle between George Trevelyan and Lytton Strachey, both members, in which Lytton Strachey was on the whole victorious. Since his time, homosexual relations among the members were for a time common, but in my day they were unknown.'

From going through the Society's papers in his role as secretary, Lytton had become convinced that many past Apostles were in fact secret and non-practising homosexuals. But some of them had not even been aware of their predilections, while other more introspective brethren had steadfastly suppressed all such inclinations and lived out lives of miserable, twilight celibacy. Now, in the new uninhibited age of reason heralded by Moore, all this was to be altered. From his personal influence on his contemporaries, Lytton hoped to ease forward the gradual advance of civilized opinion in the country as a whole. Reconstituting the Society was a first essential step along this road. But he was not alone. In Maynard Keynes, who had been elected an Apostle during February 1903, there existed a worthy if rather more cautious lieutenant. Within the voluminous correspondence which passed between these two during the next five years, Lytton expounds some of the special virtues and advantages of that love which passes all Christian understanding. Its superiority to the humdrum heterosexual relationship lay, so he believed, in the greater degree of sympathy and the more absolute dual-unity which it could command. Between opposite sexes there must always be some latent residue of doubt, ignorance, perplexity; so often intelligence was matched with stupidity, talent paired off with mediocrity. But through homosexual love, which aimed at duplicating or replacing the self rather than complementing it, one could inhabit the body and assume the personality of one's choice. And so, instead of extending, unsatisfactorily, the burdens of adulthood, one escaped into a vicarious existence at once stimulating to the intelligence and imagination, and nourishing for the imprisoned, frustrated will.

Of all Lytton's new friends at King's, Maynard Keynes was to play the most significant part. At Eton he had been both scholastically and socially successful, impressing those who liked his company as astonishingly mature, and those who did not as regarding himself as a privileged boy with rather more than the standard quota of cerebral conceit. Though he commanded a beautifully modulated speaking voice, he was not handsome. A long spoonbill nose, slightly *retroussé*, which had earned him the nickname of 'Snout' at school, was surmounted by a pair of brilliant, amused eyes. Dark-haired, still fairly slim, with a receding chin and thick sensual lips partly camouflaged by a trim moustache, he looked infinitely and amusingly sly. He had also a tremulous, supple look. Like a cat in a bush, he watched everything, yet was very forthcoming too. There was something of Homer's Ulysses about him. His extremely lively countenance conveyed great charm and animation; he was most ambitious and impatient. His own health, however, like Lytton's, was never good, and he suffered too from an unutterable obsession that he was physically repulsive. Like Lytton again, he could charm or dismay an audience with unusual power; but he showed his displeasure not merely by withdrawing into himself, but by projecting a terrible punitive ray which seemed to shrivel up all opposition. Along with this greater violence and more active ruthlessness went a higher degree of caution. After their first meeting Lytton described him as 'stiff and stern'; but under this reserved surface manner, Sir Roy Harrod has assured us, his emotions ran strong. During his first year at Cambridge especially, he felt the need of understanding friends, and in Lytton, who had previously experienced something of the same difficulties, he soon found someone in whom he might trustingly confide; for to the intellectual affinity which existed between 'Scraggs' and 'Snout' was added a deeper, secret communion of spirit.

Already, by the time he was elected to the Apostles, Keynes's cleverness was prodigious, and his intellect, in the opinion of Bertrand Russell, 'was the sharpest and clearest I have ever known'. In spoken argument only Russell himself could match the young undergraduate. Keynes, however, seemed colder, more detached and clinical. Whereas Russell was prone to attributing motives of the blackest villainy to those who disagreed with him, Keynes merely dismissed his opponents as dismal idiots. And yet, for all the extraordinary speed of his brain, the lightning rapidity with which he sucked in and devoured information, there was some imaginative quality lacking in his make-up of which he himself seemed obscurely aware and to which he drew others' attention by his uncharacteristically humble prostration before the altar of the arts. His mind was so restless and quick that his more turgid, watchful emotions never caught up with it, were never quite in step. The brilliant sparkle of his writing is not superficial, but rather icy. Like a barrister, he was often bent on putting over a point of view at one remove from himself, and his stated opinions seemed on occasions to be oddly vicarious. His retrospective exposition of an initially false premiss was sometimes brilliant, extending his ingenuity to the full; and round this central untruth the satellites within his orbit would spin brightly and with incredible velocity.

Bertrand Russell has confessed to wondering sometimes whether the degree of cleverness which Keynes possessed was incompatible with depth, but decided that his suspicions were unjustified since Keynes was perpetually so overworked that he had not the time to give of his best in his books. Yet Russell's intuition may be a surer guide to Keynes's character than his impartial reasoning. The constant overwork which pressed in on Keynes all his life did not create itself accidentally from without, but was attracted by some urgent, personal necessity. He went through life as if he had to fill an eternal vacuum within himself, and appeared scarcely capable of relaxing. Above all, he was stimulated not chiefly through his emotions, but by problems which acted directly upon his brain. With all his great charm, his view of things remained cold and almost mechanical. Sometimes, his computer-mind could be a source of considerable irritation to Lytton. Everything, even making love, he evaluated in statistical terms, and he was fond of making absurd mathematical comparisons between people's affections — one person was two point five per cent happier than someone else, and so on. For several years Lytton's intimate personal life was bound up with that of Keynes, so that it was not until after the First World War, when Keynes had grown into a more benign personality, plumper and balder, that Lytton was able to assess his character impartially. 'An immensely interesting figure' was his verdict delivered to Ralph Partridge in 1920, ' – partly because, with his curious typewriter intellect, he's also so oddly and unexpectedly emotional.'

For some considerable time at Cambridge, Keynes's superficial aloofness repelled Lytton. Desmond MacCarthy once said of him that his object in life was to impress men of forty, and Lytton felt inclined to agree. 'I don't believe he has any very good feelings', he wrote to Leonard Woolf (December 1904), ' – but perhaps one's inclined to think that more than one ought because he's so ugly. Perhaps experience of the world at large may improve him. He has been ill, and I have been twice to see him in Harvey Road.[32] Really the entourage is shocking. Old ladies call, and gossip with Mrs Keynes. He joins in, and it flashed upon me that the real horror of his conversation is precisely that it's moulded on maiden aunts.'

Despite Keynes's prematurely spinsterish manner, Lytton became increasingly friendly with him. 'Keynes is the best person to talk to,' he admitted to Leonard Woolf later that

32. No. 6 Harvey Road, Cambridge, was Keynes's home.

same month, 'for he at any rate has brains, and I now believe is as kind as his curious construction allows him to be.' When Woolf had sailed for Ceylon six weeks earlier, he had left vacant the role of confessor in Lytton's life. Keynes was an obvious possibility as his successor, and by the beginning of the Lent term of 1905 the substitution had been completed. 'You are the only person I can speak to,' Lytton now told Keynes. And to Leonard Woolf he wrote (February 1905), making amends for previous slighting observations: 'There can be no doubt that we are friends. His conversation is extraordinarily alert and very amusing. He sees at least as many things as I do – possibly more. He's interested in people to a remarkable degree. N.B. He doesn't seem to be in anything aesthetic, though his taste is good. His presence of character is really complete. He analyses with amazing persistence and brilliance. I never met so active a brain (I believe it's more *active* than either Moore's or Russell's). His feelings are charming, and, as is only natural, in perfect taste ... he perpetually frightens me. One can't be sentimental about a person whose good opinion one's constantly afraid to lose. His youth chiefly makes itself obvious by an overwhelming frankness, and of course often by a somewhat absurd naïveté.'[33]

The frankness which Lytton and Keynes exchanged in their letters from this time onwards seems, at a first reading, to uncover a state of affairs within Cambridge which would have provoked curiosity in Gomorrah and caused the inhabitants of Sodom to sit up and take note. A more careful examination, however, suggests that, especially during these early years, there was a good deal more talk than action. A special glossary is really required in order to reduce to some verisimilitude the actual meanings of the words so freely employed. To 'propose' would seem to indicate little more than an invitation to use Christian names; to 'rape' or even to 'bugger' usually means a peck on the cheek, or a dubious embrace. For, in a society which regarded homosexuality as

33. 'My disease is that I am so frank that nobody believes me and takes it for wickedness.' (Maynard Keynes to Lytton Strachey, April 1905.)

244

more grave than murder, what Lytton and Keynes were looking for almost as urgently as love itself, was a discreet and sympathetic source of disclosure. For a time they found this in each other, and, not unexpectedly, made the most of what was for both of them something of a luxury. What does emerge very clearly from between the lines of this correspondence is that it was not the younger Keynes who appeared so absurdly naïve, who stood in need of experience of the world at large, but Lytton himself, since it never occurred to him until it was too late that they were not just secret confidants, but also rivals.

By the autumn of 1904 Lytton and Keynes had already established themselves in joint ascendancy over the Apostles. A visiting Oxford contemporary that Michaelmas term, J. D. Beazley,[34] recorded nearly fifty years later that 'when I went over to Cambridge at that time I thought Keynes and Strachey were the two cleverest men I had ever met; and looking back over the years, I still think they are the two cleverest men I ever met'. Sir Roy Harrod, to whom he was speaking, then asked him whether he received the impression that one was leading or dominating the other. 'No,' he replied, 'they seemed to me to be equals, peers, different and complementary.'

Although Lytton saw more and more of Keynes at this time, he was leading something of a solitary existence. A receiver of confidences, he had none of his own to impart, only other people's. Now that all those with whom he had originally come up were gone, the place, life itself, seemed empty. Cambridge had nothing fresh to offer him; he had seen it all. 'I have had practically every experience,' he wrote. 'Nothing can come to me new again.' And to Leonard Woolf he morbidly philosophized (January 1905): 'Illness itself haunts me, but I dare say that by being always on the edge of the grave, one manages to avoid falling into it. Our bodies are like Comets' tails, trailing behind us as we whirl towards the stars; when we

34. Professor Sir John Davidson Beazley (b. 1885), the distinguished archaeologist and author of many works on ancient sculpture, painting and pottery, who was at this time an undergraduate at Christ Church.

lose them we turn into dead coals and drop into the earth.'

Towards the end of November 1904, just as the mists of depression seemed about to enfold him absolutely, a new star appeared on the Cambridge horizon which, as if by magic, dispersed the clouds and filled his whole world suddenly with its light. This was (Sir) Arthur Hobhouse, known then as 'Hobber', a freshman at Clare College, which nestles, appropriately enough, between King's and Trinity, though more closely to the former. Here, so it seemed to Lytton, was the perfect embryo to fill that vacancy in his life created by Sheppard's stubborn sentimentality. The Society – Lytton himself – was saved. 'Hobhouse is fair, with frizzy hair, a good complexion, an arched nose, and a very charming expression of countenance,' he wrote to Leonard Woolf (30 November 1904). 'His conversation is singularly coming on, he talks a good deal, in a somewhat ingenuous way, but his youth is balanced by great cleverness and decided subtlety in conversation. He's interested in metaphysics and people, he's not a Christian, and sees quite a lot of jokes. I'm rather in love with him, and Keynes, who lunched with him today at Lamb's is convinced that he's all right . . . He was at Eton, but at 17 he insisted on going to St Andrews to learn medicine, which he does up here. This in itself shows a curious determination. But he doesn't look determined; he looks pink and delightful as embryos should.'

For some months the task of securing Hobhouse's election to the Society occupied much of Lytton's time. There was among the Apostles a common practice that no freshman might be admitted. Undeterred, Lytton went to see Jackson, who carried great weight in the Society, and persuaded him that this custom, like all traditions, needed the odd exception to establish its general efficacy, and that, in any case, 'two years at a Scotch University' corresponded to a full year at Cambridge. Once this had been accepted, Lytton set about introducing the new embryo to other Apostles. 'Our embryo Hobhouse is still as satisfactory as ever,' he reported to Moore (13 December 1904). 'I had arranged that MacCarthy should meet him at lunch last Friday, but at the last moment

that evil person telegraphed to say that he couldn't come. . . .
I should like to talk to you. I feel rather like a buzzing Chimaera, but Hobhouse is a *vast* encouragement.'

By the end of the Michaelmas term almost all Lytton's canvassing seemed to have been successfully completed. For a moment, his attention was diverted from this absorbing affair by the dramatic emergence of a figure from his past. 'Marie Souvestre – the eminent woman – is ill with no one knows what,' he wrote to Leonard Woolf (21 December 1904). 'She refuses to let any doctor examine her – no one knows why – but they guess it may be because she's afraid she's got cancer – and writhes in agony. They think she hasn't got cancer – but can't tell. It would be a sad loss if so eminent a person were to die.' In fact her instinct was surer than that of her doctors, and within three months she was dead. All her friends, the Stracheys included, visited her in these last months, and though the hand of death showed on her face, she seemed quite as passionately alive in spirit as ever. 'Veracity, an undeviating directness of intelligence, faithfulness and warmth of affection, were her most delightful qualities; dignity of manner and brilliancy of speech her chief ornaments,' wrote Beatrice Webb in her diary for 31 March 1905. 'An amazing narrowness of vision for so intelligent a person; a total inability to understand religion; a dogmatism that was proof against the spirit of scientific investigation; a lack of charity to feelings with which she did not sympathize – in short, an absence of humility was, perhaps, the most disabling of her characteristics. It narrowed her influence to those whom she happened to like and who happened to like her.'

Shortly after the new year, Lytton left London and went to stay with his brother Oliver, G. E. Moore, and a contemporary of his at Trinity, Ralph Wedgwood – 'a sort of railway person'[35] – at Howe Hill, near Harrogate. Oliver, rather peremptorily removed from Balliol, had been hastily sent on a

35. Ralph Wedgwood became chief general manager of the London and North-Eastern Railway, 1923–39, then chairman of the Railway Executive Committee, 1939–41. He was knighted in 1924, and created a baronet in 1942. His daughter is C. V. Wedgwood, the historian.

tour round the world under the tutory of Robert Bridges, the poet. On his return, he successfully persuaded his mother to let him study the piano under Leschetizky in Vienna, where he had been one of only two Englishmen at Brahms's funeral. From Vienna he returned once again in disgrace to England, his piano playing not being up to concert standards, and was at once dispatched to India, to join the East India Railway. Recently he had returned home yet again, this time with a Swiss wife,[36] and set up home with Ralph Wedgwood, who had procured him a job. This was Lytton's first visit to their house, where Moore was a frequent guest. Despite some very violent arguments leading directly on to a correspondence between Oliver Strachey and Bertrand Russell, which considerably influenced the latter's philosophical views, Lytton remained mostly sleepy and almost bored. Compared with the illuminating reality of Hobhouse, who would be elected in a few short weeks, all these dialectical discussions seemed dim.

'The household consists of Oliver and Ruby and Julia[37] (his wife and child), and Wedgwood,' Lytton wrote to Leonard Woolf (January 1905). 'Moore has been here since Saturday, and I expect he goes to Edinburgh tomorrow. Wedgwood is a quasi Goth, large, strong, ugly, and inordinately good natured. He is rather stupid, but argumentative and jocose; and much better than it's possible to convey in description. His face is often positively wreathed in kindness of a strange fatherly sort. He likes music and has no perceptions. Moore has been much the same as usual, and of course rather wearing – especially with his damned Turnerisms. He has sung a good deal and played very violent duets with Oliver. I find it rather difficult to talk to him, and he has said nothing of much interest to me. Tonight he came out in a grand discussion with W and O with all the usual forms and ceremonies – the

36. Ruby J. Mayer.

37. Julia Strachey, who married Stephen Tomlin, the sculptor, and subsequently Professor Lawrence Gowing, the painter. She is the author of *Cheerful Weather for the Wedding* (1932) and *The Man on the Pier* (1951).

groans, the heaves, the tearing of hair, the startings up, the clenching of fists, the frowns, the apoplectic gaspings and splutterings.'

Nevertheless, the party seems to have been sprightly enough. Moore and Oliver play Schumann pieces with great verve and abandon, and in between tea and dinner everyone takes part in playing games of Pit, the infant Julia joining in the yells. Domestic calamities are numerous. The pipes freeze, and both the water and the gas have to be turned off. But no one – except Lytton – appears perturbed by the damage. 'The vagueté is undoubtedly too great,' Lytton comments. 'Wedgwood, however, does a great deal, I expect, in the way of taking steps.'

The Lent term of 1905, to which Lytton had so impatiently looked forward – which was to witness the glorious, unprecedented election of a freshman and mark, perhaps, the consummation of a new and perfect friendship – in fact turned out to be the most volcanic of his entire six years up at Cambridge.

The first shock exploded in his face during the last week of January. Lytton was sitting in his room reading the *Essays of Elia*, when the secretary of the Shakespeare Society came in and, handing him a card, murmured something about one of the visitors that night being unable to attend. Automatically and without interest Lytton inquired who and why. 'Oh,' came the answer, 'a man called Hobhouse smashed himself up last night on a bicycle.' When the man had left, Lytton remained sitting inert, and hours seemed to elapse before he summoned up enough nerve to cross-examine his bed-maker as to the dangers, generally speaking, of this type of accident. She, however, was reassuring. So, venturing out, he hovered about the Great Court for a time, then at last plunged into Hobhouse's room. He was in bed, being read to by a friend. In answer to Lytton's frantic questionings he declared that the doctor had been and pronounced him to be only bruised. 'Oh dear!' Lytton wrote to Keynes (2 February 1905). 'The appearance. He was flushed, embarrassed, exquisite. I fled after three seconds, cursing everything and everybody ... and wondering how soon the news would spread abroad, and how many people his bedroom would be able to hold. These thoughts still agitate and blast me. I am consumed by terrors. We live upon a cataract; and at any moment, while we are yawning at the Decemviri, or maundering at McT's, the Hope of the World may be crushed to smithers by a cart in Trinity Street.'

After tottering back to his own rooms, weak with shock, Lytton gave expression to his turbulent emotions throughout the long night in verse:

> O the darkness! O the stillness!
>   All our world is closed in sleep.
> I in sadness, you in illness
>   Solitary vigil keep.
>
> You, with happy head and tired,
>   Lie around your silent room,
> Feel your heart still vaguely fired
>   Paint with splendour all the gloom ...
>
> Ah! You bring to gentle sleeping
>   Smiles that once were my smiles too;
> Now I smile no more, but weeping,
>   Lonely, write these songs for you.

This incident, the prelude to a far greater shock, immediately confirmed the strength and fervency of Lytton's feelings towards his new embryo, whipping them up to an unprecedented pitch. But the second unforeseen event, more profound in its effects and itself the overture to a later, even more dynamic disaster, was to prove equally clearly that these feelings were not returned. Quite by accident Lytton stumbled upon the fact that his friend and confidant, Maynard Keynes, was also enamoured of Hobhouse. At once a bitter rivalry broke out which took the outward form of a struggle to determine which of them should act as sponsor for his Apostolic election. All, it is said, is fair in war, and Lytton's half-hearted guile proved no match for the greater ruthlessness of Keynes. By the third week of February it was all over. Keynes, in victory, embraced the new Apostle, and Lytton was left to brood abjectly over 'my own unutterable silence – my dead, shattered, desiccated hope of some companionship, some love.'

Never, it seemed, had his loneliness, his desire for affection, been so violent as in the next few weeks. 'Hobhouse ... was duly elected last Saturday,' he wrote to G. E. Moore (21 February 1905). '... Oh Moore! I feel like a primeval rock, indifferent and venerable. I am too old ever to take wings. The only passion I have left me is the Black Rage. My stomach struggles through endless sloughs of dyspepsia. Alas!'

Some relief he did obtain by channelling his despair into a series of unhappy love poems after the style of John Donne – 'The Conversation', 'The Speculation', 'The Situation', 'The Resolution', 'To Him', 'The Category', 'The Reappearance', 'The Exhumation' – which examined the whole affair in detail and from every possible angle. Like many of the poems he composed in later life, they are written for the most part in a strain of subdolorous insipidity, the unspecific language seeming at the same time to record and conceal the secret moments of his emotional life. Common to several is a peculiar, pervading fascination – partly made up from a sense of revulsion – for the cruder sexual actualities of life, which is offset to some extent by an ecstatic longing for some unknown, delirious state of self-oblivion. Of those which emanated directly from his unhappy infatuation for Hobhouse, probably the most interesting is 'The Two Triumphs', in which he contrasts the immediate joys of lust with the final unsullied triumph, the masochistic rapture, of unrequited love. Writing in the first person, Lytton imagines his rival tasting the sweet fruit of carnal passion to its bitter core. In this 'wrong world' lust has always been triumphant; but his own purer and more spiritual love is not blotted out. On the contrary, it flourishes in platonic adversity:

> Yet listen – you are mine in his despite.
> Who shall dare say his triumph mine prevents?
> My love is the established infinite,
> And all his kisses are but accidents.
> His earth, his heaven, shall wither and decay
> To naught: my love shall never pass away.

In the final verse Lytton drifts into a mood of erotic mysticism, not uncommon to many of the most rationalistic humanists, momentarily consumed by the fires of intense feeling. Also, in several of the other poems belonging to this sequence, Lytton's semi-aversion from sexual intercourse, mixed with phrases which bear witness to a thorough classical education and to its dubious benefits in the context of twentieth-century poems, is repeatedly exemplified. The theme running through them all is the decay of physical love. In 'The Exhumation', for example, the once beautiful body is seen as a corpse, and sexual desire is equated with death and the grave. Here, too, as in 'Knowledge' and other verses, the word 'lust' is significantly made to rhyme with 'dust'.

For some two months following the election of Hobhouse, Lytton was filled with an almost demented hatred of Keynes. On 25 February, only a single week after the election, he launched an extraordinary onslaught upon Keynes before the assembled Apostles: 'For it is one of his queer characteristics that one often wants, one cannot tell why, to make a malicious attack on him, and that, when the time comes, one refrains, one cannot tell why. His sense of values, and indeed all his feelings, offer the spectacle of a complete paradox. He is a hedonist and a follower of Moore; he is lascivious without lust; he is an Apostle without tears.'

By March he could endure neither to see nor to speak to Keynes. Their correspondence had halted and broken off. 'He repels me so much,' he wrote to Leonard Woolf that month, 'that I can hardly prevent myself ejaculating insults to his face.' But soon this harrowing antipathy underwent a subtle and curious change. All at once, and somehow in spite of himself, he was conscious of feeling closer to Keynes than ever before. The disgust which he had felt for him was perhaps only a variation of the contempt which he so often lavished upon himself. They had, after all, fallen in love with the same person; and he began to realize just how much they had in common. So it was not altogether surprising that when Hobhouse drifted apart from Keynes, Lytton should experience a genuine sense of commiseration for his late rival. 'That episode is over,' Keynes wrote to him at the end of April. '. . . I swear I had no idea I was in for anything that would so utterly uproot me. It is absurd to suppose that you would believe the violence of the various feelings I have been through.' And so, by confiding to him all his troubles and suggesting that he had not been unscrupulous but devastatingly honest and direct in his behaviour, Keynes won back Lytton's trust.

'Poor Keynes!' Lytton wrote that spring. 'It's only when he's shattered by a crisis that I seem to be able to care for him.' This was just the beginning of a new lease of friendship. Soon their correspondence started up again and their recipro- cal affection grew for a time increasingly warm. Indeed, so close was their spirit of companionship that they sometimes wondered whether they might not, just possibly, be in love with each other!

7

SALE VIE AND A GLIMPSE OF HEAVEN

During both terms and vacations, Lytton was all the while working steadily at the second part of his mammoth dis- sertation. 'My history has been – perpetual labour, inter- spersed with an occasional Symphony,' he wrote at the beginning of April. Three weeks later he left London for Moore's Easter reading-party, held this year at the Crown Hotel, Pateley Bridge, near Middlesmoor in Yorkshire – 'A Godforsaken village inn,' as he describes it, 'eight miles away from a station, and a hundred from anywhere else.' Here, high up above the sea and civilization, the barbarous natives 'live on strange meats,' he tells Sheppard (14 April 1905). 'Yester- day we had the inside of a she-goat for breakfast, and to-day at lunch Moore found himself opposite – he didn't quite know what – it was smothered in thick white sauce – he ex- plored – yes! it was a sow's udder, trimmed with tripe and parsley. . . . Good-bye! They're serving the horse-tail soup.' As so often when there is no illness or pending infatuation to absorb his attention, he soon sinks into the sloughs of tedium. Perhaps it is only in heaven that one is never bored when other people are talking. 'Isn't it ridiculous,' he writes to Leonard Woolf, 'that after a week one should find one's dearest friends quite unsupportable.' But boredom, he notes, stimulates his appetite, and each day he devours 'vast slabs of salt bacon, chunks of mutton, plates of "tea-cake" (at breakfast), pints of foul "ale" and hot jam pudding, deluged with cream. It's sickening in the abstract; but I manage to look forward to every meal. ... We don't láugh much, and we play two games of jacoby every evening. This is a tolerable life for a fortnight.'

The Easter term at Cambridge was already well advanced by the time Lytton returned to Trinity. It was late spring, and punts and panamas and iced drinks reigned along the banks of the Cam. The laburnum and lilac were out on the backs; the roses bloomed again on King's Chapel; the early peaches dropped from the walls of the Senate House; the scorpions reared their heads once more in the sunlight of the Great Court and all Cambridge came alive with the sweet scents and pale colours of an English summer. It was to be, as Lytton must have realized, his last term. The fresh yet familiar beauty of each street and building, the glamour and high spirits of youth seen through an idealizing myth, stirred in him feelings of tremulous nostalgia. 'I am restless, intolerably restless, and Cambridge is the only place I never want to leave,' he wrote, 'though I suffer there more than anywhere else.'

The first news affecting his future which reached him after returning to Trinity was not encouraging. His 'English Letter Writers' had failed to win the fifty pounds which went with the Le Bas Prize. 'That devil the Vice Chancellor[38] had awarded the Le Bas prize to – no one,' he wrote to Leonard Woolf (May 1905). 'So here am I penniless after my titanic efforts.' Still gloomier rumours and prognostications were to follow. 'I also gather that my chance for a fellowship is now merely nil – for 2 reasons. i, There are only two to be given, and ii, Laurence[39] is to be my examiner. Amen!' Vere Laur-

38. Edmund Anthony Beck, a Trinity Hall don.
39. R. Vere Laurence, then much under the influence of G. M. Trevelyan, in those days an austere teetotaller. Laurence himself was addicted

ence, a lanky bearded history don at Trinity, was pretty well as unpropitious a choice, Lytton felt, as Cunningham had been the previous year. They had never been friendly. But hopeless though the prospects seemed, he had no alternative but to continue struggling on with his work. 'I try to write my dissertation, and fail,' he told Keynes (7 July 1905). 'I die daily, as the Scriptures have it. But then I die in so many different ways.'

By June, after an Apostolic debate on 'Is Life Worth Living?', Lytton had returned again to Lancaster Gate. It was the end of the Easter term, and three months' hard labour awaited him on the Hastings dissertation – to be crowned with almost certain failure. Unavoidably, he was wasting his time. Life, as he now knew it, was certainly *not* worth living. 'Oh lord, lord, lord!' he wrote to Leonard Woolf (June 1905). 'I do feel that I'm extraordinarily misty – a sort of coloured floating film over the vicissitude of things. The mere business of carrying on one's life seems something so overwhelming and exhausting that it's all one can do to get along from hour to hour. One sleeps, washes, dresses, eats, forths, reads, eats, walks, talks, eats, reads, eats, despairs, yawns, and sleeps again, and all one's energies have been used up, and one is exactly as one was before. If one were a disembodied spirit there'd be some sort of hope . . .'

In mid-June, he visited Balliol College, Oxford. Here he was the guest of an undergraduate, Bernard Swithinbank, who, 'tall and handsome', we learn from Sir Roy Harrod, '. . . an elegant, even exquisite schoolboy', had been Keynes's closest friend at Eton. Keynes, in fact, had introduced him to Lytton, who began to cultivate his friendship soon after Hobhouse's election to the Apostles. This he seems to have done not with any motive of personal revenge against Keynes – to whom he was now again confiding his thoughts and inner feelings – but out of an instinctive sense that should their friendship happen to develop automatically on to a more intimate level, then some natural law of justice would be properly fulfilled. He

to drinking and smoking, and before he died in 1934 had become an alcoholic.

255

was particularly anxious to get on well with Swithinbank, who was himself obviously in correspondence with Keynes, and felt apprehensive lest his natural reticence should give his new friend a false impression. 'I want to tell you that I enjoyed my visit to Oxford more than I've enjoyed anything for ages and ages,' he wrote the day after returning to Lancaster Gate (20 June 1905). 'I hope you'll believe this in spite of what I'm afraid may have seemed appearances to the contrary. It's almost impossible ever to express one's feelings properly, so that when I say that I shall always remember your rooms with pleasure, will you make allowances for my inadequate statement? It was really exciting to meet the people whom I met there.'

By the same post he sent off a letter to Leonard Woolf in Ceylon, describing his new Oxford friend who, it seems, was probably as shy as Lytton himself. They must have made an odd pair. 'In appearance he's tall (taller than me, I believe) and rather large footed and essentially solid; but by no means looks a strong and bulky person, his face is pale, ill and intellectual. The expression is often cat-like – the eyelids droop, and the mouth broadens; the features are all well-shaped, the nose arched. His hair is fair and thick, his voice rather shrill and boyish. The general impression he gives is undoubtedly one of vagueness. One sees at once that he's kind, nervous and impractical; and one's a little inclined to think that that's all. But it by no means *is* all. To begin with, there's his humour, which is always faultless and always wonderfully his own. Then his character is a real character. It's poetical – untrammelled. I mean by actualities; and quite unafflicted by contortions and affectations; it shines with a pale sincerity.'

Life at Lancaster Gate during the next few weeks consisted of slow, grinding research work interspersed with a few glittering social events – a brilliant Joachim concert: *Phèdre* with Sarah Bernhardt ('Do you know the play and the lady?' he asked Swithinbank. 'Lord! But one can't expatiate. C'est Vénus toute entière à sa proie attachée'); a visit from Desmond MacCarthy who read aloud, in his half-asleep, tumbling way, pages of Landor, and occasionally succeeded in making

256

Lytton laugh; and an introduction, through Desmond, to Harley Granville-Barker, who, like most people, made him yawn with boredom. 'I live in the bosom of a large and vivacious family,' he informed Swithinbank (1 July 1905). 'I spend my days in the British Museum; and my nights are diversified by an occasional tedious dinner-party, or by conversations with the relics of my Cambridge friends.' Together with some of his and the Stephen families he also spent a weekend at the end of June with the Freshfields, parents of Elinor Clough, down in Sussex. 'Their house is incredibly vast and new,' he wrote to Swithinbank (1 July 1905), 'and packed with priceless cabinets, rugs, china vases and pictures. I was horribly depressed by the magnificence, and by the conversation, which was always on the highest levels. We discussed Henry James and Cymbeline and the essence of Architecture from morning till night.' From the other guests he singled out one as possessing exceptional qualities – Virginia Stephen. Their reaction to the house seemed to coincide exactly, and she put into words what was for him the true cause of his depression about the place, when, in mock-horror, she exclaimed: 'There's not an ugly thing in it!' Lytton could only add: 'Except the owners.'

These weeks were largely impregnated with thoughts of Swithinbank. He wrote to his new friend, received an immediate reply, and straightway wrote off again boldly suggesting an expedition to Richmond Park. 'So today I went, and we punted (or rather he) up to Twickenham, had tea there, and came back,' he notified Keynes (7 July 1905), to whom Swithinbank was also reporting back the news. 'It was perfectly charming. I said very little and he a good deal. When I left him, I was in a condition. Lord, lord. I didn't know one could have such affection without lust. But there it is. He's unique – exquisite. Only I'm jealous of anyone else thinking so, almost. I only know one other work of the Creator equally beautiful as an aesthetic whole – the Goth. And heavens, what a difference!'

Lytton had always found it difficult to work in London and was thankful when, in the third week of July, he was able to

257

move down to a large country house, six miles from Kettering, which the Stracheys had rented that summer. Great Oakley Hall, as it was called, was a typically Tudor mansion, with gardens, bowling-greens and box-hedges, all encompassed by magnificent elm trees. Inside, the rooms were complete with family portraits, carved doors and sliding panels; and there was also a large, insignificant library which on close inspection was found to contain several yards of collected sermons, the State Trials, and an edition of Pope's Homer. The spacious and leisurely air of comfort fitted in with Lytton's temperament very well. He took to the place at once, though regretfully noting one serious drawback to it: 'The Church is on the croquet lawn,' he explained to Swithinbank (15 July 1905), 'so I'm afraid our games may be interrupted by psalms and sermons. I expect there's a family pew in the church, which my mother will occupy in state, as she insists upon going to Church in the country, in order to keep up (I believe) the Established Religion. This seems a queer form of atheism, but harmless. As for me, I think I am a Christian, who never goes to Church, in order to encourage Freedom of Thought.'

Every day of the six weeks which Lytton now spent at Great Oakley Hall was passed in hard and exacting labour over the second part of his Warren Hastings. 'I work like hell, and live a regular life,' he wrote to Leonard Woolf, but he added, 'I have no hopes' (July 1905). To Clive Bell also he complained of his life of hopeless work (28 July 1905): 'My dissertation oppresses me horribly,' he admitted, 'but I cast it off as much as I can. I read Sir Charles Grandison in the intervals between wishing I were alive and wishing I were dead.' For recreation he promenaded delicately among the flowering rose bushes, perused the back numbers of *Punch* and gossiped about Clive Bell's unsuccessful proposal of marriage to Vanessa Stephen, which he was keen one day to make the basis of a comic novel. In his leisure moments he made one exciting literary discovery — Benjamin Constant, whose little masterpiece of exquisite art and charming, subtly-blended psychology enchanted him. 'I'm here, in the ordinary condition of exhaustion, and doomed to death though fated not to die,' he wrote to Keynes (18 July 1905). 'I cannot write the English language, and spend my time doing nothing else. ... Have you read Adolphe? It's superb. The point of view is original – i.e. that of the lovee. Don't you think rather a good idea? He's so dreadfully bored, and yet likes and doesn't want to give pain. It's wonderfully done – all in epigrams.'

Encompassed about by his family with all their high-strung enthusiasms and lack of inner comprehension, and involved perpetually himself in a hellish treadmill of scholasticism, Lytton was overcome for much of this summer by hopeless melancholy. 'I feel like a condemned criminal awaiting the chaplain's visit,' he told Saxon Sydney-Turner. And to Clive Bell he wrote (28 July 1905): 'The country has closed in upon me, and I'm gasping in the vacuum. Quelle sale vie! Nothing but village school treats on the lawn, and rectors to lunch, and not a word about any part of the body that happens to come between the waist and thighs.' Maynard Keynes, whom Lytton had once convinced of the dangers of unvariegated overwork, invited him to come and stay at Cambridge where he was living with his parents preparatory to a few weeks' holiday in Switzerland. Lytton's reply, written on 27 July and almost exulting in his wretchedness, conveys very strongly the empty pessimism by which he was now entangled:

Dear Keynes
   Total cash – 1/3$\frac{1}{2}$
   "   hope – ditto. i.e. hope of finishing dissertation, of ever seeing you again, of learning how to spell correctly, and of being in anything but a damned trance. I spend hours, days, and weeks in simply staring at blank sheets of paper – hopeless, helpless, utterly incompetent, completely vague, absolutely comatose, physically morally and spiritually, DEAD. Oh my brethren! Take warning by this sad spectacle of a ruined soul. Such are the results of moral looseness. Cambridge, with its sad atmosphere of paradox and paederasty, is doubtless much to blame; but it would be idle to pretend that the fault does not mainly lie with a perverse intellect which has wantonly squandered the talents supplied by an all-wise Creator.

   Lord! This garden is wreathing and writhing with a school treat. It keeps on blowing motor horns, or things like motor horns, whose blasts pierce my entrails like so many swords. This is the quiet of the country. All I can say for it is that it gives me an excuse for not pretending to go on with my dissertation; but I don't know – my nerves are now so jangled that I doubt whether I'll be able to finish this.

I have no news, except that the rector is married, that yesterday there was a flower show at Rockingham Castle, that today we had haddock for breakfast, and that tomorrow I shall stab myself . . .

Friday. Suicide postponed. I shall risk all, and come tomorrow – so please expect me sometime or other. Also, please consider this. Shall I stay at King's? Is it against rules? Wouldn't it be much better for talking, etc . . .

In another letter written that same month to Swithinbank, Lytton examines his ever-recurring low spirits rather less theatrically. The contrast in mood and tone illustrates what is perhaps in any case well enough implied, that beneath the amusing banter which makes up so much of his correspondence – always for him the freest, easiest mode of communication – there exists a very real, baffling undertow of misery. 'Is it merely bad health, or is it the feeling of one's hopeless incapacity, or is it one's horrible loneliness?' he asked (15 July 1905), and then confessed: 'I don't know – I so often feel that all is absolutely lost. The Lord knows I take no pride in this; I'm not Byronic. I'm not even decadent; it's only the truth.'

At the beginning of August, Lytton was partly seduced away from his exigent programme when his cousin, Duncan Grant, arrived for a stay of two or three days. 'He's wonderfully nice, and nice looking,' he informed Leonard Woolf. All thoughts of Swithinbank were abruptly annulled. The lanky, shy Oxonian friend of Keynes had only been a convenient substitute for Hobber. With his diffident, nervous manner, his pale and fading countenance, his body so stalwart but frail, his expression so cat-like and comatose, his voice so shrill, he approximated far too closely to Lytton himself. A companion in loneliness rather than a means of escape from it, his company had provided consolation, not vivacity. To fall in love with him would have been like preparing for a journey to the ends of the earth – and then moving next door. But with the handsome, talented Duncan Grant, an affair might lead anywhere. Of all his associates Lytton chose Maynard Keynes to whom to confide his secret hopes, at once so wonderful and so agonized: 'As for me – I don't quite know what I'm doing – writing a dissertation presumably,' he told Keynes (3 August 1905). 'But I've managed, since I saw you last, to catch a glimpse of Heaven. Incredible, quite – yet so it's happened. I want to go into the wilderness of the world, and preach an infinitude of sermons on one text – "Embrace one another." It seems to me the grand solution. Oh dear, dear, dear, how wild, how violent, and how supreme are the things of this earth! – I am cloudy, I fear almost sentimental. But I'll write again. Oh yes, it's Duncan. He's no longer here, though; he went yesterday to France. Fortunate, perhaps, for my dissertation.'

The rest of August passed without any major deflections from work. Duncan Grant's failure to reply to his letters was the cause of some self-pity, but when at last he did receive an answer it brought on a wild, violent and supreme attack of indigestion. At the same time he was shocked to learn of the tragic death of his friend Theodore Llewelyn Davies, drowned while bathing. The two incongruous events, coming together, almost prostrated him. But apart from this, his leisure moments were made up solely of trivial incidents of the ridiculous and amusing sort that always diverted him and which he loved to describe in his letters, as in his essays and books. 'There have been no particular adventures here – except one, as we were driving with Beatrice Ch. to Kirby,' he wrote to Duncan Grant (15 August 1905). 'Three bicyclists were seen approaching; two passed us safely; then there was a shriek, and a vision of a sprawling female. Shocking! We leapt out, and found it was a young female who didn't know how to ride, out with her uncle and aunt. "For Gawd's sake, Maria," said the aunt, "don't tell your mother." She had dashed into the back wheel of our carriage, but fortunately seemed not to be hurt. We transported her to Corby station and left her reposing in the waiting-room. Of course dear Beatrice was very much to the fore. But in spite of her reassuring presence, it was an awkward affair.

'Madam Fischer arrived the other day to inspect her daughter. She is French, and both her sang-froid and her bottom are tremendous. (I think the two things always go together, don't you?) The two ladies left for Liverpool today. ... I spend my days in a horrible treadmill of Begums, etc., but hope to be out of it all in a week's time. Every day I take a stroll among the elms, and down the rose-walk.'

The dissertation forecast proved rather too optimistic, for no sooner had Lytton sent off this letter than he encountered a number of unusual difficulties, the solution to which occupied every spare moment of the next fortnight. Meanwhile, family affairs whirled and eddied around him almost totally unheeded: his mother fell ill with lumbago, his aunt Kate had a heart attack which temporarily robbed her of the power of speech, his sister Pernel withdrew into convalescence from mumps; meanwhile, Marjorie, his younger sister, departed for France, Ruby and her daughter Julia Strachey came to stay, and so did Lytton's eldest military brother, Richard, with his wife Grace. Only one fleeting appearance distracted his attention for a few brief hours – that of Hobhouse, who, since he happened to be passing near by, came to lunch with the Stracheys. By now Lytton was able to observe him with a good deal of cynical detachment. He was as vain as a woman, he noted, and obviously had feelings of the wrong sort altogether. On the whole his short visit was chiefly amusing for the effect it produced on Lytton's family – one of dazzled fascination. 'Everyone bowed before him, and talked to me after he'd gone about his hair,' he informed Keynes (7 September 1905). And to Duncan Grant he wrote (30 August 1905): 'You can't imagine how he charmed everyone. I was a good deal amused at the sight. He was as vague as usual, and I felt, as usual, that he thought I adored him.' After lunch they sat out on the lawn together and Lytton noticed that he looked rather pale, and that he also complained as usual, though not perhaps more than usual, of constipation. For much of this time they discussed, in the abstract, the question of physical love. 'Poor thing,' Lytton lamented to Keynes after he had gone (7 September 1905), 'he doesn't seem to understand much! He says he's repulsed by it – what can one reply? All the same he understands more than most.'

On 30 August, Lytton completed once and for all his encyclopaedic dissertation on Warren Hastings and dispatched it to Cambridge by the last possible post. 'The weight is now off my spirit,' he wrote to Leonard Woolf (31 August 1905). 'The last week has been one of the most unpleasant of my life. Perpetual constipation, nervous irritation, headaches even, utter boredom, desperate hurry, incapacity to think – all the most sordid nuisances the flesh is heir to. I am now more or less happy, and at any rate lazy, though a good deal wrecked.'

Lytton's eventual completion of the two-part thesis which had occupied him on and off for some two and a half years was a tremendous relief. The spell of grinding apathy was broken and he felt all at once a new energy creeping through him. Whatever the electors might decide, there was nothing more he could do about it. To all practical purposes he was at long last free from all its worries and entanglements. 'The Begums have at last been vanquished,' he wrote triumphantly to Duncan Grant (30 August 1905), 'and today they were dispatched to Cambridge, where they may rot at ease till the judgement day. Your letter came just in time to see the tail ends of them, whisking out of Great Oakley like so many witches on broomsticks. The result is that I am now considerably re-animated.'

A week after sending off his dissertation he left Kettering and went, via Oxford, to stay with the Homere sisters again near Chipping Norton, where he enjoyed a peaceful and uncomplicated twelve-hour-day routine – up at eleven, croquet in the afternoon, and back to bed again at eleven. In the third week of September, he returned to Great Oakley Hall and was visited for a few days by Keynes. 'My existence here is pretty comatose,' he informed Clive Bell (5 September 1905), 'but

263

less shattering now that my wretched dissertation is finished and done with.' He was especially keen to see Duncan Grant and conjured him to leave all, leap on a train, and come for the last few days of the summer – if not to see him again then at least to meet his great friend Keynes, whom he was sure to like. 'I think I am very disgracefully behaved not to have written before to you in answer to your invitation to stay,' Duncan Grant replied (24 September 1905). 'I am afraid I cannot manage it. . . . I should like to have seen Canes (?) very much.'

Two days later Lytton set off for Trinity, and the following evening attended, in company with the other fellowship candidates, his second ceremonial dinner with the examiners. As luck would have it he sat next to his own examiner, R. Vere Laurence, that rather prim and austere Irishman. 'Laurence was wicked as usual,' he wrote afterwards to Leonard Woolf. 'I thought at times obviously hostile – well, well. What's so curious, I find, when I talk to these people is that I simply roar with laughter at my own jokes. I suppose it's to encourage myself.'

The fellowship decisions were not to be announced for another week and in the meantime Lytton rejoined his family who had by now moved back to Lancaster Gate. The days passed listlessly, and he spent much of the time recording the trivia with which they were filled, chiefly for the amusement of Duncan Grant: 'This afternoon [2 October 1905] I visited the Times Book shop in New Bond Street. It's an awful institution. One of the lady assistants was so polite to me that I very nearly proposed.'

When the Fellowship results were at last published, Lytton had returned yet again to Trinity. 'I could see everything,' he wrote to Leonard Woolf (25 October 1905), 'and Rosy's[41] enraged disappointed red face told me at once all was over.' Although his failure did not come as a shock, he was nevertheless more dismayed than he cared to admit. His disappointment was easily understandable. The quality of writing and research in 'Warren Hastings, Cheyt Sing and the Begums

40. Rosy Haigh, Lytton's bedmaker.

of Oude' would seem quite up to Fellowship standard. Officially, the reasons given by the examiners for their rejection were exactly contrary to the type of adverse criticism — 'readable but inaccurate' — which was to be most often levelled in later years against his famous biographies. The dissertation, they said, gave evidence of conscientious work and of persevering endeavour to arrive at the truth by means of a thorough scrutiny of original records. But the style and arrangement were respectively obscure and ill-ordered. The examiners ignored altogether the specific reasons which Lytton set out in the Preface for quoting rather than paraphrasing his sources. They felt that the force of his argument was frequently spoilt by the close juxtaposition of extracts of patently unequal interest. Any extract which did not possess intrinsic significance should, in their opinion, have been briefly paraphrased or even reduced to footnotes instead of appearing verbatim. Otherwise the really telling extracts lost their effect. Moreover, the incessant breaking up of the narrative by these verbatim quotes of secondary importance rendered the whole piece unnecessarily confused and tedious to read. Some of the most telling points were so successfully buried in a mass of subordinate matter as to be discoverable only by an expert in this field of research. It was these defects that led the examiners to a verdict that Lytton's dissertation 'cannot be regarded as possessed of special excellence'.

The tone of this verdict indicates that possibly a number of ancillary matters had reduced beforehand the likelihood of Lytton's success. In the first place it is not very usual for someone who has won only Second Class Honours to be elected to a position where he may be required to urge other students to excel where he has previously failed. Lytton certainly appears to have thought that Vere Laurence disliked him personally, and, whatever the foundation was for this particular belief, it does seem possible that his unsavoury reputation as a leading decadent at Trinity — the 'brilliant wicked Mephistophelean myth' which had arisen round him — may have had an adverse effect on his chances of being admitted as one of his College's reputable Fellows. In addition, he met with unusually stiff opposition from the scientists that year. It was, moreover, rather unfortunate perhaps that, while the examiners were reading his dissertation, two new books on Hastings incorporating fresh, unpublished information should have happened to be published. Neither Sir Charles Lawson's *The Private Life of Warren Hastings* nor *The Letters of Warren Hastings to his Wife*, transcribed and annotated by Sydney C. Grier from the originals in the British Museum, actually contradicted anything that Lytton had written, but they took the edge off his scholarship and emphasized the personal aspect of Hastings's character, which the dissertation had tended to ignore.

In the long run, however, it was certainly to Lytton's advantage not to settle down at once into an academic society which had exalted the poetaster at the expense of the creative essayist by rewarding such an abstract, linguistic exercise as 'Ely: an Ode' with acclaim, while disdaining a far more remarkable composition like 'English Letter Writers'. As James Strachey was to express it, 'the Cambridge authorities had enough foresight and self-restraint to spare my brother the corrupting influences of an academic career'. But the immediate blow was severe. Once again, AGAINST HIS PRINCIPLES, he had failed in a vital examination and encountered a setback to his precarious self-confidence. 'But when Cambridge is over,' he had written to Leonard Woolf (April 1905), 'when one has been cast into the limbo of unintimacy, of business, of ugly antiquity – is there any hope? ... Supposing London kills me!' Cambridge, he felt, was his spiritual home; the only place where he had been reasonably happy. As it slowly became populated by his special friends, it had acquired almost a magic quality, unique and wonderful. 'Body and spirit, reason and emotion, work and play, architecture and scenery, laughter and seriousness, life and art – these pairs which are elsewhere contrasted were there fused into one,' wrote E. M. Forster. 'People and books reinforced one another, intelligence joined hands with affection, speculation became a passion, and discussion was made profound by love.' But hardly, it seemed, had Lytton begun to taste this sweet, comprehensive unity, when he was rudely expelled, forced to return to the portentous edifice in Lancaster Gate, and start up the old alien life there all over again.

Lytton's writings over the next twenty-five years are sprinkled with nostalgic, bitter-sweet references to Cambridge, 'whose cloisters', he remarked in *Eminent Victorians*, 'have ever been consecrated to poetry and common sense'. In an attempt to define the potent spell of Cambridge, its special atmosphere blended with personal associations, he contrasted his own university with Oxford, to the disadvantage of the latter. A foreign population of non-graduates had taken up its abode cheek by jowl with the most ancient of Oxford sanctities, he pointed out, so that the once amiable congruity of the place had departed for ever. At Cambridge the peaceful academic purity of mood had been far better preserved. 'The real enchantment of Cambridge is of the intimate kind; an enchantment lingering in the nooks and corners, coming upon one gradually down the narrow streets, and ripening year by year. The little river and its lawns and willows, the old trees in the old gardens, the obscure bowling-greens, the crooked lanes with their glimpses of cornices and turrets, the low dark opening out on to sunny grass – in these, and in things like these, dwells the fascination of Cambridge.'

Lytton had vainly hoped that this feeling of fascination might permeate and form the integral part of a new and happier period in his life; that the congenial beauty of Cambridge might supersede charmless Lancaster Gate as his home. But it was not to be. 'The wicked dons of Trinity have refused to make me a fellow,' he wrote to Duncan Grant (9 October 1905). 'I'm sorry, but resigned. I had imagined so many splendid things for us, if it had come off. Poverty, drudgery must now be faced.'

Before the start of the Michaelmas term, Lytton quitted his rooms on staircase K in the Great Court of Trinity, and returned to London. It must have seemed to him that the companionship for which he had so desperately longed at

Liverpool and cherished so deeply at Cambridge was now in danger of being forfeited altogether. For six years he had eagerly frequented doctor ` and saint, and had heard great argument, but finally, like FitzGerald's Khayyám, had gone out by the same door as in he went. His departure from Trinity marked, so he felt, the end of his youth, and the premature onset of a dull and dusty middle age. At twenty-five, nearly twenty-six, he was back almost where he had been at the age of eighteen, and in much the same style as his diary entry for the spring of 1898, his thoughts turned inwards. Infinitely elevated with long spidery legs and arms, a large nose, mild eyes, a thick moustache and calamitous equine teeth, he felt himself to be handicapped by a hideous appearance that immensely inflated his inner misery: so that he expressed his sense of failure partly in terms of physical self-denigration and disgust: 'You don't know what it is to be twenty-five,' he told Duncan Grant (11 October 1905), 'dejected, uncouth, unsuccessful – you don't know how humble and wretched and lonely I sometimes feel ... Oh God, these are wretched things to be writing.'

PART II

'The middle-aged fill me with frigid despair – they have so little to recommend them – really only their vague sense of the past. I feel that I am dimly dwindling into that terrible condition – a sort of dying process. One struggles – but one sinks.' *Lytton Strachey to Maynard Keynes* (21 January 1906)

SIX

Post-Graduate

1

BUBBLES, OYSTERS AND POTATOES

DURING the autumn of 1905, and for several succeeding years, a solitary young man, the son of an English general, was to be seen journeying between London and Cambridge. His striking figure, long and limp, with its half-languorous, half-drifting motion, gave him the aspect of an adolescent, which contrasted oddly with the mature darkness of his hair and his brown moustache. There was a similar contrast, enigmatic but unprepossessing, between his pallid complexion – the hue of a seasoned scholar – and the large brown eyes with their look of almost childlike innocence and alarm. To the intellectual inquirer he would explain, in a high, musical voice, that he was engaged in elucidating two problems – the kind of things that ought to exist for their own sake, and the kind of action we ought to perform. He believed, indeed, that he possessed the solution to these problems, as a reference to some passages in the book he was carrying would show.

This singular person was Lytton Strachey, and the book was reputed to be his bible, *Principia Ethica*.

On his arrival back at Lancaster Gate that autumn, Lady Strachey had given over to him a bed-sitting room where he was to do much of his writing over the next two years. 'I am established in a room here,' he wrote to Leonard Woolf (25 October 1905), 'with a folding bed, and all my books ranged in 2 bookshelves. It's pretty dreary, and when I'm to do any work heaven alone knows.' In this desolate upper chamber he sat, bent over a hissing gas fire, while beyond the steamed-up pink and frosted window-panes, the dreary enthralling life of London ebbed past unheeded. His heart and mind still dwelt amid the enchanted lawns and cloisters of Cambridge – yet after only a week, he was thinking of it all as strangely impalpable, a fantastic, remote place like Prospero's island, half real, half fairyland. 'I find Cambridge already hardly more than a vision,' he told Keynes (13 October 1905). Like his Shakespeare in the final period, Lytton found himself partly charmed by retrospective visions of beauty, partly bored to death. He must, he felt, be getting old.

'The refusal of the persons of Trinity to give me a fellowship has left me here, nominally a journalist, really, as far as I can see, a complete drifter, without any definite hopes, and the New Age as far off as ever,' he wrote summing up the position in a letter to Leonard Woolf. 'If I were energetic – but it's so absurd – how can one be energetic over reviews? I pray to God, though, that I may miraculously take a turn towards the practical – for a year or two – which I believe would be enough. But it's all very dull and vague and quasi-infinite.'

As always when discussing his own work, Lytton was inclined to understate the amount of conscientious effort he put into it. There was something ridiculous and undignified about hard work. Besides, he liked to encourage among his friends the notion that any piece of his which they might happen to read was thrown off lightly, thereby disarming censure. But easy writing's vile hard reading, and the consistent readability of Lytton's essays attests to the minute concentration he gave to his narrative. His overall output at this time, however, was not large. In his last two years at Cambridge he had contributed about half a dozen essay-reviews for the *Spectator* and *Independent Review*. During the following two years, that is until he was taken on to the regular staff of the *Spectator,* he produced, on average, about one article every six weeks. Although these were all of a very reasonably high standard, the labour of reviewing other people's books was far from his liking – searching about in the roots of things at three guineas a piece: all exertion and no fulfilment. 'I spend my days here trying to be a journalist,' he gloomily informed Swithinbank (15 October 1905), 'but I seem to lack the conviction and energy which I feel are necessary. Other things are much more interesting than reviews! But daily bread must be obtained somehow . . .'

Yet in some respects his existence at Lancaster Gate was not so odious. Part of the horror of giving up Cambridge was simply the actual process – which vanished once it was over. Life, at any rate, did not automatically stop, but trickled on in approximately the same old unsatisfactory way as before. He still had his friends. Above all others came Duncan Grant. He was also seeing now quite a lot of the Stephen family, gazing in rapture at the magnificent unapproachable Goth, and with curiosity at the enigmatic Virginia. Then there was Clive Bell – hopelessly, it seemed, in love with Vanessa Stephen – who had returned from Paris, and having failed to obtain a Fellowship himself, assured Lytton with robust confidence that he was well out of Cambridge. Perhaps matters might have turned out very differently, Lytton reflected, had he been able to continue directing the affairs of the Society. 'It's shocking about Cambridge,' he confessed to Keynes (8 November 1905). 'I've been having tea with Bell[1] – very dim and decadent in a blue dressing-gown in his wonderful Temple chambers – and he tells the same story. It shows how far things have gone that Lamb should be the most eminent person in Trinity. What's of course chiefly lacking is intellect, and that's lacking in Oxford too – only they make up for it by culture and indecency.'

Almost every day now he was writing to Keynes about the affairs of the Society. He was hungry for Cambridge gossip which, after extracting it from Keynes, he would pass on to Leonard Woolf in Ceylon. 'The freshmen sound most exciting,' he replied to Keynes after a few days at Lancaster Gate (16 October 1905), 'and I can hardly contain myself – I burst with impatience and curiosity.' And again, the following month (27 November 1905): 'You are my only Evangelist, and I watch the posts for news from the Only Place.'

1. Clive Bell, in fact, was never a member of the Apostles.

At first the most exciting new discovery seemed to be a freshman by the name of Goodhart,[2] whose wild, temperament thrilled Lytton. The grandson of Lord Rendel, and cousin of Lytton's eldest brother-in-law, Goodhart was reckoned to be 'possibly a genius, certainly remarkable and almost certainly nice', in Lytton's words to Leonard Woolf. 'Even James was excited when I saw him, about a "wonderful" conversation they'd had, after which Goodhart had fallen back with spasms and palpitations and had had to send for a doctor. He's violently musical and wildly architectural, he talks in torrents, and believes in medieval Christianity.' But all this excitement soon turned out to be a South Sea bubble. Goodhart was taken up by the Society like an oyster, and then, almost immediately, damned and dropped again like a hot potato after it was discovered that his Christian beliefs were not confined to medieval times. But there were always new embryos to take the place of the duds – the young Charles Darwin,[3] for example, whose election Lytton supported; and Dillwyn Knox,[4] one of the famous brothers, whom Keynes had recruited, but of whom Lytton did not approve: 'Did I tell you that I took a pretty violent zid against Knox?' he asked Keynes. 'He seemed to me too gravely inconsiderate, in the regular damned Etonian way. It's impossible not to dislike someone a little, who so obviously dislikes one so much.'

2. Harry Stuart Goodhart-Rendel (he assumed by Royal Licence the additional name of Rendel) had a distinguished career both in musical and architectural fields. Among his many official appointments were Slade Professor of Fine Art at Oxford, Governor of Sadlers Wells, president of the Architectural Association and president of the Royal Institute of British Architects.

3. Charles Darwin, seven years younger than Lytton, a younger brother of Gwen Raverat, the authoress and artist, was a grandson of the great scientist Charles Darwin. He married Katherine Pember, while his younger sister Margaret became the wife of Maynard Keynes's younger brother Geoffrey. These Darwins were the children of Sir George Darwin, Plumian Professor of Astronomy at Cambridge, and a particular friend of Lytton's parents.

4. A. D. Knox, the second of the four Knox brothers, a brilliant classical scholar, afterwards Fellow of King's College. In later years, Lytton became very friendly with him.

But among the freshmen was another less obtrusive Old Etonian, Harry Norton, destined to become a close and permanent friend of Lytton's. 'I'm sure he has a very good logical kind of mind,' Keynes gravely reported to Lytton (15 October 1905); 'his own view, however, is that he is cultured – and he is incredibly. His whole person is girt about by a writhing mess of aesthetic and literary appreciations, which I have – so far – discovered no means of quelling. He's very proud of all this, but it's really rather nonsense: what saves him is his strong comprehension – I hardly ever caught him really stupid.

'There is nothing to say about his appearance – ordinary public school.'

A public school appearance was evidently not very attractive. Norton's face was round; he had a fine forehead, a short straight nose. He was tall, but owing to short shin bones he minced along with ludicrously tiny steps. Through the spectacles he always wore after his first term at Cambridge, his eyes stared out at the world with ever-diminishing optimism. Among his Cambridge friends it was held that he possessed a remarkably 'pure' intelligence. His first years at Trinity were marked by the most violent high-spirits imaginable. He talked incessantly, rattling along with loud intermittent yells of laughter. He had, too, a gentleness and sweetness of disposition, mixed, not with any sham sentimentality, but with a genuine cerebral power that endeared him to Lytton. 'He's an Etonian,' Lytton wrote to Leonard Woolf after his first meeting with Norton (October 1905), 'and created some sensation there by being observed to read Russell's book. He's very cultured and reads poetry by the yard.' After their second meeting he recorded his impressions as follows: 'He's undoubtedly nice, though very young and rather ugly. He's obviously open and honest ... talks in fact too much because of an innocent ignorance of what other people think, but talks without restraint and is quite vaguely and ingenuously indecent. As to his intelligence it seems to me doubtful, but I could hardly tell.'

Norton was in fact suffering from what is technically

known as hypomania, and this, after some years, turned over into a quite opposite mood – one of severe depression which eventually paralysed his mental processes and led to a nervous breakdown. 'He had an extremely high-grade mental apparatus,' James Strachey told the author. 'He was one of the only three or four people I have ever known in the same intellectual category as Russell – with whom he was perfectly able to argue on equal terms.'

Lytton hoped that Norton might be able to draw out his younger brother James, an enigmatic and impassive character, much given, it was felt, to laziness. But to his dismay, James began to associate more with the much-vilified Walter Lamb, while Norton was seen on more than one occasion talking to that 'blind confused charming affectionate creature' Sheppard. As for Lytton, he was powerless to do anything about it himself, for any definite act of interference, any proffering of unsought advice would be, by Apostolic ethics, to commit the unforgivable Sin of Parentage.

There were also other potential drawbacks to Norton. Being an undergraduate of considerable means, he sometimes adopted a tone of unworldliness which the others, hoist with their own philosophical petard, found hard to match. 'D'you think there's any danger in his becoming absorbed in the phenomenal?' Lytton anxiously inquired of Keynes, who thought on the whole that there was not. In later years Norton gave Lytton crucial financial help until, with the publication in 1918 of *Eminent Victorians* – which is dedicated to Norton ('To H.T.J.N.') – Lytton was able to reimburse him in full. A mathematician of very great ability, Norton was elected to a Fellowship at Trinity in 1910. But to many of his friends he appeared to lapse into a state of inertia, and most of them were not surprised to learn when he died at the age of fifty that his work on the Cantorian theory of numbers was still unfinished. Yet he had continued in his unobtrusive way to labour intermittently at it, and his papers, even in their fragmentary condition, were found to have made important advances in a branch of pure mathematics.

Of all the new friends whom Lytton met that autumn and

who were eventually elected to the Society, perhaps the most interesting was Rupert Brooke. Some seven years younger than Lytton, he had attended Hillbrow, the same private school as James Strachey, and had later gone on to Rugby with Maynard Keynes's younger brother Geoffrey.[5] His father, William Parker Brooke, was the housemaster of School Field, the house at which Rupert was entered and where every hour, he later said, was 'golden and radiant'. Good alike at work and sport, charming, debonair and with unusually good looks of a type which are at their height in the late teens and early twenties, he was immediately successful at whatever he put his hand to. He seemed, indeed, almost too good to be true, and, like some mythical deity, attracted extreme adulation from almost all those in his vicinity. Lytton had heard much of Brooke before meeting him in September at Kettering,[6] and though his curiosity had obviously been roused, he was more than prepared to dislike him. In fact, he found this legendary schoolboy quite inoffensive. 'He has rather nice – but you know – yellow-ochre-ish hair, and a healthy young complexion,' he wrote to Duncan Grant (5 September 1905), who had also known Brooke at Hillbrow. 'I took him out for a walk round the Park this morning, and he talked about Poetry and Public Schools as decently as could be expected.' Brooke, for his part, rather took to Lytton: 'Lytton Strachey I found most amusing,' he wrote to Geoffrey Keynes, 'especially his voice.' And for some years subsequently, as Chris-

5. Sir Geoffrey Keynes (b. 1887), later to become a surgeon of the first rank and our foremost Blake scholar, whose *Job* he converted into a ballet, choreographed by Lytton's cousin Ninette de Valois, and with music by Vaughan Williams. His bibliographies include volumes on the writings of John Donne, Sir Thomas Browne, Rupert Brooke and Siegfried Sassoon. He was Trustee of the National Portrait Gallery (1942–66) and Chairman of the Board (1958–66).

6. Lytton and Rupert Brooke had in fact met before. In the summer of 1898, the Stracheys had rented a country house called Ardeley Bury, near Stevenage. During that time Rupert came to stay with James. They were both then aged between ten and eleven, and James remembers Lytton reading *Paradise Lost* aloud to him in the garden. They met again in Brighton during the Easter holidays of 1900, but the encounter was of no significance and neither of them appears to have remembered it.

topher Hassall has shown and as Brooke's own letters testify, Lytton's influence worked strongly upon him.

Lytton's attitude towards this golden-haired young Apollo is interesting. Some of the rather nonchalant indifference with which he writes of him may be assumed – a reaction from the admiration of everyone else, in particular his brother James. But while he was not insensible to Brooke's appeal, he certainly did not respect his intellectual capabilities. He may possibly have thought his looks too sugary, and on occasions he suspected that Brooke, for his part, regarded him as too avuncular. At any rate, though Brooke was then hesitating between going up to Oxford or Cambridge, Lytton did not appear very anxious about the matter one way or the other. After he had left Kettering, he wrote to Maynard Keynes (7 September 1905): 'Rupert Brooke has been with us. I wasn't particularly impressed. His appearance is pleasant – mainly, I think, owing to youth – complexion, hair, etc. Of course he's quite incredibly young, so it was rather difficult to talk. I felt he wanted to attack the subject of Platonic Love, etc. but the whole thing seemed so dreadfully commonplace that I couldn't manage it. He's damned literary, rather too serious and conscientious, and devoid of finesse. The Cambridge–Oxford question still hangs in the balance. I didn't make any great effort to obtain him. The decision rests with Dr [H. A.] James, the H. Master of Rugby.'

This lukewarm response was partly due to the lack of common ground in their background and early years. Lytton's schooldays had been overshadowed by failure; Brooke's were spent basking in the limelight of popular and academic success. 'The genius at school is usually a disappointing figure,' Lytton was to write in his essay on Beddoes, 'for as a rule, one must be commonplace to be a successful boy. In that preposterous world, to be remarkable is to be overlooked.' Rupert Brooke had never been overlooked. From the various comments which Lytton passed on to Brooke in his letters, it is not clear to what extent he may at times have felt envious of the younger man's triumphal progress through life. But it is certain that he considered him, despite his poetic appearance – his long hair, silk shirt and loosely knotted foulard tie – to be fundamentally unremarkable. Because of the reverence felt for him by their respective younger brothers, Lytton and Maynard Keynes spent a good deal of time assessing Brooke's character – especially since he later became an Apostle. At this early stage, on the basis of an hour or two's acquaintance and an examination of some of Brooke's letters to James, Lytton found him to be below the line of medium capacity – to adapt a phrase of Beatrice Webb's – mainly on account of his 'vile diction', feeble epigrams and jokes and general aesthetic tinge. He was irritated, too, by what he judged to be Brooke's 'complacent egoism'; but added, in mitigation, that he seemed to have an acute sense of character and situation, a general innocence, and an interest (though not perhaps a deep one) in interesting things. These saving factors encouraged him to believe that 'something might be done', though he remained doubtful.

Shortly after Lytton's meeting with Brooke at Kettering, Geoffrey Keynes came up to Cambridge from Rugby to try for a scholarship at Pembroke. With him he brought Brooke, who had decided to stand at the same time for a scholarship at King's. Both of them stayed with the Keynes family in Harvey Road, and Maynard's letters to Lytton reveal the fact that Geoffrey was deliberately effacing himself so that this radiant schoolfriend should shine at his most brilliant. Both of them succeeded in obtaining their respective scholarships, and next year were whirled up into the undergraduate high life.

Brooke had left Rugby with honours thick upon him. During his time there he had assumed a literary cult reminiscent of Beardsley and Dowson. This pose had considerably impressed his schoolfellows, but at university dandyism was by then right out of fashion, and it failed to win him the usual acclaim. Consequently, during his first year at Cambridge he was uncharacteristically plaintive and discouraged. King's was devoid of amusement. He liked nobody. Everyone seemed dull, middle-aged, and ugly. 'I'm filled with an hysterical despair', he wrote in his first long vacation. 'I hate myself and everyone. . . . Go back to Cambridge for my second year and laugh and talk with those old dull people on that airless plain. The thought fills me with hideous ennui.'

Yet even at Cambridge things do not stand absolutely still. A wave of Fabian socialism was soon sweeping over the new undergraduates, and politics, not psychological literature, became the principal topic of conversation among the intelligentsia. This new tide caught up many of Lytton's friends — including James, Maynard Keynes, and Brooke himself.[7] As president of the university Fabian Society,[8] Brooke was to feel more at home discussing through the night and until dawn the teachings of the Webbs with his colleague, Hugh ('Daddy') Dalton.[9] He also took part in the social life at King's, and with his namesake, Justin Brooke,[10] formed the Marlowe Dramatic Society. Despite his feeling for poetry and his enthusiasm for the theatre, Rupert was neither a good speaker of verse nor even a competent actor — he never appeared natural — and the Marlowe Society's performance of Milton's *Comus* was treated by Lytton to a rather unflattering anonymous review in the pages of the *Spectator*. Both Brooke and Lytton were fascinated by the stage, but whereas Lytton was always endeavouring to rearrange the painful disorder of living into the pattern of a neat intriguing theatrical performance, for Brooke life had seldom been anything else. This staginess enveloped him like a cocoon, through which he eventually burst to be fatally poisoned by his contact with rude actuality. Assured self-dramatization had begun with him

7. So far as the Apostles were concerned, Fabian socialism had no impact, except on James Strachey. Maynard Keynes always despised the Fabians, and Norton remained quite unimpressed. The really influential figure at Cambridge was Ben Keeling, who converted Hugh Dalton from a Conservative tariff reformer. It was only after the First World War that communism became a topic of discussion within the Society.

8. Rupert Brooke became the third president of the Cambridge Fabian Society in 1909.

9. Hugh Dalton (1887–1962), later prominent in the Labour Party. Chancellor of the Exchequer 1945–7. He preceded Brooke as president of the Cambridge Fabian Society.

10. Justin Brooke of Emmanuel College was no relation to Rupert Brooke.

as a child, whereas Lytton had slowly acquired it as a defensive equipment against failure and loneliness. In a letter to a friend Lytton wrote of 'Rupert en beauté in the stalls', a phrase which, Hugh Kingsmill commented, 'conjures up Brooke in the high summer of his triumph as the toast of King's ... [and] the hollow-eyed and desiderious Strachey whom I picture peering down from the front row of the dress circle'. Brooke, indeed, always seems closer to the stage platform than Lytton. He was like the playboy son of some fabulous financier, cashing in on a happy series of speculations, strangely determined to press his facility and good fortune beyond the furthest possible limit; while Lytton, through one or two brilliant but carefully considered investments, just succeeds in keeping the duns from the door while his once tiny capital slowly accumulates.

Like most of his contemporaries, Lytton thought as little of Brooke's early poems as of his acting ability and 'Grantchester' he later dismissed as 'a bloody affected concoction'. It has been suggested by Desmond MacCarthy and by Raymond Mortimer that the change in diction and inflexion of Brooke's verse was directly attributable to Lytton's enthusiasm for Donne and seventeenth-century poetry, and even perhaps to those poems of his own which he used to declaim to his closest Cambridge friends. Without admiration for his versatile talent, it was hardly surprising that Lytton's feelings for his young friend were so mixed. After his first mood of casual indifference had passed, it was partly replaced by a latent, nagging element of disapproval which fretted the complicated compound of his emotions and which on one or two occasions exploded in violent outbursts of temper. To some extent he was susceptible to Brooke's picturesque charm, but found him altogether too improbable a personality – the sort of glorified legendary figure, with sinister undertones of puritanism, whom, in other circumstances, he might have made the subject for a short, ironical pen portrait. 'Rupert Brooke,' he wrote to Virginia Stephen in April 1908, 'isn't it a romantic name? – with pink cheeks and bright yellow hair – it sounds horrible, but it wasn't. The conversation is less political than you think, but I dare say you would have found the jokes a little heavy – as for me, I laughed enormously, and whenever I began to feel dull I could look at the yellow hair and pink cheeks of Rupert.' Nice to contemplate as a mythical decoration, he seems to have concluded, but Lytton *knew* he must have feet of clay, weak knees – both probably. Virginia Stephen, of course, also met Brooke herself. 'He was very keen on living the "free life",' she told William Plomer and Stephen Spender. 'One day he said, "Let's go swimming quite naked." '

'And did you, Virginia?' asked William Plomer.

'Of course. Lytton always said that Rupert had bandy legs. But I don't think that was so.'[11]

2

THE LIMBO OF UNINTIMACY

On leaving Cambridge, Lytton's rooms were rather violently redecorated in apple-green and taken over by his younger brother, James. 'The room is grotesquely changed – an *art nouveau* symphony in green and white,' Lytton described it to Leonard Woolf, 'with James, very prim and small,[12] sitting in the extreme corner of the sofa, which is covered with green sack-cloth.'

Though Lytton had chosen the room's new decoration himself – a fact which he omits in his description of it to Leonard Woolf – the atmosphere seemed to him now much more louring than ever it was when he had lived there. But what maddened him was the sight of his brother, a preposterous caricature of his past self, sitting there silent, contemptuous, utterly ineffectual, impotent and dull – a mere reflection of a reflection which went by the name of Walter Lamb, whose air of wheedling superiority James seemed to

11. Fresh evidence on this subject was recently made available to the author by James Strachey. 'Rupert *had* bandy legs, all the same.'

12. 'In fact,' James Strachey pointed out, 'in our stockinged feet, we were both, at our best, exactly 6 ft 1 in. tall.'

prefer to Norton's Etonian culture. It was dreadful to see him so alone and unhappy, unable to take an interest in anything, submerged by the flatness of the world. But perhaps the Society, as soon as he was elected, would have a good effect, would widen the field of his enthusiasms and make him more cheerful. One could only hope so.

James's withdrawn nature and youthful appearance soon earned for him the name of 'the Little Strachey', while Lytton now figured as 'the Great Strachey'. At Lancaster Gate, James had been known as 'Jembeau', and even 'Uncle Baby' by some of his nieces and nephews considerably older than himself. But such nicknames were exclusively family matters, and it was owing to the difficulty of differentiating in conversation between himself and his younger brother, who now, for the first time, was fully entering his world, that Lytton suggested to his friends that they should in future address each other by Christian names. This recommendation, which was universally accepted, did not therefore constitute, as has been made out, a measure of deliberate social implication – a breaking down of formal, hidebound Victorian conventions – but was a matter of practical convenience. All his life Lytton actually preferred pet-names or nicknames to either surnames or Christian names. 'The pomposity of real Christian names', he once wrote to Duncan Grant, 'is too grinding.'

The presence of a younger enigmatic brother in his old rooms at Trinity acted as a powerful catalyst to Lytton's post-graduate reputation. 'I see you're rapidly becoming a kind of distant, eminent brilliant wicked Mephistophelian myth,' Maynard Keynes wrote to him (5 November 1905). And Lytton at once replied with a touch of prophetic foresight: 'It's rather alarming to find oneself a myth. I feel as if I ought to wear very peculiar clothes – à la Tennyson – so that people like Goldschmidt[13] shouldn't be disappointed if they

13. Ernst Goldschmidt was a freshman of sinister reputation, lately arrived from Austria. For a time Lytton and Keynes considered electing him to the Apostles, but finally decided on a more appropriate measure – an introduction to Oscar Browning. In later life Goldschmidt became a leading member of the Bibliographical Society and the author of *England's Service* by 'Sarpedon'.

happened to see me. Perhaps a fur tippet in the Verrall[14] style, a fur cap, and eyeglasses at the end of a stick. But of course the first necessity is a beard!'

Clive Bell had once again left for France, and during the late autumn and the winter Lytton saw more of Duncan Grant and Desmond MacCarthy than of any of his other friends. He would sometimes have lunch with the former at his new studio in Upper Baker Street, which appealed to his bohemian notions of how a painter should live – an almost completely bare room, ornamented solely with his sketches and drawings. 'They're superb,' he told Keynes after his first visit there (24 November 1905), 'and I've no doubt of his supremacy qua artist. He made an omelette in a frying-pan over the fire, and we ate it on the bare wooden table with bread and cheese and beer. After that we drew our kitchen chairs up to the fire, and smoked cigarettes and talked . . .'

A less romantic figure, Desmond MacCarthy was of more practical use to Lytton. He had recently become dramatic critic of the *Speaker*, and arranged for Lytton to contribute unsigned book reviews. Whenever they met, MacCarthy liked to read out loud to Lytton, who sat beside him, a languid, unappreciative audience. 'I've rarely been read aloud to so much,' he complained in a letter to Leonard Woolf, ' – and have rarely heard anyone read aloud so badly.'

Over everything hung the awful brooding regime of Lancaster Gate, which exerted itself ever more potently as the weeks passed and dissolved into months. It was not that he disliked any of his family, but that regular family life corroded family affection. 'I have a sister-in-law – she's now in the house – Lord!' he wrote to Maynard Keynes in despair (9 December 1905). 'She talks incessantly balderdash of the lowest description. She tries to flirt with me. She ogles, and

14. Arthur Woolgar Verrall (1851–1912), Greek scholar and Fellow of Trinity. A remarkable lecturer with a rich shrill voice, he was one of the first dons to treat the classics as works of art. A memoir of him by F. M. Cornford and reminiscences by Eddie Marsh (on whom he acted as a great influence) are included in *Collected Literary Essays* by A. W. Verrall (1913). His chief claim to celebrity was his *Euripides the Rationalist* – the best kind of detective story.

wonders what I can possibly mean. If you come on Thursday she'll be here to flirt with you.' Such minor irregularities seemed to emphasize his premature middle age, to convince him that his youth had belonged to Cambridge and was irretrievably left behind there. The world was a muddled worry. 'I don't believe I shall ever get back what I seem to have gained so easily and lost so vaguely,' he confessed, ' – the happy state of premonitory, half-conscious, summer passion, "the tender eye-dawn of auroran love". I wonder what it is that divides me, infinitely and eternally, from those innocences and those delights. . . . The best things come to us before we know they are coming, and vanish before we know they have come. One lives a thousand ages without ever realizing what it is to live, and then, in the moment of discovery, one finds that one's already dead. . . . Oh dear! are we really so antique?'

On every possible occasion he struggled to escape, to spend even a single night elsewhere. He thought enviously of his brother Oliver, who was on the point of departing again for India: 'How he hates it!' Lytton exclaimed to Keynes. 'How he longs to stay! Ah! how much I'd like to go instead of him.' Frequent less ambitious trips away from Lancaster Gate, however, he did manage. During the course of the Michaelmas term he visited his brother twice at Cambridge, and was introduced by Keynes to all the new embryos. But the great days of the Apostles had passed – even Keynes himself admitted so. Christianity, like a pernicious weed, was springing up everywhere again. Nevertheless, after London, the air of youthful decadence was extreme. 'The whole place seemed to me more depressed and more sodomitical than usual,' he told Swithinbank after another stay there in the Lent term (4 February 1906). 'If things go on at this present rate, I shudder to think what our sons may or may not be doing twenty years hence. But perhaps by that time the fashion will have changed, and they'll all be womanizers. Well, it will be a great triumph to be thought indecent by one's son.'

Early in November he went to stay in Oxford with the Raleighs, who took him to hear a performance of the Brahms Requiem in which one of his sisters was singing. Walter Raleigh was charming and brilliant – at the same time quite unable to talk about anything that interested Lytton personally. 'Here I am, a little shattered,' he wrote to Keynes (2 November 1905). 'Last night I spent with the Raleighs, partly at a rather dull concert, and partly listening to his consummate brilliance. It's so great that it practically amounts to a disease. But in any case he belongs to the age before the flood – the pre-Dickinsonian era – which is really fatal. He's not interested in the things which absorb us – result, dead silence on my part, and blank boredom on his – though of course there are compensating moments.'

From the Raleighs, he moved across to Balliol to spend a few days with Swithinbank. Here, at last, he seemed more in tune with his surroundings. 'The amusement has been and continues great', he told Duncan Grant (3 November 1905). 'Life here swims through a beautiful sea of gentleness and *politesse*. I was not surprised, when the door opened and someone who looked like a freshman glided in, to hear him addressed as Gabriel. The angel Gabriel, I thought, of course.' He peered at many of Swithinbank's friends – including Daniel Macmillan[15] and J. D. Beazley – went to the Union, and attended a meeting of the Pleiads – a society of seven ('perhaps too many') members founded by Swithinbank – where he heard a paper read on 'Les amours de Chopin et de George Sand'. But in comparison with the proceedings of *the* Society it seemed pretty feeble stuff. The paper itself was just dully constructive and informative, gleaned from text-books specially for the occasion, while the discussion which followed seemed hopelessly vague – questions from anybody to anybody, and developing into scattered smut and small-talk. As to Oxford in general, its cultivation and impropriety mixed made up a peculiar charm, at once gentle and cerebral, which Lytton had found lacking in the more revolutionary spirit of Cambridge.

15. Daniel Macmillan (1886–1964). Elder brother of Harold Macmillan, later prime minister. A scholar of Balliol College, he subsequently became chairman and managing director of Macmillan and Co. Ltd, the publishers.

But even here there were disappointments in store for him. He would have liked to establish a close and affectionate relationship with Swithinbank, who, he instinctively felt, would cause him less pain than Duncan Grant. But the more he saw of him, the more he came to realize the unlikelihood of any really intimate friendship such as he desired. Swithinbank was too shy – too *intellectually* shy. He needed to be drawn out by a degree of tactful insinuation, obliquely and patiently applied, which was alien to Lytton's astringent temperament. 'There are awkward silences,' he reported apologetically to Keynes (2 November 1905); 'you see we really do at present have very few topics in common – I mean easy topics; though very often it's charming, and we can giggle without restraint. But what I think is the chief horror is his incapacity to analyse. He seems almost frightened and sheers off. Is it education or nature or what? This evening I pressed him hard – on the subject of Raleigh's character. He hedged for some time, and then made some quite good though rather muddled remarks. I went on, and he seemed to collapse completely – a sort of tormented resignation.'

Later in November, Lytton again succeeded in escaping from Lancaster Gate, this time to visit Bob Trevelyan and his Dutch wife Bessie for a few cold days at Holmbury St Mary, near Dorking. But it was an aimless, unsatisfactory life he was now leading. 'I feel', he wrote, 'like the Israelites who wandered in sight of the Promised Land for forty years.' His tenuous connection with the Only Place was still being preserved primarily through Keynes, who was 'certainly now', he informed Leonard Woolf (November 1905), ' – though I hardly expect you to believe it – the most important person there. He maintains a curious aloofness.' There was, in many of his references to Keynes about this time, an undisguised note of aversion. 'Keynes sits like a decayed and amorous spider in King's,' he wrote to Clive Bell (17 January 1906), using the very imagery which he was later to apply to King Philip of Spain, the spider of the Escurial, 'weaving purely imaginary webs, noticing everything that happens and doesn't happen, and writing to me by every other post.'

The truth was that their respective circumstances had changed much since Keynes was first elected to the Society. Then Lytton had been indisputably the major figure of the two, listening to the younger man's confidences and putting at his disposal the benefit of all his magnanimous understanding. But the quick and eager Apostle soon began to develop a confidence of his own. Prince D. S. Mirsky has suggested that Keynes might have grown into 'a rather dangerous rival' in the world of letters. Undoubtedly Keynes's phenomenal, un-Apostolic success aroused in Lytton some feeling of disdain, made bitter by sexual jealousy. Whereas his own influence at Cambridge was literary, moral rather than ethical, and did not extend far beyond the inner circle of Apostles and those intimate friends at Trinity and King's, the more catholic Keynes became not only a leading Apostle, but also president of the Union and of the University Liberal Club — a person of wide authority. Lytton had only obtained Second Class Honours; Keynes, with a minimum of hard work, had won a First. Lytton half-heartedly failed to be accepted by the Education Board; Keynes went on to pass the Civil Service examination with some ease. Lytton was not elected as a Fellow of Trinity; Keynes was awarded a lectureship and then a Fellowship at King's. And when, in time, the fashionable conversation switched from metaphysics and literature to economics and political philosophy, Keynes could still more than hold his own, while Lytton, despite laughing enormously at jokes he found a little heavy, remained something of an outsider. This steady reversal in the pattern of their fortunes set up an undercurrent of strain and stress which ran contrary to the flow of their old comradeship. He felt a genuine unadulterated appreciation for Keynes's intellectual powers and for the raciness of his conversation. But although he admired the author of *The Economic Consequences of the Peace*, he despised the mechanical salt-butter rogue who treated his love-affairs statistically and took the doings of the Liberal Party with great seriousness. These two attitudes persisted all through their relations. Lytton's feelings of sexual jealousy were something separate, which nevertheless magnified at times his critical judgements. What he particularly minded in his own life during these early years was lack of money combined with a lack of comfort of all kinds. The room he had been given at Lancaster Gate (it had previously been Dorothy's bedroom) was quite remarkably squalid – enough, it seemed to him, to depress anyone. The comparison with Keynes's happier and more prosperous circumstances irritated him, and it was only when Keynes suffered momentary setbacks and could no longer be considered an object of superficial envy, that their former intimacy was re-established.

The path which their gradual, limited estrangement was to follow can be traced between the lines of those letters which passed between them in the period soon after Lytton left Cambridge. This alienation, though it only once boiled over, simmered perpetually below the outer crust of their continuing friendship. Hating London, Lytton is ever thirsty for information about Cambridge youth, anxious to absorb himself in their activities, but Keynes replies casually and with a disconcerting echo of Lytton's own exact sentiments a year earlier: 'I really believe I would leave Cambridge and come up to London at once – but for one reason. I suppose the Society must be put on its legs again – or at any rate one has to try.' Lytton's letters expatiate, often movingly, on the twists and turns of his own shadowy passions and pre-occupations. Keynes writes at length of his new satisfactory successes in economics, the flattering remarks on his papers, and his intention to study ethics for the Civil Service examination. Lytton answers with mixed feelings: 'I suppose it doesn't matter very much whether you get into the C.S. or not, does it? If you didn't, wouldn't you get a fellowship, and take rooms in the Temple? That you might do in any case – very charming. Oh dear me!' Deliberating on his course of action Keynes wonders whether he should stay on at King's as an economist. 'I could get employment here,' he writes, 'if I wanted to.' But Lytton, who hopes to leave Lancaster Gate and set up home with his friend somewhere in London, is appalled at the notion. 'Oh no, it would be surely mad to be a Cambridge economist,' he replies. 'Come to London, go to

the Treasury, and set up house with me. The parties we'd give!'
Soon, however, Lytton realizes that Keynes has no intention
of getting a flat with him in town, and reflects that in these
altered circumstances his rooms in King's might continue to
be very useful. But already it is too late. Keynes is determined
to quit the deadening, stagnant atmosphere of Cambridge and
embark on the adventure of life in London as soon as possible. He will conquer the metropolis as he has the university.
He even confesses himself a little taken with Ray Costelloe,[16]
who was later to become Oliver Strachey's second wife; he
takes up mountaineering in the company of Geoffrey Winthrop Young[17] (recently sacked from his post as a master at
Eton), and is immediately successful. Lytton's consternation
rises and he sadly admits to Duncan Grant that he has no faith
in Keynes's power of penetrating below the surface of life.

In due course the result of the Civil Service examination
comes through. Keynes is second. 'A wonderful achievement,'
his father noted in his diary. But Maynard, who has worked
only intermittently, is furious – and writes to Lytton at length
to tell him so[18] – whereupon Lytton sorrowfully confesses

16. Ray Costelloe was the daughter of Logan Pearsall Smith's sister,
who later married Bernard Berenson. Ray's sister Karin married Adrian
Stephen, and her aunt Alys was the wife of Bertrand Russell. An acknowledged leader in the Woman's Movement, she was the author of many
books, including *Millicent Garrett Fawcett* (1931). She and Oliver Strachey
had two children, Barbara, who joined the administrative staff of the
B.B.C., and Christopher, now one of the top computer wizards in
Britain.

17. Geoffrey Winthrop Young, poet and mountaineer. On leaving Eton,
he had taken up a post as one of H.M. Inspectors of Secondary Schools
(1905–13). Later he became renowned for scaling Alpine peaks after
having lost a leg in the battle of Monte San Gabrielle.

18. Lytton celebrated the occasion with some witty verses entitled:

> '*In Memoriam J.M.K. Ob. Sept. 1906*.'

> Here lie the last remains of one
> Who always did what should be done.
> Who never misbehaved at table
> And loved as much as he was able.
> Who couldn't fail to make a joke,
> And, though he stammered, always spoke;

to Duncan Grant: 'I used to tell Keynes everything, but his commonsense was enough to freeze a volcano, so now I've stopped.' At this point, however, Keynes encounters a period of adversity, and is re-admitted as the sympathetic repository of Lytton's emotional problems. For the next two years, 1907 and 1908, Keynes works in the India Office, but even before his first twelve months are up he is already consumed with ennui and thinking about moving on again. 'I'm thoroughly sick of this place,' he writes to Lytton in September 1907, 'and would like to resign. Now the novelty has worn off, I am bored nine-tenths of the time and rather unreasonably irritated the other tenth whenever I can't have my own way. It's maddening to have thirty people who can reduce you to impotence when you're quite certain you are right.' Lytton, at once responding to this familiar blend of boredom and arrogant frustration, is enthusiastically sympathetic. It is more like old times again. 'I feel it's a great mercy,' he wrote later, 'having you as Brother Confessor.' How pleasant it was being able freely to divulge what he felt! For his feelings were now centred strongly round Duncan Grant, to whom he had succeeded in introducing Keynes in the very first month of his return to Lancaster Gate. And he had much to divulge.

> Both penetrating and polite,
> A liberal and a sodomite,
> An atheist and a statistician,
> A man of sense, without ambition.
> A man of business, without bustle,
> A follower of Moore and Russell,
> One who, in fact, in every way,
> Combined the features of the day.
> By curses blest, by blessings cursed,
> He didn't merely get a first.
> A first he got; on that he'd reckoned;
> But then he also got a second.
> He got a first with modest pride;
> He got a second, and he died.

3
DUNCAN GRANT AND HIS WORLD

Duncan Grant was some five years younger than Lytton. His father, Major Bartle Grant, Lady Strachey's youngest brother, had married Ethel McNeil, a beautiful but penniless Scottish girl, and Duncan, who was born in Rothiemurchus, was their only child. His early years had been spent out in India where Major Grant was serving with his regiment. But once the boy was old enough to attend preparatory school he was shipped back to England, spending his holidays with the Stracheys at Lancaster Gate. In this strange house, among children of his own age, he was very happy. 'The paved floors, the glass-coloured dome on the staircase, the little hidden servants' staircase creeping to the top of the house, the vast drawing-room, endless bedrooms, nurseries and hidden kitchens and all sorts of basements, made it a most fascinating haunt for a child.' Destined for a military career, he had in due course been entered with James Strachey as a day boy at St Paul's, where he was placed in the army class and instructed in such subjects as mathematics, of which he understood nothing. But Lady Strachey, aware of her nephew's true artistic potentialities, at length succeeded in persuading his parents to let him study at the Westminster School of Art. 'The great excitement is about Duncan,' she wrote to Lytton in December 1901, 'who appears likely to turn out a genius as an artist, at least so the experts say. But what to do with him is the difficulty.' For, in the traditional style of genius, Duncan seemed to benefit little from orthodox teaching and eventually failed to gain admission to the Royal Academy School.

From his father, Duncan Grant had inherited a love of music and an aesthetic sensibility; from his mother, as a self-portrait painted in 1911 clearly shows, his beauty. 'His face is outspoken,' Lytton wrote to Leonard Woolf (October 1905), 'bold, and just not rough. It's the full aquiline type, with frank gray-blue eyes, and incomparably lascivious lips.' As a youth he often wore a dirty collar, usually upset his afternoon tea, and never knew what time it was. When he spoke he blinked his eyes, and generally carried on in such an irresponsible fashion as to convince his uncle, Trevor Grant, that he was a hopeless and possibly certifiable imbecile. His pleasing appearance, however, was matched by a correspondingly attractive personality for those who knew him well. He was entirely natural and unconstrained in manner, possessed a lively entertaining mind, was keenly observant, but, less happily perhaps, given to practical jokes.[19]

Lytton's feelings for Duncan Grant were very far from being just skin deep. In fact he disapproved of affiliations formed solely by physical appeal. 'I know there's a sort of passion,' he wrote, ' – an animal feeling, a passion without affection, which is merely bodily pleasure, and doesn't count.' It was certainly not this that he desired, but rather an ideal union in which lust did not destroy companionship, and where genuine affection and friendliness did not diminish passion. Only through such an immaculate relationship could the disparate elements within his own nature, the conflicting will and imagination, be satisfactorily integrated; only thus could his strange, immaterial spirit of fantasy and romance be heightened, his nagging ambitions assuaged vicariously.

In these first years of exile from Cambridge, Lytton wished above all else to be an artist – a literary artist it would have to be – yet he was racked by agonizing doubts as to his capabilities. The man of action was beginning to seem too remote and immature a vision of perfection, and as it slowly faded so it was replaced by a different breed of hero, the painter, the musician, the creative literary genius. But fears of his own inadequacy pressed in on him as he laboured over his book reviews. 'Perhaps', he wrote, 'the truth is that I'm not an artist. But what the devil *am* I?' In his perplexity he looked for

19. In D. H. Lawrence's *Lady Chatterley's Lover*, Duncan Grant appears under the name of Duncan Forbes: 'that dark skinned taciturn Hamlet of a fellow with straight black hair and a weird Celtic conceit of himself'. For an account of the meeting which took place between Lawrence and Grant, see the letter Lawrence wrote to Lady Ottoline Morrell on 27 January 1915.

someone on whom to centre his complicated emotions, and towards whom he might escape from the tightening ring of his deflated egocentricity. And it was on Duncan Grant that he fastened.

In all his infatuations, even those at school, Lytton was endeavouring to relinquish his own personality and assume in its place that of the person loved. It was therefore only to be expected that he should now fall in love with an artist. 'Let's both be great artists and great friends,' he exhorted Duncan Grant. 'Je t'embrasse de tout mon coeur.' Once he had succeeded in establishing himself as a literary exponent in the arts, the direction, though not the nature, of his desires would accordingly change, aiming once more for the impossible. After *Eminent Victorians* he would again venerate social and physical splendour, and worship blue-eyed rowing Blues and handsome young Old Etonians. But these days were still far off. For this reason, however, there was always something ingenuous about his love-affairs, a quality of most extreme urgency within the aura of ethereal day-dream, where a sort of divinity seemed to clothe his senses.

Now, while his self-confidence was at such a low ebb and he followed an aimless, lonely existence, haunted daily by the thought of failure, the figure of Duncan Grant seemed to exemplify in dazzling fashion the very reverse of all his own personal shortcomings. He was a star shining miraculously in the black vault of the heavens, to which Lytton would hitch his battered and decrepit wagon. For in his view Duncan Grant was undoubtedly a genius, and destined to triumph in one of the noblest creative spheres known to man. 'He sees everything, you know,' Lytton told Keynes excitedly (18 November 1905), 'and he's probably better than us. I have a sort of adoration. When I hear people talking about him I'm filled with a secret pride.'

The obverse of this adoration was an exultant self-abasement. All his life Lytton tended to gravitate naturally towards the role of victim. At school he had attracted bullying; and he sometimes magnified his illnesses to extract from them a rarefied contemplative pleasure – though he hated sickness in others as the dreaded evidence of mortality and decay without their more delicious symptoms. In his adult love-affairs something of this pattern repeated itself, for he manoeuvred himself without fail into acute distress. Sometimes his complaints were well-founded, sometimes they were delusions; but almost always he himself was their own architect. Duncan Grant was genuinely fond of him, but Lytton's intensive emotionalism produced in him the terror of an affection greater than he could absorb. He felt overloaded by Lytton's hypersensitive attentions, his kindnesses, his claustrophobic possessiveness. For it was not simply that Lytton longed to assimilate his body, but to take, as it were, vacant possession of his very soul. Duncan, on the other hand – and he was unlikely to have attracted Lytton's attentions had it been otherwise – felt little wish to intermingle or even surrender his own identity. The responsibility for supporting Lytton's own emotionalism was too excessive, and he set about erecting a network of defences to demonstrate that he could not be taken over in this fashion. In order to evade the full rigour of Lytton's love he went to work presenting himself as a person totally unfitted to receive such romantic affections. He tried to cut the very ground from beneath Lytton's feet by reversing the current of eulogy and self-abasement. Lytton, he wrote, was 'too good, too true, too great'. He despised himself 'for not being of the fine clay that could fly with you into limitless space for ever', though, of course, he still felt for him 'a very great friendship and the utmost regard'. Over and above this modest degree of fondness, he suggested, Lytton's sentiments were wasted. As for himself, he was little better than a brute; his affection was on a lower level – nothing more than a perverted form of calf-love; he could never match the wildness and nobility of Lytton's passion.

But to all these evasions and dissimulations Lytton had a ready answer. Duncan, he explained, had overestimated the wonder and supremacy of his emotions simply because he, Lytton, was better able to give expression to them. It was merely a matter of being older. And all the while he seemed, partially at any rate, to thrive on this self-induced ill-treatment; it gave him such an emotional kick and, above all else, it preserved intact his adoration. For Duncan Grant's tactics to dilute the strength of Lytton's infatuation, though subtle, were unconvincing. Towards anyone who was absurd enough really to think highly of him or hold him in great affection Lytton automatically felt less. He returned admiration with something of a diminution of feeling. After all, he despised himself so utterly that he could not think well of a person who was taken in over so vital a matter in human relations. What, in a sense, he demanded from those on whom he fixed his love was a contempt so powerful as to blast and obliterate his own personality without trace. He laments repeatedly that Duncan Grant is stand-offish, unkind, indifferent: and at the same time he worships him all the more. 'Duncan tortures me. But a crisis must happen soon. I find him perfect,' he wrote. He was in a torment lest the unbearable torture should cease; lest he should fall out of love, and back into nothingness.

In the intervals between these painful spasms, he reflected lingeringly on his own heightened reactions to everything around him. He was, even in the ordinary course of things, of a highly sensitive disposition, prone to dizziness whenever he was swept by any sudden gusts of emotion. At concerts and in the theatre he invariably sat at the end of the row in case he should faint; for any excess of feeling always threatened to overwhelm his fragile body. This risk of losing consciousness naturally increased when he felt himself to be in love – a condition to which he was extremely susceptible, since the image of his love was so powerful that it often betrayed him into aiming at it when the reality was not there. While in these infatuated states of mind he became hyper-emotional to an astonishing degree. Describing the sensations which would consume and ravage him, Lytton frequently couples together the words 'dim' and 'intense', to indicate that any overplus of violent feelings automatically brought about a fading away of his physical awareness. From boyhood onwards, it was precisely this wretched, hateful self-awareness that he sought to eradicate. To transfer it from his own body to that of his partner was the logical apotheosis of all his passions, and one which he never fully accomplished. Half-way he does seem to have reached – expelled out of himself but injected into no one, and so wasting away into the thin air between. Exhilarated, semi-conscious, he would float like some astral projection of himself, suspended precariously *in vacuo*, a luminous, misty and insubstantial phantom hovering on the edge of an unimaginable paradise – *Lytton Strachey in love*. But always, after each crisis of dizzying emotional high tide, he would be sucked down again into the sickening depths of his own, ultimately inescapable personality.

Lytton's friendship with Duncan Grant lasted many years, but it was probably never more intense – at least on Lytton's part – than during the winter of 1905–6. 'I have fallen in love hopelessly and ultimately,' he wrote to Clive Bell (17 January 1906). 'I have experienced too much ecstasy, I want to thank God, and to weep, and to go to sleep.' While Duncan, on the other hand, persisted in acting 'almost as though he were afraid of me, of my affection – as if he didn't dare to face something he couldn't reciprocate', Lytton grew more and more deeply obsessed with the idea of being in love with him. The affair prompted his most romantic and highflown vein: 'One feels that one might, by some extraordinary twist of the will, make everything all right; and one comes against an adamantine and irrevocable rock which no power under heaven can move. Shall one dash oneself against it? That's the only question. I generally seem to do both, which is the worst solution.' Yet this did provide some sort of temporary solution, for it kept in a state of perpetual animation the repressed vehemence of his exultation – a state in which radiant happiness and delirious misery were so strangely intertwined. 'He [Duncan] is the full moon of heaven. I rave, and you may judge of my condition when I tell you that it's 4 p.m. – the most utterly prosaic hour of the day,' he confided to Maynard Keynes (8 December 1905). '. . . At the present moment I feel capable of achieving every wonder, of rising to incomparable heights! Good heavens, last night my despair was too absolute.' Lytton's admiration for Duncan Grant developed in double harness with a corresponding dislike of himself. 'I am sometimes miserable,' he ended another letter to Maynard Keynes, 'I am often desirous, I am usually unconscious, and I am always your G.L.S.' As the ardour of his affections strengthened so he felt himself liberated from the husk of G.L.S., pushed by the sheer pressure of his emotions into a strange, new multi-dimensional existence. 'I live in a mist,' he wrote to Keynes on 21 December ' – perhaps a golden one – where most ordinary things are fluctuating and dim. My nerves have quite gone. I seem to be in direct and mystic contact with the Essence of the World. The air is full of divinity, and the music of the spheres enchants me as I walk.' And in another letter describing the occult perceptivity shed upon him by his emotional excitement, he writes: 'I feel that as long as I keep up my spirits all will be well. But we do live in a queer eminent world. Perhaps – I don't know – a trifle unreal.'

Towards the end of December an event occurred which seemed about to change the dream into a living reality. This was nothing more devastating than a 'Grand Conversation' in which Duncan Grant explained his feelings to Lytton, and convinced him of his genuine affection. Lytton was at once overjoyed, and wrote off to Keynes the next day to delineate his fresh onrush of passion: 'My own crisis – oh lord God! I hardly know what to write. All that's obvious and before my nose is that he's absolutely mine. I haven't the nerve to think of the future; and, for the present, though I'm cheered, happy, proud, perhaps even rejuvenated – I'm too battered and pale to feel the high supremacies of joy. I don't know – I can hardly believe – is it possible? ... We have reached the reign of Affection – but one can't expatiate; one can only accept.'

The swift reaction away from this new enthusiasm was characteristic. Lytton and Duncan had been invited by Lady Colvile to spend the first week of January at her home, Park Cottage, at Ledbury in Herefordshire. By all that was strictly rational Lytton should have been delighted. But he was not. Everything was going rather too well for his taste. On the face of it, he had to admit, he was in luck. What could be more pleasant than the prospect of Ledbury with Duncan? But then it was sure to be all sham – *mere* enjoyment, mere blind, spurious, moonstruck ecstasies. His accustomed role was as the victim of some bitter and hopeless passion, and any other part made him uneasy. Besides, Duncan could not have much of a brain if he in fact thought so well of him – as it really seemed he did. Either he was a fool or a consummate liar. The infatuation began to ebb, his jubilation to become marred with doubts. Love was like faith – one didn't like to lose it until one had, when one couldn't understand why one ever wanted it. 'I begin to wonder whether his [Duncan's] intellect is satisfying enough,' he confided to Maynard Keynes (31 December 1905). 'I can imagine myself bored. We're to go to the Cottage at Ledbury on Wednesday, and I almost dread five days tête-à-tête.' He was beginning to suffer the pangs of requited love.

Lytton's fears, however, proved to be unjustified. The days at Ledbury were full of turbulent and unpeaceful happiness. It was impossible not to offend someone in Lytton's tense, supersensitive condition, someone, moreover, who almost cherished persecution. 'Nothing definite has happened,' he reported back to Keynes at one stage. 'I was blissfully happy till suddenly he said something which brought it over me in a sudden shock that he didn't care for me, and wanted to escape.' On the instant Lytton relapsed into a 'wretched state'; he despaired of everything and gave himself up to thoughts of death. Duncan, in response, complained of his moodiness, of the wild incoherent terrors that afflicted his soul. And all at once Lytton was head over heels, madly infatuated again. No question of boredom now. He laments of pouring out his affection into a bottomless pit, of Duncan's total lack of reciprocation; and he reflects with terror on the possibility of their friendship coming to an end. Without Duncan he felt he was nothing. The voluntary nightmare and the dream merged into a blissful, self-obliterating fantasy: 'But how often didn't I feel that it was he who was the great person and that I was a mere ineffectual shade!' he wrote to

Keynes a few hours before leaving Ledbury (9 January 1906). 'His mind! – I didn't realize before what it was – the audacity, the strength, the amazing subtlety. . . . But please remember – he's a *genius* – a colossal portent of fire and glory. His feelings transcend all – I have looked into his eyes, and the whole universe has swayed and swum and been abolished, and we have melted into one indescribable embrace. His features were moulded by nothing intermediary, but by the hand of God itself; they are plastic like living marble, they clothe a divinity, a quintessential soul. I rave; but I weep too. Looking at his face, I imagined last night the marks of Time upon it. I saw the lines and the ruins and the desolations of Age, I saw Death too, and the face composed in Death; and I prayed that the whole world might stand still for ever.'

In the second week of January, Lytton returned reluctantly and alone to London and took up the bare threads of his old existence again. He tried hard to be cheerful during this time. His pessimism and the agitations of his spirit only upset Duncan Grant, the one person he wished to make happy. But it was little use; he was 'a damned morbid selfish idiot'. Sometimes he even welcomed minor illnesses, which enabled him, for the benefit of others, to trace his defects to a definite cause. People who experience a kind of tension over nothing, or at least nothing they can pin down, were, he knew, the ones who suffered most. It was something of a relief to be able to attach some temporary physical diagnosis to his complaints. 'I'm pretty ill,' he explained to Duncan Grant on succumbing to a cold in the head, 'and in the very highest spirits.' But the cold passed and the symptoms of debility persisted. He felt that he would like to go away by himself and forget everything for a few weeks. The long, unsatisfactory dragging on of his affair with Duncan was a sort of painless torture, but he could not bring himself to creep away. Each week he saw Duncan once or twice, no more; just enough to revive and exhaust his passion. 'I like seeing him so much, and I'm so horribly unhappy when he goes away,' he told his Brother Confessor. But perhaps the worst part of all were the blank periods between these meetings, days of lassitude, nights of agonized introspection, twilight moments of terrifying, sense-less indifference. Duncan seemed so unpredictable too; at times charming and expansive, on other occasions secretive and off-hand – more friendly, even, towards Lytton's brother James.

As the days crawled by, bringing no solution to his problems, Lytton's preoccupations concentrated inwards, and he grew pitifully maudlin: 'Don't think of me, please, as perpetually unhappy,' he implored Duncan (25 January 1906), ' – only as a muddle-headed, well-meaning, weak-kneed creature, who generally manages to get along better than one might expect, but who sometimes stumbles and lapses.' Ledbury seemed a hundred years away. By the beginning of February he despaired of ever attaining the ideal love after which he was seeking, and sank into 'a sort of utter melancholy at the hope-lessness of attainment, the impossibilities of ever reaching the complete, the absolute, the adored. One's love seems to be sometimes so far above oneself – one despairs.' The vision of a mystic reincarnation had faded and disappeared, and he was sucked back into the prison of his own feeble, ugly frame. Everything now revolted him, was tainted with his own disgusting putrefaction. 'The whole world stinks in my nostrils,' he cried out to Maynard Keynes (1 February 1906). 'I stench in my own nostrils.'

4

MEN IN LOVE

Describing himself as 'a little shattered' in the months after leaving Cambridge, Lytton seemed to nourish no real appetite for life. He felt no desire to enter the roar and turmoil of the London circus on just *any* terms; he wanted to excel, to impose upon its vivid animal chaos the kind of manufactured coherence that is to be found in his best books. His ambitions, like his love, were rooted in a sense of personal insufficiency. Just as his passions came to him as an imaginative form of envy, so his quietly assertive will fed on frustration and was reinforced by his inability to escape from envy through fantasy and infatuation. Like many homosexuals, too, he felt somehow outside the common social run of humanity, and this sense of dissociation stimulated his determination to succeed.

But in 1906 he was unknown. The busy metropolis passed him by, and he hated it. London was a hideous, unaesthetic muddle; the grotesque existing in such close proximity to the plain, squalor rubbing shoulders with overloaded luxury, a lack of all reasonable satisfying order, a disconcerting unnatural alternation of beauty and shabbiness, and running through it all the senseless tempest of noise, corruption and vulgarity. It was not simply a matter of architecture and acoustics. London presented to him a spectacle of the adult world, the complexities of whose relationships appalled him. He shrank from all its heedless, cruel confusion. Even Bethlehem, and all it stood for, was preferable to this raucous, twentieth-century capital, for at least Jesus Christ hadn't been a typical city hypocrite, a brutal money-maker and womanizer. 'I want to go back to childhood,' he confessed to Duncan Grant (5 February 1906), 'to be two years old, like Ethel Melville's baby, who has been lunching here, and as exquisite, charming and divine. Talk of the feelings of dogs! Pooh! All goodness seems to me to dwindle into nothing when I look at a child of two. I'm willing to forgive our friend J.C. for all his delusions, stupidities, and wickednesses, because he really did understand so thoroughly that *they* are Heaven itself.'

Duncan had recently been given by his aunt, Lady Colvile, a hundred pounds for his twenty-first birthday, and with this sum he proposed to continue his artistic education in Paris. Staying on at Lancaster Gate while Duncan was enjoying himself on the other side of the Channel was, for Lytton, a pretty bleak prospect, and he secretly hoped that, to make this separation easier, Lady Colvile would invite him down to her villa in Menton.

Early in February Lady Colvile did write to Lady Strachey suggesting that Lytton should pay her a visit. 'I'm going to the

South of France in a few days,' he wrote happily to Swithinbank (4 February 1906). 'This I feel to be wicked, as I've positively no excuse, and I can't see why I should bask in sun and roses, and other people not. However I suppose the world is arranged on these principles.' Yet, although Lytton felt that his flight to Menton might, as he put it to Keynes, 'save me from utter death', his mood was not one of unmixed elation. He knew, of course, that he must in any event part temporarily from Duncan, but as the date of their departure drew nearer he was filled with fresh agitation. 'I'm sad because I'm so futile and incompetent,' he explained to his cousin (5 February 1906), 'and because the thought of parting from you is a dull agony. I feel like a schoolboy at the end of his holidays, who knows that tomorrow he must go away from home. How dreadful to be an exile!

'. . . I don't see that there's anything to prevent my going as soon as possible. I think it may save me. Sun, flowers, Dorothy, and comparative comfort! Don't you think so? Please be sympathetic, for I am very sad, almost in tears.'

Since both Duncan and Lytton were going to France, Lady Strachey decided that the two of them had better travel together. Accordingly they set off on 18 February by train to Paris, and stayed one night at the Hôtel de l'Univers et du Portugal. The next day, Lytton left Duncan 'up 42 flights of stairs in the hotel', a little alarmed, but glad to be in France, and continued his gloomy journey south, alternately sleeping and writing long regretful letters back to Paris. 'It's very nice now – gliding along by the shore in a demi-trance. I often turn round to say something to you; why aren't you here?'

On his arrival at Menton, Lytton was met by Lady Colvile and Trevor Grant, 'a dowager aunt and a vagabond uncle', as he described them to Swithinbank, '(they're brother and sister not husband and wife)', who took him up to their home, Villa Henriette. 'This is a very small house,' he wrote to his mother (20 February 1906), 'but charmingly placed, the front rooms looking over olive-trees to the sea.' As so often, the sea-climate and scenery acted as a solace to the wear and tear of human affairs. The landscape seemed to blend into and become a condition of his spirit. Basking under the sun he could dissolve and quite forget the enervating confusion of his emotional life, could submerge himself beneath the mighty impersonal forces of Nature. The rocks and mountains appeared to draw out and absorb his personality, which evaporated into the quivering, fathomless air above. It was far from being the ideal process of bodily transubstantiation to which he would always aspire, but it was restful and recuperative. 'The sun and general exhilaration is wonderful,' he told Maynard Keynes immediately after his arrival (21 February 1906). 'I have high hopes of regaining health . . . I can hardly believe anything any more, I pass along in a dream, looking at peacock-blue seas, and talking to imbecile dowagers, and eating artichoke omelettes . . .'

And so the first days passed slowly by in health and apathy. He bought himself a rather dashing pair of green-yellow gloves and a very splendid and very cheap Monte Carlo hat, and would sit for long motionless hours on the terrace looking at the blue blur of the sea and sky through palms, olives and cypress trees. In a sense he almost ceased to exist as a separate entity, losing all count of space and time, and becoming part of the fixed, lunatic landscape. 'Imagine, if you possibly can, my infinite silence,' he wrote to Keynes. 'I've become at one with the rocks and trees. I respond if I'm spoken to, I give out reciprocal sounds; voilà tout! I've lost count of everything, the day of the week, the number of reviews I ought to be writing, the length of time I've been without seeing Duncan, the name of the founder of the Society – all, all has gone. I can only think of whether the Protestant Church ought to have a new organ loft, and of how much Mrs Trollope loses per week at bridge. The word reminds me – I believe I was once – I have some memory – I don't know though – *was* I once at Cambridge? Are you there now? I wonder. No, no, I think it must be the colour of the sea that I'm thinking of – if it really is sea and not scenepainting. – But after all, what can one expect of one's state of mind when one's reduced to reading the works of W. W. Jacobs? – "The captain turned in his chair and regarded his daughter steadily. She met his gaze with calm affection.

' "I wish you were a boy," he growled.

' "You're the only man in Sanwick who wishes that," said Miss Nugent complacently.'

Lytton was as happy during these early days as it was possible for him to be, cut off from Duncan Grant. He thought about him constantly. Their few days together in Paris on his return journey would be the happiest of his life. Meanwhile his happiness was suspended, lying remote in the back of his mind. 'Now that I've sunk into middle-age,' he wrote to Maynard Keynes (7 March 1906), 'a quiet married life is all I look forward to, for myself, and for everyone else.'

But as his 'shattered nerves' mended, so his latent discontent began once more to mount. The sky and the sea were all very well, but after a while they grew infinitely tedious. Together they might form a beautiful background, but as things stood, it remained a background for nothing in particular, an empty stage. He missed his youthful talented friends and felt a good deal in the wilderness, discovering no one at Menton to take their place. The local boys too were rather disappointing. Their olive complexions and bare necks looked at first sight promising, but on closer inspection they nearly all turned out to be too dirty and too stupid to be tolerated. 'I have seen no one of even respectable looks for almost a week,' he complained to Keynes (24 February 1906), 'and I am becoming a little impatient ... I suppose I ought to be thankful for what I've got – sun, comfort and plenty of books – and I am, but Lord! the flesh is weak, and it's difficult not to think sometimes of what *might* be. However, it's no good talking.'

Some distraction was provided by the antics of Lytton's aunt and uncle, both of whom were, by all his accounts, highly extravagant characters. About Lady Colvile, a figure apparently of Elizabethan force and colour, rich, musical and refined, he would recite stories in his letters to Duncan Grant – the kind of amusing trivia which always appealed to his sense of the ridiculous. 'La tante Elinor has so far been fairly well under control,' he reported back during

305

the first week of his visit. 'There is a wretched imbecile of a French maid called Nina whom she worries at meals rather, but that's all. I relapse into the pathetic silence of a delicate youth, whenever I see anything like a crisis approaching. This has an excellent effect, and Nina (who deserves it) is immediately blown up for serving the currie before the rice, or for not putting the Oriental Pickles on the table.' But a week or two later 'Aunt Lell' began to suffer from *twinges* and retired to her bed. Even in illness she struck Lytton as quite magnificent: 'Aunt Lell is exquisite – perhaps tragic,' he wrote (6 March 1906). 'Her hands are enough in themselves to prostrate one; and even her face I find absorbing. I saw her the other day in bed, without her wig. You can't conceive the difference. She looked terribly old.'

As a result of Lady Colvile's sickness, Lytton was thrown together rather more with his uncle. Trevor Grant was an ex-Indian civilian, vague, well-intentioned and somewhat cranky. To keep out the heat he wore an enormous overcoat (even in winter) and spent most of his waking hours in all seasons noisily draining down cups of coffee, reminiscing about the past, and reading the day before yesterday's copy of *The Times*. Lytton was half fascinated, half repelled by this grotesque spectacle and he described his uncle in the terms of some freakish zoological specimen. 'We get on pretty well,' he assured Duncan Grant, ' – he talks, and I do my best to listen appreciatively – it's not very difficult, as it's all about old Indian days, and fairly amusing. . . . He's rather trying in some ways. He makes the most disgusting swilling and squelching noises when he's eating, and I sometimes feel that I shall shriek if it goes on for a second longer. It does, and I never do – such is my virtue, or cowardice. The truth is that he is a vagabond, not an ordinary civilized human being accustomed to live in houses, behave at table and so on. He ignores all that, and floats dimly on in his dim self-centred way. Sometimes I see him at dusk prowling along the seashore in his long flapping overcoat – a mystic solitary figure. What can he be thinking of? His sons? His photography? Old Indian days? Clementina? Death? Nothing at all? . . .'

Not long after Lytton's arrival in Menton, Trevor Grant returned to England, and his place at the Villa Henriette was taken by another of Lady Colvile's brothers, George – the complete antithesis of Trevor, very spruce and haughty and English. Removed from his natural habitat to the South of France, he seemed pathetically out of place, and no one – certainly not Lytton – could find anything to say to him.

Presently another member of the family joined the household. This was a cousin of Lytton's, Alfred Plowden, a magistrate of Marylebone Police Court.[20] Most of his holiday was spent at Monte Carlo, where he went for the sake of the tables and his smart friends, all of which Lytton austerely deplored – though it is evident that at times he felt something of the attraction of this bright tinsel life. 'Everything there [at Monte Carlo] is made out of painted cardboard,' he told Swithinbank (9 March 1906); 'the palm-trees are cut out of tin, there is always a band playing, and one feels as if one ought to be in tights and spangles.' As for Alfred Plowden himself, he struck Lytton as being one of the silliest creatures he had ever come across – 'a sort of hopelessly non-existent character who simply walks about on the stage and vanishes into space when no one else is there', he described him to Duncan Grant (7 April 1906). 'A Personnage de Comédie, I think, pure and simple.' And in a letter to Maynard Keynes he remarked (2 April 1906): 'It's really quite painful to feel as superior as I do to him. He even feels it himself. Poor man!'

Shortly before Alfred Plowden left, an incident which took place on the railway platform suggests that the glimmerings of some mute sympathy might have arisen between them. 'I saw him to the station the other evening,' Lytton recounts (8 April 1906), 'and as we waited for the train the fearful noise of the croaking frogs made him say, "I wonder what they can

20. Alfred Plowden, a first cousin of Lady Strachey's, was a tremendously celebrated figure in the popular press during the early years of the century. Like Mr Justice Darling, he was famous for the jokes he made in court, and readers of the halfpenny papers could find them quoted almost every day. His daughter Pamela, a great beauty and the first love of Winston Churchill, married the second Earl of Lytton who was for a time acting-viceroy of India.

be doing?" I couldn't help bursting out with, "I think they *must* be copulating." The Police Magistrate did smile.'

Undisturbed by the comings and goings of his various relations, Lytton spent 'the days here pretty lazily', he informed G. E. Moore (28 March 1906), 'though I have breakfast at a quarter to eight. I write a few reviews, and spend the rest of the day having tea with ladies of sixty.' In fact he wrote just two pieces for publication in these weeks – his essay on Blake which appeared in the *Independent Review*,[21] and a long review of Augustine Birrell's *Andrew Marvell* for the *Spectator*. Much of his morning was given over to the writing of letters – to G. E. Moore on Society matters, filial and fraternal letters to the family assuring them that Dorothy Bussy, then about to bear her first child, was being properly looked after, patriarchal letters reassuring his aunt, Ethel Grant, about the supposed degenerative influence of Paris on her son Duncan, love letters to Duncan Grant, and letters about love letters to Maynard Keynes. But perhaps the most surprising part of his correspondence on this holiday was with Edmund Gosse. Lytton's critical essay on Sir Thomas Browne, which had given him so much trouble to compose during December, had been based on a volume of Gosse's, recently issued in the 'English Men of Letters' series. In January he had written a second anonymous review of this book, rather more disparaging to Gosse, for MacCarthy's *Speaker*. It was the substance of these two articles that formed the basis of their

21. Published in May 1906. On 7 April, Lytton wrote to Duncan Grant: 'With some difficulty and agitation I finished my review of Blake. It is for the Independent, and will I hope appear in the May number. It annoys me to think of the poor result of so much effort. After it was finished I felt worn to the bone – a "poor, pale, pitiable form", as he says himself. But I'm now more or less cheerful again. My dear, he's certainly equal to the greatest of poets – though I somehow failed to say this properly in my damned review. His poems are the essence and sublimation of poetry.

> Poor, pale, pitiable form
> That I follow in a storm;
> Iron tears and groans of lead
> Bind around my aching head.

Isn't it a triumph? And almost too much?'

ensuing correspondence. In Lytton's view Browne's works, unlike those, say, of Byron, were not of the kind which needed, in order for them to be properly appreciated, a biography of the author to serve as commentary. 'The Glasgow merchant who read through *Don Juan*,' he wrote, 'and asked at the end whether the author was a married man was surely in need of some enlightenment.' For writers like Browne, on the other hand, it was sufficient to know that they had lived, and Gosse's book would have gained if it had told its readers 'a little more about Sir Thomas's style and a little less about his sons'. Chronologically, Browne belonged to the seventeenth century but his idiom had much in common with the Elizabethans. What could be more futile, then, than to seek for simple constructions and homely words in the pages of Browne's prose? In attempting to do just this Gosse, so Lytton maintained, had attacked the central principle of Browne's style, 'its employment of elaborate and gorgeous latinisms'. Gosse was like a man who admired the beauty of a butterfly but did not care for the wings: 'To the true Browne enthusiast, indeed, there is something almost shocking about the state of mind which could exchange "pensile" for "hanging" and "asperous" for "rough", and would do away with "digladiation" and "quodlibetically" altogether. The truth is, that there is a great gulf fixed between those who naturally dislike the ornate, and those who naturally love it.'

As a correspondent Lytton found Gosse no less uncongenial than as a critic. Perhaps the most amusing aspect of their letters is that Gosse, in defending the use of biography as a legitimate aid to literary criticism, seems to be upholding a far more enlightened principle, which is nevertheless partly contradicted by the example of his own too tactful life of Browne and partly by his over-polite and somewhat cloying epistolary style; while Lytton, dealing deftly with all points of the controversy, writes in a livelier, more amusing and up-to-date manner in order to defend a notion which is incomplete and, in the most deadly sense, academic. In the end perhaps Gosse had the best of the exchange, if only because each of his letters, its contents dull as night, was written on House of

Lords cream-laid, extra thick, imperial octavo notepaper, and brought with it an excess charge of fifty centimes. 'I think of replying on an unstamped postcard,' Lytton told Keynes after paying out several francs in instalments, ' "this correspondence must now cease." '

Besides writing reviews and letters, Lytton did a lot of reading, sometimes for his work, sometimes for pleasure, but always with the curiosity and fastidiousness of a born bibliophil. 'I'm now reading Lockhart's *Life of Scott*, Blake's poems, and the Correspondence of Voltaire,' he wrote to G. E. Moore (28 March 1906). 'It's a frightful mixture – but if one's a JOURNALIST what can one do? I read the first because I want to have read it, the second because they do me good, and the third because I like it – or because I think I might. How charming it would be to "tear the heart out" of books, like Dr Johnson! That's to say, if one liked hearts. I think I prefer the spinal marrow.'

Of these books, and indeed of all the books he read during this time, his favourite was Voltaire's Correspondence. Letters, he once told Lady Ottoline Morrell (31 October 1916), were 'the only really satisfactory form of literature', because they gave one the facts so amazingly and drew one right into the world from which they had been written. The kind of enjoyment he derived from Voltaire's letters, the gossip and illuminating if often petty idiosyncrasies which brought to life the figures from the past, is well conveyed by a *risqué* passage in one of his own letters to Maynard Keynes (27 February 1906). 'I'm reading Voltaire's Correspondence,' he wrote, 'which is the greatest fun to me imaginable. There's a poor Abbé Desfontaines whom he hated like hell because he criticized his wretched tragedies, and he works himself up into a splendid fury. At first he merely says the Abbé had been in prison; then that it was for Sodomy; then that it was for Sodomy with a chimney-sweeper's boy for Cupid – and so it goes on in letter after letter. At last there comes a little poem describing the rape, and how the Abbé was seized by the police in flagrante delicto, stripped and birched – 20 strokes for sodomy and 30 for his bad verses. It's really all very scandalous; and I think it's pretty clear that Voltaire himself had had affairs.'

One other book which he read during these two months deserves mention. This was *Henry Sidgwick: A Memoir* by A. and E. M. Sidgwick, which had just then been published and was the main subject of conversation among all Apostles. Their impatience with the lack of intimacy in its tone, of boldness in its thought, and of lucidity and crispness in its style, epitomized the dawning twentieth-century revolt against the approved standards of the nineteenth. The free-thinking Sidgwick was certainly a most eminent Victorian, and the Apostles' sharp revaluation of him as man and philosopher has been seen by some as a key to the general change in attitude among all thinking people at about this time. Yet, perhaps because the break with the Victorian age was not complete, the *Memoir* provoked an involuntary fascination in most Apostles. 'I have never found so dull a book so absorbing', Keynes told Swithinbank. The same note of paradoxical interest is more elaborately sounded by Lytton in a letter to G. E. Moore: 'My last great intellectual effort was the perusal of Sidgwick's life. I wonder if you've read it. I found it extraordinarily fascinating – though I can't think why, as *every* detail was inexpressibly tedious. I never realized before what a shocking wobbler the poor man was; but my private opinion is that his wobble was not completely honest – I believe he did it because he wanted to, and not because he thought it reasonable. Really his ethical reason for postulating an Almighty is a little too flimsy, and I don't see how an intelligent and truly unbiased person could have swallowed it. His letters irritated me a good deal – but perhaps you wouldn't find them so. The conscientiousness and the lack of artistic feeling combined occasionally drove me wild. Also the tinge of donnishness – however, I suppose one must forgive a good deal quia multum amavit.'

With Maynard Keynes, who had already read the book and written to him about it, Lytton felt freer to discuss its full implications, the peculiar remoteness which it lit up of those past times from their own new age of reason. Sidgwick was, of course, very Apostolic, but how different he was from them! Obviously Victorianism had incapacitated him. 'What an appalling time to have lived!' Lytton exclaimed in horror. 'It was the Glass Case Age. Themselves as well as their ornaments, were left under glass cases. Their refusal to face any fundamental question fairly – either about people or God – looks at first sight like cowardice; but I believe it was simply the result of an innate incapacity for penetration – for getting either out of themselves or into anything or anybody else. They were enclosed in glass. How intolerable! Have you noticed, too, that they were nearly all physically impotent? – Sidgwick himself, Matthew Arnold, Jowett, Leighton, Ruskin, Watts. It's damned difficult to copulate through a glass case.'

After mornings spent reading and writing, Lytton would pass the rest of the day in more social pursuits. 'Both Aunt Lell and Uncle Trevor apparently live in a whirl of tea-parties,' he wrote to his mother in the first week of his holiday. 'Uncle Trevor I believe adores it, though he pretends to groan and moan.' Lytton too, while groaning and moaning quite as loudly, seemed to derive some amusement from them, and like a well-conducted person allowed himself on every possible occasion to be taken to all the tea-parties, lunches and picnics. He went almost daily to the Bussys at La Souco, where he had stayed two years before, and the house seemed, if anything, even more delightful. 'You can't imagine how exquisite their tiny garden is – all intricacies, covered with every variety of growing things,' he wrote in a letter to Duncan Grant (5 March 1906). 'There are brilliant orange and lemon trees quite close to the house, and a large cluster of large white daisies, and clumps of wallflowers. Too divine, and all seen at a glance in the brilliant sun.'

The Bussys themselves appeared radiantly happy. But Dorothy's pregnant state disgusted Lytton, and he was vastly relieved once he had successfully been delivered of a niece, Jane Simone, in the first week of March. He had always liked and admired Dorothy, though he had not, until now, thought very highly of her husband. The sudden reversal in his attitude was another instance of that feeling which so influenced these post-graduate years – a veneration of the true artist, accompanied by a complementary abasement of himself as an instinctive yet hopelessly unfulfilled artist. This new response, quite different from anything he had felt in the spring of 1904, is most clearly conveyed in a passage from one of his letters to Duncan Grant, a passage which also reveals by implication the twin source of his envious admiration for the unlettered man of action – another form of self-contempt which had been paramount at school and university, and would rise again in later life. 'I admire Simon very much,' he wrote (25 February 1906), 'and I wish I could speak to him. I think he thinks me lazy – and I am – and he can't bear the idea of people being lazy. He urged me to begin a great work. It was a curious moment or two, in the twilight, at the window, looking out over the splendid Monte Carlo bay. I didn't know what to do, I couldn't speak French, and, even in English, what could I have said? – "Allons, Lyttone, allons!" – He was superb, and I was perfectly out of my depth. How could I explain – oh! what I can hardly explain to you – my utter inability to take "art" and "literature" and the whole bag of tricks seriously?[22] ... I nearly burst out to him – "Je suis obsédé! Obsédé par les personnages!" Only I didn't, because it couldn't have done any good, and the French seemed more than doubtful. So it ended up in an awkward silence and I went away half in tears.'

With Simon Bussy, too, he discussed in detail the problem of whom Duncan Grant should elect to study under in Paris, and how he should plan his year there. It was as a result of their deliberations that he became a pupil of that excellent teacher, Jacques-Emile Blanche.

Before the other inhabitants of Menton, Lytton could resume his mask of incredulous superiority. The English resi-

22. In a later part of this letter, which was written the following day, Lytton added a significant amendment. 'I find that I didn't quite say what I meant last night, about my not taking "art" seriously. I suppose I do, in some way or other, though not in the way that "artists" do. But I can't quite make out what exactly I mean.'

dents in particular used to give him many fits of the giggles. In a mad helpless sort of way, the congregation of 'characters' struck him as really too grotesque – fit only for the pages of Flaubert. Never had he come across such an appalling corporate mass of dullness, especially at those tea-parties which the dowagers of the place gave twice an afternoon with unfailing zest. As if unable to credit his senses, he went again and again. Perhaps he was 'seeing life'; perhaps it might all prove good material for some dramatic comedy he would later compose and which would carry all before it, making him and his friends millionaires.

'Oh heavens!' he wrote to Duncan Grant after staggering away from the first of these gatherings (25 February 1906). 'All the females were so much alike that I hardly knew whether I was talking to complete strangers or to the Countess [Pallavicino] or Harriet [Codrington] herself. Mrs Hodgson is a relief, as her nostrils are apparently amputated, so that I can recognize her pretty well. But Miss Scott, and Miss Egerton, and Miss Duparc! – They have all long red noses, they are all 45, they are all hopelessly respectable and insufferably cheerful.' Most eccentric of all these bright-nosed quadragenarians was Lady Dyer, a cross between a vicar's wife and an ex-governess, invariably dressed in a long velvet cloak with fur edges and a round yellow straw hat trimmed with pale mauve chrysanthemums. Lytton rather recoiled from the forceful personality which went along with this bizarre uniform, and 'came to the conclusion finally that she is a complete vulture. Her red pointed nose and her moulting fur added to the effect.' But from out of this matronly gynaeceum, it was Miss Egerton – 'a pretty terrific female, 38 wishing to be 28, with a long red nose which shoots triumphantly over the abyss' – who finally established herself as the most formidable. She took to reading Lytton's palm, and to conducting him on forced marches along the coast. Having heard of, though not read, Bernard Shaw, she soon confessed to being cleverer than most people in Menton, and graciously allowed that Lytton might be almost as clever as herself. This, however, may only have been flattery, since she had written an article on the 'Holy Land' which she had illustrated with photographs of her own, and she hoped with Lytton's aid to get it accepted by the *Strand Magazine*.

The men of Menton were even odder than the women — mostly plain, old, paralysed majors. By far the most redoubtable of this troupe were Mr Bax Ironside, a distant cousin of Lytton's nicknamed 'Mr Iron Backside'; a doddering inhabitant by the name of Stainforth who collected spiders; and Major Horrocks who, though blind, always spotted the lurking figure of Lytton from the very opposite end of every crowded drawing-room, and compelled him like some infinitely decrepit Ancient Mariner to listen to descriptions of his many diseases, eczema especially. Lunacy among the men though was not confined to the English residents, but extended, in an inarticulate fashion, across the Italian border — or so at least Lytton deduced from an encounter with an Edward Lear-like character on one of his few excursions into Italy: 'I strolled into Italy the other day — I honestly believe there's something different in the atmosphere over the border,' he wrote to Duncan Grant (5 March 1906). 'At any rate it's a great change to go from the dreary respectable villas of this side to the cabarets, guitars, singings, and dancings of the other. The comble was reached when I met a highly respectable personnage in overcoat and felt hat, who suddenly drew up in the middle of the road opposite me, and began to jump. The dear man! I really believe I should have joined him, if I had happened to have the wherewithal.'

When he was not flirting with virgins of fifty or encompassed by the military, he took himself off for solitary patrols along the shore, side-wise, like a crab, with his face to the sea and his back to the mountains. At other times he would lie out on the terrace at the Villa Henriette, gazing blankly over the still, blue limitless Mediterranean — 'any colour from peacock to an incredible *pâleté*' — in a state of the merest collapse and too lazy even to feel ashamed of himself. Below, in the bay, he watched a huge steam yacht belonging to the Rothschilds, and dreamt of owning it himself, of christening it *La Belle Espérance* and floating out in it over purple seas for ever and ever, with his chosen companions, reading Voltaire and drinking champagne. His weariness with humdrum reality and with the humdrum people round him quickly stimulated his appetite, which, once gratified, brought on recurrent attacks of dyspepsia. 'I can think of nothing nowadays but the next meal,' he confessed to Keynes; yet after only a boiled egg and a cup of coffee he suffered acutely. Though his general health had certainly improved since leaving London, his digestive system, for no obvious reason, remained 'indescribably infamous'. He enjoyed good food tremendously, yet he was now meticulous as to what and how much he ate, even to the point of giving up the delicious French coffee which he loved so much, for cocoa, which he did not like and which, in addition, did him no good. In fact none of his gastronomic sacrifices seemed to help. Indigestion stubbornly persisted. Each morning he woke starving, and at night went to bed famished.

In his brooding state, Lytton grew anxious for more Cambridge gossip, eager to exert some distant influence, revivifying to himself, on the Apostles. His letters to Keynes, Ainsworth, Moore and others are written as from an imaginary outpost to the central point of Reality. Yet despite this anxiety for news, he felt little wish to quit the torpid amenities of Menton for the cold, Christian shores of England. 'I gather from the papers that it's snowing in England,' he wrote to Keynes on 14 March. 'Why does anyone stay in that blasted country? I have had to draw my chair under the shade of an olive tree, for fear my complexion might be ruined. Venez, venez vite!'

Keynes, in fact, was then on the point of leaving England. Both he and Lytton had been invited by the Berensons to 'whirl through Italy in a motor-car' and to put up at their villa, I Tatti, at Settignano. Lytton had 'judiciously declined', but Keynes accepted with alacrity, and the two of them arranged to meet for a few preliminary days in Genoa before Keynes went on to join his hosts. And so, in the third week of March, Lytton boarded a steamer at Monte Carlo, which, he told his mother (20 March 1906), 'was packed with Germans who talked at the tops of their voices to each other without intermission; but there was an old American who came up and talked to me, telling me his life history, etc. How he had made his pile, and was now travelling with his wife and daughters. He told me that he thought Europe was a very interesting place, and that he reckoned the Mediterranean was one of the oldest seas on this planet. I agreed; but when he went on to say that in his opinion the gambling rooms at Monte Carlo exemplified Our Lord's saying as to the danger of building houses on the sand, I felt obliged to demur. His final conclusion was that I was "a lord in disguise", and I didn't deny it.'

The only completely satisfactory moment of the whole expedition was the steamer's entrance into the harbour of Genoa, the weather being brilliant and the spectacle very splendid and gay. For the remainder of the time the wind blew and blustered and the rain poured down incessantly, so that he was especially glad to have Keynes to talk to in the dark interior of the Hotel Helvetia, where they spent many hours together. On the whole Lytton preferred these hours to the hours of sightseeing, feeling that he would have been quite content to stay for ever in those Helvetian recesses, eating omelettes – which he was now able to digest properly – and discussing ethics and sodomy with Keynes. Some sightseeing, however, was deemed compulsory. 'The palaces were simply écrasant,' he wrote to Duncan Grant (26 March 1906). 'We felt like miserable marionettes, beneath their vast and endless bulks. The staircases were particularly incredible. I tried to imagine Marchionesses, etc., sweeping up them, but could hardly believe that they'd ever reach the top. The pictures were mostly of the Bolognese school, and they certainly didn't come up to the Roger Fry level. But among the 40,000 that we saw in the 40 palaces that we went into there were about 6 which it would have been delightful to have.'

These few days in Genoa with Keynes rather unsettled Lytton. On his return he felt more keenly than before the limitations of his life at Menton. Everything was so negative and spinsterish. He made up his mind to work – and did nothing. Accompanied by his invalid aunt he was solemnly driven round the 'Battle of Flowers', was pelted by every hand, and pelted back as hard as he could. But it was a depressingly chaste affair. All the while he gazed out eagerly for a decent-looking boy, and saw not one.

'I begin to talk to myself as I believe prisoners do in solitary confinement,' he confessed to Keynes (8 April 1906). Above all he longed in vain for some warm words from Duncan Grant, and felt increasingly depressed at not being able to do anything himself but express his sentimental affection by post. For all this, there was only one compensation: the calm, ominously unsensational routine of his life must, he felt convinced, be doing him a power of good. Like all restorative medicines, the taste was unpleasant, but the cumulative effect would be most welcome. The absence of all emotional strain and stress was so excruciatingly dull that it *had* to be beneficial.

That was how matters stood when, early in April, Duncan Grant did write. It was a short letter, but it had something cataclysmic to communicate, which 'I suppose I must blurt out as fast as possible. Hobhouse as you know has been staying here and I have fallen in love with him and he with me.' This, he hurriedly went on, made no difference to his friendship with Lytton, and he hoped that Lytton himself would not feel differently. He signed himself 'your ever loving Duncan'.

The immediate shock numbed Lytton. He knew that Duncan wanted to be reassured about his reaction, but he secretly believed that this mad, totally unforeseen development would in fact make a real difference to their friendship. It was true, of course, that they could like each other as before, and even go through, as before, the dreary phantasmagoria of desire. But they could never be *alone* together. In what he described twenty-four hours later as 'a hysterical letter', he wrote back to Duncan Grant: 'I think you may think me cruel, or sentimental – or both; especially, I think, if the "you" is in the plural number. – No, no! Don't be angry! Think of me, please, as a poor damned daffed human being,

318

but a human being still, who would give his ears to be talking to you. Good heavens! I occasionally burst into fits of demoniac laughter to think of the incredible muddle of everything and everybody.'

At first Lytton appears to have been overcome more by pandemonium than actual unhappiness. He wrote at once, of course, to Maynard Keynes to break the news to him in a letter which is longer and even more excitable than the one to Duncan Grant sent by the same post. 'I'm still gasping,' he admitted. 'I don't know what to feel — I only have the sensation of the utter unreality of everything, and even this blessed landscape, when I look at it, seems to waver in a wild mirage. God forgive us all! What a hideous muddle! — I have wept and laughed alternately and at the same time, wildly, hysterically, ever since I read it. Oh, how I long to talk to you! I think what I mainly feel at present is a sort of stupor. I have subsided; I'm waiting to see what will happen next.'

For some days this stupor persisted. He still didn't know what to think. Perhaps it was altogether too bizarre to take very seriously, a mere insane episode signifying no more than an added twist in the grotesque abortion of their lives, which would make no palpable difference to anything or anyone, unless, that was, he became simply a maniac in jealousy. In any case Hobber and himself hardly figured as rivals. The notion was too ludicrous. Or was it? At times he felt as if he was losing his head. The whole thing seemed lunatic from beginning to end, more vicious and chaotic than anything that ever happened in the world before. He felt as though he had heart disease. His pulse beat deafeningly through his body, and rocked him to the very spine like the recurrent vibration of a pneumatic road drill. It took his breath away. He wanted to laugh and cry simultaneously — why he scarcely knew. 'As I walk along the road here I want to collapse among the passers-by in one heaving ruin of laughter,' he wrote to Keynes; 'and sometimes I do burst out. They stare, but if they could only know the whole story — the whole incredible, impossible, inexhaustible complication — well I suppose they would collapse too.'

But after a few days the whole affair sickened him. It occurred to him that it really was a drawback to the 'New Style' of love that the chance of complications should be exactly doubled. No doubt Christians would hold that this was the right and proper punishment for unnatural emotions. However, perhaps the added amusement made it worthwhile. He still burst into uncontrollable fits – but there was little happiness in his laughter, only a stunned incredulity. At this rate no one would be able to remember off-hand who was meant to be in love with whom, or whom, indeed, they were supposed to be in love with themselves. The permutations and combinations in the constantly changing molecular structure of this kind of loving were without limit or logic. But what hurt more than anything else was the realization that Duncan Grant, who he had thought really loved him in his own strange, undemonstrative fashion, in fact felt no more for him than an amiable attachment, though this was in itself so good that it almost made up for everything. And his depression was deepened by the discovery that Duncan's more intense feeling was directed towards someone of whom he, Lytton, disapproved.

Duncan's revelation plunged Lytton back again into the baffling intrigues of human affairs from which he had originally escaped to the South of France. At one blow the soothing dullness of Menton was exploded. 'This place is so vilely relaxing that I believe it's undermining my health,' he explained to Duncan. 'I get tired very easily, and the other night I had the most horrid palpitations.' In a half-hearted sort of way he was longing to see Duncan in Paris again, especially since Hobhouse was returning to England. But he did not know whether his arrival would embarrass Duncan, and in any case doubted whether he had the courage to tell his aunt that he wanted to leave. Two days later, however, his physical and mental condition had deteriorated so markedly that it provided a legitimate excuse for his return. 'My health is completely shattered,' he wrote to Keynes (15 April 1906), 'and I cannot stay here in relaxation and solitude. . . . Anyhow it is now *certain* that D is not and was not in love with me. I dare say in our old age we'll come together again. His charm-

ingness in his letters is incredible, and I love him à
l'outrance.'

Later that same week Lytton left Menton, but on the train
northwards his fever rose dramatically. On reaching Paris he
got off and dragged himself round to the Hôtel de l'Univers et
du Portugal, where he at once retired to bed and summoned a
doctor who prescribed quinine in large doses to bring down
his soaring temperature. 'I am here,' he announced to Keynes
after a few days in bed (23 April 1906), 'I think recovering, but
I have been very ill. How I got here I hardly know; my
weakness was complete, and my depression almost absolute. I
fear my health may be appallingly weakened. But at the
moment I'm better.' Nevertheless he looked so wretchedly ill
that his sister Pippa was sent for to escort him back on the
remainder of his journey home. No sooner were the two of
them ready to depart, however, than a railway strike crippled
the whole of Paris, and they were obliged to stay on a further
week.

This was for Lytton a time of uninterrupted torment. He
woke up each morning in tears, wondering what he had to live
for. The Society? It was a poor substitute. Sometimes his
frail, supine body was convulsed with a terrible anger when he
reflected on the way things had turned out; and sometimes he
lay there too exhausted to be angry any more. In his fevered
state, he thought a lot about Hobber, and wondered what
there could be in him to damage everyone so devilishly. There
was something aphrodisiac about the role he had played in
all their lives – a grain of love-powder that worked hell. And
once again his circling imagination was drowned in a sea of
horror – his own rich ineptitude and Hobber's rewarded folly.
But why think of him? Duncan was doing enough of that. But
even as he attempted to expel these sick and infected wanderings from his mind, an unexpected letter arrived from Hobber
in England. It said nothing much; but how the handwriting
shocked Lytton, rekindling his excitement when he first saw it
on a letter addressed to himself. What a muddle it all was!
What a muddle!

Each day Duncan would come up to his room, sit at the

foot of his bed, and talk. He was kind, amusing, gentle, considerate – everything up to the very verge of what Lytton wanted. But it was not the Duncan he used to know – the boy in the orchard at Great Oakley, or during those wonderful few days at Ledbury, or the young painter in his romantic studio in Hampstead, or even, less than two months back, up those forty-two flights of stairs in this same hotel. He seemed larger and stronger, irradiated no doubt with visions of Dicker. Never could Lytton have believed that he might actually come to fear his presence, and long to escape from it. How ironic it was that every evening at Menton he had looked forward to these few days in Paris! They were to have been the happiest of his life!

But abruptly his mood would change. And 'then I know what a fool I am, what a miserable fool, for why should I be distracted and humiliated and lost? Why should I madly beg for strange unwilling kisses, and be happy for a moment amid that warmth and that diminutive sweetness? Why should I cast you from me with horror and mortal anguish, and with unsatiable adoration, and with intolerable desire? Oh yes, I know you are Duncan still.'

By the first week of May, Lytton and Pippa were at last free to return home. 'I'm rather wrecked, and fear all sorts of doctorings and wretchednesses may be necessary,' Lytton wrote to Keynes shortly before leaving. At the Gare du Nord Duncan came to see them off, and was given an embrace by Lytton. They travelled by easy stages, spent one night at Dover, and the next day were re-engulfed into the noise and gloom of London.

5

INFLUENCE FUNESTE

The doctorings and wretchednesses that Lytton had predicted continued for about three weeks. The family physician, after examining him thoroughly, came up with a new diagnosis and course of treatment. 'My health is I think improving gradually,' he was able to report by 16 May. 'Poor old Roland seems to be doing his best. He says that my disease is that there is not sufficient room in the lower part of my torso for my lungs, liver and lights, so that they are liable to press in an inconvenient way upon the heart, which is in itself superb. The cure is to be a course of terrific "exercises" of the most ghastly and depressing type, which it is hoped will expand the frame to a more reasonable size. I haven't begun this yet, but in the meantime am allowed to drink nothing at meals, as liquid'll do nothing but wash away all the nourishing matter. . . . My depression is usually pretty heavy, but I suppose it will improve with health.'

Much of this spring was spent in bed. Between the drinkless meals and terrific exercises he tried his hand at writing a short story, but his enthusiasm quickly cooled, and the piece was never completed. He wrote copiously to his friends, some of whom were able to come and visit him. But he was more amicable on paper than in person. When Desmond MacCarthy offered to introduce him to Max Beerbohm, he declined on the grounds that he had no wish to be infinitely bored. Maynard Keynes also came and visited him, staying a couple of nights at Lancaster Gate. But Lytton was critical of his friend, and when Pippa remarked that she thought Keynes was growing old too rapidly, he felt inclined to agree with her. 'I'm afraid,' he wrote to Duncan Grant with a hint of prophetic foresight (16 May 1906), 'that in three years I may find it impossible to speak to him [Keynes].' As yet, however, there was no one remotely suitable to take his place. 'You are the only person I can speak to,' he assured Keynes again in October. 'Pippa is unconscious. And my mother!'

In the final week of May, as soon as he felt robust enough to get up and go out, Lytton dashed off to Cambridge where he felt sure that he could count on some scandal to revive his spirits. Whenever he stepped into that train at King's Cross, he was reminded of some lines from Baudelaire:

> Je m'avance à l'attaque et je grimpe aux assauts,
> Comme après un cadavre un chœur de vermisseaux.

At Trinity he spent five heavenly days with all his old friends. Everything seemed more enchanting than before. Cambridge was more beautiful now than ever it had been when he was an undergraduate. But then it was always fatal to live in a place: one must keep continually on the move. At one point during this visit he caught sight of Hobber, looking, he thought, rather unhappy. Altogether, it was an entirely satisfactory week, and he enjoyed himself immensely. 'It was delightful to feel conscientiously lazy,' he wrote to Duncan Grant (31 May 1906), 'and to glide about in the canoes among the lilac and laburnum and horse-chestnuts, and to watch the cricket, and to eat strawberries, and to talk about whatever one liked.'

He was now working again, too, at his essay on Johnson, a review for the *Spectator* of J. C. Collins's *Studies in Poetry and Criticism*, and, for MacCarthy's *Speaker*, an article based on J. E. Farmer's *Versailles and Court under Louis XIV* — which, wrote the Indian scholar K. R. Srinivasa Iyengar, 'concludes with a description that could have only been inspired by a personal visit'. Lytton had found this book waiting for him on his return to Lancaster Gate and, after glancing through it, wrote off to Duncan Grant: 'I have been sent rather a fascinating book to review — on Versailles and the court of Louis XIV. It is full of plans and pictures, and I think it ought to be amusing to write about. I hope, with the aid of your descriptions, to be able to make it appear that I have constantly been there. The poor deluded public!'

Once more he bobbed back to Lancaster Gate, and once more he was off again to visit Bertrand Russell, at Bagley Wood, Oxford. 'We have been, of course, amazingly brilliant here,' he informed Pippa (9 July 1906). 'The only other guest is an American lady literature professor (also Quaker), who is nice, cultivated, etc. Bertie informs me that he has now abolished not only "classes" but "general propositions" — he thinks they're all merely the fantasies of the human mind. He's come to this conclusion because he finds it's the only way in which to get round the Cretan who said that all Cretans were liars.'

That summer the Stracheys had rented Betchworth House,

near Dorking, a large country mansion with a magnificent long gallery, and standing in park lands which enclosed a trout stream, golf course and tennis courts. Here Lytton lingered for seven painfully domestic weeks, surrounded on all sides by his family, visited by Maynard Keynes and Harry Norton, and working on his essay 'Mademoiselle de Lespinasse' for the *Independent Review*.

The thought of being drawn back to Lancaster Gate again to spend there, without interruption, the darkening autumn and winter months, was full of the usual horrors, and Lytton eventually decided to make a peregrination into the extreme north of Scotland, staying with Clive Bell and his family who had gone up there to fire off guns at Scotch animals. At least this would be a month's break from the gloom of Bayswater, an invigorating if not particularly lucid interval.

He set out from London on 9 September and stopped off for a day and a night in Edinburgh, staying with G. E. Moore and A. R. Ainsworth at 11 Buccleuch Place. 'Moore', he reported, 'was quite cheerful, and played most of the Eroica with the greatest verve.' The next day's journey north to Lairg, his eventual destination, was not without terrors. The train was so late at Inverness that there was no time for lunch, and he was able to eat nothing but a bun and a banana between breakfast at Perth, and dinner at Lairg itself. He had also given up all hope of finding his luggage, which had disconcertingly vanished at Inverness, but which, to his incredulous relief, was magically waiting for him as he rolled into the Lairg platform. He was met at the station by a gay and wonderfully golden-bearded Clive Bell, sitting, like Toad of Toad Hall, at the wheel of a dangerous-looking motor-car;[23] and together they whirled away for twenty tremendous miles over breakneck roads through absolute deserts, lakes, mountains and sunsets. 'The motor drive was somewhat terrific,' Lytton afterwards wrote to Pippa (11 September 1906), ' – the road is decidedly dim, and one bumps and leaps and shrieks as I

23. Professor Quentin Bell tells the author that Lytton was probably inexact in giving this description. Clive Bell never did and never could drive a car.

imagine one might on a buck-jumper. But the fascination of the movement is intense, and I am glad to say that every journey has to be made on it.'

The Bells appeared to be camped in a tiny 'shooting-box', set loftily on the edge of Loch Merkland. As for the family itself, Lytton's first impression of them was that they were all hearty, dumb, deaf and, except for shooting, quite blind. Yet, curiously enough, he felt that the long journey had been abundantly justified. 'We are on the edge of a loch, high up, on Ennick heights, with nothing but moors and mountains for 20 miles in any direction,' he wrote to Pippa the day after his arrival. 'Lairg is 22 miles away, and there is only one house between here and it. The country is exquisite, with vast long lakes streaming one after the other, and beautiful pale hills. It is quite unlike Rothiemurchus — far less distinguished of course, but also far more completely remote and inhuman. The house is quite small, mostly made of tin, and entirely lined with pitch-pine walls, floors and ceilings. ... I intend secretly to have a shot at a stag, or at any rate to try to, before I come away. Everyone is very "hearty", and one's appetite is too.'

After ten invigorating days at Lairg, Lytton travelled south to Feshie Bridge, to join Maynard Keynes, Harry Norton and James Strachey for what has been called 'a last wild excess ... of talk upon the old subjects'. Here, in a cottage about six miles south of Inverdruie, the four of them had found rooms, from which they would set out on terrific excursions into the mountains — one of them, to Ben Muich Dhui, being at least a twenty-five-mile walk as well as a stiff climb. Lytton also hoped to undertake a comprehensive tour of the Western Highlands, but none of his companions were keen, and he was forced to abandon the scheme. 'I could find no one adventurous enough to share the perils,' he complained to Moore, 'and what are perils unshared?' Early in October therefore he returned to England, breaking his journey again at Buccleuch Place.

Presently he was back at Lancaster Gate, and his old routine of life re-asserted itself at once — an occasional theatre, a general state of debility, and frequent encounters with his friends, chiefly MacCarthy, Norton and Sanger. 'What a vale of desolation is No 69!' he exclaimed in a letter to Keynes; but there seemed no further way of escaping it. He quickly resumed his essay-reviews – on Walter Scott for the *Speaker*, on W. P. Ker's *Essays on Medieval Literature*, and Sidney Lee's *Shakespeare and the Modern Stage, with Other Essays* for the *Spectator* – and at the same time recommenced his shuttling back and forth between Cambridge and London. 'I have been to Cambridge once this term,' he wrote on 12 November to Moore, whom he had agreed to accompany to the great annual feast, Commem, 'and am going there again next week. The Society seems to be going on all right: Keynes is constantly there. No very promising embryonics seem to have appeared yet, though I have some secret hopes of the young Charles Darwin.'

The even tenor of his life was abruptly shattered, when on 21 November he read an announcement of Thoby Stephen's death in *The Times*. 'I am stunned,' he wrote immediately to Keynes. 'The loss is too great, and seems to have taken what is best from life.' The following week he was invited by Vanessa and Virginia Stephen to their home at 46 Gordon Square and told all the details: how Thoby on holiday in Greece had been suffering from what was supposed to be pneumonia, but how his illness had turned out to be the fatal typhoid. To all three of them, who had known him so very well, such a fate seemed even now impossible. The monolithic, the immortal Thoby dead – it did not, despite their certain knowledge, ring true. But Maynard Keynes, who had known Thoby mainly through Lytton's legendary accounts of him, wrote: 'He seems to me now, I don't know why, the kind of person who is doomed to die.'

Lytton was now seeing a lot of Keynes, who had just come down from King's convinced that he was far and away superior to the examiners who had dared to place him only second in the Civil Service examination. At the end of November he stayed a few days with Maynard and the Keynes family at their home in Harvey Road. The two Cambridge exiles planned to spend part of December together in Paris, where Keynes could get to know Duncan Grant better, but since Lytton would not receive payment for his last batch of reviews until January and Keynes had not enough money to pay for them both, they decided instead to go for a week to Rye, putting up at the Mermaid Inn where Lytton had some years previously taken Sheppard. 'The inn is comfortable,' Lytton wrote to Saxon Sydney-Turner, 'but the weather cursed cold. We go out for duty-walks in order to get up appetites for too-constant meals. I am halfway through the Brides' Tragedy; as you said, it's not a patch on the Jest Book[24] – but it has some superb things. – "I've huddled her into the wormy earth!" '

Shortly before Christmas, Lytton returned to Lancaster Gate. After finishing *The Brides' Tragedy,* he now turned for the first time to Charles Darwin, and was enthralled. During the next month or two he read nothing but the works of Darwin, whom he came to consider one of the greatest stylists in English literature. Huxley, whom they all praised so, was a signboard painter in comparison. 'I'm reading the Descent of Man,' he wrote to Duncan Grant on 30 December, ' – it's most entertaining, with any number of good stories about Parrots, Butterflies, Capercailzies and Barbary Apes. The account of how the Peacock grew his tail is a masterpiece. But the chief charm is Darwin's character, which runs through everything he wrote in a wonderful way. I should like to show you some passages in his Autobiography – really magnificent! He was absolutely good – that is to say, he was without a drop of evil; though his complete simplicity makes him curiously different from any of us, and, I suppose, prevents his reaching the greatest heights of all.'

This discovery of Darwin was the single bright spot to a year which closed for Lytton in much confusion and anguish. His sickness during these final days of December came as the last and mildest of a series of indigestion attacks, palpitations of the heart, high fever and piles which had plagued him on

24. *The Brides' Tragedy* (1822) and *Death's Jest Book* (1850), both by Thomas Lovell Beddoes.

and off throughout the autumn. These ailments seem to have been closely associated with his emotional upsets, the cause of them being, once again, the presence of Duncan Grant, who had returned to England for a few weeks' Christmas holiday. Lytton's feelings on seeing him again fluctuated wildly, he told Keynes, between '(1) Excitement, (2) Spiritual affection, (3) mere lust, (4) Intellectual interest, (5) jealousy, (6) Boredom, (7) Despair, (8) Indifference'. And of all these moods the most prevalent was despair. They were seldom if ever alone together. Nevertheless, at many of these meetings, Lytton felt that he showed with horrible transparency the repressed and surging effervescence of his emotions. He tried to speak to him about important things which concerned them both, but failed miserably. And all the time Duncan appeared utterly uninterested, perhaps even unaware of the hideous turmoil going on within him. From the cruel phlegmatic way in which he seemed to avoid his company, Lytton felt sure that he must still, after all these months, be enraptured with Hobber. He found it difficult to understand how someone of such intelligence could have lost his judgement so completely. His faith was being put to a severe test, and his hopes dreadfully postponed. But then, he reflected, perhaps he was wrong to think of it in this light. It was the nature of one's passions, not their object, that counted. Then, once more, his mood would shift, and such philosophical evaluations would appear superficial and irrelevant. Everyone seemed to possess some strange compound element within him, which baffled analysis and turned intellectual judgements into dreams. He and Duncan and Keynes were like characters in Shakespeare – the Hamlets and Cleopatras, whom no one could fix down with thumb-nail definitions.

As the days and weeks of autumn slipped by, merging into winter, the weather grew colder, the attacks of one illness or another more acute, the emotional frustration increasingly desperate, and Lytton felt that he had reached about the end of his forces. He was weak, and his torments of mind and body were more than a strong man could bear. He could neither sleep nor work, and physically he was reduced to a wreck. 'I am really ill,' he insisted from his sick-bed in a letter to Keynes, ' – too ill to go round to you, as I should like to do. What will happen to me? My body was hideously bouleversé and still is. Oh God! I have suffered too much.'

But even in the lowest depths of his unhappiness he did not regret his feelings because they had brought him sorrow. That was the sin against the Holy Ghost – to blaspheme one's best affections, which were one's Holy Ghost. His outpourings to Maynard Keynes were cries for comfort from the agony of a paradise lost:

> Me miserable! which way shall I fly
> Infinite wrath, and infinite despair?

There was the true meaning of his question. How to extricate himself from the seemingly inescapable trap into which he had fallen? His infatuation flourished under a disillusion continually deferred. Duncan Grant's apparent coldness inflamed his unhappy passion which was at some moments sublimated in renunciation, at others overcome by a frenzied desire kept in circulation through perennial restraint. His impotent wrath and despair intermingled and formed the main content of his letters to Keynes: 'That that little devil should despise me, and with justice, is my lowest infamy,' he wrote on 28 November. 'That he should register my tears, and dishonour my abandonments, my failures, the miserable embraces I can't withhold! – That he should say that he pities me perhaps! – I want to shake the universe to dust and ashes! Hell! Hell! Hell!'

In dramatic contrast to the wild, stormy emotionalism which rose behind the dams of his everyday self-discipline and flooded over the pages of his almost everyday letters to Keynes, is the circumspect, diffident moderation of his correspondence over these same weeks with Duncan Grant himself. From these two concurrent and complementary sets of letters one is given not only a reflection of Lytton's peculiar duality, but also unequivocal evidence of the vain, obsessive shyness in his outward manner which has helped to spin the popular misconception of him as a dry, passionless, sublimely detached cynic, someone set aside from the current of life. He could never convey his love directly by statement or expostulation to the person loved. Instead of railing at his cousin's cryptic unresponsiveness, he merely expresses a vague and somewhat timorous wish that he could talk to him more. Of course, he adds hastily, it is no one's fault – the world itself is hardly made for talking.

Once this tone is set, the correspondence swiftly slides into a welter of mutual self-recrimination. After one unsuccessful encounter – at a family dinner at Lancaster Gate – Lytton writes to apologize in case he may inadvertently have said something – anything – during the course of the long dismal meal to offend his feelings. If he has been hurt, Duncan must forgive his, Lytton's, insensitive stupidity; if not, then he must forgive these superfluous and troublesome apologies. Whatever the case, Lytton demands forgiveness. Duncan, however, doesn't remember being pained, and is sure that Lytton would never hurt or offend him. Perhaps, he suggests, he had failed to comprehend something. Incomprehension can, physiognomically speaking, resemble pain – doesn't Lytton agree? In any event he himself intended to write to apologize about his beastly behaviour the previous week at a picture gallery they had visited together. He had felt out of sorts – and the pictures hadn't helped. But probably Lytton, with that incomparably generous nature of his, had already forgiven him. Anyway, it was of no special significance and Lytton must not, he begs, bother to answer this note.

Lytton's reply comes by return of post, expressing his gratitude both for the letter itself, and for the knowledge that his mania for inferences has led him astray. But he is horrified at Duncan referring to his earlier behaviour as beastly. On the contrary it was he, Lytton, who was at fault. He ought to have overcome his wretched sensitiveness – no, *selfishness* – and saved Duncan from feeling that he had been beastly. There had been nothing wrong at all except circumstances acting on his ridiculous nerves.

The tussle for forgiveness and for the onus of blame now warms up. Duncan at once counters Lytton's claim of selfishness with the plea that he himself is without a sense of humour. Not alone that, but he had got into the absurd way of crediting Lytton with special powers of telepathy, of knowing things automatically without being told them. This had, in fact, once led him to be enraged at a joke Lytton made about Hobber, with whom he was still hopelessly in love, but whom he was trying to forget. He saw now though that, even if Lytton had known the truth, it was foolish of him to have done anything but laugh. In his answer Lytton once again quickly shoulders all the available blame. He had got into the habit, he explains, of making jokes at serious things; it relieved (to his mind) the heaviness of existence; it was like the drops of lemon on a pancake. He was truly sorry for what he had said, and was pained at Duncan having been – legitimately – enraged with him. Was it only a blind tantrum? Perhaps the whole affair was more complicated than that. 'I'm afraid,' he wrote, 'that it may have been something more – that you may have thought, perhaps, that I didn't really care. Your not being certain that I realized that you were still in love with him makes me think this too. I don't want you ever to think of my feelings, but I did hope that you simply *knew* how much I cared.'

The last unforgiving word in this particular series of exchanges belongs to Duncan Grant: 'My brutality was rather a bitter return for your perfect goodness. When I look back and see what I have ever given you in return for it, I nearly collapse at my perfect unworthiness. O! Lytton I really mean it, when was there anyone so unselfish and noble as you. If it weren't for you I am sure I should not be able to bear life now.'

The labyrinthine pattern of Lytton's emotional life seemed to be set irrevocably in the original passions and inspirations of the past. True, Thoby had gone – but his need for a distant pedestal-hero was now less urgent than before; and besides, Thoby would later be replaced by George Mallory, the handsome mountaineer also fated to die young, who, so the unlikely story goes, once prevented the Trinity bloods from ducking Lytton in the college fountain. The brief reappearance in London of Duncan had proved to him, if proof were needed, that the other figures remained as dominant as ever – fixed points between which he was suspended, and the sudden disappearance of which could quite possibly bring about his own extinction. At any rate he could see no one as yet to take their place. 'What will happen to me?' he had asked Keynes; and so far as he himself could tell, the answer was, Nothing. He would continue living with the family at 69 Lancaster Gate; he would continue visiting Cambridge; he would continue his career as journalist, writing occasional articles and reviews for various papers; and, above all, he would continue revolving like a half-dead satellite round the far-off Duncan Grant and sending out incoherent messages to Keynes. That was all. What else could there be?

Duncan Grant had disappeared back to Paris on 19 January without saying good-bye. The next day Lytton wrote to him: 'Last night, when I came down to dinner and saw that you had taken away grandpapa's portrait, I knew that you had gone, and was utterly crushed. It was all I could do not to burst into tears at dinner, and afterwards Mama asked me if I was ill, and I nearly gave way altogether.' A few days later his misery, bewilderment and sense of loss arranged themselves into a sonnet, 'The Enigma', which he composed while walking between Piccadilly and the Charing Cross Road. It is highly characteristic of all Lytton's versifications in its form, rhetoric and the type of outspoken innuendo which he was so fond of using to record the crises of his love life:

> Oh, tell me! – I have seen the strangest things:
> I know not what: beginnings, threads and shears.
> And I have heard a moaning at my ears,
> And curious laughter, and mysterious wings.
> Have friends or angels tricked me? Oh, what brings
> This river of intolerable tears
> Over my soul? And all these hopes and fears?
> These joys, and these profound imaginings?
>
> Will no one tell me? Ah! Save me, it seems,
> The puzzle's plain to all. I am as one
> Who wanders in an unknown market-place,
> Through bustling crowds with business to be done.
> Vain are my words, and my conjectures dreams.
> I cannot greet the unremembered face.

SEVEN

Intentions

'The dangers of freedom are appalling!' *Lytton Strachey to Duncan Grant* (12 April 1907)

1
JOURNEYMAN WORK

THE year 1907 was to see the first successive links in a tightening chain of events that, during the course of the next eighteen months, would completely split apart Lytton's old routine. No sign of these dramatic changes, however, was evident in the quiet, predictable beginnings to this year. Soon after Duncan Grant had returned to Paris – 'that DAMNED TOWN' as Lytton called it – he himself left for the Homeres at Chipping Norton. Here he was given a little upstairs sitting-room and, alone with 'Venus',[1] he remained quietly working at a memorial essay on his godfather, the first Earl of Lytton, his various *Spectator* reviews, and of course, his correspondence to Duncan Grant, without whose 'incredibly kind' letters he felt he would fade away into nothingness. As it was, he had become little more than 'a doddering old hermit, . . . the Diogenes of Kingham – to whom Cambridge is a dream and even London no more than a tale that is told'. Why were dreams, he wondered, so much more heavenly than actual life? Crouching over the hot gas fire, carrying on his involved epistolary conversations with Duncan instead of pounding on for the *Spectator*, his spirit seemed to vaporize and re-form into someone else, someone who could do and say all the things a woman was able to do and say. If only he had been a

---

1. 'Venus' was the name of Lytton's fountain-pen, so called because, to make it write, he had to twist the bottom of it, which caused the nib to rise from the waves.

woman! But alas ...! Yet, in these misty, androgynous trances he was perfectly contented. He wanted nothing else from the world, 'and I really think that if I had three wishes, I should wish for three fires – one behind me and one on each side of me – as hot as the one in front'.

His methodical seclusion at Kingham, however, was repeatedly invaded in the most unplanned and disturbing fashion. The Homere sisters, noticing his wistful expression, concluded that he must be unhappily in love with the beautiful Vanessa Stephen who, shortly after the death of her brother, had become engaged to Clive Bell. It was Ianthe – 'who always talks about interesting things' – who came out with their suspicions. Lytton shrilled with amazed laughter, at the same time secretly wondering whether it ought not to be as they imagined. But then, what was one to do? These distant meditations were soon brought up short by the passionate advances of Angelica Homere, the nymphomaniac youngest sister and a prime beauty, who, inflamed by a sudden, pointless jealousy, flirted with him so boldly that Lytton grew terrified lest she might get carried away to the point of actually launching a physical assault upon him. He was thus obliged to play an unaccustomed though ironically familiar role – that of Duncan Grant to her Lytton Strachey. Indeed, he believed that it was only by the most stringent severity that he managed to ward off a scene à quatre diables. Even so, the things she insisted on saying, despite his so visibly expressed fury! The dialogues he failed to avoid!

Angelica: Will you be in London when I'm there in March?

Lytton: I'm afraid I shall be in the country on a visit.

Angelica: Oh dear! I had looked forward to seeing you so much. ... D'you know that you're perfectly beautiful?

Lytton (casual and unmoved): Of course. I've always known that.

Angelica (in tears): Do you hate me very much?

Towards the end of his stay in 'Homereland' he wrote to Keynes: 'I have done no work but my health has improved tremendously. I can't go to C. this week, as I must commit myself to my godfather with the utmost stringency. What a bore!'

While he was still at Kingham, a letter arrived from Desmond MacCarthy announcing that later in the year he expected to be appointed literary editor of a periodical to be called *The New Quarterly*. This was excellent news, and spelt out the first real change for Lytton in his career as journalist. He would, MacCarthy told him, earn about one hundred pounds a year from his commissions, and the work would be pleasant – that is, he would not have to write about anything or anybody who did not interest him, and there would not be much to do. The time, Lytton felt, might then come for a bold stroke – if he could muster up the courage. He wanted to sever altogether his rather loose connections with the *Spectator* and, in the intervals between his *New Quarterly* contributions, devote himself to some major literary work. He would reconstruct his *Warren Hastings*, and, more exciting, compose a play – a tragic masterpiece on Queen Elizabeth. And then, of course, he would have to live apart from the family, on whom, at the same time, he must still remain to some extent dependent financially. The trouble was that the family prospects were in a worse way than they had ever been. The Secretary of State for India, 'honest John Morley', had refused pointblank to grant Sir Richard Strachey a pension, and no one knew what was to happen. Things were certainly breaking up. Yet MacCarthy's letter, in spite of all the problems and obstacles which it spotlighted, cheered Lytton immensely. It was the starting-point of something new, something for which he must even now prepare himself. 'I am trying to shake myself free of most of my entanglements,' he wrote to Dorothy Bussy, 'and when I've succeeded in doing so – ho! for the chef-d'oeuvre! At times, though, I feel as if I shall never be free. My hope is to eke out a subsistence with the aid of a New Quarterly Review which MacCarthy is going to bring out, and by that means to have time for masterpieces in the intervals.'

Soon after his return to London, Lytton saw Desmond MacCarthy and they discussed in more detail the new paper which MacCarthy hoped to edit. 'It's probably to be called the London Quarterly,' Lytton wrote to Duncan Grant after this meeting (11 February 1907), 'and may possibly come out in July. I had a long talk with MacCarthy about it the other day, and I'm to lunch with him today for more. He's a very wild editor, but he's cheerful and seems to believe in me. The publisher is Dent, who will do it free of charge in order, MacCarthy thinks, to get the reputation of dealing with first-class literary gents.'

Although nothing was yet firmly settled, Lytton felt that he ought to inform St Loe Strachey, his cousin and editor of the *Spectator*, of these plans. 'I interviewed him in his office,' he wrote afterwards to Duncan Grant (21 February 1907), 'and told him that for the present I should not review any more books for him – the first step towards Liberty! He was most gracious, and said that if ever I wanted to begin again he'd be charmed to let me.' He also invited Lytton to call on him at Herbert House, his London home – a large, archetypal Victorian mansion, with faded carpets, red plush curtains and coloured glass chandeliers – where he lived with his wife 'Oriental Amy' and where he was visited by a *bourgeois* group of hangers-on including the 'dull and vulgar' Sidney Lee. 'Poor dear old St Loe strikes me now as a trifle *épuisé*,' Lytton commented to James shortly afterwards, 'with moustaches more than ever fading, and even spectacles (when no one's there). Amy is *une matrone* in blue silk with amber necklaces. ... I went in some trepidation to call at their grand Belgrave Square mansion, but when I got there found such a *bourgeois* little group – Sidney Lee, and Mr and Mrs Skinner – all in laced boots, and hardly a frock-coat between them.' Finally, as a result of these meetings, it was mutually agreed that Lytton should, after all, continue his occasional reviews for the *Spectator* until his appointment as a regular contributor to MacCarthy's new paper actually came into effect.

2

CAMBRIDGE PEOPLE RARELY SMILE

As if to emphasize his new hopes of liberation and literary achievement, Lytton at once embarked on a succession of London gaieties – lunch at the Savoy, dinner at the Carlton and the Ladies' Athenaeum, a French play, a performance of *The Gondoliers* and *The Marriage of Figaro*. The hostess on all these occasions was that noble woman, Lady Colvile, who succeeded in introducing into Lancaster Gate while she was staying there this spring a new air of festivity. 'In the intervals of these orgies,' Lytton confided to Duncan Grant, 'I hope to finish my review of Lord Lytton for the Independent, but it's damned difficult. I lay on the butter as thick as I can – there's such precious little bread.'

The one topic of conversation among the Stracheys at this time was the first large-scale demonstration which the Society for Women's Suffrage was to stage in their nation-wide campaign for emancipation – three thousand ladies proceeding from Hyde Park Corner flanked by mounted police, to be harangued by leading zealots at Exeter Hall, in what subsequently became known as the 'Mud March'. Lytton's sister Pippa, who was later to win fame and distinction as the dynamic secretary of the Fawcett Society,[2] had succeeded in commandeering the services of both family and friends to assist with the organization of this parade.[3] James Strachey and Harry Norton were summoned from Cambridge to waft the ladies to their places in the hall; Keynes was conscripted to help marshal them in the park; and even the ineffectual

2. For her work as secretary of the Fawcett Society, Pippa was awarded the C.B.E. in 1951.

3. Mrs Fawcett was leader of the constitutional movement in favour of women's suffrage – a movement going back to John Stuart Mill. It was only fairly recently that Mrs Pankhurst and her supporters had started up a society which employed non-constitutional methods to gain the same objective. The Stracheys were old friends and colleagues of Mrs Fawcett, but they deplored the behaviour of Mrs Pankhurst and the Women's Social and Political Union.

Swithinbank was fetched up from Oxford to act as a supernumerary volunteer. Pippa controlled all, and interviewed the police at Scotland Yard daily. She actually persuaded the apprehensive Lytton to join the men's league for the promotion of female suffrage, even though he considered the whole thing rather a bane, and, at its worst, distinctly alarming. 'I believe the ladies will try to forbid prostitution,' he complained fearfully to James; 'and will they stop there?'

The grand procession was held on the second Saturday in February. As the crucial date approached, Lytton realized that he was not going to be able to face it, and fled away to Cambridge for the week-end. But here, too, he was solicited by inviting women, being asked to tea at Newnham with Mrs Sidgwick,[4] 'a faded monolith of ugly beauty, with a nervous laugh, and an infinitely remote mind, which, mysteriously, realizes all'. He also saw those of his friends who had managed to escape Pippa's vigorous enlistment – Sheppard, Walter Lamb, and Dilly Knox, about whom he had by now completely changed his mind. 'His beauty was transcendent, and his feelings seemed to me superb,' he wrote after seeing him just once during this week-end.

Under Pippa's astounding management the Suffrage procession went off without a hitch, and once it was safely over, Lytton felt safe to return again to Lancaster Gate. His quick, bird's-eye view of Cambridge had rather depressed him. He really must not allow himself to go there again until it was warmer. The cold had been preternatural – arctic nights, and days of frost and slush – he was not warm once the whole time. And the discomfort and untidiness of James's room which he occupied! – fires faint and few, draughts from every quarter, and the appalling sight of James's half-demolished breakfast with its broken eggshells and spilt tea over the table to greet him on arrival and again each morning when he rose

4. E. M. Sidgwick (1845–1936), the widow of Henry Sidgwick, who became president of the Society for Psychical Research, a body concerned with making scientific investigations of such phenomena as telepathy and séances. Though not a spiritualist, she eventually became convinced of the probability of survival after death.

at twelve from his icy bed. Left unaided to put the coals on the fire, he was unable to find a shovel, the tongs broke, and he was finally obliged to bend down and prise out each black lump with his long, trembling fingers. It was a nightmare. Even the miraculous divinity of Knox had not atoned.

For once then he was happy to go back to London. The round of dissipations started up again with Aunt Lell, and for a short time Lytton was 'as cheerful as a Kangaroo'. Life could really be exciting! Those waiters, for instance, at the Carlton! He almost fainted when they bent over to serve him with vegetables, brussels sprouts and peas and roast potatoes. Back at Lancaster Gate, however, everything was drab and dim. The lack of conversation grew increasingly over-powering, especially after the family dinner when there seemed no prospect ahead but silence until one tottered to an untimely bed. That silence, that grim, grey, arid silence, was so heavy that he was seriously tempted to make another mad dash for Cambridge. But the force of inertia and a sense of duty combined to keep him steadily at work. Result: a *Spectator* review on Herbert Spencer.

A subject of much worry now was the reluctant decision of the family to leave Lancaster Gate. The news left Lytton feeling curiously empty. Liberation had come too late. For twenty-five years the place had lain like an incubus upon his spirit until it had now become an indissoluble part of his whole scheme of things, interwoven with the very fabric of his nature. To leave Lancaster Gate and all that it stood for — such a thing seemed scarcely possible. As with the death of Queen Victoria herself, it appeared as though some monstrous reversal in the course of nature was to take place. He had never known a time when the great brooding mansion was not looming over him. But now he was simply told that the upkeep was too expensive for the family to sustain with their depleted fortunes — a common-sense explanation which hardly matched the significance of the change. Lady Strachey had decided that they should move later that year to a spacious, dilapidated house in Belsize Park Gardens, Hampstead. 'There is a basement billiard-room,' Lytton wrote to

Duncan Grant after inspecting the new house for the first time, ' – the darkest chamber I've ever seen in my life, and without a billiard table. Your mother, mine and I found ourselves locked into it, and thought we'd be discovered three crumbling skeletons – forty years hence. Fortunately I was able to leap a wall and attract a caretaker.'

Towards the end of February Lytton did return again to Cambridge. Following several long conversations with the serious-minded Norton, he came to the conclusion 'that he's DOOMED. It seems to me that he lacks will (just as I do, of course, and James, only it takes us in a different way) and that the end of it will be simply the Solicitor's Office, a wife, and £60,000 a year. He hasn't the will to disentangle himself from his own webs – just as J. and I haven't the will to entangle ourselves in any web at all.' It was queer how helpless everyone was about everyone else. People were unimpingeable units whirling on fated courses, and one could no more deflect them than a ghost. Their souls were so solid that flesh and blood seemed shadows compared to them, and an outstretched hand in contact with a moving spirit melted to nothing.

In company with Knox, on the other hand, Lytton at first seemed to make contact with something more substantial. It was a relief to talk to him after the DOOMED Norton. What struck him immediately about Knox was his resemblance to Swithinbank; and he was confronted with all the same difficulties in their relationship – the embarrassments, the lack of keen cerebral grip, the tantalizing fascination. To take just one example: one evening they held a discussion on the relative merits and demerits of sapphism and sodomy – a fruitful subject, Lytton should have thought, under almost any circumstances. And yet, though it was taken up as the most natural thing in the world, it simply petered out after a time into a dim miasma. Knox was as charming as ever – but it just wouldn't do. Lytton could see his future all too clearly; he'd be elected a Fellow of King's soon, and waste away his life in blind academicism. It came to this: he simply wasn't *intellectual* – and even Bob Trevelyan, *even Walter Lamb* was

341

that. It was a relief to talk to the DOOMED Norton after one of his discussions with Knox.

Lytton's failure to strike up any new important friendships, or to extend the boundaries of his old associations during these Cambridge weeks, came as a serious setback. The world was one vast negative, he reflected, and he was its full stop. Why then did he still hang about Trinity? There was no startling new embryo, no Rupert Brooke. 'I linger on vaguely from day to day,' he confessed to Maynard Keynes (27 February 1907), 'partly in the dim hope of excitement, and partly from being too lazy to pack. I see now, though, very very clearly that nothing will ever happen, and that life is all a cheat.'

But if there existed no positive excitements, there was still a fairly continuous stream of activity. Apart from day-to-day conversations, some solitary writing, a few lectures by McTaggart and other old familiar figures, and lightning week-end visits by Charles Sanger, Bertrand Russell and others, Lytton prepared and read out before the Society two long papers. The first of these, 'Was Diotima right?', is a reasonably orthodox analysis of the relation of truth and beauty to the nature of reality, and demonstrates once again, that, though Lytton might be a revolutionary in sociological matters, he remained pretty conservative in his attitude to the arts. The same basic division is revealed, too, in his second and more interesting paper, 'Do Two and Two make Five?', in which he contrasts the Platonist and Aristotelian views of the world. Coleridge has held that every man is born an Aristotelian or a Platonist. He did not think it possible that anyone born an Aristotelian could become a Platonist; and he was sure no born Platonist could ever change into an Aristotelian. They were two classes of men, beside which it was next to impossible to conceive a third. Plato considered reason a quality or attribute; Aristotle considered it a power. With Plato ideas were constitutive in themselves; with Aristotle they were but regulative conceptions. He could never raise himself into the higher state which was natural to Plato, in which the understanding is distinctively contemplated, and, as it were, looked down upon from the throne of actual ideas, or living, unborn, essential truths. Dryden, says Coleridge, could not have been a Platonist – Shakespeare, Milton, Dante, Michelangelo and Raphael could not have been other than Platonists. And Lytton Strachey? He does not seem to have known Coleridge's dictum and goes some way to setting himself up as the third, to Coleridge inconceivable, type of man – the Aristonist or Platotelian. Strachey, the scathing iconoclast and anarch, came down firmly on the side of Aristotle, equating reason with power; Strachey, the delicate impressionist critic and biographical craftsman, favoured the more imaginative Plato. As William Gerhardie has advocated, the term 'Aristotelian' might justly and with literary advantage become pejorative; and since Lytton, too, never believed that the primary value of literature was to the state as opposed to the individual, the two irreconcilable attitudes continued in their uncertain joint possession of his mind. On the whole, however, since it is much easier – intellectually speaking – to be a revolutionary than an artist, his Aristotelianism predominated, though deep within him there lay obscure immortal longings – faintly echoed in his essays on Blake, Beddoes, even Gordon and elsewhere – which this ruthless, matter-of-fact creed never touched.

The Apostles had entered one of their usual phases of crisis. No unanimous decision could be reached about new embryos, and there seemed every likelihood of Norton and James being the only undergraduate members in the next year. It was a doleful prospect – the DOOMED Norton; and James, sunk in appalling gloom and radiating an atmosphere of apathy and oppression that ate into one's very bones. His fundamental disease, in Lytton's estimation, was that he could rouse himself to take no interest in anything but the few people he admired or was in love with – which, of course, was simple Death. Phlegmatic as a sponge, he just sucked up unending pain and despondency. It was dreadful to visit him in his rooms, like coming across one's past self, horribly parodied. The poor creature seemed quite unable to think, or read or work at all. Instead he spent all his time dreaming over a solitary fire, which eventually went out because he was too dilatory to put on more coal. There was not much to deserve all this agitation, to Lytton's mind – he wished there had been! Yet how easy for good looks and fair hair to stir up passion, if one hadn't the energy to overcome it. Laziness had become an inveterate habit with James. The very contemplation of anything difficult was poison to his system and brought on a complete collapse. It was at any rate a mercy, Lytton often reflected in his own moments of adversity, that one was not a mere machine of nerves, that one possessed, after all, something of an intellect. This, he felt, was the great stand-by, perhaps in the long run, when desire would fail and the voice of the grasshopper would become a burden, the *only* worthwhile thing – though one hardly liked to dwell on that.

It was all pretty sickening, yet Lytton felt as if he could never drag himself away from Cambridge. The beauty and the sunshine and the comfort were entrancing. But perhaps the real fascination of the place lay in the endless possibilities of adventure which might come off – and never did. Probably he took too black a view of the New Cambridge, with all the fresh and likely young men taking up politics and leaving the Apostles high and dry. In any event the one significant effect on Lytton of this change in the university climate and of his failure to enter into the life of the freshmen with their open-air socialist zealotry, was to strengthen his determination to lead a new independent life of his own, a life of literary dedication. 'As for me,' he wrote to Keynes (16 March 1907), 'I am thinking of retiring, once and for all, into Private Life. I am going to pull down the blinds and put up the shutters, and commit my mind to the manufacture of chefs d'oeuvre. I shall appear sometimes of an evening, and make a jest or two very much à la Adolphe himself, and then I shall retire, as the clock strikes twelve, to my lucubrations. The truth is the Younger Generation is too much for me. I don't pretend to understand it any more, and it can do very well, I must imagine, without me. If I let my mind dwell on some things, I get into a state – I don't [know] what – I feel almost as if I . . . was out of date. However, it's very easy to pull down the blinds, and that's what I shall do. And it's not only easy, it's delightful. I am unimpassioned, I am free, I am Adolphus.'

At last, in the third week of March, he tore himself away from Cambridge and went on for a few days to stay with Desmond and Molly MacCarthy in their country house, the Green Farm, Timworth, near Bury St Edmunds. This turned out to be a large farmhouse, partly uninhabited, with a somewhat decayed garden, and fine flat sweeping fields of turnips and cabbages all around. The newly married MacCarthys had only recently taken possession of the place so that things were not as comfortable as Lytton had hoped. The meals, for one thing, were never punctual; and the fires, for another, were always going out. It was exasperating – and yet somehow he managed to amuse himself. Poor dear Desmond, of course, was incomparably dim, but his affable company was pleasing enough for a short duration. They talked much about the new periodical, about Bernard Shaw, and modern poetry, and whether the *Nation* was better than the *Speaker*, and in the evenings they strolled round the splendid park near by, with its great lake and wood. This was the part of each day that Lytton enjoyed best, the domestic inconveniences forgotten amid the beautiful dream-like landscape – the wide stretch of water with the light on it, and the surrounding forms of trees vanishing away in haze. He was enchanted. His walks there during these warm, gentle evenings were like precious moments stolen from the rush of Time; and, being timeless, they would remain for ever in his memory.

Indoors there were distractions from boredom of a more trivial and humorous kind. Molly MacCarthy's mother, Mrs Cornish,[5] was also staying with them, a capricious eccentric of iron whim, some description of whom, Lytton reasoned, might amuse Duncan Grant. She was, he wrote (23 March 1907), 'incredibly affected, queer, stupid and intelligent. She

5. Blanche Warre-Cornish, daughter of William Ritchie, was the author of two long novels and a rather tame monograph of R. H. Benson – Corvo's 'Bobugo Bonsen' – the Catholic writer and apologist.

flowed with reflections on life, and reminiscences of George Eliot, and criticisms of obscure French poetesses who flourished in 1850. She was damned difficult to answer though. What is one to say when a person says – "Ah, isn't it delightful to think of all those dear animals asleep around us?" Do you know her remark to an Eton youth when he was introduced to her? "Oh, Mr Jones, has it ever occurred to you how very different a cow is from a thrush?" I dare say she's mad, and I'm pretty sure she's a minx, and a minx of sixty. "Can't one tempt you to Eton, Mr Strachey? You'd find all Walpole's letters in the library, and a great many delightful boys." What was one to say to that?'

3

HEART OF DARKNESS

From the MacCarthys, Lytton hurried back to Lancaster Gate – but not for long. He was already deep in complicated negotiations with G. E. Moore about another Easter reading-party. The problems were endless. Where should they go? Yorkshire would almost certainly be too cold; Lytton could still vividly recall the snowstorms of two Easters ago, and those vast slabs of salt beef at the Crown Hotel. What about the Lizard once more? 'I long to see the charming place again,' he wrote to Moore. But Penmenner House had unfortunately been snapped up by a party of Christian young men, and so was quite out of the question. Eventually they engaged rooms at Court Barton, in the village of North Molton, near Exmoor in Devon. The intricacies of choosing 'the elect of the elect' were even more difficult than usual. Too many people would distress Moore; too few would distress the landlady. And they must be the *right* people. Moore would naturally bring Ainsworth, as always; and, as always, Lytton would bring James. But after that the composition of the party was uncertain. How could they make sure that Duckworth, for example, was given the impression – without any actual lies being told, which would be unethical – that there was to be no reading-party that year? How to ensure that Bob Trevy did not stay the full three weeks? Would Mac-Carthy come at the last minute? Then what of Saxon Sydney-Turner and Ralph Hawtrey? And how, on top of all these dilemmas, to fit in Norton and Keynes?

This last question was simply one of timing. Norton and Keynes could only join them for the last ten days, since they had decided to spend a week beforehand in Paris, together with James. Lytton thought this an excellent scheme. They ought, he said, to do the thing *en grand seigneur,* and put up at the St James Hôtel in the rue St-Honoré. This would be comfortable, close to the Louvre, fairly cheap, and frequented by friendly English people. What could be better? Norton and James were silent, but Keynes gently demurred. Perhaps, he suggested, it might be even cheaper, even more comfortable to stay with Duncan Grant at 22 rue Delambre near the Boulevard Raspail. And Lytton was at once enthusiastic. What a splendid idea! Why hadn't *he* thought of it? – especially since that very week he had written to Vanessa Stephen urging her 'to look up my little cousin, when you're in Paris'.

He saw the three of them off at Charing Cross station, and returned home to dream of the wonderful holiday they would be enjoying together. It gave him a stab of keen vicarious pleasure, this day-dreaming, heightened by just a shade of mild melancholy. He was particularly anxious that Keynes and Duncan should get on well, that Keynes with his dry, unim-passioned aloofness should not bore or irritate poor Duncan. What a party they might have! He saw visions of them all crowding through in the Louvre, or lingering among the fountains and the oranges, the bronzes and the marble gods which he had described but never seen at Versailles, or perhaps looking over the Pont Neuf at the Seine, or again, if it was warm and the sun was shining, wandering in the Tuileries Gardens where Mademoiselle de Lespinasse walked not so very long ago and in the evening went to hear the same *Che farò* that they might listen to that very night. Lytton's only fear, so he told Duncan Grant, was that they might fall into the hands of the police. If they did, then of course they must at once telegraph him so that he might busy himself collecting certificates of character and of good conduct from various people – Duckworth, Walter Lamb, himself and others. In any case Keynes, with his multifarious connections, would be quite safe, as he could get the son of a bishop to swear to his exemplary behaviour while at Eton. Duncan would be let off as an artist; and no one could look at James and find him guilty of any conceivable crime. So that poor Norton was really the only one of them in danger, and he, very probably, would be excused as an *Anglais fou.*

Such titillating speculations delighted him. Now that Keynes had quitted King's and was languishing on his stool at the India Office, Lytton certainly felt more kindly towards him. Poor old Keynes! It really was more like the old times now that he was suffering under adversity. He felt closer to him than for many months. Yet this was to be the last flicker of a largely extinguished affection. The check to Keynes's progress was only momentary, and soon enough good fortune was to blaze down on him again. More successful mountain-climbing would follow, and, if that were not enough, more golf. By June 1908, when he resigned from the India Office to take up a lectureship at Cambridge, his role as Lytton's Brother Confessor had already been partly taken over by James. And before the following March, when Keynes was elected a Fellow of King's, the substitution had been completed. The triumph of Keynes was assured, and the old intimacy between the two friends never fully recaptured – another shift in the pattern of Lytton's life that even now during this trip to Paris was, with amoeba-like slowness, moving into place.

The reading-party at North Molton opens in the final week of March and lasts three weeks. Within its limitations – of comfort, warmth, good company but no love – it is one of the most agreeable gatherings Lytton has ever attended. 'This country is in the region of Exmoor (except that there is no moor to be seen),' he writes to Duncan Grant, 'and I like it, with its rolling hills vanishing away to the horizon, and its valleys with streams and trees in them, and its general air of health. We are in a farmhouse, touching a church, and there are some rather nice turkeys to be seen strutting about and gobbling outside my bedroom window, and there is plenty of Devonshire cream at meals, and there are a good many amusing (and instructive) books, and there is a piano which Moore plays in the evening.'

In short, the mild tranquillities of Court Barton are all that mild tranquillities can ever be – there is the happy certainty of a 'surplusage of beef and Devonshire cream' to be disposed of by country walks; there is a village shop with bull's-eyes in it; there are two sitting-rooms and a garden; and upstairs there are feather beds and books. Perhaps the Apostles are made for mild tranquillities and second-hand regrets. Perhaps their business is to read novels and to go to sleep in the sun dreaming of masterpieces they will never create. 'In a few minutes we shall all be tramping through the sun. And then more cream, and then more beef, and then somnolence, and then bed – solitary bed.'

Lytton has taken with him to North Molton his Warren Hastings dissertation, intending to prepare the typescript for some future publication. It will, he hopes, form a solid, scholarly cornerstone to his new career in literature. On the average he spends, during these three weeks, one hour a day emending, polishing and re-writing parts of it – much less than he has originally planned. Some of the time which should have been allocated to this work is given over to composing verse, and among the pieces he writes is his longest if not most ambitious poem to date – of about a hundred lines. This composition, which is more readily enjoyable than many of his verses, relates a simple story with an ironic, Pope-like wit and point. Long ago, we are told, a great dearth of things to say afflicted the human race. The situation baffled human intelligence until one day a young quick-minded shepherd put forward a startling innovation. His empty volubility, which illustrates as he speaks the gist of the suggestion he is making, is nicely caught by Lytton.

> O mortals! Would you know the one sure way
> Of saying much when there is naught to say?

Imitate me! Construct the flowing line,
With numbers' art your syllables entwine,
Swell out the pompous verse with stress and pause,
And govern all by metre's mystic laws!
Then shall your wandering words move sweetly on
When the last shred of meaning has quite gone,
Then empty feet transport you where you will,
And simple rhythm waft you forward still,
Then rhyme, self-spun, shall wrap you round and round
And all your folly vanish in a sound.

This speech, Lytton recounts, was considered at the time to be rank blasphemy, and the shepherd was straightway hanged from the nearest tree by an angry crowd of righteous and indignant citizens. Generations later, however, an altar is erected where this tree stood to the poor shepherd's martyrdom. An amusing description then follows of the new, articulate religion which subsequently flourished there – a mock-exaltation of the staleness and concealed boredom to which Lytton always felt so personally susceptible – in lines which show his aptitude for non-romantic, satirical rhyme.

Here maudlin lovers seeking how to spin
Poetic cobwebs from their faint and thin
Imaginations, found inspirèd aid,
Murmuring nonsense in the holy shade.
Here many a pompous simpleton pursued
Through its dull coils the eternal platitude,
Found out that what was fated came to pass,
That mortal beings perished like the grass,
That all the world was subject to decay,
That he who gave might likewise take away,
That much was known to men, yet more was not,
And naught was certain in the human lot.
Here too would hired laureates fill their lays
With ever-fresh incontinence of praise,
Proclaiming in the same insipid breath
A royal birth, or victory, or death,
Then hymn aloud in strains as void as air
The copulation of a princely pair.

Whenever he is not versifying or labouring away at the

Warren Hastings, he will write long letters to his friends describing, for their amusement, how the reading-party was being conducted. 'At this moment Keynes is lying on the rug beside me,' he tells Swithinbank (31 March 1907), 'turning over the leaves of a handbook on obstetrics which seems to keep him absorbed. Norton is next to him on a camp-stool, and it is he who is writing mathematics. Next to him is Bob Trevy, under an umbrella, very vague and contented, and planning out his next *chef-d'oeuvre*. I should have mentioned that I am on a basket chair (with plenty of cushions in case of accidents), and that I am perfectly happy, as I am writing to you instead of doing what I ought to be doing, viz., composing a preface to Warren Hastings . . .'

Most of the time during these first sunny days the party sits out in the garden, Lytton in a panama hat (also in case of accidents) and a flannel open-neck shirt, with a red beard half an inch long, feeling very hot and idle, glancing round him at the others and then continuing his interminable letters; Bob Trevy fast asleep dreaming of his opera on Bacchus and Ariadne which he has just written for Donald Tovey to set to music;[6] Ainsworth with a pair of blue spectacles to ward off the sun, reading Plato; Keynes under the umbrella, reading Galsworthy; Sanger, flat on his back on the grass, studying law; James Strachey crouched in the shadows, reading nothing; Norton for ever absorbed in his mathematics; and Moore, reclining full length on a rug, making pencil notes in the margin of Locke's *Essay on Human Understanding*.

So, for the first fortnight, the mild tranquillities drift along pleasantly enough. Then, one day, everything breaks up. Keynes and Norton leave for London, the weather abandons its habit of cloudless, demi-tropical splendour and deteriorates into vile and ceaseless rain, Sanger retires upstairs to his feather bed with a severe and persistent cold, and James collapses with toothache. The world is a vale of tears again.

6. It was at this time that Sir Donald Tovey began work on his only opera *The Bride of Dionysus*, the libretto of which was written by R. C. Trevelyan. Not completed until 1918, it received its first performance in Edinburgh on 23 April 1929.

Lytton is left huddled in the smaller sitting-room with Ainsworth and Moore, who, intoxicated by the surfeit of beef and cream, appears to be in the throes of an abstruse ethical revolution, from which he finds relief in declaiming out loud the novels of Captain Marryat. 'Has the rumour reached you of the astounding news?' Lytton asks Keynes. 'Moore has shivered his philosophy into atoms, and can't for the life of him construct a new one. He "doesn't know what to think" — about *anything* — propositions, eternal being, Truth itself! In fact he's pretty well chucked up the sponge. Isn't it shocking? Christ denying Christianity! Hegel gapes for him, and shuddering worlds hide their horror-stricken heads. He's a great man, and if he's not got water on the brain he'll come through, and soar to even more incredible heights. But has he got water on the brain? Shall we ever know?' Moore's volte-face is in fact the outcome of a succession of growing doubts and qualifications with which he has been wrestling since Christmas. But by the end of the reading-party he already seems to be moving onwards again out of his dire perplexity into the obscurely obvious. 'The Yen has discovered that when you say "So and so is so and so's father," the word "father" in the sentence has no meaning whatever. It's a rather important discovery; but I suppose it'll be blasted soon enough.'[7]

The reading-party dispersed on 18 April. 'London is a shocking-place as far as people go,' Lytton complained to James the following month. But a few distractions, mostly pictorial, did lighten the gloom, including an exhibition of Simon Bussy's paintings at Leighton House which he advised Clive and Vanessa Bell to see — 'They are all pastels, and most of them dreams of beauty' — also a private view at the New Gallery more remarkable for the onlookers than the pictures — 'That astounding creature Pinero[8] was there. ... Large red

7. In an explanatory postscript to this letter, Lytton added: 'When you say "So and so is so and so's father", you mean "So and so occupies a relation towards so and so to which the word 'father' may be properly applied" — and that's all; you needn't (and probably don't) know what "father" means.'

8. Sir Arthur Wing Pinero (1855–1934), prolific playwright much influenced by Ibsen. His best-known play is *The Second Mrs Tanqueray* (1893).

face, immense black eyebrows, rolling eyes, vast nose, theatrical manner, bandanna handkerchief, trousers creased *à la rigueur*, and patent leather boots with brown fronts' – and finally, at the Carfax Gallery, 'a charming collection of Max Beerbohm's caricatures – many of them really beautiful, and some like Blake – all (to my mind) the height of amusement.'

During the spring and early summer Lytton did very little but read the reminiscences and letters of Carlyle – 'a psalm-singing Scotchman with a power of observation which knocks you flat' – and the novels of Joseph Conrad whom he described as 'very superb – in fact the *only* superb novelist now, except old Henry James, etc. – and Lord Jim is full of splendid things. The Nigger of the Narcissus is another very wonderful one, and perhaps the best of all is a shortish story called Heart of Darkness in a book called Youth.' Among recently published books there was his friend E. M. Forster's *The Longest Journey*. 'I don't think you know Forster,' he wrote to Duncan Grant (30 April 1907), ' – a queer King's brother, and a great friend of Hom's.[9] He's just written his second novel, and there's a rather amusing account of Cambridge in it, and Cambridge people. One of the very minor characters is asked to breakfast by one of his friends and replies by putting his hand on his stomach, to show that he's breakfasted already. MacCarthy thinks that this is me. Do you? But the rest of the book is a dreary fandango. After the hero (who's Forster himself), the principal figure is Hom.'

As for his own writing, he was planning two major essays, one biographical, the other critical. The first of these, his final contribution to the *Independent Review* which had now re-formed under the name of the *Albany Review*, was on Lady Mary Wortley Montagu. The attraction which this subject held for him – something akin to an adopted filial pride – is very clearly indicated in a passage from another of his letters to Duncan Grant (13 May 1907): 'I am going to write an

9. H. O. Meredith, known as 'Hom' among his Cambridge friends, a Fellow of King's who later became professor of political economy at Queen's University, Belfast.

article on Lady Mary Wortley Montagu (Have you heard of her?) – a magnificent 18th-century lady, who wrote letters, and introduced inoculation into Europe. She was sublime, and no one knows it nowadays. I shall try and show that she was and how. She had only two tastes – intellect and lust. Imagine her pessimism! But her honesty and courage were equal to every emergency, and she never gave into anything or anybody, and died fighting. Great Lady Mary!'

The second of these essays reflects the complement of his enthusiasm for such splendid, prepotent females – a taste for men of vulnerable, superfine sensitivity. He had been introduced to the writings of Beddoes by Saxon Sydney-Turner, and soon became both fascinated by his personality and spellbound by his poetry. Like Lady Mary Wortley Montagu, Beddoes was an unjustly disregarded figure on the literary stage, a sad state of affairs that Lytton hoped to correct, by means of a long re-appraisal of his work in the opening number of MacCarthy's *New Quarterly*, now due out in the autumn.

There were other, more distant plans, too, in his mind for critical and biographical essays. Meanwhile, 'I regret to say that I go to sleep after lunch more often than not,' he admitted to Duncan Grant (18 June 1907). 'The other day I actually did it after breakfast! But that undoubtedly was a sign of disease – I wonder, though, of *what* disease? – "The disease, sir, of sloth!" a vicar would probably say. But one need pay no attention to vicars.

'I am in my room. James is opposite, reading Chinese poetry. I'm sure I must have shown you the book – one of the most charming in the world.[10] I want to write about it, and so gain a little cash. And I want to write about Madame du Deffand,[11] and Baudelaire, and Beddoes, and Marivaux and God knows who. Why on earth don't I? "Sloth, sir, sloth!" '

10. A collection of poetry translations from the Chinese made by Professor H. A. Giles of Cambridge, and originally published in 1898. Lytton was to write an appreciation of this book in the summer of 1908, printed that autumn in the *New Quarterly* and the *Living Age*.

11. Lytton's essay on Madame du Deffand was not in fact composed until 1912.

4

NOTHING TO LOSE

On 22 May, Lancaster Gate was put up for public auction. Lady Strachey was determined that the place should not go for less than three thousand pounds, but Lytton, who liked to imagine that they could let it furnished for the season to some wealthy American 'and live on the proceeds in lodgings for the next ten years', thought this too unrealistic a price to ask, and his view seemed to be proved right when the auction came to nothing. However, it soon turned out that there was a prospective purchaser hanging in the wind, with whom Lady Strachey eventually succeeded in coming to reasonable terms – though, as a result of this man's hesitancy, the family were obliged to postpone their move until September.

While these hectic and prolonged negotiations were being argued out, the ordinary day-to-day life at Lancaster Gate took on an even more chaotic air than usual. 'I now read through all meals steadily,' he told Maynard Keynes two days after the abortive auction, '. . . I think I may have spoken three sentences today.' And to Duncan Grant he grumbled: 'I really haven't the vaguest idea what I've done since I came back to London. The only certain thing is that I've done no work. Oh, devils! devils! – I've been to no plays, and heard no music, and hardly talked to anyone but Keynes (and him I believe only twice). On Thursday I had dinner with Clive and Vanessa in Gordon Square. They seemed somewhat less insistent on the fact that they were in love with each other, which made it easier to talk to them, and I enjoyed myself pretty well.' Such a passage, with its grudging, almost unintentional admission of enjoyment is very characteristic of Lytton at this time. In fact his everyday life was, as he would say, fairly tolerable. But he felt keenly his failure to blaze a glorious trail through the world. Secretly impatient for success, he was fearful that his friends, insensible to the pulsing ambitions so long constrained within him, would underrate his discontent. It was perhaps to indicate the force of this discontent as well as to draw in the uncritical sympathy which he felt it demanded, that he exaggerated the hardships of his existence.

Among the most interesting of his social engagements was a dinner-party with William Rothenstein, his wife, and Isabel Fry, the younger sister of Roger, later to win fame as a brilliant educationist. 'The dinner was remarkable,' Lytton wrote to Duncan Grant (13 May 1907), 'chiefly because Rothenstein and his wife were there. It was *the* Rothenstein – very Jewish and small and monkey-like; I believe the one who was at the Friday Club,[12] and who annoyed me, must have been his younger brother, because wasn't he rather podgy and hubristic? At any rate, I was annoyed almost as much this time – and by very much the same style of vagueness. I rather peevishly dissented, and I fear he was offended! He was nice, and extraordinarily meek, but oh! the rot he talked! Madam[13] was a blonde, somewhat devoid of [undecipherable], worshipping him, and enraged with me for daring to disagree with him! My philistinism was increased by the frightful fact that I alone of the party was in evening dress! A haughty and exclusive aristocrat was what I appeared to be, no doubt, trampling poor artists underfoot as if they were so many beetles! And I unfortunately let out that I lived in Lancaster Gate! "Horribly rich," I'm sure she murmured to him, or rather "Orribly rich". Shall I call on them, when we've settled in bijou residence in Hampstead, dressed in my third best brogalines and without a collar? But even then I should never be able to agree that Nature was only one aspect of Art, that Beauty was the expression of True Emotions, and that Music, Poetry, and Painting were the plastic embodiments of Life.'

William Rothenstein has also left a description of this encounter in his *Men and Memories*, which enables one to draw

12. Vanessa Bell's Friday Club was not founded by her until June 1910. Lytton was probably referring to Virginia Stephen's 'Friday Evenings' in Fitzroy Square.

13. Alice Knewstub, who had married William Rothenstein in 1899. According to her son, John Rothenstein, she was 'an inflammable compound of Toryism and anarchy'.

an interesting comparison between the impression which Lytton made and imagined he made on chance acquaintances – though the account here is somewhat qualified by judicious afterthoughts. 'Lytton Strachey's look in those early days was very unlike his later appearance,' Rothenstein recalled. 'Long, slender, with a receding chin, that gave a look of weakness to his face, with a thin, cracked voice, I thought him typical of the Cambridge intellectual. Dining one night with Isabel Fry, I recollect saying that poetry, usually regarded as a vague and high-falutin art by many, was in fact the clearest expression of man's thoughts. Strachey replied acidly. Who, indeed, was I to talk of matters with which I was not concerned? And I thought that here was the cultured University man, who lies in wait, hoping one may say something foolish, or inaccurate, and then springs out to crush one, in high falsetto tones. But I was mistaken. Of course Lytton Strachey was much more than a cultured Cambridge man; he was to become a master of English prose; and with reputation came a beard, and long hair, and a cloak and sombrero, which gave weight and solemnity to an appearance previously not very noticeable. I think Lytton Strachey was of so nervous a temper, that he needed some defensive armour to cover his extreme sensitiveness, and a weapon with a sharp edge, with which to protect himself. He suffered fools less genially than Max [Beerbohm], to their faces at least.'

While preparations for the move to Hampstead were being made, Lytton felt obliged to remain in London.[14] But in the

14. Among the plays he went to in these months was Herbert Beerbohm Tree's production of Wilde's *A Woman of No Importance*. 'It was rather amusing', he told Duncan Grant (2 June 1907), 'as it was a complete mass of epigrams, with occasional whiffs of grotesque melodrama and drivelling sentiment. The queerest mixture! Mr Tree is a wicked Lord, staying in a country house, who has made up his mind to bugger one of the other guests – a handsome young man of twenty. The handsome young man is delighted; when his mother enters, sees his Lordship and recognizes him as having copulated with her twenty years before, the result of which was – the handsome young man. He replies that that's an additional reason for doing it (oh! he's a *very* wicked Lord!). She then appeals to the handsome young man, who says, "Dear me! What an abominable thing to

course of May and June he did manage to get away twice – for one week-end to Cambridge and another to Oxford. The Cambridge visit was particularly refreshing. The lilacs were in full bloom, the horse-chestnuts flowering, 'the backs and river pullulating with undergraduates in flannels, and prostitutes in tights and spangles – the whole thing really delightful'. The usual group of Apostles met in Sheppard's rooms to discuss Christianity – much to Lytton's amusement; but the chief event of this visit was the sight of Knox wearing heavy black spectacles. The shock was considerable, and one that could not be erased from Lytton's mind. From this time on Knox was eliminated from even a subsidiary role in his life. As for considering him a rival to Swithinbank – why, it was laughable!

Another shock awaited him on his week-end at Oxford. As at Cambridge, everything seemed very pleasant at first, and he was enchanted by the variety of the scene. He dined off cold duck and champagne with the governor of the Seychelles; he breakfasted with Granville Proby,[15] a fat, aristocratic Old Etonian friend of Keynes's, with Humphrey Paul,[16] 'a merry

---

do – to go and copulate without marrying! Oh no, I shall certainly pay no attention to anyone capable of doing *that*, and –" when suddenly enter (from the garden) a young American millionairess, shrieking for help, and in considerable disorder. The wicked Lord Tree, not contented with buggering his own son, has attempted to rape the millionairess, with whom (very properly) the handsome young man is in love. Enter his Lordship. Handsome Y.M.: "You devil! You have insulted the purest creature on God's earth! I shall kill you!" But of course he doesn't, but contents himself with marrying the millionairess, while his mother takes up a pair of gloves and slashes the Lord across the face. It seems an odd plot, doesn't it? But it required all my penetration to find out that this *was* the plot, as you may imagine. Epigrams engulf it like the sea. Most of them were thoroughly rotten, and nearly all were said quite cynically to the gallery. Poor old Tree sits down with his back to the audience to talk to a brilliant lady, and swings round in his seat every time he delivers an epigram. The audience was of course charmed.'

15. Granville Proby, later Clerk to the House of Lords and Lord Lieutenant of Huntingdonshire (1946–50).

16. Humphrey Paul, son of the historian and biographer Herbert Woodfield Paul.

farceur, with four thousand anecdotes at his command', with Geoffrey Scott,[17] 'a bad character, all egoism and love of amusement and importance for their own sakes ... clever, and amusing and extremely scandalous', with Dillwyn Knox's younger brother Ronnie,[18] 'a christian and a prig, and a self-sufficient little insignificant wretch!' and with James Elroy Flecker,[19] who made no particular impression on him; he lunched with Swithinbank on strawberries and cream, and saw Jack Beazley, resplendently beautiful with high complexion, curling red-golden hair and charming, affectionate manners; he had tea with the Raleighs, and met a professor of Greek and a doctor who had recently examined a notorious murderer. Everything was as entertaining and as agreeable as he could have wished. The beauty of the colleges amazed him. In the evening he strolled with Swithinbank round the Magdalen College Cloisters, wondering at the strange medieval atmosphere. It was not difficult to imagine, where the Blues and Beazley and Swithin now walked among those dark old stones and brooding antiquity, monks and novices of the Middle Ages traipsing about with their *pater noster*'s, their atonements, penances, secret preoccupations. How sinister it

17. Geoffrey Scott, the notable Boswell scholar, and author of *The Architecture of Humanism* and *The Portrait of Zélide*.

18. The Rt Reverend Monsignor Ronald Arbuthnot Knox (1888–1957), whose biography has been decorously written by Evelyn Waugh (1959). Author of many books on Roman Catholicism, and of *Studies in the Literature of Sherlock Holmes*, a work that gave impetus to the Holmes-eology 'which has since become rather tiresome'. Translator of the Vulgate. When Lytton met him he was up at Balliol College and reputed to be the wittiest president of the Oxford Union within living memory.

19. James Elroy Flecker (1884–1915), poet and dramatist, who left Trinity College, Oxford, in 1906 with only a third in Mods and Greats, and returned the following year in an abortive attempt to live through writing. Agnostic and tubercular, he became an accomplished linguist, a great traveller and keen bibliophil. His finest poem is usually considered to be *The Golden Journey to Samarkand*, much admired by Eddie Marsh, but which D. H. Lawrence declared 'only took place on paper – no matter who went to Asia Minor'. His chief drama, *Hassan* (published posthumously in 1922), was produced with a ballet by Fokine and music by Delius. Reconverted to Christianity, he received communion on his death-bed at Davos in the first week of 1915.

all was! Had he been alone there in the fading twilight he might have felt quite frightened. But he was with Swithin, at the sight of whom, if the Universe were conducted as it should be, Magdalen would vanish like a dream when the sun comes in at the window and one wakes up. How lucky he was to have a friend like Swithin!

As the two of them walked in the evening sun, Swithinbank suddenly announced that he had applied for the post of sanitary inspector in the Fiji Islands, a job for which, he believed, there was little ardent competition. Once he had been convinced that this was not some new style of joke, Lytton did all in his power to dissuade his friend from such a scatterbrained course. But Swithinbank was curiously adamant. 'He has taken it into his head', Lytton wrote to James with what, it seemed to him, was only slight exaggeration, 'that there is only one thing for him to do – viz. to become Inspector General of Brothels in the Fiji Islands. Did you ever hear of such a thing? Nothing will induce him to change his mind; and he hopes to sail in July!'

Lytton's consternation was all the greater since, by a freak coincidence of timing, the now heavily bespectacled Knox – the only possible successor to Swithinbank, waiting in the wings of his life while Duncan Grant still performed in mid-stage – had been eliminated as a competent understudy that very month. The absurdity of it was that Swithinbank could quite easily become a master at Winchester which he would thoroughly enjoy, whereas the drainage system of Fiji really *couldn't* please him. He only did it from sheer indecisiveness, yet there was, of course, every reason to suppose that he would be given the job. And that, so far as Lytton was concerned, would be the virtual death of him. Something must be done!

Hurrying back to London, he conferred with Keynes, and both agreed that here was a matter for decisive intervention and counterplot. After some debate they embarked on a bold policy. Lytton went off to see his cousin, Sir Charles Strachey, in the Colonial Office and asked him what he thought of Swithinbank's plan. After making certain inquiries and confirming that the post was very far from being considered a coveted one, he condemned the whole idea as being utterly absurd. Armed with this official verdict, Keynes then wrote off to Swithinbank's father, a clergyman, imploring him in the name of God to prevail upon his son not to go, and painting all the vices and horrors of Fiji in their most lurid lights. A silence followed, during which Keynes and Lytton waited in some trepidation. Then came a telegram from poor Swithin — 'Fijis are off!' And so the situation, for the time being, was saved.

While this crisis was being sorted out, another one affecting Lytton even more directly had arisen. Towards the end of June, St Loe Strachey wrote to Lytton asking him to join the *Spectator* staff. He proposed that, with effect from October, Lytton should review a book each week for a salary of one hundred and fifty pounds per year. It was a difficult and depressing decision for Lytton to have to make. The emolument was not great, but with MacCarthy's *New Quarterly* starting up at the same time, it would, at a single blow, amount to a livelihood. For a few days he deliberated. He asked Keynes, who advised him to accept: 'It is hardly possible to overestimate the importance of money.' He asked James, who was later to become a member of the *Spectator* staff himself, and who strongly advised Lytton to refuse the offer. Acceptance, he warned his brother, would be tantamount to selling himself to 'the Mammon of Unrighteousness'. Sooner or later pressure was pretty certain to be put on him to become a regular, full-time journalist — *et voilà tout*. Once he had started this kind of work, he would not be able to resist when the time came, and all his dreams of *chefs-d'oeuvre*, plays, novels, even biographies, would have to be abandoned.

In the end Lytton accepted. 'It seemed on the whole the wisest thing to do,' he explained to Duncan Grant (25 June 1907), 'though I'm still not sure whether it wasn't simply the most cowardly. I had hoped to begin doing something worth doing, but the money, and the obvious fact that Mama wanted me to accept it, and the conceivable possibility that I might at least *think* of things, and the certainty that I could always chuck it when I liked — these considerations turned the melancholy balance, and shattered my dreams of ease and comedy. However, the splendid thing is that I shall be wonderfully rich next year (if I survive the stress and strain of composition!) and, as there's no particular reason why I should be pinned to London, I shall be able to travel.'

In July the only certainties for the future were increased wealth, decreased time, and no contractual compulsion to go on with reviewing if he found that he really could do nothing else. As for James's objection, Lytton hoped he had not sold himself but merely made friends with the Mammon of Unrighteousness. If pressure were applied in the way James had gloomily prophesied, then they would see who was right, whether he would have the strength to decline. One thing was definite. The *Spectator* appointment was another link in the chain pulling asunder his old, aimless and unproductive life. But was it at the same time forging another bondage for him? Only time would tell.

5

DUMB ASSUAGEMENTS

Three months of ease and comedy still awaited him, and Lytton was determined not to waste them. As soon as the *Spectator* appointment had been ratified, and his 'Lady Mary Wortley Montagu' completed, he began to make plans for spending a week with Duncan Grant at Versailles. This was something he had often dreamed of doing, and had indeed already done by proxy. Now, before it was too late, before his freedom was too strictly curtailed, he would make his dream reality.

After some delay, he set off in the second week of July, and for seven idyllic days he lived with Duncan in La Bruyère's house, passing most of their time in the wonderful gardens — those of the Grand Trianon for choice, for they were more retired. Though he had been prepared for much, the beauty of the place took his breath away. 'What I want to know is why anyone lives anywhere else,' he wrote to Clive Bell. 'I suppose one wouldn't be up to it for more than a week or so at a time. The ghosts would begin to grow more real than oneself.'

Surrounded by these splendid gardens, and enchanted by the company of Duncan, Lytton was content to pass his days lazily. 'We spend most of our time beside a basin in the Trianon,' he informed James, 'but one day was given to Paris, on which I looked at every picture in the Louvre, and every statue, and then went off and had a blow out, and we viewed a farce in the Boulevard Montmartre, and then we steamed back to Versailles.'

He returned to London on 17 July and almost immediately left again with James, Pernel and Marjorie for Burley Hill, which Thena Clough had once more lent the family. Here all was silence, regularity and health. After the wild exhilarations of Versailles, Lytton soon sank back into a benevolent trance which must be 'middle-age, as I seem to be remarkably contented', he told Keynes who visited him for a few days, and who was, so he informed Duncan Grant, 'rather uglier than usual'.

Whenever he felt that family life was growing too much for him, he would prescribe for himself a letter from *Les Liaisons Dangereuses* before going to bed, and a Fleur du Mal the first thing in the morning. It seldom failed. 'I've just got a book,' he told Clive Bell (9 August 1907), 'in which some notes by Baudelaire on the Liaisons Dangereuses are printed – do you know them? They're really splendid – all his wonderful sanity, precision, and grasp of the situation are finely displayed. He says, comparing modern life to the eighteenth century – "En réalité, le satanisme a gagné. Satan s'est fait ingénu. Le mal se connaissant était moins affreux et plus près de la guérison que le mal s'ignorant. G. Sand inférieure à de Sade." '

But after some three weeks the bitter, controlled pessimism of Baudelaire, and the general lack of quickening imagination which characterized so much French writing despite all its virtues of style, lucidity and order, began to deflate him, and instead of prolonging the happiness of his idyll at Versailles, these books only consolidated his familiar English apathy. 'Is literature the dullest thing in the world?' he asked Swithinbank (21 August 1907). 'At the moment I can think of nothing duller. Let's all become painters and musicians, and embark for Cythera.'[20] He wanted to engrave his mark upon the age, like a lion with its claw; but he had got nowhere, and looked like getting nowhere in the future. What on earth was he doing? Little more, it seemed, than twiddling his thumbs while his hair turned grey. And after all, wasn't that a just summary of all life – gradually, *contentedly*, to subside into a mummified state of putrefaction? The human race grubbed along like hedgehogs, sniffing and snouting, and for ever turning up its pettifogging roots. Yet possibly this view of mankind, occasioned by his study of the French Swift of poetry, was unnecessarily dismal. Surely *somewhere* there was *something* that was enormously important, some divine solution beyond analysis? And if there were, then really everything was all right after all. It sounded almost religious, such speculation, but weren't they all religious *au fond*? Not, of course, Christians – whose social virtues of obedience to duty and self-sacrifice reduced all men to the proportions of ants and termites – but religious in the proper, intellectual way, with a faith or hope that their Unknown God would help them to devote their energies to something other than merely perpetuating the futile cycle of human existence – to irradiating and enlarging the ambit of individual awareness.

These reflections were stirred not only by his casual reading, but also by his daily struggles at Burley Hill to apply himself to some writing. 'I have been grunting and sweating over a filthy article on Beddoes the whole time,' he wrote to Swithinbank towards the end of his stay there. The conditions of authorship being what they inevitably were, the actual processes of writing could hold few attractions. Why then write at all? It was surely not just a matter of vanity, of mere blind hedgehog grubbing. The best answer would seem to be that the practice, however execrable and precarious, of the craft in

20. This refers to *The Embarkation for Cythera*, a diploma piece painted by Antoine Watteau in 1712 for the Académie Royale de Peinture et de Sculpture. This painting, now in the Louvre, depicts an imagined voyage to a destined island of love and blessedness.

which one found one's deepest fulfilment was to some extent a happiness, in so far as the denial of it would be a misery. As a labour of love, the composition of his Beddoes was exhausting. At the same time his curiosity was more than usually provoked by the mysterious undertones in Beddoes's life. Here was a strangely distant character – a throwback to the Elizabethan age – yet in some ways Lytton felt remarkably close to him. For, as with General Gordon, he was not slow to perceive the special affinity which lay between them. 'I am trying to write on Beddoes,' he told Keynes (30 July 1907), 'and become daily more persuaded that he was a member of our sect. What do you think? It occurred to me yesterday that Degen[21] is probably still alive, and that we've only got to go over to Franckfort and inquire for a respectable old retired baker, aged seventy-seven, to hear the whole history! Won't you come?'

At the end of August, 'The Last Elizabethan', as he entitled his Beddoes essay, was finished and he left Burley Hill, not alas for Frankfurt but London. The family's furniture was now being transferred from Lancaster Gate across to 67 Belsize Park Gardens, and Lytton was temporarily billeted with his eldest sister Elinor's father-in-law, Sir Alexander Rendel, at 23 Russell Square. He could be of little practical use in the complex business of moving house, and so, after only a few days, he left London to spend a week at Hurst Court, in the village of Hurst near Twyford in Berkshire, which Harry Norton's family had rented that summer. This visit was not a success. Surrounded by his mother and sisters, his only respite the smoking-room and the last number of the *Mathematical Journal*, Norton was reduced to a condition of gibbering inanity. It was impossible to believe that, in the whole course of his life, he had ever addressed one single sensible word to them. In any case what would be the use? All of them indulged endlessly in aimless jokes and mad, trilling laughter which was sustained throughout a series of senseless meals repeating themselves *ad infinitum*, like something in the *Inferno*. And

21. Degen was the nineteen-year-old baker with whom Beddoes lived in close companionship for six months at Frankfurt.

the cumulative coincidence of family ugliness! At moments during his stay Lytton began to despair of the whole human race. No wonder Harry was so pitiably crushed.

'The poor fellow!' he lamented to Keynes (10 September 1907). 'Never did I see anyone so utterly done for – beyond reach of human aid. He's submerged in the ocean of stupidity and dullness which that terrible family existence of his has created. Oh! The horror of Sunday! And to see him appearing at breakfast, rather ashamed of being four minutes late, dressed in the complete vulgarity of "best clothes" with a dreadful fancy waistcoat and a revolting tie! Oh, oh! And then "church" – ugh! Fortunately no attempt was made to induce me to go – I think if there had been I should have said something gross. As it was, I hardly opened my mouth once. He is a weak-willed creature, very good-natured and very clever, but content to be his mother's puppet, and the rest of the family's buffoon.'

After his week was up at Hurst, Lytton fled to the Homere sisters at Kingham. By now he felt too exhausted to do anything but sit out in the more or less comfortable garden 'among my Greek ladies', Chopin in the distance, no reading, no writing. Middle age had descended upon him for ever. 'I have lost count of time, and have fallen into a sea of dullness, health, and decent conversation that's too shocking to think of,' he wrote hopelessly to Swithinbank (13 September 1907). 'I can dimly remember that I saw Keynes for a minute or two some years ago, but what he said to me or I to him, and why and where we met – swallowed, swallowed by the waters of female oblivion . . .

'. . . I can't help it. Could you, if you were where I am on a deck-chair (very uncomfortable) in a misty garden, looking at nothing but a tree or two, and listening to a Greek Lady (very fine and fat) practising scales on a grand piano ten yards off? I feel as if I were hardly more than a scale myself, or at least an arpeggio. Here comes a glass of milk for me, and a couple of rusks. I believe I am perfectly happy.'

On 20 September, he emerged from this contented, enervating seclusion to stay with Clive and Vanessa Bell at

Curfew Cottage in Watchbell Street, Rye, close to the Mermaid Inn where he had put up with Sheppard and Keynes. He had always loved Rye, with the mysterious unseen presence of Henry James brooding over it, and it was especially enjoyable to be there among friends – real friends, that was, with whom one could do as one pleased – come down late for breakfast, go to sleep on the drawing-room sofa, and even succumb to fits of annihilation. Virginia and Adrian Stephen were also there. 'They *are* nice,' he told Duncan Grant, 'and Bell, too, really, if one isn't put off rather by a thick layer of absurdity.' As for Vanessa, now that she was safely with child, he felt that he could almost have married her himself.

While at Rye, he shrugged off his lethargy and began writing once more – an essay on Rousseau which was not actually published until some three years later, and an eight-stanza poem, 'Knowledge', which was inspired by the prospect of seeing Duncan Grant, who had just returned from France.

> For I have seen in half-extinguished eyes
>   The dumb assuagements of immortal grief,
> Infinitudes of exquisite surprise,
>   Looks beyond love, and tears beyond belief.
>
> And subtle transmutations I have seen
>   Upon a dreaming face subtly unfold
> As when in autumn heaven's purpureal green
>   Gradually melts to opalescent gold.

After some five days in Rye, Lytton finally returned to London, moving in for the first time to the new family home in Hampstead. Number 67 Belsize Park Gardens was a smaller house than Lancaster Gate, but still quite fair-sized enough to cater for the rather depleted numbers of the family now living together. As before, Lytton was assigned a bed-sitting-room where he was to compose his reviews and articles. 'Rousseau and his bag of tricks have absorbed me,' he wrote to Clive and Vanessa Bell at the end of the month. 'I spend my days in the British Museum, and my nights in my Hampstead chamber, poring over Grimm. Madame D'Epinay, Mr John Morley, and

Mrs Frederika Macdonald,[22] and trying to determine which is the silliest. It's a dreadful occupation, and I shall probably end by being the silliest of all.'

6

WILD MAN OF THE WOODS

Lytton's brief, full-time career as journeyman of letters began on 1 October, the date on which his duties for both the *Spectator* and the *New Quarterly* commenced. Of these two jobs, the one for the *Spectator* occupied far more of his time, and in the next nineteen months he contributed to the literary section of the paper no less than seventy-five articles of one kind or another – mostly long book- and theatre-reviews.

At first he found this employment rather invigorating. It was something new; it helped to deflect his morbid inward gaze; and it gave some immediate focus to his existence. Once a week he called at the *Spectator* offices to collect some book or other, wondering desperately all the while whether he could possibly complete his piece on it in time. It was a straightforward challenge to his capabilities, and as such spurred him to new effort. Overcoming the hurry and the drudgery of hebdomadal journalism acted as a tonic to his system. He could do it! And not alone that, he could do it

22. 'The Rousseau Affair' was based on a two-volume publication *Jean Jacques Rousseau: a New Criticism* by Frederika Macdonald (1906). The principal revelations of this work related to the *Mémoires et Correspondances de Madame d'Épinay* (1818), the concluding quarter of which contains an account of Rousseau's quarrel with his friends, written from the anti-Rousseau point of view. This hostile narrative, as Mrs Macdonald showed, was in effect composed by Diderot and the Baron de Grimm. Lord Morley had published an earlier biography of Rousseau, taking the accuracy of the *Mémoires* for granted. Lytton's essay (incorrectly dated as 1907 in *Books and Characters*) did not in fact appear in the *New Quarterly* until 1910. 'What is going to happen to that appalling paper?' he wrote to Desmond MacCarthy (7 June 1910). 'I was furious to see my old Rousseau hash served up in it, and I shall never speak to you again if you don't pay me for it. I am dead for want of money, so I insist on being saved by £5.'

better than most others. His apathy and premature middle age were temporarily shaken off. He was reinvigorated. 'I walk on the Heath pretty nearly every afternoon and feel amazingly young and cheerful', he wrote to Keynes towards the end of October. 'I do really feel seventeen – with all the tastes of that age, and all the vices. Very queer indeed.'

But all too soon the inspiriting novelty of journalism wore off and the mechanical, devitalized nature of the job began to tell on him. After a month or two, once his first anxieties had been composed, he grew fretful. It was no more exciting than taking up his weekly essays to the history tutor at Trinity. 'What a filthy life this is!' he complained to Keynes (14 January 1908). 'Full of such silly horrors, and enjoyments sillier still. A taximeter is about as near to heaven as one's likely to get.' Such contemptuous sentiments were not assumed but deeply felt, yet, since he could not bear to fail at anything, he did his job so well that before four months had passed he was already being tempted by the Mammon of Unrighteousness in just the sort of manner that James had predicted. To deny this temptation proved a comparatively easy matter. In a letter dated 18 January 1908, he wrote to James to say that he had been offered the editorship of the *Spectator*, and had refused on the grounds that his business was literature, not politics. St Loe had replied that on consideration, though he regretted Lytton's decision in the interests of the paper, he was bound to say that he considered it to be the right one. 'D'you think', Lytton asked James, 'le pauvre homme realizes the depths he's got into, and wishes that he too had chucked it? I wonder. It's odd.'

With the money he was now beginning to earn, Lytton was able to repay various small loans which he had been made by Keynes and Norton, and to take them to lunch at Simpson's in the Strand, for many years his favourite London restaurant, and conveniently placed just round the corner from the *Spectator* office in Wellington Street, almost on Waterloo Bridge. Otherwise his life went on for the most part much as before – the odd play with MacCarthy, the periodic evening with Clive and Vanessa Bell, with Virginia and Adrian Stephen, the occasional week-end dash to Cambridge where James was endeavouring against odds to get Rupert Brooke elected to the Apostles, a brief visit from Ainsworth who had now moved down from Edinburgh to London and whom Lytton found more entertaining than Keynes, and from the benign and patriarchal Saxon Sydney-Turner who was less entertaining than almost anyone he had ever encountered. What had they ever found to talk about in those studious cloisters of Trinity, he and Woolf and Turner and the others? 'We reviewed old days, of course,' he wrote to Duncan Grant, 'as you may imagine, and said what we always have said for the last hundred years. Friendship is a queer business.'

The monotonous rigmarole of London life during these autumn months was once more overshadowed by the enigmatic presence of Duncan Grant. It was the old story: another resurgence of that rotating cycle of misery, rage and bewilderment that had welled up in Lytton a year ago. Almost at once the sorry deluge of letters started again, letters of flaring anger and abject apology, of self-pity and obsequious gratitude. Frightened of losing his cousin's affection altogether, he ricocheted from one overwrought mood to another. Sometimes he was reduced to utter despair, paralysed and incoherent, by Duncan's insouciance; at other times a wild exasperation swept over him; and then again he would wonder meekly whether, after all, everything was not his own fault. In one important respect, however, the situation differed from that of the previous winter. By now the figure of Hobber had faded altogether from the scene. So what could be the explanation of his present indifference? They had got on so well together at Versailles. And at Belsize Park Gardens Lytton had looked forward to seeing much more of Duncan, who was living with his family a few hundred yards away in Fellows Road. And yet, with the most implausible excuses, he continued to avoid him – or so it appeared.

'I'm in a most unholy state – ill and worse,' he wrote on 23 November. 'I'm really frightened sometimes, you've no idea of the horrible things. And then such nightmares as I had last night! Duncan, it's not you that's the cause. I have a devil inside me – perhaps seven. I occasionally feel that I'm done for, and that I shall really smash up, and "go under", as they say, like a decadent poet. It's my imagination, my awful imagination. I should like to go to sleep for ages and ages. Oh God, what a miserable thing is a human being! There's no hope for a human being outside love. That I shall never get now, and it's all I want.'

This whole hideous emotional *déshabillé* had coffined him – without hope, it seemed, of even visionary resurrection – in a maudlin world of vanity and illusion. Beauty, truth, intelligence – these were mere trifles, he reflected, dimly expressive of the single inner truth of love; and all his activities, such as travelling, talking, scribbling, and so on, were no more than unsuccessful efforts to keep this truth suppressed, to render life liveable without it. The moment his desires failed to find someone on whom to fix, everything flew to dust and ashes, and he was swallowed up in a void of self-centred tedium. Yet never for long. Each time, the cord attaching him to those points where his heart was focused drew him up out of these dull, vacuous caverns and re-established him as a prisoner of all the familiar longings for amatory reincarnation, so hopeless and unrealizable. Refreshed by the miraculously renewed surge of love and lust which flowed like an incoming tide over the dry sands of his loveless existence, the uprush of buried emotions would crush and desiccate him. In recoil from its unfulfilled unification with another being, his body felt as weak and unresistant to physical sickness as a baby's.

After a few days in bed Lytton floated down to Brighton where his health and frame of mind were soon cheered up wonderfully. Notwithstanding Christmas, everything seemed more sanguine on his return. Duncan was in a more friendly vein, and they read *Mansfield Park*, went for walks on the Heath, and caught mild influenza together.

It was while convalescing at 23 Russell Square that he heard the news that his father had fallen very seriously ill. He returned home at once. A few days later, on the morning of 12 February, Sir Richard Strachey died in his sleep. Although Lytton had never succeeded in getting close to the old man, he had always remained extremely fond of him, greatly admiring his scientific ability. For a time he contemplated writing a biography of him. There were plenty of facts, especially relating to Sir Richard's Indian career. But the plan never materialized. It would have meant, he told James, writing the whole history of India in the nineteenth century. His father had been, and would always be, not so much a tantalizing enigma, challenging curiosity and interpretation, as a remote and shadowy personage with whom it was almost inconceivable to deal except on formal terms. Their close accord on the mathematical problems which were sometimes debated in their letters to each other, had marked the limits of their lifetime intimacy. And, in retrospect, Lytton came no nearer to this distant paternal spirit. Though he had long ceased to reach out to him as any kind of confidant or companion, his father's silent presence in the house had acted as a loadstone, drawing him back from his frequent but never very long trips out of London. Now that magnetic power was switched off for ever. The focal point of the family, a rock of impregnable masculinity standing out from the eternal sea of females, had finally submerged and vanished. Somehow, and some time soon, Lytton resolved, he too must leave, and set up home elsewhere.

Towards the end of February Lady Strachey set out with her brother Trevor for the South of France. Lytton and Pippa accompanied them as far as Calais and saw them into their train. Then they went on to Boulogne where they remained for a few days at the Hôtel Bristol et Christol. The trip did them both good, especially Pippa, who needed a change and some rest urgently. Soon after their return to England, and while their mother was still abroad, they both went down for a short visit to St Loe Strachey's country house at Newlands Corner, near Guildford. 'A most gorgeous newly-painted scarlet motor-car took us to and from the station,' Lytton wrote to his mother (11 March 1908), 'and St Loe insisted on my wearing one of his numerous fur-coats, so I felt very grand. In the evening we all went to the Parish room in the village, where Amy's "Masque of Empire" was performed – mainly by village boys and girls. Amabel[23] was Britannia, which was the leading part. She looked nice but her acting was too much in the regular affected "recitation" style, which Pippa thinks she must have learnt from Amy. I can't imagine anyone acting so by the light of nature. . . . Amy was most affable and not at all prononcée. When I went she insisted on my taking away the Masque to suggest any improvements that might occur to me. It is in the main quite harmless – the chief blot to my mind is that at the end Britannia and all the Colonies and Dependencies fall on their knees, repeating R.K.'s poem "Lest we forget" and praying for mercy, etc. . . . One thing annoyed me. She talked of Queen Victoria as Britain's "greatest queen". I begged her to put "long-lived" instead – or any other disyllabic adjective – pointing out that that could only apply to Queen Elizabeth. But she wouldn't hear of it.'

By now it had become Lytton's chief object in life to escape on every possible occasion from the distractions of the new family regime. Its discomfort, its intense solitude without privacy, depressed him beyond measure, blighting alike all his attempts at work and pleasure. In numbers the family was greatly reduced. There was his mother, his sisters, Pippa who was always ready to talk about fascinating subjects, Marjorie, high-spirited, often shocking with her outrageous opinions, and occasionally Pernel, quiet, observant and witty. Ever since the earliest Lancaster Gate days, Lady Strachey had been given to reading at lunch and dinner, not books, but copies of *Home Chat* and *Tit Bits*, from the pages of which, with cries of laughter, she would shout out jokes. Everyone deprecated this practice, and she would indignantly protest at the lack of enthusiasm with which these readings were greeted all round the table. The arguments between Lady Strachey and her daughters, in particular Marjorie, were high-pitched and con-

23. Amabel Strachey (b. 1894), who later married B. C. Williams-Ellis, the architect and man of letters, was the eldest child of St Loe and Henrietta Amy Strachey. She is the author of many books for children, including *Darwin's Moon* (1966), a biography of Alfred Russel Wallace.

tinuous. Very sensibly, Lytton became in time a little deaf to all this din. But Marjorie's voice was especially raucous, and the noise was often nerve-racking.

Earlier in the year, before his father's death, he had declined an invitation from Moore to join his Easter reading-party, to be held this time in the Green Dragon at Lavington on Salisbury Plain. But in the altered circumstances he now quickly changed his mind, and in the third week of April hurried down to Wiltshire. There, despite the magical charm of Moore himself – still 'a colossal being' as he describes him to Virginia Stephen – who plays the piano and sings in the old inimitable way with the sweat pouring down his face, this gathering of his friends only seems to add to his growing sense of isolation. Hawtrey, Sanger, Bob Trevy – it is the same crowd as always; but, individually, they are changing. And perhaps he, too, is changing. The nostalgia he feels for Cambridge now intermingles with a new bitterness, born out of three years' aimless wandering in the wilderness of London. He has become more than ever sharply critical of the dons, their dull caution and dry-as-dust attitude to living; and only that month, in the columns of the *Spectator*, has launched a slashing attack on the fifth volume of *The Cambridge Modern History*, likening its learned authors – one of whom is his old tutor, Stanley Leathes – to 'the barbarians of the Dark Ages'.

In any event, whether it is he or his Cambridge companions who have changed, Lytton feels himself left out of things – an estrangement which comprised a vague and as yet obscure sense of rivalry with Keynes, and hardly any contact at all with the younger undergraduates headed by Rupert Brooke. Even his own brother, James, appears 'very mysterious and reserved, and either incredibly young or inconceivably old'. In retreat from the whole complex shifting problem of human relationships, he spends much of his time re-reading Racine, who, unlike the Apostles these days, occupied himself with the only real and permanently worthwhile subject in the world – the human heart!

'Oh, adventures! Does one ever have them nowadays?' he exclaims in a letter to Virginia Stephen. '. . . Do you? Is the

Atlantic enough for you? I am the wild man of the woods, I often think, and perhaps inexplicable to civilized people ...' Unfortunately Lytton's physique is not up to supporting such claims, which are perhaps no more than outward expressions of that shifting ambition which burns and gnaws and consumes him inwardly like a physical malady. Even these 'congregations of intellect upon Salisbury Plain', as Virginia Stephen describes the reading-party, proved too adventurous for him. He travelled back to Belsize Park with a violent cold and once there confined himself to his room, crouching over a fire 'snivelling and cursing and drinking quinine'.

May was an atrocious month. He was desperately overworked with his continuing *Spectator* and *New Quarterly* articles. Sometimes he felt absolutely sick at the thought of going on much longer in the coils of this present phase. He detested the Hampstead regime, at least as much as Keynes hated the India Office; and alas, there was no King's to receive him. 'I am almost completely lost – for the time being,' he wrote on 8 May. 'DEATH has set in. Articles to be finished in the twinkling of an eye! Horror! Horror! ... Don't come near me or attempt to speak to me for several days. No Simpsons I fear on Tuesday. Only rain and mortification.'

In addition to this regular work he had recently been asked by the Oxford University Press to write a long introduction to any book of his choice, to be published in the same series of reprints as *Blake*, which had been brought out in the previous year by Walter Raleigh – through whose personal recommendation Lytton had received this commission. For several weeks he racked his brains in vain for something that was both suitable and worth republishing, and after discussions with the publishers and with Raleigh he at last decided on *A Simple Story* by Mrs Inchbald. By May he should already have been well into this work, but could find no time to fit it in and was obliged to write off to the publishers begging for a short extension. Yet, whatever happened, the 'dreadful introduction' could not long be delayed.

And as if all this were not enough, Duncan had again been off-hand, immediately plunging Lytton down into the blackest troughs of despair. Would this torture and confusion never end? Only, he decided, when he could quit Belsize Park Gardens for good and live elsewhere; for only then could he hope to face things calmly and see them in proportion. 'I am having an acute fit of family fever, and the world is black,' he wrote to James later that same month. 'Certes, plus que je médite, the less it appears tolerable to lead the sort of hole-and-corner, one-place-at-table-laid-for-six life I do at present. It's impossible to think and impossible to breathe. Oh! Oh! I have serious thoughts of flight. But how? Where? – Could I ever face poverty, journalism, and solitude? The whole thing's sickening. It's bad luck that Duncan should be so singularly hopeless as a companion – what a great difference a little difference would have made! And now, too, just now, when I seem to see clearly that I ought to go, Keynes makes up his mind to go too, so that that avenue is cut off from me. I've a good mind to take rooms at Cambridge next term.'

Since Keynes had now removed from his flat at 125B St James's Court, preparatory to settling into King's where Alfred Marshall had offered him a lectureship in economics with a salary of a hundred pounds a year; and since Duncan was so vague and unreliable as a friend, with whom else could he possibly share a flat? To live alone was impracticable – unthinkable. But perhaps even now something might be worked out with one or other of them. Either would be preferable to his Hampstead home.

Some temporary respite from this problem came in June, almost all of which he spent in very pleasant rooms at King's. Between *Spectator* reviews, and when the weather was fine, he entertained himself with a variety of simple pleasures – gazing out of his windows at the divine Backs, or gliding up and down the river very slowly in a punt which James worked with a paddle, or eating too much, or just wandering along Trinity Street with a fixed lack of purpose. 'The only disadvantage of this place are the beauties,' he confided to Swithinbank (5 June 1908), 'who are everywhere and ravish one's heart in the most unpleasant manner. . . . I write a review a week for the *Spectator* . . . and spend all I get in reckless luxury.

It's the only way of consoling oneself for the ruins of life.'

Among his old friends Lytton saw much of Sheppard and Norton, who seemed to revive whenever he was away from home for any length of time, and became particularly charming, amusing and on the spot. Of more interest though were his impressions of Rupert Brooke, with whom his relationship was complicated by the single-minded and depressing infatuation of his brother. 'As for Rupert', he told Duncan Grant (12 June 1908), ' – I'm not in love with him, though it's occasionally occurred to me that I ought to be – but there really are too many drawbacks to him, though of course there are charms and pleasantries too. His self-conceit is écrasant, and his general pose merely absurd. He's also, I *think* – but I'm not sure – rather brutal to me, who'm an innocent friendly person, and no fool. Not the ghostliest shadow of a dream of a rapprochement. It's disappointing – a little – but certainly my heart's not broken – only rather pricked.'

Lytton was also encountering some of the other younger men now up at Cambridge – in particular Gerald Shove,[24] Hugh Dalton and James Elroy Flecker ('whom we now don't much like'), but with none of them was he able to communicate freely. How different it had been when he was up! In those delightful far-off days things were less ambiguous and therefore more exciting. One's soul could discharge itself in covert glances, allusions, delicate hints. It was easy enough to be personal, intimate, amused, even to make implications about *amours*, when one was twenty, and life was an affair of plain sailing. But when 'middle age', Spectatorial responsibilities and a ruined digestive system combined to harness and perplex one, what could be expected? 'My story is now quite unfit for publication,' he wrote to Clive Bell (12 June 1908), ' – not because of its decency, but because of its muddles – it's aesthetically very poor indeed. ... So far my successes among the younger generation have

24. Gerald Frank Shove (1887–1947), the economist, who became a lecturer in economics at Cambridge and a Fellow of King's, was at this time a keen left-wing socialist and syndicalist.

not been remarkable. Am I altogether passé? But I occasionally find myself shattered, and I *have* embarqued on various
intrigues. But it won't do, it'll none of it do. Beauty is a
torment and a snare, and youth is cruel, cruel! Today I drove
in a barouche to the races with a select assortment of undergraduates. Doesn't it sound romantic? But it was merely
rather nice. Yesterday I drank champagne from 11 to 1, and
discussed love and friendship, and the day before I went to the
A[mateur] D[ramatic] C[lub] ... and was bored – or amused?
– I really can't make up my mind.'

For long hours he would sit closeted in a small inner sanctum working at his verses, solitary but not altogether undisturbed. For so often he heard – or seemed to hear – the door
of the outer room open, and someone enter, and – did he
advance and come towards the inner door? Or was it the
bedmaker? Or the wind outside? Or simply imagination –
spectres from the old days? Lytton could not tell; only the
inner door never opened and he sat on alone and silent,
listening, and then re-applying himself to his work, striving
to arrange in some poetic pattern the muddled and tormented moments of his past. Much of his verse during the last
three years was spun round the idealized figure of Duncan
Grant, and perhaps the most successful one – because it is
least pretentious – catches something of the shrouded, insubstantial quality of their relationship.

> One day you found me – was I there?
>   Perhaps it was my ghost you found –
> I know not; but you found me fair
> And love was in my lips and hair
>   And in my eyes profound.
>
> You kissed me, and you kissed me oft.
>   – Was it my ghost or was it me? –
> Your kisses were so sweet, so soft,
> The happy cherubim aloft
>   Wept that such things should be.
>
> You vanished then – I know not why;
>   But that you vanished 'tis most true.

Yet did you vanish? — Till I die
Methinks I'll doubt (my ghost or I)
If 'twas your ghost or you.

But in view of the dramatic events now about to burst upon him, perhaps the most fitting comment and summary of the whole affair is contained in a couple of casual sentences which he had addressed earlier that year in a letter to Duncan Grant. 'The world is damned queer — it really is', he wrote. 'But people won't recognize the immensity of its queerness.'

7

A POCKET HANDKERCHIEF ON MONT BLANC

On his return to Hampstead at the beginning of July, Lytton discovered that for some time past Duncan Grant had been deeply in love with Maynard Keynes, and that his affection was returned.

Of all the darkly amorous crises sprinkled throughout his life, this was perhaps the most wretched. It came as an explosive shock, a kind of death. Like the violent eruption of an earthquake which alters every feature in the surrounding landscape, this sudden revelation destroyed in a few moments the whole structure of his last three years. The two fixed points upon which his unstable emotional existence had been so delicately suspended were instantly rooted up. He could not be sure that he would ever recover from the calamity, though reason told him that he eventually must. Yet, overwhelming all this agony of bitter disenchantment and regret was the aching realization that he had been made to look impossibly ridiculous. As he retraced the pattern of events in his mind, it was this thought which harrowed and excruciated him most. How inconceivably blind he had been! No wonder he had felt swamped by so much muddle and confusion. Now that he knew the simple truth, everything slipped neatly and obviously into place. In the first instance it had been he who had driven the two of them together, almost against their will.

And to think that all the time he had been confiding to Keynes about Duncan's childish irresponsibility and inexplicable elusiveness, and joking with Duncan on the subject of Keynes's irremediable lack of passion (*lack of passion!*), they could well have been comparing notes. How they must have laughed at him! And then, too, while he was cautiously meditating on the relative merits of living with either Keynes or Duncan, they had gone off – so he now discovered – and found accommodation together in Belgrave Road.[25] God! What a total fool he had made of himself. The world was indeed more immensely queer than even he had recognized!

There was nothing for it now but to put the best possible face upon it all. At any rate he resolved that by no word or action should he in any way swell his past accumulation of foolishness. To expend his mounting fury and remorse in pointless recrimination would only tend to emphasize all his previous stupidity. Nor must he break off diplomatic relations. For one thing this affair of Duncan's and Keynes's might still only be a brief flash in the pan; and for another, any pompous reaction could only make him appear even more inane – always providing, of course, that that were possible. Instead then he must treat it as a comparatively small incident, and so, by minimizing everything, reduce the magnitude of his own idiot cuckoldry. If supremely civilized, supremely controlled, his behaviour might win him back some of the esteem which he had shed, and at the same time prompt feelings of guilt in his treacherous friends.

To Keynes, whom he detested now more than at any other moment in his life, he wrote: 'Dear Maynard, I only know that we've been friends far too long to stop being friends now. There are some things that I shall try not to think of, and you must do your best to help me in that; and you must believe that I do sympathize and don't hate you and that if you were

25. After a short tenancy at Belgrave Road, they moved to 21 Fitzroy Square. Then, in 1911, they shared a house at 38 Brunswick Square with Adrian and Virginia Stephen, Gerald Shove and Leonard Woolf. Later still they moved to 46 Gordon Square which they shared with Clive and Vanessa Bell.

here now I should probably kiss you, except that Duncan would be jealous, which would never do!'

Keynes's response to this magnanimity was all that Lytton could have desired. 'Your letter made me cry,' he wrote back, 'but I was very glad to get it.' He wished very much to write something more, the letter went on, but he did not know what to say. Might he come to Hampstead? This proposition, naturally enough, was the very last thing to appeal to Lytton, who was always far surer of himself on paper than in person. All sorts of disasters might ensue from such a visit. Keynes would eloquently put his case and make himself appear to be innocent and upstanding; the mere sight of him might well stir Lytton into losing his temper and making a further ass of himself. Far better to keep Keynes at some distance where he remained permanently at a disadvantage. He therefore replied saying that on the whole – if Keynes did not mind – he thought it best that he should *not* come and see him at present. He was still most horribly *accablé* with the Inchbald introduction, and this combined with the general chaotic situation had reduced him to such a state of ruin and confusion that he would really have nothing whatever to say at an interview. Soon perhaps he would be going away – he did not know where or with whom. He was rather ill, too.

But Keynes still pressed resolutely for a meeting and postponed his journey to Cambridge in order to force one. Would Lytton, he inquired, like to go with him to see *Isadora* Duncan dance, and forget the real Duncan, whom no one in the world could help but adore?

Lytton, however, ignored altogether both the pun and the invitation in his answer. He had, he wrote, sent Keynes a present of some books to adorn *his rooms at King's*. Doubtless they were waiting for him now. He asked his friend to examine carefully the binding which, he believed, was of a quality and type that he particularly admired. He hoped that Maynard would be pleased with this little gift; the book on walking-sticks was especially entertaining.

And so there was nothing that Keynes could do but concede a tactical defeat, quit London and pick up his books at

Cambridge. They were delightful, he wrote back on his arrival there: 'Dear Lytton, why have you given them me? They show something you couldn't write, and they make me feel a great deal which you must understand without my saying it. Oh Lytton, it is too good of you to behave like this.'

To wrest from his opponent the very last trick of beneficence, there now only remained one final card for Lytton to play – he thanked Keynes lavishly for the letter thanking him for the books. 'Thank you,' he replied, 'dear Maynard, for what you wrote about the books. I'm glad you liked them, and it's very nice of you to feel what you say. Duncan is very kind, too. I'm sure of one thing, and that is that affection makes everything right. So I'm really extraordinarily happy now.'

In his simultaneous dealings with Duncan Grant, towards whom his attitude was more complicated, Lytton was unable to sustain the same impassive front of dignity. He began, however, on quite the loftiest note of altruism yet struck. Duncan, he knew, was considering taking art lessons in London with a certain Dr Bach. What gesture could be finer than to offer to pay for these lessons? It was an inspired stroke, which drew from his cousin an almost identical response to that from Keynes. 'Lytton you're *too* kind,' he told him, 'you make me burst into tears; I cannot bear your being so completely good and generous. I think it cruel of you to plunge me into such contradictory emotions.'

And there, perhaps, Lytton should have been content to leave it. But he could not. Remembering the past – Ledbury and Versailles in particular – it was impossible not to believe that Duncan had once felt something for him, and that everything might so easily have turned out altogether different. Duncan had praised him now for his kindness, and he could not forbear to send off a somewhat rueful answer: 'Oh, Duncan, I have thought of unkind letters, unkind words – and heaven knows you may have them from me yet; but now it is not with that in my heart that I want to speak. It is not for you that I am feeling, but for myself; and I should like you to know my thoughts . . .

'Concealment would have been easier now too, as you may guess, since if I am to speak all it must be to one more than I want to speak to. He [Keynes] will tell you, no doubt, that I am wrong, that I am foolish because I am jealous, and that I am to be pitied because I am in love. I am ready to face even pity, even the pity of both of you, on the condition that Duncan knows my mind.

'There are things in me, I knew very well, which are beastly; and there are things in you Duncan, which irritate me, which pain me, which I even dislike. If you understand that, will you understand this besides – that I am your friend? It would be irrelevant to say more.'

But once this much had been said it was impossible not to say more. The dams of absolute self-restraint had been opened a crack, and the voluble waters of self-pity, of anger, recrimination and humility cascaded through. On the evening of the day – 17 July – that Duncan received this letter, he called round unannounced at Belsize Park Gardens. Lytton could not refuse to admit him, but said very little and did not attempt to stop him when, after a brief, uneasy session, Duncan rose to leave. Later that night he sent off a short note, saying that he had thought it best that Duncan should leave when he did. Otherwise 'I might have been stupid'. Whatever happened, he concluded with a familiar refrain, they were still friends.

What really pained Lytton, however, was Duncan's ensuing silence. Unlike the persistent Keynes, he did not write for days on end to expatiate on his, Lytton's, angelic and self-effacing goodness. After the first, rather short letter, there was nothing – no consistently renewed and visible evidence of Duncan's contrition. What was he thinking? Lytton's imagination kept churning away until, after a fortnight of waiting, he could no longer contain his doubts. The urge to set down and to explain his own thoughts and injuries grew too strong for him to resist. But he was clutching at straws in the wind, begging for the kind of pity he professed so much to abhor – pity of himself, not for his grief. And so, though he painfully insists. yet again, that nothing need greatly have changed, that their sublimated friendship is still intact, the letter does not, significantly, conclude with a mere *à bientôt*.

Dearest Duncan

I want to say something, though I'm afraid it may annoy you, and I daresay I've said it already – but I feel an uneasy suspicion that I may not have made myself quite clear. It is this – though I like Maynard, I cannot think of him as you do, or else, I suppose, I should be in love with him too! The result is that I don't take your affair as seriously as you do either, and therefore imagine that you will some day or other return from Cythera. But that, I feel, is neither here nor there, and so long as you *are* in Cythera, I don't see why that fact should prevent my liking both of you as much as I always have. Please realize what I mean, if it's not too vilely expressed, and forgive me if it's all obvious and I'm merely harping on what you know. I can't bear to think that other people may think I think what I don't, and this must be my excuse for writing what I know will give you some pain. It looks rather bleak, and I wanted to say it, but there was no opportunity when you were away. When you write, it would be very kind if you would say that you understand – I'm sure you won't think I *feel* bleakly. Dear me, this seems to be about nothing but myself, which is so unimportant!

... Oh lord, lord, why do we live in such a distorted coagulated world? I feel all topsy-turvy and out of place, as if I were a pocket handkerchief that somebody had dropped on the top of Mont Blanc. It's all too preposterous, and what's worse, I'm well aware that I do very little but add to the preposterousness. But I believe that a just God – a *really* just God – would completely bear me out. Oh! You're laughing.

This is an absurd kind of letter, you must admit; I'll write again perhaps more sensibly, from somewhere or other. And you must write to me. It'll be forwarded. Adieu!

Your
Lytton

Early in August, Lytton travelled up to Scotland on a voyage of recovery. Accompanied by James, who himself hoped to wear off the ill-effects of his 'dumb deaf and blind adoration' of Rupert Brooke, he went first to the Isle of Skye, putting up for a week at the Sligachan Inn. Sligachan was a strange and desolate place, some nine miles from Portree, the nearest centre of civilization. On all sides lay deserts of bumpy green morass, sea-lochs, and, farther off, distorted blunt black mountains bulging into the sky and wrapped in a pale wet mist – a magnificent but dehumanized spectacle that seemed to act upon Lytton as a recuperative force. From the absence of all jostling humanity he derived a wonderful solace; while from the great vegetable processes of Nature going on all around he drew fresh incentive for a renewed existence. The miserable past was largely obliterated and he was remade. A new feeling of his separate, unique and indestructible identity flooded through him, finding its strength, paradoxically, from the recognition of his anonymity and entire submergence in some vaster, grander organism. Occasional blazing sunbursts would light up within him unsuspected wells of hope; and even the perpetual rain was soothing and merciful, like a gentle antiseptic washing away the stench and stagnation of human intercourse. His long sickness of living had now begun to mend, and nothing brought him all things.

Such was the amazing physical energy released in them that the two brothers were able to make a couple of expeditions on foot and through the almost impenetrable deluge to Portree, which stirred in Lytton faint tremors of his old emotions. The youth of the place seemed to him resplendent – even the women were good-looking! After a week at Skye he felt ready, if not to be re-embedded in the horrors of London, at least to make his first step back south. He was beginning to grow more critical and complaining – a sure sign of improvement. The second trip to Portree convinced him that, far from being attractive, the population was uniformly ugly beyond his wildest nightmares. And the mountains, hotels and local inhabitants appeared to him to be all on a par – all highly eccentric. The Sligachan Inn was filled to bursting point with fat ladies, fishers and climbers, who canted endlessly on about fishing and climbing, and threw sly apprehensive glances at the two thin-legged, bespectacled monstrosities sitting paralysed by the fire. After some days of torture in the smoking-room, the pressure of continual scrutiny from this crowd of burnt and weather-beaten Alpinists and fishers of fish drove them into a private sitting-room, where they could relax by themselves in luxurious and intelligent silence. So, at least, Lytton told Maynard Keynes. Yet even here, the mounting curiosity which their presence seemed to excite telepathically communicated itself through the walls to them, and they decided to flee south to Rothiemurchus.

They arrived at Rothiemurchus in the second week of August and for the next month put up in a tiny cottage with only one room and a 'cave' at their disposal. 'The "accommodation" is, as people say, rather primitive,' Lytton explained to Swithinbank (13 August 1908), '... a smallish sitting-room, where I have to sleep, and a sort of cave adjoining it, where brother James sleeps ... and there is an exceedingly amiable Scottish matron who does everything; and that's all.' Yet the place was everything that could be desired. The beauties of the countryside were truly awe-inspiring. To be among them once again made Lytton feel that life was definitely worth living after all. The beauties of humanity were rarer, though the cottage – almost touching the road to Loch an Eilein[26] – was in a strategic position for observing them. All day and every day the world swept past his window in carriages, brakes and motors; and as the road divided just in front of the house, many of them stopped to ask the landlady the way to the loch, so that Lytton could press his nose against the glass and stare his fill. It was, for the time being, as close as he wished to be to mortal men.

While at Rothiemurchus, Lytton continued to lead what was, for him, a very healthy and virile life – unceasing walks and sittings-out in the sunlight and brushing-away of flies. He was out of doors so much that his nose soon grew red and raw as Bardolph's. It was all very fortifying. On one boiling day, he told Swithinbank, 'I returned to savagery and plunged

26. 'Loch an Eilein' is a Gaelic place-name meaning 'the loch of the island'. A famous beauty spot, it is incredibly romantic and much reproduced on tourist picture postcards. The island-fortress in the middle of its placid waters was, as legend has it, the lair of the notorious Wolf of Badenoch, who in fact died several years before it was put up. The fortifications, now in ruins, were erected in the fifteenth and sixteenth centuries,

wildly into a mountain pool, lost my eyeglasses, and very nearly perished miserably of exposure. Imagine the fearful scene. I tore over hill and dale, and then lay out in the sun having erections. It was very odd.' 'We are tapis here (brother James and I)', he wrote to Clive Bell (13 August 1908), 'in a hut near a lake, like so many lop-eared rabbits. The beauties of nature satisfy me (for the moment); I go out before break-fast in pumps and brood over the lake; I walk in the heat of the day on to the summits of mountains.'

He was also writing again – things other than his *Spectator* reviews, which he had somehow managed to keep up throughout the crisis. Over these weeks, in a long series of letters to Maynard Keynes, he fabricated a highly ingenious and quite imaginary love-adventure – the most inspired of all his fictional compositions. Keynes – now passing two leisurely months in the Orkneys with Duncan Grant and work-ing at *A Treatise on Probability* while having his portrait painted[27] – was by turns curious, amazed, *almost* incredulous. Then at last came the catharsis. Not a single word of it was true. Everything had been recounted in the lightest, most amusing manner; but there can be no doubt as to the motive – deliberate or unconscious – behind this skilful and extraordi-narily elaborate piece of invention, with all its enticing scandal and controlled melodrama. Keynes had been used as a Brother Confessor to something that never took place; his old role had been falsified, and Lytton had got a little of his own back in fiction for the way he had been deceived in fact. From now on, James, who had helped him each evening over their peat fire to concoct this plot, would be his confidant in real life.

During July, when the crisis first broke, Lytton had felt up to reading little except Voltaire's correspondence which, he told Swithinbank, was 'the only completely satisfactory thing in the world'. But it was another favourite volume he took up with him to Scotland – Professor Giles's anthology of

27. This portrait, which was exhibited at the Duncan Grant Tate Gal-lery retrospective exhibition of 1959, and again, in 1964, at Wildenstein's 'Duncan Grant and his World', now belongs to the Provost and Fellows of King's College, Cambridge.

Chinese Poems, in which he now entirely immersed himself, writing a long appreciation of them for MacCarthy's *New Quarterly*. He had had a surfeit in the last weeks of high emotional drama, and his strength and stamina were seriously impaired. He wanted to avoid anything that involved him too painfully in raw passion and direct suspense. Instead he looked for simplicity, tenderness, consolation — emotions faintly recollected in tranquillity. To allay his remorse, to escape from the self-consuming rage, the nausea and suffering which welled up out of his recent tribulations, he abandoned the inconsequent world of reality for a magic sphere of pure art, where every loose end, that weighs on the heart like a broken assignation, was satisfactorily tied up, where tragedy was smoothed and rounded into song, and love and lust were no more than a bewitching interplay of syllables. In Professor Giles's anthology he found the perfect dreamy and pervading melancholy to chime in with that medley of old emotions moving beneath his surface aloofness. The peculiar enchantment of these poems which caught, through a hundred subtle modulations, all the sadness in the fragility of human relations and transmuted it into something delicate and profound and lasting, was like a balm to his wounded spirit. Fragmentary, allusive, evanescent, they seemed to compel reminiscence and romance, to redeem all the horrors of the past, changing its sorrow and vanity, misunderstanding and sentimentality from pettiness into something universal and other-worldly. It was comforting to reflect that morbid affairs of the heart such as his had been going on for centuries, and had so often been overcome. And now he, in his turn, was weathering the storm and sailing into smoother waters.

Just how Lytton associated his own personal story and blended it in with the charm and antiquity of the Chinese poems can best be demonstrated by quoting the final long paragraph of his essay, which concludes not with a translation, but with some of his own verses:

'Our finest lyrics are for the most part the memorials of

passion, or the swift and exquisite expressions of "the tender eye-dawn of aurorean love". In these lyrics of China the stress and fury of desire are things unknown, and, in their topsy-turvy Oriental fashion, they are concerned far more with memories of love than expectations of it. They look back upon love through a long vista of years which have smoothed away the agitations of romance and have brought with them the calm familiarity of happiness, or the quiet desolation of regret. Thus, while one cannot be certain that this love is not another name for sublimated friendship, one can be sure enough that these lovers are always friends. Affection, no doubt, is the word that best describes such feelings; and it is through its mastery of the tones and depths of affection that our anthology holds a unique place in the literature of the world. For this cause, too, its pages, for all their strange anti-quity, are fresh to us; their humanity keeps them immortal. The poets who wrote them seem to have come to the end of experience, to have passed long ago through the wonders and the tumults of existence, to have arrived at last in some mys-terious haven where they could find repose among memories that were for ever living, and among discoveries that were for ever old. Their poetry is the voice of civilization which has returned upon itself, which has achieved, after the revolution of ages, simplicity. It has learnt to say some things so finely that we forget, as we listen to it, that these are not the only things that can be said.

> We parted at the gorge and cried 'Good cheer!'
> The sun was setting as I closed my door;
> Methought, the spring will come again next year,
>   But he may come no more.

The words carry with them so much significance, they produce so profound a sense of finality, that they seem to contain within themselves a summary of all that is most important in life. There is something almost cruel in art such as this; one longs, somehow or other, to shake it; and one feels that, if one did, one would shake it into ice. Yet, as it is, it is far from frigid; but it is dry – dry as the heaped rose-leaves in a porcelain vase, rich with the perfume of how many summers! The scent transports us to old gardens, to old palaces; we wander incuriously among forsaken groves; we half expect some wonder, and we know too well that nothing now will ever come again. Reading this book, we might well be in the alleys of Versailles; and our sensations are those of a writer whose works, perhaps, are too modern to be included in Professor Giles's anthology:

> Here in the ancient park, I wait alone.
> The dried-up fountains sleep in beds of stone;
> The paths are still; and up the sweeping sward
> No lovely lady passes, no gay lord.
>
> Why do I linger? Ah! perchance I'll find
> Some solace for the desolated mind
> In yon green grotto, down the towering glade,
> Where the bronze Cupid glimmers in the shade.'

The composition of this literary essay seemed to purge Lytton of much of that faintness and frailty that had eclipsed his being, especially during those first wet days at Sligachan. The only drawback was the encircling presence of his family. Pippa and Pernel Strachey came up to stay with Trevor Grant in Rothiemurchus, swelling the copious number of Lytton's relations already there. Their persistent and rather alarming propinquity during the four weeks of his holiday grew increasingly irksome to him. 'My only consolation,' he wrote to Virginia Stephen, 'is that my health, as a matter of fact, is almost tolerable. I am sunburnt and I digest. Do write to me if you can. Pippa and Pernel are in a cottage half a mile away, and hundreds of dread relatives lurk behind every bush. They are of all varieties – countesses, country cousins, faded civil servants, and young heirs to landed property – and all eminently repellent. I think I shall make an Encyclopaedia of them. It would be enormously large.'

By the second week of September Lytton's only consolation was rudely snatched away from him, when he was attacked 'by a most disgusting internal disease which seemed to be a chill on the entrails', as he diagnosed it to Clive Bell.

'... It was unpleasant, as you may imagine, struggling with this among the rigours of a Scotch summer and the sanitary arrangements of a Scotch cottage.' As soon as he was able to travel, he fled southwards on a journey which, he told Moore, 'very nearly killed me'. Moore had now moved from Scotland to a house at Richmond, and Lytton wrote to tell him, in words which reflect something of his own dilapidated condition on re-entering England, that he had visited his old home. 'I spent two nights in Edinburgh, and took a walk to look at Buccleuch Place – it seemed very deserted and grey.'

8

CUL-DE-SAC

'Deserted and grey' – this was certainly how Lytton saw himself on his return that September to the home influences of Hampstead. Looked after by his sisters and fed on a special preparation of meat-juices, he lay in hope of a quick recovery and a quick escape elsewhere. It was not a happy time. But he was well cared for and temporarily too sick to be actively discontented. 'I think I'm still rather ill,' he wrote to Clive Bell (17 September 1908), 'and I'm certainly lazy, but I have projects for an infinitude of things. I've begun to read Condorcet, and it's charming, and I should like to go straight through his two volumes – but the time! the time!'

As he became stronger, he again grew more adversely critical of things; and his change of mood appears this time to have been mirrored in his reading. No longer was he content to meditate dreamily over those gentle Chinese lyrics, which seemed in his more aggressive moments to be rather too insipid and over-polite. 'I've also read for the first time the correspondence between Voltaire and D'Alembert,' he wrote off to his mother (2 September 1908). 'Don't you think there's a good deal to be said in favour of a war à outrance with the infâme. I think France is on the whole a more civilized place than England, and it seems to me that may be the result of their having had their superstitions and prejudices rooted up once and for all by the philosophers. What a disgrace that the education of the country should depend upon the squabbles of nonconformists and anglicans! But what else can happen so long as everyone goes on taking these people at their own valuation?'

This spirit of simmering revolutionary ferment was as yet relatively infrequent, and Lytton soon returned obediently enough to the placid broken-down routine, as he rather too disparagingly put it, 'of a literary hack'. He attended second-rate plays, devoured solitary lunches at Simpson's, visited St Loe and Charles Graves[28] to collect further consignments of books and to be assured that the *Spectator* was never complete when there was nothing by him in it, went by taxi to the London Library for more books to help him with these reviews, and divided his remaining hours between Hampstead and Bloomsbury. 'There are moments – on the Heath, of course – when I seem to myself to see life steadily and see it whole,' he wrote to Virginia Stephen, who was in Paris with Clive and Vanessa Bell, 'but they're only moments; as a rule I can make nothing out. You don't find much difficulty, I think. Is it because you *are* a virgin? Or because, from some elevation or another. it's possible to manage it, and you happen to be there? Ah! there are so many difficulties! So many difficulties! I want to write a novel about a Lord Chancellor and his naughty son, but I can't for the life of me think of anything like the shadow of a plot, and then – the British public! Oh dear, let's all go off to the Faroe Islands, and forget the existence of Robin Mayor and Mrs Humphry Ward,[29] and drink rum punch of an evening, and live happily ever after!'

Though he stayed at King's for one week-end late in Oc-

28. Charles Graves, assistant editor of the *Spectator*, who had worked with St Loe on the *Liberal Unionist* and *The Cornhill*, and who was a contributor to *Punch*.

29. Mrs Humphry Ward (1851–1920), popular novelist and author of *Robert Elsmere*. A niece of Matthew Arnold and a strong reactionary, her novels, especially the earlier ones, examined problems of faith and ethics with a solemn and unsmiling sentimentality that was taken at the time for high intellect.

tober, Lytton did not visit Cambridge again during the final four months of this year. There were too many people there whom he had little inclination to see. 'Cambridge has become a complete myth to me,' he wrote to James in November, '– with all the mystery and importance of a myth. I imagine it such a wonderful place.' To preserve this illusion intact he continued to stay away, but the urge to leave London was strong upon him: he went for a few days to live with Moore at 6 Pembroke Villas, on the Green at Richmond; he made plans to visit his Greek ladies where, he told Clive Bell, 'I shall probably be loved'; and when Virginia Stephen returned from Paris, he arranged to go off with her and Adrian, her brother, not on a reckless expedition to the Faroe Islands, but quietly down to Penmenner House, at the Lizard in Cornwall, where he had passed some of his happier hours with Moore's special congregations of Apostolic intellect. After a few peaceful days together spent reading, walking and talking, the Stephens left, and Lytton, who wished to postpone his return to London for as long as possible, stayed on 'in extraordinary solitude, willing to sell my soul for a little conversation. How long I shall bear it I haven't the faintest idea. There have already been moments in the long evening when I've shuddered, but Saint-Simon supports me, wonderful as ever.'

He arrived back at Hampstead towards the end of November for the last time that year. It had been for him a bad, perhaps even his worst, year; but it was not over yet. Now, finally, the time had come for Swithinbank, the understudy, to step into the principal role in his life. For long he had been a mere auxiliary, a recruit; but this winter he should at last be promoted from the reserve to the Front Line. Lytton could at least congratulate himself on not being entirely deserted, for having successfully scotched that mad venture to the Fiji Islands, and for having groomed Swithinbank as a fitting companion. He wrote off to him an affectionate letter, only to receive in reply the news that his friend was making arrangements to take service in India. It was a painful shock, and Lytton at once exerted himself to change Swithinbank's mind again. The letter he now sent off (20 September

1908) was written in an unusually urgent and even earnest tone, and is particularly interesting in someone who, not so long ago, used to envy his brothers for their active, Anglo-Indian careers. 'I believe as strongly as I believe anything that you oughtn't to go,' he wrote. 'Have you thought enough of the horror of the solitude and the wretchedness of every single creature out there and the degrading influences of those years away from civilization? I've had experience – I've seen my brothers, and what's happened to them, and it's sickening to think of. Oh! You've got your chance – your chance of being well off and comfortable among the decent things of life, and among your friends.'

But this time there was no dissuading him from his folly. He had decided; and Lytton was forced to capitulate. 'But go away,' he exclaimed in hopeless irritation, 'and be a great man, and rule the blacks, and enjoy yourself among apes and peacocks.' For Lytton, this departure – like that, apparently, of Leonard Woolf four years before – spelt out his final extinction, his DEATH. Their correspondence lingered on to the following year and then shut down altogether.

Life is a synonym for desire, and all that Lytton desired in happiness and success had eluded him, and now seemed farther off than ever. His few accomplishments appeared trivial when set beside his vague and limitless aspirations. The truth was that his move towards a new life had not been bold enough. The dangers of absolute freedom had proved too intimidating, so that he had merely replaced the chains of his past with the shackles of the present dim and misty existence. All that he had wanted fundamentally to alter remained in essence the same as before; all that he had wished to develop and perfect was destroyed and lay in ruins about him. The tumour of frustrated desire throbbed and swelled within his head. His buoyant faith in the ultimate, though perhaps distant, arrival of a Voltairian millennium of reason, had locked in conflict with his devitalized apathy. Though no one could deny that he had full cause for grief and pessimism, he simply could not submit to the destiny of a mere journeyman. On the contrary, he would do such things – what they were yet he knew not – but they would be the wonders of the earth!

But for the time being his powers could find no all-absorbing purpose to harness them satisfactorily. Oppression descended upon him like an airless cloud. It had been a terrible year, and at the end of it, here he was, left alone with projects for an obscure infinitude of things, but no likelihood of bringing any of them to fulfilment. Deserted and grey: the words which had come to him as he stood before Buccleuch Place, dismal and uninhabited in the autumn wind and rain, epitomized the predicament in which he had landed up after almost twenty-nine years of struggle.

EIGHT

The Wrong Turning

'My heart ... it seems strange that things should still be so singularly active – and at such an age too (106 last birthday). Well! perhaps this time . . ., Only, so different, so different . . . like all other times, in fact.' *Lytton Strachey to Leonard Woolf* (1911)

1
A PROPOSAL OF MARRIAGE

FOR the Christmas festivities of 1908 and the New Year celebrations Lytton fled down once again to the Mermaid Inn at Rye. 'This is a scene of complete desolation,' he wrote to James (31 December 1908), '– rain, snow, fog, dimness unimaginable.' Nevertheless there was absolute rest, which was something, and he was able to read his Mérimée, his Voltaire and his Saint-Simon unimpeded. He even had dreams of writing poetry.

For the first week, he appears to have had the place entirely to himself. At least there was no one else who *counted*; no one he could talk to or even look at for long. He sat on there alone 'in a semi-stupor among mists and golfers', he told Virginia Stephen. '. . . Their conversation is quite amazing, and when I consider that there *must* be numbers of persons more stupid still, I begin to see the human race *en noir*. Oh God! Oh God! The slowness of them, the pomp, and the fatuity.' But early in the New Year the Mermaid Inn received two visitors of note – R. Vere Laurence, his old enemy from Trinity who had rejected his Fellowship dissertation, and his old literary hero, Henry James. Both arrivals were amusingly observed and reported by letter to his brother James (4 January 1909): 'The other day as I was snoozing after lunch I had a surprise, looked up and there was Laurence, in furs and beard complete; fortunately only passing through. My final reflection was that if I were to grow a beard we should be indistinguishable.

'I've also seen Henry James – twice. Both times exceedingly remarkable, but almost impossible to describe. He came in here to show the antique fireplace to a young French poet and you never saw such a scene – the poor man absolutely *bouche béante*, and all the golfers and bishops sitting round quite stolidly munching buttered buns. He has a colossal physiognomy, and it's almost impossible to believe that such an appearance could have produced the Sacred Fount. I long to know him.'

Even more impressive was the second vision of Henry James – at a window of Lamb House. He had just appeared there as Lytton passed by, to examine more minutely some momentous manuscript, a silent but masterly performance – the polite irony of it! He looked immensely serious, and quite extraordinarily slow. 'So conscientious and worried and important,' Lytton described the scene to Virginia Stephen, ' – he was like an admirable tradesman trying his best to give satisfaction, infinitely solemn and polite. Is there any truth in this? It has since occurred to me that his novels are really remarkable for their lack of humour. But I think it's very odd that he should have written precisely them and look precisely so. Perhaps if one talked to him one would understand.'

These were the only highlights of Lytton's visit to Rye, and he returned to London two days later. Virginia had invited him to dine at Fitzroy Square on the evening of 7 January. He was to meet her cousin, H. A. L. Fisher, the historian and Oxford don whose father had married into the Stephen family. 'Summoned from the writing of history,' as one of his pupils at New College described his subsequent elevation to the post of president of the Board of Education, 'to a share in muddling it,' his paroxysms of awe and homage before the men who had converted him into a subject for future historical research, in combination with the book learning he was anxious to put at their disposal, gratified those politicians who might otherwise have regarded a history don with distaste. But in achieving this modest eminence, he had succeeded only in transferring the burden of hostility from his political to his literary associates. 'You are going to meet the Fishers on Thursday,' Virginia had written to Lytton (4 June 1909). 'You and Herbert must talk about Voltaire, and I shall say how I have been seeing his waxwork at Madame Tussaud's. I can't help thinking he is rather a fraud (H.F. I mean). He is impossibly enlightened and humane. She is a bright woman.'

'I shall be able to speak of nothing but cleeks and greens,' Lytton wrote back from the Mermaid, 'though no doubt Herbert would be very well able to cope with that. Besides the golfers there are some of the higher clergy — bishops and wardens — and two lawyers at the chancery bar. Of course these are all golfers as well, so it all comes to very much the same thing.'

H. A. L. Fisher turned out to be less interested in golf than riding, and after some false starts, the conversation switched to the subject of French literature, about which everyone professed to know something. Lytton, as was customary in front of strangers — especially Oxford dons — was mainly unresponsive. But luckily Fisher, not unaware that his father had been a distinguished general, refused to be unimpressed. 'I well remember my first interview with Strachey,' he recollected over twenty years later, 'a sensitive ungainly youth; awkward in his bearing, and presenting an appearance of great physical debility, as if he had recently risen from the bed of an invalid. His voice was faint and squeaky. His pale face was at that time closely shaven. The long red beard of Lamb's portrait which has made him so familiar, was a thing of the future. He was very silent, but uncannily quick and comprehending.'

The impression which Lytton made that evening on Fisher was favourable and long-lasting. And although no one present realized it at the time, this meeting was in due course to lead to a crucial development in Lytton's career.

Meanwhile his routine continued on much as before — labouring over *Spectator* reviews; lunching whenever possible at Simpson's; dining at Fitzroy and Gordon Squares; and the sporadic week-end foray to Cambridge where, released from polite family inhibitions, he could enter into the social life around him and speak his mind more plainly. 'On Sunday at breakfast,' Maynard Keynes reported to Duncan Grant (19 January 1909), 'Sheppard delivered an indictment on poor Rupert [Brooke] for admiring Mr Wells and thinking truth beauty, beauty truth. Norton and Lytton took up the attack and even James and Gerald [Shove] (who was there) stabbed him in the back. Finally Lytton, enraged at Rupert's defences, thoroughly lost his temper and delivered a violent personal attack.'

Lytton's letters over these weeks are full of dismal complaints – about the bad weather, about the 'ghastly solitude' of Belsize Park Gardens, and the feverish colds which seemed persistently to assail him. Some of his days were spent up in his bed, dosed with Sanatogen and quinine; and others, huddled in front of the fire, reading amongst other things the notebooks of Samuel Butler and an eighteenth-century life of Madame de Maintenon. One thing alone he looked forward to; and that was a journey he was planning later in the year to Italy. There, in the warm and friendly climate, he felt confident of shaking off his depression. In the meantime, he must live as economically as possible, save every penny. He even had to refuse Moore's invitation to the Lizard for that year's Easter reading-party: 'If I had a little more money it would be different,' he explained (5 February 1909), 'but I'm poor, and I've got to choose one thing or the other.'

Between colds, he emerged into the outside world like a mole from below ground, and suffered himself to be taken to the random concert or picture gallery. At such moments, London, for all its incursive horrors, would hold him enthralled. There were so many amenities, opportunities, people of interest and attraction. Accidentally he would forget his own ailments and become absorbed by all the curious and entertaining sights around him – in particular by glimpses of the aristocratic world of high fashion and artistic culture.

'I looked in for an hour at the New Gallery,' he wrote in

one letter to Duncan Grant (21 February 1909), '... and was carried away with excitement. It's packed with the most interesting things of the most varied kinds. ... There are Whistlers and Reynoldses, and a divine Gainsborough, and Wattses that even I found charming, and amazing Monticellis, and a superb Manet, and a John à faire mourir de peur. The Simon [Bussy] I found rather a difficult affair to take in at the first go off, but I seemed to be making progress as time went on. The excitement was increased for me by the immense distinction of the audience. – Among others, Mrs Carl Meyer was present, in ermine, the Duchess of Portland and Lady Ottoline Morrell, the Marquis de Soveral, accompanied by Señor Villaviciosa, Lord Musk and Master Musk. Mrs George Batten was talking to Lady Strachey, while Mr Lytton Strachey, who was wearing some handsome Siberian furs, was the centre of an animated group. Mr E. Marsh came in later with the President of the Board of Trade[1] – to say nothing of Mr Edmund Gosse and Mr Sidney Colvin. – The Rothenstein woman, even more painted than usual, flowed in your praises to her Ladyship.'

This world of eminent personages and splendid upper-class names held him spellbound. Intellectually he repudiated it and, as his deliberate caricature style indicates, mocked his own feeling of fascination. Nevertheless it seemed to defy all reason and satire, and persisted in its romantic hold over his imagination. He was like a child enraptured by some fabulous Arthurian legend. But part of the allure lay in his preoccupation with prestige and with personal success, its trappings and rigmarole; and part again in his devouring curiosity over the more exaggerated aspects of human nature.

Another indication of this potent and childlike spell is provided by *Lord Pettigrew*, a novel which Lytton had begun to work on that winter. Written after the style of Anatole

1. The President of the Board of Trade at this time was Winston Churchill. Edmund Gosse had worked as a translator in the Board of Trade with Austin Dobson, the poet. Sidney Colvin, who had been Slade Professor of Fine Art at Cambridge and Director of the Fitzwilliam Museum, was now keeper in the Department of Prints and Drawings at the British Museum

France's *M. Bergeret à Paris*, it is ostensibly a satire directed against the snobbery and the intrigue of fashionable society and reactionary politics.[2] Altogether he completed four chapters, that is between eight and nine thousand words, before giving it up. In this surviving fragment there are some good observations, and the narrative runs along smoothly enough. But because Lytton could not conceive of the aristocracy as being composed of real people like himself, his characters remain mere mouthpieces and never really come to life. For a time, though, he felt excited about the book's possibilities. He would lie in bed in the morning imagining its various dramatic incidents, and each day they would grow more extraordinary. 'You have never heard such conversations or imagined such scenes!' he wrote to Virginia Stephen, who had urged him to continue with it. 'But they're most of them a little too scabreux, and they're none of them written. What's so remarkable is the way in which I penetrate into every sphere of life. My footmen are amazing, and so are my prostitutes. There's a Prime Minister à faire mourir de rire. But it's impossible to get any of it together.'

Lord Pettigrew, so far as it went, was a fantasy which his mind fertilized with ideas as far removed as possible from customary experience, and it may be regarded as a symptom

2. In 1909, the House of Lords rashly rejected the Liberal reforms implemented by the budget. Asquith then dissolved Parliament and, in January 1910, won the election. Soon afterwards he introduced proposals for altering the powers of the House of Lords, but at that moment Edward VII died, and in the new reign a constitutional conference was held between the parties. This broke down in the autumn and Asquith dissolved Parliament a second time and held a second election in December 1910. Having won this too, he introduced the Parliament Bill, at the same time threatening to abolish the Lords' veto by advising the Monarch to create, if necessary, some five hundred new peers sympathetic to his measures. Rather than be flooded out in this manner, the Upper House gave way. Lytton bought *The Times* booklet reporting in full the historic debate in the House of Lords on the second reading of the Finance Bill of 1909, and marked a number of the more extreme effusions to assist him with the dialogue of his novel. This whole constitutional affair was perhaps the start of Lytton's serious political interest. He became strongly anti upper class – an attitude that was the obverse of his pseudo-snobbery.

of his desire to escape from the familiar drudgery of life in London. There were several other such symptoms, since his need for independence was now more urgent than ever before. His letters from the country have a natural melancholy about them; but those he wrote from Belsize Park Gardens are steeped in adolescent romanticism, a day-dream sentimentality released by the surrounding pressure of prosaic realism. 'If I could have my way,' he wrote after returning from Rye. 'I should go out to dinner every night, and then to a party or an opera, and then I should have a champagne supper, and then I should go to bed in some wonderful person's arms.'

Another aspect of Lytton's longing for liberty, leading to a most improbable moment of crisis, is shown in his letters to Virginia Stephen, of which there were an increasing number over this period. The relationship between these two gifted writers is interesting. Their correspondence, especially in these early years, has a self-consciousness, a stiltedness, which was entirely typical of neither, and which, in the opinion of both Leonard Woolf and James Strachey, was due to their mutual respect and admiration. But it was probably more than ordinary respect that accounted for this awkwardness. It was, at least partly, a lively apprehension of each other's power of criticism. Virginia Stephen distrusted Lytton's Cambridge education, with its overtones of ethical and intellectual superiority. Easily discouraged, she feared his quick irony – so reminiscent of her father's – his ridicule that could instantly disintegrate the vague shadows and shapes which she was trying to crystallize into something palpable. To some extent also she envied and resented his apparent self-assurance which tended to make her follow where he led; and she was always distressingly susceptible to his 'hints and subtleties and catlike malice' which could pierce the web of delicate, protective speculation, and leave her numbed and solitary.

As for Lytton, his apprehension of her was more indirect. His assumed self-confidence came from creating a fictitious image of himself which he dramatized with an elegant sureness of touch. Virginia Stephen's greater doubts suggested a more disturbing introspective honesty. Though she might follow the tune that he played, he was always looking back over his shoulder, aware that she could see through the paraphernalia of his acting. And although, too, she may have envied his earlier and more popular success as a writer, she considered his reputation rather exaggerated. To Lytton himself she was highly, almost implausibly, flattering; but to others she could criticize his work rather spitefully. He was the hare in the race for fame and she the tortoise who, with greater patience and imaginative endeavour, would eventually catch up and overtake him at the winning-post. Meanwhile, like eternal correctives, each brought out a latent feeling of inferiority in the other, raising doubts as to his or her intrinsic capabilities and achievements. Was she deluding herself with worthless, twittering phantoms, peopling her novels with airy ghosts? Was he exploiting a verbal felicity in facile and frivolous story-telling, scattering his biographies with shallow caricatures? Such uncertainties helped to confuse and unsettle their relationship.

They shared, however, much in common. To a large extent literature held a similar appeal for them. They welcomed with relief the lush, unrestrained articulation of the Elizabethans, and on the whole preferred to contemplate writers who had themselves lived in comfortable, independent circumstances – Horace Walpole, Gibbon, Henry James. Through the eyes of such men, the past might be convincingly transformed into an attractive sanctuary from the present. In addition to these special preferences, they shared several literary attributes – a vein of refined feminine malice, a sharp eye for salient facts and an intense curiosity about human nature. But the comparison between them can be extended little further than this. For all their sensitivity and unstable passion they were both somewhat removed from the quickening flow of humanity; but whereas Virginia, attracted like a moth to the light, was always trying to warm herself dangerously close to the fire of life, Lytton, like a man who has been scalded once too often, draws back, affecting to find warmth in the cold. She was absorbed by the spectacle of London; he was largely appalled by it. Her sense of character, if less vivid and clear-cut, is more genuinely subtle, and the transforming process of the past was less complete with her than with him. Her novels were the fluttering butterfly wings with which she set out on an impossible journey over the ocean to some far-off shore. His biographies were the gorgeous sweetmeats with which he consoled himself for never having attempted the journey. Writing, which fatally concentrated her self-absorption, dispersed his; and though her work is neither so perfect nor so readable as Lytton's, yet it retains the fragile, uneven pulse of original genius, while, by comparison, his is the successful achievement of a man of high talent and refinement.

The spirit of half-amused, diffident rivalry which existed between Virginia and Lytton was created as much by their similarities as by their differences in character, and below it ran a smoother undercurrent of real affection. 'Love apart, whom would you most like to see coming up the drive?' Lytton asked Clive Bell one rainy afternoon in the depths of the country. Clive Bell hesitated a moment and Lytton replied to his own question: 'Virginia, of course.'

Admiration and great affection, not love, were, then, what Lytton felt for her. Physically she did not appeal to him, and as a confidante she could not be trusted. His relationship with her was unique. He saw in her the presiding chatelaine of Bloomsbury, and in 29 Fitzroy Square a possible alternative to his mother and Hampstead. What else was there – loves apart? Now that Duncan and Maynard, the two emotional and intellectual props of his life, had collapsed, his platonic friendship with Virginia had been promoted to a new and unexpected importance. He knew, of course, that they were far from being ideally suited to each other, yet her extraordinary percipience and sensibility might prove vastly preferable to the communal incomprehension, the loving lack-of-understanding of his female relatives. This thought germinated inside him until on 17 February, despite a heavy cold, he boldly made his way across London to Fitzroy Square and, on the spur of the moment, proposed to Virginia – who, to his immediate horror and consternation, accepted him. The vague, escapist day-dream was instantly hardened into impossible reality. It was an awkward moment, especially since he realized, the very minute it was happening, that the whole thing was repulsive to him. 'As I did it, I saw it would be death if she accepted me, and I managed, of course, to get out of it before the end of the conversation,' he wrote to Leonard Woolf (19 February 1909). 'The worst of it was that as the conversation went on, it became more and more obvious to me that the whole thing was impossible. The lack of understanding was so terrific! And how can a virgin be expected to understand? You see she is her name. If I were either greater or less I could have done it and could either have dominated and soared and at last made her completely mine, or I could have been contented to go without everything that makes life important. ... Her sense was absolute, and at times her supremacy was so great that I quavered. ... I was in terror lest she should kiss me.'

In a letter to James, he describes the proposal as a decided reverse 'in my efforts to escape'. The escape he was so desperately looking for was not only from his family at Belsize Park Gardens, but also from his two most persistent visitors there, Duncan Grant and Maynard Keynes. Although it was now almost eight months since the crisis between them had exploded, still nothing was properly resolved. Lytton, fluctuating between a wide variety of moods and emotions – anger and resignation, curtness and magnanimity and sexual jealousy – presented a formidable face to Keynes who, that February, had broken down and cried in front of James. The mounting tension deepened for Lytton the unhappiness of this 'black period' of his life. His sudden proposal to Virginia, arising from an uprush of despair, was partly an effort to break this circle of intrigue, and amounted, as Professor Merle has argued, to a renunciation, hurriedly withdrawn, of his homosexual ties and of homosexuality itself. All this he confided at the time to Vanessa Bell 'who's quite unparalleled,' he told Leonard Woolf, 'but she doesn't see the real jar of the whole thing – doesn't take in the agony of

Duncan, and the confusion of my states. I copulated with —
again this afternoon, and at the present he's in Cambridge
copulating with Keynes. I don't know whether I'm happy or
unhappy.'

The next day, 20 February, the affair with Virginia was concluded, and Lytton could write to Leonard Woolf that 'I've
had an éclaircissement with Virginia. She declared she was not
in love with me, and I observed finally that I would not marry
her. So things have simply reverted.'

But perhaps the most extraordinary part of the whole
business was that, at the time Lytton was proposing to Virginia, Leonard Woolf was writing to Lytton stating that *he*
intended to propose to her. His letter was almost a vicarious
offer of marriage. Lytton was delighted. 'You are perfectly
wonderful, and I want to throw my arms round your neck,' he
replied (19 February 1909). '... Isn't it odd that I've never
been really in love with you? And I suppose never shall. ... If
you came and proposed she'd accept. She really would. As it
is, she's almost certainly in love with me, though she thinks
she's not. I've made a dreadful hash, as you see, but it was the
only way to make sure of anything. I was brought to it by
the horror of my present wobble and the imagination of the
paradise of married peace. It just needed the *fact* of the prospect of it to show me that there simply isn't any alternative
to the horror, that I must face it, and somehow get through
or die.'

Lytton advised Leonard Woolf that 'there's no doubt
whatever that you ought to marry her. You *would* be great
enough, and you'd have too the immense advantage of physical desire.' He then passed on the proposal to Vanessa, but it
seems to have been decided that, especially if Virginia was
secretly in love with Lytton all the time, Leonard had better
wait till he returned from his buffaloes and propose in
person.

This epidemic of proposals is made all the more ludicrous
by the fact that Virginia appears to have found Lytton so
physically unattractive that the prospect of their marriage was
almost as repulsive to her as to him. For both of them it

represented part of a psychological escape, a way out from something worse. He had proposed in an endeavour to cut free from Belsize Park Gardens; and she had at once accepted him as a means of dragging herself out from under the imaginary shadow of her dead father. At the same time she was not searching for a husband; rather the reverse. Marriage was a condition of life which held only limited appeal to her. Walter Lamb, who was supposed to be courting her at one time, received scant encouragement; and when Hilton Young proposed to her in a punt on the Cam, he was told that she could only marry one person – Lytton Strachey, and this though she did not love him. But what she did value above all other men was his understanding, his diplomacy, his kindness. These were the only sort of qualities that had any relevance to her. Nevertheless both she and Lytton must have realized almost simultaneously that so far from solving their separate problems, such a union could only add new mutual ones. Each was inadequate for the other's peculiar purpose.

At this time Virginia Stephen was already working at her first novel, *The Voyage Out*, which was eventually published in 1915, and which contains a portrait of Lytton under the name of St John Hirst. Naturally cautious, irretrievably intellectual, a devoted admirer of Gibbon and a confirmed misogynist, Hirst cherishes his memories of Cambridge but finds the company of his own family intolerable: 'They want me to be a peer and a privy councillor.' His appearance and mannerisms are closely observed. When he leans against a window-frame his figure looks like 'some singular gargoyle' – a shrewd use of one of Lytton's own favourite epithets. When, in sprawling relaxation, he subsides into a chair, he seems 'to consist entirely of legs'. Overhearing a group of ordinary people in ordinary conversation, he feels nauseated by their stupidity. But though he tries to isolate himself from these ignorant persons, telling another character that 'there will never be more than five people in the world worth talking to', yet he is prevented from sealing himself off completely by his thwarted ambition, and is forced to confess at one point: 'I hate everyone. I can't endure people who do things better than I do –

perfectly absurd things too.' At another stage in the narrative, when he stings Rachel Vinrace, the heroine based on Virginia Stephen herself, with some sharp and sober criticism to which she can find no quick repartee, she reflects to herself that he is 'ugly in body, repulsive in mind'.

For the most part, St John Hirst presents an unflattering likeness to Lytton, and Virginia was probably reflecting on the inaptitude of a marriage between them in a passage which describes some party at which they attempted to dance together.

'We must follow suit', said Hirst to Rachel, and he took her resolutely by the elbow. Rachel, without being expert, danced well, because of a good ear for rhythm, but Hirst had no taste for music, and a few dancing lessons at Cambridge had only put him in possession of the anatomy of a waltz, without imparting any of its spirit. A single turn proved to them that their methods were incompatible; instead of fitting into each other their bones seemed to jut out at angles making smooth turning an impossibility, and cutting, moreover, into the circular progress of the dancers.

'Shall we stop?' said Hirst. Rachel gathered from his expression that he was annoyed.

Despite his uncomplementary nature and the physical aversion she felt for him, Virginia liked Lytton; she pitied him for the unmelting, cold kernel of loneliness he carried within, and for his outward show of phoney romantics; and she admired at the same time his 'mind like a torpedo'. She sums up her compound impressions of him near the end of *The Voyage Out*, in a passage which brings together his morbid sensitivity and isolation, his envy and contempt, arrogance and self-absorption, his unhappiness and the restless fretting of his ambition:

But St John thought that they were saying things which they did not want him to hear, and was led to think of his own isolation.These people were happy, and in some ways he despised them for being made happy so simply, and in other ways he envied them. He was much more remarkable than they were, but he was not happy. People never liked him. ... To be simple, to be able to say simply what one felt, without the terrific self-consciousness which possessed him, and showed him his own face and words perpetually in a mirror, that would be worth any other gift, for it made one happy. Happiness, happiness, what was happiness? He was never happy. ... But it was true that half the sharp things he said about them were said because he was unhappy or hurt himself. But he admitted that he had very seldom told anyone that he cared for them, and when he had been demonstrative, he had generally regretted it afterwards.

The danger of identifying actual people in the creations of novelists is that, through a too literal transposition of the event-plot, the critic will misread not so much the character as the situations in which that character is involved. *The Voyage Out*, and that later and more subjective novel, *The Waves*, give some testimony of what Virginia really felt and thought of Lytton, and the manner in which her feelings for him developed.

'The characters in *The Waves*', Leonard Woolf cautiously tells us, 'are not drawn from life, but there is something of Lytton in Neville. There is no doubt that Percival in that book contains something of Thoby Stephen, Virginia's brother.' J. K. Johnstone, with more temerity, also affirms that 'there is much of Lytton Strachey in Neville', and he goes on, 'though Neville's intellect is so splendid and brave, he is too timid in some respects. He is very like St John Hirst of *The Voyage Out*. His body is ugly, and, he fears, disgusting. He wonders whether he is "doomed always to cause repulsion in those [he] loves". He loves Percival, who is intensely his opposite, with an "absurd and violent passion" which he is afraid to expose ... for he is one of those who love men more than women. At moments his emotions inspire him to write poetry, but then his intellect draws him up short, and ends his inspiration.' St John Hirst's uncommunicative misogamy has flowered in the fifteen years which separate *The Voyage Out* from *The Waves* into the fruitless, romantic homosexuality of Neville. And the lyrical yearning relationship depicted in this later novel accurately reproduces Lytton's physical and emotional susceptibility to the whole class of person whom Percival represents – in his own life

Thoby Stephen, George Mallory, and, to a large extent, Ralph Partridge – 'the normal English Public School type', as David Daiches describes Percival, 'neither intellectual nor particularly perceptive, but well adjusted and at ease in life'.

Although the character of Neville was never intended to be taken as a photographic representation of Lytton, it does provide an interesting fictional portrait, incomplete but nevertheless containing several intimate aspects of Lytton's personality as Virginia Woolf was shrewdly to interpret them – as opposed to the more shallow flattery or denigration of her letters and reported conversations.[3] The bleak, dehumanized arrogance revealed in *The Voyage Out* has softened and is now more sympathetically presented, and his contempt for the complacent mediocrity of others is seen as a stimulant to his own superior, yet precarious, sense of individuality. Precise and neat as a cat, he seeks to oppose the chaos and hubbub of the world with his love of order and exactitude. But he is never at home in this world, never at ease as Percival is, in the random company of others, feeling their presence 'like a separating wall'. Whenever he attempts to transmute his emotions of love into poetry, he automatically heightens the effect, becoming insincere, so that, as he confesses in one of the recitative lyrical monologues of which the book is made up, 'I shall be a clinger to the outside of words all my life.' Though successful, his wide literary reputation has, in itself, brought him no real happiness, and only applies a balm to soothe the pangs of his envy. 'Yet we scarcely breathe, spent as we are,' sighs Neville near the end of *The Waves* when, tired by his continual opposition to the natural forces of life, he expresses something of Virginia Woolf's own sickness of living. 'We are in that passive and exhausted frame of mind when we only wish to join the body of our mother

3. The portraits of Lytton in Virginia Woolf's novels undoubtedly give an accurate reflection of what she felt about him. However, James Strachey notes that 'so far as my observation goes she never had any real notion of what other people were like. She had some very crooked ideas.'

from whom we have been severed. All else is distasteful, forced and fatiguing.'

Their affection for one another persisted and even perhaps deepened after Lytton's proposal of marriage to Virginia. The letters which they exchanged became, too, a little less stilted and protectively self-conscious. Writing over fifteen years later to Victoria Sackville-West, Virginia Woolf described Lytton as 'infinitely charming, and we fitted like gloves'. But they were both gloves for the same hand, differently styled yet a duplication rather than a complement of each other. They could never have made a pair.

After his proposal, Lytton hurried back again across London to Hampstead, from where, that same evening, he dashed off a note to Virginia: 'I'm still rather agitated and exhausted ... I do hope you're cheerful! As for me, I'm still of a heap, and the future seems blank to me. But whatever happens, as you said, the important thing is that we should like each other: and we can neither of us have any doubt that we do.'

2

ON GRAY AND PURPLE SEAS

'I'm more exhausted than it's easy to imagine,' Lytton wrote to Duncan Grant a few hours after the disastrous proposal of marriage to Virginia Stephen. 'I've been having an agitated day, but it can't be explained yet, and don't mention it, only I do sometimes wish that I was hundreds of leagues away from everything, and everybody, floating alone on purple seas.'

Pending Italy, the nearest approximation to this dream of romantic escape was to purchase a large bottle of medicine and take himself off for a week-end to the grey, wintry seas of Brighton. He spent much of his time there writing poetry, which was a pleasant therapeutic occupation – even though he dared not show it to anyone. Far removed from the sort of idyll he had in mind, this brief week-end none the less helped repair his shattered nerves and on the last day of his visit (Sunday, 21 February 1909), he was able to report back to Duncan that 'my health so far is flourishing. I suppose the combination of Brighton and Sanatogen has done the trick!'

In the third week of March, Lytton heard that Maynard Keynes had been awarded a Fellowship at King's, and wrote off at once to offer his congratulations. He had been looking for an excuse to correspond with Keynes for some weeks. His reversal with Virginia Stephen – a full realization of the practical limits to *that* association – had produced two immediate effects: first, that of re-emphasizing the value of his old friendships; and second, that of reviving temporarily his passion for Duncan Grant. Who else was there? Perhaps, even now, he might salvage something from the shipwreck of that divine friendship. Duncan and Maynard were still on the very best of terms, so it would be impossible to re-establish his intimacy with Duncan without regenerating his amiable feelings for Maynard, and attributing the estrangement that had grown up between them to trivial, involuntary causes for which he himself was largely to blame. Probably nothing would come of it, but he was in no frame of mind to ignore even the faintest chance of happiness. His letter to Maynard was a difficult one to write, and 'I think it's hardly necessary – only to say that you must always think of me as your friend. I shall think of you in the same way. But I've been rather afraid that lately you may have felt things had become different. I don't think it's the case. The only thing is that I'm sometimes uneasy and awkward perhaps, partly I suppose because of my nervous organization which isn't particularly good – but I don't see how it can be helped. I can only beg that you'll attend to it as little as you can, and believe me to be a sensible decent person who remembers and knows.'

Lytton's nervous organization during these weeks had in fact been surprisingly, even embarrassingly, steady. For no reason whatever he felt wonderfully well, and, more incredible still, cheerful – ominously so. It must, he believed, all be due to the astonishing quantities of Sanatogen he was consuming.

But it was all very extraordinary. 'By every rule,' he explained to Duncan Grant (4 March 1909), 'I ought to be shivering on the edge of moral and physical annihilation, and I find I'm a healthy, energetic, efficient and resourceful member of society. How dreadful it sounds! I expect before the week's out I shall have joined the territorial army, and become a tariff reformer. However in the meantime I pass the time of day pleasantly enough.'

The most important outcome from this inexplicable bonus of vitality was another vigorous drive to embark on an independent way of life. The old domestic solitude-without-privacy was no longer to be endured. This time he must be more severely practical and down-to-earth, for if he failed yet again, he might never escape at all. He had three concurrent plans in mind. The first, most positive and long-term, was a scheme to set up house with his brother James somewhere in London – possibly Bloomsbury. The obstacles and perplexities of putting this move into operation seemed to him enormous, but he was firmly determined that somehow they must be overcome. 'I've practically decided to leave the house,' he wrote to James (9 April 1909), who had gone off to join Moore's reading-party at the Lizard. 'My last few days have been terrible – from every point of view. I hardly know where I am or what I'm doing; and it's quite uncertain whether I shall be any better anywhere else. But it seems clear that the time has come for trying. As far as I can see my fate is mere touch and go. The probabilities are I suppose against me. Oh heavens! What infernal horrors one has to face!

'Why shouldn't you come back on Tuesday? Is there any point in staying longer? The solitude here is accablant, and if you come it would be amusing to do a little house-hunting . . .

'. . . The grave or the lunatic asylum – which will it be? I daresay both. How unfortunate it is that the only woman who behaves with decency and propriety in this house is Pippa, and that she's never in it.'

To discover and then occupy a suitable house with James would, of course, take several weeks, perhaps even months. Meanwhile, Lytton put into effect his second interim plan, which was to follow the example of his sister Pippa, and spend as much time as conveniently possible away from 67 Belsize Park Gardens. With this idea in mind, he decided to join the Savile Club, then in Piccadilly.[4] But his first appearance there was a fiasco, the preposterous details of which he amusingly recounted to James (6 April 1909): 'My adventures on Friday, when I arrived here for the first time, were extremely painful. After having been certified as a member by a purple-bottle-nosed servitor in a guichet in the hall, I didn't in the least know what to do. There was a door, a staircase, and a notice-board; I was in my hat and coat, carrying an umbrella; the servitor merely stared from his guichet. In a moment of weakness I began to read the notices on the notice-board, and while I was doing so the servitor became involved in an endless conversation with an imbecile Major. I was therefore lost. I couldn't ask him where I was to put my hat, coat and umbrella, I had read every notice six times, and there seemed no hope. At last I made a wild plunge at the door – opened it, entered, and found myself in the dining-room, nose to nose with a somewhat surprised and indignant waiter. I then fled upstairs, and so managed to get here* safely. But there are further mysteries still to be explained – the second floor? – dare I penetrate there? . . .

'*The Smoking room, overlooking Green Park.'

A more serious proposition was his third plan – a new bid to liberate himself from the clutches of the *Spectator*. 'Perhaps Duncan has told you of my probable abandonment of the *Spectator*,' he wrote to Maynard Keynes (29 March 1909). 'At present it had better not be mentioned. I think it's the only thing to do, though it terrifies me out of my wits.'

4. In the Savile Candidates Book No. 3, it is recorded that Lytton was proposed by J. E. McTaggart on 13 February 1908 and elected on 31 March. His referees were H. L. Stephen, W. H. C. Shaw (who had married Frances, younger sister of St Loe Strachey), H. G. Dakyns, Hilton Young, John Pollock, A. Chichele Plowden (Lytton's cousin), J. B. Atkins (a friend of St Loe Strachey's and his second in command as assistant editor of the *Spectator*), and (the Rev.) H. F. Stewart, a Trinity don, friendly with Lytton and with Pernel who was then a Newnham don in the same modern languages department.

Keynes, as usual, agreed. 'I think you're much to be congratulated on getting rid of the *Spectator*,' he replied (4 April 1909), ' – if you're prepared to risk poverty and pawn your coat.' It was, he implied, easy to overestimate the importance of money. Nevertheless, Lytton's apprehensions were very understandable. It was a brave decision, and one that James had predicted he could never have the will to make. From the *Spectator* he received almost all his independent means of livelihood. Yet while he continued to expend so much of his time and precious store of energy working away for it, there could be little or no chance of composing the literary masterpieces on which he had set his sights. Most men spent all their time amassing money, but *he* wanted money in order to buy him more free time – and it had not worked out like that. Still, it was not too late. He was now twenty-nine years of age – surely not too moribund to emerge from his anonymous, journalistic obscurity and start a new career in literature. Molière, for instance, had not written his first play until he was twenty-nine, and he was as ancient as thirty-five before he began to be eminent. Lytton felt fortified by this example. The *Spectator* was like a millstone round his neck; but to cut free was tantamount to loosing anchor and setting one's sails irretrievably towards some limitless, uncharted ocean. 'I fancy myself alone before eternity', he exclaimed.

The last of his regular pieces for the *Spectator* – a rather indifferent article on Carlyle's letters – appeared on 10 April; though in the course of the next five years he did contribute five more long essay-reviews to the paper, which were specially commissioned by James – then working as St Loe Strachey's private secretary. The decision to terminate his employment with the *Spectator* was hastened by a sudden crisis in health. For a week he lay in bed feeling wretched. 'My health', he wrote to James (12 April 1909), 'has collapsed rather more seriously than usual. I've been attacked by some unpleasant diseases, among which is vertigo! The man Roland has been called in, and has ordered a complete cessation of work, and absolute mental rest. – How am I to get that, I wonder? It would be a great thing to have someone to talk to. I'm not even allowed out, for fear of falling down in the middle of Piccadilly, and I sit all day trying to read, and not succeeding very well.'

And so, once more, his plan for establishing himself on some permanent basis apart from his family had been undermined by illness, and would have yet again to be postponed. As soon as he was allowed out of doors, he left Belsize Park Gardens and went to stay for two weeks at King's. Here he was whirled into the throbbing vortex of undergraduate romance. The colleges seemed thick with amorous crises and stupendous rumours, and Lytton rolled from one to the other in fits of laughter and floods of sentimental tears. But eclipsing all else was his first meeting with the mythical George Mallory, a figure cut authentically in the heroic mould. Next to the shadow of Mallory's muscular strength, Lytton seemed to shrink back into child-size. As with Thoby Stephen, everything about him appeared larger than life – the manly shoulders, the magnificent torso, the wide open smile, white teeth and blue eyes – so large he felt he could curl up within its shadow, and sleep. He had heard of Mallory earlier from James, who was said to treat him rather severely, and from Duncan Grant, who placed him 'easily first' of all the handsome young men there. But their stories, Lytton decided, had conspicuously failed to do him justice.[5] From the start, he was swept off his feet by the sight of this splendid, godlike phenomenon. Mallory was not so much a

5. Mallory was constantly abashed by having to endure these 'disconcerting reminders' of his good looks, David Robertson, his latest biographer, tells us. He seems, at least before others, to have been disconcerted by Lytton's mixture of irreverence, indecency and outrageous coyness, but was somewhat in awe of his candour and intellect, and consistently amused by his wit, even when exercised at the expense of those 'simply absurd' objects, mountains. 'He [Lytton] is very, very queer,' Mallory wrote defensively to his fiancée, Ruth Turner (23 May 1914), ' – not to me, of course, because I know him as a friend, but to the world. He must be very irritating to many people. My profound respect for his intellect, and for a sort of passion with which he holds the doctrine of freedom, besides much love for him as a man of intense feelings and fine imagination, make me put up with much in him that I could hardly tolerate in any other.'

416

person with whom one slipped into an intimate, lasting friendship as someone whom one worshipped humbly from afar, someone whose very existence seemed to justify all the pain and perplexity of this world – the perfect human specimen. Something of the peculiar quality of his feelings towards Mallory – which, like those for Thoby Stephen, were more idealistic than sensual – are described in a very articulate letter which he wrote to Clive and Vanessa Bell (21 May 1909):

'Mon dieu! – George Mallory! – When that's been written, what more need be said? My hand trembles, my heart palpitates, my whole being swoons away at the words – oh heavens! heavens! I found of course that he'd been absurdly maligned – he's six foot high, with the body of an athlete by Praxiteles, and a face – oh incredible – the mystery of Botticelli, the refinement and delicacy of a Chinese print, the youth and piquancy of an unimaginable English boy. I rave, but when you see him, as you must, you will admit all – all! The amazing thing, though, was that besides his beauty, other things were visible, more enchanting still. His passion for James was known, but it so happened that during my visit he declared it – and was rejected. ... Poor George! I met him for the first time immediately after this occurrence, and saw in my first glance to the very bottom of his astounding soul. I was écrasé. What followed was remarkable – though infinitely pure. Yes! Virginia alone will sympathize with me now – I'm a convert to the divinity of virginity, and spend hours every day lost in a trance of adoration, innocence, and bliss. It was a complete revelation, as you may conceive. By God! The sheer beauty of it all is what transports me. ... To have sat with him in the firelight through the evening, to have wandered with him in the Kings Garden among violets and cherry blossom, to have – no, no! for desire was lost in wonder, and there was profanation even in a kiss. ... For the rest, he's going to be a schoolmaster, and his intelligence is not remarkable. What's the need?'

Early in May Lytton left Cambridge and moved to Burley Hill, which Thena Clough had lent him for the month and where he was soon joined by Pippa. The comfort and the fine spring weather were very wonderful at first. 'I've grown used to annihilation,' he admitted to James, 'and have at last learnt the art of not expecting very much.' Calm was not life's crown, but calm was best. In this mood of tranquil renunciation, he felt happy simply to sit out in the sun, flowers carpeting the ground, birds packed tight upon the trees, and *The Faerie Queene* (unopened) within reach. If only his physique had been more robust, everything would have been perfect, for then he could have explored the depths of the New Forest, and composed perhaps a century of sonnets enhaloing the resplendent beauty of George Mallory, every line of which would breathe the purest spirit of idealistic and exotic love – wafted over seas of amaranth, plunged up to the eyes in all the spices of Arabia, and lulled in the bosom of eternal spring. As it was, he had to content himself writing letters, to George Mallory of course and to his other friends. 'I can never have been in the country before at this time of year – it's all most amazing, and I'm beginning to understand the sentimentality of poets on the spring,' he told Duncan Grant (7 May 1909), delineating his placid and ethereal convalescence. 'Their preposterous descriptions are here, actually existing, under my very nose. Beds of violets, choirs of birds, blossoms and butterflies and balmy breezes and scents and everything else.'

So the days slipped by in charming vagueness and contentment. Why should it not always be so? He had declared a truce on his passions, and from this sanctuary the world of the emotions appeared farcical. Besides which, he had to think carefully about his future. He possessed, he felt sure, the two essential qualities that in the long run ought to give him success – a decent competency and the capacity and desire for doing work of importance. Love might be the very devil in disrupting one's plans, but it *was* Time's fool; and once it had flown out of the window, one was always astonished to find just how well one could get along without it.

Lytton's hopes of escaping to the sunshine of Italy had by this time been altogether relinquished. But his mother, worried over his inexplicable bouts of sickness, felt strongly that he needed some sort of restorative holiday. It was therefore decided that he should spend a few weeks in Sweden, a clean, enlightened country, notorious for its up-to-date clinics, where he might at last find some explanation and remedy for his perpetual invalidism. Lytton did not greatly look forward to this trip which was something of an anticlimax after his Roman dreams, but he felt obliged to go through with it. At least he would be out of Hampstead. And if the Swedish doctors could work some miraculous cure, perhaps he might then build up the vigour and vitality to make a successful bid for liberty, for happiness and a new career.

In any event, it was worth a shot.

3

THE SWEDISH EXPERIMENT

Lytton started out on his quest for health in mid-July, spending one day and a night in Copenhagen before arriving in Sweden. With him went two female attendants – Daisy McNeil, an eccentric aunt of Duncan Grant's who ran a private nursing home in Eastbourne for the infirm members of well-to-do families; and one of her elderly, affluent patients, a woman by the name of Elwes, 'a poor dried-up good-natured old stick with an odd tinge of excitability, alias madness I suppose, but always absolutely insipid'. These two ladies were not perhaps ideal travelling companions, but they both turned out to be very obliging, constantly offering to mend Lytton's socks, presenting him at all times of the day with cups of weak tea, and insisting that he read the out-of-date newspapers before themselves. In return for this hospitality, he could only repay them by cracking polite jokes and elaborately admiring, for their benefit, the scenery. 'Even La Elwes's conversation has its charms,' he reported back to Duncan Grant (1 August 1909). 'At first I was terrified by her hatchet nose and slate-pencil voice – and I still am occasionally – but on the whole I now view her with composure. Never have I met a more absolutely sterile mind – and yet how wonderfully

419

cultivated! It's like a piece of flannel with watercress growing on it.'

On their arrival in Stockholm, Daisy McNeil, who spoke Swedish, arranged for Lytton to have some medical tests performed by a Dr Johanson. These turned out to be rather fearful encounters, chiefly because they had to be carried on in broken French. 'Pas de laxatifs, monsieur!' were the doctor's first and last words; and he sent Lytton down with his retinue of old ladies to Badanstalten, a health sanatorium for 'physical therapeutics' at Saltsjöbaden, by the sea, not far from Stockholm. This sanatorium specialized in the treatment of heart conditions, nervous illnesses, stomach, intestine and digestive complaints and was presided over by a charming, cello-playing Dr Zander, himself a heart-and-nerve specialist, who attended personally to Lytton.

About Saltsjöbaden itself there seemed very little to fire anyone. Everything appeared infinitely negative. The water was undoubtedly the best feature of the place, and if he had only owned a small sailing boat, life might have been perfect. As it was he saw a great many boats going about, but unfortunately they were all private, and it seemed out of the question to hire one. The rest of the surroundings struck Lytton as rather second-rate, though he courteously refrained from saying so. They were very much built over, and to his eye quite shapeless. The woods were scrubby, the inhabitants more middle-class than could easily be imagined, the whole atmosphere distinctly hydropathic. However, he did feel really extraordinarily contented. By dint of never thinking, he managed to pass through the invariable daily life there pretty comfortably. It proved, no doubt, how appallingly degraded his character had become – to be able to spend week after week after week without a murmur of discontent in the company of two inconceivably dull old maids. The flatness of their trio conversations was inexpressible, and on all sides boredom reigned supreme.

'I believe I'm the only person of our acquaintance who could do what I'm doing,' he boasted to James. 'The dullness is so infinite that the brain reels to think of it, and yet I might almost be called happy. The whole place is too unimaginably bourgeois. I had quite a shock when I entered the dining-room for the first time and saw the crowd of middle-aged and middle-class invalids munching their Swedish cookery. For complete second-rateness this country surpasses the wildest dreams of man. I sometimes fear that it may be the result of democracy, but I imagine really that it's inborn, and brought to its height by lack of cash. All the decent Scandinavians, no doubt, left the place a thousand years ago, and only the dregs remain. Yet they're amazingly good-looking; and the sailors in Stockholm, with their décolletté necks, fairly send one into a flutter. The bath-attendants, however, so far, have not agitated me, and this in spite of the singular intimacies of their operations. Even the lift boys leave me cold. My health seems to be progressing rather well, but my experiences have been more ghastly than can be conceived, medical experiences, I mean – oh heavens!'

It was the sustained and startling improvement in his health that made the overall tedium supportable. The subject of health absorbed and dominated existence, and so long as it continued on the upgrade Lytton believed that he could put up with anything. He had started off the first week with nothing more strenuous than some insignificant baths ('Finsenbad'), but almost immediately he began to gain in weight, his digestion improved – also his temper – and other departments. 'Conceive me if you can a healthy and pure young man,' he wrote to Maynard Keynes (13 August 1909). 'My only terror is that none of it'll last.' But this apprehension appeared quite groundless. After the first successful week he graduated from the bathroom to the gym. 'I hope when I get on to the mechanical gymnastics, etc., that I shall swell out of my clothes,' he told Duncan Grant. And so it actually came about! His appetite increased still further, and the female attendants were asked to let out his waistcoats.

Lytton's regime at Saltsjöbaden, though not complicated, was certainly formidable, and his various cures occupied him on and off for almost the whole day. At eight o'clock each morning he was called by Sister Fanny who brought him a

421

glass of 'Carslbad water' – a mild tonic. Half an hour later he breakfasted off a locally concocted simulacrum of porridge and sour cream. At nine-thirty he paraded at the gym for a thirty-minute period of mechanical exercises. These operations took place in a large hall decked out with gadgets and appliances of the most gruesome and medieval appearance, which were worked partly by electricity, partly by the patient. In spite of his quota of electricity, Lytton found them sufficiently exhausting. All the collaborative, semi-mechanized apparatuses on which he and the other invalids performed were made up, so Lytton explained to his mother (3 August 1909), of 'most singular arrangements, by means of which the various muscles are worked without being tired. The hall where one does them [the exercises] looks exactly like a torture chamber – terrific instruments of every kind line the walls, and elderly gentlemen attached upon them go through their evolutions with the utmost gravity.'

After these exertions were over, Lytton was allowed nearly two hours of freedom and relaxation. When the sun shone, the air would glow miraculously light and clear, and he was able to sit out on his special deck-chair among the pines, and the fat and perspiring Swedish patients, wonderfully comatose, idly dreaming and idly doing nothing whatever, all with the greatest satisfaction. To his tired mind everything might seem dubious, anaemic and uncertain; but at the back of every dream and every expectation was the heroic figure of George Mallory. To everyone he poured out a constant stream of letters which amusingly describe the rigours and incongruities of this 'Swedish experiment'. And when he had wearied of writing, he would read Tolstoy, Saint-Simon, Voltaire and Swinburne. 'I only regret that I forgot to bring a copy of the Holy Bible', he wrote to his mother. But to make up for this deficiency he eagerly devoured the *Daily Mail* – two days late – and the *Gloucester and Wilts Advertiser*, in many ways the more interesting, and he began to get quite heated over far-off local affairs. Swedish politics also claimed his attention when, early in August, a general strike was called. However, the alarmist reports in the newspapers seemed purely fictional. There was, at any rate, no symptom of any strike or even the mildest ripple of a disrupting influence in those placid, medicinal halls at Saltsjöbaden.

It was during these morning periods of dreaming, reading and writing letters, that Lytton conceived a plan for compiling an anthology of English heroic verse. 'I think it might be very interesting, and that one might get a great many good extracts which people don't know of', he wrote to his mother (21 August 1909). 'The interest would be to trace the development up to Pope, etc., and then the throw back with Keats and Shelley. I think Pope made more advance on Dryden – in the mere technique of the line – than is usually recognized. Dryden's line, though of course it's magnificent, lacks the weight of Pope's. I once analysed some passages in the Dunciad, and found that the number of stressed syllables in each line was remarkable – sometimes as many as seven or eight. It's difficult to believe that this is the same metre as Epipsychidion which rushes along with three stresses to a line at most. I've written to Sidgwick[6] proposing to do this. I hope he'll accept.' Unfortunately nothing came of this plan, though fifteen years later Lytton incorporated some of these reflections on the heroic couplet into his Leslie Stephen lecture on Pope.

Shortly before midday, the treatment was resumed with a vigorous session of massage which in turn was followed up with a warm undoctored bath, superintended by various Scandinavian stewards and officials. Lunch was at one o'clock, and two hours afterwards, once the patient had properly digested his food, he was plunged into a medicinal bath. These were rather strict, inaudacious affairs, even more meticulously supervised by attendants, but never very varied and always too cold for pleasure. After tea at four, Lytton was again allowed two hours' rest until dinner, which, much to his disgust, was

6. Frank Sidgwick, the publisher, best remembered perhaps for his collaboration with Eddie Marsh on Marsh's Memoir of Rupert Brooke, and selections from Brooke's poetry. He was also responsible for bringing out Brooke's first book, Poems, which the house of Sidgwick and Jackson published on 4 December 1911.

served at the unbelievably *bourgeois* time of six o'clock. Communal walks were generally taken after dinner, under the pallid sky and among the mangy conifers of the so-called 'English Park'. It was a shocking experience to be encompassed by all the other inhabitants on these slow, pedestrian expeditions. There were *millions* of them – all either Swedes or Finns – and, despite their regrettably middle-class habits, secretly believed by Lytton to be counts and countesses incognito. Wherever he went they surrounded him in hordes – fat, old, ugly and imbecile – dotted across the shapeless nondescript countryside, or bobbing about in boats, or streaming endlessly through the corridors to their various meals and cures, or chattering over their symptoms in the 'Salong'. There was no escaping them.

In the later evening, after promenading about in the park, Lytton usually played a few games of billiards with the ever-faithful and kind Daisy. Soon, much to his amazement, he discovered that he had somehow gained an immense reputation as a billiards expert among the other inmates of the clinic. 'Directly we begin to play,' he informed his mother (21 August 1909), 'crowds enter the room, and take seats to watch the Englishman playing "cannon-ball" as they call it. As the table is very small and the pockets are very large I occasionally manage to make a break of 15 or 20 which strikes astonishment in the beholders. Apparently the Swedish game consists entirely of potting the red ball with great violence, so that cannons and losing hazards brought off with delicacy appear to these poor furriners wonderful and beautiful in the extreme.'

At half-past nine play was interrupted while Lytton was brought a large evening bowl of pseudo-porridge. An hour later he retired upstairs to his bedroom, drew down his special blinds and went off into a long and dreamless sleep.

He had originally intended to leave Sweden at the end of August, but though he was anxious not to miss all the English summer, his health was going up to such an extent in the spick-and-span, disinfected atmosphere of Saltsjöbaden that he felt obliged to extend his stay there for another fortnight.

He had, in fact, become attuned to this ingeniously monotonous existence, and could, so he said, hardly believe in any
other mode of living which did not comprise dinner-at-six,
mechanical gymnastics, porridge and sour cream, hot and
cold baths, and communal perambulations with dubious
Scandinavian countesses. It was not the unremitting hell it
sounded, but rather a purgatory where he had absolved himself through suffering.

Early in September Daisy McNeil and 'La Elwes' gave up the
struggle and fled to England; but James bravely came out to
stay with Lytton for the remaining days of his treatment. 'It
was very fortunate,' Lytton explained to Maynard Keynes (17
September 1909), 'as otherwise I should have been alone and
moribund in this ghastly region.' But then, at about the same
time, he was quite suddenly and inexplicably struck down by
illness, losing much of the weight which he had spent the
previous seven weeks so carefully amassing. By the third week
of September he had recovered, but decided to remain on for
a further ten days to re-establish 'my now normal condition
of corpulence' and to swell out again into his enlarged clothes,
which for a time hung round him in folds.

Eventually, Lytton and James left Saltsjöbaden on 23 September, arriving back in London two days later. After a week
at Belsize Park Gardens, suffering acutely from piles and carrying with him everywhere an air cushion which he had hired for
the fee of one-and-six a week, Lytton travelled down with his
mother and Harry Norton to Brighton, where, at the Queen's
Hotel and subsequently at the Belvedere Mansion Hotel, he
set about trying 'to recover from the effects of Sweden'.

4

FOR TRAVEL'S SAKE

No sooner was Lytton safely installed back in London than
he evolved a new scheme to ensure his future independence.
This entailed going to live at Grantchester as a neighbour of
Rupert Brooke's, in 'my moated grange' as he called it in

happy anticipation of his tenancy. From Saltsjöbaden he had already written to Brooke inquiring after the Old Vicarage, next to The Orchard where Brooke was then living. This house, which Brooke himself later occupied and made famous with his Grantchester poem, was owned by a Mr and Mrs Neeve, who were at that time anxious to find lodgers. 'So far they have been singularly unsatisfied,' Brooke reported in an epistolary style that bears many similarities to Lytton's own. 'Mr Neeve is a refined creature, with an accent above his class, who sits out near the beehives with a handkerchief over his head and reads advanced newspapers. He knows a lot about botany. They keep babies and chickens; and I rather think I have seen both classes entering the house. But you could be firm. The garden is the great glory. There is a soft lawn with a sundial and tangled, antique flowers abundantly; and a sham ruin, quite in a corner; built fifty years ago by Mr Shuck-brugh,[7] historian and rector of Grantchester; and *most* attractive. . . . There are trees rather too closely all round; and a mist. It's right on the river.'

James was sceptical about this plan. 'I gather Lytton's corresponding with you about a house in Grantchester,' he wrote. 'Would you hate anyone being near you? though I suppose you both dislike one another too much to meet often.' But Brooke was quite unaware of disliking Lytton; and Lytton himself felt enthusiastic about the venture. 'If I can, I shall stay there for ever,' he told Virginia Stephen (13 October 1909), 'but I suppose I can't. My health still seems to be something of a Mahomet's coffin. However, vogue la galère!'

All this, however, was before he had gone down to reconnoitre the place. In order to do this in comfort, he spent one night as Brooke's guest at The Orchard where he was observed 'to have a habit of sitting with his back against the

7. In his biography of Rupert Brooke, Christopher Hassall noted that this actually referred to Samuel Widnall, 'author and printer of several topographical books, and pioneer in photography; he was never ordained but affected the appearance of a clergyman, and in 1853 erected a Folly at the bottom of his garden, the ruinated fragment of what might be a medieval nunnery.'

book-shelves, reaching a hand over his shoulder, and bringing forward without looking the first book he touched, reading a snatch of it, putting it back, and grabbing another, all without turning round'. On first inspection, the Old Vicarage seemed fairly tolerable and even in some respects charming, so he decided that he would definitely try this experiment, at least for a short while – one of the advantages being that it was very cheap. Everything seemed fixed for a new phase in his life, but, as with so many of his previous projects, it all fell through at the last moment when Brooke casually explained to him the reason for the inexpensive rental – that the house was easily and frequently flooded in all seasons, and impossibly frigid in the winter. Perhaps James's intuition had been right in the first place. In any case, with his Mahomet's coffin, the Old Vicarage was obviously no place for Lytton; and so yet another scheme had hastily to be abandoned.

He had almost resigned himself to a further arid stretch of family life, when George Mallory came miraculously to the rescue, telling him that he was going to stay with Arthur Benson[8] and that his old rooms in Cambridge were consequently empty. Lytton hurried round there at once, and after some agitating negotiations secured the place for a relatively cheap sum. He settled down there at once, writing to explain the summary change of plan to his mother (18 October 1909). 'I have now found some other rooms on the outskirts of Cambridge (much nearer than Grantchester) which I have taken for the term at 35/- a week for board and lodging. I think they will do very well, but I can only have them for this

8. Arthur Christopher Benson (1862–1925), possibly the least talented of the three gifted Benson brothers, sons of E. W. Benson, Archbishop of Canterbury. A. C. Benson was the Master of Magdalene and a copious and indifferent author of sugar-and-water verse and prose. At the suggestion of Edward VII, he wrote the words for the air in Elgar's Pomp and Circumstance March No. 1: 'Land of Hope and Glory'. After the death of Henry James in 1916, he went to live in Lamb House at Rye, replacing Percy Lubbock, who had lived there in the intervening half-dozen years, but who was then 'cast out to seek for rest in dry places – his own mind, for instance.' (A. C. Benson to George Rylands, 26 December 1922.) The unsuspecting Lubbock later edited Benson's Diaries for publication (1926).

term. It's rather a piece of luck my getting them – the real tenant is ill, and cannot use them, so that they are perfectly civilized in the way of furniture. The people who keep them I know to be trustworthy. I hope now to be able to do some writing. My health appears to be quite satisfactory. . . .

'I forgot to mention the charming name of my new abode – Pythagoras House.'

Pythagoras House became Lytton's headquarters for the next ten weeks – almost to the end of the year. 'I'm wonderfully comfortable and healthy here – also at present shockingly lazy,' he wrote to Duncan Grant (1 November 1909). 'I occasionally wish that I could glide on here for ever, but no doubt in a week or two I shall be horribly sick of the whole place.'

But for once his doleful prognostications were not to be fulfilled. Every day Cambridge grew more gay and debonair. How delightful it was to linger among such memories! Such leisure! Such repose! And then, too, the weather was still warm enough for the occasional morning in the garden. 'I find the beauty of the trees and the country quite divine,' he wrote to Clive Bell (21 October 1909). 'The view from the King's bridge this morning – you should have seen it! Certainly this is the most beautiful time of the year for Cambridge. Won't you come up for a week-end?'

Clive and Vanessa Bell did come and visit him the following month, and so did Virginia Stephen. Lytton also attended several meetings of the Apostles, and saw much of Rupert Brooke, Harry Norton, Sheppard, Gerald Shove, Saxon Sydney-Turner and the non-Apostolic Walter Lamb. Most notable among his new and younger Cambridge associates was Francis Birrell:[9] 'I have made the acquaintance of Mr Birrell's small son, who is at King's,' he informed his mother. 'He is very gay, and has apparently never heard of Ireland.'[10]

9. Francis Birrell (1889–1935), journalist and dramatic critic, who after the war started a bookshop with David Garnett.

10. Francis Birrell's father, Augustine Birrell, the politician and man of letters, was Chief Secretary for Ireland in Asquith's Cabinet. He resigned after the Easter Week Rebellion in Dublin in 1916.

During his stay at Pythagoras House, Lytton composed a blank verse tragedy for a Stratford-upon-Avon Prize Play Competition. From the sixteenth century onwards nearly every would-be poet has attempted to write at least one blank verse drama, and the unlikely chorus of praise accorded such a playwright as Stephen Phillips has only shown up the dearth of really effective blank verse theatre in the last hundred years. *Essex: A Tragedy*, as Lytton's production was entitled, embodies several of the characteristic shortcomings one would expect to discover in modern blank verse. It is competently, even ingeniously constructed, but rather lifeless. Where the verse needs to be strong and concentrated, it is often merely windy; where it should communicate the more subtle shades of emotion, it reveals instead the naked machinery of the plot or merely etches in by conversational reference and allusion the historical background. Perhaps the most interesting lines are those given to Queen Elizabeth as she reflects on the difference between her own advanced age and that of the youthful Essex. There is a pathos and tenderness in her monologue which conveys something of Lytton's own worship of splendid masculine youth, and the sense of premature middle-age which sometimes overcame him in his blacker moods.

> For I was old
> Ere he was young, and years before he breathed
> These locks had worn the coronet of a queen.
> Rather it was that in my age I knew him,
> And to my setting skies he came to lend
> The freshness of a star. Am I a dotard
> Dreaming on fantasies? Or is it true
> That frozen years can snatch from fiery youth
> Some palpable warmth and the reflected radiance
> Of life's meridian splendour? No, 'tis no dream;
> For often in the midst of my dull days,
> My councils, and my creeping policies.
> I have known a look from Essex light the clouds,
> And make earth glory.

Such soliloquies were to play a large part in *Elizabeth and Essex*, which Lytton subtitled 'A Tragic History'; and the chief interest that *Essex: A Tragedy* now holds lies in its relationship to that later work. The action of the play is spread only over some four chapters — XIII to XVI — of the book, and it opens very dramatically with Essex's unannounced and forbidden return from Ireland on 28 September 1599. The last passage of Chapter XII in *Elizabeth and Essex* is in fact an exact description of the opening scene, and reads in places like the stage and costume directions for it:

'A quarter of an hour later — it was ten o'clock — the Earl was at the gate. He hurried forward, without a second's hesitation; he ran up the stairs, and so — oh! he knew the way well enough — into the presence chamber, and thence into the privy chamber; the Queen's bedroom lay beyond. He was muddy and disordered from his long journey, in rough clothes and riding boots; but he was utterly unaware of any of that, as he burst open the door in front of him. And there, quite close to him, was Elizabeth among her ladies, in a dressing-gown, unpainted, without her wig, her grey hair hanging in wisps about her face, and her eyes starting from her head.'

The prior composition of *Essex: A Tragedy* shows that Lytton believed that the enigma of the Queen's relationship with her famous courtier was ideally suited to a theatrical treatment, and helps to explain why *Elizabeth and Essex* was aesthetically conceived in a dramatic form, unlike all his other books — even *Queen Victoria* — which, though visually dramatic, are in construction successions of cleverly interrelated essays. The play is yet another pointer also to the fact that Lytton had a long-standing interest and thorough knowledge of the Elizabethan age; and it reveals that his attitude towards Essex and Elizabeth herself, notwithstanding the added Freudian interpretations incorporated into the biography, remained pretty well consistent throughout his adult life.

During the autumn evenings at Pythagoras House, Lytton would read out scenes from his competitive tragedy to several friends. Shortly before Christmas the play was completed and sent off to Stratford in the vain hope that it would be performed there during the Festival Week. 'When it's acted,' he optimistically wrote to Moore, 'I'll send you a box.' But the occasion never arose.

Life at Pythagoras House had been wonderfully luxurious, and in his last week or two it grew if anything more so, full of charm and sweetness and that warm humanity which was for Lytton the essence of Cambridge – 'I suppose the result of the end of term,' he told James. 'People seem to draw closer.' One constant pleasure was the proximity of George Mallory. 'It's a surprising thing, after the experience of – I won't tell you how many years – to find oneself with someone who really likes things.' But, as he had dreaded from the first, Mallory's good looks were beginning to deteriorate. The hand of Time had already started to work its havoc. He was growing fat, and his complexionless face was becoming rather washy and bulbous, its contours too lunar – like a cheese. Lytton turned away in despair. He still thought him exquisite as an ideal human concept, but it was now easier to picture him as such if he forgot, or at least blurred over, certain physiognomical and corpulent developments. Sometimes, of course, this was not possible, and he would feel heartbroken by the agony of human relationships, by those awful shadows of mortality – the inevitable melancholy end of all that is beautiful, all that is lovely on earth. His pessimism, shot through with iridescent irony and laughter, was deepened by the news that Mallory was planning to go off on one of his dangerous Alpine expeditions.[11] 'It's not only the love affairs that are bound to fail!' he wrote to James in explanation of the low spirits which recurrently sucked him down. 'And now I shall never see him again, or if I do, it'll be an unrecognizable middle-aged mediocrity, fluttering between wind and water, probably wearing glasses and a timber toe.'

In the last week of January he set off for Daisy McNeil's private nursing home at 12 Devonshire Place in Eastbourne, just two hundred yards from the front. He had expected to find Daisy alone, and was horrified on discovering that the house was full of muttering old invalid hags, among whom he

11. 'The imagination cannot create,' Lytton wrote, 'it can only reconstruct and on this occasion mine has no materials, except a snow mountain, laziness, energy, George, and a perfectly absurd companion aged 15½ – and I can make nothing out of them.'

felt like Orpheus surrounded by the Scythian women, about to tear him to pieces. 'The place is rather bizarre,' he wrote to James (26 January 1910). 'I arrived at teatime – entered a room almost pitch dark, and apparently full of females – one of them I gathered a hospital nurse – the others being presumably morphine maniacs. I don't at all know whether I'm a guest or a patient.' Lytton had rarely been so gloomy as in these demure surroundings; but even here there were slight compensations – good food and an attractive German waiter to serve it.

He returned to Hampstead at the beginning of February, but succeeded almost at once in escaping again, for 'a dream of a week' to Clive and Vanessa Bell in Gordon Square. 'Dignity, repose, and medical consolations,' he wrote to them after leaving (15 February 1910), ' – I feel that I shall never find the divine conjunction again.' Apart from the occasional poem, he wrote nothing. James had by now started full-time work as St Loe Strachey's private secretary, and most of his friends – Clive and Vanessa Bell, Ralph Hawtrey, Bertrand Russell, C. P. Sanger, Gerald Shove, R. C. Trevelyan, and Virginia Stephen (who was suffering from a nervous breakdown) – had gone down to Cornwall, so that instead of spending his afternoons and evenings in Bloomsbury, he would wander dispiritedly off to the Savile Club to sit among the intolerable old gentlemen there and gaze forlornly at the footmen. In an endeavour to revive his cheerfulness, he took himself off for a solitary few days to the Old George House, a private hotel in Salisbury. But it was no use. 'My health has become quite filthy, and the future seems very black,' he wrote to Duncan Grant (4 April 1910). 'I think I shall *have* to give up living here – which points to Cambridge – oh dear! it's very melancholy. I've been almost perpetually ill here since I came back in December – and there seems now no possible reason, except the place and entourage, for this happening. If I was well, I should like London far better than Cambridge; but it's too much never to be able to work for more than a fortnight at a time. I've been too feeble to do a stroke . . .'

The prospect of staying anywhere alone appalled him and

he wrote off diffidently to Rupert Brooke to ask if he might consider accompanying him (31 March 1910): 'Is there any chance of your being able to go with me, only, for a week or so? James thinks there may be, and says that you know of a cottage on Dartmoor. ... My health seems to be giving way, and I want to go off somewhere; but I fear its hardly possible that you're still free. If you were I could go as soon as you liked, with songs of Thanksgiving.'

Rupert Brooke at once agreed to go, but as the Dartmoor cottage, Becky House, was not vacant, he made arrangements for them to spend the second week in April at the Cove Hotel, at West Lulworth in Dorset. No sooner was this irrevocably fixed than Lytton received an invitation from George Mallory urging him to come to Paris. Since he was now obliged to spend all his available money on his 'change of air', this infinitely preferable holiday had to be put out of mind. Far from sounding off songs of Thanksgiving, therefore, he felt particularly embittered, cursing himself for having written off to Brooke in the first place simply because no one else seemed free. The expectation of West Lulworth now singularly failed to thrill him, but on his arrival there all this bitterness quickly melted away. Rupert was a charming and decorative companion, and the hotel was warm and cosy. 'Rupert read me some of his latest poems on a shelf by the sea,' he wrote to James, 'but I found them very difficult to make out, owing to his manner of reading. I could only return the compliment by giving him the first act of Essex to read – he didn't seem quite so bitter about it as you; but that may have been his politeness. I found him, of course, an extraordinarily cheerful companion. I only hope though, that he won't think me (as he does George Trevy) "an old dear". I thought I saw some signs of it.'

The two of them had never been on friendlier terms, and Lytton was always to remain grateful to Brooke for helping to pull him out of the troughs of his melancholia. Health was the order of the day at the Cove Hotel, frequent jumpings in and out of cold baths, and a pulley for developing the biceps which both poet and dramatist worked at very vigorously.

After their week together Lytton set about searching for

new lodgings at Cambridge. It was almost a month before he succeeded in engaging suitable rooms at 14 St John Street for two pounds a week. That summer he went back again to Hampstead where he was soon engulfed in the Suffrage Movement – 'demonstrations and petitions in every direction', as he described it to Maynard Keynes (7 July 1910). 'I hope to get a seat in the House for Tuesday, and if I do, of course, I shall have to shriek and be torn to pieces. An uncomfortable, but no doubt noble death.'

'Such is my low ebb,' he admitted to Saxon Sydney-Turner, 'that I'm reduced to reading the life of Cardinal Manning!' Lady Strachey had run out of new ideas to contend with his illnesses, and the only possible remedy that anyone could think of was another sojourn in the Saltsjöbaden sanatorium. Lytton's previous course of treatment there, though ultimately disastrous, had almost been successful. But for that freak setback at the end, he had looked like benefiting enormously and might have been able to avoid what had turned out one of his worst years of sickness. This time, with reasonable luck, the venture ought to pay off, making up to his body for the horrors it would certainly inflict on his mind. At any rate he could only hope so. Accordingly he set off in the second week of July for another ten weeks' spell in Sweden. This time the female cortège consisted of his sister Pernel and Jane Harrison, the fifty-nine-year-old classical anthropologist, who was using this pharmaceutical holiday 'to get new heart' for the writing of *Themis,* her celebrated study on the social origins of Greek religion.

As the journey progressed Lytton's spirits sank rapidly. What a very plain, featureless country Sweden was! Nearly everyone was good-looking, but there was a monotonous chastity about the type that was mortifying. Even the Swedish sailors, with their pretty *décolleté* necks, now failed to agitate him. And when he arrived back at the Saltsjöbaden clinic, there, to welcome him, was that same veteran brigade of patients going through the same hectic and idiotic programme of porridge and baths. Nothing had changed, and Lytton himself quickly settled down again to the old routine. 'I already feel as if I'd been here for twenty years,' he began a letter to James written on his first day (18 July 1910), 'and should be quite put out if dinner was later than six or the porridge was made of porridge.'

His regime was almost identical to that of the previous year. Instead of the *Daily Mail* he took *The Times*, studying with great interest the Minority Report on the Poor Law; and he also read Dumas's *Memoirs* and Lecky's *Eighteenth Century*. While Jane Harrison took advantage of her stay to learn Swedish principally from the writings of Selma Lagerlöf, Lytton, rather perversely, concentrated on mastering Italian – for his dreams had revived of going south to the more sympathetic climate of Italy. He still, of course, went through the same pantomime of billiards, gymnastics and massage, but this time the medical treatment was if anything rather more stringent. He was placed under the care of the unmusical Dr Olof Sandberg, the specialist in digestive complaints, who favoured a liberal use of the stomach pump. At the same time he insisted that Lytton should eat a great deal – 'as much as possible and sometimes a little more'. This drastic dietary and emetic treatment, however, appeared to pay dividends, and by the middle of August he could report to Pippa: 'My cure has been going very well.'

For Jane Harrison, suffering under a similar course of treatment, there were no such redeeming features. Unlike Lytton she could not attune herself to the colourless oddity of the place; and Pernel fared little better. 'They both find the place very singular,' Lytton explained to his mother (5 August 1910), 'and I should think the place returns the compliment so far as Jane is concerned – she makes a strange figure among the formal Scandinavians, floating through the corridors in green shawls and purple tea-gowns, and reciting the Swedish grammar at meals.'

Suddenly, in the third week of August, the weather became piercingly cold, unlike anything he had experienced on his previous stay there, 'so I fear that the summer is now over', he lamented to Pippa (17 August 1910). 'As the Salong is the only hot room, I spend most of my days in it, among a shrieking crowd of foreigners, who discuss their symptoms in every language from Chinese to Peruvian. At the present moment I'm accablé by three fat women talking Esperanto.' Despite an occasional day of heavy sunshine, the cold persisted and proved too much for Lytton's two companions who soon hastened back to England. 'This is the last anyone will hear of my health,' remarked Jane Harrison ruefully.

Lytton's invalidism, however, was made of sterner stuff, and for him the rigorous cure continued on unchecked. He felt as if he had become lodged in Saltsjöbaden for the next century. 'One leads such a sheltered life!' he reminded James. 'Nothing but meals, torpor, and senselessness.' His apathy was relieved for a time by the arrival of Pippa, but even she could only endure a fortnight of the sanatorium before retreating to England. Yet still Lytton stayed on. His health, meanwhile, had improved, though not so noticeably as on his first visit. Then, just as before, he suffered a sudden relapse, the cause of which none of the specialists could diagnose. Once again all his suffering and patience had been to little or no purpose. 'I've stayed on here week after week,' he complained to Maynard Keynes (26 September 1910), 'lured by the hope of attaining eternal health: on Friday I shall drag myself away. . . . I feel that this has been a wasted summer for me.'

To wile away the long hours at the clinic Lytton had been working spasmodically at a rather heavy *facétie* on the Suffrage Movement. 'I fear, even if it's finished, that it will never see the light of day,' he confessed to Pippa. 'The scene is the infernal regions, and the principal character so far Queen Victoria.' More serious was the work he had now resumed on his Warren Hastings dissertation. If he was to get anywhere in the literary world, he felt that he must produce a book. And he was still sure that *Warren Hastings* would be his first *magnum opus*. After all, what else was there? But now, in these last days at Saltsjöbaden, his literary horizon was suddenly transformed when, out of the blue, he received a letter from H. A. L. Fisher asking him to write a brief panoramic study of French literature for a series that he and Gilbert Murray were editing. Lytton at once accepted, though he felt sure the project would prove difficult chiefly owing to its restricted length – not exceeding fifty thousand words. 'Herbert Fisher and Gilbert Murray have asked me to write a history of French lit for upperclass citizens,' was how he announced the news to James on a postcard (21 September 1910), 'and I shall accept. It will amuse me, and perhaps pay better than reviews. "If", Herb says, "75,000 are sold you will get £290." Isn't it a bright prospect? But at any rate I gather I'll get £50.'

Lytton returned to England at the beginning of October and quickly succeeded in arranging his autumn and winter programme to such effect that hardly more than a week of it was to be passed in Hampstead. His continuous peregrinations about the countryside at this time have about them an air of desperation. He whisked and shuttled from one place to another, visiting old friends and his old rural haunts, and always avoiding London. Waiting for him on his arrival back from Sweden was an invitation from Maynard Keynes to spend a couple of days at the Little House at Burford (Oxon.) which Keynes had hired the previous year as a haven where he might concentrate undisturbed on his *Treatise on Probability*. Desmond MacCarthy too had invited him for a week's visit, but on arriving from Burford, Lytton found that his host had absent-mindedly left for Paris. However, he passed a very agreeable and comfortable time with Molly MacCarthy in the Cloisters at Eton waiting for Desmond's unannounced return. 'After a few happy quiet days in the Cloisters London fills me with terror and disgust', he confided to James. It was not in London, however, that he next turned up, but at Charterhouse, where George Mallory had taken up a temporary post as schoolmaster.[12] From here he went for a further week to the Homere sisters at Kingham 'in a state bordering on collapse – mental and physical', he told Duncan Grant (19 October 1910), adding all the same that 'in spite of the hounds, the piano, and the intellectual annihilation, I'm now beginning to pull round.'

12. 'I wonder where Charterhouse is,' he wrote on contemplating this venture into the unknown. 'I think probably in some semi-detached Surrey region.'

During these itinerant weeks he squeezed in an afternoon's discussion of his projected history of French literature with Herbert Fisher, 'who struck me as an Academic Fraud', he informed Keynes (9 October 1910), echoing Virginia Stephen's earlier view. Fortunately, Fisher's opinion of Lytton was unrepentantly high. When, earlier that summer, the editors of the Home University Library, casting round to find the right person to compose a short one-volume survey of the literature of France, asked him for his nomination, he had at once recalled his conversation in Fitzroy Square eighteen months previously. The favourite candidate for the authorship of this book was Edmund Gosse, then an established oracle on the subject. But Fisher submitted Lytton's name, recommending him as the writer of 'Two Frenchmen', his first contribution to the *Independent Review*. In urging Lytton's particular merits, he pointed, with justification, to the superior versions of the original French which, in the course of his long review, Lytton had offered in order to bring out various fine and subtle shades of meaning in the work of La Bruyère and Vauvenargues which Elizabeth Lee, a conscientious though clumsy translator, had altogether missed. Fisher also drew the attention of the editors to Lytton's own prose style, and the aesthetic cohesion of his essay-review, reminding them that the avowed policy of the Home University Library was to select authors not for academic distinction alone, but also for their literary skill in combining learning with artistic lucidity. The editors were impressed by Fisher's advocacy, and soon agreed to his candidate.

It was at this autumn meeting that Fisher explained the details of their proposition to Lytton. He was to receive from Williams and Norgate, the publishers, the sum of fifty pounds down for the copyright, and a royalty of one penny per copy sold. 'I told him that I wanted him to write a sketch of French Literature in fifty thousand words,' Fisher later recorded, 'and showed him J. W. Mackail's *Latin Literature*, with which he was not then acquainted, as a model which he might be content to follow. He assented to my proposal with rare economy of speech, and with none of the usual expressions of diffidence, which an editor is accustomed to hear from an untried author to whom he has offered a task of exceptional difficulty.'

The result of this interview was that Lytton finally committed himself to the writing of *Landmarks in French Literature*, once and for all abandoning his *Warren Hastings*. His plans now took on a fresh practical immediacy and resolution. During the autumn he would intensively read and reread a large number of French classics; while for the winter he decided to go off and live with Simon and Dorothy Bussy down at Roquebrune, where he believed that he stood the best chance of escaping the psychosomatic illnesses of the preceding year, and where, from past experience – having written part of his Fellowship dissertation and several of his more elaborate essays at La Souco – he knew he could work in comparative tranquillity. With the commission of this first book, his years of obscurity and pessimism had reached their end, and to coincide with the new emergent phase, his social and emotional life were also about to undergo some dramatically involved variations of pattern. The composition of *Landmarks in French Literature* injected into him a long-sought-after burst of self-confidence which, like an expanding spring, released him from the lugubrious routine of the past, its frustrations and lethargic aimlessness, and led on to what he himself described as his 'Spiritual Revolution'.

So that now, in the autumn of 1910, he stood on the perimeter of a new and ultimately happier world.

PART III

'I suppose I ought fo feel ... a general sense of lament-
ation – but somehow I don't. My spirit refuses to be
put down.' *Lytton Strachey to David Garnett* (23 June
1915)

NINE

The Changing Past

'The past seems to me the only thing we have which is not
tinged with cruelty and bitterness. It is irrevocable; its good
and its evil are fixed and done with; we can look at it dispassionately, as if it were a work of art. For my part, when I
think of our few happy Summer days together – how many
years ago now, I wonder? – the only pang I feel is the pang of
approaching age.' *Lytton Strachey to John Sheppard* (17
March 1906)

1
'CHÈRE MARQUISE AND CHER SERPENT'

DURING the autumn of 1910, two people, who between
them were to dominate the next few years of Lytton's life,
emerge for the first time into prominence. Lady Ottoline
Morrell he had encountered casually some years earlier at
Haslemere, where his mother had taken him to see the
Berensons. Their initial response to each other had been amiable, but lukewarm. 'His tall, bending figure and a rather long,
cadaverous face, with long nose and a drooping moustache,
made him then a not very attractive figure,' recalled Ottoline,
who was on a visit to Logan Pearsall Smith at the time, 'but I
found him most sympathetic and everything he said was of
interest.'

In Lytton's earlier correspondence there are occasional references to Ottoline after this meeting which suggest a latent
curiosity about her. But it was not until they met as fellow
guests of C. P. Sanger and his wife Dora, that the real beginning to their long and unusual friendship was formed. The
Sangers were living near the Strand, high up above the noise
of the traffic in a flat where, once a week, they would give a
party for their friends. Amid this intellectual group of young

people – many of them from Cambridge – Ottoline felt rather inadequate; but her timidity was soon dispelled by Lytton, who was in his most forthcoming mood. 'I see him now,' Ottoline wrote of that evening, 'sitting in a long basket-chair by the Sangers's gas fire leaning forward as he would still do, holding out his long, thin hands to warm. I think he had just come from one of Bernard Shaw's plays. Altogether I enjoyed my first evening at the Sangers immensely and came home quite excited.'

Lady Ottoline Morrell had felt herself to be something of a misfit, and in the plush and sunless land of Edwardian society, her prodigal, Gothic figure always stood out as a curious anomaly. Some seven years older than Lytton, she was the daughter of General Arthur Cavendish-Bentinck and his wife, Lady Bolsover. Her childhood had been lonely, lavish and discontented, and even before the age of eighteen she had shown herself to be deeply unconventional in her determination to escape from her upper-class, philistine background of material comfort and débutante dullness. The progress of this struggle was erratic: first she plunged into evangelical religion; next she persuaded her embarrassed family to allow her to travel to Italy, absorbing the beauties of art and nature; and finally she had fallen hopelessly in love with Axel Munthe. Returning to England, she determined briefly on a career of academic study at the University of St Andrews, but soon secured her freedom through marrying Philip Morrell, the Liberal member of Parliament.

It was only now, as a married woman, that she was able to find a satisfying outlet for her egregious energies – in the political activities of her husband, and, more completely, in those realms of art and intellect that represented everything antagonistic to her prim, aristocratic upbringing. Her entrée into this exciting world came largely through Virginia Stephen, whose Thursday evenings in Fitzroy Square she now began to frequent. Here she would regularly come across Lytton, and though she did not yet get to know him well, the impressions of him which she carried away from these gatherings and which she subsequently put down in her memoirs, are exact and acute. 'Of Lytton Strachey I used to feel most shy,' she wrote, 'for he said so little and he seemed to live far away in an atmosphere of rarefied thought. His voice so small and faint, but with definite accentuations and stresses of tone, giving a sense of certainty and distinction, appeared to come from very far away, for his delicate body was raised on legs so immensely long that they seemed endless, and his fingers equally long, like antennae. It was not till I knew him better that I found how agile those long legs could be, and what passion and feeling lay in that delicate body, and how rapidly those long and beautiful antennae could find passages in Racine or Dryden, and the strength and vigour of his voice when he read these passages aloud to me.'

It was not long before Ottoline constituted herself as the fashionable London hostess to a wide and varied circle of writers and artists. Once a week she would invite a select company of them to her home at 44 Bedford Square. Here, in a great double room on the first floor, decked with modernistic pictures, pale grey walls, yellow taffeta curtains, soft lights and banks of flowers, they would talk over their coffee and cigarettes, listen to chamber music or dance in their pullovers and corduroy trousers. During the four or five years before the war, Lytton was among the most frequent of her guests at these functions, and also at the more formal and distinguished dinner-parties which she gave.

Ottoline Morrell has been described as an impresario rather than a creator, but her submerged creative instincts did come to the surface as a genuine flair for spotting original artists before they had made their reputations. In Lytton she rightly detected a figure destined to make his mark on the literature of the day, and she took him up as part of a determined effort to gate-crash her way into the secret world of the artist – a world with which, so her intuition proclaimed, she possessed more affinity than with her own unenlightened background. The dilemma in which she now found herself was unenviable. Without being able to command enough natural talent to develop into a creative artist in her own right, she was nevertheless of too wilful and individual a nature to remain content with the inert traditions of her past. Her exertions to absorb vicarious nourishment from the intellectual milieu of which she had made her home the vortex took a curiously literal form in their unorthodoxy and directness. Loudly sucking and crunching between her prominent equine teeth a succession of bull's-eye peppermints, she would subject some of the shyer poets and more inarticulate painters to a series of insistent questions concerning their work and the specific details of their love-affairs. 'M-m-m. Does your friend have *no* love-life?' she once complained in her drawling, deep, resonant voice to a poet who had brought some particularly reticent friend to tea. Frustrated, almost inevitably, in these attempts to find full satisfaction from literary gossip, she sometimes despaired of ever achieving fulfilment by such ruthless ques-tionnaire tactics. Many of her friendships exploded into violent terminating quarrels, in the aftermath of which she could expect to see herself savagely caricatured in her late friend's next novel – possibly as Priscilla Wimbush in Aldous Huxley's *Crome Yellow*, or as Hermione Roddice in D. H. Lawrence's *Women in Love*.[1]

Though her sensibilities were undisciplined and over-elaborate, and she was not always very sensible, something of the extraordinary qualities of those people she mixed with did rub off on her. She had, too, the power to make artists and writers feel that their ideas were immensely exciting and im-portant to her. She was therefore, in some respects, par-ticularly well-suited to act as Lytton's confidante and to give him the literary encouragement he needed. 'Ottoline has moved men's imaginations,' wrote D. H. Lawrence, 'and that's perhaps the most a woman can do.' Certainly she moved Lytton's imagination. He found her alternately stimulating

1. Most of the spiteful stories about Ottoline emanated from her old friend turned enemy, Logan Pearsall Smith. He believed, incorrectly, that she had been responsible for seducing Bertrand Russell away from Alys Russell, his, Logan Pearsall Smith's, sister, and a woman of pedagogic saintliness. He also resented her marriage to his close friend Philip Mor-rell. 'Ottoline likes to eat people up,' he complained. And with sly insin-uations and fantastic distortions of the truth he proceeded to blow up around her personality a mist of pernicious wickedness.

and embarrassing, sometimes gloriously larger-than-life, on other occasions unendurably trivial. But the quality that appealed most to men's imaginations was the homeless pathos which underlay her baroque and flamboyant personality. Her eccentricities were the practical means by which she tried to unify and assert an essentially heterogeneous character. For the fantastic side of her temperament found expression not only in the striking décor of Bedford Square, but also in her own appearance, which seemed to have been artificially grafted on to the rest of her nature, and which at once tickled Lytton's sense of the ridiculous. Beside her outlandish get-up, his own elongated oddity almost faded into conventional insignificance. 'She was a character of Elizabethan extravagance and force,' wrote Lord David Cecil, 'at once mystical and possessive, quixotic and tempestuous.' Many other writers have testified to the bizarre impression she made upon them. David Garnett describes her as 'extremely handsome: tall and lean, with a large head, masses of dark Venetian red hair, . . . glacier blue-green eyes, a long straight nose, a proud mouth and a long jutting-out chin made up her lovely, haggard face'. Peter Quennell, who got to know her several years later, was particularly struck by the lines of her features which 'had a medieval strength, a boldly baronial, high-arched nose being accompanied by a prominent prognathous jaw. Her hair, arranged in seventeenth-century curls, was darkened to a deep mahogany red, which the pallor of her face and neck made at first sight all the more surprising; and from this strangely impressive mask proceeded a sonorous nasal voice, which drawled and rumbled, and rustily hummed and hawed, but might subside, if she were amused or curious, to an insinuating confidential murmur.' Less sympathetically, Osbert Sitwell described her as resembling 'a rather oversize Infanta of Spain or Austria', while her chameleon-like luminescence reminded Virginia Woolf of nothing more garish than a mackerel swimming in an aquarium tank. In her later years, by which time she had become a literary legend, Stephen Spender used to observe her sporting a shepherd's crook with a number of Pekinese dogs attached to it by ribbons. Her dress, too, was at least as unpredictable as her behaviour or the colour of her hair. George Santayana, arriving at Garsington for the first time, came across his hostess attired in bright yellow stockings crossgartered, like Malvolio; while Siegfried Sassoon saw her as grotesquely overpainted and powdered, with her hair dyed purple.

It was at these parties in Bedford Square that Lytton now renewed his acquaintance and began to develop a close friendship with another of Ottoline's protégés, Henry Lamb. Lamb came from a family of mathematicians, and had been educated at Manchester where his father was professor of mathematics at the university. He himself was without any trace of mathematical ability and wished fervently to be an artist. His father, however, would not hear of this, and a compromise had been reached whereby Henry agreed to study at medical school. Encouraged by his friend Francis Dodd,[2] he had nevertheless persisted in drawing in his spare time, and when in 1905 he unexpectedly won an art competition, he at once threw up his studies – though he had by then almost completed his time as a medical student – and travelled south to London, where he was introduced into the Bloomsbury world by his elder brother Walter. It was now, at the Stephen home in Gordon Square, that Lytton first set eyes on him. 'He's run away from Manchester, become an artist, and grown sidewhiskers', he reported to Leonard Woolf (October 1905). 'I didn't speak to him, but wanted to, because he really looked amazing, though of course very very bad.'

But at that stage Lytton had had no opportunity of getting to know him, since Lamb suddenly married his first wife, Euphemia, a wild, unshy art student at Manchester; and together they eloped to Paris. Here Henry had embarked upon his serious artistic training in company with Augustus John. These were crucial years in his life, and Lytton used occasionally to hear something of them from Duncan Grant, who was

2. Francis Dodd (1874–1949), the etcher and painter of landscapes, who, in 1895, had gone to live in Manchester, and nine years later moved to London where he eventually became a Royal Academician and a trustee of the Tate Gallery (1928–35).

also, of course, studying in Paris. Now, as later, Lamb was largely overshadowed by the figure of John, modelling much of his work and behaviour after John's style. A superb if rather clinical draftsman, his partial failure to match or excel his master's high standard of achievement often vexed his spirit, making him a touchy companion. Under John's exotic influence, he also clothed himself in gipsy fashion and increased his womanizing, a first conquest being one of John's own girl friends. Their liaison so alienated Euphemia that she never forgave her husband and separated from him there and then, though their actual divorce was not arranged for another twenty years.[3]

It was the whimsical, divergent element in both Ottoline and Henry that at first roused Lytton's curiosity, and for a while he appears to have been unable to distinguish clearly between the very different attractions that each held for him. 'Ottoline has vanished to her cottage, but tomorrow she begins her parties again, and I shall drag myself there if I can', he wrote to Duncan Grant (4 April 1910). 'My last view of her was at a dim evening party full of virgins given by the Russells in a furnished flat. I was feeling dreadfully bored when I sud-

3. In later life Euphemia took up with the painter James Dickson Innes (1887–1914). John Rothenstein, in his *Modern English Painters, Volume 2: Innes to Moore* (revised edition 1962, pp. 29–30) writes: 'But his [Innes's] last and deepest attachment was to Euphemia Lamb. They met in a Paris café, and Innes at once responded to the beauty of her pale oval face, classical in feature yet animated by a spirit passionate, reckless and witty, and the heavy honey-hued hair: a beauty preserved in many paintings and drawings by her artist friends, most notably, perhaps, in a tiny drawing in pen and ink by John, but even now not extinct. Together Innes and Euphemia made their way, largely on foot, to his favourite resorts on the foothills of the Pyrenees, and back to London, he contributing to their support by making drawings in cafés and she by dancing. Their attachment lasted until his death.' When he was dying in a nursing-home at Swanley in Kent, Horace Cole and Augustus John took Euphemia to see him. 'The meeting of these two was painful,' John records in *Chiaroscuro* (1962 edn., p. 180). 'We left them alone together: it was the last time I saw him. Under the cairn on the summit of Arenig, Dick Innes had buried a silver casket containing certain correspondence. I think he always associated Euphemia with this mountain and would have liked at the last to lie beside the cairn.'

denly looked up and saw her entering with Henry. I was never so astonished, and didn't know which I was in love with most. As to *her*, though, there seems very little doubt. She carried him off to the country with her under my very nose, and I was left wishing that Dutch William and his friends had never come to England.'[4]

Eight months later Lytton himself was invited to stay at Peppard, Ottoline's cottage near Henley-on-Thames. One Sunday in October, they had met at a tea-party given at Newnham by Jane Harrison. Ottoline, half-laughingly, suggested that Lytton should come and visit her, adding that Henry Lamb would be the other guest. Lytton appeared to ponder this suggestion very deeply, drifted away for a few minutes, then came back to ask: 'Do you really mean me to come to Peppard?' 'Of course I do,' replied Ottoline without hesitation, all at once dreading the responsibility of entertaining him at her home. And so it was settled.

Ottoline's fears over providing for Lytton's well-being soon proved to have been groundless. Away from the fogs of London and the noisy General Election fever that autumn, enjoyment came quite spontaneously to him, and he remained there for over three consecutive weeks. Peppard was extraordinarily comfortable, the country charming, the climate bracing. He could find no fault with anything. He ate enormous meals, went for enormous walks through the beech-woods, and had his portrait painted by Henry, who had set up his studio in the stables. 'This is altogether exquisite,' he wrote rhapsodically to James Strachey (18 November 1910). 'Such comforts and cushions as you never saw! Henry, too, more divine than ever, plump now (but not bald) and mel-

---

4. Ottoline's ancestor, Hans William Bentinck, first Earl of Portland (1649–1709), had entered William of Orange's household at the age of fifteen, becoming the Prince's loyal companion of a lifetime, his favourite, and his confidential agent. At William and Mary's coronation he was deluged with honours and rewards, but remained rather an unpopular figure in international politics. He married three times, his numerous children settling partly in Holland, partly in England. He himself died at his seat of Bulstrode, near Beaconsfield, following an attack of pleurisy.

lowed in the radiance of Ottoline. The ménage is strange. Fortunately Philip is absent, electioneering in Burnley. Henry sleeps at a pub on the other side of the green, and paints in a coach-house rigged up by Ottoline with silks and stoves, a little further along the road. She seems quite gone – quite! And on the whole I don't wonder. But his attitude is rather more cranky. No doubt it's a convenience, and a pleasure even – but then – Meanwhile Philip electioneers at Burnley.

'... I'm afraid I have now been permanently spoilt for country cottage life. How does the woman do it? Every other ménage must now seem sordid ...

'Ah! She is a strange tragic figure. (And such mysteries!)'

It was during these happy weeks at Peppard that the future pattern of a complicated triangular relationship was finally fixed and defined. Briefly stated, both Ottoline and Lytton had fallen uncompetitively in love with Henry Lamb, who returned their attentions with a mixture of affection and callousness. Lytton's infatuation is easily enough accounted for: Lamb had now come to occupy in his scheme of things that position recently vacated by Duncan Grant. He offered him the same humble accolade, showered on him the same lavish praise of his artistic accomplishments – 'that he's a genius', he wrote to his brother James (30 November 1911), 'there can be no doubt, but whether a good or an evil one?' This romantic speculation held its appeal for Lytton, who, half-cherishing the role of unrequited lover, was still drawn to people whom he instinctively felt might use him badly. Lamb was exclusively heterosexual, and of a charming, highly-strung, volatile disposition, a prey to feelings of morbid insecurity that were constantly being inflamed by his pessimistic, one-sided rivalry with Augustus John. All this made him a tricky and unpredictable inamorato: 'He is the most delightful companion in the world,' Lytton once confessed to James (November 1911), '– and the most unpleasant.' Above all, Lamb resented any suspicion that he was being imposed upon. The intense possessiveness of both Lytton and Ottoline, which his own mercurial temperament did much to stimulate, often irritated him immeasurably, hardening his heart and making him behave in a deliberately unfeeling manner. Nor did he attach the same high priority to human relationships as did the Bloomsbury Group or the Cambridge Apostles, and his egocentricity caused Lytton much misery and bewilderment. 'His [Lamb's] state of mind baffles me,' he admitted to James (August 1911). 'He seems to be completely indifferent to everything that concerns me, and yet expects me to be interested in every trifle of his life.'

Despite these formidable disadvantages, Lamb's appeal was very potent. He offered both Ottoline and Lytton admission into an unknown, superbly bohemian set – the world of all-night Chelsea parties, gay and easy-going, and of dedicated exotic artists such as Augustus John and the Russian mosaicist Boris Anrep,[5] both of whom rapidly assumed in Lytton's mind the proportions of myths. He was, too, a man of sala-mander-like good looks, rather dashing and debonair, pale, slim, with long flowing hair, a sylphic physiognomy, evil and bewitching goat's eyes and long thin lips that curved into the kind of grin one sees transfixed on the skeleton faces of some prehistoric monsters. Lamb's sinister, Pan-like beauty en-tranced and captivated Lytton. Ottoline, so close to the pair of them, was able to observe their friendship at first hand. The

5. After studying law at St Petersburg and travelling widely through Europe, Boris von Anrep (b. 1883) had gone to Paris where he studied Byzantine art. In 1910–11, when Lytton first encountered him, he had moved to the Edinburgh College of Art. In 1916 he joined the Imperial Guard and appeared, a terrific figure, in full Russian Guard uniform, claiming that a battle at the Front wasn't nearly so alarming as one of Ottoline's parties. After the war he was to live for a time in Hampstead, but returned to Paris in 1926 and devoted himself to the revival of mosaic as an independent art. His chief public commissions in Britain include the mosaic pavement at the Tate Gallery, the floor, vestibule landing and pavement at the National Gallery (which depicts, among others, Virginia Woolf, Mary Hutchinson, Clive Bell, Osbert and Edith Sitwell, T. S. Eliot and Bertrand Russell), and mosaics for Westminster Cathedral, the Bank of England and the Royal Military College chapel, Sandhurst. In 1918 he married Helen Maitland, who later left him to live with Roger Fry, whose wife had become incurably ill with a mental dis-ease in 1910 and died in 1937.

description of it which she gives in her memoirs catches perfectly the mood and spirit of Lytton's romantic fascination.

At this time his [Lytton's] devotion to Henry Lamb was very great, and tossing him about on a sea of emotion. Lamb enjoyed leading him forth into new fields of experience. They would sit in pubs and mix with 'the lower orders', as Lytton called them, picking up strange friends. And so great is the imitative instinct in the human breast that he even altered his appearance to please Lamb, wearing his hair very long, like Augustus John, and having his ears pierced and wearing earrings. He discarded collars and wore only a rich purple silk scarf round his neck, fastened with an intaglio pin. They were a surprising pair as they walked the streets of London, as Lamb wore clothes of the 1860 period with a square brown hat, Lytton a large black Carlyle felt hat and a black Italian cape.

Lytton's relationship with Ottoline was at least as picturesque, but psychologically less straightforward. A rumour had spread through Bloomsbury that he was romantically inclined towards her – a piece of gossip which Virginia Woolf, who had pictured the great hostess when absent from Lytton as 'languishing like a sick and yellow alligator', may well have helped to popularize. There were, too, scraps of prima facie evidence to lend credence to this diagnosis. Lamb once came upon them unawares, fixed in a fierce embrace from which they abruptly sprang free, so that he could witness blood trickling down Lytton's lip. Yet the basis of their intimacy was never really sexual or aggressive, and though romantic in the imaginative sense, it remained platonic. The flirtation at which they played was all good pseudo-robust Elizabethan stuff, flighty and rollicking and always more stagy than real. But that they did feel some affinity for each other is beyond question. Ottoline belonged also to that breed of overruling, imperious women – a breed which included Florence Nightingale, Lady Hester Stanhope, Queen Victoria and Queen Elizabeth – that invariably fired Lytton's imagination. Her personality was so expansive, so spontaneous and affectionate that it would frequently sweep him off his feet. Beside her, everyone else seemed only half awake. He admired intensely her undaunted, indiscreet courage, her resolution in supporting enlightened causes, her incontestable disregard for unthinking conventions.

'What a pity one can't now and then change sexes!' Lytton had once written to Clive Bell (21 October 1909). 'I should love to be a dowager Countess.' In the company of Ottoline, such a desire was partly gratified. Her unquenchable, aristocratic air appealed immensely to his eighteenth-century respect for noble birth; and left to themselves they carried on like a couple of high-spirited, teenage girls – all giggling and high heels and titillating gossip. Occasionally they would step outside the drawing-room to play at tennis in Bedford Square Gardens, their slow, huge lobs over the net being accompanied by such convulsive shrieks of laughter that a large crowd of passers-by and residents would quickly assemble to behold these hysterical performances.

Each seemed to fulfil a real need in the other; one hungering after secret confidences, the other so eager to impart them. By themselves they were natural and gay; but introduce a third person into the room and their friendship was immediately made subject to an uneasy strain. To Lytton's eyes, Ottoline would then shed her charmingly unaffected demeanour, and change from a beautiful, stately woman of genuine artistic sensibility into a fancifully bespangled and festooned monstrosity, embarrassingly effusive and artificial. This metamorphosis was partly an hallucination. Once, coming from a particularly sportive tête-à-tête with Ottoline, he began to extol her virtues in the most extravagant language to Duncan Grant and Vanessa Bell. 'She was majestic!' he cried. 'She was splendid! Magnificent! Sublime!' But when Duncan Grant and Vanessa Bell demurred at so excessive praise, he quickly amended his sentiments, adding a string of well-considered qualifications that in due course far outweighed the opening eulogy. Owing to his quite justified mistrust of Ottoline's malicious tongue, Lytton did not use her at any time as his sole confidante, apportioning the part equally between her and his brother James, who was less encouraging but more reliable.

Lytton had gone to Peppard expecting to stay on there

only a few days; but the atmosphere of pugs, cushions and erections held him there, the days dissolved into weeks, November slipped by and December came – and still he lingered on. Every day was delightfully lazy, comfortable, refreshing. Some of this time he spent reading up for *Landmarks in French Literature*, and also, in French, the novels of Dostoyevsky, to which he had been introduced by Lamb.[6] In spare moments he would diligently transcribe his poems in a manuscript book, beautifully bound in orange-vermilion vellum, with which Ottoline had specially presented him. Towards the end of November she went off to help her husband's electioneering in Lancashire, and Lytton was left with Lamb, dressed in Cossack boots and an amazing maroon suit, as his sole companion. Almost daily they wrote charming and affectionate letters to her, telling her of all they were doing.

I felt he [Lytton] came more to see Henry Lamb than to see me [she wrote afterwards]. In my journal I say that 'he terrified me' at first, but I found him more sympathetic than I had imagined, but there is something wanting in him: a perfect Epicurean without large or generous instincts, but from his exceedingly fine brain he sees light and has appreciation of nobility, but shrinks back, partly from pose, and from prejudice and nervousness. He is indeed delicate in his health and that helps to encourage self-indulgence. He too is one of those in whom feminine characteristics are strong.

He and Lamb sat up until very late at night in the little sitting-room underneath my bedroom, and I heard the duet of their voices underneath, laughing and joking, Lytton playing with him like a cat with a mouse, enjoying having his own sensations tickled by Lamb's beauty, while his contrariness adds spice to the contact. I call him the Polish count, for he seemed to me as if he was a character out of a Russian novel.

6. As a matter of speculation, the recommendation of Dostoyevsky may have come originally or indirectly from Augustus John. In August 1909, John dined with James Strachey, and in the course of their conversation made a long speech in favour of the Russian novelist, about whose work only a few intellectuals knew at this time. Lytton sent Lamb his essays on both Dostoyevsky and Stendhal, and Nicolette Devas records that Lamb used to mark them in the margin with the intials F.R., meaning Foreign Rot, or C.E., meaning Child's Essay.

For his part, Lytton realized that he had entered upon a distinctly new and invigorating phase of his life. 'Extraordinary,' he exclaimed in a letter to James (30 November 1910). 'My existence here is something new. I tremble to think of what an "idyll" it might be, if only – and even as it is – in fact I really have no notion *what* it is. It seems to me more like Country House Life in the thirties than anything else. I feel like George Sand – shall I write an Indiana?'

2

MUMPS AND A BEARD

Shortly before Christmas, Lytton left England and set off for the South of France to stay with the Bussys, where he was to remain for the next four months. At Roquebrune he hoped to avoid the hardships of the English winter, and, in the more amenable climate, to forge ahead with his writing of *Landmarks in French Literature*. But no sooner had he arrived at La Souco than he was prostrated by 'une légère attaque de cholerine'. Unable to digest anything but vile and noxious slops, he grew every day weaker and thinner and more despondent. 'I've been having chills and general ruin for the last three weeks or so,' he complained to Maynard Keynes (6 February 1911). 'I hope I may now be recovering, but I'm rather shattered and in a very bad temper – at my having come all the way to escape getting ill, without any result.' A month later he could only report: 'My condition is wobbly still.'

To many of his friends he would write off, begging for some news with which to fill the vacuity of 'this lugubre exile'. Now that he was in France, England seemed infinitely desirable. 'You can imagine how I long to be at Peppard,' he assured Lamb (21 February 1911), 'and rejoice in the honest warmth of an English winter – it all sounds so heavenly that I hardly dare to think of it.' One of his few consolations were the French translations of Dostoyevsky. He read *L'Idiot*, *Le Crime et le Châtiment* and *Les Possédés*, which he liked best of all. 'I'm as converted as you could wish about Dostoievsky,' he declared in another letter to Lamb (5 January 1911). 'The last half of Vol 2 of the Possédés quite knocked me over. Colossal! Colossal! It's mere ramping and soaring genius, and all possible objections are reduced to absurdity. I shudder to think that I might never have read it, and I never should if it hadn't been for you. ... As for my objections, some of them do remain – mitigatedly.' In due course, even this solitary comfort was exhausted – 'I'm now reduced to the Bible, which I find has a good deal of merit, in one way or another.'

At the beginning of March the Bussys left for Sicily, and Lytton's sister Marjorie came down to look after him and his child niece, Jane Simone. This reorganization hardly affected Lytton. His life went on much as before, 'a mere blank of utter nothingness punctuated by a few horrors and rages here and there'. In spite of this evergreen lassitude, he had been pressing doggedly on with his book, and completed what amounts, perhaps, to its best chapters, those on 'Louis XIV' and 'The Eighteenth Century'. 'I am in an almost complete stupor,' he admitted to James. 'Have been trying to write the history of French Literature without much success.' This estimate of his progress, infected by a kind of Mediterranean despondency, did himself less than justice. Out of the grim struggle to advance with his work was born a greater spiritual resilience and sense of freedom. 'I feel quite reckless,' he wrote to James, ' – more I think than I ever have before. It came to me quite suddenly the other day – how little anything matters ... and then that really, after all, one has a confidence.'

Early that April, Lytton returned to Hampstead. Sanatogen, which he seems to have swallowed nearly every half-hour, had apparently once more saved his life – aided on this occasion by Dr Gregory's noisome manipulation of rhubarb – and he soon felt strong enough to start away on his wanderings again. 'I should like to go on a sailing voyage for fourteen months,' he told Henry Lamb (9 April 1911). Three days later he travelled down by train to the Dog Inn, near Henley, for a week with Lamb. 'Order several beef-steaks,' he exhorted him before setting off (10 April 1911), 'and light all the fires. I am (at present) not ill, but cowardly.'

After eight pleasant days among these so-called 'lower orders',[7] Lytton left Lamb's lodgings at the Dog Inn, and went down with James to Corfe Castle in Dorset, putting up at the Greyhound Inn. The evening of their arrival, a Friday, he complained of being ill. James took his temperature with the thermometer he always carried about with him and saw that it was 104. Next day, to the general relief, an attack of mumps declared itself. James looked after him to start with, but had to go back to the *Spectator* on Tuesday morning. So Oliver was ordered to take his place at Corfe. He was furious. He had just arrived in England from India on short leave, and was longing to rush around in the social life he so much enjoyed. For some reason, possibly expense, they were obliged to transmigrate from the relatively comfortable Greyhound to the poky little Castle Inn. The two of them crammed themselves into a small closed carriage piled high and wide with luggage, balancing every sort of treasured object in their arms – oil cans, ink bottles, safety-razors and the novels of Dostoyevsky – and arrived there on the afternoon of 21 April. Because of the risk of infection, Lytton was entombed in his bedroom at the Castle Inn for almost three weeks, attended by Oliver who, very kind and very incompetent, endeavoured to look after him without succumbing to the disease himself. While Oliver sat downstairs writing love-letters to his fiancée Ray Costelloe, upstairs in his bed Lytton lay composing affectionate epistles to his '*très-cher* serpent' Henry Lamb, who had gone off to stay with Boris Anrep in Paris. During all this time the only book he had to read was a French edition of Dostoyevsky's letters which, in spite of a certain number of good things, disappointed him and tended to deepen the gloom of his quarantine. 'For one thing his [Dostoyevsky's] portrait – most infinitely abattu – with eyes – oh! – but almost, I thought, as if he had been too much crushed – which

7. James Strachey advised that although Ottoline referred to 'lower orders', Lytton in fact never did. The phrase he always used was 'lower classes'.

was also the effect of the letters,' he reported to Henry Lamb (4 May 1911). 'His life was perfect hell till six years before he died; and his letters are almost entirely occupied with begging for money – always "pour l'amour du Christ". At last whenever you see Christ on a page you skip it because you know that an appeal for 125 roubles will follow. It's deplorable and it's impossible not to have rather a lower opinion of the man. He was not at all souterrain – very simple and at all times silly. On Christianity he writes the most hopeless stuff.'

The tedium of these bed-ridden weeks was occasionally relieved by a visit from one of his friends. Clive Bell came for a day and waved up cautiously towards the invalid's window; and Ottoline Morrell blew an elaborate kiss at him from the roadway as she motored from Studland *en route* for London. 'It was very touching,' he commented, 'but insubstantial.'

It was now, during these weeks of illness at Corfe, that Lytton grew his beard[8] – that most striking token of the metamorphosis which was changing him into a mature personality, in due course to grow famous throughout Britain, America and the Continent. At first he was doubtful as to its merits. Did it, for example, make him appear *too* ridiculous? 'The beard question is becoming rather dubious – but you shall judge,' he wrote to Ottoline. She, and all his other friends, begged him to keep it, since it made him look so well; and soon enough he agreed to do so. 'The chief news is that I have grown a beard,' he informed his mother (9 May 1911). 'Its colour is much admired, and it is generally considered extremely effective, though some ill-bred persons have been observed to laugh. It is a red-brown of the most approved tint, and makes me look like a French decadent poet – or something equally distinguished.'

The growing of this celebrated beard may be regarded as a manifestation of Lytton's reinvigorated attitude towards the world. Though he still remained outwardly diffident, and tended to exaggerate his setbacks almost to the point of invention, a hard, inner kernel of self-assurance was expand-

8. 'A red-brown-gold beard,' he described it in a letter to George Mallory, 'of the most divine proportions.'

ing. In the past he too often allowed his heart to rule his head; now, for the first time, his intellect was beginning to take over control. Under the influence of his brother James he had, since leaving Cambridge, grown more interested in politics, and was in the gradual process of rejecting his vague, high-bred Conservatism in favour of a more combative, left-wing position, mildly socialistic and violently anti upper-class. 'Have you noticed there are three classes of human beings?' he asked Sheppard, ' – the rich, the poor and the intelligent. When the poor are serious they're religious, when the intelligent are serious they're artistic, but the rich are never serious at all.'

Something of this changing attitude is already implicit in a most interesting paper which Lytton delivered to the Apostles (20 May 1911) at Cambridge, where he and Oliver had gone after leaving Corfe Castle. Near the opening of this paper, Lytton confesses his idyllic sentimentalism and the rather conservative form which it took: 'I even have a secret admiration for the typical Englishman – the strong silent man with the deep emotion – too deep – oh! far too deep ever to come to the surface; I can't help being impressed.' Against this high emotional susceptibility he sets a more objective mental estimate of such a man's worth. The strict, Victorian conventions seemed to have slipped in the seven years since he had come down from Trinity; but with the dawning freedom, there was emerging a somewhat prosaic, matter-of-fact world. He deprecated the earnest pomposity with which it had become the fashion to treat matters serious and laughable. For instance, now that the bishops had started going to the music halls the community seemed to be faced not, unfortunately, with a growing sense of humour among the clergy, but an increasing solemnity on the variety stage. The managers of those places had taken to writing to newspapers to assure everyone that no *risqué* jokes were to be heard in their establishments – one could only hope they were not telling the truth. Again, eminent literary critics would pull long faces over the more outspoken classics, wondering how, to take the case of Boccaccio for example, a book of such merit could also be so scandalously immoral. Soon one would not be able to dip into *Tristram*

Shandy without being arraigned for impurity by the National Council of Public Morals. In Lytton's view it was high time that some light-hearted jester shook his cap and bells a little in the faces of such intruding Malvolios. Did they think that because they were virtuous there should be no more cakes and ale? In short, Lytton's comic and romantic sensibilities warmed to the exaggeration, the fantasy and the rhetoric of the more outspoken picturesque past; but his intelligence applauded that sober, slowly developing social justice and enlightenment which releases confidences of a more intimate humane kind – those voices which had lain pathetically inarticulate under all the Victorian gush of words. And so, rather regretfully, he comes down on balance in favour of the unpoetical Age of Criticism:

'With us, at any rate, the old rule of the curt Englishman, who feels (so he says) that his emotions are too sacred for him to dare to do anything but hint at them – that old rule has broken down. Even in my memory there has been a change. Five years ago – the things that *didn't* happen! That's what, from the modern standpoint, strikes me now. And then – five years hence! – what a subject for a poem! – but no, we've given up poetry – we've reduced ourselves to prose.

'To prose? A queer sort of prose, I think. But really, in this so-called universe, what else can one expect? To be sure, to be sensible, to view things from the ordinary standpoint of the educated man – I've tried that, and found it really rather painful. For a moment, under the pressure of *The Times* newspaper, of the Home University Library, of the Ladies, and the rest of the phenomenal world, I've succeeded in feeling sensible, and then, looking back on my previous reflections I have seen quite clearly that they were simply the crude and crazy vaporizing of an eccentric in a dream. Perhaps that's what they are. So I think for a moment; but, opening the biography of our brother Maitland, I have a revulsion. Oh dear! the grey horror of those letters to our brothers Pollock, Verrall, and Jackson! The brave concealment of tragedy! The profound affection just showing, now and then, with such a delicacy – between the lines – "I am sorry indeed that the part of your letter to which I looked so anxiously contained such bad news – and having said that I think I won't say more – it is so useless." – "I feel good reason for hoping that long before now you have become reasonably comfortable. What I wish you know." – "I do very earnestly hope that things go fairly well with you and that you have not much pain." – What a world, what a life, passing in these dimnesses! I see once more the bleak and barren plain, and the dreadful solitary castles, with their blinds drawn down.'

Lytton's manner too, as well as his appearance and his political opinions, was undergoing some change. The long and elastic body, which had for years proved such an embarrassment to him was to be coordinated by this expanding confidence, his natural ungainliness stylized and welded into part of an elegantly synthetic, physical personality. And that curious scarecrow figure too was in the process of being shaped and transformed by the same alchemy into strange, symmetrical proportions that radiated a spidery fascination and beauty. Of course, some people – Angelica Homere and Topsy Lucas among them – would always find his looks pleasing and remarkable; others – Wyndham Lewis and Dorothy Brett, for example – were constantly revolted by the sight of him. Lytton himself, from the beginning, had sadly accepted this second view. Now, for the first time, he did so less readily. To some extent, his external appearance *had* changed; but there were also crucial internal changes to account for his more optimistic attitude and to influence the way in which others regarded him. Among his friends he began to speak and act with more assurance. Like all sensitive egocentrics, he seemed timid among strangers, easily bored and only intermittently sociable. To avoid the risk of being spoken to in trains, he always, even when most badly off, travelled first class (though probably a more important reason for this luxury was his piles). And Harold Nicolson remembers seeing him later on, hiding in agony behind a door on the other side of which a party was in progress. But though still prone to boredom and acutely subject to implosions of shyness, he was better able to retaliate and reflect embarrassment back on others. Shortly after his beard had grown to its full magnificent length, a lady came up and asked him: 'Oh, Mr Strachey, tell me, when you go to bed, do you keep that beard of yours inside or outside the blankets?' Adopting his most insinuating tone – which always reminded Desmond Mac-Carthy of the gnat in *Alice in Wonderland* – he piped: 'Won't you come and see?' At another party, the conversation turned to the question of which great historical character the people there would most have liked to go to bed with. The men voted for Cleopatra, Kitty Fisher and so on, but when it came to Lytton's turn he declared shrilly: 'Julius Caesar!'

Ottoline Morrell, whom he visited at Peppard for a few days that June, also observed some change in him.

He was franker with me than he used to be [she wrote] and I was less timid and nervous with him than I had been. . . .

It is hard to realize that this tall, solemn, lanky, cadaverous man, with his rather unpleasant appearance, looking indeed far older than he is, is a combination of frivolity, love of indecency, mixed up with rigid intellectual integrity. . . .

The steeds that draw the chariot of his life seem to be curiously ill-matched: one so dignified and serious, and so high-stepping, and of the old English breed, so well versed in the manners and traditions of the last four centuries; the other so feminine, nervous, hysterical, shying at imaginary obstacles, delighting in being patted and flattered and fed with sugar.

In general he takes little part, rather lying in wait than giving himself away – only occasionally interrupting, throwing in a rational and often surprisingly witty remark. But tête-à-tête he is a charming companion – his feminine quality making him sympathetic and interested in the small things of life, and with those who know him well he is very affectionate.

Leaving Peppard early in June, Lytton returned once more to Cambridge, where he installed himself, with Oliver, in lodgings at 12 King's Parade. He had arranged to have sent on to him a trunk full of extra clothes so that there was no need to go back to Hampstead, and he was able to make Cambridge his headquarters for some time longer. Oliver soon left to marry Ray Costelloe, Gerald Shove took his place as Lytton's chief companion, and life jogged on along its amiable, enchanted course. He hardly knew why he felt so happy. The greater part of every day he spent lying in a punt near King's, 'propped up by innumerable cushions, and surrounded by innumerable books which we never read'. From this vantage point he held a sort of pastoral court among the undergraduates floating down to the bank while he passed – smoking cigarettes, talking, and eating *langues-de-chat* as they sat, row upon row, on the grass in the sunshine. The willows, the parasols, the blue skies, the white flannels – everything conspired to make these months into an elysium. At week-ends he would tear himself away to visit Lady Lytton at Knebworth, or, 'to avoid the terrors of the Coronation', George Mallory at Charterhouse, or, once again, his 'Chère Marquise' Ottoline Morrell at Peppard, 'where it was all very idyllic, dining out in the moonlight with purple candle-sticks'.

But Cambridge, though delightful, was not conducive to hard work. At the beginning of July, Lytton reluctantly decided to leave King's Parade, and travelled down to Becky House, near Manaton in Devon, which Rupert Brooke had recommended for its peace, inexpensiveness and comfort. A largish country cottage, primitive and remote, set by itself in a desolate rocky Dartmoor valley next to a waterfall and a small rushing stream, it was lived in by a working-class man and his family, who let lodgings – a large sitting-room and a few bedrooms. 'It is very agreeable,' he told Maynard Keynes, '– incredibly hot and exhilarating.' He now settled down to write the final chapters of *Landmarks in French Literature*, working not less than four hours every day, and describing himself as 'extraordinarily healthy and industrious'. His good health and general competence during this month proved to him what he had always instinctively believed: that the country was the one place for him in which to live if he wished to create some enduring work of literature. Open air, fresh food and strict, regular hours propped up his fleeting vitality and made possible his best and most sustained literary compositions.

While at Becky House, he was joined for a week by two old friends, G. E. Moore and Leonard Woolf – recently returned from Ceylon, his ascetic features burnt up by the tropical sun. 'He has a long, drawn, weather-beaten face,' Lytton rather morosely observed in a letter to James (15 June 1911), 'and speaks (when he does) very slowly, like one re-risen from the tomb – or rather on the other side of it.' As the time approached for their arrival he began to dread the prospect of their company. Why had he ever asked them? So much had happened in the six or seven years since they had been really close; he was a different, even an unrecognizable person now. Apprehensively he wrote off to Henry Lamb (5 July 1911): 'My heart quails at the thought of their conversation. Oh dear! How things must have changed since the days when I thought it was the absolute height of pleasure and glory! But now there is something cold and dry – I don't know what – the curiosity of existence seems to vanish with them: it's not that I don't like them – only that they are under the sea.' Then he had a brainwave – leading on to a very typical denouement. He invited Lamb to come and stay, at the same time apologizing to Moore and Woolf that another, possibly incompatible guest appeared to be arriving. He had invited him, he went on to explain, in a moment of unaccountable frenzy, thinking that he would certainly refuse, and had been astonished to receive a reply saying that he would be delighted to accept. But then, to his genuine surprise, Lamb cancelled this acceptance because of a trip to France; and Lytton was obliged to face his friends alone.

The visit of Moore and Woolf, however, turned out to be less submarine than Lytton had predicted. While his life and personality had been changing, theirs had not remained entirely static. 'I find them – oh! quite extraordinarily nice – but ... if they are no longer under the sea, perhaps it's I who am somewhere else now – in the clouds, perhaps,' he told Lamb (14 July 1911); 'at any rate I find myself dreaming of more congenial company. However we are very happy, and go out for walks, and discuss this and that, and do a great deal of work. My health is a great success ... fatness increasing and peevishness at breakfast almost unknown.' It was, in fact, Leonard Woolf to whom this old Apostolic atmosphere seemed most foreign. After his unintellectual, colonial career in Ceylon, the uncommunicative company of Moore and Lytton at Becky House was pretty astringent. 'In the morning Lytton used to sit in one part of the garden, with a panama on his head, groaning from time to time over his literary constipation as he wrote *Landmarks in French Literature* for the Home University Library,' he recalled, describing the everyday scene there; 'in another part of the garden sat Moore, a panama hat on his head, his forehead wet with perspiration, sighing from time to time over his literary constipation as he wrote *Ethics* for the Home University Library. Lytton used to complain that he was mentally constipated because nothing at all came into his mind, which remained as blank as the paper on his knees. Moore on the contrary said that his mental constipation came from the fact that as soon as he had written down a sentence, he saw that it was just false or that it required a sentence to qualify the qualification.' In the afternoons the three of them would set off for long walks across Dartmoor, and Moore, who had a passion for bathing, would strip off his clothes whenever they came to one of the cold, black, rock pools, and plunge in. 'Nothing would induce Lytton to get into water in the open air,' Leonard Woolf records, 'and so I felt I must follow Moore's example. It nearly killed me.' Later on, in the evenings, 'Moore sang Adelaide, Schubert songs, or the Dichterliebe, or he played Beethoven sonatas. It was good to see again the sweat pour down his face and hear his passion in the music as he played the Waldstein or the Hammerklavier sonata'.

Three weeks' hard work called for two weeks' holiday. After a night of wild unreality at the Russian ballet ('the audience for it contained everyone I knew in Europe'), he set sail for a mad Scandinavian adventure. 'We went up the coast from Gotenberg towards Norway and stayed in a village in Bohusland which is bare rock broken into innumerable islands and fjords by the sea,' he wrote to Leonard Woolf (2 August 1911). '. . . It was pleasant to sit on deck reading *Les Frères* [*Karamazov*] at the rate of a page an hour, gliding past the shores from which the fair haired naked men and women perpetually waved their hands to us ... the people are mostly good-looking and are very often wearing no clothes. They are all very stupid and perpetually talk about art and culture. They collect facts without ever understanding them in the least. They are exactly what novels, newspapers and foreigners think that we are but what we are not at all. We are the only intelligent people in Europe, I am convinced.'

By the middle of August he had returned to 'the only race which really understands things', and was staying at 82 Woodstock Road, Gilbert Murray's house in Oxford, which Lady Strachey had taken for the month. While Pippa typed out the previous chapters, he pressed on with his writing of *Landmarks in French Literature*. 'The book has become rather distasteful to me,' he confessed to James (22 August 1911), 'but it's drawing to a close. I've only seven more centuries to do.' The dankness and oppression of family life and of Oxford in August, however, proved almost too much for him; and his work slowed. He was now in terror lest he should fall seriously ill at the last moment, overrun his contract date and see all his formidable efforts wasted. The fifty pounds he was to be paid on receipt of the typescript had already been almost all spent in advance. 'I'm told the series is a great success,' he wrote to Maynard Keynes (24 August 1911), 'and that so long as there isn't a Crippen Case this winter, I ought to net at least £100.'

He had hoped to complete *Landmarks in French Literature* by the end of the month, but having failed to do this, he fled back to the solitude of Becky House for another fortnight during which he was to finish off Chapter VII – 'The Age of Criticism' – and his short 'Conclusion'. Every morning here was given over to writing; the afternoons to scrambling among the rocks in company with his brother James, Rupert Brooke and Gerald Shove (who put in a rather sombre appearance for a day or two) until the muscles of his legs hardened into iron, causing him acute pain; and the warm evenings to sitting out in a somewhat indecisive garden overlooking the moor. By 10 September he was able to report to Maynard Keynes: 'I am feeling very lazy, as I've just this minute finished my poor book, after a solid two months of perpetual labour; and the thought of more such inventions is not attractive.'

A few days later, he set off for a week's holiday at Harbour View, Clive and Vanessa Bell's house at Studland. In spite of the sunshine, the beach, the general salubriousness and relaxation, he did not altogether relish this visit. Virginia Stephen was very nice, but so shrivelled up internally that she had hardly any real being at all; Roger Fry was also there, like some medieval saint in attendance upon Vanessa Bell, who seemed quite unconscious of him and everyone else around her. The atmosphere was made worse by the presence of Julian, her son, since Lytton found most children tedious and impossible to get on with – 'When Lytton comes,' Desmond MacCarthy used to tell his wife, 'the children must go.' And then of course, as if all this were not enough, there was Clive Bell. 'Clive presents a fearful study in decomposing psychology,' he wrote off to James (24 September 1911). 'The fellow is much worse – fallen into fatness and a fermenting self-assurance – burgeoning out into inconceivable theories on art and life – a corpse puffed up with worms and gases. It all seems to be the result of Roger, who is also here, in love with Vanessa. She is stark blind and deaf. And Virginia (in dreadful lodgings) rattles her accustomed nut. Julian is half-witted.'

Not wishing to return immediately to Hampstead, Lytton decided on the spur of the moment to make a mad dash to see Henry Lamb in Brittany. He wrote off at once to Pippa in order to borrow five pounds, and then, on receiving it, started out on his adventure, travelling by G.W.R. boat from Plymouth to Brest, and the following day from Brest by train to Quimperlé. From the very first this impetuous and ill-judged expedition was marked by disaster. Almost at once he fell sick. The food turned out to be infinitely worse, the discomforts infinitely greater than he could have dreamed possible. Not alone this, but the countryside and Henry's models were far less beautiful than he had been led to expect. 'I felt', he told Ottoline (15 October 1911), 'like a white man among savages in Central Africa.' Although Henry struggled to be kind and patient with him, he was obviously put out by his guest's invalid querulousness, so that Lytton judged it best to escape after only three or four days there, and head for Paris. At the end of a night journey through Nantes he arrived at the Hôtel des Saints-Pères. After breakfast he walked, in an ecstasy of wonder, through the lovely Luxembourg Gardens. Here, in the brilliant morning light, was the very essence of France and all that he loved best in France – crowded, happy, well-ordered. The trees were beginning to turn; it seemed he had never known a scene more vivid and alive, and his spirits soared again to unprecedented heights. After the vicissitudes of his Brittany trip, the hardship, illness and emotional failure, an extraordinary sense of excitement came upon him; a spring of self-confidence gushed up; he felt able to face, to outface, the world – it was delightful and astonishing. He had finished his book on French Literature, he was thirty-one, and the best years of his life were still before him.

3

THE STRANGE CASE OF RUPERT BROOKE

While waiting for the publication of his book, Lytton spent the next three months with his family at Belsize Park Gardens. 'My days pass (so far) in infinite idleness,' he wrote to Henry Lamb (15 October 1911). 'I'm engaged in refurnishing my room, and arranging my books and imagining where pictures can go – as if I was going to stay in the poor old shooting-gallery for the next forty years or so. Perhaps I am. Perhaps at the age of 71, I shall still be marching up there after the bed's made, and looking out of the window through the fog, and sitting down pen in hand to begin my masterpiece, every morning.'

London that winter was grim and misshapen after the invigorating glory of Paris, but life there still had its pleasures. He passed these weeks idly wandering from cocoa parties in Fitzroy Square to the more effulgent hospitality of Bedford Square. Much of this time, too, was spent with Henry Lamb, who in November had returned from France to work at the Vale Hotel Studios in Hampstead. And there were other friends, other activities: 'I have been having an exhausting day with Woolf looking for lodgings in Bloomsbury. Like everyone else he doesn't know where to live; but the rooms we saw to-day were enough to make one despair of all human habitations. Filth, darkness, and hideousness combined – I quite sink back with a sigh of relief among the new cretonnes of the poor old shooting-gallery. Otherwise I've been correcting my proof-sheets, which I find a very soothing occupation. But the printers seem to sniff vice everywhere. As there's so much talk about "literature", I sometimes use the phrase "letters" as a variation – "men of letters" and so on. And once or twice I refer to "French letters" – So and so "inaugurated a new era in French letters" – and the words are underlined and queried. My innocent mind failed at first to grasp the meaning of it. So you see there are singular pitfalls for unwary authors.'

Towards the end of December, Lytton went down for two weeks to a reading-party which was being held at Lulworth in Dorset. Other friends who came and went during the fortnight included Henry Lamb, Maynard Keynes, Justin Brooke, Harry Norton, Gerald Shove, Rupert Brooke and Katherine Cox, or Ka as she was known.[9] The weather was marvellous, so hot that some people bathed, Lamb and Ka vanishing for most of one Sunday together. The events of these few days, which led directly to Rupert Brooke's estrangement from Lytton and, through him, from the entire Bloomsbury Group including Virginia Stephen and even Ottoline Morrell, were later to become the subject of much scandalous rumour and speculation. One author, for example, repeats in his recently published memoirs a story which, it seems, he picked up third-hand by way of Stanley Spencer, to the effect that Lamb, as a callous practical joke, persuaded Katharine Cox to spend an allegedly platonic night in his room and, for the next day's amusement of Lytton and his friends, teased the hopelessly lovesick Rupert Brooke. 'Naturally he [Brooke] was very

9. Afterwards Mrs Will Arnold-Forster.

upset, but Lamb thought it was a splendid joke and pretended he was saving Rupert Brooke and bringing the two of them to a sense of reality.'

Ka was the orphan daughter of a gentleman-stockbroker of radical opinions, a hefty young woman and a robust Fabian, fond of tweeds and riding, whose large squashy appearance had once been likened by Brooke himself to that of a vegetable.[10] Like practically everyone else, she had been in love with Rupert, but he was not, it seems, more than mildly flattered by her attentions until she went off with Lamb. Suddenly he felt attracted irresistibly by her indifference to himself. Bored by the endless adulation with which he had become so familiar, he was only excited by other people's lack of interest; and Ka's unaccountable unconcern soon convinced him that he was seriously in love with her. At Lulworth that winter, her obvious preference for Lamb inflamed this illusory love into a pathological jealousy, and he went into a paranoiac episode. He implored her to marry him then and there; she refused; and in the irrational ferocity of his humiliation he looked round for someone on whom to pin the blame – and selected Lytton. Had he selected Lamb – a more logical choice – his vanity would have been subjected to further injury; but by fixing on a homosexual as the chief culprit he was able to give vent to all his submerged puritanical horror and disgust. He saw Lytton as Lamb's evil genius, the instigator of all his own misfortunes; and the far-fetched stories he concocted out of the delirium of his fantasy were accepted by many at their face value.

From the private correspondence that passed between Lytton and Lamb immediately following these dramatic events, a rather different picture comes to light. Lamb, who had arrived at Lulworth after a few days at Parkstone with Augustus John, did, it appears, make some rather tepid advances towards Ka – little more than an automatic reflex in

10. This joke was evidently intended partly to describe her mental appearance. To many – even to James Strachey – she was an attractive person to look at, in the same way perhaps that Miss Joan Hunter Dunn attracted John Betjeman's subaltern.

his determined role as a womanizer – but she, to the surprise of all and to the mortification of Brooke, whose own repulsed advances were to be far more desperate and intense, at once fell passionately in love with him – 'like a fish fascinated by the glitter of some strange bait'.

By the time her feelings had developed and become obvious to all, Lamb had already left for London, unaware that he had occasioned any quite such grand passion. It was, in fact, to Lytton that Ka first confessed her infatuation; and it was Lytton who immediately wrote off to inform Lamb (4 January 1912): 'Ka came and talked to me yesterday, between tea and dinner. It was rather a difficult conversation, but she was very nice and very sensible. It seemed to me clear that she was what is called "in love" with you – not with extreme violence so far, but quite distinctly. She is longing to marry you. She thinks you may agree, but fears, with great conscientiousness, that it might not be good for you. I felt at moments, while she was with me – so good and pink and agreeable, – that there was more hope in that scheme than I'd thought before. But the more I consider, the more doubtful it grows. I can't believe that you're a well-assorted couple – can you? If she was really your wife, with a home and children, it would mean a great change in your way of living, a lessening of independence – among other things a much dimmer relationship with Ottoline. This might be worth while – probably would be – if she was an eminent creature, who'ld give you a great deal; but I don't think she is that. There seems no touch of inspiration in her; it's as if she was made somehow or other on rather a small scale (didn't you say that?). I feel it's unkind to write this about Ka, and it's too definite, but I must try and say what I think. . . . Henry, I almost believe the best thing she could do now would be to marry Rupert straight off. He is much nicer than I had thought him. Last night he was there and was really charming – especially with her. Affliction seems to have chastened him, and he did feel – it was evident . . . they seemed to fit together so naturally – even the Garden-City-ishness.'

This letter patently exonerates Lytton himself from any

472

charge of plotting against Brooke or encouraging Lamb's flirtation with Ka. Though he evidently felt rather double-faced about receiving her confidences and then making use of them to dissuade Lamb from marriage, and though it is just possible – if unlikely – that this advice was partly coloured by his own feeling of attraction for Lamb, there can be no doubt that he was endeavouring to act honourably, and to state in an objective manner what he thought to be the truth. One fact which appears to have been forgotten by everyone is that Lamb was himself still married. Ka certainly seems to have believed that she would marry Lamb, since, she explained, he had the same Christian name as her father. Surely here was a clear omen? But Lytton, far from recommending marriage, strongly advised both of them against even having an affair, on the grounds that it might break up Ka's much more suitable relationship with Brooke. Somehow he managed to prevent Ka from following Lamb up to London; while to Lamb himself he wrote (6 January 1912), 'If you're not going to marry her, I think you ought to reflect a good deal before letting her become your mistress. I've now seen her fairly often and on an intimate footing, and I can hardly believe that she's suited to the post. I don't see what either of you could really get out of it except the pleasures of the obelisk. With you even these would very likely not last long, while with her they'ld probably become more and more of a necessity, and also be mixed up with all sorts of romantic desires which I don't think you'ld ever satisfy. If this is true it would be worth while making an effort to put things on a merely affectionate basis, wouldn't it? I think there's quite a chance that ... everything might blow over, and that she might even sink into Rupert's arms. Can you manage this?'

Although Lytton's intellectual assessment of Brooke had evidently not risen, he felt far closer to him in his present misery and frustration. 'The situation, though, seems to be getting slightly grim,' he told Lamb in another letter (5 January 1912). '... Rupert is besieging her – I gather with tears and desperation – and sinking down in the intervals pale and shattered. I wish I could recommend her to console him ...

'As for Rupert – it's like something in a play. But you know his niceness is now certain – poor thing! I never saw anyone so different from you – in caractère. "Did He who made the Lamb make thee?" I sometimes want to murmur to him, but I fear the jest would not be well received.'

Ironically, now that Brooke was turning so violently against him, Lytton had begun to soften, to experience some genuine sympathy and fellow-feeling for him. Consumed by an insane jealousy, Brooke had convinced himself that Lytton was secretly scheming to discredit him in the eyes of Ka, and to bring about her marriage to the satanic Henry Lamb.[11] No one was able to persuade him otherwise; he refused to speak to Lytton, and, one by one, cut dead all his old Bloomsbury friends, who, he began to suspect, were abetting this Machiavellian plot. This condition persisted in an acute form for several months, but was cleared up manifestly by a complete change in character. The melodramatic climax in this process of alienation was staged in July 1914 in the crowded foyer at Drury Lane, where, coming unexpectedly upon Lytton, he refused the proffered hand, executed the movement known as 'turning on one's heel', and strode away. With Lytton at the time were several other old friends including Ottoline, and Brooke's impetuous and irrational behaviour caused something of a sensation. 'The number of beastly people at Drury Lane is the only good reason for going there,' Brooke later wrote to a friend. 'One can be offensive to them.'[12] The late Christopher Hassall, Rupert Brooke's definitive biographer,

11. After the Lamb episode was over, Ka's real love for Rupert Brooke re-emerged. And when that happened he had another revulsion of feeling and backed away.

12. About this incident at Drury Lane, James Strachey told the author: 'It was the first time I had met him [Rupert] since he came back [from America] and he talked to me in a perfectly friendly way. I then noticed that Lytton was standing just beside me, and I said jocosely to Rupert "I believe you know my brother Lytton." That was when he said "No" and "turned on his heel". It was decidedly awkward because it happened in an extremely visible place, with everyone one knew standing round. I believe it was a performance of Diaghilev's version of the Coq d'Or – a marvellous show. But this showed very plainly Rupert's paranoia, though I was so ignorant then that I had no notion of it.'

told the author: 'The thing to bear in mind is that R.B. was easily jealous, and at that time he was under a very great strain from overwork (on his Fellowship Dissertation for King's) and in a state where he could well allow a petty grievance to develop into an irrational obsession.'

This irrational obsession was in fact a symptom of Brooke's worsening paranoiac condition. The world of his youthful ideals had turned sour. Suffering from insomnia, dejection and nervous exhaustion, he succumbed to the sick fever of his delusions, and underwent a complete volte-face from the Fabian intellectual to the chauvinistic fugleman of 1914. The obverse of his exaggerated, schoolboy wish that everyone should love him was a curiously inverted form of vanity – the uneasy suspicion that people were planning his downfall. It was from this sickness that he had convalesced partly in the South Seas, to re-emerge an apparently changed personality, the author of a series of War Sonnets that stand oddly segregated from the earlier, main body of his work.

4

A SPIRITUAL REVOLUTION

Landmarks in French Literature, when it came out, was reviewed not widely but well. By April 1914 some twelve thousand copies of it had been sold in the British Empire and America, and after Lytton became famous at the end of the war it took on a new lease of life: four more impressions were printed between 1923 and 1927, and the demand has continued steadily up to the present day.[13] A number of critics, among them Guy Boas, Nancy Mitford, Harold Nicolson and H. A. L. Fisher himself, regarded it as Lytton's finest book, his critical *tour de force*. The most severe dis-

13. There are two editions now in print in Britain, the original one in the Home University Library series, and another in the uniform Collected Works of Lytton Strachey which, with the permission of the Oxford University Press, Chatto and Windus first brought out in 1948.

paragement that can legitimately be levelled against it was indicated in a letter which D. H. Lawrence sent to Ottoline Morrell in the summer of 1915: 'I still don't like Strachey,' he wrote, '– French literature neither – words – literature – bore.' Beneath the unaffected finesse and facility, the significant form, the cultivated refinement of taste, there was little cogent involvement with the condition of the human soul. At another level, the best that may fairly be said of it has been eloquently put by John Lehmann, who praised it as a 'luminous little masterpiece of interpretative criticism'. In *The Whispering Gallery*, the first volume of his autobiography, he recounts a conversation which he had during a train journey from France to England with an unknown travelling companion who identified herself on reaching Calais as Dorothy Bussy. 'It taught me, as no other book could have,' he told her, 'how to find excellence in the French tradition even if one were a devoted believer in the English tradition, and why Racine was a great poet and dramatist even though his greatness was so totally different from Shakespeare's.'

Among Lytton's personal friends the response to his book seems to have varied widely – even allowing for his own exaggerations. To Dorothy Bussy, who thought highly of its merits, he wrote (6 February 1912): 'James of course says that it's rubbish, Ottoline that it is a work of supreme genius, Virginia that it's merely brilliant, Woolf that it is bluff carried a little too far for decency, and Clive that it is almost as bad as "Sainte Beuve" (I haven't heard him say so, but I'm sure he must have).'

The writing and publication of *Landmarks in French Literature* marks a major point of transition in Lytton's career. Later in the same letter to his sister he observes: 'For the last year I have been going through a Spiritual Revolution – which has been exciting and on the whole pleasant. I had feared that after 30 one didn't have these things, Ah! – But now I shall be glad of a little recueillement – though it's rather doubtful whether I shall get it between Bloomsbury and Hampstead.' He was determined, he added, to do some real 'creative work', and this he still believed would be in the field of poetic drama.

This phrase, Spiritual Revolution, was intended by Lytton as a joke – but a joke with a serious meaning behind it. Over the last twelve to fifteen months, he had found himself pitched into an entirely unfamiliar environment that represented a break with Cambridge and was far less respectable than Bloomsbury. This was the world of Chelsea, of Augustus John and Boris Anrep – artists of a type utterly dissimilar to Roger Fry and all he stood for. It was like a transformation scene at a pantomime. Precipitated by Henry Lamb and Ottoline, this change was also influenced by a number of other events. His brother Oliver, for instance, who had always led a knock-about sort of life – travelling round the world, studying under Leschetizky in Vienna, starting an Anglo-Indian career in India, marrying, divorcing and so on – had returned to England in the spring of 1911. He was constantly badgering Lytton for being too cooped up: 'You spend all your life between Cambridge and the Reading Room of the British Museum,' he used to complain. And then, there was the effect of Dostoyevsky, whose novels presented Lytton with a completely new attitude to human beings and opened his mind to some things going on in himself.

This new liberation enabled Lytton to experience something he had always wanted to experience, a firm belief in the writer's essential worth within the hierarchy of the world's values; a creed implicit in so much of his earlier work from the *Warren Hastings* up till now. He had entered upon a period of his literary development which, beginning with a rhapsodic acclamation of men of letters, would lead up to his flank and rear attack on the legendary reputation of men of action and affairs. It was a time of self-justification and gathering confidence in the successful application of his own powers, a time when he would turn the tables on that type of wilful person who set out to govern the world, and by intolerance and prejudice added to the world's stock of avoidable inhumanity.

Scattered throughout the pages of *Landmarks in French Literature* are several signs and assurances of this new emergent faith. In a passage, for example, describing the formation and influence of the French Academy, he goes out of his way to explain his opposition to that official and popular indifference, even contempt, shown by England towards the arts – an attitude which deprived the writer particularly of his rightful status in society. 'On the whole, perhaps the most important function performed by the Academy has been a more indirect one. The mere existence of a body of writers officially recognised by the authorities of the State has undoubtedly given a peculiar prestige to the profession of letters in France. It has emphasised that tendency to take the art of writing seriously – to regard it as a fit object for the most conscientious craftsmanship and deliberate care – which is so characteristic of French writers. The amateur is very rare in French literature – as rare as he is common in our own. How many of the greatest English writers have denied that they were men of letters! – Scott, Byron, Gray, Sir Thomas Browne, perhaps even Shakespeare himself. When Congreve begged Voltaire not to talk of literature, but to regard him merely as an English gentleman, the French writer, who, in all his multifarious activities, never forgot for a moment that he was first and foremost a follower of the profession of letters, was overcome with astonishment and disgust. The difference is typical of the attitude of the two nations towards literature . . .'

Throughout this book, too, Lytton seldom misses an opportunity for asserting that literature can express more richly than any form of transitory action the characteristic and abiding genius of a nation. The sword, he is repeatedly avowing, is less mighty than the pen. 'Montesquieu's great reputation', he writes, 'led to his view of the constitution of England being widely accepted as the true one; as such it was adopted by the American leaders after the War of Independence; and its influence is plainly visible in the present Constitution of the United States. Such is the strange power of good writing over the affairs of men!'

Elsewhere, he takes a surprising dip into the biography of Voltaire to recount, with evident satisfaction, the great wave of general popularity which greeted his sudden last appearance in Paris, the like of which is reserved in England for military and political figures. Lytton presents this scene as gloriously dramatic, a fitting curtain-call to Voltaire's incredible career. 'One day, quite suddenly, he appeared in Paris, which he had not visited for nearly thirty years. His arrival was the signal for one of the most extraordinary manifestations of enthusiasm that the world has ever seen. For some weeks he reigned in the capital, visible and glorious, the undisputed lord of the civilized universe. The climax came when he appeared in a box at the Théâtre Français, to witness a performance of the latest of his tragedies, and the whole house rose as one man to greet him. His triumph seemed to be something more than the mere personal triumph of a frail old mortal; it seemed to be the triumph of all that was noblest in the aspirations of the human race. But the fatigue and excitement of those weeks proved too much even for Voltaire in the full flush of his eighty-fourth year. An overdose of opium completed what Nature had begun; and the amazing being rested at last.'

The gradual preparation for Lytton's Spiritual Revolution had been going on since he came down from Cambridge. Now almost complete, it was to be hurried to its full flowering by the war. But already he was filled and elated by a new assurance in his ultimate success. Like Voltaire he would live to be eighty-four, and devote most of his years to a humane and polemical art. His destiny was not, he felt sure, to be an unobtrusive Donne, penning tiny volumes of exquisite, unpublished verse for the delight of a few discriminating friends; it was more practical, and in its attainments more resounding and contentious. He felt, too, the need to expound this sense of vocation which underlay his misleadingly flippant and languid manner, to disabuse his friends of any possible misconception. 'You understand a great deal, and very wonderfully,' he wrote to Ottoline (24 February 1912). 'But perhaps there's one thing that you don't quite realise about me – I mean what I feel about my work. Perhaps you don't see that the idea of my really not working is simply an impossibility. Sometimes you have admonished me on the subject, and I think I have been rather curt in my answers; it was because I felt so absolutely sure of myself – that you might as well talk of my not breathing as not writing. It's so happened that just the last month or two, when we've been getting to know each other, I've been having a time of transition and hesitation. ... And then my health has been a vile nuisance – You see I'm making quite a case for myself! But I want you to understand this. From my earliest days I've always considered myself as a writer, and for the last ten years writing has been almost perpetually in my thoughts.'

In the past Lytton had tended to equate writing with obscurity whenever he thought of it in relation to himself. Writers, he sometimes felt, were men of action *manqués*, second-class heroes at best. Now, for the first time, he sensed that his appetite for success could be satisfied in a practical manner by means of his natural literary gifts – a kind of will to power, through the imagination. In the seventeenth century he might have found some sort of fulfilment as a Caroline mystic; but the religious motive had quietly dropped out of the modern world. If only one could still live for the glory of God, and find eternal crowns and reconciliations hereafter! But that type of thing was no longer done. Crowns were never worn, and heaven itself was out of fashion. To court success one had to be either in, or ahead of fashion.

In an address which he delivered to the Apostles that spring (11 May 1912), entitled 'Godfrey, Cornbury or Candide', Lytton makes the most explicit statement of his newly-developed beliefs. Essentially, the new faith was a method of eradicating his past sense of morbid self-abomination. He had failed, in the love of men, imaginatively to reincarnate himself in the body of some heaven-born hero; now he sought to transform his own being into the sort of person he could admire, or at least respect, for his courage and achievements. In the course of his paper he points to three main motives which shape our ends – the thirst for pleasure, the desire to do good, and the need for self-development. Though sensitive to the force of these first two impulses, Lytton places himself in the third category of human being, those whose chief aim is self-development, adding that the mainspring of his life is really ambition. 'It seems to me that I live neither for happiness nor for duty,' he told the Apostles. 'I like being happy. I scheme to be happy; I want to do my duty, and I sometimes even do it. But such considerations seem to affect me only sporadically and vaguely; there is something else which underlies my actions more fundamentally, which guides, controls, and animates the whole. It is ambition. I want to excel, to triumph, to be powerful, and to glory in myself. I do not want a vulgar triumph, a vulgar power; fame and riches attract me only as subsidiary ornaments of my desire. What I want is the attainment of a true excellence, the development of noble qualities, and the full expression of them — the splendour of a spiritual success. It is true that this is an egotistical conception of life; but I see no harm in such an egotism. After all, each of us is the only person who can cultivate himself; we may help on our neighbour here and there — throw him a bulb or two over the garden wall, or lend a hand with the roller; but we shall never understand the ins and outs — the complication of the soils and subsoils — in any garden but our own.'

Something of this revolutionary new creed was reflected in Lytton's presence which, always striking, had by this time grown positively challenging. With the possible exception of William Empson, he developed into the most photogenic and preposterous-looking figure in twentieth-century English literature. In May 1912, Max Beerbohm, who had recently returned to England after a two-year stay in Italy, was lunching at the Savile Club when he caught sight of Lytton for the first time, seated at a table with Duncan Grant. Even allowing for the looking-glass quality to the description which Max later wrote of this first visual impression, Lytton's appearance must obviously have riveted his attention to the exclusion of all the other unknown faces in the club —

an emaciated face of ivory whiteness [he recalled] above a long square-cut auburn beard, and below a head of very long sleek dark brown hair. The nose was nothing if not aquiline, and Nature had chiselled it with great delicacy. The eyes, behind a pair of gold-rimmed spectacles, eyes of an inquirer and cogitator, were large and brown and luminous. The man to whom they belonged must, I judged, though he sat stooping low down over his table, be extremely tall. He wore a jacket of brown velveteen,[14] a soft shirt, and a dark red tie. I greatly wondered who he was. He looked rather like one of the Twelve Apostles, and I decided that he resembled especially the doubting one, Thomas, who was also called Didymus. I learned from a friend who came in and joined me at my table that he was one of the Stracheys; Lytton Strachey; a Cambridge man; rather an authority on French literature: had written a book on French Litera-ture in some series or other; book said to be very good. 'But why,' my friend asked, 'should he dress like that?' Well, we members of the Savile, Civil Servants, men of letters, clergymen, scientists, doctors and so on, were clad respectably, passably, decently, but no more than that. And 'Hang it all,' I said, 'why *shouldn't* he dress like that? He's the best-dressed man in the room!'

These clothes – no less than the beard – were worn partly as a token of his new liberation, partly for the joy of provoking the too hidebound and conformable. In time his presence grew still more commanding. During these early winter and spring months of 1912, Henry Lamb embarked on a series of portraits.[15] It is interesting to compare two of these, both

14. Max's memory or observation was faulty. James Strachey has pointed out that Lytton never in his life wore gold-rimmed spectacles and never a velveteen coat – unless this is meant to include corduroy, which he did go in for during his Augustus John period.

15. Lamb was obviously fascinated by Lytton and did a great number of portraits of him. The best-known one (oil, 90 × 70 in.), for many years in the collection of Mr and Mrs Behrend, was bought in 1958 by the Tate Gallery under the terms of the Chantrey Bequest and is now on per-manent loan to the National Portrait Gallery. A painting of the back-ground of this portrait, 'Hampstead Heath from the Vale of Health', belongs to Mr Richard Carline. An earlier version, painted in 1912 (oil, 20 × 15½ in), was bought in 1923 by Siegfried Sassoon who wrote to Sydney Cockerell (24 November 1923): 'The other day I committed an extrava-gance and bought Henry Lamb's first small oil picture of Lytton Strachey (the study for the big one). It is delightful, and, I think, of historic value,

painted at Hampstead, the first in 1912, the second more celebrated one — now owned by the Tate — two years later. In both pictures there are many familiar, almost identical characteristics — the same boneless, inert, interminable legs, with their look of having been made of wax which has somehow elongated extraordinarily; the same exotic slippers of brown felt; the same spade-like beard; the same astonished eyebrows; the same furled umbrella and Homburg hat, insignia of upper-middle-class respectability, pushed to one side but still in the picture. But there are differences too, not just attributable to the less impressionistic treatment of the later famous portrait. The face has become less thin and wasted; the figure appears a little less enfeebled; the eyes, though not so sad, are more alarming; the pince-nez has been replaced by a pair of spectacles. Lytton still reclines, apparently without an ounce of energy in his fragile body, on the edge of a basket-chair, a green and black plaid rug over its arm, against

---

(I gave £60). Some day I will transfer it to the Fitzwilliam (L.S. being a Cambridge man it should be there). You can take this as a promise.' In fact Siegfried Sassoon gave this portrait to Lady Ottoline Morrell; it was exhibited at the Leicester Galleries in 1956 ('Pictures from Garsington', No. 32 in the Catalogue) and bought by Lord Cottesloe, who has shown it recently in Leningrad at a British Council Exhibition of British Painting. The Fitzwilliam Museum, Cambridge, have a bust, painted in 1913 (20½ × 16 in.) in which the head and shoulders exactly correspond to the Tate Gallery portrait. This was formerly owned by C. K. Ogden, and by J. E. Vulliamy, who presented it to the Fitzwilliam in 1945. The Ashmolean Museum, Oxford, have a 'Study for Portrait of Lytton Strachey', a preliminary drawing for the canvas now owned by Lord Cottesloe and purchased in 1961; and the Victoria and Albert Museum acquired in 1962 a pencil drawing of Strachey seated in a chair. A red chalk drawing was sold at Christie's on 4 July 1958. Mrs Gilbert Russell has another early portrait similar to that in the Fitzwilliam Museum and Mrs Julian Vinogradoff, daughter of Lady Ottoline Morrell, a painting of the head and shoulders (recently exhibited at the Café Royal Centenary Exhibition, 1965, and at the Arts Council Gallery, 1966, 'Vision and Design', commemorating the life, work and influence of Roger Fry).

Lamb's earliest known portrait, a drawing done before Lytton grew his beard, is owned by the author. And in rather a different vein, Lamb also did a caricature sketch of Lytton and Clive Bell, shown at the Henry Lamb Memorial Exhibition in 1961 at the Leicester Galleries, and bought by Mr Roger Senhouse.

a view of ordered parkland. But he is no longer quite alone. Outside, in the background, two figures have emerged from behind a tree and are wandering along a path away from the house – perhaps Mrs Humphry Ward and St Loe Strachey, having called to inquire after his well-sounding new book, *Eminent Victorians*. In both portraits Lamb displays that mingling of respect, affection and irony which several of his acquaintances felt for Lytton and which he mirrored back to the world at large. This second picture especially is sharp but subjective, and in the opinion of James Strachey too vulgarly caricatured. The lofty room and the unusual landscape seen through the vast window gives the impression of a cage in which Lytton is preserved for us as a rare specimen of the species *homo sapiens* – an amiable and bizarre botanist or an eccentric ecclesiastic. Several other people, however, who met Lytton during this period of his life but did not know him so intimately as his brother, have testified to the verisimilitude of Lamb's likeness, among them Osbert Sitwell, who stressed the unorthodox effect which this recently manufactured personality produced upon his contemporaries. In 'an age when people tended to look the same', he wrote, 'his (Lytton's) emergence into any scene, whether street or drawing-room, lifted it to a new plane, investing it with a kind of caricatural Victorian interest'.

The affection and malice in Lamb's painting catches something of his own peculiar relationship with Lytton, who, though violently attracted sexually, sometimes disapproved of him on ethical and intellectual grounds. He saw Lamb without much self-deception, the ambience of his tough, mercurial and slightly satanic vitality infected him with a dark zest. He was stimulated at times – and by the most trivial happenings – to a state of ecstasy bordering on coma. Lamb's tantalizing smile, his expression in profile of complacent and intensified mockery, could almost make him faint with pleasure. Just so arrogantly self-willed might an angel look in repose – *an angel of the devil!* In his delirium of heightened fantasy, he began to see Lamb as a demon, a mythical creature of the woods, a satyr. His slyness and cleverness made him all the more attractive. He was inaccessible too, yet the strain and paradox imposed by this impossible situation sharpened the excitement, preserved undimmed its illusory aura of beauty and romance. In his company Lytton was customarily quiet, docile, serviceable and, of course, chaste. It was often incomprehensible to him how he could go on desiring Henry, how the magnetism and tension between them did not slacken, rather that it approached snapping-point only to ease slightly and then agonizingly expand again. In all Henry's humours, whether grave or mellow, he was such a touchy, testy, pleasant fellow, so amusing, so irritable, there seemed no living with him, none without him. Sometimes the luxurious enjoyment of Lytton's indulged frustration changed to genuine misery, for heated altercations regularly broke out between them. Yet, because his new creed and confidence lent him an extra reserve of strength, Lytton was never so prostrated as he had been during the most bitter moments of his relationship with Duncan Grant. He still desperately wanted true companionship and affection, but this longing was partly mitigated by his paramount desire for power, for an honourable prestige which, he felt, would somehow bring with it the ideal love of his dreams. Before the Spiritual Revolution, his dependence upon those few whom he loved and admired had been absolute. Now he was less wholly vulnerable. A new facet of his character had grown up which was unaffected by this volatile susceptibility. As his intellectual assurance in his own abilities and potential attainments developed, so correspondingly his enhaloment of the artist gradually diminished. And so, after the terrors and quarrels between them came, not the abject, cringing apologies he addressed to Duncan Grant, but explanations and excuses that tended to place their emotional dissensions in a less hysterical context.

'I know I'm exaggerated and maladif in these affairs,' he wrote to Henry Lamb after one early reconciliation (19 February 1912). 'I wish I could say how I hate my wretched faiblesses. But I think perhaps you don't realise how horribly I've suffered during the last 6 or 7 years from loneliness, and what a difference your friendship has made for me. It has been a gushing of new life through my veins – enfin. I sometimes get into a panic and a fever, and a black cloud comes down, and it seems as if, after all, it was too good to be true . . .'

And, similarly, he would write off to his confidante, Ottoline Morrell (25 January 1912): 'He [Henry Lamb] has been charming, and I am much happier. I'm afraid I may have exaggerated his asperities; his affection I often feel to be miraculous. It was my sense of the value of our relationship, and my fear that it might come to an end, that made me cry out so loudly the very minute I was hurt.'

These letters to Ottoline are not so full of violent perdition and panting recrimination as those to Maynard Keynes. While they eloquently celebrate the value of Lamb's affection, which Lytton was never absolutely sure of retaining for long, yet one is made aware of a feeling – as one seldom was in the Duncan Grant affair – that, when the final separation comes, life will not altogether cease; that, however inevitable it may be that things will turn out unhappily, Lytton was still young, and every kind of fresh and unexpected development lay in wait for him.

TEN

Town versus the Country

'Why is London the only place to live in ... ?' *Lytton Strachey to Virginia Woolf* (8 November 1912)

'My theory is that if only I could get a cottage on these Downs, and furnish it comfortably, I could live and work in comparative happiness.' *Lytton Strachey to James Strachey* (September 1912)

1
THE ANGEL, THE DEVIL AND *A SON OF HEAVEN*

IT was during the spring and summer months of 1912 that Lytton wrote his only play to be performed on the London stage. *A Son of Heaven*, as it was called, was a full-length tragic melodrama, the action of which passes on two August days in 1900 at the Imperial Palace, Peking. After a month of plotting and planning the first act, he reported his progress in rather dismal terms to Ottoline Morrell (18 March 1912): 'I'm proceeding with my play, but rather slowly and rather gloomily. The difficulties are too horribly great; and about half the time I feel simply incompetent. Well! Racine wrote two bad plays before Andromaque – so I suppose there's some hope.'

He attributed the chief cause of these difficulties to his lack of *recueillement* shuttling back and forth between Bloomsbury and Hampstead. To try to remedy this condition, he left Belsize Park Gardens late in April, spending the next six weeks in Cambridge, this time at number 10 King's Parade, Sydney Waterlow's rooms on the second floor front.[1] 'You should

1. Sir Sydney Philip Waterlow (1878–1944), diplomat and author. A prodigy at Eton and a brilliant classical scholar at Trinity, his career, which took him as British Minister to Bangkok, Addis Ababa, Sofia and

see my solitude!' he wrote plaintively to Ottoline (30 April 1912). 'It is only equalled by my insensibility. The most ravishing creatures (or at least so I'm told) pass by me all day, and I remain icy. Well! I came for peace and I have found it.'

He was now able to work at his play with unbroken concentration. Before the end of May he had completed the first act and almost finished the second. When not writing, he passed much of his solitude in reading – Flaubert's letters, Maupassant's *Bel-Ami* ('a profoundly depressing book') and in particular *The Brothers Karamazov*,[2] which, he liked to tell the severely atheistic James, nearly converted him to Christianity. After his first rush of enthusiasm for Dostoyevsky in French, he had begun to take Russian lessons; but it was the recently issued Constance Garnett translation into English which now absorbed him. 'It's been very exciting,' he told Henry Lamb (30 April 1912), 'but on the whole I was – disappointed! I don't think it's better than the other great ones – I hardly think it as good ... I think it's the *ablest* – the mass and the supremacy of the detail, and the concatenation of the whole thing – the mastery of the material is complete. But the material itself – those tremendous overwhelming floods of unloosed genius that pour out of Les Possédés and L'Idiot – that was what I missed. Of course there are great heights, but only once, at the very end, did I feel the knife really in between my ribs, and turning. For one thing, I think there's too much of the detective-story apparatus. The Christianity also is slightly trying at times.'

Athens, was 'in some ways stranger than fiction' (Leonard Woolf). Among his books are a biography of Shelley (1912) and a translation of the *Medea* and *Hippolytus* of Euripides (1906).

2. 'Les Frères Karamazov is one of the greatest of novels. I cannot refrain from giving you this information,' Lytton wrote to Leonard Woolf. 'But I don't think that people really do think or feel like they do. Have you read it and the extraordinary speech of Ivan about Christ and Christianity and socialism which goes on without stopping for about 50 pages? I am halfway through. The Agamemnon is childish compared to it. I read it in trains slowly, as befits it, in perpetual sunshine; I shall never finish it I think or perhaps it will never end.'

In the last week of May, Lytton started off with Henry Lamb on a ten-day walking holiday up to Cumberland. After a final tremendous trek of thirty miles across mountains and moors from Carlisle to the country town of Alston, they settled down together for a few days of rest and relaxation at Handy House, a lodging-house 'with a Scotch mist out of the window, plush brackets on the walls, furniture draped à la Roger [Fry] and Henry in the middle of it all, fuming over a picture'.

The Alston trip did them both good; but despite brilliant weather, good food and delightful country ('hills are ranged round on every side; and various streams rush by') its success was always precarious. Lytton, invariably affected by illness in other people, was distressed by Henry's erratic health, and the low spiritual state which, he believed, was directly associated with it. His position was in consequence always tricky. He longed to help Henry, to try to assuage his angry melancholy; but, knowing so well how he resented interference, dreaded bringing down on his own head his friend's fierce castigation and scorn. 'At times,' he confessed to Ottoline (7 June 1912), 'I feel terrified when I think of him – he seems like some desperate proud fallen angel, plunging into darkness and fate. Oh why? Why? He nourishes himself in bitterness, and wraps himself up in his torments as if he loved them.'

Rather unrealistically, Lytton believed that the horrors which tormented Henry would dissolve, and his temperament grow more placid, once they could set up house together, preferably somewhere in the country. Several schemes were considered. For a while he thought of moving to Milton Cottage in Rothiemurchus, with both Henry and James; and at various other times that summer he inspected houses in Gordon Square, Mecklenburgh Square and Woburn Square. But in every case there was some overriding objection – either the unsuitable location combining too close a proximity of relations and too great a remoteness of friends, or else simply the noise, the expense and the hopeless gloom. Once again his endeavours seemed to lead nowhere.

From his northern trip, Lytton appears to have accumulated such a store of energy that he was able to work at Belsize Park Gardens with unusual resolution, forging well into the third act of *A Son of Heaven* by the end of June. Nor were his spirits unduly dampened down by the failure of any new *ménage* to materialize. Wearing a great deerstalker hat, tortoiseshell spectacles, a carnation in his button-hole, he would stroll down Piccadilly with his nimble, elastic tread, swinging his cloak and imagining himself a gay London spark, whirling along in taxis, drinking tea at Rumpelmayer's, striding through picture galleries with the best of them. Perhaps London was the most satisfactory place in which to live after all ...

Certainly it was the most exciting. Extraordinary things were always happening there. A lady by the name of Marzials had got in touch with him asking whether he would write a life of St-Évremond, with the aid of material collected by her late husband. 'I don't think I shall,' he told Ottoline (12 June 1912), '– unless the materials turn out to be very exciting; and that is unlikely. St Évremond was a pleasant gentleman; but that was all, I fancy. If I must write somebody's life, it had better be Voltaire.'[3]

More exciting still was the news that his friend Leonard Woolf was at last engaged to be married to Virginia Stephen, who some people had thought would end up as the wife of Walter Lamb. Such a curious event occasioned the sort of gossip which Lytton always particularly relished, full of improbable conjecture, and enlivened with humorous malice. 'I am *very* glad,'[4] he wrote to Ottoline (12 June 1912). 'I've not seen either of them yet; but I know that he's in ecstasies of happiness. He had to besiege her a good deal before she accepted him. I feel rather a fool because I kept on urging him

---

3. Among other non-fiction books that he considered writing was one on the work of Augustus John. He was approached in the early summer of 1913 by J. C. Squire and John himself about this project, but replied that he thought such a volume would be premature and that, in any case, he was not the right man to do it.

4. 'It is magnificent,' Lytton wrote to Leonard Woolf (6 June 1912). 'I am very happy; and je t'aime beaucoup.'

to propose, while he was doing it all the time; but why didn't he tell me? I suppose he thought I wouldn't be discreet enough. There's a story that a week or two before the engagement he proposed in a train, and she accepted him, but owing to the rattling of the carriage he didn't hear, and took up a newspaper, saying "What?" On which she had a violent revulsion and replied "Oh, nothing!" — She was very much disappointed at everyone taking the news so calmly. She hoped that everyone would be thunderstruck. Duncan alone came up to her expectations — he fell right over on the floor when she told him: and of course really he had been told all about it by Adrian before.'

By the beginning of July his unexpected bonus of London energy had been used up, and he hurried off back to Becky House for a month's enforced exile. The solitude here was very salutary, and his play progressed well. Every day he rose at seven, worked all morning, dozed, dreamed and read in the afternoon, walked during the evening, and read a little more at night, absorbing himself in Peking politics. 'My brain seethes like a witch's cauldron,' he wrote to Henry Lamb (13 July 1912), ' — I keep ladling out the contents into my Chinese, but it continues to boil and bubble and sometimes I hardly know whether I'm on my head or my heels ... I see that I should have been ruined if I hadn't come here. As it is, I've now finished my 3rd Act, and so only have one more to do. It ought to be the most exciting and therefore the easiest, and I hope to reel it off in a week, and then proceed to the grand revision.'

For relaxation he read Anatole France, Gray, *La Maison des Morts* (not yet translated into English), Van Gogh's letters, and Lanfrey's life of Napoleon, which drew from him a spirited tirade in one of his letters to Ottoline (6 July 1912). 'I think he [Napoleon] was the embodiment of all that is vilest in the character of man — selfishness, vulgarity, meanness, and falseness of every kind pushed to the furthest possible point. The *lowness* of him! If he had had one touch of the eminence of vice that Milton's Satan had, he would not have been utterly damnable; but the wretch was base all through. That so many people should have admired him so much seems to me one of the bitterest satires on humanity. It is the ape adoring its own image in the looking-glass.'

After two weeks of unrelieved solitude, G. E. Moore came down to stay. On fine days in the afternoons they would go off for terrific walks together along deep, narrow, aromatic Devonshire lanes, thick with summer flowers, and then up high on to the moor, bowling away into far horizons, with the heather under their feet and great piled-up rocks on the tops of the hills. In the evenings they read aloud to each other from Froude's *Short Studies on Great Subjects* and Mahan's *Influence of Sea Power upon the French Revolution and Empire*; and sometimes Moore would warble Beethoven songs at the piano.

Some of Lytton's time during these weeks was occupied in devising and drafting a petition on behalf of the sculptor, Jacob Epstein. Early the previous year Epstein had been commissioned to carve the tomb of Oscar Wilde. For over nine months he had laboured in his London studio at an immense monolith weighing some twenty tons. Eventually this work was transported to Paris, and had recently been erected over Wilde's remains in the Père Lachaise cemetery. The Préfecture of the Seine, however, had considered the tombstone indecent, and immediately ordered it to be covered with a tarpaulin. In an effort to reach some compromise, Robert Ross, the trustee for the monument and Wilde's literary executor, had without consulting Epstein (who, in any case, would never have sanctioned his action) arranged for a large plaque to be modelled and cast in bronze; and this was then applied to the offending regions of the sculpture in the manner of a fig-leaf. But one night, soon after its appearance, the plaque was removed by a marauding band of artists and poets; whereupon the tarpaulin had been quickly replaced over the tomb by the authorities, and a gendarme stationed on duty near by.

At once a protest went up in the French newspapers – a protest supported by many famous artists and men of letters. Lytton had been drawn into the affair by Francis Dodd and

Ada Leverson.[5] It was the kind of situation that would always incite his most combative qualities – the fight against philistinism and prudery. About the Préfecture of the Seine there was little enough that a relatively unknown Englishman could do; but there were other ways in which he thought that he might help Epstein. His efforts and the language in which they were expressed, like those of most effective crusaders, were commendably reasonable. The actual petition that he composed took the form of a modest proposal to the French Government, asking them to refund the money which Epstein had been obliged to expend on the customs duties in order to take the monument to France. It comprised little more than a formal statement of facts. One copy was then sent to Dorothy Bussy who translated it into French and forwarded it to Auguste Bréal with an informal letter explaining the circumstances of Epstein's poverty, and asking him to get up a small committee to see the thing through. The second copy was presented from the English side. It was hoped to obtain some official representation from the Foreign Office, but this failed. Many names were considered by Lytton to act as signatures for his statement, names which were well-known in France and which, he thought, might impress the Government – among others Henry James, W. B. Yeats, Charles Ricketts and C. H. Shannon: 'As to the English signatures,' he very properly concluded, 'Holroyd would of course be the very thing.'[6] But in the end none of these people were to be associated with the venture. The final version, which Lytton completed early in August, reads as follows:[7]

'Mr Epstein, the sculptor, has now completed the tomb of

5. Ada Beddington (1862–1933), author of six epigrammatic novels, who had married Ernest Leverson, the son of a diamond merchant. She became one of the closest and most loyal friends of Oscar Wilde, who always called her 'the Sphinx'.

6. Sir Charles Holroyd (1861–1917), Director of the National Gallery and first Keeper of the Tate Gallery, had four years previously lent his support in favour of Epstein's Strand statues. He is no relation of the present author.

7. A slightly different and shorter version of this statement appears in Jacob Epstein's *An Autobiography* (revised edition, 1963, pp. 53–54).

Oscar Wilde, which will shortly be placed in the Père Lachaise cemetery. It is estimated that the duty, levied by the French customs on the importation from England of the large blocks of stone composing the tomb, will amount to at least £120. The monument is a serious and interesting work of art, it is to be erected in a public place in Paris and it is dedicated to the memory of an English poet and littérateur of high distinction. In consideration of these facts, it has been suggested to us that the French Government might be approached with a view to the remission of the customs duty. The aesthetic merit of Mr Epstein's sculpture and the public interest attaching to it lead us to hope that he may be relieved from a considerable financial burden, which falls upon him owing simply to the commercial value of the mere stone of which his work is composed. The granting of the proposed remission of duty would, we feel, be in accordance with those traditions of enlightened munificence in all matters connected with the arts, for which the French Nation is so justly famed. George Bernard Shaw, H. G. Wells, John Lavery, Robert Ross, Léon Bakst.'

The French Government, however, was unmoved by this piece of rhetorical flattery, and showed itself to be no different from the bureaucracy of any other country. The petition failed; but two years later, at the outbreak of war, the tarpaulin was removed from the tomb without remark, and has never been replaced.

By the end of July, Lytton had finished and completely revised his Chinese play. All that remained to be added were the numerous and elaborate stage directions for the benefit of actor-managers, and then it would be ready for typing. In style it owes something to the dramatic and psychological methods of Racine, and although Lytton did not take it altogether seriously, he had intended it as a possible spectacular production in the manner of Beerbohm Tree. Meanwhile, he put the manuscript to one side and left Becky House to embark on an ambitious holiday with Henry Lamb, whose vicious torments of the spirit would, he promised himself, simply melt away with the open air, the light of day, and his own congenial companionship.

With the highest expectations – 'a map, a hat, a pair of pants' – they set off for Scotland, spending a couple of days in Edinburgh with the Ainsworths. Then they travelled north into Inverness-shire, where they put up with some tenants of the laird, the Glasses, in the small cottage near Loch an Eilein where Lytton and James had stayed in August 1908. And here, at this famous beauty spot, they encountered the first of a culminating series of misfortunes. The weather was cold and wet, and Henry's health at once took a turn for the worse. In sickness, his bad-temper and selfishness deepened, and under the stress of his sullen inattentiveness, his undeviating and contagious invalidism, Lytton too grew irritable and then ill. Nor was this all. The discomforts of the cottage soon proved beyond their endurance. Early each morning, they had to light the kitchen fire and make their own breakfast; but this they were happy to do, since they had already been woken at four o'clock by solos on the violin. 'Willie Glass would play the violin outside our bedroom from 4 to 5 a.m. in the morning,' Lytton complained in a letter to his mother (24 August 1912), 'and Annie never by any chance had a meal ready within 2 hours of the appointed time. ... Willie told endless stories dated usually 1450, and was otherwise very cultured and agreeable – but the horrors were too great in the long run – especially as the weather was disgusting also.'[8]

The hardships of this cottage life were not to be borne for long, and after a few enervating days they departed for the Alexandra Hotel in Inverness. 'So far the journey has not been a great success,' Lytton admitted to Ottoline (7 August 1912). But already he was cheered by a new brainwave – they would go to a fishing village called Helmsdale

8. James Strachey remembered that Willie Glass was little more than a gillie, though, like all highlanders, exceedingly cultured. He was also mad, and said to be, like so many others, a descendant of an illegitimate son of Laird William, Lytton's great-uncle, a notorious loose liver. 'Glass' in fact is another version of 'Grant'.

on the east coast of Sutherland. This was sure to be amusing, and on the bracing North Sea shores Henry's state of mind should improve rapidly, 'We shall probably be there', he informed Ottoline, 'for a few days at least.' Twenty-four hours later they set off, arrived at Helmsdale in the evening – and, by the first train next morning, they fled! Lytton had imagined a romantic little village between the mountains and the sea, filled no doubt with young fishermen in earrings; but what he found was a place not merely desolate and gloomy, but unimaginably hideous – nothing but a squalid street or two with equally squalid scenery round about: and not an earring in sight! His distress mounted as Henry at last broke silence to claim that this was precisely what he had expected all along.

Amid terrible agitations they hurried off on an appalling journey via Glasgow, Belfast and Londonderry to Middletown, on the north-west coast of Ireland. For four mortal days they were perpetually on the move, their money pouring out in bucketfuls, their tempers badly fretted and frayed. Absolutely exhausted, they at last came to rest at a small detached house, McBride's Hotel, which seemed a satisfactory habitation. At any rate they could go no farther. 'At present I am almost killed with various fatigues,' Lytton lamented to his brother James (12 August 1912). He expected to stay on at Middletown, he added, for a minimum of two or three weeks – he doubted whether he would be up to travelling again any earlier. But once more his hopes were reviving. Perhaps, their tribulations over, the holiday would have a long and glorious conclusion. After all, they were comfortably housed, and the countryside was wonderfully beautiful, facing the Atlantic and of a kind to which Henry was particularly responsive – vast stretches of desolate, treeless, peaty land covered with multitudes of small cottages, remote mountains in the background, and, on the other side, the sea, with island upon island, sand-dunes and shores and bays and creeks innumerable; the unified impression was huge, full of complexity and coloured in those vivid browns and greens that Henry was so fond of using in his pictures. Surely he must now be happy.

And, at first, it must have seemed as though Lytton's recurring optimism was finally to be justified, Henry, in ecstasies over the country, had started to regain his spirits. But not for long. Within two days, the clouds of his expiring animosity had reassembled and grown darker. The brief truce was over, and with it their joint afflictions redoubled and multiplied. The rain, it rained every day and the wind, it blew; Lytton, who seldom needed much encouragement in this direction, fell ill with a severe chill; and tempers once more grew strained – Henry relapsing into iciness and the blackest sulks, while Lytton, tired, miserable and bewildered, took to his bed and in despair read through the complete works of Tennyson. 'Henry I suspect is daft,' he wrote to Ottoline (14 August 1912), ' – that's the only explanation I can see for his goings on. . . . And then, of course, when he's not a devil, he's an angel – oh dear, what a muddle of a world we drag ourselves along in, to be sure! I sit here brooding over the various people – Woolf and Virginia, Duncan and Adrian, Vanessa and Clive and Roger, and James and Rupert and Ka – and the wildest Dostoyevsky novel seems to grow dim and ordinary in comparison.'

In the course of the same long letter, he warned Ottoline: 'Don't be surprised if I suddenly arrive at Broughton pale and trembling – I should send a telegram first.' Yet even now he had not given up all hope of effecting some miraculous transformation to the holiday. It was, of course, rash to be too confident, but perhaps Henry was at long last really settling down more peacefully, ascending from devil to angel again. He thought he saw signs of it. And if their turmoils were in fact over and past, then there was no reason why they should not stay on in Ireland together until the end of August, until September. . . . Four days later the final embers of this hope had been ruthlessly extinguished, and he telegraphed to Ottoline:

Shall arrive tomorrow wire train later in need of your corraggio as well as my own.

What then happened has been described by Ottoline herself.

He arrived soon after the telegram and fell into my arms [she recounted], an emotional, nervous and physical wreck, ill and bruised in spirit, haunted and shocked. I comforted him and diverted him as

497

much as I could. It was difficult to contend with the appalling weather; we gave him a sitting-room to write in, and he stayed some time. I had many an enchanting talk with him and we grew very intimate. He read aloud to me, poetry – Shakespeare, Racine and Crashaw (who carried me away by his intense passion). We took long walks together and went to see Broughton Castle where Lady Algernon Lennox was living . . .

At night Lytton would become gay and we would laugh and giggle and be foolish; sometimes he would put on a pair of my smart high-heeled shoes, which made him look like an Aubrey Beardsley drawing, very wicked. I love to see him in my memory tottering and pirouetting round the room with feet looking so absurdly small, peeping in and out of his trousers, both of us so excited and happy, getting more fantastic and gay.

The atmosphere at Broughton was all that Lytton could have wished for in the way of convalescence. His recuperation was gradual, however, for he was full of vain and painful regrets. 'I seem to have been moving ceaselessly and quite pointlessly for the last 3 weeks,' he confessed to James (21 August 1912). 'Among other things I am almost ruined financially.' During the next fortnight with Ottoline he did no work in the sitting-room which had been set aside for him, feeling altogether too sick and exhausted. 'I am constantly relapsing into indigestions and internal disorders which, though not acute, are enough while they last to make work almost impossible,' he wrote in a letter to his mother (3 September 1912). 'I think that I am not in a really healthy and competent state for more than half my days.'

In this state of mental and physical prostration, he ruminated long hours over the miserable débâcle with Lamb, gradually working himself round to a more equable frame of mind. Poor Henry had not been to blame. Lytton knew only too well what a tiresome and objectionable companion he himself could be when sunk in a depressed mood. Really it was quite natural that Henry should have got so cross with him – even so, the extent of his rage and enmity, the virulence and vile brutality of his expression of feeling still bit deep into Lytton's memory, defying all the analgesics with which he nursed his wounds. In future he resolved that, if this love were to be worth anything, he must try to retain more self-command, more strength for both of them. He must never again let his outward conduct fail. He must try harder: for the griefs and afflictions of mortal men were as nothing beside their loves.

Almost every day he wrote agonized letters to Lamb which did little to endorse this new striving after self-command. What had gone wrong between them? he asked. Perhaps he might return to Ireland and try again? Was it possible that, depressed by his cold, he had exaggerated the whole wretched business? Next time, in any event, they might sleep in separate bedrooms — how would Henry like that? Undoubtedly everything had been his own infernal fault. And so the correspondence drifted on, page after apologetic page. Shamelessly submissive, Lytton took upon himself the entire responsibility for the failure of their holiday. His letters intersperse passages of excruciating self-immolation with others of affected and effete cajolery, that pass into sexual fantasy and sexual infantilism, and are added as saccharine to Henry's bitter tantrums: 'Won't you take me back under your charge again, and cure me with the severest of your régimes? ... I feel like a naughty child. Am I one? — At any rate a whipped one. Perhaps one who has been flogged hard for some mysterious naughtiness he hasn't understood, and then been shut up in a dark room to repent — Well, there is no trace of rancour in my heart now. Won't my papa come and open the door, and take me into his arms again?'

But in the hard core of his mind Lytton could not and did not believe that Henry was entirely blameless — despite all the pathetic, little-me flummery and coyness of these letters. The most moving sentences are always those which state quite simply his bewildered sense of failure in the whole field of human relationships, a failure bound up with some ineradicable part of his being, cutting him off from the intimate conviviality of his friends: 'The longer I live the more plainly I perceive that I was not made for this world. I think I must belong to some other solar system altogether.'

By the time he returned to London, Lytton was able to take

some interest again in the general run of human activity – the people in the streets, the respectability of the Savile, the amenities of Bloomsbury. A fortnight earlier his whole future had seemed blank; now it began to fill up again with various schemes and propositions. He was composing a 'solid and stiff' review of Constance Garnett's translation of *The Brothers Karamazov* for the *Spectator* – his first published piece of writing since *Landmarks in French Literature* and his first book review after an interval of nearly two and a half years. Then Constable, the publishing company, had also approached him with an offer to write an integrated history of French social life and literature, a work that would attempt to define what France means and has meant in the history of European civilization. Though assured that he might make three hundred pounds out of this venture, Lytton was not particularly anxious to undertake it – the subject struck him as rather dreary and too similar to his other book. With nothing to lose, he felt able in the publisher's office to play the part of the Great Author. He employed, so he told Ottoline, 'all the signs of genius – a rolling eye, a melancholy abstractedness, no notion of business', a charade that went down so well that the publisher begged him to send along any other of his works, completed or incomplete. But Lytton would not commit himself. He still wanted some day to write a life of Voltaire; in the meantime, he might send them, he told his mother (9 September 1912), 'the old Hastings lucubration which I should be glad to get off my hands'. More productive was an invitation from Harold Cox to write for the *Edinburgh Review*. Lytton at once accepted this offer, and in the course of the next three years contributed to the paper four of his most interesting and elaborate biographical essays.

'I *am* happy, excited, delighted, prancing, optimistic, impudent, and youthful, now I'm in London again,' he assured Ottoline only forty-eight hours after leaving her at Broughton. The next day he left town with James to spend a fortnight at Van Bridge, a cottage near Haslemere in Sussex, which Alys Russell had put at their disposal. 'James is a delightful companion,' he wrote off happily once again to Ottoline. 'It all seems a sort of Paradise – incredibly provided at the critical moment, like a conjuring trick.' Since there was a housekeeper to look after them, they were afforded almost every luxury of comfortable living, down to the last hot-water bottle at night. 'This is a very nice cottage,' Lytton informed his mother (9 September 1912), 'with only one flaw – the extreme lowness of the rooms. Most of the ceilings come down to the level of our shoulders, and we have to creep about on all fours.'

It was now that Lytton decided to put the final touches to his Chinese play. At first he had rather scoffed at the custom of appending long stage directions, a fashion which had been introduced by Shaw and developed by Harley Granville-Barker to the point where playwrights would give not only descriptions of the scenery and action but even some account of the characters and their feelings. He used to say that on this system, Shakespeare would have written: 'Lear (*angrily*): Blow, winds, and crack your cheeks.' However, James persuaded him that managers and others were so half-witted that they would never be able to make out what was going on unless he stuck in more explanations; and so, under protest, he made the necessary additions.

In the next two years there were to be many attempts to get *A Son of Heaven* produced. The agent to whom Lytton sent it thought very highly of its chances. It was an excellent play, he said, exciting and picturesque, full of dramatic appeal, certain to make money. James Barrie and John Masefield, who also read it, echoed this favourable verdict. And the long list of actor-managers to whom it was in turn submitted – Oscar Asche, Harley Granville-Barker, Frederick Harrison, Norman Wilkinson and others – cordially agreed. He had written, they all maintained, a very good and interesting play. However, it was not precisely what was *needed* – not just then. The previous year might have provided a more propitious occasion on which to stage this particular type of tragic melodrama. But the fashion was always changing. They would continue rigorously to bear it in mind; perhaps later that year ... perhaps next year ... perhaps sometime ... perhaps. ... In desperation, Lytton finally, in January 1914, gave the typescript to his brother James, then on his way to Moscow, and he handed it on to

Dudley Ward who was the *Manchester Guardian* correspondent in Berlin and had connections with Max Reinhardt. Max Reinhardt liked *A Son of Heaven*. He declared it to be an excellent play, most exciting and picturesque. Not alone that, it was, he added, full of dramatic appeal, certain to make money. Unfortunately he was already committed for some time, and it would not be fair to the author under such circumstances to hold on to his work. He therefore returned it. After a while, Lytton grew resigned. It seemed, if one were to believe all that these distinguished men had written about his melodrama, that *A Son of Heaven* was fated to be the finest play never performed: and with that he would have to be content. He put it in a drawer and for several years forgot about it.

Meanwhile, acting on what he called an 'inspiration', Lytton shouldered a knapsack and marched off alone to Salisbury. The next few weeks he spent trudging obstinately over the Wiltshire and Berkshire downs, to Amesbury, Marlborough and Wantage. 'It was really a heavenly experience,' he afterwards enthused in a letter to Henry Lamb (9 November 1912). 'I recovered my health and spirits – but not only that: I found that there were joys in solitude that I'd hitherto hardly dreamt of.'

He was by this time sporting a conspicuous, bright yellow coat worn over a beautiful new suit of 'mouse-coloured corduroys' and an orange waistcoat; and his outlandish, heavily-haversacked figure caused some stir among the local populace as he stepped out gaily along the roads and fields, especially since he was also wearing golden earrings. These, he told James, were a great solace to him, though evidently outraging the good citizens of Wiltshire. 'They eyed me with the greatest severity,' he wrote from Amesbury (21 September 1912), 'but I bearded them.' He soon, however, elected to compromise on this outfit, skilfully arranging his long locks so as to conceal from the vulgar gaze all signs of his flashing *bijouterie*. One of the highlights of this journey – certainly the most exotic spectacle that it provided – was Lytton's raid on Stonehenge. From his hotel at Amesbury he stole out at dusk, and with the moon bright and rising behind him, approached the monument – a dark cluster of awkward shapes standing isolated in the empty plain, as if they had somehow been forgotten and left behind there. At a distance it all looked disappointingly small and squat; but then, drawing nearer, he realized that in this peculiar compactness lay its unique power and beauty. He thought of the fallen gods in *Hyperion* – the great old stones seemed to have come huddling together in a melancholy little group, like the last fragment of an army. They had that ominous look of blackness and contraction which extreme old age alone can give. The barbed wire fence was easy to negotiate, and on entering the ring, Lytton discovered that the effect from within, under the gathering twilight, was altogether different, inexplicably awe-inspiring. Each stone was in reality a gigantic bulk dwarfing him into insignificance, while, in the darkness which stretched away beyond the pillared circle, the twentieth century appeared all at once immeasurably remote.

After inspecting the Wiltshire Downs, Lytton turned north towards Churn where Ottoline, having temporarily taken up water-colour painting, was residing at a little farmhouse lent to her by her brother Henry. He had already warned her at the start of his tour that he might be travelling in this direction. 'So if one fine morning,' he had written (18 September 1912), 'you perceive a dishevelled tramp, with melancholy marked upon every limb, wearing a small black hat, a ragged beard, a pair of odd-looking spectacles, and for all I know fisherman's earrings – if you see such a figure come creeping upon a stick over your airy down – it may be ... a certain eminent young literary gentleman.' Ten days later Lytton did make a flying descent upon Churn. Ottoline noted his hurried arrival and departure in her diary, like the first brief entrance and exit of some character from a classical novel.

September 28th

Lytton arrived from Wantage with a huge pack on his back, young and gay and debonair, after two or three days' walking. He was as excited as a boy, for he had had his ears pierced and was wearing gold earrings, which he kept hid under his long hair, and he was

503

wearing his new suit of corduroys, which were very short in the legs. What squeals of laughter and giggles and fun we had about it all.

... Lytton stayed some days and fell so much in love with the little house that he wanted to take it. I was sad when he left, he was so well and full of fun and life and youth, adorable; and he and I and Philip had such delightful talks together. I watched his tall, thin back striding off with its rather quick nervous walk, vanishing into the distance. What a solitary figure he seemed then, seeking rather timidly and nervously for human adventures. I stood and waved to him and quite felt hurt that he didn't turn back.

From Churn Lytton retreated to a temperance hotel in Wantage. He had enjoyed his unscheduled pilgrimage across Berkshire and Wiltshire so much that he feared something must be very wrong. Happiness was so inexplicable, the way it came and went, like the wind. All one could ever do was to seize it when it did come, and hold it as close as possible. All August he had actively pursued it over England, Scotland and Ireland, emerging bruised and broken; now, in September, when he had almost grown resigned to failure, when his plans and movements were completely haphazard, happiness had came bubbling up, catching him unawares. These last two months presented a kind of microcosm of all his years since Cambridge – an illogical mixture of boredom, pain, and enthralling excitement. So much of his life had been spent rushing around in a void, escaping from or chasing after something. He was a wanderer on the face of the earth, and had come increasingly to feel the need of some permanent habitation and society to substitute for Belsize Park Gardens and fulfil the past role of Cambridge. Ottoline had suggested marriage, recommending Ethel Sands as the most eligible partner. She was rich, sociable, lesbian, and owned a lovely house in Chelsea.[9] But could one really marry a house?

9. Ethel Sands, painter and 'rich ugly elder spinster' (Mark Gertler), had migrated to Paris to live with her inseparable companion Nan Hudson, and only returned on the death of her mother. For a time she lived at Newington, a square grey stone house inaccurately attributed to Inigo Jones, with exquisitely decorated rooms, a forecourt, formal garden and great stone gates. By the time Lytton got to know her she was living at 15 The Vale, Chelsea. The dining-room here had mural decorations by

On the whole, Lytton thought not. Sometimes, however, as a respite from the uncertainty of his bachelor life, he did toy with the idea of marriage. 'Is this a fearful muddle?' he asked James from his temperance hotel. 'It's too sickening to be trammelled up in these wretched material circumstances to the extent I am. I suppose a wife would settle such affairs for one – oh dear! the length of time this wobble has been going on – five years at least, I believe. I suppose I'm extraordinarily incompetent. . . . Oh for a little rest! – A little home life, and comfort, and some soothing woman! Supposing one married Ka? –'

Such moments of weakness, however, were comparatively rare. If he had been irretrievably middle-aged, then he might have settled for marriage with hardly a qualm. It was, he felt, his unassuageable youthfulness that held him back from surrendering to such a second-rate solution – his youthful craving for ideal companionship, for affection and the sharing of joys. And there was something else too that now gave him an added determination and stamina – his ambition. The universe might cavort like a wild horse, but he would not be thrown – not just yet. For at times, the vision of some splendid achievement, still a little way off, would rise up and mantle his brain. If he could but seize it, firmly possess himself of it, and stand strong and secure, then all those miserable weaknesses and futilities would melt away for ever. 'Do you know how passionately I desire to do this?' he wrote to Ottoline (6 September 1912). 'To achieve something – not unworthy of my hopes, my imaginations, and the spirit that I feel to be mine? Only the difficulties and terrors are so great – overwhelming sometimes. Oh, to bound forward and triumph!'

Duncan Grant and paintings by Sickert, and in the hallway there were to be mosaics by Boris Anrep, one of which showed Lytton looking out from a cottage window towards Carrington, depicted from another fanciful mosaic window, looking up at him.

2

THE CHESTNUTS

Tired of temperance, Lytton departed from Wantage at the beginning of October and marched on the Bear Inn, some fifteen miles away at Hungerford. His perambulations about the countryside now took on a more definite purpose. The old nomadic life, which so quickly drained away his reserves of energy, could no longer go on, he had decided; at the same time he was in terror of being forced back, *faute de mieux*, into the bosom of his family. There was only one practical solution. He would avail himself of a standing offer from Harry Norton of a hundred pounds, and settle down for a time in some modest farmhouse in Berkshire or Wiltshire – like the one where Ottoline was living at Churn. 'My theory is that if only I could get a cottage on these Downs,' he explained to James, 'and furnish it comfortably, I could live and work in comparative happiness. I believe it would cost very little, and I should be able to afford another rat-hole in Hampstead, to fly to when the solitude became oppressive. . . . It seems to me my health *must* get all right in this air, which is amazing; and if I was really settled down properly with my books, etc. etc. I believe I should be able to work – and then people would come down for week-ends, and I could go up from time to time and gallivant – oh! it strikes me as a paradise.'

After several disappointments, Lytton's choice fell on The Chestnuts, a small farmhouse in the village of East Ilsley, set high up on the edge of the Berkshire Downs, and owned by a racehorse trainer and his Norwegian wife, Mr and Mrs Lowe. He moved in on 10 October, and remained there for the next three months.

Cut off from the distractions of London, he was now able to concentrate wholly on writing. His published output during this time was not large – a Spectatorial review of H. J. C. Grierson's *The Poems of John Donne*, and his long essay on Madame du Deffand for the *Edinburgh Review*. These months, however, do form a particular landmark in his literary career. 'Madame du Deffand' heralds the opening of a new phase in his development as a writer – the transition from the critical to the biographical essay – and one symbolized by his use of a new combination of names. No longer was he to contribute anonymously or as 'G. L. Strachey'. From this time onwards he saw 'Lytton Strachey', a name – 'rather theatrical, I think' – soon to grow more famous than he could have dared to hope.

This change, trivial in itself, was another indication of the new personality he wished to assume, supported by a new treatment and attitude towards his work. He wanted to write with more force and with less superficial emphasis than before – less reliance on the adjective and more on the verb. Already he felt a greater exhilaration at tackling the problems and complexities thrown up by his subject-matter, and at sorting out the maze of disordered rubble into a satisfying, coherent, literary pattern. When Henry Lamb asked him whether he was pleased with the Deffand essay, he replied (9 November 1912) that he was neither pleased nor displeased – 'but I notice with relief that I rather like writing it, which is something quite new'.

He expended much time and trouble on 'Madame du Deffand', reading everything about her that he could lay his hands on – far more than the three volumes of letters on which his paper was ostensibly based – before settling down to his own composition. 'I shall soon have to begin on the Deffand article – which I rather dread,' he told Ottoline (17 October 1912). 'So difficult to do well – and such a formality about it.' The more he read, the more 'difficult and alarming' his task appeared. 'I am appalled', he confessed after five days' more preliminary research, 'by the mass of matter to be digested, and by the small number of remarks that occur to me to say about it.' He almost wished now that he had never agreed to undertake the essay. No one would notice it, he thought, and the twenty pounds he was to be paid were little enough compensation for all the worry and exertion which would go into it.

Once he had started to write, however, all these subsidiary

complaints were forgotten. He became completely absorbed in his subject. 'It is a dreadful story,' he wrote to Ottoline (31 October 1912), 'and on the whole very gloomy, though wit, cold wit, plays over it almost unceasingly. There are the most déchirant moments, and as for Horace Walpole a more callous fiend never stepped the earth. It is impossible to forgive him – quite impossible. His brutality reminds one of – Henry! But he had none of the redeeming qualities; he was a thoroughly selfish and also a rather stupid man. She, au fond, was not much better; but anyway she loved much. It is a disillusioning spectacle – a woman with nearly everything that life can give – wealth, consideration, intellectual brilliance, experience of the world – reduced to such a pitch of cynicism, pessimism and despair. But it is also terribly pathetic. The last letter of all is ghastly.'

'Madame du Deffand' was completed by the end of November, and the proofs were corrected the following month in collaboration with the latter-day Horace Walpole – Henry Lamb. 'I meant to suggest', Lytton wrote to his mother when he had read the whole piece through again (20 December 1912), 'the kind of nasty turn that the easy-going optimism of everyday life gets, when it comes face to face with her sort of disillusionment.'

Of even greater significance was another literary work which he was meditating while living at The Chestnuts. For it was here, in the autumn of 1912, that the first idea of *Eminent Victorians* was conceived. The scale and pattern of his original scheme were quite different from the completed work. The first title which suggested itself to him was *Victorian Silhouettes*, a book which, as he envisaged it, was to contain highly condensed biographies of about a dozen eminent Victorians – some (mostly scientists) were to be admired, others (mostly non-scientists) to be exposed. Preserved among his papers is a list of the twelve most likely candidates for this volume: Cardinal Manning, Florence Nightingale (whose official biography he had once been asked to write), General Gordon, Professor Sidgwick, Watts, the Duke of Devonshire, Charles Darwin, J. S. Mill, Jowett, Carlyle, Lord Dalhousie (who laid the foundations of modern India) and Thomas Arnold. The urgency of Lytton's feelings, greatly to be aroused by the coming war – which he interpreted as a natural climax to all the false complacency and repressed fear in the nineteenth century – later obliterated the balance of his initial plan, and the theme became a sifting of Victorian prejudice. Already something of this feeling was churning about within him. 'Is it prejudice, do you think, or is it the truth of the case?' he asked Virginia Woolf (8 November 1912) after reading through Meredith's letters. 'They seem to me a set of mouthing bungling hypocrites; but perhaps really there is a baroque charm about them which will be discovered by our great-great-grandchildren, as we have discovered the charm of Donne, who seemed intolerable to the 18th century. Only I don't believe it.' And later, as the war got under way, his indignation mounted, and the illustrious Victorians whom he had elected to portray grew more and more to resemble 'those queer fishes that one sees behind glass at an aquarium, before whose grotesque proportions and sombre menacing agilities one hardly knows whether to laugh or shudder'.

For the time being, however, his gallery of Victorian notables was to include a select number painted in attractive colours – men like his father, apostles of common sense and noble, unobtrusive achievement. The first of all, as a matter of fact, just happened to be drawn in satirical vein. 'I am ... beginning a new experiment in the way of a short condensed biography of Cardinal Manning – written from a slightly cynical standpoint,' he explained to Ottoline in his first week at The Chestnuts (17 October 1912). 'My notion is to do a series of short lives of eminent persons of that kind. It might be entertaining, if it was properly pulled off. But it will take a very long time.' The writing of 'Cardinal Manning', which is the longest of the four finished portraits in *Eminent Victorians*, proved to him that he would have drastically to reduce the number of proposed biographies, if the work were not to occupy an entire lifetime. The amount of material to be compressed together was encyclopedic. Round him at The Chestnuts he gathered the formidable engines of his new project – a suffocating assortment of treatises upon the English and Roman Church, various fat studies on Manning, Newman, Keble, Pusey and other divines. 'I can't make out what Mrs Lowe thinks me,' he wrote (17 October 1912), 'but I expect she judges that I am going into the Church – from the number of books on Cardinals, the Oxford Movement, etc, etc., that I have brought with me.'

Whatever her secret thoughts, Mrs Lowe – who claimed to be an intimate of Björnson and Grieg – looked after Lytton very well; while her husband, during the afternoons, endeavoured to teach him riding. 'To-day I had my first riding-lesson with Mr Lowe,' he wrote excitedly to Ottoline (31 October 1912). 'He is infinitely gentle and sympathetic – just what I wanted. I circled round the paddock in the mildest way, and got hardly at all tired. I shall gradually increase the dose until – hunting, steeple-chasing, polo. No Spanish Cavalier will be in it.' This was a fine and spirited beginning, but the subsequent stages in his progress were less meteoric than he had foreseen. Three times a week Mr Lowe would take him out, shaking with terror, on a small, very well-behaved black cob. Together they would proceed unsteadily across the fields, walking, and occasionally trotting, For some weeks Lytton continued to feel hopeless. Then, one afternoon, he suddenly seemed to get the hang of it, and knew that he would be able to master this new art. His first action to celebrate this access of self-confidence was to order a peaked cap and a fine pair of striped gentleman's breeches to be made for him. His letters to Ottoline, James and Henry are full of his new equestrian exploits: 'I can sometimes trot for several minutes together with absolute equanimity,' he boasted (25 November 1912). 'The joys of cantering make me turn pale with ecstasy merely to think of. . . . Mr Lowe does not say much either in approval or disapproval – except that my legs are perfect! I should never have suspected it. Full many a leg is born to blush unseen.' By the end of December he was going for frantic gallops along the Downs, his long hair and pendant *boucles d'oreilles* streaming in the wind behind him.

Despite a personal belief that 'my breeches and "leggings" are much admired', he was in fact regarded with the gravest suspicion in the village of East Ilsley. Whether viewed whirling like some mythical, four-hoofed beast across the long line of the Downs, or encountered as a pedestrian when he descended into the village itself, a bearded man, like the tall Agrippa, 'so tall he almost touched the sky', Lytton presented an intimidating spectacle, and one from which the villagers instinctively shied away. And he too paled with fear, as he walked the streets among these staring, unfriendly strangers. He wished fervently that he possessed some capacity for making friends with people. 'I am quite tongue-tied,' he admitted unhappily to Ottoline (17 October 1912). 'I think it is caused by something in the blood – some sluggish element; but oh! I do desire to expand – I really do.'

This unrelieved solitude was the chief, perhaps the only disadvantage of living far off in the country. On some days he spoke to no one at all. His only connection with the world at large, he told Maynard Keynes, was via *The Times,* which arrived just after lunch and soothed him into a *post meridiem* slumber. 'Why is London the only place to live in,' he asked Virginia Woolf, 'and why must one have the strength of a carthorse, or you, to be able to manage it? You are not to suppose from this that I am unhappy here. No, my hours pass in such a floating stream of purely self-regarding comfort that that's impossible, only one does have regrets.' Such regrets grew most oppressive in the evenings when the day's work was done and he dearly felt the want of some companion. On the whole, however, solitude seemed to suit him. His health was good; he was nearly always contented; and he was working steadily and with enthusiasm.

Sometimes, to help banish this old Adam of loneliness, he would invite a friend down to stay – his sister Marjorie, or Henry Lamb, over whose indiscretions an act of oblivion had now been passed.[10] But more often at week-ends he would

10. 'A smoothing-over of the late crisis has taken place by means of long and amicable letters,' Lytton wrote to Virginia Woolf (1 December 1912), 'so if the dear fellow should go and see you, I hope you will be

arrange to leave The Chestnuts and visit his friends elsewhere. Many of these excursions were to London, where the Second Post-Impressionist Exhibition was being held at the Grafton Galleries. On the first of several visits there he arrived rather late, and on asking the porter whether Leonard Woolf – the exhibition's secretary – was still within, was urged to 'pass through, Mr Augustus John, pass through and see!'

Once inside, there was no chance of further mis-identification, since one of the major exhibits was Lamb's first large portrait. Collected round it, more often than not, was a ring of irate old gentlemen delivering tirades of abuse on Lytton's moral character, based mainly, so far as he could overhear, upon the fact that he did not wear a linen collar. 'I suppose he does it to save his laundress's bills,' was the inspired guess of one lady. 'No, madam, no!' she was speedily corrected by an enraged white-haired escort. 'I am told that he is quite well off. It is affectation – mere affectation!' One Dublin newspaper, after describing the portrait, went on to say that even more extraordinary than any of the pictures were the people who went to look at them: 'There may be seen the autumn poet, in his long overcoat, his large Quaker hat, and his strange black tie, gazing in rapt admiration at his own portrait!'

In a different sense, Lytton too was more interested in the effect produced by Post-Impressionism than in the pictures themselves. The Matisses he did find interesting, and their colour thrilled him; otherwise the Post-Impressionists and the others appeared to him painfully anxious to paint only what was dull. Picasso was merely Futuristic and incomprehensible; Duncan a fish out of water; Vanessa rather pathetic; Wyndham Lewis execrable, utterly dreary; Bonnard and Marchand not worth a mention. What really did hold his attention, however, were the irritable buffooneries of the spec-

discreet and refrain from pouring salt on the wounds by injudicious repetitions of long-cancelled abuse. I'm looking forward to see him again, but I have the greatest fears that he's cut his hair short, which would be a severe blow.'

tators. For, to an ever-increasing extent, his mind was becoming preoccupied by the ingredients of successful publicity, by the ways and means of animating public feeling, and by the methods – in his own craft – of amalgamating literature and journalism, art and polemics, the imagination and the will. 'Why do people get so excited about art? It made me feel very cold and cynical. I must say I should be pleased with myself, if I were Matisse or Picasso – to be able, a humble Frenchman, to perform by means of a canvas and a little paint, the extraordinary feat of making some dozen country gentlemen in England, every day for two months, grow purple in the face!'

But the main feeling left by these week-ends in London, and especially at the Grafton, was that he had been wise to settle down so comfortably in the country, away from his old friends. He no longer felt quite the same towards Bloomsbury. Roger Fry, for example – 'a most shifty and wormy character' – had quarrelled outrageously with Ottoline and with Simon Bussy. Then, when Henry Lamb had injured his right hand and was prevented from painting, Fry had commiserated with him by expressing a hope that it would not handicap his piano-playing! And, so often, where Fry led, Clive Bell and the others hotly pursued. It was significant that Augustus John had thought so little of their absurdities as to send nothing at all to the Grafton. Besides which, their collective reaction to the divine Boris Anrep, on whom Lytton now had a rather schoolgirlish crush, was beyond forgiveness.[11] 'The Bloomsbury Gang have been most vile about him – including I'm sorry to say Duncan,' he told Lamb (20 November 1912). 'Their lack of prescience seems to be infectious.' Individually he still got on well with them all, especially the Woolfs, who had recently established themselves in small cosy rooms in Clifford's Inn, off the north side of Fleet Street. They seemed singularly unchanged – and it was, as always, delightful talking to Virginia, who had just completed her first novel, *The Voyage Out*. Leonard too had written a novel,

11. Boris Anrep had written an introduction to the catalogue of the Second Post-Impressionist Exhibition.

The Village in the Jungle, that had been welcomed rhap-sodically by a publisher, though not by Lytton himself, who had read it in typescript. 'Can you imagine what it's like?' he asked Henry Lamb (20 November 1912).[12] 'It's painful to see how completely he seems at home on the niveau of that Bloomsbury gang.'

But the full horror of Bloomsbury was to be experienced at the Grafton. itself, where the crowds of his friends and enemies were so overflowing that Lytton felt himself in danger of being entirely submerged. 'When last I went it was most painful,' he wrote to Ottoline (18 October 1912). 'Clive was strutting round in dreadful style, without a hat, as if he owned the place. It was impossible not to talk to him, and of course he would shout his comments, so that crowds collected – all so ridiculous and unnecessary. At last, when he began to explain the merits and demerits of the [Eric] Gill statue, and positively patted it with his fat little hand, I had to disown him, and became absorbed in a Matisse drawing. Poor Woolf sits at his table and sustains the bombardments of the enraged public – how he keeps his temper I can't think. Irate country gentlemen and their wives rush up to him purple in the face, as if *he* had painted all the pictures with the deliberate intention of annoying them.'[13]

12. Lytton could not bring himself to tell Leonard Woolf what he thought of *The Village in the Jungle* for nearly six months and until he was safely out of the country. From Paris, on 23 April 1913, he criticized the novel in a manner that perfectly catches the racialism so prevalent among the Edwardian upper classes. 'I think I'm in a particularly difficult position for judging of it, because my tastes are not at all in the direction of the blacks etc. I'm sure most people have more of a fellow feeling for them. As for me, the more black they are the more I dislike them, and yours seem to be remarkably so. I did hope for one bright scene at least with some fetid white wife of a Governor, but no doubt that would have been quite out of key. Perhaps really for everybody the blacks are not a *very* interesting subject – but it's difficult to be certain. . . . Oh Lord! how horrible it all is! – Fortunately there *are* other things in the world. . . . Whites! Whites! Whites!'

13. Leonard Woolf has given his own account of these experiences in *Beginning Again. An Autobiography of the Years 1911 to 1918* (1964), pp. 93–5.

The delirium of London was a good antidote to Lytton's solitude at The Chestnuts. Some week-ends, however, he would travel up to Cambridge instead, and stay with Maynard Keynes, or G. E. Moore, or Harry Norton. Here too there was much complicated bustle and activity, and he soon found himself being drawn into the whirlpool of Apostolic politics. The chief excitement during these months centred round the election of the Austrian philosopher, Ludwig Wittgenstein, and another undergraduate named Bliss. Having studied engineering for a period at Manchester, Wittgenstein had come to Cambridge, where he was greatly impressed by Bertrand Russell's lectures on Mathematical Logic. A friendship had quickly sprung up between the two men – a friendship that, in the opinion of G. E. Moore, Desmond MacCarthy and others, Russell had tried to make exclusive of the rest of Cambridge. But then Maynard Keynes had interceded, and it was mainly through his efforts that Wittgenstein was elected to the Society. 'The poor man [Russell] is in a sad state,' Lytton reported to Saxon Sydney-Turner (20 November 1912) in a letter that conveys very well the flavour of these proceedings. 'He looks about 96 – with long snow-white hair and an infinitely haggard countenance. The election of Wittgenstein has been a great blow to him.[14] He clearly hoped to keep him

14. Bertrand Russell, in a letter to the author (14 September 1966), makes it clear that, to the best of his recollection, he was never worried about Wittgenstein and the Apostles. Lytton's account of this episode, he writes, 'completely surprised me, and I know nothing whatever about the matter concerning which you write. I knew nothing at the time about Wittgenstein's relations with the Society, nor had I any strong views as to whether he should be elected or not. I was interested in his intellectual potentialities, but I should have been glad of any outside influences that distracted him from the long monologues, lasting sometimes through the night, well into morning, during which he examined his own mind and motives. I do not think that I ever "worked myself into a frenzy" or "got quite ill" with any private worry, and, though I had anxieties at that time which were severe, they had nothing to do with the Society. I cannot imagine how the people whom you cite got these impressions of me, unless they thought the affairs of the Society were more important than I did at that time. I never felt any "mortification" at Wittgenstein being elected, nor can I think why I should have felt any such emotion.'

all to himself, and indeed succeeded wonderfully, until Keynes at last insisted on meeting him, and saw at once that he was a genius and that it was essential to elect him. The other people (after a slight wobble from [Ferenc] Békássy[15]) also became violently in favour. Their decision was suddenly announced to Bertie, who nearly swooned. Of course he could produce no reason against the election – except the remarkable one that the Society was so degraded that his Austrian would certainly refuse to belong to it. He worked himself up into such a frenzy over this that no doubt he got himself into a state of believing it: – but it wasn't any good. Wittgenstein shows no signs of objecting to the Society, though he detests Bliss, who in return loathes him. I think on the whole the prospects are of the brightest. Békássy is such a pleasant fellow that, while he is in love with Bliss, he yet manages to love Wittgenstein. The three of them ought to manage very well, I think. Bertie is really a tragic figure, and I am very sorry for him; but he is most deluded too. Moore is an amazing contrast – fat, rubicund, youthful, and optimistic. He read an old paper – on Conversion – very good and characteristic. Hardy[16] was there – p.p. and quite dumb. Sheppard was of course complaining that nobody liked him . . .'

Wittgenstein, whose work was to be exposed by Russell to an extraordinarily patient misunderstanding, had not fully appreciated the complex human reaction that would be set off by his election. A few days later he offered to resign from the Society. Lytton was at once sent for and succeeded in per-

15. Ferenc Békássy, the Hungarian poet, educated at Bedales, who had recently come from Budapest and made his mark as a Cambridge undergraduate.

16. Godfrey Harold Harvey (1877–1947), Fellow of the Royal Society and later Sadleirian professor of pure mathematics at Cambridge. Lytton had first met him when an undergraduate at Trinity. 'I played bowls on the Fellows' Bowling Green which is behind the chapel and most charming,' he wrote to his mother (2 May 1901). 'Only fellows and their friends are allowed there – ours was Hardy, who got the Smith's Prize last year – he is *the* mathematical genius and looks a babe of three.' In 1940 he published a short book, *A Mathematician's Apology*, that is generally voted a masterpiece stylistically as well as in content.

suading him to remain an Apostle. It was thus partly owing to him and Keynes that Wittgenstein widened his circle of friends and eventually found his home at Cambridge. After the war, during which he did duty in Austria as a soldier and school-teacher, he was to return to the university, becoming a Fellow of Trinity and eventually professor of philosophy, and exercising a potent influence on the younger generation of philosophers.

3

OSCILLATIONS

The Chestnuts had never been anything more than a temporary solution to Lytton's domestic problems. But it gave him a permanent taste for country-cottage life. Without disrupting the flow of his work he was able to see quite a lot of his friends, especially Henry Lamb, who came down to ride with him on the Downs, and who, as an especial mark of favour, allowed Lytton to trim his hair; and Ottoline, who was now encamped some ten miles off at Breach House, Cholsey, and who plied him with a continuous stream of letters and bewildering, upper-class gifts: a massive bottle of hair water ('I haven't yet dared to use it, as I've no notion how to. ... A tooth-brush. But how does one apply a tooth-brush to the head?'); a garish stock ('How on earth does one put it on?'), a tortoiseshell snuff-box to match his spectacles ('I shall have to take to snuff, in order to be able to produce it with a rap and astound the world'); a voluminous embroidered red handkerchief ('I haven't yet dared to use it – it seems a profanation'); or simply a batch of sweet-smelling leaves to act as book-markers, which he put to use with more courage.

All this was very agreeable, and Lytton soon determined to find a furnished cottage or farmhouse somewhere in the neighbourhood, where he could settle down permanently. The practical business of arranging such a move left him feeling weak with helplessness. 'I perceive that the path of the cottage-finder is not strewn with roses,' he wrote to Hilton Young (24 Octover 1912), who was helping him to clear away some of the thorns and who had invited him down for a few days to his own cottage, The Lacket, Lockeridge, near Marlborough. Here, Lytton was told, there existed the most propitious centre in the whole county for discovering what he wanted, something small, cheap and attractive. The Lacket was situated on a large estate belonging to a horse-trainer who took little interest in the property value of his land and was ready to let his houses without complex and protracted negotiations.

Lytton did not look forward to his stay at The Lacket. He hated the drudgery of house-hunting with its fearful dislodgement of his quiet mode of living; but, at the same time, it had been borne home to him that if he wished to perpetuate his amiable, sequestered existence, then all this introductory disturbance was unavoidable. Besides, Hilton Young was so kind and obliging that he could not find it in his heart to refuse the invitation. There were too, as he soon saw, many pretty cottages in the vicinity that made his mouth water. As for The Lacket itself, this was disappointing, chiefly because of the staid manner in which Hilton Young had done it up. 'Dear me! the poor fellow has not been brilliantly successful', he wrote to Ottoline (22 October 1912). 'It is all so correct – so scrupulously in the dullest and flattest taste – and, mon dieu! the drab dullness – the lack of inspiration – of colour even. I find myself feasting my eyes on my orange waistcoat. And in the country what gay clean and bright colours one might have. He himself was here for the weekend – exactly like his cottage. Is it Cambridge, or is it England that makes some of one's friends so spiritually anaemic? The bounce has quite gone – if they ever had any. I felt like a Spanish bull-fighter, prancing round him, and sticking darts into his hide. And the good-natured old bull came up mooing, and positively liked having them put in. His kindness was extraordinary – showing me round everywhere, and making endless enquiries. He begged me to stay on here as long as I liked. I am longing to be off, but it is difficult to move. . . . I don't see why I shouldn't stay here for the rest of my life; I'm sure Hilton wouldn't venture to raise any objections. I might begin re-decorating. It would be a nice surprise for him when he next came down, to find the place done up in orange and magenta!'

Though Lytton could not have guessed it then, The Lacket was to play a considerable role in the next few years of his life. But at this time, the few days he spent there seemed a complete wash-out. The estate agents whom he consulted in Marlborough were unhelpful; the rain came down in a way that looked eternal; he caught a chill which he tried unsuccessfully to quell with whisky; he did no writing; and he was bored. The only surprising item of his visit was the discovery of an article by Wyndham Lewis among some back numbers of the *English Review*, which Hilton Young very properly took in and preserved. By an odd coincidence this article contained an elaborate description of the innkeeper with whom he and Henry Lamb had stayed during those few, disastrous days in Brittany. This was, too, the first piece of writing by that arch-enemy of Bloomsbury that Lytton had come across. 'It was cleverly done – I could no more have written it than flown – fiendish observation, and very original ideas,' he told Ottoline (22 October 1912). 'Yet the whole thing was most disagreeable; the subtlety was curiously crude, and the tone all through more mesquin than can be described. ... It seemed to me that Henry had picked up some of his beastly mean notions from that source. Ugh! the total effect was affreux. Living in the company of such a person would certainly have a deleterious influence on one's moral being. All the same I should like to see more of his work – though not his paintings ...'

In the second week of January, his landlady, Mrs Lowe, suddenly collapsed and was taken to a nursing-home, suffering from consumption. For some weeks Lytton had been eyeing the poor woman with mounting apprehension. Could it be dangerous, he nervously inquired of James, to remain in the house with her? Was consumption (which he already suspected) contagious? Now, after three leisurely

months there, he fled hurriedly away, and having found no
other suitable cottage, was forced to return to Belsize Park
Gardens.

'My vision of the future is dim,' he admitted to Henry
Lamb. He could see not a single ray of hope on any horizon,
and he wanted, so he said, to bury himself 'under fifty oceans'.
For a week he cut himself off in Hampstead from all his
friends, feeling too gloomy to communicate with anyone.
His new confidence temporarily faded. *Victorian Silhouettes*,
on which he had built up such lofty aspirations, would
take him years to complete — even now he had hardly
begun the Manning biography. It would be a colossal undertaking — just how colossal he had only come to appreciate
since beginning to get to grips with it. He was under no illusions: the work was arduous, the prospects remote — could
he ever stay the course? Of one thing he was certain: he
would achieve nothing so long as he stayed at Belsize Park
Gardens. But, all of a sudden and quite unexpectedly, the
clouds lifted, when Harry Norton promised to make over to
him some sort of quarterly allowance pending his literary
success. With this support he should be able to find some
cottage after all, he reasoned, and there, slowly and to the
best of his ability, realize his ambitions. 'At the present
moment,' he wrote to Ottoline (18 January 1913), 'you may
be glad to hear that I'm almost ready to believe there may be
something in me after all.'

He was also ready now to face the world again, to see his
friends. For a few days he went down to visit Ottoline at
Breach House, but the recovery of his spirits, she discovered,
was only partial and intermittent. 'I had a long talk with
Lytton last night as I was on my way to bed,' Ottoline noted
in her diary (24 January 1913). 'I sat on my bed and he stood
beside me, looking so dejected and despondent, for he seems
to feel baulked in his life, doubtful about his writing: he says
that he is no good at conversation so that he could never be a
social success, that his small voice would prevent his going
into politics, which he would rather like to do, but how could
he ever make speeches with his thin tiny voice? I did my best

to encourage him with his writing, as I am sure that is his real *métier*. Poor Lytton, how dejected he becomes, and yet he is really very ambitious.'

His spirits and moods continued to oscillate violently. Back in London again, he was greatly cheered by Henry Lamb's good temper and sweet reasonableness. He was 'angelic'; he was 'divine'; not a trace of those inanities and animosities that had marred so many of their previous encounters. Since they were both living in Hampstead, they met frequently, though Lytton felt himself to be under no illusions as to Henry much wanting to see him. But that, he told Ottoline, 'makes me feel more grateful for his friendliness. I do really feel it intensely.' Part of this nobleness on Lamb's part may be traced to his celebrated portrait of Lytton, for which, by early March, he had begun to make his preliminary sketches. 'The last two days have been spent almost solid in sitting for Henry for the big portrait,' Lytton wrote plaintively (13 March 1913), ' – the result is rather shattering.'

There were other activities and events, too, that helped to disburden Lytton while he was living with his family. His letters during these two months show him caught up in a round of sociality – theatres, parties, interviews and meetings of all kinds. There were 'hilarious' lunches at Simpson's with James, Harry Norton, Gerald Shove and others; teas in solitary pomp at the Savile, or in overcrowded Bloomsbury, or again with Ethel Sands in her magnificent Chelsea house where (13 February 1913) 'I found George Moore ... Miss [Gertrude] Stein and others. I spent most of the time talking to a Spanish-Jew-American lady[17] – a friend of Miss Stein ... and I gleaned a certain amount of information about Picasso, which interested me; but I wanted to listen to George Moore, and couldn't manage it, which was vexing. ... G.M. I

17. Evidently Alice B. Toklas. Describing Lytton as 'a thin sallow man with a silky beard and faint high voice', Gertrude Stein wrote of this meeting in her *Autobiography of Alice B. Toklas*: '... we had been invited to meet George Moore at the house of Miss Ethel Sands. Gertrude Stein and George Moore who looked like a very prosperous Mellon's Food baby, had not been interested in each other. Lytton Strachey and I talked together about Picasso and the russian ballet.'

rather liked. He reminded me of one of those very overgrown tabbies that haunt some London kitchens.' And finally, in the evening, there were dinners with Henry Lamb and his patrons, J.L. and Mary Behrend – 'mostly very dull – but with amusing moments from the psychological point of view. They move in a queer stratum – I think rather like the sort of world that Wells describes in some of his novels – Fabian, and cultured, and oddly aimless and unsatisfactory. But the personal shades are many, and I think Mrs Behrend is really nice.'

Among the highlights of these weeks was an announcement that the Russian Ballet was due to arrive in the country, and that they would be dancing *Petrushka*. Was there any chance of seeing the gorgeous Nijinski? Lytton asked Ottoline (13 March 1913), who had met him in Paris and promised to introduce them. In eager preparation for this encounter he bought a new suit of dark purple ('no frills') and a fine orange stock. Meanwhile, between meals and visits to his tailor, there were plenty of other distractions. With Leonard and Virginia Woolf – she 'looking very pink and very attractive', he, in a yellow beard, somewhat less so – he went to Shaw's *John Bull's Other Island* 'and was positively rather amused. But I console myself with the reflection that, after all, the play was second rate.' With James he went to the first performance in England of Richard Strauss's *Der Rosenkavalier* and then, to James's indignation, walked out after the first act, complaining there were no tunes in it. 'I was bored to ... death,' he told Henry Lamb the next day (30 January 1913). 'There seemed so many points, and so little point, as Zarathustra might have observed. ... The discomfort of my seat, and the heat, which was far greater than any Turkish bath, contributed to my agony – Also a side view of Adrian. ... Oh mon dieu! the interminability of it all!'

Almost equally interminable, though only intermittently dull, was a visit to the Aristotelian Society, where Karin Costelloe was reading a paper. It was an odd affair – Karin rather too feminine and boring; Bertrand Russell very brilliant; Moore supreme; Ethel Sands, having come for the sake of Karin's *beaux yeux*, silent and watchful. The atmosphere was

stifling; the scene, a saturated mixture of the eccentric and the
sublime in proportions that particularly appealed to Lytton's
fancy, united his intellect and sense of comedy in an amusing,
reverential description. 'There was the strangest collection of
people,' he wrote to Lamb (4 February 1913), ' – sitting round
a long table with Bertie in the middle, presiding, like some
Inquisitor, and Moore opposite him, bursting with fat and
heat, and me next to Moore, and Waterlow next to me, and
Woolf and Virginia crouching, and a strange crew of old
cranky Metaphysicians ranged along like half-melted wax
dolls in a shop window and – suddenly ` bserved in the ex-
treme distance, dressed in white satin and pearls and thickly
powdered and completely haggard ... Miss Sands! – the incorrigible old Sapphist – and Karin herself, next to Bertie,
exaggeratedly the woman, with a mouth forty feet long and
lascivious in proportion. All the interstices were filled with
antique faded spinsters, taking notes. ... Bertie, no longer the
Grand Inquisitor, but the Joconde, with eyelids a little weary,
delivered some pungent criticisms, but the excitement came
with Moore. I wish you'd been there. I think you would have
been converted. As for me I became (for the first time for
ages) his captive slave. The excitement was extraordinary, and
the intellectual display terrific. But display isn't the right word.
Of course it was the very opposite of brilliant – appallingly
sensible, and so easy to understand that you wondered why
on earth no one else had thought of it. The simplicity of
genius! But the way it came out – like some half-stifled geyser,
throbbing and convulsed, and then bursting into a towering
gush – the poor fellow purple in the face, and beating his
podgy hands on the table in desperation. The old spinsters in
the background tittered and gasped at the imprévu spectacle.
He is really really a grand maître.'

At week-ends Lytton would desert London to press on with
his quest for a rustic sanctuary somewhere near Marlborough.
Often he went to stay at The Lacket with Hilton Young whom
he described (27 February 1913) as 'my main prop in life. ...
The good fellow has again offered me his cottage, and is making
all sorts of efforts towards getting me one.' And a fortnight

later he told Ottoline: 'My plans for a cottage are developing, and Hilton is becoming more and more of a guardian angel.' But despite all Hilton Young's efforts, these house-hunting excursions were never successful, and the prospect of finding some place to suit his fastidious if modest requirements grew increasingly dark. When not staying at The Lacket, Lytton would usually put up near by at Lockeridge Farm, a very draughty and primitive farmhouse, considerably less comfortable than Hilton Young's place. His search was impeded, too, by a multitude of minor inconveniences – among them the attentions of a housekeeper who turned out to be an ex-cook of Desmond MacCarthy's, and who had picked up from her past employment something of Desmond's style. 'The lady in charge', Lytton wrote to Ottoline during one week-end at Lockeridge (17 February 1913), 'is exceedingly vague, and can only remember occasionally that I'm staying here. When she does, she brings in a few wet sticks which she places on the fire. The result is not encouraging. ... My chief fear, however, is that she's got – consumption!'

In his leisure hours between house-hunting expeditions, Lytton was reading the works of Strindberg, and also his old friend G. M. Trevelyan's three-volume life of Garibaldi. About the latter work his feelings were mixed. The story itself was wonderfully thrilling, and Garibaldi's tempestuous career made his own problems shrink drastically in size until they appeared altogether trivial; yet he did not really enjoy this biography. 'There is much interest in it,' he informed Henry Lamb (15 February 1913), 'but tiresomely told.'

The urge to write was ever with him, though he shrank from making a full assault upon *Victorian Silhouettes* until the conditions of work were more favourable, until the summer had begun, by which time he hoped to be comfortably installed in the country. Meanwhile, during the months of February and March, he composed a highly successful and amusing *conte drolatique* entitled 'Ermyntrude and Esmeralda'. 'Will you believe me when I tell you that I have begun and got well under way with a new facétie?' he asked Henry Lamb, to whom the piece was dedicated (18 February 1913). 'Don't I deserve at least a lead medal for this? I'm actually enjoying it; but I see all too clearly that it's a mere putting-off of the worst moment – but enough!'

'Ermyntrude and Esmeralda' was written as an exchange of letters between two fancifully naïve, nubile and inquisitive seventeen-year-old girls, one – Ermyntrude – living in the country, the other in town. At school they had both pledged themselves to discover as much as possible about the untold and manifold mysteries of sex, and in their holiday correspondence they report to each other the dramatic results of their investigations.

Everything from babies to homosexuality is ingeniously touched upon with an amusing air of innocence, piquancy and wonderment. But soon their investigations take a more practical turn, leading to some remarkable experiences that culminate for one – Esmeralda – in a proposal of marriage from a fifty-year-old general, and for the other in nightly copulation with the footman. Implicit throughout this lightly-written story is a scathing criticism of those repressive procedures and taboos that govern the upbringing of most adolescents, especially young girls. Though 'Ermyntrude and Esmeralda' was not intended for immediate publication, it is Lytton's most entertaining fiction and a genuine work of pornography.[18]

4

GRAND TOUR

'Ermyntrude and Esmeralda' was completed in March, by which time Lytton had decided upon a further means of 'putting off the worst moment', that is, of postponing his serious assault on *Victorian Silhouettes*. To avoid unnecessary disappointments, he liked to return for his holidays to places which he had already visited, which held all the allure of past associations, and which he knew beforehand were to his taste. But for several years he had dreamed of travelling

18. *Ermyntrude and Esmeralda* was published in 1969 by Anthony Blond.

through Europe, and through Italy especially, visiting many of the famous towns and cities of which he had read and heard but never seen for himself. Now he determined to make this dream a reality, to spend two months on his grand tour and then return in the late spring or early summer, bursting with health and buoyancy, and straining to be at his work again. This trip, he realized, might prove immoderately expensive, but he had made up his mind to go whatever the cost, and to live, if need be, on crusts and water for the rest of the year. He hoped also to persuade someone to accompany him – his brother Oliver, or Henry Lamb, or even Maynard Keynes – but no one was free to come, and he was obliged to plan his itinerary alone. He intended to spend a day or two in Paris, and then travel south to Marseilles, Turin, Palermo and Syracuse where he hoped to remain a few weeks before returning via Naples and Rome. It was an ambitious solo programme, but he made careful preparations. He wrote to E. M. Forster to find out about *pension* life in Italy, and received a favourably discreet reply; he also sent off for information about Sicily to Maynard Keynes who, a little less discreetly, provided him with the names of the cheapest comfortable hotels, and recommended him to go on to Tunis where 'bed and boy' were also not expensive.

On the morning of 15 March, Lytton set off from Hampstead to Folkestone, where he was put on a boat sailing to Boulogne. To amuse himself during this solitary voyage – and also on the train between Boulogne and Paris – he wrote up an account of the trip, describing in particular the fellow passengers who caught his fancy. This fragment of diary records his wondering preoccupation with the British upper classes, whom he regarded now, and for most of the remainder of his life, in much the same equivocal spirit as he had the Cambridge 'bloods'. His incredulous attention was taken especially by two young men from Eton, aged about seventeen or eighteen, both of whom were wearing single eye-glasses.

'Their faces', he wrote, 'were like joints of mutton – so full-blooded and fleshy. . . . A casual observer might have thought they were dressed shabbily . . . but really everything they had on – their cloth caps, their short waterproofs, their old flannel trousers, and their old brown shoes – was impregnated with expensiveness. There was a look in their faces which showed both that they were born to command and that none of their commands would ever be of any good to anybody.'

Apart from these two Etonians there was a 'plutocrat' on board – possibly Sir James Mackay[19] – followed everywhere by four or five women in furs, for whom he took cabin after cabin, into which they eventually retired one after another, while he himself, spied on by the ever-attentive Lytton, stood stonily on the deck outside, in a yachting cap, 'looking like an old cock with his hens in the background'.

To Lytton's eyes there were still other eccentrics on board, notably two aristocrats remarkable for their overcoats. 'The first was perhaps a baronet,' he noted, 'about 35, with ginger hair and high colouring, and a blonde wife with ineffectual diamond earrings, who no doubt was considered pretty. He fussed a great deal as we were getting near Boulogne, about his luggage, walking to and fro, and instructing stewards – with that queer, pointed, almost German-goose-step walk which must be the right thing when one's travelling, because James and I saw Lord Portsmouth doing it in exactly the same way, on the platform at Inverness in his tailcoat of grey flannel. But what was particularly striking about the Baronet was his very big and very thick and very brilliant ultramarine overcoat, which one had to look at as much as one could whenever he passed, so that it was only after he'd passed several times that one noticed that he was wearing spats and that his brown boots were almost incredibly polished. At the buffet at Boulogne afterwards, sitting with his wife next to him and the maid opposite, he seemed to be quite frightened by the foreign language.

'The second man was no doubt a Lord – tall, dark and angular – rather like Victor Lytton; and *he* had on an immense *white* overcoat. The odd thing about both overcoats was that

19. Sir James Mackay, first Earl of Inchcape (1852–1932), the ship-owner; director and chairman of numerous shipping companies.

they had evidently been got for effect, and yet there was only one thing about them over which any care had been taken – and that was the quality of the material. The blue one was a bad blue, and the white one was a poor white; and neither had any shape; and each was provided with the vulgar strap and button at the back that happens to be common now. ... Perhaps it is this inability to be interested in anything but the mere quality of materials that has made the English what they are. One sees it everywhere – in their substantial food with its abominable cooking, in their magnificent literature with its neglect of form, in their successful government with its disregard of principle.'

There were many other classes and other nations represented among the passengers on the boat – a number of very seasick Polish young ladies, some pedantic French youths, a young don from Oxford and, on the upper deck, an academician (or possibly a Russian prince) retching systematically into a basin – but none of these roused Lytton's curiosity for long. It was a rough and windy crossing. By the time the boat had reached mid-channel Lytton too felt a little sea-sick, and as his soul began faintly to grow disembodied, so all these lesser breeds without the titles, spats and overcoats seemed to suffer a strange diminution.

But the British Upper Classes remained life-size to the end.

Lytton stayed only one full day in Paris, during which he went to *King Lear* at the Odéon – a bad translation, feebly acted, which seemed to fill the French audience with amazement. 'C'est d'un romantisme!' they repeated incredulously to each other. He also found time to see an exhibition of Renoir's pictures. 'Some of the early things were exquisite,' he wrote to Ottoline (17 March 1913), 'but the late ones are too horrid for words. I gather the poor old man's hand has grown very shaky. It seems a shame to show them'.

From Paris he travelled by train to Dijon. He had planned to move more quickly farther south, but the thick snow and the cold intimidated him, and he decided to make his journey in shorter hops until the skies had cleared, the temperature risen. There was, he noted, a kind of dishonesty about *foreign* bad weather that particularly dismayed one. Sometimes, too, he felt lonely. 'I wish I had a companion,' he confessed to Ottoline (17 March 1913). 'It's slightly grim to be wandering all alone. But there are compensations.' He remained in Dijon for two days, at the very modern Grand Hôtel de la Cloche in the Place Darcy, which he described (19 March 1913) as 'splendid – with masses of food and wine, and such delightful rotund Burgundian fellow-guests – all with hooked noses and light eyes'. As for the town itself, Lytton was charmed by it and went everywhere with a Kodak camera which Henry Lamb had lent him, snapping old buildings and young boys. 'I felt', he wrote to Henry (19 March 1913), 'as if one could well live and die in one of those heavenly "hôtels", in some street off the tramline, wrapped in infinite repose. Probably one could get one for the cost of a country cottage! – They are not large, but the proportions are perfect and the feeling of space supreme. But I suppose one would really have to be a 17th Century Magistrate to carry it off properly – and on the whole I don't think I am.'

The next stage of his journey took him through Avignon to Marseilles, a bright and bustling town, whose whole population seemed to be continually passing and re-passing him in an endless, frantic hurry as he sat, with Kodak uncertainly poised, inspecting them all from a café table outside the Grand Hôtel de Noailles et Métropole in the rue Noailles-Canebière. 'I've tried some snapshots,' he reported back to Henry, 'but I find it very difficult to manage. It's such a business getting the machine into play. I've wasted several plates already.' In the evenings he would retire up to his bedroom and read Samuel Butler's *The Way of All Flesh*: 'To my surprise I find it cheering.'

As his expenses had already mounted far above the original conservative estimates he had made back in Hampstead, he decided to miss out Tunis and sail, via Toulon, to Naples. From Marseilles he set sail on Thursday, 20 March, and arrived in Naples after 'a very painful sea passage' on Easter

Saturday. Although by this time utterly weary of travelling, he had made up his mind during the voyage that Naples would not suit him and that he would have to hurry on almost immediately to Palermo. But within twenty-four hours of landing there, he thought that he would never be able to tear himself away. The atmosphere was pure romance – infinitely long streets; sudden vistas solid with flowers; and over everything the beaming sun. During the daytime he would rattle about the place in taxi cabs, 'with my eyes bursting out of my head and my brain in a whirl of ecstasy', he told Ottoline (24 March 1913). 'I try to take snapshots, but my hands shake so with excitement that no doubt they're all failures.' In the evening he would return, fatigued but happy, to Parker's Hotel which, to his constant surprise, was crowded with *bourgeois* English majors and their ladies, all in evening dress and all listening stonily to Italian love-songs warbled by smiling Italian minstrels with mandolins.

'Everything is extraordinarily large,' he wrote to James shortly after his arrival, 'especially the town, which is infinite, and packed with wonders – people, not things. In spite of my deathly exhaustion I took two excursions through it to-day in cabs – the rattling and the surrounding hubbub and general remuement are indeed intoxicating. Then you look up at Vesuvius – (not erupting! I had fully expected a tuft of smoke). . . . One of the oddities is this hotel, quite filled with English of the most English – what on earth are they doing here? I look at them, and look at them, but it remains an impenetrable mystery.'

For the most part Lytton was content simply to ride or wander about the town itself. He did practically none of the proper things on the sightseer's itinerary – scarcely stepped into a church, never went to Capri, and only hurriedly visited the museum. The mere effort of existing in those astonishing streets among that wonderful population of people was enough for him. But one excursion he eventually did make to Pompeii. 'It was an enchanting experience,' he eulogized in a letter to Ottoline (26 March 1913). 'The heat of an English July – can you imagine it – and the hills all round – and that

530

incredible fossilisation of the past to wander in. What a life it must have been! Why didn't we live in those days? Oh! I longed to stay there for ever — in one of those little inner gardens, among the pillars and busts, with the fountain dropping in the court, and all the exquisite repose! Why not? Some wonderful slave boy would come out from under the shady rooms, and pick you some irises, and then to drift off to the baths as the sun was setting — and the night! What nights those must have been!'

In spite of a good deal of bad taste, Lytton concluded that there must have been much beauty in the houses at Pompeii — walls of deep reds, yellows and blacks seen between white pillars in the brilliant sunshine, green-blue figures round square fountains, flowers of all colours in the courtyards, and a vision of Vesuvius at the end of a street. Most disappointing to him were the bawdy pictures, so feeble and anaemic, on some of the walls. These were concealed from the public and only unlocked by winking custodians for the benefit of respectable bachelors such as himself. Some, however, they would not unlock, even in the face of Lytton's most eager imprecations; after which his interest palled. The heat was so intense during this expedition that he drank off several pint bottles of beer, and while drinking them, was persuaded by his guide to make a further excursion some way up Vesuvius. This climb drained him of his last drop of energy, all the more so since politeness obliged him to follow up his beer with several glasses of Lachryma Christi in a village inn. 'If I were a carthorse,' he commented to Ottoline, 'existence here would be perfect.'

His plans had by this time grown vague and unsystematic; the original route was finally abandoned, and since he had heard alarming reports of overcrowding in Sicily, he proposed instead to go off for some days to Ravello, which Hilton Young had recommended to him as being quiet and sequestered.

On the morning of Sunday, 30 March, after a drive of three-and-a-half hours along the shores of the Mediterranean, he arrived at Ravello, set in the precipitous high hills above

Amalfi and over a thousand feet above the sea, which lay, almost directly below his *pension*, perfectly blue and smooth. Hilton Young had not misled him. Ravello turned out to be a fairly small village, wonderfully peaceful and unsophisticated. Beyond the sea, looking south over the Gulf of Salerno, lay distant misty mountains with Paestum at their foot; and inland, steep cliffs covered with chestnut woods and fruit trees in full bloom; and in the foreground, Norman and Saracen church towers, terraced gardens and wild flowers of every colour and variety – hyacinths and freesias, wallflowers and red roses. What adventures he might have had in this divine place if only he had spoken the language!

In another letter to Ottoline (4 April 1913) he describes Ravello as 'a heavenly spot', and continues in a vein reminiscent of his earlier letter (11 March 1906) to Maynard Keynes depicting 'My Castle in Spain' – the dream, now revised in the light of seven years' further experience, of a newly constituted Bloomsbury Group, rejuvenated and removed to Ravello. 'Why not come here?' he asked. 'We could collect a société choisie in this pleasant place – and dream away 2 years delightfully. Henry would be given a studio in the extreme end of the village. Desmond and Molly would have an apartment in the very centre. Duncan would lie out among the fruit-trees. Virginia would prance in after dinner. And even John might occasionally appear. I should insist on having James, but not Henry James – except for a week-end once a year. Don't you think it would do very well?'

The Pension Palumbo, where Lytton put up, was a plain lodging-house without any of the pretensions of a large city hotel. Originally it had been built as a Bishop's palace. Lytton's room was in the annexe, opening on to a spacious platform with views in every direction, and reached by a marble staircase. Since he had this annexe practically to himself, there seemed an admirable opportunity for settling down to some not too arduous work. He had brought with him several books on Cardinal Manning, but no sooner had he started to write than his health gave way. The cause of this collapse was the weather. He had arrived in intense heat, 'a blazing sun,' he told Henry Lamb (31 March 1913), 'and such a mass of light reflecting and refracting – and one can sit for indefinite hours with one's head in the shade and the rest of one grilling'. His health was barometrically dependent to an extraordinary degree upon the climate. When the skies were open and blue, the sun hot, he was sprightly and well; but the passing of a single cloud could bring on internal apprehensions, indigestions, or even worse. And so, when the rain began to fall in Ravello and the temperature suddenly dropped, Lytton was at once reduced to his bed. After a week of this, he decided that, since there seemed no prospect of a return to summer conditions, he must leave for Rome. 'I hope Rome may improve me,' he wrote to Lamb (5 April 1913). 'It's very annoying to have such a futile inside.'

He arrived in Rome on Monday, 7 April under a clear, warm sky, and feeling quite revitalized. For three days he stayed at a small hotel which did not offer many facilities for repose. 'One's fellow-travellers are death indeed,' he complained to James, 'the human race at its lowest ebb – mon dieu! Fit only for Forster's novels, but he hasn't got them. Oh!' On Thursday he moved to the Pension Hayden, in the Piazza Poli, which was more comfortable but 'pretty thick with Americans'. He was nursing a certain grudge by now against E. M. Forster, who, he felt, had completely misinformed him about Italian accommodation. 'My experience of Pension life is most painful,' he grumbled in a letter to Saxon Sydney-Turner (14 April 1913), 'and I find that Forster has quite misrepresented it – whitewashed it absurdly. For sheer, stark ignorance, imbecility, and folly the conversations here can't be beaten. I'm rapidly becoming a second Flaubert under these influences. I can think of nothing but la Bêtise Humaine.'

Rome offered, so he discovered, all the allures of Cambridge – the same sort of surprises in the street, and an air of fancy-dress. The Forum and the Palatine seemed like capricious college gardens thrown about among the wild enormities of ancient magnanimity. The town itself continually astonished and delighted him; the variety of attractions was so vast that he could not help being cheerful. For years he had imagined the architectural beauties of Rome, and now at last he could stare his fill at them. He went to the Pantheon; to the Castle of St Angelo (a Piranesi engraving of which had hung on the wall of his nursery at Lancaster Gate, and which he had always longed to see); to the Janiculum to look at the exquisite Bramante Tempietto; to St Peter's, the huge exterior of which took his breath away; to Hadrian's Villa; to the Colosseum; to the Medici Gardens, and the lake of Nemi and the Baths of Caracalla, 'like some strange impossible dream materialised'. He also went to the Sistine Chapel which, he told Henry Lamb, 'quite désorientéd me at first. In the end I think I liked it – but it's very queer. As an effort of constructive skill the ceiling is terrific, but it seems rather thrown away. I believe if each morceau could be taken away separately and framed, it would be better. The difficulty of seeing any of it is very great. There are some lovely other frescoes round the walls, by Perugino, Botticelli, etc.' But of all the wonders that he beheld, the most marvellous was the Forum, so very large, covered with green trees and shrubs, with lilac and wistaria, and whole choruses of singing birds – altogether different from anything he had expected.

Every morning and afternoon Lytton busied himself inspecting the curiosities of the town. And then he would repair to an appalling English tea shop to read the Continental edition of the *Daily Mail*. Between tea and dinner he usually wandered over to the Pincio and after listening to the band playing Rossini, strolled in the Borghese Gardens and meditated on Cardinal Manning. After dinner, and with the utmost regularity, he dashed off to the cinema. One afternoon, by way of a change, he went to hear Beethoven's Pastoral Symphony, conducted by Richard Strauss, and described it (13 April 1913) as 'dreadfully dull. Strauss looked like a prematurely-aged diplomat, and I thought did his best to add somnolence to an already somnolent affair. After that came his own things – Hero etc., but I didn't stop.'

When not off seeing a particular building or monument, he was quite happy to wander at will, looking in on an art gallery, or, like a decadent poet, sipping fatal drinks from café tables as the youths ambled by in squadrons, or just floating up some fascinating street or other past so many lovely small piazzas and splendid palace façades in the general direction of an obelisk or a church. There was a peculiar luxury in having only oneself to please, and being able to savour one's own sensations by degrees and to the heart's content. Yet unremitting solitude carried its disadvantages too. 'I feel that I shall have left a multitude of things unseen,' he wrote to Ottoline (17 April 1913). 'I should like to linger on for weeks and weeks – but the expense is really getting too great, and also the silence! I haven't spoken one word to an intelligent human being for a month, and I'm beginning to feel it.'

Lytton had hoped to go on to Florence for a few days, but a financial seal was set on this scheme when he purchased a large and expensive Piranesi print – 'I think it's rather magnificent,' he concluded in his last letter from Rome to Ottoline. 'Well, someday we *must* come here together, that's certain, isn't it? What fun it'll be! . . . The Pope is dying. Shall I apply for the post? Then you could come and stay with me at the Vatican.'

5

PEREGRINATIONS AND ANGOISSES

Because his finances had 'been reduced to chaos by the voyage', Lytton resigned himself to spending most of the remaining spring and the summer with his family. His days, however, despite this penury, seem to have been far from monastic; and he plunged back almost immediately into the gyrations of London life – theatres, music-halls, parties. To assist in the cure of a chill that he had caught on stepping ashore in England, James dragged him off to a performance of *Tristan and Isolde* which, to his own surprise, he enjoyed and which effectively killed off his diseases. He also went, under James's direction, to *Ariadne on Naxos*, which bored him, and to hear Paderewski play the Emperor Concerto, and Nikisch conduct the Eroica. But by far the most exciting musical experience during these months was *The Magic Flute*, which he had not heard before and which he went to twice. The first time, he told Henry Lamb (5 May 1913), 'I went quite vaguely thinking it was a short light affair of no great importance – and I was overwhelmed. . . . I think it gives a new conception of Music itself. It seemed to me Perfection made manifest – an intarnishable vein of beauty, and a grandeur before which one fell prostrate. It is too abominable that it has not been done in London for years and years, and it is now only done by the poor Carl Rosa Company at the Coronet with all the draw-backs of bad scenery and poor singing and feeble acting. How can the English pretend to care for music? I go again on Friday.'

Most of the social entertainment in these first few weeks was provided by 'Our Lady of Bedford Square' as he now called Ottoline, at 'Throne Hall'. The turns within her flower-decked drawing-room were even more varied and numerous than usual, and of all the principal stars there, the one to interest Lytton most was the novelist, Gilbert Cannan. 'The poor fellow must have a dim time of it with his wife, who's 20 years older than him, and very distressing,' he remarked after their first meeting. Mary Cannan had formerly been married to J. M. Barrie, who still gave her an annual allowance of money on which the couple largely subsisted and which was handed over each year at a tête-à-tête dinner held, at Barrie's whim-sical suggestion, on the divorced pair's wedding anniversary. Lytton at first confessed himself to be 'furiously prejudiced against G.C.'; mainly, it appears, on account of a certain cool-ness which had temporarily sprung up between Ottoline and himself, and which he diagnosed as being due to her recent patronage of Cannan. When, early in May, Ottoline left Eng-land with her family for Lausanne, a whole month passed without the exchange of a single letter between them – an unprecedented silence. Meanwhile, Lytton declared himself to be quite converted to Cannan, owing partly to his honesty and openness of mind, but chiefly to his attractive statuesque appearance. Tall and handsome, Cannan had known Henry Lamb at school in Manchester, had gone to Cambridge after Lytton had come down, and was dramatic critic of the *Star*.

He had also written several plays and three novels, the last and best of which — *Round the Corner* — Lytton now attempted to read. 'Perhaps it would have been wiser not to,' he confided to Henry Lamb (5 May 1913), 'as it would be difficult to conceive anything duller and more completely lacking in the joie de vivre. I stuck to it, and read every word of the blasted thing, but while I was doing so I felt a cloud over my life. The poor fellow is so modern and broad-minded too! But oh! the taste! — and the pointlessness.' He still hoped, however, that Cannan would appeal to him personally and 'in a moment of épanchement' invited him over to tea at Belsize Park Gardens. At that time the megalomania which was to drive Cannan into a mental home had not fully asserted itself, though already he was moody and disdainful, his embittered humour — a verbal assuagement of this latent desire for power — reminding some of his literary-minded friends of Hamlet. His visit to Lytton's home went off fairly well, though it was quite evidently not the preliminary to a really close friendship. 'He is very very dull,' Lytton informed Lamb after Cannan had left (17 May 1913), 'though good — an empty bucket, which has been filled up to the brim with modern ideas — simply because it happened to be standing near that tap. The good thing about him is a substratum of honest serviceableness — but that is not enough in my line to excite me. *He* no doubt found me far too rarefied for him. I daresay if I took the trouble I could induce in him a culte for me which would replace the one he at present has for Rupert [Brooke]. But of course I shan't.'

After Ottoline had departed for Switzerland, most of Lytton's social entertainment came in the form of Bloomsbury evening parties. These were very wild, unprincipled affairs, if one may judge from Lytton's description of a typical one given by his brother Oliver. All the guests were in fancy-dress — among them Saxon Sydney-Turner got up as a eunuch. 'Karin [Costelloe] was the leading figure,' Lytton wrote to Lamb (16 June 1913), '— in white flannel cricketing trousers and shirt. Duncan was appalling as a whore great with child, and Marjorie incredible as a post-impressionist sphinx. Oliver

537

was a Harlequin, Roger a Brahmin, and I Sarastro. The gambols were extraordinary and in the middle of them Gerald [Shove] appeared, drunk, in evening dress and a top-hat. He and Karin sang a Vesta Tilley song together and carried on a good deal. I was considerably in love with both.'

Such parties were invigorating to Lytton, but sometimes, when he was in his more fragile moods, their rowdiness jarred upon him. 'The dissipations of our circle are approaching a vertige,' he reported to Lamb the week following Oliver's entertainment (23 June 1913). 'The last party was at Adrian's. Owing to an accident I couldn't bring myself to go – further than the door in the square – whence I heard such a Comus uproar that I slipped away again. I had been having dinner with the Sangers, and felt that my condition was too hopelessly inadequate. The accounts of the proceedings made me glad I didn't venture. The nudity reached a pitch – Duncan in bathing-drawers, and Marjorie with nothing on but a miniature of the Prince Consort. Next time – next time is on Thursday, at Karin's, 10 o'clock. If you started at once, couldn't you be there?'[20]

Lytton himself was very much there at Karin's party, during the course of which a one-act farcette that he had written called *The Unfortunate Lovers or Truth Will Out* – fashioned rather in the slight, fantastic manner of a Chekhovian burlesque – was given its première. Set at a country inn during the year 1840, the fun of the piece resides in the improbable interrelationships assumed by the Bloomsbury actor-guests, the entire cast comprising two pairs of elopers – Duncan Grant playing a young boy disguised as a woman (a part originally intended for Molly MacCarthy), Clive Bell apparently his homosexual lover and dressed initially as a male, Marjorie Strachey as a girl wearing the clothes of a man, and Vanessa Bell attired simply, but misleadingly, as a woman. In the final scene, most of the characters were revealed to have been in double-disguise, men originally got up as men later assuming women's clothes and vice versa, and so complicated were the metamorphoses, the sequence of split-second acci-

20. Henry Lamb was then staying in Ireland.

dents uncovering one layer of masquerade after another, that before the end no one could remember who was what.

To win a little recuperation from frenzies such as these, Lytton now made the first of many agreeable week-end visits to Asheham, a lonely Sussex farmhouse which Leonard and Virginia Woolf had lately rented, and which lay among great trees in a meadow in a corner of the South Downs. The other guest on this occasion was Desmond MacCarthy, 'with his eternal dispatch-box, from which he produced the first chapter of a novel on school life – not very inspiring. He can't make up his mind, he says, "how far to go"'[21]

Lytton's own literary plans were equally indecisive. On his arrival back from the Continent the entire scheme of *Victorian Silhouettes* had presented itself clearly to his mind. 'An idée has suddenly crystallised,' he told Henry Lamb (5 May 1913), 'and I mean to attack it immediately.' But once again his programme was disrupted, the scheme faded, and he blamed his unproductiveness on the irritations of *la vie de famille*. 'As to work,' he reported only twelve days later (17 May 1913), 'the crystal that formed itself so suddenly and beautifully has melted into a sticky little puddle at the bottom of my brain.' He dreaded having to pen some hasty, uncongenial hack work for money, and quickly devised a compromise solution which he put up to Constable. This was a book on Racine – a subject which appealed to him for several reasons. Because of his familiarity with and understanding of Racine's work, and his previous writings on it in the *Spectator* and in *Landmarks in French Literature*, such a project might be completed with considerable speed and ease. He also believed in his own ability to produce an original and worthwhile volume of criticism that might command a very fair sale. The Constable directors, however, were more doubtful, and at a meeting held in the last week of May vetoed the proposition

21. MacCarthy in fact never completed this novel on school life. But a short story, *The Mark on the Shutter or A Small Boy's Conscience* – 'for me, the best short story ever written about a school' (Lord David Cecil) – may have been a distillation of his original idea. It is included in *Humanities* (1953).

on the grounds that Racine was too unpopular in England for a book about him, however meritorious, to make money. Several other subjects were suggested as alternatives, but none of them sympathetic to Lytton, who left the office without any agreement having been reached.

He now resigned himself to the drudge of literary journalism, and wrote off to Harold Cox proposing an article in the *Edinburgh Review* on Samuel Butler. But Harold Cox was dubious about so untopical a contribution, and, in the manner of editors, succeeded, without ever rejecting the idea, in postponing a definite decision about it *sine die*. And so, between January and November of this year, Lytton published nothing, not even a review, though of course he composed a few unpublished pieces and contemplated several more. One of these latter was a satire on Roger Fry's Omega Workshops[22] and the whole fashionable, exclusive nonsense, as he saw it, talked about Post-Impressionism — a sketch to be thrown off quickly and light-heartedly in the Molière vein. 'A crank always wanting to be up to date — in the hands of a pseudo-impostor who would put him through all sorts of paces, and try to have his daughter,' was how he explained it in a letter (28 July 1913) to Henry Lamb, whose work had recently been criticized by Boris Anrep for being too far re-

22. The Omega Workshops had officially opened in July 1913 at 33 Fitzroy Square, these premises serving as showroom, design studios and actual workshops. The driving force behind the scheme was Roger Fry, who was helped by two directors, Vanessa Bell and Duncan Grant. Among the young artists they employed part-time at thirty shillings a week to design and produce textiles, dress fashions, furniture and pottery were Wyndham Lewis, Edward Wadsworth, William Roberts and Gaudier-Brzeska. Several of their fabrics were hand-painted with dyes. In some cases local carpenters were employed to do basic joinery in white wood which the artists would then decorate; in others, designs were placed in the hands of large firms — furnishing fabrics sometimes printed in France, carpets sometimes woven by Royal Wilton, stained glass produced in Fulham. Amateur and experimental in execution, their products — which could be bought or made to order — aimed at educating the public taste to radically new aesthetic ideas. It was not wholly a success. In June 1919, Fry closed the workshops and the company was forced into voluntary liquidation.

moved from Post-Impressionism. 'The 2 Academicians, always coming in together and talking in unison – and all sorts of other cranks – Miss Stein, Rupert perhaps, and others – A General whom it was important not to offend, because of legacies, coming in at the critical moment while all the queer creatures were parading about, reciting poems, painting pictures, etc. – in the midst of a room newly furnished in the P-I manner – they in desperation having to dash into the said furniture, to conceal themselves from his wrath – Rupert into a commode, and Miss Stein into the Grand Piano. Then perhaps after all the General himself getting impressed and converted by the arch-impostor – and so on.'

Leonard and Virginia Woolf's success in finding Asheham had stimulated once again his own desire for an agreeable country cottage. 'My existence is chiefly dominated just now by the housing question,' he told Henry Lamb (5 May 1913). Since it appeared that there was not a single unoccupied farmhouse ready to be rented in the whole of Wiltshire, Hilton Young had recommended Lytton to build a small cottage to his own requirements and pay for it gradually over the years. Lytton at once took up this idea and developed it. His plan was to establish this place as a week-end retreat for his friends, who would all contribute some amount towards its cost. After a great deal of cautious reconnaissance, Hilton Young had spied out a likely plot of land, and Lytton persuaded George Kennedy, the architect, to come down, inspect the ground and examine local conditions. Apart from the price, which was steep, everything seemed set fair: the situation was excellent; Kennedy agreed to design the building himself; and to celebrate the new venture they all three drank warm champagne at eleven o'clock one May morning on the platform of Marlborough railway station. But then, when Lytton had finally nerved himself for every risk and effort, a surprising discovery was made: the land in question, so carefully selected, happened to belong to the National Trust and was therefore not for sale. This was a severe blow, and for several weeks Lytton was reduced to 'a trance of slothful désespoir'. Rallied once more by the miraculous Hilton – 'I shall have to write him a poem in Heroic Couplets' – he then resumed his quixotic search for land. Soon a new, rather inferior site was located, but this time Kennedy only sent down his second-in-command, William Park, who in due course produced a plan which struck Lytton as mediocre. By now everyone's enthusiasm had waned, and, since it was obviously a mistake to proceed with anything so permanent as actual construction work in this half-hearted mood, it was generally agreed, with a sigh of relief, to let matters drop.

To superintend all these fruitless negotiations Lytton had spent much of May, June and July down at The Lacket, during which time he read almost every book there and evinced a particular appreciation for the gay absurdity of Chekhov, which seemed to catch so much of the wry, comical futility of his own life. 'The more I think of them [Chekhov's plays],' he wrote to Lamb (23 June 1913), 'the more eminent they seem.' Gradually, too, the internal atmosphere of The Lacket came to appeal to him rather more. 'I find myself quite beginning to like the matting on the walls,' he admitted (1 June 1913), 'and in a day or two I foresee that I shall be seeing some merit in Arnold-Forster's water-colours.' This change of mood was all the more fortunate since, towards the end of July, Hilton Young suddenly announced that he was not going to use his cottage for a year, and that, from the end of September, Lytton was free to move into it and remain there till the following autumn at a rent of thirty pounds. For an extra sum, the housekeeper, the excellent Mrs Templeman, would also stay on and look after him. This was tremendously good news and Lytton joyfully accepted the offer. 'I was in the greatest doubt as to how I could conveniently dispose of myself in the coming year,' he wrote to Hilton Young (28 July 1913), 'and I never dreamed that such a piece of good luck would come my way. It ought really to save my life, I think – temporarily if not permanently; and the most distinguished life-saving apparatuses can do no more. Of course Mrs Templeman must be included. Is she frightfully expensive? But it doesn't matter – I would sell out all my East India Stocks to keep her.' Although, inevitably, his first six winter months would be rather ice-bound, their solitude would give him a perfect opportunity for some consecutive literary effort – the most vital consideration of all. 'I'm rather terrified by the prospect,' he confessed to Ottoline (16 August 1913), 'but I think on the whole it's a good thing. I ought to be able to do some work there, and get up a good dose of health. But I dread the bleakness of the wintry downs, and shall have to rush up from time to time and fling myself into the arms of the yellow drawing-room.'

Released from the pressure of endless doubt and indecisiveness, Lytton could spend the intervening weeks in a gregarious, holiday spirit. In mid-July he again visited Asheham, this time for a full week, feeling 'infinitely more cheerful – in fact altogether perky and insouciant'. The only cloud in the sky was the illness of Virginia Woolf, who, shortly after his departure, was struck down by violent headaches, sleeplessness, and an acute fit of despondency, and had to be removed to a nursing-home.

Back in London, Ottoline was again the focal point of all Lytton's entertainments, having returned from Switzerland and quickly resumed her succession of Bedford Square parties. These, as always, were crowded with celebrities, and carried off with a panache which, to Lytton's eyes, made the lamentable old Bloomsbury milieu appear like a subterranean world of fishes. At one of these fine parties he at last met the legendary Nijinsky who was 'certainly not a eunuch' and who, he told Henry Lamb (24 July 1913), 'was very nice, though you won't believe it, and much more attractive than I'd expected – in fact very much so, I thought. . . . Otherwise he did not seem particularly interesting – as the poor fellow cannot speak more than 2 words of any human language it's difficult to get very far with him. As it was, there was another Russian who acted as interpreter and the conversation was mainly conducted by Granville Barker.' The previous week, before retiring down to Asheham, Lytton had gone to see Nijinsky's latest ballet, Le Sacre du Printemps,[23] 'one of the most painful

23. Nijinsky was the choreographer of Le Sacre du Printemps. He did not dance in it.

experiences of my life', he described it. 'I couldn't have imagined that boredom and sheer anguish could have been combined together at such a pitch. Stravinsky was responsible for
this.' Yet at moments he still found the performance pleasing,
and Nijinsky dazzled and delighted him: 'I sent him a great
basket of magnissime flowers, which was brought on to the
stage and presented to him by a flunkey.'

After a week-end in Manchester with Henry, who had been
commissioned to paint an official portrait of his father, Professor Lamb, Lytton hurriedly fled to the remoter country,
fearing that Henry's tribulations over trying to combine filial
sentiments, municipal expectations and the call of high art,
all on one small canvas, might easily result in a mood of
irritability directed, for want of any better target, against
himself. On Wednesday, 23 July, he arrived at the Plough
Inn, Holford, a lovely little village at the foot of the
Quantock hills, and here he put up for almost three weeks. He
had not intended at first to remain for more than a few days,
but Henry's portrait occupied him longer than had been anticipated, and the Plough Inn was so *soigné*, the weather so
radiantly hot and fine, the food so sumptuous ('Sir Walter
Scott alone could describe it properly, and even my greed
finds itself nonplussed'[24]), the country so green and undu-
lating, that he seemed to fall into a kind of trance where time
slipped by unnoticed. During the mornings he would go for
walks, often to Alfoxton House which Wordsworth had
rented for seven pounds a year less than The Lacket, and
where he and Coleridge first collogued together until, suspected of being secret agents of the French Revolution, they
were obliged to quit the place and go and live in the Lake
District. Then, after returning to a lunch of smoked ham,
mountains of fresh green peas, raspberries and Devonshire
cream, he slumbered contentedly throughout the afternoon
over a somniferous copy of *The Times*, roused himself for
tea, wrote a few crepuscular letters to his friends – including

24. A fine description of this food, and of the inn itself, is given by
Leonard Woolf in *Beginning Again. An Autobiography of the Years 1911
to 1918* (1964), pp. 153–4.

Clive Bell, who had recently been appointed buyer for the Contemporary Arts Society and whom Lytton was now urging to purchase some pictures by Stanley Spencer and, after dinner, finished up the day with a little light reading of Dutch history and an early bed 'dreaming of Nijinsky'.

At last Henry successfully completed his portrait and Lytton was able to join him down at Poole, in Dorset. After a week-end here, the two of them travelled north to the Lake District – a destination probably determined by Lytton's recent reflections on Wordsworth. For a week they stayed at an inn at Brampton, in Westmorland, and every day went off for fifteen-mile walks, sweating and toiling in the August haze, in their pockets sandwiches which they would eat under a hedge, talking and sketching until by the afternoon they had arrived at some place for tea; then home again over the mountains, Henry generally barefoot.

'I have practically no money left,' Lytton confessed complacently to James (18 August 1913), 'and I shall be ruined by these absurd journeys backwards and forwards across England, but it can't be helped.'

On Monday, 19 August, Lamb returned again to Ireland, and Lytton, having once more gathered up his strength, travelled south in the first week of September to spend several days with Clive and Vanessa Bell at Asheham. Many of the Bloomsbury Group were also down there, including Adrian Stephen – who turned up from Dieppe where he had been staying with Wyndham Lewis and Frederick Etchells – Duncan Grant, Saxon Sydney-Turner – rather eerie with his rheumatic silences and indecisive flittings to and fro – Roger Fry, encamped with his children in a field, and Maynard Keynes, who tended to dominate the party. Despite this, and despite catching a heavy cold on his very first day, Lytton managed to distil a good deal of amusement out of his visit. He sat for portraits to Roger Fry, Duncan Grant and Vanessa Bell,[25] and in the intervals played, with great vigour, at badminton – a far more agreeable game,

25. The Vanessa Bell portrait – 'a more truly *fauve* Strachey than Henry Lamb's now canonical image of 1914' (Ronald Pickvance) – is now in the collection of Mr Richard Carline. Mrs Barbara Bagenal owns the Duncan

he thought, than tennis, which was merely a matter of brute agility. In the evenings they would all sit about and talk. 'Conversation, as you may imagine, eddied and swirled unceasingly,' he wrote to Ottoline (14 September 1913), 'so that even if my head hadn't been obfuscated it would hardly have kept its equilibrium. I was reminded of that verse in the Apocrypha about "a roaring voice of most savage wild beasts, or a rebounding echo from the hollow mountains" – but I managed to survive, and actually at the last moment succeeded in winning 30/- from them all at poker – which has come in very conveniently!'

Suddenly the gaiety and entertainment of this week were extinguished by the shocking news that Virginia Woolf had attempted to commit suicide. 'There has been a horrible occurrence,' Lytton wrote to Lamb (13 September 1913). 'Virginia tried to kill herself last Tuesday, and was only saved by a series of accidents. She took 100 grains of veronal and also an immense quantity of an even more dangerous drug – medinal. The doctors at one time thought there was very little hope. But she recovered, and is apparently not seriously the worse for it. Woolf has been having a most dreadful time for the last month or so, culminating in this. . . . The doctors all agree that the only thing required is feeding and rest, so really now the prospect seems to be pretty hopeful. George Duckworth has lent them his country home in Sussex, and they intend to go there in about a week.'

Remembering, perhaps, his own proposal of marriage to Virginia, Lytton felt an acute commiseration for Leonard Woolf, whom he visited briefly after leaving Asheham on his way north to Redcar in Yorkshire for the week-end with his old Liverpool friend Lumsden Barkway, now a vegetarian and fully-fledged Presbyterian clergyman, dressed in pitch black. After a couple of days of cold vegetable fare, he struggled on farther northwards to Milton Cottage, Rothiemurchus, where James had set up house with two of the Olivier sisters, Noel

---

Grant portrait. The Roger Fry painting was until recently in the Strachey house at Gordon Square.

and Brynhild,[26] together with the latter's husband, Hugh Popham. No sooner had he joined them than he subsided into a dismal decrepitude. Scotch rain pelted down outside; discomfort hounded him within. 'The arrival was worst of all,' he reported to Lamb (24 September 1913). 'A DOG! – One of those dreadful vast ones, standing higher than a table – ugh – belonging to the young woman – imagine my anguish, cooped up in the pouring rain in the tiny sitting-room with four other persons, and IT coiled about my ankles – day after day – Splitting headaches, nerves racked, yellow eyes revolving wildly in despair – and then at night having to make my way through the mist to a dark wooden outhouse where a bed had been rigged up for me, and where my agonised soles were pierced with icy oilcloths.'

Luckily the four others were not oppressed by Lytton's infirmities, and once James had prescribed a quantity of Dr Gregory's malodorous rhubarb tablets, he soon recovered and was able to take some interest in the Oliviers. 'I liked the Popham couple,' he told Henry. 'Noel is of course more interesting, but difficult to make out: very youthful, incredibly firm of flesh, agreeably bouncing and cheerful – and with some sort of prestige.'

At the end of the month the party broke up, and Lytton returned to London. 'Of course I've done not a stroke of work in these peregrinations and angoisses,' he admitted to Henry Lamb (24 September 1913). 'It's very annoying. I shall make for Lockeridge as soon as possible and sit down steadily there.' After a few days in Hampstead collecting together his belongings, he moved down to install himself at The Lacket where, feeling that his wanderings were now to be left behind, his long-cherished ambitions would at last be submitted to some practical test, and all his dreams of true eminence either made good or extinguished altogether.

26. Daughters of Sir Sydney (Lord) Olivier (1859–1943), civil servant, statesman, and at that time governor of Jamaica.

ELEVEN

The Lacket

This is an age whose like has never been
Since Jahveh made the world, and lo! 'twas green.
Through all the mouldy chronicle of Time
Scribbled in prose, or furbished up in rhyme,
Or in the pomp of monuments expressed
(Like some plain woman who is over-dressed).
Where shall we find, ye grim and dreary Powers
Of Human Folly, folly such as ours?
The bronze age and the iron age, we're told,
Were once; and was there once an age of gold?
Perhaps: but now no learning of the schools
Need we to know this age the Age of Fools.

Lytton Strachey (1915)

1
ALONE WITH A WIDOW

THE Lacket was a compact, romantic-looking, thatched cottage, rather isolated, and sheltering behind a huge box hedge, with a boulder-strewn hillside rising directly behind it.[1] A few hundred yards away lived the philosopher and mathematician A. N. Whitehead and his wife, with both of whom Lytton became very friendly. Although his tenancy was to last for one year only, he eventually stayed on until the end of 1915; and it was here that he wrote, besides a number of his best-known literary and biographical essays, two of the four portraits which make up *Eminent Victorians*.

After moving in during the first week of October, he was immediately taken charge of by Mrs Templeman – a 'discreet

1. 'Small' was the epithet Lytton used when describing the cottage. Maire Lynd, who stayed there, remembers it as having at least five bedrooms.

old lady', as Virginia Woolf described her, 'who is as noiseless as an elephantine kind of mouse'. To his relief this formidable old woman seemed entirely to comprehend all his wishes, and was especially reassuring on the matter of economy. He still had a little of the hundred pounds that Harry Norton had given him, and to this sum his mother had added a further hundred. With what he could earn from contributions to periodicals, he hoped to pay for sufficient free time in which to complete his *Eminent Victorians*. The solitude was, of course, comfortless at times – especially in the evenings; and Mrs Templeman, for all her massive qualities of discretion and practical competence, could be appallingly severe. 'She places the vegetables upon the table with a grimness ... an exactitude ...,' he complained to James (April 1914). 'When she calls me in the morning she announces the horrors of the day in a tone of triumph:– "Rain, as usual, sir." – "Oh, Mrs Templeman, Mrs Templeman!" – "Yes sir; old fashioned weather; that's what I call it." ' Otherwise the two of them got on very well, though Mrs Templeman evidently believed that the 'darkness' was bad for Lytton. 'When I observed that the darkness in London was worse,' he wrote to Hilton Young (9 January 1914), 'she said "Yes, sir, but then in London you have the noise" – to which no reply seemed possible.'

Yet despite the severities and non-sequiturs of his housekeeper, the bleakness of this winter in the country, and the recurrent incapacities that came upon him, Lytton was content. 'I wish the place were mine,' he told Henry Lamb (27 October 1913), 'that I might mould it nearer to my eyes' desire.' And he implored Hilton Young to have an 'owl stuffed with wings outspread, so that I may hang it up over my bed and confuse it with the Holy Ghost in my last moments'. To Duncan Grant he wrote (28 October 1913) explaining that 'I lead a singularly egotistical life here, surrounded by every luxury, waited on by an aged female, and absorbed completely in Eternal-Peace. In the intervals of my satisfaction I struggle to justify my existence by means of literary composition, but so far the justification has not been so convincing as might be wished.'

The main literary composition during these first winter months was not 'Cardinal Manning', but some minor pieces for the *New Statesman*, and, for the *Edinburgh Review*, his long literary essay on Stendhal. 'Henri Beyle', as this paper was called, had been commissioned by Harold Cox early in October as a reply to Lytton's previous application to write on Samuel Butler. The subject was not altogether agreeable to Lytton, since it necessitated, he felt, a return to the adjectival, flamboyant style of *Landmarks in French Literature*, as opposed to his new, more incisive biographical approach (which he nevertheless managed partly to incorporate). He feared that the contrived emphasis of his treatment might not retrieve the essay from ultimate tedium, but he had no hesitation about taking it on, and, having assembled his library at The Lacket, began in the third week of October reading through the whole of Stendhal's work. 'I am beginning to gird up my loins for the wrestling bout with Stendhal,' he announced (27 October 1913) after ten days of intensive reading; and by 10 November he was able to report that 'I have plunged into the writing of the Stendhal affair and find it far less unpleasant than I'd expected – in fact I'm so far enjoying doing it very much'.

Concurrently with this he had also dashed off a much shorter, lighter composition on the subject of toleration entitled 'Avons-nous changé tout cela?' His first notion had been to send it off to A. R. Orage of the *New Age*, but because he did not have that paper's address readily to hand, he dispatched it instead to J. C. Squire at the *New Statesman*. To his mingled pleasure and alarm, the article was immediately accepted for the sum of three guineas. 'As for the New Statesman,' he wrote to Lamb (17 November 1913), 'I am getting to loathe it; and the worst of it is I now seem to be in imminent danger of becoming a regular contributor to its pages. The fellow Jack Squire, who is its editor or sub-editor, is most unpleasant, and I am trying hard to pick a quarrel with him, so as to escape having anything further to do either with him or it.' In fact the quarrel between Lytton and Squire was not to break out for almost another five years, and in the meantime

Lytton continued to contribute infrequent articles, totalling about a dozen in all. In a number of these he is evidently spoiling for a fight, especially in his various pieces on toleration, which carry references to the Bible, for instance, that he felt sure *must* prove too strong for the editor, who, by demanding their excision, would show up his paper's fundamental spirit of intolerance, and provide him with a legitimate excuse to sever his connections with it. What actually happened was far less satisfactory. His contributions appeared with all their more audacious comments and implications perfectly intact, but marred by many smaller changes, omissions of quite trivial words or insertions of Squire's own, almost always fractionally inferior to the original text, and, though intensely irritating, never drastic enough to supply Lytton with a sufficiently high-principled reason for cutting off this small but valuable source of income.

Lytton's life at The Lacket was strictly regulated. Every morning, when not overpowered by illness, he wrote at his desk; every afternoon, when it was not raining, he would set off in a thick overcoat, gloves, scarf and earrings, to trudge through the desolate idyllic woods, whose gamekeeper, 'a grimy old fellow with a nice bare breast', would engage him at great length in talk about football; every evening he would either read – usually books involving the subject on which he was then working – or study manuals on the Italian language, or perform various muscular exercises designed to regulate his digestive system.

At week-ends he sometimes went up to London, staying either at Belsize Park Gardens or with the Bells in Gordon Square, and timing his visits to coincide with some interesting concert, art exhibition, lecture or theatre. One more irregular week-end he spent with the St Loe Stracheys at a spectacular house-party in Surrey, full of reactionary ambassadors and their ladies, of superior journalists and distinguished K.C.s, and garnished with immense meals of the choicest kind, and an exquisite footman. There was plenty of 'copy' for his letters, but, he decided, no discoverable intelligence or romance. The ambassador and his wife were, he told Pippa, 'the acme of unimportance'; and much of the conversation was taken in charge by Leo Maxse, 'a mere spider in mind and body', who was still raving obsessionally on about the Marconi scandal and discharging his venom against the cabinet.[2] Among the guests was a couple whom he was to get to know better once he himself was better known – the Colefaxes.[3] 'He is a dreadful pompous lawyer and politician with a very dull large face pétri with insincerity,' he wrote to Lamb (4 November 1913). '. . . She too is a thoroughly stupid woman.'

The unmitigated hostility of these observations indicates clearly what an awkward and unsuccessful figure Lytton still cut socially. In the fashionable, phoney world of the upper classes he was a complete nonentity. People who, a mere half-dozen years later, would entreat him to lunch or dine with them, now viewed him with unconcealed distaste or overlooked him altogether. And he returned their air of contemptuous, empty-headed superiority with scathing disdain.

Yet he could not suppress a growing desire to enter this extraordinary world, and be courted by it. These mediocre performances in society tended to disrupt his peace of mind, and 'the result of it all is that I'm now feeling singularly solitary,' he confessed to Ottoline (6 November 1913) on his return to The Lacket. 'But as I'm trying to work, it's so much the better.' At such hangover moments, the lack of human distractions deepened his gloom and the voice of duty would sound with particular asperity in his ear. Less disturbing in their after-effects were the week-ends when, instead of going

2. Leonard James Maxse, editor and proprietor of the *National Review*, was drawn into the Marconi affair through some articles written in his paper by W. R. Lawson which suggested that certain ministers in the Government were guilty of corruption. Maxse's statement before the Select Committee of the House of Commons was largely responsible for flushing out those ministers concerned and making them face public opinion. In due course he became the butt of the Liberal press, and himself highly excited and obsessional about the whole matter. See *The Marconi Scandal* by Frances Donaldson (1962).

3. Lady (Sybil) Colefax, a middle-class fashionable hostess and campfollower of the arts, who managed an ambitious social career with military self-discipline. Her husband, Sir Arthur Colefax, a pillar of the law, haunted her splendid entertainments like a smiling but silent spectre.

off himself, he invited down one or two of his friends. His guests during these first four months at The Lacket included James, Pippa and Pernel, Duncan Grant, Maynard Keynes and Henry Lamb, whose arrival exactly coincided with one of Lytton's more severe attacks of flu, so that 'he [Lamb] had to perform the functions of sick-nurse – which pleased neither of us'. Leonard Woolf also came down a couple of times, with reports that, though Virginia's condition was still so serious as to warrant constant attendance by a team of four nurses, the doctors were confident that in time she would fully recover. 'Poor Woolf!' Lytton wrote to Ottoline (4 October 1913). 'Nearly all the horror of it has been and still is on his shoulders. Ka gave great assistance at the worst crisis, but she is now in London. Apparently what started this attack was anxiety about her novel coming on top of the physical weakness. The Doctors say that all depends upon rest and feeding-up.' Leonard himself had by this time finished a second novel, the typescript of which he sent to Lytton early in the New Year. After carefully going over every page, Lytton came to the conclusion that he could not with sincerity recommend his friend to publish it. By nature, he felt sure, Woolf was not a novelist. Probably he ought to have been an administrator, in a fairly subordinate position – or possibly even a member of the Stock Exchange like the rest of his family. He was wonderfully nice, but a trifle lost, which made matters all the more difficult when he arrived down at The Lacket asking for a candid opinion on his typescript. 'He was very sympathique, as ever, but there were some thorny moments during the discussion of his novel,' Lytton admitted to Lamb (19 January 1914). 'I don't think the poor fellow is in his right assiette – though what the right one is I can't imagine. Perhaps he should be a camel merchant, slowly driving his beasts to market over the vast plains of Baluchistan. Something like that would I'm sure be more appropriate than his present occupations of Fabianising and novel-writing, and even than his past one of ruling blacks.'

So frequent were these guests to The Lacket that Mrs Templeman soon began to display alarming symptoms of disintegration. Before each new arrival, her conscience would totally lose its head and she would insist on sweeping all the chimneys, scrubbing all the floors and spreading a general air of ruin throughout the house. For a few weeks it looked as if she might succumb to a fit of apoplexy, and sink altogether under her load of self-imposed, unnecessary duties. But Lytton's tact and resourcefulness – qualities not popularly credited to him in his dealings with *hoi polloi* – eventually carried the day, and after several confidential chats, the handsome tip of a golden sovereign at Christmas, and the promise that whenever he was away her sister might come over from Newbury and stay at The Lacket, she seemed to muster new strength and a very real disaster was averted.

'I am enjoying myself very much here,' he wrote to his mother, summing up his life at The Lacket after two months (7 December 1913), 'and feel as if I should like never to move away. The solitude is complete and the weather (just now) appalling, but it doesn't seem to matter. My old woman looks after me very well and very economically. I try to write a certain amount every day, and the rest of the time is spent in eating, sleeping, walking and reading. In the evenings I struggle with Italian. My occasional wish is for a wife – but it is not easy to be suited in that matter.'

So many of his best laid schemes had previously come to nothing that he could now scarcely believe his good fortune. Daily he waited for some calamity to descend and wreck everything, but to his mild surprise 'it continues very idyllic here', he informed Ottoline (9 October 1913). 'Whoever thought that I should end my days alone with a widow?'

2

SCENES FROM POST-EDWARDIAN ENGLAND

For the first seven months of 1914, Lytton's life continued to conform to the same simple pattern of daily work at The Lacket, surrounded by his books and his detestable medicines, and interspersed with frequent stimulating sallies up to town.

One unlooked-for effect of residing in this rustic chastity was the change of attitude it engendered within him towards London itself. Only recently it had been somewhere from which to escape, a stale and unprofitable place that devitalized its inhabitants and impeded their ambitions. When, some years later, David Cecil asked him how he had spent his time in the metropolis, Lytton replied blankly: 'I walked about the streets, and sometimes I took a taxi.' Now, in the seclusion of emptiest Wiltshire, he was at times submerged by the most abject melancholia – a regurgitation, as he saw it, of the green-sickness of his youth. And with the onset once more of this shocking, but divine discontent, London became transformed into an exciting area where no encounter was impossible and every adventure was for the asking.

Such adventures as did come his way were inconclusive. 'After I left you I went to the Tube,' he recounted one incident to Lamb (20 February 1914), 'and saw there a very nice red-cheeked black-haired youth of the lower classes – nothing remarkable in that – *but* he was wearing a heavenly shirt, which transported me. It was dark blue with a yellow edge at the top, and it was done up with laces (straw coloured) which tied at the neck. I thought it so exactly your goût that I longed to get one for you. At last on the platform I made it an épreuve to go up to him and ask him where he got it. Pretty courageous, wasn't it? You see he was not alone, but accompanied by two rather higher-class youths in billycock hats, whom I had to brush aside in order to reach him. I adopted the well-known John style – with great success. It turned out (as I might have guessed) that it was simply a football jersey – he belonged to the Express Dairy team. I was so surprised by that I couldn't think what other enquiries I could make, and then he vanished.'

Fragmentary encounters of this kind helped, in some sense, to strengthen his resolve to excel at writing; for it was only on paper, he reflected, that he could carry things through to a successful conclusion. When it came to a platform, a black-haired youth and a football jersey, he failed manifestly to exhibit the sterling qualities of a man of action. London, however, continued to radiate an illusory aura, and if it provided no rhapsodical, consummating romances, there was always during his visits there plenty of breathless activity of a more humdrum sort. In January he went up and stayed with his family, who were then making preliminary arrangements to move from No. 67 to No. 6 Belsize Park Gardens. When not in conclave over this affair 'I flew from Square to Square, from Chelsea to Hampstead Heath with infinite alacrity,' he told Duncan Grant (6 February 1914). 'I even went to the Alpine Club.[4] I could not look much at the pictures there, as I found myself alone with [Nina] Hamnett,[5] and became a prey to the desire to pass my hand lightly over her mane of black hair. I knew that if I did she'd strike me in the face – but that, on reflection, only sharpened my desire, and eventually I was just on the point of taking the plunge when Fanny Stanley[6] came in and put an end to the tête-à-tête.'

Early in February he again went up to London, 'my excuse being that Swithin has just returned from Burmah,' he explained to Duncan Grant (6 February 1914), 'but the truth is that I can't resist Piccadilly – though how it's spelt I've never been able to discover.' Swithinbank, however, gave him a

4. The Second Grafton Group exhibition was being held at the Alpine Club Gallery, where Duncan Grant, Vanessa Bell and others were showing pictures.

5. As an art student Nina Hamnett (1890–1956) had been encouraged by Sickert who spotted in her drawings a fine talent that she later never quite succeeded in developing. Instead of becoming a great artist, she set herself up as a great cicerone to the art world of Paris and London and a leader of the *vie de bohème* which she described in her two volumes of autobiography, *Laughing Torso* (1935) and *Is She a Lady?* (1955). Among her many friends were Modigliani, Gaudier-Brzeska, who did a sculpture of her body (now in the Victoria and Albert Museum), and Roger Fry, who employed her – together with her husband Roald Kristian – in the Omega Workshops, and who painted her portrait (in the collection of Mrs Roger Diamond). Among her enemies was Aleister Crowley, the Beast No. 666, against whom she successfully defended herself in 'one of the most extraordinary trials of the first half of the 20th century' (John Symonds). She died in poverty.

6. 'Aunt Fanny Stanley', though not really an aunt, was a proverbial figure of a faithful elderly female relative, on the Grant side of the family.

magnificent lunch at Simpson's, with such quantities of Burgundy that he was ill for a week afterwards. He had not seen Swithin for nearly five years, and the change in his friend was very remarkable. They behaved at lunch almost like two strangers, and were quite unable to recapture their old intimacy. Was this the young man whom he, Lytton, had once thought so handsome, and with whom he had seriously contemplated falling in love? It seemed scarcely possible to him as he now sat regarding the 'very benevolent, medical man' lunching opposite him, so quiet, so respectable, so dazed. 'All youth gone,' he lamented in a letter to James (14 February 1914). ' – and so sad – so infinitely sad and gentle: I suspect some tragedy – or would suspect one if there was anything in his character to allow of such a thing. Perhaps he's simply become a Buddhist. As for talking to him, it was quite impossible, and he was pained by my get-up.'

Another old friend whom he met by chance that same week at the Savile Club was E. M. Forster, whom he seems to have found just as unsatisfactory as Swithinbank. 'We went all over London together,' he told James (3 February 1914), 'wrapped in incredible intimacy – but it was all hollow, hollow. He's a mediocre man – and knows it, or suspects it, which is worse; he will come to no good, and in the meantime he's treated rudely by waiters and is not really admired even by middle-class dowagers.'

Not all his engagements up in town were social. On the same day as he encountered Forster, Desmond MacCarthy had fixed up for him to lunch with a Mr Kenneth Bell 'half-wit and publisher',[7] at the Devonshire Club in St James's Street. 'It was a singular function,' he observed to James (3 February 1914), 'chiefly in my honour, as Mr Bell, the young and advanced partner of the old-fashioned firm of Bell, wished especially to get in touch with me. I accordingly thought it would please if I appeared in a fairly outré style – cord coat, etc. – and the result was an extreme nervousness on the part of Kenneth. However, he suggested that I should write one of

7. Kenneth Bell (1884–1951), Fellow of All Souls and of Balliol, who five years before his death was ordained a priest in the Church of England.

a new series of biographies of modern persons, to be written in a non-official manner; I suggested Cardinal Manning as a good subject; he appeared to be enthusiastic at the notion; but now I don't know (a) whether he really wanted it done by me, or (b) whether I really want to do it. I hope to find out when I interview him in a few days' time – if possible at his office; these club lunches with claret and kummel flowing through them in all directions don't make for lucidity.'

The second discussion took place ten days later at the Savile Club. On both occasions, though subjected to great pressure, Lytton could only be induced to propose schemes that amounted to slight variations of what he was already writing or planning to write. By this time he had been ruminating too long over his Victorian portraits to abandon them altogether; and he felt, in any case, too mentally exhausted to tackle some entirely fresh scheme of work. His real idea was to persuade Bell to forget his own project and fix up a contract for *Eminent Victorians*. For this second meeting he decided to adopt a very peevish, arrogant tone, in the hope that this would impress the publisher; but he was soon disarmed by the almost reverential manner in which he was received, and which brought to the surface his natural modesty. 'It's very queer how they're all after me so frantically,' he remarked to James (14 February 1914). 'I interviewed Mr Basil Williams at the Savile (he's the editor of the new Biographical Series) and he fairly crouched.[8] It was plain that the series – "Creators of the 19th Century" – would not suit me, so I was firm and resisted all his pleadings. He begged me to write on Victor Hugo, Pius IX, Ibsen, and I really forget how many others, but I only smiled mysteriously, and a great deal, and so left him. However, at tea, Mr Bell appeared and pretty well bowled me over with his bonhomie (B. Williams is a sad, cheerful, compact and strangely uninspired little man, I forgot to mention.) The result is that I was led to suggest a series of

8. Professor A. F. B. Williams (1867–1950), historian and barrister. He was the biographer of Cecil Rhodes and William Pitt, author of Volume XI of the Oxford History of England, *The Whig Supremacy 1714–60*, and editor of 'Makers of the 19th Century'.

19th century essays on great men, in one volume, which he (K.B.) eagerly seized upon — though so far the financial arrangements are in the vague.'

For some weeks these negotiations dwindled on, then finally broke off altogether; and Lytton was left still working at his volume of Victorian essays, but without a definite contract or a publisher. Would his *Eminent Victorians* ever attract *any* publisher? His doubts multiplied and stirred up a growing fear within him that the book might not appear in print for many years.

On the whole, Lytton's visits to London were made purely for pleasure. He would hurry off to the usual run of theatres, concerts and operas, and whenever possible went to hear the music of Mozart who, he declared after a performance of *Don Giovanni*, was 'the greatest artist that ever lived'. Some entertainment of a more unusual kind was provided by a meeting which he attended of *New Statesman* subscribers. This was held towards the end of April at the Kingsway Hall, and since he happened to be in town at that time Lytton turned up there out of simple curiosity. 'The so-called editor was "in the chair",' he told James, 'a most nauseous creature,[9] I thought — with Mr and Mrs Webb and B. Shaw on each side of him. I've no notion of what the point of the meeting was — no information of any kind was given, and I could only gather from some wails and complaints of the Webbs that it wasn't paying. B. Shaw made a quite amusing speech about nothing on earth. I'd no idea that the Webb fellow was so utterly without pretentions of being a gentleman. *She* was lachrymose and white-haired. Altogether they made a sordid little group. At the end there were "questions" from the audience — supposed to be addressed to the Editor qua Chairman, but the poor man was never allowed to get in a word. The three Gorgons sur-

9. The first editor of the *New Statesman* was Clifford Sharp, the other permanent members of the staff at this stage being Desmond MacCarthy (dramatic critic), J. C. Squire (literary editor) and Emil Davies (City correspondent). The paper, a brain-child of the Webbs, had been founded in 1913. Shaw, a part-proprietor, was expected to be the star contributor, his articles, the Webbs estimated, being likely to attract up to a thousand new readers.

rounding him kept leaping to their feet with most crushing replies.'

Most of Lytton's entertainment came in the form of evening parties. The spring and early summer months of 1914 were unusually gay, as if the atmosphere had been charged with something electric, imbuing all that went on with a miraculous lightness. Distinguished foreigners flocked to London, which seemed to be enjoying a season such as it had not known for many years. The new Russian ballets, the operas at Covent Garden, the social and sporting calendar appeared more spectacular than ever before. Everything moved with an odd ease and brilliance, gorgeously illuminated like the dying moments of a fine day before the sun sinks finally from sight.

Although there were many wild Bloomsbury parties, Lytton tended to dissociate himself from them in the belief that he now belonged to a world outside the Bloomsbury Group. Yet the dislike that he often expressed for these gatherings was partly an extension of his own self-dislike, and pointed to his real affiliation there. For the time being, however, he found more enjoyment in other social intercourse – at the bohemian celebrations, for example, provided by the Augustus John set. That May, John had moved into the vast square studio in Chelsea which he had had specially constructed for him; and it was here that he gave a magnificent all-night house-warming party in fancy dress, to which Lytton was invited. 'The company was very charming and sympathetic, I thought,' he wrote to James, ' – so easy-going and taking everything for granted; and really I think it's the proper milieu for me – if only the wretches had a trifle more brain. ... John was a superb figure. There was dancing – two-steps and such things – so much nicer than the waltzes – and at last I danced with him – it seemed an opportunity not to be missed. (I forget to say I was dressed as a pirate.) Nina Lamb was there, and made effréné love to me. We came out in broad daylight.'

But undoubtedly the most urbane sociality of these months was to be found at the *salon* in Bedford Square, which by this time had reached the height of its fame as a centre for artists and writers. Among the most frequent *habitués* besides Lytton himself were the Gilbert Cannans; the handsome, volatile, Jewish painter Mark Gertler; Stanley Spencer, tiny and uncivilized; Desmond MacCarthy, soporific, reclining on a peripheral sofa; Bertrand Russell, rather priggish and uncomfortable; Harry Norton, now pink and fat, but very bright; and, of course, Nijinsky ('that cretinous lackey') with whom Lytton had become thoroughly disenchanted, but who still enthralled Ottoline 'gaping and gurgling like a hooked fish'. Her friendly advances were by this time causing much merriment among her friends. For though she plied him constantly with her most sentimental attentions, Nijinsky remained inexorably unresponsive and uncomprehending. On one occasion the two of them were sitting together in a tiny inner room when Lytton entered the house. As he advanced down the drawing-room he overheard Ottoline's husky voice, with its infinitely modulated intonations, utter the words: 'Quand vous dansez, vous n'êtes pas un homme – vous êtes une idée. C'est ça, n'est-ce pas, qui est l'Art? . . . Vous avez lu Platon, sans doute?' – The reply was a grunt.

The principal guest at the largest, most glittering of these Bedford Square receptions was Asquith, the prime minister. This party, held early in May, represented Ottoline's last bid to secure an under-secretaryship for her husband, and might ultimately have proved successful had they not both embraced militantly pacifist convictions at the outbreak of the war three months later. The gathering itself was brilliantly successful. Lytton's head spun alarmingly round and round at finding himself pressed cheek by jowl with so many celebrated personages. Ottoline had warned him in advance that the prime minister was to be there, 'but I was rather surprised', he told James, 'to be rushed, the very minute I arrived into the dear man's arms. It was most marked; someone else whom he was talking to was scattered to the winds, and we were then planted together on a central sofa. He was considerably less pompous than I'd expected, and exceedingly gracious – talked about Parnell and such reminiscent matters at considerable length. I could see no sign of the faintest spark of anything out of the common in cet estimable Perrier Jouet. He seemed a pebble worn smooth by rubbings – even his face had a somewhat sand-papered effect. He enquired about my next book, and I gave him a sketch of it. At the end he said with slight pomp "Well, you have a difficult and interesting task before you." I said "*You* have a difficult and interesting task before *you*!" He grinned and said, "Ah, we do wha twe can, we do what we can," on which we parted, and I found myself involved in a tête-à-tête with the Lady Howard de Walden.[10] The company was most distinguished and the whole affair decidedly brilliant. Henry James of course loomed in the most disgusting way. The Raleighs were also there, and – very extraordinary – Sir M. Nathan . . .[11] Ottoline was in a vast gold brocade dress, and seemed remarkably at her ease, and in fact at moments almost tête-montée. In the middle of it all she fell upon me, and charged me with infidelity, breaking her heart, etc.'

In the political sphere it was then the height of the Ulster crisis, and Asquith had just dramatically taken over the War Office. His graciousness on this occasion struck Lytton as being partly that of a genuine good humour, and partly the professional manner of a man whose business in life it was at all times to create a favourable impression. Apart from discussing Lytton's writing they also talked about various public figures – Lord Randolph Churchill among others – and Asquith then turned the conversation back to Parnell who, he declared, was the most remarkable man he had known. Lytton wished later he had suggested that Gladstone was surely even more remarkable; then, after Asquith recounted how he had met Parnell in the Temple one morning when the divorce pro-

10. Margerita Dorothy van Raulte, who had married Lord Howard de Walden, the professional amateur sportsman and patron of the arts, the previous year.

11. Sir Matthew Nathan (1862–1939), civil servant and soldier, at this time chairman of the Board of Inland Revenue. He was later appointed governor of Queensland. In pristine days, he had been one of Dorothy Strachey's unsuccessful suitors.

ceedings had just become public and how Parnell had shown that he had no notion of the hubbub this would produce, the talk pausing a moment with a slight embarrassment, he got up, cordially shook Lytton's hand, and walked off into another room. The entire meeting had lasted about ten minutes. 'If I hadn't known who he was,' Lytton afterwards wrote of this encounter in an unpublished essay (May 1918), 'I should have guessed him to be one of those Oxford dons who have a smattering of the world – one of those clever, cautious, mediocre intelligences, who made one thank heaven one was at Cambridge. Two particulars only suggested a difference. His manner was a little nervous – it was really almost as if he was the whole time conscious, with a slight uneasiness, that he was the Prime Minister. And then, though his appearance on the whole was decidedly donnish – small and sleek and not too well made in the details – his hands were different. Small and plump they were too; but there was a masterfulness in them and a mobility which made them remarkable.'

Because Lytton could only feel relaxed with a single individual – and was therefore incomparably more eloquent in his correspondence than in his general conversation – it is easy to forget that in full company, however enjoyable and distinguished, he could still be refractory. His presence was felt by many acquaintances – even those he quite liked – to be coldly watchful. 'He doesn't say anything, except tête-à-tête,' Walter Raleigh wrote to Logan Pearsall Smith describing the personal impression he had received after seeing Lytton that June at Newington. 'I wish he would write a book called *Life Among the Man-Haters*, or *Out Against God*.'

In fact, during these weeks and months, Lytton was busy distilling some of this simmering animosity against God and man into his 'Cardinal Manning'. He laboured steadily and meticulously at this long essay, and his letters reveal something of the progress of his work, its complexities and amusements.

Lytton Strachey to Clive Bell, 22 February 1914

'I'm at present devoting 3 hours a day to Cardinal Manning, and as I'm not yet Voltaire I find there's precious little time left over for extraneous philanthropy.'

Lytton Strachey to Henry Lamb, 22 February 1914

'I sit here buried in books on Cardinals and Theologians, and am rapidly becoming an expert on ecclesiastical questions. For instance, I now know what Papal Infallibility means – or rather what it doesn't – the distinction is highly important. I think that dogmatic theology would make a much better subject for a Tripos than most. Fine examination papers I could set. – Discuss the difference between "definitionists" and "inopportunists". – Explain with examples the various meanings of "minimism". – Give a brief account of *either* Newman's attitude towards the Syllabus *or* Dollinger's relations with the Vatican Council. State clearly the interpretations put by (a) W. G. Ward, (b) Veuillot, (c) Dupanloup, upon the words "Ex cathedrâ". Doesn't it sound entrancing?'

Lytton Strachey to Henry Lamb, 14 March 1914

'I'm enjoying my Manning a good deal so far; the chief drawback seems to be that it's such a slow business. And of course I'm quite prepared to find when it's done that it's all a fantasia; but the only way of knowing that is to go through with it to the bitter end, and hope for the best.'

Lytton Strachey to Ottoline Morrell, 27 March 1914

'I'm trying to work, and even succeeding to some extent. My task is rather a strange one. I think it may have some vestiges of amusement in it – but it's difficult to say as yet. I won't, I fear, be quite as bright as the Chartreuse de Parme, though, in any case!'

When immersed in the actual process of writing, which stimulated his mind both imaginatively to construct cohesive literary patterns and journalistically to sharpen up interviews and conflicts and to embroider background settings, Lytton was happy at his work. But whenever he tried to evaluate 'Cardinal Manning' more dispassionately as a vehicle of his personal ambitions, to look at it as a fraction of the long journey he had undertaken in search of an uncertain Holy Grail, his vision dimmed and he grew impatient. The whole enterprise looked too improbable. Writing was such a solitary business; it was impossible for him to relate his work to the outside world, to judge its effect on other people, and it assumed at times an illusion of unreality. Besides, this exacting project might lie beyond his physical powers. 'If one had the thews of a bull,' he wrote to James that April, 'and the pen of a ready writer, one might get something done. As it is everything takes such a devil of a time. One has to sleep, eat, digest, take exercise – and after all that, one has to squeeze out one's carefully moulded sentences.'

His rate of progress on 'Cardinal Manning' was further decelerated by several other literary commitments over these months. At the beginning of the year he had applied again to Harold Cox asking whether he might write for him two articles, one on Dryden and the other on Byron. The reply was flattering but unspecific. His 'Henri Beyle' had been generously praised, and he was now asked to become a regular contributor to the *Edinburgh Review*; but no mention was made of Dryden and none of Byron. Six months later, however, he published in that paper the first of two long essays on Voltaire. Meanwhile he composed a couple of shorter pieces for the *New Statesman* – one of them a highly controversial reassessment of Matthew Arnold – and, as his very last contribution to the *Spectator*, a leading review of Constance Garnett's translation of *The Possessed*.

'A Russian Humorist', as this review was called, provides an eloquent testimony to the veneration in which he still held Dostoyevsky at this time. Not being the work of a writer of great linguistic subtlety like Chekhov or Gogol, Dostoyevsky's novels were all the easier to appreciate in translation, and had lately been gaining wide popularity in England. Lytton disapproved of the Constance Garnett versions. The first impact of Dostoyevsky had, of course, come to him some three years earlier, when he had read the novels in French. That first impact had lasted, possibly even strengthened, as the less well-known books came his way. He was particularly fascinated by the inspired psychological effects that were grafted on to a conventional, clumsily constructed plot. With their complex 'feel' of life, their fondness for the abnormal, these novels embodied a peculiar strangeness of form and spirit that greatly excited him. Beforehand he had believed, as he wrote in a *Spectator* review of 1908, that 'those writers succeed best who are least anxious to combine the conflicting elements in their material'. Dostoyevsky's example proved to Lytton the falsity of this earlier dictum, and had converted him to a more catholic and comprehensive point of view. So taken was he by Dostoyevsky's 'strong psychology' that he attributed concealed virtues to the often careless and conservative method of narration. The apparent lack of balance which characterized the Russian novelist's work was, he reasoned, an illusion produced by his unbounded genius, the interior presence of which gave each book a unique, if concealed, aesthetic coherence. 'The strange vast wandering conversations, the extraordinary characters rushing helter-skelter through the pages, the far-fetched immense digressions, the unexplained obscurities, the sudden, almost inconceivable incidents, the macabre humour with its extravagant exaggerations – all these things, which seem at first little more than a confused jumble of disconnected entities, gradually take shape, group themselves, and grow at last impressive and significant.'

A number of critics in recent times have alluded to what Professor C. R. Sanders calls 'the extremely important influence' of Dostoyevsky on Lytton's work, and especially on *Eminent Victorians*. There can be no doubt that, at the time of writing this book, he was greatly impressed by Dostoyevsky's originality in combining so many heterogeneous elements. But essentially the appeal was more emotional than technical. 'The frenzy of Dostoievsky', his abandonment of all tasteful artistic restraint and careful symmetry, acted upon him as upon other writers of the age with whom he had

little in common, T. S. Eliot and James Joyce, as a release
from the calm sobriety, the limiting, predictable common
sense of the great tradition of English literature. Dostoyevsky
commanded an unparalleled insight, Lytton believed, into the
workings of the human mind. At first sight it might appear
that the actual tenor of his own personality had little enough
in common with the tortured spirit of the great Russian
novelist. But these novels showed the unconscious processes
at work in all human beings and came to Lytton as a revelation. It was precisely because the events in Lytton's mind
were, in fact, underneath, very similar to Dostoyevsky that
the novels produced such an effect on him – and on his writing of *Eminent Victorians*. On the surface, the well-balanced
arrangement of his colloquial romantic style with its compact
classical construction owes nothing to the digressions and
prolixities of *The Idiot* or *The Possessed*. But Dostoyevsky's
extravagance, his exaggeration and comic fantasy (which
Lytton was the first critic to recognize), his untraditional
complexity and indifference to the commonplace, undoubtedly emboldened Lytton to experiment with the forms
of traditional biography, to mix the ingredients of drama,
irony and psychological innuendo after a fashion never previously attempted.

On the sixth and seventh days of each week Lytton rested
from his labours, and turned his attention to entertaining and
being entertained by his friends. One of his first week-end
visitors to the country was his landlord Hilton Young, bringing with him Desmond MacCarthy who, a few years earlier,
had himself rented The Lacket. 'Desmond is a great study,'
Lytton wrote to James (9 February 1914). 'I've never seen
anyone so extraordinarily incapable of pulling himself
together. He'll never write anything, I'm afraid, in that hopeless miasma. He rode eighteen miles yesterday with Hilton,
came back almost dead, and stretched his now vast bulk on a
chair in a stertorous coma. At last we somehow got him to
bed. He rose at 11.30 this morning, refused to have anything
for breakfast, and then ate the whole of a pot of marmalade
with extreme deliberation. He's wonderfully good-natured,

affable, and amusing, but there are moments when dullness seems to exude from him in concentrated streams.'

Other friends continued to besiege him at The Lacket throughout the spring and summer, including his brothers James and Oliver, Henry Lamb, Swithinbank, Harry Norton, and Leonard Woolf who stayed a full week. 'He has been having a nervous breakdown in a mild way,' Lytton told Lamb (12 March 1914), 'and seemed to want repose. He says he's now much better, and goes away on Saturday. Virginia is apparently all right now, and there are no nurses any more. I've been able to work in spite of his presence: but it's I fear going to be rather a long job.'

So Lytton's life at The Lacket ambled amiably on – supported by his friends on Saturdays and Sundays, and by Cardinal Manning, Dostoyevsky, Voltaire and others during the rest of the week. It was not an entirely smooth existence: cold, illness and the pangs of temporary solitude constantly confronted him. Yet he was never unhappy, since his work now gave this existence some sense of progress and direction. Of course he still had a long way to go, but there seemed no reason why this present, settled mode of living should not continue on its quiet passage indefinitely. After all those wandering, disordered years since Cambridge, what could possibly disturb the calm, sensibly variegated flow of his days, the simple pattern of dedicated labour and civilized entertainment?

But on 4 August, war was declared with Germany, and the last brilliant afterglow of Edwardian England flickered out for ever.

3

TWO TYPES OF PATRIOTISM

Much that is fundamentally misleading has been written of Lytton's attitude to the First World War. It is assumed by some that he was almost totally unaffected, and this view is *prima facie* sustained by previous synopses of his career. 'His activities', wrote Lord David Cecil in the *Dictionary of National Biography*, 'were not interrupted by the war of 1914–1918, for he was a conscientious objector.' For much of this time he remained living in the country, Cecil goes on to recount, preserved in a state of financial independence by his family and friends, who, together, sedulously subscribed to foster his delicate literary talent.

The implications of such telescopic sketches are very far removed from the truth. Besides affecting his literary work, war cast over his private life a deep shadow that coloured much of his writing, both published and unpublished. With his invalid health, there was absolutely no question at any stage of the war of Lytton being called up for active service, or even participation of a more subsidiary kind. Logically, therefore, the wisest course he could take would have been to cut himself off entirely from political and military affairs. Yet this he could not do. Painfully and unwillingly he found himself involved in the whole wretched business. It filled the horizon wherever he went, blighting his days and troubling his nights.

> Last night I dreamt that I had gone to Hell.
> I seemed to know the *milieu* pretty well.
> The place was crammed as tight as it would hold
> With men and hatred, folly, lust and gold.
> And lies? Ah, I'd forgotten: without fail
> Red hot for breakfast came *The Daily Mail*.
> Well, thought, they say, is free. I wish it were!
> Can you think freely in a dentist's chair?
> Then so can I, when, willing or unwilling,
> All Europe on my nerves comes drilling, drilling.
> I do my best; I shut my eyes and ears,
> Try to forget my furies and my fears,
> Banish the newspapers, go out of town,
> And in a country cottage settle down,
> Far from the world, its sorrow and its shame;
> But, though skies alter, still the mind's the same.[12]
> What comfort, when in every lovely hour
> Lurks horror, like a spider in a flower?

12. '*Coelum non animum*', the Strachey family's motto, comes from Horace – '*Coelum non animum mutant qui trans mare currunt*' – which

The inescapable anguish of this time was not the symptom of a bellicose form of patriotism. Far from it. Most patriots, while paying polite lip-service to the excellence of peace, welcomed the outbreak of war with chauvinistic rejoicing. Lytton's hatred of it was never assumed, but deeply felt; he was not excited by the fighting. Though he loved the English countryside dearly, feeling that he could never be happy living anywhere else in the world, he was not tempted to inflate this fondness into a fulsome national prejudice, an exclusive pride. 'On the whole I don't care much about England's being victorious (apart from personal questions),' he wrote to James (27 September 1914). ' – but I should object to France being crushed. Mightn't it be a good plan to become a Frenchman?'

France, to his mind, was the most civilized country in the world and therefore the one least likely to provoke a war. All war was a return to barbarism, and, in a modern world, all wars should be – *were* – avoidable. They plunged civilization back overnight into dark medievalism, away from the bright new age of enlightenment and detached toleration for which he had been quietly working, and whose dawn, not very long ago, he had so confidently proclaimed. In place now of these emergent virtues, warfare substituted insensitivity, injustice, cruelty, hypocrisy – vices that always flourished with much more frenzy and unreasonableness at home than at the front. And by this substitution, too, it disrupted at a blow all that made life worth living: art degenerated into infantile propaganda; friendships were callously wrenched apart.

Several of Lytton's friends were quickly infected by the mounting war fever. Throughout the country an unashamed howl went up for conscription, but the Liberal Government

Lytton translated for this line of his poem. This motto was subject to some variation. In the eighteenth century, when it was the fashion to get dinner services made in China, the Stracheys at Sutton Court sent orders to the East for a set to be made with the motto on each plate. The whole dinner service arrived eventually, inscribed COBLUM NON ANIMUM. Pieces of Coblum china still survive at Sutton Court.

remained firm and in an official statement in *The Times* of 15 August, Kitchener, newly appointed Secretary of State for War, announced that voluntary territorials were to be divided into two categories – those serving abroad and those at home. This announcement stressed the importance of home defence and made it clear that the Government 'does not desire that those who cannot, on account of their affairs, volunteer for foreign service, should by any means be induced to do so'.

Lytton himself seems to have believed that all physically fit intellectuals should be prepared to defend the shores of England, but with this reservation: no intellectuals were in fact physically fit. His highly personal views on military service were frankly set out in a letter which he wrote to James early that September. 'I think one must resist,' he explained, 'if it comes to a push. But I admit it's a difficult question. One solution is to go and live in the United States of America. As for our personal position, it seems to me quite sound and coherent. We're all far too weak physically to be of any use at all. If we weren't we'd still be too intelligent to be thrown away in some really not essential expedition, and our proper place would be – the National Reserve, I suppose. God has put us on an island, and Winston has given us a navy, and it would be absurd to neglect those advantages – which I consider exactly apply to able-bodied intellectuals. It's no good pretending one isn't a special case.'

At this stage of the war Bloomsbury was less resolutely pacifist than is popularly supposed. That September, Clive Bell, whose *Peace at Once* (1915) was to be publicly burnt by order of the Lord Mayor, wrote to James Strachey asking for information as to how to join the Army Service Corps or some other non-fighting unit, since his health prevented him from going into the fully combative forces. Duncan Grant immediately entered the National Reserve. Rupert Brooke spoke unceasingly of his intention to go to Belgium. 'I cannot see the use of intellectual persons doing this,' Lytton commented on hearing the news, 'as long as there are enough men in any case, and the country is not in danger. Home defence is another matter, and I think I should certainly train if I had the strength.' But of all his friends the one most violently caught up by the call to arms was, to his great grief, Henry Lamb. For weeks he had repeatedly threatened to join up, and then, after prolonged hesitation, enrolled as an assistant at Guy's Hospital – an odd result, Lytton reflected, of Austria declaring war on Serbia. 'He's so fearfully undependable,' he sorrowfully complained to James (27 August 1914). 'Also his words have no connection with his feelings, nor his acts with anything; and he's constitutionally incapable of constancy. ... It seems to me that really – from any point of view – it's grotesque for a person of his health to go into the army: and I don't think this has been sufficiently emphasised. I hope to goodness he'll get fixed into something fairly harmless before long, as otherwise there'll always be this terror.'

Despite the columns of militant journalism that were every day being poured out in the press, Lytton did not believe that the feeling among ordinary men and woman in the country was especially warlike. He blamed the newspapers – particularly those of Lord Northcliffe – for deluding credulous people like Henry Lamb who did not know their own mind, and for trying to whip up a blind, evil animosity against the Germans. Disregarding the press, the condition of things seemed perfectly calm during these first weeks. In the remoteness of the country there was no detectable change at all, but within London it was obvious from the grave faces of the people in the streets that something grim was happening. Their expressions denoted no intoxication, no lust for national conflict, but sorrow and despondency. 'So far as I can make out there isn't the slightest enthusiasm for the war,' Lytton reported to Dorothy Bussy (21 August 1914). 'I think the public are partly feeling simple horror and partly that it's a dreadful necessity. But I think there will be a change when the casualties begin – both in the direction of greater hostility to the Germans and also more active disgust at the whole thing. Though of course a great deal will depend on the actual turn of events.'

Lytton tended at this stage to dissociate himself from the

more belligerent pacifists, not so much because he disagreed with what they said, but because he believed their general fulminations, directed for the most part against the Foreign Secretary, Sir Edward Grey, to be a bad error of tactics. 'Those anti-Grey people are really too senseless,' he wrote to James (18 August 1914). 'Can't they see that they do nothing at this moment if they appear as pro-Germans? The only hope is to appear anti-German and also pro-peace. The more they worry Grey the more rigid he'll become. I agree that the Japanese and Polish affairs are very bad – especially the latter, it seems to me. I didn't expect those Muscovites would show their hand so soon. That manifesto was a wonderful piece of blatant hypocrisy. Is it possible that the Poles will be such fools as to put their faith in the Tsar? Also won't it be plain pretty soon even to E. Grey that the war's being run for the aggrandisement of Russia? I don't believe the English public would stand that.'

The English public, Lytton considered, should be stirred up about peace. Instead of wasting energy blaming the Government, as Bertrand Russell was busy doing in the *Nation*, intelligent people ought to institute a Stop the War party in the cabinet, backed by public opinion. Far from canvassing this support, Russell's passionate denunciations were, in Lytton's view, wantonly alienating the populace. Nevertheless, there remained a residuum of fundamental good sense about people's attitude to the war which he found heartening. 'I haven't seen anyone,' he wrote to James (16 August 1914), 'who hasn't agreed on the main lines – viz: that we should take nothing for ourselves, and insist on ending it at the earliest possible moment.'

There seems little doubt that in his interpretation of the public's feeling at large Lytton was being too optimistic. In the early days of most international wars, the word 'peace' is likely to fall on deaf ears, and certainly never stimulates the popular imagination. Before the carnage gets under way, the idea of war is simple and inspiriting, not horrific. Though it is true that Bertrand Russell's activities resulted in more personal hardship than public good, Lytton's orderly, democratic schemes were equally ineffectual, for in order to change the *status quo* you must unfortunately break the laws that barricade it. The House of Commons would have had no debate at all on the question of England entering the war had not Philip Morrell courageously got to his feet and made a protest. His speech, by all accounts the finest he ever made, did no good and put an end to his political career – though nothing had so become that career as his leaving of it. 'I can never forget seeing him standing alone,' Ottoline noted in her diary (3 August 1914), 'with nearly all the House against him, shouting at him to "Sit down!" '

Momentarily, even Lytton himself would feel the faint vibration of war fever, instantly to be checked and objectified by his intelligence. Yet feeling it, he understood something of its appeal, and the force with which it was soon surging through the country, unerringly picking upon the female sex and those whom age exempted from service. 'I walked into Marlborough to-day,' he wrote to James (18 August 1914), 'and found there the news of the continued French advance in the Vosges, and the "confusion" of the German army. Is this possibly the beginning of a great turning movement? It is appalling to have to *wish* for such horrors – but now it's the only way.

'. . . . Yesterday I felt for the first time a desire to go out and fight myself. I can understand some people being overcome by it. At any rate one would not have to think any more.'

For the most part, however, the war affected him as a personal tragedy. One of his sisters was in Germany and he was worried about getting her out. But when Evelyn Whitehead advised him to appeal to the British ambassador in Germany, he was nonplussed. 'But how can I?' he protested in his most penetrating voice. 'I have never met him.'

On a more public level he was equally incredulous. He followed the news carefully, growing more amazed and disgusted at each new communiqué and report. His political attitude in these early days of the war is nicely caught and summed up in a letter he wrote (21 August 1914) to Dorothy Bussy, after reading through a macabre White Paper that reproduced the official dispatches which had passed between Sir Edward Grey and the ambassadors. 'It's like a puppet-show, with the poor little official dolls dancing and squeaking their official phrases, while the strings are being pulled by some devilish Unseen Power. One naturally wants to blame somebody – the Kaiser for choice – but the tragic irony, it seems to me, really is that everyone was helpless. Even the Austrians were no doubt genuinely in terror of the whole regime being undermined by Slavism, and the Russians couldn't allow the Austrians to get hold of the Balkans; the crisis finally came when the Germans found out that the Russians were secretly mobilizing – that frightened them so much that the war party became supreme, and all was over. The real horror is that Europe is not yet half-civilized, and the peaceful countries aren't strong enough to keep the others quiet.'

4

BUSINESS AS USUAL

For the time being Lytton continued his quiet existence at The Lacket, 'living the life of a complete St Anthony', as he described it to Ottoline (24 October 1914), 'with Mrs Templeman in the role of the Queen of Sheba – and I can't say she plays the part with conviction'. On most evenings now he would spend a solitary hour or two, crouched over the fire 'knitting mufflers for our soldier and sailor lads,' he informed Clive Bell, 'but I expect that by the time I've finished them the war will be over, and they'll be given to Henry and Duncan'. Acknowledging the possibility of the country being overrun by the enemy, and feeling that at all costs it was essential to be ready with words of propitiation, he gave up Italian and began to take lessons in German.

For the next four years, of course, there was to be no more travelling abroad to France, or Italy, or even Sweden; but his perpetual oscillation between Wiltshire and the metropolis went on much as before. In London, there were still the Thursday evening parties at Bedford Square, where the pressure of worry and unhappiness could be relieved for a few hours in the company of other sympathetic artists and writers. To assist in the pretence that things were otherwise than they were, to liberate them from themselves and from their cares, the guests at these parties would robe up in fancy dress and, while Philip Morrell played Hungarian dances or fiery Russian ballet music at his pianola, throw themselves into fantastic dances. 'Now and then,' recalled Ottoline, 'Lytton Strachey exquisitely stepped out with his brother James and his sister Marjorie, in a delicate and courtly minuet of his own invention, his thin long legs and arms gracefully keeping perfect time to Mozart – the vision of this exquisite dance always haunts me with its half-serious, half-mocking, yet beautiful quality.'

There were also the Bloomsbury parties to which Lytton had now started going once again. One of the most spectacular of these affairs, which conveys the peculiar flavour of them all, was arranged at 46 Gordon Square by Clive and Vanessa Bell. After listening to some Mozart played by Adila and Jelly D'Arányi (who, as Hungarians, were looked upon with hostile suspicion by most Englishmen, but to whom Bloomsbury, for this reason, was now particularly hospitable) the guests all went upstairs to witness a performance of the last scene from Racine's *Bérénice*, acted by three huge puppets eight feet tall, painted and cut out of cardboard by Duncan Grant.[13] The words of the play were declaimed solely by members of the Strachey family, whose fearful Gallic mouthings before 'several eminent frogs' were as remarkable in their way as the puppets themselves.[14]

At moments the whirl of London gaiety was almost too extreme, the ingenuity needed to conjure forth these high

13. 'We like Duncan Grant very much,' D. H. Lawrence wrote to Ottoline Morrell (27 January 1915). 'I *really* like him. Tell him not to make silly experiments in the futuristic line, with bits of colour on a moving paper. Other Johnnies can do that. Neither to bother making marionettes – even titanic ones. But to seek out the terms in which he shall state his whole ...'

14. A rather different account of a second showing of this play, performed before an English audience, is given by David Garnett in *The Flowers of the Forest* (1955), pp. 22–3.

1. The Strachey Family. *Back Row*: Pippa, Dorothy, Richard, Oliver;
Middle Row: Ralph, Lytton, Lady Strachey (holding Elinor's daughter
Frances), Sir Richard (with Marjorie between his knees), Elinor
(holding her daughter Elizabeth); *Front Row*: Pernel (with racket) and
Elinor's son, William

2a. Mark Gertler

2b. Henry Lamb

2c. Roger Senhouse

2d. Gerald Brenan

2e. Bernard Penrose

2f. David Garnett

3a. Raymond Mortimer, Frances Marshall,
Dadie Rylands

3b. Ottoline Morrell

4a. The Lacket

4b. The Mill House, Tidmarsh: painting by Carrington

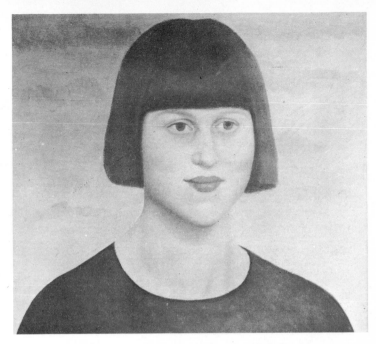

5a. Carrington: a portrait attributed to Mark Gertler

5b. Duncan Grant and Maynard Keynes

6. The Banana Tree: facsimile of a letter (written probably late in 1916) from Carrington to Lytton

7a. Carrington as a
Slade student: from a
design by Albert
Rutherston, 1915

7b. Lytton and
Carrington at Ham
Spray

8a. Lytton and Marjorie Strachey playing chess

8b. Lytton Strachey by Carrington

spirits too preposterously far-fetched. Practical jokes abounded. One of the most skilful was successfully played by Duncan Grant on Lytton himself. At breakfast one morning, while he was staying with his family in Hampstead, he received through the post a poem in French purporting to come from a rather taciturn French actor named Delacre, a man whom he had met at several of Ottoline's parties and whose conversation seemed to consist entirely of long, sombre stories, usually beginning: 'Figurez-vous, mon cher ...' This poem, composed in rhymed couplets, implied that the writer had recently seen Lytton in some extremely compromising situation. It was inscribed on a single sheet of paper, in ominous, anonymous capital letters.

> SI UN VIEUX
> VEUT BAISER DANS LA RUE
> UN JEUNE HOMME
> VAUT MIEUX
> PRENDRE UN FIACRE
> AVANT QU' APRES
> TON AMI DELACRE
> DEMEURE TOUT PRES
> DE KNIGHTSBRIDGE CHER MAÎTRE?
> CA BIEN PEUT ETRE.

Although he was quite honestly at a loss as to what indiscretion Delacre was claiming to have observed, Lytton felt terrified that the story might gain currency with his friends and that he would quickly become the butt of their slanderous humour. His imagination began to run away with him. Perhaps, once started, the rumour would spread far beyond the immediate circle of Bloomsbury. Already he could see the garish newspaper headlines – 'Astonishing Accusation!' In panic he rushed round at once to Delacre's hotel, and implored him not to show it to anyone.

What subsequently took place Lytton confided to David Garnett at tea that same afternoon. 'Delacre had then behaved in a most extraordinary and alarming manner,' David Garnett recounts. 'He had listened to Lytton's little speech without making any comment whatever. He had then excused himself and left the room. After waiting three-quarters of an hour Lytton had asked a waiter to find Delacre and had been told that he had left the hotel. Lytton was completely baffled by this behaviour and felt that he had not improved matters by his *démarche*.'

After listening with great amusement to Lytton's account of this strange imbroglio, David Garnett read the lines again and pointed out that it was highly improbable that M. Delacre, who was presumably a vain as well as a serious actor, should select the word *fiacre* as a rhyme to his own name. 'You don't think that Duncan wrote it by any chance?' he hazarded.

Lytton stared in dismay. The notion had briefly occurred to him, but he had dismissed it, being unable to believe that Duncan was capable of such fiendish cleverness. The French seemed so idiomatic; and it rhymed, too, so ingeniously. But now, hearing the very same suspicion voiced by David Garnett, he suddenly recognized it as the obvious explanation.

'What, that monster!' he exclaimed. 'Of course! He's a devil! I believe if the truth were known all the preposterous predicaments in the Universe might be traced back to him.'

To all appearances therefore the Bloomsbury milieu was the same as ever; but appearances were misleading. Beneath the forced-up gaiety and manufactured high spirits there lay a darker side. This gloom was soon deepened by news of the first fatalities. 'For myself I am absolutely and completely desolated,' Maynard Keynes wrote to him from King's (27 November 1914). 'It is utterly unbearable to see day by day the youths going away first to boredom and discomfort and then to slaughter. Five of this College, who are undergraduates or who have just gone down, are already killed, including to my great grief Freddie Hardman, as you may have seen from the papers.' Lytton had seen Hardman only a month or two earlier at one of Ottoline's parties. 'I think what the Greeks meant by that remark of theirs about those who die young was that they escape the deterioration of growing old; and perhaps if Freddie had gone on living he could hardly have gone on being so nice,' he wrote in his reply to Keynes (1 December 1914). 'But I'm afraid this reflection isn't much of a consolation to you.'

The war also put an end to Lytton's intimacy with Henry Lamb, who, after joining the R.A.M.C., was sent abroad to serve in France – where he was awarded a Military Cross – then to Macedonia and Palestine. For a while their flow of correspondence trickled on, but by the end of 1915 it had ceased altogether; and after the war they met only occasionally. There was no one, during these war years, who really commandeered Lamb's special place in Lytton's affections. He was always entering into trivial romantic affairs – 'a violent, short, quite fruitless passion' for the twenty-one-year-old painter Geoffrey Nelson, for example, and a romantic affection for Ted Roussell, a young plough-boy from Sussex, who enlisted in 1917 and was killed in the last week of the war[15] – but these attachments, though sometimes highly-charged, were of little lasting significance and merely reproduced on a greatly reduced scale the lineaments of his more serious intimacies, those that created in themselves some precedent, some extension to the emotional pattern of his life.

Something of a new variation in this pattern did gradually come about, however, at this time. This was the emergence of a dual, half-reciprocated relationship that comprised in part ordinary affectionate friendship, and in part homosexual flirtation. On the whole, it was a happy development for Lytton. Two men in particular of whom he soon grew especially fond were Francis Birrell and David ('Bunny') Garnett, themselves very close friends. Both were younger than himself, but he did not idolize them as he had Thoby Stephen, Duncan Grant, Henry Lamb or even Sheppard. He rejoiced in their company, and with each of them felt a warm affinity, though his fond-

---

15. 'Dear Ted,' Lytton wrote to him on 13 November 1918, 'I wonder how you are. I haven't heard from you for a long time – and I hope you are well and flourishing. Now that the war's over, I expect you'll be coming back quite soon – which I daresay you won't be sorry for. Let me hear from you when you have time to write. Always your friend, L. Strachey.' This letter was returned to Lytton, its envelope marked 'Deceased'.

ness was seldom without some austere qualifications. 'I think he's a nice fellow at bottom,' he wrote of Francis Birrell to James (21 January 1915), 'but the overlaying paraphernalia are distinctly trying. He seems a sort of secondary Clive – and in the Dostoievsky style, half knows it.' While the innocent, bumptious Birrell chattered on so inexhaustibly, Garnett would remain exasperatingly silent. He enunciated his thoughts with a sort of rustic slowness and deliberation, his speech being pock-marked with 'ghastly pauses', as Lytton once complained to Roger Senhouse (2 February 1929), ' – each long enough to contain Big Ben striking midnight – between every two ... words.' Nevertheless, Lytton quickly developed an even closer friendship with him than with Birrell, a friendship which did much to lighten the burden of these war years. 'No, the world is not agreeable,' he wrote to James six months after meeting Garnett (11 June 1915). 'And then again I think of dear Bunny – and the fact that such a person should exist in it fills me with delight. Charming!'

It was Francis Birrell who in December 1914 had introduced Lytton to David Garnett. That Christmas, Lytton held a large party at The Lacket. Daphne and Noel Olivier, James Strachey and Duncan Grant came down to stay with him in the cottage, while Birrell and Garnett took rooms at a local inn. David Garnett has given a description of this first meeting with Lytton and of his impressions over this holiday, which vividly evokes the peculiar atmosphere of the place. 'Lytton was tall and rather emaciated,' he recalled, 'with a reddish beard and lank dark hair which hung in a long lock over his forehead and was cut off squarely, in pudding-basin fashion, at the back of his head. His nose was large with a high bridge; he wore spectacles and was obviously rather short-sighted. I was struck first of all by his gentleness and his hospitality. Then I could see he was very much alive and very responsive. That evening the response may sometimes have concealed boredom, for Lytton was easily bored and the prospect of Christmas with two young women in the house – one of whom often spoke in tones of indignant emotional idealism – may have seemed rather appalling. James had let him in for them, and his curiosity and affection for Frankie [Birrell] had let him in for the shy, but good-looking hobbledehoy he had brought with him.'

On Christmas Day, David Garnett continues, the animal spirits of the low-brow members of the party got out of hand, and he and Daphne Olivier, after exchanging a wild glance, dived into the soft, round, springy box hedge which encircled the garden. Noel Olivier, Francis Birrell and eventually Duncan Grant followed them. But their sport was checked by the sudden appearance of their disconcerted host, who, in high-pitched and despairing tones, forbade them to continue. 'We realised', wrote Garnett, 'that Lytton was really a little upset and, sorrowfully, we desisted and for the rest of the day accepted Strachey canons of behaviour, though some of us passed up our plates for second helpings of turkey and plum pudding.

'Once again I was struck by the rigidity of the Strachey outlook. We had to conform to Strachey views and Strachey habits: the Stracheys would not even try to pretend to adapt themselves to manners or customs which were not their own.'[16]

This brand of forbidding, kill-joy severity, Garnett soon discovered, was only one side of Lytton's moral attitude, which, on a plane less rowdy and athletic, expressly sanctioned certain tentative deviations in human intercourse. Garnett, whose career was perhaps remarkable for the multitude and ambivalence of its emotional experiences rather than the depth of feeling that these experiences engendered, was fascinated by this unusual blending of strictness and unorthodox condonation, and soon made Lytton into something of a moral mentor.

That evening, after his intervention over the box-hedge incident, Lytton read out to his guests, assembled round the fire after tea, 'Ermyntrude and Esmeralda'. The witty, rather scan-

16. David Garnett appears to have misinterpreted Lytton's attitude on this occasion. He was not being old-maidish over their behaviour, but was concerned by the damage they were doing to a fine box hedge over two hundred years old.

dalous manner of this story reminded Garnett of Laclos's *Les Liaisons Dangereuses*. It was the kind of *risqué* theme which Lytton enjoyed exploring in various unpublished dialogues, narratives, poems and short stories, and which, though intended specifically for the amusement of his friends, occasionally came near to compromising his friendly relations with a few of them, notably Clive Bell. But on this occasion he was surrounded by an entirely appreciative audience, and David Garnett was so especially receptive to the message contained in this particular story that he proclaimed himself to be there and then converted for the rest of his potent life into a confirmed and industrious *libertine* – 'that is a man whose sexual life is free of the restraints imposed by religion and conventional morality'.

5

UNDERTONES OF WAR

The war, though it sharpened Lytton's critical faculties, acted as a giant encumbrance to the everyday business of writing. The magnitude of world events burst through and disrupted his concentration, and, with its cargo of painful emotional disentanglements, seemed at first to threaten the realization of all his carefully laid literary plans. 'Namur is terrible,' he wrote to James (August 1914). 'I suppose it's certain now it will be a long business. As for my private hopes, they're almost gone.'

When he did manage to settle down to some literary composition, such as 'Voltaire and England', he found it, as he told Henry Lamb (5 September 1914), 'a considerable sedative'. But by and large he felt in no mood for writing, and the Manning biography, which should have been finished by the end of August, gave him great difficulty. Twenty-seven foolscap pages of it had to be entirely rewritten, and it was not in fact completed until shortly before Christmas. His letters to his friends and family during this autumn contain repeated avowals of his determination to 're-attack the Cardinal', but it was only in the New Year that he could actually show them the fruit of his labours. Their response was immediately gratifying – all the more so because he had not expected everyone to care for it. 'I have seldom enjoyed myself more than I did last night, reading Manning,' Virginia Woolf wrote to him (January 1915). 'In fact I couldn't stop, and preserved some pages by force of will to read after dinner. It is quite superb – It is far the best thing you have ever written, I believe – To begin with, what a miracle it is that such a group should have existed – and then how divinely amusing and exciting and alive you make it. I command you to complete a whole series: you can't think how I enjoy your writing.'

Much fortified and encouraged by this and other similar letters of appreciation, Lytton now embarked on the second of his eminent Victorians.[17] Exactly one year ago he had read Sir Edward Cook's official biography of Florence Nightingale, telling his mother at the time (15 January 1914) that although the lady with the lamp was certainly a fascinating woman, he did not really like her, and that, in his opinion, her stature was not truly great. Having turned down the offer of writing this book himself, he was particularly interested to see the kind of woman whom Edward Cook had depicted. 'I have just been reading the book I might have written – the Life of F. Nightingale,' he informed James (16 January 1914). 'I'm glad I didn't, as I couldn't have satisfied anybody. She was a terrible woman – though powerful. And certainly a wonderful book might have been made out of her, from the cynical point of view. Of course the Victorian Age is fairly reeking all over it. What a crew they were!'

From the cynical point of view, he now believed that he might make a wonderful short biography of Florence Nightingale, compressing the mass of diluted information in the

17. 'Send me your life of Manning at once or I shall go mad,' E. M. Forster wrote to him (17 May 1915). 'I will disinfect it.' A fortnight later he wrote again. 'I will return the Cardinal when I have read him again – a habit you censured some 12 years back. Meanwhile I wish you would send me Mademoiselle Nightingale and some short witty stories. I am certain you have some – they will be quite safe.'

official Life into a closely wrought solid and dramatic unity. 'I'm beginning to attack Florence Nightingale,' he announced to Henry Lamb (3 January 1915). 'I want it to be very much shorter than the Cardinal, which will involve rather a different method, I think. I'm not quite sure whether the damned thing will be possible, but I hope for the best.'

The preparation and actual writing of 'Florence Nightingale' occupied Lytton for almost six months. His correspondence over the first half of 1915 is sprinkled with references to this work which tell of the arduous growing pains of its composition and his own changing moods and difficulties.

Lytton Strachey to Henry Lamb, 12 January 1915

'Florence Nightingale is progressing. I wish I didn't dislike hard work quite so much. But of course it might be worse − I think it's chiefly the starting that is so unpleasant.'

Lytton Strachey to Ottoline Morrell, 11 February 1915

'I find Florence N. rather a hard nut to crack, but I'm struggling with extraordinary persistence. Don't you think I've become wonderfully industrious lately?'

Lytton Strachey to Virginia Woolf, 28 February 1915

'I am in rather a state just now with Miss Nightingale, who is proving distinctly indigestible. It's a fearful business − putting pen to paper − almost inconceivable. What happens? And how on earth does one ever manage to pull through in the end?'

From this time on there was no question of the 'possibility' of writing on Florence Nightingale, only of the difficulty. For six weeks of the spring he was laid up with 'influenza and its consequent dilapidations', and wrote nothing. Then, in the early summer, he re-applied himself to the biography with a desperate and concentrated energy.

Lytton Strachey to Ottoline Morrell, 8 June 1915

'It is very· agreeable here − not *too* hot (it never is!) − a cool breeze perpetually blowing. I spend all day sitting out writing my étude of Florence Nightingale, in which I'm at present completely involved – I hope to get the wretched thing done before very long though.'

Lytton Strachey to James Strachey, 11 June 1915

'I've been getting into a frantic state with F. Nightingale – working incessantly until my brain spun round and round, and then in its usual dim unexplained way my health went groggy, and yesterday Lady S. arrived.

'... The F.N. affair has been much more terrific than I could have expected. I imagined originally that I'd be able to do the whole thing in a fortnight. It's still not nearly done; and I'm in terror lest after all it should turn out quite illegible – I imagine Eddie Marsh trying to read it and saying afterwards, "It bored me stiff." I feel there would be no appeal from that.'

Lytton Strachey to Henry Lamb, 13 June 1915

'I am submerged by Nightingale, which has turned out a fearful task. I'm now within sight of the end, though, I hope.'

Lytton Strachey to Ottoline Morrell, 23 June 1915

'F. Nightingale has at last been polished off, I'm glad to say. So I'm feeling very gay and chirpy—'

Illness and the dramatic events of the war continued to undermine his progress, the first making him 'feel as if my brain was lying perdu somewhere far away under the dust-heaps of accumulated generations', the second giving him the sense of living on a perpetual volcano. Yet both, while depriving him of much of the initial urge to write, also helped to pin-point his concentration once he had embarked on his work. At times, however, the political and military calamities would still split through and shatter this literary concentration. He was appalled by the lurid suggestions he read in some newspapers, notably *The Times*, about the possibility of forming a coalition Government. His head buzzed with unanswered questions. Could the rumours be true? And if they

were, what did it all mean? Why should the cabinet contemplate such a move? Had they made some ghastly blunder,
for which they were being coerced to pay this price in order
to preserve the Opposition's silence? Or had they come to the
conclusion that the war was hopeless without conscription?
If *that* were true, then all was lost, and the country would be
engulfed in a jungle of militarism. The prospect was really
frightful. Already there had been a sinister augury of the rising
mood in recent disgraceful riots directed against civilians of
Germanic extraction still living in England. The most alarming
feature of these incidents had been, perhaps, the conduct of
the authorities who, in effect, encouraged them and then
made use of them as an excuse for further maltreatment of
those miserable people. 'Doesn't it all make one want to go
and bury oneself somewhere far, far away – somewhere so far
away that even the Times will never get to one?' he asked
Ottoline. ' "Où me cacherai? Fuyons dans la nuit infer-
nale!" '

But more terrible than the political uncertainty at home
was the awful, the unbelievable finality of the news from the
front. So much seemed, abruptly, to have come to an end. In
June, his fellow Apostle Ferenc Békássy was killed in the Bu-
kovina after only two days' fighting. Two months earlier
Rupert Brooke had died. Owing to his failure to maintain
amicable relations with Brooke, the news of this particular
tragedy affected him more deeply than any other. So much of
his past was raked up by it. After their pointless estrangement,
the thought of Brooke had haunted Lytton. 'I feel his state is
deplorable,' he had written to Ottoline (22 October 1912),
'and something ought to be done to bring him back to ordinary cheerful ways of living. I hope to see James next week-
end, and talk about it. I feel it particularly because once when
I was very low – in health and spirits – Rupert helped me a
great deal, and was very charming. And then besides, how
wretched all those quarrels and fatigues are! Such opportunities for delightful intercourse ruined by sheer absurdities!
It is too stupid. "My children, love one another" – didn't
Somebody, once upon a time, say that?'

That Rupert should have ended his life on such an un-satisfactory note, with all the old quarrels and intrigues still unresolved, struck Lytton with deep pathos, and brought home to him with added force the monstrous futility of human affairs. 'I suppose by the time you get this you will have seen about Rupert's death,' he wrote to Duncan Grant (25 April 1915). 'The news came yesterday: apparently it was owing to some illness or other. He was put into a French ship, and taken to Lemnos, where he died. James is a good deal shattered, and altogether it's a grim affair. It was impossible not to like him, impossible not to hope that he might like one again; and now. ... The meaninglessness of Fate is intolerable; it's all muddle and futility. After all the pother of those years of living, to effect – simply nothing. It is like a confused tale, just beginning and then broken off for no reason, and for ever. One hardly knows whether to be sorry even. One is just left with a few odd memories – until they too vanish.

'Poor Eddie [Marsh] is quite wrecked – and busy writing an obituary notice for the Times.'

He now felt so strongly about the international situation that it was most sensible, he reasoned, not to discuss it with anyone, and if possible not to think of it himself. He opened *The Times* every morning with dread; and in the evenings tried to immerse himself in books which had little or no association with the war – the *Memoirs of Lady Hester Stanhope*, H. G. Wells's *Boon*, and *The Voyage Out* by Virginia Woolf. It seemed to him that as the years went by he was growing increasingly sensitive, instead of gradually turning, as he had once half-humorously predicted, into a solid and heartless rock of a man. At the same time he remained constitutionally incapable of wearing his heart on his sleeve for daws to peck at, and so had to seek solace from the ferment of this vulnerable inner sensitivity in hard work. The pains and anxieties of writing could obliterate for a time the greater horrors of public outrage. But the pace of such work was often agonizingly tedious. 'The slowness of my work is alarming,' he had written to Henry Lamb while still struggling with 'Florence

Nightingale' (2 February 1915). 'I fully intend to do another play when this affair is finished, and after that I daresay a novel – by which time, at the present rate of progress, I shall be 75.'

The novel he never attempted, but a Chekhovian *jeu d'esprit, Old Lyttoff,* the scene of which was set at a farmhouse which Clive and Vanessa Bell had recently taken near West Wittering, he began later that year. It was, he told David Garnett (18 May 1915), 'a horribly melancholy story, ending with a pistol-shot, of course'. On the whole, however, he was unable to concentrate on work that was so entirely removed from the military crisis. He had been approached again during February by H. A. L. Fisher who asked him to contribute another volume to the Home University Library, this one to be entitled *France.* There were several good reasons why he might have accepted. It seemed on the whole a bright journalistic notion; a mere pot-boiling job occupying some three months in all, and providing him with a useful fifty pounds in advance of royalties. But he refused. At such a time, when it was so difficult to think of anything but what actually was and what might be, the degradation, irrelevance and triviality of penning such a dainty manual for the leisured readership of the upper classes would have been insupportable.

In the intervals between literary polemics, meals and sleep, he was now re-reading *War and Peace* (in Constance Garnett's translation) with ever-increasing admiration and wonder. 'It is an amazing work,' he told Ottoline (21 August 1915), 'and I really think the best chance of putting a stop to the War would be to make it obligatory for everyone to read it at least once a year. In the meantime I think it ought to be circulated broadcast, though to be sure it would make rather a bulky pamphlet! But, oh dear me! in between whiles, what an ass the poor man makes of himself! "Matter and impertinency mixed," but luckily there's a good deal more matter than impertinency.'

Here, then, was a subject that could be turned to fine anti-war propaganda, a subject that made *France* seem vague and insubstantial. Perhaps the *Edinburgh Review* would be interested; before he was half-way through the novel, he had sounded out the editor. 'In a moment of rashness I wrote to Harold Cox, suggesting that I write an article on him [Tolstoy]', he told David Garnett (7 August 1915). 'I don't know whether he'll accept, but if he does it'll be a fearful job – rather like writing on God. Have you read "Family Happiness" – in the Ivan Ilytch book? After that, one's left wondering how anyone can dare to write anything else ever again. And then – one remembers – Dostoievsky!'

As usual, Harold Cox countered Lytton's proposal with one of his own. Tolstoy, he declared, was out of date. And Lytton, who in the meantime had been reading Aylmer Maude's biography, experienced some relief at this preposterous decision. Tolstoy was too medieval, too anti-intellectual to suit his kind of neat, Procrustean treatment. The matter and impertinency were more mixed, too, than he had originally thought, and a sense of exasperation perpetually mingled with and confused his admiration. 'I have no patience with a man who decides to commit suicide because he can't see the object of existence,' he confided to David Garnett (23 August 1915), 'and then decides not to because everything becomes clear to him after reading the Gospel according to St Mark. But I suppose one may forgive a good deal to the author of War and Peace.'

The immediate outcome of his negotiations with Harold Cox was 'Voltaire and Frederick the Great', which appeared in the *Edinburgh Review* that October. And as so often when he was productively employed, the nightmare of the war temporarily receded. 'My Voltaire-Frederick article occupies me to the exclusion of all else,' he wrote to Ottoline (21 August 1915), 'it is a fearful task, and must be finished by the end of the month. I feel like a negro slave; whenever I look up from my writing table, I seem to see Mr Harold Cox over my shoulder whirling a cat-o'-nine-tails. Lord have mercy upon us.'

When not involved in writing, and especially at week-ends, Lytton would arrange for himself various social distractions. He visited the Behrends, Ottoline Morrell, and Clive and Vanessa Bell at a small farmhouse standing some fifty yards off from the shore of Chichester Harbour, which had been rented by Professor Tonks of the Slade from his friends St John ('Jack') and Mary Hutchinson.[18] Occasionally, too, he would go up to spend a few days with his family in Hampstead. After his rustic seclusion at The Lacket, the 'Temptations of London' were very hard for him to resist, and in spite of the very best resolutions he seldom got to bed before one o'clock each morning. 'Life here seems to continue in an agreeable manner,' he wrote to David Garnett from Belsize Park Gardens (14 July 1915), 'one can't help feeling rather guilty about it, with these surrounding horrors; but there it is. It's so nice and hot for one thing, and there are so many occupations in this town. One can go from Hampstead Heath to the British Museum, from the British Museum to Gordon Square, from Gordon Square to Treviglio's, from Treviglio's to the Palace to the Café Royal, from the Café Royal to . . . in fact a beneficent Deity appears to have provided suitably for every moment of the day and night. You need not suppose that I am idling: far from it. I am working hard . . .'

Back at The Lacket there were fewer diversions so that, paradoxically, it was only in the deep peace of the country that he seemed fully vulnerable to fits of acute war pessimism. Paradoxically, too, he found himself becoming more, not less, susceptible to minor domestic inconveniences. The spring of 1914 had been idyllic – 'peonies and poppies in the garden, feathered songsters on every bough, and flannelled Marlborough boys in the middle distance'. But this year it was all very different, full of unforeseen terrors. 'The Spring has set in with all its hatefulness,' he announced to Henry Lamb (6 March 1915). 'It's cold, dank and stuffy at the same time: the birds wake one up at three o'clock in the morning with their incomplete repertories; and Mrs Templeman's fancy turns to thoughts of – I don't know what, but certainly something

18. Mary Barnes, daughter of Winifred Strachey (who married Sir Hugh Barnes), the fourth child of John Strachey (1823–1907). Her grandfather, Sir John Strachey, was a younger brother of Lytton's father. She married St John Hutchinson, Master of the Bench Middle Temple, Recorder of Hastings and a Trustee of the Tate Gallery.

pretty astringent.' Even the summer came as a total dis-illusionment. Whether or not he had as yet been transformed into a cactus, he couldn't be sure – but after all, what matter did it make if there were no one to admire him? And then, to add to his distress, they did nothing but fire off guns on Salisbury Plain – heavy, massive guns that boomed and boomed, though one knew, of course, all along that this could only be imitation artillery, cardboard cannons that acted as uncomfortable reminders of what, in any case, one could never forget. Slowly, in nervy, inconceivable dreariness, his life seemed to be ebbing past. 'It is fearful – I see that I have muddled the summer completely,' he wrote to Francis Birrell (August 1915). 'I am alone – desolate and destitute – in a country of overhanging thunder clouds and heavy emptiness. I've got so low that I can hardly bear the thought of anything else, like the prisoners who beg not to be let out of their sentence.'

The last few weeks of Lytton's tenancy at The Lacket were, however, crowded with visitors. Pippa and Pernel came down, and so did James with a new girl friend, Alix Sargant-Florence, an ex-Newnham student. Other week-end guests included Roger Fry, E. M. Forster and Clive Bell. Perhaps the most un-expected visitor of all was G. E. Moore. 'I feel that in my present state he'll reduce me to tears with his incredible reasonableness,' Lytton admitted to Francis Birrell (August 1915). 'When I last saw him I asked him whether the war had made any difference to him. He paused for thought, and then said – "None. Why should it?" I asked whether he wasn't horrified by it – at any rate at the beginning. But no; he had never felt anything about it at all.'

Lytton had originally planned to stay on at The Lacket until the beginning of October, thus completing exactly two years there. But when an opportunity arose for sub-letting the cottage for the last three weeks of his tenancy, being at this time severely worried by money troubles, he eagerly seized upon it, moving out and back to London in the second week of September. 'By a stroke of genius I got Forster to do my packing up at The Lacket,' he gleefully told James (17 September

591

1915), 'and actually to transport the 10 million packages to B.P.G. for me!'

While E. M. Forster was humping his two years' accumulation of books and belongings back to Hampstead, Lytton, with a lingering touch of nostalgia, took himself off to a succession of country house parties. 'I'm feeling some twinges of regret, too, at leaving these remote regions,' he confessed to Ottoline (21 August 1915), 'but on the whole I'm not sorry – and anyhow it must be done. Adieu, adieu, adieu, remember me

      Your
      Lytton.'

TWELVE

War and Peace

'The country is certainly the place for peaceful happiness – if that's what one wants! I think one wants it about half the time; and the other half *un*peaceful happiness. But happiness *all* the time.' *Lytton Strachey to Lady Ottoline Morrell* (24 February 1916)

1

GARSINGTON

OVER the spring, summer and autumn months of 1912, Lady Ottoline Morrell in company with a maid, her six-year-old daughter, and Bertrand Russell, made a number of trips to Lausanne to consult a Swiss doctor by the name of Combe. He had prescribed a new and drastic course of treatment out there, and made other strong recommendations governing her future life back in England – recommendations that seemed at first even more devastating to her friends than to Ottoline herself. 'I had a sad blow this morning from Ottoline (who is returning from Lausanne) to say that the Combe man has ordered her to retire to the country, and not to spend more than a week in London for the next 2 years!' Lytton wrote from The Chestnuts to Henry Lamb in Ireland (9 November 1912). 'I suppose it won't make much difference to you; to me it will be desolating. It was the one centre where I had some chance of seeing amusing and fresh people – my only non-Cambridge point of rapport in London. I was looking forward to rushing up from time to time and mingling with the beau monde! – All dashed. But I'm sure it's the only thing for her health, and I don't think she'll much mind.'

In a reply to Ottoline herself written the same day, Lytton was equally frank about the effect this move would have on

him. 'I am altogether écrasé by your new regime,' he declared,
' – chiefly from a selfish point of view – for I am sure it is the
one thing to do you real good, and I think you'll probably on
the whole enjoy the country. I had counted so enormously
on Bedford Square for the future that I feel quite shattered.
London will be almost a perfect blank now.'

From the depths of the Berkshire countryside, Bedford
Square had beckoned to him as the one illuminated focal
point in a grey metropolis. He had only recently established
himself there as one of Ottoline's most welcome visitors
when now, out of the blue, it would all evaporate into thin
air. He felt like a child cheated of some promised treat. The
overcrowded and amorphous *salon*, which had offered so
much romantic adventure, was to peter out into a mere episode, leading nowhere. For others who lived all their lives in
London, this development could not, of course, seem so ca-
lamitous. But Lytton felt utterly crushed by the news. 'I am
écrasé by the loss of Bedford Square,' he admitted to Virginia
Woolf (1 December 1912), 'but I suppose you hardly feel it. I
think you've never taken to the caviare.'

Ottoline's imminent move to the country, however, was
continually being postponed, until altogether some two-and-a-
half years had elapsed, by which time Lytton was returning to
his old life in London – a change round that, as it turned out,
suited him perfectly. From the very first, Ottoline had had her
eye on a certain house which she and Philip Morrell used to
pass when they drove out to political meetings from Oxford.
'The vision of this house as we passed it one night touched
some spot of desire,' she narrates, 'and I exclaimed, "That is
the only country house I could live in." It had a wonderful
beauty and mystery.' Accordingly, when this house happened
to come up for sale in March 1913, Philip Morrell had gone
down and bought it there and then – though he and Ottoline
were not allowed to take possession of it until the next year.
'So this day our die was cast – for better or worse,' wrote
Ottoline in her *Memoirs*. 'That which had been a misty castle
was now a solid possession.'

Garsington Manor, as their new home was named, was a

Tudor house built in Cotswold stone and set in five hundred acres of ground. Here Ottoline was to live for fourteen years, forming her famous Arcadian colony where she resolutely acted out the part of evangelical patroness to the writers and artists of her choice. It was Bedford Square all over again, but on a far more spacious, crazy and spectacular scale. The early months of 1915 she spent supervising the painting and re-decoration of the house itself, and the planting of the garden, both of which she refashioned after her own inimitable style. By June everything was more or less ready. 'I imagine wonder,' Lytton wrote to her with excitement (8 June 1915), ' – ponds, statues, yew hedges, gold paint. . . . I'm sure you needn't be afraid of my Critical Eye – for the simple reason that it won't be able to find anything to criticize!'

Ottoline, however, remained apprehensive over the reaction of her friends to this bold new venture – and with some reason. The mark of her erratic personality was soon stamped firmly and unforgettably on these surroundings, which were of great natural beauty. Situated on the slope of a hill, Garsington was screened by farm buildings, and though of noble, even grand proportions with its mullioned windows and steep-pitched roof, the front façade suggested a smaller house than it really was. Only from the ornamental garden which fell away to a converted swimming-pool, scattered with leaves and sheltered by dark yew hedges in which were set galleries of stone statues, could the full imposing dimensions of the building be properly appreciated.

Garden-statues lined the terraces; ancient trees surrounded the house [wrote Peter Quennell describing its splendid and eccentric environs]. From under the dusty shadow of an ilex would come wandering a dishevelled peacock – like all peacocks, except when they are in love and the quills of the tail, stiffly extended, rattle together with a staccato vibration, it appeared despondent and a little lost; and, after the trailing bird, the hostess might herself emerge. She seemed to trail, as did the bird she followed – in a dress of bottle-green that swept the lawn, trimmed with bands of thick white swansdown bordering the square-cut neck. The large feathered hat that she often assumed was both regal and pleasantly proletarian;

for it suggested a portrait of Queen Henrietta Maria but also recalled an Edwardian photograph of a Cockney *élégante* on Hampstead Heath.

The influence of Ottoline's demonic personality had also permeated the sumptuous decorations of the house. All the available space was littered with strange boxes of incense, cabinets, oriental china, coloured and patterned hangings. The large, low, panelled rooms, formerly' a mixture of seventeenth-century and Victorian baronial styles, had undergone a transformation. Instead of staining or pickling the wood, she had daubed it with vivid coats of paint, blue and green to match the colour of her eyes, and, in the case of the sitting-room (from the central beam of which was suspended a cardinal bird in a lacquer cage) Chinese scarlet, which occasionally matched her hair.

The oak panelling [David Garnett records] had been painted a dark peacock blue-green; the bare and sombre dignity of Elizabethan wood and stone had been overwhelmed with an almost oriental magnificence: the luxuries of silk curtains and Persian carpets, cushions and pouffes. Ottoline's pack of pug dogs trotted everywhere and added to the Beardsley quality, which was one half of her natural taste. The characteristic of every house in which Ottoline lived was its smell and the smell of Garsington was stronger than that of Bedford Square. It reeked of the bowls of potpourri and orris-root which stood on every mantelpiece, side table and window-sill and of the desiccated oranges, studded with cloves, which Ottoline loved making. The walls were covered with a variety of pictures. Italian pictures and bric-à-brac, drawings by John, watercolours for fans by Conder, who was rumoured to have been one of Ottoline's first conquests, paintings by Duncan and [Mark] Gertler and a dozen other of the younger artists.

The celebrated Renaissance court over which Ottoline presided amid this ornate, other-worldly environment was soon the Mecca of all aspiring young writers and artists. From being a highly fashionable meeting-place, Garsington was quickly transformed into a cultural legend. During the war years, and for some considerable time afterwards, Lytton was one of the most frequent guests here. At week-ends especially, he and other members of the Bloomsbury Group could withdraw from the ugly turbulence of London or emerge from the natural solitude of the country into the artificially rustic atmosphere which Ottoline cultivated. And here, by way of relaxation, they threw themselves into the plays and *tableaux vivants* which formed a regular feature of Garsington entertainment. For Lytton such pastimes held a nostalgic appeal, and in the community at Garsington he hoped to discover what he had failed to make permanent at Cambridge, a congenial home from home.

As a flamboyant extension to Ottoline's odd temperament, Garsington both disconcerted and fascinated him. From the first, its garish novelty took his breath away. It was splendid and ridiculous, admirable and exasperating; and he continued to feel half-captivated by it, half-embarrassed. Behind the silvery-grey stone front, the lofty elms and tall iron gates of Garsington, he entered an improbable world where sophistication and simplicity were incoherently mixed up. 'Only is the sunlight ever normal at Garsington?' Virginia Woolf once wrote to Barbara Bagenal. 'No I think even the sky is done up in pale yellow silk, and certainly the cabbages are scented.'

Max Beerbohm once likened Lytton's ageing mother to Madame du Deffand in the last period of her life; blind, still vivacious – though unable to understand young people – still a very fount of wit – yet profoundly sceptical – set fast in her literary prejudices and enthusiasms, and out of touch with the movement of contemporary life. In Ottoline, Lytton himself thought he recognized an approximation to Madame du Deffand at the prime of her life. In Bedford Square he had looked to find re-created the atmosphere of unparalleled amenity which reigned in the drawing-room of the Convent of St Joseph. At Garsington he pictured another Sceaux 'with its endless succession of entertainments and conversations – supper-parties and water-parties, concerts and masked balls, plays in the little theatre and picnics under the great trees of the park'. It was here especially that Lytton wished to see Ottoline come to her full maturity and establish her pre-eminent position as one of the great leaders of contemporary

English society. It was here – where Asquith (then prime minister), entering on one occasion with Maynard Keynes, was announced as 'Mr Keynes and another gentleman' – that literature and the arts could secure their true level of importance. It was here that Bloomsbury could mingle with the floating company of diplomats and aristocrats, fine ladies and their distinguished escorts, as in eighteenth-century France. And together, this élite of the nation could practise 'those difficult arts which make the wheels of human intercourse run smoothly – the arts of tact and temper, of frankness and sympathy, of delicate compliment and exquisite self-abnegation'. Through their literature, their art, their polished manners, they would be an example and an inspiration to the civilized world. Their gay company should even now hold its own as a subject for conversation with the battle of the Somme or the rout of the Germans at Jutland. At last the artist would rise to his rightful place in society. But though honoured by this world of high birth and aristocratic urbanity, he must never be its minion, so that his creations, while reflecting the finest social ideals of the times, would escape the worst faults of persons of rank – superficiality and amateurishness. His literature would be remarkable for precisely the contrary qualities – for the solidity of its psychological foundations and for the supreme excellence of its craftsmanship. Like the court of Louis XIV, Garsington was to bring into prominence the work of the profound and subtle artist who, while beneficently encircled by a select, leisured, illustrious and critical audience, yet retained the larger outlook and sense of proportion that had come to him from his own restless experience of life. This perhaps was Lytton's dream.

The reality turned out to be rather different. Long before it had moved back to London again, the company which met at Garsington seemed to have the hand of death upon it. The radiant atmosphere of Sceaux was only parodied. The gifts of tact and temper proved far beyond the placatory powers of Lady Ottoline. Her exalted devotion to the arts was too indiscriminate, too unrestrained; her humour, seldom exercised at her own expense, was too malicious; her love of power, her possessiveness, embroiled at one time or another almost everyone, and grew into a heavy obsession that hung over Garsington like a storm cloud. Instead of recapturing the graceful, easy motions of Madame du Deffand's *salon* – like those of 'dancers balanced on skates, gliding, twirling, interlacing, over the thinnest ice' – they floundered and pushed and pulled in a bedlam of conflicting egotisms, released as sudden tempests of altercation, as the cold wind of spiteful gossip or the blustering, dismal rain of envious bickering. Even in the calmer moments, it was not delicate compliment, exquisite self-abnegation that were practised, but the perpetual rumour of machination and intrigue, which bubbled and boiled below the surface of their gatherings.

Lytton first visited Garsington with Duncan Grant and Vanessa Bell in the second week of July. His Critical Eye soon found much to fix upon. 'It was not particularly enchanting,' he wrote to David Garnett (14 July 1915). 'Such fussifications going on all the time – material, mental, spiritual – and at the same time quite indefinite. *Dona nobis pacem, dona nobis pacem*, was all I could murmur. The house is a regular galanty-show, whatever that may be; very like Ottoline herself, in fact – very remarkable, very impressive, patched, gilded and preposterous. The Bedford Square interior does not suit an Elizabethan Manor house in the wilds of Oxfordshire. It has all been reproduced, and indeed redoubled. The pianola too, with Philip, infinitely Philipine, performing, and acrobatic dances on the lawn. In despair I went to bed, and was woken up by a procession circumnavigating my bed, candles in hand ... the rear brought up by the Witch of Endor. Oh! *Dona nobis pacem*!'

To Ottoline herself Lytton sent off a letter by the same post telling her how much he had enjoyed Garsington. He felt, he said, rejuvenated by the delightful company, the pleasing ambience of her new house. And to prove that this was not just formal politeness, he invited himself back there a fortnight later.

The other guests on this second visit were Clive Bell and

Mary Hutchinson, a young Slade student, Barbara Hiles, and an ex-Newnham undergraduate, Faith Bagenal. The two latter were encouraged to scamper off together for most of the time, leaving their elders to discourse learnedly among themselves on life and literature. The hurly-burly, jamboree atmosphere swirled about them even more preposterously than before, and was given full throat by Clive Bell's raucous highspirits. 'Somehow I feel horribly lonely on this occasion: a sort of eighteenth-century grim gaiety comes upon me, and I can hardly distinguish people from pugs,' Lytton confided to David Garnett (25 July 1915). 'I wish they'd all turn into embroidered parrots, neatly framed and hanging on the wall – but they won't; they will keep prancing round, snorting, and (one after another) trying to jump up into one's lap. It's most tiresome – one pushes them down in vain – the wriggling wretches! ...

'Since beginning this I've already had three visitations from the pug-world – and now I must go down on to the lawn, and have tea with them all, and practise my grim gaiety again with them, as if I were a M. le Marquis circa 1770. What fun it would be to be one really! – Or at least infinitely convenient. But I'm not. I'm circa 1915 or nothing . . .'

To Ottoline he then (31 July 1915) wrote off to express the 'gratitude and delight' with which her hospitality had overwhelmed him. His short stay had been exhilarating. 'I find even my vigorous health taking on new forces, so that I am seen bounding along the glades of Hampstead like a gazelle or a Special Constable.' He was looking forward, so he assured her, to many more adventurous week-ends at Garsington. 'I shall come again,' the letter concluded.

In the following years he did go there again, very often, and almost always left behind him the same backwash of alternating flattery and complaint. Many of these complaints, which were perfectly genuine if sometimes exaggerated, arose from invitations which he himself had sponsored quite voluntarily. For he seems to have felt that by ridiculing Ottoline as a perpetual hostess, he would avert ridicule from himself as an inexplicably persistent guest. Virginia Woolf, who was the recipient of so many of Lytton's lampoons on Ottoline, was puzzled by this behaviour. Why ever did he continue to visit Garsington? Were his feelings really so bitter and uninvolved as he liked to make out? Or was this blasé attitude merely put on so as to cover up other, more romantic feelings of which he was ashamed? Perhaps he went on turning up there out of an excess of politeness, a superficial show of kindness to someone who seemed on the verge of spiritual and physical disintegration. 'I suppose the danger lies in becoming too kind,' she wrote to him inquisitively (14 September 1919). 'I think you're a little inclined that way already – take the case of Ottoline. It seems to me a dark one.'

But really it was less dark than she liked to imagine. Part of the fascination of Garsington lay in never knowing whom you would find there. The prolongation of Lytton's visits represented a triumph of that fanciful strain within him over the more down-to-earth side of his nature. 'Mr Strachey is the eighteenth century grown up,' Aldous Huxley once wrote in a review of *Books and Characters*, 'he is Voltaire at two hundred and thirty.' But if he was a superannuated Voltaire, then Ottoline should be cast as a would-be, reincarnated Madame de Châtelet. Lytton had dreamed of resurrecting the past as it appeared to him through the magic lens of retrospect. His sustained and incessant trips to this apogee of Garsington reveal the tenacity with which he clung to these impossible dreams, to the scenes of such imagined graces and delights.

On leaving The Lacket, Lytton went off to stay with the St John Hutchinsons at Eleanor, their house at West Wittering near Chichester, where he enjoyed himself a good deal doing nothing in particular and no writing whatsoever except a single letter to Ottoline asking himself back again to Garsington. He arrived there, from Eleanor, on 16 September, 'and shall probably stay about a week', he notified Pippa (17 September 1915). 'It is deliciously hot, and it is nice sitting out on the lawn; but there are still too many pugs in the house, and Iris Tree is at the present moment reading her poems aloud to Bertrand Russell, and I feel that my turn will come next.'

To record the joys of this latest Garsington sojourn, Lytton told Ottoline, were a task beyond even 'the tongues of angels', and it was 'amid inward lamentations' that he left for the desolate regions of Ledbury. 'I wish I could rush back to Garsington helter-skelter,' he protested (28 September 1915). 'If you ever hear a faint sigh or an unusual creak when you open the door, you will know that it is my departed spirit still fluttering about, and revisiting the haunts of its youth.'

Life at Park Cottage with his mother and his aunt, the ever-vigorous Lady Colvile, was a startling change from Garsington. After Bertrand Russell, pacifism, poetry and *tout ce qu'il-y-a de plus moderne*, he was plunged into the strange antique world of county ladies and important gentry, who looked on him considerably askance, asked him whether he didn't think Russell a crank, pronounced Mrs Asquith to be in the pay of the Germans, and roundly declared that the country was going to the dogs. At the same time they fussed continuously over him with hot-water bottles and second helpings and inquiries as to whether the buttered toast was done *exactly* to his taste, and were at once so kind, and so militant, that he sensed their happiness would be made complete only when they could persuade him to have an extra egg at breakfast and be certain that all the inhabitants of Germany would shortly be massacred in torment. 'Deans, Dowagers and retired Admirals reign supreme,' he wrote to James (3 October 1915), 'with various curates, organists, and female toadies filling up the interstices. It's all very very wicked of course, and how I keep silent I hardly know – except that nobody ever dreams of imagining that I might say anything. Lady C. is indomitable – dashing for miles in motors – and the food is very good – and there are several nice dull *books* to read ... otherwise ...'

Now that he had given up The Lacket, those restless, post-Cambridge years of wandering seemed to be reasserting themselves once more. He had no home but Hampstead, and his antipathy to communal family life was as strong as ever. From Ledbury he went to stay with Augustus and Dorelia John at Alderney Manor, not very far from Henry Forde's school in Parkstone. He had hoped after this to return yet again to Garsington, but was suddenly struck down by illness and obliged to limp back to Belsize Park Gardens, 'apparently for the rest of my unnatural life', as he put it to Keynes (4 November 1915). 'The fog has descended in force and the shadow of Death reigns,' he wrote gloomily to James on his arrival there (19 October 1915). '... The comble was reached last night, when very nearly all the lights were put out, which combined with the fog produced complete darkness. In the streets of Soho one might have been on a Yorkshire Moor for all one could see to the contrary. How the human spirit manages to flicker even as faintly as it does is a mystery.'

2

SEX, CENSORSHIP AND D. H. LAWRENCE

During the autumn and late winter of 1915, the war hysteria had grown palpably more fanatical, and was being ventilated throughout London in a manner that recalled to Lytton the most septic hypocrisies of Victorian England. Truth, it has been said, is invariably the first casualty of war, and humour the second. In their place there now flourished a pugnacious sentimentality which had its root in repressed fear. Popular bigotry, widely championed by the patrio-sadistic reporting of the press, was quickly fanned to a new intensity by the engines of official war propaganda. Everywhere were pasted up posters depicting alleged and mythical German atrocities, and these had lately been reinforced by others which were designed to stimulate the militancy of civilians, and which succeeded in arousing the unmitigated scorn of the front line troops. 'Women of Britain say – GO!' one caption read; but it was hardly the sort of call to inspire Lytton. He was astonished, almost awed by the sentimental ingenuity of mottoes such as 'Go! It's your Duty, Lad' (illustrated by a proud white-haired little old lady ushering her equally proud, debonair son into the ranks of the army); or the classic 'Daddy, what did YOU do in the Great War?' (a plainly guilt-ridden, civilian paterfamilias being interrogated by his young daughter perched trustingly on his knee, while his son plays innocently at soldiers on the floor near by).

It was the autumn of the Gallipoli failure, of the first large Zeppelin air raids, of the collapse of the Asquith Cabinet. The Bishop of London, referring to the war as the greatest fight ever made for the Christian religion – 'the choice between the nailed hand and the mailed fist' – went on to state that 'there must be a kind of glorying in London at being allowed to take our little share of danger in the Zeppelin raids'. In the sphere of literature, the most dramatic event of these months was the successful prosecution and suppression of D. H. Lawrence's novel, *The Rainbow*, ostensibly on the grounds of obscenity but actually because of its denunciation of war. In times of national crisis the film of imbecility upon the ocean of life thickens appreciably, and the sentiments expressed by established men of letters do nothing to suggest that the incidence of fools among writers is any less high than in other professions. A good idea of the swollen confusion of mind now fashionable among the authorities may be gained from statements made by some notable literary figures. J. C. Squire, writing under the pseudonym of 'Solomon Eagle' in the *New Statesman*, suggested that D. H. Lawrence might be 'under the spell of German psychologists'. Augustine Birrell, the belletrist, in private conversation at Garsington, expressed surprise at so much fuss over the soldiery: 'After all,' he pointed out, 'the men out there will be returning some day.' In a public speech, however, delivered in his capacity as Chief Secretary for Ireland and a cabinet minister, his attitude was less casual, and he roundly declared that he, for one, would 'forbid the use, during the war, of poetry'. The zealotry of those proponents of war safely behind the lines – symbolized by the giving of white feathers to men in civilian clothes – and the unctuous Christian philosophizing extended to those who were risking their lives at the front, sickened Lytton. He felt himself to be more of a misfit than at any time since going up to Cambridge, and his attitude reverted to its most hostile and embittered.

The principal target for his rancour at this time was Scotland Yard's confiscation of *The Rainbow*. Though Lytton felt little affinity for Lawrence, and did not like his novel, he was compelled to support his cause. He interpreted the court case as yet another pitched battle between the powers of darkness and light, and many of his pacifist friends appeared to share this belief. Philip Morrell raised questions about the book's suppression in Parliament; and Lytton himself wrote off to the *New Statesman* an ironic letter in favour of the suppression, which was itself suppressed by the editor. 'It seems strange that they [the police] should have the leisure and energy for that sort of activity at the present moment,' he commented in a letter to David Garnett (10 November 1915). 'But no doubt the authorities want to show us that England stands for Liberty. Clive is trying to get up an agitation about it in the newspapers but I doubt if he'll have much success. We interviewed that little worm Jack Squire, who quite failed to see the point: he thought that as in his opinion the book wasn't a good one it was difficult for him to complain about its suppression. Damn his eyes! In vain we pointed out that it was a question of principle, and that whether that particular book was good or mediocre was irrelevant – he couldn't see it. At last, however, he agreed to say a few words about it in his blasted paper – on one condition – that the book had not been suppressed because it mentioned sapphism – he had heard that that was the reason – and in that case, well, of course, it was quite impossible for the *New Statesman* to defend perversity.'

Earlier that year David Garnett had introduced Lawrence to his Bloomsbury friends, and with disastrous consequences. 'To hear these young people talk', Lawrence complained to Ottoline, 'fills me with black fury: they talk endlessly – and never, never a good thing said. They are cased each in a hard little shell of his own and out of this they talk words.' To Garnett himself Lawrence confessed that these friends of his 'sent me mad with misery and hostility and rage'. Garnett had then decided that, since he could not continue to see Lawrence and still count Francis Birrell, Duncan Grant, Maynard Keynes and Lytton among his companions, he had better have nothing more to do with Lawrence. This decision was hardly surprising. For although, at first sight, he might not appear to be a very typical member of Bloomsbury, Garnett had more in common with some of this group than he could ever have had with Lawrence. His animal spirits were strong and surprisingly various, while Lawrence's doubtful claim to be *grand animal* was little more than an expression of his wish to cut free from the strangulated, back-to-the-womb atrophy of his relationship with women. The Lawrentian cult of the dark primeval wild beast, involving a loss of responsible human identity, seemed far more rhapsodically unrestrained than Garnett's humanized and domesticated animal world, which represented for him an extension, not an abandonment, of the physical province of human beings. Lawrence, had he taken Garnett's woman-into-animal metamorphosis seriously, would have found it stifling and unendurable. As it was, he later dismissed *Lady into Fox* as 'mere playboy stuff', or, in other words, more Bloomsbury verbiage, empty and meaningless.

Although Lawrence had met his brother James and two of his sisters at Cambridge, he had never in fact seen Lytton himself until, by an unexpected coincidence, they encountered each other one Friday night early that November at a party held just off the Earls Court Road, in the studio of Dorothy Brett, the painter.[1] Arriving there late, Lytton was immedi-

1. 'I really did not like Lytton Strachey', Dorothy Brett told the author (9 March 1966). 'First of all he was so unpleasant to look at, to put it mildly, and he was secretively obscene. I did not know him intimately, I used to meet him at week-end parties at Garsington, at parties in London. He was of delicate health, but as far as I could make out not delicate minded ... I can remember an amusing incident at Garsington, when Lytton complained that Ottoline was stingy with the food. So the next morning, as a sort of ironical swatt at him, Ottoline had a breakfast sent up, consisting of eggs, sausages, bacon, mounds of toast, etc. To her chagrin he ate it all!! From that day he was stuffed with food. ... The Bloomsburies scared me to death. I was much closer to Lawrence, Murry, Katherine, Gertler, who were not Bloomsburies. Virginia Woolf was the only one at all nice to me. I was a great nuisance with my deafness. I

ately thrust into the centre of a large and very miscellaneous crowd – Brett herself, looking, with her *retroussé* nose and childish hands, about seventeen (less than half her age), and spoken of as the 'virgin aunt' of her two constant companions, the wild and energetic painter Mark Gertler, who rushed about the room acting as assistant-host, and Dora Carrington 'like a wild moorland pony', as Ottoline once described her, 'with a shock of fair hair, uncertain and elusive eyes, rather awkward in her movements', standing speechless next to a large silent dog. While poor Brett, terribly deaf, laboured energetically at the pianola, her drunken guests disported themselves round the studio. 'Some seemed strangely vulgar,' Lytton afterwards told James (8 November 1915), 'dreadful women on divans trying to persuade dreadful men to kiss them, in foreign accents (apparently put on for the occasion).'

Among this jumble of humanity D. H. Lawrence and his German wife Frieda, claimed Lytton's particular attention. 'There were a great many people I didn't know at all,' Lytton wrote to David Garnett (10 November 1915), 'and others whom I only knew by repute, among the latter, the Lawrences, whom I examined carefully and closely for several hours, though I didn't venture to have myself introduced. I was surprised to find that I liked her looks very much – she actually seemed (there's no other word for it) a lady: as for him I've rarely seen anyone so pathetic, miserable, ill, and obviously devoured by internal distresses. He behaved to everyone with the greatest cordiality, but I noticed for a second a look of intense disgust and hatred flash into his face ... caused by – ah! – whom? Katherine Mansfield was also there, and took my fancy a good deal.'[2]

---

missed so much which irritated everybody. ... There was something to me creepy about Lytton. I have no objection to homosexuals, no prejudices whatsoever, maybe it was just his looks, I don't know.'

2. On 3 October 1919, Lytton wrote Katherine Mansfield a fan letter. 'Dear Katherine, The Government tells one only to write letters that are necessary – so be it! This is the letter of a loyal subject, because I can think of nothing more necessary than to tell you how much I admire your

Lawrence's and Lytton's mutual aversion seems to have been aggravated by their many points of apparent similarity. With their reddish beards and their puny bodies, their crippling physical infirmities, their irritated contempt for ordinary men and women and intense internal envy of those vaulted up into high positions, their love of travelling – of 'moving on' – and their years of struggle to disburden themselves from the very different but pervasive influence of their mothers, each one seemed to stand as a painful caricature of the other's least admirable qualities. But it was their wide dissimilarity, especially of background, which cast their work into such opposing forms, and which has posthumously led to the seesaw of their literary reputations. At any point in time, when one is venerated, the other, as if by some natural law of physics, will always be underrated. 'The poetic inspiration of an age', Lytton wrote in one of his *Spectator* reviews, 'seems to follow what may be called, for want of a better term, a nation's "centre of gravity". With the Elizabethans the centre of gravity was among the middle classes – the country gentleman like Drake or Raleigh, the country yeoman like Shakespeare, and the university scholars like Marlowe and Ben Jonson. After the Restoration the centre of gravity moved more and more rapidly towards the aristocracy, until at the beginning of the eighteenth century it became fixed in the great Whig families who had achieved the Revolution. And simultaneously literature took on the qualities of aristocracy, grew refined, brilliant, and ordered, and concerned itself exclusively with the life of London drawing-rooms.'

It is in just such an atmosphere of ordered refinement and aristocratic glitter that the main body of Lytton's work has been most readily appreciated. His natural medium as a writer was the essay, that drawing-room form of literature quaintly supposed these days to have been accompanied by a tinkle of tea-cups and the titter of well-bred amusement. The centre of

Athenaeum reviews, and how grateful I am to you for such charming weekly titillations ... I should be very glad to hear any news of you – but I don't want to give trouble – only let me have a word or two some day.'

gravity since and even during Lytton's time has moved away again from the drawing-rooms of the aristocracy, and taken new root in the industrial surroundings of the lower-middle and working classes. The democracy of Dickens, considered so vulgar in his own life, was made acceptable, even popular, by the inspired advocacy of G. K. Chesterton. The social 'message' of Lawrence himself has been disseminated through the schools and universities by the overwrought punditry of Dr Leavis and his educationist disciples, and has culminated in a mood of strident 'moral' attitudinizing that would probably have been unpleasing to Lawrence and anathema certainly to Lytton.

The war, which crumbled the cement of Victorian standards into disused rubble and opened up unmendable fissures in the gilded Edwardian way of life, had the effect of quickening and distorting an inevitable upheaval of existing habits and traditions. A new dispensation slowly emerged. The political emancipation of women, the equalizing tax structure, the consolidation of the working class, the rise of collectivism and State control, the growth of the Labour Party, the changes in dress, manners and public attitudes to questions of morality, all helped to reform the fabric of class-relationships. These were the raw materials, so chaotically thrown together, for the architecture of a reorganized system of society. Yet in the immediate aftermath of the war, during the early 1920s, it seemed as if the poetic inspiration might again reside with the upper-middle class. The old order began to re-establish itself – but only briefly. The restoration of the aristocracy was never accomplished. Instead, an enormous, shapeless social transformation gradually came about, and history became increasingly a matter controlled by a heterogeneous group of men – the so-called meritocracy. By the time of his death, Lytton had already lost some of his high literary prestige, for he had gained his brilliant success by those very qualities that were to ensure his equally swift downfall. Marx and Freud, the two chief opposing influences on the humanities over the next thirty years, were both really inimical to Lytton's talent, and his belated endeavour to align himself with the latter in his *Elizabeth and Essex* may partly account for the comparative failure of that book.

Under such conditions the reputation of Lawrence has swollen disproportionately; that of Lytton shrivelled away too far. For Lawrence was like a man digging up with careless frenzy huge trenches of black useless earth, but every so often coming across a whole, rough nugget of gold. While the meticulous and skilful Lytton, crouched over a stream, pans with methodical precision his few ounces of precious metal, peering all the time through his spectacles to assure himself that not even the faintest yellow speck has escaped his vigilance.

It was appropriate, however, that Lawrence and Lytton should meet during the war, the artificial conditions of which had temporarily made them into wary and grudging allies. In reaction from their smashed-up hopes and ideals, both sought to promote the same sort of revolution – a fierce, undismayed assertion of social and personal liberty – and subscribed to a short-lived, scatter-brained venture in the form of a fortnightly periodical entitled *The Signature* – fathered on the luckless and quixotic Middleton Murry. It was fitting, too, that as fellow guests at Brett's party they should never speak to each other or be formally introduced. They had come, momentarily and coincidentally, to the same point from two altogether different directions, and after this intersection the graph of their careers was again to veer off on two totally divergent courses. And so, though he carefully observed Lawrence, Lytton had nothing to do with him personally, and left the party surrounded by his own gay set. 'When it was time to go, we went with Iris [Tree],' he wrote to James (8 November 1915), 'and emerged upon the pitchblack Cromwell Road at half past one, Iris wildly whistling with her fingers in her mouth for taxis, rushing in front of them to stop them, and then, when they turned out to be full, leaping on to the footboard, and whirling off . . . it was a wild scene.'

3

CONSCRIPTION

'My life here has been rather dissipated of late,' Lytton wrote to David Garnett from Belsize Park Gardens (8 November 1915), ' – and very idle.' One of his chief dissipations during these doldrum days was the reopening of his German lessons, now under the supervision of an astringent English spinster in Mecklenburgh Square, whom he called on once a week. In the intervals he would struggle with Heine; but it proved uphill work. He was too indolent and naturally inept at speaking languages to make much headway – besides which, German was a horribly difficult tongue to master. Apart from this 'I am also engaged on a short life of Dr Arnold (of Rugby),' he wrote to his mother (12 December 1915), who was spending the winter in Menton, 'which is a distinctly lugubrious business, though my hope is to produce something out of it which may be entertaining. He was a self-righteous blockhead, but unlike most of his kind, with enough energy and determination in him to do a good deal of damage – as our blessed Public Schools bear witness!'

His progress with 'Dr Arnold' during this winter was scarcely more spectacular than his German tuition, and except for two *New Statesman* reviews he wrote little for publication. Yet it was an active, if unproductive winter. Political worries agitated and exhausted him, and his moods of melancholy were further deepened by various pestilential diseases which crowded in upon him and an unfortunate accident when, in a moment of distraction, he walked straight into a lamp post, crashing his forehead against it with maximum velocity.

To shake off his feeling of apathy he now embarked on a wild life of entertainment, hurrying from party to party, his late hours growing ever later night by night. Soon, this social life had become almost too exigent – but he could not resist it. 'The London whirlpool is, as usual, very trifling when looked at in detail, but none the less absorbing on the whole,' he told Francis Birrell (November 1915). 'I rush from Hampstead to Bloomsbury, from Bloomsbury to Chelsea. I go to concerts, Music Halls, and the Café Royal. I attend lectures by Maynard and Mr Shaw. The latter function was an odd one. Bertie in the chair, and a large audience eager for a pacifist oration and all that's most advanced – and poor dear Mr Shaw talking about "England" with trembling lips and gleaming eyes, and declaring that his one wish was that we should first beat the Germans, and then fight them again, and then beat them again, and again, and again! He was more like a nice old-fashioned Admiral on a quarter-deck than anything else. And the newspapers are so stupid that, simply because he's Mr Shaw, they won't report him – instead of running him as our leading patriot.'

The murky streets of London, so invitingly blacked out now at night, had grown extraordinarily attractive to him. 'How I adore the romance and agitation of them!' he exclaimed in a letter to Ottoline (21 January 1916). 'Almost too much I fear!' Periodically he would feel the need for the more peaceful enjoyments of the country, and he spent several week-ends with Clive and Vanessa Bell at Eleanor, and with Leonard and Virginia Woolf down at Asheham. But most of his country visitations were to Garsington. Although he seldom stayed for longer than a single week, his retreats there at this time were particularly frequent. The fresh country air, the luxurious living, good food and sympathetic quietude (at least during the weekdays) were, so he apologetically informed his friends, beneficial to his health.

It came as no surprise, then, that it was with Ottoline that he chose to spend the Christmas holidays. 'There has been a nice party here, including the Bells and Keynes,' he wrote from Garsington to his mother (28 December 1915); 'it is a comfortable house, and the country round about is most beautiful – very hilly and romantic – and very unlike the dull flat expanses in the immediate neighbourhood of Oxford. On Christmas day there was a grand festivity in one of the barns, which was rigged up with decorations on a Christmas tree, and all the children in the village came and had tea there. It was really a wonderful affair. There were over a hundred children, and each one had a present from the tree; they were of course delighted – especially as they had never known anything of the kind before, since hitherto there haven't been any "gentry" in the village. Every detail was arranged by Ottoline, whose energy and good-nature are astonishing. Then in the evening there was a little dance here, with the servants and some of the farmers' daughters, etc. which was great fun, her Ladyship throwing herself into it with tremendous brio. It takes a daughter of a thousand Earls to carry things off in that manner.'

'How very kind Lady Ottoline is,' Lady Strachey replied. 'I am most grateful to her.'

Much of the talk during these winter weeks centred around conscription. To solve the difficult task of bringing enough men to the colours, within a country the bulk of whose population was still believed to be hostile to the idea of universal military service, the Government had, in October 1915, started the notorious Derby Scheme. This was a voluntary plan, on the continental pattern, the purpose of which was to persuade men of serviceable age to 'attest' – that is, to undertake to join up whenever called upon to do so – by means of a moral and not a legal obligation. At Asheham and Garsington, the Bloomsbury Group would assemble at week-ends to debate the situation, the nucleus of these gatherings consisting of, besides Lytton himself, Clive Bell, Vanessa Bell and Duncan Grant and Maynard Keynes, David Garnett, and Harry Norton. Almost all of them were opposed to the type of blandishment and blackmail on which the Derby Scheme operated, and felt alarmed by the compulsory conscription that was threatened if this scheme failed. 'The conscription crisis has been agitating these quarters considerably,' Lytton wrote to James from Garsington as early as 23 September; 'but the comments have not been particularly illuminating. Some say that Lloyd George is verging towards the madhouse cell. Others affirm that E. Grey is "immovable" against conscription. Personally I feel despondent – about that and most other things.'

By December, the Derby Scheme had failed, and, in the first

week of January, the Government introduced their Military Service Bill, under which all single men were automatically deemed to have enlisted and been transferred to the Reserve, from which they could be called up when needed. The Labour members of the Coalition Government threatened resignation – then withdrew their threat. Nothing then stood in the way of the Bill – yet Lytton still hoped for some last-minute miracle, some nationwide uprising against it. 'Philip [Morrell] now seems to think that it may take a fortnight or even 3 weeks getting through the Committee stage,' he informed James; 'and in that case isn't it still possible that something should be done? Surely there ought to be a continual stream of leaflets and pamphlets. Also if possible meetings all over the country, and signatures collected against the Bill.'

To help disseminate this type of anti-conscription propaganda, Lytton at once joined the No Conscription Fellowship or N.C.F. as it was usually called, and the National Council against Conscription, or N.C.C. – the two societies that had been formed to resist the Act, to campaign for pacifism, and, subsequently, to urge that out-and-out conscientious objectors, or 'absolutists', should be given unconditional exemption from participating in the war, instead of being forced either into prison or into government occupations. Several other members of Bloomsbury including James Strachey – recently sacked from the *Spectator* by the militaristic St Loe – assisted at the N.C.C. offices in Bride Lane, addressing envelopes, sticking on stamps, and writing leaflets. One of these, which stated that the Government's motive for bringing in compulsory service was to prevent strikes and crush labour, created a considerable stir. This was Leaflet No. 3, drawn up by Lytton, who, as so often when dealing with an immediate practical situation, resorted to allegory.

CONSCRIPTION

WHY they want it, and why they say they want it.
THEY SAY THEY WANT IT to punish the slackers
THEY WANT IT to punish the strikers.

THEY SAY THEY WANT IT to crush Germany
THEY WANT IT to crush labour.
THEY SAY THEY WANT IT to free Europe
THEY WANT IT to enslave England.
DON'T LET THEM GET WHAT THEY WANT BECAUSE THEY
KEEP SAYING THEY WANT SOMETHING DIFFERENT.

The Cat kept saying to the Mouse that she was a highminded person, and if the Mouse would only come a little nearer they could both get the cheese.

The Mouse said 'Thank you Pussy, it's not the cheese you want; it's my skin!'

Shortly after this leaflet had been printed, H. W. Massingham[3] saw it, decided it was seditious, and rushed round to the Bride Lane office to get it withdrawn from circulation. Sir John Simon, who had resigned from the Cabinet to lead the opposition to the Military Service Bill, and who, according to Maynard Keynes, was rather regretting his hasty decision, also disapproved very violently of this piece of propaganda. And so it was agreed to send out no further copies, though, since half a million had by then been distributed, this decision came rather late in the day. The *Morning Post*, in any case, had already got hold of a copy and blazoned a long, angry article about pacifist propaganda in general. After quoting some sentences from Lytton's leaflet, the paper demanded: 'Would it be possible to imagine a more wanton and malicious indulgence in false witness?' There seemed no intelligible point of contact between the two sides. On reading the article Lytton commented with quiet indulgence to Ottoline: 'Queer fellows they are.'

Amid all the infuriated pessimism of this losing campaign, it was a great comfort for Lytton to find himself in a solid phalanx of agreement with his friends. Bloomsbury, as a whole, believed that the war had been started to refute militarism, and that to establish it now in England expressly contradicted our original and honourable intentions. Distrusting deeply the political management of the war, they favoured,

3. H. W. Massingham (1860–1924), the famous editor of the *Nation*.

from 1916 onwards, the policy of a negotiated peace settlement.

Lytton's own views, which surreptitiously found their way into much of what he wrote during these years, were strong and uncompromising. In his prepared statement as a conscientious objector, he explained his attitude in language that is well-defined and explicit. Before 1914, he declared, 'I was principally concerned with literary and speculative matters; but, with the war, the supreme importance of international questions has been forced upon my attention. My opinions have been for many years strongly critical of the whole structure of society; and after a study of the diplomatic situation, and of the literature, both controversial and philosophic, arising out of the war, they developed naturally into those I now hold. My convictions as to my duty with regard to the war have not been formed either rashly or lightly; and I shall not act against these convictions whatever the consequences may be.'

Among the men in command of political operations, none were any longer moved by philosophical ideals towards noble aims. Woodrow Wilson meant well, but was a simpleton; Clemenceau appeared to be no more than a worldly and ambitious cynic; and as for Lloyd George, Lytton's one ardent desire, he told Francis Birrell, was that, once the war had ended, the prime minister should be publicly castrated – if possible at the foot of Nurse Cavell's statue. Nor did Churchill inspire him with any confidence – a fact which he recorded in a Blakean epigram:

> Though Time from History's pages much may blot,
> Some things there are can never be forgot;
> And in Gallipoli's delicious name,
> Wxxxxxx, your own shall find eternal fame.

Asquith, too, though in some ways more appealing than Churchill, was equally unprincipled, and, Lytton had come to feel, of even greater incompetence. 'Nothing is more damning than his [Asquith's] having told Maynard (who told me of it at the time) that "the Conscriptionists were fools", and that he was giving them "enough rope to hang themselves by", three weeks before he was himself forced by them to bring in a bill for Conscription,' Lytton later commented in an unpublished biographical portrait of Asquith (May 1918), 'If it was true (as Maynard assured me it was, on what I gathered was the best authority) that in December 1916, after he had been turned out with ignominy and treachery by Lloyd George and Bonar Law, he was willing and in fact anxious to act under them as Lord Chancellor, his wits must have sunk even lower than his sense of decency. I think eventually he must have grown too positively fuddled – with too much food and drink, too much power, too much orotund speechifying, too many of those jovial adventures of the "lugubre individu".'

Ultimately, Lytton believed, the world was governed not by extremists, not by flagrantly unreasonable fanatics, but by moderate men. The sight of these men, with their seductive plausibility, in full control of events, posed for him a profoundly menacing spectacle. Their inflated sentiments and headstrong actions presented a terrifying revelation of what the multitudes of ordinary respectable men and women were thinking. By invoking the lowest common denominator within society, such leaders were able to exert a powerful brake upon the natural advancement of civilization, and to give dominion to the basest, most egotistical elements in human nature.

Amid the fevered bigotry and hysteria of war, people on both sides, Lytton felt, relinquished their individual detachment and with it their humanity, so that, as hostilities were prolonged, the opponents came to resemble each other ever more exactly. The British Government, for example, had, even before conscription, undertaken to improve recruitment by means just as discreditable as the Germans themselves. 'Is your "best boy" wearing Khaki? ... If your young man neglects his duty to his King and Country, the time may come when he will NEGLECT YOU!' This was the type of advocacy, 'limited neither by the meagre bounds of the actual nor by the tiresome dictates of common sense', that Lytton particularly abhorred. He did not believe that everything should be sacrificed to the safety of the State; he did not believe that truth should be sacrificed. This twisted, repellent form of patriotism, which justified mendacity and tyranny to ensure national unity, spread like a rampant disease caused not by too much love of one's country, but by too little. A propagandist now himself, bent on persuading others not just by personal example but public exhortation, he employed methods similar to those used by the authorities to popularize his own convictions. In 'The Claims of Patriotism', an article published towards the end of the war in *War and Peace*, he wrote: 'The lover who loved his mistress with such passionate ecstasy that he would feed her on nothing but moonshine, with disastrous consequences – did he, perhaps, in reality, not love her quite enough? That, certainly, is a possible reading of the story. And it might be as well for patriots ... to reflect occasionally on that sad little apologue, and to remember that nothing sweetens love – even love of one's country – so much as a little common sense – and, one might add, even a little cynicism.'

To Lytton's common-sense and cynical mind, the passing that spring of the new universal Conscription Bill for compulsory National Service made Britain as ardent a supporter of the principle of militarism as Germany herself. 'What difference', he used to ask, 'would it make if the Germans *were* here?' Human beings had a value that was independent of any national or temporal processes, and individual human standards must never therefore be jettisoned to make room for the requirements of empirical transactions and passing circumstances. His own quarrel was with the whole militarist point of view, whether expressed by allied or enemy officialdom. 'L[loyd] G[eorge] is a sharper,' he wrote to Pippa. The prime minister's refusal to 'explore every avenue of peace' exposed him, and others in his Cabinet, as militarists pure and simple, who believed that eternal peace was just a sentimentalist's dream. For such men the actuality of peace held no excitement or romantic appeal; it was attractive only as an illusory concept which paradoxically justified the pursuit of war to attain it.

Lytton saw himself as one in a long line of crusaders. During the eighteenth century Voltaire had waged a constant fight against religion – then the dominatiñg factor in human affairs. Stendhal had continued this struggle into the nineteenth century with his attacks upon the powerful forces of Roman Catholicism. But by the end of that century, with the sudden tremendous upsurge of scientific interest and discovery, the social power of organized religion had slumped, until it now ceased to represent any vital part of the national consciousness. The 'powers of darkness' were no longer led by theologians, but by their modern counterparts, the secular and political warmongers. It was with this breed of men that the Voltaire of the twentieth century had to do battle. Yet, despite the wartime rash of intolerance, Lytton believed that the odds were not set quite so heavily against him as they had been against his prototype two hundred years back. War did not obsess or unnerve the human mind so ceaselessly as the age-long, pernicious hocus-pocus of religious superstition. The powers of light were gradually advancing; for human nature, Lytton considered, had changed and was still changing for the better. To moderate men with their limitations of average passions and average thoughts, it might still appear that 'militarism and the implications of militarism – the struggles and ambitions of opposing States, the desire for national power, the terror of national ruin, the armed organisation of humanity – that all this seems inevitable with the inevitability of a part of the world's very structure; and yet it may well be, too, that they are wrong, that it is not so, that it is the "fabric of a vision" which will melt suddenly and be seen no more'.

If, as Lytton believed, war was justifiable only as a means, the last means, of defence, and never as an assertion of nationalism, then the days of this pristine and aggressive type of patriotism, on which the wilful politician and ambitious diplomat so abundantly thrived, were already numbered. Lloyd George stalked the political arena like some prehistoric monster, doomed to extinction. At the end of the war Lytton wrote to Keynes: 'To my mind the ideal thing would be to abolish reparations altogether – but of course that is not practical politics – at any rate just yet; perhaps in the end it will become so.'

These were opinions on which nearly all Bloomsbury, from Keynes to Bertrand Russell, were in general agreement. But it was not so on all matters connected with the military operations. 'Bertie was most sympathetic,' Lytton wrote to Ottoline (31 December 1915) on the eve of the introduction of the first Military Service Bill. 'I went to see him this morning and we had lunch with Maynard in an extraordinary underground tunnel, with city gents sitting on high stools like parrots on perches, somewhere near Trafalgar Square. Maynard is certainly a wonder. He has not attested, and says he has no intention of doing so. He couldn't tell us much – except that McKenna is still wobbling; but he seemed to think it not unlikely that he and Runciman would resign – in which case he would resign too, and help them to fight it.'

But after compulsory military service had been introduced Reginald McKenna, chancellor of the exchequer, made no move to resign; nor did Walter Runciman; and nor did Keynes. Maynard, it seemed, was rather less of a wonder after all. Certainly both Lytton and Russell felt that he had 'ratted', and, individually, they both pressed him to quit the Treasury, reasoning that it must be impossible to reconcile his avowed sympathy for conscientious objectors with the job of demonstrating how to kill Germans as cheaply as possible: 'the maximum slaughter at the minimum expense'. Keynes now found himself situated awkwardly, midway between his Bloomsbury friends and his friends at the Treasury. But there was no chance of resignation. 'He obviously enjoyed the way the war had brought him up in the world,' observed Alan Wood, 'and had given him friends among important people, including Asquith when he was Prime Minister.' This opinion is supported by the letters which Keynes wrote to his family during these years. He did not, however, feel entirely easy over his decision, and to appease Lytton and Russell made a token gesture of support. 'He announced for their benefit that, although he was not a Conscientious Objector, he would conscientiously object to compulsory service,' Roy Harrod explains. 'Accordingly, when he received his calling-up notice, he replied on Treasury writing-paper that he was too busy to attend the summons. This appears to have quelled the authorities, for he was troubled by them no more. On the other hand, he did not carry this policy through to its final conclusion, for a year or two later the Treasury discovered a gap in its records. In the file there was no notice of exemption against his name. And so, to placate the Treasury Establishment Officer, he walked quietly round and went through the formalities of obtaining exemption.' In the meantime, however, he had interceded to support, with great effectiveness, several of those conscientious objectors among his friends – notably James Strachey, Duncan Grant and David Garnett – on whose behalf he gave telling evidence before the Military and Appeal Tribunals.

Although at one in their repudiation of Keynes's vacillation, Lytton and Bertrand Russell harboured differences of temperament and of opinion that became increasingly obvious as the year 1916 progressed. The passing of the Military Service Bill, which took the wind out of Lytton's sails as a political crusader, redoubled the force of Russell's pacifist propaganda. Even by the third week of January, Lytton was confessing to Ottoline (21 January 1916) that 'the anti-Conscription movement has been rather fading out as far as I'm concerned'. Russell, by contrast, was embarking on a series of pacifist lectures, later published under the title *Principles of Social Reconstruction*. These turned out to be a great success, crowded with ladies of fashion and intellectual young men attending earnestly to his every word. Lytton too went to all of them and was unstinted in his praise. 'Bertie's lectures help one,' he wrote (16 February 1916). 'They are a wonderful solace and refreshment. One hangs upon his words, and looks forward to them from week to week, and I can't bear the idea of missing one – I dragged myself to that ghastly Caxton Hall yesterday, though I was rather nearer the grave than usual, and it was well worth it. It is splendid the way he sticks at nothing – Governments, religions, laws, property, even Good

Form itself – down they go like ninepins – it is a charming sight! And then his constructive ideas are very grand; one feels one had always thought something like that – but vaguely and inconclusively; and he puts it all together, and builds it up, and plants it down solid and shining before one's mind. I don't believe there's anyone quite so formidable to be found just now upon this earth.'

Two months later, Russell's campaigning reached a crisis over the Everett affair. On 10 April, Ernest F. Everett, a conscientious objector and member of the N.C.F., was sentenced to two years' hard labour for disobedience to military orders. Nine days afterwards the N.C.F. issued a leaflet protesting against this sentence, whereupon six men were arrested and imprisoned for distributing it. On learning this Russell immediately wrote off a letter to *The Times* declaring that he was the author of the leaflet and that, if anyone should be prosecuted, it ought to be himself as the person primarily responsible. This letter, of course, made prosecution unavoidable and Russell duly appeared before the Lord Mayor, Sir Charles Wakefield, at the Mansion House on 5 June 1916, charged with making, in a printed publication, 'statements likely to prejudice the recruiting discipline of His Majesty's forces'. A. H. Bodkin[4] appeared for the prosecution; Russell defended himself; and the proceedings were brightened by the startling arrival of Lytton, and Ottoline Morrell dressed in a brilliant hat and cashmere coat of many colours. 'B.R. spoke for about an hour,' Lytton recorded, '– quite well – but simply a propaganda speech. The Lord Mayor looked like a stuck pig. Counsel for the prosecution was an incredible Daumier caricature of a creature – and positively turned out to be Mr Bodkin. I felt rather nervous in that Brigand's cave.' Russell was found guilty and fined £100 (with £10 costs and the alternative of 61 days' imprisonment), a sentence that was confirmed on appeal.[5]

4. Later Sir Archibald Henry Bodkin (1862–1957) who between 1920 and 1930 was Director of Public Prosecutions.

5. This appeal was heard before the City Quarter Sessions, at the Guildhall, on 29 June 1916. Russell declined to pay the fine, but there was

Disgusted by what he considered to be Lytton's defeatist attitude, Russell despised his inability to persevere with the cause of pacifism, to stick at nothing. But Lytton suspected that Russell, like so many professional reformers, wanted bad conditions of one sort or another, so that he might have the personal joy of altering them. Conscription filled Lytton with no such joy. 'It's all about as bad as it could be,' he wrote to Vanessa Bell from Garsington (17 April 1916). 'Bertie has been here for the week-end. He is working day and night with the N.C.F., and is at last perfectly happy – gloating over all the horrors and the moral lessons of the situation. The tales he tells make one's blood run cold; but certainly the N.C.F. people do sound a remarkable lot – Britannia's One Hope, I firmly believe – all so bright and cheery, he says, with pink cheeks and blithe young voice – oh mon dieu! mon dieu! The worst of it is that I don't see how they can really make themselves effective unless a large number of them do go through actual martyrdom: and even then what is there to make the governing classes climb down? It is all most dark in every direction.' Towards the end of 1917 Russell himself decided to withdraw from active pacifist agitation, believing – as did Lytton – that it was by then more important to wait and work for a constructive post-war peace. Yet he could point to some solid achievements as a propagandist. In the Everett case, for example, his own leaflet and the ensuing trial had caused the Government to commute the original sentence to a hundred and twelve days' detention.

Lytton had no triumphs of this sort to his credit. He much preferred to campaign indirectly, even anonymously, rather than expose himself to the vulgar brawling of wind-and-winter combat. At first the various limitations imposed by the new Act appear to have released his mind from its baleful absorption in his own ill-health, and to have conferred upon

---

never any question of imprisonment since he owned valuable books that could be seized and sold. These books were saved by the action of Russell's friends, who subscribed the necessary hundred pounds and bid that sum for the first volume put up for sale at the auction.

him once more that simulacrum of vitality and bubbling humour that sparkles so brightly through the pages of *Eminent Victorians*. 'I seem to be rising a little out of them [low spirits] now,' he told Virginia Woolf (25 February 1916). 'I don't know why – perhaps because the horrors of the outer world are beginning to assert themselves – local tribunals, and such things – and one really can't lie still under *that*.' And to Ottoline Morrell he wrote (16 February 1916): 'At moments I'm quite surprised how, with these horrors around one, one goes on living as one does – and even manages to execute an occasional pirouette on the edge of the precipice!'

The view from the precipice, however, did not fire him as it did Russell, but increasingly filled out his thoughts with a cumulus of worry. After the two Military Service Acts had been passed he at once appealed for absolute exemption on the grounds of health and conscience, expecting that, after a medical examination and an interview with the tribunal, he would be placed in Class IVb, and made liable for clerical work. Once this had happened he intended to appeal, and, in the eventuality of this appeal failing, he was prepared to be sent to prison – though with little confidence in his capacity to resist prolonged hardship. 'The conscience question is very difficult and complicated,' he wrote to James who was in a similar predicament to himself (28 February 1916), 'and no doubt I have many feelings against joining the army which are not conscientious; but *one* of my feelings is that if I were to find myself doing clerical work in Class IVb – i.e. devoting all my working energy to helping on the war – I should be convinced that I was doing wrong the whole time; and if that isn't a conscientious objection I don't know what is. ... I'm willing to go to prison rather than do that work.'

Lytton was subject to much nervous strain while waiting for the Hampstead Tribunal. 'I am still in a most half and half state – with a brain like porridge, and a constant abject feeling of exhaustion,' he reported to David Garnett. 'However, I am now on a diet, and drink petroleum o'nights, and even try now and then to do a Swedish exercise or two – so I hope I shall really soon begin to recover. I wish I could go away from this bloody town and its bloodier tribunals – I should like to go to sleep for a month; but it's no good thinking of moving till the first stage of the affair, at any rate, is over.'

His depression was deepened by a number of visits he made, as an ordinary member of the public, to watch the proceedings of the Hampstead Tribunal. 'It was horrible, and efficient in a deadly way,' he told Ottoline (March 1916). 'Very polite too. But clearly they had decided beforehand to grant *no* exemptions, and all the proceedings were really a farce. It made one's flesh creep to see victim after victim led off to ruin or slaughter.' And to Dorothy Bussy he declared (25 March 1916): 'I believe the name of the tribunals will go down to History with the Star Chamber.'

The amount of suppressed ill-feeling these tribunals were raising by this time all over the country was very considerable. Made up of ageing local worthies, they had become a means of venting public horror at the mounting slaughter on the Western Front, vicariously, upon the 'shirkers' who came up before them. Very few of the papers dared to refer to them, and the debates in the House of Commons were scarcely reported at all. It was really only by reading Hansard assiduously that one could discover what was going on. Perhaps it was not surprising that such scratch bodies, composed of miscellaneous Borough Councillors, without any judicial training, without any defined procedure, armed with immense powers and subject to the most violent animus, should find it difficult to interpret the conscience clauses of a fairly complicated Act of Parliament. Yet it was not just with conscientious objectors that they abused their powers; they were almost as unrelenting with cases of hardship. The accounts which Lytton got to hear from his friends of other tribunals were sometimes hair-raising. 'I don't think that even if you had mentioned God in your application it would have had much effect,' he wrote to Francis Birrell (March 1916), ' – he is quite out of fashion; and as for Jesus he's publicly laughed at. Odd that one should have lived to find oneself positively on that fellow's side.'

On 7 March Lytton appeared as a claimant for exemption

before the local Advisory Committee. These Advisory Committees had no legal basis, though in effect they controlled the administration of the law, at the same time shrugging off admitted responsibility. When an applicant appeared before one of these bodies, he was not allowed to argue his case, since the Committee maintained that it existed for advice, not decision. Yet the Tribunal almost invariably carried out the recommendation of the Committee, so that, when each applicant subsequently came up before it, he would find its mind already made up on the motion of a body that had refused to consider his case judicially. Lytton at once stated that he had an ineradicable conscientious objection to assisting in the war.

'I have', he said, 'a conscientious objection to assisting, by any deliberate action of mine, in carrying on the war. This objection is not based upon religious belief, but upon moral considerations, at which I have arrived after long and painful thought. I do not wish to assert the extremely general proposition that I should never, in any circumstances, be justified in taking part in any conceivable war; to dogmatize so absolutely upon a point so abstract would appear to me to be unreasonable. At the same time, my feeling is directed not simply against the present war: I am convinced that the whole system by which it is sought to settle international disputes by force is profoundly evil; and that, so far as I am concerned, I should be doing wrong to take part in it.

'These conclusions have crystallised in my mind ... and I shall not act against those convictions whatever the consequences may be.'

To all this the Committee listened politely. At the end, they made no comment whatever. They did not attempt to dispute what Lytton had said, but they at once informed him that they would recommend the Tribunal to grant him 'no relief'. The only logical assumption he could make was that they had spontaneously decided, for reasons unexplained, that his objection was fraudulent. He bowed coldly and left the room.

Between these court appearances, his social life billowed

on much as before, helping to drown the apprehension that had settled on him. 'Ottoline has been up this week, receiving a series of visitors in her bedroom at Bedford Square, in a constant stream of exactly-timed tête-à-têtes – like a dentist,' he wrote to David Garnett (10 March 1916). 'Yesterday there was a curious little party at Maynard's, consisting of her ladyship, Duncan with a cold, Sheppard with a beard, James and me. There she sat, thickly encrusted with pearls and diamonds, crocheting a pseudo-omega quilt, and murmuring on buggery.

'I have also met Mr Ramsay MacDonald lately – not I thought a very brilliant figure, though no doubt a very worthy one. He struck me as one of Nature's darlings, whom at the last moment she'd suddenly turned against, dashing a little fatuity into all her gifts.'

Nourished by special foods, fortified by Swedish exercises, Lytton prepared for his examination before the Hampstead Tribunal with all the thoroughness of a general laying plans for some military offensive. The exaggerated conduct of the Advisory Committee had given him an opening, he felt, for saying something really scathing, and he spent his days, so he told James, drawing up imaginary cross-examinations of Military Representatives. But although, as he wrote to Ottoline (11 March 1916), 'I am beginning to tighten my belt, roll up my sleeves and grind my teeth', he at no time relished the idea of putting his case without the aid of Counsel, and without any real hope of justice being done or even the elementary rules of fairness kept. 'I don't care much for the prospect,' he admitted to Francis Birrell (March 1916). 'I don't feel as if I had sufficient powers of repartee, and sufficient control of my voice, or my temper; and public appearances of any kind are odious to me.'

However he steeled himself for the ordeal. The spectacle he presented was even odder than his appearances at previous oral examinations, for entry to Balliol and to the Civil Service. For his eccentricity was now far more assertive, and he was out to vindicate himself before an acknowledged enemy.

The proceedings, especially in view of his unfitness for soldiering or even manual work in a farm or factory, soon grew farcical, as each side endeavoured with all possible ingenuity to make his opponent feel acutely silly.

'There was a vast crowd of my supporters surging through the corridors of the Town Hall, and pouring into the council chamber,' Lytton described the scene in a letter to Pippa (17 March 1916). 'My case was the very last on the list. They began at about 5, and I appeared about 7.30, infinitely prepared with documents, legal points, conscientious declarations etc.' His friends and family now put in a strong appearance. First there entered Lytton's character witness, Philip Morrell, bearing a light blue air cushion. Following him innumerable brothers and sisters, including James, Elinor, Marjorie, Pernel and Oliver, trailed in and lined themselves up opposite the eight members of the Tribunal, seated at a long table. Meanwhile, in other parts of the small courtroom, some fifteen attendant spirits, Bloomsbury painters and pacifists, took their seats amid a miscellaneous sprinkling of the general public. Finally, the applicant himself, suffering, among other disorders, from piles, and carrying a tartan travelling rug, made his entrance. Philip Morrell gravely handed him the air cushion which, to the astonishment of the chairman, he applied to the aperture in his beard and solemnly inflated. Then he deposited this cushion upon the wooden bench, lowered himself gingerly down upon it facing the mayor, and arranged the rug carefully about his knees.

The examination could now commence. In the course of it the military representative attempted to cause him some embarrassment by firing a volley of awkward questions from the bench.

'I understand, Mr Strachey, that you have a conscientious objection to all wars?'

'Oh no,' came the piercing reply, 'not at all. Only this one.'

'Then tell me, Mr Strachey, what would you do if you saw a German soldier attempting to rape your sister?'

Lytton turned and forlornly regarded each of his sisters in

628

turn. Then he confronted the Board once more and answered with ambiguous gravity: 'I should try and come between them.'

His sense of the dramatic and the absurd had carried the day. The Tribunal, however, were not amused, and his application for absolute exemption on the grounds of conscience was adjourned pending an examination by the military doctors. This examination was held only a few days later at the White City, where Lytton turned up, this time equipped with sheaves of doctors' certificates and an inventory of his medical symptoms. From eleven in the morning until half-past three in the afternoon he sat among a crowd of rowdy and promiscuous young men, silently perusing Gardner's *History of England*. But for once, in compensation for past trials, his disabilities stood him in good stead. He was rejected as medically unfit for any kind of service and formally pronounced a free man. 'It's a great relief,' he confessed to Ottoline that same evening. '... Everyone was very polite and even sympathetic — except one fellow — a subordinate doctor, who began by being grossly rude, but grew more polite under my treatment. It was queer finding oneself with four members of the lower classes — two of them simply roughs out of the streets — filthy dirty — crammed behind a screen in the corner of a room, and told to undress. For a few moments I realised what it was like to *be* one of the lower classes — the appalling indignity of it! To come out after it was all over, and find myself being called "sir" by policemen and ticket collectors was a distinct satisfaction.'

Now that there was no call to return to the Tribunal, Lytton straightway set off for Garsington, where he spent the next three weeks recuperating. 'I am still infinitely délabré,' he declared in a letter to Virginia Woolf (15 April 1916), 'in spite of the infinite solicitudes of her Ladyship. It is a great bore. I lie about in a limp state, reading the Republic, which I find a surprisingly interesting work. I should like to have a chat with the Author.'

A few days later he left Garsington to spend Easter at Asheham with the Woolfs. 'Virginia is most sympathetic, and even larger than usual, I think,' he wrote back to Ottoline (23 April 1916); 'she rolls along over the Downs like some strange amphibious monster. Sanger trots beside her, in a very short pair of white flannel trousers with blue lines, rattling out his unending stream of brightness. Woolf and I bring up the rear – with a couple of curious dogs, whose attentions really almost oblige me to regret the charms of Socrates.'[6]

Lytton returned to Belsize Park Gardens at the end of the month. He had by now laid up such a store of bucolic health that he felt ready to face the constant *brusquerie* of London without flinching. There was the National Book Sale – a quiet affair – a performance of *The Magic Flute*, James's appearance before the Appeal Tribunal, and – a delightful novelty – a ringside seat at a boxing match featuring the handsome and legendary Jimmy Wilde, the 'Tigerstown Terror'; all of which he took in his stride.

This month, too, his mother returned from wintering in Menton. Lady Strachey was now in her seventy-fifth year and had recently lost the sight of one eye. 'The news of Mama is very appalling,' Lytton had written to Pippa (10 February 1916). 'The only hope is that in spite of everything it will be possible to read with the other eye. The whole thing is the most sickening piece of bad luck.' For the time being this other eye remained quite all right, and the light of Lady Strachey's vigorous spirit continued to shine out unimpaired. 'I have now passed the "mezzo del cammin di nostra vita",' Lytton announced to her on his thirty-sixth birthday, 'and am rather surprised to find that existence continues to be highly interesting in spite of that fact. I used to think in early youth that one's development would come to an end in one's thirties – but I don't find it so – on the contrary, things if anything seem to grow more interesting instead of less. Also, they grow more satisfactory. One seems, as one goes on, to acquire a more complete grasp of life – of what one wants and what one can get – and of the materials of one's work, which give a greater sense of security and power. I think I now

---

6. Ottoline's chief pug dog.

see where my path lies, and I feel fairly confident that, with decent luck and if my health can go on keeping its head above water, I ought to be able to get somewhere worth getting to. Really I consider, apart from illness, and apart from the present disgusting state of the world, that I'm an extraordinarily happy person. One other reflection is this – that if I ever *do* do anything worth doing I'm sure it will be owing to you much more than to anyone else.'

Shortly after his return to London, Lytton took his mother down to Durbins, Roger Fry's house at Guildford, which Oliver and Ray Strachey had rented, and where Lady Strachey was to pass most of the next eighteen months. Before very long, the odd distinctive Strachey regime was in full swing. 'Several members of the Strachey family were staying there,' wrote Nina Hamnett, another guest that summer. 'In the evening Lady Strachey would read us restoration plays and we would play games. Everyone would choose a book from the library and hide the cover. They read a passage from their books and the others had to guess who had written it.'

After a few days at Durbins, Lytton left for another long spell at Garsington, which had recently been converted into a reserve for pacifist intellectuals, dons *manqués* turned farm labourers who, after digging in the fields during the day, would withdraw into the Manor House by night to 'puff churchwarden pipes by the fire', as Siegfried Sassoon put it, 'and talk cleverly in cultured and earnest tones about significant form in the Arts and the misdeeds of the Militants'. These nightly goings-on quickly excited the suspicions of the authorities, and the local police, taking it into their heads that the Member of Parliament for Burnley and the Duke of Portland's sister were German spies, spent much of their time nosing around the midnight shrubbery and trying to detect signals to Zeppelins.

Lytton did not greatly relish being incorporated into this flock of shaggily attired, argumentative critics and artists over which Lady Ottoline moodily presided as pastoral shepherdess. But amid this 'assemblage of Bloomsbury and Crankdom' he did come across a few interesting personalities – Katherine Mansfield 'very amusing and sufficiently mysterious'; Aldous Huxley 'young and peculiarly Oxford'; and the beautiful refugee, Maria Nys, daughter of a Belgian industrialist, later (1919) to become Aldous Huxley's wife, whom Lytton was now coaching in Latin for her entrance examination to Newnham.[7] Both Katherine Mansfield and Maria Nys, with her vulnerable and defenceless look of a child with a mature body, stirred in him some indecisive, easily quenchable feelings of sexual attraction which exercised his imagination for a while before rapidly coming to nothing. 'Why on earth *had* I been so chaste during those Latin lessons?' he asked himself in an autobiographical essay written later that year (26 June 1916). 'I saw how easily I could have been otherwise – how I might have put my hand on her bare neck, and even up her legs, with considerable enjoyment; and probably she would have been on the whole rather pleased. I became certain that the solution was that I was restrained by my knowledge that she would certainly inform "Auntie" of every detail of what had happened at the earliest opportunity.'

When the week-end parties and entertainments broke up, the days between slipped by calmly and serenely. All over the country there were rumours of conscientious objectors being shut up in underground cells, fed on bread and water, and transported as cannon fodder to the front line. But in the early summer stillness, from behind those high yew hedges and the placid aloofness of that grey stone façade, these rumours dwindled into distant echoes that hung in the air, vague and improbable. 'It's been unusually peaceful,' Lytton wrote to Maynard Keynes (10 May 1916), 'and I'm lying out under my quilt of many colours in the sun. I hope soon to have accumulated enough health to face London again for a little. It is horrid to sit helpless while those poor creatures are going through such things. But really one would have to be God Almighty to be of any effective use.'

7. Also living at Garsington was Sir Julian Huxley's future wife, Juliette Baillot, to whom Lytton was giving instruction in English verse.

4

THE VIRGIN AND THE GYPSY

During the autumn of 1915, Lytton had spent with the Bells at Asheham a certain week-end which set in motion seismic repercussions that were to reshape the entire story of the last sixteen years of his life.

Besides various Bloomsbury guests, including Duncan Grant and Lytton's cousin Mary Hutchinson, two ex-Slade student girls, Barbara Hiles and Dora Carrington, had been invited down. Barbara Hiles, 'a nice springing and gay girl', as Ottoline described her, was pretty and lively, considered by some of the Bloomsberries to be rather tiresome but kind.[8] Her friend Carrington was altogether different, and far more difficult to describe. She was not really pretty, and certainly not beautiful − her body being made for action, like a boy's. But she radiated an extraordinary aura of attractiveness. Her mind was intuitive rather than intelligent, and she had not been well educated. Nor did she talk particularly well, her voice being unusually flat and only in moments of emotion taking on a more melodius tone. Although not erudite herself, she had the charming gift of making others feel clever, drawing them out and listening with rapt attention to every syllable they spoke. Her manner was naturally flattering; she had a dazzling smile; and she invariably made up to − almost flirted with − everyone she liked. The strong emotions she provoked in many men − among them Mark Gertler, Ralph Partridge and Gerald Brenan − were chiefly aroused by her strange and enchanting vivacity. She was alive at every point, consumed by the most vivid feelings about people, places, even things. One way or another she cared about everything, and the strength and variety of her feelings

8. Several members of the Bloomsbury Group were to have reason to be grateful to Barbara Bagenal, as she later became. With great devotion she nursed Saxon Sydney-Turner through his declining years, and, after the death of Vanessa Bell in 1961, looked after Clive Bell, whose life she certainly helped to prolong.

confused her and wore her out. 'You are like a tin of mixed biscuits,' Iris Tree once told her. 'Your parents were Huntley and
Palmer.' Yet, all her life, she remained a giver not a receiver
and so uniquely herself that every look, every word, every
gesture was unlike that of any other person.

Always an elusive subject for the camera, no photograph
catches the sparkling colour, the impetuosity and dynamism
of her physical personality, or conveys much idea of the impression she created on others. At first sight there seemed
something childish about her – rather chubby round cheeks,
and clear eyes, so false-innocent, but full of light. To casual
acquaintances she was most easily recognizable by her thick,
light-brown hair, tinged with gold, and worn short and perfectly straight, like a Florentine page-boy's. But perhaps her
most striking features were her smooth milk-white skin, her
hands which had a peculiar independent character of their own,
and a pair of large, intensely blue eyes, rather sunk in their
sockets, and carrying an unforgettably tragic look that would
suddenly light up with quick mischievous amusement.

In the course of this week-end at Asheham, Lytton and
Carrington went off one afternoon for a walk along the
woods, and Lytton, being momentarily drawn to Carrington's
boyish figure, suddenly stopped and embraced her. Astonished, she broke away; and later that same day complained
bitterly to Barbara Hiles that 'that horrid old man with a
beard kissed me!' Her friend tried to reassure her that his
advances would probably proceed no further, but she naïvely
refused to understand what was implied until the giggling
Barbara spelt out the word H-O-M-O-S-E-X-U-A-L. 'What's
that?' she answered. And no amount of explanation seemed
able to mitigate the fierce resentment which had welled up in
her. Planning to pay him out at the first possible opportunity,
she tiptoed very early the next morning into Lytton's bedroom, taking with her a pair of scissors with which she intended to snip off his beard while he slept. It was to be one of
those simple, devastating practical jokes of which she was so
fond – a fitting revenge for his horrible audacity. But the plan
misfired. As she leant over him, Lytton suddenly, quietly,

opened his eyes and looked at her. The effect was instantaneous. She seemed to become hypnotized, and fell, there and then and for the rest of her life, violently in love with him.

To understand the nature of Carrington's all-consuming attachment to Lytton, to define the poignant centripetal role she was to occupy in his future career, and to explain the complicated emotional entanglements in which Lytton became enmeshed, some short account of Carrington's previous history is essential. One of five children, she was the daughter of a retired Indian railway engineer who had married a governess. She loved her father, but detested her mother who still retained all the tutorial, bullying mannerisms of the governess, and who demanded from her children an endless, fussy attention. Carrington responded passionately to the English countryside in which she was brought up, but disliked her schooling at Bedford – a town much favoured by ex-colonels for its cheap education, and which retained some of the puritanism of Bunyan – and hated her home, which was entirely saturated by her mother's odious presence. Her parents she once likened to those of H. G. Wells's Anne Veronica. They were commonplace and material: she was a *new woman* striving to be liberated. 'It's just like being in a bird-cage here,' she told Mark Gertler, 'one can see everything which one would love to enjoy and yet one cannot. My father is in another cage also, which my mother put him in, and he is too old to even chirp or sing.'

With her sister, who was older than herself and who had escaped from their humdrum home into a humdrum marriage, Carrington preserved little contact. On the whole she was always far closer to her brothers, the rather conventionally-minded Noel, who later became a publisher with the Oxford University Press and an editor of *Country Life*,[9] Sam, a pretty

9. Noel Carrington is the author of *Design in Everyday Life* and *Popular Art in Britain*, and editor of *Mark Gertler: Selected Letters*. For several years he was editor of the Penguin series *Puffin Picture Books*, but in 1946 decided to change to farming in Berkshire, where he now lives.

hopeless character who looked after dogs, and whom in later life she never mentioned except as a joke, and Edmund, her 'sailor-brother' shortly to be killed during the battle of the Somme.[10] Soon hardened and forced into independence by the rough-and-tumble world of these brothers, she reacted strongly against the callow, filial sentimentality ceaselessly exacted of her, and came increasingly to feel that she ought to have been born a boy. Her correspondence is full of disgusted complaints at her loathsome femininity. 'How I hate being a girl!' she exclaimed in an early letter to Mark Gertler. And in another: 'Today I have been suffering agonies because I am a woman. All this makes me so angry, and I despise myself so much.' As she grew up, this feeling of revulsion began to assert itself in various practical ways. She became an ardent supporter of women's emancipation. For many years, too, she kept intact an unremitting virginity complex, and found, once this had eventually been overcome, that she could derive pleasure from loving several people, of both sexes, pretty well concurrently. Not being strongly sexed, however, she never regarded her unpredictable, sporadic love-making in the customary light of a series of stereotyped 'affairs': each relationship was something completely *sui generis*.

At school Carrington had been considered odd, rather

10. Carrington often spoke of her brother 'Teddy' as a sailor and gave many of her friends the definite impression that he had been drowned at sea. A year or so older than she was, E. A. Carrington had just finished his time at Cambridge when war was declared. With a group of rowing friends he had decided to volunteer for a minesweeper, and joined the Navy as an A.B. After about eighteen months the Admiralty for some reason broke up his unit. He then put in for a commission in the Wiltshire Regiment, where his eldest brother Sam had served as a regular officer some years before the war, and where Noel had been serving since 1914. After a short training course he was sent out to France in 1916 and posted missing early in the battle of the Somme. There are other references in Carrington's letters to Sam, wounded in August 1914, and to Noel, wounded in June 1915. But the loss of Teddy was a great blow and did much to confirm her in her pessimism and pacifism. Her relations with him were not close, but he was the first young man she knew to be killed in the war and she felt passionately his loss. The last time he came on leave he was in sailor dress, and she made several drawings of him.

dreamy, careless and in perpetual need of discipline. Her
reports stated that she was no good at anything except drawing, and, since she also caused trouble at home, her mother
packed her off to the Slade School of Fine Art, where she won
a scholarship.[11] Once there, rejoicing in her new freedom, she
cut her hair short and dropped the use of her feminine baptismal name Dora – 'a sentimental lower class English name'
as she once described it to Noel (27 December 1916), which
she hated and by which only her mother continued to call her.
For the rest of her life, even after her marriage, she was
known as Carrington, *tout court*.[12]

From the moment she left home, 'there was a constant
struggle to avoid returning for holidays and to evade by some
ruse maternal discipline and inquisition', her brother Noel remembers. Their mother never ceased to regret this independence and her own loss of control over her daughter. It
was at the Slade that Carrington had first been introduced by
C. R. W. Nevinson[13] to the talented painter Mark Gertler. The
son of devout, impoverished, Jewish parents, Gertler had
spent a miserable childhood in the slums of Whitechapel.
From his earliest years he had been determined to become an

11. There are at the Slade two fine life paintings by Carrington, one of
which won her a first prize in 1912–13. She was also awarded second
place in the Melvill Nettleship Prize for Figure Composition (1911–12),
and, in her last year, a first prize for a painting from the cast. Visual art
and perceptions played a vitally important part in her existence, making
up for much of what was otherwise unhappiness. She enjoyed visual experiences, for instance, during the course of an ordinary walk, that most
people would never appreciate or even be aware of.

12. After the suppression of her baptismal name, Carrington attempted
to find a substitute, signing some of her letters 'Doric' or 'Kunak'. But
none of these inventions lasted for long. It was only very secretly that
Lytton eventually called her 'Mopsa'.

13. C. R. W. Nevinson (1889–1946), later a member of the London
Group and the New English Art Club. His most memorable paintings,
with their semi-cubist technique, record the sufferings of the First World
War, in which he was an official artist. As a student he was in love with
Carrington; after she left him for Gertler he married Kathleen Knowlman,
the daughter of a businessman. In 1937 he published an autobiography,
Paint and Prejudice, which reveals something of his despondent sense of
the world's ill-will towards him.

artist. In the autumn of 1908 he was sent to the Slade by the
Jewish Educational Aid Society, acting on the advice of William Rothenstein. Like Carrington, he wrestled with an inability to adapt himself to Slade standards, and stood out
from the uniform heap of students, among whom he soon
gained a considerable reputation.

Gertler was immediately attracted to Carrington. With her
short honey-coloured hair, now shaped pudding-basin
fashion, her big blue forget-me-not eyes, delicate pale complexion, shy and diffident manner, she appeared to him as
fragile and sublime as a piece of priceless First Period Worcester china. Her superior middle-class birth, emphasized by a
rather mincing precise accent and punctuated between sentences by a little gasp, enhanced her distinctive feminine
appeal – so utterly unlike the run-of-the-mill Jewesses, shop-
girls and models with whom Gertler had previously carried on
casual love-affairs. He was captivated by her air of simplicity,
her extraordinary childlike innocence, her passionate love of
beauty, her generous trustfulness and odd, unexpected impulses.

But appearances and early impressions were deceptive. She
herself was not deeply in love with him. According to
D. H. Lawrence, a close friend of Gertler's, who took Carrington as the prototype of Ethel Cane in his short story
'None of That', she was incapable of real love.[14] 'She was
always hating men, hating all active maleness in a man. She
wanted passive maleness.' Lawrence's explanation of Carrington's virginity complex, based mainly on what he had
heard about her relationship with Gertler and subsequently
with Lytton, was that what she chiefly desired was not love,
but power. 'She could send out of her body a repelling
energy,' he wrote, 'to compel people to submit to her will.' In

14. Aldous Huxley also made some use – and to rather different ends –
of Carrington's personality in his portrayal of Mary Bracegirdle in *Crome
Yellow.* 'Pink and childish,' Huxley describes her. 'Her short hair, clipped
like a page's, hung in a bell of elastic gold about her cheeks. She had
large blue china eyes whose expression was one of ingenuous and often
puzzled earnestness.'

Lawrence's view, Carrington was searching round for some epoch-making man to act as a fitting instrument for her evil and daemonic energy. By herself she could achieve nothing. Only when she had a group or a few real individuals, or just one man, could she 'start something', and make them all dance in a tragi-comedy round her, like marionettes. 'It was only in intimacy that she was unscrupulous and dauntless as a devil incarnate,' Lawrence wrote, giving her the standard paranoiac qualities of so many of his characters. 'In public, and in strange places, she was very uneasy, like one who has a bad conscience towards society, and is afraid of it. And for that reason she could never go without a man to stand between her and all the others.'

Although she did not passionately love Gertler, Carrington admired him and had what, to his chagrin, she termed 'an honest affection' for him. She wanted to value him as a brother, to be 'just friends'. 'I do not love you physically, that you know,' she wrote to him the same month as she met Lytton (November 1915), 'but I care for you far more than I do for anyone else.'

But for Gertler this was not enough. Dark and handsome, he was, in fact, more physically attractive to Lytton than to Carrington – a state of affairs that really satisfied no one. There was indeed something striking and unforgettable about his presence – the shock of hair, the amazing vitality, the versatile gift for mimicry and extravagant humour, and the romantic excitement he communicated was given depth by a contrasting look of profound suffering in the eyes, 'the vivid eyes of genius and consumption'. Tempestuous and aggressive in his behaviour, he gave the impression of having schooled himself in the rudiments of polite society only through a most supreme effort of the will that might disintegrate at any second. He plunged into every activity which took his fancy with unrestrained violence, and was an exacting friend, a demanding and jealous lover.

Undoubtedly Carrington felt excited by Gertler's wild personality. He held her spellbound with the ardent flow of talk that poured from his lips. His eager response to the movement and colour of life found an immediate echo in her own heart and filled her with elation. Chaotic and newly alive, he seemed composed of elements which knew no tradition, which were as far removed from her own dull background as it was possible to imagine.

In time their friendship developed into a fierce, intimate struggle of wills in which Carrington proved herself to be by far the more subtle and intransigent of the two. A vein of high and unconscious comedy ran through their harrowing relationship. Gertler impatiently declared his total love, and urged her without delay to become his mistress or his wife. She, finding herself unable to speak of such matters in any but the most oblique terms, reassured him that he was the mainland from which she made expeditions across the seas to remote islands, but to which she would always return. And when, growing tired and puzzled at these vague metaphorical evasions, he tried to cross-question her more precisely as to the date on which he might expect to be accepted as her lover, she would murmur 'next summer' or 'next winter', depending upon whether it was autumn or spring. Hope sprang eternal in Gertler's breast. Yet whenever the season appointed duly arrived, Carrington would slide off once more into evasions. He was the mainland . . . Finally, when Gertler's cries of anguish rose to fever pitch, she felt obliged to inform him that he was not ready yet for her 'corporeal body'.

He had almost despaired of ever winning her love, when, out of the blue, she would send him a parcel of spotted ties or a jar of honey together with a letter stating her determination in the future to be less selfish, to make him happier. And so he would be encouraged to take up the struggle once more. Her repeated exhortations to him to be happy, bewildered and depressed Gertler. What could she mean? What was she implying? He could never make her out. When she smiled, he imagined she was mocking him and stood amazed at the strange emotional dependence he felt upon everything she thought and did. But what exactly she was thinking and what she would do next he could never tell. It was hopeless. He had almost decided to give her up when, suddenly, yielding to his demands, she did go to bed with him – once. His predicament now seemed even worse than before. Still, somehow, she eluded him; still he had not really possessed her. She loved him – she swore she did – but the contact of his body 'made me inside feel ashamed, unclean. Can I help it? I wish to God I could. Do not think I rejoice in being sexless, and am happy over this. It gives me pain also.'

There was no deliberate intention on Carrington's part of torturing Gertler. On the contrary, she liked him immensely – but not in the way he wanted. Her independent nature could not submit to his bullying advances. Toughened by her fight to break away from the web of meaningless family gentility, she held this hard-won freedom very dear. From the experiences of her childhood, too, she had learnt never to abandon herself completely for any length of time to a single emotion; and it was this defensive measure which accounted for her inconsistencies, her minor deceptions, her aptitude for broken engagements, and which gave her ascendancy over the highly vulnerable enthusiasms of Gertler. Although, therefore, she was drawn to his exuberant personality, she sensed, through that part of her which remained detached from all she did and felt, that he represented a menace to her liberty. Consequently she was determined that their valuable friendship should evolve only as a blending of individual freedoms.

Yet, at a certain level of intercourse, the two of them were deeply incompatible. Neither was prepared or even able to forgo his or her own aims. Gertler, in particular, bitterly resented the inexplicable hold that this sturdy doll-faced girl could exercise over him. 'If only you could give yourself up in love,' D. H. Lawrence counselled him (20 January 1916), 'she would be much happier. You always want to dominate her, which is no good. One must learn to relinquish oneself, not to bother about oneself, but to love the other person. You hold too closely to yourself for her to be free to love you.'[15]

15. Gertler was almost certainly D. H. Lawrence's model for the sculptor Loerke in *Women in Love*, and the original of the painter Gombauld

Advice of this sort, always more pleasant to give than to receive, Gertler considered he could only hope to follow once he and Carrington were regular lovers. And when she point-blank refused this, he tried to talk himself out of his infatuation. She was, he reasoned, perfectly true to type; impulsive without being sensual, kind without being affectionate, with all the raw red passion for life decorously bred out of her. He was bewitched by this type simply because he was unused to it. She was the *lady* and he the East End boy. To take her seriously just because he was suffering an uncharacteristic setback would be to make an utter fool of himself. So he reasoned. But his eloquence, so efficacious in making others prisoners, had not the power to release him from his own captivity. For still she seemed to him like no other woman in the world, and without her life was 'awful and black'.

A one-time admirer of Nietzsche, Gertler held an opinion of women in general that followed superficially that of the German philosopher. An artist such as himself, he believed, needed women as he needed food. They were useful, perhaps even essential to him when he had time to spare for them. If one could not do without them, then one must dominate them – that, in any case, was what they liked. Carrington's apparent self-sufficiency wounded his vanity and contradicted his Nietzschean beliefs. In spite of himself, he had started to feel subservient to her; and this he could not tolerate – especially since her insidious influence disrupted the process of his art and corroded his creative faculties.

Carrington, on the other hand, believed that art derived from and was a distillation of personal experience. Gertler must be made to accept her at her own estimate, instead of treating her as a mere embryo to be incubated in a man's passion, hatched out into a common sluttish mistress or submissive dowdy wife and helpmate. Realizing that if she surrendered herself to his desires she might also have to

---

in Aldous Huxley's *Crome Yellow* – 'a black-haired young corsair of thirty, with flashing teeth and luminous large dark eyes'.

relinquish her hold over him, she refused to comply with his authority. His crude insensibility, his trick of plunging into intimate life without waiting for the natural ripening of intimacy, his rough and tyrannical rages repelled her and roused her own fighting qualities, so that she gathered all her forces to resist him. By the late autumn of 1915, when Carrington first encountered Lytton, their arduous affair seemed to have reached a deadlock from which neither side could advance or retreat.

But it was not to be so.

When Carrington returned from Asheham, she wrote to Gertler describing something of her visit, but saying nothing of the feelings over Lytton which had sprung up in her. 'I have just come back from spending three days on the Lewes downs with the Clive Bells, Duncan, Mrs Hutchinson and Lytton Strachey. God knows why they asked me!! It was much happier than I expected. The house was right in the middle of huge wild downs, four miles from Lewes, and surrounded by a high hill on both sides with trees. We lived in the kitchen for meals, as there weren'T any servants, so I helped Vanessa cook. Lytton is rather curious.'

Gertler himself had met Lytton a year earlier at one of Ottoline's parties. At that time Lytton seems to have cherished some modest hopes that the young painter might succeed Henry Lamb as the artist in his life. He put himself out to be kind and gallant to Gertler, pressing on him copies of Virgil's Pastorals, *Tristram Shandy*, *Hamlet*, the poems of Thomas Hardy, Keats's letters and the novels of Dostoyevsky. Gertler, flattered by these educational attentions, read hard and widely. He did more: responding with invitations to tea, going off for walks with Lytton in Kensington Gardens, staying at The Lacket and Belsize Park Gardens. Often they were uphill work, these poems and tea-parties. Yet he was genuinely very taken with Lytton and, being grateful for his kindness, slightly in awe of his urbanity, always remained on his best behaviour. On one occasion Lytton sent him some of his own poems and a typescript of 'Ermyntrude and Esmeralda'. These pieces were not exactly to Gertler's taste, but he replied with commendable diplomacy: ' "Ermyntrude and Esmeralda" I thought extremely amusing. But the poems I thought were fine. I wonder if you have any more work you could let me read? I should like to.'

What author could resist such an invitation? More poems quickly followed – interspersed with volumes of Shelley – and these helped to establish Lytton in Gertler's mind as a man of enlightened sexual views and serious artistic intent. It was now, in the late winter of 1915, that a plot of astonishing craftiness occurred to him. His estimate of Lytton's character had suggested a subtle and peculiar scheme for breaking down Carrington's resistance. He had tried, on his own behalf, every trick in the book: he had left her for three months at a time; he had bombarded her with his extremest attentions; he had spoken openly and honestly of his love for her; he had lied to her; he had lost his temper; he had reasoned; he had pleaded – all in vain. The odd conclusion to which his hysterical thoughts now impelled him, was that Carrington did not sufficiently esteem him as a painter. If his talent and the significance of his work could be authoritatively impressed upon her by a third, impartial being, then, he seems to have reasoned, the complicated knot of her sexual reserve might at long last be unravelled. After all, what girl would not give herself freely to a genius, to a superman?

The proper person to be entrusted with this vicarious task, Gertler decided, must undoubtedly be Lytton. He was the perfect catalyst. For it appeared from certain casual questions and comments which Carrington had let fall about him since her week-end at Asheham, that she shared Gertler's own respect for Lytton's culture and intelligence. The more he thought about it the more this scheme recommended itself to him from every conceivable aspect. Lytton, he felt sure, regarded him highly as a painter. And besides, although he very evidently believed in sexual licence and might well convert the impressionable Carrington to these incontinent beliefs, he would obviously have no interest in replacing Gertler himself in her affections. The plan seemed completely foolproof.

In pursuance of this plan, Gertler therefore saw to it that, while in London, Lytton and Carrington came regularly in contact with each other, tactfully absenting himself from these meetings so that his own artistic accomplishments might be fully eulogized without inhibition.

The result produced by these circumspect tactics was decisive. Carrington's infatuation for Lytton, which might in less propitious circumstances have wasted away into nothing, gained enormously in strength and purpose. Part of January 1916 she spent painting his portrait, and her diary entries for this month show the awe and veneration in which she already held him. 'I would love to explore your mind behind your finely skinned forehead', she wrote on 5 January. 'You seem so wise and so very coldly old. Yet in spite of this what a peace to be with you, and how happy I was to-day.'

Her happiness in his company redoubled every time they met. She could not contain it, and soon she determined somehow to make herself indispensable to him – without at the same time relinquishing Gertler's friendship. The obstacles in her way must have appeared almost insurmountable. The anticipated hostility of the terrifying Bloomsberries, of her formidable mother, and, worst of all, of Gertler himself – all of whom must consequently be kept in ignorance of her devotion to Lytton for as long as possible – would have sufficiently deterred most women. Not so Carrington. For her they acted less as a cause for despair than a spur to renewed endeavour. An even more discouraging problem with which she had to contend was Lytton's brand of avuncular lassitude, so kindly and oh! so apathetic. She quailed before his giraffe-like aloofness, and so frightened of him was she that she would seldom even risk a telephone call, since he sounded 'so very frigid and severe on that instrument'. How then could she seduce him? Often he exasperated her by his silence, his bland unresponsiveness. But though she sometimes felt like bullying him out of this passivity, she never actually dared to do so for fear of alienating him altogether.

For Lytton's own feelings towards Carrington were more mixed, changing as their relationship progressed. At times he felt flattered by her adoration; and at other times it alarmed him. He admired her zest for life, but her total lack of education and intellectuality bored him dreadfully. He could make her feel her ignorance most acutely, and her apprehension before him was so great that she scarcely dared to open her mouth in his presence. Nevertheless, in some moods, Lytton derived a good deal of enjoyment from instructing this raw and eager recruit in the delights of English literature – lessons which she very willingly absorbed and then liked to pass on to the still waiting, still vainly attentive Gertler, who thus received a double quota of prose and poetry.

Lytton's liaison with Carrington was more or less platonic, and the few attempts which were made later on to extend their relationship on to a physical plane were not successful. There seems little doubt that, on her account rather than his, Lytton regretted this failure to make Carrington his mistress. As Samuel Butler has written of a similar predicament:

> A man will yield for pity if he can,
> But if the flesh rebels what can he do?

About this incompatibility there was little enough, of course, Lytton could do, and his slight sense of guilt really derived from another failure on his part. Though at first Carrington liked to recognize in her protracted insecurity a safeguard to her independence, in time her uppermost desire became to marry Lytton, to look after him as his wife. But since they never married, their unorthodox relationship was always very volatile. Lytton's rather flimsy sexual attraction to her did endure for a time, but his association with the other sex was always of a fragile or filial kind. That image of the ideal which most men seek in women, appeared in a masculine form to Lytton, whose youthful hero-worship – a result of his adolescent feeling of ostracism – did not dissipate itself in more natural emotions as he grew up. Girls, who had no place at school and very little in the university, consequently did not fill any place in his imagination except in a domestic setting. Carrington therefore found herself being unconsciously manoeuvred into a maternal role, in time succeeding Ottoline as the chief confidante in Lytton's emotional life, instead of becoming the chief object of his love. It was not ideally what she would have wished – more than ever now she hated her womanhood and poignantly regretted not having been born a boy – but since it preserved her nearness to him, she willingly accepted the part.

This, then, was the capacity in which she set about making herself absolutely indispensable to him. Her extraordinary success can be measured in terms of the very deep and enduring affection for her which sprang up in Lytton. In the last year of his life, he wrote to her expressing his gratitude with a moving humility that hints at the sense of inadequacy he felt in matters where she was concerned. 'Your behaviour to me is indeed miraculous,' he told her (May 1931), ' – how you put up with my petulance and vagueness I hardly know. Existence without you would be altogether impossible.'

The kind of selfless love which he, in all his romances, had never quite attained, she succeeded in lavishing upon him without even trying. She almost lost her own identity, caring for him as other people care for themselves. When he was with her, she was alive; when he was away for a week-end, a day, she ceased to exist; and when he died, she ended her life.

Carrington's devotion is not easy to account for by any common-sense standards. Those few who knew of her attachment to him were incredulous. When Arthur Waley asked her what on earth there could be about Lytton to appeal to her, she exclaimed lyrically: 'Oh, it's his *knees*!' – an explanation which left Waley more dumbfounded than ever. This answer, however, does, very obliquely, indicate a certain similarity between her and Lytton. The fantastic, slightly disconcerting sense of humour which they shared was an expression of their peculiar, half-audacious, and highly sensitive non-conformity. In some respects they were the same type of person, emotional to a degree, yet awkward, giving the superficial impression of being cold and remote, insular and egotistical. Carrington seems to have felt that she had discovered in

Lytton a father-substitute with whom she could establish an intimate relationship free from the pernicious presence of her mother, which had so effectively destroyed her real father. Since her love for Lytton was never really consummated, she never met with the disillusionment common to such cases, the acute neurotic tension and recoil symptoms of fear. Instead, her attachment grew stronger until it came to infect every particle of her being. Thus, it would seem that both Lytton and Carrington were in search of some place of rapport away from their homes, where they might settle down with a parent-substitute – a mother to one, a father to the other – both pursuing their separate sexual lives free from any parent-fixation.

A somewhat scatterbrained and less sympathetic interpretation of their attachment has been put forward by Percy Wyndham Lewis, who diagnosed it simply as a father–daughter association, which Lytton embarked on in order to assert his revolutionary spirit of pseudo-manhood, and Carrington to establish, rather belatedly, the parental dominance which had been absent from her childhood. In his novel, *The Apes of God*, this arch-enemy of Bloomsbury culture – or of the 'Pansy-clan' as he liked collectively to call its tribesmen – has given a maliciously distorted and hilarious caricature of Lytton under the name of Matthew Plunkett. The crane-like Plunkett walks with an affected anarchical gait, adopts mannerisms reminiscent of his father, puts on in front of strangers an owlish ceremony of regulation shyness, and articulates with two distinct voices, one a high-piping vixenish shriek, the other of a more fastidious percussion – 'a nasal stammer modelled upon the effects of severe catarrh'. Being a modern man much taken up with modern psychology, this hero conceives the intensely original idea of submitting himself to psychoanalytical treatment in the Zürich consulting-den of the Jewish Dr Frumpfsusan – an extravagant notion obviously suggested to Wyndham Lewis by the career of James Strachey, Freud's pupil and English-language translator. Plunkett's aim, expressed in Jungian terms, is to get himself extroverted so that he can overcome a 'virulent scale complex

648

of psychical-inferiority'. Dr Frumpfsusan explains that he must falsify nature to his own personal advantage. 'Inferiority-feeling', he flatteringly suggests, 'may result from an actual superiority! The handicap of genius, isn't it?' He tells Plunkett that, for successful extroversion, he must seek to dominate the scene, that he should contrive to be a Gulliver in Lilliput. 'For that truly uppish self-feeling,' he concludes, '... you must *choose your friends small!* ... believe me, *you cannot choose your lady friend too small* ...'

It was therefore on doctor's orders that Plunkett took up with Betty Blyth, his Carrington-like girl friend, a petite doll-woman. Of the magical puppet prescription, her preternaturally tiny figure was dwarfed by the fairy giant of this Bloomsbury legend, who, towering far above her, would strive to assume the swaggering, buccaneering manner of the more flamboyant extrovert. When she calls on him one afternoon, he solemnly and with portentous concentration caresses one of his dollie's flaxen curls with the extreme fingertips of an extended tapering hand and arm, and feeling at last 'a distinct vibration, in the recalcitrant depths of his person', he swoops down and picks her up 'as though she had been a halfton feather'. With some difficulty, his knees bent and trembling, he staggers against the wall and then into his bedroom, only to drop Betty on the floor at the sudden shock of seeing, stretched out fast asleep on his bed, his last year's boy friend.

The explanation of Lytton's attachment to Carrington implied in this farcical drama is ingeniously malevolent. The acquisition of an awed and submissive girl friend, like the growing of a beard, was meant to conceal his dandified homosexuality and to establish him as a man of open virility, like his father, whom he unconsciously mimics. But this theory, which might plausibly enough be made to account for certain psychological factors in Lytton's character, does not follow the biographical course of events in his relationship with Carrington, either in the manner in which this relationship started up or in the extraordinary fashion in which it later developed. The basic triangular pattern of Lytton's emotional life was not, at its centre, altered by his association with Carrington. But, on the periphery, it became immensely complicated by the introduction of unlooked-for inter-relationships which sprang up between lover and confessor, and which sucked in and fatally involved fourth and fifth and sixth parties who all contributed, from time to time, something real and unique to Lytton's life.

Wyndham Lewis does, however, spot Carrington's father-fixation, of which she herself was unaware. The mysterious peace and happiness she experienced in Lytton's company, she put down, reasonably enough, to the very different nature of their friendship from the stormy affair she was still carrying on with Gertler. Lytton made no demands upon her, and did not seek to interfere with her freedom. In contrast to the tortured and tempestuous Gertler, he was at all times gentle and courteous. With him she felt safe.

And she felt more positive emotions too. At the prospect of spending some days with him at Garsington, she wrote to Lytton (20 April 1916) – 'mon chère grand-père' – confessing her 'incredible internal excitement'. Her letters to Gertler over this same spring period are less simple and consistent. Written in her childlike, illiterate, eloquent scrawl, freely illustrated with drawings not always relevant to the text, these letters are frequently undated and from their emotional content could be placed in almost any order. In one she suggests parting from Gertler at least temporarily 'as it nearly sends me mad with grief, at seeing you so miserable'. In another she urges him to read Keats. Yet another contains a lethal analysis of their incompatibility: 'You are too possessive, and I too free. That is why we could never live together.' But in a pencil note, written that May, she sounds a more optimistic chord. 'You will not love me in vain,' she promises him (16 May 1916), '– I shall not disappoint you in the end.'

Perhaps, at long last, Gertler thought, the plan was beginning to work. And so, containing his impatience, he waited on, wondering what would happen next.

The last ten days of May Lytton and Carrington spent together at Garsington during one of Ottoline's most strenuous and rowdy house-parties. Other guests included Philip Snowden[16] and his wife, H. W. Massingham, Bertrand Russell, Maynard Keynes and various young ladies either deaf or French. 'The Snowden couple were as provincial as one expected,' Lytton wrote to James (31 May 1916), '– she, poor woman, dreadfully plain and stiff, in stiff plain clothes, and he with a strong northern accent, but also a certain tinge of eminence. Quite too political and remote from any habit of civilized discussion to make it possible to talk to him – one just had to listen to anecdotes and observations (good or bad); but a nice good-natured cripple . . .'

Into this powerful anti-Cabinet conclave, during the Sunday afternoon torpor and while the peacocks were setting up their continuous shrieking about the garden, the prime minister and party arrived, just in time to rescue a servant maid from drowning. The atmosphere was more like a campaign in Flanders than an English country garden-party, but when the excitement had died down and tea was served, Lytton was able to observe at leisure Asquith's entourage. 'They *were* a scratch lot,' he reported to James. 'Lady Robert Cecil, stone deaf and smiling most sweetly at everything she didn't hear, a degraded Lady Meux (wife of Admiral Hedworth[17]) with a paroqueet accent, and poor old [Sir Matthew] Nathan, in walrus moustaches and an almost Uncle Trevor air of imbecile and louche benignity.'

But it was the prime minister himself who chiefly interested Lytton. Asquith seemed to have changed, grown redder and

16. Viscount Snowden (1864–1937), then member of Parliament for Blackburn and champion of the conscientious objector. Later he became chancellor of the exchequer (1924; 1929–31). He had been one of the chief founders of the Labour Party, and second in the Party only to Ramsay MacDonald.

17. Sir Hedworth Meux (1856–1929) who, the previous year, had been made Admiral of the Fleet. In 1910 he married Mildred, the third daughter of the first Baron Alington, and widow of Viscount Chelsea (d. 1908), and a few months later changed his name from Lambton on coming into a large fortune under the will of his mother-in-law. On his death he left the very pleasant sum of £910,465. His widow later married Lord Charles Montagu.

bulkier, since their last encounter in the summer of 1914. Then they had met at the height of the Ulster crisis; now they met again only a few days after the Irish Rebellion. 'I studied the Old Man with extreme vigour,' Lytton wrote to James, 'and really he is a corker. He seemed much larger than he did when I last saw him (just two years ago) – a fleshy, sanguine, wine-bibbing, medieval Abbot of a personage – a glutinous lecherous cynical old fellow – oogh! – You should have seen him making towards Carrington – cutting her off at an angle as she crossed the lawn. I've rarely seen anyone so obviously enjoying life; so obviously, I thought, *out* to enjoy it; almost, really, as if he'd deliberately decided that he *would*, and let all the rest go hang. Cynical, yes, it's hardly possible to doubt it; or perhaps one should say just "case-hardened". Tiens! One looks at him, and thinks of the War. . . . And all the time, *perpetually*, a little pointed, fat tongue comes poking out, and licking those great chops, and then darting back again. That gives one a sense of the Artful Dodger – the happy Artful Dodger – more even than the rest. His private boudoir doings with Ottoline are curious – if one's to believe what one hears; also his attitude towards Pozzo struck me – he positively shied away from him ("Not much juice in *him*", he said in private to her ladyship . . . so superficial we all thought it!). Then why, oh why, does he go about with a creature like Lady Meux? On the whole, one wants to stick a dagger in his ribs . . . and then, as well, one can't help rather liking him – I suppose because he does enjoy himself so much.'

Enjoyment was the keynote of his personality, Lytton afterwards reflected. A big, sanguine, jovial man, he had clearly just enjoyed a good lunch with several glasses of good red wine. 'There was a look of a Roman Emperor about him (one could imagine a wreath on his head),' Lytton wrote in his unpublished pen-portrait of Asquith (2–6 May 1918), 'or a Renaissance Pope ("Well, let me enjoy the world, now that I am Vicar of Christ."). . . . Standing beside him on the lawn, in the brilliant sunshine, with the house behind us and the landscape below us, I reflected that since I had last seen him a change had come over the world, as well. It was disgusting; and yet, such was the extraordinary satisfaction of the man that, in spite of everything, one could not help feeling a kind of sympathetic geniality of one's own.'

In the calmer moments of his stay at Garsington, Lytton went 'for some enormous walks', he told James, '– "expeditions" – with, precisely, Carrington. One was to the town of Abingdon, a magical spot, with a town-hall by Wren perhaps – a land of lotus-eaters, where I longed to sink down for the rest of my life, in an incredible oblivion. ... As for Carrington, she's a queer young thing. These modern women! What are they up to? They seem most highly dubious. Why is it? Is it because there's so much "in" them? Or so little? They perplex me. When I consider Bunny, or Peter (he's close by, at Magdalen) or even Gertler, I find nothing particularly obscure there, but when it comes to a creature with a cunt one seems to be immediately désorienté. Perhaps it's because cunts don't particularly appeal to one. I suppose that may be partly the explanation. But – oh, they coil, and coil; and, on the whole, they make me uneasy.'

Part of this unease was due to Carrington's idolatry of him. But he also felt some disquiet on behalf of Gertler who, in reply to one of his own letters earlier that month, had written back a despairing account of himself. Apart from his other worries, it appeared that he was nearly bankrupt. Something, Lytton decided, must be done. 'I've just heard from Gertler, who says he's on the brink of ruin,' he wrote from Garsington to Clive Bell (12 May 1916), '– has taken his last £2 out of the bank, and will have nothing at all in another week. Do you think anything can be done? I'm sure £10 would make a great difference to him, and I thought perhaps you might be able to invest some such sum in a minor picture or some drawings. Or perhaps you could whip up somebody else. If you do anything, of course don't mention me, as his remarks about his finances were quite incidental, with no idea of begging.'

On the same day Lytton wrote a somewhat stilted but kindly and generous letter to Gertler himself. 'I have long wanted to possess a work by you – so will you put aside for me either a drawing or some other small piece, which is in your judgement the equivalent of the enclosed [£10] – And I'll carry it off when I'm next in London. I only wish I could get one of your large pictures – what idiots the rich are! And how I loathe the thought of them swilling about in their motors and their tens of thousands, when people like you are in difficulties. What makes it so particularly monstrous is that the wants of artists are so very moderate – just for the mere decencies of life. All the same, though I'm very sorry that you're not even half as well off as an ordinary Civil Servant, you may be sure that I don't pity you – because you *are* an artist, and being that is worth more than all the balances at all the banks in London.'

Carrington was delighted that her friends, especially Lytton, were aiding the impoverished Gertler, and wrote enthusiastically to say how happy she was to hear that he was at last selling some of his pictures. Her letters from Garsington, being written on the spur of the moment and not for the eyes of posterity, contain no references to the prime minister or the other important personages, except Augustus John who, she assures Gertler, had 'made no attempt on my virginity last Tuesday' when they were alone together in a taxi. Her comments on Lytton are deliberately unrevealing. He is *very* serious, she remarks, but interesting when one gets to know him better. He has been reading poetry to her. Otherwise, she prattles on about the countryside, about 'the wonderful blue flowers, and so many birds singing all day'. She has been painting tulips, she writes, and instead of returning to meet Gertler in London she will stay on longer at Garsington – 'you could not but be happy if you were here now I think' – in order to paint more tulips – 'such tulips I feel weak with excitement'. She has also swum in the swimming-pool twice before breakfast. 'The children wear no clothes and run over the grass, and stand in the tulips, thigh deep in yellow tulips. It has made me depressed for they are so beautiful and I wished for the impossible to be more like them, and I hated this bulk of a body which surrounds my spirit, and yet I feel so lovely! Are you happy now because I love you.'

But somehow Gertler was not happy. His next meeting with Carrington had been summarily postponed, and all he got instead were descriptions of flowers and birds. It was more than human patience could endure. Sometimes he thought that she must be deliberately teasing him. Moreover, he had begun to suspect that she was concealing something from him, and accused her of being too friendly with Gilbert Cannan – then busy writing *Mendel*, his novel built round the Gertler–Carrington love-affair. Carrington, with literal justice, repudiated this accusation. Once, before a room full of people, Cannan had given her a brotherly kiss on the cheek – like a handshake – when she was about to leave. Nothing more. 'I care so little for anything except making you happy that I will promise not to kiss anyone since it causes you pain,' she reassured Gertler. Really, she went on, the incident was not worthy of discussion – though she nevertheless saw in it the opportunity for delivering a homily on trust: 'But do you not see that you cast a cloud of doubt on our trust in each other, by thinking for one moment that anything else or anyone could interrupt it? we shall always live in one sense apart. But I feel always come back to each other. There is nothing, absolutely nothing which can affect us now.

'You must cease being miserable at once, and believe me. What do I care for anyone else?, and you know it – '

Gertler's jealous suspicions had acted as a warning to her, and after this burst of self-exoneration she veered hastily towards harmless topics. How lovely the weather was; how lovely Dorothy Brett was looking. She wished that she could share with Gertler her love of Rimbaud, but it was all too new and enthralling for her to speak about yet. Finally she fell back once again to marine allegory: 'It has felt like a lock on the river, with our two boats up against the lock. Now it is open, and we can rush so swiftly down the river. and you won'T be impatient If my little craft is not quite so fast and sticks in the reeds. The great and lovely thing is that we are on the same river.'

But Gertler's suspicions were only partly allayed.

5

UNREGARDED HOURS

At the beginning of June, Carrington reluctantly dragged herself away from Garsington to join Gertler as a fellow guest of St John and Mary Hutchinson at Eleanor. Lytton meanwhile stayed on, grateful for the sudden influx of peace. Since his ordeal before the tribunals his health had not been good and he had been forced to lead rather a hole-and-corner life 'like a sick dog', he described it to Gertler (10 May 1916), 'dragging about from cushion to cushion, or creeping out into the sunshine to lie there dreaming'. Now that the rag-time of house guests, bustle and excitement had died down, Garsington was converted into a perfect Home of Rest. Even Ottoline herself had departed, and Lytton was free to sit out alone in the kitchen garden, idling, reading, and writing letters. 'I feel as if I were gradually turning into a pear-tree on a South Wall,' he told Vanessa Bell (2 June 1916), 'and unless you come and pull me up by the — root, before long, I shall very likely be doomed for the rest of my life to furnish fruit for her ladyship's table.' Even so the prospect of struggling out into the world again, of facing train journeys and the buffetings of London, filled him with palpitation and alarm.

When, in the third week of June, he eventually did leave, it was not back to the horrors of London, but for a remote Suffolk farmhouse, Wissett Lodge, which Duncan Grant had temporarily rented in order to set himself and David Garnett up as official fruit farmers, thereby discharging their obligations under the National Service Act. After the pugs, cushions and erections of Garsington, the atmosphere of bees and blackberries exactly suited his mood, and he hesitated here until the end of the month, with Harry Norton as the other guest. 'Is it the secret of life or of ... something else ... I don't quite know what? ... Oblivion? Stupor? Incurable looseness? — that they've discovered at Wissett?' he asked Virginia Woolf (28 July 1916). 'I loved it, and never wanted to go away.'

These summer days at Wissett rolled by very lazily, and he sucked in an added strength. Most of the time he spent reclining under the rambler roses and laurel bushes composing poetry, wandering from gooseberry-bushes to easels, listening to Norton on Prime Numbers, crouching over a wintry fire looking at old magazines, eating huge meals and sitting up into the early hours of each morning arguing about art. Their only adventure occurred one Sunday morning – the farmers' day off – when the four of them set out for a long walk towards the sea – not a very wise direction, as they discovered when an agitated corporal rushed up to them and nearly flung them all into a military gaol owing to their collective Germanic appearance and the incorrect Suffolk accent in which they answered his questions.[18] Apart from this episode, their life was unbrokenly smooth. 'Everything and everybody seems to be more or less overgrown with vegetation,' Lytton informed Ottoline (20 June 1916), 'thistles four feet high fill the flower garden, Duncan is covered with Virginia (or should it be Vanessa?) creeper, and Norton and I go about pulling up the weeds and peeping under the foliage. Norton is in very good spirits, having evolved a new theory of cubic roots.'

During their long evening talks, Lytton, in strictest confidence, told his friends something about Carrington. Their curiosity was understandably roused, and since Duncan Grant had been joined at Wissett by Vanessa Bell, Lytton was encouraged to invite Carrington down. But, on this occasion, she was unable to abandon Gertler, and a temporary lull settled over their triangular affair.

Lytton filled in this lull by writing an unpublished autobiographical essay[19] which was by way of being a new literary

18. The German spy question used recurrently to cause Lytton some embarrassment, especially in the country. 'It is distinctly unfortunate being so noticeable a figure,' he complained to Vanessa Bell (6 August 1917). 'Ought I to shave my beard for the period of the war? But would even that lull the suspicions of the yokels?'

19. Like 'Lancaster Gate', this autobiographical essay was intended for, and subsequently read to, the Memoir Club.

experiment, exposing to view a side of his character usually latent in his writing. Abandoning his familiar technique of a neatly integrated compression of material set in a pre-fabricated form, he deliberately employed a more diffuse style and consecutive, linear mode of composition, to describe in considerable detail the minutiae of a single not extraordinary day, Monday, 26 June, and the spontaneous self-observations called forth by them. Such a digressive manner does not really suit Lytton's pen, though he manages the exercise very cleverly. The experiment, however, also reveals a few minor disturbances in his emotional life – a slight breach with Ottoline, which, though quickly healed, sounded the overture to a wider, more permanent dissidence later to break out between them; an uneasiness with Vanessa Bell over their mutual attraction to Duncan Grant, and some hint of awkwardness with Duncan Grant over their mutual attraction to Vanessa Bell; a tremulous flirtation in the garden with David Garnett; and, arising from this last incident, a confession that although he was singularly fortunate in knowing so many friends, he could never be sure if any of them quite liked him.

On leaving Wissett, Lytton called on Gertler at his studio in Rudall Crescent to choose the drawing for which he had already paid. The description of this visit which he gives in a letter to Ottoline (3 July 1916) emphasizes the real lack of affinity existing between them. Gertler had shown him his 'latest whirligig picture', Lytton wrote. 'Oh lord, oh lord have mercy upon us! It is a devastating affair isn't it? I felt that if I were to look at it for any length of time, I should be carried away suffering from shellshock. I admired it, of course, but as for *liking* it, one might as well think of liking a machine gun. But fortunately he does all that for himself – one needn't bother with one's appreciations. He said it reminded him of Bach – Well, well!'

While Lytton was staying at Belsize Park Gardens, Carrington came over one afternoon to tea and told him that, later in July, she had been invited down again to Garsington – this time with Gertler. Lytton himself was expecting to return there about the same time, and now promptly wrote to Ot-

toline confirming his visit. 'I want to get my Arnold life done,'
he had told her earlier from Wissett (20 June 1916), 'and I
think under your peaceful shades it might be accomplished.'
His few days in London, though entertaining, had quickly
tired him, and he was eager for the repose of the country
once more. 'I am accumulating writing material,' he wrote
(3 July 1916), ' – and mean to be very industrious for the next
month or so.'

A week later he arrived down at Garsington, where he was
able, over a period of rather more than a fortnight, to do no
work whatever. Presided over by an apoplectic Ottoline, her
face almost entirely covered by peeling flakes of white chalk,
tightly swathed in a stiff gown of peacock silk, her slender
throat encased in baroque pearls, a continuous whirlpool of
a party surged about him – numberless guests all spiralling
round one another in the house, and overflowing into a cottage and the village inn. To make it worse, Lytton complained
to Mary Hutchinson (10 July 1916), most of them – including
Clifford Allen,[20] Eva Gore-Booth,[21] H. W. Nevinson[22] and
Lady Constance Malleson[23] – were 'so damned political and
revolutionary that I got quite sick of the conscientious objector and the thought of Ireland's wrongs'. But there were
plenty of other, less political guests within the crowd, among
them Evan Morgan,[24] 'a tall bright-coloured youth with a

20. Clifford Allen (1889–1939), created Lord Allen of Hurtwood in
1932. For his leadership of the resistance to military conscription he was
several times put in prison and his health seriously weakened.

21. Eva Gore-Booth, sister of the rebel Countess Markievicz, and noted
for her nerve and dash riding to hounds. Her gazelle-like beauty enraptured W. B. Yeats, who commemorated her in a poem. A minor poet
herself, she later lost her way amid the coils of philanthropic politics.

22. H. W. Nevinson (1856–1941), journalist and essayist, who during
the war won fame as the *Guardian*'s correspondent at the Western Front
and particularly at the Dardanelles, where he was wounded. His three
tomes of autobiography have been abridged into one volume, *Fire of Life*
(1935), by Ellis Roberts. His son, by his first marriage, was the painter
C. R. W. Nevinson.

23. Lady Constance Malleson, actress and writer. Youngest daughter of
the fifth Earl of Annesly, she had recently married Miles Malleson, the
actor, from whom, in 1923, she obtained a divorce.

24. Later Viscount Tredegar (1899–1949) who founded the Tredegar

paroqueet nose, and an assured manner, and the general appearance of a refined old woman of high birth'; and, once again, the alluring, impassive Katherine Mansfield – 'an odd satirical woman behind a regular mask of a face ... She was very difficult to get at; one felt it would take years of patient burrowing, but that it might be worth while.'

'The week-end is over – true enough – but ... the party still goes on,' he lamented in another letter to Virginia Woolf (17 July 1916). 'Carrington and Brett are here (ever heard of *them*) and now, a few minutes ago, Gertler (ever heard of *him*) turned up. The rag-time has begun again. I have fled into the garden – but one might as well try to fly from the Eye of the Lord.'

Lytton's disinclination to be drawn into this mixture of conviviality and altercation, as expressed to Virginia Woolf, was partly a device for concealing his growing attachment to Carrington. Yet it was also a very authentic apprehension that he voiced. The Gertler–Carrington situation struck him as gloomy and complicated, he confided to Mary Hutchinson (23 July 1916), 'but complicated in a dull way. The poor thing [Carrington] seems almost aux abois with Gertler for ever at her, day in, day out – she talks of flying London, of burying herself in Cornwall, or becoming a Cinema actress. I of course suggested that she should live with me, which she luckily immediately refused – for one thing, I couldn't have afforded it. And there she is for the present at Garsington, with Mark gnashing his teeth in the background, and Brett quite ineffectual, and her Ladyship worming and worming for ever and ever, Amen.' But at the same time, Lytton noticed that Carrington still rather admired Gertler, and he sympathized with him over the virginity question – 'unless she's the most horrible liar'.

But whatever the truth, the whole situation was growing too hectic, blowing up, he felt sure, into an incredible hurricane of an affair, and he soon decided to fly beyond the

---

Memorial Lecture at the Royal Society of Literature, and who was at this time an undergraduate at Christ Church, Oxford.

garden, into the arms of Oliver and Ray Strachey at their suburban haven at Durbins. 'I came here with the notion of working,' he wrote from Garsington to Barbara Hiles (17 July 1916). 'Mon Dieu! There are now no intervals between the week-ends – the flux and reflux is endless – and I sit quivering among a surging mesh of pugs, peacocks, pianolas, and humans – if humans they can be called – the inhabitants of this Circe's cave. I am now faced not only with Carrington and Brett (more or less permanences now) but Gertler, who ... is at the present moment carolling a rag-time in union with her Ladyship. I feel like an open boat in a choppy sea – but thank goodness the harbour is in sight.'

His anchorage at Durbins was a complete contrast to Garsington. Since Oliver only returned in the evenings from the Foreign Office to play Bach at the piano, Lytton was left with his mother, Ray and his sister Pippa, who all conspired to look after him and make him totally comfortable. The days were warm and sunny and he would sit out in the garden, now strewn with hollyhocks and lavender, working on his 'Dr Arnold' and recruiting after the agitations of the previous weeks. The only interruptions were provided by the occasional brief appearances of middle-aged visitors. Among these was Ray Strachey's uncle, Logan Pearsall Smith, who, Lytton told Ottoline (21 August 1916), 'is really now *more* than middle-aged – senile, one's inclined to say, poor old fellow – doddering on with his anecdotes and literature, which, in spite of the efforts of a lifetime, remain alas! American. I was rather amused by his view of Vernon [Lee], "I think on the whole she's the best talker I know" – I gave paralysed assent, and then ventured to add, "But perhaps at times she tends to be slightly boring" ... He wouldn't have it though. Well, well, de gustibus non est disputandum, which may be translated:

'Tastes differ: some like coffee, some like tea;
And some are never bored by Vernon Lee.'[25]

25. Violet Paget (1856–1935), the lesbian bluestocking who wrote books on aesthetics, politics and Italian art under the pseudonym of 'Vernon Lee'. In later life she grew rather deaf and was obliged to resort

Another visitor to Roger Fry's house was Walter Raleigh, who also seems to have struck the rejuvenated Lytton as being senile, though very pleasant. For the first time Lytton was feeling some sense of superiority over his distinguished seniors. 'He was far less outré and bloodthirsty about the war than I'd expected – chiefly just childish; rather timid too, it seemed, on controversial questions; and really I liked him more than I ever had before.'

Virginia Woolf had invited him down to Asheham after leaving Guildford in mid-August, but he had to refuse this invitation 'as I have engaged myself to go [to] Wales then, with a small juvenile party' (28 July 1916). He would, he added, be at large again in September, when he hoped to visit Leonard and Virginia in Cornwall.

The journey to North Wales was occasioned by Nicholas Bagenal, who had just then come out of hospital after recovering from a wound in the hip. He was in love with his future wife, Barbara Hiles, who persuaded Lytton to act as chaperon during a fortnight's holiday they were to spend together at her father's cottage, before Nicholas returned to the front. In agreeing to this Lytton had inquired whether he in turn might be accompanied by Barbara's friend, Carrington. And so the juvenile party was formed – 'though really', Lytton confessed to Mary Hutchinson, 'I sometimes begin to wonder what the diable I am doing in this galère of grandchildren'.

Difficulties and anxieties abounded. Lytton felt apprehensive over the inherent amenities of North Welsh cottages, and almost regretted that he had not chosen instead the known qualities of Asheham. Barbara too began to wonder whether she had done the right thing by including the finicky and censorious Lytton Strachey on such an out-of-the-way expedition. 'Oh Lytton I'm so excited and so afraid you will be unhappy, or bored,' she wrote to him (5 August 1916). In his

---

to an ear trumpet which she employed only when talking herself. She was famous also for appearing in the first line of a poem by Browning: 'Who said "Vernon Lee"?' There is a recent biography of her by Peter Gunn (1965),

reply he endeavoured to set her mind at ease, though because of his own doubts the note is a little forced and pessimism gleams clearly through. 'I pray for this weather to last,' he answered (8 August 1916). 'But if it doesn't, we can always shut the doors and windows, and cook and eat and cook and eat indefinitely. In the intervals we can hum tunes and recite ballads. But if it's fine we must scale the mountains with gazelle-like tread. . . . I'll bring some books.'

The chief difficulties, however, were provided by Carrington, whose fears outmatched the sum of Lytton's and Barbara's and possibly, too, those of the wounded Nicholas Bagenal. The invitation had originally been extended to her at the end of July, while she was still at Garsington, and her excitement was at once shaken up by doubts. 'How much do you all really want me to come?' she asked Lytton (30 July 1916). She was penniless and too 'proud' to accept money from another woman, namely her friend Barbara, who was almost as poverty-stricken as herself. On the other hand, considerations for Gertler do not seem to have strayed into her mind. After her lecture on trust, surely he would not dare to object. She therefore resolved to *walk* to North Wales, or possibly to bicycle there. But was it all going to be worth such a tremendous effort? How could she tell? 'It would be awful to walk so far,' she admitted to Lytton (30 July 1916), 'and then be met with the chilly eye of criticism!' But her prevailing fear was that, under adverse conditions such as they might well come up against in Wales, her tenuous attachment to Lytton could be subjected to new strains and stresses, might snap altogether. Well, she could only do her best. She was, so she assured him, assiduously reading her Donne, and in order to please him had begun to take lessons in French. The rest of her news was gossip in the Strachey manner. 'Ottoline insists on trying her best to get my state of virginity reduced, and made me practically share a bedroom with Norton!! And Poor Brett got sent out four times in one morning with Bertie for long walks across remote fields by her Ladyship!!'

Early in August, her famous and refurbished virginity still intact, Carrington went off to stay with her parents at

Hurstbourne Tarrant. She was in a fiercely rebellious mood, vanishing out of the house during the day for long walks over the hills with a dog named Jasper, and at night sleeping out on the roof under the open sky. Her mother, so she complained to Gertler, 'was more awfull than ever', and her father more pitifully ill and old: 'I hate him for living as he does or rather I hate life for making him live,' she raged. 'It is so undignified an end like this.'

Meanwhile negotiations over the holiday were growing daily more involved. Lytton had offered to pay for Carrington's travelling expenses, but, possibly from a sense of delicacy, did not write to her at her parents' home to tell her so. Instead he communicated with Barbara Hiles. 'I am rather rich just now, I find,' he lied (8 August 1916), 'so it would be absurd for her [Carrington] to go by foot, or worse, for lack of money.' This news was speedily relayed on to Carrington, but still she hesitated, until her mother, learning of her projected journey now for the first time, absolutely forbade it. Her mind was then very simply made up. She would go.

At last the complicated preliminaries were at an end, and it was arranged that at four o'clock on the afternoon of Saturday, 12 August, the four of them would converge on the platform of Llandudno Junction – Barbara and Nicholas having travelled from Westbury-on-Severn in Gloucestershire, Lytton from Guildford in Surrey, and Carrington from Andover in Hampshire.

On the day beforehand Lytton left Durbins for Belsize Park Gardens to prepare for his journey. Late that Friday afternoon, as he was wandering down the Haymarket, all at once he sensed, pervading the atmosphere, an extraordinary spirit of cheerfulness, of bonhomie. Puzzled, he glanced round. 'The streets were empty ... and I was vaguely strolling, when, (without exaggeration) I became aware of a curious sensation of "bien-aise" in the air,' he later recounted, describing the incident. For a moment or two he was at a loss as to how to account for this feeling. Then, 'looking round I saw a motor coming up the hill; it was open, and in it was Asquith, alone, with a look of radiant happiness upon his face – happiness which was indeed literally radiant, for I had actually felt it when my back was turned. He passed on without seeing me – he really looked too happy to see anything. I think there was a portmanteau in the car, and I suppose he was off somewhere for the week-end.'

As the prime minister, glowing with joy, floated off from this singular unperceived *rencontre*, away into the distance, – the simile is Lytton's – a seraph in a heavenly ecstasy, the immanent euphoria flooding the Haymarket drained away, and Lytton was left with a sense of amused and astonished envy. How the devil did the old boy manage it? He wished that he could feel one half so buoyant over his own week-end. The good-humoured incredulity he felt was all the more remarkable since he strongly disapproved of Asquith's conduct over the recent Roger Casement trial. 'Casement, I don't take much stock of, somehow or other,' he had written to Ottoline (3 July 1916), 'though I perceive the romantic bravery of the man; yes, I do perceive it, but the absence of Wisdom refrigerates me – and something sentimental and cheap in his phraseology too. I could have imagined some much grander speech. Of course I should be very glad if they didn't hang him, but I can't believe there's much chance of that – especially with Asquith prime minister. That old buffer has certainly been distinguishing himself lately. Is he a coward, or a fiend, or simply a dunderhead I wonder?'

Whichever he was, Asquith continued, off and on, to fascinate and perplex Lytton, and, whenever they met, to instil within him a humorous grudging amiability. If only *he* could derive so much pleasure from life!

The fortnight in Wales on which he now embarked turned out, however, to be far more pleasurable than he had dared hope. Everything was perfectly civilized – bees-waxed parquet floors, spring mattresses, air cushions, delicious meals and 'an old hag to wash up'. The cottage itself, very small and sequestered, painted white outside and with a tiny garden filled with flowers, was perched half-way up one of the chain of mountains which on all sides shut them in, while along the flat valley directly below there ran a broad and shallow river – the sort of wild precipitous country that agreeably reminded Lytton of Rothiemurchus. 'I enjoyed the Welsh fortnight very much indeed,' he afterwards told David Garnett (2 September 1916). 'You can't think how kind they all were to me – and how wonderfully nice. Barbara managed the cottage, and the cooking with the greatest skill ... Nick was really charming – his gaiety of spirits never ceased. It will be too horrible if he is forced back into that murderous whirlpool. As for Carrington – we seemed to see a great deal of each other. But this let me remark at once – my attitude throughout in relation to *all*, has been of immaculate chastity, whatever the conduct of others may have been.'

As always, and increasingly as time went on, Lytton loved to be surrounded by men and women younger than himself. The high spirits and energy of young people infected him in such a way that he seemed able to shrug off his own inhibiting 'antique spirit', as he used to call it. One half of him, he once told Ottoline, felt as if it had gone back ten years or twenty, while the other half, he was pretty sure, had moved forward by about the same amount; so the result was – 'me voici, a mixture of 18 and 52'.

Although a teenager for most of this time, when things went wrong he would rapidly revert to a quinquagenarian. On the very day of their arrival at the railway station, an icy wind started up which persisted non-stop for the next two weeks. Every hour great bundles of cloud would come toppling down the mountains and envelop the cottage; and not a single day passed without some rain. But there were warm intervals. during which the party, released from their hideout, sprang up into the mountain fastnesses with maximum agility. They also made expeditions to Conway and Llandudno, where the three younger members bathed while Lytton, according to Carrington, 'wandered aimlessly gasing at beautiful faced youths. Which in truth there were but few of.' Inevitably on one of these excursions, he fell victim to a chill, which reduced him to bed for most of the second week. Carrington sat at his bedside painting his portrait as he lay there, and listening to him declaim Shakespeare's sonnets and the poems of John Donne.

One highlight of the holiday was a bottle of champagne. Nick withdrew the cork with a pop – and Lytton, flinging his arms wildly in the air, shrieked: 'God! What the war must be like!'

In the final week of August the party broke up and Lytton and Carrington went off together for a few days to Bath – 'a most charming town', he informed David Garnett (2 September 1916). 'How one bounds along those elegant streets, and whisks from Square to Circus and Circus to Crescent! One almost begins to feel that one's on high heels, and embroidery sprouts over one's waistcoat. And then – the infectious enthusiasm of my youthful companion . . . you smile; but you are mistaken.'

Something of this infectious enthusiasm and the manner in which they both swept through these days is conveyed by a letter which Carrington innocently sent off to Gertler. 'Yesterday we investigated the whole town,' she wrote to him (29 August 1916). 'Every house nearly! and sat for about two hours in a 2nd hand book shop. I discovered accidently an early Voltaire which gave Lytton great joy. as he had been looking for it a long time. After tea we walked through the city upon to a high hill because we had seen in one of the books on architecture, (that I studied all Sunday), a wonderful house. Called "Widcomb House". and indeed it was beautiful! – Fielding lived in this village also – We boldly asked the maid if we might go over the garden. She fetched after a long time an incrediably old lady. Who said we might. But seemed utterly bewildered why anyone should want to see her house! The garden with a deep valley very big with high trees, distant hills gave me strange emotions. It was a sad morbid place. and deadly quiet – Lytton read the Voltaire to me. an account of Frederick the Great, and Voltaire's relationship with his son.'

After a highly diversified couple of days in Bath, Carrington regretfully parted from Lytton and returned to Andover.

She had been with him for three consecutive weeks, had lived with his moodiness, his invalidism, and loved him more than ever. 'I did enjoy myself so much with you,' she wrote back to him, ' – you do not know how happy I have been everywhere, each day, so crowded with wonders ... Dear Lytton. I have been so happy, incredibly happy.'

Lytton himself, his money and adventurous feelings still not wholly eliminated, had by this time journeyed on to Wells, a town quite as charming as Bath. 'What a pity it is that it should now be the fashion for clergymen to believe in Christianity,' he wrote to his mother (3 September 1916). 'I should have so enjoyed being Bishop of Bath and Wells!' For a week he lingered on at 6 St Andrew Street, 'sunk down into lodgings under the eaves of this somewhat démodé Cathedral'.

He had done little writing during these 'unregarded hours' of wandering; but a short poem which he now composed gives some clue as to how, at this stage in its development, he liked to see his semi-platonic, oddly romantic association with Carrington a wholeheartedly half-and-half affair, so far removed from her own primary involvement.

Who would love only roses among flowers?
    Or listen to no music save Mozart's?
Then why not waste life's unregarded hours
    With fragile loves and secondary hearts?

Ah! Exquisite the tulips and the lilies!
    The Schuberts and the Schumanns, how divine!
Then kiss me, kiss me quickly, Amaryllis!
    And Laurie, mix your wantonness with mine!

6

FRAGILE LOVES AND SECONDARY HEARTS

Something had gone wrong.

No longer could Gertler place any reliance on Lytton. As his unknowing champion in the tilts of love, he had proved himself totally inefficient. Gertler felt, also, a mounting irritation at the inexplicable friendship that had grown up between the two of them. This juvenile party in Wales was the last straw. He was not jealous of Lytton – that would be absurd – but he felt he had been cheated.

For already strange and disturbing rumours had begun to percolate through Bloomsbury. Ottoline Morrell, indignant at the thought of losing Lytton to Carrington, whispered mischievous scandal in his ear, echoed by Dorothy Brett who, almost equally possessive, feared the loss of her 'virgin niece'.[26] At the same time, none of Carrington's letters did anything to clear up the mystery. With implacable irrelevance she wrote to Gertler of Andrew Marvell, of Shakespeare and of John Donne 'who excites me to such a pitch. that I can think of nothing else some days'; and, in a more esoteric style, of how wonderful and extraordinary it was to wear trousers and feel like a young and eager boy 'not tied – with female encumbrances, and hanging flesh'. She also described, ecstatically. the 'Cezannesque' Welsh landscape, and very plaintively, the pygmy inhabitants of Wales – 'the most vilely ugly human beings I have ever seen. The women gave one actual pain to look at, with their crooked teeth and red shining faces and bleary bulbeous brown eyes!' Most depressing of

26. 'How and why Carrington became so devoted to him [Lytton] I don't know,' Dorothy Brett told the author. 'Why she submerged her talent and whole life in him, a mystery. ... Gertler's hopeless love for her, most of her friendships I think were partially discarded when she devoted herself to Lytton. ... I know that Lytton at first was not too kind with Carrington's lack of literary knowledge. She pandered to his sex obscenities, I saw her, so I got an idea of it. I ought not to be prejudiced. I think Gertler and I could not help being prejudiced. It was so difficult to understand how she could be attracted.'

all she dwelt on her expansive upsurge of happiness – an un-discriminating happiness which seemed altogether to exclude Gertler. 'I am excited over everything lately. The fullness of life. So many people alive who one doesn't know, so many wonders past which one finds everyday, and then the things to come. oh the wonder of it all!'

Gertler had by now grown intolerably weary of this blithe cultural correspondence. On those matters about which he really wanted to know, she told him nothing. He chided her for her secrecy, and she replied by blaming his egotism. Ab-ruptly he switched his attack to Lytton's character, singling out, with paradoxical logic, his homosexuality as the chief cause of complaint. But to his surprise Carrington rushed to his defence, saying that she had recently come to change her views on that subject, since 'one always has to put up with something. pain or discomfort, to get anything from any human beings. Some Trait in their character will always jar. But when one realizes it is there, a part of them, and a small part – it is worth while overlooking it. for anything bigger and more valuable – ' And in conclusion she added: 'Lytton sends you *his* love. you must like him because I do so very much.'

Ironically, so it seemed to Gertler, Carrington's views on heterosexuality still appeared unchanged, and on her return to Andover, his vexation and disappointment overflowed into a long despairing cry, a bitter tirade of pleas and re-criminations. The letter he now wrote (4 September 1916) summarizes very powerfully all the agony of frustration that had welled up in him over the past months and years.

God I ask only one thing of you – one little tiny prayer. Let me love and be loved. Create an inseparable bond between some being and myself. God, I am lonely – so lonely. I can't bear my loneliness. ... Do you love me? Can you love? Is there nothing between us except my own fiery love? ... Have you any concentrated passion at all? ... You are impossible – impossible to love. You are so incon-sistent too, God save me from this Hell that I have been living in for so long. Save me soon, I can't bear it much longer! Your body seems most beautiful to me. Most painfully I Long for it. ... How can you bear to let your beauty pass by, when you know there is a man dying for it! Have you a Heart. There is only one period of Youth in our life time – Don't waste it! And me, Take me off the Rack of Torture soon. ... You have had Lytton with you and he easily made up for my absence. He did well enough, Ugh! Ugh! Ugh! How I hate the coldness of life! It is not your fault Carrington Life is so arranged. Life has made you cold. You can't come close – you can't nestle. You are too weak! You say in your letter you are 'a wild Beast never to be tamed'. For me you are not wild enough, You are too spread out – You are not concentrated – That's what I hate about you! Your ego has never been surpassed! You are frightened – Frightened always, of soiling yourself! ... you are not a 'wild' Beast but a frightened Beast and a timid Beast – Please don't flatter yourself. If you had known many men – had had many lovers then you could boast of this 'Wildness' and this flightiness of your soul! But my poor Virgin, you have known *no* man yet. ... I hate your Virginity!

Although Gertler was right in supposing Carrington to be drifting away from him, the situation between them was not yet so abysmally bleak as, in his despair, he had imagined. Indirectly, Lytton's influence on her was having something of the effect that Gertler had originally looked for. The author-poets of 'Venus and Adonis', 'To his Coy Mistress', and 'The Extasie' were, in fact, accomplishing more by way of over-coming Carrington's virginity than all Gertler's impassioned exhortations. Even though Lytton was to mean incomparably more to her than any other human being – perhaps already did so – his importance in her life in no way coincided with the part Gertler played, and in no way diminished her affection for him. As a fellow painter he could appreciate certain sides of her character far more intimately than any writer, so that, while she admitted to being 'incredibly happy' with Lytton in Wales, Carrington could still, with what she thought to be perfect honesty, write back to Gertler that 'the intimacy we got at lately makes other relationships with people strangely vacant, and dull'.

Another of Carrington's peculiarities, which to some extent strengthened Gertler's position, was that she could never bear to give anyone up. Even when she feared to see someone, she loved to think and dream of him, and to write him letters. After her return home to Hurstbourne Tarrant, she sent off copious letters to Gertler, along with which went various tokens of her abiding affection – presents of flowers and plums, and all the more ordinary endearments. Even her allegorical effusiveness – 'We will always be twin souls, but separate souls. mounting together' – and her most irritating literary tutelage – 'My admiration grows daily for John Donne. (you must pronounce it like the verb "Done". as if his name was spelt Dunn. I have only Just mastered it. But it is correct.)' – were often oblique indications that she sincerely valued Gertler's friendship and wanted to share more with him.

About this time Carrington began to make arrangements to live in London, so that she might be nearer Lytton and farther away from her parents. Towards the end of September she moved into an apartment with Dorothy Brett, on the second floor of No. 3 Gower Street. Above them in the same building lived Middleton Murry and Katherine Mansfield; and below, Maynard Keynes, Gerald Shove and Sheppard, who had been taken on as a translator by the War Office. For several weeks prior to this move Carrington had been writing to Gertler saying how much she was looking forward to seeing him more frequently. But when they did meet, Gertler flew into a rage, and on leaving him Carrington wrote from Gower Street to tell him that 'I simply must be alone for a little while – do you mind. It is *not* that I am in any way angry with you ... only I could not see you and think at the same time as I want to. – And in my distantness which you would interpret as coldness, we will disagree and possibly quarrell.' Always prone to feelings of guilt, she could not bear anyone to reproach her. Gertler's anger and jealousy, which had brought about so many of their temporary estrangements, were soon to lead to her token submission and, only then, when that failed, finally and regretfully, her complete renunciation of him.

There were, however, hidden reasons to account for her 'distantness' and her inability over these autumn and winter months to see quite as much of Gertler as she had promised.

While in Wales, it had been decided that a country cottage should be rented for Lytton, where he could work in peace. Since he could not afford this kind of gracious retirement on his own, the scheme was to be promoted on something like a company basis – various of Lytton's Bloomsbury friends taking shares (that is, paying an annual sum of money) in return for which they might use the cottage (which would be inhabited and vicariously looked after by Lytton himself) as their own occasional country retreat. 'Have you heard of the scheme for a country cottage?' Lytton asked Maynard Keynes (14 September 1916). 'Would you be willing to join? Barbara has already found something that sounds as if it might be suitable. Oliver and Faith [Henderson] are going to take shares – also perhaps Saxon. I don't know about Harold. Oh, Carrington, too.'

Barbara Bagenal's find was an unfurnished house in Hemel Hempstead, at an annual rent of forty-eight pounds and with 'a loft for conscientious objectors'. When this fell through, the quest was vigorously taken up by Carrington. 'I boldly went into all the estate agents in Newbury yesterday, and enquired about houses,' she reported to Lytton at the beginning of her search (16 September 1916). '... I have maps of every square inch of the country now! And correspondence with every auctioneer in Newbury Marlborough, and Reading!' Sometimes accompanied by Barbara, she would bicycle all over the countryside, often travelling fifty miles in a day. But though unflagging, she was, as both Lytton and Barbara came to realize, a highly impractical house-hunter. Her notions of what would accord with Lytton's literary genius were so extremely grandiose that, as time went by, the scheme seemed to enter the realms of elevated fantasy. 'Our country cottage still floats high in the air,' Lytton commented to Ottoline (1 October 1916), ' – a cottage in Spain.'

In the meantime, Lytton was obliged to carry on as best he could. From Wells he had gradually and with great indecision drifted back, via Park Cottage, Ledbury ('among my dowagers'), Garsington and Eleanor, to London, which 'I found horrible – stuffy and chilly at the same time, and packed full and flowing over, with inconceivably hideous monstrosities. They push one off the pavements in their crowds, they surge round every bus, they welter in the tubes – one dashes wildly for a taxi, but there are no taxis left. In the night it's *pitch* dark; one walks wedged in among the multitudes like a soldier in an army – one peers in vain for some vestiges of beauty – all in blackness – but one can't help hoping; then at last somebody strikes a match to light a cigarette – and a seething mass of antique Jewish faces is revealed. No! London is decidedly *not* a place to be in just now.'

Nevertheless, it was in London that Lytton was to remain fairly continuously over the next fifteen months. On arriving back at Belsize Park Gardens, he at once settled down to work, and by the last week of October he was able to announce that 'cet épouvantable Docteur Arnold est fini – praise be to God!' Almost immediately he began reading and making notes for 'The End of General Gordon', but progress, he informed Ottoline, was very slow.

The winter passed by uneventfully. While he was working, there was little time for anything else. His existence, however, was never so dire or solitary as he liked to make out. There were parties at Barbara's studio in Hampstead and at Augustus John's in Chelsea, dinners at the Café Royal with Keynes, teas with Carrington and Katherine Mansfield at Gower Street, luncheons and occasional theatres with Boris Anrep ('very fat and friendly') or with Sheppard 'and a party of young men'. He also took Carrington over to Hogarth House in Richmond to see Leonard and Virginia (shortly to set up their Hogarth Press, for which Carrington did woodcuts);[27] he paid several visits to the new Omega Club in Fitzroy Square, where he met Arnold Bennett and W. B. Yeats; and inspected the Bloomsbury decorations at No. 4 Berkeley Street, 'which I found extremely depressing. They're in a very small room at the top of the house, and consist of colossal figures plastered on the walls, like posters, but without the gaiety of

27. The first publication of the Hogarth Press, *Two Stories* (1917) – now a collector's item – has four woodcuts by Carrington, for which she received the sum of fifteen shillings.

posters.[28] In the middle of the room stood Margot [Asquith], very stiff and straight, in a very short black dress and a white veil.'

He was by now being mildly courted by a retinue of hostesses, among them Dorelia John, Ethel Sands and Mary Hutchinson, of whom the last was soon to emerge as the second woman of his life, whose intermittent role was largely overshadowed by that of Carrington. 'She is indeed a wonderful creature,' Lytton wrote of her some years later to Roger Senhouse (21 September 1927), 'and I am delighted that you should have experienced the activity and enthusiasm of her affections. It is very rare to find such a spontaneous warmth, isn't it? Such a generous appreciation of life! — I can realise what a comfort a talk must have been to you.'

After a week-end at Asheham in November, Lytton succumbed to a series of winter illnesses which greatly slowed down his work, and he decided to convalesce over Christmas at Garsington, immune from the newspapers and other vulgarities of London. Ottoline herself was none too well that winter, and as a fellow sufferer Lytton would send her letters full of compassion and solicitous advice. To Virginia Woolf he at the same time (21 February 1917) wrote to say that 'Lady Omega Muddle' as he sometimes referred to the unhappy woman, 'is now I think almost at the last gasp — infinitely old, ill, depressed, and bad-tempered — she is soon to sink into a nursing-home, where she will be fed on nuts, and allowed to receive visitors (in bed).'

He had now started again his occasional articles and reviews for the *New Statesman* and this added to his customary winter discontent, which he tried to assuage by reading and re-reading *Gargantua and Pantagruel*. 'Yes, Rabelais has surged over me altogether,' he assured Ottoline (6 February 1917). 'I read very little else. I find him far the best antidote yet discovered against the revolting mesquineries de ces jours. I read him in the tube, and he is a veritable buckler

28. The decorations at No. 4 Berkeley Street had been specially commissioned from Roger Fry, who made, as part of them, a large circular rug and some tables in inlaid wood.

of defence, warding off those miserable visages, with their miserable newspapers. What an adorable giant, to drop into the arms of! And then the interest of the book, from so many points of view, is so great. I am glad I never really read it before; it is intoxicating to get a fresh enthusiasm when one's over eighty.'

By the end of March, he had begun to feel again something like his actual age – now thirty-seven. The weather brightened and grew warmer. Spring was in the air once more, and with its coming the old desires for all manner of exploits and adventures revived within him. With a sigh of relief he gave up his contributions to the *New Statesman*, and determined to press ahead with his serious writing. 'I have been dawdling horribly lately over reviews – and now I feel that I really must set to and seriously attack the General,' he told Ottoline, who had invited him again to Garsington (23 March 1917). 'I'm afraid it would be fatal to leave my stool until I've captured his first line of trenches.'

Meanwhile, Carrington's dual relationship with Lytton and Gertler had slowly been moving towards a crisis. To Gertler, at any rate, her inconsistency had never been more baffling. At times she was closer and more intimate with him than she had ever allowed herself to be in the past; and then, on the spur of the moment, she would turn sulky and cold. She praised him for his wonderful patience with her (January 1917); and raged at him for his impetuosity (January 1917). From a Lawrentian 'Wild Beast' she would suddenly dwindle into one of Katherine Mansfield's defenceless, petite heroines – 'so young and rather little against the bigger issues', as she described herself (November 1916) – and then, alarmingly, evolve back again into uncompromising savagery. She blamed Gertler for not talking to her seriously; she blamed herself for failing to build up 'a descent relationship between us'. She told him something about the poet 'Marloe', and that she was painting portraits of Lytton and of her friend, the strange, austere, intellectual Alix Sargant-Florence – already in love with James Strachey, whom she later married. For weeks she would see

Gertler almost every day; then, without warning, she would
vanish for more weeks still with Barbara Bagenal and Saxon
Sydney-Turner (then impotently in love with Barbara)[29] to
Asheham, where, like children, they spent much of the time
tobogganing on tea-trays across the Downs.

Her prolonged exhortations to Gertler to be happy, which
run like a Greek Chorus through the pages of her letters, had
become a means of salving her own conscience for the
wretchedness which she seemed destined to inflict upon him.
'I want you to love people more,' she instructed him; then
followed this up by throwing herself passionately at him, and,
when in delight he responded, freezing into distant immobility. In the course of her many apologies to him during this
period, she describes herself as 'possessed of a devil' which
she was powerless to exorcize. She felt, she said, in a vile
mood, nervy, and strangely contaminated within. 'You cannot
think how I hate myself sometimes – often,' she confessed
(January 1917). 'I will try and get this over soon and will
come and see you then . . . I've no more to say to you now.
Except do not be unhappy – '

There were several good reasons for Carrington's remorseless discontent this winter. First, she had been disgusted by the
publication of Gilbert Cannan's *Mendel*. 'How angry I am over
Gilbert's Book,' she had complained to Gertler (1 November
1916). 'Everywhere this confounded gossip, and servant-like
curiosity Its ugly and so damned vulgar.' In the same letter she
laments over the loss of her brother. 'I am losing hope rather
of Teddy. Its beginning to depress me terribly sometimes.' But
four months later, when it was officially confirmed that her
brother was dead, she turned for support not to Gertler, but
Lytton. 'You will not mind if I want to see you often,' she
wrote to him (26 February 1917). 'For its wretched being
alone and knowing how he went – without ever having been

29. For very many years Saxon Sydney-Turner professed to be in love
with Barbara Bagenal, his ardour carrying him to the extent of sending
her every week a large box of chocolates, but not to the point of discovering that she didn't eat chocolate.

seen or loved. He had the independence of a child like Poppet,[30] all his joys contained inside himself – made by himself.'

Lytton's kindness to her at this time, his compassion and gentleness, was her one source of relief. Only with him did she feel content, free from pain. Her adoration of him deepened. Of course, she knew that there must always be precise limits to their relationship, but it was satisfaction enough simply to be with him whenever that was possible; and when it was not, to receive and memorize his marvellous letters. She thought that she understood him better than anyone. In his reply to her from Alderney Manor, where he was staying with Augustus and Dorelia John,[31] Lytton ruefully apologizes for his inability to do more for her. 'I fear I *am* at times a trifle – unsatisfactory,' he admits (8 March 1917). 'Is it age, sex, or cynicism? But perhaps it's really only appearance – of one sort or another. The fellow, as they say, (only they don't) is good at heart. I wish I could be of more avail – I often think that if the layer of flesh over my bones were a few inches thicker I might be. But that is another of the tiresome arrangements of the world. ... Ma chère, I'm sure I do sympathise with your feelings of loneliness. I know what it is so horribly well myself.'

Lytton's understanding increased, to some extent, the tension within Carrington. For much of her incalculable moodiness these months had sprung from a sense of guilt – a feeling that she was betraying Gertler with her affection for Lytton.

30. Poppet John, the daughter of Augustus John.
31. In her memoirs, *Two Flamboyant Fathers* (1966), Nicolette Devas records that she used to meet Lytton and Carrington with the Johns 'at Fordingbridge and neighbouring gymkhanas. A gymkhana was an incongruous place to find the drooping, indoor plant aesthete, with his limp hair undignified in the wind. ... If you saw Strachey in a wilting pose on the periphery of the coconut shies, or drifting across the field on his long frail legs, Dora Carrington was his shadow, a pace behind, at heel, devoted, worshipping. ... We called her the "North Wind" for the way she poked her face into the wind; her long black [sic] hair, cut with a square fringe, swished out at the back in a dark pennant, while her black skirt, too, always seemed to be under the influence of the wind, blown against her gaunt figure.'

If only Gertler were in some ways more like Lytton! Somehow she could not reconcile her attachment to both of them. She shrank from making an unreal, cut-and-dried decision between them – they were so dissimilar she could not possibly consider them as rivals or even alternatives. During the latter part of 1916, in an attempt to form some honest, mutually satisfactory relationship with Gertler and banish all traces of self-reproach, she permitted him to start having full sexual intercourse with her – but only infrequently. 'I do not love passionately everyday and night,' she explained to him (1 February 1917). 'It comes over me with sweeps, and then sometimes I find myself so detached from the world and everybody that I hate any intrusion mental or physical at these moments you get aggravated, and I admit with reason because I am not consistant with what I was previously. If you try to force me to be perpetually consistant, we shall quarrell. I will try, and make you happy. Since I want to, as you suffer so much I know by my beastliness, therefore do not get depressed.'

Four days later she again assured him: 'I am going to be less selfish, and make you happier.' For Gertler, she knew, was still far from happy. This unpredictable, piecemeal love-making had stimulated his sense of frustration. It was neither one thing nor the other. The quarrels between them grew more violent, and he repeatedly scorned her for trying to look like a boy – with her short hair, her lack of make-up and her fondness for wearing trousers.

Early in April, Carrington went down to stay at Lord's Wood, her friend Alix Sargant-Florence's home near Marlow – 'a very nice house', as she described it to Gertler, 'one of the best sort. with great comforts and a most beautiful bathroom you ever saw with coloured tiles.' The other guests were Lytton and James, Harry Norton and Maynard Keynes. It was a wholly agreeable party; the sun shone, Carrington, happily dressed in breeches, roamed the great woods and commons all round, read Plato 'and was very excited over it', and in the evening listened to James playing Bach and Beethoven at the pianola. Sometimes, too, they would all sit round reading plays – Vanbrugh's *The Relapse* and Shakespeare's *Troilus and Cressida* – 'which was great fun', Carrington wrote. 'Only I was so agitated when it came to my part that I could hardly enjoy it as much as I should.'

In his 'Collins' to Alix (10 April 1917), Lytton afterwards wrote: 'It was very sad coming away. I wish I could have stayed for ever, quaffing Chianti twice a day, gorging Périgord Pie, dreaming by the fire and perpetually putting off the Grande Expédition. But such things must end, though your noble hospitality made me feel as if I were an Adam wilfully taking my departure from the Garden of Eden.'

For Carrington, these few days at Lord's Wood produced a decisive effect. The last vestiges of her doubts were dispelled. She was certain now that, with Gertler, she could never experience such serenity, and that it would be largely withheld from her until she had told him everything – which would probably mean breaking with him altogether. Only by such drastic measures might she purge herself of that poisoning sense of sinfulness which had so lowered and demoralized her lately. On her last day at Marlow, therefore, she wrote two letters, one to Gertler telling him something of her conclusions and arranging to meet him on the following Monday afternoon, and the other to Lytton – who had just left Marlow – asking to see him the evening of the same day. On Sunday she travelled up by train to London, and the next morning woke from a disquieting dream of her brother Teddy drowning at sea. After lunch she took a bus to Penn Studio, where she found Gertler, very calm, but pale as a ghost. At first they both, rather nervously, talked about his pictures – a copy of Cézanne he was then painting and his Merry-Go-Round.[32] In the middle of their conversation he turned and quietly asked her what exactly she intended doing in the future, how she wanted to plan her life. She had been prepared for all sorts of insane rages and titanic fits of anger, and his

---

32. This famous picture – 'the best *modern* picture I have seen' (D. H. Lawrence) – shown at the London Group Jubilee Exhibition, 'Fifty Years of British Art', at the Tate Gallery in the summer of 1964, is now in the Ben Uri Gallery, London.

perfect control disarmed her. 'I became more and more wretched and wept,' she scrawled in her diary. 'It seemed like leaving the warm sun in the fields and going into a dark cold wood surrounded by trees which were strangers. I suddenly looked back at the long [time] we had had between us of mixed emotions. But always warm because of his intense love and now I had to leave it all and go away.'

At this moment, too, for the first time Gertler seems to have become aware that Carrington really meant this meeting to signal the end between them, their final good-bye; and he broke down and sobbed. His tears were more terrible than any eloquence or melodrama and made Carrington feel more and more hateful to herself. It was an agonizing, hopeless scene, 'for he wanted to die and I thought how much this love mattered to him,' she wrote, 'and yet in spite [of] its greatness I could not keep it, and must leave. His loneliness was awfull.'

Shortly afterwards they left the studio and had tea together in a café, hardly speaking at all. He asked her in a subdued voice whether she intended to go and live with Lytton as his wife or mistress, and she told him that she did not.

'But he may love you,' Gertler protested.

'No, he will not,' she answered flatly.

This last denial, she sensed, made their separation easier for him to accept. But he still begged her to go on seeing him as a friend, a brother, though both of them knew that any such arrangement must be quite impractical. As the time came for them to part, they grew all at once embarrassed with each other, as with a stranger. Carrington felt as if she had already left for some distant country from where communication was impossible. 'How very much I cared for him suddenly came upon me,' she recorded. 'The unreality, and coldness of Lytton ... I left – frightfully ill – with a bad pain in my side.'

She then returned to her rooms, which she was now sharing with Alix Sargant-Florence, had a hot bath and dressed for the evening. Lytton was already downstairs having tea with Alix and her mother. Carrington joined them, but felt too ill to pay much attention to the conversation, though she observed with a mixture of fascination and contempt how, in the mêlée of this great emotional drama, Lytton 'sat there quite calmly, quibbling and playing lightly with his words'. Later, the two of them went out to dinner, and Carrington was glad to prolong the conversation about other things — Lytton's many friends and illnesses. But soon, the weight of what was being left unspoken began to press upon her unbearably. The time they took over each separate course was appalling. Should she speak up now in the restaurant or wait until Lytton took her home? In her bewilderment she fell silent, but Lytton himself appeared totally unaware of any uneasiness.

After he had escorted her back to her flat, and they had settled down in front of the fire, he at last broached the subject burdening her mind. Briefly he asked her what she had wanted to tell him, and she tried to explain.

'I thought I had better tell Mark as it was so difficult going on,' she said.

'Tell him what?' Lytton politely inquired.

'That I couldn't go on. So I just wrote and said it.'

'What did you say in your letter?'

Carrington hesitated. 'I thought you knew.'

'What do you mean?'

'I said that I was in love with you. I hope you don't mind very much.'

'But aren't you being rather romantic?' Lytton asked. 'And are you certain?'

'There's nothing romantic about it,' she answered wryly.

'What did Mark say?'

'He was terribly upset.'

Lytton looked alarmed. 'Did he seem angry with *me*?'

'No, he didn't mention you.'

'But it's too incongruous,' he protested. 'I'm so old and diseased. I wish I were more able.'

'That doesn't matter.'

'What do you mean? What do you think we had better do about the physical?'

'Oh, I don't mind about that.'

Lytton paused. 'That's rather bad,' he commented.

As their discussion progressed, Lytton again brought up

their apparent incompatibility, especially their physical in-compatibility. He was 'so very ancient' — wasn't she being rather too romantic, that is, rather too *unrealistic?* But Carrington firmly repeated that she knew what she was doing. 'I wish I were rich,' Lytton remarked at one stage, 'and then I could keep you as my mistress.' This angered Carrington, and she told him that no amount of money could alter the incompatibility he had mentioned; and to this he rather ruefully agreed. 'Then he sat on the floor with me,' Carrington wrote, 'and clasped my hands in his and let me kiss his mouth, all emeshed in the brittle beard and my inside was as heavy as lead, as I knew how miserable it was going to be.'

Secretly Carrington hoped that he might stay the night with her, but after some further talk he got up and left. Alone, she was suddenly overpowered by a maundering chaos of sensations — 'the misery at parting and my hatred of myself for caring so much. And at his callousness — He was so wise and just.'

A little later she wandered downstairs to Alix, and began talking with her, long into the night — of how to cope with her incontrovertible worship of Lytton, of how to arrange their lives together, of how to avoid the necessity for secrecy, for deception, anxiety and tribulation. Only now, after all the years with Gertler, did she know what it was to love — for the first and last time. It seemed incomprehensible that there should be this painful barrier between them: as if two mated birds on their peregrination were caught and forced to live apart in separate cages. How could they be set free? How?

And although no answer presented itself, she felt some relief at being able to discuss the problem with someone who comprehended so well. And as she talked on and on, later and later, it seemed as though in a little while a solution must be found, and then a new and wonderful life would begin. And it was clear to her that the end was nowhere yet in sight, and that the most tortuous and difficult part of it was only just beginning.

THIRTEEN

Tidmarsh

Suppose the kind gods said, 'Today
You're forty. True: But still rejoice!
Gifts we have got will smooth away
The ills of age. Come, take your choice!'

What should I answer? Well, you know
I'm modest – very. So no shower
Of endless gold I'd beg, nor show
Of proud-faced pomp, nor regal power.

No; ordinary things and good
I'd choose: friends, wise and kind and few;
A country house, a pretty wood
To walk in; books both old and new

To read; a life retired, apart,
Where leisure and repose might dwell
With industry; a little art;
Perhaps a little fame as well.

Lytton Strachey (1 March 1920)

1

DRAMA AND UNCERTAINTY

CARRINGTON'S decision in the spring of 1917 to abandon
Gertler for Lytton redirected the entire course of her life. Yet,
although ultimately so momentous, her resolution was anything but quickly conclusive. As if eager to extract the maximum melodrama from this strange emotional nexus, she
arranged to have dinner with Gertler on the very day following their 'final' interview. They were to meet that Tuesday
evening at the Eiffel Tower restaurant in Percy Street. Gertler
turned up a few minutes late, and for a brief while after he had
joined her they exchanged stiff pleasantries across the table.

Then, suddenly, Carrington blurted out that the two of them had really better not see each other any more. Gertler at once agreed, adding that he had come to the same conclusion himself. They fell silent. Then, not knowing what to say, she referred to her interview with Lytton the previous night.

'How did that go off?' Gertler asked, curious about Lytton's reaction.

'All right.'

'Then what did you do?'

'Went to my rooms,' Carrington replied; and added: 'I told Lytton then.'

'What did he say?'

'He was sorry.'

'Was that all he said?' Gertler laughed incredulously.

Carrington felt slightly indignant. 'Well, it wasn't his fault. What more could he say?'

'Fancy just saying that. Nothing more?'

'No.'

'Good God! And he doesn't care?'

'No. I knew he didn't.'

This seemed to disquiet Gertler greatly. 'I never want to see you again', he told her. 'So will you mind if I leave you directly after dinner?'

'No.'

The conversation up to this point had been subdued. But all at once Gertler exploded: 'To think after all these years, in three months you should have a man like Strachey, twice your age, emaciated and old!'

There was a long silence following this outburst. Shortly afterwards Gertler got up and left, and Carrington walked back to Gower Street alone. From there, the last thing before going to bed, she wrote him a letter (14 April 1917):

Thank you very much for treating it as you have – and for your very great love in the past few years I thank you. I shall never forget it.

Would you mind not Telling anyone (except your friend Monty[1]

1. Montague Shearman, barrister and connoisseur of pictures. He was one of Gertler's most loyal friends and patrons, often lending him his

or Kot[2] if you wish to) about it. anyway for the present. As it was
too great a thing to let them know about, and jeer.

I will return your EL GRECO very soon, and any other books, if I
have them – I hope you will soon be happy again. And forgive, for
causing you so much sorrow your

friend   carrington.

This letter, evidently intended by Carrington at the time to
be her very last word to Gertler, in fact turned out to be the
prelude to a more intimate, if no happier, spell between the
two of them. After only a fortnight they were seeing each
other again, and exchanging a stream of letters. What appears
to have happened was this: Gertler soon found himself unable
to keep up his initial renunciation of Carrington. His sexual
vanity had, understandably, been mortally offended by her
preference for an ill-defined union with Lytton. Moreover,
he disapproved of their friendship, he told himself, on moral
grounds. The very thought of it revolted him to the marrow of
his bones. Sickened and excruciated as he was by jealousy,
the latent antipathy he had always felt for Lytton now emptied
itself into a violent protesting, poignant letter he sent to
Carrington.

I am afraid that I cannot support you over your love for Lytton [he
declared] ... I do believe in *you*, but nothing on earth will make me
believe in Lytton as a fit object for your love – The whole thing in
fact is most disappointing to me, even nauseating. I am sorry Carrington, but nothing will ever make me change my mind ... I hate
the whole business ... If you had com[e] and told me that you

---

rooms in the Adelphi. An exhibition of Shearman's collection was held at
the Redfern Gallery in 1940.
   2. Samuel Solomonovitch Koteliansky, who, in 1910, had come to England on a scholarship from Kiev to do research in economics for three
months, and stayed for life. Swarthy, with a pale sensitive face and fierce
black glance, he was, as his friend D. H. Lawrence once said, 'a bit Jeho-
vah-ish'. He made a career for himself as a fine translator of the works of
Bunin, Chekhov, Gorky, Kuprin, Tolstoy and others, sometimes in collaboration with his friends Lawrence, Katherine Mansfield, Middleton
Murry and Leonard Woolf, who used to render his strange English into
their own prose style.

thought L.S. was a wonderful man and that you had an admiration for him, I should have tried to dissuade you because I do not think that he is, I think very much to the contrary in fact. But you came and told me that you *loved* him ... You have by your love for that man poisoned my belief in love life and everything, you by that love turned everything I once believed in and thought beautiful into ridicule ... for years I wanted – you only tortured me, then suddenly you gave your love to such a creature, and you yourself said that had he wanted your body you would without hesitation have given it to that emaciated withered being, I young and full of love, you refused it. Tell me Carrington what am I to think of life now, you say you are happy, yes you are *But I am not.* I long to fly to another Carrington where I shan't smell the stench that fills my nostrils constantly from the combination of your fresh young self with that half dead creature who is not even man enough to take your body – your beautiful body – But thank God he cannot, because if that happened, I should be sick all day.

I do not believe in [the] L.S. kind – His atmosphere is as thin as his body – he is merely learned and scholarly but fundamentally empty ... He will deaden you in time and that is what hurts me so, You are absolutely at his feet. You follow him about like a puppy, you have lost all self respect, I shudder to think of it ... Why do you not at least control yourself a bit, must you be so Slavish and abject Surely there is in me also Something to Study, if only my Art, You sicken me with your devotion ... Having told you this Please let us leave the subject *once and for always,* I cannot discuss it because it hurts me so, And Please dont be hard on [me] now because of my opinion Remember that I love you still ... I never change my mind. And if you hate me now please don't give me up at once, as I couldn't bear it.

Incalculable as ever, Carrington actually felt less like giving up Gertler just then than she had done for months. She had expected her anguished decision in favour of Lytton to simplify her state of mind and deliver her from the harrowing chaos of the winter. But in the last fortnight of April, which she described as a 'nightmare', her confusion was only aggravated by a terrifying sense of isolation. Never had she felt so alone, so cut off from the glow of ordinary human warmth. It was as if she had exiled herself to some bleak, uninhabited island, where no ships passed. The astringency and reticence of Lytton's character chilled her. At times she could get no-where near him. Of course, he was unfailingly *kind* to her, but emotionally quite incapable of being demonstrative – especially when, as now, his affections were not greatly stimulated by sexual passion. His spidery stillness and riveting silences – only occasionally would he stir to unfold and reorganize his complicated angular limbs – unnerved and hypnotized her.

Although he did his best to aid Carrington, Lytton still thought she was being alarmingly unrealistic in her attitude towards him, and so as not to deceive her, he made no attempt to play a part which he felt he could not keep up. She had, he reasoned, better know the worst from the start, before it was absolutely too late. The misery and frustration engendered within her by this scrupulous attitude naturally made her more sympathetic to Gertler's similar bygone agonies over herself. By the end of April, less than two weeks after their series of final farewells, the two of them were back together on very much the same footing as before. They met frequently; he sent her flowers; she wrote (28 April 1917): 'I will try and make you happy. all I can. I have just been reading King Lear by Shakespear. I think it his best work.' In his relief at having her back again, Gertler was unusually tactful and undemanding, and she responded to him sympathetically: 'I wonder why I am agitated already in case you are not happy,' she wrote to him early in May. '... I did so love our day at Hammersmith. you see how contradictory it all is. But I love seeing you so much more now.'

By an ironic, circuitous route, something of the ends that Gertler had first sought through bringing Carrington and Lytton together had actually come to pass. She had at last become his mistress, originally out of a sense of guilt, and now in order to keep him close to her, so that his companionship might provide consolation against the chaste severity of her foredoomed life with Lytton. 'I am really certain I could never live with you sexually day after day,' she told him. But the occasional night, week-end, even week maybe, she might be able to manage. Yet though, with qualifications, Gertler seemed to have attained his long-held aim, he was still very far from satisfied with the state of affairs. Seldom had Carrington appeared to him more tantalizing and seductive. For really what she had done was to pass on to Gertler, in a slightly variegated form, the elusiveness which, in Lytton, so tortured and perplexed herself. In their most intimate contact, Carrington even now seemed curiously remote from Gertler. And though she sometimes complained of Lytton's 'cynical frigidity and discipline', he knew that his own incendiary passion must play a miserable second fiddle to Lytton's most casual whims, to all of which Carrington reacted with such breathless and servile promptitude. It was infuriating. He tried not to censure Carrington, but his loathing for Lytton grew intense.

Clear evidence of the corrupt influence Lytton was exercising over poor Carrington was presented to Gertler in the second week of May when he was invited by her and Alix down to Lord's Wood – only to find on his arrival there that Carrington was on the point of leaving for a hastily-convened country party with Lytton, Barbara Bagenal and Saxon Sydney-Turner. The four of them were hurrying off to spend a week at Chilling, Logan Pearsall Smith's house at Warsash on the Hampshire coast, which Oliver and Ray Strachey were then renting. On their way down by train, they stopped off for some hours at Winchester, and went round to explore the city, the cathedral and school. 'That's one of the few things Lytton is rather good at. Exploring,' Carrington explained to her brother Noel (15 May 1917). They arrived at Warsash in the evening. Chilling, an old but modernized farmhouse situated on Southampton Water and commanding a splendid view of sea and ships to the far horizon, was, according to Carrington, 'quite the decentest place you ever saw ... it's quite in the country miles from any village or houses. a very old Elizabethan Farm house black half timbered house – with a huge garden and orchard behind. and only two wheatfields separate it from the sea. and Marvellous little woods full of primroses and bluebells ...'

To Gertler in particular she was at considerable pains to

689

convey something of her idyllic, pastoral happiness. Chilling, she assured him, was one of 'the most lovely houses and places' she had ever beheld. 'It's Elizabethean, very old. in the fields with an orchard outside. and lambs. and nightingales at night. and an orchard behind the house with trees in blossom. Dear friend I am so happy because it is all very beautiful. . . . Did you enjoy staying with Alix!'

Almost every day, she went on, she bathed naked in the sea with Oliver and Barbara, while the antediluvian members of the party, Lytton and Saxon, observed them from the safety of the beach. Otherwise there was not a single human being to be spied – only sea-planes in their squadrons swooping down low over the waves where they swam and then high up into the heavens. Lytton was still working intermittently at 'The End of General Gordon', and Carrington herself spent some of the time painting and doing woodcuts. At other times the two of them would go off together for long walks along the sea-shore, Lytton reciting Keats's poems, *Romeo and Juliet* ('which I thought very beautiful'), *Henry IV*, and 'also some Greek History'.

Gertler, stranded at Lord's Wood, was enraged by these provoking stories. Some day, somehow, he would avenge these wrongs done to him by Lytton. But so happy was Carrington that all her apprehensions for the future were dissolving away. A solution to her problems, indefinable as yet, had never seemed nearer. 'If only like a magician I could frizzle up my parents into ether,' she wrote to Lytton after returning to Hurstbourne Tarrant (26 May 1917), 'and waft them to some remote town, and then encase you in the old wall nut tree so you could never escape me . . .'

2

SUMMER MANOEUVRES

On his arrival back at Belsize Park Gardens, a tedious ordeal awaited Lytton. The Government was combing out all those who, for whatever reason, had up till then been exempted from military service, and he was required to re-establish his case once again from the start. This time he hired counsel to represent him, restated in three measured paragraphs his conscientious objections to the war, and arranged for Philip Morrell to appear for him as a character witness. When the hearing took place, however, his barrister would not allow Philip Morrell into the room – 'which I'm sure was a great mistake, as if he had appeared the Chairman would have recognised him, and seen that I was "well-connected", which, as it was, he didn't grasp'. The conscience part of the case was soon adjourned pending a medical re-examination by the army doctors, and a few days afterwards, Lytton appeared again at the White City, where he was shuttled about from doctor to doctor for about six hours – 'fortunately without any clothes on for most of the time'. Although greatly fearing that on this occasion he would be ordered off at the very least to scrub tables and floors, he was once more given what amounted to absolute exemption from all kinds of service. His medical grading was confirmed as C 4, he was relegated to the reserve, and ordered to reappear every six months for further check-ups.

To recover from this 'fearful business', he hurried down to Garsington over Whitsun, 'leaving poor General Gordon alone and neglected on my writing table'. Among the other people who turned up there during the holiday was Asquith who, now deprived by Lloyd George of his premiership, looked 'a very diminished deflated figure'. But primarily he was absorbed by two other guests, Augustine Birrell and the poet Robert Graves, who together seemed to represent the very opposite poles of life. 'Old man Birrell – decidedly a Victorian product,' he wrote to Carrington (28 May 1917). 'Large and tall and oddly like Thackeray to look at – with spectacles and sharp big nose and a long upper lip that moves about and curls very expressively – white hair, of course, and also rather unexpectedly sensitive and even sometimes almost agitated fingers. Altogether, a most imposing façade! And there he sits, square and solid, talking in a loud deep voice – can you imagine it? – and being very entertaining for hour after hour – telling stories and interjecting reflections and all the rest of it – and all with the greatest gentility – taking up one's remarks most good-humouredly, and proceeding and embroidering with an impression of easy strength. Underneath – there really seems to be almost nothing. The ordinary respectabilities and virtues, no doubt, and a certain bookishness, gleaned from some rather narrow reading, and then – blank.'

Later in the same letter to Carrington, he passes on to a description of Robert Graves, then on sick-leave from the front. 'The fashion for facades has its drawbacks,' he remarks. 'For instance there is the youth Graves, with one lung shot away, keeping himself going on strychnine, and with strange concealed thoughts which only very occasionally poke up through his schoolboy jocularities. Terribly tragic I thought. I found him (I need hardly say) attractive – tall and olive-brown complexioned, with a broken nose and broken teeth (the result of boxing) – dark hair and eyes.'

From this time on, whenever they were apart, Lytton would be punctilious in dispatching to Carrington the long chatty and amusing letters to which she always looked forward so eagerly. She would write to him herself, tirelessly, on page after page of foolscap paper or the roughly torn-out leaves of children's exercise books, half-illegible, bewitching scribbles, overlaid with caricatures, telling him all she was doing each day and of her deep love for him. 'Do you know everytime I see you now I love you even more,' she wrote to him that summer. And again: 'More beloved than any creature please come next week again. I could kill you dead with my hugs to-day.' More than ever she felt keenly her lack of formal education, knowledge and literary finesse. 'I wish I could write properly to you,' she exclaimed (June 1917), 'but you know its almost too hard.' Resolutely she went on trying, wrestling with the inarticulate sensations which congregated within her, imitating Lytton's phrases, copying his French *mots* and expletives which somehow helped to fashion and enrich her own mongrel style, and always begging him to send back just one more of his wonderful letters. To these pleas Lytton responded nobly, his meticulous, anecdotal communications, with their vertiginous avoidance of deep feeling, contrasting strongly with Carrington's sprawling and unpunctuated pastiche. Over the next fifteen years they built up between the two of them an oddly fascinating correspondence, extraordinarily voluminous considering how much time they spent in each other's company.

Lytton's side of this correspondence, carefully informal, carefully light and dismissive in tone, smoothly and easily constructed, catches some part of his charm and humour, but steers clear of other more serious aspects of his character – in particular his rigorous seeking after truth. Carrington's letters are completely different. For all their lack of coordination, they form a kind of unconscious improvised poetry, creating a life of their own where things flow in and out of each other perpetually and where objects, events and persons are all touched with vibrant personal meaning, threats or blessings, pleasure or pain. They were, Gerald Brenan, another superb letter-writer, once told her, like a 'gesture, speech, walk, expression, seen through a medium of words; like the rustling of leaves, the voices of birds, the arrangement of natural forms. Education has not deadened in you this mode of expression, has not, as it has for nearly all of us, reduced speech and writing to the level of a vulgar formula, through which we can barely let our own natures be recognised. You have not got this horrible stickiness of civilised people, that makes everything they come in contact with – clothes, opinions, manners, morals, relationships, adhere to them, however inappropriate these things may be to them, however little they may be able to absorb them. You have a kind of virginity about you.'

Carrington was especially anxious that those who knew of her attachment to Lytton should not pity her. She felt their sympathy to be undignified, and did everything to discourage it. 'You must not think I am unhappy,' she wrote to Barbara Bagenal at the end of May. 'For I am often very happy only it is just that I cannot bear sometimes not seeing him even for a day ... If it is fine I am going for a jaunt to Cambridge with him, Barbara, I am so excited.'

At Cambridge, early in June, the two of them stayed with Harry Norton. Lytton piloted Carrington all round the colleges – 'I was rather excited over King's Chapel windows,' she told Noel (3 June 1917). 'But mostly over the architecture of Wren at Emmanuel, and also the Library Trinity' – took her to the Fitzwilliam Museum, and over to the Old Vicarage at Grantchester where Rupert Brooke had lived, and where they met Miles Malleson and his wife.

On their return to London, Lytton made another effort to press ahead with his work on General Gordon. But progress was still slow, and there were frequent interruptions – theatres, a performance of *Figaro* and, most interesting of all, a private view of Augustus John's drawings at the Alpine Club. Very characteristically, Lytton seems to have interested himself more in the spectators than the exhibits. 'Such a strange well-dressed and respectable crowd,' he exclaimed in a letter to Ottoline. 'The great man appeared in the middle of it, dressed in a neat but not gaudy Khaki suit, with his beard considerably trimmed, and altogether a decidedly colonial air. On the whole, I must say I prefer him en bohème.'

What distracted him most of all from 'The End of General Gordon' was the worrying condition of his mother. For some time Lady Strachey had been experiencing pain in her defective eye, and in July she was advised to undergo an operation to have it out. While she was in hospital, and subsequently during her convalescence at Durbins, Belsize Park Gardens was shut up, and Lytton went to stay for some days with Carrington at her new lodgings at No. 60 Frith Street, in Soho. 'Lytton has been living with me this last week here since Wed.,' she wrote to Barbara Bagenal. 'He went on Sat. evening to Durbins. So I am still so happy that I thought I would write to you. Just to inform you that I've never been so happy in my *life* before. Hurray ... It was fun persuading Mrs Reekes, my housekeeper That Lytton was my uncle. But I think the general uproar that went on in the early morning in his room Rather upset her belief in me!'

Once again, however, Carrington seems to have been deliberately oversimplifying her feelings so as to keep at bay the dreaded 'sympathy' of her friend. She resented Lytton's unmitigated coldness, and the obvious fact that he could leave her for days or weeks on end without a qualm. Perhaps, for all she knew, he let out a sigh of relief at their parting. His lack of passion, she wryly remarked to Gertler, kept one pleasantly cool in the hot weather. And in her sixteenth letter to him that July, she wrote: 'Lytton will be away for two months. So you will have no more reason to curse him or me. For you will have me every night you want to. What confessions we honest people make!' As a confession this was certainly outspoken, but, as it turned out, hardly accurate. For part at least of this time, she retreated back to Hurstbourne Tarrant, writing to Gertler on literary and botanical matters, then suddenly erupting with: 'What a mess I've made of your life for you!' Even in her deepest disappointment she would permit no one else to criticize Lytton, and when Gertler sought to fix on him the blame for her unhappiness, she lectured him sternly on what his proper attitude should be: 'When anyone runs Lytton down you ought rather to say. he must be better than we think since Carrington loves him. Do you not see that if you love me, you *must* believe in what I love, and not agree with the public who are stupid, and prejudiced in saying It is ill sorted and I am mislead.'

At Durbins, the atmosphere was more subdued. Lady Strachey, 'attended by a pub-faced nurse', was still very weak after her operation, and needed a good deal of attention from everyone. 'Marjorie is my principal companion,' Lytton told Mary Hutchinson (24 July 1917), 'and we seem to get on very well – in the kind of way in which brothers and sisters do, when they're not in love with each other.' Over the summer Roger Fry's house provided a convenient sanatorium for Lady Strachey. Fry himself was away for most of the time, so that there was ample accommodation for her own friends and family to visit her, especially since she was so near London. Lytton too found it a suitable base for his purposes – the writing of General Gordon. 'For he is still around my

neck, the old albatross!' he told Ottoline (14 August 1917).
'But he won't be much longer, I'm thankful to say.' By the
third week of August it was evident that his mother was well
on the mend, and he prepared to leave Durbins and join Leonard and Virginia Woolf at Asheham. 'I find myself plunged in
the gulf of Gordon, from which it is impossible to emerge for
2 or 3 days', he wrote to Virginia. 'Then I hope the crisis will
be over — though there'll still be some finishing paragraphs to
be applied. Please expect me on Thursday.'

'The End of General Gordon' was completed later that
month at Asheham, where he read it over to his friends. From
Asheham he moved on to Charleston, a house not far off, in
Sussex, which Clive and Vanessa Bell were then sharing with
Duncan Grant and David Garnett. In the neighbourhood of
Lewes, and beneath the northern slope of the South Downs,
Charleston provided a permanent country home for these
Bloomsbury non-combatants, where they could peaceably
discharge their wartime obligations under the Military Service
Act. It also gave the Bells' three children, Julian, Quentin and
Angelica (later to marry David Garnett) a reasonably secure
place outside London in which to live, and became Maynard
Keynes's chief refuge during week-ends until his marriage to
the ballerina Lydia Lopokova some eight years later, when he
set up house near by at Tilton.

On this, Lytton's first visit to Charleston, he read out the
first two essays of *Eminent Victorians* — 'Cardinal Manning'
and 'Florence Nightingale'. The response within this Bloomsbury sanctum varied enormously. Duncan Grant fell asleep
and Vanessa Bell was rather critical, not of Lytton's treatment
of his subjects, but of the prose style, which she thought too
brim-full of clichés. Clive Bell was more appreciative, and
David Garnett seemed highly impressed, realizing, as he later
wrote, 'that Lytton's essays were designed to undermine the
foundations on which the age that brought war about had been
built.'

Garnett's eager absorption of Lytton's writing was a striking factor in the friendship between them which had ripened
rapidly through these war years, and was slowly to decline

during the 1920s. Their intimacy was closely bound up with Garnett's youthful attractiveness and every year that passed interposed a certain added distance between them, making their relationship more casual and uncomplicated. In a sense, Garnett was a genuine disciple of Lytton's. Though in no way homosexual, he looked up to him as something of an emotional and literary mentor. Yet Lytton could scarcely believe in this young and gifted man's admiration of him. 'Do you think that he likes me *really?*' he had once questioned Barbara Bagenal (17 July 1916). Though his rowdy spirits and Georgian athleticism were sometimes too excessive for Lytton's indoor tastes, yet Garnett's robust good looks, his unabashed conceit, his unselfconscious manner, his matter-of-fact imagination and vivid response to the physical and materialistic side of living, coupled with a strain of modern sensibility, were of a type to which Lytton felt himself inevitably drawn. His fair hair, broad shoulders and the very blue eyes which seemed able to mesmerize women, were as alluring to Lytton as his soothing countrified manner. This was most immediately noticeable in the slow, puzzled way of speaking he adopted, which was often most potent at 'smoothing down my fretful quills with the softest hand – when the rest of the world seemed to be conspiring against me'. At once generous and self-assured, Garnett was an easy companion, shrewd and independent, and with a strong vein of humour which he exploited very entertainingly at the expense of the vagaries of his friends.

Lytton felt great affection for Garnett as a young man, showing him many acts of imaginative and practical kindness. When, for instance, he was alone in Paris during the winter of 1915, Lytton had sent him a Shetland cardigan which, on Garnett's own testimony, had probably saved him from pneumonia, and also dispatched to him a series of letters in the hope of cheering him up. 'Mon cher,' he wrote in one of these letters which contains the essence of a message that he had been propounding in several of his wartime literary essays, 'go to the end of your Rue de Beaune and look for the house at the corner, on the Quai where Voltaire died, at the age of

84, having conquered both the Rulers of this world, and of the next – and where (though the inscription doesn't say so, I think) he had lived fifty years before as a young poet. Consider that life and take courage.'

In his autobiography David Garnett has recorded that 'Lytton would often make devastating comments on people he did not like, but he had an astonishing patience and sympathy with those he did. He often had an intuitive understanding of what I was feeling.' In exchange for these telepathic confidences, Lytton felt safe in discussing with Garnett some of his own personal problems, which, for fear of ridicule, he could seldom disclose to other of his Bloomsbury friends. As the sympathetic repository of Lytton's troubles, Garnett had been one of the very first to hear about Carrington. What could possibly be the outcome of this astonishing affair? Lytton asked. But neither Garnett nor anyone else could yet tell.

Although Lytton had finished his draft of 'The End of General Gordon' shortly before arriving at Charleston, the revisions he needed to insert within the essay were extensive, and to his dismay he found that further work had still to be done. 'That terrible General isn't yet done with,' he complained to Pippa (23 August 1917). He had been joined at Charleston now by Carrington, and together the two of them planned to travel westwards, via Salisbury, to Devon and Cornwall, during which Lytton hoped to add the final touches to his fourth eminent Victorian.

They set out early in September and soon arrived in North Cornwall, putting up for three weeks with a Mrs Elford, at Beeny Farm, three miles from Boscastle.[3] With them went James Strachey and Noel Olivier, the young girl who had once figured as the ideal virginal heroine of Rupert Brooke's antiseptic fantasies. The accommodation, according to Lytton, was rather severe – 'a small and dirty farm-house, with an old

3. This cottage had been recommended to James Strachey by a Quaker lady in the Society of Friends office where he was doing Work of National Importance: distributing milk to German wives.

lame hag and a couple of cats to look after us'. Carrington's description of their life at the farm, recorded in a letter she sent to her brother Noel, is more graphic, and shows the obvious influence of Lytton's way of looking at and expressing things. 'This remote house,' she calls the place, 'Kept by an old hag. daughter, son, and old ancient farmer. All rather ramshackle. and decayed ... The sea is quite near. But unfortunately un-get-at-able as theres a precipace of grey stone some 400 feet in height ...

'It's a bit rough, no hot water in the morning, or conveniences. Just vast quantities of food and cream and long walks along the top of the coast cliffs. Lytton's reading the tempest to me. and in the evenings Mottley's Dutch Republic and last night Gibbon on the Emperor Claudius who was no doubt about it a bad fellow.'

When not walking or reading aloud to Carrington, Lytton spent his time indoors working on his book. By the third week of September his revisions were complete, though he still feared that further amendments might prove necessary after he had read the recently published two-volume Life of *Sir Charles Dilke* by Stephen Gwynn and Gertrude Tuckwell, which was to provide him with a useful summary of events concerning Gordon's assignment in the Sudan.[4] 'I am glad to say that Gordon is at last finished,' he wrote to Pippa (27 September 1917). 'In spite of every effort, he is about half as long again as Florence N. I think the four will fill a good-sized book – but perhaps a very short one ought to be added. I'm afraid the Life of Dilke will contain information on the Gordon affair, and make alterations necessary, which will be a nuisance. I'm now reading Creighton's Life – have you read it? I thought he might do for number 5; but I find he's not sufficiently unlike Manning – though full of interest.

'The post-horsewoman approaches. Farewell! Give my love to Mama, and all the other Durbinians.'

While Lytton worked, read and wrote letters, Carrington

4. Part V of 'The End of General Gordon' owes something to Gwynn and Tuckwell's volumes.

would go off into the cornfields and paint landscapes, having with difficulty extracted from the authorities a permit to do her painting near the coast. When it was wet or cold, she would sit 'like a poached egg' in front of the wood fire, reading and penning her long, muddled letters. Sometimes she was stricken by loneliness and a perverse jealousy over the fact that Gertler seemed to be able to manage quite well without her – at least, he had hardly written and appeared to be rather too adequately looked after by Dorothy Brett and Lady Ottoline Morrell. 'I long to be back with you and Brett,' she wrote to him. 'Theres a confession! But when I was at Charleston it was so good to be with artists who talked about painting, and sometimes I feel strangely isolated having lost my companions. Do not leave me Mark.' She implored him to write more often to her to put her mind at rest. She was, she said, longing for his forgiveness, and promised that when she returned to London in October, they would at least be *true* friends. 'I have learnt so much now,' she told him. 'I am humbled like the man in the Psalms even unto the dust – and do not hate me for my cruelness. it was impossible I should have known what you felt.' She was full of joint schemes for her return. They would work together. Perhaps they might read history one to the other in Monty Shearman's flat? What about Sir Thomas Browne? And why shouldn't they teach each other French? After the war, too, they must certainly spend some time in Devon and Cornwall.

At the end of some ten days at Beeny, all four of them 'were about at the ends of our endurance what with flea bites and the horrors of a real pigsty of a farmyard', and they decided to move elsewhere. Wires were dispatched to various outlying farms, and after several refusals, acceptance was signalled back from a Mrs Box, an unknown woman living some thirty miles north of them at Home Farm, Welcombe, near Bude. On Saturday, 20 September, they therefore set off for this new farmhouse with some trepidation. 'I imagined of course a new bungalow farm, with a methodist female with spectacles and no food to eat!!' Carrington wrote to Barbara Bagenal (21 September 1917). 'After a 14 mile drive from Bude in a motor car we arrived here. It's simply perfect. A big grass paddock and walled garden and, a small farmhouse. We have a room each, two sitting-rooms, an unlimited supply of food and cream, and big double beds.'

This luxury, the fine weather and beautiful country round about put everyone in the best of spirits, and they remained on there for three weeks, idle and contented. The farm was perched on the tip of a steep hill rising between two deeply-cut green valleys, one of which formed the frontier between Devon and Cornwall, and along both of which streams ran to sea beaches. It was surrounded by animals – four black and white cats, a collie dog, a big pink pig and two smaller black ones, all very well behaved and all of whom Carrington named after her friends. The country with its immense sea-cliffs and rocks, its inland woods and brooks was so vast and strangely foreign to the tamer traditional English landscape that she felt she was living in a different country. She would wander off for long walks with Lytton, paint by herself, bathe in the sea with Noel Olivier, or lie alone in one of the swift silver rivulets under the hot sun and let the water rush over her body, as cold as knife blades. How good it was simply to be alive! Like all the others she ate enormously; when indoors she would either study Tolstoy and Dostoyevsky, or else paint the 'veille mère Box' in her kitchen, and most evenings she sat gazing in rapt attention at Lytton as he read aloud from Gibbon or from his own work. Never – not even at Chilling – had she been happier. She felt she could go on living here for the rest of her life – and wrote to Gertler to tell him so. Some of her letters at this time are ecstatic.

Barbara I am so happy here [she told her friend Barbara Bagenal 21 September 1917]. Almost a headache every morning because I get so tired and exhausted. Simply loving so hard! . . .

The sea has yellow sands and big rocks and there are valleys such as you never saw with rivulets which flow down to the sea and green forests on the hills. It is surely one of the best places in England. I am painting old Mere Box who is 70, an amazing old Lady, who wears a pink bonnet and curious garments. Miss Box and her sister and brother keep the farm. I have swum in the sea twice with Noel.

Today is so hot and the flies buzz round our heads. I like Noel very
much, She is very gay and amusing. Lytton also finished his Essay on
General Gordon and read it to us. I think it is very masterly.

By the time Carrington arrived back at Andover later in
October, she was once again sure that the solution to her
problems was imminent, and that a permanently new and
wonderful life was at any second about to start up. All her
instincts told her so. Devon and Cornwall had been a radiant
prelude to their lasting life of happiness together. It was the
first anniversary of her brother Teddy's death, and her parents
had seldom seemed more remote to her. Only Lytton could
offer real comfort. Already, on their first evening apart, she
was impatient to be back with him again, to be seated once
more near his lean and benign figure, gaze up at those calm
geometrically composed features, those soft eyes, and hear
once more his voice – his jokes, his reading, the wit and pith-
iness of his conversation on which he bestowed all the charm
of some musical design. It was no longer he but other people
who seemed distant, odd and uninteresting. She missed him
painfully, and in desolation her heart overflowed with gratitude. 'Oh its wretched having lost you,' she wrote. 'And not
to have you tonight to talk to. Dearest Lytton I can never
thank you enough for these weeks. I did not relize how happy
I had been until this evening ... If only you were here –
and so many wishes – you have spoilt me for too long. and
now I feel as if suddenly I had walked into a greenhouse in the
winter ... Forgive me for writing but I wanted you so badly –
one is not left alone to cry – Dearest Lytton I love you so
much.'

Such artless intensity stirred within Lytton faint tremors of
his old apprehensions, and his reply, as so often, was guarded
and apologetic to the point of formality. 'I'm very glad you
enjoyed the summer and so did I – very much indeed,' he told
her, 'but I fear I am too crabbèd. I wish, too, I could be more
effectual in other ways; but I am old, debilitated, and floating.
However, you know all this.'

3
THE MILL HOUSE

Carrington's determination to secure a country cottage where she and Lytton could live had never seriously wavered. During the summer and early autumn of 1917 she had written to David Garnett and other friends who already knew of her liaison with Lytton, asking them to search round for somewhere suitable. She herself bicycled everywhere, stopping pedestrians and other bicyclists in the streets to inquire if they knew of any empty farms or small houses. The vague plan which had been hatched a year before to rescue Lytton from Belsize Park Gardens was now fixed in all its details, and ready to be put into operation. Oliver Strachey, Harry Norton, Saxon Sydney-Turner and Maynard Keynes had all agreed to participate in a scheme whereby each of them, together with Lytton himself, was to put up twenty pounds a year in order to rent and maintain a decent country house. In its practical effects, this represented a subsidy to Lytton, who was to act nominally as caretaker and, with Carrington, live there permanently. The others would only occasionally make use of the place, which would thus become yet another of those pastoral Bloomsbury outposts, along with Asheham, Charleston and Eleanor, and provide a welcome alternative to the crowded and baroque rusticity of Garsington.

This scheme, therefore, though chiefly to the advantage of Lytton and Carrington, seemed to suit everyone. Barbara Bagenal volunteered to act as a kind of treasurer, collecting contributions by quarterly instalments and paying off the rent.[5] Other non-contributing friends might, of course, be invited down by the caretakers whenever the shareholders (who naturally took priority) were not in residence. 'I find London more and more disagreeable to work in; and Carrington also

5. Once this scheme had been put into operation, Maynard Keynes every three months or so used to take Barbara Bagenal to the Café Royal and over lunch or dinner there go through the formality of checking her book-keeping.

wants to be in the country; so it appears on the whole a reasonable project,' Lytton explained to Clive Bell (6 November 1917). 'I shouldn't be able to face it alone; female companionship I think may make it tolerable – though certainly by no means romantic. I am under no illusions. But in the present miserable, chaotic, and suspended state of affairs, it seems to me the best that can be done. A little quiet work is really almost all that one can look forward to, just now.'

Carrington's parents were planning in the near future to move from Hurstbourne Tarrant to Cheltenham, and realizing that this might be the most propitious time to break free from them, she redoubled her house-hunting expeditions. To the surprise of everyone, she was almost immediately successful. In the third week of October, while bicycling along the Thames Valley, she came upon the Mill House, in the tiny village of Tidmarsh, about a mile due south of Pangbourne, in Berkshire This discovery – later to be the subject of her most remarkable painting – overjoyed her, and she wrote off excitedly to Lytton to tell him all about it and give him the terms and conditions of the lease.

The Mill House had been built on to the end of a large weather-boarded water-mill, the mill stream of which was banked to a high level and bounded one side of the garden. Although the mill-wheel did not now work, the corn-chandler's warehouse above it was still in operation. The house itself, Carrington explained, was 'old fashioned' with gables and some lattice windows. Inside, though rather damp and in need of some renovation, it was nicely decorated, and contained modern fireplaces and 'new oakbeams'. There were three reception rooms, a kitchen, bathroom with hot and cold water, six bedrooms and a box room, all of which were fitted with electric light. The grounds belonging to it, on two sides of the house, extended over an acre and a half, and included a small orchard, a sunken Roman bath kept replenished by the gushing mill water, and a tennis or croquet lawn. It was near a church and a post office, took thirty-five minutes to reach by express train from Paddington, was being offered for three years' lease at a rent of fifty-two pounds per annum and, Carrington concluded, 'sounds too good to be alright!'

To Lytton also it sounded ideal. In such a place he might make a real home for himself. 'It's this wretched separation of everybody that makes one uncomfortable,' he told Clive Bell (6 November 1917). 'But my hope is that if the house at Tidmarsh comes into being, it may be possible by the summer to have some pleasant reunions in the old style, whether the war's going on or not.' Of course, he had not the least intention of turning his back on the pleasures of London and immuring himself without respite in agricultural retirement. Far from it. If he could have been content to live from hand to mouth, it would have been absurd ever to leave the metropolis. But he felt very strongly the urge to write, and for that 'un peu de recueillement' was essential. 'My notion is not to retire altogether,' he wrote to Clive Bell (4 December 1917), ' – but for 2 or 3 weeks at a time; and to spend happy intervals gadding about among such people as are left.' By enjoying alternately the best of both worlds, he hoped to remain industrious without becoming bored, to achieve some real literary prestige without bankrupting his personal life.

All the same, though this was what they wanted, both Lytton and Carrington had some qualms about the Tidmarsh experiment. They feared the kind of prying, malicious gossip at which, privately, they themselves so excelled. Already there was some scandalous talk about them. 'My plans for the future are quite devoid of mystery,' Lytton assured Clive Bell. And after describing the project in some detail, he ended up a little peevishly: 'This rather dreary explanation will I hope satisfy you that all is above board. Please don't believe in the hidden hand.' In the next few months he was more than once called upon to provide this same dreary explanation, since rumour and conjecture were still rife. He experienced some difficulty, too, in breaking the news to his mother. Lady Strachey did not voice her disapproval of this state of affairs – that was not her way. But her distaste was heavily implicit in everything she did not say. 'A curious scene at Belsize Park,' Leonard Woolf reported to Lytton a few weeks after the Mill

House had been taken (January 1918). 'V[irginia] and I at tea with her Ladyship. V. very innocently: "Well, Lady Strachey, and what do you think of Tidmarsh?" An awkward pause and some very indistinct remarks from her Ladyship. A pause. Then across the table to me: "What do *you* think of it all?" (She was referring to the general European situation, but I naturally thought she referred to Tidmarsh).'

The difficulties which confronted Carrington were more drastic. Back at Hurstbourne Tarrant she concocted a special story for her parents. Tidmarsh, she told them, was to be a new retreat for Slade artists – girls only – where they could put up cheaply and devote their time to painting; and this casual explanation appears for a time to have satisfied them, preoccupied as they were with their own plans. But to other people, whose opinions she cared about more, there was no such way out. The Bloomsberries at first disapproved of her, treating her coldly like a tactless intruder. By going off to live with Lytton she must have known, too, that she would antagonize some of her oldest friends – Dorothy Brett, for example, whose company she sadly missed. She was also certain, of course, to attract the rancour of Ottoline, who, much to Lytton's perplexity, showed the obverse of this rancour in a sudden flowering of her friendship with Gertler. 'What does it mean?' he asked Clive Bell (6 November 1917). 'I should have thought, a priori, that they would have found it impossible to have anything to do with each other. It's very strange. ... Perhaps they're so wildly different, that neither has any notion of what the other's like, and so they're able to mix and mingle without any difficulty – though, I suppose, after all, their interweavings don't go much further than an after-lunch pianola romp.'

The most pressing of all Carrington's worries, however, was the problem of Gertler himself. The many improbable schemes about which she had written to him from Cornwall – the history, the French, and Sir Thomas Browne – were now all forgotten, probably rather to his relief. On the surface, their friendship filtered on much as before – endless letters, the occasional dinner, cinema or bed – as if nothing had or was about to change. For Carrington simply could not bring herself to tell him that she was about to go off and live with Lytton. In fact she went out of her way to conceal the facts, so that Gertler still had no idea of what was happening.

As for Lytton himself, he still rather admired Gertler 'in a certain way'. He wanted to explain everything to him, so that they could all be friends together. Then they could invite him down to Tidmarsh in the summer. What could be more reasonable? Or more delightful? Carrington, however, soon managed to persuade him that such urbane behaviour was out of the question. She knew Gertler better than he did. He was too wild for any sort of rational, civilized treatment. If either of them, on the spur of the moment, blurted out the truth, the shock might drive him to madness, to actual physical violence, maybe. He could be dangerous, she reminded Lytton. Lytton was convinced. She must do, he said, what she thought best. He would not interfere. He could see that she thrived on dissimulation and intrigue and extracted a mischievous excitement from deceiving people like Gertler, but he was forced to acknowledge that, in order to avoid any foolish unpleasantness, it might be wise to follow her advice. Perhaps, under Ottoline's advances, Gertler would anyway soon lose interest. At all costs, violence and unnecessary pain should be avoided. 'It all rather alarms me,' he admitted to Carrington (9 December 1917). '. . . I find *him* very attractive – I really do like him – and would like to be friends with him; but the worst of it is that I can't feel any faith in him. . . . It's a nuisance to have to be on one's guard, when one doesn't in the least want to be. – And it's so silly – his way of going on – because there's no point in it. However I don't suppose it can be helped.'

Carrington's attitude was altogether different from Lytton's, and her tactics, designed to postpone rather than to eliminate trouble, were almost certain to lead to more violent repercussions later on. At first she merely tended to mislead Gertler, telling him, with partial truth, that her frequent absences from London that autumn were due to her parents' move from Hurstbourne Tarrant. But so many stories of her and Lytton had been buzzing round lately that Gertler – whom Carrington had again accused of trickery and lack of trust – was sceptical. And so, in her twenty-sixth letter of November, she boldly attempted to give the lie to his suspicions. 'No, I'm not going away with Lytton!' she stated. 'But my people are leaving Hampshire, and are going to live in a town, Cheltenham, So I've got to go home for a little while when they move to help them. and take away my goods and furniture. Then I'll be back again in London all the winter I expect.'

Within this basic misconception, once laid, it was child's play to plant the hard core of a lie. In her twenty-ninth letter of the month it is done, with a neat and logical inconsequence that seemed for the moment to carry perfect plausibility. 'Oliver Strachey has taken an old water Mill House near Reading, so I am going to let him keep all my furniture for me. Until I have a place in London of my own. Its such a nice Mill House. and it will be good to have a retreat – like you and Brett have Garsington.'

And there, in this dangerous condition, the matter temporarily rested.

Pending the final negotiations over Tidmarsh, Lytton's miserable, chaotic and suspended way of life was meanwhile jogging along much as before. Belsize Park Gardens had been opened up again, and his mother and various sisters reassembled there. The war went interminably on, his old friends seemed fewer and less accessible, he was reviewing once more for the *New Statesman*, the weather grew colder and altogether he felt pretty dejected. 'The amenities are getting so few and feeble, and the horrors steadily increase,' he complained to Clive Bell (20 October 1917). 'Last night was spent waiting in vain for a bombardment – a most gloomy proceeding; and I suppose one that must be looked forward to now as the usual thing.' His longing for the quiet and seclusion of Tidmarsh mounted daily, and to Mary Hutchinson – 'the only sympathetic person in London' – he confessed (31 October 1917): 'London fills me with disgust; and I am hoping to leave it for ever (minus a day).'

All the same there were plenty of social engagements to occupy him. He was seeing a good deal of company, chiefly of the Café Royal kind, and full of good-natured eccentricity. This swirl of conviviality culminated in a farewell party given by Augustus John, who was shortly off to France as a Canadian major. Lytton's new attitude of disapproval towards John appears to have been touched by a small element of unconscious envy. Certainly an unkind critic might point out that the more conventional position which he sees Augustus John as occupying was, in many respects, similar to one into which he himself would move a little later. 'Poor John!' he lamented to Clive Bell (4 December 1917). 'Did you by any chance go to that show of his at the Alpine Club? The impression produced by the reduplication of all that superficial and pointless facility was most painful. Naturally he has become the darling of the upper classes, and made £5000 out of his show. His appearance in Khaki is unfortunate – a dwindled creature, with clipped beard, pseudo-smart, and in fact altogether deplorable. All the same, late on Saturday night, there were moments when, in spite of everything ... mais assez! – '

Other exhibitions to which he dragged himself in these final weeks of 1917 included a show at the Omega Club – about which he mercifully kept silent – and one of Max Beerbohm's caricatures at the Grosvenor Gallery in Mayfair. He had gone there with forebodings of tedium, feeling that he had already seen enough caricatures to last him a lifetime, 'but I was quite carried away', he told Clive Bell (4 December 1917). 'He [Max] has the most remarkable and seductive genius – and I should say about the smallest in the world.'

When not out and about enjoying what he called his 'smart life', he spent his days at Belsize Park Gardens meticulously going over, for the very last time, his completed manuscript of *Eminent Victorians*. Having discarded the idea of adding a short life of Mandell Creighton, he toyed briefly with the notion of writing on Watts – one of his original twelve candidates – but this also came to nothing. The preparation, research and composition of the book had extended over some

five years, and its completion now neatly coincided with a
distinct and significant landmark in his biography, something
for which he had been vainly struggling ever since he left Cambridge – the final end to his family life in London. It was a
fitting moment to conclude his work as a tetralogy. Besides,
now that he read through, in their sequence, the finished version of these essays, he realized that, from an aesthetic point
of view, no further additions were necessary. To add even one
more paper would be a wasteful and ridiculous excess, a
pointless squandering of his small store of preciously gar-
nered creative energy. In their symmetry, their delicate balance
of mood and tone – variations on a single unifying and cohesive theme, comprising, in the opinion of Sigmund Freud, a
treatise against religion – he saw that this series of four biographical portraits corresponded, as they stood, to the four
inter-related movements of an orchestral symphony, or
perhaps more appropriately to the intimate pattern of a string
quartet:

'Cardinal Manning' – *Allegro vivace*
'Florence Nightingale' – *Andante*
'Dr Arnold' – *Scherzo*
'The End of General Gordon' – *Rondo*

His final corrections to *Eminent Victorians* were completed
by the beginning of December, at the same time as the negotiations over his lease of the Mill House at Tidmarsh were
settled. Carrington, accompanied by Barbara Bagenal, hurried
down there at once to start on the job of making it reasonably habitable by Christmas, when Lytton and some of his
guests were expected. With the aid of the local postmistress,
they set to work, painting walls, staining the floors, creating
carpets and arranging furniture, all in the most energetic
fashion. Carrington was a devotee of Cobbett, and her furnishing as well as her housekeeping expressed both the
comfort and the poetry of cottage and farmhouse life. 'Her
very English sensibility, in love with the country and with all
country things,' wrote Gerald Brenan, who visited Tidmarsh
two years later and was enchanted by the unique, un-

sophisticated atmosphere of the place, 'gave everything she touched a special and peculiar stamp.' In Lytton's bedroom, for instance – later called 'the Adam and Eve Room' – she had let herself go, painting on one wall the lifesize, naked figure of Adam, faced, on the opposite wall, by the naked Eve.

And she was happy preparing for her new life, happy as she had seldom been. 'I am so happy Because I truly Believe it will be good living here,' she wrote to Lytton. 'and you will be contented, almost – dearest Lytton, all my love to you.' Handicapped by his complicated shyness from expressing openly the gratitude he felt, Lytton sent back the kind of gossipy letters which he wrote so well and which he knew delighted her, full of his adventures, and his acid and amusing observations on the 'smart life' he was still leading – a tea party, for instance, with Ethel Sands 'in her très-soigné Vale Avenue residence. There she was in a black tea-gown . . . and a tiresomely elegant young female of the name of Enid Bagnold,[6] fresh from the Tombola Fair. It was all absurdly polite and futile, and punctuated by milk-and-water indecencies which made my heart sink in my boots, and made them rock with laughter.'

In the third week of December, Lytton went down to join Carrington at the Mill House. It was extremely cold, and many of the rooms were still in a state of wild disorder. While continuous pandemonium sounded from within, outside everything lay quiet and motionless in the stationary grip of winter. Yet whenever the sun came out, what a blessing it was to be in the country! And how pleasing was the prospect of their life together here, once all was in proper trim and the warm weather had begun.

Meantime there were many temporary horrors to be endured. A letter which Lytton wrote to Virginia Woolf on 21 December describes very bleakly the rigours of settling in, and, probably on account of a sudden frost which burst all

6. Enid Bagnold, the novelist and playwright, who had been Frank Harris's deputy on the magazine *Hearth and Home,* and whose first book, *A Diary without Dates,* had just been published. In 1920 she married Sir Roderick Jones.

their pipes, arrived in so damp a condition that it was in places totally illegible. 'Here I am in considerable agony. Nature turned crusty, the "pipes" congealed, and it has been so cold that my nose (to say nothing of other parts) dripped in icicles. ... My female companion keeps herself warm by unpacking, painting, pruning the creepers, knocking in the nails, etc. ... I try to console myself with Queen Victoria's letters ... I still have the notion that I may be able to work in this seclusion, when all the nails have finally been knocked in. Nous verrons.

'... Ah dearie, dearie me, I am nodding over the fire, and she's sowing an edge to the carpet with a diligence ... Ah, la vie! it grows more remarkable every minute.'

Lytton and Carrington's first guests at Tidmarsh were Gerald and Fredegond Shove, who dropped in for a quick gay visit. Then, on Christmas Eve, Harry Norton arrived carrying with him in a neat satchel one large turkey and four bottles of claret. For the Christmas holiday itself James Strachey and Alix Sargant-Florence joined the party. 'I am gradually settling down (amid a good deal of loose paint and calico) to a regular rural existence,' Lytton informed Clive Bell on the last day of December, 'and before long I hope to be really involved in work.' Later that day he returned to London, where he had arranged to have an interview with Messrs Chatto and Windus about the proposed publication of his *Eminent Victorians*.

Left on her own, Carrington now knew something of the way in which the next fourteen years of her life with Lytton, at Tidmarsh and later at Ham Spray House, would turn out. There would have to be many sacrifices. Already she missed some of her young artist friends, and the particular trees and fields of her home. Seldom again would she have much time for serious painting. Instead she became an excellent gardener and an erratic if conscientious housekeeper. Though she usually had a maid to help her, she did most of the cooking herself – an art for which she had had no training and only a latent aptitude. She prepared large and delicious country meals for Lytton and his friends – home-made wines, game, and raspberry jelly and good helpings of green vegetables from the garden; and teas of farm butter, honey in the comb, rich plum cakes baked in the oven, skilfully concocted marmalades and fresh warm loaves of currant bread, all neatly laid out on the table with a pink lustre tea-service. But behind the scenes, in the kitchen, there was indescribable chaos, as if a bomb had exploded. It was a wonder that Lytton was not severely poisoned, though, possibly, of course, some of his later sicknesses may not have been psychosomatic in origin at all. Several of their guests suffered acutely. Carrington's rabbit-pie, for example, though a very succulent dish, was sometimes lethal in its after-effects, and Diana Guinness (later Lady Mosley) told the author that after one devastating plateful 'I had to have the Doctor at 3 A.M. – thought I was dying – I had to stay on some more days and that was how I became so fond of Carrington.'

In her capacity as nurse to Lytton's many indispositions, she could be equally solicitous and alarming: Barbara Bagenal once preventing her in the nick of time from serving him, as a drink, half a tumbler of undiluted iodine. But she had set out to make herself absolutely indispensable to him, and gradually, detail by detail, she taught herself to be so. She was his housekeeper, his confidante, his go-between. Unable to give an order to a servant in his own home, he would tell Carrington when he wanted a cup of tea, and she would solemnly inform the maid. If he was by himself, he would go without. She enveloped him in a love and admiration which struck others as excessive, but which exactly suited him, since their union could never be a midnight, tête-à-tête affair, but was of an everyday and practical nature. Lytton needed not a mistress, as Gertler had done, but a companion to look after him and to understand him with that sensibility, that selfless tolerance and quickness of mind that neither Lady Strachey nor Ottoline had ever really possessed. Carrington was this perfectly sympathetic spirit; her artistic flair, lively and exceptional nature acted as the salt preserving their relationship from the alkaline coating of tedium.

Though they lived together for the rest of their lives, neither ever became warder to the other's captivity. By mutual consent, both retained something of their independence, even if Lytton's flights from Carrington's attentions sometimes bore the look of a schoolboy's guilty truancy. For she, it appeared, would very willingly have become his prisoner and hated his departures which, she nevertheless instinctively realized, acted as the safety-valve to their unconventional union. When left alone in the country, as in these first days of 1918, she was overcome by fear. The Mill House seemed full of strange noises, either rats or ghosts, and both equally terrifying.[7] At night she would hurry up to bed early, and listen, and long for sleep. These inexplicable night-sounds echoed the frightening insecurity which had always lurked soundlessly beneath the surface of her contentment. In spite of everything, she hardly ever felt confident that her life with Lytton would continue for very long, and secretly went on hoping that somehow he might one day ask her to marry him.

Yet with all her fears and uncertainties, it was a good life she enjoyed with him, materially and otherwise. She travelled widely and met many people. Towards Lytton's young men she felt no jealousy, and since they adored her, she basked in their playful attentions. These years at Tidmarsh were probably the happiest in both their lives. For her happiness was Lytton's happiness, and all her energies were orientated towards what they both wanted. She was certain, too, that though he might feel little sexual desire for her, yet she would be closer to him, and better for him, than anyone else could be. Never again would he be enfeebled by unnecessary illness or prostrated by secret misery and depleted vigour. She would see to it that he led a regular life supported at every turn by glasses of warm milk, reviving country walks, measured doses of quinine, Bemax and Sanatogen, and sensible clothes, and Extract of Malt, and Dr Gregory's rhubarb powder, and eucalyptus oil and all the other wholesome syrups, nourishing foods and cunning medicaments the world had to offer.

7. The corn storehouse next door was, of course, a regular breeding ground for rats. 'One morning I was awakened by yells from Lytton's room,' James Strachey remembered, 'and went in and found something moving inside the bottom of his bed – a rat, which I caught in a chamber pot.'

4

'TOUT EST POSSIBLE'

While Carrington was busy renovating and redecorating the Mill House, Lytton had been looking round for a suitable publisher for his book. Several years earlier, Geoffrey Whitworth, the art editor of Chatto and Windus, had asked Roger Fry to write for them a book on Post-Impressionism. Fry had declined, but added that his friend Clive Bell was then engaged in writing just such a work, and that he would ask him to submit it to them. In due course the book, entitled *Art*, arrived, was accepted, and became an immediate success. 'And how very strange to be published by Chatto and Windus!' Lytton had commented shortly before its appearance (9 November 1913). 'I thought they did nothing but bring out superannuated editions of Swinburne variegated with the Children's Theological Library and the Posthumous Essays of Lord de Tabley.'

But now, four years later, everyone was conspiring to urge the same strange publishers on himself — 'including Mr Robert Nichols,[8] who hurried up to me the other evening, and assured me that they were just the people for my book, with its delicate ironical flavour, etc., etc. as if he had read it all years ago'. Clive Bell, soon to bring out his *Pot Boilers* (1918) with the same firm, had recently spoken to Whitworth and his associate Frank Swinnerton about the manuscript of *Eminent Victorians*. They at once expressed interest, and so, early in December, after having arranged for it to be typed, Lytton decided to send them the completed text.

He was not confident about its acceptance. According to Raymond Mortimer, he felt that it was too strong meat to be readily digested, and that he might have to wait several years

---

8. Robert Nichols (1893–1944), the poet and dramatist, who was at this time working in the Ministry of Labour, having seen service on the Belgian-French front. His recently published book of poems *Ardours and Endurances* had been widely read and he was regarded by many as a sort of new Rupert Brooke.

for its publication, until public taste became more amenable. In any case, it would almost certainly have to be postponed until after the war was over. In a letter to Clive Bell (4 December 1917), however, he expresses his uncertainties rather differently: 'I fear it might not strike them as quite sufficiently advanced,' he wrote.

Whatever the exact reason for these doubts, he cannot have been prepared for his publishers' heady reaction. Whitworth read it first, then passed it on to Swinnerton, who, finding the typescript in its cover of crimson paper on his office desk one morning shortly before Christmas, began casually to turn its pages.

They were so enchanting [he later wrote] that I continued, and when night fell I could not leave the book, but took it carefully home. ... I had hardly taken the typescript up again after dinner when ... there was an air raid by Germans. The whirring of aeroplanes overhead, the rattle of machine-gun fire, and finally the frightful thunder of a gun in the field at the bottom of our garden, would all have served to distract a mind less happily engaged; but as it was, with curtains closely drawn to prevent the escape of light, I consorted that evening with Cardinal Manning, Thomas Arnold, Florence Nightingale, and General Gordon. The nineteenth century had come alive again.

Both Whitworth and Swinnerton were 'as excited before publication as the world was after it', especially since, outside Cambridge circles, the name of Lytton Strachey was relatively unknown. Frank Swinnerton vaguely recalled his primer on French literature, but as yet knew nothing of its author. His enthusiastic acceptance of the book reached Lytton shortly before Christmas. He replied (30 December 1917) asking for fifty pounds to be paid to him on the day of publication, as an advance against a royalty of 10 per cent of the published price – and bringing up the matter of illustrations – always a most significant and carefully chosen part of his biographies. 'I think the portraits would be an important feature of the book,' he wrote, 'but I do not know how to obtain photographic prints of them, nor can I engage to pay for their cost. The portraits I have in mind are to be found in books which

are easily procurable: would you be able to obtain reproductions of these? I should add that I think there should be
five portraits, and not four, as a portrait of Newman (there is
a very suitable one in Wilfrid Ward's biography) seems to me
indispensable.'[9]

To agree the terms of his contract, Lytton arranged to call
at the offices of Chatto and Windus early in January. The
impression which he created at this meeting was so very vivid
that Swinnerton later recorded it in *The Georgian Literary
Scene*.

[Lytton Strachey] was fairly tall, but his excessive thinness, almost
emaciation, caused him to appear endless,' he remembered. 'He had
a rather bulbous nose, the spectacles of a British Museum book-
worm, a large and straggly dark brown beard (with a curious rufous
tinge); no voice at all. He drooped if he stood upright, and sagged if
he sat down. He seemed entirely without vitality; and most people
would have mistaken him for an elderly professor of languages who
was trying to remember some grammatical rule which he had forgotten all about. Sad merriment was in his eye, and about him a
perpetual air of sickness and debility.

Lytton was delighted by Swinnerton's and Whitworth's
high estimate of his work. But in the ensuing months between
the acceptance of his typescript and the publication of his
book, he was recurrently plagued with doubts as to its merits.
Perhaps the style was too richly adorned, the adjectives too
thickly plastered on; perhaps the tone was over-emphatic;
perhaps the characters would fail to 'convince'. To reassure
himself he solicited his friends' favourable opinions. He sent a
copy of 'The End of General Gordon' to Philip Morrell, who
liked it, and another to Virginia Woolf, who thought it masterly – 'It's amazing how from all these complications, you
contrive to reel off such a straight and dashing story,' she
wrote back to him, 'and how you weave in every scrap – my
God, *what* scraps – of interest to be had, like (you must
pardon one metaphor) a snake insinuating himself through

9. In the first edition of *Eminent Victorians* there were actually six
illustrations, the last one being a photograph of Gladstone.

innumerable golden rings. . . . I don't see how the skill could be carried further.'

Wherever he went during this winter he would seize the opportunity to read aloud some pages from his book. Anxious even at this stage to iron out any minor flaws which were still undetected, always fond of reading before a sympathetic audience, he found that this was the perfect method for testing the flow and effectiveness of his rather conversational prose style. At Tidmarsh he read it to Carrington, and at Hampstead to some of his family. Over Easter he spent a few days at Asheham, where he again read some passages to Leonard and Virginia Woolf and his fellow guests, James Strachey and Noel Olivier; and early in April he went on to Charleston and, as a sequel to the Manning and Florence Nightingale essays which Clive and Vanessa Bell, David Garnett and Duncan Grant had heard the previous autumn, he read them those on Arnold and Gordon. On another occasion, visiting 'Jack' [St John] and Mary Hutchinson, he sat, a Shetland shawl draped round his shoulders, in an armchair close to the fire, and, though uncomfortably afflicted with shingles, delivered in a faint and plaintive voice several selected chapters. One of the other guests was Osbert Sitwell, who recalled that their hostess 'pressed her lively young daughter of seven to allow him to see her imitation of him. While the precocious mimic showed off, Lytton watched the child with a look of the utmost distaste, and when asked by the mother what he thought of the performance – one of real virtuosity – remarked in a high, clear, decisive voice, "I expect it's amusing, but it isn't at all *like*!" '

These first four months of 1918 were extremely busy ones for Lytton. 'My life passes almost entirely among proof sheets, which now flow in upon me daily,' he told Ottoline (3 March 1918). 'It is rather exciting, but also rather harassing. All sorts of tiresome details, and minor crises – about covers, illustrations, contracts, and so on – keep turning up; but my hope is that in about six weeks or so "Eminent Victorians" will burst upon an astonished world.' Between proof sheets he was contributing reviews to the periodical *War and Peace*, which Leonard Woolf was editing while the regular editor,

Harold Wright, was away, and experimenting with another play.

Mainly because of this work, Lytton spent a good deal of his time in London, where he had recently joined the left-wing 1917 Club. This club, evolving from some discussions between Oliver Strachey and Leonard Woolf, had started up the previous December, taking the lease of No. 4 Gerrard Street in Soho, 'in those days the rather melancholy haunt of prostitutes daily from 2.30 onwards', Leonard Woolf recalls. Its membership, which later became largely theatrical, was then a curious mixture of the political and the literary and artistic. 'It's quite a comfortable and attractive place,' Lytton assured Carrington after his first entry there, ' – very nice rooms, and tolerable furniture and tea and toast to be had.' Apart from these homely amenities, the club furnished him, in the domain of politics, with a ringside view of much that was going on, and an opportunity to study some of its more illustrious radical members, such as Ramsay MacDonald, the rather uneasy first president of the club.

While in London this winter, Lytton took time off to attend Bertrand Russell's trial at Bow Street. This trial arose out of an article Russell had written for the N.C.F. weekly, *The Tribunal*, advocating acceptance of a recent peace offer made by Germany. As a result of it, he was sentenced to six months' imprisonment in Brixton jail. Lytton felt that the more the friends who showed themselves in court, the better for Russell, but their laughter at some of the prosecution's misdirected sallies and the amusing quotes from Russell's article may well have helped to stimulate the magistrate Sir John Dickinson's ferocity.[10] 'I have never encountered such a blast of vitriolic hatred,' Russell later commented on Dickinson. 'He would have had me hanged, drawn and quartered if he could.' And Lytton echoed this view in a description of the case he sent to Ottoline (3 March 1918). 'It was really infamous – much worse, I thought, than those other pro-

10. Sir John Dickinson (1848–1933), who had taken his law degree at Trinity College, Cambridge, and who from 1913 to 1920 was Chief Metropolitan Police Magistrate, Bow Street.

ceedings before the Lord Mayor — even more obviously
unjust, gross and generally wicked and disgusting. The spectacle of a louse like Sir John Dickinson rating Bertie for immorality and sending him to prison! ... James and I came
away with our teeth chattering with fury. It makes one abandon hope that such monstrosities should occur, openly, and
be accepted by very nearly everybody as a matter of
course.'

At about the same time, Lytton had to face a smaller ordeal
of his own. Later that March he was summoned to yet
another medical examination, this time to be conducted by
the civil authorities. He had no clear notion of what to
expect, of what this change in the system might entail. The
general outlook of the war was not good, and there was little
reason to expect its end in a mere seven months' time. In view
of the tiresome possibilities that might, even now, ensue, the
prospect was a disturbing one. As it turned out, the result of
this medical board was very satisfactory, and he was declared
to be permanently and totally unfit for all forms of military
service. 'It is a great relief,' he admitted to Ottoline (20 March
1918), 'and I can now relapse into writing and reading without
that anxiety hanging over my head. The whole thing was
infinitely better managed than before — far more civilised, and
careful, and the doctors positively polite and even sympathetic. This comes of the military having nothing more to
do with it.'

Though the cause of his many trips to London was mainly
matters of business, there were still some opportunities for
'gadding and whirling'. One particular dinner-party, given by
Mary Hutchinson, led to an alarming corollary — 'the unfortunate occurrence in the purlieus of Ravenscourt Park', as
Lytton afterwards used to call it — which formed what in effect
was the final scene in Carrington's tragi-comic affair with Gertler. The two of them had continued to correspond, and
whenever she visited London — which was not very often — she
would call in at Gertler's Hampstead studio and tell him about
her lovely life in the country, the birds and the trees, and how
much better it was than living in foggy old London. He would

sit there, sullen and crumpled, as she explained to him how much lighter and more alive everything seemed in Berkshire. The people all had friendly faces, and one could walk along the roads without those snorting buses and motors on every side, and that mob of scurrying pedestrians. She loved the Mill House – and so would he. She would ask him to stay there when the others, Oliver and the rest, were away. Their friendship, she added, her tactlessness swelling in a rhapsodic crescendo, had taken on a new freedom and flexibility – 'like birds in the air meeting on a tree suddenly, conversing without discord – and knowing that we can both fly off and again meeT perhaps soon perhaps next summer and we can still go on where we left off'.

Of the true nature of the Tidmarsh *ménage* Carrington still revealed nothing. But such matters could not for ever be kept secret, and within two short months Gertler had picked up all the stories of what was going on. 'I know that you live with Lytton,' he fulminated (24 February 1918). His first reaction was explosive. On the evening of 14 February, after Jack and Mary Hutchinson's party in Hammersmith, Lytton and Carrington were walking off down the blacked-out streets, when the dark figure of Gertler loomed from the shadows, overtook them, and, with a cry of rage, launched a two-fisted attack upon the astonished Lytton. Luckily various Bloomsbury pacifists were not far off; and a number of professors and mathematicians hurried forward, succeeded in separating the two pugilists and led the panting Gertler off. 'Anything more cinematographic can hardly be imagined,' Lytton told Clive Bell (18 February 1918), 'and on looking back it wears all the appearance of a bad dream. All the same it was at the time exceedingly painful, especially as a little more presence of mind on my part might have prevented the situation; but it all came about with a speed. Poor Mark! The provocation was certainly great, and I was very sorry for him. However, as he was obviously drunk, perhaps he was rather less conscious than one supposed. Characteristically, Maynard came to the rescue, and eventually led him off, and pacified him, with amazing aplomb. Monty [Shearman] had already tried and completely failed; Carrington had fled under the protection of Sheppard. who kept on repeating, during the height of the crisis — "Who *is* it? Who *is* it?" in a most pained voice; and Harry supported my trembling form from the field. It was really an intervention of Providence that they should all have come up at the psychological moment, as Heaven knows what mightn't have happened.'

A week later Lytton was dining at the Eiffel Tower restaurant with David Garnett, when Gertler again appeared, but this time. being sober and non-violent, he came up and apologized for his earlier assault: 'I am sorry about the other night. Please forgive me.'

Lytton giggled and replied: 'It was nothing at all. Please don't worry yourself about it.'

'I don't think', David Garnett later commented, 'that was what Gertler wanted to be told.'

But if Lytton's polite diminution of this incident ludicrously trivialized Gertler's emotional upheaval, Carrington's more inconsequential attitude seriously aggravated it. She felt responsible for the whole wretched affair, and greatly upset by it. The haunting look of loneliness and despair in his face, deepened by the tubercular ill-health which was to keep him in and out of sanatoria for the rest of his life, contributing eventually, in 1939, to his suicide, testified to the suffering with which she had afflicted him. She saw this clearly, and was chafed by guilt. Her lies, devious neglect and lack of foresight had very largely been to blame. 'Please do not worry about last night,' she wrote to him the following morning. 'I am only *very* sorry if I gave you the cause of your distress. It was quite unintentional.' He must, she wrote in another letter, make new friends in London. She cared very much that he still loved her, and: 'Remember I care always very much for you. Just as much as I used to. It is in no way changed — and if you know how much I felt your Pains and griefs it would lessen them for you.'

But still it was the old story. At every crucial moment, Carrington's letters to Gertler were bafflingly irrelevant, full of unconscious irony. She appreciated that their relationship was entering a new phase, and that if this new phase were to be at all harmonious, unpoisoned by the misdeeds of the past, then she must straightway contradict the various rumours which had percolated through to him from Dorothy Brett and others. The truth was far less damaging, less injurious than these lies. A full explanation was needed to clear the air, but she shied away from it. 'I think if we are going to be friends again,' she announced, 'I had better be quite frank and tell you about what I do down here. and Lytton, and everything. or else it won'T be real.' That was what she told him: and that was all. It was an avowed Statement of Intent which hung in the air unsupported by any revelation of truth, but which, as it gently floated away into the distance, took on for her the aspect of an important disclosure.

Carrington had no talent for factual truth, and the pregnant weight of all she failed to say seemed to Gertler to consolidate his most salacious and horrible suspicions. Her silence was more potent than any deliberate provocation could have been. In his anger, he replied crudely and bitterly to her letter, and this, in one way, was what she had wanted, enabling her to transfer back on to him her unacceptable sense of guilt. His loss of temper seemed to exonerate her from responsibility. After all, she had endeavoured to make an alliance, and her attempts had been scornfully flung back in her face. 'I hardly see the use of corresponding when you are so antagonistic towards me,' she answered indignantly (28 February 1918). 'When I said I wanted to tell you more about my self, I did not mean to make that crude statement — which I knew you already knew. . . . Evidently from your last letter *We think so very differently about relative values of everything now*. Yet it is impossible for me not to care everytime I see you. Very much. This letter is not bitter; only I feel rather tireD, and perhaps disappointed about it. But *Don'T* write anymore, I would rather not start it again. . . . There is not answer to this letter.'

But, of course, there was; and for another two years the unanswerable answers and replies, inquiries, vindications, apologies, misunderstandings, concessions and rebuttals, trickled on, until eventually, sad and exhausted, they passed on out of reach of each other's lives for good.

There was much more, besides Gertler, to occupy Carrington's time and attention now. The four weeks immediately prior to the publication of *Eminent Victorians* Lytton spent at Tidmarsh. Life there was a steady stream of visitors — Oliver Strachey, who sat for a portrait by Carrington; James, who had abandoned his projected career in medicine after three weeks as a medical student to become dramatic critic of the *Athenaeum*;[11] Alix Sargant-Florence, reading Rabelais with the aid of six dictionaries; Barbara Bagenal and her husband Nick, who would sometimes stay to keep Carrington company while Lytton was away; Middleton Murry, very gloomy over the prospects of his wife Katherine Mansfield's health, and very excited over his own prospects as editor of the *Athenaeum*; Saxon Sydney-Turner, quiet and scholarly, reading Euripides; and Maynard Keynes, who, Lytton told Clive Bell (18 February 1918), looked 'very prosperous, but not very well I thought, and full of the L[loyd] G[eorge] crisis. He thought it possible that a vote of censure might be moved in the House by infuriated back-bench Tories, that the Govt. might then fall and be succeeded by a Law–Asquith combination including tout ce qu'il-y-a de plus respectable, but not pacifist, though destined to make peace. I doubt it — and I doubt still more, if it did come off, whether it would be any good. To be caught in the clutches of a second Coalition, and a respectable one this time, seems to me a dismal fate. But it's difficult to believe that the Goat won't clamber over this fence as he has so many others.'

Another less pleasant and untroubled visit to the Mill House in these first months was made by David Garnett, who

11. James Strachey had caught influenza, and never returned to his medical studies. Instead, at the invitation of Middleton Murry, he had become dramatic critic of the *Athenaeum* for about a year. He was already interested in psychology and in 1920 went to Vienna where he was psychoanalysed by Freud and became his pupil. Alix, his wife, also went out to Vienna, and also became a psychoanalyst. She is the author of *The Unconscious Motives of War* (1957).

has given an interesting glimpse behind the scenes there. Carrington's aura of disarming innocence was offset by a mischievous addiction to cruelty. Her truly appalling practical jokes had little in common with the high-spirited, extrovert hoaxes staged by Horace Cole and Adrian Stephen. *Their* chief targets were the humourless representatives of officialdom and they derived their fun from the long elaborate preparation each joke required beforehand, from the ludicrous pantomime effect of their performance and from the resulting embarrassment caused to those with an over-developed sense of responsibility. Carrington's exploits were more private matters. Like many divided natures she possessed a heightened capacity for unhappiness, and her practical jokes were often a means of revenging herself upon life. At her most unambitious, she would stop short at sewing up people's pyjamas. But often her schemes were more subtle and individual than this. Her favourite victims came from among those two types of person who had, in the past, inflicted most pain upon her – motherly women and virile, sexually adventurous young men.

David Garnett fell perfectly under this second classification. And when, in the early summer of 1918, he had almost reached breaking-point over a desperate love-affair, the opportunity presented to Carrington for wickedly exploiting the situation seemed too good to miss. She therefore sent him an invitation, asking him to come and stay with her and Lytton for the week-end, and to this she added a postscript promising him that he should find there the person he most wanted to meet. The implication was obvious. In a turmoil of excitement Garnett caught a train to Reading, hastened along the last eight miles of his journey to Tidmarsh on foot, and arrived at the Mill House late at night. Carrington was at once fully in command of the situation. 'I knew you would come tonight,' she exclaimed as she made him sit down to eat. 'I was certain of it. Lytton wouldn't believe me.'

'Where is . . . my fellow guest?' Garnett inquired as soon as he decently could.

Carrington answered that she was upstairs.

'I picked up my rucksack and went upstairs,' Garnett records, 'and Carrington followed to show me my room.

' "Which is *her* room?" I asked, for it was torture to wait another moment. I must find out if I was there with her knowledge, even at her wish.

'Lytton had come out on to the landing and looked at me with surprise. "Why, who do you think is there?" he asked.

'I stepped forward to open the door but Carrington seized my arm. "Stop! You mustn't go in!" she exclaimed.

' "Well, who is it, then?" I asked, bewildered.

' "Mrs Swanwick," tittered Lytton who was mystified by the whole affair. This was an idiotic joke, for Mrs Swanwick was an elderly feminist and socialist.

'I freed my arm from Carrington and was about to rush into the room when the door opened and a young man whom I had seen once before in my life stood in the doorway.

' "He must be her lover! That is why Carrington is trying to stop me going in!" flashed through my mind.

'But the young man was so incongruous a figure – so terribly unsuited for the part, that I realised that I must be slightly mad and I pulled myself together sufficiently to greet him civilly and then retire to bed.'

Blinded by his infatuation, it did not occur to Garnett until much later that he had been the victim of a singularly brutal practical joke. And since Carrington had told nothing of her scheme either to Lytton or to Marshall, the young man, the incident passed off without further mention and without impairing Garnett's friendship. Carrington was very warm and friendly with him all the rest of the week-end, probably repenting of what she had done.

When there were no guests to entertain or be entertained by, Carrington would vanish up into the attic, painting pictures which no one was allowed to see, or disappear outside to busy herself among the early potatoes and the hens,[12] while Lytton sat on downstairs writing or reading. He had

12. 'We are trying to grow vegetables – and hens,' Lytton wrote to Dorelia John (10 May 1918). 'Neither seem to come up with sufficient

already begun to compose his biographical essay, 'Lady Hester Stanhope', and also, during the week of 2–5 May, his revealing and rather wicked pen portrait, 'Mr Asquith'. He had, for the first time, been reading Charles Greville's *Memoirs*, the full text of which he was later to edit, and the six volumes of the Goncourts' *Journals*, which Virginia Woolf had put him on to.

Among recently published books he was reading a new study of Byron ('what a splendid subject he would be for a really modern and artistic biography!') and Sidney Colvin's biography of Keats. In spite of all the biographer's pomp and tepidity, the tragedy of Keats's short life came through to Lytton as overwhelming. 'It seems to me one of the most appalling stories known,' he declared. 'One of the worst features of it is that one gathers that he had never once copulated. Is it possible, though?' His comments on one other new book that spring are also interesting. This was *Remnants*, Desmond MacCarthy's first collection of articles from the *New Statesman*, the *New Witness*, the *Eye Witness* and *The Speaker*, which Constable had just brought out. 'I suppose you've seen Remnants – a book in the best of taste,' he wrote to Clive Bell (10 May 1918). 'But it's difficult not to think that the milk has been standing a very long time, and that, though the cream is excellent, there's not much of it. However, nowadays, it would be absurd to complain of anything that is genuinely charming. His Asquith doings fill me with astonishment. I can still hardly believe that he likes those people or can think it worth while to flatter them. Perhaps really he only finds them amusing to pass the time of day with – one can *just* imagine that – and that it may be rather fun to meet the Lord Chief Justice.'

Soon enough Lytton's own incursions into aristocratic society would give rise to a similar wonderment in his other Bloomsbury friends. But for the time being his life glided contentedly on amid the congenial company and conversation of his friends. A new optimism and buoyancy was in the air.

---

rapidity – damn them – and in the meantime living costs about £100 a minute.'

Many years before he had written to Maynard Keynes (27 February 1906): 'When I have a home of my own, I should write up "Hope" over the door.' Now that at last he had a home of his own, his motto, he told a friend, was to be: *'Tout est possible.'* There is something of this hopeful, adventurous spirit, expressed with a characteristic tongue-in-the-cheek style, in several of his letters. 'We have many projects', he wrote to Clive Bell (16 April 1918) ' – to build a fire-place, a book-case, a theatre, to learn Spanish, to attach the pump to the mill-wheel by a leather band, to buy 24 geese, to borrow a saddle from Farmer Davis and saddle the Blacksmith's pony with it and ride into Pangbourne, to write a drawing-room comedy, a classical tragedy in the style of Euripides, and the History of England during the War. But le temps s'en va, mon cher, and we are left idling in front of the fire.'

Happy in the tranquil seclusion of Tidmarsh, looked after and idolized by Carrington, surrounded by his books, visited by his friends – and visiting them – the six years during which Lytton lived at the Mill House included some of the most successful, exciting and generally satisfactory days of his career. In the spring of 1918 only three ingredients to his happiness were still missing: a new passionate love-affair; a little fame as a writer to soothe away the mortifications of his early years; and the necessary money to make this ideal way of life permanent. All these were to be granted him. Soon he would fall deeply in love once more; while fame and fortune were even now about to be showered on him in full by the publication of *Eminent Victorians*.

PART IV

'Whenever I think of old age I turn pale with horror –
the rain, the loneliness, the regret – oh dear, let's turn
away one's thoughts.' *Lytton Strachey to Duncan Grant*
(5 March 1906)

FOURTEEN

A Life Apart

At that, I'd stop. But then, suppose
   The gods, still smiling, said 'Our store
Of pleasant things still overflows,
    Look round; be bold; and choose some more.'

Hum! I should pause; reflect; then 'Yes!'
   Methinks I'd cry, 'I see, I see,
What would fill up my happiness.
   Give me a girl to dwell with me!

A girl with genial beauty dowered,
   And health, and vigorous liberty,
By supreme Nature's self empowered
   To live in loneliness and glee,

And clothe her fancies with fair form,
   And paint her thoughts with vivid hue,
A girl within whose heart, so warm,
   Love ever lingers – oh, so true!'
                   Lytton Strachey (1 March 1920)

1

SUCCESS!

LIKE Byron, Lytton awoke one morning to find himself famous. *Eminent Victorians* marked an epoch in biographical literature, and its immediate impact was tremendous. The world was weary of big guns and big phrases. To the jaded palate of the younger generation, the merits of the book – its brevity, coherence and verisimilitude, its reason and impertinency mixed – were as striking as its limitations have since become; and many could detect no faults in its entrancing pages. 'It might be described as the first book of the 'twenties,' wrote Cyril Connolly. '... He [Lytton] struck the note of ridicule which the whole war-weary generation wanted to hear, using the weapon of Bayle, Voltaire and Gibbon on the creators of the Red Cross and the Public School System. It appeared to the post-war young people like the light at the end of a tunnel.'

Lytton was astonished by the long and laudatory reviews he read everywhere. He had scored a fine success, yet he felt somewhat uneasy at the lack of attacks. Even the Catholic Press seemed to be remarkably full of Christian charity. What could be the explanation for it all? 'I'm getting rather nervous,' he admitted to Ottoline Morrell (3 June 1918), ' – the reviewers are so extraordinarily gushing that I think something must be wrong.' And in a letter to James (May 1918) he suggested: 'I fancy these good fellows [the reviewers] must think they're doing a politeness to the Editor of the Spectator.' Yet still the success rolled on, until it seemed at last as if he might also make some money from his writing. His name had become a household word; everyone was talking about the book – it was mentioned and quoted in leading articles, and before the end of the year had gone into seven impressions. 'So far it has all been sugar,' Lytton told Mary Hutchinson (30 May 1918), '. . . and I'm really rather disappointed that none of the Old Guard should have raised a protest. I did expect a *little* irritation. Is it possible that the poor dear creatures haven't a single kick left?'

He need not have worried. The custodians of popular mythology, the literary politicians, dons and bishops, were soon enough to denounce him as a bearded Mephistopheles, full of cunning and depravity, in sinister, hirsute league with such dangerous spirits as Bernard Shaw, Augustus John and D. H. Lawrence, together bent on destroying all that should be held sacred in society. This, of course, was exactly as it should have been. When the *Spectator* delivered a denunciation, he felt relieved; and he was encouraged, too, by Edmund Gosse's thundering fulminations in *The Times Literary Supplement*. 'As for Gosse,' he exclaimed, 'after having spent all his life saying disagreeable things about other people (his father included) – to turn round in self-righteous wrath,

because someone criticises Lord Cromer!' Most heartening of
all was another letter in the same paper from Mrs Humphry
Ward, angrily defending her grandfather, Dr Arnold – 'What
an old wretch! . . . But it's a triumph to have drawn her.'

But for the most part, the reception given to his book was
wonderfully favourable, and the few shrill notes of protest
were drowned in a loud chorus of praise. 'I shall soon have to
make a triumphal progress through the British Isles,' he announced to Ottoline; and he reassured Clive Bell (27 May
1918) that 'I remain calm even in the face of the praises of the
Daily Telegraph and Mr Asquith.'

The prestige and immediate sales of *Eminent Victorians* had
been greatly boosted by Asquith when, in the course of his
Romanes Lecture delivered at Oxford early that summer, he
gave the book what Lytton called 'a most noble and high-
flown puff'. The ex-prime minister was still a widely influential
figure, and no better publicity could have been looked for
than his flattering commendation. 'This must be circulated,'
Lytton wrote off to Carrington (June 1918), 'and it's to be
hoped and indeed presumed that every member of the great
Liberal Party will buy a copy.' He had happened to be staying
at Garsington on the Saturday when Asquith was delivering
his speech, and drove over with Ottoline to hear it. 'It must
be confessed that the lecture was a horribly dull one,' he
afterwards told his mother (21 June 1918), ' – but one can't be
too severe after such a noble piece of advertisement. Apparently he was very enthusiastic about the book, talking about
it to everyone. I didn't see him to speak to. The sight inside
the Sheldonian was rather splendid – with red gowns – and
Curzon (the Chancellor of the University) enthroned on a
chair of state, in the highest pomp.'

It is possible that Asquith might not have spoken quite so
warm-heartedly of 'Mr Strachey's subtle and suggestive art'[1]

1. During the course of his Romanes Lecture, entitled 'Some Aspects of
the Victorian Age', Asquith said: 'In a recently published volume – the
most trenchant and brilliant series of biographical studies which I have
read for a long time – Mr Lytton Strachey, under the modest title *Eminent Victorians*, has put on his canvas four figures (as unlike one another

had he known that, only a fortnight before, it had been applied no less trenchantly to himself, in putting together some reflections that arose from the publication of his *Occasional Addresses*:

'The fundamental material of Mr Asquith I take to have been a middle-class, North-Country solidity, eminently respectable, almost nonconformist, moderate, cautious, humdrum, and with a not unintelligent eye on the main chance. Then came the influence of Balliol and Jowett, which infused the timid Oxford culture and the timid Oxford worldliness into the virginal undistinguished mass. After that the Bar, with its training in agility of case-putting and its habit of pomposity. So far the development was ordinary enough; but the final influence brought with it some odd contradictions. The Margot set – rich, smart, showy, and self-indulgent – got hold of Mr Asquith. The middle class legal Don became a *viveur* ...

'His public career suggests a parallel with Walpole. But one gathers that under all Sir Robert's low-minded opportunism there was a certain grandeur, and that his actual capacity was supreme. In Asquith's case the inveterate lack of ideals and imagination seems really unredeemed; when one has peeled off the brown-paper wrapping of phrases and compromises, one finds – just nothing at all. And as for his capacity, it was perhaps not much more than the skill of a parliamentary tactician. He could never deal with a serious difficulty. He mismanaged Ireland; and, though it would be hardly fair to blame too severely his incompetence in the conduct of the war, his inability to cope with the internal situation was really inexcusable.'

Almost the only people from whom Lytton heard nothing after the appearance of *Eminent Victorians* were his publishers, who, in that quaint way publishers have, presumed that the author's interest in his work had automatically

---

as any four people could be). ... They are in less danger than ever of being forgotten, now that they have been re-created for the English readers of the future (not in a spirit of blind hero-worship) by Mr Strachey's subtle and suggestive art.'

ceased on publication day. Perhaps they feared Lytton's continual pestering; if so, they had seriously misjudged his character. Chatto and Windus had brought the book out at the price of ten-and-sixpence, allowing Lytton 15 per cent of this on the first thousand copies sold, and 20 per cent thereafter. They had also undertaken to pay him fifty pounds, in advance of royalties, on 9 May. But the days went by, and still no money reached him. 'It's rather awkward,' he nervously admitted to Clive Bell on 27 May. 'Ought I to write to Geoffrey Whitworth? Perhaps if I'm patient it'll come all right — but perhaps not. I should be glad of your advice.' The following day a letter from Geoffrey Whitworth did turn up. It made no mention of the advance, but, almost regretfully, explained that *Eminent Victorians* was going so well that 'we are *being forced* to *think about* a reprint'. Meanwhile, Clive Bell very sensibly advised Lytton to bring up the matter of his advance without delay. He did so, and by return of post — exactly three weeks late — received a cheque with apologies.

After this false start, the relationship between Lytton and Chatto and Windus grew to be extraordinarily cordial.[2] They are always seeking out ways and means to pay him extra money (without any prompting from Lytton), always improving the mouth-watering clauses in his contracts, and subsequently breaking them for his increased benefit. They press him not to hurry with his next book; they offer to grapple with the tax authorities on his behalf; they invite him to witness the printing of his books[3] and send him innumerable

2. Most of the correspondence concerning Lytton's work was carried out by the senior partner at Chatto and Windus, Charles Prentice, who also designed all his books. Harold Raymond, who later became chairman of the firm, remembers Lytton calling there on several occasions. 'We found him a very considerate author to deal with,' he told the author (15 November 1966). 'We knew that he would hold decided views on many of the details of book publishing and we were careful to consult him on any matter on which we thought he would like to be consulted; and whenever we did, he would reply promptly and with sound sense.'
3. On one occasion Lytton was invited to witness the printing and other machines in action. The performance was arranged in such a way that, at its conclusion, a first copy of his book would be magnificently produced

dust jackets and alternative bindings from which he is asked to select his favourite; then out of the blue they write to congratulate him about nothing in particular, and urge him to submit all negotiations to the Society of Authors for his own protection. And Lytton too is extremely courteous. He invariably makes pressing inquiries after the health of the partners, apologizes for the slightest delay or for the legitimate corrections to proof copies; he recommends a friend of his to join the firm, and on one occasion tries unsuccessfully to rescue for them his *Landmarks in French Literature* from Williams and Norgate, which, in 1927, went bankrupt.

On 16 July, a third edition of *Eminent Victorians* was issued in Great Britain, making a total of three thousand copies in all. In November the American edition came out. In both countries the book sold steadily and well, and before long it was being translated into several European languages, including Swedish, German, French, Italian and Spanish.

Lytton was particularly anxious to have a good French translation and he consulted Dorothy Bussy about this. That summer Dorothy was in England, spending much of her time with André Gide, then living at Merton House in Cambridge as the guest of Harry Norton.[4] Gide had come over with Marc Allegret, carrying a letter of introduction to the Strachey family from Auguste Bréal. During his stay, he had seen something of Lytton and rather more of Dorothy, who was helping to improve his English, and who later translated many of his books. Cambridge, in the summer holidays, half-emptied of undergraduates and half-filled with wounded soldiers, was not at its best, and Gide passed much of his time reading and bicycling about the countryside. His opinion of Lytton as a biographer was qualified. He had been strongly advised to

---

and presented to him. As he stepped into the room, however, where all this was busily taking place, the machinery broke down and came to a halt. Nothing could start it up again, publishers and printers were overcome with confusion; but Lytton was probably rather relieved.

4. Gide had begun his stay at Grape House in Grantchester, but transferred to Merton House in order to be nearer Dorothy Bussy, then living at 27 Grange Road, Cambridge.

read *Eminent Victorians* by Arnold Bennett, and he began to do so that October. 'I can endure neither the flaccidity of his thought nor the amenity of his style,' he wrote of 'Cardinal Manning'. 'But this book nevertheless seems to me of great importance' And again, in a letter to Dorothy Bussy: '*Eminent Victorians* lies on our sitting-room's table and is constantly "en lecture". . . . Yet I'm not at all sure this book may find in France many readers.'[5]

Very soon, for the first time in his life, Lytton was to become a person of independent means. During the final dozen years of his life, his average income, from all sources, must have been somewhere between two and three thousand pounds per annum. But success made little outward difference to his way of living. The first use to which he put his money was the repayment of past loans from Harry Norton and others, and the making of improvements to Tidmarsh – among them the fulfilment of an early Abbotsholme ambition, the building of an earth closet in the garden. Success suited him, emphasizing his natural modesty which had sometimes been distorted in the past by frustration and the malignant germs of envy, and making him as a companion more kindly. At no time did he feel the urge to play the great man of letters, and though he made regular trips to London meeting many other celebrated literati, he never really overcame his natural shyness and was always happy to return to the seclusion of the Mill House. Although, therefore, his appearance was well-known to the public, his retiring and secretive personality remained hidden. People could judge only from what they saw, and their deductions were hardly more than beard-deep. Wyndham Lewis has given a fanciful picture of him in his country cottage – a benevolent but rather inhuman old maid of a man, responding coquettishly to his few selected guests

5. On 29 September 1918, Gide wrote to Lytton: 'Un contretemps absurde fait que je n'ai reçu que trop tard votre aimable invitation, alors que déjà tout était décidé pour mon départ. Le plaisir que je me promettais, de vous revoir et Miss Carrington, était si vif que peu s'en fallut je me remisse mon voyage. . . . Du moins croyez la sincérité de mes regrets. Et pour me consoler, je vous lis.'

(of whom Wyndham Lewis was not one), and dragging his daddy-long-legs from room to room, languidly, like a sun-doped stork. 'The big lips under his beard were dreamy and large and a little childlike, his big brown eyes were bovine but intelligent. He knew to what "tribe" he belonged, but probably did not practise the rites of the tribe. He liked watching.'

This frigid, impassive and essentially loveless public image is corrected by the intimate personal testimony of Carrington. 'I am glad at any rate the public does not share my feelings about your appearance and character!' she wrote to him that July, while on holiday with her brother Noel in Scotland. 'Since you are bored with praise of your creations, I will tell you that I think you are the most eminent, graceful person. The most worthy, learned and withal charming character. And I shall always love you in your entirety. You know Dear Lytton it has been rather amazing living with you For so long. Now that I am alone and think or ponder on or over it. Visions steal up – of those hot days when you wore your Fakire clothes – in the orchard – The one afternoon when I saw you in the baTH. – When I lay on your bed on Thursday And smelT your hair, and broke the crackling beard in my fingers.'

Both Carrington and Lytton were glad to have escaped from 'the buffeting of London'. After all the turmoil and agitation of the past, their perplexed and tortured spirits could now find rest among the simple vegetable things they loved so well – the flowers and fields and trees. In their separate ways they were what Carrington termed 'particular-fastidious', disliking the *mélange* of living too closely against other people, yet always aware, as they grew older, of the dangers of becoming eccentric and old maidish. 'Mine is a "vita umbratilis", as Cardinal Manning said', Lytton told Clive Bell (27 May 1918), '– a life in the shade or a shady life, – whichever you prefer.' In the delicious summer heat, the Tidmarsh garden had burst out into a startling tropical refulgence, and Lytton would have been content, so he felt, to sit out there among the laburnums, lilacs, buttercups and apple-blossom, dressed in his Brahmin's robe (though with his mind not altogether Brahminical), serenely dreaming the hours away – would have been, that was, if only so many people were not still being slaughtered just round the corner. Would the war *never* end? But there was no purpose served by brooding over it – far better to return to his Sainte-Beuve.

One of the delights of living in a country cottage of one's own was the pleasure of inviting down one's friends. G. E. Moore and, and Lytton's sisters Pippa and Marjorie, his brother Oliver and a new girl friend, James who 'weeds with two fingers', and Noel Olivier avidly reading Havelock Ellis on sexual inversion, Clive Bell and Mary Hutchinson, and an odd inseparable trio made up of that 'vieillard ratatiné' Saxon Sydney-Turner, Nick and Barbara Bagenal – 'all are incredibly aged. Nick and Barbara (the one without a kidney, and the other with a child) totter and potter like an old couple in an almshouse; and Saxon is wonderfully young for eighty-seven'.

An interesting glimpse behind the scenes at the Mill House has been recorded by another guest there in the late summer of 1919, Gerald Brenan. The afternoon on which he arrived was heavily overcast. The trees and the grasses were steeped in a vivid green and the purplish clouds overhead threw the interior of the house into a gloomy shade.

Carrington, with her restless blue eyes and her golden-brown hair cut in a straight page-boy bob, came to the door [Brenan later recalled] ... and I was shown in the sitting-room. At the farther end of it there was an extraordinary figure reclining in a deep armchair. At the first glance, before I had accustomed my eyes to the lack of light, I had the illusion – or rather, I should say, the image came into my mind – of a darkly bearded he-goat glaring at me from the bottom of a cave.[6] Then I saw that it was a man and took in gradually the long, relaxed figure, the Greco-ish face, the brown sensitive

6. In a letter to the author (14 September 1966), Gerald Brenan has emphasized that this passage records 'the first impression of a young man, just demobilised from the army, in a bad light, and that it reflects more on my *naïveté* than on him. As soon as I had got over my first shock, I felt his elegance and distinction.'

eyes hidden beneath thick glasses, the large, coarse nose and ears, the fine, thin, blue-veined hands. Most extraordinary was the voice, which was both very low and in certain syllables very high-pitched, and which faded out at the end of the sentence, sometimes even without finishing it. I never attuned my ears to taking in everything that he said.

But what struck Brenan more forcibly than anything else was the minute attention Carrington lavished upon this fabulous creature. 'Never have I seen anyone who was so waited on hand and foot as he was by her,' he wrote, 'or whose every word and gesture was received with such reverence. In a young woman who in all other respects was fiercely jealous of her independence, this was extraordinary.'

Over tea, Brenan was beset by a jarring assortment of impressions. With Lytton, 'elegant in his dark suit, gravely remote and fantastic, with something of the polished dilettante air of a sixteenth-century cardinal', he could not hit it off at all. He did not dislike him, but felt as though they were trying to communicate on altogether different wavelengths. And although Carrington, with her pre-Raphaelite clothes and her coaxing voice, blue eyes and honey-mouthed mischievous smile, attracted him physically, he did not take to her there and then, because he had heard that she had made cruel fun of his close friend John Hope-Johnstone, to whom he was very loyal.

So, by the time he left late that summer afternoon, he could have had no premonition that before long he was to be whirled up into the irregular mainstream of their two lives, and that for seven long years Carrington would be the leading person in his own life.

2

THE BEAU MONDE

Life at Tidmarsh did not in itself satisfy the whole either of Carrington's or Lytton's nature. Despite her unique bondage to Lytton, Carrington preserved some strange indissoluble particle of independence; and every so often she would take herself off for solitary expeditions to the sea, where, remembering her dead sailor-brother Teddy, she seemed to shed her neurotic worries and imbibe a fresh strength and resilience.

For Lytton, the Mill House was an ideal headquarters where he could rest between metropolitan adventures. After his success, he was being taken up, much to his delight and slightly to his shame, by the aristocracy. 'The upper-classes rouse my curiosity, and for the present, I think I shall proceed with my enquiries,' he confided to Carrington (26 June 1918), who loved to hear his ironic descriptions of these forays into the beau monde. And again: 'What I really need is the Gentleman's Complete Guide to Society.'

In the weeks and months that followed – and increasingly as time went on – he found himself a week-end guest at the country houses of several brilliant society figures – of Lady Astor at Cliveden, of Lady Desborough at Taplow Court, of Lady Horner at Mells Manor in Somerset; and he was invited to luncheon- and dinner-parties by the most celebrated London hostesses of the day – Lady Colefax and Lady Cunard, Princess Bibesco and Lady d'Abernon, wife of the British ambassador in Berlin. Society fascinated Lytton partly because it was an hallucination. From a distance, it stood out as clear and well-defined – formidable or absurd according to one's angle of vision. One read about it in the newspapers, and even on its fringes, mesmerized by the whirl of self-flattery, the illusion of its reality persisted. But penetrate into its glittering vortex, and it melted away. It had existed only as a glow in one's mind; it was nothing. Yet even a bright, well-conducted nothing was an escape from the self, from the necessary solitude of the artist. Lytton hardly knew whether to be pleased or disgusted at this new state of affairs, and his confusion is implicit in many of his letters. 'I go next Saturday to the Duchess of Marlborough's', he wrote to Ottoline (7 July 1918), ' – is it the beginning of the end? Personally I don't think you or Tolstoy need be alarmed. In the first place, *they* won't like *me*; in the second place *I* won't like *them*. You know I am not altogether uncritical! Curiosity is what chiefly moves me. I want to see for myself. I met the D. of M. in Maud's [Lady Cunard's] ante-room at Drury Lane, and thought her (from a hasty inspection) more distinguished than the rest. Can you give me any tips about her? Lady Randolph [Churchill] was also there – an old war horse, sniffing the battle from afar.' Another member of this Drury Lane party was Margot Asquith who 'had the cheek' to ask Lytton for a copy of his *Eminent Victorians*, and who invited him round to tea so that he might make the presentation. Despite her deplorable manners, he seems to have thought her a more valid personality than he had at first supposed – less *exagérée* and 'even faintly civilised'. But finally he decided that, like so many of these society people, she was unsympathetic – rather like a creature in a play instead of a real human being, someone to watch but never to make friends with. Someone, also, to write home to Carrington about. 'Her mauvais ton is remarkable', he wrote (26 June 1918). 'There she sits in her box (cadged) thinks she's the very tip-top, the grande dame par excellence, and all the rest of it – and every other moment behaving like a kitchen-maid – giggling, looking round, and nudging Elizabeth [Asquith – Princess Bibesco]. As for music, of course it's never occurred to her that such a thing exists. Yet, as one looks at her small weather-beaten (perhaps one should say life-beaten) countenance, one wonders – there does seem a suggestion of something going on underneath.'

Lytton was a *succès fou* in London society; and in spite of his criticism, he was soon being afforded every opportunity to pursue his inquiries into this grand, artificial world of the upper classes. People who only half a dozen years earlier had wondered how on earth Lady Ottoline Morrell could put up with such a queer fish in her drawing-room, now began to entreat him to lunch or dine with them. In the second week of August he was invited down with Maynard Keynes to The Wharf, as house guests of the Asquiths. 'I'm not much looking forward to the outing,' he confessed to Clive Bell (10 August 1918), 'there is a certain frigidity in those altitudes.' But still, curiosity drew him on, and once he had turned up there he actually lapsed into enjoyment. Though not altogether uncritical, of course, he wanted them to like him; and to achieve this he was prepared to like them in return. His cynicism melted in the facile aura of their hospitality, to be replaced by warmer, more sentimental feelings. 'Maynard supported my tottering footsteps with great tact,' he reported to Ottoline (8 September 1918). 'Margot was extremely kind, and the Company (though not particularly brilliant) was entertaining. There were no great nobs. The Old Man was highly rubicund and domestic – also, I thought, a trifle sleepy. It was chiefly a family party – Violet,[7] Cys[8] and his wife, Anthony,[9] Elizabeth[10] – diversified by Lady Tree and one or two nonentities. Violet and I were very friendly. She certainly has changed enormously – so much more tolerant – at times almost humble, I thought, and even her appearance seems to have entirely altered, the angularity having disappeared, and something of the plenitude of the matron taken its place. ... Am I a backslider? I don't think so, and she seemed to be almost intelligent. Even Elizabeth I got on better with (isn't it shocking?) and Margot's goodness of heart rather won me. But what I enjoyed best was the family side of the party – playing foolish letter-games after dinner with the more frivolous (including the Old Man) while the serious persons – Maynard, Margot, Elizabeth and Texeira de Mattos ... gave themselves over to Bridge. You see what I have sunk to! I even enjoyed going off to Church on Sunday evening with Lady Tree – can you imagine the spectacle. And Margot gave me a volume of her diary to read, which was really very interesting, as it had a detailed account of the Cabinet-making manoeuvres of 1906, and I sat up reading it till 2 o'clock in the morning.'

7. Violet Asquith, the daughter of H. H. Asquith by his first wife Helen (*née* Melland); later Lady Violet Bonham Carter, and later still Baroness Asquith.

8. Cyril Asquith, the youngest of Margot's stepchildren.

9. Anthony Asquith, usually known as 'Puffin' within the family; later a film producer.

10. Elizabeth Asquith, Margot's daughter, who married Prince Antoine Bibesco.

His final comment on Asquith himself, too, is more nostalgic, and shows a perceptible softening of his attitude of only four months earlier. 'From what I could see, it appeared to me almost incredible that he should ever play a big part in politics again – the poor old fellow! The worst of it is he'll hang on, and block everything. Though to be sure, even if he did vanish, who could succeed him?'

After leaving The Wharf, Lytton raced straight on to yet another country house party, this time at a sixteenth-century castle perched on a rock off the Northumberland coast, the home of Edward Hudson, the proprietor of *Country Life* – 'a pathetically dreary figure', as Lytton described him, '. . . a fish gliding underwater, and star-struck – looking up with his adoring eyes through his own dreadful element. . . . A kind of bourgeois gentilhomme also.' At the end of an alarming journey undertaken in a tumble-down dog-cart, at sunset, across three miles of desert sea-sand – partly in flood and dotted with sunken posts to indicate the route – he arrived at this fortified rock, nervous, dishevelled and weary, to find the rest of the house-party already assembled there, attired in evening dress, and tucking into a banquet of lobster and champagne. Lindisfarne, however, which had been converted into a 'dream castle' by Sir Edwin Lutyens, struck him as rather a poor affair, except for its actual situation 'which is magnificent,' he told Mary Hutchinson (7 September 1918), 'and the great foundations and massive battlements, whence one has amazing prospects of sea, hills, other castles etc. – extraordinarily romantic – on every side. But the building itself is all timid Lutyens – very dark, with nowhere to sit, and nothing but stone under, over and round you, which produces a distressing effect – especially when hurrying downstairs late for dinner – to slip would be instant death. No, not a comfortable place, by any means.'

Predominant among the guests was Madame Suggia, the celebrated cellist, with whom Lytton at once made great friends.[11] She seemed to possess the two principal qualities

11. Suggia afterwards confessed to being terrified by Lytton's formidable intellect.

of which, among all women, he stood in greatest awe – a real and unaffected talent, and superabundant physical vigour. 'She is very attractive,' he informed Mary Hutchinson, 'owing I think chiefly to (1) great simplicity – not a trace of the airs and graces of the "Diva" with a European reputation – no bother about playing or not playing – almost a boyishness at times; and (2) immense vitality – her high spirits enormous and almost unceasing – which of course is a great pleasure, particularly to a quiescent person like me. I suppose, besides this, that she's a flirt; but it is difficult to say, and there are so many grades of flirtation. Certainly she is full of temperament – of one kind or another; and there was one evening when she got tipsy – tiens! Her music was of course marvellous – and I got such masses of it! I used to go with her, her mother (a pitiable old remainder biscuit) and the accompanist, to her bedroom; she would then lock the door (to prevent the ingress of Hudson, I fancy) and practise – for hours – playing Bach suites one after the other, and every kind of miracle, with explanations and comments and repetitions, until one tottered down at last to lunch (for this used to happen in the morning) in a state of ecstasy. Then in the evening after dinner she gave her full dress performances. It was really all an extraordinary joy.'

The other guests were altogether less eminent and more eccentric. There was Lady Lewis, for instance, a cosmopolitan Jewess, who slightly distressed Lytton by talking for hours on end about his wonderful *Early Victorians*; and a couple of American Negroes, crude, amiable and inconceivably rich (he played a banjo, while she pored silently all week over Lytton's book, with results that were not communicated to him); then there was Suggia's mother – 'a subject in itself for a Balzac novel' – unable to speak a single word of any known language, perpetually neglected and perpetually smiling; and a Mr George Reeves, the attractive piano accompanist, who, together with Lytton, was forced by Hudson to go off on appalling fishing excursions in the early dawn. Of more authentic interest was William Heinemann, the publisher, pouring forth his eternal reminiscences of Whistler and Ibsen, and his elaborately old-world, improper stories which never failed to make Lytton shriek with laughter. 'I found him a fascinating figure,' he confided to Mary Hutchinson, '– one that one could contemplate for ever – so very very complete. A more absolute jew face couldn't be imagined – bald-headed, goggle-eyed, thick-lipped; a fat short figure, with small legs, and feet moving with the flat assured tread of the seasoned P. and O. traveller. A cigar, of course. And a voice hardly English – German r's; and all the time somehow, an element of the grotesque.' Last, and least of all, there was Mr and Mrs Fort: 'Mr F. an ex-militaire with a voice like a megaphone and an infinite heartiness – and a simplicity of behaviour. ... One evening at dinner, after a good deal of champagne, carried away by exhilaration, he made a speech – a long, long speech, proposing the health of "our host" in heartfelt sentences – one sat gasping – the unimaginable farrago seemed to last interminably; and then, if you please, ce pauvre Hudson found himself replying, at equal length, and with an even wilder inconsequence. After that it was clear that the only thing to do was to get altogether drunk.'

After a week at this improbable castle, 'surrounded by cormorants and quicksands', Lytton made his escape and rejoined Carrington. His perambulations and adventures across Northumberland over the next ten days, 'with Carrington like a large woolly sheep trotting beside me', took them to the beautiful village of Elsdon, where they put up for a week at The Bird and Bush Inn. Then they set off once more, travelling south through Durham and York and eventually, on 14 September, arriving back at Tidmarsh. For the next six weeks Lytton settled down here, spending his days very quietly and drinking infinite glasses of milk, brought to him by Carrington with precise regularity. 'To-morrow (or perhaps to-day) our calm is to be impinged upon by the arrival of —— and —— ,' he wrote to David Garnett (24 September 1918). 'I think it very cheering to be with people who are thoroughly happy – for whatever reason.' Such a remark points to Lytton's refreshing new outlook on life, in complete contrast to those undergraduate and post-graduate days when the 'affectionateness' of the Bussys and 'couples in the road with their silly arms round their stupid waists' would irritate him by the unwitting emphasis they placed upon his own solitary condition.

One symptom of the past that still lingered on was a predisposition to sickness. Late this September, his summer dissipations suddenly subsided into 'a recurrent colic'; and he quickly took to his bed. His chief complaint that autumn was shingles, which reduced him to 'a mere wraith – a ruined spectre ... a state of deliquescence'. Carrington somehow managed to step up her manifold attentions to meet the crisis, until eventually Lytton was able to tell Mary Hutchinson that 'the worst appears to be over. Becket's tonic (a mixture of blood and chloroform apparently) is working wonders. And the infinite quietude here should be a solace for the soul. Me voici in bed, after breakfast, supported by pillows, and murmuring like Florence Nightingale "Too kind – too kind" to Carrington's ministrations.'

By the final week of October, he had recovered sufficiently to visit Jack and Mary Hutchinson at the new house they had rented in Robertsbridge. But Carrington was jealous of anyone else looking after Lytton, fearing that they would do it very much more efficiently than herself, and thereby diminish his absolute reliance on her. While he was away in Sussex, she bombarded him with packages of shortbread, bundles of flowers, and parcels of warmer and still warmer clothes; and before he left Tidmarsh, she sent a characteristic letter, full of unresolved contradictions of feeling, to Mary Hutchinson, telling her all about Lytton's convalescence.

I am sure you will be able to provide Lytton with so many more comforts – Clive says you have four handmaids to wait upon him! – Than he gets this barbaric house, that I feel I cannoT tell you of muCH. But I will go through his day 8.30 breakfast in beD 2, eggs. toast, and jam *without pips* in it. If that is possible! – 11ock glass of hot milk with biscuiTs – LunCH His doctor recommends his having rice or macaroni as vegetable with meaLs. and milk puddings – Siesta in afternoon – tea at four ock – and so on till 10.30 when he has a bowl of bread and milk before going to bed – and a glass of milk with biscuits by his bedside in case he wakes up in the night –

Lytton adds that you will then be required to sleep in the next room and wake at. one o'ck, two o'ck, five o'ck when he taps on the wall. and come in to bath his arm or sympathise with his groanings! — I will send him armed with his food booKs, and sugar BuT really his wants are few, and as I said after this rude existence. and my appaling house management, and nursing. he is bound to be happy with you! ... My constitution and appetite is that of an Ox, So nursing LyTTon hasn't exactly impaired my health! He's been dreadfully disapointed aT not being able to come to you sooner. BuT really to day for the firsT time he is much better — I am really so happy. Mary, that he is going to stay with you as I know you will care for him as noone else woulD ... I feel so moved, Mary, because you are so good to Lytton. and because Clive was so charming. I can'T write proper letters like you written. BuT I only want to thank you rather especially — for everything.

with love

yr

affec

carringTON

Lytton was still down at Robertsbridge on 11 November — Armistice Day. When the news of peace came through, he found it at first difficult to believe. After the long years of war, he could hardly recall what peace was like. What did the papers write about, for instance, when there was no war? Perhaps the weather made headlines. Carrington, who had gone up to London to see Barbara Bagenal, then in a nursing home having her baby, expresses something of the same blank bewilderment in a letter to her brother Noel, written the next day from the 1917 Club. When the guns were fired at eleven o'clock, she explains, she had thought it must be some joke, or some elaborate new bombing device thought up by the Germans.

But it soon turned out to be Peace. with a big P. instantly everyone in the city dashed out of offices and boarded the buses. It was interesting seeing how the different stratas of people took it Travelling from Hampstead. seeing first the slum girls, and coster people dancing. pathetic scenes of an elderly plumBer nailing up a single small Flag over the door. Then the scenes became wilder as one reached Campden Town and more and more frantic as one [approached] Trafalgar Square office boys and girls, officers, Majors, waacs all leaped on taxis, and army vans driving round the place waving Flags. In the Strand the uproar was appalling. I was to meet Monty Shearman in [the] Adelphi for lunCH, and it was almost impossible I found to get there! He then took me off to the Café Royal to meet some other rejoicing friends of his ... then lunch aT the Eiffel Tower restaurant.

Lytton himself came up to London to join in the orgy of patriotic euphoria. After a first stunned silence at the ill-omened booming maroons, the people had gone mad. The streets were crowded, and everywhere there was noise. In their immeasurable relief, the whole population of London seemed bent on bursting their throats in an effort to contribute to the general din. Motors hooted, handbells rang, police whistles shrilled – everyone felt the urge to do something ridiculous.

The evening was humid and rainy. Almost all Bloomsbury had assembled in Monty Shearman's flat in the Adelphi, where a large celebration party was being held. 'Everyone was THere,' Carrington wrote describing the scene to Noel, 'The halt, the sick and the lame. Even old Lytton [who] was on his deathbeD in Sussex rushed up, and joined in the merriment. ... It was a great party. I Danced without sTopping for 3 hrs.' The rooms were packed with a familiar but constantly changing company – Clive Bell, Diaghilev and Massine, Roger Fry, Duncan Grant, Jack and Mary Hutchinson, Maynard Keynes, Lydia Lopokova, Ottoline Morrell, Osbert and Sacheverell Sitwell and, of all people, Mark Gertler. While Henry Mond strummed away on the piano, David Garnett paired off with Carrington and danced and danced with her amid the jostling crowd of guests. Lytton himself was also seen to dance, after his own irregular fashion. 'I remember the tall, flagging figure of my friend Lytton Strachey,' Osbert Sitwell wrote, 'with his rather narrow, angular beard, long, inquisitive nose, and air of someone pleasantly awakening from a trance, jigging about with an amiable debility. He was, I think, unused to dancing. Certainly he was both one of the most typical and one of the rarest persons in this assembly. His individual combination of kindness, selfishness, cleverness, shyness and sociability made him peculiarly unlike anyone else. As I watched him, I remember comparing him in my mind to a benevolent but rather irritable pelican.'

Next morning, Lytton hurried back to Robertsbridge, where he stayed on a further two weeks. Carrington, meanwhile, remained up in London for several days before returning alone to Tidmarsh to paint and prepare the house for Lytton's homecoming. Though he was already held in great request by many of the London *salonnières,* Lytton passed most of the next four months of winter at the Mill House. Life was sometimes cold and damp, but never solitary. For Christmas James and Alix came down, and so did Harry Norton. 'We eat large chickens,' Lytton wrote to Ottoline (27 December 1918), 'which pretend to be turkeys not very effectively, and drink grocer's wine. Such is the force of convention.'

Immediately after Christmas, Carrington took off from Tidmarsh for Cheltenham to attend the funeral of her father, who had suddenly died the previous Saturday. It was for her a sad and even horrifying experience. 'Oh Mark I did suffer horribly,' she wrote to Mark Gertler (3 January 1919). 'It was ghastly to see a little yellow ghost. with a saint like marble face lyinG in a narrow coffin. Instead of that splendid old man in his wheelchair by the fire. And then thaT hard china faced sister – and my mother with her sentimental attitude – was almost more hurting.' She stayed on there a full week, a week of nightmare, becoming increasingly upset. So many new ideas and emotions shot through her every day, every hour. She had never felt death so cruelly before, and it sickened her by its awful indignity and ruthlessness. Her father had been so indestructibly large, so simple, so good-hearted – and now he was nothing. He had never altered his way of life to please conventions, and his big rough character compelled in her a sort of reverence. She felt guilty, now that it was too late, at not having fought for him more openly against the rest of the family. Her sister and her mother had never seemed so alien to her, so petty and female with their concern about their black dresses. She was glad once her father was actually buried away beneath the ground, for then the last connection with her mother had been effaced for all time. Unable to endure their company any longer, she travelled back to Tidmarsh, feeling tired and empty-headed. From this day on, Lytton was the only real family she would recognize; and his home would always be her home, even to death itself.

For the first ten weeks of the New Year, the two of them lived at the Mill House like a couple of hibernating animals. In refusing an invitation to go and stay with Leonard and Virginia Woolf, Lytton confessed (29 January 1919): 'I find London impossible ... Later on, later on, when the snow has vanished ... It is dreadfully dull down here, but healthy and for the moment there are fires.' He had changed into a complete St Anthony. And as for his friends in the smart set, he appeared to have abandoned them altogether – for the time being. 'The conditions of life seem hardly to be ameliorating,' he explained to Clive Bell (18 February 1919), 'and so I have decided definitely to give up the gay world, to become an anchoret, to read nothing but the various lives of the Prince Consort, to gaze out of [the] window at the snow, and to put another log on the fire.'

At the same time, through sheer *désoeuvrement* it seemed, he had started work on a new book.

3

QUEEN VICTORIA AND OTHER ESSAYS

It was at Tidmarsh that Lytton's classic biography of Queen Victoria was originally conceived and brought to life. While moving into the Mill House in December 1917, he had already begun to 'console' himself with Victoria's letters. 'I am reading Victoria's diary, when a young maid,' he noted (11 December 1917), ' – most absorbing, but not long enough.'

The first suggestion that he should make Victoria the subject of his next book had come from Walter Raleigh, shortly after the publication of *Eminent Victorians*. 'We want your method for some stately Victorians who have waited long for it,' he wrote on 13 May 1918. 'First the great Panjandrum – Victoria herself. This is obvious. How can an adjective have a meaning that is not dependent on the meaning of its substantive? ... It's really wicked of you to leave those stout volumes alone, when you could put the gist of them within reach of us.'

Nevertheless, Lytton's initial idea, following the success of *Eminent Victorians*, was, he told Philip Morrell, to write a second series of pen-portraits, treating this time the scientists who had been among his original list of twelve candidates. Very soon, however, he relinquished this notion, though it was not until the end of this year that he seems finally to have made up his mind. Queen Victoria, he informed Clive Bell (28 December 1918), was 'an interesting subject, but an obscure one ... It's very difficult to penetrate the various veils of discretion. The Prince Consort is a remarkable figure; but Sir Theodore Martin's life of him in five stupendous volumes is not to be recommended to the general public. Have you heard of Emily Cranford? There's a book by her on the queen which is not without merit – Irish and full of gossip about the forties – very disordered, but in parts distinctly good.[12] I'm beginning to think that most of the good books are overlooked. For instance the Private Life of Henry Maitland is surely highly interesting – but who mentions it? I found it the other day, quite by chance, and found it absorbing.'

By the New Year, Lytton had completed enough reading and research to feel reasonably certain that, as he phrased it to Chatto and Windus (3 January 1919), the subject of his next biography would be 'The Life of Her Late Majesty'. Writing the following day to his mother and sensing her displeasure at such a project, he is more diffident. 'I am beginning a serious study of Queen Victoria; but it's difficult to say as yet whether anything will come of it.' As he had probably expected, Lady Strachey was taken aback by this news, fearing that the venerable queen would come in for even rougher handling than her

12. Nevertheless this book is not listed in the bibliography or 'List of References in the Notes' at the end of Lytton's *Queen Victoria*.

eminent subjects. 'I don't much fancy you taking up Queen Victoria to deal with,' she replied. 'She no doubt lays herself open to drastic treatment which is one reason I think it better left alone. She could not help being stupid, but she tried to do her duty, and considering the period she began in, her upbringing, her early associations, and her position, this was a difficult matter and highly to her credit. She has won a place in public affection and a reputation in our history which it would be highly unpopular, and I think not quite fair, to attempt to bring down.

'What about Disraeli? He is near enough our own time to be topical, and too near to have been thoroughly dealt with as yet. His two reputations, the early one and the later which has developed into a legend, are quite contradictory, and until they have been welded together, are in my opinion equally false.'[13]

But Lytton was already determined to press on with this new book. All through the late summer, the autumn and winter months he had been reading copiously – biographies of Albert the Good, of Victoria herself and all manner of works on Victorian politics and history. His letters to Pippa sometimes contain lists of volumes for her to send down to him at the Mill House when he was unable to get up to London. Perhaps the most interesting of all the works he consulted was Sir Herbert Maxwell's two-volume edition of *The Creevey Papers*, on which he wrote a separate biographical essay. 'How can anyone read novels when there are Creevey Papers to be had – in which there is every variety of human, political, and historical interest, sur le vif – I don't understand,' he told Clive Bell (18 February 1919).

13. In 1920 Lytton did in fact write an article on Disraeli for *Woman's Leader*. A review of Monypenny and Buckle's six-volume biography, 'Dizzy', as it was called, consists of little more than an elegant admission of perplexity. 'The absurd Jew-boy, who set out to conquer the world, reached his destination,' ran the opening sentence. And he had little to add to this statement, since, as he told Hesketh Pearson shortly after the publication of *Queen Victoria*, Disraeli's mummy-like inscrutability baffled him. 'I can't make him out,' he admitted; 'his character is so utterly contradictory.'

As with all Lytton's major works, the preparatory reading of books on his subject took up almost twice as long as the actual writing. Over the next two years he would stay up in London – at Belsize Park Gardens, or with his brother Oliver at 96 South Hill Park, or occasionally at the Savile Club – for weeks at a time, visiting the London Library and the British Museum Reading Room, and then returning to Tidmarsh with a few pages of notes in an exercise book and some sheets of foolscap devoted to quotations. At the Mill House, huge parcels of books would arrive regularly from booksellers and libraries, and be read through day after day – six or eight or ten hours' reading a day. And at the end of each book, a dozen pencil entries on half a sheet of notepaper would represent all the salient material he had extracted. 'His critical faculty was so highly developed by the time he came to write biography that he rarely noted down a superfluous fact, and still more rarely had to return to a book once read for some fact he had previously rejected,' recorded Ralph Partridge (8 October 1946). 'Still, the reading to be done was immense; and he never skipped through books, and never trusted an index to pick out references to his subject. An outline of the book he intended to write was in his head before ever he began his course of reading, but not a word went on paper until the reading was finished. Then very likely he would take a holiday abroad before settling down to write.'

It was largely owing to this intensive method of research that Lytton found such little time to concentrate on other writing. In the five years after the publication of *Eminent Victorians* he produced only eight essays for periodicals. Two of these, 'Dizzy' and 'Mr. Creevey', were direct offshoots from his *Queen Victoria*; two others (both written in the summer of 1918) were pacifist propaganda contributions to *War and Peace*; and the rest dealt with such old favourites as Shakespeare, Voltaire and Horace Walpole.

But there were other contributory reasons, too, to account for the small output over these years. The composition of *Queen Victoria* exhausted him, and he felt that while he was working on it he dare not squander the least drop of vital energy on unrelated articles. At the same time, he could seldom resist dashing off poems and plays, not for publication but for enjoyment and the enjoyment of his friends. Some weeks, for instance, of the summer of 1918 were given over to 'Quasheemaboo' or 'The Noble Savage', a drama which he composed for Madame Vandervelde and Jack Hutchinson to act in at a charity gala. 'The first performance is to be on July 1,' he informed his mother (5 June 1918). 'The plot of the play was suggested to me by you once – probably you've forgotten all about it – A wife who has become a successful actress without her husband knowing it. When she tells him he disbelieves her, whereupon she gets up a melodramatic scene, which completely takes him in – and then she rounds upon him. So if it's taken up, and performed on the Music Hall Stage and brings in millions, you shall have half the profits!' Though never professionally performed, it is a well-constructed and amusing farce, and contains some charming rhymed couplets – for example Captain Cutts's song:

> Once in a way the sun is o'er us,
> Once in a way the sky stays blue,
> Bees are a-buzzing, and birds in chorus,
> Every rose is as sweet as you
>   – All summer delights in a single day
>   Once in a way, once in a way.

> Once in a way the twilight lingers,
> Once in a way the moon shines bright.
> Stars are lit by the angels' fingers,
> Kisses fall with the falling night.

Over his published writings Lytton was strictly cautious in what he wrote, and for which paper he contributed. In the summer of 1918 he had been approached by J. C. Squire, then acting editor of the *New Statesman*,[14] to write book reviews and articles for his paper. In refusing this offer, Lytton first objected to the rates of payment before coming to the pri-

14. Clifford Sharp, the regular editor of the *New Statesman*, had in 1917 been called up for military service, trained as an artillery officer and sent to Stockholm on an intelligence mission.

mary reason why, at this time, he could not 'feel comfortable'
in the columns of the *New Statesman*. 'Perhaps you won't
mind my also saying that the idea of contributing to the New
Statesman would be more pleasant to me if I could sympathise
rather more with its war-policy. This, so far as I can make it
out, seems to be a species of unconscious jingoism. Your
ideals are no doubt admirable but what you are really promoting is the policy of the knock-out blow – that is to say the
wicked and impossible policy of the Northcliffe Press. That
this is so is shown (to take one instance) in the tone of your
remarks this week about Lord Lansdowne.[15] Whether you
agree with him or not, you ought to be able to see that he is
an honest man, and a man who is at any rate trying to use his
reason. But evidently you see neither of these things, for you
attack him in a style for which I can really only think of one
epithet – blackguardly. It appears to me that the only possible
explanation is that, whatever you may say, and whatever you
may think, you are in fact a Northcliffian.

'I was very glad to hear that my book amused you – though
I fear it may have seemed to you not quite Christian
enough.'

15. In a letter to *The Daily Telegraph* on 29 November 1917 (a letter
previously turned down by *The Times*), the veteran Lord Lansdowne had
sought to counteract the internal propaganda of both Britain and Germany, which, he felt, was helping to prolong the war unnecessarily. 'What
are we fighting for?' he asked. The answer, of course, was to defeat the
Germans, not out of mere vindictiveness, but honourably and in such a
way as to prevent another war in the future. He defined Britain's war
aims with the aid of five guiding points. There was to be no annihilating
knock-out blow; no imposition of an unwelcome form of government on
the German people; no permanent economic sanctions after the war was
over. Britain would work for international agreement on the 'freedom of
the seas' question and help to set up a compulsory international pact to
ensure peace. This letter provoked a hurricane of abuse from the Government and in the Press. Northcliffe, for example, endeavoured to discredit
Lansdowne as a statesman, an Irish landlord, and an individual. But a
minority of people applauded Lansdowne's courage and honesty. On 31
January 1918 he received a deputation led by the ex-Lord Chancellor,
Lord Loreburn, who presented him with an address commending him for
his initiative. Among the signatories were Noel Buxton, G. P. Gooch,
Dean Inge, Gilbert Murray and Stanley Unwin.

Squire angrily repudiated these charges, but Lytton was obdurate. He did not contribute anything more to the *New Statesman* until, in 1931, under the new editorship of Kingsley Martin and as the amalgamated *New Statesman and Nation,* the paper had completely changed its political policy.

By the year 1919, he had, in any case, begun to associate himself with the *Athenaeum,* which had then reached a peculiar stage in its long and erratic history. 'It was about the end of 1828 that readers of periodical literature, and quidnuncs in those departments, began to report the appearance, in a Paper called the *Athenaeum,* of writings showing a superior brilliancy and height of aim.' So wrote Carlyle in *The Life of John Stirling.* But by the twentieth century, both brilliancy and height of aim had long since vanished, and as a monthly 'Journal of Reconstruction', the *Athenaeum* had barely survived the war. In 1919, however, it was given a drastic new lease of life when Arthur Rowntree purchased the paper and reconstituted it as a weekly 'Journal of English and Foreign Literature, Science, the Fine Arts, Music and the Drama'. By what F. A. Lea has described as 'a stroke of inspiration', Rowntree offered the editorship to Middleton Murry, then an undischarged bankrupt. The result was that during the two years that Murry reigned as editor, the paper lost almost ten thousand pounds. Its contributors over this period included a large number of men and women who were later to win leading positions in the literary world. The brilliance had been restored, but the aim was now so superior as to be right off target.

The letter which Murry wrote to Lytton (12 February 1919) rallying him to the *Athenaeum*'s happy band of regular contributors is very typical of him – almost a collector's item – showing how humility, a rather touching bewilderment, Himalayan earnestness and the dependence upon other people to make a name for him were so nicely muddled together in his character. 'I have been made editor of the new Athenaeum,' he announced, '– heaven knows what beneficent bee entered the bonnets of the owners – which is shortly to arise like the phoenix. I shall try to make it as good as I can. But to do that

it is necessary that you should become a regular contributor ...

'But, my dear Lytton, it is your duty to the coming generation. I do think that a new Athenaeum is a great opportunity,
and I know that unless you will join, we shall be unable to
make the use of it which we ought to make. Therefore,
though it will be a bother, and though the work will be no
better paid than elsewhere, please be conscientious in your
responsibilities and say you will.'

Murry's obvious sincerity, his longing to be disinterested
and his very evident seriousness impressed Lytton, reducing
the slight scepticism he felt at his lofty sense of purpose, out-
topping common sense. In any event, there could be no doubt
that he was infinitely preferable to Squire, whom Virginia
Woolf had described as 'more repulsive than words can
express, and malignant into the bargain' (26 May 1919). After
inviting Murry down to Tidmarsh at the end of February,
Lytton wrote to Clive Bell (3 March 1919): 'Talking of new
papers, Murry was here for a night, to talk about the Athenaeum, the prospects of which sounded most hopeful. I
think he ought to make a good job of it, with his extraordinary competence quâ journalist. I said I'll try and write a
little for it — I should like to write a great deal, but I'm too
slow, and then how does one put things? And perhaps on the
whole books are more important than magazines.'

When Murry left Tidmarsh, he took with him 'Lady Hester
Stanhope', and in the next six months Lytton found time to
send him four further articles — one piece of dramatic criticism, 'Shakespeare at Cambridge', and three biographical
essays. This last trio, together with 'Lady Hester Stanhope',
provide a good index to his future development as an essayist,
prefiguring his last series of minor compositions later assembled as *Portraits in Miniature and Other Essays*. They are
fashioned after two distinct styles. In 'Voltaire' and 'Walpole's
Letters' he was, of course, treating subjects for whom he felt a
close affinity. Both had been his constant reading since Cambridge days, so much so that he had come to know each of
their long-vanished faces as well as that of some living friend —

'one of those enigmatical friends about whom one is perpetually in doubt as to whether, in spite of everything, one *does* know them after all'. When he was not dealing with men who had much in common with his own character, he liked to amuse himself portraying the eccentrics, those grand, preposterous, inexplicable freaks of Nature, at once so intimidating and so delightful, whose extraordinary lives contrasted romantically with his own, and answered his inner sense of abnormality. 'Lady Hester Stanhope' and 'Mr Creevey', both minor historical figures of extreme and triumphant unconventionality, fell into the second category. As with his 'Voltaire' and 'Walpole's Letters', the accent is placed firmly upon the biographical interest. Lytton is no longer so much taken up with public achievement as with the quirks of individual personality, which he gracefully sets off against the fat pastures of social and political high life.

A fortnight after 'Lady Hester Stanhope' had appeared, Lytton wrote to Ottoline (17 April 1919): 'I find the Athenaeum a great addition to existence. Don't you? It really, as they say, "supplies a long felt want".' But over the latter term of Murry's editorship, the paper began to lose some of its early momentum. Lytton's enthusiasm then cooled, and he contributed nothing further to its columns. 'The dear Athenaeum is much the best literary paper, it seems to me,' he told F. L. Lucas (27 June 1920), 'but lately one's rather felt it was in need of "new blood". If you supply it, so much the better!'

The proprietors also felt the paper to be in need of 'new blood' in the form of a new editor. Early in 1921, Murry resigned from his post, and that February the *Athenaeum* merged with the *Nation*. Also financed by the Rowntree family, the *Nation* had been founded in 1907, and was skilfully edited by H. W. Massingham, the impress of whose personality was strongly marked upon every page. The paper's political impact, however, was weak, and, mainly for this reason, it had not expanded into a paying proposition. Moreover, a new body of ardent Liberals, known as the Grasmere Group and numbering among its members Sir William Beveridge, Philip

Guedalla, Maynard Keynes, Walter Layton, Ramsay Muir and E. D. Simon, seriously concerned over the absence of a satisfactory Liberal weekly, had started discussions with the Rowntree family, who were themselves growing restive under the mounting loss of some thousands of pounds every year. As a result of these talks, it was agreed that fresh money would be found to reduce the burden upon the Rowntrees, if some marked radical alteration was made in the political outlook of the paper. Massingham then resigned as editor and Keynes was elected chairman of the new board. Ramsay Muir and T. S. Eliot were at first proposed as editor and literary editor, but eventually these posts were filled respectively by Hubert Henderson and Leonard Woolf. The first issue of what some critics have regarded as a special pulpit for the Bloomsbury Group came out on 5 May 1923, and contained an appreciation by Lytton of Sarah Bernhardt. The literary section of the re-formed *Nation and Athenaeum* was kept independent from the political policies in the main part of the paper, and the freedom which Leonard Woolf allowed Lytton – reminiscent of that in the *New Quarterly* and *Independent Review* – exactly suited him. During the next five years he contributed eighteen signed essays which were to comprise almost the whole of his sixth published volume, *Portraits in Miniature*.

4

MEMOIR OF AN INFANTRY OFFICER

On the afternoon of 10 August 1918 there arrived at the Mill House a visitor who was to enter very intimately into the lives of Carrington and Lytton, affecting them both individually and in their relationship to each other. This was Ralph Partridge, a wartime friend of Noel Carrington. A large, powerfully built young man, with a high-coloured complexion and dancing light-blue eyes, he had left Oxford early in the war to join the army, in which he had greatly distinguished himself, being awarded a Military Cross and rising at the age of twenty-three to the rank of major, commanding a battalion. Noel

Carrington had first introduced him to his sister at the beginning of July 1918. His irresistible zest for life, fascinating good looks and easy, open ways at once delighted her, and she immediately sent off a letter to Lytton reporting the discovery of this impetuous new personality. 'The young man Partridge had just come bacK from Italy – the one I was telling you about the other evening,' she wrote (4 July 1918). '... He adores the Italians and wanTs after the war to sail on a schooner to the Mediteranean Islands and ITaly; and trade in wine without takinG much money and to dress like a brigand. I am so elated and happy. It is so good to find someone you can rush on and on with, quickly. He sang Italian songs to us on the platform and was in such gay spirits – and used his hands gesticulatinG.'

This description sent through Lytton a flutter of sentimental speculation. Of course, he was more than prepared to be disappointed; all the same he would like to interview this romantic-sounding creature for himself. 'The existence of Partridge sounds exciting,' he replied. 'Will he come down here, when you return, and sing Italian songs to us, and gesticulate, and let us dress him as a brigand? I hope so.'

And so, with Lytton's approval, it was agreed that Carrington should invite the young officer over to the Mill House. This visit, so eagerly awaited by both of them, was not a success, and gave no hint of the strange role he was soon to play in that household. With fine and unabashed tactlessness, he started off almost at once on a heated argument about the war, claiming that all the carnage did not matter one jot, that he himself had no objection to being killed fairly and squarely by the enemy, and that all pacifists were skulkers and ought to be shot. Lytton, dismayed by this exhibition of bumptious arrogance, did not join in the discussion. After all, he reasoned, this major had come to see Carrington, not himself. But Carrington, angry that Lytton should have been exposed to such rudeness, fiercely and incoherently argued the virtues of 'passifism', and finally, in despair, led him off outdoors where his militaristic views might discharge themselves harmlessly into the open air.

Partridge himself seems to have remained obstinately unaware of his *faux pas*. 'I have been initiated into the Mill House,' he notified Noel Carrington the following week (17 August 1918), 'but as a great part of the μυστήρια took place on the river, I viewed the proceedings very favourably. Old man Strachey with the billowy beard and alternating basso-falsetto voice did not play a great part.' And in a letter to his friend Gerald Brenan, he described Carrington as 'a painting damsel and a great Bolshevik who would like to strike a blow for the Cause', while Lytton is dismissed as 'of a surety meet mirth for Olympus'. Partridge's name does not crop up in Lytton's correspondence this year at all, except cursorily in one letter to Clive Bell as 'some Major Partridge or other', a friend of Carrington's. But Carrington, for her part, communicated a rather disdainful account of him to her brother, in which she pays back some of the antipathy which he had so obviously directed towards her adored Lytton (12 August 1918): 'He isn't very interested in Books or poetry or painting', she complained. '... He was surprised that Lytton had written that Book. as he said he didn't think he looked as if he could have. ... Then he didn't see very much in the book except that the style was "rather good" – Then he was prejudiced against Lytton slightly for his beard and appearance. and confessed it.'

To all outward appearances, then, Ralph Partridge had absolutely nothing in common with the Tidmarsh regime. But beneath the clash of opinions and the contrast of personalities, at a more elemental level, the three of them had already begun to form that summer the basis of an odd triangular union which, despite many complicated strains and crises, would persist over the next thirteen years, until the death of two of them.

Immediately after the war was over, Ralph Partridge returned to Oxford, where he was supposed to be completing his law studies and from where he would bicycle over the twenty miles to Pangbourne for week-ends. He had fallen deeply in love with Carrington. And she responded to some extent, partly because he was a very attractive man and she was flattered by his attentions, and partly because, much to her joy and surprise, Lytton had now taken to him strongly.

It is not difficult to account for the warmth of Lytton's feelings. Although, in these happier, more successful years, he no longer thrived on scorn and disparagement as once he had done, it did not necessarily alienate him as it would most people. The initial disapproval he felt for Partridge's cocksure insensitivity gradually gave way before a susceptibility to his more potent charms. First and foremost of these was his vigorous, physical masculinity. Like Thoby Stephen's, like George Mallory's before him, his fine Herculean torso appeared to have been fashioned after the geometry of some pagan deity. 'He seemed born to lead anything from a Polar expedition to an infantry assault,' recorded his friend Gerald Brenan. '... He was very sure of himself and did not easily submit to authority that he regarded as stupid or incompetent.' His hearty Rabelaisian laugh, his incredible blue eyes rolling wildly in their sockets like a Negro's, his rollicking high spirits, his formidable self-assurance supported by an enterprising efficiency in all practical matters, his lack of Christian feeling, all emphasized for Lytton this god-like aspect, inspiring him with a kind of hero-worship. There was, however, no question of any homosexual attachment between them, since Partridge was exclusively heterosexual. Indeed, his mind ran much on women, many of whom adored him; and he had many romantic conquests, especially among actresses and chorus-girls. He was, in fact, something of a sensualist and womanizer; yet Lytton seemed to like him all the more for this, for it was, after all, no more than a necessary part of his splendid masculine virility, and therefore to be admired.

Such were Ralph Partridge's more resplendent qualities; and had this been all, then Lytton's passion for him would have amounted to nothing new — just another item in the list of insignificant flirtations that would from time to time flare up and then die down again, like fireworks leaving no trace of their path in the skies. But this was not all. For already Lytton thought he could detect beneath the exterior beauty and bravado other traits which made him a far more complex and

763

fascinating character than, say, George Mallory could ever have been. Despite his loud conventional opinions, he was really something of a rebel, and even in his casual remarks delivered in a half-jocular, half-ironic, stylized tone of voice, Lytton was able to observe the workings of a strong if undeveloped mind. His fierce and often uncontrolled emotions would lead to loves that were extraordinarily permanent, and dislikes that were stormy. He was far more aggressive in argument than he realized, but his outlook remained completely unsentimental and realistic. He had a tenacious memory and a passion for acquiring facts that made him a rewarding pupil.

Lytton soon set about tr_ing to educate this young man, to develop his potentialities and instil into him some of his own tastes in literature and views on sexual ethics. The result was that, for all his determined individuality and disinclination to submit to authority, the burly, hot-headed man-of-the-world fell very largely under Lytton's sway. From a bluff and breezy extrovert, he slowly metamorphosed into an intelligent and cultivated man of letters, a publisher for some time with the Hogarth Press, a *New Statesman* reviewer and finally an author. In time, he developed an almost feminine interest in people and states of mind, for which reason numerous people would confide in him and ask his advice. So fundamental was the change brought about in him by Lytton's tuition that people who knew him well only later in life could scarcely credit his earlier history. 'He was a very emotional man,' Gerald Brenan wrote, 'and whenever he held an opinion he held it passionately and liked to have it out with those who disagreed with him.' This characteristic at least never altered. During the First World War he had been in his element in the front line; twenty years later, as a conscientious objector, he was attacking militarism with the same emotional abandon that he had previously hurled against Lytton and other pacifists. This conversion was directly due to Lytton, who, as it were, made a new man out of him, only to find, once he had done so, that his infatuation for the ebullient and debonair army major he first met had partly faded away. Their association over a few years completely shifted its ground. The disdain which Partridge had spontaneously experienced for this pacifist and skulker with his billowy beard and his books, was replaced by a genuine admiration and devotion; while Lytton himself became extremely fond of this new disciple, who, on and off, was to act as his secretary.

There was one other unusual trait in Ralph Partridge's make-up which from early days appealed to Lytton, for whom it sanctified all the philistine errors of taste and judgement, and this was his utter lack of worldly ambition. Though naturally athletic, he was congenitally lazy – a curious mixture of indolence and vitality. At Oxford he had, in a leisurely way, taken up rowing, but when asked to row for the Varsity eight had declined to do so on the grounds that it interfered with a holiday he was planning. Later, when invited to represent Great Britain in the Olympic Games, he again refused since the training involved too much inconvenience and hard work. This kind of disinterestedness had always attracted Lytton, and he was charmed by such refreshing indifference to fame. What it must be to have the opportunity to turn one's back on such things! Lytton was deeply impressed, and for some time Partridge embodied a new vision of his ideal self. 'Lord!' he exclaimed on one occasion to Carrington (11 July 1919). 'Why am I not a rowing blue, with eyes to match, and 24? It's really dreadful not to be.'

On most evenings when the three of them were alone together at Tidmarsh, Lytton would read aloud – this being an important part in the curriculum of schooling his young friends. Carrington still found the greatest difficulty over the longer words, but she had a feeling for poetry and came to absorb a good deal of it, particularly the Elizabethan song books. Meanwhile, Ralph too was gradually shedding his boorishness, and, with his natural intelligence, began picking up a fair education. But at this time, his attention was fixed less on the declaiming Lytton than on the rapt and enigmatic figure of Carrington. Predictably, she was still something of a mystery to him – yet all the more desirable for that. He was accustomed to quick, simple conquests over women, and to an equally precipitate loss of interest in them. Either that, or else they did not respond to him, and he did not like them. It was all cut-and-dried. But Carrington was quite different. His relationship with her baffled him. He found it impossible to understand her slavish attachment to Lytton, and although he could tell that she liked him and found him sexually attractive, he still felt her elude his reach, ever-appealing, impalpable, inexplicable. He tried everything he knew to make her his own property absolutely, but was never really satisfied. When the winter began to thaw and the warmer weather to spread through the country, he would appear in front of her stark naked and twist himself into provocative contortionist positions so that she could make sensational drawings of his strong, magnificently proportioned limbs. Carrington was touched and gratified by this artistic cooperation – he was a very thrilling partner for her, anatomically and in other more confusing ways. 'I've been drawing R.P. naked in the long grass in the orchard,' she told Lytton (May 1919) after one pastoral session. 'I confess I got rather a flux over his thighs, and legs so much so that I didn't do very good drawings.'

Throughout much of this winter Ralph had been trying to persuade Carrington to go off on a holiday with him. But she did not wish to leave Lytton, who, however, urged her to go. And so eventually, more for his sake than Ralph's, she went together with her brother Noel and Ralph's sister Dorothy. Nearly all her brief separations from Lytton were enforced in this peculiar way. 'I was never in all these 16 years happy when I was without him,' she wrote at the end of her life. 'It was only I knew he disliked me to be dependent that I forced myself to make other attachments.'

Towards the end of March, then, Carrington and Ralph, Noel and Dorothy, sailed away for a few weeks to Spain, leaving Lytton at Tidmarsh. The outcome of their trip, though it settled nothing, was to establish on a firmer basis their three-cornered relationship. Carrington's protracted absence brought home to Lytton just how much he had come to depend upon her in the ordinary but indecipherable business of running the household affairs. Without her help, he some-

times appeared hopelessly lost, comically, even wantonly so.
'This morning I visited the butcher's,' he wrote to James (7
April 1919), 'and stood for some hours among a group of
hags and every sort of "joint" and horror. At last my turn
came, and I asked if they had any mutton – of the butcher's
wife. She said "Yes". I produced my coupon, on which she
became rather mysterious, moved about, then brushed past
me murmuring "wait a minute" in lurid tones. So I did. At last,
on the departure of one of the hags, she said: "That was the
food controller's wife." So I suppose we'd been committing
some illegality, though what it can be I've no idea, as my
principle is to understand nothing of such matters.'

To avoid the mysterious rules and rigours of 'shopping',
Lytton decided to take himself off for a week to the Cove
Hotel at West Lulworth, with its memories of Rupert Brooke,
where he could be sure of being looked after properly. He
expected to see James already installed there, but could find
no sign of any brother and was obliged to 'sit solitaire, cheek
by jowl with a quite silent (luckily) and half-witted military
couple in a most higgledy-piggledy hotel', he complained to
Ottoline (27 March 1919). '... There are splendid Downs
going down into cliffs – all so pale and peaceful – into the sea,
which yesterday was a Mediterranean blue. The sun was
streaming down. I stretched myself full-length upon the grass,
and basked. It seems incredible; and indeed I thought at the
time there was some trickery about it – and so there was. As I
was basking, an old seagull swooped past, and positively
laughed in my face – a regular mocking jeering laugh – as much
as to say "you wait" – and lo and behold in the night the
weather completely changed, and now we are back in the old
story of hurricanes and deluges – ugh! And to be penned in
with the Major and Mrs Major all day – oh! I shall struggle out
and breast the elements, I think, what e'er betide.'

From West Lulworth, Lytton hurried on to Lyme Regis,
where he caught up with James and Alix, spending Easter with
them at a lodging-house in Sherborne Lane. 'Behold me basking in the sun,' he wrote to David Garnett (5 April 1919), 'on
the Marine Parade, the sun sparkling below me, aged spinsters,

discharged army youths etc. etc. floating round me.' Towards
the end of the month he left this crowded, vacuous atmosphere and returned to the Mill House to rejoin Carrington and
Ralph, now due to arrive back from Spain. He was grateful to
have them back again, happy that life could proceed once
more on its ordered course. The last few weeks, though not
wholly unpleasant, had seemed like a relapse into those aimless and nomadic days before the war.

By all accounts Carrington and Ralph had enjoyed a wonderful holiday in Spain, walking up to thirty miles a day and
travelling from Cordova to Seville, from Toledo to Madrid.
Though clouds of anxiety over Lytton's solitary welfare had
often thrown shadows across her mind, Carrington became
absorbed by the splendours of her journey, marvelling with
that extraordinary freshness of hers at every new phenomenon she beheld – the paintings, the people, buildings and
mountains. 'I have seen sights one hardly dreamt of,' she
wrote excitedly to Gertler (30 April 1919). 'And people so
beautiful that one quivered to look at them – and then those
El Grecos at Madrid and Toledo – and yet one has to keep it
all inside. I feel so strong just now and savage – But I see it
will wear off in this cold climate before many days.' Brown
and plump and healthy, lit up by a kind of Atlantic happiness,
she seemed fonder now of Ralph than ever, and fervently
hoped that he and Lytton might continue to hit it off together
as they had begun to do late that winter. As for Spain, it was a
superb country, so primitive and full of startling colours. She
longed somehow to convey all the pleasure she had received
to Lytton; he must certainly go there as soon as possible, and
she would show him round – with Ralph too, of course.

As for Ralph, this gloriously happy vacation had helped
to bring about in his mind a major decision. He knew now
that Carrington was the only girl for him. Never had he felt
like this about anyone. As soon as he came down from
Oxford, he must somehow persuade her to marry him.

5
THE T. S. ELIOT FIASCO

The spring and summer months of 1919 once more drew Lytton forth from his country hibernation, and soon he was caught up again in the superior merry-go-round of London entertainments. 'My smart life proceeds apace,' he informed Mary Hutchinson (15 May 1919). 'I find it mainly simply comic, and distinctly exhausting. No pasturage for the soul, I fear! Lady Cunard is rather a sport, with her frankly lower-class bounce; she makes the rest of 'em look like the withered leaves of Autumn, poor things. But she herself I fancy is really pathetic too. So lost – so utterly lost! – She takes to me, she says, for the sake of that dear nice Bernard Keynes, who's such an intimate friend of hers . . . after lunch, Lady C. suddenly said she must go and fetch Princess Bibesco (not Elizabeth – another) from the French Embassy opposite.[16] She dashed off to do so. Reappeared very quickly, with the Princess, and – who do you think? – George Moore. He looked too preposterous – like a white rabbit suddenly produced by a conjuror out of a hat. He was furious, of course, and went away at once. Apparently, he had told Maud [Lady Cunard] over and over again "I do not want to come" – but it was useless – he was carried off – propelled into Mrs [Saxton] Noble's arms, and then, out of Maud's clutch for a moment, vanished.'

Superficially, London was very agreeable to Lytton just now, and many of the letters he wrote over this period give amusing descriptions of his exploits there. 'To lunch with Lady Cunard today', he announced to Carrington (16 May 1919), '– the prospect leaves me blasé . . . a blasé literary man I've become, I fear.' But for all the trivial delights and absurd social scenes he depicts, Lytton was never truly at home in this milieu. The glitter of it all would titillate his fancy for short stretches of time, during which his social apprehensions and

16. Opposite Kent House. The Princess Bibesco Lytton referred to was probably Princess Marthe Bibesco, the friend of Proust and author of *Proust's Oriane* and *The Sphinx of Bagatelle*.

his inherent boredom with society would seem to mix and cancel each other out. But beneath his open-eyed, ironic philandering with the *beau monde* there lay a hard centre of disapproval that occasionally makes itself apparent – however light-heartedly – in the retrospective accounts of parties he would send to his friends. In another letter to Carrington, written two days earlier, he describes a visit to Mrs Ava Astor, the wealthy widow of Colonel J. J. Astor, soon to marry Lord Ribblesdale. 'Yesterday I went (at my own suggestion) to tea with Mrs Astor. For the first time my courage began to ooze. The immense size of that Grosvenor Square house – double doors flying open, a vast hall with a butler and two female footmen permanently established in it, vistas beyond of towering pilasters and a marble staircase and galleries – it struck awe into the heart. Then a door quite close at hand was swiftly opened, and I was projected into a large square room, in a distant corner of which, on a sofa, was a lady whom in my agitation I hardly recognised – the colour of hair seemed to have quite changed – and as I advanced three small dogs rushed out at me snapping. I at last reached the sofa and we had a long but not amorous tête-à-tête. The poor dear woman is terrified of Bolshevism – thinks Mr Smillie[17] will lead the mob against her – and asks anxiously "Do you think they'll all go red?" I read her a lecture on the inequality of wealth, and left her trembling to get ready for the Opera.'

One can detect in such a passage the unreconciled stages of Lytton's social attitude – the awe, the surprised amiability, the radical reproof. Society represented to him a direct challenge. When unknown and miserable long ago at Lancaster Gate, he had hated London for its vast anonymity, and the bland disregard it showed him. But now that it had begun to take notice of him, he wanted to assure himself that he was at least equal to its attentions. Determined not to be outfaced by the intimidating pomp, he soon found, to his innocent wonder-

17. Robert Smillie, president of the Miners' Federation of Great Britain (1912–21) who, in 1923, became Labour M.P. for Morpeth. A dour, granite-faced lowlander, he was said, by the few who knew him well, to be kind and intelligent, and was much admired by Oliver Strachey.

ment, that many of the celebrated aristocratic personalities framed by all this dazzling and ridiculous prestige were actually rather simple insensitive people.

These fashionable circles, which only a year before were gravely preoccupied with matters military and political, had recently turned their attention to the arts, and in particular the ballet. Early that summer, Diaghilev's company, with Picasso, Massine, Stravinsky and Ansermet, arrived in London to give their spectacular and triumphant performance of *La Boutique Fantasque*, *Le Tricorne* and *The Good-Humoured Ladies*. Immediately they were taken up once more by the best-known society hosts and hostesses. But Bloomsbury also shared in the festivities, and it was to introduce this odd confluence of artists, dancers and musicians into the more rough-and-tumble world of Upper Bohemia that Clive Bell and Maynard Keynes gave an informal supper-party for them at 46 Gordon Square.[18] Among the guests were Picasso, Derain, Lopokova and some forty young or youngish painters, writers and students. 'Maynard, Duncan Grant, our two maids and I waited on them,' Clive Bell later recalled. 'Picasso did not dress. We rigged up a couple of long tables: at the end of one we put Ansermet, at the end of the other Lytton Strachey, so that their beards might wag in unison.'

Most of the gatherings to which Lytton was asked were less intellectual and artistic affairs. During May he twice visited Garsington and found it on both occasions 'terribly trying'. In a letter to Virginia Woolf (27 May 1919), he wrote: 'I was often on the point of screaming from sheer despair, and the beauty of the surroundings only intensified the agony. Ott I really think is in the last stages – infinitely antique, racked in

18. Diaghilev had been taken up by London society (Lady Ripon, for example, and, of course, Ottoline) before the First World War. It is, however, a curious fact that Bloomsbury had not paid any attention to him until his reappearance after the war. This was because it was only during the war that Diaghilev became involved with Picasso and Derain. His earlier painters, such as Bakst, were despised by Bloomsbury, who took little interest in any elements other than painting. A feature of the return of Diaghilev was his new prima ballerina – Lopokova – eventually to marry Maynard Keynes.

every joint, hobbling through the buttercups in cheap shoes with nails that run into her feet, every stile a crisis, and of an imbecility ... She is rongée, too, by malevolence; every tea party in London to which she hasn't been invited is wormwood, wormwood.'

Another country house where his name regularly appears in the visitors' book was The Wharf. Twice that summer the Asquiths invited him over for week-ends, once in June, the second time in July. Here again the tedium was pretty extreme. Margot's friends now seemed to him a dreary lot, with the exception of Mrs George Keppel, who was the best of a large party, none of whom he knew. But the rich absurdity of his entrance there largely compensated for the dullness. 'My heart sank and sank – and sank still further on reaching this house, which is really a worse house than Charleston to arrive at,' he confided to Carrington (June 1919). 'No sign of Margot – only a faded group of completely unknown people. I lost my head – opened a door, and found myself projected into a twilight chamber, with four bridge players in the middle of it. Complete silence. Margot was one of them. At last, after a long time, in which nobody even looked in my direction, she said, "Oh, how d'you do?" – I fled – fled to the other house, where my bedroom is – opened another door, and there, at the end of the room, alone and dim, was the Old Man. He was as usual most cordial, and conducted me with incredible speed all round the garden, and then back again to the other house. He's a queer nervous old fellow, really.'

Altogether, it was 'one of those deplorable Wharf week-ends,' as he summarized it to Mary Hutchinson, 'after which one comes away, murmuring "never again, never again".' But a month later he was back there once more, though 'it's perhaps slightly better than the last time', he admitted to Carrington (17 July 1919). 'There's a middle-aged Scotch woman who plays chess with me while the others play bridge, and there are not quite so many absolute imbeciles. The "painters" are that creature Ranken[19] (a white haired pseudo Eddy) and a little

19. William Bruce Ellis Ranken (1881–1941), old Etonian, ex-Slade student, and for many years vice-president of the Royal Institution of Paint-

sporting fellow – an ostler – called Mullings [sic], I gather, who, I also gather, paints race-horses for his living . . .'

Among the overall second-rateness, Lytton was meeting a few people who stood out as being of some permanent interest in political and literary life. At a lunch given by Leonard and Virginia Woolf, he sat next to that curious couple, the Webbs, and, so Virginia noted in her diary, 'sported very gracefully'. She also commented: 'However one may abuse the Stracheys, their minds remain a source of joy to the end; so sparkling, definite and nimble. Need I add that I reserve the qualities I most admire for people who are not Stracheys?'

Another figure of portentous political significance whom Lytton encountered at this time was Lord Haldane[20], who, so he informed Ottoline (3 June 1919), was 'very satisfying – so incredibly urbane as to be almost a character in a French play – or as Mr Asquith suggested an Abbé. In both of them I was struck by the fact of their talking of nothing but the past; what happened in August 1914 etc. seems to absorb them still. But really nowadays there are other things to think about.'

Several of his literary acquaintances were also out of the ordinary, including W. H. Davies, 'gnome and poet', and Aldous Huxley, who 'looked like a piece of seaweed', was 'incredibly cultured' and who 'produced a very long and quite pointless poem for me to read'. Though Lytton and Huxley were always friendly, their mutual sympathy seems to have been incomplete. 'I used to see Lytton Strachey quite frequently at Garsington, in London, at one or other of the centres of "Bloomsbury" sociability, and once or twice at his

---

ers in Water Colours. He painted portraits, interiors, flower-pieces and landscapes, and was particularly known for his portraits of British Royalty – including Queen Elizabeth (wife of George VI), Queen Mary and Princess Christian – and also for his interiors of Windsor Castle and Buckingham Palace. In 1936 he was one of four painters given facilities to paint the Coronation ceremony of King George VI in Westminster Abbey.

20. The Rt Hon. Richard Burton Haldane, F.R.S., O.M., had been Secretary of State for War under Asquith from 1914 to 1915, and also Lord High Chancellor – a post which he regained in 1924, under the first brief Labour Government, having split off from the Liberals.

house in the country, when he was being looked after by poor Carrington and Partridge,' Huxley told the author. 'I always enjoyed his learning and his wit, but found his humanism rather too narrow for my taste.' On a number of occasions during this spring of 1919, the two of them would visit Osbert Sitwell, then a patient in a military hospital in London. To the eyes of the recumbent invalid, they made a startling and lugubrious couple, their 'silent elongated forms ... drooping round the end of my bed like the allegorical statues of Melancholy and of a rather satyr-like Father Time that mourn sometimes over a departed nobleman on an eighteenth-century tombstone. Lytton's debility prevented him from saying much, but what he did say he uttered in high, personal accents that floated to considerable distances, and the queer reasonableness, the unusual logic of what he said carried conviction.'

Another literary acquaintance for whom his feelings were peculiarly mixed was T. S. Eliot. They had first been introduced several years before, when Lytton appears to have registered a somewhat lukewarm response to the American poet. But after a second meeting at Garsington on 12 May 1919, he declared that 'he's greatly improved – far more self-assured, decidedly intelligent, and, so far as I could see, nice'. Two days later they met again in London, and Lytton reported to Carrington (14 May 1919): 'Poet Eliot had dinner with me on Monday – rather ill and rather American: altogether not quite gay enough for my taste. But by no means to be sniffed at.' At the same time, in a letter to Mary Hutchinson (15 May 1919), Lytton describes his friendship with Eliot as having reached a fluctuating stage. 'I do like him, though,' he added. 'He's changed a great deal since I last saw him – a long time ago. But the devitalisation I'm afraid may lead to disappointments.'[21]

---

21. A few days after their dinner together in London, Eliot wrote to Lytton (19 May 1919): 'Dear Strachey, I find that I am being sent on a tour of the provinces, by my bank, as soon as I can get off, and that I shall probably be gone some weeks. So unfortunately there is no possibility of my asking you to dine with me in the near future, as I should have liked you to have done. I only fear that when I am settled here [18 Crawford

These fears seemed well-founded. Invariably cautious, inhibited and formally polite, Eliot was an awkward person with whom to get on terms of intimacy. That month Lytton read *Prufrock and Other Observations*, which The Egoist Ltd had brought out in 1917, and although he was not altogether in tune with Eliot's profound obscurities and complicated states of mind, he sent him a letter which, he hoped, might advance their friendship. In his reply (1 June 1919) Eliot, with a characteristic blending of the precise and the nebulous, dwells on the processes of his writing.

Whether one writes a piece of work well or not seems to me a matter of crystallisation – the good sentence, the good word, is only the final stage in the process. One can groan enough over the choice of a word, but there is something much more important to groan over first. It seems to me just the same in poetry – the words come easily enough, in comparison to the core of it – the *tone* – and nobody can help one in the least with that. Anything *I* have picked up about writing is due to having spent (as I once thought, wasted) a year absorbing the style of F. H. Bradley – the finest philosopher in English – 'App.[earance] and Reality' is the Education Sentimentale of abstract thought.

Turning from his own writing to Lytton's letter, Eliot (who was then working for Lloyds Bank) comments:

You are very – ingenuous – if you can conceive me conversing with rural deans in the cathedral close. I do not go to cathedral towns but to centres of industry. My thoughts are absorbed in questions more important than ever enter the heads of deans – as *why* it is cheaper to buy steel bars from America than from Middlesbrough, and the probable effect – the exchange difficulties with Poland – and the appreciation of the rupee. My evenings in Bridge. The effect is to make me regard London with disdain, and divide mankind into supermen, termites and wireworms. I am sojourning among the termites. At any rate that coheres. I feel sufficiently specialised, at present, to inspect or hear any ideas with impunity.

Mansions, W.1] again you will be buried away in the country. Perhaps you will keep me in touch with your movements, and perhaps you will even let me have your opinions and Reviews of anything of mine you see in print.'

Lytton described this letter as 'grim', and for some time he hesitated to communicate with Eliot again. 'I do intend to spur myself up though,' he assured Mary Hutchinson (17 July 1919), 'as I don't want to drop him. Only I fear it will take him a long time to become a letter writer.' Early in August, he opened up the correspondence once more, and Eliot answered saying how propitious it was that he had written just before he, Eliot, disappeared to central France, where no letters could reach him. 'I have not been away but in London, in my office or among my books or (several times) in bed,' he went on (6 August 1919), 'and have frequently imagined you sitting on the lawn at Pangbourne or in a garden, conducting your clinic of Queen Victoria with perfect concentration. ... You have frightened me because I always expect you to be right, and because I know I shall never be able to retaliate upon your finely woven fabrics. I have lately read an article of yours on Voltaire which made me envious.' Ten days later he sent Lytton a postcard from the Dordogne, where, he was careful to point out, he had been walking the whole time and so had no address at all. London was extraordinarily difficult; very slowly one bled to death there. But wandering through the Corrèze he was happy and sunburnt, surrounded by 'melons, ceps, truffles, eggs, good wine and good cheese and cheerful people. It's a complete relief from London.'

In the months and years that followed, they met and corresponded only infrequently; and although Lytton made several overtures to a closer relationship, and although these were apparently welcomed by Eliot, there always persisted something rather reserved about their association, always something to hinder its further development.[22] While each of them, for politeness' sake, professed to admire the other's work, their reciprocal civilities never really carry great con-

22. When, for example, Lytton wrote inviting him to spend a week-end with him at Tidmarsh, Eliot replied (14 July 1920) that he was delighted to hear from him and would love to have come, 'but unfortunately I have some people motoring down for Saturday afternoon. Perhaps this is providential, as I ought to work Sunday on a book which is heavy on my conscience. How do you ever write a book? It seems to me a colossal task. *Perhaps* you will ask me again sometime?'

viction, and they felt each other to be, if not wireworms, certainly not supermen.[23]

Bloomsbury had by this time tentatively taken up Eliot – the Hogarth Press in 1919 publishing his *Poems*, and four years later *The Waste Land* – but his dry, authoritarian manner still made him something of an enigma to them. 'When we first got to know Tom, we liked him very much,' remembered Leonard Woolf, 'but we were both a little afraid of him.' In the summer of 1922, various members of Bloomsbury set up the Eliot Fellowship Fund, a scheme which was designed to release Eliot from his work at the bank, which, they felt, was injuring his health and seriously interfering with his creative powers. A circular, which was distributed to all potential subscribers asking them to contribute at least five or ten pounds a year for a minimum term of five years in return for first editions of all Eliot's future volumes, expounded the scheme as follows:

It is impossible that he [Eliot] should continue to produce good poetry unless he has more leisure than he can now hope to obtain, but his literary work is of far too high and original a quality to afford by itself a means of livelihood. For this reason it is proposed to raise a special Fellowship Fund to enable him to give up his post at the bank and devote his whole time to literary work. It is estimated that at least £300 a year for a period of not less than 5 years will be required, and it is hoped that many admirers of good literature will be glad to contribute to a fund which has for its aim the preserving of the talent of one of the most original and distinguished writers of our day.

23. Nevertheless, in a letter inviting Lytton to a small party at 38 Burleigh Mansions, Eliot wrote (10 December 1923): 'And once again – although I admire and enjoy your portraits in the Nation, it is to my interest to say that they are not *long* enough to do you justice. So – although you once refused – 2 years ago – please remember that I should like to lead off a number of the *Criterion* with you, up to 5000 or 8000 words. . . . I have thought that you ought to do MACAULAY – but anything from you would ensure the success of a number, besides the pleasure it would give me. Could you?' Lytton did not write his essay on Macaulay until 1927. Published in the *Nation and Athenaeum* (21 January 1928), it was 2,500 words long.

A committee, consisting of Ottoline Morrell, Leonard Woolf, Harry Norton and Richard Aldington, who acted as treasurer of the fund, was established in England to manage this project, and other committees in France and America were also formed to work in collaboration with the English group. But shortly after the circulars had been drafted Eliot gravely demurred, and a postscript had to be appended explaining that 'circumstances have arisen which make it necessary that Mr Eliot should be allowed to use his own discretion as to continuing or relinquishing his present work at the bank'. Nevertheless, without imposing or implying any conditions on the reluctant beneficiary, the committee decided to go ahead with the plan as best it could, since it remained beyond dispute, even by Eliot himself, that 'any addition to his income would not only remove from him considerable anxiety which the expense of illness has brought upon him, but would make it possible for him to give more time to writing than he can now do'.

And so, in its amended form, the scheme was launched, quickly petered out and finally came to nothing. As one who shared his admiration for Donne — years before it was fashionable to admire him — Lytton naturally had some qualified respect for Eliot and was prepared to help him financially. But, hedged about by Eliot's own sombre caveats and qualifications, the Fellowship Fund struck him as being a rather ludicrous proposition, and he parodied the Bloomsbury circular in a mischievous letter to Leonard and Virginia Woolf (December 1922):

THE LYTTON STRACHEY DONATION

It has been known for some time to Mr Lytton Strachey's friends that his income is in excess of his expenditure, and that he has a large balance at the bank. It is impossible, if his royalties continue to accumulate at the present rate, that he should be in a position to spend them entirely upon himself, without serious injury to his reputation among his more impecunious acquaintances. For this reason it is proposed that he should set aside the sum of £20,000 (twenty thousand pounds) to be known as the 'Lytton Strachey Donation', the interest upon which shall be devoted to the support of such persons as the Committee shall think fit to select.

All those in favour of this scheme are requested to communicate with Lady Ottoline Morrell, Garsington, Oxford, adding the sum which they themselves would wish to draw from the Donation annually. No sum less than £20 (twenty pounds) a year should be asked for, though demands for capital sums of £5000 (five thousand pounds) and upwards will be entertained.

POSTSCRIPT

Since the scheme in the accompanying circular was proposed it has come to the knowledge of the Committee that circumstances have arisen which make it impossible that Mr Lytton Strachey should be prevented from using his own discretion as to the disposal of his ill-gotten gains. It is however certain that many persons would benefit even from such small sums as 5/– (five shillings) or 2/6 (two-and-sixpence), supposing that Mr Strachey were willing to disburse them. Under these circumstances the Committee propose to continue the scheme in its present form, without, however, imposing upon Mr Strachey any conditions as to how his money should be spent.

It was through Eliot that the Hogarth Press was offered the uncompleted manuscript of James Joyce's *Ulysses*. According to Leonard Woolf, he and Virginia decided to try and publish it in about 1918, but since no English printer was willing to risk prosecution, they were eventually forced to abandon the enterprise. Leonard refers to the novel as 'a remarkable piece of dynamite', but Virginia, as often in her attitude to living writers, was malicious. When Lytton signified to her that he was willing to lend his support to their lame duck of an Eliot Fellowship Fund, she replied (24 August 1922): 'One hundred pounds did you say? You shall have a receipt. Cheque payable to Richard Aldington or O. Morrell as you prefer. My own contribution, five and sixpence, is given on condition he puts publicly to their proper use the first 200 pages of Ulysses. Never have I read such tosh. As for the first 2 Chapters we will let them pass, but the 3rd 4th 5th 6th – merely the scratching of pimples on the body of the bootboy at Claridges. Of course, genius *may* blaze out on page 652 but I have my doubts. And this is what Eliot worships, and there's Lytton Strachey paying £100 p.a. to Eliot's upkeep.'[24]

It may be that Virginia Woolf's scurrilous, semi-playful strictures were deliberately exaggerated to tune in with what she supposed Lytton's attitude to be. But it seems more probable that this criticism provided a vent to that jealous competitive spirit of hers, since Lytton, who always campaigned against censorship in any form, supported the unabridged publication of *Ulysses*. In any event, Virginia's sense of rivalry and lapse of sympathy did not prevent her from stirring up support for Eliot once again a few months later – this time over his appointment as literary editor of the *Nation and Athenaeum*. The chief strategist in putting over this plan was Maynard Keynes, who had met with great opposition from his fellow directors, none of whom had apparently heard of Eliot. The only way Keynes saw of ousting this opposition was to convince the directors that Eliot was well thought of by contemporary writers of the highest distinction – like Lytton Strachey – who would contribute to their paper should Eliot become its literary editor. It was Virginia who, on 23 February 1923, wrote Lytton a private and confidential letter recounting this state of affairs, and asking once more for his assistance. 'I have to approach you on a delicate matter – to wit, poor Tom,' she explained. '. . . As you are aware the Eliot fund business has proved a fiasco; and this certainly seems to be the only possible solution of the problem. In fact, the poor man is becoming (in his highly American way, which is tedious and longwinded to a degree) desperate. I think he will be forced to leave the Bank anyhow. So if you would write me a line giving some sort of promise that you would write, or at least would be more inclined to write for him than another we should all be very grateful.'

Lytton at once pledged his support directly to Keynes, who described the negotiated arrangement, with Eliot as assistant literary editor presumably under Leonard Woolf as 'poise and

24. It is significant to note that Lytton subscribed his hundred pounds some four months prior to writing the parody. In later years Eliot became a close friend of Dorothy and Janie Bussy.

counterpoise', adding in a private note a fortnight later (9 March 1923): 'Pretty complete victory. Ramsay Muir[25] and Guedalla have committed suicide and Mrs Royde Smith[26] has been assassinated.' Yet, from the point of view of Eliot's appointment, this announcement of victory seems to have been premature, since, as Sir Roy Harrod rather disingenuously notes in his Life of Keynes, 'At first it was hoped to secure Mr T. S. Eliot as Literary Editor, but he was not immediately available and the paper could not wait.'

At about that time, Eliot was appointed editor of the newly founded *Criterion*, a paper which, standing for Classicism in literature and religion, was almost totally alien to Lytton, Keynes and the Woolfs.

6
STRACHEY'S PROGRESS

Although, on and off, Lytton continued to work at the British Museum and the London Library during the spring and early summer months of 1919, his frequent rovings into the mansions of the great and wealthy had begun seriously to slow down his progress on *Queen Victoria*. He remained so long up in town that it was rumoured that he had taken special lodgings near the Albert Memorial to keep in the right mood for his work.[27] The truth, however, was less whimsical. London,

25. Ramsay Muir (1872–1941), historian and Liberal M.P. for Rochdale (1923–4). Chairman and president of the National Liberal Federation. Author of many books including *History of the British Commonwealth* (2 vols, 1920 and 1922).

26. Naomi Gwladys Royde-Smith, prolific professional Welsh 'women's' novelist and eldest daughter of Michael Holroyd Smith. As literary editor of the *Weekly Westminster* – a paper that, in the pre-1914 days, enjoyed a great vogue – she had published a lot of Rupert Brooke's early verse. During the First World War she and Rose Macaulay had conducted a joint salon for writers and artists, founded on that of Julie de Lespinasse, about whom she wrote a biography. In 1926 she married Ernest Milton, the actor.

27. On 1 March 1919, Lytton wrote to Vanessa Bell: 'By-the-bye, what is your view of the Albert Memorial as a work of art? It's not easy to consider it impartially – one's earliest memories are so intertwined

like a sticky spider's web, absorbed him; his wings were caught, and he fluttered, fluttered in vain. 'London continues to be very agreeable,' he admitted to Ottoline (30 May 1919), 'but I doubt whether I shall stay there much longer. A little work is really becoming necessary, and it's quite impossible to do a stroke in that charivari – I envy Harriet Martineau, whose autobiography I've been reading (rather an interesting book). She worked six hours a day writing political economy, and then every evening explored the beau monde. But in those days people were made of steel and india-rubber.'

It was not until the early part of July that Lytton succeeded in breaking free from the filigree of town life and retreating down to Tidmarsh. Here he was able to work with reasonable calm and concentration, the only respite being a week-end visit from E. M. Forster, with his 'curious triangular face, and a mind, somehow, exactly fitting'.

That month, Carrington had gone down with her brother Noel and Ralph to Welcombe, next to the Box farm she and the others had been at in the summer of 1917 – 'a very good place for painting'. They were living in a remote little cottage, West Mill. 'I do like small places like this where one can't spoil things,' she wrote to Mark Gertler, 'and the walls are white and one can sit with lovely still lives on the tables coloured jugs with flowers, bread Bottles of ink and teacups long after the meal is finished – and letters are written. outside the window one looks up a long valley with high Hills either side covered with trees, and Forests. behind the other way the cottage faces roaring sea. only a few minutes walk with huge

---

with it – surely we must have met on those steps in long clothes? – but surely there's a coherence and conception about it not altogether negligible? – Compared, for instance, to the memorial to Victoria opposite Buckingham Palace, it certainly stands out. At any rate, it's not a thing one can easily forget.' Professor Quentin Bell comments on this letter that the Albert Memorial was 'the stock joke and aunt sally of the 1920s. Then a later generation Betjeman-wise in its day discovered or rediscovered it. Now the clever jokes at the A.M. are thought particularly "20sh" and are I fancy laid at Lytton's door. It's fascinating to find Lytton in 1919 coming so close in his judgements to the views of the post-Strachey epoch.'

crags, and cliffs. Fortunately there are [no] trippers here, so one can wear what one likes, and wander about the place without meeting stupid Fat Ladies with dogs.'

While she was away, Lytton, looked after by Boris and Helen Anrep's cook, pressed on with his biography. 'Now I am fairly in it, or should I say Her, immersed, pegging away daily, and quite, so far enjoying myself,' he told Mary Hutchinson (17 July 1919). In spite of this industry, he greatly disliked being left altogether alone, and in the fine summer evenings would sit out among the rambler roses in the mill-garden and dream wistfully of London, of Shaftesbury Avenue, the Soho streets, Soho Square, the little passage into the Charing Cross Road, and the Tottenham Court Road, along and along to the trees of Gordon Square – and so on endlessly. Every shop window, every paving stone, it seemed, he could call up before the mind's eye, especially when the light began to thicken, the street-lamps and illuminations to come on, though still weaker than the fading daylight, and all sorts of lovely creatures would flit from shadow to shadow across the roads. How he had hated London in the past: how the vision of it intoxicated him now in his quiet garden! 'I can hardly bear to think of it, I love it so much – to distraction.'

The result of this secluded, self-disciplined life was that he soon finished the first two chapters of *Queen Victoria* – 'Antecedents' and 'Childhood'. 'I have been absorbed by Victoria for the last month,' he informed his mother (19 August 1919), 'and have now written the opening part – as far as her accession. So far the variety of curious characters and circumstances keeps me going – the difficulty will be much greater, I expect, after the death of the Prince Consort.'

His family were now beginning to organize their move later in the year to a new home, 51 Gordon Square. Over these years, Gordon Square seems to have been largely taken over by the Bloomsbury Group and their friends. Duncan Grant and Vanessa Bell made good use of No. 37 for a time; James and Alix Strachey lived on the top floor of No. 41, where Lytton, Ralph Partridge and Carrington also had occasional rooms;[28]

28. James Strachey and Alix Sargant-Florence had taken the whole of

into the flat below them Lydia Lopokova had moved during 1922, before her marriage to Maynard Keynes, when she transferred to No. 46; the ground-floor flat was occupied during one ballet season by Ernest Ansermet. No. 42 was in 1925 the home of Oliver Strachey and his daughter Julia. Near by, in Taviton Street, and subsequently Brunswick Square, lived Frances Marshall, David Garnett's sister-in-law, later to move into 41 Gordon Square and marry Ralph Partridge. No. 46, which had been taken by the Stephen family in 1904, was now the property of Maynard Keynes, who, during the war, shared it with Sheppard and Harry Norton – though Clive and Vanessa Bell and Duncan Grant still retained some accommodation in it. Adrian Stephen and his wife Karin, both psychoanalysts, inhabited No. 50, as did, for a very long time, Arthur Waley. And now, pure chance had decided that Lady Strachey and her daughters would dwell at No. 51. 'Very soon I foresee that the whole square will become a sort of college,' Lytton wrote to Virginia Woolf (28 September 1919). 'And the rencontres in the garden I shudder to think of. The business of packing, deciding what is to be sold, what sent to Tidmarsh, what given to the deserving poor etc. has been fearful, and is still proceeding, the brunt of it of course falling on the unfortunate Pippa. I am fit for very little more than wringing my hands. In the intervals I go to the British Museum, and try to dig up scandals about Queen Victoria. Altogether a distracting life, and the comble was reached in the small hours of Friday morning, when the policeman's wife who acts as caretaker gave birth to a baby just outside my bedroom door.'

His research work at this time, though it uncovered no

---

41 Gordon Square in January 1919, and let off various bits of it at various times to various people. 'We began by living on the top two floors, before we were married,' James told the author. 'Then we took on the second floor and then for some time·when we were rich, the first floor as well. There was even a very short period when we had the whole house, during which we gave a celebrated party with two hundred guests. Then by degrees we receded again till in our final period we had only the top three floors ... Lydia [Lopokova] was on the ground floor and shook the whole house when she practised her entrechats.' In 1956, James and Alix Strachey gave up 41 Gordon Square and went to live near Marlow.

scandals, was of particular advantage. With the help of Arthur Waley, then working in the Department of Prints and Drawings at the British Museum, and of H. A. L. Fisher, a trustee of the Museum, he had been given leave to study the manuscript of *The Greville Memoirs,* the printed version of which had omitted many passages. It was amusing to read through the old papers, and he was able to note down several points of value. On 9 October 1919, he wrote to H. A. L. Fisher: 'I have made a certain number of extracts from parts of the Memoirs that have not been published – dealing chiefly with Victoria's attitude towards the Tories in the first years of her reign. There are also a few other notes of minor importance. I should be very glad to be able to refer to these in my book (I should not want to make long verbatim quotations) – and I think you will agree with me that there is really no reason at all why I shouldn't. Greville was very cross with the Queen for taking sides in politics – snubbing Wellington etc. – and it was natural that Reeve should refrain from publishing these passages while H.M. was alive. But now the conditions are different – and the attitude of Queen Victoria in 1840 (which, incidentally, she changed a few years later) is merely a matter of historical interest and Court politics of 80 years ago.'

Lytton went on to ask Fisher whether he would speak up for him at a meeting of the Trustees of the British Museum on 11 October, and Fisher, who completely shared Lytton's sensible views, agreed to do this. The result was that he was able to tell Lytton the following week that the Trustees had decided not to impose any restriction on his use of the *Memoirs.*

At the end of September, Lytton went back to the Mill House, where he stayed 'penned down' for the next six months, working hard at his book, and, in the intervals, arranging his library, which, having been brought down from Belsize Park Gardens, now covered the walls and floors of practically every room at Tidmarsh – while he sat in the midst of this confusion, happily cataloguing their titles in various coloured inks on a series of ruled cards. In this fashion the days succeeded one another in a most orderly manner, the sole excite-

ments being an occasional week-end visitor, or an occasional
new book. Among the latter were Daisy Ashford's *The Young
Visiters* which was 'perfectly charming' and *La Porte Étroite* by
Gide, which he thought 'decidedly remarkable'.[29] But most
exciting of all were two books brought out that winter by his
friends. The first of these was Virginia Woolf's new novel,
Night and Day, which he told Ottoline (15 November 1919),
was a work not to read, but to re-read – 'there seemed so
much in it that one could only just effleurer as one went along,
and longed to return to. She [Virginia] was here last week, and
appeared to be very well and cheerful, and of course more
amusing than ever.' And to Pippa he wrote (13 November
1919): 'The visualisation of faces does makes it difficult to
judge of. But I think Mrs Hilbery is a chef d'oeuvre.' The other
highlight of these winter months was Keynes's polemical masterpiece, *The Economic Consequences of the Peace*.[30] This book
had been written by Keynes during the months of August and
September down at Charleston, and he had read passages
from it while Lytton was staying there. On his return to Tidmarsh a few weeks later, Lytton wrote to Keynes (4 October
1919): 'I seem to gather from the scant remarks in the newspapers, that your friend the President [Woodrow Wilson] has
gone mad. Is it possible that it should be gradually borne in

29. Lytton also mentions at this time Ethel Smyth's reminiscences, *Impressions that Remained* ('extremely entertaining, not to say interesting.
Curiously old-fashioned, too'), *The Education of Henry Adams* ('certainly
very remarkable, though a trifle long'), Stephen Graham's *A Private in the
Guards* which was enjoyable 'chiefly as a self-revelation, but also for
accounts of things in the war', and Festing Jones's biography of Samuel
Butler ('vol 2, after Miss Savage dies, decidedly falls off in interest, I
think. *Her* letters are really excellent').

30. This was the book that first made Keynes's name internationally
famous. On publication it was smothered, to use Keynes's own words to
Lytton (23 December 1919), 'in a deluge of approval; not a complaint, not
a word of abuse, not a hint of criticism; letters from Cabinet Ministers by
every post saying that they agree with every word of it, etc, etc. I expect
a chit from the P.M. at any moment telling me how profoundly the book
represents his views and how beautifully it is put. Will it be my duty to
refuse the Legion of Honour at the hands of Clemenceau? Well, I suppose
this is their best and safest line.'

upon him what an appalling failure he was,[31] and that when at last he fully realised it his mind collapsed? Very dramatic, if so But won't it make some of your remarks almost too cruel? — Especially if he should go and die.'

Although Keynes felt strongly that his sketch of Woodrow Wilson formed an essential part of his argument, and that, if the peace settlement was to be properly understood and the situation rectified, Wilson's character must be elucidated, he nevertheless did moderate some of his pages. The book was published in December, and on receiving a complimentary copy Lytton wrote back (16 December 1919): 'Your book arrived yesterday, and I swallowed it at a gulp. I think it is most successful. In the first place, extremely impressive; there is an air of authority about it which I think nobody could ignore. I was rather afraid at Charleston that it might appear too extreme, but I don't think this is at all the case. The slight softenings in the Clemenceau and Wilson bits seem to me distinct improvements, adding to the effect, rather than otherwise. Then the mass of information is delightful. I had never, for instance, had any definite idea as to what the Provisions of the Peace Treaty really were — it was impossible to gather from the newspapers, and the import of the Treaty itself would have been clearly incomprehensible — so that your exposé, apart from the argument, was most welcome; and of course this is only one of a great number of extraordinarily interesting sets of facts. As to the argument it is certainly most crushing, most terrible. I don't see how anyone can stand up against it. . . . One thing I doubted — and that was whether, on your own showing, even your proposed terms were not far too harsh. Is it conceivable that the Germany which you describe should be able to or in fact would pay 50 million a year for 30 years? To my mind the ideal thing would be to abolish reparations altogether — but of course that is not practical politics — at any rate not just yet; perhaps in the end it will become so.'

Work on his own book was now advancing steadily. 'It is

31. i.e. at the Paris Peace Conference, which Keynes attended as principal representative of the Treasury.

really very agreeable down here – what with one thing and another,' he told Mary Hutchinson (10 December 1919). 'Queen Victoria progresses with infinite slowness but still moves.' Every morning, alone in his library, he would labour at it for about three hours, during which time he usually put down some three hundred words in ink, with hardly a correction. He composed, so he told Ralph Partridge, in his head, not sentences but entire paragraphs before committing them to paper – which may account for the extreme fluidity of his style. Nothing, except illness, was allowed to interfere with his work. 'Queen Victoria, poor lady, totters on step by step,' he reported on 9 December. 'As she's still in her youth, what will she be like in age at this rate? I can only hope that she may proceed in inverse fashion – growing speedier and speedier as she gets older, and finally fairly bundling into the grave.'

By the following spring he had completed the chapters on 'Lord Melbourne' and 'Marriage', and possibly the fifth chapter also – 'Lord Palmerston' – though this is not certain. At any rate, he felt that he had arrived at a convenient halting-place, and that, before setting to work on the final part of the biography, he would fortify himself with a few weeks' holiday abroad.

7

SOUTH FROM PANGBOURNE

'I am curiously happy just now,' Lytton wrote to Keynes on 16 December. This was for him what he described as a 'halcyon winter'. Not only was his writing going ahead very well, but the conditions of his life appeared more propitious than ever before. He was seeing a lot of Ralph Partridge. Sometimes he would brave the winter winds to go over and watch him row at Oxford; and often Ralph bicycled across to Tidmarsh for the week-end when they would read Elizabethan poetry together, and talk about literature, art, and all manner of complicated subjects. 'Lytton gets on so much better with him now,' Carrington confided to her brother Noel (12 December 1919). 'In fact they are great friends, and have long discussions on Einstein's theory whilst I darn the socks.'

It was an odd domestic communion, but one that suited Lytton admirably. For by now he had already fallen deeply in love with Ralph. Several times a week he would write to him, and these letters reveal both the intensity of his feeling and the teasing, affectionate manner in which he treated him. 'Clive and Mary are here – in great feather,' he wrote on 11 January 1920. 'We talk and talk and talk. I wished you had been here at dinner yesterday to enjoy the jugged hare with some wonderful jelly concocted by Carrington out of the remains of the Burgundy – delicious! – When are you coming back? Truth to tell, the Auld Mill Hoose is, as they say, "not itself" sans our Master Ralph. I see that if I had any sense I should have had you nailed up by the ear in the Tidmarsh pillory, so that you couldn't have escaped until everyone was quite tired of you. I warn you this is what you must expect when you return – it won't hurt *very* much, and will be an interesting experience. Imagine me sitting up in bed, in my muffetees. The wind howls, the rain pours, and the horror of Sunday covers the earth.'

Three weeks later he is writing to him again (3 February 1920): 'If you don't appear either tomorrow or Thursday, I shan't see you for a hundred years, it seems to me. My beard will be snowy white, and your ears will have grown so intolerably perky for want of pulling that they'll have to be clipped by the executioner. . . . I am feeling very cheerful and well. My dearest creature, don't bother too much about my health. The exhaustion that shatters is the kind that's caused by miserable baffled desires – in a black period of my life I was nearly killed by it; but now, dear, I am buoyed up and carried along by so much happiness! On this subject two generalisations have occurred to me. Generalisation no. 1. – The secret of happiness is to want neither too much nor too little.

'Generalisation no. 2. – No one can master this secret, under the age of 39.'

Sometimes Lytton felt tempted to ask too much from 'my sweet Ralph';[32] and then again, in reaction from this mood

32. Partridge's actual Christian name was Reginald – Rex for short –

and especially when Carrington was not with them, he was overcome by anxiety lest Ralph should feel unnecessary disquiet, and he would hasten to reassure him – 'don't suspect darknesses, please'. Illness – any one of his 'quatre maladies mortelles' – could still swiftly deflate his high spirits. When Carrington and Ralph spent a few days together in Oxford, leaving him at Tidmarsh, the solitude closed in round him and he nearly burst into tears. 'My dear one,' he wrote on that occasion to Ralph (February 1920), 'I am feeling rather dejected and lonely, and feel that I must press your hand before I go to my solitary couch. Carrington's too. ... It seems so good when we're all three together that I grudge every minute that keeps us apart.'

From the first, then, it seemed as if an idyllic partnership had sprung up between the three of them. Carrington was delighted that her two men should have taken so well to each other. She was able now to play a still closer part in Lytton's emotional life. If she could attract the boy-friends whom he liked, then, she felt, her place with him was secure, her influence indispensable. And Lytton did not resent Ralph's passion for Carrington – indeed their happiness seemed only to swell his own. For the time being, therefore, their three-cornered affair remained curiously unselfish, all of them adhering to the first of Lytton's generalizations – not to ask for too much or too little from it – so that each one derived added enjoyment from the pleasure of the other two. There appear to have been no real moments of awkwardness or misunderstanding between them – indeed they made fun of such possibilities. 'I send my fond love,' Lytton ended one of his letters to Ralph (February 1920), 'and all the kisses and etceteras that I didn't dare to send you by Carrington for fear of their being intercepted en route.'

The situation, however, could not stay poised for ever at this finely balanced point. Ralph had been completely won over by Lytton's unwavering gentleness, his thoughtfulness, his

---

but Lytton invented the name Ralph for him, and soon everyone was calling him by this.

alert and witty mind. He was charmed by him: but he was in love with Carrington. Towards the end of this winter, he started to put pressure on her to marry him. She strongly resisted, while Lytton, who wished everything to remain exactly as it was, looked on anxiously, wondering how things would turn out, but never attempting to influence them in any way.

Thus the first sinister shadow had been thrown across their strange relationship; but almost at once it was temporarily dissolved again when, that April, the three of them took off for six weeks' holiday together in Spain. They were to stop at all the places that Carrington and Ralph had visited the previous year – Carrington was insistent upon this; for only then could she share with Lytton in retrospect all her past experiences there, transmuting them from a meaningless confusion of pleasurable sights and sounds into something really memorable. In addition to this itinerary, they planned to spend a few days with Ralph's friend, Gerald Brenan, who, the previous autumn, had sailed from England with a hundred pounds in his pocket to set up house at the primitive and inaccessible mountain village of Yegen, in Andalusia. This was to be the highlight of their journey.

Full of the highest anticipations, they started out by boat towards the end of March, stopped off for a day at Corunna, and finally disembarked at Lisbon. From here they continued their journey through the night by train across the Spanish border to Seville, Lytton travelling first class, the other two third. 'At the best of times travelling in this country is hard,' he wrote to Mary Hutchinson (11 April 1920), 'all the train journeys last for twelve hours at a minimum, and the slowness of one's advances is heart-breaking. We had a fearful night coming out of Portugal – the 1st class carriage blocked with sucking babies and drunken commercial travellers – poor Ralph reduced to sleeping on the portmanteau in the corridor, etc. etc. But still, one does progress, and the sights one sees are worth the horrors.'

These horrors rapidly multiplied as they pressed on into the wilds of Spain. By the time they reached Seville, Lytton was already quite exhausted, but Ralph's strict, almost regimental schedule, which had unfortunately neglected to take account of his companion's lack of soldierly stamina, did not allow for many periods of rest. Soon he was hurrying the party on again, this time to Cordova – 'a most wonderful town', so Lytton informed Pippa (1 April 1920). Almost all the places he was to see were more spectacular than he had expected. But Cordova he loved best of all, describing it in a letter to Mary Hutchinson as 'oriental – a network of narrow narrow streets, and a very big and beautiful mosque, in the middle of which the astonishing Christians have stuck a huge rococo church – the effect is dizzying. One evening we went in after sunset, and found a mass in progress. A full orchestra was at work in the baroque building, a tenor was singing an aria by Mozart, and all round, dimly lighted by a lamp here and there, were the pillars and arches of the antique mosque, stretching away in every direction into far distant darkness. It was incredibly theatrical and romantic, and I felt like Uncle John, very very nearly a Roman Catholic.'

Ralph's time-table permitted them to linger on in Cordova three full days. Then they were up and off again, and after more agonizing hours of Spanish travelling, came to Granada, which, Lytton declared, was 'astounding – very high up, with immense snow mountains directly over it, and the Alhambra – huge dark red walls and towers – dominating the town. Before long, one observes picture-postcard elements in this, and the detail of the Alhambra is sheer Earl's Court, but the general grandeur of situation and outline remain.'

They arrived in Granada on 2 April, Lytton describing himself on a postcard to Virginia Woolf as 'very chirpy'. But his chirpiness did not long survive. As the party had fought their way onwards and upwards, so their difficulties had steadily mounted. After reaching Granada these tribulations came to a head. Every day there was some fresh crisis or disaster – and the victim of all these catastrophes was Lytton, who became more and more alarmed the further they left civilization behind. Already it seemed to him that he had been away from England for several years. 'I am breaking S[trachey] of his

792

milksops,' Ralph had confidently predicted to Noel Carrington early on; but his optimism was ill-founded. At Granada Lytton suffered a serious relapse. The ruthless Spanish cuisine, with its emphasis on potato omelets, dried cod, and unrefined olive oil, played havoc with his delicate digestive system; he caught Spanish influenza; he nearly trod on a Spanish snake; he mislaid his pyjamas; he injured his knee and announced that he was liable to faint at any moment, though requiring no assistance to recover; and at all times he refused absolutely to exchange a word with any of the natives. Before embarking on this holiday, he had toyed for a while with the Spanish grammar, but not apparently to much practical avail. 'I began the study of the Spanish language last Thursday,' he had written to Ralph on 11 January, '– but I haven't quite completed it yet – there's still time for you to put on the finishing touches. . . . Te envio un baccio.' Such eloquence was confined to paper. And to England. On Spanish territory, nothing would induce him to order even a glass of water. Whenever he lost sight of his two companions he was seized with a sort of dumb panic and, in all matters of communication, relied on Ralph who, he admiringly wrote to his mother, 'can grapple with the Spanish language in a most talented way'.

Their nerves frayed by these setbacks, Carrington and Ralph had now begun to quarrel, and a trying emotional tangle quickly arose between them. Ralph, on whose shoulders the responsibility rested for every decision, complained with mounting exasperation that their holiday was rapidly turning into a fiasco. Carrington retorted that Ralph was insufferably dreary, that he might *look* very handsome and make a 'good bedding plant', but that he was 'not for use in the day time', and should consequently remain silent – except as interpreter. Outwardly it was a typical lovers' quarrel, but the underlying bone of contention was Lytton. Ralph felt at times that he was holding them back and spoiling their journey – which was less satisfactory than last year. Carrington seems to have felt that Ralph was using Spain like some open-air gymnasium, that he was incapable of enjoying the beauties of architecture and landscape in a relaxed and civilized manner.

At Granada their fortunes took a steep plunge. For it was here that they had arranged to join up with Gerald Brenan, who intended to escort them across Los Alpujarras – that wild tract of country between the Sierra Nevada and the hills which lie to the north of the Mediterranean – up to his small mountain cottage. Brenan, however, delayed by chronic mismanagement of his own affairs, failed to arrive on time, and so there was nothing for Lytton and the others to do but wait uncertainly in the Hotel de Paris, and in the meantime explore the town. They went to the mosque, to a bull-fight, and a concert. Carrington in a letter (undated) to her brother describes something of the unresolved stalemate in which they had landed up. 'Monday we spent trying to find Brenan who is due to meet us, and convey us over the hills to his cottage for a week. Lytton refuses to go until he has R.P.'s good word for his safety. which R.P. can't give until he sees Brenan. at present Lytton's rather ill I think with the slightly billious food of this hotel.'

Lytton himself uttered no complaints over Brenan's absence. The trip which he envisaged up vertical, zigzagging tracks and across the most primitive, out-of-the-way region of Spain, with all its incumbent trials and hardships, struck him as being the very height of folly. His spirit of adventure, so keen at the outset of their voyage, had been remorselessly worn away by never-ending mishaps, until by now he felt the strongest aversion to courting further and greater calamities. 'Partridge, the young man who is with me,' he told his mother (18 April 1920), 'has an eccentric friend who has taken up his abode in a remote village there (Los Alpujarras), and it was decided that we should go and see him.' Writing to Mary Hutchinson at about the same time, he felt able to express his feelings more explicitly, describing Brenan as 'an amiable lunatic . . . who has come to live here in pursuit of some Dostoievsky will o' the wisp or other, and whom Partridge had engaged himself to come and visit with solemn vows'. Despite the hideous prospect of this visit, he neither wanted to spoil it for the others nor to be left at Granada alone (or even with Carrington, in whose capabilities he had little confidence).

With characteristic tenacity, he determined to accompany them all should Brenan turn up.

Not to be baulked by this reverse, Ralph had meanwhile dispatched an urgent telegram to his friend reminding him of their arrival in Granada and adding that, unless he contacted them, they would be leaving again in two days. This message brought Brenan, weak with influenza, scrambling down the mountains just in time to miss them – by half an hour – at their hotel, and barely in time to catch up with them at the bus station. The four of them then boarded a motor-bus and for several frantic hours bumped along a most appalling road until they reached Lanjaron, 'a small health resort in the hills'. Here they put up at an hotel, and began to discuss the next stage of their journey. The problem of transporting Lytton up to Yegen loomed large. He sat in a cane armchair drinking cognac, silent and bearded, and betraying no sign of enthusiasm for the various ways and means that were being debated. Finally, it was decided to engage a carriage for the following morning to carry them all to a village called Orgiva, where they would procure mules to transport them along the last few miles of their trek. Brenan, however, had forgotten about the floods that spring. All went well until they reached the Rio Grande, which was so swollen as to be virtually impassable. On arriving at the ford, the mules went in almost up to their girths amid the racing water, and Lytton drew back in alarm. The party then wearily retreated to the hotel, deciding to make a fresh start by another route early the following morning.

After this day's failure everyone's nerves were more than ever on edge, and the evening passed in general low spirits and an air of recrimination – Lytton gloomy but mutely resolute, Brenan harassed and ruffled, Carrington and Ralph full of reciprocal accusations. 'The conveyance of the great writer to my mountain village began to assume more and more the appearance of a difficult military operation,' Brenan afterwards recorded. 'Carrington, caught between two fires, became clumsily appeasing and only Lytton said nothing. As for myself, I never doubted my powers to go anywhere or do anything of a physical sort that I wished to, but under my friends' bombardment I felt my unfitness for assuming responsibility for other people.'

Next morning at nine o'clock they again set off. The day was very hot, and thirty miles of difficult and precipitous country lay before them, filling them all with the darkest forebodings. No sooner had they dismounted from the carriage and descended into the river valley, than Lytton, who was suffering by this time from piles, discovered that he could not ride on mule-back. Every half-mile or so the band of them would arrive at a river, he would perilously mount his animal, be agonizingly conveyed across, and then climb off again – all the while balancing an open sunshade high above his head. This procedure repeated itself with a monotonous frequency throughout the day, so tiring Lytton and so delaying their progress that at last they agreed unanimously to break their journey and put up for the night at the small village of Cádiar. But one look at the best bed available at the *posada*, and they quickly changed their minds and dragged themselves off again along the bed of the same river which they continued, as in a nightmare, to cross and recross on their mules, and so on and so on by narrow tracks, up and up into the hills until the day began to fade and the stars appeared in the sky.

The last part of their march, straight up a mountainside of some two thousand five hundred feet, was undertaken in silent twilight. This dramatic ascent, along a steep path bordered by precipices, was made by Lytton sitting side-saddle. On reaching the top, Carrington and Brenan hurried ahead over the six miles that remained to give warning of the great man's arrival and see to it that a meal was prepared. Ralph and Lytton reached Yegen half an hour later – at about ten o'clock that night – having travelled a good twelve hours with only one halt in the middle of the day. 'Lytton and I certainly had mules,' Carrington wrote to Noel. 'But as we crossed a rapid torrent at least thirty times *on* the mules they were'nT altogether an unmixed joy! My God. I was never so glad to reach any place in my life as I was Gerald's cottage that night.' And in a letter to Mary Hutchinson, Lytton gave his comments on their adventure. 'Such a journey from Granada as you

never saw, taking three days, beginning with a frantic motor-
bus (the roads, ma chère, the roads!) and ending with a complete day on mule-back (Carrington on a donkey) winding up
and up by the bed of a river, crossing and re-crossing, the
water up to our beasts' bellies – oh it was a scene! – the sun
scorching, the wind whistling, the rain drenching, at last the
night coming on – Lady Hester wasn't in it: the emotional
crises, too, of the strangest sort – until we arrived in pitch
darkness and almost dead at our singular destination. ...
Well, I hardly guessed that I should ever live to be led to such
a spot by the beaux yeux of a Major!'

But once there, Lytton began to feel that the expedition had
almost, if not quite, been worthwhile. Brenan's cottage was
magnificently placed, very high up, the hills all round being
covered with fruit-trees and vegetation of every kind – olives,
oranges, figs and vines, chestnuts and bright green poplars. To
the north stood the towering snow-topped Sierra Nevada, far
away to the south could be seen the blue glimmer of the
Mediterranean, and all around were vast stretches of hill and
rock and chasm – an extraordinary variety of landscape on an
enormous scale, brilliantly coloured. 'Look at a map of Spain,
and find Granada,' he instructed Mary Hutchinson (11 April
1920). 'Thence draw a line of 40 miles in a southwesterly direction, across the Sierra Nevada, and you will arrive – here.
Yegen is a village among the mountains, high up with a view of
the Mediterranean in the distance, and all round the most
extraordinary Greco-esque formations of rocks and hills.
Never have I seen a country on so vast a scale – wild, violent,
spectacular – enormous mountains, desperate chasms –
colours everywhere of deep orange and brilliant green – a
wonderful place, but easier to get to with a finger in a map
than in reality!'

Lytton passed most of his days at Yegen recovering from
the fatiguing passage there and preparing himself for the
terrors of the return journey. 'I am treated with the utmost
consideration, of course,' he wrote, 'and I am enjoying myself
greatly, but I shan't be sorry when this section of our trip is
over, and we return to comparative civilization.' Only during

the last day, cheered presumably by the prospect of leaving, did he relax completely and become almost lively. The others, however, were in high spirits, bathing and going off for picnics. Despite the general strain of their visit and her unflagging concern for Lytton's health, Carrington was especially happy during this week. She was attracted to Brenan and found him an enchanting companion.[33] 'He is such a charming person,' she wrote to Noel, 'very like Teddy in his good humour and charm. But oh so vague about distances, and any idea about time! We spent some of the best days there with him that I've ever spent in Spain.'

Soon they were on their way again, this time by another route, 'beginning with a mule journey', Lytton wrote to his mother, 'then going in a delightful diligence by a horse and a mule, then in a motor-bus over another incredibly horrible road to Almeria, which is on the coast, and where civilization begins again'. From here they travelled on by train to Toledo, where, in hot sunshine, Holy Week was being celebrated with a glittering religious festival. By a strange coincidence, Osbert Sitwell, recently risen from his sick-bed, was also visiting Toledo with his brother Sacheverell, and caught sight of Lytton and Carrington on the opposite side of a narrow street leading up to the Plaza from the Cathedral. Between them, like a slow-moving stream, passed the procession of worshippers, and it was not until half of it had filed by that the Sitwells beheld a phenomenon which, because of its startling incongruity, impressed them as being far more remarkable than any that had so far been exhibited – 'the lean, elongated form of

33. 'Yes, we were none of us quite ourselves those few days at Yegen,' Gerald Brenan later wrote to Carrington (May 1920), '– not so gay nor so careless nor so witty as we generally count on being. Perhaps that's always the case. But you were admirable, you know, and so was Lytton ... Lytton was so cheerful over that appalling endless journey! Ralph was gloomy at first – he had reason to be – and I, whilst we were at Yegen, felt angry about something – about what I don't know, for no doubt it all came from my feeling ill and overtired. But you have seen Yegen and will come back again. That's the main thing. Chiefly for Lytton's sake – because he may not want to repeat that journey of approach, I wish you had stayed at least another week.'

Lytton Strachey, hieratic, a pagod as plainly belonging as did the effigies to a creation of its own. Well muffled, as usual, against the wind, and accompanied by his faithful friend and companion Carrington ... who, with fair hair and plump, pale face, added a more practical, but still indubitably English-esthetic note to the scene, he was regarding the various giants and giantesses with a mute and somewhat phlegmatic air of appreciation.'

Since Lytton did not at first notice his friends, partly concealed by the colourful throng jostling and scurrying between them, Osbert Sitwell was able to study him with some care, later recording his impressions in a volume of memoirs.

His head [he recalled] was crowned with a wide-brimmed brown hat. He had by nature a narrow, long-shaped face, and his narrow, rather long beard, which extended it in similar fashion and showed itself to be chestnut-coloured in the sun, exaggerated this characteristic. ... Humour and wit were very strongly marked in the quizzical expression of his face, and also, I think, a kind of genuine diffidence as well as a certain despair and, always, a new surprise at man's follies. ... His long nose, the colour of his face and beard, his rather arched angular eyebrows, and his brown eyes, the sense of a cultured, scholarly man that permeated his entire outward aspect, all these characteristics and qualities were, though highly individual, essentially English. It is important to look the part one plays, and he gave consummately the impression of a man of letters, perhaps rather of one in the immediate past than in the present; a Victorian figure of eminence, possibly. Yet ... it was an Elizabethan as well as a Victorian head that peered from aloft over the darker, more obviously excited people ... as he stood there, thinly towering, impressive undoubtedly, but with an undeniable element of the grotesque both in his physique and in his presentation of himself, it was at him one looked, and not at anybody else.

While Osbert Sitwell was forming these detailed impressions, Lytton suddenly caught sight of him and Sacheverell, and signalled to them with a look of amused and friendly recognition. At that moment, the two lines of spectators on either side of the road broke behind the procession, the Sitwells were whirled away in one direction and Lytton and Carrington were swept far out of sight in the other.

They did not meet again. Lytton's party were staying only forty-eight hours in Toledo, and the next day they had moved on to Madrid, 'which I think has little to recommend it besides the Prado', Lytton informed his mother, 'but that is a large exception'. They put up for several days here at the Hotel Terminus, 'rather a grand hotel above our means', as Carrington described it (26 April 1920), 'but its very enjoyable'. Almost every day they would visit the Prado to look at the Velasquez paintings 'and many other marvels'.

On 21 April, they left Madrid, travelling by train to Paris where they stayed at the Hôtel d'Orléans, in the rue Jacob. Only an hour after arriving there, they ran into Nick and Barbara Bagenal, and all five of them went off 'very cheerily' to Versailles, where Nick and Barbara were taking a course in French literature. 'I was most delighted with Versailles,' Carrington wrote to Noel. 'It's beauty amazed me every moment. Lytton was of course in his element. And gave us a superB History of the French Kings and their intrigues.' In the sophisticated atmosphere of Paris Lytton was at his best. The tribulations of the past weeks were quite forgotten and he became what Partridge termed 'an incalculable asset'. He took them to lunch at Foyot's, to a concert of classical quartets, to explore the bookshops, to see the pictures at the Louvre. He was animated, amusing, almost ebullient.

On the afternoon of Saturday 24, Ralph had to race back to England to see his mother, who had suddenly been taken ill. That evening Lytton wrote to him: 'My Angel, It was so miserable parting from you that I hardly knew what to do. After being with you for so long and so very very happily, it was dreadful to know that you had gone. But dearest we shall soon meet again – very soon after you get this – if not before! Paris is delightful – such a warm evening, and everything even more attractive under the night sky than the day one; but we miss you terribly – the little café where we dined again tonight seemed to have lost half its charm without the courier to order dinner and enjoy the wine with and to speculate over the whores. My dear one, I have enjoyed it all immensely, and how can I ever thank you enough for what you have done for me during these five weeks? It is indeed good to think of how many wonderful memories we have now between us — from the porpoises in the Bay of Biscay to the Fra Angelico in the Louvre!'

The following Tuesday Lytton and Carrington caught the Dieppe train, thankful to be returning at last to London and the Home Counties. They were met that same evening at the station by Ralph, and the three of them went off to have dinner together 'and to drink to the memory of the most glorious of holidays', as Lytton expressed it.

Such were the miraculous healing and inspiriting powers of love. But when, three years later, Leonard and Virginia Woolf were preparing to make a similar trip to Spain, and to visit Gerald Brenan, Lytton urgently warned them against such a plan. 'It's DEATH!' he shrilled. 'DEATH!'

8

THE END OF QUEEN VICTORIA

Shortly after their arrival back in England, the three of them went their separate ways — Ralph to row and complete his legal studies at Christ Church, Carrington into a London hospital for a minor operation on her nose, and Lytton down to the Mill House, where he was soon 'plunged in Queen Victoria'.

Since nearly all his research work had been finished before going on holiday, Lytton was to spend only a small part of the coming year in London. Whenever he did go up, he would usually stay at 41 or at 51 Gordon Square, where, late in 1928, he was given a self-contained, ground-floor flat. 'It would be hard to imagine a house more middle-class and more 19th century,' recorded the Italian critic Emilio Cecchi, who called on him there one summer evening. 'Victorian lithographs adorned the walls of the entrance hall, and the maid wore a crest of tulle; by the side of the twin pillars was to be found the classic tablet listing the various members of the family with the captions "In and Out".[34] ... Such impressions were heightened within Strachey's studio; accentuated in fact to the point where they seemed to be prompted by a certain mischievousness. ... It was as if one had stepped into a page of a Victorian novel. A Louis Philippe divan, a few books on a windowsill, a small desk, more lady-like than one would associate with an extremely successful author. Exceptionally, the desk bore a fair-sized Still Life of post-impressionist affiliation. Within the grate burned one of those ineffable anthracite fires which serve any purpose other than heating the room: one pace away you roast, at two paces your teeth chatter. The blue corkscrew candles, which stood on the marble fireplace, supported some prints which featured dandies of varying hues, beaus in their hats and patterned breeches, as well as blond beauties with wasp waists. Behind the muslin by the windows, the pale green of the trees of Gordon Square could be discerned in the setting sun.'[35]

The composition of *Queen Victoria* dominated the next eight months. Nevertheless, while Carrington was in hospital, he did allow himself several excursions away from the loneliness of Tidmarsh. One of the first was a visit to Ottoline. 'As for me, I feel slightly melancholy, quite worn out, from a long Garsington week-end,' he reported to David Garnett (26 May 1920). 'Though her ladyship was affable and there was almost enough to eat, it was none the less an exhausting business. Twice we witnessed the "eights" at Oxford (poor Partridge rows in them) – a horrid ceremony – crowds of dreadful women – mothers and sisters – veritable harpies – gloating

34. When the author visited 51 Gordon Square in 1964 this tablet was still in position, with the word 'Out' slotted against those members of the family who were dead. The house has now been taken over by London University.

35. Before 1928, whenever he stayed at 51 Gordon Square, Lytton would occupy Pernel's room on the second floor, while she was away in term-time at Newnham. Emilio Cecchi's published description of the flat at 51 Gordon Square, which Lytton moved into after his mother's death, must be read with extreme caution. According to James Strachey, it has 'every single detail incorrect, without exception'. It is also 'very silly indeed', serving only one purpose – 'to make fun of Lytton'.

over the young men's tortures, in extreme heat and extreme hideousness – so much effort wasted – so much pointless cruelty and vague stupidity everywhere.'

But if Oxford produced a lowering effect on his morale, Cambridge, where he next went as the guest of Maynard Keynes, was full of effervescence. He still believed London to be the most stimulating place in which to stay, but its enormous human mechanism, churning out a ceaseless round of work and amusement, soon palled, since it served only to repress the peacetime spirit of rejuvenescence. In the less anonymous atmosphere of Cambridge, the difference between war and peace was, almost literally, the difference between death and life. Once the war had ended, the place had gone through a transformation as sudden and complete as that of a Roman spring. All at once, after the icy season of sterility, the sap began to flow again, and the exuberance of youth burst out. It was almost incredible – to see college courts with caps and gowns in them, and swishing boats tearing after one another on academic streams. Youthfulness was infectious, and it became possible to believe once more in the New Age of Civilization.

'Life is more agreeable here than ever,' Keynes had assured him – though lamenting that 'my bed is depressingly disengaged all this month' – and he invited him over to King's, where he would meet Lord Chalmers. Lytton eagerly accepted, and during the week-end wrote off an account of his visit to amuse the convalescent Carrington. 'Lord Chalmers is a pussy-cat of an old buffer with white hair and great urbanity – a plum on a wall, very far gone – squashy, decidedly. He makes long elaborate speeches, likes dragging in the eminent dead, and when he does so usually turns to me with a slight bow and says – "a friend of Mr Strachey's" – how Pozzo can take such obvious absurdity at all seriously quite beats me. We had a most pompous dinner yesterday in Hall, with the "Combination Room" afterwards – the wine-bibbing dons assembled round a long mahogany table, and drinking port, slowly, glass after glass (not very good port, I thought). Then I went to Trinity, and talked for some hours with [F. L.] Lucas, who appeared to me decidedly fascinating – though exactly why I'm blessed if I know. The young, otherwise, seem to be rather in retirement, though Maynard promises me a luncheon with Spicer and Sebastian [W. J. H.] Sprott (he tells me a real person). ... Cambridge is certainly a cosy, sympathetic spot after the grim grandeurs of Oxford – quite middle-class, which is always such a relief – at any rate for a day or two.'

By early June, Carrington had left the hospital and withdrawn down to the Mill House, racked by headaches, and feeling very sorry for herself. Lytton also hastened back to Tidmarsh in order to take care of her – 'so far I have induced her to keep in her bed', he told Ralph. 'With rest and feeding-up (if these can only be administered!) I think she ought to be all right again before long.'

In less than a fortnight she was back to normal and, with her usual energy, looking after Lytton, who was thus free once more to concentrate fully on his writing. These were uneventful, industrious months. Ralph, in his last term at Oxford and heavily occupied with his rowing and his reading, was scarcely able to see them, and so there was nothing for it but to work. 'It seems melancholy here without you,' Lytton confessed to him (9 June 1920). 'Truth to tell, I miss you very much.' Though he sometimes complained of laziness, his correspondence this summer shows that he was hard at work on his biography, which was giving him a lot of trouble. 'Queen Victoria proceeds at a fine rate,' he had reported on 19 May. But on 26 July he appears more gloomy: 'Victoria drops a lengthening chain, damn her. It is not easy to be sprightly with such a Majesty.' And three days later, he wrote in a similar vein to Ralph: 'I lead a life of complete regularity and painful industry here – piling page upon page – well! I hope somebody some day may be amused by it, but I feel damned uncertain.' On 14 August he told Mary Hutchinson: 'Up to the end of this month I must be here, struggling with Victoria, who's proving a tougher mouthful than even I had expected. I must masticate and masticate with a steady persistence – it's the only plan.'

By the beginning of September he had had enough of it, and on reaching another convenient halting-place, decided to recruit with a round of visits to his friends. 'I got at last perfectly paralysed by Victoria,' he admitted to James (September 1920). 'My brain spun round and round, and I thought I was going to sink into imbecility. So it became necessary to have a rest.'

He hurried down to stay with the Bells at Charleston, sending Carrington, in exchange for various parcels of sugar, gingerbread and clean clothes, a long account of the domestic scene there, in particular a Bloomsbury Experiment with Time (4 September 1920). 'Typically, Maynard has insisted on ... you'd never guess what: altering the time! So that the clocks are one hour in advance even of summer-time, with curious consequences. For one thing Jessie disapproves, won't have it, and has let the kitchen clock run down, so that the servants have *no* time. Then Clive is fitful on the subject, and insists upon always referring to the normal time; and altogether the confusion is extraordinary. How mad they all are! Maynard, though he sees what a rumpus it causes, persists. Vanessa is too feeble to put him down, and Clive is too tetchy to grin and bear it. The result is extremely Tchekhof-esque. But luckily the atmosphere is entirely comic, instead of being fundamentally tragic as in Tchekhof. Everyone laughs and screams and passes on.'

From the topsy-turvy climate of Charleston, Lytton moved on to Monk's House, a cottage which Leonard and Virginia Woolf had recently taken after leaving Asheham, in the village of Rodmell, on the opposite bank of the river Ouse. Here, though the diet seemed extraordinary – jam and potatoes and bottled plums – the atmosphere was far more equable. 'This country seems to me the best in the world,' he wrote to Ralph (11 September 1920). 'I went for a perfect walk yesterday with Virginia. Oh, for a great farmhouse here, with many large panelled rooms and a walled garden, and barns, and horses for my two children, and a pianola, and multitudes of books, and a cellar of wine, and ... but my imagination runs away with me. Well! Some day it may occur!'

After a week at Monk's House, he travelled on to Jack and Mary Hutchinson's home in West Wittering. 'The house is minute,' he informed Ralph (16 September 1920), 'with two children at the noisiest age ramping over it, and the tête-à-tête with Mary Hutch grows difficult as time goes on. The complete absence of sex-instinct is such a bore, unless there's a great deal of intellect to make up. When there's a slight flirtation – even an infinitesimally slight one, it makes such a difference!'

His autumn peregrination over, Lytton flew back at the end of the month to Tidmarsh to be confronted once more by *Queen Victoria*. 'Here I sit,' he wrote to Mary Hutchinson (4 October 1920), 'over the fire, trying to nerve myself for the coup de grâce on Victoria: but I hesitate ... she quells me with her fishy eye.' He hoped to finish the book before Christmas, and longed to be free of it; but his hopes seemed doomed, the captivity endured, and on 11 November he admitted to Keynes: 'It seems to me still rather doubtful whether I shall kill Victoria or Victoria me.' The captivity, however, had its compensations. He was sending each chapter on to Ralph Partridge, who would type it out and correct the spelling. From one of his letters to Ralph (23 November 1920) it appears that he had to alter his description of the Prince Consort's death, and that this delayed him more than he had estimated. Meanwhile, he told Middleton Murry (22 September 1920), 'I live the life of one submerged beneath horsehair sofas and collapsed crinolines.' On 6 December, Geoffrey Whitworth of Chatto and Windus came down to Tidmarsh so that together they might plot and plan the book's publication. Lytton promised that his typescript would be completed early in the New Year, ready for Chatto's Spring List. He gauged the length to be around ninety thousand words – ten thousand words shorter than he had originally intended.[36]

Arrangements for the American edition of *Queen Victoria* were more complicated and, in the long run, less satisfactory.

36. Since Lytton's original estimate of one hundred thousand words held good until the early autumn of 1920, it seems likely that he had meant to deal with Victoria's old age at greater length, deciding on a more cursory treatment only while he was actually at work on the ninth chapter.

Keynes, whose *The Economic Consequences of the Peace* had been recently brought out by Harcourt Brace, had persuaded Lytton to relinquish his own firm. On his advice, Lytton wrote to G. P. Putnam's, who had brought out *Eminent Victorians*, politely notifying them that they would not be handling his next book — a decision which gave rise to some consternation. At the same time Keynes opened up negotiations with Harcourt, Brace, and after some exchanges of letters and telegrams, reported back to Lytton that he had secured an outright offer for the American rights amounting to seven thousand dollars — slightly over two thousand pounds — which could be safely invested to bring in something between one hundred and fifty and two hundred pounds a year for life. 'I hardly know what to advise,' he added (30 November 1920). 'But for you there seems a good deal of virtue in certainty. You would still have the whole of the English rights intact to gamble with. What shall I cable back?'

Lytton was rather doubtful whether this sum was really enough, especially since it was to include serial rights for a number of extracts in the *New Republic*.[37] Already from

37. On 27 January 1921, Lytton wrote to his brother James in Vienna: 'My state has been appalling – given over to Victoria for weeks and weeks without cessation – a fearful struggle, its horrors being increased by the "relaxing" conditions at Tidmarsh – however it's now done – typed – and actually handed over to Chatto's. The relief is enormous; but the worst of it is that various crises are still pending. The American question is acute and complicated. Maynard has been acting as an intermediary with Harcourt, his American publisher, who, after some havering, offered 10,000 dollars for all the American rights complete. At that time this was worth nearly £3000 – and I thought it would do, and accepted. But since then the wretched dollar has sunk, so that it's now worth only about £2660. But still the contract has not been fixed. There are also various difficulties about the serialisations – in England and America and their dates. The Times (also via Pozzo) is being negotiated with, but nothing has been settled yet. In the meantime, Chatto has payed me £750, as advance royalties, payable in receipt of the MS. The arrangement is that I gets 20% on the first 5000 copies, and 25% after that – viz. on the selling price of the book, which will probably be 15/–. So that the advance royalties covers the first 5000 copies. If I get £700 for the serial rights – which is conceivable – I may net something between 4 and 5,000 – which doesn't seem so bad – though I still shiver in my shoes over the

Putnam's he had received, on a 20 per cent royalty basis, over seven hundred pounds from the immediate sales of *Eminent Victorians* – and here there had been no question of a serial. On the other hand he was impressed by what Keynes had said about the advantage of certainty on an outright sale, and so he asked his friend to demand on his behalf the sum of ten thousand dollars for all rights, or up to five thousand dollars excluding serial rights. Harcourt, Brace cabled back that they were willing to make the ten-thousand-dollar payment, providing they were given the Canadian rights of the biography. Since Chatto and Windus generously agreed to this, the contract was then signed. And so, to everyone's satisfaction, was concluded a deal that over the years deprived Lytton and his literary executor of many thousands of pounds.

On 24 January, Lytton wrote to Geoffrey Whitworth telling him that the book was almost finished. There remained one more task, and that was rather peculiar. It consisted in fitting in the final paragraph, the famous death-bed scene of the queen, which was the very first paragraph he had written and towards which the rest of the book had been subtly manipulated.

Now at last he was a free man, and could roam the streets of London again. On 25 January, he came up to 51 Gordon Square, where he was to spend most of the next three months, 'leading a life of idleness and proof-reading'. His other reading included two books recently produced by his friends – Leonard Woolf's *Empire and Commerce in Africa* which he

American question which continues to hang in the wind. I suppose I shall have to invest it – which seems rather dull – and I daresay the best thing would be to buzz it all straight off. I wish to goodness you had been here to assist me in these terrific transactions. And as for the proof correcting, I shudder to think of it. C & W. say they'll have it out on April 7th. As for the work itself, I hope it's readable, and that it steers the correct course between discretion and indiscretion. I feel rather doubtful as to whether the presentment of her Majesty forms a consistent whole: the tone seems to shift so wildly – from tragedy to farce, from sentiment to cynicism: but let's hope it all forms up. It's almost impossible for me at the present moment to get an impartial view of it. The strain of such a long continuity has been extreme. I don't feel as if I should ever be able to face such a bulky affair again.'

thought 'terrific'; and the *Oedipus Tyrannus* of Sophocles translated and expounded by Sheppard.[38] He did no work, bringing out between August 1919 and May 1923 only one essay – a very indifferent piece on Disraeli, which appeared in *Woman's Leader*. 'All is well,' he assured Carrington (24 February 1921), 'and the weather so marvellous that anything but idleness seems out of place.' He had been asked by the *Nation* to review Margot Asquith's autobiography, but he so disliked it that he considered it prudent to refuse. A more fascinating volume, which had been sent to him by Hesketh Pearson, was Frank Harris's notorious Life of Oscar Wilde. 'It has a fair amount of rather new information,' he wrote to James (November 1920), 'though of course, it's not nearly detailed enough, and it isn't really *very* well done. However the story is a most remarkable one. The admirer is called Mr Hesketh Pearson, and is apparently some sort of agent for Frank Harris in England. He sent me the book in order, as he said, to find out what the greatest English biographer thought of the greatest American one – a slightly double-edged compliment, I fear. But *is* F.H. American? Or what?' Pearson's letter, partly written in parody of Lytton's dramatic prose style, had declared that there was 'no dark and sinister motive' behind his action – an assurance which only served to alarm Lytton. 'I'm rather afraid he [Pearson] may want me to write some wretched review or puff,' he complained to Carrington (3 November 1920), 'so I shall tell him that I can't do that, but otherwise will graciously accept the book.'

Released from his long imprisonment at Tidmarsh, he now set his face towards a life of easy entertainment. He went down to Cambridge, met the new embryos and Apostles, and read a paper to the Heretics. Occasionally, too, he would

38. 'I am reading the Oedipus Tyrannus in a new edition that Sheppard has just brought out, with a translation (which is what I read – with an occasional puzzled glance at the other side of the page) and an elaborate and rather interesting commentary,' Lytton wrote to Ralph Partridge. 'In the entire list of the world's masterpieces, my fancy is to place it second, though I wish I could understand the Greek better than I do – and when I think of all the hours and years I spent learning the paradigms of the irregular verbs, and construing Thucydides!'

return to the Mill House for a week-end, bringing with him
one or two of these new undergraduate friends — Sebastian
Sprott, F. L. Lucas, James H. Doggart — or some of his older
associates — Roger Fry, Desmond MacCarthy, David Garnett.
One of his pleasantest encounters over these months was with
Max Beerbohm, who, the previous June, had sent him a letter
executed after his most polished and whimsical manner —
'rather amusing and very elaborate', Lytton commented, 'but
how to answer it, Christ alone knows. Of course completely
for publication.[39] All very nice, in its way, when done by

39. In which case it had better be published here. 'Dear Lytton Strachey, Some time in 1913, at this address, my wife and I acquired a young
fox-terrier. We debated as to what to call him, and, as Henry James had
just been having his 70th birthday, and as his books had given me more
pleasure than those of any living man, I, rather priggishly perhaps, insisted that the dog should be known as James. But this was a name which
Italian peasants, who are the only neighbours we have, of course would
not be able to pronounce at all. So we were phonetic and called the name
of the dog *Yah-mès*. And this did very well. By this name he was known
far and wide — but not for long; for alas, he died of distemper. Now that
we are re-established here, we haven't another dog; dogs aren't so necessary to one as they seem to be in England, and they have an odd and
tactless way of making one feel that one *is* in England — perhaps because
they don't gesticulate and don't speak one word of Italian and seem to
expect to find rabbits among the olive-groves and to have bones of Welsh
mutton thrown to them from the luncheon table. But the other day we
were given a small kitten — charming in itself and somehow not distinctive of local colour. The old question arose: what shall we call it? Again
I laid myself open to the charge of priggishness, perhaps. And again you
will perhaps think I have taken a liberty. But — well, there it is: no book
by a living man has given me so much pleasure — so much lasting pleasure
in dipping and re-reading since I wrote to you — as your "Eminent Victorians". And the name of that kitten is, and the name of that cat will be:
Stré-chi (or rather Stré-cci). I do hope you don't mind. I am sure you
would be amused if you heard the passing-by peasants enticing it by your
hardly recognisable name. We will re-christen it if you like.'
    This letter was written from Villino Chiaro on 7 July 1920. Lytton, in
his reply, expressed his sense of honour at this appellation, and two years
later, in June 1922, Max took up the sequel to this story in another letter.
'The kitten of whom I told you last year is now a confirmed cat. He is
much larger than he seemed likely to become, and is vigorous and
vagrant, but not, I am sorry to say, either affectionate or intelligent. It is
not known that he ever caught a mouse; he dislikes rain, but has no

somebody else, but a bore, a dreadful bore, when one has to sit down oneself in cold blood, and compose.' Early in the spring, Max came to London to arrange for an exhibition of his drawings, and he asked Lytton whether he 'might professionally stare at him'. A few days later Lytton called round to see him at the Charing Cross Hotel. 'He rang me to ask me to go and see him, explaining that he drew a caricature of me, and wished to "verify his impressions" ', Lytton afterwards wrote to James (14 April 1921). 'I went yesterday, and found him, very plump and whitehaired, drawn up to receive me. "Let us come out on to the balcony, where we shall have a view of the doomed city." He begged me to turn my profile towards him, and for a minute or two made some notes on the back of an envelope. He was infinitely polite and elaborate, and quite remote, so far as I could see, from humanity in all its forms. His caricatures are to be exhibited in three weeks – "if England still exists".'

Max felt for Lytton a special sense of affinity that, in certain details, falsified his likeness. Though they were never very close friends, Max looked on him almost as a younger brother. For in an age that was busy vulgarizing art, Lytton's good taste had remained uncontaminated. Max felt that he was to Lytton what Oscar Wilde had been to him. 'You are wonderful,' he had written to him after the publication of *Eminent Victorians* (28 July 1918). He saw Lytton not as a modern figure, but as a modified edition of himself, someone who had made further advances in the fastidious and refined craft of letters. 'He was no longer velveteen-jacketed,' Max noted with surprise when Lytton arrived at his hotel. 'He was dressed now in a worldlier manner, which, I told him, seemed to me less characteristic, and he willingly agreed that he should remain velveteen-jacketed in my drawing.' What Max,

---

knowledge of how to avoid it if it falls; and if one caresses him he is very likely to scratch one. He is, however, very proud of his name, and sends his respectful regards to his Illustrissimo Eponymisto Inglese.'

In the course of this same letter Max refers to Lytton's essay 'Voltaire and Frederick the Great' as an 'abiding masterpiece', and adds: 'So is "Madame du Deffand".'

with his static and mannered ways, could not see was that Lytton had moved largely in step with the times. He was more eagerly up to date than Max allowed for or depicted in his caricatures. For Max himself, the earthquake of the war had opened up an abyss beneath his feet, cracking apart the formalized world of his youth. His pleasures – like Lytton's – were mainly those of travel and society. But during the last forty years of his life, spent in monotonous retirement at Rapallo, he severely curtailed both these cultivated pastimes. For Lytton, on the other hand, London and the Continent had ceased to exist as places of entertainment only in the war years themselves. Now that peace was restored and he had money of his own to spend for the first time, he was able to indulge more fully these favourite recreations, emerging from his Home Counties hibernation, travelling and entering society as never before. The disorganized post-war world, which so horrified Max, enlivened him and at times even tempted him into believing that an age of peace and prosperity lay before mankind. The carnage, the philistinism, the reign of terror, stupidity and press dictatorship were over. Civilized people could again lead civilized lives, and meet civilized people in other countries. A few weeks after the publication of *Queen Victoria*, and a year since his energetic expedition to Spain, Lytton set off with Pippa from England to stay with the Berensons in Florence. A month of pleasurable relaxation and amusement lay ahead of him.

But, behind him, he had left a simmering volcano.

9

MOONS AND HONEYMOONS

During the closing months of 1920, while Lytton was putting the finishing touches to *Queen Victoria*, the emotional *sonate à trois* that was being played between Ralph, Carrington and himself, had slowly spiralled to a *sforzando*. Ralph, having come down from Oxford and failed to obtain a post as assistant to G. D. H. Cole, the Fabian economist, had been engaged by Leonard Woolf to act as his secretary and compositor in the Hogarth Press. Minutely remunerated, such a job seemed hardly suitable for the burly ex-major – 'I don't see Partridge setting up the type,' Lytton commented – but Ralph himself seemed well content. This job took him a step nearer marrying Carrington – indeed, he could see no reasonable obstacle to their immediate marriage. No obstacle, that was, except Carrington herself. For she still obstinately resisted his proposals, partly because, with her feminist ideals, she rejected conventional marriage, and partly because she felt that Ralph, for all his affection for Lytton and his hastily assimilated education, did not really belong to her world. Few of her artistic friends and few of Lytton's at first liked him, though many came to do so later. Bloomsbury had been particularly sceptical about his role in the Tidmarsh regime, and resented his intrusions into Gordon Square. But despite all her opposition, Ralph was amazingly persistent, and Carrington began to fear that her own stubbornness might soon alienate Lytton, ruining their life at Pangbourne together, which she loved so much. He had said nothing, of course. She would not expect him to. But she sensed his growing disapproval of their fractious relations. As Ralph's exasperation mounted, so, in proportion, did her own anxiety.

'Lytton dear, do you know what comfort you are to me,' she wrote to him while he was staying down at Charleston that autumn. 'I feel as long as you live on this earth I can never mind anything.' Diagnosing at once the cause of her distress, Lytton answered with all his customary tenderness and concern, seeking to allay her fears. 'My dearest, I am sure that all is really well between us, which is the great thing. Some devil of embarrassment chokes me sometimes, and prevents my expressing what I feel. You have made me so happy during the last 3 years, and you have created Tidmarsh as no one else could have, and I seem hardly to have said thank you. But you must believe that I value you and your love more than I can ever say.'

Yet even now Carrington was not altogether reassured. If Ralph, becoming fed up with her uncompromising refusals, were to leave, then Lytton too, she suspected, might go. Either that, or, if his unfailing courtesy and sense of pity held him back, then he would certainly feel an involuntary resentment against her for driving away the man he loved. She therefore proposed a compromise. She would live with Ralph, on a more or less experimental basis, until Christmas. Since he had already begun working in London, this meant that the two of them must put up during the week-days at 41 Gordon Square[40] – a few yards from the Stracheys' house – going down together to Tidmarsh for week-ends. Though no one could tell at first what precisely this temporary plan would involve, all parties seemed reasonably well satisfied – in spite of the very considerable emotional complications. At least, for the time being, the worst crisis had, to everyone's relief, been postponed. 'On Fridays Carrington and the Major appear, departing again on Monday,' Lytton explained for the benefit of James (November 1920). 'How long the arrangement will last I haven't an idea. I rather fear that she may find it doesn't suit her – that the ménage at Gordon Square is too purely domestic – but I don't know. If it breaks up – but perhaps it's not much use in anticipating.' To prevent it breaking up he again tried to reassure Carrington: 'It seems to me that your trying the G. Square experiment is probably right,' he told her. 'But whatever happens you must rely on my affection.'

Nevertheless, Lytton did not believe that this emergency compact could succeed for very long. What would take its place, he had no idea – whether everything would collapse in ruins, or a new regime would arise, phoenix-like, from among the debris. Already, by the New Year, Carrington was feeling acutely miserable, shut in by the buildings of Bloomsbury, missing Lytton every day she was apart from him, longing for the open breathing country again, yet trying not to reveal her wretchedness to Ralph. But she was never adept at concealing her emotions. Ralph, well aware of her unhappiness, soon grew dissatisfied himself at their arrangement, and began urging her once more to marry him. Even though they were

40. They took over the flat previously occupied by James and Alix Strachey, who that June had left for Vienna.

living together all the time now as man and wife, he still felt
tantalized by her untouchable, uncontrollable passions, and
convinced that only official wedlock could put an end to his
torture. Marriage, he argued, would make no outward
difference to *her* life – indeed, in some respects, such as travelling abroad with him, it would make things easier for her. But
still she resisted. She was unwilling to change a proven
beneficial state of life for another unknown one. What were
the trivial difficulties of travelling abroad once a year to the
permanent, inescapable ones of being attached to a brood of
Partridges, with a mother and a father bird, for ever chirping
at one? 'Oh dearie dearie I wish one never grew up,' she complained to Noel (11 May 1921), 'or else One could live in A
land where conventions, and parents n'est existe pas.'

By May, they appeared to have reached a deadlock. The
strain between them was very great. Then, suddenly infuriated
beyond endurance by her childish evasions, Ralph threatened
that if he did not marry her he would go off to Bolivia and
become a sheep farmer. Was he bluffing, or had the moment of
decision finally arrived? Carrington could not tell. He
sounded serious, desperately serious. She did not know
whether to laugh or cry. She did not know *what* to do.

It was just as the state of affairs had come to this explosive
point, that Lytton chose to remove himself to Italy. He had
punctiliously refrained from interfering in their drama, though
its outcome would affect him profoundly, and now, by the
same token, his letters to Carrington scrupulously omitted
any reference to her drastic predicament with Ralph. Instead
he wrote of visiting the Sitwells at Montegufoni, 'a truly outstanding place'; of Geoffrey Scott at the Villa Medici,[41] a

41. Immediately before the war Geoffrey Scott had been looking after
the decorations and furniture of various new rooms at I Tatti, where he
encountered and fell in love with Nicky Mariano, later Berenson's li-
brarian and companion. Mary Berenson had planned that the two of them
should marry, live together near by and act as her husband's helpers and
advisers, but during the war Geoffrey Scott had married Lady Sybil Cutting (who later became the wife of Percy Lubbock). During his stay at I
Tatti, Lytton saw something of Nicky Mariano, who remembers that Berenson urged him to take up Pius IX as his next subject, a suggestion by

superb eighteenth-century villa higher up in the hills; of Goldie Dickinson and Harry Norton whom he also saw. But chiefly his correspondence was taken up with descriptions of his host, Bernard Berenson, and his famous villa at Settignano, I Tatti. 'The house is just what I imagined – large – full of beautiful objects one can hardly look at, and comfort that somehow is really far less comfortable than Tidmarsh. A sister of Berenson's and her husband (poor American creatures) Lord and Lady Berwick, and some female secretaries (I gather) make up the party so far. His Lordship looks like an imbecile butler, and I should think was one. Lady B. is a sad pseudo-beauty. . . . There is a distinct air of civil war about, which is slightly unpleasant. Otherwise everything seems perfect.'

In another letter, a few days later, he writes: 'B.B. is a very interesting phenomenon. The mere fact that he has accumulated this wealth from having been a New York gutter-snipe is sufficiently astonishing; but besides that he has a most curious complicated temperament – very sensitive, very clever – even, I believe, with a strain of niceness somewhere or other, but desperately wrong – perhaps suffering from some dreadful complexes – and without a spark of naturalness or ordinary human enjoyment. And this has spread itself over the house, which is really remarkably depressing . . . one is struck chill by the atmosphere of a crypt. Oooh! – And so much of it, too – such a large corpse–so many long dead corridors, so many dead primitives, so many dead pieces of furniture, and flowers, and servants, such multitudes of dead books; and then, outside, a dead garden, with a dead view of a dead Tuscan landscape . . .'

Back in England, the volcano had meanwhile started to erupt. Ralph's nerve had been the first to crack. Shortly after

---

which he seemed to be tempted. 'I was by that time familiar enough with the intricacies of the English language to catch and appreciate the witty squeaks that interrupted Lytton Strachey's silences,' she records. 'One evening we had him to dinner at the Villino [Corbignano] and there in a small circle and feeling perhaps no necessity to be on his guard he talked freely and charmingly. His inquiries about our experiences at the end of the war were so full of delicate understanding that I wondered whether he had not more heart than his usual manner would have led one to suppose.'

Lytton left for Florence, he suffered some sort of breakdown, threw himself at the feet of Leonard and Virginia Woolf and poured out his long accumulation of grievances. They advised him to marry Carrington at once, or to put his threat into execution by leaving her and Lytton altogether. Virginia, with her love of stirring up trouble, and knowing only too well that everything she said would be remembered and repeated, interposed a few poisonous comments of her own. Lytton had told her, she said, that he did not intend to go down to Tidmarsh very much after he returned from Italy. He was nervous, she explained, that Carrington would feel some sort of claim on him if he continued living in the same house with her too long. It was a wonder to everyone, she added, how Lytton had put up with her even for three years. What on earth did they find to do when they were alone together? Possibly Ralph would be best out of it. Life in Bolivia was said to be very bracing.

Carrington, by this time, had returned to the Mill House, having been commissioned to paint the signboards of some public houses in Reading, where she would spend the days working.[42] It was here, after his discussion with the Woolfs, that Ralph now caught up with her. They met in a small workmen's café. The terrible deterioration in Ralph's appearance appalled Carrington. His mouth twitched; he looked dreadfully tired and ill, and seemed to have gone completely to pieces. Seeing him in this wretched state of mind, she felt fonder of him than ever she had done in his more swaggering, self-assertive moods. Their unhappiness and confusion intermingled, and they were closer to each other than at any other moment. But Carrington felt guilty too. As with Gertler, she was the culprit. It was her selfishness that had so upset him, had caused him such anguish.

Speaking in a flat, unnatural voice, without excitement,

42. 'What good news of the Greyhound!' Lytton wrote to her (6 July 1921). 'It will be splendid if you become Sign Painter in Ordinary to the Counties of Berks, Wilts and Hants! I am longing to see it in position.' She painted several other signboards in the neighbourhood, including that of John Fothergill's inn, the Spread Eagle at Thame.

Ralph began by saying that he knew she was not in love with him, but he thought that her affections were nevertheless strong enough to make him happy. He could not go on any longer in the same uncertainty and pain. He would definitely leave the country if she would not marry him. He then repeated to her all that Virginia had told him. The effect of this on Carrington was like an electric shock. She had realized, of course, that Lytton was frightened of her becoming dependent on him, of her becoming, as she put it, 'a permanent limpet'. And she had known too, all along, that she had nothing to hope from him, that marriage between them was out of the question. But Virginia's spiteful half-truths altered her way of looking at their relationship. Always, in future, she would feel a terror of being physically on Lytton's nerves, of revolting him. Therefore she decided, chiefly for Lytton's peace of mind, but also for Ralph's happiness, that she would have to surrender. That afternoon in the café she told Ralph that she would marry him. Even now, though, she shrank from the ultimate renunciation of her principles, hoping that, having agreed in theory to become Ralph's wife, she might somehow or other indefinitely defer putting it into practice.

So, the final scene of their dramatic tragi-comedy was played out. Both of them were utterly exhausted, Ralph elated, Carrington soberly resigned, as they drove back that night to Tidmarsh. The next morning, Carrington sent off a long letter to Lytton, telling him everything that had happened. It was one of her most abandoned pieces of writing, a poignant and terrible document.

All along I have known that my life with you was limited. I could never hope for it to become permanent. After all Lytton, you are the only person who I have ever had an all absorbing passion for. I shall never have another. I couldn't now – I had one of the most self abasing loves that a person can have. You could throw me into transports of happiness and dash me into deluges of tears and despair, all by a few words. But these aren't reproaches . . . Of course these years of Tidmarsh when we were quite alone will always be the happiest I ever spent. And I've such a store of good things which I've saved up, that I feel I could never be lonely again now. Still its

818

too much of a strain to be quite alone here waiting to see you or
craning my nose and eyes out of the top window of 41 G.S. to see if
you are coming down the street, when I know we'll be better friends,
if you aren't haunted by the idea that I am sitting depressed in
some corner of the world waiting for your footstep . . .

I saw the relief you felt at Ralph taking me away, so to speak, off
your hands.

I think he'll make me happier, than I should be entirely by myself
— and it certainly prevents me becoming morbid about you. And as
Ralph said last night you'll never leave us. Because in spite of our
dullness nobody else loves you nearly as much as we do.

So in the café in that vile city of Reading, I said I'd marry him. . . .
After all I don't believe it will make much difference and to see him.
so happy is A rather definite thing. I'd probably never marry
anyone else, and I doubt if a kinder creature exists on this earTH . . .

I cried last night Lytton, whilst he slept by my side sleeping happily — I cried to think of a savage cynical faTe which had made it
impossible for my love ever to be used by you. You never knew, or
never will know the very big and devastating love I had for you. How
I adored every hair, every curl on your beard. How I devoured you
whilst you read to me at night. How I loved the smell of your face
in your sponge. Then the ivory skin on your hands, your voice, and
your hat when I saw it coming along the top of the garden wall from
my window. Say you will remember it. That it wasnt all loST. and
that you'll forgive me for this outburst, and always be my friend. . . .
Ralph is suCH a dear, I don't feel I'll ever regret marrying him.
"Though I never will change my maiden name that I have kept so
long," — so you mayn't ever call me anything but Carrington . . .

You gave me a much longer life than I ever deserved or hoped for
and I love you for it terribly. I only cried last night at realizing I
never could have my Moon — that sometimes I must pain you and
often bore you. You who I would have given the world to have made
happier than any person could be, to give you all you wanted . . .

I see I've told you very little of what I feel. But I keep on crying,
if I stop and think about you. Outside the sun is Baking and they all
chatter and laugh. It's cynical, this world in its opposites. Once you
said to me, that Wednesday afternoon in the sitting Room, you loved
me as a Friend. Could you Tell it to me again?

The pathos of this extraordinary letter moved Lytton very
deeply. It reached him in Florence on 20 May, and he wrote
back immediately the same day so that Carrington's agony of

mind should not be prolonged. He told her that Virginia, with characteristic neurotic malevolence, had lied about his feelings and intentions; that he thought her marriage to Ralph would be best for all of them. And he told her other things that made her as happy and grateful to him as the circumstances allowed. He came as near, in his reply, as his peculiar nature permitted to overcoming that 'devil of embarrassment' that choked the free expression of his feelings. All the pathos and tenderness of their relationship is conveyed in these two letters.

But I hope that in any case you never doubted my love for you [he wrote]. Do you know how difficult I find it to express my feelings either in letters or talk? It is sometimes terrible – and I don't understand why it should be so; and sometimes it seems to me that you underrate what I feel. You realise that I have varying moods, but my fundamental feelings you perhaps don't realise so well. Probably it is my fault. It is perhaps much easier to show one's peevishness than one's affection and admiration! Oh my dear, do you really want me to tell you that I "love you as a friend"? – But of course that is absurd, and you *do* know very well that I love you as something more than a friend, you angelic creature, whose goodness to me has made me happy for years, and whose presence in my life has been, and always will be, one of the most important things in it. Your letter made me cry, I feel a poor old miserable creature, and I may have brought more unhappiness to you than anything else. I only pray that it is not so, and that my love for you, even though it is not what you desire, may yet make our relationship a blessing to you – as it has been to me.

Remember that I too have never had my moon! We are all helpless in these things – dreadfully helpless. I am lonely and I am all too truly growing old, and if there was a chance that your decision meant that I should somehow or other lose you, I don't think I could bear it. You and Ralph and our life at Tidmarsh are what I care for most in the world – almost (apart from my work and some few people) the *only* things I care for . . .

. . . you seemed in your letter to suggest that my love for you has diminished as time has gone on: that is not so. I am sure it has increased. It is true that the first excitement, which I always (and I suppose most people) have at the beginning of an affair, has gone off; but something much deeper has grown up instead.

Carrington and Ralph were married on 21 May, at the registry office in St Pancras. Carrington described herself in the register book as an Artist (Painter) of Tidmarsh Mill House, Pangbourne; Ralph as a Private Secretary, living at 41 Gordon Square. The witnesses were Lytton's sister Marjorie, and a young friend, Alan MacIver. That evening the two of them left for Paris, journeying on the next day to Venice where they spent their honeymoon, and where, for an 'enchanting week',[43] they were joined by Lytton and Pippa. Early in June they all returned to England.[44]

To Lytton's mind, everything had turned out unexpectedly well. He himself was delighted with the new system, which seemed to promise just that mixture of emotional security and independence that best fitted him. Ralph too seemed quite content, and so even did Carrington. 'Rex is happy,' she told her brother Noel, 'and that is the main thing.' Her psychological reactions, however, were more complicated than she yet knew, and because she had greatly valued her liberty, she bore Ralph a secret resentment for its loss.

But, for the moment, the sun shone; and there was no trace of the storm-clouds already massing beyond the horizon.

43. 'I enjoyed Venice enormously,' Lytton wrote to Ottoline (29 June 1921). 'I think you once told me it was the perfect place, and I quite agree with you. I had no idea it was so splendid and enchanting, and I can hardly bear the thought that it is still going on in all its fascination and that I am not in the middle of it. I want to rush back to the Piazza without the delay of a moment. I want to sink into a Gondola and have myself wafted to St George. Oh dear! The beauties – of all kinds! Why did I ever leave there?'

44. It seems likely that on his return journey Lytton, finding new company, made an excursion from Milan. In a letter to the author (3 February 1968) Mr Cecil Roberts, the novelist, recalled seeing 'two most extraordinary creatures' board a steamer on Lake Como in June 1921: 'One was tall, attenuated, with a long reddish beard, about forty, dressed in a loose shirt, and trousers, carrying a small knapsack with a panama. His companion was a youth of about twenty. His shirt was open to the navel, he wore tight white trousers and sandals on bare feet. He rolled his eyes and was quite flirtatious towards the elder, who addressed him in a squeaky voice.' In Nottingham in October 1926, when Mr Roberts was having tea with Sebastian Sprott, a bearded man, whom he positively identified as the elder of the companions on the lake steamer, entered the room. Mr Roberts was astonished to learn that this was 'the celebrated Lytton Strachey'.

FIFTEEN

Eminent Edwardian

'The agitations are of course terrific. Do you think there is no enD to love affaires. and one can never say "c'est fini"?' *Carrington to Alix Strachey* (11 May 1925)

'The world grows odder and odder. I perceive that we must resign ourselves to life in a lunatic asylum.' *Lytton Strachey to Katherine Mansfield* (3 October 1919)

1
KISSING AND FISHING

THE wedding of Carrington and Ralph had been alarming for the first moment or two, and on general principles, Lytton objected to marriage. One saw such terrible examples of decent people caught like flies in the web of matrimony; one had experienced the horror that existed in most family life, and witnessed the persecution, cruelty and stupidity of that unreasonable institution. Was it surprising, then, if one disapproved of the whole paraphernalia? Besides, an artist, or any person with serious ambition, had to place his freedom and his art above everything else. Yet perhaps one ought not to hold such principles unless they could be scrapped when occasion demanded. People who did marry but who still remained individuals and did not quarrel among themselves, Lytton admired. In any case, this particular marriage, he now felt certain, would make little perceptible difference to their troika. Both husband and wife appeared perfectly satisfied, and the households at Tidmarsh and Gordon Square went on as of old. 'Private life continues to flow on very smoothly,' he assured James. 'The curious ménage or ménages work, I think, quite well. Ralph is really a charming creature, and seems quite content, and Carrington appears to be happy.'

Uncommitted to any serious literary composition, Lytton was free to make regular forays into London society, obediently reporting back to his 'Angel Guardian' any item, however disappointing to himself, that might amuse her. 'Last night [28 June 1921] the Sitwell dinner was dreadfully dull, and they took me off afterwards to an incredibly fearful function in Arnold Bennett's establishment. *He* was not there, but *she* was – oh my eye, what a woman! It was apparently some sort of Poetry Society. There was an address (very poor) on Rimbaud etc. by an imbecile Frog; then Edith Sitwell appeared, her nose longer than an ant-eater's, and read some of her absurd stuff; then Eliot – very sad and seedy – it made one weep; finally Mrs Arnold Bennett recited, with waving arms and chanting voice, Baudelaire and Verlaine till everyone was ready to vomit. As a study in half-witted horror the whole thing was most interesting. The rooms were peculiarly disgusting, and the company very miscellaneous. ... Why, oh why, does Eliot have any truck with such coagulations? I fear it indicates that there's something seriously wrong with him.'

But already, quite unknown to Lytton, the ground had been secretly prepared for every kind of ramification and intrigue. Over a year ago, when the three of them had gone out to Yegen, the first seeds of these impending complications had been planted. Although much taken up with Lytton's health at the time, and with the general strain of the visit, Carrington had felt greatly attracted to the village, the small house and its owner. Brenan, she reasoned, was a creature like herself – lawless, artistic and romantically cast adrift from the workaday world. He reminded her of her sailor-brother Teddy, and, according to David Garnett, she also spoke of him as a modern version of Trelawny's self-portrait in *The Adventures of a Younger Son*.[1] As soon as she returned to Tidmarsh, she had

---

1. See David Garnett's *The Flowers of the Forest*, p. 242. But Brenan, in a letter to the author, comments: 'Carrington's comparison of me to Trelawny is meaningless because I am totally unlike him. ... if she really said this it can only have been because she knew nothing about Trelawny but his name.'

begun writing to Brenan regularly. 'On rereading these letters today,' Brenan told the author. 'I can see that she was making up to me. There were suggestions that if her life at Pangbourne broke down she would come out and join me. But I did not take this in then, partly because I was very innocent and partly because the problems of my own life were so great that I did not want to be tied up with a girl.' Yet even at this stage he certainly felt drawn to Carrington. When she had married Ralph, he wrote to congratulate her, but added half humorously: 'I am sorry for my own sake, because have love affairs I simply must, and whom shall I ever find as charming as you?'

It was not until June 1921 that Brenan fully enters into the story, when his great-aunt, having adopted him as her heir, provided a little money for him to visit England. From his parents' house he bicycled over to the White Horse at Uffington, for a picnic with Carrington. Ralph was unable to join them because of his work at the Hogarth Press, and Lytton, who distrusted picnics, also stayed in London. Carrington and Gerald were therefore alone. It was possible that day to taste the full flavour of an English summer. The sun burnt the grass, made the air tremble around them, and sucked up the juices of the trees. Not a leaf moved, and everywhere above them the sky was a motionless dull purple. They laid out and ate their picnic on the pale crumbling slope of a hill, near a solitary haystack and a little misty wood. 'We talked and suddenly she put her arms round me and kissed me. I let her, but afterwards felt angry because I was Ralph's friend and because she meant nothing to me . . .' The following week-end Gerald went to stay at Tidmarsh. He was determined that nothing more should come of this strange episode. 'Then as I sat in an armchair I saw her move across the window with the evening light behind her, and I knew I was in love. It was like the first attack of flu to a Pacific Islander – I was completely, totally under from the first moment. I had fallen for her in the same way in which she had fallen for Lytton, and just as violently. And she was in love with me.'

Of these sudden developments Ralph Partridge suspected absolutely nothing. He had welcomed his friend's arrival in

England with the greatest amusement and delight. 'He [Brenan] is the apotheosis of vagueness in man,' he reported to Noel Carrington (17 July 1921). 'He eats, moves and sleeps, entirely unaware of the natural laws which govern these processes. He will talk anyone into a coma and withal is always interesting. Also he may very likely write a good book before he breaks his neck day-dreaming.'

Once Gerald Brenan's week-end at Tidmarsh was over, he returned to London on his way back to Spain, while the other three left for a holiday in the Lake District. 'There is no need for me to tell you how fond I am of you,' he wrote to Carrington (29 July 1921), 'for you can see that every time I look at you – nor of what kind my affection is, for that I only vaguely know myself. There are moments when you appear so entirely, so tormentingly beautiful that I begin to lose my head a little . . . [you are] a creature so beautiful that it would be a sort of madness not to fall in love with you.' A few days later a telegram arrived from Carrington asking him to follow them. Without hesitation he put off his journey to Spain and set off northwards, joining them at Watendlath Farm, near Keswick in Cumberland. By this time, the party also included Marjorie Strachey, who had suddenly turned up 'in pitch darkness and a howling tempest . . . having lost a reticule containing £6', James and Alix, recently returned for a holiday from Vienna, much in love and busy translating Freud.[2] The

2. James Strachey was to become the translator and general editor of the Standard Edition of the *Complete Psychological Works of Sigmund Freud* (24 vols. Hogarth Press), in the preparation of which he was assisted by his wife Alix and by Anna Freud (Freud's youngest daughter). Started in 1946, it was officially completed twenty years later. Although James Strachey had begun to take an interest in psychoanalysis just before the First World War, it was not until he and his wife went to Vienna in 1920 to study under Freud that he took the subject up professionally. On 9 March 1921, he wrote to Lady Strachey that he and Alix were translating 'a series of Freud's "clinical" papers. There are to be five of them, each giving a detailed history of a specially interesting case and an account of the treatment. They were written at intervals during the last twenty years – the first in 1899 and the last quite recently – so that they give a very good idea of the development of his views. Altogether the book will probably be about 500 pages long. It is a great compliment

seven of them led a crowded cottage life, herded together into the small back parlour of Farmer Wilson's sheep farm. 'I am sitting, as you may guess, rather comatose, in a small cottage apartment,' Lytton wrote to Virginia Woolf (23 August 1921), 'green mountains out of the window, the stuffed head of a very old female sheep over the window.'

For Gerald, this next fortnight sped by in a dream of surreptitious excitement. Everything that was beautiful and sad seemed crowded into these few days of his life. When the sun shone they would all clamber about over the stony hills, until Lytton's feet were covered with blisters and 'I can only wear silk socks and slippers in which I totter occasionally into the air'. After the first few days, however, the rain and cold were fairly continuous, and the two Strachey brothers would remain crouched over the fire – Lytton reading Beckford's *Biographical Memoirs of Extraordinary Painters*, and James, 'on an enormous air-cushion balanced upon a horsehair sofa', studying Dr Varendonck on the psychology of day-dreams. But whatever the weather, Ralph would go determinedly out to fish, without any cessation or luck, from morning until evening – he 'has caught two sardines so far' – and he was invariably accompanied by Carrington and Gerald, carrying fish-hooks and hard-boiled eggs wrapped up in newspaper. While Ralph sat, rod in hand, beside the river, the other two would kiss and cuddle behind a bank close by. Gerald was soon afflicted by a deepening sense of guilt about this deception. To such wild things had passion led them. Beforehand, he had envisaged a kind of platonic attachment; he had thought he would be able to divert his affection for Carrington out of dangerous channels into some literary com-

---

to have been given it to do. And he thought of the plan on purpose to be of help to us in two different ways. First of all, it'll give us a specially intimate knowledge of his methods, as we are able to talk over with him any difficulties that occur to us in the course of the translation; and we now go on Sunday afternoons specially to discuss whatever problems we want to. In the second place, our appearance as official translators of his work into English will give us a great advertisement in psychological circles in England.'

position. But within a few hours of his arrival at Watendlath Farm, he knew that this was a mirage. Everything except love was driven out of his head. He was like a man overwhelmed and drowned in the sea. That he should love his best friend's wife more than anyone else in the world became a fiendish torture. God knew how it had happened! Treachery to such a friend as Ralph seemed to him the blackest of crimes, intensely painful and discreditable. He blamed himself – and yet he could not give up loving Carrington. There was only one right course. He would go and explain to Ralph exactly what was happening. Surely, he urged, Ralph would understand that their relationship was, so they said, that of brother and sister. For in their desire not to be unfaithful to him they kept up the pretence of not being in love with each other, but simply very intimate friends. They would have been genuinely shocked to have heard their liaison referred to as 'an affair'. But Carrington, who knew Ralph better, would not agree to divulging anything. And so the kissing and the fishing continued, and there were several meetings in a barn. Carrington's happiness was stimulated by this exquisite concealment, while Gerald lived in a sort of romantic ecstasy, with few overt sexual feelings. He did not experience the least pang of jealousy, but on the contrary was infused with an increased affection for his friend. As for Ralph himself, he still suspected nothing, and felt pleased that Carrington and Gerald seemed so close. They were just like one another, he thought, vague, imaginative, hopelessly impractical.

The others too paid them little attention. 'The mysterious Brenan', as Lytton called him, was just Ralph's extraordinary friend. In one of his letters from Keswick to Mary Hutchinson, Lytton complains that the sole adventures in the vicinity appeared to be meteorological ones (25 August 1921), 'and – so far as I can see – there is precious little love-making'. The only sign from the Outer World, he informed Pippa (30 August 1921), 'has been a vision of Mr Stephen McKenna trailing over the mountain-tops in company with a lady in magenta silk'. Altogether, he concluded, their holiday had turned out pretty uneventful.

On 2 September, the party broke up, and Gerald left for Spain. Haphazard, he planned to reunite with Carrington the following year. 'Oh, if I had never come back to England,' he lamented, 'if I never had, if I never had! I should then have been living an eventless life in Spain, calling myself happy. . . . I have lain awake sometime thinking that soon I shall see you no more for 8 months, and I feel absolutely sick at the thought. I do not want, as things are, to be with you any longer; but to be without you is horrible. It is like going out suddenly into complete darkness.' Still no one had detected the least sign of their flirtation. But he and Carrington had placed a time-bomb beneath the Tidmarsh way of life – and who could tell when it would go off?

2

VIEWS AND REVIEWS

For the time being, at any rate, the bomb did not go off, and private life, on the surface, seemed smooth and unruffled. 'One wonders whether one has been quite wise in coming North,' Lytton had confided to Virginia Woolf from Watendlath Farm (23 August 1921). Now, in early September, he floated south again with considerable relief to the placid Downs and red-brick houses of Sussex. Amid these sympathetic regions he lingered on contentedly, staying with the Woolfs at Monk's House, with the Hutchinsons at Eleanor, and with the Bells at Charleston, where 'I read for the first time the (almost) complete account of Oscar's trials,' he told Carrington (September 1921). '. . . It is very interesting and depressing. One of the surprising features is that he very nearly got off. If he had, what would have happened I wonder? I fancy the history of English culture might have been quite different, if a juryman's stupidity had chanced to take another turn.'

There were plenty of other invitations to the country this autumn, among others from Ottoline and Lady Astor – who would invariably address him in her letters as 'Dear Author'. In town there were, of course, the Sitwells and the Bloomsberries, and various luncheon parties with Lady Colefax and Princess Bibesco. But by far the most rewarding of these social excursions were to Cambridge, where, as the guest of Maynard Keynes, he met the new and talented generation of post-war undergraduates, and grew absorbed once more by university and Apostolic affairs. Among those who soon became his special friends and whom he now began to invite back for week-ends to Tidmarsh were George ('Dadie') Rylands,[3] a charming, feline, fair-haired Etonian of great poise and elegance of dress, with a flair for stagecraft, then in his first year at King's and much under the influence of Sheppard; W. J. H. ('Sebastian') Sprott,[4] who had come up from Felsted to Clare College and was soon to be appointed as a demonstrator at the Psychological Laboratory at Cambridge; F. L. ('Peter') Lucas, later famous as a literary critic; the brilliant and precocious logician Frank Ramsey, whose brother has become Archbishop of Canterbury; J. H. Doggart ('the Dog'), the celebrated eye-specialist; and the three eldest Penrose brothers, Alec, 'a complete womanizer', as Lytton once called him, Lionel, the geneticist, and Roland, the art critic and biographer of Picasso. 'He [Alec] is a man of character (rare nowadays), and determined to be aesthetic,' Lytton informed James (28 November 1921), 'but I rather fear with no very great turn that way ... Lionel Penrose (younger brother) is at John's, and a complete flibbertigibbet, but attractive in a childish way, and somehow, in spite of an absence of brain, quite suitable in the Society.'[5]

3. George Rylands (b. 1902) later became a Fellow, Dean, Bursar and lecturer at King's College. He is now a governor of the Old Vic, and chairman of the directors and trustees of the Arts Theatre, Cambridge. His best-known book is the Shakespeare anthology, *The Ages of Man* (1939). He is also director of the long-playing recording of Shakespeare.

4. Since 1965, W. J. H. Sprott has been Emeritus Professor of Psychology at Nottingham University. He is the author of several books, including *Human Groups* (1958) and *Sociology at the Seven Dials* (1962).

5. Lionel Penrose, F.R.S. (b. 1898), Galton Professor of Eugenics, University College, London, since 1945, and author of *The Influence of Her-*

Towards the end of 1921, this life of recreation was miti-gated by a little work on the preparation of his next book. Shortly after the publication of *Eminent Victorians*, Geoffrey Whitworth had suggested to him that he might bring out a volume of selected essays, as an interlude between his two major biographical works. 'Such a book would be sure of success,' Whitworth wrote (4 April 1919), 'even though it might be slight in bulk.' But already by that time Lytton was deep in *Queen Victoria*, and so the scheme was dropped. Now, after his biography had appeared, Lytton's mind did not im-mediately revert to this idea, which, in any case, he felt to be uneconomic. He discussed his various biographical projects with Virginia Woolf, in particular the 'History of the Reign of George IV', which she considered to be a magnificent subject for him. But there were difficulties. 'The worst of George IV,' Lytton announced one afternoon over tea at Verreys, 'is that no one mentions the facts I want. History must be written all over again. It's all morality.' 'And battles', Virginia inter-posed.

While he was thus undecided, Chatto and Windus wrote to remind him of Whitworth's original proposition for a volume of essays, this time making him a definite offer. Lytton at once accepted. It seemed an easy method of making money. En-couraged by this, he opened up bargaining with his American publishers, Harcourt, Brace. 'I don't think you heard the end of my negotiations with Mr Brace,' he reported to James (28 November 1921), ' – they were perfectly hectic, and I spent days in which I alternated between the vast halls of the Hotel Cecil and the office of the Authors' Society, where poor Mr Thring assisted me with his advice and exclamations. Mr Brace was a very pale, worn out American, with the inevitable tor-toises, and we had a high old time, struggling and bargaining in the strangest style. I made a gallant effort to recapture the copyright of Victoria, but I found that he wanted more for it

---

edity on Disease (1934) and *The Biology of Mental Defect* (1949, 3rd edn 1963), who, as Lytton was soon to become aware, was one of the cleverest of his Cambridge friends.

than I was willing to give, and it ended by my agreeing to let him have my next book (on very good terms) and the offer of two others, in exchange for £1500 down. It was an extraordinary, prolonged and feverish battle, at the end of which Mr Brace nearly dropped dead, as with shaking hand and ashy face he drew out his cheque-book. He had begun by offering £1200; but at the last moment I was able suddenly to raise my terms, and in a jiffy I had made £300. I can only hope that in some mysterious way I haven't been let in – but Mr Thring supported my every movement.'

Once these arrangements had been settled, Lytton returned to Tidmarsh where, over the next two months, he busied himself gathering together a number of his fugitive essays, choosing those he liked best from the many reviews and articles he had written since his Cambridge days. Finally, he selected fourteen of these pieces, originally composed between 1904 and 1919, to make up this fourth volume. With the help of Ralph and Carrington, he passed each of them through a fine comb of textual emendation, making quite extensive alterations to the earlier ones such as 'Racine', for example, in which he rewrote no fewer than twenty-three passages. Some of the corrections he made were trivial – dealing merely with typographical errors and the rare grammatical slip. Others smoothed out awkward or redundant phrases which he had at first overlooked, but which stood out conspicuously when he read them aloud. 'Still others', records C. R. Sanders, who made a line-by-line comparison of the essays in the first and second versions, and documented all discrepancies, 'are motivated by the desire to convert journalistic articles and reviews into literary essays.' Footnotes were dropped or drastically reduced, adjectives were pruned, some new illustrative material and the occasional amusing comment was added, and the number of parallel constructions increased.

The most interesting revisions Lytton made were the improvements to his style. These were of two kinds: those which tightened up his prose, giving it more restraint, and those which indicated a desire to add greater force and emphasis to the original narrative. In the first category may be placed some over-long transitional passages that have either been trimmed and condensed, or thrown out altogether. Other paragraphs were also compressed, and dubious, over-bold opinions concerning living authors were toned down or occasionally qualified by the insertion of a 'perhaps'. A few long paragraphs were broken up so as to make for easier reading, but more often Lytton would fuse two paragraphs together so as to achieve an effect of greater weight. Similarly, several quotations only alluded to in the earlier text were now supplied in full, and in some cases, extra information has been given to bear out more convincingly the conclusions they were designed to support.

Since Lytton's prose style had matured early on, these revisions, though numerous, were mostly of a minor nature. A few reviewers, however, were to comment adversely on his writing. 'Here and there,' observed the critic of *The Times Literary Supplement*, 'the style falls into a mechanical vivacity: there are sentences that a more alert revision would have struck out.' Yet Lytton's revision, as has been demonstrated, was painstaking and minute. Any defects of the style accurately mirrored the man.

By the end of January, Lytton had finished the preparations for this book – all but the title. First he had thought of calling it *Views and Reviews*, but rejected this after discovering that W. E. Henley had already used it. 'Help! Help!' he implored Pippa (31 January 1922). 'The title question is pressing, and I am almost desperate. What do you think of "Books and Brains" – with "French and English" added underneath on the title page? A mixture of pure literature and biography should be indicated. Other possibilities are "Men, Women and Words" – "Books and Characters". Send a p.c. if you or Lady S. have any suggestions.' Two days later he decided on *Books and Characters* – 'tame but harmless', he told Pippa – appending 'French & English' on the title page, as he had originally wanted to do.

Most of the Press notices were favourable, notably *The Times*, whose reviewer praised Lytton's literary criticism rather at the expense of his biography. 'Mr Lytton Strachey has cleared the honour of the nation. He has repaired past sacrileges by publishing the finest essay upon Racine which has ever been written in English. ... Mr Strachey's is perhaps the finest critical intelligence at work in English literature to-day.' Middleton Murry, who reviewed the book in the *Athenaeum*, was in complete agreement, proclaiming Lytton's critical work to be of the first order, and singling out for special praise his fine sense of justice. And Aldous Huxley, in the course of a generally appreciative notice, described him as 'a superlatively civilised Red Indian living apart from the vulgar world in an elegant park-like reservation', who rarely looked over the walls at the surrounding country. 'It seethes, he knows,' Huxley continued, 'with crowds of horribly colonial persons. Like the hosts of Midian, the innumerable "poor whites" prowl and prowl around, but the noble savage pays no attention to them.'

Although *Books and Characters* was naturally not a bestseller, it earned Lytton considerable prestige in the world of letters. The following year his *Landmarks in French Literature* was reprinted, and his growing eminence as a critic as well as a biographer was marked both by the award of the Benson Silver Medal[6] and by an invitation from the Royal Society of Literature to become a member of its Academic Committee. This last offer he rejected for reasons that are interesting biographically. After sending back a polite letter of refusal, disclaiming his 'election', he then asked Edmund Gosse, himself on the Academic Committee, to act as his interpreter *vis-à-vis* the Royal Society of Literature, whose members, he feared, might misjudge his sentiments if they had nothing but his official communiqué before them. He felt especially anxious in case they might think he was declining out of superior feelings, and he wanted to stress the fact that he felt sincerely the compliment that had been paid to him. 'It would be futile to

6. Under the endowment of A. C. Benson (1 May 1916) medals were to be awarded in respect of meritorious works in poetry, fiction, history, biography and belles-lettres. A selection committee was appointed each year by the Fellows of the Royal Society of Literature, who alone had the right to recommend recipients.

argue the pros and cons of Academies and similar bodies in general,' he explained to Gosse (30 December 1922), 'and I realise that a good case may be made out for them; but so far as I am personally concerned I am convinced that I should really be out of place in one. This is as much a matter of instinct as of reason. Perhaps it is regrettable, but the fact remains that, as Saint-Simon said of himself: "Je ne suis pas un sujet académique" ...

'... So I hope you will sympathise with me in my declining the honour and I am sure that if I am ever able to do any service to Literature, it will be as an entirely independent person and not as a member of a group.'

Lytton dedicated *Books and Characters* to Maynard Keynes, who, with Sebastian Sprott, came down to spend Christmas with him at Tidmarsh. Although Lytton had earned between seven and eight thousand pounds since the spring of 1918, he had up till now escaped paying any income tax.[7] 'The authorities here seem to have overlooked my existence,' he confided to Keynes (11 November 1921), 'and if this happy state of things could continue, so much the better.' But he knew that it could not, and he asked Keynes's advice as to whether he should be paid by his publishers *en bloc* or as the royalties came in. Keynes also furnished him with a 'detailed list of stocks of every kind, in which he insists that I shall put all I have. There is no choice but to submit, and face bankruptcy.'

During the rest of the winter Lytton languished uneasily at the Mill House. 'My state has long been quite deplorable,' he confessed to Virginia Woolf (6 February 1922). 'I put it down to the Winter – the agony of thick underclothes, etc. etc.; but of course it may be sheer deliquescence of the brain. Anyhow,

7. The accounts from Chatto and Windus show Lytton to have received by the end of March 1922 £4,867 2s. 0d. on the sales of his books in the British Empire, £1,105 11s. 0d. on sales in the U.S.A. (which does not include the outright sum of £1,500 from Harcourt, Brace), and £99 in respect of French and Swedish rights. To this should be added a small amount from the continuing sales of *Landmarks in French Literature*, something from his contributions to the *Athenaeum*, etc., and possibly also an income from private investments.

from whatever cause, I am sans eyes, sans teeth, sans prick, sans ... but after that there can be no more sanses, – and on the whole I feel more like a fish gasping on a bank than anything else. It is terrible. I hope wildly that a change will come with the swallows ...'

He had recently joined the Oriental Club, of which his father had been a prominent member,[8] and this new status, he felt, suited very well his condition of premature, winter senility. The place was like a luxurious mausoleum. 'Very ormolu,' Carrington noted in one of her letters to Noel. 'Full of old Indian Dug Outs.' And Lytton, in a letter to Virginia Woolf (6 February 1922), described it as 'a vast hideous building ... filled with vast hideous Anglo-Indians, very old and very rich. One becomes 65, with an income of 5000 a year, directly one enters it. One is so stout one can hardly walk, and one's brain works with an extraordinary slowness. Just the place for me, you see, in my present condition. I pass almost unnoticed with my glazed eyes and white hair, as I sink into a leather chair heavily with a copy of the Field in hand. Excellent claret too – one of the best cellars in London, by Jove. You *must* come! I'll write again soon, if you can bear it.' But when he did write again, four days later, it was the same tale of cold and discontent. 'The horror of getting up is unparalleled, and I am filled with amazement every morning when I find that I have done it. To my mind there is clearly only one test of wealth, and that is – a fire in one's bedroom. Until one can have that at any and every moment, one is poor. Oh, for a housemaid at dawn!'

Towards the end of February, Carrington and Ralph left for Vienna to visit James Strachey and Alix, who was seriously ill with pleurisy, while Lytton, in order that he might be properly looked after, moved up to Gordon Square. 'Life here has been proceeding in its usual style of utter dullness punctuated by hectic frenzies,' he wrote to Carrington on his forty-second birthday. 'One of the latter occurred last night – a very absurd party at Lady Astor's to meet Mr Balfour – a huge rout – 800

8. There is in the Oriental Club a portrait of Sir Richard Strachey painted in about 1888 by Lowes Dickinson, the father of Goldie Dickinson.

extremely mixed guests – Duchesses, Rothensteins, Prime Ministers, Stracheys (male and female) – never did you see such a
sight! As it was pouring cats and dogs the scene of jostling
taxis and motors in St James's Square was terrific – it was
practically full up. No one could get out it was so wet – for
hours we sat ticking and cursing and occasionally edging an
inch or two nearer the portals of bliss. To add to the confusion, various streams entered the Square by the side streets,
and mingled with the cars. However the police and the good
nature of the English lower classes saved the situation. If such
a thing had happened in Paris it would have been simply Pandemonium. As it was, it was merely a great bore. The P.M. was
leaving as we entered. Horror of horrors! The Rt. Hon. gentleman did *not recognise* Lytton Strachey! – though he bowed
very politely – as did Mrs Lloyd George – an unparalleled
frump. Mr Balfour was very complimentary behind large demi-
ghostly spectacles.'

Yet despite these hectic frenzies, the London scene, Lytton
reported, was 'not very gay', and when Carrington and Ralph
returned from Vienna, he went back to Tidmarsh contentedly
enough. His own amorous adventures, and those of his
closest friends, seemed to have become suspended, and he felt
at times a little bored.

3

MADNESS

Over the past six months, since Gerald Brenan sailed away to
Spain, Carrington had been writing to him every few days; and
he had replied. Although Ralph insisted on reading their correspondence, he still suspected nothing – principally because
there were effusive postscripts attached to these letters which
he was never shown. Now, at the beginning of April, they were
all to meet again, Lytton and Carrington and Ralph and
Gerald, at Norhurst, the house of Septimus Bollard and his
wife Clare, in the Basses-Pyrénées. Norhurst faced west, was
perfectly suited for the hot weather, and, to Ralph's great joy,

overlooked a trout stream which ran just below. All around were deep valleys coated with the greenest grass, and everywhere grew bracken, tall and spreading itself into arches. Huge beech forests covered the headwaters of the streams, and above these, standing out against the blue sky, there pointed needle-sharp peaks of red and yellow rock. 'We are pretty high up among the hills,' Lytton wrote to Pippa (7 April 1922), ' – a charming house full of the local furniture – armoires and cupboards innumerable – in a small village, with steep heights on every side. Everything seems quite nice, though not exciting. There is hope of fishing, when the streams, which are at present Niagaras, subside. The health, I think, should be greatly improved after about a fortnight of mountain existence . . .

'I am writing this in a basque bed, but now I shall have to get up and go downstairs and face the family. Le père de Madame (an Anglo-Indian planter, I gather) is rather distressing. He once went out to shoot Bustards in Nagpore, but never found any . . . However, Madame herself is very agreeable and sings Italian songs very nicely after dinner.'

Clare, now married to a rather diminutive, donnish husband with military idiosyncrasies,[9] was a voluptuous, highly sexed and unstable woman. Dark and beautiful, though, with some malformation which made hearing difficult, she was also rumoured to have been Derain's mistress and was herself a painter, whom Carrington had got to know at the Slade and to whom she now began to confide her secret feelings for Gerald. A late snow had fallen on the lilac blossom, and while Ralph resolutely fished below, and Lytton sat listening in silence to Professor Bollard as he recited from a book he was then composing on Elizabethan tragedy, Gerald, upstairs in the attic, would pose for Carrington. Probably because of

9. 'Bollard . . . has mildly literary and pedantic tastes. He is dull but harmless – I fear is writing a series of sixteenth-century lives in the style of Eminent Victorians. She is rather more interesting – perhaps a Saph – much attached to Carrington – but oh, not what might be called clever. She paints – à la Modigliani, etc. The place is pretty high up in the Pyrenees – a largish village with steep hills in every direction – snow to be seen in the distance. . . . I think I should be able to last out another 10 days or so. . . .' Lytton to James Strachey (9 April 1922).

physical feelings he was as yet quite unaware of, Ralph had taken a most violent dislike to Clare Bollard, and was persistently and gratuitously rude to her, so that the atmosphere at meals, when they were all obliged to congregate, became increasingly strained. Even more unaccountably, at least to Lytton, she began, in spite of this, to make up to Ralph. Then, to everyone's astonishment, on the very last day of their visit, Ralph and Clare fell into each other's arms with all the violence that had seemed to mark his previous antipathy.

No sooner had this awkward situation been created than, the very next morning, Lytton, Ralph and Carrington packed up and departed, travelling, via Toulouse and Provence, back to England. They were hotly pursued across the Continent by the passionate Clare, and by Gerald, who waited only to collect a sleeping bag and the camping kit which he had been forced to abandon on his journey up from Yegen in the deep snow of the Roncesvalles Pass. Daily, the position seemed to grow more complicated and grave. During May, Gerald put up at Pangbourne, while Ralph proceeded openly to carry on his impetuous affair with Clare, adopting all the time a very aggressive and disparaging attitude to Carrington. For some weeks it looked as if the whole Tidmarsh regime was about to crumble and disintegrate. Carrington, in despair, appealed to Lytton, who counselled patience, and in the meantime sent off to Professor Bollard a gift of some books on the Elizabethan dramatists. Up till this time, Gerald had kept his relations with Carrington confined to a more or less platonic level, out of a rather tarnished sense of loyalty to Ralph. But under these altered circumstances he now felt no further obligation to do so, and when Ralph and Clare went off for a few days together, he and Carrington – who, in any case, had never shared his scruples about making love – resolved to do the same.

Then the storm burst. While they were away together, Clare let out to Ralph that his best friend and his wife had fallen in love. She told him of the love-making that had taken place at Watendlath Farm, and that, in the Pyrenees, Gerald, Carrington and herself had hatched 'the Norhurst Plot' by which she should flirt with Ralph so as to leave Carrington and

Gerald alone together. Ralph was thunderstruck. Being a very emotional and neurotic woman, Clare did not scruple to distort a few of the facts and put the most dramatic interpretation on others, and although Ralph believed her completely, she would no longer really mean anything to him after this. In an uncontrollable fury he rushed back to Tidmarsh. From his outraged reaction, it would seem that he considered it quite proper for him to have a love-affair with a married woman, but absolutely immoral for Carrington to take a lover. But there was more to it than this – there was the deception which burnt within him as a most wounding humiliation. For whereas he believed in complete openness at all times and about everything, Carrington cherished her secrecy closely and would even conceal small, quite unobjectionable matters to safeguard her privacy. The key to Ralph's character lay in his belief that marriage meant total trust, total communication. He had a passion for truth in love and friendship. So his unbridled frenzy on hearing Clare's news was caused less by questions of technical infidelity – though these became important – than by the dissimulation practised by his best friend and his recently married wife. This revelation of lies and deceit shattered him, and in a sense gave the death-blow to his marriage with Carrington, which no subsequent patchings-up could really resurrect.

After a furious argument with Carrington in the Mill House, Ralph dispatched a telegram to Gerald demanding to see him in London. When they met, he announced that unless Gerald could promise him that he had had no physical intercourse with Carrington, he, Ralph, would separate from her there and then and for ever. Gerald swore that he had not, for although his instinct was still to tell his friend the truth, he felt that he had no right, by doing so, to endanger Carrington's life with Lytton. Ralph, now somewhat at a loss, replied with stern uncertainty that he would have to consider what he would do, but that if he decided to go on living with Carrington, then Gerald must go back to Spain and give his word never to communicate with her again. Gerald promised. There was nothing else that he could do. The first person in Carrington's life was always Lytton, and Gerald himself could never hope to take Ralph's place with him. Also he was very poor, and for that reason any alternative arrangements would have been doubly impractical. So, briefly and for the last time, Gerald returned to Tidmarsh to tell Carrington what had transpired at his interview with Ralph. Lytton, relieved that he did not mean to rock the boat and capsize them all, was especially kind,[10] and when Gerald had sailed again for Spain on 14 June, sent after him an affectionate and encouraging letter.

Things are still unsettled here [he wrote (15 June 1922)] and the first necessity is to clear the atmosphere. Letters between you might seem ambiguous to Ralph, and all ambiguities just now are to be avoided.

... I hope you will go on writing. From the little I've seen of your work, it seemed to me to differ *in kind* from everything else going about by writers of your generation. To my mind there is a streak of inspiration in it, which is very rare and very precious indeed.

... Things have turned out unhappily; but never forget that, whatever happens, and in spite of all estrangements, you are loved by those you love best.

Yours ever affectionately,
Lytton Strachey

Besides its accuracy in detecting the future author of *South from Granada, A Life of One's Own, Jack Robinson,*[11] *The Spanish Labyrinth* and other fine books to be a writer of rare and original inspiration, this letter exhibits the compassion of someone who had himself suffered acutely in love-affairs, but who had never been embittered by his setbacks. It also illustrates just what Bloomsbury, at its best, meant by civilized behaviour in personal relations, and how difficult outsiders such as Ralph Partridge found this behaviour to accept. For Lytton, and a few others, laid great stress on such controlled

10. 'I am very sorry for him [Brenan],' Lytton wrote to Ralph Partridge about this time. 'He has injured himself very badly, and his life at the best of times was not a particularly pleasant one.'

11. Written under the pseudonym of George Beaton, and, in the opinion of David Garnett, a work equal to W. H. Hudson's *The Purple Land*.

and impeccable conduct, and their refusal to accede any rights or claims to jealousy was one of the rules they stood for most strongly – one that amounted, perhaps, to a real discovery in sophisticated, humane dealings with other people. Gerald greatly appreciated Lytton's friendship. 'Please forgive me the unhappiness I have caused to you as well as to others and do not think too badly of me,' he had written the night before his departure. 'And thank you for the kindness you have always shown me. It has been a great pleasure to me to have known you and to have caught a glimpse at Tidmarsh of people who cultivate a free, happy and civilised life. Now that I have lost my part in it, I see all its attractions.'

Everything that had happened over the past ten weeks appeared to Gerald to have been hideously grotesque. But though he certainly experienced some guilt over these tragic happenings, he was still convinced that they had been largely senseless and unnecessary. All his subsequent actions and his letters to Lytton make it clear that he did not change his feeling for Carrington or Ralph because of this crisis between them, and that, despite being extremely upset at having contributed to their unhappiness, he did not regret anything he had done.[12] 'But that, among reasonable people,' he wrote to

12. Gerald Brenan sent Carrington several long letters during the next few months via either Lytton or John Hope-Johnstone. On 11 June 1922 he declared: 'I have one request. When you are able to talk to Ralph about me, tell him what you know to be true, that my only treachery was to conceal from him my affection for you. That this affection did not begin suddenly but insensibly, that though I could not bear to end it by telling him, I tried to lead it into safe channels. That I hoped in the end, with time, seeing that my feelings are different from his and that I live so far off, to reveal it to him and that he would tolerate it. . . . My friendship with Ralph is at an end; that I accept, but what I cannot endure is that he should think it never existed. I was devoted to him as I have been, I think, to no other man; I do not believe I would willingly have injured him.'

In another letter, posted two days later, he added: 'Whatever I think of, my thoughts return to you and make me feel how much and how sweet a happiness I am deprived of. . . . You do not know how much I love you, how much I shall always love you. There is nothing about you which does not charm me or that could ever grate upon me; your face, your body, your character, your habits are perfect – not because they conform to any exterior standard of perfection but because they make up a unity of their

Lytton from Spain (14 July 1922), 'I who am fond of Ralph, can be – O wonderful irony! Too fond of C, and that without being the cause of their seeing less of each other or of their affections diminishing, and without my wishing for anything new for myself – that by these good and innocent means can be so great a source of unhappiness to all of us – is nothing less to me than madness, madness, horrible madness . . .'

4

THE AWKWARD STAGE

The task of reintroducing some sanity and spirit of affection into Tidmarsh during the next eighteen months fell predominantly on Lytton's shoulders. It was an arduous, extremely tricky exercise in patient diplomacy, and one that he played with the utmost tact. First of all he had to reconcile Ralph to Carrington – neither of whom would consent to see the other until he had engineered a face-saving peace settlement between them. He started off by assuring Carrington that he sympathized absolutely with her feelings, and that, however things might turn out, he would never desert her. Nevertheless, he insisted that she must keep this confidence to herself, and for a while at least, look with extraordinary leniency upon all Ralph's indiscretions. Ralph himself, having signified his willingness to return to the Mill House on certain conditions, had gone, pending Lytton's negotiations on his behalf, down

---

own which is good and beautiful. Am I allowed to tell you that? I may fall in love, I may have other friendships and liaisons, but I shall not forget you, because my feelings for you neither exclude other affections nor can be excluded by them. What I feel for you I shall feel for no one else, and to you I shall always be different to what I am to other people. One part of me belongs unalienably to you, and when I am with you or when I am thinking of you everything else in me is oblite ated.'

Some months later, when friendly relations between himself and Ralph had been resumed, Gerald Brenan wrote to Carrington from Yegen (15 September 1922): 'I have acted badly and foolishly, and you foolishly – but from now onwards let us be the only people to act sensibly, and with a view to the greatest possible happiness, for all concerned, in the future. Love. Gerald.'

to stay in Richmond. 'I think I was able to make her realise your feelings and point of view,' Lytton wrote to him there (June 1922). 'Of course, she was, and is, terribly upset. She said that you were essential to her – that Gerald was not at all – that this crisis had made her realise more than ever before the strength of her love for you. I explained your dread of a scene, reconciliations, etc., and said you wanted to sleep in the yellow room. She quite understood. I am sure that she loves you deeply. Be as gentle with her as you can when you come.

'We must try now to forget all those horrid details, and trust to the force of our fundamental affections to carry us through. At any rate, we know where we are now, which is a great thing.

'. . . As for me, my dear, I can't say how happy your decision to try going on here has made me. I suppose I *could* face life without you, just as I *could* face life with one of my hands cut off, but it would have been a dreadful blow . . .

'. . . My nerves are rather on the jump, and I am longing for your presence – the best restorative I know of! I sympathise with you so absolutely, so completely, my dear, dear love. Sometimes I feel as if I *was* inside you! Why can't I make you perfectly happy by waving some magic wand?

'Keep this letter to yourself.'

After the route had been paved for Ralph's difficult return, Lytton did all in his power to make life at Tidmarsh delightful. He would invite over for week-ends the most interesting and amusing guests – some of his Cambridge friends whom Ralph liked and who adored Carrington, and other older luminaries such as E. M. Forster. He also bought a car. Since neither Carrington nor himself could run it, and since 'R.P. is a born driver', this naturally increased their joint dependence on Ralph together with his sense of responsibility towards them – though Lytton was quick to assure him that 'of course you know the little car belongs to you'. A little later in the year, when Ralph complained about his job at the Hogarth Press – his poor income and prospects – Lytton immediately stepped in and tried to argue his case with Virginia Woolf. 'There have been various conversations on the Hogarth question – with rather indeterminate results,' he reported to her (19 September 1922). 'I think the poor creature is really anxious to continue, but foresees difficulties. He is already brushing up his energies! On the whole I gather that he thinks less printing and more business might be a solution. Perhaps if some department in the business could be handed over in toto to him he would fling himself into it with more zest. But this is only a vague suggestion, and so please don't draw conclusions from it. I suppose he will write himself before long. The distance-from-London question is a very trying one.' After these tentative suggestions had led nowhere, and Ralph quitted the Hogarth Press, Lytton employed him as his secretary to answer his correspondence, deal with the income tax authorities, with publishers and editors, assist with proof-reading and other duties. And so, by these means, Ralph was gradually incorporated back into the Tidmarsh life. While his and Lytton's interdependence tightened, so, more obliquely but inevitably, would his feelings for Carrington slowly revive.

Outwardly, then, their triangular *ménage* continued much as before, and to those who did not know them very intimately, life at the Mill House appeared happy. 'You have no idea what a perfect life we lead here,' Carrington wrote to Noel (25 July 1922). '3 Hives of Bees, 30 ducks, 30 chickens, a Forest of delicious raspberries, and peas, and a Roman Bath to bathe in out of doors. Annie who is a gay little girl of sixteen, exquisitely lovely, who cooks and housekeeps for us all and then Lytton who is a paragon of a friend, who buys new books for our delight. The new car is a great joy. We go lovely rides in it. ... Do you know we can sleep in the car, for the Front seat comes out and we can make it into a caravan (!). R. is a very perfect driver.'

But underneath this smooth surface of country contentment, the atmosphere remained critical. For Carrington, in particular, these summer months were miserable. Ralph still seemed completely hostile to her, and she felt that she had even lost Lytton's confidence because of her never-ending lies and subterfuges. Yet there was no alternative but to go on living at the Mill House where 'everything was completely awfull for me'. She felt strangely alone, and missed Gerald's letters and warm friendship 'more than I ever thought, in my wildest moments, I should, and when one mustn't talk of it, it keeps on tormenting my head. But I won't talk of him because it only makes me remember him more, then after all no one else can mind except me – only if I am grousy and sullen you [Lytton] mustn't think me altogether selfish . . .'

Lytton went on calming and reassuring her, but for a time it seemed as if Ralph's love had been totally expunged by her deception. He was continuing his affair with Clare in the most brash and insensitive way. 'I can tell you it was pretty intolerable,' Carrington admitted in a secret letter to Gerald later in the year (19 October 1922). In order to retain Ralph's undivided affections, Clare was always stirring up his indignation against Carrington and Gerald, keeping alive the old embers of his bitterness. Their affair was all the more tormenting for Carrington since – as if the ramifications of this story were as yet inadequate – she herself felt a strong sexual attraction towards Clare: 'It all follows,' she explained, 'from my lustful sapphism.' Yet despite this attraction, she now hated her, and was glad to see that Lytton too greatly disliked her, believing that it was impossible to include such a mischief-maker in their lives. Yet he still counselled patience, and advised Carrington not to try to coerce Ralph into giving her up. In time, he promised her, their affair would die a natural death.

Towards the end of June, Clare left England and went back to Norhurst with her new lover – Mark Gertler![13] Lytton, sensing that this might be a good opportunity for Ralph and Carrington to regain some of their lost harmony, and that this might more easily be achieved if he were not there looking on, left the same week for a fortnight in Venice. But before leaving, he summoned Barbara Bagenal down to Tidmarsh in order to keep Carrington company and see that she came to no harm.

As a holiday companion, Lytton took with him his young

13. Mark Gertler hated Ralph Partridge, whom he used to call 'the Policeman', and it seems probable that he had urged Clare to go off with Ralph in order to stir up as much trouble as possible.

Cambridge friend Sebastian Sprott, who, the previous year, had accompanied Keynes to Algeria and Tunisia. Together they journeyed in some style down to Venice and put up at the Casa Frollo in the Giudecca, a 'nice sort of broken-down place, which will just suit us', Lytton informed Pippa (22 June 1922). His own room looked out towards the Lido and on the day he arrived the weather was blue and a fresh breeze was entering the windows. Why, he wondered, did not he and all his friends live here permanently? The one drawback was a typically Venetian one – noise. 'An ice factory, if you please, is next door, and naturally chooses the hour of 3 a.m. for its most agitating operations – sounds of terrific collapses and crushes shake the earth, and I awake in terror of my life.' Otherwise there was little to complain about – everything was as beautiful as the previous year, when he had spent a week there with Ralph and Carrington on their honeymoon. 'Venice is very lovely – but oh dear! *not* so lovely by half as it was last year,' he wrote diplomatically to Carrington (July 1922). 'Such a difference does the mind make upon matter! Sebastian is really charming – most easy to get on with, most considerate, very gay, and interested in everything that occurs. . . . Of course he is young – also, somehow, not what you might call an "intimate" character – which has its advantages too. Nor is he passionate – but inclined if anything to be sentimental, though too clever to be so in a sickly style. His sentimentality is not directed towards me . . .'

Lytton's own sentimentality was directed towards a 'sublime' gondolier named Francesco, whom he had already taken to on his earlier stay there. 'Francesco carries one to the Piazzetta in about 10 minutes, according to wind and obstacles,' he wrote to Ralph (24 June 1922). 'He is exactly the same as ever. It was luck being able to have him . . . a few weeks after we went away last summer a new rule was made by which no one was allowed to hire a gondolier for more than a day at a time – except old clients – under which heading I mercifully come! Apparently Berenson last July tried to take Francesco as I did, with the result that a mob of enraged gondoliers collected booing and shouting, and he was nearly torn limb from limb. But *I* was at once recognised, and no mob assailed me ... the rule was made by the degraded gondoliers, who found they were losing all their custom. It seems to me next year they'll do away with the blessed privileges of "old clients" as well – the pigs. ... Sebastian enjoys everything very much, and keeps up a constant chatter of a mild kind, which just suits me at the present moment. I can't say he looks ultra respectable, with a collarless shirt, very décolleté, and the number of glad eyes he receives is alarming. However so far his *behaviour* has been all that could be desired.'

The news from Tidmarsh during these weeks was unsensational. But it did not sound as if Carrington and Ralph were drawing any closer. Lytton felt moments of great discouragement – 'a feeling that everything is too difficult and fearful – a feeling of the futility of life'. But such moods passed, and his letters were always trying to cement over these difficulties. To Carrington he is invariably cheerful, describing various social occasions, how, for example, he had called to have tea with some friends of Lady Colefax, 'Mr and Mrs Robinson, who have a grand palazzo with an immense garden rather far away facing the lagoon and the cemetery. It was a curious vision – the huge rooms filled with the richest furniture – marble courts, roses, fountains etc. and the two melancholy owners of it all – he a sad little nonentity, and she a large disappointed horse of a woman, grumbling incessantly, cursing Italy, the heat, the mosquitoes, the Church bells, complaining of everything you can think of that anyone could desire. ... I am to dine tête-à-tête on Sunday. She is, with all her horror, slightly intriguing. One wonders how she can have got into such a state.'

Meanwhile, Lytton's correspondence with Ralph reveals more of his secret anxieties. Was he returning from Venice too early? he asks. Would it ease matters if he stayed at Gordon Square for ten days before coming down to Tidmarsh? Had Ralph already forgotten him? The uncertainty of the last months had greatly stimulated Lytton's feelings of affection. 'I hug you a hundred times and bite your ears. Don't you still realise what I feel for you? how profoundly I love you? ... I wish I could talk to you now ... I am always your own Lytton.'

Once back, he resumed the work of patching and repairing their broken relationships, trying everything he knew to dissipate the uneasy atmosphere that still hung over the Mill House. Here was a man who detested violence and 'uncivilized' conduct, devoting months to appeasing Ralph, just as a few years earlier he, who prided himself on refusing to speak to unintelligent people, had courted and borne with the company of an uneducated girl. By any standards this behaviour shows that he was much less of the blasé, squeamish intellectual that legend has painted him.

During the month of August he sublet Tidmarsh and with Carrington and Ralph set out on a five weeks' motor tour of Devon and Wales. This, he thought, might easily help in clearing the air. But from the very first, things did not go well. After the resplendent heat of Italy, the immoderately frigid climate, with snow, ice, sleet and hurricanes of rain, nearly killed Lytton, wearing him down to a mere shadow of his former shadowy self. 'I creep about on a broken wing, hélas!' he told Mary Hutchinson. Three weeks later he was able to report to Pippa that 'so far we have had exactly two fine days, and on one of them the motor broke down, so that we spent most of it in a garage'. They were constantly on the move from one dud and exorbitant hotel to another. 'I think my next work will be a fulmination on the Hotels of England,' Lytton groaned.

Throughout these misadventures, the Partridges had kept up a rather grim humour. In the third week of August, they took rooms for ten days at Solva, near St David's. 'It is on the snout of Wales – a sea coast in the Cornwall style with rocks, coves, and islands, and would be perfect if there were any sun to see it in,' Lytton wrote to Pippa (18 August 1922). It was a relief to be settled at last in this pleasant and empty spot – for him, but not, perversely, for the Partridges. Now that there was no succession of calamities to distract them from their personal antagonisms, the tension mounted quickly; then exploded. All the time they had been driving through Devon and Wales, Carrington could sense that Ralph's thoughts were fixed far away on Clare, that he was completely obsessed by her life. At Solva, angry scenes broke out between them. Carrington declared that if he really cared for her, as he had maintained on returning to Tidmarsh, then he must see that it was becoming unbearable for her to go on living with him, knowing he was still friends with Clare. After all, she had sacrificed Gerald – why should he not give up Clare? Ralph retorted that he had no objection to her and Gerald being simply friends – and at once sat down and wrote off a letter to Gerald to tell him so. According to Ralph, Carrington had subtly imposed this law of non-communication upon herself so as to put him in the wrong with Clare. And so they argued about it and about, and as the days passed and the arguments went on, so the atmosphere between them showed signs of clearing, and, quite unintentionally, they began to grow fonder of each other.

On the first day of September, they left Wales and motored back homewards. That same day Clare Bollard came back with Gertler from Norhurst, and Carrington, dreading another period of misery leading, perhaps, to an ultimate crisis, broke down. All that she most prized in life seemed to be slipping away from her. 'I love R very much,' she burst out in a letter to Gerald (19 October 1922). 'I suppose that when a person dies, or nearly leaves one for ever one becomes very aware of all one's feelings. ... I also love Lytton and I also love our life here. when I see other peoples lives' I see how good this is ... I care enough for it to put a good Deal of energy into opposing any enemy who threatens it.' The crisis that she feared never materialized. By the end of October she and Ralph appeared to have arrived at some agreement. So long as Carrington herself did not resume relations with Gerald, Ralph promised not to see Clare. 'You say you mistrust Clare,' he told her, 'and think she is wicked. I tell you that I mistrust Gerald, and think, not from wickedness but from thoughtlessness and vagueness he may imperil my happiness.'

No one was more responsible for this new amnesty than Lytton. Carrington's life at Tidmarsh had been made endurable solely by his kindness, and that gentleness and understanding which he would always display when she most needed it.

849

'Lytton is still my Caesar, or whatever the expression is,' she exclaimed that autumn. 'Through all the scenes, the wretchednesses, he has been amazing. If it hadn't been for his friendship I should have rushed away. He makes one see that one ought never to let other people's meanesses wreck one.'

Ralph, too, had only stayed with Carrington during these awkward months because of his sense of loyalty to Lytton. That winter he gave up Clare altogether, and though he entered into some lighter affairs with women he met at London parties – with Marjorie Joad, among others – he grew in time to love Carrington again very deeply. But it was a different kind of love, less possessive, one that would later admit all sorts of further complications for them both.

5

ON THE MOVE

'I am stiff – frozen stiff – a rigid icicle,' Lytton wrote to Virginia Woolf from Pembrokeshire (22 August 1922). 'I hang at this address for another week, and slowly melt southwards and eastwards – a weeping relic of what was once your old friend.'

He had made out an elaborate schedule for his September visitings. After a week-end with Sir Philip Sassoon at Trent[14] – 'rather boring, really' – he joined Clive and Vanessa Bell at Charleston, dividing the next week between them and the Woolfs at Monk's House. 'I'm enjoying myself here very much,' he wrote from Charleston to Mary Hutchinson (7 September 1922), 'it is positively hot enough to sit out of doors

14. Sir Philip Sassoon (1888–1939), politician and connoisseur. He was Unionist M.P. for Hythe (1912–39), private secretary to Lord Haig (1915–18), under-secretary for air (1924–9, 1931–7) and first commissioner of works (1937–9). Despite this successful career, his gifts were, according to Osbert Sitwell, more those of an artist than a politician. He was a trustee of the National Gallery, the Tate Gallery and the Wallace Collection. His various houses, Trent Park, Port Lympe and New Barnet were renowned as centres of art and entertainment, always filled with politicians, painters, writers, professional golfers and airmen.

– I pretend to read, and really do nothing but chat. Clive and I go for vast walks over the downs, which have grown more beautiful than ever. Oh for a farmhouse at the foot of them, for my very own.'

In one sense he looked forward to the winter, which always seemed to bring with it a suspension of amorous adventures and entanglements. His spirit, so he confided to Mary Hutchinson (22 August 1922), had been almost broken by the perturbing events of the spring and summer. 'It would be indeed charming to see you again, and exchange confidences. But I hope you will lay in a good supply of wood, coal, mackintoshes, umbrellas and galoshes – rum punch for the evenings, too; followed, very likely, by glasses of porter in our bedrooms, warmed by red-hot pokers. I pray for Winter, when we shall be snug once more, and the sun will shine, and we will only *occasionally* shiver.'

After a short stay with the Hutchinsons, Lytton went off for a long, 'pretty grim' week-end to Garsington, the only other guests being W. J. Turner and his wife – 'a very small bird-like man with a desolating accent, a good deal to say for himself – but punctuated by strange hesitations – impediments – rather distressing; but really a nice little fellow, when one has got over the way in which he says "count" ', he patronizingly wrote to Virginia Woolf (19 September 1922). 'Ott. was dreadfully dégringolée, her bladder has now gone the way of her wits – a melancholy dribble, and then, as she sits after dinner in the lamplight, her cheek-pouches drooping with peppermints, a cigarette between her false teeth, and vast spectacles on her painted nose, the effect produced is extremely agitating. I found I wanted to howl like an Irish wolf – but perhaps the result produced in you was different.'[15]

From Garsington he took himself off to the Manor House,

15. On the same day Lytton wrote to Ottoline herself: 'It was a great pleasure to see you and to have some talks – I only wish there could have been more of them. Needless to say that I enjoyed my week-end very much. It was delightful to find Philip in such good trim, and I liked making the acquaintance of Turner. I hope your health is really taking a turn for the better at last. What a disgusting arrangement one's body does become when its machinery goes out of order.'

Mells, to put up for some days with Lady Horner, 'my only other co-guest being Eddie [Marsh], who is quickly killing me with his dreadful self- and world-satisfaction. The house is a very charming one – the true country-house style, and the Horner famille seem a cut above the ordinary run of the upper classes. Lady H. has heard of Beaumont and Fletcher, and Katherine A[squith][16] dabbles in theology.' The following week, he left for a brief visit to Berlin with James, who was attending a congress on psychoanalysis, with Sigmund Freud in the chair – 'it seems a good opportunity of being shown round'. Later, the two brothers visited Potsdam and Sansouci, and saw the Voltaire *Zimmer* prepared by Frederick the Great, its walls decorated with monkeys, and still with Voltaire's books on the shelves.

At last, early in October, he was compelled to retreat to Tidmarsh. To his deep relief, peace and happiness seemed to have been restored. In these improved circumstances, he was more than content to spend most of the winter there. 'The winter is too terrible,' he wrote with playful exaggeration to Maynard Keynes (28 November 1922). 'I can neither feel, think, nor write – I can only just breathe, read, and eat. I am impotent – my hair has turned perfectly white – my beard has fallen off . . .' But the winter, as he predicted, had brought with it a sweet cessation to all their painful emotional dramas. Over Christmas, Keynes and Lydia Lopokova came down to stay, and Lytton wrote a short playlet for Carrington and Ralph to perform for them. And so, quietly and harmlessly, the old year came to an end with Tidmarsh, like a vessel which had weathered a menacing storm, limping slowly on its course.

The new year also opened quietly. During January and February, Lytton made only two expeditions away from the Mill House. The first of these was to Cambridge, where he attended a performance of *Oedipus Rex* given by the Marlowe Society. Among the audience were many of his new undergraduate friends – F. L. Lucas, Stewart Perowne and Dadie Rylands, who had already made something of a name for himself in *The Duchess of Malfi*, acting the part of the Duchess. Another

16. Lady Horner's daughter, married to Raymond Asquith.

spectator there was Cecil Beaton, who noted down the scene in his diary. 'During the interval, the audience rushed to the club room to shout and smoke. Lytton Strachey peered at everyone through thick glasses, looking like an owl in daylight. He is immensely tall, and could be even twice his height if he were not bent as a sloppy asparagus. His huge hands fall to his sides, completely limp. His sugar-loaf beard is thick and dark, worn long in the fashion of an arty undergraduate.'

His second excursion in these months was again to Ottoline's. 'Now I am off – est-il possible? – to Garsington,' he reported to James (February 1923). There seem to have been two chief reasons why he still consented to go there. Ottoline's invitations were frequent and insistent, and despite his acid comments about her to others, Lytton remembered well her kindness to him in the past and he did not now want unnecessarily to hurt her. In her virulence, her disillusion, her life of crowded loneliness, she had grown much less sympathetic to him. Yet Garsington itself even now retained some afterglow of its old magical enchantment. Besides a core of the old Bloomsbury guard, there was usually an influx of clever, pink-and-white undergraduates from Oxford among the guests, and it was their presence which formed the most powerful inducement to Lytton. Among these younger men were Edward Sackville-West, David Cecil, L. P. Hartley, Lytton's cousin John Strachey, C. M. Bowra[17] and John Rothenstein. One hot Sunday afternoon, John Rothenstein records,

I found myself with two companions, likewise Oxford undergraduates, in a house where none of us had been before, pausing at an open french window that gave upon a lawn, at the farther end of which a tea-party was in progress. We paused because the lawn was not so large that we could not discern among the tea-drinkers the

17. C. M. Bowra, now Warden of Wadham College, Oxford, recalls that, on one occasion when Lytton was staying at Garsington, 'a party of Asquiths arrived and settled down to tea. Lady Ottoline left the room, and when she came back it was empty except for Strachey. She asked what had happened, and he said in his piping voice, "There's been a row." There had, about the war, and the Asquiths had retired in a dudgeon.'

figures of Lytton Strachey, Aldous Huxley and Duncan Grant, as well as that, so awe-inspiring upon a first encounter, of our hostess Lady Ottoline Morrell. At that moment this modest patch of grass seemed to us an alarmingly large area to cross beneath the gaze of so many august eyes. So it is that I can still picture the group: Lytton Strachey inert in a low chair, red-bearded head dropped forward, long hands drooping, finger-tips touching the grass; Aldous Huxley talking, with his face turned up towards the sun; Duncan Grant, pale-faced, with fine, untidy black hair, light eyes ready to be coaxed from their melancholy, and Lady Ottoline wearing a dress more suitable, one would have thought, for some splendid Victorian occasion, and an immense straw hat. . . . After listening to the discourse of Lytton Strachey and several others I vaguely apprehended that in this Oxfordshire village were assembled luminaries of a then to me almost unknown Cambridge world.

Early in March, Lytton went up to Gordon Square to be with his mother, who was now on the point of going completely blind. 'I hope it will not be long before I get sight of you,' she had scrawled with a shaky and uncertain hand, in what was to be her very last letter to him (February 1923). '. . . I am not able to see what I write, but I hope you will be able to read. Ever, dearest, Your loving Mama.'

As the spring approached, Lytton again grew concerned over the *status quo* at Tidmarsh. Ralph and Carrington had jogged along on friendly enough terms throughout the winter, but their new association was not yet resilient enough, Lytton judged, to withstand any further shocks. To make life as diverse as possible, he arranged for them all to travel abroad extensively that year, hoping by these means to circumnavigate the possible dangers.

In the third week of March, therefore, the three of them set off from England for a two months' holiday to the Mediterranean lands, joining James and Alex at the Établissement Thermal, a civilized hotel for invalids at Hammam-Méskoutine, a tiny inaccessible village a few miles south-west of Bône, where Alix was recovering from a serious attack of bronchitis. 'Apart from the unfortunate circumstances, it is a pleasure to be here,' Lytton wrote back to Pippa (27 March 1923). '. . . The hotel is almost by itself in very beautiful country, with mountains all round, and masses of vegetation, and wild flowers such as I have never seen before. Oranges, lemons, palms, and bananas grow in the garden, and hoopoes hop from bough to bough.' As for the Arabs, they seemed to Lytton highly romantic in their white burnouses, but oh! so unapproachable! The other inhabitants of their hotel were English couples, invalids all, who had travelled there for the sake of the natural springs – 'extraordinary boiling hot affairs, which come bursting and bubbling out of the ground, giving off steam, and literally too hot to put your finger in'.

No sooner had Lytton set foot in Algeria than an extraordinary change came over the northern African continent. Its climate altered. While the Easter crowds in London sat out over their iced drinks in Regent's Park, the Algerian population shivered round their native fires. The weather was unprecedented, as it so often is, and far worse than anything recalled even by the Oldest Biblical Inhabitant. Taken unawares, Lytton quickly succumbed to a feverish cold, and while Carrington and Ralph went off for a week to inspect Constantine and Biskra, and James looked after Alix, Lytton nursed his sickness in solitary confinement. But he was also working. On 12 April, he sent off to Maynard Keynes his essay on 'Sarah Bernhardt' for the first number of the newly reconstituted *Nation and Athenaeum.* 'She is *most* suitable,' Keynes replied (27 April 1923). He had also dispatched to him a review copy of Harold Nicolson's *Tennyson,* but at this Lytton demurred. 'I'm sorry to say I can't face Lord Tennyson,' he wrote back (16 April 1922). 'Harold N's book is so disgusting and stupid.'

On the morning of Sunday, 15 April, all five of them left Hammam-Méskoutine for Tunis, then travelled on to Palermo, in Sicily, and after a week here pursued their journey north to Naples. 'We have been having a very enjoyable though rather exhausting time,' Lytton wrote to Keynes from Parker's Hotel (5 May 1923). 'I am now recruiting in this slightly dreadful place. The sun shines, the sea glitters, the trams ting-tang along – and this evening at 6.30 St Januarius's blood will liquefy. But I fear that, like Cardinal Newman, I shan't "have time" to go and see the miracle.'

From Naples they went to Rome, and from Rome soon returned to Pangbourne. 'I am back again,' Lytton announced to Keynes from Tidmarsh (28 May 1923), 'more or less alive, but furious at having been fool enough to exchange the heats of Rome for this fearful refrigerator.' The next week he again visited Garsington for what turned out to be the most disastrous week-end of all. At all costs, he felt that he must escape another such stay there. 'It has been even worse than I anticipated,' he complained to Carrington (3 June 1923). 'Appalling! A fatal error to have come, I see now only too clearly. The only other guest a miserable German doctor – a "psychoanalyst" of Freiburg – ready to discourse on every subject in broken English for hours.[18] The boredom has been indescribable. Most of the conversation is directed towards the dog, when the doctor is not holding forth. Imagine the ghastly meals. Then Philip at the pianola, then Philip reading out loud his articles in the Spectator, then Dr Marten on mysticism – "it can be explained in a few sentences" – followed by an address for 40 minutes by the clock. After which Ottoline joins in. Horrible! horrible! ... Julian [Morrell] has become a kind of young lady – plays Bach and cuddles the dogs all day. Mr Ching came and played Bach. Pipsey is to play Bach after dinner. My brain totters. Soon I shall be playing Bach myself ... If there had been a telephone in the house, I really believe I should have rung you up and fled. I am tempted to start walking as it is.

' "Psycho-analysis" is a ludicrous fraud. Not only Ottoline has been cured at Freiburg. The Sackville-West youth was there to be cured of homosexuality. After 4 months and an expediture of £200, he found he could just bear the thought of going to bed with a woman. No more. Several other wretched under-

18. Dr Marten was one of the strangest characters Ottoline attracted to Garsington. 'Other friends of mine consulted him,' Robert Gathorne-Hardy records, 'and in later years we half suspected that he made experiments on English patients who had been so lately enemies of his country. With his practice he combined some superficial psychoanalysis. I asked Ottoline if he had found out anything peculiar about her. "I find," she droned with humorous solemnity, "that my brothers play an undue part in my life." '

graduates have been through the same "treatment". They walk about haggard on the lawn, wondering whether they could bear the thought of a woman's private parts, and gazing at their little lovers, who run round and round with cameras, snapshotting Lytton Strachey. Query, what did Ott go to be cured of? Whatever it may have been, she is pronounced by all the youths to be "better – much better". Probably after playing Bach this evening, I shall hurry to Freiburg myself. I shall certainly be badly in need of some "treatment". But I admit that I would rather receive it at the hands of P. Ritchie than of the German doctor. I must go downstairs. He will explain to me the meaning of asceticism "in [a] few sentences" – and then Ottoline will join in. The bell rings. Terror and horror!'

Philip Ritchie, the eldest son of Lord Ritchie of Dundee, soon to embark on a legal career with the novelist C. H. B. Kitchin[19] in the chambers of Lytton's old friend, C. P. Sanger, was then still an Oxford undergraduate. Together with some of his friends, he had come over to tea that Sunday afternoon and 'was the one charming element', Lytton claimed. 'He told me shocking gossip about everyone, and in my gratitude I nearly flung my arms round his neck.'

19. In his novel *Crime at Christmas* (1935), which is dedicated to Kenneth Ritchie, C. H. B. Kitchin wrote: 'It is my fate, in Bloomsbury, to be thought a Philistine, while in other circles I am regarded as a dilettante with too keen an aesthetic sense to be a responsible person.' This sentence, Mr Kitchin confirmed in a letter to the author (5 July 1965), 'has certainly an autobiographical overtone and largely sums up my social situation during the twenties. I was introduced to Bloomsbury by Philip Ritchie, who was a close friend of mine, and met most of the leading lights in that circle, but being in those days a tiresome mixture of shyness and conceit, I never felt sufficiently at home in it to form intimate contacts with its members. Strange to say, Virginia Woolf, the most formidable of them all, developed, I think, a slightly protective attitude towards me and it was thanks to her good offices that the Hogarth Press published my first two novels, *Streamers Waving* and *Mr Balcony*. I doubt if any other publishers would have considered them at that time.' Kitchin's reputation as a writer was made with his third book, *Death of My Aunt*, but Lytton, who liked his writing and who once, with his sister Marjorie, acted in a rather daring charade at a gathering in his house, preferred his first two novels and his fourth, *The Sensitive One* (1931), which he had in his personal library.

As the warmer summer weather came in, Lytton's refrigerated spirit quickly thawed, and when Virginia Woolf encountered him at about this time, she observed that he seemed buoyant. The conversation between them turned to literature, and he declared, with an embracing optimism, that they had twenty years of creative work still before them. He himself had completely recovered by this time from the long period of prostration that followed his writing of *Queen Victoria*. 'I have pledged myself to write once a month for that fiend Maynard,' he also told Dadie Rylands (14 July 1923). Though he claimed to have been 'lured' into this 'perfectly mad occupation', it proved in fact to be a most rewarding one, and one that he enjoyed performing. Keynes, whom he had visited at King's early that June, had arranged for him to be paid forty pounds for each contribution – 'a splendid remuneration', Lytton acknowledged – and had also 'made a precarious arrangement with the *New Republic*' for each of these articles to appear in America, from where Lytton would receive almost as much again.

Now that he was writing regularly once more, there was less time available for social entertainments. He did not regret this, and turned down a number of invitations, especially Ottoline's, with positive relief. Life at Tidmarsh was calm and unclouded. During the whole of July, we hear of only a single week-end house party – with the Duchess of Marlborough at Blenheim, the potent architecture of which quite ravished him. 'Nobody was particularly interesting (except, perhaps, the Duchess)', he confided to Mary Hutchinson (11 July 1923), ' – it was the house which was entrancing, and life-enhancing. I wish it were mine. It is enormous, but one would not feel it too big. The grounds are beautiful too, and there is a bridge over a lake which positively gives one an erection. Most of the guests played tennis all day and bridge all night, so that (apart from eating and drinking) they might as well have been at Putney.'

His work, however, did not prevent him from inviting his friends down to the Mill House. In the first two months of this summer there was a long procession of such visitors –

Pippa, Boris Anrep, J. H. Doggart, Frank Ramsey (twice), Sebastian Sprott, Dadie Rylands (who was soon to take Ralph Partridge's place in the Hogarth Press), and Stephen Tomlin, son of Lord Justice Tomlin, a brilliant and erratic sculptor, bisexual and deeply melancholic at times, yet perhaps the most acutely intellectual of all Lytton's younger friends.

So far there had been no sign of any friction between Carrington and Ralph, but Lytton did not intend to take any chances. His policy was still to keep them on the move. At the beginning of August he and Sebastian Sprott, together with Ralph, Carrington and Barbara Bagenal all crammed into the car and started out on an extensive motor tour of France. From Boulogne they drove first to Amiens, then on to Rouen and to Chartres, whose cathedral Lytton announced to be 'superior to any other I have seen'. From here they continued their journey south to Le Mans, then swept eastwards via Orléans to Dijon, where Sebastian Sprott left them to join up with a young friend at Basle. Lytton's destination was the Cistercian Abbaye de Pontigny, on the Yonne, where he had been invited to attend the annual 'Entretiens d'été'. At these conferences, which used to last some ten days, writers and professors from a number of countries would assemble to discuss, *ad nauseam*, a few common moral or literary problems – some of intimidating erudition and obscurity. Lytton had been asked to come by André Gide, who was himself on Le Comité provisoire des Entretiens d'été, and who had written in his all but totally illegible hand to assure Lytton that they were anxiously awaiting 'votre présence à cette réunion "d'éminents" penseurs des pays divers, qui doit avoir lieu cet été – du 16 au 27 Août, à l'abbaye de Pontigny (celle-même où Thomas Becket trouvait asile). . . . J'aurais le plus grand plaisir à vous y voir et à vous presenter quelques amis qui ont un vif désir faire votre connaissance.'

The original plan had been for Ralph to continue touring the country with Carrington and Barbara Bagenal while Lytton was stationed at this 'highbrow club' as he called it. But in response to an urgent wire telling him that his father was dying, Ralph dashed back to England, depositing the two women at an inn near Vermonton, and promising to motor out again and collect them all at the end of the month.

Meanwhile Lytton was being introduced by Gide to his fellow *penseurs*,[20] in particular the strong French contingent which included Georges Raverat, Paul Desjardins, Charles du Bos (who was later to write a long critical essay on Lytton), Jacques Rivière, Roger Martin du Gard, Jean Schlumberger and Max Lazard. They were immediately startled by his resemblance to the Henry Lamb portrait, which up till then most of them had regarded as simply a caricature. 'On the first day,' recalled André Maurois, 'we were alarmed by his tall, lanky frame, his long beard, his immobility, his silence; but when he spoke, in his "bleating falsetto" it was in delightful, economical epigrams.'

Lytton too was considerably startled by his experiences at Pontigny. The sanitary arrangements at the Abbaye were 'crushing and inadequate'; his breakfast contained not a single egg; and his cold, bleak bedroom turned out to be nothing more nor less than a monk's cell. He felt melancholy, too, at being separated from Ralph, and at his own 'constant and immense difficulty in effecting any kind of communication with the natives'. Like a schoolboy pitchforked into a new school, he was lonely and bewildered. Some of the older boys, though benevolent, were particularly aloof. 'Gide is hopelessly unapproachable,' he told Carrington (26 August 1923). 'He gave a reading last night of one of his own works – in a most extraordinary style – like a clergyman intoning in a pulpit. It was enormously admired.' In a letter to Ralph (25 August 1923) he explains that he is not really depressed, but overwhelmed by 'a sort of sentimental sunset Verlaine feeling'. He enjoys 'some secret love-affairs of course – confined, equally of course, to my own breast'. One of these secret passions was for the young and austere Blaise Desjardins – 'largish, pale, unhealthy, who sings very well – but apparently particularly dislikes me, hélas!' And there were also some pseudo-adventures in which he was the object of other

20. Among the German contingent was Heinrich Mann, brother of Thomas, and then almost as celebrated as a novelist.

people's admiration. 'La belle Américaine, with the short black hair, has already come into my life – a slight bother – she is an "artist" – has asked me to sit to her – has read my article on Racine, which she thinks wonderful – gazes at me with slightly melancholy eyes, etc. etc. . . . I shall only, I fear, turn out a disappointment. Her husband is an agreeable American-speaking Frenchman. . . . I am beginning to wonder how we shall weather through another week. Translation hardly seems to be a subject adapted for 10 days of discussion! I only wish I were translated myself, like Bottom. Sometimes I feel as if I *had* been! And my Titania? – La Belle Américaine? Peut-être. Here she comes to do my portrait.'

Invariably the best part of each day was the morning, when he was allowed to sit in the excellent library and, without superintendence, read. But even then, owing to the lack of morning eggs, the exhaustion was considerable. At moments, either from early faintness or the soporific effect of the afternoon debates, everything at the old abbey seemed like a dream. He listened to their discussions with an air of politely scornful indulgence, never volunteering an interjection of his own. 'The "entretiens" which occur every day from 2.30 to 4.30 (what a time to choose) are rather appalling', he complained to Ralph. 'Almost perpetually dull – and then the constant worry of one's being expected to speak and never doing so. Up to now I have allowed exactly three words to issue from my mouth – in public; so that I am growing very unpopular. The fatigue is fearful.'

Some of the subjects were in themselves quite sufficient to start him yawning – 'LES HUMANITÉS, sont-elles irremplaçables pour former une Élite?' or 'Y-a-t-il dans la Poésie d'un Peuple un trésor réservé impénétrable aux Étrangers?' What could one say to questions such as these? During the long and heated conference on 'THE MEANING OF HONOUR', his boredom appeared to reach its summit, and lapping one of his gigantic grasshopper legs over the other, he shut his eyes and dropped off to sleep. 'And what in your opinion, Monsieur Strachey, is the most important thing in the world?' suddenly asked Paul Desjardins. There was a long and painful pause.

861

Then from the slumbering beard there issued a tiny treble: 'Passion!' This was one of his three words, and he uttered it with such nonchalance that the solemn circle of intellectuals, relieved for an instant, broke into laughter. Pressed during another discussion on the subject of 'LES CONFESSIONS' to contribute something, he stood up, after an extended pause announced: 'Les confessions ne sont pas dans mon genre,' and sat down again. On another day, at the end of an exhaustive argument over the latest Gidean cult of whimsical behaviour and 'actes gratuits', his still small voice from the back of the hall was overhead inquiring plaintively: 'Est-ce qu'un acte gratuit est *toujours* désagréable?'

Predictably, most of the French *éminents penseurs* did not know what to make of this strange francophil in their midst. Perhaps he was too English to be interested in purely abstract problems; perhaps he was too frail to take a more active part in the proceedings; or possibly he felt their ideas were too unsubtle to hold any interest for him. 'Looking at him there,' André Maurois wrote, 'we had the impression of an almost infinite disdain, of a wilful abstraction, of a refusal ... And yet ... And yet sometimes, for one fleeting instant, a glance would flash behind his spectacles so vividly that we wondered if all this lassitude might not be the mask of a man really amused and keen, and more Britannic than any Briton.'

At the end of this month Ralph reappeared to rescue Lytton and motor them all back to England. They took this journey in leisurely stages, winding slowly up to Paris where 'anything more like Hell than the grands boulevards I've never seen,' Lytton commented in a letter to Dorothy Bussy (25 November 1923). 'We went to a revue – incredible. Nothing but very old and enormously fat and completely naked females walking about the stage. I was nearly sick. But the country towns were adorable. We had a most delightful tour back – via Vézelay and all sorts of lovely places – such a wonderful sense of civilization that at last one begins to disbelieve in the existence of M. Poincaré.'[21]

21. Raymond Poincaré (1860–1934) was then prime minister of France and minister of foreign affairs.

Back in England again, Lytton sped off for what was now his customary September trip to Charleston. The summer was almost over, and still no trouble had broken out between Carrington and Ralph. The last three months of this year they passed chiefly down at Tidmarsh, Lytton composing his *Nation and Athenaeum* essays. Occasionally, when the month's work was done, he would go up to spend a few days in Gordon Square, whirling among Bibescos, Cunards and Colefaxes. All this, however, was 'pure vapidity' and he preferred whenever practicable to visit Cambridge, which was always so 'delightfully hectic'. That Michaelmas term, he was able to make only one journey there, but this was 'perfect', he told Maynard Keynes (11 December 1923). 'So much sympathetic variety I never saw. I enjoyed myself deliriously – the only horror was going away. However, I was solaced in the train by finding myself sitting next to Sir A. Quiller-Couch, whom I was able to study out of the corner of my eye for an hour and twenty minutes. Could anything be more soothing?'

To Lytton's great satisfaction, his plan of extensive travel that year seemed to have preserved Carrington and Ralph's marriage perfectly intact. They had come through the summer wonderfully well – perhaps those wretched emotional disturbances were a thing of the past now. They had resumed marital relations, and Ralph was evidently finding it less and less necessary to see other girls. They had no quarrels, and they joked and laughed together like happy people. Then, that December, as if to flaunt the strength of the new intimacy which had sprung up between them, they went abroad again together – to visit Gerald Brenan at Yegen! Ralph now claimed that his attitude had completely changed. He was no longer consumed by any sense of bitterness, anger or humiliation – quite the reverse. In a letter from Spain (23 December 1923) he explained to Lytton that he had had a long, amicable chat with Gerald and that 'I feel no jealousy at all now seeing them together – it was only because I was certain it had passed that I came out – now they know that I know what happened in the past, the excitement has died away – I don't feel at all alarmed about it reviving, but that may be because I can't help my conviction that all nice people in the world are perfectly happy just as they are. I do hope it is true of you, dear, at least.'

Lytton, who had been worried over the possible repercussions arising out of this dangerous expedition, was overjoyed by this evident triumph of sweet reasonableness. The future looked bright.

The early winter of 1924 was, however, a particularly severe one for Lytton's health. He was forced temporarily to abandon his work, and between February and June no essay of his came out in the *Nation and Athenaeum*. 'I am in rather a low state,' he told Pippa on 27 February. 'I was attacked by flu on my return here from London. When that went off lumbago supervened – not very badly – but it has been distinctly crushing and is still lingering about. The result is a general debility, as you may imagine.' Three weeks later he was still feverish. 'I'm sorry to say I'm still bedridden,' he scribbled in a faint and wobbly letter to Mary Hutchinson (20 March 1924). 'I can *just* get up for a little sometimes, but my feebleness is beyond anything you ever saw. ... The wretched flu keeps coming back at intervals – in the form of a fever – so that I can't ever yet be sure that it's gone. But every attack is less bad than the last. A most unpleasant lingering malady!' By early April he was at last on the mend, and went down with his sister Pippa to convalesce at Lyme Regis. 'The Cobb is visited twice daily,' he dutifully reported back to Carrington, then deep in the novels of Jane Austen. 'Once there was a regular *Persuasion* accident – my hat flew off – I dashed after it – crashed to the ground – cut my trousers at the knee – but otherwise quite undamaged – except for the loss of dignity.'

The Mill House, during the winters, had proved too damp for his health, and for some time he had been looking round for a new house. That winter Carrington came across one that seemed to please them all, and Lytton now decided to buy it. 'I believe I've bought Ham Spray for £2,300 – but it still totters,' he announced to James on 4 January. By the end of this month, the contract was signed, and the deal completed. Ham

Spray House lay near the Downs between Newbury and Hungerford, and at this time had no drains or electric light, and was in need of a general overhaul. The builders started to put the place in some kind of order early in the spring, and while they were installing the sanitary and electrical fittings, Carrington would go over nearly every day to plan her decorations and the layout of the garden. 'We are beginning to be busy over our new house,' Lytton told Ottoline on 24 April. '... It is altogether rather agitating, and complete financial ruin stares me in the face. I suppose I shall have to write another masterpiece.' Even with some temporary help from a legacy which Ralph had received on his father's death, the move was turning out to be fearfully expensive, and Carrington was forced to admit that they were 'on the rocks for d'argent'.

But she was in her element painting and decorating the rooms, staining the floors and doors. Ralph was always driving her and any of their guests from Tidmarsh that spring – Leonard and Virginia Woolf, Sebastian Sprott, Dadie Rylands, Maynard Keynes and others — over to the new house, and whenever possible they would be put to work on some job that needed doing. Lytton's letters are full of the bustle and activity of these months. 'We spent yesterday at our new house,' he wrote to David Garnett (23 May 1924), 'with various persons, among them Tommy [Stephen Tomlin] and Henrietta [Bingham] – I liked her more than before. She whitewashed amazingly and never said a word.'

There was always much to do; and when they left Tidmarsh on 15 July, Ham Spray was still not really habitable. Lytton stayed away as much as possible during these first weeks, fleeing with Pippa for a fortnight to Brittany.[22] They were all

22. 'My darlings,' Lytton wrote from the Hôtel du Dauphin, Vannes, on 30 July 1924, '... Vannes is a very pleasant town largely old, with charming old houses, half-timbered, the wood painted in pale colours – grey, brown or pink – which has a very pretty effect. Unfortunately the modern frogs have built various atrocities all over it; but not enough to ruin the place. Our hotel looks over the chief square, in which the Breton boys tumble over each other in endless pleasure all day long. In the evening we sit outside the café, listening to the strains of a cultured trio as

extremely excited, but Lytton himself had been sorry to give
up the Mill House, where, despite their difficulties, life on the
whole had been so wonderfully happy. He was filled with a
mixture of nostalgia and trepidation. 'Old age I suppose, but for
whatever reason, the solid calmness of Tidmarsh exactly suits
me', he had written to Carrington during the negotiations for
Ham Spray (1 January 1924). In later years, Tidmarsh was to
retain a very special place in his memory. One night in July
1928, he almost wept as some music on a phonograph record
recalled memories of his life there. 'Among others, there was a
string quartet by Schubert, which brought back Tidmarsh to
me with extraordinary vividness. I felt the loss of that regime
very strongly, and in fact . . . nearly burst into tears. I hope and
pray that our new grandeur . . . won't alter anything in any
way – it would be wretched to lose our native simplicity!'

darkness falls. . . . At Le Mans, as we were going to our train, there were
no porters at the station, so I took up my two green suitcases and proceeded to walk down the platform. Suddenly, without a word of warning,
my back literally went crack – it was a fearful sensation – more terrifying
than painful – as if something had broken inside. I tottered to a bench,
and Pippa managed luckily to find a man who put the things into the
train. When there I felt so shattered I thought I was going to faint.
However, some food and brandy improved matters, and I was much better
by the time we reached Rennes. . . . In the train between Le Mans and
Rennes, as I lay pale and dim, a country youth with red hair, and, as they
say, "the very picture of health", got in. I longed to be him, with a body
which would do its work properly, and, well, an adequate mind. However,
in the evening, at Rennes, feeling rather better, I perceived that the
change, after all, would not have been a wise one.'
  Lytton left Pippa at the Hôtel de Londres in Paris on 7 August, writing back to her the next day that his 'journey went off very successfully.
. . . I found a perfect berth reserved in a cabin which I shared with a
discreet Scotchman. England began directly I entered the large and spot-
less ship, everyone becoming instantly polite and sympathetic. The crossing was quite good, I had breakfast at Southampton, arrived at Newbury
at 9.30, and was whisked back here in the car in time for a glass of milk
and a biscuit.'

SIXTEEN

Ham Spray House

'I lead a dog's life, between Queen Elizabeth's love affairs and my own.' *Lytton Strachey to Dorothy Bussy* (11 June 1927)

'What is love? 'Tis not hereafter – no; but it also isn't heretofore. Is it even here? Ah, well! – But the odd thing is (among all the other oddities) that one occasionally manages to enjoy oneself.' *Lytton Strachey to George Rylands* (12 August 1927)

1
PAPER-GAMES AND PUSSY-CATS

HAM SPRAY was a pleasantly modernized country house of the Jane Austen period, approached by a long straight avenue of lofty wych-elms, and with a long veranda looking south up to the Newbury Downs – a wonderful stretch of grand shapes and solitary expanses. Less picturesque than Tidmarsh, it was also much larger; and though its length and narrowness made it a difficult house to keep warm, Lytton soon ensured a reasonable modicum of comfort by introducing a number of improvements – central heating, an 'electric light engine', a hot-water apparatus, the loft at the east end converted into a studio for Carrington. At last, by his own definition, he could count himself a wealthy man, being able to boast of an open fireplace – beautifully adorned by Boris Anrep with the mosaic of a reclining hermaphrodite figure – in his bedroom. According to Wogan Philipps, the painter, he is also supposed to have fitted up an appliance by which the wires of his bed under the mattress were electrically heated, so that, lying in bed, he was agreeably grilled all night – one of the many apocryphal stories that sprang up around him.

The study, in which Lytton now did all his writing, was also upstairs. Its walls were lined with French and English authors, mostly of the eighteenth century, in their original editions; a large writing-desk stood in the centre of the room, and, hanging over the mantelpiece so that it dominated everything else, was a picture of Voltaire by Huber, showing him seated at a table, his hand raised in benediction above a group of friends. Here, during the mornings, Lytton would retire to work. He still never used a typewriter, disliked dictation, and wrote all his manuscripts out in a neat, flowing hand. In his most characteristic sitting-position at the desk, his body was completely relaxed so that the full force of his energy might be directed to the task before him. He constructed each sentence in his mind before putting pen to paper. On one occasion, some friends were discussing George Moore's extensive revisions to his novels, and one of them asked Lytton about his own amendments. 'I write very slowly, and in faultless sentences', he replied.

His daily routine at Ham Spray was simple and well-ordered. After breakfast he worked; after lunch he lay down; after tea he would usually go, stick in hand, for long walks over the Downs; and in the evening, after dinner, he either played piquet in the downstairs front drawing-room, or listened to music – usually Mozart, Beethoven or Haydn – on the ramshackle phonograph, or read out and discussed his manuscripts with Ralph and Carrington; all three of them, with Tiber the cat, seated round the fire.[1]

Under Carrington's hand, every room at Ham Spray was gradually transformed. She fashioned curious Victorian-style designs from coloured tinfoil paper, she decorated the doors and chimney-pieces, she hung pictures and made delicate paintings on glass and china. Upon the tiles, the plates, the cups and saucers, appeared passion-flowers, legs of mutton, fishes, abstract shapes and whole orchestras of cats playing cellos.[2] The atmosphere of Ham Spray, less characteristically individual than Tidmarsh, had something in common with

1. Besides Tiber (or Tiberius) there were at one time or another a number of other cats at Tidmarsh and Ham Spray, including Agrippa, Nero, Ptolemy and, christened by Carrington, Biddie.
2. Lytton always encouraged Carrington with her painting and thought

Leonard and Virginia Woolf's new house in Tavistock Square, combining a certain austerity and restraint with some less definable feeling of epicurean ease. Besides Carrington's own decorations, there were also a few of Henry Lamb's drawings, and paintings and panels by Duncan Grant, Vanessa Bell and John Banting, executed mostly in thick browns and terracottas, rusty reds, eggshell blue or pale green. The walls of many of the rooms were embellished by 'Fanny Fletcher's Papers' – hand-blocked wallpapers made with carved potatoes and again in characteristic Bloomsbury shades, mauves, olives and cloudy yellows.

Though she employed a woman to deal with the housework, Carrington still did much of the cooking, which was unusual in those days. She was also passionately devoted to the garden and had made herself into a subtle and rather learned horticulturist, collecting and tending all sorts of rare plants to which she became personally attached – in particular a special lily-of-the-valley bed. She planted May trees and vines, and created an entire tulip garden. Now that all the quarrelling with Ralph had ceased, she seemed entirely happy and absorbed in 'my mole hole' as she called the new house. 'The loveliness of this country seems to make one permanently happy,' she wrote to her friend Barbara Bagenal, soon after moving there. 'I am indifferent almost to everything except looking at the downs, and wandering in the garden. There are so many things to do, in the end I do nothing but lie on a sofa like a cat and look at Bulb catalogues, think of gardening, think of painting, contemplate writing letters, talk to Lytton, read the newspapers and gaze eternally out at the downs.'

Once Ham Spray had been bought outright, and they had all moved in there, a deeper sense of security settled on Carrington. She felt more confident that, whatever disruptions might break in upon them from time to time, her life with Lytton could never be effaced. Everything that happened in the

---

it important that she should be induced to show her pictures at various London Group exhibitions. But her shyness was inviolable and she would not be persuaded.

869

world beyond the circle of their home became of diminishing significance to her. She allowed her appearance to deteriorate, using no lip-stick or make-up, and growing rather unkempt and dumpy looking. 'It was as though she had been worn to the bone by life and love,' observed Nicolette Devas, 'eroded by her own cold North Wind.' But she was content. She never lost that quick intensity and wildness of her emotions. As she became more withdrawn, more preoccupied within herself and her immediate surroundings, so her sexual instincts grew more acutely lesbian, and in these later years, most of her closest friends were women. In particular she was at this time violently attracted to Henrietta Bingham, daughter of the United States ambassador at the Court of St James, a beautiful young girl with a perfect oval face, straight dark hair parted in the middle and long black eyelashes shading her brilliantly blue eyes. 'I dream of her six times a week dreams that even my intelligence is appalled by, and I write letters, and tear them up, continually,' Carrington confided to Alix Strachey (11 May 1925). Yet these unrequited fantasy passions do not seem to have caused her much really deep anguish, ' – in fact,' she declared, 'I have seldom felt more self-possessed, and at peace with my lower self'. Spiritually she considered herself to be composed as never before, and her past life now appeared infinitely muddled compared with the quietly flowing river of the present. Perhaps this was merely an illusion, perhaps merely the outcome of middle age, she reflected. Even so, it was 'rather a relief!' 'One of the comforts of being over thirty, I find, is at last to know what one feels, and only do the things one wants to do!' she wrote to Mark Gertler (7 October 1925). '. . . In reality I am very happy, I love the country, and house so passionately that I find nothing outside it seems to affect me very much. I do more painting than I used to, and now I have a fine studio here.'

The artistic, simple, yet sophisticated atmosphere that saturated their home formed the best and most sympathetic expression of Carrington's and Lytton's strange life together. They made an eccentric but endearing couple. 'I have the memory of them both in their pleasant, large room at evening half-shadow,' their friend Iris Tree wrote to the author. 'Books, paintings, the sweep of the Downs through the windows, an ancient gibbet on high hill tops, the garden overlooked by a weeping Ilex tree, roses outside and in. And Carrington, rose-cheeked, pouring tea, laughing upwards from under her thatch of hair, licking her lips with a delicate greediness for delicious things and topics. Lytton wrapped in a shawl, purring with delicate malice and enjoyment of thoughts succinctly worded, his hands stretched out transparent to the flames in the firelight.' In the village of Ham, Lytton was looked up to with a peculiar mixture of awe, affection and amusement. Because of his beard he was called 'God'; but he would often descend from his heights, and sit out on the village green surrounded by the village lads, dealing out forbidden cigarettes to them.

The eight years he lived here were less secluded than those at Tidmarsh, and the new regime was certainly grander. No longer did it appear to be quite the 'life retired, apart' which he had eulogized on his fortieth birthday. He entertained more, and his guests were more varied. During the daytime his personality might appear frail and apathetic as before, and he could still freeze a party with the depth-charge of his dreadful, destructive silence. But later on in the day he always seemed to wake up, delighting in the company of his young companions, and often playing the fool, putting his beard in his mouth, feigning extreme senility and acting up with fantastic highspirits. In summer there were badminton matches on a converted tennis court, or gentle games of bowls on the lawn; and indoors, unexpectedly fierce ping-pong contests. For the evening's entertainment, he would sometimes produce one-act farcical playlets for his guests to perform, in which all the men were women, and all the women men, and the ingenious plots hurried the actors into a bewildering, hermaphroditic confusion. The fun of these pieces cannot be recaptured on paper, though there is an occasional neatly inverted epigram which comes over well.

> That proverb more than once you have been told
> Which says that all that glitters is not gold.

True: but I think this proverb even fitter –
Gold's always gold, although it may not glitter.[3]

Equally successful were the amateur film shows that they would sometimes prepare. David Garnett remembers a particularly imaginative one produced by Carrington and Stephen Tomlin and filmed by Bernard Penrose. 'The setting was Dr Turner's private lunatic asylum, where the inmates were experimented upon and reduced to the condition of animals, the subject being Saxon Sydney-Turner's sinister attempts to experiment upon the innocent heroine who was played by Rachel MacCarthy,[4] wearing a daisy chain. The scene of Saxon, as Dr Turner, peering round the bathroom door at her, had a macabre quality which I have never seen achieved in any other film. My sister-in-law Frances also achieved a success as a human quadruped lunatic wearing riding-boots on her arms.'

A glow encompassed the life at Ham Spray, a bright phosphorescence of spiritual and physical well-being; but it was never an entirely happy home, for the luminous layer of sophisticated 'native simplicity' partly concealed an area of much personal disappointment and secret regret. Some visitors there sensed this undercurrent of unhappiness beneath the attractive veneer, and to one of them, the novelist Rosamond Lehmann, Lytton confessed in an agonized voice that he would willingly surrender all his literary success for the gift of physical beauty. But though he might never be handsome himself, he could at least surround himself with good-looking companions, and absorb pleasure from their beauty. As he grew older he gathered round him at Ham Spray many young men and women whose company he relished partly for their aesthetic appeal – he loved diffidently to touch their bare arms, to pinch their cheeks, to run his fingers through their hair – and partly from the satisfaction he derived from instructing and enlightening youth. The critical severity of his mind would

3. From 'A Castle in Spain', acted at Ham Spray one Christmas.
4. Rachel MacCarthy was the daughter of Desmond MacCarthy. She later married Lord David Cecil, and wrote a long library novel, *Theresa's Choice* (1958).

melt away before these young people, and, transported on the rosy clouds of sentimental speculation, he would endow them with all sorts of fine imaginary qualities. And just as he found youth irresistible, so young people responded to his enthusiasm, and adored him. In particular they loved his eager generosity, his unembarrassed zest for fun and enjoyment. 'Is there any reason why we should be bored *all* afternoon?' he once asked his seventeen-year-old nephew Richard, then on holiday from Rugby and supposed to be working at some dull holiday task. 'Let's go to the theatre!' he added, and took the youngster off to just the kind of show that would appeal most to a schoolboy, and which he very obviously enjoyed too. But he could not always hit it off with adolescents, who still found his appearance, and sometimes his manner too, formidable and perplexing. The first steps to any intimacy were painfully difficult for him, and he approached them with an hysterical bashfulness. Another nephew, the artist John Strachey, remembers him 'suddenly showing me an 18th century French print of a young woman having an enema, accompanying this gesture with a terrifying giggle. I daresay that he was trying to get on some sort of terms with me. Unfortunately the attempt was a failure and I became more scared than ever.'

As a host, Lytton was, in E. M. Forster's words, 'urbane and delightful', but his behaviour towards those of whom he disapproved could still be deadly. Raymond Mortimer records that 'he possessed an astonishing power of establishing intimacy. Of persons whom he took against (sometimes on very inadequate grounds) he could be intolerant to the point of rudeness, but he was one of the most warmly affectionate men I have known. It was a great delight to arrive at his Wiltshire home. ... He had a particular taste and gift for nonsense, and when playing some paper-game in the evening, would throw across at one an improvised quatrain about a friend or a pussy-cat. ... The mention of some writer or politician would suddenly reveal, behind the wit and the warmth, an unpardoning sense of right and wrong. The brisk assurance of his indignation would have astonished those who thought to dismiss him as an elegant trifler.'

As time went on, he filled Ham Spray with his rare personality. There was a fine library, good food and wine, comfort but not luxury, and always endless talk. Lytton regarded conversation as the pleasantest occupation in life, 'and indeed,' Lionel Penrose commented, 'with the Stracheys this ideal could be realised'. This talk revolved mostly round literature and the arts, and their literary and artistic friends. He had a gift for making the past actual as he spoke, and his knowledge never smothered conversation, but nourished it. Friendship brought out the best in Lytton, and he gradually built up at Ham Spray a private world of his own. His conversation had the merit of discovering hidden excellences in others, a quality to which Virginia Woolf paid tribute when, after Lytton's death, she remarked to Clive Bell: 'Don't you feel there are things one would like to say and never will say now?'

Because of this outspokenness, his strong moral opinions and his refusal to ingratiate himself with those whose temperaments he found objectionable, he was not liked by everyone. His passion for ribald joking, schoolboy puns and charades embarrassed some, and strangers sometimes found him quite impossible to get on with. He could be markedly inconsistent and disobliging. Stephen Spender, who used to be taken over to Ham Spray by Wogan Philipps and his wife Rosamond Lehmann, certainly thought him the most astonishing of the Bloomsbury Group. 'He combined strikingly their gaiety with their intermittent chilliness', Spender later recorded. 'Sometimes he would play childish games such as "Up Jenkins", which we played one Christmas. Often he would gossip brilliantly and maliciously. At times there was something insidious about his giggling manner; at times he would sit in his chair without saying a word.'

With more malevolence, Harold Nicolson would speak of him as a bearded and bitchy old woman.[5] Sir Herbert Read

5. Harold Nicolson's wife, Vita Sackville-West, was also antipathetic towards Lytton. On 3 August 1938, she wrote to her husband from Sissinghurst: 'The drooping Lytton must have done its [Bloomsbury's] cause a great deal of harm. I hated Lytton.'

remembered him as 'rather a wistful, querulous figure'. And George Santayana, too, remarked abruptly: 'I am not an admirer of Strachey. I knew him.'[6]

But none of these, in fact, knew him very well. Almost always the people who shunned him he wanted to shun him. Many of those who expressed really strong antipathy towards him had, it turns out, hardly ever met him. T. E. Lawrence, for example – whom Lytton himself considered a 'tawdry' character and a second-rate writer – appears to have based his aversion solely on a study of Lamb's portrait.[7] Most extraordinary of all is the inspired virulence of Wyndham Lewis, who encountered him casually once or twice in the entire course of their lives, but who nursed an obsessional hatred of him for over forty years. On 22 July 1926, he sent Lytton a letter that provides an almost perfect documentary specimen of the paranoiac disease which afflicted him. 'Dear Strachey,' he wrote from 33 Ossington Street, Bayswater. 'It is a very long time since I saw you. I should very much like to see you soon, to discuss two or three literary matters with you.' He went on to suggest that they should meet 'incognito, or rather unobserved', in an unfrequented part of the town, for dinner, 'say at the Great Eastern Hotel Restaurant, called I believe the Great Eastern Restaurant; or for tea in some obscure tea-shop – say near the Law Courts in Covent Garden Market'; and that provisionally they should not divulge their

6. 'Personally I can't bear Santayana, I confess,' Lytton complained to Katherine Manseld (3 October 1919) ' – but that must be considered as a mere personal idiosyncrasy.'

7. In a letter to Robert Graves dated 1 October 1927, T. E. Lawrence compared Lytton Strachey unfavourably with Bernard Shaw. 'It's hardly fair to bracket him [Shaw] with Lytton Strachey,' Lawrence wrote. 'The only portrait which I've seen of him, lately, (deliberate portrait) was that one of William Archer prefixed to three of Archer's plays: and it was direct and wholesome. Strachey is never direct: and not, I think, in himself wholesome. But I don't know him, and my memory of his books tangles itself with my memory of Henry Lamb's marvellous portrait of an outraged wet mackerel of a man, dropped like an old cloak into a basket-chair. If the portrait meant anything it meant that Lytton Strachey was no good.' See *T. E. Lawrence: Letters to his Biographers. Robert Graves and Liddell Hart.*

arrangements. There is no record of Lytton having kept this rendezvous, nor of Wyndham Lewis ever going down to Ham Spray; but almost thirty years later – having carefully scrutinized Lytton's physiognomy with his hostile caricaturist's eye (this undoubtedly being one of the literary matters he referred to in his letter) – he published a novel, *Self-Condemned* (1954), in which the character of Cedric Furber, a rich, lonely bachelor in his forties, strict and fussy and old maidish, is founded on Lytton. The description he gives of this heavily bearded idiot-child living down at his country home is a brilliantly perverse and distorted view of what he took to be Lytton's disintegrating futility:

> Certainly Mr Furber's mask most successfully suggested a distinct, and possibly a new zoological species. ... A long shapeless black beard ... stretched downwards from the base of his nose, and threw the onus of expression upon the eyes ...
>
> While he was with this queer creature René always felt that he was engaged in field work as an amateur naturalist. It was like being a bird-watcher, and Mr Furber a great dreary owl. ... Was he a soft, good-natured, 'impish', old shit? No: he was not susceptible of a worldly classification after that manner. One cannot speak of an owl as a shit, for instance.

Lytton's health responded well to the new environment; in his letters questions of illness began to take second place to financial topics, and a fall in the barometer was as nothing compared to a fall in the rubber market. 'Unfortunately, I am never sick now,' he complained to Virginia Woolf (11 September 1925), ' – only sterile – every Monday, and all other days of the week.'

His manner, too, grew generally gayer than in earlier times. On hot days in the summer, he would arm himself with a green-and-white parasol or an enormous wopsical sun-hat, and descend from the safety of the veranda, manipulating his elongated joints as he stepped across the lawn with the slow, calculated elegance of some spectacular secretary bird. Then he would subside into a deck-chair, a crumpled, ageless figure, his long, lanky legs tightly pressed together, his knees on a level with his head, his diaphanous hands resting on his baggy trousers; and he would begin to talk. He seemed, in all he now did, quietly, radiantly, joyful. There existed a flagrant contrast between his extreme physical passivity, and the frantic, delighted extravagance of his gestures. His immobility was apt suddenly to be disrupted by the most lavish gesticulations when he repudiated some enormity or hailed some audacity that pleased him. Lady Pansy Lamb, who married Henry Lamb in 1928 and met Lytton at Ham Spray for the first time during the previous year, was amazed to find him so happy and amusing after the stories she had heard of his perpetual invalidism before the war. Other of his new friends were unable to believe that he had passed through such a prolonged black period. To his niece, the novelist Julia Strachey, he was 'the most vivid personality I have ever seen'; to Noël Coward 'a fascinating person. I liked and admired him enormously.'

In all the tributes of his friends, two qualities stand out as exceptional: his generosity and kindness. He set no value on money, and his success as a biographer meant above all added opportunities to share pleasures with his friends. Without shedding any of his mischievousness, he continued to grow gentler, more serene. He also regained something of the romantic imperialism of his Cambridge and *Spectator* days. David Cecil recalls him in last years speaking with mild affection of the British Raj. And in a high indignant voice and with long grave face he exclaimed to Frederick Laws: 'When I read Dr Renier's book *The English – Are They Human?* I felt just like the British lion. I waved my tail and I roared!'

On the surface his religious opinions also appeared to some to have eased slightly, though this was probably not true in fact. Wogan Philipps, a devout atheist, felt disappointed, however, that he did not rigorously rule out all hope of another life. The world, he said, was so extraordinary that no one could deny the possibility of some kind of personal survival. In fact he considered that Christianity, which throughout history had been such a bitter enemy of humanitarianism, was now largely a spent force: it was no longer omnipotent, controversial or even interesting. He had helped to fight the good fight against it, but now the war was over, the victory assured;

and perhaps, for that very reason, militant and dogmatic atheists were out of date. 'One may say what one likes (more or less) on religion now,' he wrote to his nephew Richard (5 May 1926), 'but perhaps that is because no one's very much interested in it. There are other, more intimate subjects, which can't be mentioned – or only in the most recondite fashion.'

Elizabeth and Essex and all but six of the essays which make up *Portraits in Miniature* were composed by Lytton while living at Ham Spray. Much of his research, especially for the former, had of course to be done in London, and when working at the British Museum he would stay up in his rooms at 51 Gordon Square. While the younger members and second generation of Bloomsbury – later to be headed socially by Angelica Bell[8] – gave late-night parties at the studio in Fitzroy Street,[9] the old Bloomsbury Group re-formed round 52 Tavistock Square, where Leonard and Virginia Woolf lived on the top two floors above the Hogarth Press. Lytton was very seldom drawn into the rowdy Fitzroy Street parties, but he quite often turned up at the more sedate after-dinner gatherings held in Tavistock Square, and whenever he was expected, Virginia Woolf would add to her invitation cards by way of an inducement the words: *Lytton Strachey is coming*. Roger Fry, Duncan Grant, Maynard Keynes and Lytton himself were the great aces of these evenings, and, more occasionally, Desmond MacCarthy and E. M. Forster. Sometimes they would assemble at Vanessa Bell's house – congregations usually not exceeding six or seven in number, one or two of whom had been invited from the younger generation. No drinks were

8. Angelica Bell, the painter, and daughter of Vanessa Bell and Duncan Grant, who became the second wife of David Garnett.

9. No. 8, Fitzroy Street, a studio once occupied by Whistler and by Sickert, into which Duncan Grant had moved after the war. Not all the parties here, at Taviton Street, or at 46 Gordon Square were confined to Bloomsbury and Cambridge alone. David Garnett remembers seeing Picasso talking to Douglas Fairbanks senior at one gathering; and at another, everyone formed an enormous circle, while, at the centre, two particular guests were left to introduce themselves – Lytton and the film actress Mary Pickford.

provided except coffee, and although the arrangements were quite informal, the unspoken purpose of these meetings was to conduct good conversation. The mellow, harmonious effect of these late-night conversaziones was of a well-practised orchestra, its members all seeming to share a very similar attitude to life, and displaying a pleasure in their friends' performances indistinguishable from their own.

Lytton's entertaining while in London was most often done at his club. John Lehmann, who had been introduced to him by Dadie Rylands, and who saw him fairly regularly during these later years, has told how he would meet him at his rooms in Gordon Square, or at the Athenaeum, and encourage him to recount many fond and naughty stories of Leonard Woolf. 'I was in a glow of pleasure and amusement,' he wrote of their visits to the Athenaeum, 'as Lytton, in his high, thin but authoritative voice ordered an excellent wine and we settled down to a long discussion about the past of Bloomsbury and Lytton's Cambridge days, about poetry (which Lytton wrote copiously, though modestly and in secret), or modern French literature, in which he sadly found all the vices of German literature and very few of the great traditional French virtues. I also visited him at Ham Spray, and explored endlessly in his library while he worked, and afterwards would go for walks with him, during which we renewed our discussion – or rather I renewed my eager questioning and he his judicious and witty answers to the ever-unsatisfied disciple.'

Lytton was always thankful when, his researches over, he could return again to the serenity and comfort of Ham Spray. He had created there an environment exactly moulded to his temperament, and in these sympathetic surroundings, his shy personality, which was never completely liberated in his writings, could convey itself most memorably to his friends. 'One remembered afterwards his doubts and hesitations, his refusals to dogmatize, his flights of fantasy, his high, whispering voice fading out in the middle of a sentence, and forgot the very definite and well-ordered mind that lay underneath.' Gerald Brenan wrote. '... One observed a number of discordant features – a feminine sensibility, a delight in the absurd, a taste for exaggeration and melodrama, a very mature judgement, and then some lack of human substance, some hereditary thinness in the blood that at times gave people who met him an odd feeling in the spine. He seemed almost indecently lacking in ordinariness.'

His tall, lean body, the great tawny beard and high voice, the charming and impudent smile that would flit across his narrow face to greet some subtly barbed observation, the soft and steady gravity of the eyes, witty yet serious, brooding behind his tortoiseshell spectacles, all went to make up a unique physical personality that infiltrated every fibre of the house with its odd, congenial presence. Perhaps the most vivid evocation of him there has been given by another visitor, F. L. Lucas. 'That tall red-bearded figure,' he recalled, 'with the exquisite hands, delicate yet looking so young for his age, who walked the fields of Ham Spray, had a foreign touch about his appearance, as of a Russian landowner; or like some pictured Jehovah, terrifying to strangers, who would yet relax at any moment into an amused Epicurean Zeus.'

2

ATTACHMENT

When Lytton returned with Pippa from France early in August, the renovations to Ham Spray had greatly advanced, and he decided to risk moving in. But there was still plenty of work to be done, and it was not until the autumn that he felt safe in reporting to Ottoline (8 November 1924) that 'we are established here pretty solidly now, and it seems a very satisfactory place – surrounded by all that is most romantic'. By the start of the winter, the old regime seemed to be properly reasserting itself again around the new environment. Lytton was beginning to work regularly at his essays for the *Nation and Athenaeum*; and he resumed once more the familiar series of visitations[10] – to Mells, to Eleanor, to Garsington again

10. 'Lytton came back from Lady Horner's on Wednesday,' Ralph Par-

and to Clare College, where, as the guest of Sebastian Sprott, he encountered another Victorian biographer, Hector Bolitho. 'There were too many people in a small room, packed tight as asparagus in a bunch,' recorded Bolitho who had driven over to meet him, 'so I escaped to the kitchen with my drink, and a book. I had seen Lytton Strachey in the bedlam, looking like a bewildered owl released into a cage of parrots. He also wished to escape, for I looked up from my book and saw him at the door. He whispered, "Is this a kitchen?" I glanced at the stove and sink and answered, "Yes". He said, "I suppose they cook things here", and then vanished.'[11]

He was by now greatly lionized, but the vulgarity, rowdiness and sociality there quickly wore him out, and he would hurry back with evident relief to the haven of Ham Spray. For Ham Spray was unique: a most perfect and amenable vehicle for leading the contented life. Yet already, by the summer of 1925, his existence there with Carrington and Ralph had become subject to many subtle new strains and aberrations. Unlike the single crisis at Tidmarsh, there were no dramatic scenes, no sudden revelations, no exploding storms of passion and repression. Everything was quiet; quiet, open and uneasy. Outwardly, Carrington and Ralph had regained their love and affection for each other, while Lytton himself, so Carrington told Alix (11 May 1925) 'grows more and more benign, and charming, which means I suppose one is on the brink of some unseen volcanoe'.

Yet it was not an unseen volcano that was at work within Ham Spray, but an interior change in the chemistry of their

---

tridge wrote to Frances Marshall (19 September 1924). 'He had been to see Longleat with Mr [Stephen] McKenna and Lord Hugh Cecil, and had to lend them 2/6 to tip the housekeeper. He began a flirtation with McKenna, and the French governess fell in love with him and writes him admiring letters. . . .'

11. Bolitho continues: 'I thought this affected and odd until many years later when I found a paragraph in Frank Swinnerton's The Georgian Literary Scene in which he wrote of the "shuddering hand" with which Strachey "drew a curtain between himself and current vulgarity", and of his knowing, and wishing to know, "nothing at all", of whatever happens in the every-day houses of modern England.'

lives together. Much developed since the pioneer days of 'the Tidmarsh experiment', and now removed to a modern well-equipped laboratory, their central nucleus had grown strangely unstable, had started to expand and attract into its field other particles that adhered and quickly built up a molecular structure of dangerous complexity.

They were not bored with one another, the three of them; but they seemed to have explored every logarithmic variation of mutual development, and now looked outside their small triple relationship for fulfilment. Each one wanted to promote that part of his or her emotional life that was kept separate from the other two, so as to achieve happiness without disarranging the triangular union they all prized so highly. But their independent passions and adventures *did* affect this union, demonstrating how intimately, how illogically, how vulnerably, their total lives were inter-connected. Tidmarsh had provided an unorthodox common ground for their oddly assorted personalities and divergent tastes. Ham Spray should be an arena where, jointly and individually, they might sport and enjoy themselves, indulge their appetites and express their feelings without endangering each other. They were determined that the sensitive domestic cell that enclosed them so delightfully there should not imperil or limit their private pursuits; they did not think these private pursuits should interfere with the happiness of anyone else.

Ralph Partridge was the first to fret against what he felt to be the restrictive influence of Ham Spray. His devotion to Carrington and Lytton never really faltered, but he knew that the two of them could not satisfy his whole nature, and, feeling hemmed in by their demanding practical reliance on him, he was sometimes caustic over their shortcomings, their lack of self-sufficiency. This irritation had already been greatly aggravated when, towards the end of 1923, he had met a beautiful, dark-haired young woman, and gradually fallen deeply in love with her. Frances Marshall was the sister-in-law of David Garnett, very lively and intelligent, and utterly unlike the superficial type of pretty girl with whom he had been carrying on brief meaningless affairs during the last year. Though 'one of the prettiest girls one could find anywhere', she possessed a good mind, had read philosophy at Cambridge, and now worked in Francis Birrell and David Garnett's bookshop in Taviton Street, Bloomsbury. It was here that she had first encountered Ralph when he was travelling books for the Hogarth Press, and soon she was responding to his affection. But she would not permit his advances to proceed too far – a precaution that earned his respect for her and deepened his fondness. As he had begun to fall in love, so his retrospective attitude to Gerald Brenan started to soften; and it was indirectly owing to Frances Marshall's influence over him that he had taken Carrington out to Yegen. They had been determined to eradicate once and for ever the bitterness that had divided them all; and they succeeded in doing even better than this. On arriving there, they had learnt that Gerald was intending, with his great-aunt's help, to return to England in the spring, and Ralph had magnanimously given his blessing to his friend then carrying on a full affair with Carrington. This having been settled to everyone's agreement, he had felt at liberty to pursue Frances Marshall, who came to meet them in Paris that January on their way back to Tidmarsh. Lytton, worried that this encounter might lead to trouble, had also hurried out there, and the four of them spent an enjoyable few days without any trace of friction.

Even before moving to Ham Spray, the new molecule was to have Lytton at its centre, Ralph and Carrington revolving round him, and Gerald and Frances spinning in a wider orbit around the three of them. But in the months that followed, Lytton, incapacitated by persistent illness, had been unable to steer their overloaded craft through the increasingly complicated shoals and reefs. Ralph's letters to Frances over those last months at Tidmarsh had revealed very clearly his gloom and vexation, prompted by the undying sense of responsibility he felt towards both Carrington and Lytton. He was baulked by the surrounding vagaries and infirmities. 'I'm restless and uneasy without you,' he confessed to Frances that spring. '. . . It's partly because I can't get absorbed directly into the current of this life – it's not very absorbing on a squelching day like this – you seem to have attached most of my interest in anything. ... I feel silent before Lytton, and Carrington has an awful headache and stays in bed where I can only look after her and not talk to her.'

Then Lytton himself was struck down. For weeks he lay in his bedroom, with a bandage round his head, groaning, and looking like a wounded soldier. Carrington, in despair, had been worn out by her infinite duties round and around his bed, and Ralph, who tried to help, felt smothered by the sickly atmosphere. 'There have been lugubrious doings here,' he told Frances (8 March 1924). '... Pippa has come down for the week-end and we talk of diseases the whole time. Apparently Lytton used to get ill like this at the age of five and from then onwards – it is only in the last ten years that he's been free of disease. We now anticipate he will go back to this earlier condition, if we do not make still gloomier prophecies. It takes two people really to look after him, and a doctor, and we never stir out as it's too gloomy going for solitary walks. You *will* come down next weekend whatever happens, won't you? It's a grey sort of house to come to, but I do want you, if you can bear it. ... What a bloody curse illness is – it ties everyone up for nothing. I'm not really depressed, only cross ...'

But long after Lytton recovered, Ralph remained discontented. His thoughts had invariably been focused elsewhere; he could never get interested in the people or the conversations, or become re-immersed in the goings-on at the Mill House. 'I'm like a lost soul without you,' he had lamented to Frances (22 June 1924). 'I can't do anything but talk to Carrington about you.' Tidmarsh had appeared lifeless and empty, and he had felt sadly isolated from everything that happened there – as if he were watching all that went on beside him through the reverse end of a telescope. It was impossible, unnatural, for him to bisect his life into two water-tight compartments. He could not do it.

But although Ralph had experienced few difficulties over introducing Frances's name, often rather tactlessly, into their discussions at Tidmarsh, he had been assailed by un-characteristic qualms about inviting her down there, and whenever doing so had given as his excuse the fact that she would be helping Carrington with the move to Ham Spray. He had been as eager as a schoolboy for them all to get on well together, but knew in his bones that probably they would not. And as it turned out, Frances's visits were not really a success. Both Lytton and Carrington could not help but regard her as a potential danger to their way of life. Besides, she was not really their type of person – emotionally too well-balanced and unneurotic for Carrington, and imaginatively too un-fanciful for Lytton. But they had been kind to her, overkind perhaps, and tried to conceal their slight antipathy, hoping that Ralph's feelings for her would soon pass. Lytton's attitude towards her was at all times impeccable, while Carrington, who could not camouflage her prejudices so well, had gone out of her way to stress her friendship and excuse her oc-casional uncontrollable lapses. 'It is very charming of you, you know, to come and help me (us) at Ham Spray,' she had written to her about this time, 'and you must forgive my crab-idness which is only the reaction to this commotion of a move. Really I am the soul of friendliness! My love. C.'

But by the time they were ready to transfer to the new house, the state of affairs had given no signs of improving, and they had left Tidmarsh with sharply differentiated reactions that did not augur well for this fresh chapter in their lives. 'I feel completely out of it all,' Ralph had written to Frances (17 July 1924). '... I'm not intoxicated with delight to be off, or harrowed by regrets. I'm merely uprooted like a tree, and waiting to grow some more roots. Carrington has tears in her eyes very often but I'm not moved like that in the very least. ... I feel uneasy because I'm engaged on something that you can't really share with me, it's such a waste of time and an irritation to the nerves. I *shall* be glad when I get back into the world again.' For Carrington the world was Lytton, Tid-marsh or Ham Spray; but for Ralph it was London and Frances. He saw the shell of the Mill House, utterly dreary and inert, and he saw the debris of uninhabited Ham Spray – and his heart sank. What odds did it make? Both, to him, were dried-up husks of houses, and he had little enough place in either of them. His exposed and tender roots sought not this stony ground, but the fertile soil of London.

Ralph had counted on their suppressed troubles being greatly alleviated, and some amicable sense of balance restored, by the arrival of Gerald Brenan, without whom their inter-dependent community was, so far, lop-sided. Gerald reached London towards the end of May 1924, taking a flat lent to him by Roger Fry in Fitzroy Street, next to Sickert's old studio. Almost at once the new regime was put into operation. Carrington would travel up every second week-end, or else Gerald would go down to Ham Spray, and for a short time took rooms near by at Shalbourne. But the experiment did not work out as Ralph had planned. Next to Lytton, Carrington had loved Gerald better than anyone because, while he stayed in Spain, he shared with Lytton one quality that was always irresistible to her – inaccessibility. But after Gerald landed in England, her passion for him began to lessen. He had belonged to her day-dream world, and now, rather inconveniently, he had materialized as a living entity. To try and preserve the illusion of his veiled elusiveness, she made herself obstructive, out of reach, and saw much less of him than he had obviously bargained for. She had so little time, she would explain. There was her painting, and her life with Lytton; and when she did come up to London, she had many other friends to see – Henrietta Bingham, for instance, who has 'killed my desires for less jeunes garcons pretty completely'.

For Gerald, on the other hand, there was only work – a biography of St Teresa – which was going badly, and Carrington herself. During the fortnightly week-ends that they spent together in Fitzroy Street, Ralph would occasionally drop in to spend the night with them, and together the three of them would try and hit on some verbal solution to their problems. 'I was so miserable when I left you,' Ralph wrote to Frances after one such visit (4 July 1924), '. . . I went to Fitzroy Street. Carrington and Gerald in their respective beds, grunting with sleep – gloomy mutterings between us and then an uneasy tossing night of it. . . . I had a long talk with C. – but *not* about you this time, about Gerald and her and me. A sad talk that, too, because she thinks she ought not to go on seeing him like this; he doesn't settle down or try to find new friends while he thinks he is going to see her. They have decided not to meet again for a month. I hardly come into it, as it is between themselves they have decided this. Only it makes me melancholy that relations are so difficult between people who are fond of each other. That Gerald can't be happy unless he has too little of Carrington or too much for him to stand. My darling, I can't bear the spectre of unhappiness that one sees stalking about.'

So the confusion thickened, and the opportunities for un-happiness rapidly multiplied. Every tension set up in any part of the molecule, between any two of its atoms, would affect each and all of them. Carrington, with that peculiarly pos-sessive yet independent nature of hers, would not give up Gerald, who had fallen more deeply in love with her than ever. She was still leading a full married life with Ralph; but it was perfectly natural for her to love several people, men and women, at the same time, and wish to enjoy sexual inter-course with all of them; though, as she was not strongly sexed, not very often. She also particularly wanted to see Gerald for another reason – to talk to him about Ralph! Now that everything was being conducted openly, the dis-cussions between them all rolled and meandered on without end. Carrington, however, shrank from burdening Lytton with her worries. She knew how much he appreciated serenity, and so she confided in Gerald – in the same manner as Ralph confided in her – selecting the one person whom these confidences would hurt most. She was troubled, she told him, about Frances's growing influence over Ralph. Her own jeal-ousy of Frances, though suppressed, was causing her to fall in love with her husband all over again. As even her affair with Gertler had shown, she never willingly gave up anyone, and as she sensed Ralph moving slowly away from her, so her emotions over him were freshly aroused. This was hardly encouraging news for Gerald, who had, in any case, been presented with many opportunities for remarking her renewed preference for Ralph over himself. Then she was worried, too, she went on to explain, about Lytton's attitude. If Ralph were to leave Ham Spray and go off and live with Frances, how would Lytton respond? Would he stay on with her, or might he even now leave?

This last fear, at least, seemed largely unwarranted. For Lytton also had not been inactive during these months and to add to the complications at Ham Spray now felt that he too was falling in love again. The person to have awakened these emotions in him was Philip Ritchie, the young Oxford undergraduate whom he had first met and liked so well at Garsington. Each time he saw him after that, Lytton's admiration grew, until he pronounced Ritchie to be 'one of the nicest people in the world'. He was not a handsome boy but he had a peculiarly inverted kind of charm which his irregular features helped to bring out. He was gauche, but his manner was consistently endearing; he was absolutely unsentimental, but noticeably warm-hearted; he was lively company, intelligent and unpretentious; and, when Lytton got to know him, he was being pursued by Princess Bibesco. It was not difficult for Lytton to see in him a younger, perhaps a superior version of himself, and his feelings of amiability soon deepened into love. 'I assure you he's a great rarity,' he wrote to Carrington (17 October 1924). 'It's true he's not immediately attractive to look at, and that he probably has no taste in pictures; but he's intellectual (a good point); and he's sensual (also good); and he gives not the slightest value to anything but what is really valuable (very good indeed).'

While on one of his visits to Garsington, Lytton had been introduced by Ritchie to his closest friend, another Oxford young man called Roger Senhouse, a romantic creature of extremely good looks, 'with a melting smile and dark grey eyes'. The two of them, Ritchie and Senhouse, were practically inseparable, and Lytton soon formed with them both a very intimate triangular friendship.

And so, quite early on, the new molecule formed round

Ham Spray. By the spring of 1925, Philip Ritchie and Roger Senhouse had become almost permanent week-enders there, while Gerald Brenan and Frances Marshall would also come down once or twice a month. The outer structure of this molecule, for the time being, remained firm, but within it there raged ceaseless pushing, pulling, quivering, throbbing commotion. Part of this activity was set up by Stephen Tomlin, who, though not as yet sucked into its circumference, spiralled around the outer rim emitting shock waves to which each of the atoms would react differently but always with an electric sensitivity. A frequent visitor to Ham Spray, he was devoted to Lytton, whom he came to regard as something of a substitute for his aloof and magisterial father. Lytton returned this affection; but Ralph, who thought him a born troublemaker, distrusted him, while Carrington's emotions were more mixed because of his being, like herself, unhappily infatuated with the enigmatic Henrietta Bingham.

These anomalies churned up a constant air of pending and indefinable crisis, a perpetual expectation of the unexpected. The position seemed to change almost hourly. One day, for example, Gerald and Carrington were pronounced to be getting on much better; twenty-four hours later, out of the blue, Gerald wrote to announce that he was not going to see Carrington again for at least two years – then, the following week-end, he turned up as usual without explanation. Occasionally, too, Ralph might suspect Frances of favouring some rival to himself, and ventilate his ill-humour on Lytton's friends. Meanwhile Lytton himself, caught in a 'semi-embrace' with Philip Ritchie, would wander off to deliberate as to whether in fact he was really in love after all, and if so, with whom. Carrington responded violently to every shift, especially when she and Lytton were apart, now appearing ecstatic and open-hearted, now solitary, fearful.

And over everything, like a balm, there flowed a river of conversation. From Friday night to Sunday night they swapped a mixture of analysis, gossip, scandal and advice; and from Monday back to Friday again they continued the exchanges on page after page of writing-paper. These colloquies, passionate and amused, would leap from general propositions to private speculation and back again with startling rapidity. As they sat in the garden, paced the veranda or pursued one another round the ping-pong table, the talk of psychoanalysis and masturbation, of jealousy, inquisitiveness, the prevalence of homosexuality, the peculiarities of their friends' love-affairs, sped on and on, suspended only occasionally by some universally recognized *pièce de résistance* – a recitation by Lytton, for example, from Stendhal's *Psychologie de l'Amour*, or a charade by Sheppard giving an imitation of poor Ottoline pretending to be as *petite* as Lydia Lopokova, or a performance by Marjorie Strachey singing nursery rhymes, hymns and traditional songs in a way that, without altering the words, made them sound extraordinarily obscene.

These cabarets and conversations often helped to relax the underlying tension, reducing the magnitude of their problems and temporarily dissolving their perplexities into laughter. Yet the spectre of a pervading unhappiness still stalked the rooms and grounds of Ham Spray, and Lytton was occasionally glad to escape for a week-end elsewhere. Early in 1925 he made the first of several attendances at David Garnett's new Cranium Club,[12] at the opening meeting of which his name had been proposed and 'carried by acclamation'. Here many of the younger Bloomsberries would meet once a month and, according to Carrington, 'try and discuss Einstein but actually sing "Rendel my son" at the Piano'. Early in March, too, he went to stay for the very last time at Garsington, which Ottoline was then preparing to leave on her return, a little later that year, to London. He had also planned a trip to Sicily in April with Carrington, but an attack of neuritis supervened, putting him against Sicily and in favour of the convalescent airs of Lyme Regis. Here he retired with Sebastian Sprott, while Carrington set off with Ralph, Frances and Harry Norton's sister[13] for a walking tour of Provence. 'We saw

12. The Cranium Club was named after Thomas Love Peacock's Mr Cranium in *Headlong Hall*, who personifies the cult of phrenology.

13. J. E. Norton, the Gibbon scholar and author of *A Bibliography of the Works of Edward Gibbon* (1940).

Arles, Nîmes and the Pont du Gard, Saint Remy, Carvillon and Tarascon,' she recorded afterwards. 'I climbed a mountain 2,500 feet high, and walked 20 miles the same day, I came back with no voice, a sore throat, and completely exhausted. But I think in spite of the exhaustion, it set one up rather. Spiritually I feel very composed and tranquil. ... In Paris I completely collapsed to an Exquisite Spanish actress Raquel Meller. Fortunately she is inaccessible.'

Lytton, also recovering his composure, in Lyme Regis, was enjoying a more sedentary holiday. He and Sebastian Sprott would play piquet, read the trial of Leopold and Loeb, brave the remorseless east wind, and sit up talking late into the night – Lytton dreading to go to bed since he had brought his hot-water bottle without its stopper. 'There seems to be hardly another soul here,' he reported to Pippa (29 March 1925), ' – except the town crier; and the Cobb is desolate.'

Separated from Carrington and Ralph, he was better able to indicate those feelings that he was constitutionally incapable of showing face to face – feelings which, even now, they might be tempted to overlook. 'Among other things I've felt a certain inability to express my feelings properly,' he admitted in a letter to Ralph (3 April 1925), ' – I don't know why – and I've been afraid you may have thought, or dimly imagined, that they might have changed in some way – owing to Philip, perhaps, or other things. But it is not in the least so. All I feel for you is exactly the same, only strengthened by the passage of time; and it would be useless for me to try to say how much you and Carrington are to me. I can hardly imagine how I would exist without you both. Perhaps all this is unnecessary, and merely the result of the depression and fear of low vitality. But in any case you will understand.'

Love, that convenient monosyllable, was what Lytton hinted at – though he could not bring himself to write it down. But another, less rhapsodic term defines his attitude far more precisely – *attachment*. They were attached to one another by many ties of understanding, mutual affection, need. Ralph had become an essential part of Ham Spray. And though Lytton might from time to time wish to escape from its

891

enervations, he cherished his home, and wanted above all to pursue his ideal way of life there, now being threatened by the bombardment of so many exterior forces. In Gerald Brenan and Frances Marshall he saw two particularly dangerous and disruptive influences; but he recognized their right to enter into the life there along with Philip Ritchie and Roger Senhouse. If the present unwieldy molecule, its atoms dedicated to eternal motion, could be held together by the gravitational pull of his own love and affection, then he could be counted on to do all in his power to preserve its equilibrium.

But he feared for the future. How long could their 'singular amatory arrangements' continue? How long could this vibrating level of intensity persist without rending asunder the whole perilous architecture of their lives? If he could himself be happy, then perhaps he might spread the bond of that happiness to the others, and entangle them in a magic web of love. More than this he could do nothing but watch and wait as the entire structure shook, twisted and jerked in a restless, unending inner ferment.

3

A MODERATE SUCCESS

The most exciting event of this summer was the first public performance of his old 'Chinese concoction', *A Son of Heaven*. Since 1913, when this 'tragic melodrama' had initially been planned as a stage thriller in the hope of making him a quick fortune, Lytton had allowed it to remain idly in his desk. But now that he had won money and fame with his biographies, the theatre managements, which had been so enthusiastically unhelpful in the lean years, wanted to consider the play afresh. The right time to stage it, they declared, had finally arrived: the right time for them, that was, but not for Lytton. He could no longer take this juvenile pot-boiler with any seriousness – his only real concern, in any case, had been with the machinery of constructing a play. His interest revived briefly on learning that the Lord Chamberlain objected to certain passages, but when the Stage Society approached him with an offer to produce it, he turned them down. Harcourt, Brace, however, determinedly set themselves up in America as agents for the play, and the impecunious Desmond MacCarthy confidently predicted that, once turned into a film, it would make Lytton a millionaire. Mrs Patrick Campbell, too, seems to have taken some interest in Lytton as a playwright, and on being assured by him that there was no suitable star part for her in *A Son of Heaven*, begged him to write another play especially for her, providing him as she spoke with a detailed description of her role in it. But Lytton stared at her with such a depth of silence and incredulity that for a second the thought crossed her mind that he might have died of a sudden stroke. 'Well, will you, Mr Strachey?' she at last urged him after a long pause, whereupon he turned and piped up in his tersest, most emphatic treble: 'No!' But to another, more humble request he felt himself obliged to accede. This was to allow two public charity performances at the Scala Theatre, put on in order to raise funds for the London Society for Women's Service, of which his sister Pippa was the secretary.

The action of *A Son of Heaven*, which takes place in the Winter Palace of the Chinese imperial court at Peking during the Boxer Rising, is sustained by an orderly yet ingenious progression of dramatic surprises, enriched by some colourful palace intrigues and subterfuges, and a full array of oriental magnificence – an Empress who speaks like a later version of Elizabeth I, a diffident, sensitive Emperor, Princes, Ministers, Courtiers, amorous Generals, Manchus, mobs and bodyguards, and a masked executioner played in the Scala production by Ralph Partridge. These historical materials Lytton welded together with a nice dramatic licence, inventing episodes to fit in with the theatrical development.

The Scala production of *A Son of Heaven* has been described by K. R. Srinivasa Iyengar as 'a moderate success'. Considering the quality of the acting and the violent altercations which, right up to the opening night, were being furiously waged between the cast and the producer, even a moderate success seems remarkable. The leading part of the Empress Dowager, which Lytton had originally created for the comic actress Fanny Brough, was taken by Gertrude Kingston, at that time a very well-known performer of the old professional school – intelligent and efficient, but perhaps slightly ham.[14] The producer was Lytton's Cambridge friend, Alec Penrose, who, being avant-garde and much influenced by the work of Edward Gordon Craig, felt that the whole play should be presented as a kind of ballet. Inevitably these two principal figures took great exception to each other, and since neither was willing to concede anything, the result was an appalling clash of styles and a succession of ear-splitting rows. Gertrude Kingston thought the producer's theatrical notions amounted to so much new-fangled nonsense, and utterly disregarded all his instructions. He was furious, but powerless to do anything with her since she was obviously the mainspring of the whole affair. During rehearsals a crisis would break out every few days that would threaten to capsize the entire production, and Lytton, in his now familiar role as mediator and diplomat, would hurry up to London to sort things out.

These rehearsals were not made any easier for anyone by the rest of the cast, which comprised young amateur actors from Cambridge and the neighbourhood of Gordon Square, and included three future academic professors. Many of them had little notion of how to act. Professor Geoffrey Webb[15] played the part of Wang Fu, a provincial official, and also a European soldier; Sheppard was got up as a Manchu; Pro-

14. It was for Gertrude Kingston that Bernard Shaw had written his one-act piece of buffoonery *Great Catherine* (1913), a music-hall divertissement, set at the court of the Empress Catherine, that displays his generosity rather than his genius. As well as being an actress and founder of the Little Theatre in London, Gertrude Kingston devoted herself to giving conferences on Political Speaking, getting up illustrated books for children and painting in lacquer.

15. Geoffrey Webb (b. 1898), who had been at Magdalene College, was to become Slade Professor of Fine Art at Cambridge (1938–49) and a member of the Royal Fine Arts Commission (1948–62). Among his books are a biography of Sir Christopher Wren (1937), *Architecture in Britain: the Middle Ages* (1956), and an edition of the letters of Sir John Vanbrugh (1928).

fessor Dennis Robertson[16] was Li, head eunuch in the palace, whose retinue of lesser eunuchs included Lytton's artist-nephew John Strachey. Lytton's niece, Julia, who took the part of Lady Ling, chief lady-in-waiting, dressed in Chinese court costume, with red lips like two aces of hearts set tip to tip, fluttered through her part very prettily, but Gerald Brenan, a palace guard, who only had to say 'Yes, your Majesty!' was so nervous on the first night that he said, 'No, your Majesty!'

Most of the actors had parts that were singularly ill-suited to their characters in actual life, and were obliged to play love-scenes opposite people to whom they felt a particular aversion. From the very first, then, there was much competition for certain roles, much bartering of parts, much carping and rivalry. At Ham Spray nothing but the play was talked of for several weeks. 'Do you want a super part?' Ralph asked Frances (25 May 1925). 'I am put down to be a Russian, a Boxer, an executioner and a Eunuch – fellow eunuchs are to be Adrian [Stephen] and Frankie [Birrell] and Mouldy [Webb]. Alec takes it all very seriously. Lytton tries hard not to show any interest but is unmistakably excited. . . . I anticipate a great deal of bother and very slight fun in the end.'

By 7 July, with only a few days to go, it looked as if the production might have to be called off. Alec Penrose had threatened to resign, and Gertrude Kingston was preparing to walk out unless he did so. 'There's a Pirandello plot going on in Lytton's play,' Ralph explained ' – the Empress together with the chief Eunuch are plotting against Bea Howe in real life as on the stage, and wish to turn her out together with Alec. Lytton was telephoned for and had to rush up yesterday afternoon to get at Dennis Robertson and the conspirators. There is ferment at 51 Gordon Square – Pippa and Ray at their

16. Sir Dennis Robertson (1890–1963), then a Fellow of Trinity College, Cambridge, afterwards Sir Ernest Cassel Professor of Economics in the University of London, adviser to the Treasury (1939–44) and president of the Royal Economic Society (1948–50). As a past president of the Cambridge Amateur Dramatic Club, he was the only really good performer in *A Son of Heaven*.

wits' end, how to appease Gertrude and yet maintain Alec. Lytton went up swearing to maintain the constitution, but also in great sympathy with the rebellion.' Once again a crisis was averted, the actors and producer appeased; and the play was at last ready for production.

Perhaps the best features of the Scala version were the Incidental Music, composed by the young William Walton,[17] the vivid costumes and the sets — of the Throne Hall of Heavenly Purity in the Winter Palace, the palace garden and the courtyard in the palace precincts — designed by Duncan Grant rather after the style of a D'Oyly Carte *Mikado*. The general atmosphere was of a pleasant teashop, James Agate commented, 'and one reflected that Sir Arthur Sullivan would have turned the whole thing into a delightful entertainment'.[18] The programme cover, 'A Son of Heaven' executed in Chinese characters, was done in mauve and red by Vanessa Bell.

The worst feature, undoubtedly, was the mutilation of Lytton's text. Enormous cuts had been made, including some of the chief speeches, in such a way that the original faults of the play were glaringly paraded, its merits concealed. The handling of the scenes was still commendably expert, and the long monologues incorporated many clever devices to forestall boredom. But the smooth development of the play had been seriously damaged by the excisions so that that warring duality which is at the centre of so much of Lytton's work was here crudely exposed. 'Mr Strachey himself appears to have been in two minds about the mood of his play,' wrote *The Times* critic, and most of the other dramatic critics noticed two opposing strains within the drama. The first, a rattling melodrama, reached its climax in the final act, amid a staccato profusion of tremendous moments. This romantic cres-

17. This music, Sir William Walton wrote to the author, 'has long ago disappeared. If I remember rightly, he [Lytton] was not very interested in "A Son of Heaven", in fact I suspect he was against it being put on at all.' The tympanist in the scratch orchestra was Constant Lambert, who later became famous as a conductor.

18. Other critics have taken strong exception to this description of James Agate's, pointing out that the designs were more in the style of a Diaghilev-Picasso ballet.

cendo, strongly influenced by Elizabethan drama, alternated with a softer air of modern poetic tragi-comedy, somewhat after the style of Chekhov. Mixed with the dramatic plot were many jokes about eunuchs and Queen Victoria, and much splendid regal absurdity – the Empress Dowager, for instance, indulging a royal whim by bidding the guns cease fire on the enemy because they disturbed her picnic. But the realism and the romanticism were never properly fused together as they appear to be in Lytton's biographies and essays, where supreme technical dexterity keeps them in a state of invisible suspension.

Desmond MacCarthy also sensed some disunity in the fabric of the play, which he ascribed to a muddling of two inharmonious themes. The one realistic character, he observed, was the Empress Dowager, 'The Old Buddha', always vital but violently inconsistent, cautious yet courageous, shrewd though ignorant, regal and vacillating. Lytton had, in fact, built up her character from the biographical portrait by J. O. P. Bland,[19]

19. J. O. P. Bland (1863–1945), the writer on Chinese affairs, who had worked in China since 1883 and been a representative of the British and Chinese Corporation Ltd. As a journalist, he was correspondent successively in Shanghai and Peking (1897–1910) for *The Times*. Among his many works was *China under the Empress Dowager* which he wrote in 1910 with Sir Edmund Backhouse, and a biography of Li Hung-Chang (1917) which Lytton reviewed in *War and Peace* and which was of use to him in 'The End of General Gordon'. During the early 1920s, Lytton wrote to Bland asking whether, in his opinion, he ought to allow *A Son of Heaven* to be produced, and Bland, replying as though the Shavian revolution in the theatre had never taken place, advised against it, 'for the reason that you have a big reputation, and this play would, I fear, give the heathen cause to blaspheme. You have followed the historical course of events so precisely, and reproduced the chief actors in the Boxer Crisis in such a manner, as to necessitate, I think, accuracy in depicting them; and this is lacking. A Chinese Empress who talks of kissing (oh, la-la!) and of masked balls at court would never do! – and no Chinese woman would say the things Ta-hé says. The play, in fact, whilst interesting and picturesque, is to me unconvincing, because it lacks the correct oriental atmosphere, and the characters talk like Europeans – I've always thought the Pearl Concubine's [Ta–hé] tragic life would make a grand basis for a Puccini opera, and I once sent him a synopsis of a three-act scenario based on it – but as Pierre Loti's "Fille du Ciel" proved (I think) it doesn't lend itself to the purposes of a European dramatist. The only way it could

and she was the only figure to come fully to life upon the stage. Beside her, the helpless young Emperor was a waxwork. Yet it was he who occupied the centre of the stage. MacCarthy explained: 'Mr Lytton Strachey, I like to think with youthful, though certainly with mistaken diffidence, was not content with one rich theme, namely, the struggle of this ruthless, adroit, ill-informed old bundle of passions and patriotism against "foreign devils" without and palace intriguers within. He brought the Son of Heaven right to the front when he ought to have remained part of the background ... The Old Buddha should dominate the play completely. Even if the second theme had been able to rival in interest the other, it would have only pulled the play out of its proper centre of gravity, for the secret of good play-writing is the elaboration of a single theme, not the ingenious dove-tailing of two.'

All the major London critics gave the play leading notices that were in the main favourable. St Loe Strachey, much reconciled to his cousin's work since *Queen Victoria,* described the occasion and the audience as highly distinguished, and in his *Spectator* review demanded that the play be transferred to the West End. But though Gertrude Kingston wanted to try and put it on in America, and Sybil Thorndike, who saw it at the Scala, was 'enormously impressed' and eager to follow up her triumph as Shaw's St Joan by acting the 'very wonderful part of the "Old Buddha" ',[20] nothing came of these plans during Lytton's lifetime.[21]

---

be made effective for the English stage would be in the high-serious, tragic vein – like Masefield's "Faithful", only more so.'

20. 'I wonder if you would allow me to read your play?' Sybil Thorndike inquired. 'There are not many such parts this year for women – men get all the tremendous parts – (except in the Greek plays) I want to play a Queen Elizabeth one of these times. I've read 8 different plays and have been offered them – Bernard Shaw says she's too successful for him to tackle with interest – I hope that somebody might do her.'

21. Lytton's attitude to *A Son of Heaven* seems to have undergone some change after the Scala production. In a letter to Frances Marshall (9 August 1925), Ralph Partridge wrote: 'Lytton said he was struck by the highbrowness of all his dear friends, as shown about his play, the way they scorned anything that didn't aim at "the heights" of Art (though all

But twenty-four years later, in the spring of 1949, *A Son of Heaven* was revived for a run of three weeks at the New Lindsey Theatre, where it was produced by Vera Bowen, a sensitive and intelligent Russian producer and a close friend of Lydia Lopokova. By all accounts, this wholly professional presentation was far superior to the Scala version, more smoothly integrated, and, in the crucial scenes, very moving.[22]

4

A NEW EXPERIMENT

The opening performance of *A Son of Heaven*, a brilliant social occasion, took place on the evening of Sunday 12 July. But Lytton was not there. A few hours before the curtain went up, having successfully steered the company through their last turbulent scenes, he fled the country, travelling through the night to Innsbruck, where he was to link up with Sebastian Sprott. Together they had planned an extensive walking tour of the Dolomites. But on only the second or third day, loaded down by an enormous pack strapped across his narrow shoulders, Lytton subsided into a crumpled heap in the middle of an empty road between two precipitous cliff walls sighing shrilly: 'I can't go on! I simply can't go on!' They then returned a few yards down the road to a café filled with noisy young German girls selling freshly picked bunches of edelweiss. But when they offered one to Lytton, he brushed it aside with a tired wave of

---

writing for *Vogue* themselves); he wants to write another play now, but thinks they'll all be severe on him if he's not as lofty as Shakespeare, as serious as Ibsen.' When Gertrude Kingston tried to get the play performed in America, he wrote to her (14 July 1926): 'I really don't mind what cuts or alterations are made, if you approved of them. I have always thought that what was needed was a hero – a young, clean-limbed Englishman (or whatever they're called) in the English Embassy, who would rescue Ta-Hé at the critical moment, etc., etc – but I don't see how that's to be added now.'

22. In 1950 and 1951, *A Son of Heaven* was successfully transmitted by the B.B.C. several times on various home and overseas programmes in a version arranged by Mr Harold Bowen.

his hand – 'Cotton wool,' he whispered. 'Just cotton wool.'

The expedition quickly degenerated into a commonplace bus tour, which pleased neither of them. By the time they had arrived at Cortina, they were both heartily sick of buses. 'It's a most wearing method of travelling,' Lytton complained in a letter to Carrington, ' – there are crises at every turn – one never knows whether one will get a seat – then one's packed in with countless Germans got up like escaped convicts – and finally the machine breaks down on the top of a mountain 10,000 feet high and 18 miles from anywhere. This is what happened to us. There we sat, as night fell, among the convicts, the rain thundering down on the canvas roof – horror on horror! However, we got in safe at last. ... Sebastian is charming, and makes existence possible by his command of the German tongue.'

On Wednesday, 5 August, while Sebastian hurried on to Florence, Lytton set off by an early train for London, arriving back the following day. At the week-end he returned to Ham Spray. 'He seems very much the same,' Ralph admitted with disappointment (9 August 1925), 'rather worn by his journey from Munich, and very pleased to be back.' Carrington, who still minded his departures abroad dreadfully, was enraptured at seeing him again. While he was away, her life had been deprived of all colour. Now, though the disagreeable domestic drudgeries went on, she could take enjoyment once more in the pleasant things around her – 'a very hot sun all day, the exquisite beauty of the downs, Lytton's very supporting affection'. He was so kind to her, she told Ralph (20 September 1925). 'He has such finesse of tact that he responds very quickly to one's moods.'

While Ralph spent most of the early autumn book-binding and dreaming of Frances, and while Carrington cooked, painted and wrote long letters to Gerald, Lytton settled quietly down to catalogue his library. He did no writing, and the only new books which gave him pleasure were those of his friends, especially Keynes's brilliant memoir of Alfred Marshall.[23] The domestic scene appeared calmer, less tormented

23. On 21 October 1924 Lytton wrote to Keynes: 'It was very kind of

than for many months. Philip Ritchie had disappeared to Monte Carlo and never wrote to him. 'I confess at the moment I am depressed,' he confided to Mary Hutchinson. 'Such a lull everywhere.' James and Alix came to stay, and E. M. Forster and J. R. Ackerley. Also Henry Lamb, who seemed rather 'faded', Carrington observed. 'He positively crouched, and begged for the crumbs that fell from Lytton's beard. Rather ironical. ... That he should now beg to be allowed to come over again, when 10 years ago *he* made Lytton cringe at a LooK.'

Another old friend to visit them this autumn was David Garnett, who brought with him a copy of his new novel, *The Sailor's Return*. 'I think it is a beautiful work of art,' Lytton wrote to Garnett after he had left (20 September 1925), ' – most skilful in its conception and treatment. Your power of omission seems to me particularly remarkable. I only wish (personally) that the subject had been rather different – I am slightly rubbed the wrong way by simple domesticity, babies and rattles. However, of course, this is a mere idiosyncrasy and does not affect the real value of the book.' He also tried to read Aldous Huxley, but, he told Ottoline, ' "Those Barren Leaves" fluttered from my hands before I had read more than four of them.' *The Tales of Genji*, translated by Arthur Waley,

---

you to send me your Life of Marshall, which I have read with the greatest interest and admiration. It seems to me to be one of your best works, and I only regret that it should be buried in an addendum to the Economic Journal. I wish there were more such things – just the right length and esprit – written in English. What a world it opens up! What strange people were the married monks of the nineteenth century! By-the-bye you don't say – perhaps in the circumstances you couldn't – whether he used French letters. Or was he (or she) naturally sterile? That they should have no offspring seems to have been an essential part of their system of existence. I am alarmed, horrified, impressed – almost over-awed – by such a life. Mon dieu! how wildly different are one's own experiences! The emotions and embraces in which I found myself involved as I read your Memoir – what, oh what, would the subject of it have said of them? After all, he took what was really an easy road to Heaven. And did he get there?' In his answer Keynes said that he didn't think that Marshall 'used letters', but that he became sterile soon after marriage.

was faintly pleasurable – 'very beautiful in bits – Country wine, made by a lady of quality – Cowslip brandy'.

On 20 September, Lytton once again started off on his 'Autumn Manoeuvres', missing out Monk's House this time, and going straight to Charleston. 'Clive, whose clothes are really too shabby even for me – sprouting bits of cloth at the shoulder-blade, – buttons hanging on threads from the trousers – is an indefatigible walker,' he wrote to Carrington (24 September, 1925), ' – out we go for hours over the downs. In the evenings we sit up till half past one chatting.'

The subject of almost all these chats was Maynard Keynes's sensational marriage to Lydia Lopokova. On 25 August, they had been married at a London registry office and gone off for a couple of weeks' honeymoon to Russia, where Maynard could meet Lydia's parents. Bloomsbury was 'shocked'. They had all been given plenty of opportunity to inspect Lydia, and few of them really approved of her. How could Maynard, Lytton wondered, have brought himself to marry such 'a half-witted canary'? There was nothing to her. She bobbed and flitted about the furniture, chirruping away to everyone, and failing in every way to conceal her incomprehension of even the most coherent English speech. It was a disaster! What ever could have possessed Maynard? Why had he done it? they wondered. Of course some people might cynically suggest that being able to show off a brilliant ballerina as his wife would prove a great asset in his aspiring career. But it was not this. He actually seemed to be in love with her – and she with him. Extraordinary! Before long they would be taking marriage to the ultimate absurdity of having children – but that, on second thoughts, was *too* improbable. And so the idle and mis-informed gossip went on at Charleston late into the night.

Lytton shared some of these ridiculous misgivings. He was never personally impolite to Lydia or to Maynard himself and would often invite them down to Ham Spray. The general hostility to their marriage within Bloomsbury, however, was very obvious, and nowhere more so than down at Charleston. For many years Maynard had been part of a very close three-cornered relationship with Duncan Grant and Vanessa Bell. Now he was transferring the centre of his personal life away from them. They had no right, by Bloomsbury ethics, to object; but they resented his departure and released their emotional resentment in all sorts of petty ways. Maynard, for example, laid claim to a certain picture by Duncan; Vanessa argued that it was hers, and Duncan, called in to adjudicate, naturally supported her. Passions rose high. Maynard, they maintained, didn't *need* the picture. He had no aesthetic taste and he was, in any case, *far* too rich. Besides, he had other pictures. So they planned to remove it with their other belongings from 46 to 39 Gordon Square. But Maynard, foreseeing what might happen, had screwed the picture to his bathroom wall and so frustrated their plot. Vanessa was furious, but still determined not to be outwitted. Appearing to be mollified, she invited Maynard for a week-end to Charleston, and while he was on his way down, herself travelled up to London armed with her old latchkey to No. 46 and a screwdriver. She unscrewed the picture, carried it across to No. 39, and then returned quietly to Charleston that afternoon without a word. These were not actions that could easily be forgiven, and Maynard's association with several of his old Bloomsbury friends was severely compromised.

But not with Lytton, who, whatever his private convictions, invariably remained, so Lydia Lopokova told the author, 'very kindly and amiable'. He had a chance to judge the new *ménage* when, after leaving Charleston, he visited Tilton for a few days – and he did not judge it very highly. 'The Keynes visit was rather lugubrious, somehow or other,' he told Carrington (29 September 1925). 'For one thing the house was so hideous. Then Lydia is a pathetic figure, to my mind – and so plain. Maynard is as engrossed as usual in his own concerns. He was very interesting on Russia and Wittgenstein; but there is a difficulty of some kind in one's intercourse with him – he seems rather far off. . . . Would you believe it? Not one drop of alcohol appeared. The Charlestonians declare that il gran Pozzo is now immensely rich – probably £10,000 a year. I can believe it – and water, water everywhere! Such is the result of wealth.'

Eleanor, where Lytton next went to stay with Mary Hutchinson, was much more congenial – appetizing food, claret of an evening, and entertaining literary gossip about T. S. Eliot, who 'is giving up the Criterion, and is to edit a newspaper – the Nursing Gazette'. Clive Bell turned up, now 'a martyr to the piles – is it the result of his pulling up his trousers so very, very high?' But best of all was the sudden reappearance of Philip Ritchie, whom Lytton carried off back with him to Ham Spray early in October.

The momentary lull here was now at an end: the brief summer amnesty within the household waned, and they began moodily to pitch and flounder towards a fresh crisis. While Lytton anxiously hovered, blowing hot and cold over Philip Ritchie and alternately cold and hot over his companion, Roger Senhouse, tension between the other semi-permanent incumbents at Ham Spray tightened to snapping point. There was no question of ill will, but they were all more touchy, more dissatisfied than ever with the status quo. Their carping sensitivity seemed to be unilaterally reserved for giving voice to their own grievances, slights and misfortunes. Skilful at analysing the effect that others were capable of producing on them, they discounted the effect they produced on others. When E. M. Forster, for example, in a querulous outburst to Gerald Brenan, complained that he did not intend to return to Ham Spray again because of Ralph Partridge's inattentive attitude, Ralph was genuinely astonished, and hastened to repair the breach.[24] Ought they all to take more interest in out-

24. Forster had rather fallen for Ralph Partridge. 'I had a long walk with Morgan [Forster] to the Gibbet and on to the top of Walbury Camp', Ralph wrote to Frances Marshall (undated); 'there was a terrific wind and the country looked bleak but sympathetic. I could hardly manage to talk to Morgan, though I tried *earnestly* – that's the word. I like him for liking me, but I'm completely in the dark as to his real character. His language is so linked up with his mother and his aunts that it's like a dialect which I can't talk. I agreed that I'd behaved badly to him on his previous visits, and said that that made me inclined to have a grudge against him. We talked about friendship but not with conviction or much interest. He likes it without intimacy, I with, otherwise it seems to me almost too mild ... he likes so much and I so little that it's hard to agree.'

siders? he asked. Did their behaviour in public do them credit? The question was quickly taken up, and became one for general debate.

But the weakest link in the Ham Spray molecule appeared to be that connecting Carrington with Gerald Brenan. She was at her most perverse, unable to relinquish him, half-loving him, but terrified by the violence of his passions which her own perversity was doing so much to inflame. Her tormenting habits had driven him more wildly eccentric than ever. He was almost at the end of his tether. Vainly he tried to break his jealous obsession over her. He seized upon Ralph, interrupted his book-binding, implored him to tutor him in ping-pong, made him practise three, four and five hours a day, then suddenly contracted tennis elbow and had to give it all up. Still he had not set down a word of his biography of St Teresa. Instead he would take down twenty books at a time from the shelves, read half a page here and there, put them back and then, half an hour later, return, take down the very same books again and go through an identical performance. Every day he wandered in distraction from room to room, and from book to book. After an hour spent indoors extolling the glory of the open English country which he alone appreciated, he would pass another hour walking in the fields describing the architectural beauties of Fitzroy Street and the advantages of a grimy environment for the literary temperament. Either he treated everything with a terrible microscopic earnestness or with the utmost triviality, according to his mood. Testy and cantankerous for much of the time, he also started to worry about his health and to worry others about it. He was the soul of indiscretion among visitors, and when there was no one else to abuse, would launch upon long denunciations against the cat Tiber – its lack of character, its bad manners, its ugliness, its inexplicable habit of scratching him when he tormented it. One way and another he unsettled everyone, worked himself up into dizzy and terrific states – but even so could not shake off his obsession.

This rising tension soon produced some unlikely feuds and alliances between the colliding atoms. Lytton tried hard to be sympathetic to all but was heard on one occasion to declare that people in love should never live together, since they either drove each other mad or out of love. Gerald was certainly never out of love, and neither, wholly, was Carrington. Each now had made a particular ally of Ralph, monopolizing his time with his or her private confidences and complaints. To all these he would give ear with a sublime detachment, afterwards passing on any items of amusement to Frances. By taking all Gerald's more unpleasant utterances quite literally, Carrington buried herself into an even deeper state of bewilderment and guilt. How could she deal with him? He was so unreasonable, demanding at a moment's notice that she should drop whatever she was doing in order to see him whenever – and for whatever reason – he felt unhappy about her, which was almost every other day. Her head spun round in confusion.

As for Gerald, his old friendship with Ralph, which had up till then been poisoned by unreasonable jealousy over Ralph's past married life with Carrington, began to mend. The current appeared to go in reverse, and the two men grew increasingly fond of each other, bound together by all they had suffered over her. Gerald's despair reminded Ralph of his own position some three and a half years ago. 'He [Gerald] is far more bitter about her than I am,' he wrote to Frances. 'The wounds are fresh in him, but scars in me.' The convulsions of Gerald's passion at times shocked Ralph. He would pour out all his long accumulation of rage against her maddening ways – her broken promises, her indifference when pursued, her ardour when pursuing. Yet how dreary she made other, better-behaved women seem! It was dreadful to think that her bewitching charm should depend upon so much pain; her power to hurt was perhaps her greatest fascination. In a panic, Gerald begged Ralph to restrain his wife from taking any other lovers. But at the same time he affected to be contemptuous of more peaceful love-affairs, and for that very reason, Ralph feared, might abuse Frances.

It was, in fact, from this less tempestuous love-affair between Frances and Ralph that the real danger threatened. The crisis sprang upon them suddenly that autumn. In the middle of September, Frances and Ralph had gone off for a month's holiday in Spain, become lovers, and on their return decided that they wanted to spend their lives together.

But how could they extricate themselves from this intolerable, clinging web of human relationships? How? Taking advantage of a week-end trip by Lytton to F. L. Lucas's home in Cambridge, Ralph treated Carrington to a prolonged discourse about the problems involved and his thoughts on solving them. For many months now, so he informed her, they had seemed to be travelling on divergent courses. Left to themselves, they might easily exasperate each other beyond endurance. The truth was, he had discovered, that the two of them were incompatible. She always liked getting her own way, and that way had to be different from everyone else's; while he could not bear letting her have it without a protest, which was his attempt to get *his* own way. Neither of them, in his opinion, was very yielding to the claims of the other. When he felt drawn to her, she drew back; and when he drew himself in, she felt wounded by his apparent hardness. It was an impossible set-up. From this time onwards, therefore, they should be to each other as brother and sister, not husband and wife. He could not part from Frances, whom he loved, he went on to explain, but must take steps to put their liaison on a more permanent basis. Since Frances obviously could not come and live at Ham Spray, he must go up to London.

Carrington stood before him, awkward and miserable, her toes pointed inwards, like a schoolgirl being reprimanded by a headmaster. She begged him not to abandon his life at Ham Spray altogether. If a complete separation between them could be avoided – even if it meant only seeing each other at infrequent but regular intervals – then his new life with Frances would be much easier for her to accept. Much upset, and with great emotion, she emphasized again and again the difficulty she would have in keeping Lytton once he thought Ralph no longer took any interest in her and wanted to sever all connections. But he unequivocally denied that this was his intention. He could not bear to abandon her and Lytton, while

Frances, he added, fully respected his feelings over this. What, then, should be done? The time had come to admit Lytton into the secret, for much depended on how he would react to the news.

After he had returned from Cambridge, a long interview was staged between the three of them. Ralph, who had been dreading this ordeal, mechanically repeated all he had said before. Carrington, now that Lytton was beside her, 'was calmer but so sad'; while Lytton himself listened carefully to everything, but without any comment or the least sign of emotion. His position was an extremely tricky one. Although he was no longer in love with Ralph, he depended upon him and was desperately anxious that he should not leave Ham Spray. Ralph's practical efficiency was indispensable. Without him, Carrington and himself would be constantly exposed to all manner of disasters from fused lights to unlighted fires. It would be shipwreck! They had come to rely on his great ability for controlling situations, for knowing what to do at all times. 'But does Ralph *always* know what to do?' E. M. Forster had once queried. 'Yes,' Lytton replied. 'He has an instinct which tells him how other people are going to behave. He never does the wrong thing.' The present situation, however, was clearly beyond Ralph's control, and Lytton was inhibited from saying everything he wished by the presence of Carrington. His best tactics, he reasoned, might be to approach Frances, who should prove less intransigent than Ralph. To her, he felt that he could say anything he liked. He therefore announced, at the conclusion of Ralph's speech, that he would be going up next day to London, where he would discuss the matter with Frances. He hoped he might be able to clear up his own and the Ham Spray problem with her more easily, he added cryptically, than with the others.

The meeting between Lytton and Frances Marshall took place the following evening at the Oriental Club. Lytton at once made his own views clear. If Ralph were to go and live permanently in London with her, he said, then he could not guarantee staying indefinitely on at Ham Spray alone with Carrington. The Ham Spray molecule might disintegrate entirely, and Carrington would then be left desolate. To all this Frances answered that she had no wish to drive a wedge between Ralph, Carrington and Lytton, and that if Ralph did decide to come and live in London with her, she would not prevent him constantly revisiting them, and would like to do so herself.

Lytton then hurried back to Ham Spray. He could do no more. He told Ralph that Frances had been admirably forthright in explaining what she wanted, and the next move must lie with him. Without being unfair, he wanted to bring home to Ralph and Frances their full responsibility for any action they might take. He had explained to them the possible consequences: beyond that he would neither help nor hinder them. It was their own decision.

By December, Ralph had decided. As an experiment, he would take a flat with Frances in London; but the two of them would go down practically every week-end to Ham Spray, he always spending at least one day and night alone with Carrington and Lytton before Frances arrived. Early in 1926, they arranged with James and Alix Strachey to rent rooms in 41 Gordon Square. Lytton, Ralph told Frances, 'seems very pleased that we are going to 41 and did not say a single crabbing word except that if he had known they were so cheap he would have taken the rooms himself'.

In fact, Lytton was vastly relieved that the split had not been more drastic. Really, this solution was the best he could reasonably have expected: he would still see Ralph every week and the continuity of Ham Spray was safely ensured. Now that everything was agreed to, he intimated that, whatever had happened, he would never have deserted Carrington.

Carrington herself was rapturous. She was keeping Ham Spray; she was keeping Lytton; and she had not lost altogether her hold on Ralph. Her letters convey a rush of hysterical relief. The appalling winter days of suspense were drawing to an end. Spring was already in the air, with all its sense of wonder and renewed promise of joy to come. 'Today the hot sun,' she wrote to Ralph (13 February 1926), 'the innumerable birds singing, the flowers which suddenly have all come out made me so happy I couldn't work indoors. I had to run about in the garden and put down sods on the empty flower bed, but in reality running round the garden out of high spirits. Lytton came out and pretended to be an old gentleman tottering on the esplanade. . . . Lytton suddenly said last night as I was reading over the fire "A game – or have you gone up the spout?" For some reason it made me laugh today every time I thought of it.'

In March, while Ralph and Frances were preparing to move into their new flat, Lytton took Carrington away to the Green Bank Hotel at Falmouth. On their return, Ralph had left Ham Spray for London, and the new experiment was ready to begin. The house felt strange without him. 'In another year I suppose and hope I shall be as indifferent as Alix is to people,' Carrington wrote to Ralph (30 March 1926). 'But you must see that although everything is for the best in the best of all possible worlds for you and F., if you chose to live one day in Lytton's life or mine you would realise the difference . . .'

5

ELIXIR No. 145

'How long were the pauses between his books!' Desmond MacCarthy exclaimed in his essay, 'Lytton Strachey and the Art of Biography'. But Lytton thought constantly and deliberately about his literary future in these pauses. What should he do next? There was no lack of suggestions, or of his objections to them. When Siegfried Sassoon, for example, asked him why he did not write about Dickens, he weakly protested: 'But I should have to *read* him!' He still often contemplated a biography of Voltaire, and used to say that he put aside this project because the subject would have been too sympathetic to exercise all his critical faculties – though the real reason may well have lain in those rows and rows of correspondence and thousands of as-yet-unpublished letters.[25] He already

25. Lytton had, in fact, read the whole of Voltaire's correspondence (or as much as had then been published) many years before in his mother's 'complete' edition.

knew so much about Voltaire that he was appalled by the prospect of what he would have to read and handle. He kept the chessboard of literary success in the corner of his study and would, so to speak, often stroll indolently over to it, amused at his own hesitation, and wonder which piece would be the best to move next – a queen, a bishop, or a knight? Or what about a little attack meanwhile with pawns against the public?

Since moving into Ham Spray, his output had been remarkably slight – only four *Nation and Athenaeum* essays and the Leslie Stephen Lecture. For several months he deliberated half-seriously over writing a Life of Christ. But since the spring of 1924, he seems actually to have written little else but love poems to Philip Ritchie. Then, in the spring of 1925, he decided that he would not, after all, go through with his biography of Christ. 'Quite a good book has just arrived – Le Mystère de Jésus, by Couchond,' he told Ralph (3 April 1925), ' – it finally relegates the poor fellow to the region of myth, and seems to me to be the last nail in the coffin of my book. What a nuisance! I think I shall have to take definitely to the drama.'

Again he studied the chessboard; and it was not a stage drama that he finally fixed upon. For in October, a completely new idea came to him. He would compose, he thought, a book of love-affairs: Queen Elizabeth and the Earl of Essex; Voltaire and Madame du Châtelet; Byron and his half-sister; Mr and Mrs Browning; and lastly, if he had the courage, Verlaine and Rimbaud. Such a scheme would yield admirably to the principles of biography formulated by Dr Johnson in his *Lives of the Poets*. A biographer's first business was not to deal with those of a man's actions that had become part of history; the biographer ought to 'pass slightly over those performances and incidents which produce a vulgar greatness, to lead the thoughts into domestic privacies and to display the minute details of private life'. And this precisely was what Lytton had in mind to do. He was determined now to proceed with this project – in any case he needed, so Ralph told him, the extra money to pay his colossal super-tax. To demonstrate his determination, he started reading about Queen Elizabeth at once.

Two months later his plans had entirely changed. The story of Elizabeth and Robert Devereux, Earl of Essex, so absorbed him that he decided to devote a whole volume to it. He would follow up his portrait of one queen by this study of another. But it was going to be an altogether different sort of book, an experiment to transform biography from the solid craft and classical style of his *Victoria* into the more exciting, impalpable spheres of poetic drama – that elusive world that moved between fact and fiction, fantasy and reality, and that was the world of his own love-affairs.

Lytton began work on *Elizabeth and Essex* on the morning of 17 December. The following day, Carrington wrote to Ralph: 'He [Lytton] has written two pages of Queen Elizabeth. He says he has forgotten how to write and finds it almost impossible!' During the next month he would work at the book nearly every day. 'I have been having quite a tussle with the Virgin Queen,' he admitted to Ralph (6 January 1926), 'and am feeling at the moment perfectly exhausted.' Of all his major works, *Elizabeth and Essex* was to be the most ambitious, and none gave him so much difficulty or wore him out so completely. For over a year he had serious doubts as to whether he could pull it off at all. His stamina seemed more vulnerable than ever, and he often needed to interrupt his work with short recuperative holidays. Early in June, after several months' slow grinding labour, he took himself off with Pippa for a few days to Paris where 'the great, the exciting, the absorbing news was that – Cocteau had become a Roman Catholic', he afterwards wrote to Ottoline (10 June 1926). 'Compared with that the collapse of the franc was nothing.'

The following month, at the end of another short burst at *Elizabeth*, he travelled up to Hexham, in Northumberland, to spend a few days with the novelist Rosamond Lehmann and her first husband, Leslie Runciman. 'Mr and Mrs R. share the establishment with a young man called Wogan Philipps – quite nice – and then there was Dadie – and that was the party,' he wrote to Carrington (19 July 1926). 'Leslie is to me extremely

attractive – in character, even, as well as appearance. But I
don't suppose many would agree with this. He is pompous,
moody, flies into tempers, and is not mentally entertaining by
any means. Perhaps you would be bored by the poor fellow.
But oh! he's so strong, and his difficulties are so curious – and
his eyelashes . . . there's a childishness about him that – I daresay all grown-up people are childish in some way or other – I
find endearing. Rosamond is a much brighter character . . .
though not as good-looking – gay, enthusiastic, and full of
fun. She and Dadie get on like a house on fire. Wogan lies
vaguely and sympathetically at their feet. And dear Leslie
makes a pompous remark, to which no attention is paid,
looks divine, scowls, until I long to fling my arms round his
neck.'[26]

On 18 July, he continued his journey northwards into Scotland, where he was to be awarded an honorary doctorate in
Law by the University of Edinburgh. He stayed at 16 Moray
Place as the guest of Sir Alfred Ewing.[27] Everything was
gloomy beyond words, a terrible descent into a middle-class,
unromantic purgatory after the lost paradise of jokes and fluttering eyelashes at Hexham. 'I shan't exchange a sensible word
with a single soul till I depart,' he complained to Carrington.
'. . . Sir Alfred is a pawky little Scotch body, his wife a very
plain, unfortunate, high-minded individual, without a spark of
humour. Lord Allenby – a large, stupid man – is my fellow
guest in the house.[28] It was certainly very wise of me to refuse

26. Walter Leslie Runciman (b. 1900), afterwards Viscount Runciman
of Doxford, who became director-general of B.O.A.C. (1940–43), had his
marriage to Rosamond Lehmann dissolved the following year (1927). In
1928, Wogan Philipps (afterwards Baron Milford), a communist, farmer
and painter, became Rosamond Lehmann's second husband.

27. Sir Alfred Ewing (1855–1935), a distinguished scientist noted for his
researches into magnetism, was principal and vice-chancellor of the University of Edinburgh (1916–29).

28. Viscount Allenby (1861–1936) – formerly Field-Marshal Sir Edward
Allenby and nicknamed 'the Bull' – was later made rector of the University of Edinburgh. On this occasion he was being awarded an honorary
doctorate in Law. On 20 July 1926 Lytton wrote to Rosamond Lehmann:
'Lord Allenby was in the train with me, and is in the house with me now –

the dinner, which is going on at the present moment, and where they all are, poor creatures, drinking bad champagne and listening to facetious speeches. This is a fine 1800 house, in a beautiful circle, – but oh! the taste of its internal decorations! How deplorable are the well-off!'

Two days later, after a laureation address by the Dean of the Faculty of Law, Professor James Mackintosh, the honorary doctorates were formally awarded.[29] 'The musical chairs went off very quietly this morning,' Lytton wrote later that day to Rosamond Lehmann, ' – since then there has been a lunch and garden party, and in a few minutes a dinner party begins. What is left of me will return to-morrow – to face Lady Astor – and her son Bobbie (who is not so bad). Nothing could be more complete than the contrast between this and Anick Cottage.'

By the end of the month he was back at Ham Spray and working again. The love-story of Elizabeth and Essex was already involving him far more emotionally than his *Queen Victoria*. He seemed implicated in it personally, and it kept prompting memories of those early love-affairs and mingling with the fantasies that hovered over his present infatuations – especially for Roger Senhouse. In the days when he was occupied with this 'tragic history' as he called it, he appeared

---

a large, stupid man, whom one would like to stick pins into – but it would be useless – he would never feel them.'

29. In this laureation address, Professor James Mackintosh referred to Lytton as 'an eminent Georgian who first made his mark in contemporary literature by his witty and subtle biographies of Eminent Victorians. The book was the outstanding literary triumph of the last year of the war; its acid analysis of character and its brilliant irony delighted a generation grown somewhat weary of the ideals and idols of its forerunner. Three years later his *Queen Victoria* made a still more favourable impression by its sympathetic and illuminating portraits of the revered Queen and the Prince Consort and its penetrating and suggestive criticism of the spirit of the time. Although he disclaims the role of historian, Mr Strachey has blazed a trail through the thicket of this crowded epoch for which every future explorer passing that way will have reason to thank him. He is eminently worthy of our Order of Merit in the department of letters, if only for restoring to the delectable but almost forgotten art of biography its proper style, proportion and attitude.'

like a creative novelist, to enter the dim, visionary world, neither wholly embodied nor disembodied, of his own imagination. At moments, it was difficult for him to disentangle what was the real from unreal, what belonged to *Elizabeth and Essex* from what belonged to himself. Sometimes his whole being was suffused with a thrill that could hardly be defined. His senses grew faint. He was a poet – a dramatic poet. And then another flood of feeling suddenly swept upward and engulfed him: he was something more – he knew it. What was it? Was he a woman? A queen? And for a second he might fancy himself, in some half-conscious day-dream, possessed of something of that regal femininity – while before him stood the young and spirited Essex! Then the feeling fled away, and all was vacancy and a sense of effort. In the aftermath of these periods of strange spectral concupiscence, he would feel drained of all energy, bereft almost of any positive identity, as if floating in the bubble of some somnambulistic trance. 'A kind of dreaminess has descended upon me', he confided to David Garnett (11 August 1926), ' – only momentarily, I fancy – but there it is – I drift and drift; very pleasant, though shocking for my morale. ... Circumstances have slightly changed, but hardly feelings, I think. As for me, so far as I can see I have always been identically what I was at the age of two. Rather monotonous for the rest of the world, perhaps!'

During this autumn, he seldom passed more than two consecutive weeks down at Ham Spray. For now that Ralph came down only at week-ends – and almost always with Frances – and he was faced in the weekdays with the solitary ordeal of *Elizabeth and Essex*, he welcomed all the more the society of his friends. He needed their company to bring back a stronger awareness of his own personality and reaffirm the reality of the external world. The first of a long succession of invitations came from Edward Sackville-West (later Lord Sackville), whom he visited at Knole for a few days at the end of August. 'Knole was interesting – beautiful on the whole externally, with College-like courts and charming gardens and park,' he afterwards told Roger Senhouse (2 September 1926), 'but the inside was disappointing – too much hole-and-corner Elizabethanism; one longed for the spaciousness of the 18th Century; and the bad taste of countless generations of Sackvilles littered it all up. Eddie, it seemed to me, continued the tradition in his ladylike apartments. . . . We had quantities of music, both on piano and gramophone – interrupted from time to time, rather characteristically I thought, by – a cuckoo-clock! I found the self-centredness of my host a little chilling; and am very glad not to be the heir of Knole.'

On his return to Ham Spray, he 'rather scandalously dropped Elizabeth for the moment', in order to write a semi-serious essay on Racine which set out to prove that Racine displayed homosexual tendencies,[30] and, more incredible still, a long poem about a mouse. Once these two *oeuvres* had been polished off, he veered off northwards to visit Sebastian Sprott, who had recently left Cambridge to take up the post of Lecturer in Psychology at University College, Nottingham. 'I arrived here[31] on Friday with R[oger],' he notified Mary Hutchinson (11 October 1926). '. . . Nottingham is the oddest, grimmest place in the world, but with a certain hideous grandeur – Enormously large.' And in a letter to Pippa sent the same day, he described the town as being 'grim and vast in a way I had hardly expected. The Explanation of England, probably.' There was little to do except sit on the edge of the gas-fire reading Elizabethan books, or wander without purpose through the dismal streets where 'so far I've seen nothing either in the shops or out of them, to deserve more than passing attention'. Fellow lecturers of Sebastian's came to tea, but they seemed a melancholy crew, particularly Professor Weekley, Frieda Lawrence's ex-husband – 'a pompous old ape, "You keep a manservant, Sprott?" and so on'.

At last, after a couple of days with F. L. Lucas and his wife

30. This essay was accidentally destroyed shortly after Lytton had completed it. On 17 June 1927 he wrote to Topsy Lucas: 'My writings are not in luck just now. A MS on Racine, that I'd written (to prove he was homosexual – not *very* seriously) has just been burnt by a housemaid in London. The only copy too!'

31. 29A Clumber Street, Nottingham.

'Topsy' in Cambridge, he came to rest at Ham Spray. The year seemed to be holding its breath before taking its final dive into winter, and he knew that he should now be bracing himself to do some hard work on *Elizabeth and Essex*. Yet he could not seem to settle down to it. A terrible lethargy encompassed him after even the smallest effort. 'It seems to me that the world has stopped going round,' he confessed, 'but I am too lazy to bother about it.' He even gave up reading books on Elizabethan subjects, and turned instead to Emil Ludwig's *Life of the Kaiser* 'which is quite well done – interesting and fairly intelligent, though the translation might be better', to a new edition of *Les Fleurs du Mal* 'with a most interesting Preface by Valéry [who] . . . persists in maintaining that Poe is a genius of the front rank', to the letters of Walter Raleigh which had 'some good things in it' but were rather too 'provincial', and to Arnold Bennett's *Lord Raingo* – 'distinctly neolithic; but, *qua* flint spearhead, quite well done'.

It was now exactly a year since he had embarked on *Elizabeth and Essex* and his progress was extremely discouraging. 'Nobody can be more disgusted by my delay than myself,' he admitted to Chatto and Windus (13 December 1926). 'I am in hopes that I may be able to finish something on Queen Elizabeth before very long – certainly in less than a year – I hope much less. . . . The Elizabeth book would be a very short one – dealing with her love-affair with Lord Essex at the end of her life. I should of course wish you to publish it if you liked the idea; but I feel rather doubtful about the whole thing.'

This loss of confidence lowered his spirits immeasurably. 'Comfort and conversation – it is my ideal of existence,' he wrote to Topsy Lucas (21 October 1926), '. . . but to be sure the Comfort department is not all that it might be in this arctic region as the Winter draws on.' He had, so he believed, become 'run down' during the course of the year and now planned on a fortnight's holiday in Rome with Roger Senhouse – 'a short jaunt with a divine creature!' as he described it to David Garnett (21 December 1926). 'I believe the breezes of the Channel and the sunlight of Rome will set me up com-

pletely,' he confidently predicted (16 December 1926). Accordingly, on Wednesday, 22 December, the two of them set off
from London to arrive forty-eight hours later under a blue
sky and brilliant sun. They had booked a big double room in
the Hotel Hassler, 'the best in Rome', as Lytton proclaimed it
to be (2 January 1927), 'high up over the steps that go down
to the Piazza di Spagna ... so that everything is spread before
us – St Peter's dome and a hundred churches. ... We live in the
height of luxury – private bathroom, etc., for £1 each day,
including food. R. is a perfect companion – appreciates everything, and is continuously charming to me. He says he is enjoying himself very much, and I think he is – certainly I am.'

Now that he was far removed from *Elizabeth and Essex*,
Lytton was soon feeling wonderfully re-invigorated. The holiday went so well in fact that he began to fear some unforeseen snags. Something, surely, *must* go wrong – a slight
chill on the entrails at the very least. But no, the days sped
blithely past, full of miraculous sunshine and unbroken happiness – it was really quite disturbing. 'Everything has equalled
my wildest hopes,' he announced to Ralph (3 January 1927).
'... We lounge in the Forum, pant grilling up to the Coliseum,
sit toasting on the Pincio. – I hardly dare describe the generous heat. ... On Friday we took our lunch with us and
motored out into the Campagna, and ate among ancient
tombs on the Appian Way and the cypresses and pines with
their spreading tops, drinking chianti in the blazing sun, while
lizards crept out of the Roman masonry and flicked their green
tails at us.' In the evenings they would return to 'this dowdy
German Hassler, where old Morganatic English females crouch
and creep', to play piquet and read Dante. They also went to 'a
delightful Roman opera', and on one notable day Lytton was
entertained as guest of honour at a luncheon given by Princess
San Faustino, who treated him throughout the meal to an
involved explanation of a scheme she had recently devised to
assist the unemployed. This scheme evidently revolved round
the cultivation of the soya bean, from which magic substance,
the princess assured Lytton, everything from factories and
cars to synthetic chocolates and bath salts could be manu-

factured. After working this idea up, as course followed course, to an exciting climax, she turned at the very end of the meal to her principal guest and appealed: 'Mr Strachey, what do you think of my scheme?' But he, in his highest, most discouraging key, only answered: 'I'm afraid I don't like beans.'

After the delights of Rome, Ham Spray presented a vista of snow and desolation. But Lytton quickly acclimatized himself, and was soon extolling the beauties of the surrounding country – the enormous Downs in their perpetual shadow, and the opalescent fields and trees. The weather seemed to be surpassing itself, positively showing off, as if 'to demonstrate that, after all, there's not much to choose between England and Italy'. While Carrington spent most of these days out of doors, snowballing with Ralph or riding her new 'flea-bitten mare' Belle, Lytton would sit for long hours in his study 'busy with Elizabeth'. 1926 had been an appallingly unproductive year. He was determined to take himself in hand and achieve something worthwhile before the end of the summer. Yet even in these near-ideal conditions, he still seized every reasonable opportunity to turn aside from *Elizabeth and Essex* to some less exacting theme. During the last part of January, he made a characteristic divergence to compose another portrait-in-miniature for the *Nation and Athenaeum* on a seventeenth-century Master of Trinity – 'The Life, Illness and Death of Dr North'. 'It's rather comic,' he explained (31 January 1927), 'and will I hope have the additional merit of bringing me £40.'

But for the next few months he struggled assiduously with *Elizabeth*. 'I can only write nonsense to-day,' he confessed to Roger Senhouse on 7 February. 'I wish I could write Elizabeth as well. If only she could be reduced to nonsense – that would be perfect. The whole of Art lies there. To pulverize the material and remould it in the shape of one's own particular absurdity. What happiness to do that! I must try again.'

During the late winter and spring he wrote nothing else for publication, and the only literary distraction he permitted himself was to read a number of books whose topics were very far removed from his own. Dadie Rylands, 'to pamper my

passion for Eton', had sent him M. R. James's reminiscences –
'a dim affair', he described it (26 January 1927), 'vapid little
anecdotes and nothing more. Only remarkable as showing the
extraordinary impress an institution can make on an adolescent mind. It's odd that the Provost of Eton should still be
aged 16. A life without a jolt.' He also read Emil Ludwig's
Napoleon – 'interesting though really second-rate'. But the
books which chiefly occupied him were three modern novels
by his friends. The first of these, chronologically, was David
Garnett's *Go She Must!* which he considered to be 'beautifully
written, and some of the descriptions exquisite – the whole
thing, so far as I can see, wonderfully well done – only – it's
almost impossible to read. At least so *I* find. There seems to
be no interior tide flowing through it, to carry one along. But
that may only be because of some personal disability on my
part. I only know that I suffer agonies of boredom – and
admiration – on every page.'

Rosamond Lehmann's first novel, *Dusty Answer*, he found
more readable. 'It seemed to me to have decided merit,' he
wrote (11 May 1927), 'and for a first novel remarkable. The
disadvantage to my mind is that it is too romantic and
charged with sunset sentiment. A youthful fault, I suppose.
Not sufficiently "life-enhancing". But very well and carefully
done – without horrors in taste (a rare thing nowadays) and
really at moments moving.'[32]

By far the most original of all, however, was Virginia
Woolf's *To the Lighthouse*, which he greatly preferred to her
previous novel, *Mrs Dalloway*. 'But it really is a most extra-

32. In conversation with Rosamond Lehmann, Lytton remarked on the
gusto and forward sweep of *Dusty Answer*. But to Topsy Lucas, who may
have felt envious of Rosamond Lehmann's success, he wrote (7 May 1927):
'I positively read it – every word. It seemed to me to have certain merits,
and to escape certain horrors. But I found it lowering on the whole –
which can't be a good sign. Only of course I am hopelessly inexpert in
modern novels. I am now in the middle of Virginia's [*To the Lighthouse*]–
which I like, so far, much better than Mrs Dalloway. It really is most
unfortunate that she rules out copulation – not the ghost of it visible –
so that her presentation of things becomes little more, it seems to me,
than an arabesque – an exquisite arabesque, of course.'

ordinary form of literature,' he expostulated to Roger Senhouse (11 May 1927). 'It is the lack of copulation – either
actual or implied – that worries me. A marvellous and exquisite arabesque seems to be the result. I suppose there is some
symbolism about the lighthouse etc. – but I can't guess what it
is. With anyone else, the suggestion would be fairly obvious,
but it won't fit into the sexless pattern by any manner of means.'

Over the first five months of the new year, Lytton very
seldom left the countryside. But he was careful never to
overtax his stamina, and would lay aside all work during the
week-ends to build up fresh reserves of strength against the
coming week, and to relax in the company of his friends.
These were very numerous, for besides the almost permanent
platoon of visitors to Ham Spray that winter, there were
many other more occasional guests – Dadie Rylands 'reading
Shakespeare with a violent cold in the nose', the 'very whimsical and charming' E. M. Forster, James and Alix arguing 'on
Dr Freud and the Artist', Raymond Mortimer and Francis Birrell 'whirling like loquacious windmills', Julia Strachey 'so
vague and amusing', John Lehmann who 'with quite a slight
adjustment of his features might have been a great beauty',
Pippa 'a most sympathetic character', and Saxon Sydney-
Turner 'a crane-like figure, for ever smoking – pipe in hand on
one leg – or else perched on the arm of a chair, reading Plot-
inus in the original', who typically succeeded in avoiding the
cab sent to meet him at the station, and walked the whole way
from Hungerford, bag in hand – 'the sort of thing he
thoroughly relishes!'

Once in a while, too, there were more spectacular invasions
by strangers. 'As I was returning from my walk in the afternoon,' Lytton narrated in one of his letters to Roger Senhouse (9 February 1927), 'an aeroplane was seen to be
gyrating round the house. 3 times it circled about us, getting
lower and lower every time. Intense excitement! The farm
hands, various females, Olive[33] and her mother, all the cats,
and myself, rushed towards it, and Carrington was left solitary

33. Olive Martin, who helped Carrington with the cooking and housework and remained at Ham Spray until her marriage in the 1930s.

in her bed, like Antony "whistling in the air". Finally the machine came down in a field exactly opposite the lodge gates at the end of the avenue. There I found it – a group of rustics lined up at a respectful distance. I took it upon myself to approach – but in a moment perceived that the adventure would end in a fizzle. No divine Icarus met my view. Only a too red and stolid officer together with a too pale and stolid mechanic. They had lost their way. I told them where they were, asked them to tea which they luckily refused, and off they went. It *might* have been so marvellous! – What surprised me was the singular smallness and compactness of the contraption – not nearly as big as a motor bus.'

Early in February, Lytton had told Roger Senhouse that 'my own work goes fairly well, though slowly'. As the month advanced, and the weather grew colder, so his work went less well and even more slowly. 'The rain descends in spasmodic bucketfuls, and life here proceeds on its accustomed course,' he reported glumly on 23 February. 'I sit with books and papers. Carrington wanders endlessly up and downstairs, dressed in bright scarlet pyjamas and a cerulean dressing-gown, the cats grow more and more intolerable.' In the cold, his ideas solidified; he subsided into a spiritual palsy and by mid-March his work slackened to a complete halt.

There was nothing for it, he decided, but to rush up to London and try to drown his inertia in a sea of parties. After his long abstinence, the social scene came to him with a certain freshness. He had lunch with Lady Curzon and her daughter, dinner with Ethel Sands, tea with Lady Horner with whom he met 'old Haldane, as urbane as usual, talking of Newton and Einstein in such a style that it was impossible to make up one's mind whether he understood a word of what he was saying'. He saw a production of *No Gentleman* 'and was rather struck by Owen Nares's acting to my surprise', and attended a lecture delivered at the Queen's Hall by Roger Fry. 'The hall was completely full – about 1800 people – and the lecture lasted from 8 to 10.30! – It was full of interest of course, the best thing being a quotation from Michael Angelo on Flemish art – really brilliant – I'd no idea he was a wit.'

By the time he went back to Ham Spray, spring had begun, and with it there came a renewed keenness for work. 'Wonderfully enough I have begun to work again with new vigour – such a mercy!' he exclaimed. Steadily, but at a gradually declining pace, he struggled on until Easter. 'I am still lazy,' he confessed to Roger Senhouse (17 April 1927), 'but feel that at any moment I may plunge into hectic work.' After the oasis of the Easter holiday, his rate of progress across the desert of *Elizabeth and Essex* decelerated still further, and he began to feel the need increasingly to slip away from Ham Spray for brief interludes. At the end of May he visited Peter and Topsy Lucas at The Pavilion, their house at Cambridge, and on his return he wrote to them (6 July 1927): 'I am trying to work. It is not very easy. Truth to tell, I am almost in complete despair.' For a time he even considered abandoning *Elizabeth* altogether and restarting 'my novel of the Judge'. Surely that would be more amusing to do? But perhaps that too was by this stage beyond his powers. He must take up *Elizabeth* once more; he must try again. But first there was another smaller oasis at Whitsun, and then a few days' spree in London – a meeting with Emil Ludwig, a hectic evening as guest of honour at the 1917 Club, dinner with Douglas Davidson and Dadie Rylands at Boulestin's, tea with Lady Lavery, and an amusing luncheon-party with Lady Aberconway where he encountered Osbert Sitwell, 'distinctly charming', and Somerset Maugham, 'a hang-dog personage, I thought . . . with a wife. Perhaps it was because I've eschewed such things for so long that I was amused – the odd mixture of restraint and laisser-aller struck me freshly – but eventually it's just that that becomes such a bore.'

Once more the gaiety of London seemed to inject him with new energies. 'My state is I believe ameliorated,' he allowed (17 June 1927). 'I have written a fair amount, and hope to continue – a most unpleasant form of occupation in my opinion – but one simply has to!' In spite of his best efforts, it soon became obvious that he could never finish the book by the end of the summer. After more than eighteen months of laborious exertion at it, he had actually written only 25,000 words – barely over a third of what would be the final narrative. 'I am afraid I cannot give a very satisfactory report of Her Majesty,' he told Charles Prentice of Chatto and Windus (5 July 1927). 'It seems impossible that she should be finished off before October, and I hardly think it would be safe to think of publishing before Christmas – and perhaps really the Spring would be a more likely time.

'So far as I can judge the affair is nearly half-done, and should come to about 50,000 words; but I am extremely vague about this. My experience has always been that things grow longer and take more time than one expects beforehand.

'. . . Please do not expect too much! "Rather a dull production", *I* expect!'

For a further ten days he continued to 'crouch in my writing-room fiddling with Elizabeth'. Then, feeling the springs of inspiration to be drying up again, he dashed off to London for a dinner at Philip Sassoon's and a nautical party – 'several creatures I'd not seen before – a few flirtations – drink and comfort – a sensation of being quite at home as an Admiral – perfect contentment in fact', he confided to Mary Hutchinson (15 July 1927). 'It was sad leaving London yesterday, but I have no money and must work.'

But this time the trick was not effective. Back at Ham Spray he experienced no renewal of vitality, but 'one of those fearful collapses [that] sometimes overtake me', as he described it in a letter to Dadie Rylands (18 July 1927). Jack and Mary Hutchinson came down for a few days, and so did Peter and Topsy Lucas, and there was much talk about the old subjects – Freud and Sainte-Beuve, love and Cambridge. Lytton's convalescence passed. But his will to write seemed to have been fatally impaired, 'I cannot work,' he wrote in despair to Topsy Lucas (27 July 1927), 'perhaps tomorrow I shall be able to – but I've been idle for days and days. It's a wretched state of affairs, but useless to talk about.'

Carrington now eloped for a fortnight to stay with James in Munich, and Sebastian Sprott, who came down to keep Lytton company, busied himself sorting out and arranging in a series

924

of concertina files the enormous number of old letters which Lytton had preserved.[34] His industry – from which the present biographer has benefited – was 'quite unparalleled', Lytton remarked (8 August 1927). For weeks he laboured away 'with terrific diligence'. Lytton could seldom resist leaving his desk to bury himself in these sheaves of old correspondence, gliding back on a river of nostalgia past Ottoline's 'gigantic mountain', and 'an exquisite, though too small collection' from Virginia Woolf, past the vanished visions of Sheppard and Woolf, through the cloud of years to older and still older memories of Keynes and Hobber, Papa and Mama. 'Oh, such a plunge into the past! – and so many pasts! Hectic undergraduate days – absurdly melodramatic,' he exclaimed in a letter to Mary Hutchinson (27 July 1927). 'George Mallory later – rather sweet. A bundle from Rupert Brooke – nice, decidedly. Some vague Duncan letters – very amusing. The Bunny [David Garnett] budget. And so on – until the present seemed to fade into some kind of mirage, and unreality reigned. I'm afraid my biography will present a slightly shocking spectacle! In the middle of it all, as I was dreaming over a snapshot of George I'd forgotten all about – so alluring! – the door opened, and who should come in but – Henry! Yes – that ghost. But accompanied, this time, by a far from spectral entity – his Pansy – a gay, sturdy, light-haired, dark-eyed young lady – positively attractive! (Her brother, so Henry says, is no less so – oh! oh!). He seems set up – perhaps that will end happily – perhaps she will be able to quell his evil spirit. Though I fear she'll never make him a good painter. But that hardly matters, I suppose!'[35]

34. The only letter of interest which seems to have been missing – and which the author has been unable to find elsewhere – was one sent to Lytton by Thomas Hardy.

35. 'Dadie has been here, and now Henry Lamb and his Pansy are with us for 2 nights,' Lytton wrote to Roger Senhouse (4 September 1927). 'Rather lugubrious, though I like her – she is a sister of Longford's – perhaps you knew him at Oxford? – very pretty, strong and gay – but so young that it's difficult to discover what's inside her, and I hardly think that H.L., who seems to be surrounded with an aura of pale purple depression will do much to open her out.'

These next six weeks were unspeakably wretched. For no apparent medical reason, he told Ralph (3 August 1927), he was confined to his sick-bed suffering from 'one of those fits of lassitude with slightly swollen glands in the throat'. For ten days he continued to feel unaccountably 'wobbly', 'feeble', 'in a sad state'. It was a great nuisance. Gradually, through the second week of August, he began to mend. 'My health is apparently recovered,' he informed Dadie Rylands (12 August 1927), 'though I still feel a little chancelant – and when shall I ever again do any work? Sebastian toils away in the most exemplary manner. Order rises out of chaos. Correspondence after correspondence is sifted, arranged, and bound up. I feel when it's all finished the only thing left for me to do will be to sink into the grave – it's all so neat and final.'

His tall and bony frame had become increasingly subject to strange weaknesses. The lurid unreality of the past now seemed to enfold him, absorbing and dissipating his precious store of energy, leaving him pale and wan. Though his serious illnesses were few, a long succession of minor maladies, a host of morbid, unspecified diseases held Carrington in a state of alarmed suspense. Our knowledge, both of the laws of physiology and of the actual details of his disorders, is too limited to allow a reliable diagnosis as to their cause. In some respects, like nearly all the Stracheys, his constitution was very sound. Fundamentally he was strong – he would often walk his friends into the ground over ten or twelve miles – yet his curiously unstable temperament remained vulnerable to a multitude of abnormal agues and fevers. With the approach of middle age, the emotional excitements that assailed him scarcely diminished, and while he was at work on *Elizabeth and Essex* they may actually have increased. He complains often in his letters that 'my nerves seem so edgy and disordered'. Why? What could be the special cause of those acute nervous infirmities that so shook and humbled him? Possibly an explanation lay in the fact that, like Elizabeth's, some of his ailments were of an hysterical origin, and that his probing into her odd, neurotic condition had aggravated his own kindred diseases. It seemed almost as if this original neurosis was posthumously contagious, that it had, in part, been passed on to him. In his peculiar, rarefied manner, Lytton was living more intensely within Elizabeth than in any of his previous subjects, and from the mixing of their thoughts and feelings he emerged tainted with some of Elizabeth's sexually warped characteristics. Certainly his prolonged study of her taut, audacious temperament – nourished as it was not by a healthy physique, but by an immense will and a highly-strung nervous system – emptied his own bodily resources as no other book had previously done.

As a consequence of this exhaustion, everything came to a standstill by the end of August. With immeasurable relief he turned away from *Elizabeth* to some of his old favourites – Montaigne's essays, the *Confessions* of Rousseau in a 'first edition [that] omits some vital passages owing to prudery', and Swift's poems – 'that man certainly had a dirty mind, in the literal meaning of the word. But no doubt if he liked one it would have been extremely exciting.' His investigations into sixteenth- and seventeenth-century England had greatly whetted his appetite for 'the singular punishments they went in for in those days'. Much of his correspondence over this period contains exultant descriptions of these practices, which thrilled his naturally ribald and prurient imagination,[36] and influenced his choice of reading – of an eighteenth-century French Penal Code, for instance, in which he observes that 'the

36. 'I must tell you a curious tale of the 17th century that I've just come upon – à propos of what I told you of the singular punishments they went in for in those days,' Lytton wrote to Dadie Rylands (8 September 1927). 'It was discovered by Archbishop Laud that the Headmaster of Westminster had written a letter to a Bishop in which he referred to "that little meddling hocus-pocus". The letter was found among the Bishop's papers, and Laud (rightly) flew to the conclusion that it referred to himself. He had the Headmaster arrested and taken before the Star Chamber, where he was condemned to be fined £5000, and ... to have his ears nailed to the pillory at Westminster in the presence of his scholars! – Can you imagine a more marvellous half-holiday for the whole school? Only conceive of it! – But, most unfortunately, the Headmaster made off, and the sentence was never carried out, and the dear boys were disappointed. If one had lived in those gay days how careful one would have had to be! – even more so than now I fancy.'

punishment for blasphemy was curious. For the first time, offenders were fined; for the second, third and fourth times, more and heavier fines; for the fifth time the pillory; for the sixth time, the upper lip was cut off; for the seventh time, the lower lip cut off; "et si par obstination et mauvaise coutume invétérée, ils continuent" . . . the tongue cut off. After that, the imagination of the law gives out. There is also a section on "Délits commis dans les Bois" . . .' He had collected an entire shelf of obscene literature entirely on buggery, including a dissertation by a seventeenth-century Jesuit in Latin on how women can commit sodomy with one another. His other reading included *The Rodiad*, 'a very amusing Regency poem (reprinted) on a highly shocking theme', and among the new books, Katherine Mansfield's *Journal* edited by Middleton Murry, which he described as 'quite shocking and incomprehensible. I see Murry lets out that it was written for publication – which no doubt explains a good deal. But why that foul-mouthed, virulent, brazen-faced broomstick of a creature should have got herself up as a pad of rose-scented cotton wool is beyond me.'

'I am, I think, rather better in health – feeling, at any rate at the moment more cheerful, and with a faint prospect of being able to do a little work,' he reported to Mary Hutchinson on 12 September. But it was not at *Elizabeth* that he planned to work – not just yet. Instead, during the next six weeks, he added to his collection two further portraits-in-miniature, on Carlyle and Gibbon – and contributed a long review of the second volume of Sidney Lee's *King Edward VII* to the *Daily Mail*.[37] He was by now feeling much stronger, his health and spirits 'positively bouncing upwards', he told Virginia Woolf (16 September 1927). In the third week of September he and Carrington visited Augustus and Dorelia John in their 'curious establishment on the other side of Salisbury. You never knew anything quite so singular,' he assured Dadie Rylands, ' – so vague – so utterly lacking in amenities – so (every now and

37. 'A Frock-Coat Portrait of a Great King', *Daily Mail*, 11 October 1927, page 10. For this review Lytton was paid fifty pounds. It has not been reprinted in any of his collected volumes.

928

then) fascinating. There were two girls – two boys – some sort of governess – such silences and driftings! Dorelia herself is a most wonderful person. I am fondly attached to her – but she moves on an unfortunate plane.'

A few days later, on 20 September, he left Ham Spray again for a week at Charleston. 'Clive is nice, as he invariably is when not feeling the need to show off,' he reported to Roger Senhouse (22 September 1927), ' – Vanessa very superb – and Duncan of course charming as ever. There is a youth too, Julian, whom I haven't seen since he was quite a boy – he's now on the brink of going to Cambridge. He's a very nice creature, was once most beautiful, but all now is ruined by a most unpleasant fatness. A Socialist – despises Art – so I'm told . . .[38] Inside the house is rather ramshackle – a regular farmhouse, not done up in any way – but very beautiful in parts, owing to the taste and skill of Duncan and Vanessa's decorations. They paint most of the day in a studio they have built at the back, but I haven't yet been allowed inside. Clive spends the mornings writing his Great Work on Civilization.[39] After dinner we gossip and play the gramophone.' One day while he was staying there, the Woolfs came over

38. 'Clive and Vanessa's boy, Julian is here,' Lytton wrote to Topsy Lucas from Charleston (23 September 1927), ' – he goes to King's next term. Obviously very nice – fat and rather plain – socialistic I fancy, and rather ponderous, as the young are apt to be, at moments.' At Cambridge, Julian Bell became an Apostle, also turning his talents to poetry, womanizing and left-wing politics. Deeply attached to his mother, he was yet reacting against the liberal milk-and-water humanitarianism and the out-and-out pacifism of Bloomsbury, and tried to escape from the clash between his sense of loyalty and his unsqueamish instincts by taking, in 1935, the job of professor of English at the Chinese National University of Wuhan. Two years later, his problems still unresolved, he returned home, where Vanessa Bell was trying to secure for him the post of company director, at a hundred pounds a year, of a family business importing feathers from China. He himself was eager to fight in the Spanish Civil War, and so a compromise was reached whereby he drove an ambulance with the Loyalist Forces in Spain. He was killed on 18 July 1937 at Villanueva de la Canada, in the battle of Brunete.

39. The revised edition of Clive Bell's *Civilization* was published in 1928.

from Rodmell, and Virginia, 'looking very young and beautiful', declared that they must all write their memoirs, on an enormous scale, and have them published in volume after volume in ten years' time.

By the time he came to leave Charleston, Lytton was completely well again. But he was taking no chances, and decided to go off with Carrington for a week in Weymouth. 'I feel sure I shall like Weymouth,' he announced as soon as he had arrived there. The streets were full of rare beauty, and the whole town, he thought, was entirely without pretensions, 'hardly altered, one feels, from the dim days of old George III'. Everything seemed to interest or amuse him. He bought a very large and heavy Kodak camera, and sauntered about snapping 'enormous photos' – of the wishing-well at Upwey, of 'an absurd statue of George III, with a sort of Piazza del Popolo effect behind it', and of the lighthouse at the end of Portland Bill, 'a desolate region, extremely suitable for convicts'. His beneficence embraced all he saw. Even the lodging house where he and Carrington were staying delighted him. 'Our landlord is the Mayor of Weymouth,' he boasted. '. . . Life in lodgings is really very fascinating, it seems to me. Everything is fixed – so unconnected with real existence – so comfortably hideous. I could go on here for weeks and weeks.'

He was also being highly entertained by the work of a young novelist he had come across – William Gerhardie. On the whole, he tended to feel nonplussed by the style of contemporary fiction. 'I don't know whether I'm hopelessly classical, or simply out of date, or an irredeemable purist, or what,' he wrote to Topsy Lucas (30 October 1927). '. . . There are so many modern writers I can't see the point of, whom so many other people like very much, that it looks to me as if there were certain qualities I'm impervious to.' Whenever the intelligence of an author outstripped his artistic talent, Lytton would feel out of step with his work, and he preferred to be lulled by a surfeit of aesthetic sensibility. In Gerhardie's novels, especially his Chekhovian masterpiece *The Polyglots*, sensibility and intellect were finely balanced, and the result he found 'really very amusing, in the Dickens-Dostoyevsky-Douglas style'.

As for his own writing, it was going remarkably well. He had finished 'Carlyle', was half-way through 'Gibbon', and planned two more portraits-in-miniature, on Macaulay and Hume. But *Elizabeth and Essex*, which he had not looked at since the middle of August, still awaited him. Even in his buoyant holiday mood, he could not make light of this undiminished ordeal. Chatto and Windus were becoming increasingly anxious over the protracted delay. This pause separating his books had already lengthened far more than anyone expected: how much farther still was it to be extended? 'I have been unwell all this summer,' Lytton explained to Charles Prentice (4 October 1927), 'and the result is that Elizabeth is not nearly so far advanced as I had hoped. It is most annoying; but I seem to have recovered now.' Under these improved conditions, he estimated that he might have a typescript ready before the end of the winter, in which case the book could be published some time in the late spring. He would be overjoyed finally to have got rid of it.

For, over the past year, his life had been jolted by a series of numbing emotional shocks. He had lived under a shadow of obsessive anxiety. But, this autumn, his problems had begun to resolve themselves. The shadow slowly lifted. As he was driven back from Weymouth to Ham Spray, his prospects appeared brighter than for a long time. He was strangely happy.

He was in love again.

6

TWO IN THE CAMPAGNA

Once Ralph Partridge set up flat with Frances Marshall in the spring of 1926, the cloud that had hung so low over Ham Spray quietly dissolved. Yet the sky was subtly altered. For almost two years, Lytton had wavered in his affections between the two friends, Philip Ritchie and Roger Senhouse, and wavering, had committed himself deeply to neither. Of the two, Philip Ritchie seemed to be his favourite: his endearing ugliness had suggested somehow a more tangible, various and available being than the beautiful and romantic Senhouse. But for all his charm, Ritchie had in some ways turned out to be a disappointment. It was impossible to get properly involved with someone who so often disappeared abroad without any word of explanation, who never wrote letters, and who seldom encouraged Lytton to the exclusion of other admirers.

Circumstances too had favoured a sentimental attachment with Senhouse. In August, the young man had come down to stay with him at Hungerford for three or four crucial days. After he had left, Lytton wrote excitedly to Mary Hutchinson (11 August 1926). 'Ma chère, I have just had a most unexpected piece of good fortune – a free gift from Providence. The other day I gave a slight push to a door which I had longed to turn the handle of for about two years but hardly dared even to touch. To my amazement, it opened; and I found myself in an exquisite paradise. I am still in it, so to speak. Nothing more charming could be imagined. Perhaps you will guess the initial of the door – if so, you will see at once that this is an extremely confidential communication!'

These few days marked the start of what was to be the very last of Lytton's major love-affairs, one that, with all its attendant crises, miscalculations, and moments of disillusionment, persisted until his death nearly six years later.

The personality of Roger Senhouse dominated these final years. The world of course still believed Lytton to be an icy, passionless intellectual – a 'Bloomsbury' cut-out. Yet even in middle age, the very opposite seemed to be the truth. Nature had implanted within him an amorousness so odd and irrepressible as to be always obvious and sometimes even shocking to his friends. His susceptibility to Roger Senhouse was plain for them to see – the handsome, elegant youth, with his open manner, his boyish spirit, his words and looks of admiration, fascinated Lytton. The descendant of a long line of Senhouses of Maryport in Cumberland, and recently come down from Magdalen College, Oxford, to work for a large import-export firm at Hays Wharf in the London Docks, Roger Senhouse exhibited a medley of inherited traits and purely personal proclivities that, in their strange juxtaposition, Lytton found peculiarly compelling. The melodious accents of Eton sounded sweetly in his ears and aroused something of that exaggerated loyalty which non-Etonians sometimes feel for the old school. Also, Roger was a connoisseur of books – later to be the first partner of Fredric Warburg in the firm of Secker and Warburg, and a sensitive translator of Colette; he was unambitious yet adventurous, a creature of curious taste and fantasy. His invariable manner of gentle, unruffled calm concealed a nature of hectic and bewildering eccentricity. His powerful physique, steel-blue eyes and firm jaw, all promised a certain decisiveness in action that was also wildly misleading; he was swept hither and thither by the breezes of his moods and the accidents of circumstance. His spirit, so vague and wayward, combining the cross-currents of learning and lasciviousness, lived and moved in a superb uncertainty. Something about him – his dark-brown hair, perhaps – reminded Lytton of George Underwood, the second of his 'desperate passions' at Leamington College. There was, he concluded, a marked resemblance between his feelings for Roger and for that freckled, red-haired schoolboy of over thirty years ago. Recently he had noticed Underwood's name in an Army List and reflected that by now he must be a senior officer of nearly fifty, with a wife and family – bald, with a few tufts of fading ginger hair – a short, podgy, good-natured figure, very popular in the mess. But when he glanced across at Roger, the years peeled away and his vital forces flowed again, bringing with them the feverish excitements and jealousies of youth. To be away from the struggle of adult life, away from the fame, complexity and division; to be back in the simple unchanging past, a boy again at Leamington; to escape irrevocably into the prolonged innocence of boyhood, and insignificance, and dreams! – That was love.

Lytton was now in his late forties, approaching fifty, while Roger was only in his early twenties – a dangerous con-

catenation of ages. Yet for the moment – it was the autumn of
1926 – all was well. There were long talks, long walks across
the Berkshire Downs, and in the evening more talk and more
laughter, and then there was music, until at last the rooms of
Ham Spray were empty, and they were left, the two, playing
cards together. When he was in London, Lytton would often
drop in on Roger at his flat, and every week they exchanged
affectionate letters. There was a tender, playful quality to their
friendship. Lytton liked to compose for him special love-
poems, and in a more flippant vein even addressed his envelopes in verse:

> Deliver this to SENHOUSE (Roger)
> I prithee, postman debonair!
> He is the handsome upstairs lodger
> At number 14 BRUNSWICK SQUARE.

In October, when the two of them had gone up to stay with
Sebastian Sprott in Nottingham, Lytton wrote to Mary Hutchinson (11 October 1926), 'How to describe my happiness? It
is simply shocking – that's all that can be said. Sebastian is
charming, but ignorant.' There was, in these first few months,
a particular reason for trying to preserve the secrecy of their
affair. Neither of them knew what would be Philip Ritchie's
reactions once he found out. They dreaded hurting him. After
all, it was he who had first introduced them. And was not
Lytton now working the very same trick that Maynard Keynes
had pulled on him twenty years back with Duncan Grant? Not
quite, perhaps, but it could be something very close to it.

The news, however, could not be withheld from Ritchie
indefinitely, and once the two of them had decided to go off
to Rome together in the new year, there was no choice but to
tell him something. Even so, for all their sakes, they allowed
him to know no more than was completely necessary.
'R[oger] has told P[hilip] about it – as vaguely as possible,'
Lytton informed Mary Hutchinson (17 December 1926).
'P[hilip] was extremely charming and sympathetic, R[oger]
says, and didn't bother with cross-examinations. Please, if he
talks about it to you, don't know much more than the bare
fact. The details are so harrowing – to him and everyone else.

Don't even know anything about dates. He's coming here tomorrow. Rather agitating! Really rather a singular, not to say shocking, situation.'

This fortnight in Rome sounded the topmost note to the early part of their relationship. Seldom had Lytton felt happier. His happiness was such that he could scarcely believe in it, that he seemed scarcely conscious from day to day. If only time could have stood still for a little and drawn out those halcyon weeks through vague ages of summer! But there is no respite for mortal creatures. Human relationships must either move or perish. After they had left the sun and blue skies of Italy, this sweet prologue to their friendship came to an end, and the first scene of the ensuing drama opened against the wintry climate of England.

As his memories of George Underwood suggest, the quality of Lytton's love-affairs did not greatly alter throughout the course of his adult life. Spasmodically, Lytton did experience some degree of sexual attraction towards women – the plump and innocent Maria Nys, for example, Katherine Mansfield, Nina Hamnett and, of course, Carrington herself – but these moods were always short-lived, and his customary emotional attitude to the opposite sex was one of instinctive and incapacitating alarm. In any event, since the way to heterosexual happiness was blocked[40], he naturally returned for his most satisfactory love-affairs to the adolescent period of his life, so that the character of all his infatuations – with their common ingredient of awe-struck hero-worship – remained to a large extent permanent, static. Because the very core of his homosexual affection was imbedded in a sense of unsureness and was, in effect, a natural regression to the sunlit days of his youth, there could obviously be little real chance of a ripening development in these affairs, except in the realms of fantasy. Yet they were not all identical. With a common

40. In a letter to Sheppard (7 April 1903), Lytton hints at an incest taboo: 'I think of when I was a child, when I rushed headlong to my mother and clasped her and kissed her with all my strength, and wonder whether I shall ever again love anyone as much as that, with as wild an ecstasy as that, and with as many tears.'

emotional pattern there was room for a surprising variation of feeling. The people he fell in love with were still, generally speaking, the type of men he would himself like to have been, or who possessed specific attributes in which he felt himself to be woefully deficient. But the attributes he admired were various, often contradictory, and fluctuating.

The evidence of his love-poems points to other changes in psychological emphasis. In these poems written at or immediately after leaving Cambridge, his sad obsession and revulsion from the physical act of love-making accurately reflects the mood of this black period of his life. His later poetry, however, tends to divide lust from love, treating most manifestations of the former with a ribald wit and humour, and true passion as something chiefly phantasmagorical, not subject to the decay of physical deterioration or the anti-climax of fully indulged intercourse. Lust is no longer a 'guttural voice' that rhymes with 'dust' to signify the grave of man's nobler aspirations: it is something far less earnest and more thrilling. Very characteristic of the lighter vein in which he presents erotic themes are some lines of verse which he sent to Roger Senhouse in the summer of 1929.

> How odd the fate of pretty boys!
> Who, if they dare to taste the joys
> That so enchanted Classic minds,
> Get whipped upon their neat behinds;
> Yet should they fail to construe well
> The lines that of those raptures tell
> –It's very odd, you must confess –
> Their neat behinds get whipped no less.

This verse, of course, is written primarily to provoke sexual amusement, not to express a disgusted aversion from concupiscence. They are the lines of a happier, freer and more pleasure-loving man. He needed sexual stimulation not so much to arouse and then gratify desire between himself and another man, but to pacify those awful pangs of prurient yearning which had so often in the past made a dungeon of his isolation. Once this need had been met, he was released from the cage of his physical passions into the misty and impalpable region of the spirit where love alone dwelt. It is this delirious universe of ecstatic self-oblivion that his later love-poems celebrate. Happiness was a narcotic, inducing symptoms which were the very obverse of that nausea summoned up in Lytton by the actual, unromantic, strenuous processes of love-making – a nausea that combined something of the relish and exigency of hypochondria. In 'The Haschish', which he composed before the outbreak of the war, he pictures himself liberated from what he again describes as 'this wrong world', and admitted into a disembodied world, not encumbered by the bonds of logic and reason, but strangely ambiguous, inconsequential, rapturous.[41] Here he can find the happy ending to man's laborious terrestrial journey, his promised peace. Despite many lines that seem to imply the occult and immortal nature of this dreamlike realm, the seance is not imbued with any real mystical glow, and consists principally of a shedding of mundane egotism and vanity. He does not seek through love to discover any state of heightened awareness, or any awakening into a new vibrant dimension of life, but to attain a condition of gently melting unconsciousness, an ineffable ebbing away from the reach of a muddled, ugly world. For this reason, the most touching lines of the poem are those in which Lytton expresses his intense longing for self-forgetfulness, for a deliverance from out of the cocoon of his sick body and the hateful London life that walled him in, a life of pain and tribulation.

> Oh, let me dream and let me know no more
> The sun's harsh sight and life's discordant roar;
> Let me eclipse my being in a swoon,
> And lingering through a long penumbral noon,
> Feel like a ghost a soft Elysian balm,

41. James Strachey has urged that there was never any question of Lytton actually being a hashish eater. In those days, in England, hashish was not so much a drug (*Cannabis Indica*) as a purely literary substance – from the *Arabian Nights* (though later celebrated in France in more realistic fashion by Rabelais and Baudelaire). Lytton, in any case, was 'far too respectable ever to *dream* of going in for that sort of thing', and would have disapproved of the journalistic existence the drug now enjoys.

A universe of amaranthine calm,
Devoid of thought, forgetful of desire.
And quiet as joined hearts which still suspire
Love's ultimate tenderness, while faint bliss
With pale mandragora drowns the accomplished kiss,
So shall I find, inextricably sweet . . .
— Looks that are felt, and lusts as light as air,
And curious embraces like September flowers
Vanishing down interminable hours,
And love's last kiss, exquisitely withdrawn,
And copulations dimmer than the dawn.
Who now shall fret?

It is only when chloroformed and emasculated in this way that the passions of lust and love could unite to the complete satisfaction of Lytton's fastidious nature. The entranced and guiltless vision he evokes becomes highly conventional, taking on the classical poetic diction of later Victorian sentiment, as soon as he tries to conjure forth a more palpable picture of homosexual bliss, and sees the

forms of golden boys
Embraced seraphically in far lands
By languid lovers, linking marvellous hands
With early Virgins crowned with quiet wreaths
Of lily, frailer than the air that breathes
The memory of Sappho all day long
Through Lesbian shades of fragmentary song . . .

As he had grown older, so his health had become more robust, his temperament less squeamish. Already in 'Happiness', written while he was at work on *Eminent Victorians*, there is a definite regeneration of energy. As in 'The Haschish', the sensations of joy and multitudinous gladness are described as if they have been provoked by some drug — not an aphrodisiac, but an anodyne or opiate inducing drowsiness. An insidious music haunts his inward ear with harmonies that leave behind them a timeless refrain quivering in the air. The pre-war feeling of listlessness between these celestial crescendos to his romances is now replaced by something more resilient. Sometimes, Lytton explains, the ruthlessness of our fate seems to relent, and our destiny shines before us, marvellous and benign. Such inspiriting glimpses into the future, he implies, are bestowed upon those who have mastered their impatience, and whose senses are no longer drenched with elemental desire, either for lust or power. They are

> oftenest known
> To those in whom the waiting soul has grown
> A little weary, and whose deep desires
> (As in black coal sleep unextinguished fires)
> All joy's rich possibilities ignore
> And, not despairing, not expect no more.

He had reached the stage of expecting no more from love when Roger Senhouse suddenly and wonderfully re-ignited these unextinguished fires. The new flame burnt brightly, erratically, almost without control, giving out a rather different light from earlier conflagrations. During his Cambridge days, Lytton had, in schoolboy fashion, associated sex with excrement and been much obsessed by the idea of sodomy. Among his post-Cambridge writings, however, can be traced the development of more sophisticated sexual deviations, and the suggestion that he could become erotically aroused by other parts of the body, especially the ears. There are a few references to ears in the Duncan Grant correspondence, and, a little later, a curious pleasure in contemplating 'the strange divine ears, so large and lascivious – oh!' of George Mallory. But it is not until his infatuation for Ralph Partridge that ears crop up regularly in his letters, and by the time he is writing to Roger Senhouse, they seem to have taken on a magical, lickerish significance. He is always threatening to tweak or pinch Roger's ears for some slight misdemeanour, or slice off one or possibly both as punishment for some imagined crime; and he describes with horrified delight the mutilations to ears practised in the sixteenth and seventeenth centuries.

Such fetishes were an offshoot of the rich fantasy life to which, for the first time, he now seems to have abandoned himself. In his affair with Duncan Grant he had tried to force a reality out of his day-dreams by assuming, almost literally, the form and personality of the man he loved. With Henry Lamb, he had resorted to moods of sexual infantilism only in moments of crisis or reconciliation, so that fantasy and actuality had run alongside in a makeshift partnership that was bound eventually to break apart. With Ralph Partridge he had not attempted to transmute himself in an imaginative way, but to alter the object of his love so that they might be closer in everyday life – with the result that, once he had partly succeeded in this conversion, his initial amorousness was watered down into more ordinary friendship. But in the company of Roger Senhouse, he stepped into a wish-fulfilment world where both of them could adopt fictitious identities and play out vicarious roles. It was a more imaginative method of escaping from his own limited personality, of merging more intimately with his loved one – a method that was evolved out of Roger Senhouse's surrealist and capricious nature. Together they would pretend they were David and Absalom, Nero and his slave, a member of Pop (The Eton Society) and his fag, a parent and child – the invention was inexhaustible, the variety endless. And it was Lytton who took the lead. In a revulsion from arid intellectuality, he would call for a flight back to nature. 'Why can't we return to our primeval forest, and swing from the boughs entranced in happiness?' he demanded (13 March 1927). 'We should live on three nuts a day, and sleep together, far up, in the middle of some marvellous palm. Never to touch the ground, Roger – how divine! Wouldn't that alone be worth all the intellect of humanity?' At other times he would visualize some more cosy domestic scene to act as a refuge from his present self. 'Won't you take me on as your servant instead of Peel?' he begged (December 1926). 'I have always longed for such a job. To have no will of one's own, no importance, no responsibility, hardly even a soul – how very satisfying it would be. If I shaved off my beard nobody would recognise me. "Disappearance of a well-known Author" – and it would be delightful.'

For Lytton, the knowledge that he could be drawn away from his pallid environment and absorbed into a multitude of imaginary-historical scenes and forms and places was an extraordinary boon that added to his love-life a wholly unexplored and enchanted territory, into which he might be liberated almost at will. Gradually, by means of certain aberrant experiments, he learnt how to rise above the murk and haze of the passing day into this fugitive wonderland. The aesthetic tastes which he and Roger shared – especially for literature and music – became invested with strange sexual properties. Books and their bindings began to haunt Lytton's dreams. 'One's feelings towards certain books certainly approach the libidinous, as Dr Freud would say,' he observed. In Rome, during their fortnight of intense happiness together, they had read Dante, and afterwards Lytton discovered that simply by touching this book with lingering hands he could conjure up a wonderful sensuality. To trail his finger-tips over the delicious morocco bindings sent through him a shiver of delirious, throbbing excitement – 'for which I am sure Dante would have reserved a particularly ingenious circle of Hell – If only such a vice could have occurred to him.' Even reading together from a French first edition that had belonged to the 'Grand Dauphin' – the eldest son of Louis XIV – transported Lytton. No longer was he a middle-aged, twentieth-century author, but the heir apparent to the French throne; and there beside him sat – not a handsome, Etonian bibliophil – but the king himself! It was an experience too improbable for the most exaggerated novel. 'I fear I am almost too happy when I am with you,' Lytton confessed to Roger (February 1930). '. . . Oh dear, the intricacy and intensity of existence reduces me to a shadow. Every moment is peculiar beyond words.'

Music too could work the same strange spell between them, dissolving the walls of this too solid world, softening Lytton's heart, unlearning his mind, and stirring, with trembling compression, his whole being until it seemed to float, weightless and unsubstantial, like the airs that crept so softly upon the harp-strings and filled the silence of the spheres with their legendary echoes. He had always loved music, but this special sensitivity was quite in excess of anything he had felt before. Music *really was* the food of love, and all of heaven that we had on earth. It seemed to breathe voluptuous visions into the warm air, making him giddy with expectation, whispering unheard-of joys to his weary spirit, whirling him round and round and drenching his senses with an imaginary relish, sharp and sweet. Mozart he preferred. Bach was too religious. And as for Vaughan Williams, 'I have an instinctive feeling that he must be South Kensington – but I expect that's only because I once knew his female relatives'. Almost always he liked to hear string music. Such harmonies as those of the Beethoven Last Quartets lay in immortal souls, and it was only when he was uplifted beyond the muddy vesture of decay which ordinarily encloses us that he could become sensible to their full beauty. For it was to the fleeting strains of fine music that lust and affection could melt into one, a pale and tender union, assimilating all other passions. What was that shuddering sensation that swept through his body as he listened? It was almost as if he and Roger were the instruments themselves – the violin, its very strings and bow, with its exquisite taut movement, rhythmically back and forwards, in and out, so subtly potent, so ravishing.

Such experiences were beyond the range of words, but when, at the end of the first chapter in *Elizabeth and Essex*, he describes the highest point of rapture in the queen's love-affair with her courtier, it is with a musical metaphor that he awkwardly tries to evoke it. 'When two consciousnesses come to a certain nearness the impetus of their interactions, growing ever intenser and intenser, leads on to an unescapable climax. The crescendo must rise to its topmost note; and only then is the preordained solution of the theme made manifest.'

Less psychological, and more successful as literature, is a poem he composed for Roger Senhouse in the late winter of 1926, conveying something of the exaltation that invested their sessions of reading and music together.

> Then such delight the enchanted spirit knows
> As when in June on a red-bosomed rose
> A golden rosebud leans an amorous chin;
> Or when all's hushed – breath's held – the strings begin!
> And with an answering harmony there flows
> O'er the rapt bass a thrilling violin.

The rapture which Lytton felt he had discovered with Roger could not be perfectly fitted into the rest of his life. It was unique and indivisible, neither wholly a part of Ham Spray nor any part at all of the Strachey household at 51 Gordon Square. In March 1927, therefore, he decided to take extra rooms somewhere else in London. After a consultation with James, he committed himself to renting a flat in 41 Gordon Square – the very house that Ralph and Frances had gone to a year earlier! Here he hoped to be able to see Roger more easily, and repay the hospitality of their mutual friends – Mary Hutchinson, Dadie Rylands, Raymond Mortimer and others.

This spring, Lytton stood at the very top of happy hours. Before Rome he had never really been able to credit his good fortune – his 'free gift from Providence'. But then the lure of unprogressive satisfactions had entrapped them both, engulfing Lytton in an air of indulgent and delusive ease. A seal seemed to have been set on his happiness. The fleeting hour stood still so that tomorrow always promised a miraculous renewal of today – what could be more natural, then, than to plan for the future? But when he wrote off to Roger telling of his new rooms, the reply was vacillating, indecisive. For so caught up had Lytton become with images from his make-believe world that he had misconstrued the facts. He expected to see his own sentiments exactly mirrored back to him by Roger. What he actually saw was something far more blurred, more formless and diffuse. 'It's really rather a wonderful combination of things we seem to have discovered, or perhaps invented,' Lytton had written to him. But Roger was not so sure. He felt frightened of being shifted into a false and untenable position, where his own bland affection would fail in opposition to such heady passion. By consenting to go to Rome with Lytton – who had paid for everything – he found himself bound by something more than airy friendship or flirtation, by the ties of gratitude for a very real benefit. All these further plans might tie him tighter still. So he began to struggle and seek refuge in dissimulation.

Lytton was at once bewildered and hurt. Roger's apparent inconsistency and lack of concentration gave him the feeling

943

of trying to make an impression on cotton wool. What could be the explanation? He was uncertain of how to treat the situation in which he found himself. On an impulse, while in London, he telephoned him 'feeling like a detected murderer'. But to his surprise Roger sounded extremely friendly, and they arranged to go to *Così Fan Tutte* together. The reconciliation was delicious, but even so Lytton remained puzzled. 'I feel a good deal happier, though rather alarmed,' he told Mary Hutchinson (25 March 1927), '– I don't quite know why – please support me!'

Although Lytton could not have known it until a day or two later, there were good reasons for this alarm, and much need, during the next weeks and months, for the support of his friends. Even as the two of them sat listening to Mozart that evening, a letter was in the post on its way to Ham Spray which set out many of Roger's apprehensions. Where were these flights of fantasy, these adventures of mind and imagination, leading them? he nervously inquired. Lytton would contrive roles and situations which were so gripping, so enjoyable, that he, Roger, was completely swept up by them. They were so amusing too, and since they gave Lytton such evident pleasure, pleasurable to him also. But reality kept breaking through, plunging Lytton down a terrifying abyss. It was these sudden dizzying descents, when the knowledge, born of disaster to all his aspirations, would come to him that fiction is not fact, the image not the substance, earth not a timeless paradise – it was these agonizing, heart-sinking moments of transition that terrified Roger. He did not himself experience this dreadful recoil, for he had not the same craving for make-believe, but he saw their effect on Lytton and was sucked into the complicated passage of emotions. Although not fully understanding what was going on, he still felt lost, nervous, upset, and in some degree responsible for the anguish that played so horribly upon Lytton's spirit. What should he do? Their physical needs and inclinations proclaimed themselves as being so very different. It was all right when Carrington was there, and it was not so bad when Lytton came up to London, at which times Roger would, in some degree, take Carrington's place. But he was apprehensive about going down to Ham Spray alone. Quite literally, he feared that Lytton might go mad. There seemed to be no culmination to his feelings. That strange wild passion that inflamed his being burnt within him to a white-hot intensity, but, discovering nothing to ignite, devoured itself. In his excitement, he would urge Roger to more and more extravagant measures, would grow extraordinarily worked up: yet the pressure could find no exterior release. Even in his most extreme states, he was somehow still inhibited. Roger knew, of course, that Lytton's attitude towards him was not one of simple sexual desire. Their relationship was rather one of limitless sympathy – and he was frightened of anything that might impair it. Most of all he dreaded paining Lytton, who was at all times very vulnerable, who remembered everything one happened to say and gave it an unmeant significance.

'Lytton, I cannot bear to wound you in any way at all,' he wrote, ' – it has an instantaneous effect upon me – and yet I am continually finding myself upon the point of doing so by some inconsiderate word or action, and if I hurt you and see that I have, I feel a sense of shame that makes me nervous. I want always to feel entirely open, straightforward and undisguised in front of you, but I discover too often that I have cloaked my proper feelings, and that I am falling into a part that is not true to my nature. ... You are, Lytton, so overwhelmingly charming and considerate to me that I am quite at a loss to know how to reciprocate it, for were I to mention at any time dissatisfaction with what was taking place, I know the pains you would devote to amend it. ... I know you say that you get all that satisfies you from things as they have existed for the last months, but I who keep watch, as it were, can only realise that what I have loosely termed "things" might be so very much better.'

The effect of this letter upon Lytton was unexampled. A blackness and a void closed in upon him, and the blood drained from his head. He could not conceal his agitation. 'I am in almost complete despair,' he lamented to Mary Hutchinson (1 May 1927). 'All is shattered!' He read only one meaning into Roger's hesitant words: that he did not feel for him what Lytton had taken for granted he felt – that he did not love him. And he had been so certain of this love, too! Just when happiness seemed within his grasp, when he had practically been able to see with Roger's eyes, adopt his will, set their two hearts beating in unison, and catch the very warmth from his soul, the good moment had fled. Where was the thread now? He was falling, falling into a blind desolation, while Roger, like a thistle ball, floated onwards and upwards, far beyond his reach, wherever light winds blew. The old trick! – and he had been taken in by it once again. Had he really forced Roger out of his true nature, or was he simply being irresponsible? Surely it must be irresponsibility, that delinquent, frivolous, incalculable irresponsibility which lay at the very root of his fatal charm. 'Yes, Roger's charm. But what pray is charm, I should like to know?' Lytton ruefully inquired of Mary Hutchinson. His character was so fluid and indefinable, so deceptively soluble that it appeared to take colour from whatever it touched. From day to day, he was never the same person – now tender and affectionate, now politely offhand as if faintly embarrassed to find himself the idol of an ageing invalid. No wonder Lytton had been misled!

The next four-and-a-half months were overhung with hideous uncertainty. Lytton's thoughts rushed round, confused and crowded, from disappointment to regret, from rage to repentance with brief flashes of febrile exhilaration. Unreasonable jealousies agonized his brain. Like someone deranged, he was driven by a harrowing restlessness hither and thither. Kindness and company were what he sought, to numb the shock and to distract his mind from morbid, endlessly rotating preoccupations. He could not bear to be left alone, but hurried from Carrington to Mary Hutchinson and Topsy Lucas, from Dadie Rylands to Stephen Tomlin, frantically drinking in their words of comfort and reassurance.

In these friends, at least, he was fortunate. All that friends can do in such circumstances, they did. 'I am surrounded by infinite kindness and devotion,' he wrote to Dadie Rylands (18 July 1927), 'but how can I not sometimes feel lonely?' At Ham

Spray a new orientation of human affairs was spinning into place, and involving all the complexity that had by now become *de rigueur* in that ambiguous household. In reaction from his disappointed passion for Roger, Lytton turned momentarily back to Ralph Partridge. Memories of their old intimacy – 'so intensely romantic and moving – rushed back upon me, and I felt strangely upset', he confided to Mary Hutchinson (9 August 1927). 'There he was, downstairs, the same person, really, I couldn't help feeling; but six years or seven had gone – and where were we now? – I longed to say something – but it was impossible to do more than murmur some vague word or two, and he returned to London.'

Throughout this summer, Lytton tried to ease the heartache by a few light flirtations with young men. 'Yes, love is tiresome,' he admitted to Topsy Lucas (27 July 1927), 'but life goes on, and things do happen – quite fresh and exciting – even though one is chucked by some R[oger] or other.' The most abiding consolation and companionship, however, came from his other two friends, Dadie Rylands and Stephen Tomlin. The latter, for a brief spell, occupied a uniquely bipartite position in the Ham Spray regime. After months of mutually inflicted torture, Carrington and Gerald had temporarily split up, and Tomlin at once stepped into Gerald's place upon the stage. Being completely bisexual, it seemed that he ought to have been nicely suited to perform a sort of virtuoso solo *pas de deux*, and for a time he did just this. But his influence between Lytton and Carrington was never a very stable one, for though equally attractive to both, his personality was far too moody, too brightly painted, too brittle – like that of a lunatic putting on an inspired charade of normality. Besides – and this was later to be of tragic importance – Ralph strongly, if rather illogically, objected to his having a love-affair with Carrington. The relationship between the two men had always been rather variable. Ralph admired his outstanding intelligence and legalistic pleasure in argument. But he considered him to be essentially dishonest and corrupt, someone more likely to destroy than to create happiness – and he feared what this influence, acting upon Carrington, might lead to. At the end of July, however, their tenuous affair lapsed when Tomlin was married off to Julia Strachey. 'I am leading a decidedly queer life,' Lytton apprised Mary Hutchinson (19 July 1927). 'Both T[ommy] and D[adie] are devoted to me – and I to them; they please me in every way – though, to be sure, the ways are different! ... My relation with T[ommy] is exciting – there is strength there – and a mind – a remarkable character; – but there is a lull in the proceedings, for he is to be married on Thursday (I believe). There is also a lull with D[adie], who has gone to Cambridge – a delightful, gay affair that one. So you see altogether I have plenty to think about in my seclusion. ... Was there ever such a world? Such lives? Such peculiarities?'

Despite these moments of excitement, his seclusion this summer was generally 'dank and cheerless'. For once he could find no escape from his troubles within his work, for imbedded in the story of *Elizabeth and Essex* he saw much that poignantly reflected back his own tragic history. This may largely have been the cause of his painfully slow progress at the book. He had been unhappily in love before, yet managed to carry on steadily with his writing because it afforded him relief, even forgetfulness, from his emotional problems. But *Elizabeth and Essex* only exacerbated this pain.

The withdrawal of Roger's radiant presence gradually became insupportable to Lytton. There was no satisfaction anywhere. At the end of June, Philip Ritchie came down to stay with him at Ham Spray in order to recruit after an attack of tonsillitis, and a momentary calmness fell upon Lytton. But soon all was gloom and hesitation once more. The estrangement between him and Roger was never complete. At all times the outward forms of affection and respect were maintained, and sometimes they appeared as close to each other as ever – disagreement vanished, the gloom lifted, hope returned. But Lytton could never tell how things would turn out from one meeting to the next. 'As for my young man, whom I went to on leaving you,' he wrote to Mary Hutchinson (15 July 1927), '– he was unexpectedly delightful – really most coming on – the villain!'

For a while, there did seem some detectable pattern to
Roger's behaviour – or so Lytton believed. The farther apart
from each other they were, the more affectionate he appeared.
'I think of R[oger] still – no doubt too much – I wish I didn't,'
Lytton confessed to Mary Hutchinson (27 July 1927). 'Things
must take their course and it seems unlikely that I shall see
him again before the autumn. There must no doubt be something tiresome about me, when seen very near at hand; but his
reactions have I think been a trifle extreme.'

Whatever the attitude Lytton adopted in order to protect
himself, Roger would counter with a fresh surprise. His
actions were quite unpremeditated, quite unpredictable, uncomprehending, incomprehensible. He was psychotic, neurotic, erratic, erotic. In desperation, Lytton even tried to interest
him in another of his friends – at least there would be some
certainty, some rest, in losing him altogether. But it was no
use. His mood of philosophic fatalism lasted about a week
before it was wrenched apart by a totally unforeseen visit
from Roger to Ham Spray. By a strange coincidence, the day
of his arrival marked an exact year since the visit on which
Lytton first 'found myself in an exquisite paradise' – and Roger
now 'kept the anniversary by sleeping, for the first time, by
himself', Lytton told Mary Hutchinson (9 August 1927).
'However, such coincidences are ridiculous. ... He looked far
from well – pale and puffy – no beauty that I could see – really
almost someone different. So dreadfully fat! – All went well,
he was most amiable. I behaved with the highest propriety, he
seemed to enjoy himself, and positively on going away gave
me an entirely unsolicited kiss. A queer creature, certainly.
Decidedly charming. ... We spent a happy hour comparing
Rabelais in the original with Urquhart's translation. He picked
wild flowers and branches from shrubs on our morning walk –
more flowers in the garden – and went back with a huge armful
– to my mind a sympathetic thing to do, and what no one else
I know (except Carrington) would dream of doing. Aren't
things strangely – exasperatingly – mixed? What does one
want? What does anyone want? – Really? Ah! – so little – and
so much – '

The search for this lost, complicated quality of love jolted him up and down a tortuous and exhausting switchback of emotions. 'The Lytton-clock needs winding up,' he wrote to Dadie Rylands (15 August 1927). 'The hands remain immovable in mid-career, and Ham Spray is the Realm of Chastity.' Their relationship had become totally inexplicable to him – though 'I suppose Time will make all things clear'. Early in September, Roger left for a holiday in Germany, dispatching back to Lytton a stream of postcards and long letters that 'positively sent his love!' But what, after all, was love? The contradiction of Lytton's state of mind grew more extreme than ever. Difficulties, dangers, griefs there might be in their singular friendship, but now absence momentarily made all things clearer. A feeling of vast relief spread over him after Roger had left – at least he could enjoy some peace for the next two or three weeks. But even this proved untrue. All too soon he started to wonder what Roger was doing, whether he himself occupied any place in his thoughts and emotions. Life was dull, colourless, almost non-existent without him. 'Do you think of me sometime?' he asked, '. . . are you beginning to forget that I exist? As for me, I can hardly believe that I do – exist I mean.'

This disturbed frame of mind might have been prolonged indefinitely, had not, that September, a catalytic tragedy struck at them both. After an unexpected relapse from his tonsillitis, Philip Ritchie suddenly died. For his friends, the news came as a complete shock. 'I had imagined him well and possibly in Scotland,' Lytton wrote to Dadie Rylands (15 September 1927). '. . . It is crushing and miserable. Carrington too feels it terribly – she is infinitely sweet and good. Roger is not back yet . . . I feel very troubled about him. Fate has been unkind to him, certainly. I wish to be with him and comfort him, but it is an added irony that he may feel unable now to make use of my devotion.'[42]

42. Ritchie had developed a cold before his operation, but the surgeon decided to go ahead. Two days afterwards a severe haemorrhage occurred. He then underwent a second operation to stem the bleeding. A London specialist was called in; but the poison had already got into his

Yet the real irony was that, even in this tragic adversity, Roger could not abandon his capacity for surprising Lytton. Far from being unable to make use of Lytton's devotion, he relied upon it absolutely. The death of Philip Ritchie wiped out at a blow all the previous months of estrangement and cruel suspense. Unhappiness might endure for a spell, but joy quickly superseded it. The two of them met as soon as Roger arrived back in London. He was in a wretched state, full of morbid self-reproaches, which Lytton tried to dispel by showing him how disproportionate they were. 'It is such a great mercy, Dadie,' he afterwards wrote to George Rylands (21 September 1927), 'the cloud that was between us has gone away, and it was possible for me to do all I could to console him and show him my affection quite naturally; and he was perfectly charming and affectionate.'

For the next two weeks, while Lytton was away at Charleston and Weymouth, they corresponded practically every day. They had never been closer. They were held together by the deepest ties of affection, and sorrow had given a new fibrous strength to this contact. 'But you know, my dearest,' Lytton had written to Roger before returning from Weymouth that October, 'it is impossible not to feel an undercurrent of sadness – more than before; about Philip; and about more general things – the dangers and difficulties of all human life – the miserable pain of separations and misunderstandings – the wicked power of mere accident over happiness and goodness – I know you feel all this and as for me, when I reflect upon these things, I can't help crying, and then Roger, I sink into our love which comes like the divine resolution of a discord, and all is well.'

7

TOGETHER

'All is well' sounded a cheerful refrain to many of Lytton's letters over the following six months of the winter. 'It is de-

---

lungs and some seven weeks later, on 13 September, he died of septic pneumonia.

lightful to find oneself down here again,' he wrote from Ham Spray to Topsy Lucas (29 January 1928), 'in freedom and comparative comfort, in spite of the incredible barbarity of the weather. Roger continues to be perfectly charming, and I am curiously happy.' Because of this contentment, because he again felt confident of Roger's devotion, health and spirits flowed back into his capricious organism, and his life became productive and well-balanced once more. 'All is well now between Roger and me,' he notified Dadie Rylands (15 October 1927). 'I am feeling so very happy about it. He is perfectly charming – and I have complete confidence in his affection. In all ways, too, I am much calmer. It is the greatest relief ... thank you for all your sympathy, and kindness during that miserable time.'

Roger spent much of his available time at Ham Spray this winter, and he and Lytton made two trips to Brighton before the end of the year. Since Lytton's work was 'terribly behindhand', his visits to London and elsewhere, he told Ottoline (4 October 1927), 'will have to be more truncated than usual'. Even so, he found time to spend a couple of 'altogether perfect' week-ends with Peter and Topsy Lucas, to go and watch Dadie Rylands play Volumnia in a Cambridge production of *Coriolanus*, and make a number of dashes up to London to see Desmond MacCarthy, Sybil Colefax, Cynthia Asquith and the 'charming boy' Rex Whistler,[43] 'rather à la Philip IV of Spain in appearance – "maussade" perhaps is the word: but he seemed serious and unconceited'.

Back at Ham Spray, he would either 'sit mewed up, struggling with Gibbon', or 'sit reading the whole of Hume's History as mum as a mouse'. By 2 November he had finished Gibbon and 'am pegging away at Macaulay', he told Roger,

43. Rex Whistler (1905–44), the English artist who, with great linear resourcefulness and wit, specialized in the rendering of eighteenth-century life in the rococo style. A versatile painter, he is particularly known for his book illustrations, murals (including 'The Pursuit of Rare Meats' at the refreshment room in the Tate Gallery) and designs for the theatre and ballet. But he also produced textiles, bookplates, china, carpets and even luggage labels for Imperial Airways. There is a biography of him by his brother, the poet and designer Laurence Whistler.

' – Hume, you see, left to the last – and hope to dispatch him (mac) before Friday'. A week later he reported: 'I plod on with Hume'; and three days later still he wrote to Dadie: 'I have been working like ten cart-horses lately, and have now finished all four of those bloody historians. A great relief! – And now once more I find myself face to face with that moblèd queen.'

His diligence over these weeks was impervious to all temptations, among them a most strange eruption of unexpected visitors from the expensive classes, including Osbert Sitwell, Christabel Aberconway, Siegfried Sassoon and Stephen Tennant, all of them entirely occupied with 'dressing up'. Lytton described the scene in a letter to Roger (27 October 1927). 'The night before they had all dressed up as nuns, that morning they had all dressed up as shepherds and shepherdesses, in the evening they were all going to dress up as – God knows what – but they begged and implored me to return with them and share their raptures. When dressed up they are filmed – and the next week-end, I suppose, the film is exhibited. Can you imagine anything more "perfectly divine"? One would have expected them to come in a vast Daimler, but not at all – a small two seater (open) with a dickey behind was their vehicle – they came very late, having lost their way on the Downs, and I shudder to think of the horrors of their return journey. Strange creatures – with just a few feathers where brains should be. Though no doubt Siegfried is rather different.'

In the last week of November, Lytton finally restarted work on *Elizabeth and Essex*. Earlier that month he had met his American publisher, Donald Brace, in London, and told him that it now seemed unlikely that he could finish the book before March. Brace in any case wanted the British publication delayed until the autumn. 'He said that this would make it much easier to prepare the way for the American sale,' Lytton explained to Charles Prentice (6 November 1927), 'which apparently is necessarily a long business – partly because of the size of the country – but also, I cannot help thinking, because of the slowness of the wits of its inhabitants.'

For the next three months he laboured steadily and with hardly an interruption at *Elizabeth* 'who marches forward with infinite slowness'. Frances Marshall, who, with Ralph, still came down to Ham Spray most week-ends, notes in her journal at this time that Lytton was constantly 'busy writing'. She also communicates something of the peculiar happiness which then irradiated the whole house – Carrington invariably charming, Lytton amiable and animated, discussing Wittgenstein, logic, the difference between *a priori* and empirical knowledge, or the theory that literary genius and children were incompatible; then joking until everyone burst out with laughter; playing chess, paper-games and drawing competitions; reading 'two little Gerhardie volumes', *Futility* and *Donna Quixote*,[44] T. S. Eliot on Shakespeare – 'interesting remarks, but not quite enough' – and Peter Lucas's edition of Webster in four stupendous volumes, a most noble work of astonishing erudition, though 'in some ways a juvenile book'.

One entry in Frances Marshall's journal catches very sympathetically the wonder and contentment of these winter days. 'Arrived at Hamspray with the black kitten. Roger Senhouse the only visitor. Lytton seems very much in love with him. Philip's death seems in some way to have brought them together. The effect on Lytton is to make him very gay and charming. Walked in the fields while Carrington galloped about on Belle. In the evening we let off some fireworks – an exquisite display of pink and green fountains under the pampas grass.' This same day (12 November 1927) Lytton wrote to Dadie Rylands: 'He [Roger] gives me so much happiness that I hardly know what to do about it. I sometimes feel inclined to stand on my head, and do cart-wheels all down the Downs. Do you think that would be a good plan?'

44. *Futility*, William Gerhardie's first novel on Russian themes, sponsored by Katherine Mansfield and later to be taken up and praised by Edith Wharton, Arnold Bennett and numerous other writers, was published in 1922. 'Why was there no shouting,' afterwards inquired H. G. Wells, ' – shouting to reach the suburbs and the county towns?' *Donna Quixote* (1927) is a play by William Gerhardie, of which the first act is a farce, the second a comedy and the third a tragedy.

Over Christmas, Stephen and Julia Tomlin came down, with Frances and Ralph, and they were shortly joined by James. A Christmas tree was reared in the back room for the 'petit peuple' from the village who held a boisterous party round it – while, a little way off, like a beneficent shadow, Lytton moved among his books. Over night a heavy fall of snow filled the ditches and lanes with immense drifts and extraordinary shapes, like giant mushrooms, columns and sand-dunes. A brilliant sun shone in the white fields and trees, and a transparent blue sky extended from horizon to horizon, without a cloud. The horses in the farmyard cantered about jumping imaginary obstacles in their efforts to keep warm. Within Ham Spray too every psychological cloud seemed to have evaporated. 'Lytton, who had an assignation with Roger, was anxious to get away in spite of all difficulties,' recorded Frances Marshall (28 December 1927), 'and a procession set out to walk in to Hungerford. Lytton in a fur coat and waders, R[alph] in top boots, a ruck-sack and a crimson hat trimmed with monkey fur, James with his head entirely enveloped in a scarf, we must have looked a bizarre collection. The scene was fantastically beautiful; after Inkpen the roads were full to the top with snow; the blue sky brought out curious pink lights in it and deep blue shadows, cottages were grotesquely hung with post-card icicles, and the snow was marbled all over with ripplemarks made by the wind. At Hungerford the world seemed suddenly ordinary again; people stepped into the train wearing bowler hats, and gaped to see a troupe of Bulgarian peasants, headed evidently by their Prime Minister in his fur coat.'

The new year opened with undimmed radiance. 'Good Queen Bess' slowly trundled forward; Roger's charm, in its unaccountable fashion, continued unabated, while alongside it ran Lytton's own curious happiness. On the week-end of 11 February, the two of them made a lightning trip to France, crossing the Channel in a gale and terrific thunderstorm from Tilbury to Dunkirk, and hurrying on to Paris where they were to meet Norman Douglas. This meeting was the outcome of almost five years' intermittent correspondence between the two writers. Lytton, who had read nothing of Douglas's work before 1923, was first introduced to it that year by Carrington – a passionate admirer of all his novels and travel books. Two years later he confided to Ottoline (16 February 1925) that Norman Douglas 'seems to me an attractive figure. I've become a great admirer of all his works; though I hardly dare say so, owing to the scoffs of the cultured.'

Under pressure from Carrington, he had opened up the correspondence between them in October 1923, writing to say how much he had admired and enjoyed *Siren Land* (1911), *Old Calabria* (1915), *South Wind* (1917), *Alone*[45] (1921) and *Together*, which had come out earlier that year.[46] This letter soon led the way to a long sequence of those reciprocal civilities to which authors are so poignantly prone. 'I value your opinion more highly than that of any English writer,' Douglas eulogistically answered (9 November 1923). 'In these decidedly lean years it is the fatness of your kine that is so particularly striking. Your books are so full; there is so much of so many things in them – so much experience, so much learning, so much art, so much humour, so much philosophy, and so much proof that there is so much, so very much, more underneath, that is unexpressed . . . in fact for me, your opinion is a thing apart from that of others, even as your writings belong to

45. 'I have a special love of *Alone*. How did you manage to fill it with that romantic beauty? The variety of moods in it is indeed extraordinary; and yet the totality of the impression is completely preserved,' Lytton wrote to Norman Douglas. 'I am delighted to hear you like *Alone*!' Douglas replied. 'So do I. What you discover in it to please you is no doubt the result of that ridiculous war, driving me into myself. I really felt *alone*, surrounded by a legion of imbeciles hacking each other in pieces. An exhilarating sensation; and one that has not quite faded away. May it never do so.'

46. 'We are reading a new novel by Norman Douglas in the evenings,' Carrington wrote to Dorelia John (10 February 1928). 'Tell me, have you got it? It's rather Greek, and very lecherous. I've been doing some designs for some rooms at Cambridge. Panels for doors. I think I shall go over there and paint them soon. Its a Hideous gothic room in Kings, belonging to a sweet canary Don called. Rylands. So I'm doing Hideous Gothic pictures of roman emperor heads, and Greek urns to make a nice job of it.'

a category by themselves ... do let me thank you for the real pleasure – joy, I should say – which I have derived from your books. A thing of art, unquestionably.'

By the end of this year they had already exchanged photographs – 'his [Douglas's] photograph seems to me much more prepossessing than I had expected', Lytton admitted in a letter to Dorothy Bussy (25 November 1923). 'I had imagined something large, Scotch and coarse.' Douglas had also sent Lytton the revised edition of *Siren Land* and Lytton had responded with 'a charming letter of thanks and appreciation', lamenting only the absence of a map.[47] Not to be outmatched in the offering of literary garlands, Douglas straightway dispatched back 'a very nice letter' of his own. 'I wish you would write a biography of Heliogabalus, for example, drawn from new sources discovered yourself during a recent visit to Egypt,' he wrote (3 December 1923). 'Come here, and we'll do it together. Or the private journal of the Emperor Claudius.'

The heady compliments and mild whimsy trickled amicably on throughout the next year and, in February 1925, Douglas forwarded Lytton four copies of his privately printed brochure *D. H. Lawrence and Maurice Magnus. A plea for better manners*,[48] a theme nicely in harmony with the tone of their

47. A revised edition of *Siren Land*, Norman Douglas's first serious book, was published by Martin Secker this winter. 'As for Siren Land,' Douglas wrote to Lytton (9 November 1923), 'seven of its twenty chapters were cut out by the publisher as being "too remote from human interests". *Without consulting me*, he also pulped the entire edition save what had already been sold, which is an infamous proceeding, as one would gladly have bought a copy or two to give to friends. It cannot be helped; one is in the hands of these brigands. Secker has now brought out a new one; the copies reached me last night and I am sending you *one* right away. You will find it stodgy in places, and precious, and unintelligible here and there; but it testifies to an appalling industry.'

48. This pamphlet was written in 1924 as a reply to D. H. Lawrence's Introduction to *Memoirs of the Foreign Legion* by Maurice Magnus. Lytton forwarded one of his copies to Ottoline Morrell. 'I think it may amuse you,' he wrote (11 February 1925), 'even if you haven't read the book à propos to which it is written; for years I've thought that some such protest was wanted; and N.D., it seems to me, has done it effectively, in his own particular style. But I doubt whether "friend Lawrence" will see the error of his ways.' In the *New Statesman* (20 February

own correspondence. 'I hope you will not dislike it,' he wrote (4 February 1925). 'It is the first thing I have written since October 1923, so you see you are not the only person afflicted with the complaint of non-productivity. . . . I heard a rumour that William Beckford, Esquire, might soon be engaging your attention. That would be wonderful. You are the only person who could handle that proposition. A lovely subject!'

Throughout this time the two of them had never met, though there had been several tentative arrangements to do so. 'Now come here if you can,' Douglas wrote from Italy on 25 September 1927. 'Florence is taboo for me also, at present. I am living at Prato and only go in for an afternoon now and then, thickly veiled and wearing blue glasses and a carroty beard. This will last, I daresay, till after Christmas. But there is no reason why you shouldn't come to the neighbourhood, anyhow.' When eventually they did come face to face some four months later, the suggestion had again come from Douglas. 'Now just think if you can't run (or fly) over to Paris for a week-end,' he urged Lytton (31 January 1928). 'I have to go there about the 10th, and have some 58 teeth pulled out, and 63 new ones put in, and I am sure you are the very person to hold my hand. Besides we can go to Pruniers in the intervals. Nancy Cunard is there: I hope you like her?[49] So do come along.'

After so much epistolary warmth, Lytton felt rather nervous of actually encountering Douglas man to man, and was glad to have Roger Senhouse with him. The week-end was, he confessed beforehand to Dadie Rylands (9 February 1928), 'a truly frantic project. . . . I am excited and terrified, as you may imagine. Good God! The crossing! The cold! The streets

---

1926) Lawrence, 'weary of being slandered', defended himself against Douglas's charges.

49. After the First World War, Nancy Cunard had gone to live permanently in France, set up her own Hours Press at Réanville and published (1928–31) some twenty volumes of contemporary authors. A journalist for the *Manchester Guardian*, a wide traveller and a poetess, she later wrote her memories of Norman Douglas and some reminiscences of George Moore.

of Paris! And – most serious of all – Norman Douglas! Will he be charming, vulgar, too talkative, too vague, or what? – Perhaps a womanizer after all! Who knows? And what, oh what, shall I say? How *am* I to carry it off? A silent owl in an ivy bush. I shall beg Roger to wear a false beard, and shave mine off, so that we may change parts. And I'll let you know the upshot.' These preliminary fears were soon whipped to a frenzy by a series of last-minute calamities, as Carrington recounted to Dorelia John (10 February 1928). 'There is great agitation as his [Lytton's] drawers, and vests haven'T come back from the wash and the wind roars so fiercely that he is terrified all the ships will sink. But I expect it will be great fun boozing at Foyots.'

Before Lytton set off for Paris, Douglas had written to ask whether he could put him on to someone who might help him collect 'the obscenest and most blasphemous Limericks (university or Stock Exchange?)', since he wished to make a full anthology 'for scholarly purposes of course', which would be privately printed some day 'with copious notes'. It was in this capacity, as adviser on limericks filthy and profane, that Roger Senhouse travelled out with Lytton.[50]

50. Roger Senhouse, as it turned out, was of no practical use to Douglas over the limerick book. On 30 July 1928, Douglas wrote to Lytton from the Abruzzi mountains, where he had fled with 'two youngsters', asking whether 'our young friend' could be induced to send him some limericks. 'I should be ever so glad, as the book is under weigh (? way) and I want as much variety as possible.' On 12 September 1928, he again wrote: 'I have *finished* the limerick book. It will shortly be printed and bound, and a copy shall go to you. So you needn't bother the poor Roger (appropriate name).' A little later that year one hundred and fifty copies of *Some Limericks* were privately printed in Florence for subscribers only. They were all signed, bound in handsome amber-coloured canvas, and sold at five and even ten guineas each – after which all sorts of other private editions have been brought out. Douglas planned two sequels – *More Limericks* and *Last Limericks* – but because the police court in Florence, stirred up, it was commonly believed, by the British Home Office, threatened to take criminal proceedings, he judged it wiser to publish no further limericks. As to *Some Limericks*, Nancy Cunard has commented: 'They have to be seen to be believed, rollicking, scatological and dire, as they are, in their schoolboy mirth, stockbroker or Army-wit, and all of them frightfully funny. But not so funny as the

Their meeting, despite Lytton's apprehensions, was remarkably successful. After the rough passage, Lytton arrived feeling like 'a mere piece of wet brown paper', and now dreading more than ever their *rencontre*. Douglas, however, turned out to be most sympathetic, speaking with an amusing pseudo-Scotch accent and behaving not at all in the bohemian, florid manner that his letters had somehow suggested. He seemed to understand at once Lytton's aversion to 'those trailing café parties', and brushed it all aside, declaring that he too did not care for them. Then, so that Lytton should have an opportunity to recover, they arranged to meet at Foyot's for dinner. That evening, Douglas arrived, very punctually, wearing a sombre black coat. But as soon as they started to discuss the limerick anthology, there was no black coat on his conversation. 'N.D. was rather older than I expected,' Lytton afterwards narrated in a letter to Mary Hutchinson (22 February 1928), ' – not flamboyant (as I had rather feared) – in fact rather the opposite – very neat – something (as Roger said) of a schoolmasterish effect in *appearance* – one of those odd benevolent unexpectedly broad-minded schoo'masters one sometimes comes across. Superb in restaurants, ordering food, and so on. A curious, very marked accent – partly Scotch, perhaps, partly – I don't know what – distinctly fascinating. The talk was mainly on a certain subject. Roger played up admirably, quite admirably, and made everything go much more easily than would otherwise have been the case. He seemed to be not particularly literary – which was slightly disturbing; and I think just a trifle too old – I mean belonging to a generation almost too distant for really intimate approach – a touch of Sickert – but perhaps I'm wrong. ... A slight effect you know of having been not very well treated by life. He's been very unlucky with publishers, and has made hardly anything out of his books. One would like to surround him with every kind of comfort and admiration and

---

learned note that accompanies each (and its variants), where the author (or collator) examines them closely, often in a pseudo-scientific manner. ::: The Index is a gem in itself.' (*Grand Man*, pp. 286–7).

innumerable boys of 14½.' In the course of their conversation Douglas said he might be coming to England that summer, and Lytton at once replied that he would give him a party at Boulestin's. 'I hope you will come to Ham Spray, too,' he added. 'Oh, shoorly, shoorly' was the answer.

The following day, Lytton and Roger went over to the Hôtel d'Isly in the rue Jacob, where Douglas was staying with Victor and Nancy Cunard. 'Their relations were not very easy to disentangle,' Lytton reported. 'Christian names reigned – and they were all three living in the same hotel. N.D. insisted on coming to the station to see me off – insisted on paying for every meal – and eventually tried to tip the porter!'

The more Lytton thought of Douglas on his arrival back in England, the more he felt that there was something pathetic about him. He was a kind man, and he lived in want. It was particularly abominable that his books should have brought him so little reward. In return for his hospitality over the week-end, he immediately tried to interest Chatto and Windus in Douglas's work, especially his novel on religion, *In the Beginning*, a limited edition of which had been privately printed in Florence the previous year. 'Of course I don't know in the least whether such a thing would be possible for you,' he admitted to Charles Prentice (15 February 1928), '(nor did I say anything to him about it), but the suggestion seemed worth making, and I hope you won't mind my doing so. I feel he is exactly the sort of writer your firm would like to be connected with, and that he on his side would benefit greatly if this could happen. In my opinion he is a most distinguished person, and it's a scandal that his last three books should produce no more than £12 a year in royalties.' As a result of this letter, Chatto and Windus became Douglas's publishers, bringing out *In the Beginning* later that year, and subsequently a number of his other books, including his autobiography, reprints of his earlier works, and *An Almanac* (1945), a volume of Douglas's favourite passages from the whole corpus of his work.

From now on, Lytton decided, until *Elizabeth and Essex* was finally off his hands, he must go nowhere. Determinedly he refused all invitations – including one to a Birth Control Ball and another to a charity performance of a play said to be dictated from the Other World by Oscar Wilde. 'I feel I must stick to this wretched grindstone, or all will be lost,' he explained to Mary Hutchinson (22 February 1928). 'Its serpentine prolongation is getting past a joke.' He had reached the thirteenth chapter, and all was proceeding well. 'I am getting on with old Bess as fast as I can expect,' he had informed Roger (20 February 1928). A fortnight later, he wrote: 'Here I am all alone – it is wonderfully peaceful – a faint mist hangs about – but so far I have managed to keep it out of my head. The Bess crisis is pretty serious – a regular death-grapple![51] But I hope the worst will be over by the end of the week. . . . Bemax supports me.'

After two-and-a-half years of intermittent struggle, he was within sight of the long-prepared last paragraph of his book. An uncharacteristic fit of impatience now seized hold of him. Every day he worked longer and longer hours – until, suddenly, his stamina gave way. Depression and a series of terrible headaches racked him, and for a fortnight he was unable to write anything. With her customary devotion, Carrington nursed him through this illness, and by Easter he felt well enough to go and stay with Dadie Rylands at his home in Tockington, near Bristol. Here, to assist in his recuperation, he would read aloud each morning from the plays of Molière; and after tea he permitted himself to do just a little work, arriving back at Ham Spray with four closely written sheets of paper – another chapter done!

Very slowly the narrative edged forward, until once again

51. Lytton uses this same phrase in a letter (3 March 1928) to Lumsden Barkway, who had written to him on his forty-eighth birthday. 'I am in the death-grapple with a vile book on Queen Elizabeth, and dare not relax my grip. It was delightful and astonishing of you to remember my birthday. Yes – I am 48 – it seems absurd, and I should suggest that there must be a mistake of twenty years in my birth certificate, if it were not that *you* would arise as a witness against me! . . . The odd thing is that my hair refuses to give any evidence – so far as I can see – it remains preposterously brown. But I always felt I was a kind of Samson – *all* my strength is in my hair! . . .'

there came a death-crisis. 'At the moment I am almost dead with exhaustion from this fearful tussle with the Old Hag,' he told Roger (19 April 1928), 'and I think tomorrow I shall have to take a complete rest.' Finally, on the very last day of the month, the agony came to an end. 'I am glad to be able to tell you that my book is finished,' he announced triumphantly to Charles Prentice, 'and the last bit is being typed now.'[52]

The next week he travelled up to London and called on Prentice to deliver the completed typescript and to discuss its probable date of publication and the title. It was the first Thursday in May. When at last he left the office, late that afternoon, all the details had been agreed. The sun shone in the streets as he stepped out jauntily on his way back to Bloomsbury. He was a free man again.

8

END OF AN ERA

Elizabeth and Essex utterly prostrated Lytton – far more so than *Queen Victoria* had done seven years earlier. 'It was a terribly exhausting book to write,' he confessed to Ottoline (29 November 1928) ' – I don't know why – I was sadly depressed most of the time.' He was to live for almost four years more, but over much of this final period the pulses of creative work seemed to have grown feeble, while over his love-life the clouds of weariness and suspense were perpetually forming and dissolving again. After *Elizabeth and Essex*, he published only four new essays – besides compiling a number of the notes to *The Greville Memoirs*. To some of those nearest him it appeared occasionally as if the inner spring had lost its elasticity, and the mechanism continued to act by the mere force of momentum. 'I had not realised what a weight Elizabeth had been on me – especially for the last few months,' he confided to Roger (25 May 1928), ' – and the relief of getting rid of it – of really being mentally free again – is very great. My spirits are beginning to bounce about again as they

52. The typing was done by Ethel Christian's of Southampton Street, to whom Lytton would send batches of his manuscript at intervals.

ought.' Once, during the last, hardest months of his work, he had told Topsy Lucas (30 October 1927) that he wished 'I never had even to pretend to do any work – I believe I should whirl round in a perpetual circle of pleasure'. For the remaining two thirds of the year there was no further need either to work or to pretend to work, and he was at liberty to revolve to his heart's content in a smooth ellipse of travel and sheer indolence. There was nothing whatever to do – and he was just the man to do it. Laziness, he told Lumsden Barkway, was 'an accomplishment which I have thoroughly mastered! I could give you lessons in the art.'

But now came over him the absolute necessity to move. A few days after having relinquished the typescript, he and Carrington set off on a four-week tour of Provence, spending the first ten days at Aix – 'a truly delightful place – utterly dim – with house after house of extraordinary beauty'. They put up at the Hôtel Nègre-Coste, and each day, in architectural ecstasies over the house fronts and doorways, they would wander through the fascinating streets, or explore the antique shops where they bought, among other items of furniture for Ham Spray, a large chest-of-drawers – 'Oh dear, oh dear! The gigantic packages!' One morning they motored over to Cassis to have lunch with Duncan Grant and Vanessa Bell in their small house 'La Bergère'. 'They seemed very cheerful, but wouldn't show us any pictures,' Lytton remarked in a letter to Roger (17 May 1928). 'Rather a singular ménage.'

From the first all went well. Already 'that horrid feeling of exhaustion has passed away', he wrote to Dadie Rylands. Aix was definitely a town to come to again. Carrington was behaving like an angel. 'We have enjoyed Aix enormously. C. has been a charming and infinitely accommodating travelling-companion. Luckily her propensity for wild-cat actions has calmed down, so it's all been plain sailing.'

On 18 May they left and were driven – 'by a perfect driver who steered his course with complete aplomb round all the precipices' – through Les Baux, to Arles, where they met Brian Howard,[53] apparently sent out there to write an

53. Wit, poet, critic and friend of the famous, Brian Howard dazzled

article on the great gathering of gipsies at Saintes-Maries.

He cottoned on to Lytton [Carrington wrote to Ralph (20 May 1928)], but mercifully we were just starting off in our automobile, so we were spared his company. I can't imagine anything more awful than having that chattering mouldy crow (a better name) at meals. ... Of course I should love to go to the great concourse of gypsies next Thursday at Santa Maria. Where they offer a sort of Fête to their patron saint, Saint Sara, but Lytton I can see *dreads* the gypsie world, so I don't feel I can ask to go = They say the gypsies allow nobody to their revly rites in the cathedral, and *tear* Foreigners limb from limb, if they are discovered at the ceremony. When Lytton asked Brian Howard if he would mind (being torn to pieces), He replied in a décrepid voice, – 'well – I suppose it might have its fascination and attractions'. He hopes to secret himself in the Cathedral and take some photographs by the help of an introduction from 'Country Life' to the Archbishop. He seemed very dim and had never taken a photograph before.

After two grey days in the Hôtel Forum, Baedeker in one hand, Kodak in the other, they hurried on to Nîmes, where the buzz and gaiety was extraordinary after the decayed droning of Arles. They arrived at the Hôtel du Cheval Blanc, where 'there are no men servants – only females. Except one very old walrus waiter. Lytton was rather agitated when he found himself having his trunks carried by a female!' In spite of being extremely tired, they went out at once to inspect the theatre and the arena. 'Very remarkable both,' Lytton noted in a letter to Roger, 'but the latter seemed oddly small after the Coliseum ... the central space seemed too constricted to hold any crucified miscreants at all comfortably – hardly room for a lion to turn round in – and besides rows of neat green garden chairs were ranged about in preparation for some horrid concert business tomorrow.'[54]

Eton, Oxford and London during the twenties and thirties by his exotic manner of living and of conversation. In the opinion of Evelyn Waugh, who pilloried him as Anthony Blanche in *Brideshead Revisited* and Ambrose Silk in *Put Out More Flags*, he was like Byron 'mad, bad and dangerous to know'. He committed suicide in 1958.

54. Carrington, in a letter to Ralph (21 May 1928), gives a fuller description of their adventures: 'Lytton's impatience to see everything the

The last stage of their holiday took them, via Pont du Gard, to Avignon. For days they had been journeying against a bitter, incessant wind that cut to the bone. But now a sultry heat settled over the country, reducing Lytton to a wraith. He and Carrington battled up through this motionless weather to Paris where, to their dismay, the heat was even more torrid. After booking into the Hôtel Foyot, Lytton crept out, half dead with giddiness, to try and get a little air under the trees in the Luxembourg Gardens. But it was no use. After an hour he limped back again and subsided on to his bed where, for the next four days, he was fed by relays of food from the restaurant.

He longed passionately now for the soothing grey English skies, the mild and gentle – the inevitable – English rain, confident that once he had quitted the artificial hot-house of Paris and set foot once more 'on the soil of Old England, I shall be well again'. Yet the prospect of further arduous travel made him shrink back in alarm, and eventually it was Ralph, driving a large new Sunbeam which Lytton had just bought, who came out to rescue him.

It was a relief to be back amid the cool and quiet of Ham Spray. For a few days he pondered over whether he might

---

moment he arrives, is always extraordinary! Inside the arena we found a curious Bull fight going on. A young bull entered the arena to the sound of Buggells; and about a dozen young men – not drest up – just in shirts, and cotton trousers started darting from side to side, in front of the Bull. At last one braver than the rest, (very attractive with light red shoes . . .) rushed up to the Bull and seized a red cocKade off its head between its horns, and got away with it. Then they all tried to touch the Bull's horns. It was a curious game. I found it difficult to believe there was any danger. The Bull seemed so bewildered, and slow, like a very poorly cross old widow, having to play "Touch" with a gang of little scaramouches.'

When this performance was over, they went off to have a large tea in the Boulevard Hugo, and Carrington 'ate so many cakes I felt almost ill'. After which they walked to the gardens which were 'crowded with all the nobility of nîmes in their grandest clothes', and Lytton climbed the Hill of Pines to look at the monument at its summit – 'all monuments look their best about 5 o'clock, I've noticed' – and finally, before retiring to their hotel, the two of them sat by one of the lakes, listening to the evening music from the Pavillon, and sipping vermouth – 'It was a BosKy scene.'

compose a complex idyllic poem about Eton — 'a mixture of Tennyson and T. S. Eliot', but decided against this once the proof sheets of *Elizabeth and Essex* arrived — unexpectedly early — from Chatto and Windus. With meticulous care he read through these three times — besides having them checked separately by Goldie Dickinson and Roger Senhouse — and it was at this stage that he inserted the Essex poem at the end of Chapter VII. There was also the endless enmeshment of making the index, fussing over illustrations and preparing a special, limited, American edition of the book — 'I spend my days signing my name at 4 guineas a signature for the Americans.'

Among contemporary novels that he was reading were two that have become particularly well-known — Aldous Huxley's *Point Counter Point* and D. H. Lawrence's *Lady Chatterley's Lover*, neither of which he greatly liked. 'I have bought — I hardly know why — *Point Counter Point*, and am making a heroic effort to read every word of it,' he wrote to Topsy Lucas (7 October 1928). 'So far it seems to me worthy but not at all interesting. Is this my fault?' By the time he had finished the book, he felt more certain that the fault must principally lie with the author. It was, he told Dadie Rylands, 'a bad book, in my opinion. The man can't write; his views are rotten; and the total result of his work is a feeling of devitalisation and gloom.'

About *Lady Chatterley's Lover* his feelings were more mixed. 'In many ways I liked it,' he wrote to Roger (23 October 1928), '— the ordinary Lawrenceisms were less in evidence — and it was excellent to attack that subject frontally. But I complain of a sad lack of artistic intention — of creative powers thrown away — of an obsession with moralising. To say nothing of a barbaric, anti-civilization outlook, which I disapprove of.' He had been persuaded to read Lawrence's novel in the first place by Norman Douglas, who also wrote asking him for his opinion of it (30 July 1928), adding that 'I liked it on the whole'. After finishing it, Lytton set out his reactions in much the same words as he used to Roger Senhouse, drawing from Douglas some approving qualifications

(12 September 1928). 'As to Lawrence (D.H.) – you are perfectly right,' he answered. 'He writes too quickly; a perfect diarrhoea, or rather cholera; besides he can't control his impulses. Lady Chatterley is better than I expected.'

On 3 August, Lytton finished correcting his proofs, sent them back to the publishers, and the following day started out with Roger Senhouse for a short Scandinavian holiday. At the end of 'a highly successful journey' they arrived in Copenhagen, whose charming eighteenth-century houses in the rococo style reminded Lytton of Aix. 'We have had all sorts of meals in all sorts of restaurants – have spent hours in second-hand bookshops, with no result – have walked through endless streets and gardens – and so far have seen no sights,' he wrote to Carrington (8 August 1928). '. . . The inhabitants are pleasant, but oh! so lacking in temperament! Duty seems to guide their steps, and duty alone.'

On their very last day in Copenhagen, Raymond Mortimer appeared, having arrived the night before from Berlin and put up in the Phoenix Hotel where they were staying. 'We spent the day with him,' Lytton told Carrington (14 August 1928), 'he was in rather a flutter what with one thing and another – not in his best mood – talked of Venice and those delightful things one went about in there – those charming motor-boats – etc. etc. so that I nearly shrieked. However he was mainly pathetic – and it seemed cruel to leave him alone in that strange city . . .'

At the end of the week, Lytton and Roger moved on to Stockholm. The fearsome medicinal halls at Saltsjöbaden, to which Lytton paid a brief nostalgic visit, appeared totally unchanged from when he had been a patient there eighteen years ago, but Stockholm itself had altered. It had grown in size, was more evidently a capital city, yet still retained its charm. 'There is a great deal of water in every direction – broad limbs of the Baltic permeating between the streets – so that there really *is* some resemblance to Venice,' he wrote to Carrington (14 August 1928). 'The blueness of the water in this northern light is often attractive, and there are quantities of white steam ferry boats moving about, which adds to the gaiety of the scene. The best building to my mind is the royal palace, which stands on the central island of the town – a large severe square pale brown 18th century structure, dominating the scene. Then, slightly remote, on a broad piece of water, is the new Town Hall[55] – distinctly striking – very big – and of an effective bigness, built in dark red brick, with one very high tower at the junction of two wings – one (facing the water) longer than the other. . . . . The worst of it is, however, that in spite of a certain grandeur of conception, there is no real greatness of feeling about it. It is extremely clever and well thought out, but the detail is positively bad – in bad taste, and sometimes actually facetious – and there is no coherency of style – classical, gothic, oriental, byzantine, modern Viennese, etc. etc., so that one has no sense of security or repose. It is a pity, as the site is so good, and the hulk *is* impressive – which is certainly something; but the more I looked the more certain I became that it was infinitely far from real goodness. One longs for some of the severity of Kennedy – and more still for the splendour of Bramante.'

The days sped by all too quickly and soon they were returning. Back at Ham Spray, a desperate band of workmen, under Carrington's leadership, was making alterations to the house. Every hour their activities grew more frenzied, leaping upward in a dreadful crescendo of noise and confusion. 'No peace, no repose on this earth I plainly see,' Lytton grumbled (30 August 1928). 'One rushes out of doors to escape from the eternal maelstrom only to find oneself set upon by ten million wasps, who, having demolished every particle of fruit in the garden, now begin to devour human beings.' While the pandemonium lasted, Lytton fled up to London where he continued to lead 'a shockingly lazy life. But,' he added to Topsy Lucas, 'I find it very good for my health, which is something.' There were lunches at the Ivy, dinners at Boulestin's, long conversations in the Oriental Club – strawberries – asparagus – cider cup. And there were copious parties. At Argyll House, one of his fellow guests was A. J. Balfour. 'I like watching

55. This celebrated Town Hall was built between 1911 and 1923 after drawings made by R. Östberg.

him,' Lytton told Roger Senhouse, '– the perfection of his manners – the curious dimness – the wickedness one catches glimpses of underneath. But of course any communication of ideas is totally out of the question. One might as well talk to the man in the moon.'

In Bloomsbury, he went to the evening gatherings of the 'Woolves' and Bells, Duncan and Maynard, and special literary afternoons, with tea, given by Ottoline at her new house in Gower Street. This was the last, least brilliant phase in her career as patroness of the arts, and not even the presence of W. B. Yeats – 'with grey coat-tails and wide-ribboned pince-nez that recalled an old fashioned American politician' – could quite dispel the atmosphere of mediocrity. On Lytton's first visit there, the guests included Aldous Huxley and the Irish poet and chatterbox James Stephens, 'a little gnome-like Irishman,' he described him to Roger Senhouse (9 November 1928), 'with a touch of the nautical, quite nice, but gassing away thirteen to the dozen with endless theories and generalisations. One of those essentially frivolous minds that mask themselves under a grand apparatus of earnestness and high-mindedness. On and on he went – inveighing against "destructive criticism" (that tedious old story), pointing out that no one could write about love, but only about sex, lamenting that there were no epics, etc., etc. Aldous didn't say much – he was very agreeable as usual. I enjoy his company, partly because (I can't help it) I somehow feel so definitely his superior! A question of astral bodies, or auras, I think. "Son génie étonné tremble devant le mien" – or something of that sort. Do you believe in those magnetic influences? I almost do – how otherwise to account for the mysterious aversions, engouements, dominations etc. that seem to have no reasonable explanation? Ethel Sands filled up gaps with her appreciative shiny teeth, and Pipsey interrupted and floundered as usual. . . . I was suddenly asked to give my opinion upon some long-winded dictum of Mr J.S's on medieval clothes – the differences between the sexes – beauty of women – love – and all the rest of it. I was rather at a loss and could only shriek.

"Armour! I'm in favour of armour!" ... Mr J.S. condemned me, of course, as destructive.'

Lytton's second visit to Gower Street went off rather better, except for a painful circumstance at the beginning. 'I made a pompous entry – late – everyone sitting round at the table – a general remuement, etc. and some slightly dazed looks', he wrote to Senhouse (8 January 1929). 'I didn't know why, but on at last taking my seat found that *all* my front buttons were undone, from top to bottom. ... There was also cet éternal Stephens, Max [Beerbohm] himself was most quiet – like a great round pussy-cat. He was snowed under by the Irishman, though.'

At week-ends, he liked to go down to Cambridge, and once he went to a 'slightly alarming' house-party at Rushbrook Hall, near Bury St Edmunds, a large, very handsome redbrick Tudor building, with a moat, converted into a Queen Anne Renaissance style – the seat of Lord Islington.[56] He had been invited there out of the blue, and thinking that if he refused, it would mean that he had lapsed into a permanent hermit, accepted – only to regret his decision the minute he arrived, convinced that a permanent hermit was what he really ought to be. The sight of a small neatly prepared bridge-table, as he passed through an enormous sitting-room on the long march to his bedroom, confirmed his very worst fears. All the old sensations returned; his exasperation at the elegant vapidity of the upper classes, made more acute by the difficulty of putting his finger on the actual spot of degradation – perhaps, after all, it was something wrong with the glands. How could he shine in such company? 'I had envisioned some sort of crowd, into which one could disappear,' he wrote to Topsy Lucas (7 October 1928), '– but there are only 2 other guests –

56. Sir John Poynder Dickson-Poynder (1866–1936), politician and administrator, who had been governor of New Zealand (1910–12) and was created first Baron Islington (1910). Among his later appointments had been under-secretary of state for the colonies (1914–15), parliamentary under-secretary for India (1915–18) and chairman of the National Savings Committee (1920–26). In 1926 he had officially retired.

Lord Hugh Cecil and Evan Charteris.[57] The conversation is ceaseless, impossible to join. Lord I. is a country gentleman of about 60. Lady I. an ex-beauty, a brilliant mimic (oh dear!) and a featherhead. Evan C. is a middle-aged man about town — mild, pungent, dull and amusing. Lord Hugh — you can imagine — a very unreal figure with all the regulation Cecil charm. During a long discussion last night on the pros and cons of capital punishment, his view was that there was only one objection to it — that (as at present arranged) it involved a voluntary executioner. Medievalism itself! —'

Down at Ham Spray, there were the usual stream of visitors — E. M. Forster, Raymond Mortimer and Francis Birrell, Lytton's niece Janie Bussy, Gerald Heard,[58] who delighted everyone by his 'unexpected intensity', Arthur Waley, 'admirable, triumphant, talking away like anything and rather less remote than usual', Saxon Sydney-Turner, who strolled about 'looking very shrewd and nervous, amiable and ill, and reading

57. Sir Evan Charteris (1864–1940), the barrister and biographer, who later became chairman of the trustees of the National Portrait Gallery (1928–40), chairman of the Tate Gallery (1934–40) and a trustee of the National Gallery (1932–9). Among his books are a biography of John Sargent (1927) and *The Life and Letters of Sir Edmund Gosse* (1931).

58. Gerald Heard (b. 1899) was at this time the author of *Narcissus: An Anatomy of Clothes*, a book which attempted to work out historically the connection between architecture and costume. Later, as H. F. Heard, he gained fame as the writer of mystery stories, and, as Gerald Heard, as the author of studies in theological and scientific subjects. In 1937 he was to leave England for America where he became a close friend of Christopher Isherwood and Aldous Huxley, who portrayed him as the mystic William Propter in *After Many a Summer* and, possibly, Bruno Rontini in *Time Must Have a Stop*. Bishop Barkway, in a letter to the author (20 May 1963), writes of a side of his [Lytton's] nature which he kept tightly concealed from others, but it is characteristic of the many conversations he had of the deepest of all mysteries. Once in the "Backs" he confided to me how much he was attracted to the oriental point of view. It was then a fore-shadowing of the interest in the Indian religions such as is manifested by Gerald Heard and others like him in this time.' But Gerald Heard has recorded that 'L.S. never said anything to my knowledge re Oriental Religions. He did once suggest he would write a Life of Christ but in a Queen Victoria key, and one did suggest it wouldn't be a successful composition.'

Isocrates in the original', the ebullient Boris Anrep, who 'bubbled along in a perpetual fountain of amusement', and another friend who told 'an absurd story of William Jowitt in Paris ... that solemn handsome personnage. He confessed that his one pleasure was whipping women, but he didn't know how to manage it – could G. tell him what to do, and where to go? G. handed him over to one of his numerous friends, who had every renseignement at his finger tips. W.J. announced that he had only 4 hours – had to leave Paris after that. They sat in a café discussing every possibility. W.J. could not quite make up his mind what he would like best. The friend described a certain lieu, where the naked ladies entered the room on all fours, pecking grain from the floor like chickens, while the customers lashed their behinds. W.J. was struck by this ... and yet ... did not after all feel *quite* sure that it was exactly what he wanted. And so it went on, until at last the four hours were up, and he went back to England. The poor fellow's debauches are always of this nature.'

The year, which had opened in such a brilliant glow of happiness, ended sadly. Early in December, Lady Strachey, now in her eighty-ninth year, developed bronchitis. There was little hope of a recovery. Almost to the last she had retained her extraordinary zest for life. But gradually, though the vigour of her mind was as phenomenal as always, it had seemed to withdraw from the contemporary world and focus itself ever more distantly on the past. She could not clearly remember what had happened the day before, but incidents from her London life of over fifty years back lived vividly in her imagination – Browning's indignation at being called 'Robert' by a troop of unknown and unintroduced American women; Tennyson reciting his poetry in a surging, monotonous voice; the night Salvini lost his shaven wig in the middle of Alfieri's *Samsone*; George du Maurier singing French songs with a meticulous accent in his tiny, mosquito voice; the quiet and serious manner of George Eliot and Carlyle's Homeric shouts of laughter. And farther back, and more vivid yet, her mind retraced the incredible voyage out to India – the water-spouts, the flying fish, the albatross wheeling overhead, the tremendous storms, the unearthly sea calms, and her mother playing the cottage piano on board the *Trafalgar*. Those far-off days in India were more real and dear to her than ever – there was Lord Lytton, the viceroy, in his blue silk dressing-gown, and Lord Roberts mending her sewing-machine; she could re-experience the excitement of the amateur theatricals in Calcutta, and remember the time she chased a leopard with a croquet mallet.

Blindness had been a great deprivation, seeming to emphasize her natural remoteness from post-war England, the emptiness of her declining years. Old age was an uneven patchwork of bright memories. 'It is like looking out on a garden once filled with life in all its variety and emotion', she wrote at the close of her memoirs, 'children frolicking, youth in all its vigorous activity, lovers meeting in the shade, friends eagerly discussing every aspect of humanity, exquisite music rising and falling, artists at work on the heavenly beauty around them; and now all has vanished, nothing is left but a space, empty of all but graves, among which wander a few time-worn figures; while the faint echoes of once familiar sounds, reaching the ear, tell us of a new-crowded space outside our ken.'

This autumn, her strength was already beginning to fail. She was subject to alarming fits of fainting, and had grown too frail to walk more than a few steps without assistance. Leonard and Virginia Woolf, strolling along the pavement of Gordon Square one November day, happened to glance up at her window, and saw her blind and silent figure sitting on the balcony, with Pippa close behind. They waved up, and on being told of their gesture, she leant forward and opened her arms in an unforgettable signal of affection, a vast maternal benediction.

It was the last they saw of her. Death came fairly peacefully. For two weeks she lay in bed, fitfully conscious, looked after night and day by Pippa. Lytton visited her often, and tried to take some of the strain off his sister. 'I have been rather numbed and exhausted with this wretched business,' he admitted to Roger Senhouse on 14 December, 'and at the same time emotionally perturbed and chaotic.' Each day she grew a little weaker, a little more sequestered and forlorn, though she had curious bursts of energy almost to the end. On the afternoon of Friday, 15 December, she died, quite quietly, in her sleep. Although her death had been expected (and, being so very old, it was not possible in any case that she could live much longer), her loss was a great sadness to Lytton. He felt the shock deeply. 'It is impossible to escape the grief, though one has discounted it so long,' he wrote to Topsy Lucas (21 December 1928). 'The prospects of old age are indeed miserable. Yet some manage to keep a hold on life till the last moment – and then vanish suddenly; but they are the lucky few.'

SEVENTEEN

Another World

'Human life in its last stages is certainly a miserable affair.
And yet we are horrified when Death comes to put an end to
it.' *Lytton Strachey to Carrington* (19 November 1931)

1

THE LOST GIRL

HE was rich, but impenetrably exhausted. For the next six
months a low fever and the universal presence of unhappiness
sat upon his enfeebled spirit, reducing him on and off 'to bed
and ashes'. He was seldom acutely miserable, but often
during this period his life appeared to have become simply a
long process of getting tired. He felt tired of himself, tired of
sustained composition, tired above all of tears and laughter.[1]

Ham Spray, that season, rang to the sound of tears and
laughter. Roger Senhouse came and Roger Senhouse went,
very much as usual – 'sweetness and vagueness incarnate'. And
very much as usual Lytton's dubitations multiplied, were deliciously melted away, and returned again in greater numbers.
'I feel it's my métier to accept his [Roger's] peculiarities and
peccadilloes,' he stoically remarked to Topsy Lucas (14 July
1929).

The other eruptions at Ham Spray he accustomed himself

1. Although it did not manifest itself openly until the last four months
of his life and was not, even then, recognized for what it was, the disease
which finally killed Lytton must, according to present-day medical knowledge, in all probability have affected his health in various indirect ways
(such as pernicious anaemia) for something like two years before his
death. It was this, combined probably with a change-of-life period and in
addition to the normal mental prostration which followed the writing of
a full-length book, that seems to have so influenced these years.

to treat with equal stoicism. The new living experiment which he had helped to inaugurate in the spring of 1926, with Frances and Ralph spending the weekdays away together in Gordon Square, was not turning out as he had hoped. Increasingly he found it impossible to see Ralph except in the company of Frances. Every time Ralph came down to Hungerford he brought her; and at the end of their stay there they would leave together. Lytton did not dislike Frances, but he could not easily get on with her, and nor could Carrington. The two women had never been real friends. Frances, it is true, felt a deep admiration for Carrington, never thought her tiresome, and spoke of her as a unique person, unlike anyone else in the world. But the most that Carrington felt for Frances was a genuine gratitude for having accepted so readily Ralph's links with Ham Spray. Their outward manner was usually polite, complimentary, apologetic, lukewarm. They strove to outdo each other in diffident civilities. Carrington's reactions were also complicated by a lesbian attraction for Frances, her feelings shot through with sudden rushes of tenderness, moments of despair. They were therefore not simply rivals for Ralph's love, but two people who, because of odd quirks of circumstance, found the independent lines of their happiness knotted together in a way that no one could unravel. They kept their distance, not wanting to tamper too boldly with this knot for fear of damaging themselves. Somehow it all seemed beyond them.

The situation was particularly awkward for Carrington. She never complained to Lytton about this latest arrangement, in case it should alter for something worse. But he could sense from her fretful, nervous manner, and from the recognition in it of his own secret reactions, the inner discomposure that was troubling her. Both of them resented Frances's habitual presence which fanned the embers of their fading emotions in the most painful way. The atmosphere between the four of them at week-ends had consequently become forced and uneasy, heavy with a weight of unspoken feeling which all Ralph's parades of jocular friendliness could not dispel.

Eventually, in the autumn of 1928, Lytton decided to try

and remedy this ticklish state of affairs. His approach was characteristically reasonable. After one particularly grim week-end, he wrote to Ralph (6 November 1928) a long, tactful, undemanding letter: 'My dearest, I am writing this without telling Carrington, and perhaps you may think it best not to show it to Frances, but of course you must do just as you like. I have felt for some time rather uneasy about F. – but have been unable to bring myself to say anything. What worries me is her coming down here with you so much, and staying for so much of the time you are here, so that we see so little of you alone. It is not quite what I had expected would happen – and I think not exactly what you intended either. I am afraid you may suppose that this indicates some hostility on my part towards F.; but this is far from being the case. Can you believe this? I hope so. I hope you will trust that I am telling the truth, and believe in my affection for you, which is something I cannot describe or express. I feel it too deeply for that. I know that this must be painful to you, but it seems better that I should tell you what is in my mind than that I should continue indefinitely with a slight consciousness of a difficulty not cleared up between us. Perhaps it can't be cleared up – but at any rate I think it's better open than secret. I don't want to force you into anything unwillingly. If you feel that you can do nothing – then it can't be helped. If you feel that you cannot answer this either by writing or in talk, do not do so, I will say nothing more about it, and all will be well between us. But conceivably it might be possible for you to suggest to F. that it would be better if she came down rather less often – and if that could be managed the situation would be very greatly eased. It is for you to judge what you can do. I trust your judgement. I only feel that you may perhaps have allowed things to drift from an unwillingness to take an unpleasant step. I don't know. And please do not do anything under a sense of "pressure" from me. I press for nothing. I only ask whether perhaps it may be possible, without too much pain, to make me happier.'

It was impossible for Ralph to turn his back on such a modest appeal. The two of them met the following week on neutral territory – 37 Gordon Square – to disentangle the problem. And, as a result of their discussion, circumstances did grow a little less congested down at Ham Spray, though the atmosphere there was never entirely cleared.

No sooner, however, had the tension in one part of the molecule relaxed slightly than, dramatically, it tightened up elsewhere. The weakest link in its structure had long been that securing Carrington to Gerald Brenan. After their temporary break-up, when Stephen Tomlin had briefly become Carrington's lover, there was a final attempt at reconciliation in 1928. But by then their relationship had already grown explosive. Gerald's inability to affect Carrington permanently and profoundly was an endless exasperation to him. She seemed by her very character to be armour-plated against his emotional assaults. And although his rushes of bitterness and anger had made her frightened of seeing him, she still could not countenance the thought of giving him up. It was the old problem. They seemed therefore to have reached a stalemate, since neither, for the sake of his own peace of mind, could leave the other in peace.

The end came over a ludicrously trivial incident involving a bundle of old ties. Carrington, going through Lytton's clothes one day, had come across the ties in his wardrobe. He no longer wanted them – she did not want to throw them out. Then a brainwave had occurred to her – a solution that would please everyone. She liked making parcels – firm, neat, satisfactory objects. And she liked to delegate certain articles to certain particular people – it ministered to some peculiar sense of order and justice in her. She therefore wrapped up the bundle of Lytton's used ties and sent it off to Gerald. Being hardly able to afford a tie himself, he was sure, she reasoned, to be overjoyed by this gift.

But Gerald was outraged. To be handed Lytton's cast-off clothes symbolized cruelly, even cynically, the second-hand place he had for so long occupied in Carrington's affections. She took no account of his own tastes, his individuality. He and Lytton had practically nothing in common with each other, yet he was obliged continuously to live under Lytton's shadow, to rely upon his constant beneficence and hospitality, to listen to stories about him when he was not present and now, as the final indignity, to walk about dressed up in his old clothes. It was the last straw. His anger flared out, and Carrington, terrified and bewildered by this vitriolic reaction to her present, tried vainly to reason with him. He was finding, she said, a quarrel in a straw. There was nothing at stake. But for him honour was at stake. The incident had all at once clarified matters, the clouds parted and he saw everything in a hard perspective. Their love-affair had led nowhere, could never do so. He reproached her scathingly. They parted and did not see each other again until after Gerald's marriage to the American poetess, Gamel Woolsey, in 1930. 'She [Carrington] could not bear anyone to reproach her because she was all too prone to feel guilty,' he explained to the author, 'and that was how I lost her.'

Over the last four years of her life, that is from 1928 to 1932, Carrington kept a sort of random, uncoordinated diary – spasmodic and disjunctive entries in no particular sequence, sometimes undated, ranging from brief notes to fierce, unchecked outpourings that ramble repetitiously on over the scrawled unpunctuated pages, full of ravening pathos, tiresomeness, deep despair – on the stiff beige-coloured cover of which she inked in, with her child's hand, a title: *D. C. Partridge:* HER BOOK. This unique volume records with shocking and melancholy vividness the vast disorganization of her life, the unlocated muddled agitations that so upset her peace of mind.

These last years were seldom calm, seldom happy. Her days, especially when Lytton was absent from Ham Spray, were often long and dismal, racked by headaches and ill thoughts of death; and at night she was plagued by hideous dreams – dreams of decapitation and dripping blood, of young boys being drowned on rafts, of making violent lesbian love to girls. Her solitary and promiscuous nature, like that of a cat, with its awkward quirk of virginal integrity, refused to be at ease with other people, with 'bouncy groups', yet dreaded isolation from humanity. Whenever Lytton left her side, she felt the draught, and like an anxious mother she feared for his safety and for her own. Lytton, who appreciated much of what she was silently feeling, would try to reason away these apprehensions, minimize her terrors. 'What absolute despair can seize one without warning or apparent cause,' she wrote at one point in her diary. 'Lytton maintains it is the adrenalin glands not working.'

Lytton's nearness brought some order and cohesion to her chaotic incomplete existence. Otherwise she could only find serenity and meaning in her painting, and here infrequently. Every year since 1918 she had made a resolution to paint more, but every year her human relationships had complicated this resolve. Sometimes she could not bear the thought of anyone touching her, of even coming close to her – yet she needed desperately to love people. All her passions and affections were attempts to re-create some childish situation. If Lytton may be said to have represented to her a father, then the affairs she entered into with many young men were chiefly endeavours to find a substitute for her dead brother. Her love for Gerald Brenan had long been one attempt to replace him – but as she got to know Gerald better so he filled the part less and less convincingly. He was too articulate, too much, unblinkingly, himself. But now after he had left, she took up with someone else who was better fitted by character to approach her ideal. This was Bernard Penrose, nicknamed Beacus. Like Teddy, Beacus was rather a quiet man, who in spite of private means had lived some time as able seaman and second mate before the mast, and sailed the clipper route round the Horn in one of the last of the British wind-jammers. To look at he was generally considered attractive, having a square muscular body and a brick-red face. But in literary terms he was limited, by Bloomsbury standards.

It might seem surprising that a woman of Carrington's individuality should have allowed herself to become deeply involved with such a conventional person. In fact Beacus's incurious nature seems to have been especially pleasing to her. She was better able to recapture the lost, yearning sensations she had experienced for her rugged and reserved brother. To be with him had all the advantages of being alone. There was an uncomplicated morning light that played about their love, casual and blameless. 'His [Beacus's] remoteness just suits me,' she recorded in HER BOOK. 'For I feel I am not being "observed" all the time, that No reactions are expected. That whatever happens is alright. a moon shining in the window across the beD. – In the morning seeing a tousled face lying beside me. and then embraces, and more Love. But the sky is light, it has to come to an end and reality must return.'

Fleetingly this reality did return, and the man she had thought so beautiful would appear dull. One episode in the love-affair, which probably took place early in 1929, catches brilliantly the beat of her mixed sensations – the desire, indifference, excitement, anxiety, disillusion, obsession.

A short love affair. Then a month of thinking about little else. a weekend to Cornwall. The pleasure of leaving London invisibly in the rain, like a ghost, curious how little interest anyone takes in one's movements. The tedium of the journey and the slowness of trains, and then a sudden panic as usual. 'I am too old, it is ridiculous. Probably it is all a mistake'. at Exeter the car outside and thens later on the Platform. And my misgivings returned. as I felt it would all be a delusion. One of my own day dreams which had No relation in anybody else's head. at Oakhampton. the disappointment because the bedroom wasn'T exactly as I had imagined. I had 'seen' a big tester bed, a large low room with Dark mahogany furniture, and burning fire . . . Instead a neat spare room in my Mother's style with No fireplace and everything white and polished. I felt Nothing can survive this. But curiously enough, it did. In the cinema he held my hand. and I teased him . . . I lay in bed and read Tristram Shandy, while he drank in the bar. When I said it doesn'T matter tonight He never questioned, or enquired. Not very much curiosity. Yet that is probably the main attraction. Perhaps the most beautiful moment with a shirt in dark close fitting trousers and a brass belt. Do men know the beauty of their appearances as exactly as females do?

Over the next two years her obsession became fiercer, mounting into a violent passion that was all the more unrestrained for being so mildly reciprocated. She was ten years older than Beacus, and always painfully aware that their attachment could not last for long. Each day was important.

After they had become friends, she went about with him occasionally and ordered his ship's stores down at Southampton where he sometimes had his converted Brixham trawler.

In 1930, after Beacus had been at sea for some months, Carrington became pregnant. Her horror and disgust at the process of childbearing had always been overwhelming. She used to maintain that only by Lytton could she endure to give birth to a child. And so she arranged to have the pregnancy terminated. Lytton himself did not conceal his disapproval of this affair. Though Lytton had made little point of contact with either Frances Marshall or Gerald Brenan, he was always perfectly tolerant of Ralph's and Carrington's friends, and never jealous of their attachments to younger men and women. In the past he had made an exception only of that *femme fatale*, Clare. But now, not unreasonably, he found himself objecting to some of her friends. Yet what could he do? For over a dozen years she had been making persistent sacrifices for his welfare, had sought and willingly endured privations. No one so self-willed and independent as she was could for so long have immolated herself to another person without many unconscious longings for liberty. Had he therefore the right to complain now these secret longings were taking a form inconvenient to himself? On the whole he thought not. Yet inconvenient this state of affairs certainly was for Lytton. On one occasion Carrington brought Beacus to the house when he was suffering from jaundice, nursing him there for a whole month while Lytton crept noiselessly about in the next room. On any previous occasion such an event would have been unthinkable.

Then Beacus sailed to the Mediterranean and it seemed to Carrington that with him had gone her last connections with youth and beauty. In some ways she was relieved. She had been attacked by pangs of remorse at neglecting Lytton on certain occasions in favour of her lover. But now that this last adventure was over, now that she was less restless and her 'lusts had run dry', she would start to make it up to him. By the summer of 1931 she was already painting more and look-

ing forward with deeper contentment to a serene and happy
life with Lytton among the rooms and gardens she had created
for them both at Ham Spray.

2

PORRIDGE AND SEALING-WAX

'It is really shocking, I am becoming a nature-lover and observer – fatal!' Lytton had exclaimed to Roger Senhouse early
that winter (12 November 1928). 'The intellect fades in proportion.' The most potent attraction holding him down at
Ham Spray was the climate of almost compulsory idleness
that hung about there. In the aftermath of *Elizabeth and Essex*,
idleness had become the chief refuge of his fading intellect. Of
course there were always plenty of improbable schemes in the
air for a new *magnum opus*. On one occasion he spent three
hours discussing with Francis Greenslet the suggestion that he
might try his hand at a historical biography of Julius Caesar –
'immaculately dressed, curled up into a double knot, in a big
armchair, presenting his views on Caesar as a man, lover, historian, general and emperor' – but it all came to nothing.
Robert Nichols vainly urged him to tackle Louis XIII – 'one of
the most extraordinary beings who have ever lived'. J. B.
Pinker equally vainly petitioned him to write a secret Life of
Shakespeare. Peter Davies, the publisher, offered him a contract to write a short book on Edward VII, but this Lytton
refused on the grounds that his Life, without such details as
could only be touched upon after the death of certain people
still living, would not be of sufficient value. As an antidote to
the huge but dubious success of *Elizabeth and Essex*, he then
considered writing a biography of more limited appeal, on
General Booth perhaps, or even Benjamin Jowett. And he also
toyed for a while with the idea of a book on George Wash-
ington, from which he was apparently dissuaded by the voluminous mass of material that was unhappily written 'in that
almost incomprehensible and quite intolerable language – American'.

Throughout the year he published only two pieces, one of them a review of Walter Raleigh's *Discoveries of Guiana*, being his final contribution to the *Nation and Athenaeum*. Hubert Henderson was then preparing to give up his editorship of the paper on being appointed, together with Keynes, to the staff of the Economic Advisory Council. There was talk of a new Bloomsbury weekly to take its place – which Lytton proposed should be called the *W.C.1.* – and from this time on he switched his allegiance to Desmond MacCarthy's newly formed *Life and Letters*.

MacCarthy had first approached Lytton that March asking him to write something for this periodical, and Lytton replied giving him as his choice of subject either *King Lear* or Bishop Creighton. MacCarthy selected the latter, and Lytton set to work early in April, describing himself in a letter to Roger Senhouse (9 April 1929) as 'in rather a state, as ... I am now faced with the necessity of writing the affair out of my head apparently, as the blessed London Library, deaf to my frenzied shrieks, has refused to send me any books'.

To *Life and Letters* Lytton was also to contribute his essay on Froude (originally entitled 'One of the Victorians'), this being the last of his series 'Six English Historians', and 'Madame de Lieven', the last but one of his portraits in miniature. His final essay did not come out until April 1931 – only a month before its reappearance in the collected volume, *Portraits in Miniature and Other Essays* – and was printed in the amalgamated *New Statesman and Nation*, which had recently come under the editorship of Kingsley Martin, for whom Lytton had promised to write regularly.

In this final period of his life, Lytton was the most unprolific of authors. But he was still infected by an inveterate and incurable itch to read. He seemed to be reading constantly, and almost always had a book in his hand. Every time he travelled up to London, he would scour The Times Book Club, finding there that spring only Hugh Kingsmill's *Matthew Arnold* and I. A. Richards's manual of his laboratory methods of literary study, *Practical Criticism*, which he thought 'fascinating'. Soon he returned again to his old favourites, to Chesterfield, to Virgil, to Moore's *Principia Ethica* – 'such pleasant reading' – and out-topping all, Gibbon. 'My laziness is becoming more scandalous than ever,' he happily informed Roger (13 September 1929). 'I do nothing but read Gibbon – first in the quarto – then in Bury's edition.' The dearth of contemporary literature, he complained to Topsy Lucas, was 'serious'. But later that year three new books did manage to win his favour. The first of these was Richard Aldington's celebrated war novel, *Death of a Hero*. "I've got Death of a Hero from the Times, and am quite enjoying it so far,' he told Roger (14 October 1929). 'I like the brightness of the fellow, rather to my surprise. But I really don't understand why he should have deliberately made such an ass of himself on the "comradeship" question. Most unnecessary!'

His admiration for Virginia Woolf's *A Room of One's Own* was unqualified, and in a letter to Dorothy Bussy he described it as 'a masterpiece'. Also a masterpiece was Richard Hughes's first novel, *A High Wind in Jamaica*, about which he wrote to many of his friends, including Norman Douglas, in terms of the very highest praise. 'My chief conversation will be, now and henceforward, on the subject of a High Wind,' he notified Roger Senhouse (1 October 1929), 'insisting that everyone should read it who hasn't and that everyone should admire it who has.' Eighteen months later, Lytton met Hughes briefly one afternoon at Ham Spray. 'Yesterday there was an incursion in the shape of Richard Hughes, who arrived with Faith Henderson, with whom he was staying,' he notes in a letter to Roger (5 May 1931). 'Slightly sinister, we thought – but perhaps only timid under a mask.' To Richard Hughes's eyes it was Lytton who appeared sinister. 'My first impression was of the extraordinary beauty of the inside of the house,' he wrote to the author, '– a beauty based on little original architectural distinction. Lytton, I think, spent most of his time deep in a chair – he was certainly ill at the time – but I was too frightened of him to look at him closely: my general impression, however, was that he looked as if he had been designed as the perfect objet d'art to go with the background of the house.' Characteristically, Lytton did not mention his admiration for

A High Wind in Jamaica, and Hughes never suspected it. 'How cock-a-hoop I should have been at the time had I known it!'

If he was still idle, at least he was not solitary. The blue weather continued to fasten him down at Ham Spray, where he was visited for a time by Pippa. The two of them had been appointed joint-executors and trustees of their mother's will, a long and complicated document, under which Lytton himself was left two thousand pounds, minus any sum which he had received from her during her lifetime.[2] Later this year, Lytton arranged with Pippa to move back into 51 Gordon Square, taking over the ground floor which he converted into a self-contained flat. On 13 June, he also made what was to prove his own last will, in which he bequeathed ten thousand pounds together with all his pictures and drawings to Carrington, and a further one thousand pounds to Ralph, the residue of the property – with the exception of the books given to Roger – being left to his brother James, whom he also appointed his executor.

Slowly, as the days lengthened and grew warmer, Lytton's round of idleness became more strenuous. It was impossible to enjoy his leisure thoroughly unless there was plenty to do. He went up to London to watch Edith Evans act in Reginald Berkeley's *The Lady with the Lamp*, a play about Florence Nightingale which 'seemed to me entirely based on E.V. except for some foolish frills added by the good gentleman', and to lunch, unsuccessfully, with Lady Cunard who 'talked the whole time, so that Max [Beerbohm] was never once allowed to open his mouth. Idiocy! Idiocy!'[3]

The weeks slipped by as in a recurring dream. While Car-

2. Lady Strachey's estate had been valued at £36,810 11s. 8d. Twenty years earlier Sir Richard Strachey had left only £6,470 16s. 8d. – possibly because he had made over some of his capital to his wife. Lady Strachey had also, in the meantime, inherited the estate of her sister Elinor (Lady Colvile).

3. 'That blasted woman wouldn't let Max open his mouth once – a ceaseless stream of pointless babble, really too maddening! In a few asides edged in between her blitherings, he seemed charming – but of course resigned.' (Lytton to Mary Hutchinson, 2 March 1929.)

rington went to France and Ralph dealt with his publishers and managed his finances, Lytton returned to King's – 'such sunshine – such crowds of young gents – such benignity', was invited to still more lunches, more enormous tea-parties. Soon he recovered, then, like a spent taper, went out again. He seemed to have caught an everlasting cold and lost his voice most irrecoverably – 'at present it takes the form of a frog in the throat. Croak! Croak! Most tiresome!' There was nothing for it but to hibernate within Ham Spray and be nursed by Carrington. After a month's convalescence, his fell disease subsided, he felt 'almost like a human being again' and well enough to go off for 'a perfect week-end with Roger' to Bath. They stayed together at the Pulteney Hotel, in Laura Place – 'a perfect spot – and quite a sympathetic établissement,' he told Carrington (3 June 1929), 'with a lift boy no less sympathetic, who at last said to me (in a broad West Country accent) "Excuse me, zurr, bout are you the zelebrated author?" ... We inspected all the favourite sights – including Prof. Saintsbury at No. I. the Crescent – his white hair and skull-cap were visible as usual through the window.'[4]

Early the next month, Lytton, Carrington, Ralph and Sebastian Sprott set off for a fortnight's holiday in the flat, phlegmatic land of Holland. It was a peculiar trip. On board ship the four of them huddled together cheerlessly drinking gin and watching their Dutch and German fellow passengers who sat, for six hours at a stretch, in long rows of deck-chairs, moving only twice a day for heavy meals, and otherwise just staring stonily at the horizon as it tilted gently above one rail and

4. George Saintsbury (1845–1933), historian and literary essayist, friend of Mandell Creighton and noted especially for his writings on French literature. On retiring from his post of Regius Professor of Rhetoric and English literature at the University of Edinburgh, he had gone, in 1916, to live at 1 Royal Crescent, Bath, where among several other works, his *Scrap Books* and *Notes on a Cellar Book* were written – the latter leading to the foundation of the Saintsbury Club. He was an adulator rather than a critic, a romantic with high Tory prejudices and a slightly snobbish fastidiousness. His attitude to criticism and biography in general may be adduced from one sentence: 'Let us also once more rejoice in, and thank God for, the fact that we know nothing about Homer, and practically nothing about Shakespeare.'

then slipped gently below it, in an endless ding-dong fashion.

They arrived at Rotterdam, examined the zoo, then hurried on to The Hague. Most of their thirty-six hours here were spent looking at the Van Goghs, and visiting the Municipal Museum 'with twenty rooms containing every sort of broken pot and dug-up coin, and the Prison with instruments of torture and engravings of prisoners being castrated by the mob', Ralph wrote to Frances Marshall (3 July 1929). 'Apart from the sights, Lytton rushed into a bookshop and found it was exactly like Maggs, so grand that it was quite out of the question to buy anything except a novel by H. G. Wells.' That night was Gala Night, and Lytton sought to entertain his party at the Royale Restaurant, where a deafening band of Ruritanian Jews scraped the strings of their instruments and ogled the guests, while two impassive Dutch couples danced interminably, and immense quantities of food were served. The tone of all four of them was still curiously sombre, and, hoping for a rapid uplift in their spirits, they left next day for Leyden, which Nancy Cunard had told Lytton was 'wonderful' – though exactly in what way she had not specified: *just wonderful*'. But once again they were disappointed, and quickly made their way to Amsterdam, where they remained a week, 'looking at cheeses'.

Their mood continued generally irritable and cheerless. 'I have been rather maddened by the sporadic behaviour of the party,' Ralph burst out in one of his letters to Frances (4 July 1929), '. . . all are piano, piano, I don't know why. Perhaps we are all very old indeed, or perhaps we are growing a little Dutch.' Ralph himself was anything but piano, bubbling over with small grievances, disgruntled, quick to quarrel. Each member of the party seemed buried in his own distant thoughts, yet slightly resentful of what Ralph termed the 'selfish egotism of the others'. He himself was severely missing Frances, wondering why he had consented to come on this dull and purposeless journey; Sebastian, though pleasant, was unfathomable, unforthcoming; Carrington tiresome and wayward, her thoughts reeling back across the sea to the absent

Beacus; while Lytton, lonely and fastidious, concerned over Roger, contributed to the unfestive spirit his most alarming silences. Their holiday was thus strangely unreal. A pall of apathy seemed to have settled on them, choking their normally acute faculties. Beside each one moved the unseen presence of another, a loved-one, whose company he kept more closely than that of his companions: so that the four of them appeared to travel among a world of spectres, feeling themselves the shadows of a dream, unable to make fresh contact with the foreign sights and sounds that slowly passed them by.

In a letter to Mary Hutchinson written from Amsterdam (4 July 1929), Lytton, more charitable than Ralph, conveys something of this miasma, of the painless, bewildering shadow that fell between his actions and his preoccupations. 'Have you ever been to this hydroptic country?' he queried. 'My days pass pleasantly enough, though amid the discomforture of travelling and the dubious recollections of love. I have *three* companions! – Rather a multitude; but they are very charming, and I have no right to feel lonely – none at all – and yet – it is idiotic – I keep imagining what it might be with – almost saying to myself, if only —— were here! Almost, because I'm really not quite so silly as all that, and enjoy everything – pictures, houses, canals, even barges, just as they come. It makes an odd mixture of impressions. The few days before I left England were curiously filled with experiences, and they are as much present with me as the beautiful seventeenth-century doors and windows – so solid, so rich – that line the waterways, and the Rembrandts and De Hooghes in the picture galleries, and the delicious dinners at a pound a head that one stumbles into quite accidentally, having intended simply to have a snack at an A.B.C. . . . but it is true that I am troubled about Roger – in an unexpected way. It is not easy to know one's own mind – not easy to balance instinct and reason – not easy to be sensible and in love. Do not mistake me, though – I am *not* unhappy – only speculative, a little dubitative, faintly uneasy, perhaps. I wake up at three o'clock in the morning and lie awake for an hour, trying drowsily to disentangle the puzzle of my mind and heart – and then sink to sleep again, having accomplished nothing and not in the least put out. I wish I could write poetry; but the mould seems to be lacking into which to pour the curious fluid – melted silver? porridge? gilded sealing-wax? – of my emotions. I have found no solution in these antique masterpieces – another world! another world! With them everything is fixed and definite and remote; but with me there is nothing but hazard, intensity, and interrogation.'

When Lytton returned from Holland he found that Roger had abruptly left with a friend for the south of France. Days passed in silence and speculation. A week-end, on which they had planned to go away together to the country, came and went – and still there was no news. Lytton, quite in the dark, did not know what to feel – anger, jealousy, fear, indifference. 'I am in rather a state about R., as you may imagine,' he confessed to Mary Hutchinson (25 July 1929). 'The possibilities are so various – the poor thing may be ill – or the wretch may be dreaming – or the little devil may have sailed for Greece in Mr B's yacht. In any case there's nothing to be done, but twiddle one's thumbs, and seek such consolations as are available.'

A few days later, a letter at last arrived from Cannes, written in Roger's most cramped style, and answering practically none of Lytton's queries. He had come down for a 'rest', Roger explained, had stayed on an extra ten days or so 'through weakness', but regretted it now, and would be back in England on the same day as his letter. Lytton immediately rang up Brunswick Square – but there was no Roger. Next day there arrived a further letter, which mentioned that he had been obliged to postpone his return because of – constipation! 'Surely, surely, something better might have been thought of as an excuse for another week in the South of France,' Lytton complained to Dadie Rylands (29 July 1929), ' – but such are our friend's strange fancies. I ... have grown inert – cannot really bother any more ... I shall twiddle my thumbs like an aged Barbary Ape.'

All further speculation became futile. Roger was so irresponsible that one could not take anything he did very seriously. Even so, until these mysteries could be elucidated, Lytton knew that he must go on living in a state of suspense. Though he still could not hope to unravel the puzzle of his own mind, he determined to let things pass, to act sensibly even in love, and shake off the heartache by involving himself in some literary work – *The Greville Memoirs*, perhaps, which he had for long been putting off. To his friends who visited him at Ham Spray that August he seemed 'rather low and flat', but 'this does not mean that I am depressed or worried – quite the reverse', he assured Dadie Rylands (2 August 1929). 'I feel extremely cheerful, and seem to have emerged on to some upper plateau from which I can contemplate all the eventualities with equanimity. It is something of a miracle, and a great relief.'

This state of calmness was not perhaps a very natural condition. But while it lasted, he was happy, and more than happy, to turn back to his work, and absorb himself, at last, in *The Greville Memoirs*.

3

AMBITIONS

There is a passage in one of Lytton's letters to Roger Senhouse that is crucial to the full understanding of his character. 'Do you know how ambitious I am?' he asked (16 January 1929). 'Don't breathe a word of this to anyone, but I long to do some good to the world – to make people happier – to help to dissipate this atrocious fog of superstition that hangs over us and compresses our breathing and poisons our lives. – But it can't be done in a minute.'

Lytton was not wholly an observer, nor a participant, but a sufferer of life. His gentleness and generosity prevented these sufferings from turning sour within him, so that, for the most part, his cynicism stopped short at common sense. He wished to infiltrate his humanitarian principles, subtly, through literature, into the bloodstream of the people, and in such a way that they accepted it all quite naturally, if need be, without at first realizing what it was to which they were agreeing. He wanted to seduce his readers to tolerance through laughter and sheer entertainment. Never keen on scoring quick debating points, he sought to write in a way that would contribute to an eventual change in our ethical and sexual *mores* – a change that couldn't 'be done in a minute', but would unobtrusively bend the more flexible minds of young people. Unlike some professional moralists and reformers, his general theories were not held at the expense of private conduct, but represented an extension of it. His humanitarianism was not, therefore, an assumed ethical attitude, to be worn and taken off again like a coat, and always cut to fashion, but a normal, instinctive expression of his kindness. Twice in the 1920s, for example, he had anonymously helped out Desmond MacCarthy with gifts of money. His support of many *avant-garde* and philanthropic causes, from birth control to the relief of war victims, came from the same desire to prevent avoidable suffering and, more aggressively, to obliterate those misguided forces that caused this suffering. This was the real success he had been striving for.

Eminent Victorians had, of course, been his fiercest and most influential piece of polemics, dissipating the atrocious fog of Victorian sentiment and exposing much of its sham folklore. But he was never a propagandist in the political or revolutionary sense. He admitted to being 'left wing', yet repudiated any description of himself as a socialist. He had no wish to regulate personal behaviour or add further restrictive actions to the natural obstacles that must always prevent mankind from reaching its dreams of enjoyment. Since Cambridge, he had largely been out of step with the established order. The incursive post-war tendency to interfere with the private life of the individual was due, both directly and more obliquely, to the Great War itself, which had subordinated the individual entirely to the State – that is nearly fifty million persons to a few thousands. In the ensuing years of peace, this desire to regulate others still persisted, though its expression varied in each country according to the traditions of that country and to its good or bad fortune in the war. In America, where the war fever had been most virulent and the losses of men smallest, and where the dragooning of vast masses of fellow citizens had come as a new experience, the cessation of conscription had left a want which was supplied by the enforcement of prohibition. In Italy, Germany and Russia autocracies were formed, the unconscious aim of which was to recover in another war the national prestige lost in the Great War. France alone left its citizens in peace, for France, unlike America or Britain, knew conscription before the war, and unlike Italy, Germany and Russia, emerged from the war with its prestige enhanced.

The position in Britain during the 1920s was peculiar. The country had suffered very grievously during the years of hostilities, and was further safeguarded from the lunacy of American prohibition by a certain balance in the national character. Yet State interference with the individual had for many the charm of novelty. The Defence of the Realm Act lingered on, vexing the ordinary man and encouraging empty and energetic busybodies to plan more penetrating attacks on the individual. It was this type of governmental officiousness that particularly exasperated Lytton.

One example was the Oscar Levy affair. Dr Levy, a distinguished philosopher, scholar and man of letters, had left England in 1914 and returned again in 1920 on business, staying on because of ill-health. After a few months he was threatened with deportation under the Aliens Restriction Act – a law that was due to expire at the end of 1921. In the early autumn of that year, Lytton had joined the Semitic Bloomsbury Committee which was making protests against his expulsion, and signed a petition to Lloyd George pointing out that Dr Levy had relinquished his German citizenship and had nowhere to go. 'The police expulsion of so eminent a man,' this petition concluded, 'is surely a grave reflection on English civilization.'

By this time all sorts of rumours were being broadcast – that Levy was connected with espionage during the war, that he was in counter-intelligence or the secret service. The

Government confirmed or denied nothing, though granting a short delay of the deportation order for him to recover his health and for them to re-examine his statements. But Lytton was not optimistic. He disliked joining movements and committees, much preferring to work for what he believed by himself. The secret springs of his ambition were not nourished by belonging to anonymous, dry groups of improvers. He thirsted after an effective dual role as poet and reformer. But one had to be effective, and collectivism bred collectivism. As so often amid the pitched battles between light and darkness, he felt ill at ease among his allies, his foul-weather friends. 'I have become involved in the great pro-Dr-Oscar-Levy movement,' he reported to Ralph (5 October 1921). '. . . I was summoned this afternoon to the headquarters of the movement at 34 Gordon Square, one of the principal props of which turned out to be Mr [David] Bomberg, painter. . . . Another Jew welcomed me, and I rather gathered that I too was a Jew – which made me uneasy. At last I tore myself away, but I am in dread of being pursued for the rest of my life by this strange collection. As for poor Dr Oscar Levy I can't believe that with such supporters his chances are very good.'

And so it turned out. On 25 October, Dr Levy left England for France, the French Consulate having given him permission to enter the country and stay there without time limit. Once again French civilization had shown itself to be superior to the English.

One of the chief dangers to the liberty of the individual was the rising popularity of autocratic controls. Autocracies, whether they were called Fascism, Bolshevism or Puritanism, claimed that they subordinated the selfish, prurient desires of the individual to the service of the community. To Lytton's mind, they in fact subordinated these individual desires to the passion for power of a few emotional misfits with enormous vigour and no internal resources. He objected to autocracy for much the same reason as he had objected to militarism. For all autocracies, however excellent the ideals with which they started, inevitably move towards war, partly because war is the simplest and most comprehensive expression of power, and partly because the suppression of the man-in-the-street cannot continue for ever. If the State must add artificial restrictions to those restrictions on enjoyment inherent in the nature of things, then the pressure of unsatisfied desire must eventually be eased, and war is the most effective way to ease it – removing fear of unemployment and modifying, in the near neighbourhood of death, the severe tenor of private and public opinion.

In Britain, the most threatening form of autocracy was Puritanism. In the field of literature and the arts, this Puritanism took the form of a prudish censorship exercised by those substantial citizens who permanently seemed to fear that society would at any moment flounder into a quagmire of vicious iniquity, but for some swift and drastic steps designed to restore to the community a proper, biblical sense of sin. All through his career as a literary critic, Lytton waged a continuous offensive against the expurgated text. In reviewing the first four volumes of Mrs Paget Toynbee's sixteen-volume edition of Horace Walpole's letters, he complained vehemently against certain omissions. 'The *jeune fille* is certainly not an adequate reason, and, even if she were, the *jeune fille* does not read Walpole. Whoever does read him must feel that these constant omissions are so many blots upon perfection, and distressing relics of an age of barbarous prudery.'

Some fifteen years later, in 1919, Lytton reviewed Paget Toynbee's two-volume *Supplement to the Letters of Horace Walpole*, and protested with even greater vigour at the numerous passages dropped on the score of propriety. 'Surely,' he exclaimed, 'in a work of such serious intention and such monumental proportions the publication of the *whole* of the original material was not only justifiable, but demanded by the nature of the case.' Paget Toynbee was quick to defend his policy in the correspondence columns of the *Athenaeum*. Great care and forethought, he assured his readers, had been taken over his responsibilities as editor. Improprieties would be too mild a word with which to describe the excised passages, which might be compared 'to the grossest of the avowals contained in the unexpurgated editions of Rousseau's

Confessions'. In any event, the manuscripts had been deposited under sealed cover in the Bodleian 'where they will be available to any future editor of the letters at the discretion of the Delegates of the Clarendon Press'.

The following week Lytton returned to the attack in a letter that stated his views with uncompromising allegorical force. 'If a surgeon were charged with having made an unnecessary amputation,' he pointed out, 'and were to answer that after all the limb was still in existence, carefully preserved, under a sealed cover, and that, if need arose, it might be sewn on again by another surgeon, at a future date, the patient's friends would hardly feel that the reply was reassuring.' After expressing wonder at the type of literary man who would, presumably, wish to see Rousseau's *Confessions* reproduced only in a hideously truncated version, Lytton passed to the general problem of personal censorship: 'It is, moreover, extremely hard to see what good purpose is served by the deletion of passages which, in the opinion of individual editors, are indecent. ... Literature is inundated with improprieties and grossnesses of every kind; the mischief – if mischief it be – has been done already. It is too late to be prudish: Catullus, Rabelais, and a hundred others stare us in the face; the horse is gone, and no locking of the stable door will bring him back again.'

When, in 1926, Paget Toynbee brought out a further supplementary volume of Walpole's letters, there were again expurgated pages. 'The editor', complained Lytton, 'is still unable to resist meddling with the text. The complete edition is incomplete, after all. Apparently, we should blush too much were we to read the whole of Walpole's letters; those privileges have been reserved for Dr Toynbee alone. It was impossible not to hope that, after so prolonged tête-à-tête with his author, he would relent at last; perhaps, in this latest volume at any rate – but no! the powers of editorship must be asserted to the bitter end; and the fatal row of asterisks and the fatal note, "passage omitted" occur, more than once, to exacerbate the reader. Surely it would have been kinder not to reveal the fact that any deletion had been made. Then one could have read on, innocent and undisturbed. As it is, when one's irritation has subsided, one's imagination, one's shocking imagination, begins to work. The question must be asked: do these explicit suppressions really serve the interests of the highest morality? Dr Toynbee reminds one of the man who . . .[5] But enough; for, after all, it is not the fly but the ointment that claims our attention.'

Lytton, however, was continually spotting this fly in the ointment, and grew increasingly vexed by it. Not only Walpole's correspondence, but Blake's poems, Pepys's Diary and Boswell's letters had been mutilated by earnest professors who claimed at the same time to be rehabilitating the author's original text. 'When', Lytton demanded, 'will this silly and barbarous prudery come to an end?'

In one particular instance he saw an opportunity for defeating such prudery. *The Greville Memoirs* is not listed among the four bibliographies of *Eminent Victorians*, but on 6 November 1917, while still at work on 'The End of General Gordon', Lytton had written to Clive Bell: 'I spend most of my time reading Greville's Memoirs (do you know them?) — very dry, and as they are dry — just the kind of book that pleases me. He was a slow-going medium member of the governing classes of those days — the days of Sir Robert Peel and Lord Melbourne — and he writes with a restraint and a distinction.'

When Lytton had come to compare the complete manuscript in the British Museum with the Silver Library edition — which he included among the 'Works Referred to in the Notes' at the end of *Queen Victoria* — he had been disgusted to discover just how badly tampered with even the fullest published version was. He drew attention to this state of affairs both by a preliminary note in *Queen Victoria* acknowledging his indebtedness to the Trustees of the British Museum for their permission to make use of certain unpublished passages from the memoirs, and in the text of the biography itself, where he tells of Victoria's indignation at seeing the contents of the abridged version that came out during her reign. Two years

5. Passage omitted [Lytton's footnote.]

later, in 1923, Lytton published his essay 'Charles Greville' in the *Nation and Athenaeum,* stating his opinion that Greville's diary was good enough 'to make him certainly famous and possibly immortal'. Throughout this essay, which gave the background history of the diary, he very sensibly resisted the temptation to exaggerate its merits in the hope of securing immediate publication, comparing it, unfavourably, with Saint-Simon. Very many of its pages, he explained, were rather metallic in style – a reflection of one side of Greville's nature – and in political matters, its information was not always reliable. Yet, he added, it was of extreme value, since the sheer quantity of Greville's knowledge was enormous, and it was first-hand. 'He was not exactly a gossip, nor a busybody; he was an extremely inquisitive person, in whom, somehow or other, it seemed natural for everybody to confide. Thus the broad current of London life flows through his ample pages, and, as one turns them over, one glides swiftly into the curiously distant world of eighty years ago. A large leisureliness descends upon one, and a sense that there is plenty of room, and an atmosphere of extraordinary moderation. Reason and instinct, fixity and change, aristocracy and democracy – all these are there, but unaccountably interwoven into a circumambient compromise – a wonderful arrangement of half-lights ... So Greville unrolls his long panorama; then pauses for a little, to expatiate in detail on some particular figure in it. His portraits, with their sobriety of tone and precision of outline, resemble very fine engravings, and will prove, perhaps, the most enduring portions of his book.'

Lytton went on to present a summary of the brighter incidents in Greville's own life. This was the sort of thing at which he always excelled, and here he admirably succeeds in whetting the reader's appetite for the full, unexpurgated version. 'Perhaps', he modestly suggested, 'the time has now come when a really complete edition of the whole work might be produced with advantage; for the years have smoothed down what was agitating and personal half a century ago into harmless history. When the book first appeared, it seemed – even with Reeve's tactful excisions – outrageous. The later Victorians were shocked. .... To turn from their horrified comments to the Greville Memoirs themselves is almost disappointing. In those essentially sober pages the envenomed wretch of the Victorian imagination is nowhere to be found.'

Quite unknown to him at this time, a copy of the diaries made by a clerk employed by the original editor, Henry Reeve, had found its way, after the death of Reeve's widow, to the United States. Shortly after the appearance of Lytton's essay in the American magazine *New Republic*, this unabridged manuscript fell under the notice of P. W. Wilson, formerly a writer on the *Daily News* and a Liberal member of Parliament, who, in 1927, brought out in two volumes a collection of extracts from it, containing some information that had never hitherto been printed. This publication gave rise to an even more anomalous situation than before. The manuscript diary, which filled ninety-one small quarto books bound in red morocco, had originally been published in three instalments, totalling eight volumes altogether, in 1874, 1885 and 1887. Reeve had silently made excisions of three kinds – 'scandalous stories, which might give pain to persons then living; observations upon the writer's private affairs; and reflections upon the character and conduct of Queen Victoria'. P. W. Wilson's compilation, while apparently supplying these omissions, contained only a series of rearranged fragments from the diary, and provided no means of distinguishing the new material from the old. The result was that the public were still without a satisfactory text.

In a letter to *The Times* on 12 November 1927, Lytton proposed that, in order to resolve 'this curious state of affairs', a full and accurate edition of the diaries should at once be prepared. 'The old version,' he wrote, 'purporting to be complete, has been shown to be mutilated; and the new publication, though it divulges some suppressed passages, bears little resemblance to the original work. Two conclusions suggest themselves:

'(1) It can no longer serve any useful purpose to put obstacles in the way of public access to the original manuscript in the British Museum;

'(2) The time has now come when the Greville Memoirs should be published in their entirety, with all the editorial care which a document of such historical and literary importance deserves.'

The following day, Lytton received a wire from Allen & Unwin, the publishers, asking him to edit a complete version of the memoirs. The task commended itself to him on several grounds. He was already well familiar with the social and political world between 1814 and 1860, having studied it in great detail for his *Queen Victoria* (for which, of course, he had consulted the diary in manuscript). The job, too, would come as a relief from the rigours of *Elizabeth and Essex*. He might look forward to many absorbing, civilized hours of methodical occupation – work that would bring with it a curious comfort of its own.

It seemed now as if he were within reach of achieving the end for which he had been campaigning ever since 1921. But after a month of indecisive negotiations, the Trustees of the British Museum at length washed their hands of the whole business. Greville's niece, Lady Strafford, then aged ninety-seven, would probably institute proceedings, they informed Lytton, were any uncorrupted narrative brought out. In these circumstances they could not be a party to his scheme. 'What a world!' Lytton exclaimed to Carrington in exasperation.

For the time being there was nothing more to be done, and his negotiations with Allen & Unwin lapsed. Then, the following summer, Lady Strafford died. Almost immediately Lytton applied again to the Trustees, who, this time, opposed no obstacles. Work began late in August. 'It is very agreeable here,' Lytton wrote to Carrington from London (11 September 1928). 'The weather is most soothing – and so is the work in the British Museum. We have been so far most industrious. I enjoy it very much and R[alph] is an excellent work-companion. The only question is whether I shall ever be able to give it up. It seems to me an ideal way of spending the hours – and we can hardly bear to tear ourselves away from the beloved MS at a ¼ to 5, which is closing time.'

Another aspect of this state of affairs is given by Frances

1001

Marshall. In her diary entry for 15 September she wanly noted: 'R[alph] has now become to all intents a business man, going to the British Museum every day until 5, and as he lunches at present with Lytton I don't see him from morning till evening, which is the strangest sensation.' The very next week, however, Frances herself was to change into a business woman, joining the others at work in the manuscript department. 'R[alph] and I are both now working on the Greville MSS in the British Museum,' she wrote (21 September 1928). It becomes more fascinating each day.'

Lytton's plan was that Ralph and Frances should transcribe the missing and disputed pages of the memoirs, and that every so often Ralph should come down to Ham Spray bringing with him the material they had prepared, which he would then annotate. 'I have been working with Ralph nearly every day at the British Museum,' he told Roger Senhouse (19 September 1928). 'Now Frances takes my place in the afternoons, and before long she will altogether I think. It is very pleasant work. Various amusing details keep turning up, sometimes in a childishly easy cipher.'

Presently, as he had predicted, Lytton ceased going to the British Museum almost entirely, Frances taking over from him in the mornings also. This arrangement, besides freeing Lytton so that he might compose occasional essays, enabled him and Carrington to see rather more of Ralph by himself, and so helped to ease the feeling of tension at Ham Spray. Already, by the end of January, the three of them had made considerable headway. Ralph 'brought an enormous quantity of Greville MSS', Lytton wrote to Roger Senhouse from Ham Spray (2 February 1929), 'and I see that the moment is rapidly approaching when I shall have to plunge into that ocean in good earnest'.

Even so, he judged, this moment had not yet properly arrived. First there was the problem of interesting some publishers. 'I am beginning to fear that I may have some trouble with the publishers about printing *everything* – which is what I want to do,' Lytton confided to Roger Senhouse (19 September 1928). Although no publisher could deny that it was of great historical importance, there was little sensational appeal in such a book, and the sale could hardly be large. On the other hand, Lytton reasoned, all the public libraries and educational institutions would have to possess it, and his edition – if it did contain *everything* – would never be replaced. The firm which stood most to gain was Heinemann, having been responsible for bringing out the English edition of P. W. Wilson's two piecemeal volumes. Early this year, Ralph called at the Heinemann offices and persuaded them to agree, in principle, to bringing out the full text.[6] A few months later, Harcourt Brace wrote to Lytton inquiring whether they might

6. The firm of Heinemann did not eventually publish these volumes. P. W. Wilson's version of the diaries had been so ill received that the publishers felt obliged to offer to undertake a complete edition of the text, which, they agreed, should be entrusted to Lytton Strachey. When Lytton died, the negotiations fell through. What happened then has been described to the author by Mr Roger Fulford. 'Some time after my first book was published – which was in 1933 – I was approached by Mr James Strachey to know if I would complete the book and, if need be, find another publisher. Mr Thomas Balston, who had been responsible for the publication of my first book and was at that time the active mind in Duckworth's, agreed that his firm would publish it, and it may well have been that he suggested my name to Mr James Strachey. Plans with Duckworth advanced and, owing to the cost of production, we contemplated doing it in the old-fashioned way with subscribers' copies. When Mr Balston left Duckworth (I think in 1934) that firm declined to complete the project. Mr Balston most generously put me in touch with Mr Daniel Macmillan and Macmillans agreed to publish it, and carried out their undertaking. The cost of the finished book and the numbers printed were nothing to do with me. It is obvious that the commercial hazards at that time were very great and, if Macmillan's book was expensive, at least it was published.

'Part of the explanation for the high price which this book fetches in the second hand market is that it was beautifully produced by the Cambridge University Press. Mr and Mrs Ralph Partridge behaved with great generosity; they had done a great deal of work on the text and on the footnotes, this was neither acknowledged financially nor on the title page of the finished book.'

Mr Balston writes that 'I am still very proud of my small part in its production, and of having immediately realised how very great its importance would be to the many historians who would be working on that period in the next fifty years or so ... I am also glad that I thought it so important that I sent it to the C[ambridge] U[niversity] P[ress], then with Walter Lewis as their typographer the best printers in England, and of course, very expensive.'

publish the American edition. 'It is very interesting to hear that your firm contemplates the publication of the new and complete Greville,' Lytton replied to Donald Brace (24 October 1929). '. . . no doubt it would be a serious undertaking; I think it will take about ten large volumes; probably it would bring you more glory than profit! From my point of view, nothing would please me better than that you should undertake it. Our relations have been so pleasant that I would welcome any extension of them, and there is the minor point that a republication of the introduction would be facilitated . . . It is really the size of the affair that is the vital point – both from the point of view of the publisher and from that of the reader, who will not buy it unless he is a serious student: the plums of scandal and surprise – and there *are* some – are too few and far between to allure anyone else.'

From the summer of 1929, despite a few 'sad interruptions', he devoted a regular part of his time to *The Greville Memoirs*, and his correspondence over the next two years carries intermittent remarks about 'getting down to' and 'continuing to grovel in Greville'. This year, too, saw the publication of *Leaves from the Greville Diary*, a potted version in one volume, with an agreeable introduction by Lytton's old friend, Philip Morrell. This book, by drawing attention to the need for a complete and authoritative edition, acted as a spur to Lytton and his team. In 1930, Lytton arranged with Gabriel Wells of New York for the American manuscripts to be transferred back to England and placed in the Bodleian Library at Oxford. By the time of his death, early in 1932, all the passages omitted from Reeve's edition, including those in cipher and those scratched out with a pen, had been transcribed from the original manuscripts. 'The latest and best edition by Reeve,' Roger Fulford tells us, 'that in the Silver Library published by Messrs Longmans in 1888, had been collated with the manuscripts and his frequent liberties with the text corrected. The notes are almost all Mr Strachey's – though here and there it has been found possible to add to them in the light of information published since his death.'

After Lytton's death, the work was carried on by Ralph and

Frances, who collaborated in the thankless and monumental task of preparing a full index volume, and Roger Fulford contributed a Preface to the edition. Eventually, in 1938, seventy-eight years after Greville had concluded the last page of these diaries, they were given to the public in their entirety. Yet not even then was this definitive edition to be easily accessible, costing fifteen guineas and being limited to only six hundred and thirty copies – of which six hundred were for sale. 'When so much labour and learning have been expended upon this edition,' Raymond Mortimer commented, 'it is deplorable that the ordinary reader should still be obliged to use the old mutilated text.' And he went on to express astonishment that Macmillan, the publishers, 'should have condescended to this method of publication, against which Lytton Strachey himself would certainly have been the first to protest'.

In attacking censorship and celebrating sex in literature among contemporary authors, Lytton was equally forthright. He identified himself, for instance, with that faction opposing the prosecution of Radclyffe Hall's lesbian novel, *The Well of Loneliness*, though he does not seem to have thought very highly of the book's merits. And when, on 23 March 1929, Gilbert Murray wrote a letter to the *Nation and Athenaeum* deploring the cult of obscenity in modern writing, which he claimed, had a peculiar power for destroying the higher imaginative values in its vicinity, Lytton at once replied, calling up in evidence to refute this statement two classical writers, Rabelais and Swift. 'Both in "Pantagruel" and in "Gulliver" it is obviously this very element [obscenity] which acts as a stimulus to the authors' most profound observations and most astonishing flights.'

His opinion of D. H. Lawrence had not altered much since they had encountered each other at Brett's studio during the war. He saw him as a kind of Puritan standing on his head, an evangelist of sexual obsession, a confused mind allied to a disordered temperament, one who wrote in bouts of happiness but more often in despair. 'Above all, the fact is that I cannot abide prophets,' he told Emilio Cecchi. Yet in the past he had petitioned against the suppression of *The Rainbow*, and now, most unwillingly, found himself supporting Lawrence once again. On 14 June 1929, an exhibition of Lawrence's pictures, organized by Philip and Dorothy Trotter, had opened at the Warren Gallery in Maddox Street, London. For three weeks this exhibition had continued, then suddenly, after some thirteen thousand people had already been to the gallery, the police swooped down and carried off thirteen of the pictures, which, preparatory to having them burnt, they stored away in a cellar of the Marlborough Street Police Court. 'I suppose you heard about the police raid on Lawrence's pictures at the Warren Gallery?' Lytton wrote to Roger (15 July 1929). 'I saw Dorothy and her spouse at Boulestin's one evening, and heard her account of it. The police appear to have been singularly idiotic, but D. herself, it seems to me, was almost equally so. They were on the point of seizing a drawing by Blake of Adam and Eve as obscene, and she was silly enough to tell them it was by him, and so make a cheap score; but if she had only let them do it, there couldn't have been a better exposé of their methods. Next day I had lunch with Mary [Hutchinson] and she showed me the book of reproductions from his pictures. They are wretched things – no drawing or composition so far as I could see – and in fact no point – not even that of indecency; there were some pricks visible, but not a single erection, which one naturally supposed would have caused the rumpus.'

To make sure that he was not being unfair to Lawrence, Lytton shortly afterwards went round to the Warren Gallery with Geoffrey Scott. But his low opinion was only confirmed by what he saw, he dismissed the exhibits as 'poor' and declared that in his view the whole show had been a mistake. 'At least you think the pictures respectable?' queried Scott in the context of the impending trial. 'Much too respectable!' Lytton answered.

Respectability, or the absence of it, however, was not the real issue. It was a question of law. Immediately after the police seizure, Philip and Dorothy Trotter had started to get up a petition, but sensed, as Philip Trotter wrote, 'a winter wind from Bloomsbury in the dudgeon of Lytton Strachey and the silence of Roger Fry'. This petition, which they asked Lytton publicly to support, was embodied in the following formula:

'Since many pictures of admittedly great artistic value contain details which might be condemned as "harmful to the morals of those who are unstable or immature", we protest in principle against the destruction of pictures on that ground. The burning of a book does not necessarily destroy it, and condemned books have sometimes taken their places among the classics, but the burning of a picture is irreparable.'

The Trotters were careful to emphasize that they were not inviting Lytton's judgement about Lawrence's ability as a painter. The matter went far beyond the question of the merits of any individual artist's talent. They were seeking to change a law that, as it stood, permitted an anonymous informer, spurred on by the sensationalist section of the press, to put into action the machinery by which a serious painter's work was placed in peril of total destruction. After a brief hesitation, Lytton signed, to help 'protect contemporary art from the grave menace implied in the terms of the summons issued in regard to Mr Lawrence's work'. Probably to his relief, however, this issue was never pressed, since at the trial St John Hutchinson, acting on Lawrence's instructions, offered to withdraw the offending pictures and assured the court that they would not be shown again.

Because of its special wording and the wider purpose implied by this petition Lytton felt his course of action to be reasonably straightforward. His moral and aesthetic principles had not been brought into open conflict with one another, but were able to operate in an uneasy partnership. He longed amicably to reform the world, and could not logically ignore any chance that was presented to him to help bring this about through ordinary legal processes. But the amelioration that really interested him was less a matter of laws than of the attitudes to which these laws were meant to give social expression. What he in fact sought, to appease his secret ambitions, was not simply a civilian reformation, but a spiritual renaissance, not just a precedent in the Statute Book, but a place in literature.

4
'DEAREST DADIE . . .'

51, Gordon Square. July 29, 1929.

'Dearest Dadie,

'My drive to London I enjoyed very much. . . . I arrived at exactly the right moment at the Oriental, where I found Ralph. He was *most* helpful, and completely set me up (at any rate for the time being) and I think all may be well in that direction. . . . I went round to Bernard Street, and chatted with Helen [Anrep], whom I found as usual very stimulating. *Her* Roger [Fry] is in a gloomy place in France, drinking water like urine and surrounded by scenery so hideous that even he can't paint it – but his health is steadily improving . . .'

Ham Spray House, August 2, 1929.

'I am occupied most of the day sitting to Tommy [Stephen Tomlin] – luckily I am allowed to read. We go for a long walk after tea and I must say I enjoy his conversation very much – Ralph, Frances, and James arrived to-day – Julia [Tomlin] is also here . . .'

Ham Spray House. August 9, 1929.

'The prodigal [Roger Senhouse] returned on Monday, and I have had a letter in his most winning style, so I am feeling for the moment very happy, and wish at any rate for the time being to pass an act of oblivion. He comes to-morrow for the night. . . . I sit all day to Tommy who is creating what appears to me a highly impressive, repulsive, and sinister object.[7] Perhaps it is the pure truth. Otherwise, we argue up hill and down dale (literally as well as metaphorically).'

Union Club, Carlton House Terrace. August 16, 1929.

'Stephen Tennant and Siegfried Sassoon have just been

7. Stephen Tomlin's head of Lytton may now be seen at the Tate Gallery. After it was finished, Lytton gave a sherry party at 51 Gordon Square so that his friends could inspect it. 'It seemed to me very successful,' he wrote of the sculpture to David Garnett (3 November 1929).

having dinner with me here — accidentally. The former asked after you. Extremely beautiful — but frail beyond imagination. S.S. seems to be his garde malade. . . . I'm off to Lady Horner's to-morrow till Tuesday — it won't be very exciting. I fear the sick-room atmosphere that always pervades that sort of society.'

Salt Mill House,[8] *Fishbourne, Chichester, August 29, 1929.*

'It's charming down here — on the very edge of Chichester harbour, whose waters creep and gurgle at the bottom of a lawn mown by countless guinea-pigs. A strange, romantic, flat country, with a cathedral spire in the distance. Mary [Hutchinson] is delightful, and Jack [St John Hutchinson] mostly away, failing to get off homicidal motorists at country-town police courts. . . . No adventures — except with the local doctor, to whom I went in a panic over crabs. A young, a positively non-hearty, an almost good-looking individual. Some dim excitement, during the examination, as you may imagine. Then — "are you any relation to Mr *Lytton* Strachey?" — "I *am* Mr Lytton Strachey". — "Oh! Indeed!" Mutual blushes — a climax clearly approaching — it came in the shape of — "I am to be married on the 16th". For the rest, no crabs.'

Charleston, Firle. Lewes, Sussex. September 19, 1929.

'The inevitable dolce far niente reigns. It is as beautiful as ever. One walks, one talks, one drinks, one thinks, one writes idiotic letters.'

Royal Albion Hotel, Brighton. October 12, 1929.

'This hotel seems to be quite unchanged — the same rooms, the same food, the same appalling band after dinner — and so life floats away . . .'

Ham Spray House. November 4, 1929.

'It was rather amusing — I took [E] Morgan [Forster] and Carrington — a lovely drive. When we got there [Stephen Ten-

8. The Salt Mill House was 'a small abode, owned by an Admiral', which the Hutchinsons had taken for the summer.

nant's house], we found ... no Siegfried, but Arthur Waley, Willie Walton and Rex Whistler. We had lunch on the lawn, in such blazing sun that our host was given an excuse for sending for a yellow parasol for himself and a series of gigantic plaited straw hats for his guests. We were filmed almost the whole time by a footman (a dark young man in spectacles). We inspected the aviary – very charming, with the most wonderful parrots floating from perch to perch and eventually from shoulder to shoulder. Finally we went indoors, and in a darkened chamber were shown various films of the past, worked by the footman, who also turned on a gramophone with suitable records. Stephen was extremely amiable, though his lips were rather too magenta for my taste; Arthur was positively gay; Morgan shone as required; W.W. said absolutely nothing; and I, sitting next to Rex Whistler, couldn't make up my mind whether I was attracted or repelled by his ugly but lust-provoking face ... Morgan was charming at the weekend – full of accounts of Africa from bottom to top. He read two stories to C. and me – improper – quite amusing – but there always seems to be a trace of Weybridge in his style, whatever the subject may be.'

Extract from Frances Marshall's Journal – December 3, 1929.

'At the weekend there were only Lytton, R[alph], C[arrington] and I and it was spent very quietly. R. went for walks with Lytton and I worked at my Plutarch in the back room. On Sunday Beacus turned up after lunch, but his Bentley soon carried him away, and then came Mozart and Beethoven quartets on the wireless and after dinner Lytton reading Hamlet aloud to us. That was very enjoyable. He read with obvious excitement in a trembling fiery voice, his eyes piercing, and making pouncing movements with his long right hand.'

Ham Spray House. December 23, 1929.

'How I wish you were coming to Little Kidlington for Christmas! ... The drear months are now beginning, and we shall all of us have to give each other the support, love, lust, etc. that we can. There can be no doubt about that. In the meantime an immense cargo of wood absolutely wringing wet has entered this house, and every fire is quite black and cold, with a faint singing note added. Oh dear, oh dear! Where are the heats of next July?

'all my love
'Lytton'

5

MISADVENTURES

Early in April 1930, Lytton left England for a holiday in Rome with Dadie Rylands.

Ever since Carrington's thoughts became taken up with Beacus, Dadie had stepped forward as the principal confidant of Lytton's heart. Whenever the love and lust he desired from Roger were being withheld, it was Dadie who chiefly provided the support he so badly needed. Exquisitely sympathetic to all Lytton's varying bouts of ill-fortune, Dadie was none the less critical of the weakness that would again and again lead Lytton back into those secret, unbridgeable lands of ecstasy, where he, Dadie, could not follow. Irritably he complained of the absurd and dismal pattern into which Lytton's relations with Roger seemed to have drifted. And Lytton, obliged to defend his conduct, would reply with just the lightest hint of reproof (20 November 1929): 'People must gang their ain gait. ... And I also feel that it's specially my business to understand and make allowances for that peculiarly sweet creature. So you see ...'

But Dadie could not be expected to see. During the spiritless months of winter, he was very close to Lytton. Then, once the heats of July had returned, and Lytton was again very much happier, their friendship sagged a little with the indefinable weight of guilt. There were moments when Lytton felt slightly ashamed of having to confess that, for the time being, he had no further absurd or dismal indiscretions to unburden. He suspected that Dadie was envious of the undivided love which he and Roger shared. Intermittently that summer, the vision of Roger spread across the whole horizon, obliterating all other friends. 'To me our relations have always been among the greatest blessings of my life,' he wrote to Roger (30 July 1930), ' – that I have never doubted. The truth is I'm gorged with good fortune, and really if I can't be extremely happy it's a scandal.'

The early winter and spring of this year were overloaded with scandalous, lacklustre moods, holed by brief emotional crises, and pitched into the troughs of desolation. His vitality reached its very lowest ebb. 'I am at the moment sunk in sloth,' he admitted to Topsy Lucas (2 January 1930), 'which I believe is very good for the health, though perhaps not very good for the morals. So I shall say no more.' The effects of even an attack of 'collywobbles' or 'a wuzzle buzzle of a cold' upon him were now so devastating that he felt it essential to watch over his every symptom with the greatest caution, and he went about carrying a small pouncet box loaded to the brim with an assortment of coloured tablets which he would slip into his mouth at the conclusion of every meal. He was also feeling the cold more. According to reports in the London press, he had been advised one winter by a friend to wear a body-belt, and this advice he followed with the utmost satisfaction. But when the milder weather had arrived he had felt unable to discard his comforter, and so kept it on all through the summer. When the next winter came and the weather turned colder, something had to be done to meet the emergency, and what Lytton did was to wear two body-belts. Again the summer came and again it was too tepid for the shedding of clothes. All through this second summer Lytton wore two belts. And so, as the seasons alternated, this process had gone on.

Whatever the small element of truth in this story, Lytton undoubtedly suffered most acutely this winter, and being unable to wait for the far-off heats of July, decided to break out of his freezing hibernation and escape for a few weeks to Rome. This idea immediately brought him to life. The perturbations over clothes and hotels were tremendous. Roger, after prolonged indecision, came to the conclusion that he

could go, and then that he could not. At last Lytton invited
Dadie, 'a charming and conscientious companion', to accompany him. They booked in at the Hotel Hassler and New
York – where Lytton had previously taken Roger – Dadie
carrying with him a portable edition of Shakespeare, and
Lytton some novels of Trollope and most of Proust's À la
Recherche du Temps Perdu. As it turned out, once they had
done The Times crossword each day, there was little opportunity for reading. When the sun shone, they would march off
on long sightseeing expeditions. 'The beauty of everything is
very great,' Lytton wrote to Carrington (13 April 1930), 'but it
is a rigorous vigorous life one has to lead – so difficult ever to
dream in Italy – and the Italians, one gathers, do nothing else!
I don't understand it.'

They were thrown back on social life, which proceeded in a
kind of caricature of the London scene – 'upper-class vagueness and unreality, American frenzy, intellectual sodomy etc.
etc.', as Lytton described it all in a letter to Ralph (19 April
1930). 'It is rather amusing, but it would be much nicer to lie
under a tomb in the Campagna, or linger among the cypresses
of Tivoli.' One afternoon the two of them went to have tea
with an old countess who inquired whether Dadie was
Lytton's son; another day they encountered Lady d'Abernon
who, 'poor soul, appeared out of space, and disappeared
again after a slightly painful interchange of civilities'; they
dined at the British Embassy with Maurice Baring; they met
Beverley Nichols one evening and his American millionaire
companion, Warren Curry, both of whom 'after wandering in
despair over Europe and Africa, now openly quarrel standing
in the street outside hotels'.[9] The climax to their social life
took the form of 'a particularly mad lunch party at Lord

9. This description is a very typical piece of Stracheyesque extrava-
ganza and has, Beverley Nichols assures the author, 'little basis in fact. It
is true that I knew a young American called Warren Curry who came over
to England to study for a short while and stay with me. But we certainly
never wandered "in despair over Europe and Africa". We never went near
Africa, and our only excursion abroad was a brief trip to Rome where, far
from quarrelling, we had a very enjoyable week-end.'

Berners'.[10] A desperate antique hag (by marriage an Italian Princess), dressed in flowing widow's weeds, and giving vent to a flowing stream of very dimly veiled indecencies, kept the table in a twitter.'

Almost all May he stayed down at Ham Spray since (11 May 1931) 'I feel as if I *must* stick to Greville for this month and get it done (more or less) . . . [and] in order to read in peace'. At week-ends he was visited by relays of relatives and friends – the Bussys, the James Stracheys, the Tomlins, the Guinnesses, the Lambs, the MacCarthys, Sheppard, Norton and Doggart, Clive Bell 'who chirps away with swinging legs which reveal a strange span of drawers below the knee, as ever', and Boris Anrep who never ceased to pace the rooms like a maniac, exhausting and amazing everyone with the fertility of his ideas, playing boisterous games of chess, plotting Lytton's future career in all its distant details, and then going off on long descriptions of the enormous fishes he had seen off the coast of Brittany, some round as footballs, others rhomboid, and one with a cruel triangular mouth which, if you wedged a brick into it, gave a crack! – and spat it out as powder.

Once he had finished off this next section of *The Greville Memoirs*, Lytton abandoned himself for the rest of the summer to a varied social life. Living for much of this time at his flat in 51 Gordon Square, he would turn up occasionally at select and fashionable dinner-parties, or at Boulestin's, or The Ivy or Bellometti's in Soho Square. William Plomer, meeting him in Tavistock Square for the first time, has etched a vivid profile of what he must have looked like in this last phase of his life. The beard and spectacles, Plomer observed, made him appear older than his real age of fifty. 'Although he was lanky and Edward Lear was rotund, I imagine that Lear's beard and spectacles may also have seemed to create a certain distance between himself and others. About Strachey's eyelids, as he

10. Sir Gerald Tyrwhitt-Wilson, fifth baronet and fourteenth Baron Berners (1883–1950), musician, artist and author, whose ballet music 'Luna Park' was this year being performed in C. B. Cochran's revue. He had been honorary attaché in Rome (1911–19) and after the war often stayed at 3 Foro Romano, his house overlooking the Forum.

looked out through the windows of his spectacles over the quickset hedge of his beard, there was a suggestion of world-weariness: he had in fact just two more years to live. To me he did not seem like a man in early middle-age, and although his beard made him look older than he was, I did not think of him in terms of a sum of years but as an intelligence alert and busy behind the appendage of hair and the glass outworks. A glint came into his eyes, the brain was on the move as swiftly as a bat, with something of the radar-like sensitivity of a bat, and when he spoke it was sometimes in the voice of a bat.'

This strange Byzantine spectacle had puffed up around the shy and kindly personality of Lytton the clouds of a prodigious, awesome reputation. He was more than ever in demand at London social events. To these he submitted with a characteristic mixture of enthusiasm and malice, curiosity and goodwill. 'I've been plunging in the oddest manner among the Upper Classes,' he reported to Dadie Rylands (8 July 1930). Among the very oddest of these functions was an unconventional tea-party given by the Duchess of Marlborough, the purpose of which was to assemble the most eminent living writers in the land and record photographic groups to correspond to Conversation Pieces. If these proved sufficiently exciting, it was planned that paintings should be made of them. A most miscellaneous crowd assembled in the gilded salons of Carlton House Terrace – including Harold Nicolson, David Garnett, Raymond Mortimer, Francis Birrell and Augustine who 'seems extraordinarily vigorous, and in fact younger than anyone else'. While the duke, who absolutely forbade the use of a spiked tripod on his parquet floor, or of flashlight bulbs in case their smoke discoloured the ceiling, argued to a position of stalemate with an American photographer, the writers interminably waited in their formal group. 'The exhaustion was terrific,' Lytton complained, 'the idiocy intense. Oh dear, oh dear, oh dear!'

London society swirled and bubbled about him this year more crazily than ever before, and his attitude of boredom and amusement is nicely conveyed in a letter he wrote to Carrington (28 May 1930) after a dinner-party at the London home of Bryan and Diana Guinness. 'I had quite an interesting time last night, though I started off in a fit of depression to No. 10 Buckingham Street. On the way I fell in with the endless stream of motors going to the "Court", each filled with a sad bevy of débutantes – and an occasional redcoat. A considerable crowd lined the Mall, gaping at this very dull spectacle. I found again a large party – about 18 – with Eddie Marsh, but not Lady Cunard – again sat next to Diana [Cooper]. Once more Harold Acton figured – I feel myself falling under his sway little by little. At last, after a rather dreary dinner, we reached Rutland Gate, where, as I'd feared, Pa and Ma Redesdale[11] were in evidence. However, it was really a pleasant and a very young party – everyone looked very nice and behaved very well, it seemed to me – such good, gentle, natural manners – no stiffness – no blatancy – more like a large family party than anything else. The effect was rather like a choice flower-bed – each tulip standing separately, elegant and gay – but a ghostly notice glimmered – "Please do not pick".'

His criticism, though often severe, is never ill-tempered. Its purpose was to amuse people rather than to ease some interior pain. For the old corrosion had lost its bite, envy and bitterness had been washed away. Throughout all his experiences, however, Lytton never seemed to lose that youthful capacity of attracting to himself the most ludicrous situations. One misadventure that summer concerned his trousers and a firm of invisible menders. Discovering early one morning that there was a disastrous rent in his trousers, he put on a large ulster overcoat and made his way to an invisible-mending shop near Piccadilly. On arriving there he surveyed the young person behind the counter and asked in his high-pitched voice: 'Can you mend trousers?' On being reassured, he turned round, and, after considerable commotion beneath the ulster, produced the trousers. But upon examination it was

11. The parents of the celebrated Mitford sisters, Diana, Jessica, Unity and Nancy who, in her novel *The Pursuit of Love*, caricatured her father as the crazy and uncontrolled Uncle Matthew, a man who 'knew no middle course, he either loved or hated, and generally, it must be said, he hated'.

decided that the tear was too severe to be invisibly mended and would have to be tacked. Lytton said he would return that afternoon. He then walked off and lunched at the Oriental, still clad in the ulster, his legs lapped tightly one over the other. After lunch he returned and there was a similar pantomime with the ulster. Then, safely trousered once more, he strode off back to Gordon Square.

Another, scarcely less preposterous incident took place early that June. 'I had a curious adventure at the National Gallery where I went yesterday to see the Duveen room – a decidedly twilight effect: but spacing out the Italian pictures produces on the whole a fair effect,' Lytton told Carrington (10 June 1930). 'There was a black-haired tart marching round in india-rubber boots, and longing to be picked up. We both lingered in the strangest manner in front of various masterpieces – wandering from room to room. Then on looking round I perceived a more attractive tart – fair-haired this time – bright yellow and thick hair – a pink face – and plenty of vitality. So I transferred my attentions, and began to move in his direction when on looking more closely I observed that it was the Prince of Wales – no doubt at all – a Custodian bowing and scraping, and Philip Sassoon also in attendance. I then became terrified that the latter would see me, and insist on performing an introduction, so I fled – perhaps foolishly – perhaps it might have been the beginning of a really entertaining affair. And by that time the poor black-haired tart had entirely disappeared. Perhaps he was the ex-king of Portugal.'

To recover from excitements such as these, he fled down to stay with Dadie at King's where everything should have been delightful, and he could enjoy himself greatly in the company of Goldie Dickinson, Gerald Heard – now literary editor of the *Realist*[12] – and Steven Runciman, whose *The Emperor*

12. For the period of a year Gerald Heard edited what he describes as 'a monthly effort which, backed by a number of writers and scientists, was to advocate Scientific Humanism. It called itself the *Realist*, but as it had no money backing, its title was as ill-chosen as its history was brief.'

Romanus Lecapenus he had recently read and much admired.[13] Poetic fields, gay gilded scenes and shining prospects encompassed him; but very soon the pace of life in Cambridge, with its river-parties and dinners, theatres and young men, had grown almost as hectic as that of London. Fearing to be reduced to a mere wraith, he hurried on for a few days to Taplow Court, a large mansion in the French château style, set high amid green lawns overlooking the sparkling reaches of the Thames − the home of Lady Desborough, perhaps the most celebrated and brilliant hostess of the age. The names of the guests staying with her over the previous week-end would appear on Monday mornings in *The Times*: a long list of statesmen, diplomats, proconsuls, fashionable beauties, terminated generally with one or two men of learning or letters. Lytton, however, does not appear to have been very impressed by this distinguished clientele which included, on that occasion, 'a knot of dowagers and [J. M.] Barrie. Also Lord D[avid] Cecil, who struck me as being too much at home among the female antiques. Desmond was there too − a comfort; but I came away feeling pretty ashy. Lord Desborough[14] himself was really the best of the crew − a huge old rock of an athlete − almost completely gaga − I spent

13. 'I used to see him [Lytton] quite often from the time that I first went up as an undergraduate to Cambridge in the autumn of 1921,' Sir Steven Runciman told the author (3 July 1965). 'He was always immensely kind and friendly; but I was horribly shy in those days and must have been very unrewarding company. He really much preferred my brother, who was not a striving intellectual as I (alas) was, but was remarkably good-looking − and was much flattered by Lytton's friendliness, though embarrassed by what his rowing friends might think of it.

'My most vivid memory of him is at a dinner-party given by Maynard Keynes in, I suppose, 1924, W. J. H. Sprott and myself being the other guests. I thought then, − rightly, − that I was unlikely ever again to listen to such brilliance of talk. But I have to admit that, brilliant as Lytton was, Maynard was the more brilliant.'

14. Lord Desborough, the father of Julian Grenfell the poet, was one of the most esteemed all-round sportsmen of his generation. He swam the Niagara pool, slaughtered a hundred stags in a single season, played cricket for Harrow and ran the three-mile for Cambridge, ascended the Matterhorn three times by three alternative routes and fenced in the Olympic Games.

the whole of Sunday afternoon with him tête-à-tête. He showed me his unpublished books — "The History of the Thames" — "The History of the Oar" etc., etc. He confessed he had read the whole of Shakespeare. — "And, you know, there is some pretty stiff stuff in him"!'

A visit to Ireland a few weeks later gave him the opportunity for several more social misadventures. He had been invited by Bryan and Diana Guinness to Knockmaroon, in Castleknock, a large comfortable house on the farther side from Dublin of the enormous Phoenix Park. In preparation for this holiday, he had purchased a very splendid and aggressive suit of orange tweeds, and happily attired in these he travelled by a luxurious train over the smooth obedient sea to Kingstown, where, 'owing to the incompetence of the idle rich', there was no one to meet him. He was then obliged to board another, uncomfortable train to Dublin, and next a lawless taxi which 'wandered for hours in the purlieus of the various Maroons and Knocks — the rain all the time pouring cats and dogs'. At an advanced hour of the evening he arrived, to be met with looks of faint horror from the large assembly of guests. 'Oh dear me!' he exclaimed in a letter to Roger (9 August 1930). 'My new tweeds were far too loud, and, when I burst in rather unexpectedly, quite horrified (I could clearly see) Lady de Vesci — but no matter, she left for England almost at once (whether in consequence of my tweeds or for some other reason) accompanied — this I regretted — by her son (or so I gathered) Lord Rosse,[15] a foolish young man, but not unattractive.'

The company, which rapidly diminished the longer Lytton stayed on (until, after ten days, there seemed to him to be no one else there) included Nancy Mitford, the sister of Diana Guinness and 'amusing', whom he made 'shriek with laughter all the time and [think] how adorable' he was, Henry Yorke[16]

15. Now a pro-chancellor of Trinity College, Dublin. Much of his work has been associated with the National Trust; but perhaps his main achievements were as vice-chancellor of Trinity College, in which capacity he is still remembered by his friends as having borne the heat and burden of the day of the library appeal, etc.

16. Henry Green, the novelist, who had already published both *Blind-*

and his wife ('rather nice, I think') and a 'pretty but non-existent' Peregrine Willoughby. Besides these, of course, there were
the 'little Guinnesses', his hosts. 'He is so small . . . as to be
almost invisible; but she is I suspect more interesting, but
probably too young to provide any real sustenance.' Dominating this company, looked up to by all and evidently enjoying everything tremendously was Henry Lamb, who had come
with his 'very agreeable' wife, Pansy. The change that had
taken place in him was extraordinary. 'Henry will obviously be
my great support in this gathering,' Lytton wrote to Carrington (9 August 1930). '. . . [He] is a great success. They all
adore him, and he is evidently quite happy. A strange unlooked-for transformation. Great play was made of his having
hired an evening rig-out for the ball – 7/6 the night. . . . How
curious to be thrown together with Henry after all these
years, and in Ireland, too, where such a fearful crisis was once
enacted between us.'

'Everything is pretty much as I'd expected,' Lytton soon
decided. Even so, he informed Mary Hutchinson (9 August
1930) 'the grass doesn't grow under one's feet at Knockmaroon'. In rapid succession he was whisked off to a ball at
the Viceregal Lodge, assisted along a mountain-climbing expedition, escorted round the Dublin National Gallery and
taken to the Abbey Theatre, 'where Diana G. grew so restive
over the brogue and the boredom that she swept out in the
middle of the performance with the whole party at her heels'.
Some aspects of this drawing-room life, in particular its mixture of decorum and impropriety, did come as a surprise to
him. 'The state of civilization here is curious,' he reported to
Roger, ' – something new to me. An odd betwixt-and-between-

---

ness and *Living*. Mr Yorke remembers (1967) Lytton as being extremely
well dressed, 'as bright as a button', invariably courteous, amiable: 'a
real charmer'. In particular he was struck by the fact that Lytton always
listened very attentively to what everyone said, would encourage them to
speak, then, when they had finished, gently utter just two or three words
that might completely deflate them. His technique was superb. Yet
people did not feel aggrieved; for there was always more humour than
malevolence in his remarks.

ism. The indecency question, for instance – certain jokes are permissible, in fact frequent – but oh! there are limitations. And I must say I am always for the absolute. And the young men invariably leap to their feet when a young woman enters the room.'

On his return to Ham Spray, Lytton began to write again. 'A sudden inspiration has come upon me,' he confided to Roger (2 September 1930), 'and I am dashing off an article on Froude ... Quite a pleasure to be working again! A sudden influx of energy!' He completed this essay on 4 September, though it was not until December that it appeared in *Life and Letters*. Meanwhile, he tried his hand at a 'sadistic story' and then, his zeal still not abated, the long essay on Madame de Lieven which 'absorbs me'. This burst of creative industry, after months of semi-idleness, astonished him. 'I only wish I could send you some of my own bouncing strength,' he told Roger (23 September 1930). ' – I never thought in days gone by that I should have any to spare for other people.'

He had energy to spare, too, for somersaulting once more through the endless hoops of social entertainment. Among the authors whom he met for the first time this autumn were Caradoc Evans, the short-story writer from Wales, the young Italian novelist, Alberto Moravia, and the English poet and critic, Stephen Spender. 'Such a scene last night at the Ivy when Caradoc Evans, rather the worse for drink, apostrophised me in Anglo-Welsh for ¾ of an hour,' he told Roger (23 September 1930). 'But I daresay that name conveys even less to you than it does to me. "Truly to God" was one of his favourite phrases – "Truly to God, Mr Strachey, you can write English – English – you know what I mean – you *know* – yes, Mr Strachey, English, truly to God!" It was only ended by his mistress, a vast highly coloured woman in the Spanish style, taking the whole party in her car to this house [51 Gordon Square] – where I cleverly escaped, without letting the others in. So you see one does have a certain sort of adventure even in this deserted London.'

His encounter with Alberto Moravia, whose *Gli Indifferenti* had recently been brought out in Italy, was a far more sober and fastidious affair, and took place in 'that palace of faded grimness', the Reform Club, to which they had both been invited by E. M. Forster. 'E.M.F. assured me that he [Moravia] really was good-looking,' he related to Roger (15 November 1930), ' – however (knowing the peculiarity of his taste) I wasn't surprised to find a human weasel awaiting me under the yellow-ochre Ionic columns of the central hall. Otherwise he wasn't so bad, as foreigners go. He's apparently written a novel that is so shocking that even Beryl de Zoete refuses to translate it. "I deescra-eeb nékeed weemin" was his explanation. (Rather a disappointing one!).'[17]

It was at Ipsden House, some forty miles from Hungerford, near Wallingford, where he had been invited for a Christmas Eve lunch by 'Ros and Wog', that Lytton first met Stephen Spender 'whom I liked very much', he afterwards confided to Roger (27 December 1930). The young poet's red cheeks, blue eyes and romantic expression delighted him, and he described him as 'a gay, vague lively creature – youthful and full of talk. Has written a homosexual novel, which he fears will not be published. Thinks of living in Germany with a German boy, but hasn't yet found a German boy to live with. Writes poems after lunch, and reads them aloud to Rosamond.' On Boxing Day, 'Ros and Wog' and Stephen Spender motored over to Ham Spray for dinner, at which the other guests were Clive and Vanessa Bell, Carrington's brother Noel, Ralph and Frances. 'It was a curious little party, but I enjoyed it,' Lytton wrote. 'Got some talk with S.S. who was very amusing and nice. Then we played Up Jenkins – rather a fearful game. Then the wireless was turned on, and dancing took place – Clive tottering round with Frances, Wogan gyrating like a top with Carrington – and for a moment with me! . . . The latest scandal is that the Woolves (aided and abetted by Dadie, of all people) are trying to lure John Lehmann to join the Hogarth Press, and put all his capital as well as to devote his working hours

17. *Gli Indifferenti* was not translated and published in England until 1935, when it appeared under the title *The Time of Indifference*. Alberto Moravia's regular English-language translator is Lytton's old friend Angus Davidson.

to doing up parcels in the basement. And the large ape is seriously tempted.'[18]

In the second week of January, after a few days at Gordon Square, Lytton returned to Ham Spray, feeling unaccountably happy and light-headed. A new book of his, *Portraits in Miniature*, was shortly to be published, and he busied himself making the final corrections to his typescript.

He had just one more year to live.

6

STRACHEY'S FINAL PERIOD

Perhaps the most acute criticism of *Portraits in Miniature*, and in particular of Lytton's handling of the death scene, has come from Carrington. In the summer of 1931, *The Week-End Review* ran a competition for the best profile of Lytton Strachey – done in his own manner. After briefly reminding its readers of the group of essays entitled 'Six English Historians', the preamble went on: 'Let us suppose that to these a seventh is added – that of Mr Strachey himself.' Signing herself 'Mopsa', Carrington submitted an imaginary death scene of Lytton, easily winning the prize in a contest that the organizer, Dyneley Hussey, described as having inspired competitors to the best efforts he had ever seen in the course of his experience as a judge. 'If Mopsa be thought cruel,' he wrote, ' – and I was in two minds whether on that score she might not have to be ruled out – the victim is, after all, only getting as good as he gives.' Carrington's almost unknown parody, with its quoted *mots*, its contrived suspense, its characteristic turns and twists of phrasing, its jokes, cryptic insinuations and, above all, its flippant, 'thrown-away' moment of extinction, is a wickedly apt mimic of Lytton's style, of the affectations and peculiarities of his personality. Not a word is out of place. It is a perfect caricature, composed with the loving malice of

18. A full account of how John Lehmann joined the Hogarth Press and of his subsequent career there as a publisher is given in the first volume of his autobiography, *The Whispering Gallery* (1955).

someone who had become utterly immersed in his life, but was moved at times by a fierce, unconscious drive to escape from him.

Crouching under the ilex tree in his chaise longue, remote, aloof, self-occupied and mysteriously contented, lay the venerable biographer. Muffled in a sealskin coat (for although it was July he felt the cold) he knitted with elongated fingers a coatee for his favourite cat, Tiberius. He was in his 99th year. He did not know it was his last day on earth.

A constable called for a subscription to the local sports. "Trop tard, trop tard; mes jeux sont finis." He gazed at the distant downs; he did not mind – not mind in the very least the thought that this was probably his last summer; after all, summers were now infinitely cold and dismal. One might as well be a mole. He did not particularly care that he was no longer thought the greatest biographer, or that the Countess no longer – or did he? Had he been a woman he would not have shone as a writer, but as a dissipated mistress of infinite intrigues.

But – lying on the grass lay a loose button, a peculiarly revolting specimen; it was an intolerable, an unspeakable catastrophe. He stooped from his chaise longue to pick it up, murmuring to his cat 'Mais quelle horreur!' for once stooped too far – and passed away for ever.

This, the least practical of Carrington's jokes, was to rebound upon herself with tragic consequences, throwing her neurotic temperament fatally out of equilibrium. Some six months afterwards, when Lytton actually died, she became convinced that somehow she had helped to kill him. The unconscious motives behind this parody came to the surface as a fantastic, tormented sense of guilt that assisted in her own pitiable self-destruction – a haunting belief that her fictitious obituary notice had been responsible for Lytton's untimely death.

Death was much in Lytton's thoughts over these last few years. The necrology of those who had been close to him makes melancholy reading. Apart from Philip Ritchie and Lady Strachey, whose deaths had affected him most sombrely of all, many of his best and most admired friends had died. Several of them were Apostles.

How fast has brother followed brother,
From Sunshine to the sunless land.

In the spring of 1922, he had gone to the cremation service of one of the eldest and most eminent brothers – Walter Raleigh. Lytton had not seen Raleigh for two or three years, but the occasion prompted many memories of the old days at Liverpool and Cambridge, and filled him with a sad nostalgia.

The previous year, one of the most brilliant undergraduates, Michael Davies, was drowned bathing at Oxford in almost exactly the same circumstances as his uncle, Lytton's old Trinity friend, Theodore Llewelyn Davies. The pointless annihilation of such a promising young man greatly upset Lytton, bringing back something of the sense of futility that had overpowered him during the holocaust of the war. 'Michael Davies's death was a dreadful tragedy,' he wrote to Ottoline (29 June 1921). 'He was a charming creature – and what is rarer, an intelligent one. Last year he seemed to me to be the only young man at Oxford or Cambridge with real brains, and I am sure if he had lived he would have been one of the remarkable people of his generation. The uselessness of things is hideous and intolerable.'

Lytton's objection to death was not one simply of humanitarian sentiment. It had something in common with the idea behind Shaw's *Back to Methuselah*. Expectation, not experience, controlled human behaviour. It followed that men and women would only work for a happier world if they could look forward to a longer span of life in which to enjoy it themselves. Above all, it was the purposelessness of death, its indiscriminate desecration, that riled Lytton. The brevity of our lives was such that the thinking few did not have sufficient time to cultivate science, to improve their intellect to its furthest point, or to produce the noble works of creation of which they were capable. Death had incalculably slowed down the advance of civilization, and robbed mankind of untold masterpieces. When Jane Harrison, the classical anthropologist, died in the spring of 1928 aged seventy-seven, Lytton mourned not just the demise of an old friend, but the deprivation to the whole world of a fine talent, a talent that ought to have been permitted to conceive still further ideas, and to continue with her invaluable teaching. 'I've been feeling rather sad about Jane Harrison's death,' he told Roger (18 April 1928). 'She was such a charming rare person – very affectionate and appreciative, very grand, and very amusing. Her humour was unique ... I had not realised that she was quite as old as 77. What a wretched waste it seems that all that richness of experience and personality should be completely abolished! – Why, one wonders, shouldn't it have gone on and on? – Well! there will never be anyone at all like her again.'

How unreasonable was even the extinction of an old person when his faculties were still intact! One short period of waking past, and we slept for ever – the arrangement seemed ridiculous; it irritated him. There were, in any case, so very few people of genuine talent that the death of any one of them seemed to diminish him personally. Geoffrey Scott, for instance, who died in August 1929, he had never particularly liked. But he respected his intelligence and felt that the loss to English scholarship was considerable – especially in view of the fact that his work on the multi-volume *Private Papers of James Boswell from Malahide Castle in the Collection of Lt-Colonel Ralph Hayward Isham* had not been completed. Justifiably, Lytton feared that the Boswell papers would be exported from Europe to some pottling old transatlantic professor – a dismal fate. 'One doesn't see who can grapple with them,' he wrote to Roger (18 August 1929). 'I only hope they won't be handed over to some wretched American.'

The most serious shock of these years was the sudden death of that precocious mathematical logician and philosopher, Frank Ramsey. He had been suffering from an undiagnosed disease of the liver, had entered hospital for an operation, but never recovered. The loss to Cambridge was immense. He was just twenty-six years old, perhaps the most brilliant man of his generation, and the main body of his work as yet hardly begun. Already, like Moore at the turn of the century, he had revived the Society, acting as a tremendous stimulus on his contemporaries and starting up a vintage, Apostolic era. He was the same stamp of man as Moore, with the same unassuming, natural manner about him, the same good-natured, unselfseeking character, illuminated by an air of divine vocation. 'I am terribly distressed about Frank,' Lytton wrote to Dadie Rylands (19 January 1930), who had also known him well. 'It is truly tragic. He was one of the few faultless people, with a heavenly simplicity and modesty, which gave a beauty to his genius such as I have never known in anyone else. He had all the charm of childhood, and yet one never doubted for a moment when one was with him that one was in the presence of a very great mind. The last time I spoke to him was – do you remember? – when we met him coming out of the Provost's Lodge, and he told us, with those delightful fits of laughter, about the cat that came into his lecture room. I am miserable – miserable – to think that I shall never be able to make him laugh again, never hear him again at the Society, never again be able to say to myself, after reflecting on the degradation of humanity – "Well, after all, there is Frank". The loss to your generation is agonising to think of – and the world will never know what has happened – what a light has gone out. I always thought there was something of Newton about him – the ease and majesty of the thought – the gentleness of the temperament – and suppose Newton had died at – how old was he? – twenty-six? – I am afraid Richard [Braithwaite][19] will be particularly upset – will you please give him my love?'

The following month, another pre-eminent Apostle had

19. In 1931, Professor Richard Braithwaite (b. 1900), at that time University Lecturer in Moral Science (now Knightsbridge Professor of Moral Philosophy at Cambridge), edited and introduced a volume of Frank Ramsey's posthumous papers entitled *The Foundations of Mathematics* – 'mostly quite incomprehensible', Lytton claimed (7 October 1931), 'and even those recommended (by Braithwaite in his introduction) to the "general reader" seem to me alarmingly obscure. I'm glad to see that G. E. Moore (in a preface) confesses that (owing no doubt to his stupidity) he can make neither head nor tail of them. One *can* see an extraordinary eminence, though, showing through the fog.'

collapsed and died after a short illness – Lytton's friend, C. P. Sanger. He had belonged to that class of men, aspiring yet unambitious, whom Lytton most unenviously admired. Like Ramsey, like Moore, and very few others, he had combined great talent with natural modesty, and in his qualities of sincerity, of humour and humility, he fulfilled the highest ideals of the Apostles. Sanger was one of the most penetrating intellects and one of the most truly noble characters, Lytton once declared, he had ever encountered. His kindness in the far-off days at Trinity had been a wonderful benefit for a young man, and their friendship ever since had remained a cherished possession. He was one of those men whose extraordinarily great attributes were never, because of their very greatness, properly appreciated by the world at large. For some days beforehand, Lytton had realized that the end was probably inevitable. 'A nervous breakdown was the apparent cause,' he explained to Roger (11 February 1930). 'I fear it was the result of a long process of over-work, underfeeding, and general discomfort – a wretched business. He had an astonishing intellect; but accompanied by such modesty that the world in general hadn't any idea of his very great distinction. And he was so absolutely unworldly that the world's inattention was nothing to him. I knew him ever since Cambridge days, when he constantly came for week-ends for the Apostles' meetings – and then in London, when, at first, they lived in a little set of rooms at Charing Cross – and afterwards by a curious chance, Philip [Ritchie] became an added link between us. How he loved Philip, and how often he used to talk to me about him, with mild expostulations over his illnesses! – And so all that is over now, and I shall never go to New Square again.'

The deaths of these friends prompted within Lytton many bitter-sweet memories over the past, and these were given a new twist and impetus by Sebastian Sprott, who had again come down to Ham Spray to arrange and file away the last of Lytton's vast bundles of correspondence. As before, Lytton could not resist dipping into these papers, though they aroused in him a whole range of complicated sensations. Why, he wondered, should it sometimes depress him so much to go through old letters? Perhaps there was some false illusion attached to it, like the putting on of a pair of distorting spectacles, some hallucination that persuaded one to view distant episodes as other than they were.

For assuredly the past seemed more exciting than the present. Ottoline had written him a letter that April which recalled many incidents now long closed and half-forgotten. He seldom saw Ottoline these days – just occasionally in Gower Street, where she presided as the faded relic of a great hostess. In her prime, she had been a splendid figure, he remembered; but disaster seemed to have spread over her relationships like a winter blight. Even in her best days she had possessed no control over her vigorous contradictory instincts. She referred in her letter to the ashes and poisonous vapours scattered on what might have been too good; yet the ashes and vapours, alas, had been of her own making. Lytton experienced some uneasiness over answering this letter. After all, one could not get milk when the udder had run dry. Clearly a certain amount of sentiment was called for, and a little sincerity too – but how tactfully to provide it? After ten days' hesitation, he replied in what was to be the last long communication to pass between them, kind, partly truthful, agreeably clouded with metaphor, the conclusion to a long friendship, now obsolete. 'For me,' he wrote (18 April 1931), 'getting to know you was a wonderful experience – ah! those days at Peppard – those evenings in Bedford Square! I cannot help surmising that if H[enry] L[amb] had been a *little* different – things would have been *very* different, but perhaps that is an impossible notion. Perhaps we are all so deeply what we are that the slightest shift is out of the question. I don't think I want to go back. It was thrilling, enchanting, devastating, all at once – one was in a special (a very special) train, tearing along at breakneck speed – where? – one could only dimly guess – one might be off the rails – at any moment. Once is enough! ... I have been astonishingly happy now for a long time – if only life were a good deal longer – and the sunshine less precarious!'

Something of the sober mood of Lytton's thoughts at this time may be glimpsed from an entry made by Carrington in *D. C. Partridge*: HER BOOK, dated 20 March 1931. 'At tea Lytton said to me. "Remember all the bird Books and flower Books are yours". I said "Why". "Well, after I am dead it would be important". Then I said, and "all my pictures, and objects are yours". and he said "Really?" almost as if he didn't believe me. I said "but if you died first — " but I felt suddenly serious, and gloomy, and Lytton noticing the change, like a wind sweeping across the lawn through the laurels, changed the conversation.'

But the interior dialogue persisted. He did not expect to die, and looked forward like most of his family to a long life. Yet there were other reasons, besides the deaths of his friends, to account for these vague forebodings. Throughout 1931 he was almost perpetually ill. These illnesses did not in themselves appear to be very serious, but they seldom left him in peace and their cumulative effect was very enfeebling. Of course, he had been familiar with sickness all his life. But in the past, it seems probable that part at least of his bad health had been self-induced. Now, when, unknown to himself, he was in the clutch of an insidious and lethal disease, his condition appeared, paradoxically, less real to him. The sensation was very odd. As if anaesthetized, he felt that his physical awareness of things was being painfully wrenched apart from his emotional or spiritual consciousness, as though he had become strangely suspended, almost stationary as in a dream, between two orbits of existence, swimming lightly between them while all the other solid entities of the universe rushed about him on their well-coordinated courses. It was not so much a vivid pain that attacked him as the blurred, invading presence of some internal discomfort that he could not precisely locate, and which made all movement unpleasant, and sitting or bending curiously difficult. At first his physician, Dr Starkey Smith, diagnosed internal piles and prescribed some suppositories. Later, changing his diagnosis, he arranged for Lytton to be attended by a professional masseuse and treated with an ultra-violet lamp. The wandering symptoms came and went, and came again in a more complicated form, accompanied by headaches, a slight temperature and a buzzing in the ears that made him slightly deaf. 'I feel inclined to retire into a monastery,' he concluded after four months of these disorders (31 April 1931), 'but on second thoughts that couldn't be much good really – a nunnery, possibly . . .'

In his letters, Lytton invariably makes light of his illness, is invariably eager to report the least symptom of a recovery. He admits that he feels weak, describes his condition as 'tiresome', but, always hopeful of a quick improvement, predicts that, within a few days, he will be brisker again. Yet the truth is that this long series of attacks had bankrupted his physical resources so that he found it more and more difficult to sustain a period of resuscitation. Occasionally he comes near to admitting this deficiency and its darker implications: 'I suppose I am gradually recovering,' he wrote to Roger (26 January 1931), 'but there are still moments when I feel as if I were at the bottom of a well with only the dimmest chance of getting out.'

Rather uncharacteristically, too, since his ailments demanded so much supervision, Lytton was frightened of appearing fussy and over-tedious to his friends. Especially he feared, through seeming a liability, to incur the disapproval of Roger Senhouse, whom he nevertheless issued with regular hebdomadal bulletins of his progress – often in the form of optimistic pronouncements which had to be quickly corrected by disappointing statements of fact. 'As for my health,' he wrote on 20 March 1931, the same day as his recorded conversation with Carrington, 'it's now becoming the Grand Bore of Christendom, and I fear to refer to it. However, I'll just remark that I'm perhaps rather better – but not yet right. I feel quite well – and then seem to sink back into a buzzing ineptitude.'

Because of his invalidism, Lytton was restricted for most of this year to an unusually subdued mode of life down at Ham Spray. He seemed to exist in something of a trance. Winter gave way to spring with its lovely pale afternoon colours spreading across the Downs, its friendly unemphatic shapes, its gently falling rain and bright watery sunbursts; and spring soon merged into summer, turning the trees into a lush green, and the field in front of the house to a brilliant yellow, up to the eyes in buttercups. In the long twilight evenings, he would wander off, sometimes alone, sometimes with Carrington, for walks across the country, to gaze over the calm crepuscular landscape and reflect upon how English it all was and how admirably it suited him. While his multiplying ailments continued to nag and gnaw at him, he turned increasingly to exterior comforts, to the company of his oldest friends, to the soothing solitude of Nature. He was reading Keats, 'who is perfect', and whose poetry always seemed to heighten his awareness of the slumbering mystery of the vegetable world, making him feel at one with it. 'C. and I are left alone in this vague garden with its weeds and roses – ah! one draws a long breath, and looks out dreamily at the dreaming downs,' he wrote to Roger on 29 June. 'Last night, just after sunset, an extraordinary light, as of some vast motor car appeared behind the trees on the top of the downs – a blaze between the trunks – we gazed – and then realised that it was the moon, that was just there – it moved rapidly upwards and sideways – a surprising and romantic spectacle, until at last it was balanced – a golden circle on the edge of the hill.'

They were unexciting but seldom boring, these first seven months. 'Life trundles along here in the quietest style,' he told Roger (17 April 1931), ' – the question of the next book to read is the only pebble that ruffles the surface of the pond. Yesterday there was an event though – 2 visitors by aeroplane – viz. Dorelia and Kaspar John. The latter took C. up for a turn – she adored it; but *I* refrained – the attraction, somehow or other, was not sufficient.' After her flight, Carrington again tried to coax Lytton into going up, but he seemed not at all keen, and Caspar John felt that he must be cursing him under his breath. Mentally and physically he recoiled from Carrington's entreaties to 'have a go'. 'No,' he said. 'It is too violent – too alarming – too positive – too demanding an experience for me to contemplate.' Carrington replied that she knew him well enough to tell him that it would be none of these things, and Caspar chipped in to say that he would certainly deal gently with one of so gentle a nature. Dorelia then asked him how, in the future, he would be able to discipline Carrington if he wilted where she had braved, and the argument continued until they had reached, what was for Lytton, the safety of the house. The dreaded two-seater aeroplane was now out of sight in the field beyond the trees, and with renewed confidence he rounded on his tormentors, and in high-pitched words declared that he was the wrong *shape* for flying and that his beard presented a hazard that was likely to foul the controls. Exhausted, he coiled himself down into an armchair. There was no more to be said, and so ended the story of his non-flight with a future admiral of the fleet.

Social events now appeared to him as lacking in attraction, and he had little wish to meet new people. When he stayed up in Gordon Square among the Bloomsbury crowd he had 'to clench my teeth in preparation for the infernal boredom of the next few weeks'. He went down to King's, by affinity, though not by topography, an extension of Bloomsbury, and tried to persuade C. P. Snow to take snuff. But although there was certainly no diminution of social life, 'it's the social life of a preparatory school to my mind'. With Alan Searle – 'my Bronzino Boy' as he used to call him – he visited Oswald Balfour[20] at the White House, in Thorpe-le-Soken, Essex, but was not sorry to leave after two nights. The Bronzino had behaved very tiresomely, to his mind, getting himself bitten in the stomach by their host's bulldogs, and then collapsing into hysterics; an intolerable Dickensian charwoman called Mrs Scroggins had appeared and bearded Lytton from morning to night with tales of village politics; and the rest of the house guests seemed sorry figures all of them, a painful crew – Nature's second fiddles. Towards Oswald Balfour himself, the first violin, Lytton did not feel the least attraction at all 'except physically in a very odious way. The English upper

20. Lieutenant-Colonel Oswald Balfour, who had been military secretary to the governor-general of Canada (1920–23) and who, before his death in 1953, became a prominent industrialist, chairman and director of several steel companies.

class characteristic of going in for character as opposed to mind is annoying,' he commented to Roger (4 July 1931), 'even when it crops up in such queer (in every sense of the word) surroundings.'

It was a relief after paltry adventures such as this to return from the queerness and the bulldogs of the White House to the cats and queerness of Ham Spray, where the only complication was a certain hesitation over what book to read. George Trevelyan's *Queen Anne* was 'very good and instructive', and the ex-prime minister A. J. Balfour's *Chapters of Autobiography* he thought 'very well done in its way – that is the way that tells you nothing of any real interest – curiously 18th century, in fact – so clear and limited. But the silly fellow was a Christian, and that I cannot forgive.' Philip Guedalla's Life of Wellington, *The Duke*, he could not finish – 'after going through the Peninsular War and Waterloo, I've given up,' he told Roger (7 October 1931), ' – the way of writing is too tiresome and the mentality too thin to make 500 gigantic pages endurable. Queen V[ictoria]'s letters are much better in every way – so full of incident and feeling, and so idiotically to the point.'[21]

Among recent fiction, there was a new novel by Somerset Maugham – to whom he had once been introduced by Alan Searle – the notorious *Cakes and Ale*. This book, he explained to Dorothy Bussy (November 1930) 'is causing some excitement here as it contains a most envenomed portrait of Hugh Walpole, who is out of his mind with agitation and horror. It is a very amusing book, apart from that – based obviously on Hardy's history (more or less) – only marred, to my mind, by some curious lack of distinction.' In other contemporary novels he could, as usual, find little merit. 'I don't know what

21. Lytton, in fact, had never thought well of Guedalla's work. Professor John Dover Wilson, in a letter to the author (18 May 1964), recounts that when, in about 1926, 'I saw him [Lytton] off at King's, I said, "There's a lecture going on in the Hall as you go by. You might like to go and listen, incognito." "What!" he said. "In this beard?" The lecturer, I replied, was also a famous figure, Philip Guedalla. "One of my imitators?" was his comment.'

to read,' he complained to Roger (27 June 1931), ' – except perhaps Mr Gerhardi.'[22]

Eventually, for want of anything better, he fell back on Proust, determined finally to get to the end of his great *roman à clef*. Everyone had urged him to read it – in particular Clive Bell – but oh! the effort required to restart that heavy, shapeless monstrosity, with its labyrinthine analyses, its endless subjective digressions, its infinitely protracted involutions of prose. In the second volume of his fine biography of Proust, Mr George Painter has listed Lytton's name among the earliest admirers of Proust's work in Britain. Certainly the Bloomsbury Group as a whole appear to have taken him up, convinced that, since he dissected life at a different angle from his predecessors, he would alter our attitude to life. But Lytton could never really be termed a Proustian.[23] For him, books were like friends, and reading an extension of companionship – a way of expanding beyond the circumference of time and place the circle of one's kindred acquaintances. For Proust, on the other hand, art was the only purpose and justification of life. Worldly pleasures caused the kind of ailment provoked by the ingestion of abject nourishment; at best friendship, which was always a simulation, could throw up fresh material to be distilled off into his life's work; at worst, by wasting valuable time, it represented a sacrifice of reality – that sole reality that was his novel. This vocational spirit was quite foreign to Lytton, who strove to combine the truth of his writing with some extraneous entertainment, and so, by adding to the sense and gaiety of nations, enrich our *savoir vivre*. Proust gave no quarter to entertainment for entertainment's sake. À

22. *Pending Heaven*, William Gerhardie's fourth novel, about two men treading the donkey-round of paradise deferred, their literary friendship strained to breaking-point by rivalry in love, had been published a few weeks beforehand.

23. But he liked Proust more than Joyce. In a letter to his brother James (7 May 1922) he had written: 'My only serious occupation is the reading of Proust, and that I do find a pretty strenuous business. As for Ulysses, I *will not* look at it, *no*, NO.' After he had read *Ulysses*, he criticized it for not containing a single idea, or showing any signs of intelligence.

la Recherche du Temps Perdu is not a book to read, but to re-read — yet Lytton could hardly read it at all. Had literature, even fine literature, he wondered, got to be so dull? What, in any case, was this subtle quality of unreadability which Proust possessed in such an astonishing degree? No wonder he had felt himself unable to provide an Introduction to C. K. Scott-Moncrieff's matchless translation of *Swann's Way*. And so he grimly struggled on, boredom clogging admiration on every magnificent, laborious page. Then, with a sigh of relief, he turned to other more amiable books — Diderot's letters, and the verses of that 'supreme poet' Burns. 'I now spend all my spare time reading Burns,' he had told Dadie Rylands (26 November 1930), '— an unfashionable occupation, no doubt; but personally I prefer him to T. S. Eliot. I was led on to this by the new life of him, by a woman called [Catherine] Carswell[24] — not at all badly done and full of interest.'

Because of the dearth of new reading matter, he soon came back to some of his old favourites, in particular to the sixteenth century. 'So here I am in my solitude,' he wrote from Ham Spray to Roger (12 May 1931), 'buried in books — chiefly about old atheists — such strange stories are told of them! The Elizabethans grow more and more peculiar. In Norwich, about 1580, a unitarian was burnt alive, but as a preliminary had his ears cut off! — Because he had said things about the Queen as well as about Christ! Then there was a superb Dutch Inquisitor, about 1500, who suddenly had a revulsion, and declared in public that Christianity was idiocy, Christ a scoundrel, immortality a delusion, and that there was no God. He was imprisoned for 10 years, and then, as he was unrepentant, burnt alive. Perhaps on the whole we live in better times, but it's difficult to calculate.'

Possibly some compromise, he thought, between the sixteenth and twentieth century would have suited him best. And

24. 'I still go on with Burns. Do you?' Lytton asked Dadie Rylands (28 December 1930). 'There is an essay on him by Walter Raleigh in "Some Authors" which is worth reading, and contains a superb quotation from one of Keats's letters. It reminded me of what one sometimes forgets — that Keats was far the most delightful person who ever existed.'

this, in a sense, was what he evolved. For the fantasies which these old stories gave rise to in his mind acted as a make-weight in his emotional life, a deviation through which he sought to make up for the satisfaction he had failed to extract within his own person and from his own times. They were the excitements of a man partly and permanently disappointed in his aspirations of forming an actual, ideal intimacy. For some years the sado-masochistic imagery of this make-believe, taken largely from the randy and savage days of Elizabeth, and framed in total contrast to his kindly, gentle behaviour in practice, had not altered very much. But the fantasies persisted and grew in strength while the relationship upon which they had been constructed dwindled, and from acting as a stimulation of love, they were becoming a substitute for it. By this time he had known Roger for seven years – perhaps too long, since his capacity for being surprised by him, for some months on the wane, seemed finally to have been exhausted. Roger's dogged unpredictability no longer enlivened him; he expected it, and it wearied him. Tenderness and great affection certainly he still felt, but the gross adulation he had directed towards him had too often in the past dispersed itself into the empty spaces left by Roger's elusiveness; and the spell of vacuity had ceased to entrance him. Even Roger's virtues could be singularly exasperating. Always unmercenary, he never bartered affection for gifts. Naturally, Lytton did not want this; but there is no doubt that he would have liked to barricade him round with presents.[25] Besides, he enjoyed spending money on him, taking him to places that he knew beforehand he would like and watching his pleasure. He did not ask for gratitude, but resented Roger's vague distaste for accepting too much. After one reconciliation, for instance, Lytton had offered to buy him a Citroën car – but Roger simply did not want it. Lytton's fears, too, of six months ago were now being realized. Earlier in the year, Roger had been 'simply angelic' about his illnesses. But gradually his attitude seemed to change. 'My mood lately has been a new one for me,' Lytton

25. Of his lovers he once said: 'I would like to throttle them with luxury.'

wrote to him on 18 August. 'I've had the feeling that our relationship was coming to a dead end – or perhaps just fading away.'

7

FAREWELL TO FRANCE

From the fatigue and disillusion of love, Lytton escaped back into writing. That summer he began a long essay on *Othello*, but it was never completed and was below his best standard. The unreality of 'Othello' was partly a consequence of steadily worsening health and a worried antipathy arising from his relationship with Roger Senhouse. The essay was written with his last reserves of strength, and they were exhausted before he could finish it.

A less arduous flight from reality, he seems to have felt, would be to leave England for a while, and travel gently abroad. He wanted to cut adrift from people, from common sense. He was tired: tired of humanity, tired of real life, tired, in fact, of everything except poetry and poetical dreams. Solitude alone could relieve his weariness – solitude, plenty of comfort, good food, and travel from one palliative place to another. He wished to console his spirit with beauty, to be uncomplicated, uninvolved. For the time being, his problems seemed too universal to unburden upon any confidant. Carrington, in any case, had parted only recently from Beacus and was too full of her own guilt-ridden worries to be overloaded with his. And Dadie Rylands could never be trusted as a brother-confessor with matters that concerned Roger. And so, for the first time since 1902, Lytton resorted to keeping a diary. 'A Fortnight in France', as he labelled the exercise book to which, each night, he committed his reflections and the impressions of his journey, is one of the best and most unselfconscious of his autobiographical pieces, and before the end of September, when he returned to England, it had helped to purge much of his temporary distaste for life.

He started out for Paris on 3 September, arriving at the

Hôtel Berkeley, in the Avenue Matignon, later that day. After many weeks of strangely febrile tension, he could at last take a long breath, pause and look round. More than once that summer, his visionary existence had seemed more real than the physical world around him. He was drowsy with a nervous highly-strung defatigation that seemed to recall and to include all the bodily and love-sickness of the past. Nostalgia soothed and confused him with mixed feelings – a distant reminder of that brief interlude in Paris some twenty-five years ago with Duncan Grant, up those forty-two soaring flights of stairs in the Hôtel de l'Univers et du Portugal, and other visits, the most recent and most vivid of them with Roger. He was alone this time, but not lonely. Places, not people, exercised the forefront of his mind. By the time he returned to his hotel that night, satisfaction and sleepiness blanketed all other sensations.

'I am sleepy after the journey and the excitements of Paris, he wrote on the first page of his diary late that night, '– after the hideous examination of so many horrid people – after the doubts and alarms which will even still attack me about my luggage and the non-appearance of porters – after the enormous lunch in the train – after several chapters of Lord Salisbury – after the Lord knows what besides.' 'After the decidedly dreary and by no means cheap dinner at the restaurant here, I struggled out to a glass of coffee at the Rond Point . . . and then, not very conscious, strolled down the Champs Elysées towards the Place de la Concorde, in the darkness. Lights in the distance caught my eye, and then I remembered the new illuminations. I went on, beginning to be excited, and soon came to the really magical scene; the enormous Place – the surrounding statues – the twin palaces on the North side – and in the middle the astonishing spectacle of the obelisk, a brilliant luminous white, with black hieroglyphics, clear as if drawn by ink all over it. A move to the right revealed the Madeleine; and then, looking back, I saw the Arc de Triomphe, brightly lighted, with the avenue of lamps leading to it. A most exhilarating affair! It was warm, the innumerable motors buzzed, the strollers were many and – so it seemed – sympathetic.'

The next day he left Paris by train for Rheims – literally 'a godforsaken city'. He was dismayed at seeing the large areas of the original town that had been hopelessly wiped out by the war, including, of course, the cathedral. 'Naturally with the cathedral bashed God goes,' he observed; 'but what's more serious is that nearly everything else has gone as well. I had imagined a few neat German bombs had blown up the sacred building and that that was all. Far from it – the whole town was wrecked. A patched-up remnant is all that remains – the patches dated 1920. Miserable!'

The next morning it was drizzling with rain, and Lytton set off with overcoat and umbrella to explore the town more thoroughly. 'The Cathedral, what with pre-war restorations, war destructions, and post-war restorations, presents a deplorable spectacle,' he noted down in his diary. 'I doubt whether even in its palmiest days it was anything very much – except, probably, for the glass. I tottered away from it to lose myself in dreary streets, jumping sky-high at one moment before the startled gaze of an elderly inhabitant – an attack of the Strachey twist.'

Like a true hypochondriac, he scrutinized, half-relished and pencilled down his spasms and convulsions with sensuous care. All his adult life he had dreamed of breaking out from the prison of his wretched body, to which his ailments acted as the pin-pricks of an unwelcome reminder. And recently, in the last months, these dreams had begun to obtrude over reality, so that he felt himself to be moving along two unconnected planes of existence – one, the familiar yet oddly remote part of Lytton Strachey; the other, vacuous and undefined, just beyond the gross envelope of his physical being. It was as if these attacks of the 'Strachey twist' were the literal, premature straining of his spirit to wriggle free from the dying carcass in which it was incarcerated. And because this escape was partly successful, he could look upon himself now more objectively, from the outside, no longer overwhelmed by the humiliation and remorse of youth. Still pre-occupied with his appearance, he had learnt to accept it with resignation, with humour, and with a kind of shocked detachment that made it appear as if he were regarding someone else. Even the inexorable advance of middle age did not affect him so sharply as once he thought it must. Passing down the rue St-Honoré one day, he inspected his own image mirrored back to him in a shop-window, philosophically, like some sophisticated woman *d'un certain âge* before her dressing-table. 'I saw for the first time,' he recorded, 'how completely gray my hair was over my temples. So that has come at last! I was beginning to think it never would. Do I feel like it? Perhaps I do a little – a very little. A certain sense of detachment declares itself amid the agitations that continue to strew my path.'

This, then, was the consolation of a middle age he had once so dreaded. A numbness had spread over his being, cushioning him from the awful heartache and the pain that only a short time ago could plummet him into such terrifying despair. It was an agreeable change. Buoyed up by a curious composure in the region of the heart, he felt that he could never again be much upset by romantic trials. The indiarubber ball, having been bounced up against a brick wall an infinity of times, had finally sunk quietly to the floor. As on a previous occasion some two years back, Roger had gone off with his friends to the Riviera in preference to travelling with Lytton. But 'I hardly feel as if I *could* now be shattered by him as I was,' Lytton reflected. '. . . I am really calm – that dreadful abysmal sensation in the pit of the stomach is absent. What a relief! Whether this means that I am out of love or not I can't pretend to say. I hope it means that my feelings are at least more rational. The inexpressible charm of his presence, the sweetness of his temper, his beautiful affectionateness – why should these things make it difficult for me to accept the facts that he must be allowed to have his own tastes, and that his tastes happen not to be what I would have wished?'

Every renunciation should be followed by regret; and it was this placid absence of regret that perplexed Lytton. Could it be maturity? Could his chloroformed fading away of awareness be what was termed 'the prime of life'? Thoughts of age led him unavoidably back to thoughts of death. Maybe death itself was merely an extension of this agreeable anaesthesia that had invaded him. But what, in that case, was his attitude to death? Dying, perhaps, would be, as people said, like leaving a party, and it must all depend on what party one was leaving. 'If one's in love with life,' he wrote, 'to leave it will be as terrible as the dreadful moment when one has to leave one's beloved one – an agony, long foreseen – almost impossibly fearful – and yet it inevitably comes. And really it is a kind of death whenever the beloved object goes; which is why sleeping together is such a peculiar solace – death is avoided – one loses consciousness deliciously alive.'

He was not ready yet to return to England. His antipathy to life in general had centred upon the English. One had only to see them here, in Rheims, among the French – their shapeless features, their desiccated self-conscious expressions, their idiotic little clipped moustaches ... but enough! Presently he would be working himself up into a rage. And no doubt the French too were just as bad in their own way. One evening at a restaurant in Rheims, he noticed a sober, white-haired, rather indigent Englishman at the next table, undoubtedly an admirable example of the race. A schoolmaster, perhaps, – no, a cashier – with his unfortunate wife. Quiet, dim, but able to speak to the waiter with complete efficiency. Lytton envied him – except that he had made that fatal mistake of a wife. How did one speak to waiters? One of the main problems of existence, he sometimes thought.

On Monday, 7 September, he caught a train at Rheims station, stopped off at Châlons for an hour or two to inspect the cathedral, and then travelled on to Nancy, 'a perfect town', like a miniature rococo Bath, laid out with the most enchanting squares, all sorts of vistas, a triumphal arch or two, the most lovely gilded iron-work done by a resident bearing the propitious name of Lamour, and a delightful little park called the Pépinière, completely in the French style – regular alleys of charming trees, amateurish lawns, neat flowerbeds, a fountain, some statues. Yet, in the first hours after arriving there in the rain, his heart had shown a tendency to sink. The Grand-Hôtel in the Place Stanislas, where he had booked in, was moribund. Nothing worked; the lift never moved; the hot water was cold; even the door-key dropped to pieces. But he resolved to stay on for a few days. Perhaps tomorrow would be fine, and he might linger and loiter all over the place – in that glorious rococo square, under those triumphal arches, along the alleys in the Pépinière – and sip vermouth on the cobblestones, and dream of Voltaire.

And so it turned out. The time slipped by very agreeably in eating, idling and walking. The only out-of-the-way episode took place over dinner on his first evening. It was one of those trivial incidents that set off Lytton's powers of acute and humorous observation in their best vein, and indicated a slowly reawakening interest in his fellow beings, still struggling with his general distaste. 'The table next to me was reserved for one,' he narrated that night in his diary. 'Presently the guest arrived – one of those thin-lipped intellectual epicures, who correspond exactly to some of our friends who interest themselves in art. Enjoyment the one thing that is *not* present. With my neighbour, the severity and pedantry of taste was carried to its most ascetic pitch. He ate his melon like a scrupulous rabbit, and then, in flawless French, entered into elaborate and distressed dissertations with the waiters. 'Où est le maître d'hôtel?'' etc. The French was in fact so flawless that I decided he must be an Englishman. The clothes seemed certainly English. No decoration in the button-hole. The only slightly suspicious object – and this really ought to have decided me – was a rather effeminate wrist watch. But I came to the conclusion that he must be some distinguished member of the Civil Service – one of those infinitely cultivated and embittered eunuchs who, one must suppose, govern the country, and perhaps afford the most satisfactory explanation of its present plight. But really the wrist watch ought to have shown me that I was wrong. However, at last I determined, coûte qu'il coûte, to satisfy my curiosity. After a great deal of complicated manoeuvring of orders and counter-orders, he ate a fig. I also had figs; but before eating mine, I turned to him and said, in the most off-hand and idiomatic English style possible

— "Are these all right?" I calculated that if he'd been French he would have been quite at sea. As it was, there was a moment's hesitation, and he answered, with the precise politeness that one expected. "They're excellent." The question seemed solved, and I ate my fig, which, as a matter of fact was not very good. But then doubt suddenly assailed me. Giving way to the instinct of the moment, I very rashly said — "May I ask you another question? Are you an Englishman who speaks French very well, or a Frenchman who speaks English very well?" A faint — a very faint smile — appeared (for the first and last time) and he answered "I'm Italian." This completely ruined me. The eventuality had never occurred to me; and I saw at once that he belonged to that dreariest of classes, the cosmopolitan, that he was doubtless merely a diplomat. At the same time — naturally, given his status — not the remotest sign of unbending: he coldly continued with his cigar. I had got into an impossible position — was being tacitly told that I was a tiresome intruder — and all I could do was to depart in silence as soon as I could and with whatever dim dignity I could muster.'

Three days later, Lytton went for the night to Strasbourg. The contrast between eighteenth-century France and medieval Germany was very striking. 'I'd no idea how thoroughly teutonic this town was, ' he noted, 'everyone speaks German in the streets — everybody is German — the place is simply German — and how the French managed to get up such a hullabaloo about it I can't understand.'

After walking about the streets for about two hours, he was glad to get back to the Hôtel de la Maison Rouge and have a bath before dinner. What a blessing it was to be able to afford such comforts! Of course it meant as a rule, in those days of inflation, paying twelve shillings a day for one's room, instead of about eight shillings; but even so, it was well worth it. Whether these luxuries would be available very much longer remained to be seen. The inter-war depression in England and the world at large made it seem doubtful. Following the Wall Street crash of October 1929, the blizzard of a financial crisis had sprung up from the west. That September, Britain abandoned the Gold Standard and prohibited the export of gold from the country. Unemployment rose; poverty and dissatisfaction grew; a split developed within the Government and a General Election was imminent. To avoid a slump the second Ramsay MacDonald administration had instigated what Keynes described as 'a policy of Bedlam', and public confidence in Britain's stability quickly diminished. How much longer, then, could expensive pleasures, such as Lytton was treating himself to, be maintained? Surely not for long. 'All the more reason to snatch at them while one can,' he decided, ' – to plunge into a hot bath immediately, before the revolution comes and all the water's permanently cold!'

The following day, he journeyed back to Nancy. During this, his second three-day visit, Lytton explored the remoter and more unfashionable quarters of the town. The dingy outskirts, the smelly and decayed streets reminded him strongly of the slums of Liverpool. Yes, another revolution would, regrettably, have to come. 'France, with all her gold, seems pretty poverty-stricken,' he commented. 'The beggars here are such as I've rarely seen – they look as if they'd all sat to their fellow townsman Callot – visions of utter horror and degradation. The soldiers are uncouth rustics with red noses and (about half of them) wear spectacles – which doesn't seem quite the thing.'

One morning in Nancy, as he was sitting outside a café drinking a glass of grenadine and seltzer, 'my mind pleasantly blank', a passing motor slowed down and a woman, slightly fashionable in appearance and slightly familiar too, looked in his direction, then seemed to whisper his name to her male companion. 'The motor stopped, and I automatically got up, thinking it might be Diana Cooper, but – such is my vagueness for faces – not at all sure.' Only after she had introduced her companion as Dr Rudolph Kommer – that spherical, remorselessly shaved, enigmatic 'dearest friend' – did Lytton's hesitation disappear. 'The truth was that she was looking younger,' he observed, 'more cheerful, and less like the Madonna than usual.[26] They got out and insisted on my

26. Lady Diana Cooper had played the role of the Madonna in Max Reinhardt's famous New York production of *The Miracle* in 1924.

moving with them to the Café Stanislas – more expensive. There we sat for some time.' After Duff Cooper's return to London in August to be made under-secretary of state for war, Diana Cooper explained to Lytton, she had stayed on in Venice with Laura Corrigan at the marvellous Palazzo Mocenigo, enjoying the wild and festive season there and meeting many younger people who, as she put it, frolicked her along with them. Now she was driving back to London ' – with this ghastly-looking dago – an odd couple, but somehow or other not in the least compromising. But why?' Lytton questioned. 'Perhaps he was paying . . . She was very agreeable; but I had, as I always do for some mysterious reason with her, the sensation of struggling vainly to show off that I'm not a fool – mysterious, because really her own comments are very far from being out of the ordinary. K (or C) was polite. They admired Nancy; but it was too early for lunch and they had to hurry on to catch the boat to-morrow [September 12] at Calais. They went to their car, and I then observed that there was another member of the party – a kind of chauffeur, who sat in the dicky behind. He grinned a good deal – rather tendenciously I thought; perhaps he was K (or C)'s man – in every sense, – and I daresay the brightest of the three.'

Two days later, Lytton returned to Paris, putting up this time at the Hôtel Foyot. On his second day here, he wandered off to the Musée de L'Orangerie in the Tuileries, to look at an exhibition of portraits by Degas. 'The pictures were fascinating,' he wrote that evening in his diary, '–so exquisite, witty, and serious; and there were admirable sculptured studies too, in bronze. Then a stroll down the Tuileries Gardens – how supremely enjoyable it all was! My old dread and dislike of Paris melted into nothing in the shining sun. A rainbow in the fountain – the long alley beyond – the magnificent Louvre closing in the distance – nothing but radiance and exhilaration.'

The truth was that Paris had become for him a city of nostalgia, of *le temps retrouvé*. He went once again into the lovely Luxembourg gardens, in the brilliant morning light. The trees were beginning to turn, and he remembered that time –

almost exactly twenty years ago (but at the very end of September 1911) – when he had strolled along these same happy, well-ordered avenues after his visit to Henry Lamb in Brittany, following a night journey through Nantes, and felt an extraordinary current of vitality and excitement push through him. This morning he was happy, though less excitedly so. As he walked on, he remembered, too, another curious visit, not so long ago, with Carrington, in the intense heat, when, half-dead with exhaustion, he had crept out to try and get a little air under the trees, but, not succeeding, had then limped back again to that same Hôtel Foyot where he remained in bed until Ralph came and rescued them.

Carrington and Ralph. For two weeks now he had been cut off from them both without a word of news. Meeting two old friends, Peter Morris and the artist and illustrator John Banting, in a Paris street one afternoon, he suddenly realized how he had come to miss England, and all the pleasures of Ham Spray. What kind of life had he been leading this last fortnight? A visionary one certainly, subjective and evanescent. The complete absence of letters had produced a strange vacuum round him. Yet it had been a fine relaxation, stimulating his appetite again for the rigours and complexities of human relationships, for work, and all that made up life itself. He longed to be back in England. Carrington, Ralph, Ham Spray – it would be delightful! And when the winter came, perhaps they could all set up somewhere in Africa or southern Spain. The torture of the English climate was getting past a joke now that he was over fifty, nearly fifty-two.

And so he prepared to return home, took a final farewell of his beloved France, and made the last entry in his diary. 'Well, I must pack, and tell them to get my bill ready. I wish I was like K (or C) and had a man! But even that would impinge upon my freedom – which has been so absolute. And now it's dwindling, dwindling. The flèche d'or awaits me. I must get in and roll off – to what? – London, Ham Spray, the London Library, the Oriental, notions of work, notions of Love, R[oger], and, in short, ordinary life!'

8

THE FINAL SILENCE

For a further two months after his return to England, Lytton was able to sample the pleasures of ordinary life. There were few notions of work, but plenty of social junketings. He dined with Somerset Maugham, and with Lady Cunard, Desmond MacCarthy and Noël Coward. He met William Gerhardie and Victor Cazalet at a party given by Syrie Maugham in the King's Road,[27] and Charlie Chaplin at one of Ottoline's Gower Street receptions. In the country he saw 'Ros and Wog' and a good deal of the 'little Guinnesses' at Biddesden, their large country house near Andover.[28] That September, Diana Guinness had given birth to her second son and Lytton bravely went over to visit her while she was still in bed at 10 Buckingham Street. 'In those days one did not put a foot to the ground for 3 weeks after the birth,' she wrote to the author. 'I told the nurse to take the baby to her room "because Mr Strachey can't abide babies". However, when Lytton and I

27. Syrie Maugham, daughter of Dr Thomas Barnardo the celebrated physician and philanthropist, was one of the most fashionable interior decorators of her day. In 1927 she had been divorced from Somerset Maugham, who was her second husband, her first being Sir Henry Wellcome, a noted American scientist. William Gerhardie, who remembers this party, writes to the author that 'I asked Cazalet, since he knew everybody, to introduce me to the most glamorous débutante present. He confessed that as she was rumoured to be engaged to a royal duke, and was highly sought after, he must seek an appropriate moment; meanwhile fobbing me off with Lytton Strachey. When Strachey was in the heat of relating his experience of driving in a taxi into the courtyard of Buckingham Palace, and the anti-climax of being fobbed off with the king's secretary Lord Stamfordham, Cazalet came back to say that the débutante was now available, and Strachey was left mournfully alone. I never saw him again. ... As for poor Cazalet, he crashed to death in an aeroplane accident (suspected of political sabotage) in his capacity of dispenser of affectionate reassurance to the Polish wartime leader, General Sikorski, sitting beside him.'

28. Biddesden has a window painted by Carrington which depicts a girl peeling an apple. This was done by her in September 1931 as a surprise for Diana Guinness when she returned from London after having her baby,

were in the midst of our chatting she came in with the child in her arms and insisted on holding it practically under poor Lytton's nose. He said politely: "What a lot of hair!" To which she replied in a rather scornful way: "Oh, that will all come off." Lytton gave a faint shriek: "Is it a wig?" '

His well-known nervousness with infants had on this occasion been aggravated by the doleful sick-bed atmosphere. 'Poor dear Lytton. He had an absolute horror of sickness,' Alan Searle remarked, 'but he used to come and visit me in a nursing home when I was recovering from an operation, and used to bring me bunches of dead flowers – it had evidently taken him days to get up the courage to come.'[29]

He himself had fallen ill about this time with what was apparently just a winter fever, and despite feeling unusually 'low and dim' he could not believe it to be anything exceptional. The cure, really, was more shattering than the disease, and 'no doubt in a day or two I shall be all right again'. Before very long he did seem better, and was greatly cheered at having made everything up with Roger. The following month, the two of them went down for a happy week-end together to Brighton, staying this time at the Bedford Hotel since 'it seemed to me rather unadventurous not to try something new'.

At the beginning of November, Aldous Huxley and his wife Maria came down to spend a week-end with him at Ham Spray. 'The Huxley visit went off quite well,' he reported to Roger (7 November 1931). 'For one thing the weather was really perfection, and they were evidently out to be agreeable – especially Maria, who hasn't quite got over her early Ottoline bringing-up. Aldous is certainly a very nice person – but his conversation tends to be almost perpetually on high levels with a slightly exhausting effect.'

29. In a letter to the author (29 January 1963) Mr Searle also wrote: 'Lytton was an old friend of mine. I introduced him to Mr Maugham . . . I can tell you that Maughan and Strachey liked each other very much. We used to talk about him a great deal to his sister Madame Bussy. . . . On one occasion I gave him a number of letters that had passed between Queen Victoria and the Iron Duke, and in return he gave me a silver tea caddy that had belonged to Samuel Butler.'

This exhaustion, which came over him very easily now, he put down to 'too much wit and too little humour perhaps'. Even so, despite feeling drained of all energy, he was suffering from a restless sense of impatience – 'one of the worst cares of life!' He had little wish to work, but an overpowering urge to enjoy himself, and he rushed up to the idle and idyllic whirl of London. Dining with Clive Bell one evening shortly after arriving in Gordon Square, he complained of feeling off colour, and left early, saying that they must meet again soon when he was well. The following Friday they dined once more. This time he appeared to be better, and Clive Bell 'enjoyed one of those evenings which Lytton contrived to turn into works of art'. The next day, Saturday, accompanied by Pippa and some other relatives, he travelled down by train to Ham Spray. At Paddington he discovered by chance that Clive Bell was journeying to Wiltshire in the same coach. 'He came to see me in my compartment,' Clive Bell recorded, 'where I was alone, and we had some talk, mostly about my tussle with the Commissioners of Inland Revenue, who, as usual, were behaving disagreeably. At Reading he rejoined his party. At Hungerford I watched him walk along the platform on his way out. That was the last time I saw Lytton.'

Several of his other friends, too, were never to see him again. Shortly after his return to Ham Spray, he retreated up to his bed with what appeared to be a bad attack of gastric influenza. On 4 December, in one of his very last letters, he wrote to Roger: 'I'm sorry to say I'm still sadly pulverised – have been for some days in bed – now creep about, but in an enfeebled semi-miserable condition. I cannot feel that I'm really on the mend yet. A sudden reversion to a state of affairs that I thought had gone about 15 years ago! ... This is a gloomy recital, I fear! – In a way particularly annoying because there doesn't seem to be anything serious the matter. Only an eternal lack of equilibrium inside. Hélas! Luckily there are a lot of books to read.'

The books with which he lightened these hours included Margaret Kennedy's novel *Return I Dare Not* – 'mediocre' – Somerset Maugham's *The Painted Veil* – 'class II, division I' –

Burns's Letters to Mrs Agnes Maclehose – 'an amusing, curious book, published in the '40's' – and Leonard Woolf's first volume of *After the Deluge* – 'on Civilization, History, Humanity, Life etc. . . . I find it quite readable'. Virginia, too, had recently sent him a copy of her latest novel, *The Waves*, but he shrank from immersing himself in it. 'It's perfectly fearful,' he admitted to Topsy Lucas (4 November 1931). 'I shudder and shiver – and cannot take the plunge. *Any* book lying about I seize up as an excuse for putting it off – so at the moment I'm in the middle of Lucien Leuwen (Stendhal) – said by the French to be one of *the* masterpieces . . . well, well! –'

During the last week of November and the first two weeks of December, there were days when he seemed to start a recovery, but the general drift was downwards, and soon he was hardly able to read anything more. The attacks of diarrhoea, to which he had always been prone, became much more severe and unremitting. Although his pulse stayed remarkably steady between 100 and 120, his temperature fluctuated wildly, sometimes soaring to 104, and then tumbling down again to 96 within the space of a single day. He was able to retain practically no food, and, for week after remorseless week, could only be fed on what Carrington termed 'sparrow's food' – rusks, mashes, Benger's Food and tumblers of brandy. He lost weight and strength rapidly. For almost two months the appalling struggle went on, bringing into play all the visceral toughness of Lytton's character, his iron determination. Though no one allowed himself to consider the likelihood, he was in fact already dying, and with the help of too many physicians – at one time or another four specialists, two general practitioners and three nurses. Dr Elinor Rendel, Lytton's niece, who was not officially called in, pronounced his case to be one of typhoid, due to the 'deep well water' at Ham Spray. But his regular consultant from Hungerford, Dr Starkey Smith, appeared more doubtful. There was, he assured everyone, no cause for alarm. Nevertheless he admitted the possibility of Lytton's illness being either a bad attack of colitis or one of four groups of paratyphoid.

Meanwhile the only treatment that Lytton could be given

was a strict diet and constant nursing. A trinity of professional nurses moved into the house and took it in turns to look after him. One was named Mooney, another McCabe, and the third, who had St Vitus's Dance and was as deaf as a post, Philipps. Lytton, however, made up nicknames for all three of them: Clytemnestra; Old Mother Hubbard; Mousie. Pippa had also come down to join Carrington and Ralph at Ham Spray, and the routine of a long illness now set in. The Bear Hotel at Hungerford was packed with Stracheys – Oliver, Marjorie, Pernel and many others. Frances Marshall went to live close by at Ham post office, and soon friends were coming down almost every day from London.

The brunt of the prolonged and sickening anxiety fell on Ralph, Carrington, Pippa, and James, who were there regularly over these weeks. Ralph attended to the electric light, the water supply, the fetching and carrying from Hungerford or Newbury. Carrington, who could only respond to the situation emotionally, was also, in a sense, a patient, and it was with her that Ralph felt he had to deal. Every minute she was eaten up by a terrifying dread. She would not stir beyond the garden, and avoided seeing all callers. At nights, she hardly slept at all, or if she dozed off, woke every few minutes from ghastly nightmares. 'I feel nothing as bad can happen again,' she told Mary Hutchinson. By day she would sit at Lytton's bedside, sponging his face with syringa scent or eau-de-Cologne. Whenever she left his room she would burst into tears, then fling herself into the running of the house, the cooking, even painting. Enormous glass-pictures found themselves hastily brought into the world. For hours on end Ralph, who was none too controlled himself, would talk to her and attempt to restrain her from rushing into needless panics. Pippa, much calmer than Carrington, alternated with her at Lytton's bedside, and it was she whom he probably liked to see most. As he sank deeper and deeper into his illness, his mind reverted, like Queen Victoria's, to scenes from his childhood, and these he was best able to communicate to his sister, who had nursed him through several early illnesses. She adored Lytton, and never betrayed her grief or thought of herself. Her screeching laugh, too, seemed to cheer him. Once, when his temperature had reached 104, Ralph entered the bedroom to find him weakly but coherently discussing with her the merits of McTaggart's philosophy. James also was a great support. Admirable in all emergencies, less alarmist than Ralph yet unexcelled by anyone except possibly Carrington in his devotion to Lytton, he sat reading detective stories by the fire when there was nothing practical to be done. His pink unruffled presence reassured Carrington. 'James is such a truthful *exact* person,' she noted, 'that I believe everything he says and Looks.'

On 9 December, the eminent bacteriologist and Physician-Extraordinary to George V, Sir Maurice Cassidy – 'very grand specialist, bluff, 50, toothe-moustache', as Carrington described him – took over the case. He was called in by Starkey Smith, who had been with him at medical school and knew him personally. After driving down from London, he examined Lytton with great thoroughness, concluded that he was suffering from ulcerative colitis – adding that his heart lungs and pulse were all satisfactory – and carried off with him two samples of blood. His cheerful matter-of-fact manner inspired everyone with fresh confidence. The following night, his report came through via Starkey Smith: the samples had shown nothing. At various stages over the next week he examined six more blood cultures, but they too proved negative. Nevertheless, he felt convinced that Lytton was suffering from some sort of enteric fever. On 17 December, Ralph took him further samples to be analysed – but with the same result. By now Cassidy's optimism had begun to ebb, and the state of affairs seemed more inexplicable and more grave than at practically any other time. On the advice of Lionel Penrose, the family also consulted Leonard Dudgeon, professor of pathology at the University of London, superintendent of the Louis Jenner Clinical Laboratory at St Thomas's Hospital, and reputed to be about the best diagnostician in the country. After the most elaborate examination, he definitely confirmed the ulcerative colitis verdict. Throughout these weeks, this diagnosis was on the whole maintained, though, round about

Christmas, the possibility of paratyphoid was again admitted, and everyone in the house was instructed to be very scrupulous over all forms of hygiene.

Meanwhile, Lytton continued to get steadily worse. The real danger which Cassidy and the other doctors feared was the risk of perforation, which is constantly present in enteric fever. The worst of this condition was that it might go on for months. It had no curve and no crisis; the danger period might be almost as lengthy as the sickness itself. The critical stage gave no warning usually of its approach, Cassidy declared, and could occur at any time, day or night, regardless of temperature or pulse or any haemorrhages. An immediate emergency operation would then become essential. Plans for this operation had already been made. If Lytton were to collapse entirely and his temperature sink well below normal, Ralph was to telephone Starkey Smith, who had instructions to summon John Ryle, the surgeon at Guy's Hospital specializing in gastro-intestinal illnesses, down to Ham Spray at once. The operation would then be performed in Lytton's bedroom. At some moment an injection of blood would be needed, not a transfusion, and Ralph was shown how to provide this. Since no anti-toxins and scarcely any treatment were then known for this complaint, nothing more could be done.

The house was submerged in ponderous gloom. Carrington and Ralph, Pippa and James were obliged to conduct an entirely defensive campaign. The continual strain reminded Ralph of the worst days of the war. 'I feel back in the trenches myself,' he wrote to Frances (13 December 1931), 'there are the same orders for the day to carry out, telephone messages from headquarters, visits from the Colonel and Staff, N.C.O.'s to question and tell to carry on with what they do infinitely better than you could, and at the back of one's mind the anxiety at night, the possibility of something unexpected being sprung upon one. I sleep as lightly as a feather. During the dark hours I breathe with only the top half of the lungs, and when I see daylight I take a deep breath and eat a hearty breakfast.'

It remained to be seen whether Lytton, with all his tenacity, could withstand the double strain of prolonged high fever and low diet. For a further week his tough constitution held out. He knew that a great deal depended upon his own efforts, and so long as there was hope of recovery he concentrated every particle of his strength and will-power upon this objective. But each day his symptoms remained unaltered or grew worse, and his strength slowly declined. He knew about the possibility of enteric, from which his cousin, Sir Arthur Strachey, had died, nursed by Pippa out in India, and the question of whether the struggle was worth continuing, of whether recovery was at all possible, must have occurred to him. The crisis came, very alarmingly, on Christmas Eve. His condition sank swiftly and he appeared to be dying. Cassidy, Ryle and an anaesthetist were sent for from London, but everyone had by this time given up hope. Everyone except Carrington. 'I simply wouldn't believe that he could be defeated,' she said, 'and I still can't.'

Then, when it appeared almost impossible that he should do so, he rallied. The doctors now decided to administer injections of a new serum. Lytton was told that if he could maintain the fight a little longer, there was every hope of his fever subsiding. He did his best. He took up the fight once more. Miraculously, by the evening he had grown a little better, and over the next few dangerous days he somehow managed to hold his own.

At the end of the year he was still maintaining this advantage, and having once escaped death so narrowly, his fight for life fired all his friends with a new spirit of hope. Describing the new year celebrations at Ipsden, Rosamond Lehmann wrote to her brother John: 'That evening was the first for a week when the feeling of being in a bad dream lifted a bit – as we had just heard that a miracle had happened and Lytton pulled round after being given up by everybody. I now feel he will live, though the danger is still acute. The bottom would fall out of the world for us if Ham Spray were no more.'

Incredibly, this slight improvement was sustained over a further fortnight. At all times Lytton was a model patient. Although always in discomfort and sometimes in pain, he never complained, but lay, day after day, without moving, eating everything he was given and swallowing his 'vile black medicines' without a murmur. His courage, constant high spirits and the undimmed clearness of his mind amazed the doctors. 'D'you know,' remarked Cassidy, 'I'd quite dote on that chap if I saw much of him.' He appreciated the awful strain his illness was imposing upon the others and strove to lighten it by his own wry and unfailing cheerfulness. He was too weak to speak very much, but towards Carrington he was especially careful to remain optimistic, always greeting her with some joke. At night he had to be given sleeping draughts and these, he claimed, induced a whole series of amusing dreams. 'I've spent the whole night skipping,' he told her one morning, 'so curious. I didn't know I could skip. It was rather delightful.'

He thought about literature all the time, not so much about people. He talked of Shelley's youth; and with deep satisfaction, he would recite lines of poetry:

> Lorsque le grand Byron avait quitté Ravenne ...

It was the music of such lines, like a river of sound, noble and slow-moving, that soothed him. But sometimes, as with Villon's unanswerable refrain, with its despairing intimations of mortality, the lines that came into his mind would have a poignant aptness to his own predicament:

> Mais où sont les neiges d'antan?

He tried also to compose poems of his own. 'But it's so difficult,' he sighed. 'Poetry is so very difficult.'

'Don't think about poetry,' Pippa advised him, 'it's too tiring. Think of nice simple solid things – think about teapots and chairs.'

'But I don't *know* anything about teapots and chairs.'

'Well,' replied Pippa, 'think of people playing croquet, moving quietly about on a summer lawn.'

Lytton seemed pleased. 'Ah yes, that's nice.' Then a pause. 'But I don't remember *any* reference to croquet in French literature.'

Once, in the early hours of the morning, when he was alone

with the night-nurse, Clytemnestra or Old Mother Hubbard –
stupid women, whose stupidity vexed him – he began trying
under his breath to compose a new poem.

'Don't you weary yourself, Mr Strachey,' she commanded.
'*I'll* write all the poetry that has to be written.'

There was a long silence. Then the puzzled nurse overheard
two whispered words, incomprehensible to anyone who did
not recognize the slang of thirty years before: 'My hat!'

The poems of these last two months Lytton transcribed,
very faintly in pencil, into a small exercise book. For the most
part they celebrate and expound the nature of his agnosticism,
his fastidious epicurean appetite for life, his resignation to the
mysterious inevitability of death, and his acceptance of things
as they are – calm, incurious, inexplicable:

> Let me not know the wherefore and the how.
> > No question let me ask, no answer find;
> I deeper taste the blessed here and now
> > Bereft of speculation, with eyes blind.
> What need to seek or see?
> It is enough to be.
>
> In absolute quiescence let me rest,
> > From all the world, from mine own self, apart;
> I closer hold the illimitable best,
> > Still as the final silence, with calm heart.
> What need to strive or move?
> It is enough to love.

Love was his real religion, and he could only envisage and
worship a god who would sanctify those loves which had
formed the deepest and most enduring passions of his life. A
puritan, Old Testament God he could neither believe in nor
understand. If God was anything, God was love – actual love
as he had experienced it. Another of these poems, cast in the
simple and traditional mould of a prayer, is really a hymn to
sexual passion and love, addressed to a personal, officially
unknown god:

> Lord, in Thy strength and sweetness,

> Be ever by my side
> Close as the foot to fleetness
>   The bridegroom and the bride.
>
> Through sickness and through sadness
>   Still let me see Thy face;
> Bestow upon my gladness
>   Thy consummating grace;
>
> Fill with a golden clearness
>   My crowded hours of light;
> And hallow with Thy nearness
>   My most abandoned night!

With its unexpected last line, this poem acts as a satire of the orthodox Christian concept of a God of married love. Yet the agnosticism he proclaims is swept aside by the intensity of his feeling in these final poems, especially in the last one of all:

> Insensibly I turn, I glide
> A little nearer to Thy side . . .
> At last! Ah, Lord, the joy, the peace,
> The triumph and the sweet release,
> When, after all the wandering pain,
> The separation, long and vain,
> Into the field, the sea, the sun,
> Thy culminating hands, I come!

The days passed: the position remained the same. On 6 January, Pernel Strachey wrote from the Bear Inn at Hungerford to Lumsden Barkway: 'We are still very anxious about Lytton though on the whole he is better than in the Christmas week when things were almost desperate. ... It is really a question of whether his strength can hold out against the high temperature – but the consultant who saw him on Sunday after a fortnight's interval was pleased with his condition in spite of his weakness and thought him better than when he saw him last. But we cannot feel anything but great anxiety while he is like this. His mind has been absolutely clear all through and his calmness most wonderful.'

While he lay motionless in his bedroom, willing himself to live a little longer, a little longer, letters of condolence from his friends poured in, and these were read out to him by Pippa and Carrington. The last one which he was able to read for himself came from Virginia Woolf. To her friend Vita Sackville-West she now wrote: 'I should mind it to the end of my days if he died, but they think he may get through now. Like all the Stracheys he has a fund of Anglo-Indian tenacity, besides which remains perfectly calm, collected and cheerful and likes to argue about truth and beauty – you must admit that this is admirable.'

The newspapers too were taking a great interest in his illness, and Ham Spray was besieged by reporters' telephone calls until, through an arrangement which combined the Strachey administrative common sense with their odd quirk of humour, unreliable reports were made up each day and issued to all newspapers through the Ham village post office.

By the second week of January, another celebrated specialist had been called in on the recommendation of Ottoline Morrell. This was Sir Arthur Hurst, 'a weird little man', Carrington told the Guinnesses. 'I feel great confidence in his queer excited manner, and he looks extremely intelligent.' Hurst, who inclined to Cassidy and Dudgeon's original diagnosis though admitting the possibility of paratyphoid, recommended certain variations in Lytton's treatment, and said he had seen similar cases recover. And by 15 January, it actually did appear as if Lytton was getting better. Hurst confirmed this improvement. But by now Lytton had shrunk to such a shadow of himself that to those who were visiting him for the first time since November and who saw the extraordinary fragility of his appearance, worn down by weeks of illness, it seemed scarcely possible that he could ever get well again.[30]

30. Visitors to Ham Spray over the final weeks of Lytton's illness were generally discouraged. Lytton himself was usually too weak to see them, and Carrington had not the heart to speak to anyone. Since everything possible was being done for him, callers or guests, however close to him, could be of no practical help and might even increase the strain within the house. Roger Senhouse, for example, did not go down at all – though this was partly because his brother-in-law was also fatally ill at the time. He exchanged many letters with Carrington, however, asking for news and trying to distract her from worrying. After Lytton's death, Car-

His weakness was so great that he seemed barely conscious at all; he could seldom speak, though occasionally he would murmur something about Málaga, where he wanted to go later that winter with Carrington and Ralph. The doctors, however, since they believed the ulcers to be abating, still gave every hope – if only Lytton could hold out. He tried; but the last frail fabric of stamina was already leaving him.

Three days later, his condition began to deteriorate once more. By this stage his friends and family did not know what to believe. The doctors' wavering bulletins and diagnoses filled them with uncertainty. Following the various symptoms, hour by hour, they lived on an endless switchback of alternating hope and despair. Whether there was any real chance of a cure or not, they could not tell. One new anxiety had been added to the previous ones. They had discovered from a paper Carrington had written, intended to be opened only upon her death, that should Lytton die, she meant to follow him. Ralph had not the least doubt that she was set on this course, and if allowed to, would kill herself. Who, that knew her, could doubt the violence of even the least of her desires or her absolute determination, in spite of all obstacles, to carry them out? Ralph felt certain, however, that she would choose certain ways of suicide and reject others – those, for example, which were disfiguring. James openly accused her of planning suicide, and she denied it. But her denial meant nothing. They secretly searched her studio and took away a medicine that was poisonous.

On the afternoon of Wednesday, 20 January, while Carrington was bathing his face, Lytton suddenly whispered: 'I always wanted to marry Carrington, and I never did.' It was not true; but he could not have said anything more consoling to her. Later he fell asleep for an hour, his mouth open, and

---

rington, who was especially fond of Roger, wrote to him: 'Darling, Nothing can be said to make anything better. But I wanted to tell you, that Lytton loved you so much always, and talked so often to me of all the happiness he had with you. You altered his Life more than anyone, and it was marvellous that his last evening with you was so completely happy. . . . Your loving Carrington.'

she watched him, as she had done so often, with terror in her heart, thinking that if he died, she could not live. At a quarter to three, she observed a change in his face. 'I suddenly noticed his breathing was different although he did not wake up, and I thought of the Goya painting of a dead man with the high light in the cheeK bones.' She ran out and called the nurse, who at once asked her to telephone Dr Starkey Smith and find out how much strychnine Lytton might be administered. After telephoning, Carrington rushed back and held his arm while the nurse injected the prescribed dose. Presently his breathing deepened, and Carrington ran off to tell James and Pippa. When Lytton regained consciousness, Pippa told him that the doctor would soon be calling again. 'I shall be delighted to see him,' he said weakly. 'But I'm afraid I shan't be able to do much socially.'

That afternoon, for the first time, Carrington gave up hope. 'It became clear to me that he could Not live,' she scrawled in HER BOOK. Dr Starkey Smith arrived shortly afterwards and gave him another injection. 'I saw from his face he had no hope', Carrington noted. 'He slept without any discomfort or pain. Hatred for nurse Philipps came on me. I cannot remember now anything except watching Lytton's pale face, and his close shut eyes lying on the Pillows and Pippa standing by his bed.'

At four o'clock, Ralph returned from a late picnic with Gerald Brenan, whom Carrington had specially invited over to tea, saying she wished to see him. Hardly were the two of them at the door when James came out. There had been a fresh crisis, he told them, and Lytton was sinking fast. Ralph hurried in, and Gerald drove to the post office to send off telegrams, since James did not want to use the telephone in the house for fear of being overheard by Carrington. Then he motored back, went in, and sat waiting in the drawing-room. Presently he heard Carrington's low and musical voice, more exquisitely modulated, more caressing than ever. They had not met since Gerald had gone back to live in Spain. He did not feel able to look at her, but she came up behind him and took his hand.

It had been decided, in the event of a crisis occurring, to send for Stephen Tomlin. This was Ralph's idea, who was eager to mobilize anyone who might help to ensure Carrington's safety. They had got in touch with him and he was standing by. While Tommy was in the house, it was felt, she would not attempt to take her own life. It was a cruel but subtle expedient, for its success depended upon the fact of his already being so unbalanced and neurotic, so prone himself to suicide, shattered by his brother Garrow having been killed flying only the previous month, the failure of his own marriage to Julia Strachey and by all the supports in his life tottering, that Carrington's sense of responsibility would be aroused, and that she would pull herself together to attend to him. In addition to this, of course, there would be the shock of Lytton's death. Stephen Tomlin's principal relations with other people contained always a strong element of dependence. Lytton was not merely one of his closest friends; he relied, in some almost filial way, upon his existence. Carrington would have to control herself and him.

Stephen Tomlin having been sent for, Gerald drove off to Hungerford station in Ralph's car to meet him. 'He stepped out of the train looking more than usually undecided and pale and we set off in silence for Ham Spray,' Gerald Brenan recorded in his diary. 'But D.C., though apparently glad to see him, would not hear of him staying there and declared she could not understand why he had come.' So the two of them went back to the Bear Inn at Hungerford, where they sat up late, talking. 'When at last we went upstairs to bed, he asked if he might sleep in my room, since he could not face the idea of sleeping alone,' Brenan continued. 'I consented and then, instead of lying down in the other bed, to my embarrassment he got into mine and like a child that is afraid of the dark and cannot bear to be separated from others, burst into tears. It was impossible not to be touched by his misery and I regretted that I was not a young woman so as to be able to console him more effectively.'

At Ham Spray that night special watches were arranged by Lytton's bedside. Pippa was to remain there till midnight; Carrington, it was planned, would replace her until three o'clock; Ralph would then relieve her and carry on for the next three hours, until James took over for the last three. At three o'clock Carrington passed James on the landing on her way to Lytton's bedroom. Neither of them had slept. During the early part of her vigil, Carrington had asked Nurse Mooney whether there was any chance of Lytton living. She seemed surprised at the idea. 'Oh no – I don't think so now,' she said. Carrington leant over the bed and gave Lytton a kiss on his forehead: it was damp and cold. Ralph, also unable to sleep, came in with a cup of tea, and sat down by the fire. Carrington went over and kissed him too, told him she was going to her bedroom and asked him not to wake her, since, after weeks of her 'non-sleeping disease', she was worn out. James, she noticed, had gone downstairs to the front room. She walked quickly along the passage and down the back stairs.

It was half-past three. The house was very quiet, and outside the moon shone in the yard through the elm trees and across the barns. She walked over to the garage. The door was stuck fast open, and she could hardly move it. Every jerk seemed to shriek through the still night air. At last she scraped both doors closed. She got into the car, and accidentally touched the horn. 'My heart stood still, for I felt R[alph] must have heard As the landing window was open. I stood in the yard watching for a light to go on in the passage. after some time I crept back again, and made every preparation all Ready that I could start up the car directly the milking engin started in the Farm yard.'

Then she waited, feeling very cold in her dressing-gown. Outside there was not a sound. Her plan was to stay there until half-past four, at which time every morning the farmers started up the milking-machine, the noise of which would drown the humming of the car engine. Half-past four came by the car clock, and still nobody stirred. Then she remembered it ran ten minutes fast. She went outside again and continued patiently to wait, her resolution unfaltering. At half-past five she suddenly heard sounds from across the yard, and movements in the milking-shed. She ran back to the garage, shut the door once more, and a few moments after the milking-machine had started up, switched on the car engine.

'I was terrified by the noise once it nearly stopped so I had to turn on the petrol more. There seemed no smell. I got over in the back of the car and lay down, and listened to the thud of the engin below me, and the noise of the milking-machine puffing away outside. at last I smelt it was beginning to get rather thick. I turned on the light in the side of the car and looked at the clock only 10 minutes had gone. However Ralph would probably not come exactly at 6 ock. The windows of the car looked foggy, and a bit misty. I turned out the light again, and lay down, gradually I felt rather sleepy, and the buzzing noise grew fainter, and further off. Rather like fainTing I remember thinking ... I thought of Lytton, and was glad to think I shouldn'T know any more. Then I remember a sort of dream which faded away.'

Shortly before six o'clock there was yet another serious crisis in Lytton's condition. Thinking that this time he must be dying, they sent for Carrington, and when they could not find her in her bedroom, searched the house. Going out to the garage, Ralph saw her lying behind the exhaust pipe of the car, the engine still running. She was unconscious. He carried her up to her room and immediately summoned Dr Starkey Smith. Had he found her ten minutes later, she would have been dead.

The doctor gave her an injection: there was a terrible buzzing in her ears, she woke up, saw Dr Starkey Smith still holding her arm with the syringe, and cried out: 'No! No! Go away!' pushing his hand off, until he seemed to vanish 'like a cheshire cat'. Then she looked up and saw her bedroom window. It was daylight. 'I felt *angry* at being back after being in a very happy dream. Sorry to be awake again a Buzzing in my ears and something wrong with my eyes. I couldn'T see my hands or focus on anything.' Ralph was there. He held her in his arms, and kissed her, and said: 'How could you do it?' It had never occurred to him that she would attempt anything with Lytton still alive. She would wish, he thought, at all costs to be there at the last moment, and that was why, when Lytton was apparently on the point of death, he had gone in search of her. She had solemnly promised him not to try anything. But she must have been aware that, the moment Lytton died, she would be closely guarded, and that Stephen Tomlin, waiting a few miles away with Gerald Brenan, would be brought into the house. By some obscure train of feeling, she had hoped, through the offer of her own life, to rescue Lytton's. 'It is ironical,' she scribbled in HER BOOK, 'that Lytton by that early attack at 6 'ock saved my life, when I gave my life for his. he should give it back.'

But Lytton was not dead. Although everyone had tried to keep from him the gravity of his illness, he was not deceived. He accepted the idea of extinction with a quizzical and diminutive humour, very typical of him. 'If this is dying,' he remarked quietly, just before falling into unconsciousness, 'then I don't think much of it.'

Early that morning, Stephen Tomlin was urgently called to the house. Other friends and relatives arrived, their cars crunching backwards and forwards on the gravel. The fine frosty weather that had gone on without a break since Christmas still lasted. It was intensely still – the sort of weather Lytton had always loved. A soft golden mist lay over the green meadows and enfolded the elm trees. The sunlight, sprinkling through their branches, seemed to linger and delay, before touching the walls of the house, and streaming through the windows. It was impossible for those who waited not to contrast this beauty with Lytton dying, or to wonder what result might follow for the three, bound together in precarious balance, whom he left behind.

At midday, Carrington got up and went into Lytton's room. He was still sleeping, breathing very deeply and fast. Pippa sat near his bed. 'I went up and sat in a chair, and watched him,' Carrington wrote. ' "So this is death" I kept on saying to myself. The two nurses moved about behind the screen. Ralph came, and sat on the floor I felt completely calm. His face was very pale like ivory. Everything seemed to be transfixed. The pale face of nurse MacCabe standing by his bed in her white clothes, Pippa watching with those sweet brown eyes all tear stained, her face mottled. The noise of the electric light machine outside. I sat there thinking of all the other mornings in Lytton's room. . . . It seemed as if time had lost all its properties. as if everything was marked by Lytton's [heart] beating Not by the Ticks of the clock. Suddenly I felt very sicK, and ran out to my bedroom, and was violently sicK into the chamber Pot. . . . I went back to Lytton's room, and sat on the chair. about 2 o'clock or 1.30 Lytton grew worse, and his breathing became shorter. I stood holding Pippa round the waist. Lytton never opened his eyes. I could Not cry . . . sometimes his breathing almost stopt. But then he breathed again fainter. suddenly he breathed no more and nurse MacC. put her hand on his heart under the clothes and felt it. I looked at his face it was pale as ivory. I went forward and Kissed his eyes, and his forehead. They were cold.'

Epilogue

He first deceased, she for a little tried
To live without him, liked it NOT, and died.[1]

Final entry in 'D. C. Partridge: HER BOOK'

A POST-MORTEM, carried out at James's insistence on the afternoon Lytton died, revealed that his stomach was practically eaten up by cancer. A malignant growth had formed, completely blocking the intestine and actually making a perforation (through which food must have been passing) into the colon. From the first, he had had not the slightest chance of recovery. His body was left for a day lying on the bed. Carrington placed on his head a crown of evergreens which she had picked in the garden. He looked incredibly tired and frail, the lines of awful fatigue and infirmity frozen deeply into his face. The next day the body was removed for cremation at Golders Green,[2] and a bronze plate commemorating him was later placed in the Strachey Chapel, at the church of St Andrew, Chew Magna, in Somerset.

Meanwhile, at Ham Spray, the routine of life went on much as usual. James and Pippa having left for London, there were now, briefly, five of them staying there – Carrington, Ralph, Frances Marshall, Stephen Tomlin and Gerald Brenan. The main function of the last-named, it seemed, was to lend support to the others – to go for long walks with Ralph and to sit up late talking to Stephen Tomlin. Frances Marshall found relief to her feelings in running the house. It seemed

1. 'Upon the Death of Sir Albert Moreton's Wife' by Sir Henry Wotton.
2. Apart from the functionaries, the only people present at the cremation were James Strachey and Saxon Sydney-Turner, who insisted on coming. 'There was, of course, no ceremonial of any kind,' James reassured the author.

surprising, after all that had happened, that there should still remain in these people assembled here the ordinary needs for eating, conversation, sleep. Carrington alone did not leave her room. She stayed in bed, where she would pass most of the day and night in tears. Even with the strongest sleeping draughts, she scarcely slept. The long nights which never seemed to end, and the days which ended all too soon, prostrated her with grief and weariness. Tormented by hideous nightmares about Lytton and 'terribly deformed faces cut in half', she felt each morning as if he had died afresh: and each day his loss was harder to bear. 'I am not facing things,' she admitted to Rosamond Lehmann, 'I can't for a bit . . . I find it difficult to go on with ordinary life, and I almost hate anybody else who can, although I know it's unreasonable to expect the world to stand still.'

Ralph was in and out of her room all the time. Stephen Tomlin too saw her a good deal, and it was he who appeared to be the most successful in halting her from making another immediate attempt to destroy herself. 'He persuaded me that after a serious operation, or fever, a man's mind would not be in a good state to decide on such an important STEP,' she wrote in HER BOOK. '– I agreed – So I will defere my decision for a month or two until the result of the operation is less acute.'

To Stephen Tomlin, also, she liked to read poetry, some of the verses she and Lytton had shared, and especially from a favourite Elizabethan anthology he had once given her. One short poem in this volume, 'Misery' by Thomas Howell, she had heavily marked, turning down the page on which it was printed:

> Corpse, clad with carefulness:
> Heart, heaped with heaviness:
> Purse, poor and penniless:
> Back, bare in bitterness:
> O get my grave in readiness,
> Fain would I die to end this stress.

On the second day after Lytton's death, Carrington asked

to see Gerald. 'I had been somewhat dreading this,' he wrote in his diary, 'for – besides the pain of seeing her in such distress – I guessed beforehand that our past estrangement, present uneasy terms and above all the fact that in the past it was Lytton who had really come between us, must at present make any real communication impossible. Besides we now belonged to different countries and had no common language: she was excessively unhappy and I was the opposite: she must feel chiefly hate where I felt chiefly guilt, and no pretence could conceal this.

'I sat in the chair by her bed: and she began to question me about my life, about our cottage, about Gamel; her tone was not unkind nor even insincere, but so remote, indicating such a gulf between us, that it was clear that no natural form of conversation was possible. I asked her about her plans – she answered vaguely. It seemed to me that she was cut off not merely from myself but from everyone, and that for the time being neither sympathy nor pity were acceptable.'

She wanted to suffer. Into the random, hysterical pages of *D. C. Partridge:* HER BOOK, she poured out her agonized emotions, not in order to unburden herself of them, but to set them down in such a way that she should never permit herself to forget even the very least of them. The whole structure of her unstable life had depended on Lytton, and his disappearance took away all meaning, all purpose. 'Oh darling Lytton you are dead,' she scrawled, 'and I can tell you nothing.' The house, the fields and trees they had known and loved together meant nothing to her alone. She could not rouse herself to care about anything, could not apply her mind to anything but the living past. 'He [Lytton] was, and this is why he was everything to me, the only person to whom I never needed to lie, Because he never expected me to be anything different to what I was. and he was never curious if I did not tell him things. . . . No one will ever know the utter happiness of our life together. The absurd and fantastic jokes at meals and on our walks, over our friends – and his marvellous descriptions, and then all his thoughts he shared with me.'

Pain was the only link she still preserved with Lytton, and

she could not bear the thought that she might get over her pain. To this natural affliction was added remorse – remorse imposed upon herself as a punishment for having (as she thought of it) neglected him over the last year or two for Beacus Penrose. Yet even had there been no Beacus, there must necessarily have been guilt. The result of the autopsy, which showed that Lytton's condition, even if properly diagnosed, was inoperable, had come as some slight relief to her. But guilt was threaded into her personality. Had she not felt a premonition that Lytton might die after writing that parody death-scene for *The Week-End Review*? She blamed herself, not for overt acts, but secret thoughts; for moments of depression or bitterness, and hours spent needlessly away from him in the company of others.

On all these accounts, it appeared doubtful whether she could be persuaded to continue living. Stephen Tomlin and Ralph had made her promise to attempt nothing for a month or two, hoping that, if she could be got through a few months, there would be many things that might help to attach her to life. But the foundation was gone, nothing could really mitigate that, and for years to come there would always be moments of depression when she might easily decide to end it. The one essential was never to allow her to be at Ham Spray by herself. Arrangements were therefore made by which she would always be surrounded by friends. When Gerald Brenan left, Julia Tomlin came down, and the vigilant, compassionate supervision of her life went on.

Up in her bedroom Carrington would scribble out innumerable letters in a quivering, shapeless handwriting, to her friends – Barbara Bagenal, Diana Guinness, Rosamond Lehmann, Mary Hutchinson, Dorelia John and others. Many of these friends were helpful; others were less so. The unresolved problems of this desperate transitional period at Ham Spray gave plenty of scope for those who liked to find some roundabout vent for the hostile feelings which death arouses in almost everyone. A few, showing great injustice and a complete misconception of the true state of affairs, sought to blame Frances Marshall, declaring that 'but for her everything would be different'. The majority tried to insist that Carrington should at once sell Ham Spray and 'make a fresh start' elsewhere. They did not understand that, in her eyes, this would be almost tantamount to killing Lytton a second time; they could not sense the cold and melancholy consolation that the house afforded her. 'I have a longing to immesh myself in his [Lytton's] relics,' she confided in HER BOOK, 'that craving for death which I know he disapproved of, and would have disliked. If I could sit here alone just holding his clothes in my arms on the sofa with that handkerchief over my face I would get comfort, but I know these feelings are bad.'

Practically the only people whose company did not jar on her during these first weeks were Dorelia John, and Stephen and Julia Tomlin. Even Ralph's presence distracted her. 'No death,' he had written to Charles Prentice (11 February 1932), 'has ever hurt me more than his.' His grief and despondency, which at times were almost too much for him to bear, only made Carrington worse. He was ready to give up his entire time to her, for his position – a subject for much ambiguous rumour and concern to others – was to himself perfectly well-defined. He considered himself married to Frances in all except name, yet loved Carrington, no less deeply, as a sister. 'I cared for Carrington in a way I've never cared for anybody and I know I could never care again,' he told Rosamond Lehmann (March 1932), 'she was an obsession to me – once she got into anybody's blood she was ineradicable.' Carrington herself, though certainly jealous of Frances, probably did not want Ralph, with all the inconveniences this would entail for her, back as a husband. As for Frances, she was ready to do almost anything that would best fit in with the situation. She would not give up Ralph, but she was prepared to continue sharing him with Carrington, and to allow them, if necessary, to go on a long holiday together.

Progressively this situation grew worse. The atmosphere at Ham Spray, brittle, full of tension, after the departure of Gerald Brenan became steadily more explosive. Ralph's very natural and unavoidable suspicions vexed Carrington, and his anxieties helped to inflame hers. Consequently his own presence by no means acted as a reliable guarantee against another suicide attempt, and it was therefore imperative that the Tomlins – or Stephen Tomlin alone – should remain in the house. Ralph was the only person who could arrange this, but he had come greatly to resent the superior power of persuasion that Carrington's former lover was exercising over her. His old irritation broke out, and he could hardly bring himself to speak to him. Stephen Tomlin's attitude, too, was not especially mollifying; and Carrington's daemon could not, even at this time of abject misery, resist playing on the bad feeling between the two of them. Nervy and irritable, Ralph's aggressiveness discharged itself daily on Stephen Tomlin who, in February, returned with Julia to London.

Any precipitate crisis that might have resulted from their departure was staved off by an invitation from Dorelia John, asking Carrington to go and spend some days at Fryern Court. It had been planned that Dorelia should afterwards come back to Ham Spray, taking the Tomlins' place there for a time. But Augustus John fell ill and she had to cancel this visit. However, she arranged with Carrington that they should all three go off on a holiday to France in the middle of March.

On her return from Fryern Court, Carrington seemed rather better. She was, it appeared, pulling herself together. In the kitchen garden at Ham Spray she made a bonfire, dropping on to it a miscellaneous collection of Lytton's personal belongings, clothes, pyjamas, and lastly his spectacles – without which no one ever saw him – and watching them vanish in the curling smoke. Her immense activity in tidying the house, in arranging books and papers, reassured everyone. The piece of waste ground under the ilex-tree and the Portugal laurels was cleared out, new trees planted, a seat put up facing the Downs. Desmond MacCarthy came down to see her, and tried to interest her in the publication of Lytton's unpublished essays and letters; and this, though premature, was a good plan. She started to read through these miscellaneous writings, and to connect Lytton's memory with the future.

Yet, inwardly, she still pined for him as before. Five weeks had passed since his death, and the period of immunity she had

promised Stephen Tomlin was almost up. Still she could see
no hope for the future; her existence was empty, bleak. 'Every
hour some habit we had together comes back and I miss you,'
she wrote to Lytton in HER BOOK, '– at night I dream of you
in the day you are wiTH me –. I read over and over again our
favourite poems but there is no one to talk about their beauty
now. No use now devising surprises to please you. You were
more dear to me every year – What is the use of "adventures"
now without you to tell them to? It is all wrong, there is no
sense in a life without you.' The good days were past, the sun
had gone out, and before her stretched an eternity of dull
blank skies. Lytton had been 'more completely all my life than
it is possible for any person to be'. She was unfit to go on
living. Nothing and no one could keep her. She was not young
enough to start afresh – besides what was there to start? She
had no one – not even Ralph. She was alone. Soon she would
be thirty-nine. Old age, which she had always dreaded, lay
before her – wrinkles, hollow cheeks, disease, feebleness,
decay – things far more horrifying than death. From her
Elizabethan anthology she cut out two of the beautiful
stanzas which Chidiock Tichborne[3] had written in the Tower
before his execution, and pasted them into HER BOOK:

3. Chidiock Tichborne (1558?–86) had joined the Babington conspirators and agreed at a meeting held in St Giles's-in-the-Fields in June
1586 to be one of six to whom the deed of killing Queen Elizabeth was
specially allotted. He was seized in St John's Wood on 14 August and
lodged in the Tower. At his trial on 13 and 14 September he pleaded
guilty. Six days later he suffered the full penalty of the law, being disem-
bowelled before life was extinct. But his final speech and noble demeanour before being hanged moved many to compassion, as did the
pathetic letter he wrote to his wife Agnes on 19 September. In addition to
the two stanzas which Carrington pasted into HER BOOK, there is a
third one:

> I sought my death and found it in my womb,
>   I look'd for life and saw it was a shade;
> I trod the earth and knew it was my tomb,
>   And now I die, and now I was but made;
> My glass is full, and now my glass is run
> And now I live, and now my life is done.

My prime of youth is but a frost of cares;
  My feast of joy is but a dish of pain;
My crop of corn is but a field of tares;
  And all my good is but vain hope of gain;
My life is fled, and yet I saw no sun;
And now I live, and now my life is done.

The spring is past, and yet it has not sprung;
  The fruit is dead, and yet the leaves be green;
My youth is gone, and yet I am but young;
  I saw the world, and yet I was not seen;
My thread is cut, and yet it is not spun;
And now I live, and now my life is done.

On the last day of February, Carrington and Ralph, Frances Marshall and David Garnett, went over to visit some friends living not far off. While there, Carrington asked if she might borrow a gun to shoot the rabbits that were destroying her garden. Ralph was present at the time and heard her make this request, but his powers of vigilance were at an end, and he wearily accepted at face value her explanation. For six weeks, in an agony of mind night and day, he had been plotting and devising schemes to fasten her to life. The signs of improvement he thought he detected in her recently had encouraged him to relax too far. A week after this, Carrington demanded that she be left alone at Ham Spray. Ralph remonstrated with her, begged her to let him stay by her side. But she insisted, reassuring him that she was much better. In any case, she would be off with the Johns in a few days, she pointed out. Her calm and reasonable manner allayed his suspicions, and he left for London.

It may be that Ralph's actions over this final week or two – his renewed antipathy to Stephen Tomlin, his extraordinary and very untypical negligence over the gun and now his weakness in giving way to Carrington's dangerous demands – were guided by unconscious motives. Things could not go on for ever as they were. Undoubtedly, at some level, he must have longed for almost any end to these weeks of anguish, any solution to his entangled domestic and emotional problems.

Carrington's manner had not, in fact, altogether taken him in. In a letter to Gerald Brenan early that March, he wrote that, while welcoming the visible signs of her improvement, he still did not trust her. She had some secret up her sleeve, he believed. And he had noticed also that she was giving away too many of her possessions.

Nevertheless, he left. And since Olive, the cook, was away with flu, for the first time since Lytton's death Carrington was alone in Ham Spray. On Thursday, 10 March, Leonard and Virginia Woolf came down to see her. Though the day itself was sparkling and sunny, the interior of the house felt bitterly cold. Carrington gave them tea, and talked a lot of Lytton, his ways, his friends. There was a look of dead pain in her great blue eyes, and she seemed, as Virginia said, 'helpless, deserted, like some small animal left'. At first she appeared calm, but there came a moment when she kissed Virginia, and burst into tears. Just before they left, Virginia asked her to come and see them in a few days, and Carrington replied: 'Yes, I will come, or not.'

Next morning she woke – as she always did now – very early, made herself a cup of tea and ate an apple. When the post came, she opened her letters and read *The Times*, which was later found crumpled up in her cupboard. Then she put on Lytton's yellow silk dressing-gown, which no one had ever known her to wear before, and took up the gun. It was nearly eight o'clock. She moved towards the window and saw, walking on the lawn below, two partridges – it would have been like her to find a joke, a bitter pun, in shooting not one of them, but herself.

She had thought out her preparations carefully. First she removed her favourite rug so that it should not be spoilt by the blood, and laid down another inferior rug in its place in such a way that it might appear that she had slipped on it. Next she turned and stood with her back to the window, facing a tall mirror in which she could see her position. Then she placed the butt of the gun on the floor and the barrel against her side. Finally she pulled the trigger.

Nothing happened.

She had forgotten to release the safety-catch. Now she did so, but this must have put her aim out, for when she pulled the trigger a second time, the gun was not pointed correctly, and the shot, though taking away part of her side, missed her heart.

The gardener had heard the noise, and coming under her window, caught what he thought was the sound of groans. He hurried to the foot of the stairs and she called out to him, said that she had slipped on the mat and asked him at once to fetch the woman who lived in the lodge at the end of the drive, and to summon the doctor. When the woman came, she repeated to her the same story and told her to telephone Ralph. To Dr Starkey Smith, she again said the same thing, and, since she was in acute pain, he injected morphia. He seemed upset – he had known her for several years – so she sent him down to get the key of the cellar and help himself to a drink. She also apologized for giving so much trouble. Although he could not examine her properly for fear of increasing the flow of blood, he saw that she was probably too seriously injured to recover.

Ralph had been to a party the night before, had slept heavily and late in his rooms at Great James Street, and was awakened by the telephone message giving him this news. David Garnett, who was sleeping upstairs at the Nonesuch Office, luckily had his car, and drove him and Frances down. They arrived about 11 o'clock, and found Carrington lying on the floor of her bedroom where she had fallen, still conscious and, in spite of the morphia, in pain. She told them that she hated life, that she wished to die – but even this she had bungled. Then on seeing how distraught Ralph was, she changed her story, claimed that it had all been an accident, and promised him that she would try, for his sake, to live.

Partly because of these conflicting stories, there was some question in her friends' minds later on as to whether this act had been premeditated from the first. In Frances Marshall's opinion, she had never wavered. 'Nothing,' she wrote to Rosamond Lehmann, 'I do believe, would have shaken her determination.' Certainly, since Lytton died, she had been obsessed by death. Like a prisoner who earns remission through good conduct, her pretended amelioration had been a manner put on to earn for herself the opportunity she needed. No doubt, having made her preparations, the knowledge that she could do away with herself at almost any moment acted as some sort of reserve of strength. Yet there were also signs — unfinished letters, a diary filled up ahead with future appointments and so on — which seemed to indicate that she was half ready to go on living. These, however, were inconclusive. Perhaps suicide can only be premeditated up to a certain point, and Carrington did not definitely make up her mind until the last minute. Perhaps, too, since she was not an accomplished actress, she really was beginning to get over the worst of Lytton's death, and was driven to kill herself by some fear of gradually weakening intentions. Ralph was coming down to join her that evening; and the following week she was due to go off to the South of France with Augustus and Dorelia John. This day, then, was her very last opportunity. There was, too, some element of spite in her action, a wish to show those friends who had tried so diligently to nurse her back to life that they meant absolutely nothing to her. No possibility of anything resembling recompense existed for her on the wide, wide earth, since she could no longer talk with Lytton; since of all the scenes around her, of all her favourite pursuits, of whatever delighted her ear, her eye, and her understanding, his society was the vivifying soul.

As the pain increased, the doctor again injected morphia. Towards midday she became unconscious, and at a quarter-past two, she died. 'I went into the room and saw her dead,' David Garnett wrote. 'There was a very proud expression on her face.'

Presently David Garnett left and Gerald Brenan arrived to find Ralph 'scarcely able to control his feelings or speak coherently'. Alix Strachey, Carrington's oldest friend, had also come down by train and was the greatest support imaginable to the other three.

Carrington had left a letter for Ralph in which she said that she hoped he would marry Frances and have children. A long list of presents she wished given to her friends followed, and instructions that her ashes were to be buried under the Portugal laurels, with Lytton's close by, she hoped, under the ilex. Her activity in the garden, which a month ago had so heartened everyone, had therefore been the preparation for her grave. She also set aside one hundred pounds for Stephen Tomlin to design her tombstone, but Ralph suppressed this altogether, perhaps because he saw the disadvantages, so near to the house, of any monument. This letter was not produced at the inquest, held on Monday, 14 March, which found her death to have been due to a 'gun shot wound in the left side caused through accidentally slipping when holding a loaded gun in her hand'. There was no post-mortem.

Ralph and Frances, Alix Strachey and Gerald Brenan stayed on at Ham Spray until the inquest was over. 'Before they took her away, I saw her,' Gerald Brenan recorded in his diary, '– or rather the terrible changes wrought in her by death. The same hard frost, the same icy weather prevailed as when Lytton had died, seven weeks before. As I lay awake in his room – for they had put me to sleep in his bed – I could hear the rooks calling all through the night among the frozen trees. It was not possible, even by walking into the next room where her body lay, to understand it.'

SELECT BIBLIOGRAPHY

There is a helpful Chronological Check List of Lytton Strachey's books and published essays at the end of Professor C. R. Sanders's *Lytton Strachey: His Mind and Art* (1957). The following books I have consulted for literary and biographical information.

Allen, B. M.: *General Gordon.* London: Duckworth, 1935.
  Gordon and the Sudan. London: Macmillan, 1931.

Altick, Richard A.: *Lives and Letters.* New York: Knopf, 1965.

Annan, Noël: *Leslie Stephen: his thought and character in relation to his times.* London: MacGibbon & Kee, 1951.

Beaton, Cecil: *The Wandering Years.* London: Weidenfeld & Nicolson, 1962.

Beaverbrook, Lord: *The Decline and Fall of Lloyd George.* London: Collins, 1963.

Beddington-Behrens, Sir Edward: *Look Back – Look Forward.* London: Macmillan, 1963.

Beerbohm, Max: *Lytton Strachey* (The Rede Lecture). Cambridge University Press, 1943.

  Letters to Reggie Turner, edited by Rupert Hart-Davis. London: Hart-Davis, 1964.

Bell, Clive: *Euphrosyne* (anonymously edited). Cambridge: Elijah Johnson, 1905.

  Old Friends: Personal Recollections. London: Chatto & Windus, 1956.

Bell, Julian: *Essays, Poems and Letters,* edited by Quentin Bell (with contributions by J. M. Keynes, David Garnett, Charles Mauron, C. Day Lewis and E. M. Forster). London: Hogarth Press, 1938.

Bell, Quentin: *Bloomsbury.* London: Weidenfeld & Nicolson, 1968.

Bennett, Arnold: *Journals,* vol. 2, *1911–1927;* vol. 3, *1921–1928,* edited by Newman Flower. London: Cassell, 1932, 1933.

Benson, E. F., *As We Are.* London: Longmans, 1932.

Birrell, Augustine: *More Obiter Dicta.* London: Heinemann, 1924.

Bloomfield, Paul: *Uncommon People: A Study of England's Élite.* London: Hamish Hamilton, 1955.

Boas, Guy: *Lytton Strachey* (An English Association Pamphlet). London: 1935.

Bolitho, Hector: *My Restless Years*. London: Max Parrish, 1962.

Bower-Shore, Clifford: *Lytton Strachey: An Essay. London: Fenland* Press, 1933.

Bradford, Gamaliel: *The Journal of Gamaliel Bradford, 1918–1931*, edited by Van Wyck Brooks. Boston, Mass.: Houghton Mifflin, 1933.

　The Letters of Gamaliel Bradford, 1918–1931, edited by Van Wyck Brooks. Boston, Mass.: Houghton Mifflin, 1934.

Brenan, Gerald: *South from Granada*. London: Hamish Hamilton, 1959.

　A Life of One's Own. London: Hamish Hamilton, 1962.

Britt, Albert: *The Great Biographers*. New York: McGraw-Hill, 1936.

Brookfield, Frances M.: *The Cambridge 'Apostles'*. London: Pitman, 1906.

Campbell, Roy: *Light on a Dark Horse: An Autobiography 1901–1935*. London: Hollis & Carter, 1951.

Campos, Christopher: *The View of France from Arnold to Bloomsbury*. Oxford University Press, 1965.

Cannan, Gilbert: *Mendel: A Story of Youth*. London: T. Fisher Unwin, 1916.

Carrington, Dora: *Carrington: Letters and Extracts from her Diaries*, chosen and with an Introduction by David Garnett. London: Jonathan Cape, 1970.

Carver, George: *Alms for Oblivion*. Milwaukee: Bruce Publications, 1916.

Cecchi, Emilio: *Scrittori Inglesi e Americani*, revised edition. Milan: Mondadori, 1947.

Cecil, Lord David: *Max*. London: Constable, 1964.

Clemens, Cyril: *Lytton Strachey* (International Mark Twain Society, Biographical Series, No. 11). Webster Groves, Mo., 1942.

Clifford, James L. (ed.): *Biography as an Art: Selected Criticism, 1560–1960*. Oxford University Press, 1962.

Connolly, Cyril: *Enemies of Promise*, revised edition. London: Routledge & Kegan Paul, 1949.

Cooper, Lady Diana: *The Rainbow Comes and Goes*. London: Hart-Davis, 1958.

Dalton, Hugh: *Call Back Yesterday: Memoirs 1887–1931*. London: Muller, 1953.

Devas, Nicolette: *Two Flamboyant Fathers*. London: Collins, 1966.

Dobrée, Bonamy: 'Lytton Strachey', in *Post Victorians* edited by W. R. Inge. London: Nicholson & Watson, 1933.

Du Bos, Charles: *Approximations*. Deuxiéme Série. Paris: Éditions G. Crès et Cie, 1927.

Dyson, A. E.: *The Crazy Fabric*. London: Macmillan, 1965.

Edel, Leon: *Literary Biography*, revised edition. London: Hart-Davis, 1959.

Elton, Lord: *General Gordon*. London: Collins, 1954.

Epstein, Jacob: *Let there be Sculpture*. London: Michael Joseph, 1940.

Forster, E. M.: *Goldsworthy Lowes Dickinson*. London: Edward Arnold, 1934.

Abinger Harvest. London: Edward Arnold, 1936.

Two Cheers for Democracy. London: Edward Arnold, 1951.

Fry, Roger: *Duncan Grant*. London: Leonard & Virginia Woolf, 1930.

Garnett, David: *The Flowers of the Forest*. London: Chatto & Windus, 1955.

The Familiar Faces. London: Chatto & Windus, 1962.

Garraty, John A.: *The Nature of Biography*. London: Cape, 1957.

Gerhardie, William: *Memoirs of a Polyglot*. London: Duckworth, 1931.

Resurrection. London: Cassell, 1935.

Gertler, Mark: *Selected Letters*, edited by Noel Carrington, and with an Introduction by Quentin Bell. London: Hart-Davis, 1965.

Glenavy, Beatrice: *Today We Will Only Gossip*. London: Constable, 1964.

Goldring, Douglas: *The Nineteen Twenties*. London: Nicholson & Watson, 1945.

Gordon, George: *The Lives of Authors*. London: Chatto & Windus, 1950.

Gosse, Sir Edmund: *Some Diversions of a Man of Letters*. London: Heinemann, 1919.

More Books on the Table. London: Heinemann, 1923.

Leaves and Fruit. London: Heinemann, 1927.

Grant, Patrick: *The Good Old Days*. London: Thames & Hudson. 1956.

Graves, Robert: *Goodbye to All That*. London: Cape, 1929.

Guiguet, Jean: *Virginia Woolf* (translated by Jean Stewart). London: Hogarth Press, 1965.

Hamnett, Nina: *Laughing Torso*. London: Constable, 1932.

Harrod, Roy: *The Life of John Maynard Keynes*. London: Macmillan, 1951.

SELECT BIBLIOGRAPHY

Hassall, Christopher: *Rupert Brooke: A Biography*. London: Faber, 1964.

House, Humphry: *All in Due Time*. London: Hart-Davis, 1955.

Huxley, Aldous: *Crome Yellow*. London: Chatto & Windus, 1921.
On the Margin. London: Chatto & Windus, 1923.

Iyengar, K. R. Srinivasa: *Lytton Strachey: A Critical Study*. London: Chatto & Windus, 1939.

John, Augustus: *Chiaroscuro: Fragments of Autobiography*. London: Cape, 1952.

Johnson, Edgar: *One Mighty Torrent*. New York: Stackpole Sons, 1937.

Johnstone, J. K.: *The Bloomsbury Group*. London: Secker & Warburg, 1954.

Kallich, Martin: *The Psychological Milieu of Lytton Strachey*. New Haven, Conn.: Yale University Press, 1961.

Kendall, Paul Murray: *The Art of Biography*. London: Allen & Unwin, 1965.

Keynes, John Maynard: *Essays in Biography*. London: Macmillan, 1933.
Two Memoirs, with an Introduction by David Garnett. London: Hart-Davis, 1949.

Kingsmill, Hugh: *The Table of Truth*. London: Jarrolds, 1932.
The Progress of a Biographer. London: Methuen, 1949.

Köntges, Günther: *Die Sprache in der Biographie Lytton Stracheys*. Marburg: Hermann Bauer, 1938.

Lawrence, D. H.: 'None of That', in vol. 3 of *The Complete Short Stories* (Phoenix Edition). London: Heinemann, 1955.
Women in Love. London: Martin Secker, 1920.
Selected Letters, edited by Aldous Huxley. London: Heinemann, 1932.
Collected Letters, 2 vols., edited by Harry T. Moore. London: Heinemann, 1962.

Lea, F. A.: *The Life of John Middleton Murry*. London: Methuen, 1959.

Lehmann, John: *The Whispering Gallery*. London: Longmans, 1955.
I am My Brother. London: Longmans, 1960.

Leslie, Seymour: *The Jerome Connexion*. London: John Murray, 1964.

Lewis, Percy Wyndham: *The Apes of God*. London: Nash & Grayson, 1930.
Self-Condemned. London: Methuen, 1954.

Lunn, Sir Arnold: *Roman Converts*. London: Chapman & Hall, 1924.

MacCarthy, Sir Desmond: *Memories*. London: MacGibbon & Kee, 1953.

Mais, S. P. B.: *Some Modern Authors*. London: Grant Richards, 1923.

Martin, Kingsley: *Father Figures: A Volume of Autobiography*. London: Hutchinson, 1966.

Marwick, Arthur: *Clifford Allen: The Open Conspirator*. Edinburgh: Oliver and Boyd, 1964.

Maurois, André: *Aspects of Biography*. Cambridge University Press, 1929.

Poets and Prophets. London: Cassell, 1936.

Mirsky, Prince D. S.: *The Intelligentsia of Great Britain*. London: Gollancz, 1935.

Moore, G. E.: *Principia Ethica*. Cambridge University Press, 1903.
Ethics. London: Williams and Norgate, 1911.

Moore, Harry T.: *The Intelligent Heart: The Story of D. H. Lawrence*. London: Heinemann, 1955.

Morrell, Lady Ottoline: *Ottoline: The Early Memoirs of Lady Ottoline Morrell 1873–1915;* edited and with an introduction by Robert Gathorne Hardy. London: Faber, 1963.

Mortimer, Raymond: *Channel Packet*. London: Hogarth Press, 1948.

Duncan Grant. Harmondsworth: Penguin, 1948.

Muir, Edwin: *Transition*. London: Hogarth Press, 1926.

Nathan, Monique: *Virginia Woolf* (translated by Herma Briffault). New York: Grove Press, 1961.

Nehls, Edward: *D. H. Lawrence: A Composite Biography*. 3 vols. Madison, Wis.: University of Wisconsin Press, 1957–9.

Nicolson, Sir Harold: *Tennyson*. London: Constable, 1923.
Some People. London: Constable, 1927.
The Development of English Biography. London: Hogarth Press, 1933.

'Olivia' (pseudonym of Dorothy Bussy): *Olivia*. London: Hogarth Press, 1949.

Oman, Charles: *On the Writing of History*. London: Methuen, 1939.

Pearson, Hesketh: *Modern Men and Mummers*. London: Allen & Unwin, 1921.
Ventilations. Philadelphia, Pa.: Lippincott, 1930.
Thinking it Over. London: Hamish Hamilton, 1938.

'About Biography' (The Tredegar Memorial Lecture, 1955); included in *Essays by Divers Hands, Being the Transactions of the Royal Society of Literature*, vol. xxix, 1958.

Pippett, Aileen: *The Moth and the Star: A Biography of Virginia Woolf*. Boston, Mass.: Little, Brown, 1955.

Plomer, William: *At Home*. London: Cape, 1958.

Quennell, Peter: *The Singular Preference*. London: Collins, 1952.

The Sign of the Fish. London: Collins, 1960.

Quiller-Couch, Sir Arthur: *Studies in Literature*. Second Series. Cambridge University Press, 1927.

Raleigh, Sir Walter: *Letters 1879–1922*, edited by Lady Raleigh. London: Methuen, 1926.

Rantavaara, Irma: *Virginia Woolf and Bloomsbury*. Helsinki: Annales Academiae Scientiarum Fennicae, Series B, tom. 82, 1, 1953.

Raymond, John: *England's on the Anvil*. London: Collins, 1958.

Reddie, Cecil: *Abbotsholme 1889–1899, or, Ten Years' Work in an Education Laboratory*. London: G. Allen, 1900.

Robertson, David. *George Mallory*. London: Faber, 1969.

Robertson, Graham: *Letters from Graham Robertson*, edited by Kerrison Preston. London: Hamish Hamilton, 1953.

Roosevelt, Eleanor: *This is My Story*. London: Hutchinson, 1937.

Rothenstein, John: *Modern English Painters*, 2 vols. London: Eyre & Spottiswoode, 1952, 1956.

Summer's Lease. London: Hamish Hamilton, 1965.

Rothenstein, William: *Men and Memories*, 2 vols. London: Faber, 1931, 1932.

Russell, Bertrand: *Portraits from Memory*. London: Allen & Unwin, 1956.

The Autobiography of Bertrand Russell 1872–1913. London: Allen & Unwin, 1967.

Rutherston, Albert: *Contemporary British Artists: Henry Lamb*. London: Benn, 1924.

Sanders, Charles Richard: *The Strachey Family 1558–1932*, Durham, N. Carolina: Duke University Press, 1953.

Lytton Strachey: His Mind and Art. New Haven, Conn.: Yale University Press, 1957.

Sassoon, Siegfried: *Siegfried's Journey*. London. Faber, 1945.

Scott-James, R. A.: *Lytton Strachey* (Writers and their Work, No. 65). London: Longmans, 1955.

Sherburn, George: *Selections from Alexander Pope*. New York: Thomas Nelson & Sons, 1929.

Simson, George Kuppler: 'Lytton Strachey's Use of his Sources in

Eminent Victorians': a thesis submitted to the Faculty of the Graduate School of the University of Minnesota (unpublished), 1963.

Sitwell, Edith: *Taken Care Of.* London: Hutchinson, 1965.

Sitwell, Sir Osbert: *Laughter in the Next Room.* London: Macmillan, 1949.

Spender, Stephen: *World within World.* London: Hamish Hamilton, 1951.

Squire, Sir John: *Books Reviewed.* London: Hodder & Stoughton, 1922.

Stansky, Peter, and Abrahams, William: *Journey to the Frontier: Julian Bell and John Cornford: their lives and the 1930s.* London: Constable, 1966.

Stein, Gertrude: *The Autobiography of Alice B. Toklas.* London: John Lane, 1933.

Stephen, Adrian: *The 'Dreadnought' Hoax.* London: Leonard & Virginia Woolf, 1936.

Stone, Wilfrid: *The Cave and the Mountain.* A Study of E. M. Forster. Oxford University Press, 1966.

Strachey, Julia: *Cheerful Weather for the Wedding.* London: Leonard & Virginia Woolf, 1932.

Strachey, Lytton: *Landmarks in French Literature.* London: Williams & Norgate, 1912.

Eminent Victorians. London: Chatto & Windus, 1918.

Queen Victoria. London: Chatto & Windus, 1921.

Books and Characters: French and English. London: Chatto & Windus, 1922.

Pope (The Leslie Stephen Lecture). London: Cambridge University Press, 1925.

Elizabeth and Essex: A Tragic History. London: Chatto & Windus, 1928.

Portraits in Miniature and Other Essays. London: Chatto & Windus, 1931.

Characters and Commentaries (with a preface by James Strachey). London: Chatto & Windus, 1933.

Spectatorial Essays (with a preface by James Strachey). London: Chatto & Windus, 1964.

This volume contains thirty-five of the essay-reviews that Lytton wrote for the *Spectator*, less than half of his total contributions to that paper. The essays in *Books and Characters, Portraits in Miniature* and *Characters and Commentaries* have been regrouped into two volumes in the Chatto & Windus Uniform Edition of the Collected Works of Lytton Strachey: *Biographical Essays* and *Literary Essays*, both first published in 1948.

Ermyntrude and Esmeralda. London: Anthony Blond, 1969.

Lytton Strachey by Himself: a Self-Portrait, edited and introduced by Michael Holroyd. London: Heinemann, 1971.

Strachey, Lytton, and Fulford, Roger (eds): *The Greville Memoirs*, 8 vols. (Joint editors: Ralph and Frances Partridge.) London: Macmillan, 1937–8.

Strachey, Lytton, and Woolf, Virginia: *Virginia Woolf and Lytton Strachey: Letters*. London: Chatto & Windus, 1956.

> This volume has several cuts, deletions of names, and omissions of whole letters. The present biographer has had access to the full correspondence.

Strachey, St Loe: *The Adventure of Living*. London: Nelson, 1922.

Swinnerton, Frank: *The Georgian Literary Scene*. London: Dent, 1938; rev. ed. 1951.

Figures in the Foreground: Literary Reminiscences 1917–40. London: Hutchinson, 1963.

Thurston, Marjorie: 'The Development of Lytton Strachey's Biographical Method': a dissertation submitted to the Graduate Faculty of the University of Chicago (unpublished), 1929.

Toklas, Alice B.: *What is Remembered*. London: Michael Joseph, 1963.

Trevelyan, G. M.: *Autobiography and Other Essays*. London: Longmans, 1949.

Trevor-Roper, Hugh: *Historical Essays*. London: Macmillan, 1957.

Trilling, Lionel: *E. M. Forster: A Study*. London: Hogarth Press, 1944.

Unwin, Sir Stanley: *The Truth about a Publisher*. London: Allen & Unwin, 1960.

Warburg, Fredric: *An Occupation for Gentlemen*. London: Hutchinson, 1959.

Webb, Beatrice: *My Apprenticeship*. London: Longmans, 1926.

Our Partnership. London: Longmans, 1948.

Wilson, Edmund: *Axel's Castle: A Study in the Imaginative Literature of 1870–1930*. New York: Charles Scribner's Sons, 1931.

The Shores of Light: A Literary Chronicle of the Twenties and Thirties. London: W. H. Allen, 1952.

Wood, Alan: *Bertrand Russell: The Passionate Sceptic*. London: Allen & Unwin, 1957.

Woolf, Leonard: *Sowing: An Autobiography of the Years 1880–1904.*
London: Hogarth Press, 1967.

Beginning Again: An Autobiography of the Years 1911–1918.
London: Hogarth Press, 1964.

Downhill All the Way: An Autobiography of the Years 1919–1939.
London: Hogarth Press, 1961.

Woolf, Virginia: *The Voyage Out.* London: Duckworth, 1915.

Jacob's Room. London: Hogarth Press, 1922.

The Waves. London: Hogarth Press, 1931.

A Writer's Diary. London: Hogarth Press, 1953.

Roger Fry. London: Hogarth Press, 1940.

The Death of the Moth and Other Essays. London: Hogarth Press,
1942.

Granite and Rainbow. London: Hogarth Press, 1958.

Young, G. M.: *Victorian England: Portrait of an Age.* Oxford University Press, 1960.

FOR THE BEST IN PAPERBACKS, LOOK FOR THE 🐧

In every corner of the world, on every subject under the sun, Penguin represents quality and variety – the very best in publishing today.

For complete information about books available from Penguin – including Pelicans, Puffins, Peregrines and Penguin Classics – and how to order them, write to us at the appropriate address below. Please note that for copyright reasons the selection of books varies from country to country.

In the United Kingdom: For a complete list of books available from Penguin in the U.K., please write to *Dept E.P. Penguin Books Ltd, Harmondsworth, Middlesex, UB7 0DA*

In the United States: For a complete list of books available from Penguin in the U.S., please write to *Dept BA, Penguin, 299 Murray Hill Parkway, East Rutherford, New Jersey 07073*

In Canada: For a complete list of books available from Penguin in Canada, please write to *Penguin Books Canada Ltd, 2801 John Street, Markham, Ontario L3R 1B4*

In Australia: For a complete list of books available from Penguin in Australia, please write to the *Marketing Department, Penguin Books Australia Ltd, P.O. Box 257, Ringwood, Victoria 3134*

In New Zealand: For a complete list of books available from Penguin in New Zealand, please write to the *Marketing Department, Penguin Books (NZ) Ltd, Private Bag, Takapuna, Auckland 9*

In India: For a complete list of books available from Penguin in India, please write to *Penguin Overseas Ltd, 706 Eros Apartments, 56 Nehru Place, New Delhi, 110019*

In Holland: For a complete list of books available from Penguin in Holland, please write to *Penguin Books Nederland B.V. Postbus 195, NL – 1380 AD WEESP Netherlands*

In Germany: For a complete list of books available from Penguin in Germany, please write to *Penguin Books Ltd, Friedrichstrasse, 10 – 12, D 6000, Frankfurt a m, Main 1, Federal Republic of Germany*

In Spain: For a complete list of books available from Penguin in Spain, please write to *Longman Penguin España, Calle San Nicolas 15, E – 28013 Madrid, Spain*

FICTION AND THE READING PUBLIC

Q. D. Leavis

First published in 1932, Mrs Leavis's crackling analysis of fiction and its readers from the Elizabethan era to the 1930s has survived as a 'fresh, lucid and vigorous' classic of literary criticism. She convincingly puts to flight the notion that only 'literature' and 'the few who can talk intelligently of Stendhal, Proust and Henry James' have been important in shaping the human spirit and its concerns. As a social and critical document, this work is sensible and pungent; as a book, it is a source of unmitigated pleasure.

THE DIARY OF VIRGINIA WOOLF

Volume 1 1915–19   Volume 3 1925–30
Volume 2 1920–24   Volume 4 1931–35
Volume 5 1936–41

Edited by Anne Olivier Bell

'Three qualities of the great diarists – Pepys, Greville or Kilvert – she certainly has. She is interested in everything she sets down she writes for, and talks to, each reader directly . . . she moves back and forth between the ridiculous and the sublime with no loss of authenticity or humour . . . She offers rich and inexhaustible companionship' – Michael Ratcliffe

'As an account of the intellectual and cultural life of our century, Virginia Woolf's diaries are invaluable; as the record of one bruised and unquiet mind, they are unique' – Peter Ackroyd in the *Sunday Times*

Lytton Strachey

QUEEN VICTORIA

Virginia Woolf (once she had swallowed her envy) wrote: 'In time to come Lytton Strachey's Queen Victoria will be Queen Victoria, just as Boswell's Johnson is now Dr Johnson. The other versions will fade and disappear. It was a prodigious feat.' And Harold Nicolson, after detailing the overwhelming mass of materials facing the biographer, commented: 'To produce a book in which there is no trace of artificiality or strain – this, in all certainty, is an achievement which required the very highest gifts of intellect and imagination.'

EMINENT VICTORIANS

'*Eminent Victorians* is the work of a great anarch, a revolutionary textbook on bourgeois society written in the language through which the bourgeois ear could be lulled and beguiled, the Mandarin style' – Cyril Connolly in *Enemies of Promise*

Lytton Strachey's desire 'to lay bare the facts . . . as I understand them, dispassionately, impartially, and without ulterior intentions' gave him, in an age of panegyric, the reputation of an iconoclast. In his famous study of four Victorian figures, in fact, only the essays on Cardinal Manning and Dr Arnold are consistently severe: his portrait of Florence Nightingale, though it exploded the fable of the Lady of the Lamp, is often admiring, and the tragedy of General Gordon is retailed with a note of tenderness.

YOUNG THOMAS HARDY

Robert Gittings

Highly praised for *John Keats*, Robert Gittings repeats his success with his award-winning (James Tait Black Memorial Prize and the W. H. Heinemann Royal Society of Literature Award) two-volume biography of Thomas Hardy.

The first for a quarter of a century, it cuts through the specula-tions and half-truths to give an outstanding and evocative account of the important first thirty-five years of one of our major poets and writers.

'Really Mr Gittings's talent for biography is astonishing. His sureness of touch . . . the terse interrelating, scrupulous lack of over-emphasis, and frequently noticed excellence of the writing, give us a splendidly rich, suggestive and always controlled pic-ture of the young Hardy' – *The Times Higher Education Supplement*

The Older Hardy by Robert Gittings is also published by Penguin

SECRETS OF A WOMAN'S HEART

The Later Life of Ivy Compton-Burnett 1920–1969

Hilary Spurling

'A biographical triumph . . . elegant, stylish, witty, tender, immensely acute – dazzles and exhilarates . . . a great achieve-ment' – Kay Dick in the *Literary Review*

Ivy Compton-Burnett was one of this century's most individual novelists. In this second volume of her magnificent biography, Hilary Spurling shows that this enigmatic and formidable figure was not only a writer of outstanding wit and devastating insight, but a woman capable of great affection, generosity and friendship.

'Even more enthralling than the first . . . we can congratulate Hilary Spurling on having extended the boundaries of the art of biography' – Hugh Brogan in the *Sunday Times*

'Absorbing, moving, at times helplessly funny' – Anthony Powell in the *Daily Telegraph*

'An admirable biography. One of the very best I have ever read' – Sybille Bedford in the *Guardian*

Winner of the Duff Cooper Memorial Prize

AUGUSTUS JOHN

Michael Holroyd

Archetypal bohemian, man of heroic energies, Augustus John was the very model of the brilliant and unruly artist-reprobate that is so fascinating to read about and so dangerous to know.

'Mr Holroyd has made a great name for himself as a biographer of this period . . . he has brought to this task the same rare gift of acute sympathy which he had already bestowed on Strachey' – Philip Toynbee in the *Observer*

'Mr Holroyd's outsize portrait is both vastly informative and hugely entertaining . . . perhaps Holroyd's most delightful talent is a combination of eye and tone of voice that we more readily associate with novelists than with biographers' – *Newsweek*

'Mr Holroyd, in addition to his gifts as a biographer, shows himself in this book to have keen insight into works of art' – Kenneth Clark in *The Times Literary Supplement*

'He has an enviable ability to deal with the intricacies of multiple relationships, with the tensions and developments of complex human situations . . . the gradual, sometimes comic and sometimes tragic, developments of what became known as "the John tribe" is excellently rendered' – Quentin Bell in the *Spectator*

Michael Holroyd 'writes with something of Augustus's own bravura and attack and with a vigour that puts one in mind of Max Beerbohm on Bernard Shaw' – Hilary Spurling in *The Times*